The Collected Courses of the Academy of European Law
Series Editors: Professor Gráinne de Búrca,
Fordham Law School, New York
Professor Bruno de Witte, and
Professor Francesco Francioni,
European University Institute, Florence
Assistant Editor: Barbara Ciomei, *European University Institute, Florence*

VOLUME XVI/1
EU Administrative Law

The Collected Courses of the Academy of European Law
Edited by Professor Gráinne de Búrca, Professor Bruno de Witte, and Professor Francesco Francioni
Assistant Editor: Barbara Ciomei

This series brings together the Collected Courses of the Academy of European Law in Florence. The Academy's mission is to produce scholarly analyses which are at the cutting edge of the two fields in which it works: European Union law and human rights law. A 'general course' is given each year in each field, by a distinguished scholar and/or practitioner, who either examines the field as a whole through a particular thematic, conceptual, or philosophical lens, or who looks at a particular theme in the context of the overall body of law in the field. The Academy also publishes each year a volume of collected essays with a specific theme in each of the two fields.

EU Administrative Law

PAUL CRAIG

Academy of European Law
European University Institute

OXFORD
UNIVERSITY PRESS

OXFORD
UNIVERSITY PRESS

Great Clarendon Street, Oxford OX2 6DP

Oxford University Press is a department of the University of Oxford.
It furthers the University's objective of excellence in research, scholarship,
and education by publishing worldwide in

Oxford New York

Auckland Cape Town Dar es Salaam Hong Kong Karachi
Kuala Lumpur Madrid Melbourne Mexico City Nairobi
New Delhi Shanghai Taipei Toronto

With offices in

Argentina Austria Brazil Chile Czech Republic France Greece
Guatemala Hungary Italy Japan Poland Portugal Singapore
South Korea Switzerland Thailand Turkey Ukraine Vietnam

Published in the United States
by Oxford University Press Inc., New York

First published 2006

British Library Cataloguing in Publication Data
Data available

Library of Congress Cataloging in Publication Data
Data available

Typeset in Adobe Garamond
by RefineCatch Limited, Bungay, Suffolk
Printed in Great Britain
on acid-free paper by
Antony Rowe Ltd, Chippenham

ISBN 978–0–19–929681–1

3 5 7 9 10 8 6 4 2

This book is for Anita and Ciaran

Preface

This book deals with EU Administrative Law and is divided into two parts. Part I is entitled 'Administration and Law' and considers the different ways in which the EU delivers policy. This is a complex topic in its own right, as will become apparent from the chapters within Part I. The objective is to explicate, analyse and evaluate these modes of policy delivery, assess the role of law therein, draw conclusions about their relative efficacy and the extent to which they meet basic precepts of accountability. The approach is contextual and draws on different disciplines.

The focus in Part II shifts to 'Law and Administration' with analysis of the principles of judicial review as they have been developed by the Community courts. The chapters consider in-depth the principles of judicial review that are applied to control and structure EU administration and that of the Member States when acting in the sphere of EU law. The discussion examines the legislative and political initiatives that are relevant to particular issues, as well as the contribution made by the Community courts. The analysis of positive law in each of the areas studied is complemented by normative analysis, which takes full account of the relevant academic literature.

I have made certain assumptions concerning the primary materials that are relevant to this study. I have assumed that the Constitutional Treaty is unlikely to enter into force, given the negative votes in the referenda in France and the Netherlands. I have nonetheless drawn on material from the Constitutional Treaty when it is pertinent to discussion of particular topics. The Charter of Fundamental Rights is not formally binding at the time of writing. I have nonetheless examined this in detail in the chapter on Rights, in part because there is a greater likelihood that it will become binding in some later Treaty revision and in part because it is in any event an interpretative tool drawn on both politically and legally.

I have learned much from friends and colleagues over the years, in the UK, Europe and the USA, and I have benefited greatly from academic discussion at Conferences and the like.

I would like to thank Dr Alexandros Tsadiras for writing the chapter on the Ombudsman and Hanna Wilberg for research assistance on the chapter on Shared Management. I am very grateful for the help from all those at Oxford University Press, who have done an excellent job in seeing the book through production. Many thanks also to Anita and Ciaran for being there and bearing with me when writing this book.

The law is as stated on 30 April 2006.

PAUL CRAIG
St John's College, Oxford

Contents—Summary

Table of Cases xxix
Table of Legislation lxxv
List of Abbreviations xciii

Part I—Administration and Law

1. Crisis, Reform, and Constitutionalization 3
2. Centralized or Direct Community Administration 31
3. Shared Management 57
4. Comitology 99
5. Agencies 143
6. Open Method of Coordination 191
7. Social Partners 235

Part II—Law and Administration

8. Foundations 263
9. Courts 283
10. Access 313
11. Process 349
12. Competence and Subsidiarity 401
13. Law, Fact, and Discretion 429
14. Rights 483
15. Equality 545
16. Legal Certainty and Legitimate Expectations 607
17. Proportionality I 655
18. Proportionality II 687
19. The Precautionary Principle 717
20. Remedies I: The Community 749

21. Remedies II: Member States 789
22. The Ombudsman 829

Index 857

Contents

Table of Cases xxix
Table of Legislation lxxv
List of Abbreviations xciii

Part I—Administration and Law

1. Crisis, Reform, and Constitutionalization 3
1. Introduction 3
2. The Fall of the Santer Commission 3
A. The Committee of Independent Experts, Its Origin and Criteria of Operation 3
B. The Committee of Independent Experts' Detailed Critique 6
C. The Committee of Independent Experts' Conclusions 11
3. Service Delivery and Accountability: Reflections on the Committee's Report 12
A. Ascription of Responsibility for Taking on Policies Where There Were Staff Shortages 13
B. The Legitimacy of Contracting Out as a Method of Service Delivery 15
4. The Prodi Commission and Institutional Reform 16
A. The Initial Prodi Reforms 16
B. The Second Report of the Committee of Independent Experts 18
C. Reforming the Commission: The White Paper 21
5. Implementation of the Reforms 23
A. A Culture Based On Service and Ethical Standards 23
B. Priority Setting and the Efficient Use of Resources 24
C. Staff Policy 25
D. Financial Management, Control, and Audit 25
6. Conclusions and Assessment 28

2. Centralized or Direct Community Administration 31
1. Introduction 31
2. Direct/Centralized Management 31
A. The Rationale for Direct/Centralized Management 31
B. Delivery of Direct/Centralized Management and Contracting Out 32

3. The New Financial Regulation 33
   A. General Principles 33
   B. Five Choices 34
4. Management by the Commission: Recasting Responsibility for Projects 34
5. Management by Executive Agencies: Policy and Implementation, Power and Responsibility 37
   A. Establishment, Winding-up, Legal Status, and Staffing 37
   B. Tasks 38
   C. Financial Arrangements 39
   D. Damages Liability and Review of Legality 40
   E. The First Executive Agencies 43
      (1) The Intelligent Energy Executive Agency 43
      (2) The Education, Audiovisual and Culture Executive Agency 47
      (3) Executive Agency for the Public Health Programme 49
6. Management by Networks of National Agencies 50
7. Management through Contracting Out: Contract Award, Contract Specification, and the Allocation of Contractual Risk 52
8. Conclusions and Assessment 53

3. Shared Management 57

1. Introduction 57
2. The Common Agricultural Policy 58
   A. Treaty Foundations 58
   B. From Price Support towards Income Support 58
   C. The Framework of Shared Management 60
3. The CAP, Shared Management, and Law 62
   A. The Delineation of Legislative Objectives: The Tension between the Collective Interest and the Interests of Individual Member States 62
   B. Legislative Design and Content: Incentives for Compliance 63
   C. The Undermining of Formal Law: Pressure from the Member States and Acquiescence by the Commission 64
   D. The Law Attempts to Catch Up: Formal Legal Change and Its Effectiveness 64
   E. The Conciliation Procedure: Bargaining in the Shadow of the Law 65
   F. The Contribution of the ECJ: Teleological Interpretation in Support of the Commission 66
   G. The Reformed CAP: Looking to the Future 68
4. The Structural Funds 69

A. The Treaty Foundations 69
B. The Genesis of Structural Fund Policy 70
C. The 1988 Reforms 72
D. The 1993 Reforms 74
E. The 1999 Reforms 75
F. The 2007 Reforms 76
G. The Framework of Shared Management 78
5. The Structural Funds, Shared Management, and Law 78
A. The Delineation of Legislative Objectives: The Tension between the Collective Interest and the Interests of Individual Member States 78
B. Legislative Design and Input: Project Selection 80
C. Legislative Design and Output: Payment and Incentives for Compliance 83
D. Legislative Design and Output: Control Systems, Reporting, Checks, and Incentives for Compliance 84
E. Legislative Design and Output: Correction of Irregularities, Sanctions, and Incentives for Compliance 88
F. The Contribution of the ECJ: Teleological Interpretation in Support of the Commission 91
G. Formal Law and Efficacy 93
H. Soft Law and Reform 94
6. Conclusions and Assessment 96

4. Comitology 99
1. Introduction 99
2. The Nature of the Problem 99
3. Rule-making in the EU: A Short Guide to a Complex History 102
A. The Ambiguous 'Original Intent' 102
B. The Birth of Comitology 104
C. Judicial Imprimatur 105
D. The Single European Act and the First Comitology Decision 106
E. The Treaty on European Union, Amsterdam, and the Second Comitology Decision 108
F. The Nice Treaty and the Proposed Amendment to the Second Comitology Decision 111
G. The Constitutional Treaty 112
H. Three Approaches to Comitology 113
4. Deliberative Supranationalism, Rule-making, and Comitology 114
A. The Thesis 114
B. Deliberative Supranationalism and Consensual Deliberation 116
C. Deliberative Supranationalism and the European Parliament 117
D. Deliberative Supranationalism and Participatory Rights 119

5. Technocracy, Rule-making, and Comitology 121
6. A Hierarchy of Norms, Controls, and Comitology 124
A. A Constitutional Hierarchy of Norms 124
B. Regulations, Delegated Regulations, and Implementing Acts 126
(1) Regulations, Delegated Regulations, and Comitology 126
(2) Delegated Regulations, Implementing Acts, and Comitology 127
C. The Effectiveness of the Controls over Delegated Regulations 128
(1) Control *Ex Ante* 128
(2) Control *Ex Post* 129
7. Rule-making, Democracy, and Efficiency 131
A. Legislative Mandate and Control: Legitimation from the Top 131
B. Legislative Mandate, Control, and Committees: Legitimation from the Top 132
C. Participation Rights: Legitimation from the Bottom 134
(1) The Legal and Political Status Quo 134
(2) Participation Rights and the Public Law Regime 136
(3) Practical Implementation and Cost 137
(4) The Courts and Judicial Review 138
8. Conclusion 140

5. Agencies 143
1. Introduction 143
2. The Rationale for Agencies in the Nation State 143
3. The Rationale for Agencies in the EU 145
4. Evolution 148
5. Classification 152
A. The Commission View 153
B. An Alternative View 154
(1) Regulatory Agencies 154
(2) Decision-making Agencies 155
(3) Quasi-regulatory Agencies 155
(4) Information and Coordination Agencies 156
6. Limits 160
A. Legal Limits 160
B. Political Limits 162
7. Legal Accountability 164
A. The Agency Regulation 164
B. The Treaty 165
C. Targeting Judicial Review 167
D. Applying Judicial Review 168
8. Political Control and Accountability 168

A. Agency Tasks, Criteria, and Reporting 169
B. Agency Composition 170
C. Agency Work Programme 173
D. Agency Transparency 175
E. Agency Networks 176
F. Agency Participation 179
9. Financial Accountability 180
10. The Existing Agency Regime 182
11. The Future Agency Regime 183
A. The Rationale for EU Agencies 183
B. Legal Constraints 185
C. Political Constraints 186
(1) Agency Tasks and Specification 186
(2) Agency Appointments and Reporting 187
(3) Agency Composition 187
(4) Agencies and Regulatory Impact Assessment 188
(5) Agencies and Legislative Veto 189
12. Conclusion 190

6. Open Method of Coordination 191
1. Introduction 191
2. Launch and Relaunch: Lisbon, Nice, and Brussels 191
3. Economic Policy, Employment Policy, and Social Exclusion 195
A. Economic Policy 195
B. Employment Policy 201
C. Social Exclusion 205
D. Streamlining the Procedures 208
E. The Open Method of Coordination: Two Sets of Issues 209
4. The Open Method of Coordination and the Traditional Community Method 209
A. Soft Law v Hard Law 209
B. The Open Method of Coordination v the Traditional Community Method 213
5. The Open Method of Coordination: An Evaluation 215
A. Transparency 217
B. Public Debate 218
C. Parliamentary Involvement 218
D. Participation 221
E. Deliberation and Learning 224
F. Peer Pressure 227
G. Substantive and Procedural Impact 228
6. The Open Method of Coordination: Future Prospects 229

A. The Relationship between the Economic and Social Order 229
B. Reforming the OMC Process 231
7. Conclusion 233

7. Social Partners 235
1. Introduction 235
2. The Emergence of the Social Dialogue 235
3. The Treaty Framework 237
A. The Social Partners and Implementation of Directives: Article 137 EC 238
B. The Social Partners and Consultation: Article 138 EC 238
C. The Social Partners, Agreements, and Law: Article 139 EC 238
D. The Social Partners, Process-Oriented Texts, and Joint Opinions 240
E. The Social Partners and the Open Method of Coordination 241
F. The Tripartite Social Summit for Growth and Employment 241
G. The Social Partners and the European Council 242
4. The Social Partners, Agreements, and Formal Law 243
A. Rationale and Legitimacy: Representation 243
B. Rationale and Legitimacy: Better Governance as Social Subsidiarity 247
C. Rationale and Legitimacy: Better Governance, Functional Attribution, and Democracy 248
(1) The Community Democratic Model 249
(2) Participatory Democracy 251
(3) Associative Democracy 252
(4) Directly-deliberative Polyarchy 253
(5) Neo-Corporatism, Functional Participation, and Democracy 254
D. Rationale and Legitimacy: Conclusions 255
5. The Social Partners, Autonomous Agreements, and the Shadow of the Law 257
6. The Social Partners, Process-Oriented Texts, Joint Opinions, and the Sectoral Social Dialogue 258
7. Conclusion 260

Part II—Law and Administration

8. Foundations 263
1. Introduction 263
2. Justification 263
3. Sources 264

4. Grounds 265
5. Reviewable Acts 266
6. Background Principles 270
A. The Rule of Law 270
B. Institutional Balance 273
C. Effectiveness and Cooperation 277
D. Administrative Efficacy 278
7. A General Code of Good Administration 279

9. Courts 283

1. Introduction 283
2. Central Structural Features 284
3. Central Jurisdictional Features 285
4. Caseload 286
A. The Rationale for the Caseload Problem 287
B. Judicial Mechanisms for Limiting Caseload 288
5. Reform Objectives 291
6. The Relationship between the ECJ and CFI 292
A. Direct Actions 293
B. Preliminary Rulings 296
7. The Relationship between the Community Courts and National Courts 299
A. Limitation of the National Courts Empowered to Make a Reference 300
B. The Introduction of a Filtering Mechanism 301
C. The National Court Proposes an Answer to the Question 304
D. The National Court Gives Judgment 305
E. The Creation of Decentralized Judicial Bodies 307
8. The Constitutional Treaty 310
9. Conclusion 312

10. Access 313

1. Introduction 313
2. Access, the Initial Determination, and the Courts 314
A. Access, Individual Decisions, and the Right to be Heard 314
B. Access, Legislative Norms, Consultation, and Participation 316
C. Legal Access, Principle, and Policy 318
3. Access, the Initial Determination, and the Political Process 322
A. Rights to be Heard Accorded by Community Legislation 322
B. Rights to Participate or be Consulted Accorded by Community Legislation 322
C. Participation, Consultation, Soft Law, and the Commission 324

D. Participation, Consultation, and Agencies 327
E. Access and the Political Process: Politics, Law, and Participation 328
4. Access to Judicial Review: Standing 331
A. *Locus Standi*: The Background 331
B. *UPA*: The Advocate General's Opinion 335
C. *UPA*: The ECJ's Reasoning 337
D. *Jégo-Quéré* 339
E. A Complete System of Legal Protection: Indirect Challenge? 340
F. A Complete System of Legal Protection: Direct Challenge? 342
G. The Constitutional Treaty and the Charter 344
5. Conclusion 347

11. Process 349

1. Introduction 349
2. Process and Transparency 350
A. The Values Served by Transparency 350
B. Transparency and the EU Treaty 351
C. Transparency and the Community Courts 353
D. Transparency, Regulation 1049/2001, and the Community Courts 354
(1) Protecting the Reality of Access 355
(2) Interpretation of the Exceptions 356
E. Conclusion 359
3. Process and Hearing 360
A. Applicability 360
B. Content: General Approach 361
C. Content: Notice and the Right to Respond 363
D. Content: Access to the File 365
E. Content: Cross-Examination 369
F. Content: Separation of Functions 370
G. Content: Causation 372
4. Process and the Duty of Care/Diligent and Impartial Examination 373
A. Recognition of the Principle 373
B. Application of the Principle to Competition 375
C. Application of the Principle to State Aids 376
D. Development and Limitation of the Principle 378
5. Process and Reasons 381
6. Process and the Charter of Fundamental Rights 385
7. Process and Sector-specific Legislation 387
A. Competition 388
(1) Individual Process Rights 389

(2) Procedural Rights and Powers Accorded to the Commission 390
B. State Aids 392
(1) Individual Process Rights 392
(2) Procedural Rights and Powers Accorded to the Commission 393
8. Process, Care, Reasons, and Dialogue 393
9. Process and Substantive Review 396
A. Process Rights Facilitating Substantive Review 396
B. Process Rights as a Means to Consider the Substance of the Case 397
10. Conclusion 398

12. Competence and Subsidiarity 401
1. Introduction 401
2. Internal Competence 401
A. Competence, Shared Competence, and Uncertainty 401
B. Treaty Articles, Interpretation, and Disagreement 404
C. Power, Implied Power, and the Scope of Implication 406
D. Power, Community Objectives, and Necessity 407
3. External Competence 410
A. The Early Case Law, Express Power, and Judicial Implication 410
B. The WTO Case, External Competence, and the Limits of Exclusive Competence 412
C. The Open Skies Cases, the *ERTA* Ruling, and Exclusive External Competence 413
D. Shared Competence, Mixed Agreements, and Cooperation 415
E. The Constitutional Treaty, External Competence, and Exclusivity 416
4. Subsidiarity 419
A. The Meaning of Exclusive Competence 420
B. The Subsidiarity Calculus 422
C. The Role of the Court 425
5. Conclusion 427

13. Law, Fact, and Discretion 429
1. Introduction 429
2. Law, Fact, and Discretion 429
A. Introduction 429
B. Law 431
C. Fact 431
D. Discretion 433
3. Review of Legal Issues 435

A. The General Approach: Substitution of Judgment 435
B. The General Approach: Qualifications 438
4. Review of Fact and Discretion: The Early Case Law 439
A. Classic Discretion 439
B. Jurisdictional Discretion 440
C. Jurisdictional Discretion Plus Classic Discretion 442
D. Contrast and Similarity 444
E. Discretion: Positive and Normative Reflections 445
5. Review of Fact and Discretion: Constancy and Change in the Modern Jurisprudence 446
A. Manifest Error: *Pfizer* 447
(1) *Pfizer* and Factual Error 448
(2) *Pfizer* and Discretion 450
B. Manifest Error: *Airtours* 452
C. Manifest Error: *Tetra Laval* 453
(1) *Tetra Laval*: The CFI 453
(2) The Commission: The Limits of Review 455
(3) Vesterdorf: The Defence of the CFI 455
(4) *Tetra Laval*: The ECJ 457
D. Manifest Error: Common Policies, State Aid, and Structural Funds 457
(1) Common Policies 458
(2) State Aids 460
(3) Structural Funds 462
E. Misuse of Power 462
6. Fact, Standard of Proof, and Standard of Review 464
A. The Standard of Proof Required of the Primary Decision-maker 465
B. The Standard of Judicial Review applied by the Court 466
C. The Standard of Judicial Review applied by the Court: The Meaning of Manifest Error 467
D. The Standard of Judicial Review for Fact: Future Prospects 470
(1) Standard of Proof 470
(2) Standard of Judicial Review 471
(3) A Differential Standard of Judicial Review 471
(4) Judicial Review and Institutional Capacity 473
7. Discretion, Manifest Error, and Hard Look 474
A. Substantive Review and Judicial Choice: Two Techniques 474
B. Substantive Review and Judicial Choice: US Law 475
C. Substantive Review and Judicial Choice: Manifest Error 477
8. Conclusion 481

14. Rights 483

1. Introduction 483
2. The Evolution of Fundamental Rights 484
   A. The Judicial Contribution 484
   B. The Political and Legislative Contribution 486
3. Concerns Prior to the Charter of Fundamental Rights 488
   A. Community Rights and National Differences 488
   B. Taking Rights Seriously 489
   C. Rights and General Principles 490
   D. The Relationship between the EC and the ECHR 490
   E. The Need for a Coherent Human Rights Policy 491
4. The Charter of Fundamental Rights of the European Union: Genesis 492
5. The Charter of Fundamental Rights of the European Union: Content 494
6. The Charter and the Constitutional Treaty 497
7. The Reach of the Charter: Union Institutions, Verticality, and Horizontality 498
   A. The Distinction 498
   B. The Normative Argument 499
   C. The Distinction Qualified 501
8. The Reach of the Charter: Member States, Verticality, and Horizontality 502
   A. The Meaning of Implementation 502
   B. Scope of Application 504
   C. Verticality and Horizontality 505
9. The Reach of the Charter: Existing EU Law and Competence 506
10. Charter Interpretation: Rights and Principles 508
    A. The Rationale for the Divide 508
    B. The Nature of the Divide 509
    C. The Consequences of the Divide 511
11. Charter Interpretation: The General Limitation Clause 512
12. Charter Interpretation: Existing EU Law and Consistent Interpretation 517
    A. Charter Rights and Treaty Rights 518
    B. Charter Rights and Community Legislation 518
    C. Charter Rights, Treaty Rights, and the Courts' Jurisprudence 520
    D. To Replicate or Not 522
13. Charter Interpretation: The Relationship with the ECHR 523
    A. Charter Rights that Correspond to ECHR Rights 523
    B. Charter Rights To Be Given the Same Meaning and Scope 524

C. Relationship between the EU and the ECHR in the Absence of Accession 525
(1) The ECJ's Perspective 525
(2) The ECHR's Perspective: The General Approach 525
(3) The ECHR's Perspective: Qualification to the General Approach 527
(4) The ECHR's Perspective: The Concurring Opinion by Judge Ress 530
D. Relationship between the EU and the ECHR if the EU Accedes 531
14. Charter Interpretation: The Relationship with National Constitutions 532
A. The Interpretative Obligation 533
B. The Substantive Obligation 533
15. Charter Interpretation: The Relationship with International Law 535
16. The Charter, Rights, and Remedies 537
17. The Legal Status of the Charter 538
18. Human Rights Policy for the European Union 539
19. Conclusion 543

15. Equality 545

1. Introduction 545
2. The Four Freedoms, Nationality, and Equal Treatment 546
A. Economic and Social Rationales 546
B. Discrimination and Equal Treatment 547
C. Equal Treatment and the Interplay between the Economic and Social Rationale 549
(1) The Definition of Worker 549
(2) The Benefits Given to Workers 551
(3) The Public Service Exception 555
3. Article 12 EC, Nationality and Equal Treatment 559
A. Economic and Social Rationales 559
B. Article 12 EC as an Interpretative Device in Relation to the Four Freedoms 560
C. Article 12 EC as Protector of the Objectives Underlying the Four Freedoms 562
D. Article 12 EC and the Implementation of Community Legislation 564
E. Article 12 EC, Gravier and the 'Scope of Application' of the Treaty 565
F. Article 12 EC, Citizenship and the 'Scope of Application' of the Treaty 567

(1) The First Juridical Technique: *Martinez Sala* and *Trojani* 569
(2) The Second Juridical Technique: *Grzelczyk* and *Bidar* 572
(3) The Third Juridical Technique: *Collins* 575

G. Conclusion 576

4. Common Policies, Equal Treatment, and Constraints on Regulation 578
A. The Regulatory Role of Equal Treatment 578
B. Comparability and Objective Justification: *Ruckdeschel* and *Royal Scholten-Honig* 581
C. Comparability, Objective Justification, and Arbitrariness 582
D. Conclusion 585

5. Article 141, Sex Discrimination and Equal Treatment 585
A. Economic and Social Rationales 585
B. Equal Pay 588
C. Equal Treatment 593
(1) The Limits of Equal Treatment: Affirmative Action 595
(2) The Limits of Equal Treatment: Sex and Sexual Orientation 599

6. Article 13 EC, the Race and Framework Directives and Equal Treatment 600
A. Economic and Social Rationales 600
B. The Race and Framework Directives 602

7. Conclusion 603

16. Legal Certainty and Legitimate Expectations 607

1. Introduction 607
2. Legal Certainty and Actual Retroactivity: Procedural and Substantive Constraints 607
3. Legal Certainty, Legitimate Expectations, and Apparent Retroactivity: Types of Case and Rationale for Protection 610
4. Revocation of Lawful Decisions 614
A. The General Principle: Favourable Decisions Bind 614
B. Qualifications to the General Principle: Consent and Fraud 617
C. Qualifications to the General Principle: Conditional Decisions 618
D. Qualifications to the General Principle: Change of Policy 619

5. Revocation of Unlawful Decisions 621
A. The Nature of the Problem: Legality v Justice 621
B. The Divide between Illegality and Legality 622

C. Retroactive Revocation: Balancing 623
D. Prospective Revocation: Balancing? 626
6. Departure from Individual Representations 627
A. The Nature of the Representation: Precise and Specific Assurance 628
B. The Conduct of the Representee: The Prudent Trader 631
C. The Conduct of the Representee: The Legitimacy of the Claim 633
7. Representations and Changes in Policy 635
A. The General Principle: Mutability and No Legitimate Expectation 635
B. The Exceptions: Bargain, Assurance, and Legitimate Expectation 637
C. Overriding Public Interest: The Balancing Exercise 639
8. Departure from Existing Policy/Guidelines 641
A. The General Principle: Guidelines Bind 641
B. Application of the General Principle: Judicial Construction of Guidelines 644
C. Qualification to the General Principle: The Scope of the Guidelines 647
D. Qualification to the General Principle: Discretion Inherent In or Left By the Guidelines 648
9. Representations, the Balancing Exercise, and the Legal Test 649
A. The Nature of the Legal Test 649
B. The Application of the Test 651
10. Unlawful Representations 652
A. Positive Law 652
B. Normative Considerations 653
11. Conclusion 654

17. Proportionality I 655

1. Introduction 655
2. The Meaning of Proportionality 655
3. Proportionality and Discretionary Policy Choices 658
A. Common Policies: Agriculture and Fisheries 658
B. Common Policies: Transport 664
C. Anti-Dumping 665
D. Inter-institutional Controls 666
E. Evaluation: Suitability, Necessity, and Manifest Disproportionality 668
F. Evaluation: *Stricto Sensu* Proportionality, the Third Limb of the Test 670

4. Proportionality and Rights 672
   A. Rights Enshrined in the Treaty or Community Legislation 672
   B. Discretionary Policies, Fundamental Rights, and Proportionality 674
   C. Evaluation 678
5. Proportionality, Penalties, and Financial Burden 681
   A. The General Approach 681
   B. Proportionality, Penalties, and Legislative Objectives 682
   C. Penalties and Unlimited Jurisdiction 684
   D. Evaluation 684
6. Conclusion 685

18. Proportionality II 687
1. Introduction 687
2. Positive Law: The Four Freedoms 687
   A. Goods 689
   B. Workers and Persons 692
   C. Establishment and the Provision of Services 692
3. Positive Law: Equality and Discrimination 695
   A. Equal Treatment 695
   B. Equal Pay 698
4. Positive Law: Application of Community Legislation 701
5. Positive Law: The Impact of Article 10 EC 703
6. Normative Considerations: The Intensity of Review 704
   A. Justification for Strict Proportionality Scrutiny 704
   B. Proportionality and Sensitivity to National Values 706
   C. Proportionality and Sensitivity to Differences in National Values 708
7. Normative Considerations: The Role of the National Courts and the Complexity of the Proportionality Inquiry 711
8. Conclusion 715

19. The Precautionary Principle 717
1. Introduction 717
2. A New General Principle of EU Law 718
   A. Foundations 718
   B. Development 719
3. The Precautionary Principle and Review of Community Action 722
   A. *Pfizer* 722
      (1) Interpretation of the Precautionary Principle 722
      (2) Application of the Precautionary Principle 724
   B. *Artegodan* 727
      (1) Interpretation of the Precautionary Principle 727
      (2) Application of the Precautionary Principle 728

C. *Monsanto* 730
4. The Precautionary Principle and Review of Member State Action 731
A. Member State Compliance with Environmental Directives 731
B. Member States and the Four Freedoms 733
C. Member States and the Interpretation of Community Legislation 735
5. The Precautionary Principle, Politics, and the Commission Communication 735
6. The Precautionary Principle, Academic Discourse, and the EU 738
A. The Academic Discourse 738
B. The Precautionary Principle and Political Decision-Making in the EU: An Evaluative Strategy 741
C. The Precautionary Principle and Political Decision-Making in the EU: Food Safety 743
D. The Precautionary Principle and Legal Decision-Making in the EU 746
7. Conclusion 748

20. Remedies I: The Community 749

1. Introduction 749
2. Interim Measures 750
A. Direct Actions 750
B. Indirect Actions 752
C. Assessment 754
3. Annulment 755
A. Direct Actions: Articles 231 and 233 EC 755
B. Direct Actions: Article 231 EC 756
C. Direct Actions: Article 233 EC 758
D. Indirect Actions: The Analogous Application of Articles 231 and 233 761
E. Assessment 763
4. Damages Liability: Scope 764
5. Damages and Annulment 765
6. Damages Liability: Discretionary Acts 766
A. The *Schöppenstedt* Test 766
B. Superior Rule of Law 767
C. Flagrant Violation/Serious Breach: The Early Case Law 769
D. Flagrant Violation/Serious Breach: The Current Test 771
7. Damages Liability: Non-Discretionary Acts 773
A. The Test 773
B. Discretionary and Non-Discretionary Acts 774
C. The Meaning of Illegality 774

8. Damages Liability: Causation and Damage 775
A. Causation 776
B. Damage 777
9. Damages Liability: Community Servants 780
10. Damages Liability: Lawful Acts 781
11. Restitution 782
12. Joint Liability of the Community and the Member States 784
A. Procedural Issues 784
B. Substantive Issues: Wrongful Authorization of National Action 785
C. Substantive Issues: Application of Unlawful Legislation by a Member State 785
13. Damages Liability: Assessment 787

21. Remedies II: Member States 789
1. Introduction 789
2. National Remedial Autonomy: The Initial Limits 789
3. National Remedial Autonomy and Effectiveness of Community Law 791
A. Effectiveness and 'New' Remedies 791
B. Effectiveness of Community Law: Proportionality and Adequacy of National Remedies 793
C. Effectiveness of Community Law: The Temporal Effect of Preliminary Rulings 794
4. National Remedial Autonomy and Effectiveness of Community Law: Judicial Expansion 795
A. The Adequacy of the National Monetary Remedy 795
B. Substantive Conditions Attached to the National Remedy 796
C. Sustainability of National Time Limits 797
5. National Remedial Autonomy and Effectiveness of Community Law: Judicial Retreat 799
A. The Limiting of *Marshall II* 799
B. The Limiting of *Emmott* 800
C. The Implications for *Marshall II* 803
6. National Remedial Autonomy and Effectiveness of Community Law: A Nuanced Approach 803
A. National Courts and Consideration of Community Law at their own Motion 804
B. Limitation Periods 806
C. Recovery of Interest 808
D. Recovery of Sums Unduly Levied 810
E. Recovery of Sums Unduly Paid 811
F. Cause of Action 812

7. National Remedial Autonomy and Effectiveness of Community Law: An Assessment 813
8. State Liability: The *Francovich* Foundations 815
9. State Liability: The *Brasserie du Pêcheur/Factortame* Criteria 817
A. The Three Part Test 817
B. The Relevance of Discretion 819
C. Interpretation and Application: The ECJ's 'Guidance' 820
10. State Liability Post *Brasserie du Pêcheur/Factortame*: Judicial Acts 821
11. State Liability Post *Brasserie du Pêcheur/Factortame*: Serious Breach 822
A. The Serious Breach Test: The ECJ Resolves the Issue 822
B. The Serious Breach Test: The ECJ Leaves the Issue to the National Court 824
12. State Liability Post *Brasserie du Pêcheur/Factortame*: The Relationship with National Remedial Regimes 824
A. Who Pays 825
B. Equivalence and Effectiveness 826
13. State Liability: An Assessment 827

22. The Ombudsman (by Dr A. Tsadiras) 829
1. The Institutional History of the Ombudsman 829
2. The Powers of the European Ombudsman 832
A. The Initiation of Inquiries 833
(1) The Reactive Role: Responding to Complaints 833
(2) The Proactive Role: Own Initiative Inquiries 838
B. Investigative Powers 840
C. Remedial Powers 843
3. The Notion of Maladministration 847
4. The European Ombudsman and the Community Courts 851
5. Conclusion 855

Index 857

Table of Cases

Cases are listed in alphabetical order

COURT OF FIRST INSTANCE

ABB Asea Brown Boveri Ltd v Commission (Case T-31/99) [2002] ECR II-1881 .... 376, 636
Aden v Council and Commission (Case T-306/01) [2002] ECR II-2387 750
AFCon Management Consultants v Commission (Case T-160/03) judgment of 17 March 2005 779
Afrikanische Frucht-Compagnie GmbH v Commission (Cases T-64–65/01) judgment of 10 February 2004 .... 636, 782
Agrana Zucker and Stark AG v Commission (Case 187/99) [2001] ECR II-1587 .... 376, 382
Air France v Commission (Case T-2/93) [1994] ECR II-323 652
Air Inter SA v Commission (Case T-260/94) [1997] ECR II-997 .... 315, 316, 361, 519
Airtours plc v Commission (Case T-342/99) [2002] ECR II-2585 ..... 452, 454, 456, 465, 466, 469
AIUFFASS v Commission (Case T-380/94) [1996] ECR II-2169 318
Aloys Schröder v Commission (Case T-390/94) [1997] ECR II-501 ... 774
Alpharma Inc v Council (Case T-70/99) [2002] ECR II-3495 .... 317, 438, 447, 629, 633, 662, 722, 746
Antillean Rice Mills NV v Commission (Cases T-480 and 483/93) [1995] ECR II-2305 .... 759, 767
APOL and AIPO v Commission (Cases T-61 and 62/00) [2003] ECR II-635 683
Archer Daniels Midland Company and Archer Daniels Midland Ingredients Ltd v Commission (Case T-224/00) [2003] ECR II-2597 .... 684, 759
Area Cova SA v Council (Case T-196/99) [2001] ECR II-3597 635
Arizona Chemical v Commission (Case T-369/03), judgment of 16 January 2004 752
Armement Cooperatif Artisanal Vendeen (ACAV) v Council (Case T-138/98) [1999] ECR II-1797 335
Artegodan GmbH v Commission (Cases T-74, 76, 83–85, 132, 137 and 141/00) [2002] ECR II-4945 .... 115, 167, 397, 478, 720, 721, 727, 729, 746, 747, 748

Asia Motor France SA v Commission (Case T-7/92) [1993] ECR II-669 .... 376, 382, 397, 479
Asia Motor France SA v Commission (Case T-154/98) [2000] ECR II-3453 376
Asia Motor France SA v Commission (Case T-387/94) [1996] ECR II-961 .... 376, 382, 759
Asociacion Espanalo de Empresas de la Carne (ASOCARNE) v Council (Case T-99/94) [1994] ECR II-871 134
ASPEC v Commission (Case T-435/93) [1995] ECR II-1281 318
Assidoman Kraft Products AB v Commission (Case T-227/95) [1997] ECR II-1185 616
Associacao Comercial de Aveiro v Commission (Case T-81/00) [2002] ECR II-2509 462
Associazione delle Cantine Sociali Venete v European Ombudsmen and Parliament (Case T-103/99) [2000] ECR II-4165 854
Astipeca SL v Commission (Case T-180/00) [2002] ECR II-3985 683
Atlantic Container Line AB v Commission (Cases T-191, 212, 214/98) [2003] ECR II-3275 .... 376, 648, 759
Atlantic Container Line v Commission (Case T-395/94) [1995] ECR II-2893 751
Automec Srl v Commission (Case T-24/90) [1992] ECR II-2223 375
Azienda Agricola 'Le Canne' Srl v Commission (Case T-241/00) [2002] ECR II-1251 .... 375, 382

Banan-Kompaniet AB and Skandinaviska Bananimporten AB v Council and Commission (Case T-57/00) [2003] ECR II-607 .... 772, 777
Banatrading GmbH v Council (Case T-3/99) [2001] ECR II-2123 768
BASF AG v Commission (Cases T-79, 84–86, 89, 91–92, 94, 96, 98, 102, 104/89) [1992] ECR II-315 268
BASF Lacke & Farben AG v Commission (Case T-175/95) [1999] ECR II-1581 367
Bayer AG v Commission (Case T-41/96) [2000] ECR II-3383 435
Bocchi Food Trade International GmbH v Commission (Case T-30/99) [2001] ECR II-943 .... 463, 660
Boehringer Ingleheim Vetmedica GmbH and CH Boehringer Sohn v Council and Commission (Cases 125 and 152/96) [1999] ECR II-3427 .... 660, 671, 675
BPB Industries plc and British Gypsum Ltd v Commission (Case T-65/89) [1993] ECR II-389 366
British Airways plc and British Midland Airways Ltd v Commission (Cases T-371 and 394/94) [1998] ECR II-2405 375

British Airways plc v Commission (Case T-219/99) [2003] ECR II-5917 684
British American Tobacco International (Investments) Ltd v Commission (Case T-111/00) [2001] ECR II-2997 358
Browet v Commission (Cases T-576–582/94) [1994] ECR II-677 633
Bureau Européen des Médias de l'Industrie Musicale (BEMIM) v Commission (Case T-144/92) [1995] ECR II-147 .... 375, 758
Bureau Européen des Unions Consommateurs and National Consumer Council v Commission (Case T-37/92) [1994] ECR II-285 .... 134, 375

C v Council (Case T-84/98) [2000] ECR IA-113 779
Camar Srl and Tico Srl v Commission (Cases T-79/96, 260/97, 117/98) [2000] ECR II-2193 .... 773, 774, 775, 778
Camar Srl v Council (Case T-260/97) judgment of 13 July 2005 778
Campo Ebro v Commission (Case T-472/93) [1995] ECR II-421 767
Carvel and Guardian Newpapers Ltd v Council (Case T-194/94) [1995] ECR II-2765 353
CEMR v Commission (Cases T-46 and 151/98) [2000] ECR II-167 .... 619, 620, 628, 630
CETM v Commission (Case T-55/99) [2000] ECR II-3207 683
CEVA Sante Animale SA and Pharmacia Enterprises SA v Commission (Cases T-344–345/00) [2003] ECR II-229 .... 463, 777
Chomel v Commission (Case T-123/89) [1990] ECR II-131 615
Cobrecaf v Commission (Case T-514/93) [1995] ECR II-621 777
Comafrica SpA and Dole Fresh Fruit Europa Ltd & Co v Commission (Cases T-198/95, 171/96, 230/97, 174/98 and 225/98) [2001] ECR II-1975 .... 773, 775, 778
Comafrica SpA and Dole Fresh Fruit Europe & Co Ltd v Commission (Case T-139/01) judgment of 3 February 2005 .... 773, 778
Communita Montana della Valnerina v Commission (Case T-340/00) [2003] ECR II-811 .... 92, 683
Conserve Italia Soc. Coop rl v Commission (Case T-186/00) [2003] ECR II-719 683
Conserve Italia Soc. Coop rl v Commission (Case T-305/00) [2003] ECR II-5705 .... 683, 684
Consorzio Gruppo di Azioni Locale Murgia Messapica v Commission (Case T-456/93) [1994] ECR II-361 628
Cordis Obst und Gemuse GrossHandel GmbH v Commission (Case T-18/99) [2001] ECR II-913 .... 635, 637, 768, 787
Corus UK Ltd v Commission (Case T-171/99) [2001] ECR II-2967 .... 757, 783, 784

Danielsson v Commission (Case T-219/95) [1995] ECR II-3051 752

Dieckmann & Hansen GmbH v Commission (Case T-155/99) [2001] ECR II-3143 .... 640, 651
DIR International Film Srl v Commission (Cases T-369/94 and 85/95) [1998] ECR II-357 .... 162, 643
Dorsch Consult (Case T-184/95) [1998] ECR II-667 .... 777, 782
Dubois et Fils SA v Council and Commission (Case T-113/96) [1998] ECR II-125 675

Eduardo Vieira SA, Vieira Argentina SA and Pescanova SA v Commission (Cases T-44, 119, 126/01) [2003] ECR II-1209 765
Efisol SA v Commission (Case T-336/94) [1996] ECR II-1343 .... 632, 639, 773
Embassy Limousines & Services v European Parliament (Case T-203/96) [1998] ECR II-4239 630
Emesa Sugar (Free Zone) NV v Council (Case T-43/98) [2001] ECR II-3519 635
EnBW Kernkraft GmbH v Commission (Case T-283/02) judgment of 16 March 2005 .... 628, 773
Enso Espanola SA v Commission (Case T-348/94) [1998] ECR II-1875 371
ENU v Commission (Cases T-458 and 523/93) [1995] ECR II-2459 774
Eridania v Council (Case T-168/95) [1995] ECR II-2817 751
Estabelecimentos Isidore M.Oliviera SA v Commission (Case T-73/95) [1997] ECR II-381 634
Etablissments Biret et Cie SA v Council (Case T-210/00) [2002] ECR II-47 777
Eugenio Branco Ld v Commission (Case T-347/03) judgment of 30 June 2005 634
Euroagri Srl v Commission (Case T-180/01) judgment of 28 January 2004 617
Europe Chemi-Con (Deutschland) GmbH v Council (Case T-89/00) [2002] ECR II-3651 760
European Night Services v Commission (Cases T-374, 375, 384 and 388/94) [1998] ECR II-3141 .... 389, 479
Eyckeler & Malt AG v Commission (Case T-42/96) [1998] ECR II-401 .... 364, 365, 367

Féderation Française des Sociétés d'Assurances (FFSA) v Commission (Case T-106/95) [1997] ECR II-229 435
Ferriere Nord SpA v Commission (Case T-176/01) judgment of 18 November 2004 646

Firma Leon Van Parys NV and Pacific Fruit Company NV v Commission (Case T-160/98) [2002] ECR II-233 786
Forde-Reederie GmbH v Council and Commission (Case T-170/00) [2002] ECR II-515 782
France-Aviation v Commission (Case T-346/94) [1995] ECR II-2843 .... 315, 364
François v Commission (Case T-307/01) judgment of 10 June 2004 .... 759, 779
François Vainker and Brenda Vainker v European Parliament (Case T-48/01) judgment of 3 March 2004 779
Frank Lamberts v European Ombudsman (Case T-209/00) [2002] ECR II-2203 855
Fresh Marine Company SA v Commission (Case T-178/98) [2000] ECR II-3331 .... 765, 773, 774, 775, 777

GE Betz, Inc, formerly BetzDearborn Inc v OHIM (Case T-107/02) judgment of 30 June 2004 628
Graphischer Maschinenbau GmbH v Commission (Case T-126/99) [2002] ECR II-2427 .... 460, 758
Grynberg and Hall v Commission (Case T-534/93) [1994] ECR II-595 628

Hameico Stuttgart GmbH v Council and Commission (Case T-99/98) [2003] ECR II-2195 .... 765, 778, 782
Hercules Chemicals NV v Commission (Case T-7/89) [1991] ECR II-1711 .... 373, 481, 628
Hijos de Andres Molina SA (HAMSA) v Commission (Case T-152/99) [2002] ECR II-3049 .... 432, 435
Hirsch, Nicastro and Priesemann v ECB (Cases T-94, 152 and 286/01) [2003] ECR II-1 761
Holcim (Deutschland) AG v Commission (Case T-28/03) judgment of 21 April 2005 .... 759, 783
Hyper Srl v Commission (Case T-205/99) [2002] ECR II-3141 367

ICI v Commission (Cases T-36–37/91) [1995] ECR II-1847 367
Industrias Quimicas del Valles, SA v Commission (Case T-158/03) judgment of 28 June 2005 660
Industrie des Poudres Spheriques SA v Commission (Case T-5/97) [2000] ECR II-3755 376
Innova Privat-Akademie GmbH v Commission (Case T-273/01) [2003] ECR II-1093 628

Interhotels-Sociedade Internacional de Hoteis SARL v Commission (Case T-81/95) [1997] ECR II-1265 .... 618, 619, 620
International Express Carriers Conference v Commission (Cases T-133 and 204/95) [1998] ECR II-3645 463
International Potash Company v Council (Case T-87/98) [2000] ECR II-3179 65
International Procurement Services v Commission (Case T-175/94) [1996] ECR II-729 773

Jego-Quere v Commission (Case T-177/01) [2002] ECR II-2365 339
JFE Engineering Corp v Commission (Cases T-67, 68, 71 and 78/00) judgment of 8 July 2004 648

Kaufring AG v Commission (Cases T-186, 187, 190, 192, 210, 211, 216–218, 279–280, 293/97) [2001] ECR II-1337 .... 364, 367
Kuijer v Council (Case T-211/00) [2002] ECR II-485 354
Kusterman v Council and Commission (Case T-201/94) [2002] ECR II-415 764
Kyowa Hakko Kogyo Co Ltd and Kyowa Hakko Europe GmbH v Commission (Case T-223/00) [2003] ECR II-2553 .... 628, 648, 684

La Cinq SA v Commission (Case T-44/90) [1992] ECR II-1 ...... 397, 479
Ladbroke Racing Ltd v Commission (Case T-67/94) [1998] ECR II-1 758
Laga v Commission (Case T-93/95) [1998] ECR II-195 765
Lagardere SCA and Canal SA v Commission (Case T-251/00) [2002] ECR II-4825 .... 615, 622, 625, 627
Lamberts v Commission (Case T-209/00) [2002] ECR II-2203 764
Lenzing AG v Commission (Case T-36/99) judgment of 21 October 2004 432
Les Laboratories Servier v Commission (Case T-147/00) [2003] ECR II-85 .... 721, 735
Lilly Industries Ltd v Commission (Case T-120/96) [1998] ECR II-2571 268
Limburgse Vinyl Maatschappij NV v Commission (Case T-305–7, 313–6, 318, 325, 328–9 and 335/94) [1999] ECR II-931 .... 756, 761
Lisrestal v Commission (Case T-450/93) [1994] ECR II-1177 ... 315, 316, 361
LR AF 1998 A/S v Commission (Case T-23/99) [2002] ECR II-1705 636

Malagutti-Vezinhet SA v Commission (Case T-177/02) judgment of 10 March 2004 722

Martinez, Charles de Gaulle, Front National and Emma Bonino v EP (Cases T-222, 327 and 329/99) [2001] ECR II-2823 .... 630, 673
Maurissen v Court of Auditors (Case T-23/91) [1992] ECR II-2377 ... 463
max.mobil Telekommunikation Service GmbH v Commission (Case T-54/99) [2002] ECR II-313 .... 379, 385
MCI, Inc v Commission (Case T-310/00) judgment of 28 September 2004 .... 628, 630
Medici Grimm KG v Council (Case T-7/99) [2000] ECR II-2671 .... 608, 783
Mehibas Dordrselaan BV v Commission (Case T-290/97) [2000] ECR II-15 .... 373, 628
Merck & Co Inc, NV Organon and Glaxo Wellcome plc v Commission (Case T-60/96) [1997] ECR II-849 318
Metropole Television SA v Commission (Case T-206/99) [2001] ECR II-1057 .... 376, 382, 760
Meyer v Commission (Case T-72/99) [2000] ECR II-2521 628
Meyer v Commission (Case T-333/01) [2003] ECR II-117 777
Moccia Irme v Commission (Case T-164/96) [1996] ECR II-2261 751
Montan Gesellschaft Voss mbH Stahlhandel v Commission (Case T-163/02) [2002] ECR II-3219 .... 751, 752

NMB France SARL v Commission (Case T-162/94) [1996] ECR II-427 665
Nolle v Council (Case T-167/94) [1995] ECR II-2589 .... 374, 787

Odigitria v Council and Commission (Case T-572/93) [1995] ECR II-2025 777
O'Dwyer v Council (Cases T-466, 469, 473, 474 and 477/93) [1996] ECR II-2071 .... 632, 768
Olivieri v Commission and EMEA (Case T-326/99) [2003] ECR II-6053 729
Opel Austria GmbH v Council (Case T-115/94) [1997] ECR II-2739 608
Organizacion de Productores de Tunidos Congelados (OPTUC) v Commission (Cases T-142 and 283/01) judgment of 28 January 2004 632

P & O European Ferries (Vizcaya) SA and Diputacion Foral de Vizcaya v Commission (Cases T-116 and 118/01) [2003] ECR II-2957 812
Partex-Companhia Portugesa de Servicos SA v Commission (Case T-182/96) [1999] ECR II-2673 463
Peix, SA v Commission (Case T-125/01) [2003] ECR II-865 758

Petrie v Commission (Case T-191/99) [2001] ECR II-3677 .... 352, 853
Petrotub and Republica SA v Council (Cases T-33–34/98) [1999] ECR II-3837 .... 315, 361, 519, 665
Pfizer Animal Health SA v Council (Case T-13/99) [2002] ECR II-3305 .... 115, 184, 317, 333, 381, 438, 439, 447, 448, 450, 451, 469, 479, 662, 663, 671, 675, 719, 720, 721, 722, 725, 746, 747, 752
Pfizer Ltd v Commission (Case T-123/03) judgment of 2 June 2004 .... 268, 396, 397
Philip Morris International Inc v Commission (Cases T-377, 379, 380/00, 260 and 272/01) [2003] ECR II-1 .... 268, 438
Pollmeier Malchow GmbH & Co KG v Commission (Case T-137/02) judgment of 14 October 2004 .... 433, 644
Primex Produkte Import-Export GmbH & Co KG v Commission (Case T-50/96) [1998] ECR II-3773 .... 315, 316, 361, 364, 367

Regione Autonoma della Sardegna v Commission (Case T-171/02) judgment of 15 June 2005 633
Regione Autonoma Friuli-Venezia Giulia v Commission (Case T-288/97) [2001] ECR II-1169 .... 460, 683
Regione Toscana v Commission (Case T-81/97) [1998] ECR II-2889 268
Rica Foods (Free Zone) NV and Free Trade Foods NV v Commission (Cases T-332 and 350/00) [2002] ECR II-4755 463
Ricosmos BV v Commission (Case T-53/02) judgment of 13 September 2005 367
Riviera Auto Service Etablissements Dalmasso SA v Commission (Cases T-185, 189, 190/96) [1999] ECR II-93 375
Rothmans International v Commission (Case T-188/97) [1999] ECR II-2463 .... 110, 354

SA Cimenteries CBR (Cases T-10–12, 15/92) [1992] ECR II-2667 268
SA Hercules Chemicals NV v Commission (Case T-7/89) [1991] ECR II-1711 366
Saint v Council (Case T-554/93) [1997] ECR II-563 268
Salzgitter AG v Commission (Case T-308/00) judgment of 1 July 2004 460
Scan Office Design SA v Commission (Case T-40/01) [2002] ECR II-5043 776
Schneider Electric SA v Commission (Case T-310/01) [2002] ECR II-4071 761
Schultze v Council and Commission (Case T-261/94) [2002] ECR II-441 .... 764, 777

Scippacercola v Commission (Case T-187/03) judgment of 17 March 2005 357
Sgaravatti Mediterranea Srl v Commission (Case T-199/99) [2002] ECR II-3731 .... 92, 462, 634, 683
SIC-Sociedade Independente de Communicacao, SA v Commission (Cases T-297–298/01) judgment of 19 February 2004 759
Siemens v Commission (Case T-459/93) [1995] ECR II-1675 376
Sison v Council (Cases T-110, 150, 405/03) judgment of 25 April 2005 356
Smets v Commission (Case T-134/96) [1997] ECR II-2333 642
Société Français de Transports Gondrand Frères v Commission (Cases T-104/02) judgment of 21 September 2004 758
Solvay Pharmaceuticals BV v Council (Case T-392/02) [2003] ECR II-4555 .... 721, 746
Solvay SA v Commission (Cases T-30–32/91) [1995] ECR II-1775 .... 367, 373
Sonasa-Sociedade de Seguranca Ld v Commission (Case T-126/97) [1999] ECR II-2793 .... 619, 634
Stadtsportverband Neuss eV v Commission (Case T-137/01) [2003] ECR II-3103 619
Stahlwerke Peine-Salzgitter v Commission (Case T-120/89) [1991] ECR II-279 771
Stichting Greenpeace Council (Greenpeace International) v Commission (Case T-585/93) [1995] ECR II-2205 .... 134, 318
Sumitomo Chemical (UK) plc v Commission (Case T-78/04) judgment of 2 July 2004 .... 750, 751, 752
Svenska Journalistforbundet v Council (Case T-174/95) [1998] ECR II-2289 354
Sytraval and Brink's France v Commission (Case T-95/94) [1995] ECR II-2651 .... 377, 395, 396

Technische Glaswerke Ilmenau GmbH v Commission (Case T-198/01) [2004] ECR II-2717 .... 379, 380, 383, 395, 462, 750, 751
Territorio Historico de Alava-Diputacion Foral de Alava v Commission (Cases T-127, 129 and 148/99) [2002] ECR II-1275 435
Tetra Laval BV v Commission (Case T-5/02) [2002] ECR II-4381 .... 367, 453, 454, 455, 456, 457, 458, 466, 468, 469, 470, 472, 473
Thessalonikis v Commission (Case T-196/01) [2003] ECR II-3987 .... 93, 759
Tideline Signal Ltd v Commission (Case T-211/02) [2002] ECR II-3781 .... 379, 385, 685, 760, 761

T. Port & Co KG v Commission (Case T-52/99) [2001] ECR II-981 .... 463, 635, 778
Tremblay v Commission (Case T-5/93) [1995] ECR II-185 384
Turco v Council (Case T-84/03) judgment of 23 November 2004 .... 357, 358
TWD Textilwerke Deggendorf GmbH v Commission (Cases T-244 and 486/93) [1995] ECR II-2265 462

UEAPME v Council (Case T-135/96) [1998] ECR II-2335 .... 134, 245, 246, 255, 257, 260, 317
Unifruit Hellas EPE v Commission (Case T-489/93) [1994] ECR II-1201 .... 628, 632
Union Francaise de l'Express (Ufex), DHL International, Service CRIE and May Courier v Commission (Case T-77/95) [2000] ECR II-2167 376
UPS Europe SA v Commission (Case T-127/98) [1999] ECR II-2633 758

Van den Bergh Foods Ltd v Commission (Case T-65/98) [2003] ECR II-4653 628
Vela Srl and Tecnagrind SL v Commission (Cases 141–142, 150–151/99) [2002] ECR II-4547 619
Ventouris Group Enterprises SA v Commission (Case T-59/99) [2003] ECR II-5257 684
Verein fur Konsumenteninformation v Commission (Case T-2/03) judgment of 13 April 2005 .... 355, 673
Vereniging van Exporteurs in Levende Varkens v Commission (Cases T-481 and 484/93) [1995] ECR II-2941 .... 757, 767, 771, 773
Vlaams Fonds voor de Sociale Integratie van Personen met een Handicap v Commission (Case T-102/00) [2003] ECR II-2433 .... 315, 316, 361
Vlaamse Gewest v Commission (Case T-214/95) [1998] ECR II-717 643
Vlaamse Televisie Maatschappij NV v Commission (Case T-266/97) [1999] ECR II-2329 363
Volkswagen AG v Commission (Case T-62/98) [2000] ECR II-2707 376

Westdeutsche Landesbank Girozentrale and Land Nordrhein-Westfalen v Commission (Cases T-228 and 233/99) [2003] ECR II-435 .... 376, 379
Williams v Court of Auditors (Case T-33/91) [1992] ECR II-2499 642

Wirtschaftsvereinigung Stahl v Commission (Case T-244/94) [1997] ECR II-1963 463
WWF UK (World Wide Fund for Nature) v Commission (Case T-105/95) [1997] ECR II-313 .... 353, 354

Yassin Abdullah Kadi v Council and Commission (Case T-315/01) judgment of 21 September 2005 .... 535, 536, 677, 678

EUROPEAN COURT OF JUSTICE

Aalborg Portland v Commission (Cases C-204–205, 211, 213, 217, 219/00) [2004] ECR I-123 .... 364, 368, 369, 370, 373, 398, 684
Aannemersbedrijf P.K.Kraajeveld BV v Gedeputeerde Staten van Zuid-Holland (Case C-72/95) [1996] ECR I-5403 806
Abertal v Commission (Case C-213/91) [1991] ECR I-5109 751
Abrahamsson v Fogelqvist (Case C-407/98) [2000] ECR I-5539 598
Abrias v Commission (Case 3/83) [1985] ECR 1995 633
Acciaieriere Ferriere e Fonerie di Modena v High Authority (Case 16/61) [1962] ECR 289 582
Adams v Commission (Case 145/83) [1985] ECR 3539 777
Adoui and Cornuaille v Belgian State (Cases 115 and 116/81) [1982] ECR 1665 708
Aerpo v Commission (Case C-119/88) [1990] ECR I-2189 .... 767, 768
Affish BV v Rijksdienst voor de keuring van Vee en Vlees (Case C-183/95) [1997] ECR I-4315 .... 61, 641, 651, 670, 671
Ahlstrom Osakeyhitio v Commission (Cases C-89, 104, 114, 116, 117, 125–9/85) [1993] ECR I-1307 470
Aktien-Zuckerfabrik Schöppenstedt v Council (Case 5/71) [1971] ECR 975 .... 765, 766, 767, 769, 787
AKZO Chemie BV v Commission (Case 53/85) [1986] ECR 1965 268
Al-Jubail Fertilizer v Council (Case C-49/88) [1991] ECR I-3187 .... 315, 317, 361, 519
Albany International BV v Stichting Bedrijfspensioenfonds Textielindustrie (Case C-67/96) [1999] ECR I-5751 .... 260, 586
Albert Heijin BV (Case 94/83) [1984] ECR 3263 689
Alfons Lütticke GmbH v Commission (Case 4/69) [1971] ECR 325 777
Algera v Common Assembly (Cases 7/56 and 3–7/57) [1957] ECR 39 .... 614, 620, 623, 626
Allonby v Accrington & Rossendale College, Education Lecturing Services, Trading as Protocol Professional and Secretary of State for Education and Employment (Case C-256/01) [2004] ECR I-873 ... 699

Allué and Coonan v Università degli Studi di Venezia (Case 33/88) [1989] ECR 1591 557
Alonso-Pérez v Bundesanstalt für Arbeit (Case C-394/93) [1995] ECR I-4101 802
Alpha Steel v Commission (Case 14/81) [1982] ECR 749 .... 616, 626
Alpine Investments BV v Minister van Financien (Case C-384/93) [1995] ECR I-1141 708
Ambulanz Glockner v Landkreis Sudwestpfalz (Case C-475/99) [2001] ECR I-8089 586
Amministrazione delle Finanze dello Stato v San Giorgio (Case 199/82) [1983] ECR 3595 .... 791, 810
Amministrazione delle Finanze dello Stato v Simmenthal SpA (Case 106/77) [1978] ECR 629 .... 285, 286, 792
Amministrazione delle Finanze dello Stato v Srl Meridionale Industria Salumi (Cases 212–217/80) [1981] ECR 2735 609
Ampafrance SA v Directeur des Services Fiscaux de Maine-et-Loire (Cases C-177 and 181/99) [2000] ECR I-7013 669
Amylum NV and Tunnel Refineries Ltd v Council and Commission (Cases 116 and 124/77) [1979] ECR 3497 .... 770, 777
Analir v Administracion General del Estado (Case C-205/99) [2001] ECR I-1271 694
Angelo Ferlini v Centre Hospitalier de Luxembourg (Case C-411/98) [2000] ECR I-8081 569
Angelo-pharm v Freie und Hansestadt Hamburg (Case C-212/91) [1994] ECR I-171 .... 115, 450, 725
Angestelltenbetriebsrat der Wiener Gebietskrankenkasse (Case C-309/97) [1999] ECR I-2865 590
Anker, Ras and Snoek v Germany (Case C-47/02) [2003] ECR I-10447 559
Annibaldi v Sindaco del Commune di Guidonia and Presidente Regione Lazio (Case C-309/96) [1997] ECR I-7493 .... 486, 503, 504
Anomar v Estado Portugues (Case C-6/01) [2003] ECR I-8621 709
Antillean Rice Mills NV v Commission (Case C-390/95) [1999] ECR I-769 .... 458, 767, 774
Aprile v Amministrazione delle Finanze dello Stato (Case C-229/96) [1998] ECR I-7141 .... 802, 807
Arbeiterwohlfahrt der Stadt Berlin v Bötel (Case C-360/90) [1992] ECR I-3589 .... 592, 700
ARCO Chemie Nederland Ltd v Minister van Volkshuisvesting, Rumtelijke Ordening en Milieubeheer (Cases C-418–419/97) [2000] ECR I-4475 732
Arnold Andre GmbH & Co KG v Landrat des Kreises Herford (Case C-434/02) [2004] ECR I-11825 660

Asociasion Espanola de Empresas de la Carne (Asocarne) v Council (Case C-10/95) [1995] ECR I-4149 .... 318, 332, 334
Associacao dos Refinadores de Acucar Portugueses (ARAP) v Commission (Case C-321/99) [2002] ECR I-4287 631
Association Greenpeace France v Ministere de l'Agriculture and de la Peche (Case C-6/99) [2000] ECR I-1651 .... 718, 730
Associazione Italiana per il World Wildlife Fund v Regione Veneto (Case C-118/94) [1996] ECR I-1223 290
Asteris AE and Hellenic Republic v Commission (Cases 97, 99, 193 and 215/86) [1988] ECR 2181 760
Asteris v Greece and EEC (Cases 106–120/87) [1988] ECR 5515 784
ASTI v Chambre des Employés Privés (Case C-213/90) [1991] ECR I-3507 557
ATB v Ministero per la Politiche Agricole (Case C-402/98) [2000] ECR I-5501 .... 635, 636
Atlanta AG v Commission and Council (Case C-104/97) [1999] ECR I-6983 .... 316, 317, 635
Atlanta Amsterdam BV v Produktschap voor Vee en Vlees (Case 240/78) [1979] ECR 2137 682
Atlanta Fruchhandelsgesellschaft mbH v Bundesamt fur Ernahrung und Forstwirtschaft (Case C-465/93) [1995] ECR I-3761 .... 752, 753
ATRAL SA v Belgium (Case C-14/02) [2003] ECR I-4431 688
Austria v Council (Case C-445/00) [2001] ECR I-1461 .... 750, 757
Azienda Agricola Giorgio v AIMA (Case C-495/00) [2004] ECR I-2993 611
Azienda Agricole Ettore Ribaldi v AIMA (Cases C-480–2, 484, 489, 490–1, 497–9/00) [2004] ECR I-2943 689

Bactria Industriehygiene-Service Verwaltungs GmbH v Commission (Case C-258/02) [2003] ECR I-15105 .... 317, 346
Badeck v Landesanwalt beim Staatsgerichshof des Landes Hessen (Case C-158/97) [1999] ECR I-1875 .... 597, 598
Banchero (Case C-157/92) [1993] ECR I-1085 289
Banco de Credito Industrial SA (Banco Exterior de Espana SA) v Ayuntamiento de Valencia (Case C-387/92) [1994] ECR I-877 435
BAT and Reynolds v Commission (Cases 142 and 156/84) [1987] ECR 4487 444
Baumbast and R v Secretary of State for the Home Department (Case C-413/99) [2002] ECR I-7091 692
Bayerische HNL Vermehrungsbetreide GmbH & Co KG v Council and Commission (Cases 83, 94/76, 4, 15, 40/77) [1978] ECR 1209 .... 769, 778

Behn Verpackungsbedarf GmbH v Hauptzollamt Itzehoe (Case C-80/89) [1990] ECR I-2659 .... 632, 633
Bela-Mühle Josef Bergman KG v Grows-Farm GmbH & Co KG (Case 114/76) [1977] ECR 1211 682
Belgium v Commission (Case C-75/97) [1999] ECR I-3671 435
Belgium v Commission (Case C-110/03) judgment of 14 April 2005 609
Belgium v Commission (Case C-142/87) [1990] ECR I-959 .... 373, 683
Bellio F.Iii Srl v Prefettura di Treviso (Case C-286/02) [2004] ECR I-3465 735
Bettray v Staatssecretaris van Justitie (Case 344/87) [1989] ECR 1621 550
Beus v Hauptzollamt München (Case 5/67) [1968] ECR 83 .... 384, 579
Bilka-Kaufhaus GmbH v Karin Weber von Hartz (Case 170/84) [1986] ECR 1607 .... 592, 593, 698, 699
Binder GmbH v Hauptzollamt Stuttgart-West (Case C-205/94) [1996] ECR I-2871 384
Birke v Commission (Case 543/79) [1981] ECR 2669 765
Bleis v Ministère de l'Education Nationale (Case C-4/91) [1991] ECR I-5627 557
Bonifaci and Berto v Instituto Nazionale della Previdenza Sociale (IPNS) (Cases C-94–95/95) [1997] ECR I-3969 826
Booker Aquacultur Ltd and Hydro Seafood GSP Ltd v Scottish Ministers (Cases C-20 and 64/00) [2003] ECR I-7411 676
Bosphorus Hava Yollari Turizm Ve Ticaret AS v Minister for Transport, Energy and Communications (Case C-84/95) [1996] ECR I-3953 .... 526, 527, 528, 529, 530
Bozetti v Invernizzi (Case 179/84) [1985] ECR 2301 790
BP Supergas v Greece (Case C-62/93) [1995] ECR I-1883 802
BPB Industries and British Gypsum v Commission (Case C-310/93) [1995] ECR I-865 366
Brasserie du Pêcheur SA v Germany, R v Secretary of State for Transport, ex p Factortame Ltd (Cases C-46 and 48/93) [1996] ECR I-1029 .... 711, 771, 772, 787, 817, 818, 819, 820, 821, 822, 823, 824, 825, 826, 827, 828
Bresle v Prefet de la Region Auvergne and Prefet du Puy-de-Dome (Case C-257/95) [1996] ECR I-233 289
Briheche v Ministere de l'Interieur, Ministere de L'Education and Ministere de la Justice (Case 319/03) [2004] ECR I-8807 599
Brinkmann Tabakfabriken GmbH v Skatteministeriet (Case C-319/96) [1998] ECR I-5255 .... 820, 822, 823
British Steel plc v Commission (Case C-1/98) [2000] ECR I-10349 647

British Sugar plc v Commission (Case C-359/01) [2004] ECR I-4933 684
Brown v Secretary of State for Scotland (Case 197/86) [1988] ECR 3205 .... 550, 566, 574
Brunnhofer v Bank der Osterreichischen Postsparkasse AG (Case C-381/99) [2001] ECR I-4961 .... 590, 699
BSM Geraets-Smits v Stichting Ziekenfonds VGZ (Case C-157/99) [2001] ECR I-5473 694
Buitoni v Forma (Case 122/78) [1979] ECR 677 .... 681, 682

Caballero v Fondo de Garantia Salarial (Fogasa) (Case C-442/00) [2002] ECR I-11915 .... 503, 505
Calpak SpA and Societa Emiliana Lavorazione Fruita SpA v Commission (Cases 789 and 790/79) [1980] ECR 1949 .... 332, 333
Campus Oil Ltd v Minister for Industry and Energy (Case 72/83) [1984] ECR 2727 .... 548, 689
Canal Satelite Digital SL v Aministacion General del Estado and Distribuidora de Television Digital SA (DTS) (Case C-390/99) [2002] ECR I-607 694
Cargill BV v Commission (Case C-248/89) [1991] ECR I-2987 625
Cargill BV v Produktschap voor Margarine, Vetten en Olien (Case C-365/89) [1991] ECR I-3045 625
Carlo Tedeschi v Denkavit Commerciale S.r.l. (Case 5/77) [1977] ECR 1555 106
Carlos Garcia Avello v Belgium (Case C-148/02) [2003] ECR I-11613 569
Carpenter v Secretary of State for the Home Department (Case C-60/00) [2002] ECR I-6279 .... 485, 693
Casagrande v Landeshauptstadt München (Case 9/74) [1974] ECR 773 553
Caturla-Poch v Parliament (Case C-107/89) [1989] ECR 1357 751
Centre public d'aide sociale de Courcelles v Lebon (Case 316/85) [1987] ECR 2811 554
Cereol Italia v Azienda Agricola Castello (Case C-104/94) [1995] ECR I-2983 681
CIRFS v Commission (Case C-313/90) [1993] ECR I-1125 .... 628, 643, 652
CNTA SA v Commission (Case 74/74) [1975] ECR 533 .... 639, 640, 779
Codorniu v Council (Case C-309/89) [1994] ECR I-1853 .... 333, 339
Coenen v Social Economische Raad (Case 39/75) [1975] ECR 1547 693
Cofidis SA v Fredout (Case C-473/00) [2002] ECR I-10875 806
Colegio de Oficiales de la Marina Mercante Espanola v Administracion del Estado (Case C-405/01) [2003] ECR I-10391 559

Collins v Secretary of State for Work and Pensions (Case C-138/02) [2004] ECR I-2703 .... 549, 550, 568, 575, 576
Comateb v Directeur Général des Douanes et Droits Indirects (Case C-192/95) [1997] ECR I-165 .... 791, 810
Comet BV v Produktschap voor Siergewassen (Case 45/76) [1976] ECR 2043 790
Commission and France v Ladbroke Racing Ltd (Cases C-359 and 379/95) [1999] ECR I-6265 375
Commission v Akzo Nobel Chemicals Ltd and Akros Chemicals Ltd (Case C-7/04) [2004] ECR I-8739 751
Commission v Artegodan GmbH (Case C-39/03) [2003] ECR I-7885 .... 168, 478, 727
Commission v AssiDoman Kraft Products AB (Case C-310/97) [1999] ECR I-5363 .... 760, 765
Commission v Atlantic Container Line AB (Case C-149/95) [1995] ECR I-2165 750
Commission v Austria (Case C-147/03) judgment of 7 July 2005 692
Commission v Austria (Case C-203/03) judgment of 1 February 2005 697
Commission v Austria (Case C-475/98) [2002] ECR I-9797 414
Commission v BASF AG (Case C-137/92) [1994] ECR I-2555 .... 268, 269
Commission v Belgium (Case 35/97) [1998] ECR I-5325 548
Commission v Belgium (Case C-173/94) [1996] ECR I-3265 558
Commission v Belgium (Case C-217/99) [2000] ECR I-10251 690
Commission v Belgium (Case C-278/94) [1996] ECR I-4307 548
Commission v Belgium (Case C-355/98) [2000] ECR I-1221 548
Commission v Belgium (Case C-471/98) [2002] ECR I-9681 414
Commission v Belgium II (Case 149/79) [1982] ECR 1845 .... 555, 557
Commission v Camar Srl and Tico Srl (Case C-312/00) [2002] ECR I-11355 .... 766, 767, 772, 773
Commission v Council (Airport Transit Visas) (Case C-170/96) [1998] ECR I-2763 269
Commission v Council (Case 16/88) [1989] ECR 3457 .... 103, 107
Commission v Council (Case 22/70) [1971] ECR 263 .... 267, 412
Commission v Council (Case 45/86) [1987] ECR 1493 .... 383, 408
Commission v Council (Case 81/72) [1973] ECR 575 757
Commission v Council (Case 165/87) [1988] ECR 5545 409
Commission v Council (Case C-27/04) [2004] ECR I-6649 199
Commission v Council (Case C-122/94) [1996] ECR I-881 384
Commission v Council (Case C-176/03) judgment of 13 September 2005 269
Commission v Council (Case C-209/97) [1999] ECR I-8067 409

Commission v Council (Case C-257/01) [2005] ECR I-345 .... 107, 111
Commission v Council (Generalized Tariff Preferences) (Case 51/87) [1988] ECR 5459 757
Commission v Denmark (Case C-192/01) [2003] ECR I-9693 ... 692, 734
Commission v Denmark (Case C-467/98) [2002] ECR I-9519 414
Commission v European Central Bank (Case C-11/00) [2003] ECR I-7147 .... 666, 667, 668, 669
Commission v European Investment Bank (Case C-15/00) [2003] ECR I-7281 .... 166, 666
Commission v European Parliament and Council (Case C-378/00) [2003] ECR I-937 .... 109, 111, 758
Commission v Finland (Case C-469/98) [2002] ECR I-9627 414
Commission v France (Case 21/84) [1985] ECR 1356 549
Commission v France (Case 307/84) [1986] ECR 1725 558
Commission v France (Case 318/86) [1988] ECR 3559 ...... 590, 595, 696
Commission v France (Case C-24/00) [2004] ECR I-1277 .... 692, 734, 735
Commission v France (Case C-212/03) judgment of 26 May 2005 692
Commission v France (Case C-262/02) [2004] ECR I-6569 707
Commission v France (Case C-265/95) [1997] ECR I-6959 513
Commission v France (Case C-280/02) [2004] ECR I-8573 .... 731, 732
Commission v France (Case C-334/02) [2004] ECR I-2229 689
Commission v French Republic (Case 68/76) [1977] ECR 515 548
Commission v French Republic (Case 167/73) [1974] ECR 359 547
Commission v Fresh Marine A/S (Case C-472/00) [2003] ECR I-7541 .... 766, 772, 773, 855
Commission v Germany (Case 12/74) [1975] ECR 181 548
Commission v Germany (Case 178/84) [1987] ECR 1227 .... 689, 690, 706
Commission v Germany (Case C-62/90) [1992] ECR I-2575 ..... 689, 690
Commission v Germany (Case C-103/01) [2003] ECR I-5369 426
Commission v Germany (Case C-467/98) [2002] ECR I-9855 .... 414, 417, 418
Commission v Germany (Case C-493/99) [2001] ECR I-8163 694
Commission v Greece (Case 68/88) [1989] ECR 2965 .... 703, 793
Commission v Greece (Case C-140/03) judgment of 21 April 2005 692
Commission v Greece (Case C-185/96) [1998] ECR I-6601 555
Commission v Greece (Case C-290/94) [1996] ECR I-3285 .... 558, 559
Commission v Hellenic Republic (Case C-185/96) [1998] ECR I-6601 547
Commission v Hellenic Republic (Case C-187/96) [1998] ECR I-1095 548
Commission v Ireland (Case 45/87) [1988] ECR 4929 548

Commission v Ireland (Case 113/80) [1981] ECR 1625 548
Commission v Ireland (Case 249/81) [1982] ECR 4005 548
Commission v Ireland (Case C-354/99) [2001] ECR I-7657 .... 703, 793
Commission v Italy (Case 154/85) [1987] ECR 2717 548
Commission v Italy (Case 225/85) [1987] ECR 2625 557
Commission v Italy (Case 270/02) [2004] ECR I-1559 690
Commission v Italy (Case C-129/00) [2003] ECR I-4637 811
Commission v Jégo-Quéré & Cie SA (Case C-263/02) [2004] ECR I-3425 .... 317, 318, 331, 339, 340, 342
Commission v Lisrestal (Case C-32/95) [1996] ECR I-5373 .... 315, 361
Commission v Luxembourg (Case C-111/91) [1993] ECR I-817 555
Commission v Luxembourg (Case C-472/98) [2002] ECR I-9741 414
Commission v Luxembourg (Case C-473/93) [1996] ECR I-3207 .... 556, 557, 558, 559
Commission v Luxemburg (Case C-455/03) [2004] ECR I-10191 693
Commission v Netherlands (Case C-41/02) [2004] ECR I-11375 .... 691, 734
Commission v Netherlands (Case C-299/02) [2004] ECR I-9761 692
Commission v Solvay (Cases 287–288/95) [2000] ECR I-2391 269
Commission v Spain (Case C-45/93) [1994] ECR I-911 562
Commission v Sweden (Case C-468/98) [2002] ECR I-9575 414
Commission v Sytraval and Brink's France (Case C-367/95) [1998] ECR I-1719 .... 315, 361, 377, 378, 379, 383
Commission v T-Mobile Austria GmbH (Case C-141/02) [2005] ECR I-1283 .... 380, 539
Commission v Tetra Laval (Case C-12/03) [2005] ECR I-987 .... 455, 457, 466, 469, 471, 473
Commission v UK (Case 124/81) [1983] ECR 203 689
Commission v UK (Case C-6/04) judgment of 20 October 2005 733
Commission v UK (Case C-359/97) [2000] ECR I-6355 795
Commission v UK (Case C-383/92) [1994] ECR I-2479 .... 703, 793
Commission v United Kingdom (Case 40/82) [1982] ECR 2793 706
Commission v United Kingdom (Case 61/81) [1982] ECR 2601 590
Commission v United Kingdom (Case 165/82) [1983] ECR 3431 595
Commission v United Kingdom (Case 207/83) [1985] ECR 1202 548
Commission v United Kingdom (Case C-466/98) [2002] ECR I-9427 414
Compagnie d'Approvisionnement de Transport et de Crédit SA et Grands Moulins de Paris SA v Commission (Cases 9 and 11/71) [1972] ECR 391 .... 765, 782
Compagnie Francaise de l'Azote (COFAZ) SA v Commission (Case 169/84) [1986] ECR 391 .... 134, 318

Compagnie Industrielle et Agricole du Comté de Loheac v Council and Commission (Cases 54–60/76) [1977] ECR 645 782
Compagnie Interagra SA v Commission (Case 217/81) [1982] ECR 2233 786
Compagnie Maritime Belge Transports SA v Commission (Cases 24–26 and 28/93) [1996] ECR I-1201 464
Comptoir National Technique Agricole (CNTA) SA v Commission (Case 74/74) [1975] ECR 533 .... 442, 768
Conegate v Customs and Excise Commissioners (Case 121/85) [1986] ECR 1007 708
Connolly v Commission (Case C-274/99) [2001] ECR I-1611 .... 516, 679
Conserve Italia Soc. Coop. arl v Commission (Case C-500/99) [2002] ECR I-867 .... 625, 683
Consorzio Cooperative d'Abruzzo v Commission (Case 15/85) [1987] ECR 1005 624
Consten & Grundig v Commission (Cases 56 & 58/64) [1966] ECR 299 373
Coote v Granada Hospitality Ltd (Case C-185/97) [1998] ECR I-5199 794
Corsica Ferries Italia Srl v Corpo dei Piloti del Porto di Genova (Case C-18/93) [1994] ECR I-1783 289
Corsten (Case C-58/98) [2000] ECR I-7919 693
Costa v ENEL (Case 6/64) [1964] ECR 585 286
Cotter and McDermott v Minister for Social Welfare and Attorney General (Case C-377/89) [1991] ECR I-1155 798
Council v Hautala (Case C-353/99) [2001] ECR I-9565 672
Courage Ltd v Crehan (Case C-453/99) [2001] ECR I-6297 812
Cowan v Le Trésor Public (Case 186/87) [1989] ECR 195 562
Criminal Proceedings against Attila Vajnai (Case C-328/04) judgment of 6 October 2005 486
Criminal Proceedings against Bernaldez (Case C-129/94) [1996] ECR I-1829 290
Criminal Proceedings against Bickel and Franz (Case C-274/96) [1998] ECR I-7637 569
Criminal Proceedings against Bordessa, Mellado and Maestre (Cases C-358 and 416/93) [1995] ECR I-361 694
Criminal Proceedings against Burmanjer, Van der Linden and de Jong (Case C-20/03) judgment of 26 May 2005 690
Criminal Proceedings against Carra (Case C-258/98) [2000] ECR I-4217 586
Criminal Proceedings against Jean Monteil and Daniel Sammani (Case C-60/89) [1991] ECR I-1547 528

Criminal Proceedings against John Greenham and Leonard Abel (Case C-95/01) [2004] ECR I-1333 734
Criminal Proceedings against Keck and Mithouard (Cases C-267 and 268/91) [1993] ECR I-6097 .... 431, 713, 714
Criminal Proceedings against Leon Motte (Case 247/84) [1985] ECR 3887 719
Criminal Proceedings against Linhart anf Biffl (Case C-99/01) [2002] ECR I-9375 702
Criminal Proceedings against MacQuen (Case C-108/96) [2001] ECR I-837 .... 709, 710
Criminal Proceedings against Maria Pupino (Case C-105/03) judgment of 16 June 2005 .... 269, 486
Criminal Proceedings against Max Rombi (Case C-107/97) [2000] ECR I-3367 611
Criminal Proceedings against Nunes and de Matos (Case C-186/98) [1999] ECR I-4883 .... 703, 793
Criminal Proceedings against Paolo Lirussi and Francesca Bizzaro (Cases 175 and 178/98) [1999] ECR I-6881 718
Criminal Proceedings against Richardt and Les Accessoires Scientifiques SNC (Case C-367/89) [1991] ECR I-4621 711
Criminal Proceedings against Saddik (Case C-458/93) [1995] ECR I-511 289
Criminal Proceedings against Sivio Berlusconi (Cases 387, 391 and 403/02) judgment of 3 May 2005 .... 703, 793
Criminal Proceedings against Sofia Skavani and Konstnatin Chryssanthakopoulos (Case C-193/94) [1996] ECR I-929 693
Criminal Proceedings against Sunino and Data (Case C-2/96) [1996] ECR I-1543 289
Criminal Proceedings against X (Cases C-74/95 and 129/95) [1996] ECR I-6609 485
Crispoltoni v Fattoria Autonoma Tabachi and Donatab (Cases C-133, 300 and 362/93) [1994] ECR I-4863 .... 60, 635
Cristini v SNCF (Case 32/75) [1975] ECR 1085 711
CT Control (Rotterdam) BV and JCT Benelux BV v Commission (Cases C-121–122/91) [1993] ECR I-3873 759

D and Sweden v Council (Cases C-122 and 125/99) [2001] ECR I-4319 600
Da Costa en Schaake NV, Jacob Meijer NV and Hoechst-Holland NV v Nederlandse Belastingadministratie (Cases 28–30/62) [1963] ECR 31 .... 284, 285
Daewoo Electronics Manufacturing Espana SA (Demesa) v Commission (Cases C-183 and 187/02) [2004] ECR I-10609 634

Dansk Rorindustri A/S v Commission (Cases C-189, 202, 205, 208 and 213/02) judgment of 28 June 2005 ... 609, 611, 636, 642, 643, 644
Data Delecta Aktiebolag and Forsberg v MSL Dynamics Ltd (Case C-43/95) [1996] ECR I-461 ... 562
De Boer Buizen v Council and Commission (Case 81/86) [1987] ECR 3677 ... 780
de Peijper (Case 104/75) [1976] ECR 613 ... 689
De Vos v Bielefeld (Case C-315/94) [1996] ECR I-1417 ... 554
Defrenne v Sabena (Case 149/77) [1978] ECR 1365 ... 485, 587, 589, 594
Defrenne v Société Anonyme Belge de Navigation Aérienne (Case 43/75) [1976] ECR 455 ... 561, 587, 588, 589, 594
Dekker v Stichting voor Jong Volwassenen (VJV) Plus (Case C-177/88) [1990] ECR I-3941 ... 796, 815
Delacre v Commission (Case C-350/88) [1990] ECR I-395 ... 632
Demo-Studio Schmidt v Commission (Case 210/81) [1983] ECR 3045 ... 375
Denise Richez-Parise v Commission (Cases 19, 20, 25, 30/69) [1970] ECR 325 ... 775
Denkavit Futtermittel GmbH v Finanzamt Warendorf (Case 139/77) [1978] ECR 1317 ... 583
Denkavit International BV v Kramer van Koophandel en Fabrieken voor Midden-Gelderland (Case C-2/94) [1996] ECR I-2827 ... 802
Denkavit International v Bundesamt für Finanzen (Cases C-283, 291 and 292/94) [1996] ECR I-5063 ... 823
Denkavit Italiana (Case 61/79) [1980] ECR 1205 ... 795
Detti v ECJ (Case 144/82) [1983] ECR 2439 ... 628
Deufil GmbH & Co KG v Commission (Case 310/85) [1987] ECR 901 ... 443
Deuka, Deutsche Kraftfutter GmbH, B.J.Stolp v Einfuhr-und Vorratsstelle für Gertreide und Futtermittel (Case 78/74) [1975] ECR 421 ... 442
Deutsche Milch-Kontor GmbH v Germany (Cases 205–215/82) [1983] ECR 2633 ... 811
Deutsche Paracelsus Schulen fur Naturheilverhafen GmbH v Grabner (Case C-294/00) [2002] ECR I-6515 ... 710
Deutsche Post AG v Gesellschaft fur Zahlungssyteme GmbH and Citicorp Kartenservice GmbH (Cases 147–148/97) [2000] ECR I-825 ... 586
Deutsche Telekom v Schröder (Case C-50/96) [2000] ECR I-743 ... 589, 794
D'Hoop v Office National de l'Emploi (Case C-224/98) [2002] ECR I-6191 ... 569

Di Leonardo Adriano Srl and Dilexport Srl v Ministero del Commercio con l'Estero (Cases C-37 and 38/02) [2004] ECR I-6911 .... 635, 636
Dietz v Commission (Case 126/76) [1977] ECR 2431 787
Dilexport v Amministrazione delle Finanze dello Stato (Case C-343/96) [1999] ECR I-579 .... 807, 810
Dillenkofer v Federal Republic of Germany (Cases C-178–179/94, 188–190/94) [1996] ECR I-4845 823
DIR International Film Srl v Commission (Case C-164/98) [2000] ECR I-447 .... 162, 756
Distillerie Fratelli Cipriani SpA v Ministero delle Finanze (Case C-395/00) [2002] ECR I-11877 .... 315, 361
Dorsch Consult Ingenieurgesellschaft GmbH v Council (Case C-237/98) [2000] ECR I-4549 782
Dounias v Ypourgio Oikonomikon (Case C-228/98) [2000] ECR I-577 794
Douwe Egberts NV v Westrom Pharma NV (Case C-239/02) [2004] ECR I-7007 690
Driessen en Zonen v Minister van Verkeer en Waterstaat (Cases C-13–16/92) [1993] ECR I-4751 633
Du Pont de Nemours Italiana SpA v Unita Sanitaria Locale No.2 Di Carrara (Case C-21/88) [1990] ECR I-889 548
Duff v Minister for Agriculture and Food Ireland and the Attorney General (Case C-63/93) [1996] ECR I-569 635
Dumortier Frères SA v Council (Cases 64, 113/76, 167, 239/78, 27, 28, 45/79) [1979] ECR 3091 .... 771, 776

Eau de Cologne and Parfumerie-Fabrik Glockengasse No 4711 KG v Provide Srl (Case C-150/88) [1989] ECR 3891 289
Eco Swiss China Time Ltd v Benetton International NV (Case C-126/97) [1999] ECR I-3055 806
Edeka v Federal Republic of Germany (Case 245/81) [1982] ECR 2745 635
Edis v Ministero delle Finanze (Case C-231/96) [1998] ECR I-4951 .... 802, 806, 807
Einfuhr-und Vorrasstelle für Getreide und Futermittel v Koster, Berodt & Co (Case 25/70) [1970] ECR 1161 .... 103, 105, 106
Einfuhr-und Vorratsstelle für Getreide und Futtermittel v Firma C.Mackprang (Case 2/75) [1975] ECR 607 635
Elliniki Radiophonia Tileorassi AE v Dimotiki Etairia Pliroforissis and Sotirios Kouvelas (Case C-260/89) [1991] ECR I-2925 ... 485, 503, 504, 505, 533

Emesa Sugar (Free Zone) NV v Aruba (Case C-17/98) [2000] ECR I-675 472
Emmott v Minister for Social Welfare (Case C-208/90) [1991] ECR I-4269 .... 797, 798, 800, 801, 802, 803, 815
Enderby v Frenchay Health Authority and the Secretary of State for Health (Case 127/92) [1993] ECR 5535 .... 592, 593
Eridania SpA v Azienda Agricola San Luca di Rumagnoli Viannj (Case C-289/97) [2000] ECR I-5409 .... 458, 582
Eridania Zuccherifici Nazionali v Ministere de l'Agriculture et des Forêts (Case 230/78) [1979] ECR 2749 581
Etablissements Consten SaRL and Grundig-Verkaufs-GmbH v Commission (Cases 56 and 58/64) [1966] ECR 299 444
EU-Wood-Trading GmbH v Sonderabfal-Management-Gesellschaf Rheinland-Pfalz GmbH (Case C-277/02) [2004] ECR I-11957 709
European Ombudsman v Frank Lamberts (Case C-234/02) [2004] ECR I-2803 855
European Parliament v Commission (Case C-156/93) [1995] ECR I-2019 109
European Parliament v Council (Case 302/87) [1988] ECR 5615 274
European Parliament v Council (Case C-41/95) [1995] ECR I-4411 757
European Parliament v Council (Case C-70/88) [1990] ECR I-2041 274
European Parliament v Council (Case C-93/00) [2001] ECR I-10119 757
European Parliament v Council (Case C-259/95) [1997] ECR I-5303 109
European Parliament v Council (Case C-295/90) [1992] ECR I-4193 .... 409, 757
European Parliament v Council (Case C-392/95) [1997] ECR I-3213 757
European Parliament v Council (Case C-417/93) [1995] ECR I-1185 109
European Parliament v Council (Government Procurement) (Case C-360/93) [1996] ECR I-1195 757
European Parliament v Council, Re the Edicom Decision (Case C-271/94) [1996] ECR I-1689 408
European Parliament v Council (Road Taxes) (Case C-21/94) [1995] ECR I-1827 .... 757, 759
European Parliament v Council (Telematic Networks) (Case C-22/96) [1998] ECR I-3231 757
European Parliament v Gaspari (Case C-316/97) [1998] ECR I-7597 383

Evans v Secretary of State for the Environment, Transport and the Regions and the Motor Insurers' Bureau (Case C-63/01) [2003] ECR I-14447 .... 805, 809, 824
Executif Régional Wallon and Glaverbel SA v Commission (Cases 62 and 72/87) [1988] ECR 1573 443
Extramet Industrie SA v Council (Case C-358/89) [1991] ECR I-2501 334

Falck SpA and Acciaierie di Bolzano SpA v Commission (Cases C-74 and 75/00) [2002] ECR I-7869 .... 378, 379, 395, 608, 631
Fantask A/S v Industriministeriet (Case C-188/95) [1997] ECR I-6783 802
Fazenda Pública v Camara Municipal do Porto (Case C-446/98) [2000] ECR I-11435 806
Fédération Charbonnière de Belgique v High Authority (Case 8/55) [1954–56] ECR 292 .... 406, 579, 656
Fédération Nationale d'Agriculture Biologique des Regions de France v Council (Case C-345/00) [2001] ECR I-3811 276
Fédération Nationale du Commerce Exterieur des Produits Alimentaires v France (Case C-354/90) [1991] ECR I-5505 812
Ferring SA v Agence Centrale des Organismes de Securite Sociale (ACOSS) (Case C-53/00) [2001] ECR I-9067 435
Finanzamt Bergisch Gladbach v HE (Case C-25/03) judgment of 21 April 2005 701
Finanzamt Goslar v Brigitte Breitsohl (Case C-400/98) [2000] ECR I-4321 609
Finsider v Commission (Cases C-363–4/88) [1992] ECR I-359 777
Fiorini (neé Cristini) v Société Nationale des Chemins de Fer Français (Case 32/75) [1975] ECR 1085 554
Firma A. Racke v Hauptzollamt Mainz (Case 98/78) [1979] ECR 69 .... 441, 444, 445, 446, 580, 608
Firma A. Racke v Hauptzollamt Mainz (Case 283/83) [1984] ECR 3791 580
Firma Foto-Frost v Hauptzollamt Lubeck-Ost (Case 314/85) [1987] ECR 4199 .... 285, 306, 336
Firma Kühlhaus Zentrum AG v Hauptzollamt Hamburg-Harburg (Case 79/77) [1978] ECR 611 581
Firma Wilhelm Fromme v Bundesanstalt für Landwirtschaftliche Marktordnung (Case C-54/81) [1982] ECR 1449 811
Fiskano v Commission (Case C-135/92) [1994] ECR I-2885 .... 316, 364
Flemmer v Council and Commission (Cases C-80–82/99) [2001] ECR I-7211 611

Foto-Frost v Hauptzollamt Lübeck-Ost (Case 314/85) [1987] ECR 4199 752
France v Commission (Case C-235/97) [1998] ECR I-N7555 67
France v Commission (Case C-301/87) [1990] ECR I-307 363
France v Commission (Case C-393/01) [2003] ECR I-5405 730
France v Commission (Case C-456/00) [2002] ECR I-11949 462
France v Commission (Re Pension Funds Communication) (Case C-57/95) [1997] ECR I-1627 267
Francovich and Bonifaci v Italy (Cases C-6 and 9/90) [1991] ECR I-5357 .... 277, 538, 815, 816, 824, 826, 827, 828
Freers and Speckmann v Deutsche Bundespost (Case C-278/93) [1996] ECR I-1165 .... 592, 700
Freistaat Sachsen and Volkswagen AG and Volkswagen Sachsen GmbH v Commission (Cases C-57 and 61/00) [2003] ECR I-9975 461
Frico v VIV (Cases 424–425/85) [1987] ECR 2755 628
Fux v Commission (Case 26/68) [1969] ECR 145 778

Garage Molenheide BVBA v Belgische Staat (Cases C-286/94, 340 and 401/95, and 47/96) [1997] ECR I-7281 701
Gebruder Lorenz GmbH v Germany (Case 120/73) [1973] ECR 1471 .... 373, 377
Geitling, Mausegatt and Prasident v High Authority (Cases 16–18/59) [1960] ECR 17 373
Geitling v High Authority (Cases 36, 37, 38 and 40/59) [1960] ECR 423 484
Georgios Orfanopoulos v Land Baden-Wurttemberg (Cases C-482 and 493/01) [204] ECR I-5257 692
Germany v Commission (Case 24/62) [1963] ECR 63 .... 382, 383, 384
Germany v Commission (Case 34/62) [1963] ECR 131 579
Germany v Commission (Case 84/82) [1984] ECR 1451 377
Germany v Commission (Case C-54/95) [1999] ECR I-N35 67
Germany v Commission (Case C-239/01) [2003] ECR I-10333 758
Germany v Commission (Case C-301/96) [2003] ECR I-9919 383
Germany v Commission (Case C-399/65) [1996] ECR I-2441 750
Germany v Commission (Case C-426/93) [1995] ECR I-3723 670
Germany v Commission (Cases 281, 283–285, 287/85) [1987] ECR 3203 406
Germany v Council (Case C-280/93) [1994] ECR I-4973 ... 472, 585, 675
Germany v European Parliament and Council (Case C-233/94) [1997] ECR I-2405 .... 405, 425, 426
Germany v European Parliament and Council (Case C-376/98) [2000] ECR I-8419 .... 405, 675
Giuffrida v Council (Case 105/75) [1976] ECR 1395 464

Granaria BV v Hoofdproduktschap voor Akkerbouwprodukten (Case 116/76) [1977] ECR 1247 ... 682, 769
Grant v South-West Trains Ltd (Case C-249/96) [1998] ECR I-621 ... 600
Grau Gomis (Case C-167/94) [1995] ECR I-1023 ... 289
Gravier v City of Liège (Case 293/83) [1985] ECR 593 ... 565, 566, 567
Greece v Commission (Case C-259/87) [1990] ECR I-2845 ... 783
Greece v Commission (Case C-278/00) [2004] ECR I-3997 ... 634, 683
Grifoni v EAEC (Case C-308/87) [1994] ECR I-341 ... 778
Groener v Minister for Education (Case 379/87) [1989] ECR 3967 ... 548
Groupement des Hauts Fourneaux et Acieries Belges v High Authority (Case 8/57) [1957–8] ECR 245 ... 583
Groupement des Industries Sidérurgiques Luxembourgeoises v High Authority (Cases 7 & 9/54) [1955–56] ECR 53 ... 579
Grundstuckgemeinschaft SchollBstraBe GbR v Finanzamt Paderborn (Case C-396/98) [2000] ECR I-4279 ... 609
GruSa Fleisch GmbH & Co KG v Hauptzollamt Hamburg-Jonas (Case C-34/92) [1993] ECR I-4147 ... 608
Guerin Automobiles v Commission (Case C-282/95) [1997] ECR I-503 ... 268

Haahr Petroleum v Havn (Case C-90/94) [1997] ECR I-4085 ... 802
Haim v Kassenzahnarztliche Vereinigung Nordrhein (Case C-424/97) [2000] ECR I-5123 ... 819, 825, 826
Handels-og Kontorfunktionarernes Forbund i Danmark v Dansk Arbejdsgiverforening, acting on behalf of Danfoss (Case 109/88) [1989] ECR 3199 ... 590, 591
Hauer v Land Rheinland-Pfalz (Case 44/79) [1979] ECR 3727 ... 485, 675
Hauptzollamt Bremerhaven v Massey-Ferguson (Case 8/73) [1973] ECR 897 ... 408
Hauptzollamt Munchen-Mitte v Technische Universitat Munchen (Case C-269/90) [1991] ECR I-5469 ... 315, 374, 375, 377
Hautala v Council (Case C-353/99) [2001] ECR I-9565 ... 354, 355
Hayes and Hayes v Kronenberger GmbH (Case C-323/95) [1997] ECR I-1711 ... 562
Heineken Brouwerijen BV v Inspecteur der Vennootschapsbelasting (Cases 91 and 127/83) [1984] ECR 3435 ... 377
Hellmut Marschall v Land Nordrhein Westfalen (Case C-409/95) [1997] ECR I-6363 ... 596, 597
Henri de Compte v European Parliament (Case 141/84) [1985] ECR 1951 ... 369, 627
Henri de Compte v European Parliament (Case C-90/95) [1997] ECR I-1999 ... 615, 616, 624

Hercules Chemicals NV v Commission (Case C-51/92) [1999] ECR I-4235 .... 367, 756
Herpels v Commission (Case 54/77) [1978] ECR 585 618
Hill and Stapleton v Revenue Commissioners (Case C-243/95) [1998] ECR I-3739 .... 592, 626
Hoekstra (nee Unger) v Bestuur der Bedrijfsvereniging voor Detailhandel en Ambachten (Case 75/63) [1964] ECR 177 549
Hoffmann-La Roche v Commission (Case 85/76) [1979] ECR 461 314
Hoffman's Stärkefabriken v Hauptzollamt Bielefeld (Case 2/77) [1977] ECR 1375 585
Höfner and Elser v Macrotron GmbH (Case C-41/90) [1991] ECR I-1979 586
Holtz & Willemsen v Council (Case 153/73) [1974] ECR 675 ... 585, 768
Hoogovens v High Authority (Case 14/61) [1962] ECR 253 .... 272, 623
Hortiplant SAT v Commission (Case C-330/01) [2004] ECR I-1763 93
Humblet v Belgium (Case 6/60) [1960] ECR 559 .... 790, 796
Hupeden & Co KG v Hauptzollamt Hamburg-Jonas (Case C-295/94) [1996] ECR I-3375 682

IFAW Internationaler Tierschultz-Fonds GmbH v Commission (Case C-168/02) judgment of 30 November 2004 357
Ijssel-Vliet Combinatie BV v Minister van Economische Zaken (Case C-311/94) [1996] ECR I-5023 643
Industrie des Poudres Spheriques v Council and Commission (Case C-458/98) [2000] ECR I-8147 .... 315, 361, 519, 760
Industrie-en Handelsonderneming Vreugdenhil BV v Commission (Case C-282/90) [1992] ECR I-1937 771
Interhotel v Commission (Case C-291/89) [1991] ECR I-2257 .. 315, 361
Intermodal Transports BV v Staatssecretaris van Financien (Case C-459/03) judgment of 15 September 2005 284
International Business Machines Corporation v Commission (Case 60/81) [1981] ECR 2639 267
International Chemical Corporation v Amministrazione delle Finanze dello Stato (Case 66/80) [1981] ECR 1191 .... 285, 762
International Express Carriers Conference (IECC) v Commission, La Poste, UK and the Post Office (Case C-449/98) [2001] ECR I-3875 375
International Fruit Company v Produktschap voor Groenten en Fruit (No 2) (Cases 51–54/71) [1971] ECR 1107 548
Internationale Handelsgesellschaft v Einfuhr-und Vorratstelle für Getreide und Futtermittel (Case 11/70) [1970] ECR 1125 ...... 485, 656

Interporc Im-und Export GmbH v Commission (Case C-41/00) [2003] ECR I-2125 .... 355, 760
Inzirillo v Caisse d'Allocations Familiales de l'Arrondissement de Lyon (Case 63/76) [1976] ECR 2057 554
IPK-Munchen GmbH v Commission (Cases C-199–200/01) [2004] ECR I-4627 760
Ireks-Arkady v Council and Commission (Case 238/78) [1979] ECR 2955 779
Irish Farmers Association v Minister for Agriculture, Food and Forestry (Ireland) and the Attorney General (Case C-22/94) [1997] ECR I-1809 635
Italian Republic v Commission (Case 13/63) [1963] ECR 165 581
Italy v Commission (Case C-372/97) [2004] ECR I-3679 683
Italy v Commission (Case C-91/01) [2004] ECR I-4355 .... 462, 645
Italy v Commission (Case C-99/99) [2000] ECR I-1535 460
Italy v Commission (Case C-253/97) [1999] ECR I-7529 67
Italy v Commission (Case C-298/00) [2004] ECR I-4087 631
Italy v Council (Case C-120/99) [2001] ECR I-7997 458
Italy v Council (Case C-340/98) [2002] ECR I-2663 .... 635, 637

JämställdhetsOmbudsmannen v örebro läns landsting (Case C-236/98) [2000] ECR I-2189 592
Jenkins v Kingsgate (Clothing Productions) Ltd (Case 96/80) [1981] ECR 911 .... 591, 592
Jippes v Minister van Landbouw, Natuurbeheer en Visserij (Case C-189/01) [2001] ECR I-5689 661
Job Centre coop.arl. (Case C-55/96) [1997] ECR I-7119 586
Johnson v Chief Adjudication Officer (Case C-410/92) [1994] ECR I-5483 802
Johnston v Chief Constable of the Royal Ulster Constabulary (Case 222/84) [1986] ECR 1651 .... 485, 504, 595, 695, 794
Julius Kind AG v EEC (Case 106/81) [1982] ECR 2885 .... 583, 768

Kalanke v Freie Hansestadt Bremen (Case C-450/93) [1995] ECR I-3051 .... 596, 597, 605
Kali & Salz, France, SCPA and EMC v Commission (Cases C-68/94 and 30/95) [1998] ECR I-1375 .... 465, 466
Kalliope Schöning-Kougebetopoulou v Freie und Hansestadt Hamburg (Case C-15/96) [1998] ECR I-47 548
Kamer van Koophandel en Fabrieken voor Amsterdam v Inspire Art Ltd (Case C-167/01) [2003] ECR I-10155 693
Kampffmeyer v Commission and Council (Cases 56–60/74) [1976] ECR 711 .... 778, 779, 785, 787

Karner Industrie-Auktionen GmbH v Troostwijk GmbH (Case C-71/02) [2004] ECR I-3025 707
KB v National Health Service Pensions Agency and Secretary of State for Health (Case C-117/01) [2004] ECR I-541 600
Kemikalieinspektionen v Toolex Alpha AB (Case C-473/98) [2000] ECR I-5681 .... 690, 719
Kempf v Staatssecretaris van Justitie (Case 139/85) [1986] ECR 1741 550
KG in der Firma Hans-Otto Wagner GmbH Agrarhandel v Bundesanstalt für Landwirtschaftliche Marktordnung (Case 8/82) [1983] ECR 371 580
Kjell Karlsson (Case C-292/97) [2000] ECR I-2737 .... 503, 512, 514
Klockner v Commission (Cases 303 and 312/81) [1983] ECR 1507 653
Kobler v Austria (Case C-224/01) [2003] ECR I-10239 .... 821, 823, 828
Kol v Land Berlin (Case C-285/95) [1997] ECR I-3069 634
Koninklijke Nederlandsche Hoogovens en Staalfabrieken NV v High Authority (Case 14/61) [1962] ECR 253 373
Konle v Austria (Case C-302/97) [1999] ECR I-3099 825
Kowalska v Freie und Hansestadt Hamburg (Case 33/89) [1990] ECR 2591 .... 592, 700
Kramer (Cases 3, 4 and 6/76) [1976] ECR 1279 412
Kreil v Bundesrepublik Deutschland (Case C-285/98) [2000] ECR I-69 .... 595, 696
Kremzow v Austria (Case C-299/95) [1997] ECR I-2629 .... 486, 504
Krohn & Co Import-Export GmbH & Co KG v Commission (Case 175/84) [1986] ECR 753 786
Kruger GmbH & Co KG v Hauptzollamt Hamburg-Jonas (Case C-334/95) [1997] ECR I-4517 753
Kuhl v Council (Case 71/72) [1973] ECR 705 783
Kuijer v Council (Case C-353/99) [2000] ECR I-1959 354
Kunqian Catherine Zhu and Man Lavette Chen v Secretary of State for the Home Department (Case C-200/02) [2004] ECR I-9925 701
Kuratorium für Dialyse und Nierentransplantation v Lewark (Case C-457/93) [1996] ECR I-243 .... 592, 700
Kutz-Bauer v Freie und Hansestadt Hamburg (Case C-187/00) [2003] ECR I-2741 700
KYDEP v Council and Commission (Case C-146/91) [1994] ECR I-4199 773

Laara, Cotswold Microsystems Ltd and Oy Transatlantic Software Ltd v Finland (Case C-124/97) [1999] ECR I-6067 .... 516, 709

Laboratoires Pharmaceutiques Bergaderm SA and Goupil v Commission (Case C-352/98) [2000] ECR I-5291 .... 766, 771, 773, 774, 787, 788, 815, 819, 820, 828
Lair v Universität Hannover (Case 39/86) [1988] ECR 3161 .... 566, 574
Land Nordrhein-Westfalen v Beata Pokrzeptowicz-Meyer (Case C-162/00) [2002] ECR I-1049 611
Land Nordrhein-Westfalen v Uecker and Jacquet v Land Nordrhein-Westfalen (Cases C-64/96 and 65/96) [1997] ECR I-3171 569
Land Rheinland-Pfalz v Alcan Deutschland GmbH (Case C-24/95) [1997] ECR I-1591 812
Landbrugsministeriet-EF-Direktoratet v Steff-Houlberg Export (Case C-366/95) [1998] ECR I-2661 811
Landelijke Vereniging tot Behoud van de Waddenzee and Nederlandse Vereniging tot Bescherming van Vogels v Staatssecretaris van Landbouw, Natuurbeheer en Visserij (Case C-127/02) [2004] ECR I-7405 .... 732, 733
Landesamt für Ausbildungsförderung Nordrhein-Westfalen v Lubor Gaal (Case C-7/94) [1996] ECR I-1031 553
Larsy v INASTI (Case C-118/00) [2001] ECR I-5063 824
Lawrie-Blum v Land Baden-Württemberg (Case 6/85) [1986] ECR 2121 .... 550, 557
Leifer (Case C-83/94) [1995] ECR I-3231 711
Lemmerz-Werke v High Authority (Case 111/63) [1965] ECR 677 615
Leon Van Parys NV v BIRB (Case C-377/02) judgment of 1 March 2005 768
Levez v Jennings (Case C-326/96) [1998] ECR I-7835 .... 802, 807
Levin v Staatssecretaris van Justitie (Case 53/81) [1982] ECR 1035 .... 550, 551
Limburgse Vinyl Maatschappij (LVM) v Commission (Cases C-238, 244, 245, 247, 250–252 and 254/99) [2002] ECR I-8375 .... 367, 525, 684
Lommers v Minister van Landbouw, Natuurbeheer en Visserij (Case C-476/99) [2002] ECR I-2891 697
Louwage v Commission (Case 148/73) [1974] ECR 81 642
Ludwigschafener Walzmühle Erling KG v Council (Cases 197–200, 243, 245, 247/80) [1981] ECR 3211 .... 448, 580
Luhrs v Hauptzollamt Hamburg-Jonas (Case 78/77) [1978] ECR 169 632
Luisi and Carbone v Ministero del Tesoro (Cases 286/82 and 26/83) [1984] ECR 377 562

Maas & Co NV v Bundesanstalt fur landwirtschaftliche Marktordnung (Case 21/85) [1986] ECR 3537 682
Maatschap Toeters and M.C.Verberk v Productschap vee en Vlees (Case C-171/03) [2004] ECR I-10945 660
Magorrian and Cunningham v Eastern Health and Social Services Board (Case C-246/96) [1997] ECR I-7153 800
Mannesmann AG v High Authority (Case 19/61) [1962] ECR 357 656
Maria Martinez Sala v Freistaat Bayern (Case C-85/96) [1998] ECR I-2691 .... 568, 569, 570, 571, 573, 577, 578
Marks & Spencer plc v Commissioners of Customs & Excise (Case C-62/00) [2002] ECR I-6325 611
Marleasing SA v La Comercial Internacional de Alimentacion SA (Case C-106/89) [1990] ECR I-4135 711
Marshall v Southampton and South West Area Health Authority II (Case C-271/91) [1993] ECR I-4367 ..... 795, 796, 799, 800, 803, 809, 810, 815
Maso and Gazzetta v INPS (Case C-373/95) [1997] ECR I-4051 826
Masterfoods Ltd v HB Ice Cream Ltd (Case C-344/98) [2000] ECR I-11369 481
Mattila v Commission (Case C-353/01) [2004] ECR I-1073 355
Maurin (Case C-144/95) [1996] ECR I-2909 486
Maurissen v Commission (Cases 193–4/87) [1989] ECR 1045 40
MedioCurso-Etabelecimento de Ensino Particular Ld v Commission (Case C-462/98) [2000] ECR I-7183 .... 315, 361
Meganck v Commission (Case 36/72) [1973] ECR 527 783
Meiko-Konservenfabrik v Federal Republic of Germany (Case 224/82) [1983] ECR 2539 609
Merci Convenzionali Porto di Genova SpA v Siderurgica Gabriella SpA (Case C-179/90) [1991] ECR I-5889 586
Merkur GmbH & Co KG v Commission (Case 43/72) [1973] ECR 1055 .... 584, 768
Meroni & Co v Industrie Metallurgiche SpA v High Authority (Case 9/56) [1958] ECR 133 .... 42, 160, 161, 162, 164, 183, 184, 185, 186, 190, 276
Metallgesellschaft & Hoechst v Inland Revenue (Cases C-397 and 410/98) [2001] ECR I-1727 .... 808, 809, 826
Metro-SB-Grobmärkte GmbH & Co KG v Commission (Case 26/76) [1977] ECR 1875 .... 134, 318
Michel S v Fonds National de Reclassement Handicapés (Case 76/72) [1973] ECR 457 .... 553, 554
Miethke v European Parliament (Case C-25/92) [1993] ECR I-473 268
Milac GmbH v Hauptzollamt Hamburg-St Annen (Case 8/78) [1978] ECR 1721 545

Ministère Public against Xavier Mirepoix (Case 54/85) [1986] ECR 1067 719
Ministère Public v Even and ONPTS (Case 207/78) [1979] ECR 2019 554
Ministère Public v Marchandise (Case C-332/89) [1991] ECR I-1027 713
Ministère Public v Muller (Case 304/84) [1986] ECR 1511 690
Ministero della Salute v Codacons (Case C-132/03) judgment of 26 May 2005 735
Ministero delle Finanze v Spac (Case C-260/96) [1998] ECR I-4997 .. 807
Ministero delle Politiche Agricole e Forestali v Consorzio Produttori Pompelmo Italiano Soc. Coop arl (COPPI) (Case C-271/01) [2004] ECR I-1029 92
Moccia Irme v Commission (Case C-89/97) [1997] ECR I-2327 752
Molkerei Wagenfeld Karl Niemann GmbH & Co KG v Bezirksregierung Hannover (Case C-14/01) [2003] ECR I-2279 459
Monin Automobiles v France (Case C-386/92) [1993] ECR I-2049 289
Monin Automobiles-Maison du Deux-Roues (Case C-428/93) [1994] ECR I-1707 289
Monsanto Agricultura Italia SpA v Presidenza del Consiglio dei Ministri (Case C-236/01) [2003] ECR I-8105 .... 730, 731, 735
Morellato v Unita Sanitaria Locale (USL) n. 11 di Pordenone (Case C-358/95) [1997] ECR I-1431 688
Mulder v Council and Commission (Cases C-104/89 and 37/90) [1992] ECR I-3061 .... 771, 778
Mulder v Minister van Landbouw en Visserij (Case 120/86) [1988] ECR 2321 .... 638, 640, 649, 779
Mulligan v Minister for Agriculture and Food, Northern Ireland (Case C-313/99) [2002] ECR I-5719 689
Musik Metronome GmbH v Music Point Hokamp GmbH (Case C-20/96) [1998] ECR I-1953 675
Musique Diffusion Française v Commission (Cases 100–103/80) [1983] ECR 1825 .... 364, 370

Nachi Europe GmbH v Hauptzollamt Krefeld (Case C-239/99) [2001] ECR I-1197 761
Nachi Fujikoshi Corporation v Council (Case 255/84) [1987] ECR 1861 665
Nashua Corporation v Commission and Council (Cases C-133 and 150/87) [1990] ECR I-719 268
National Power plc and PowerGen plc v British Coal Corporation and Commission (Cases C-151 and 157/97) [1997] ECR I-3491 335

Netherlands and Koninklijke PTT Nederland NV and PTT Post v Commission (Cases C-48 and 66/90) [1992] ECR 565 363
Netherlands and Leeuwarder Papierwarenfabriek v Commission (Cases 296 and 318/82) [1985] ECR 809 383
Netherlands v Commission (Case 11/76) [1979] ECR 245 67
Netherlands v Commission (Case C-278/98) [2001] ECR I-1501 .... 67, 68
Netherlands v Commission (Case C-452/00) judgment of 14 July 2005 .... 463, 660
Netherlands v Commission (Cases C-48 and 60/90) [1992] ECR I-565 316
Netherlands v Council (Case C-58/94) [1996] ECR I-2169 .... 354, 642
Netherlands v Council (Case C-110/97) [2001] ECR I-8763 ...... 635, 639
Netherlands v Council (Case C-301/97) [2001] ECR I-8853 .... 463, 472
Netherlands v Parliament and Council (Case C-377/98) [2001] ECR I-7079 .... 405, 406, 409, 426, 750
Nicoli v Eridania SpA (Case C-87/00) [2004] ECR I-9357 460
Nimz v Freie und Hansestadt Hamburg (Case 184/89) [1991] ECR 297 .... 592, 700
Nold v Commission (Case 4/73) [1974] ECR 491 485
Nolle v Hauptzollamt Bremen-Freihafen (Case 16/90) [1991] ECR I-5163 374
Norbrook Laboratories Ltd v Ministry of Agriculture, Fisheries and Food (Case C-127/95) [1998] ECR I-1531 .... 819, 824, 826
Northern Ireland Fish Producers' Association (NIFPO) and Northern Ireland Fishermen's Federation v Department of Agriculture for Northern Ireland (Case C-4/96) [1998] ECR I-681 .... 448, 660
NV Algemene Transporten Expeditie Onderneming van Gend en Loos v Nederlandse Administratie der Belastingen (Case 26/62) [1963] ECR 1 285

Océano Grupo Editorial v Rocio Murciano Quintero (Cases C-240–244/98) [2000] ECR I-4491 806
Oelmühle Hamburg v Bundesanstalt für Landwirtschaftund Ernährung (Case C-298/96) [1998] ECR I-4767 811
Office National de l'Emploi v Joszef Deak (Case 94/84) [1985] ECR 1873 554
Officier van Justitie v Koniklijke Kassfabriek Eyssen BV (Case 53/80) [1981] ECR 409 689
Officier van Justitie v Sandoz BV (Case 174/82) [1983] ECR 2445 .... 689, 706, 719

O'Flynn v Adjudication Officer (Case C-237/94) [1996] ECR I-2617 .... 548, 555
Oleifici Mediterranea v EEC (Case 26/81) [1982] ECR 3057 773
Olli Mattila v Council and Commission (Case C-353/01) [2004] ECR I-1073 672
Olmuhle Hambourg AG v Hauptzollamt Hamburg-Waltershof (Cases 119 and 120/76) [1977] ECR 1269 682
Omega Spiehallen-und Automatenaufstellungs-GmbH v Oberburgermeisterin der Bundesstadt Bonn (Case C-36/02) [2004] ECR I-9609 .... 516, 708
Openbaar Ministerie v Van der Veldt (Case C-17/93) [1994] ECR I-3537 688
Opinion 1/76, On the Draft Agreement Establishing a Laying-up Fund for Inland Waterway Vessels [1977] ECR 741 .... 412, 413, 414, 417
Opinion 1/94, Competence of the Community to Conclude International Agreements Concerning Services and the Protection of Intellectual Property, WTO [1994] ECR I-5267 .... 412, 413, 415, 416, 417
Opinion 2/00, Opinion Pursuant to Article 300(6) EC, Cartegena Protocol [2001] ECR I-9713 .... 411, 415
Opinion 2/91, Re the ILO Convention 170 on Chemicals at Work [1993] ECR I-1061 .... 412, 415, 416
Opinion 2/92, Competence of the Community or one of its Institutions to Participate in the Third Revised Decision of the OECD on National Treatment [1995] ECR I-521 413
Opinion 2/94, The Accession of the Community to the European Human Rights Convention, Re, [1996] ECR I-1759 .... 408, 412, 486, 491, 531
Orfanopoulos v Land Baden-Wurttemberg (Cases C-482 and 493/01) [2004] ECR I-5257 485
Osterreichische Unilever GmbH v SmithKline Beecham Markenartikel GmbH (Case C-77/97) [1999] ECR I-431 .... 702, 703

P v S and Cornwall County Council (Case C-13/94) [1996] ECR I-2143 .... 587, 589, 599
Palmisani v INPS (Case C-261/95) [1997] ECR I-4025 .... 826, 827
Papiers Peints de Belgique v Commission (Case 73/74) [1975] ECR 1491 383
Parti Ecologiste 'Les Verts' v European Parliament (Case 294/83) [1986] ECR 1339 .... 40, 165, 166, 167, 854
Pasquale Foglia v Mariella Novella (Case 104/79) [1980] ECR 745 .... 289, 290, 302

Pasquale Foglia v Mariella Novello (No.2) (Case 244/80) [1981]
ECR 3045 .... 289, 290, 302
Pastoors and Trans-Cap GmbH v Belgian State (Case C-29/95)
[1997] ECR I-285 701
Pauvert v Court of Auditors (Case 228/84) [1985] ECR 1973 653
Pesqueria Vasco-Montanesa SA (Pevasa) and Compania Internacional
de Pesca y Derivados SA (Inpesca) v Commission (Cases C-199 and
200/94) [1995] ECR I-3709 765
Pesquerias de Bermeo SA and Naviera Laida SA v Commission
(Cases C-258 and 259/90) [1992] ECR I-2901 773
Peter, Paul, Sonnen-Lutte and Christel Morkens v Bundesrepublik
Deutschland (Case C-222/02) [2004] ECR I-9425 818
Peterbroek, Van Campenhout & Cie v Belgian State (Case C-312/93)
[1995] ECR I-4599 .... 799, 804, 805
Petrides Co Inc v Commission (Case C-64/98) [1999]
ECR I-5187 774
Petrotub SA and Republica SA v Council (Case C-76/00) [2003]
ECR I-79 383
Pflucke v Bundesanstalt für Arbeit (Case 125/01) [2003]
ECR I-9375 808
Phil Collins v Imtrat Handelsgesellschaft GmbH (Case C-92/92)
[1993] ECR I-5145 .... 560, 564
Philip Morris Holland BV v Commission (Case 730/79) [1980]
ECR 2671 .... 433, 434, 443, 444, 445
Pietsch v Hauptzollamt Hamburg-Waltershof (Case C-296/94) [1996]
ECR I-3409 682
Pinna v Caisse d'allocations Familiales de Savoie (Case 41/84) [1986]
ECR 1 762
Plaumann & Co v Commission (Case 25/62) [1963] ECR 95 .... 332, 333,
337, 338, 342, 345, 765
Pontillo v Donatab (Case C-372/96) [1998] ECR I-5091 635
Pool v Council (Case 49/79) [1980] ECR 569 584
Portugal v Commission (Case C-150/95) [1997] ECR I-5863 ..... 581, 585
Portugal v Commission (Case C-365/99) [2001] ECR I-5645 682
Portugal v Commission (Case C-159/96) [1998] ECR I-7379 757
Portugal v Council (Case C-149/96) [1999] ECR I-8395 768
Portugal v Council (Case C-268/94) [1996] ECR I-6177 416
Portuguese Republic v Commission (Case C-89/96) [1999]
ECR I-8377 755
Portuguese Republic v Commission (Case C-159/96) [1998]
ECR I-7379 268
Portuguese Republic v Commission (Case C-240/92) [2004]
ECR I-10717 268

Portuguese Republic v Council (Case C-268/94) [1996] ECR I-6177 486
Preston v Wolverhampton Healthcare NHS Trust (Case C-78/98) [2000] ECR I-3201 .... 800, 807, 808
Procureur de la République Besançon v Bouhelier (Case 53/76) [1977] ECR 197 548

Questore di Verona v Zenatti (Case C-67/98) [1999] ECR I-7289 709

R, ex p Centro-Com v HM Treasury and Bank of England (Case C-124/95) [1997] ECR I-81 689
R (on the application of Alliance for Natural Health and Nutri-Link Ltd) v Secretary of State for Health (Cases C-154 and 155/04) judgment of 12 July 2005 .... 161, 359, 426, 734
R (on the application of Bidar) v London Borough of Ealing and Secretary of State for Education (Case C-209/03) [2005] ECR I-2119 .... 568, 573, 574, 575, 577, 578
R (on the application of Omega Air Ltd) v Secretary of State for the Environment, Transport and the Regions (Case C-27/00) [2002] ECR I-2569 664
R (on the application of Swedish Match AB and Swedish Match UK Ltd) v Secretary of State for Health (Case C-210/03) [2004] ECR I-11893 658
R v Bouchereau (Case 30/77) [1977] ECR 1999 692
R v Henn and Darby (Case 34/79) [1979] ECR 3795 708
R v HM Treasury, ex p British Telecommunications plc (Case C-392/93) [1996] ECR I-1631 .... 711, 820, 822
R v Immigration Appeal Tribunal, ex p Antonissen (Case C-292/89) [1991] ECR I-745 .... 549, 550
R v Intervention Board, ex p E.D.& F.Man (Sugar) Ltd (Case 181/84) [1985] ECR 2889 .... 681, 682
R v Lomas (Cases C-38, 151/90) [1992] ECR I-178 762
R v Minister for Agriculture, Fisheries and Food, ex p Fedesa (Case C-331/88) [1990] ECR 4023 .... 610, 659, 661, 662, 670, 671
R v Ministry of Agriculture, Fisheries and Food, Commissioners of Customs and Excise, ex p National Farmers' Union (Case C-157/96) [1998] ECR I-2211 719
R v Ministry of Agriculture, Fisheries and Food, ex p Hedley Lomas (Ireland) Ltd (Case C-5/94) [1996] ECR I-2553 .... 819, 824
R v Secretary of State for the Environment and Ministry of Agriculture, Fisheries and Food, ex p Standley (Case C-293/97) [1999] ECR I-2603 675

R v Secretary of State for the Environment, Transport and the Regions, ex p Omega Air Ltd (Cases C-27 and 122/00) [2002] ECR I-2569 459
R v Secretary of State for Health, ex p British American Tobacco (Investments) Ltd and Imperial Tobacco Ltd (Case C-491/01) [2002] ECR I-11453 .... 406, 426, 658, 667, 675, 676
R v Secretary of State for Health, ex p Richardson (Case C-137/94) [1995] ECR I-3407 795
R v Secretary of State for the Home Department, ex p Kondova (Case C-235/99) [2001] ECR I-6427 485
R v Secretary of State for Social Security, ex p Eunice Sutton (Case C-66/95) [1997] ECR I-2163 .... 799, 809
R v Secretary of State for Transport, ex p Factortame Ltd (Case C-213/89) [1990] ECR I-2433 ..... 753, 772, 787, 791, 792, 793, 798, 817, 819, 820, 821, 822
R and V. Haegman Sprl v Commission (Case 96/71) [1972] ECR 1005 785
Ragusa v Commission (Case 282/81) [1983] ECR 1245 642
Ramondin SA v Commission (Cases C-186 and 188/02) [2004] ECR I-10653 463
Raulin v Minister van Onderwijs en Wetenschappen (Case C-357/89) [1992] ECR I-1027 .... 550, 567
Razzouk and Beydoun v Commission (Cases 75 and 117/82) [1984] ECR 1509 .... 587, 589
Rechberger v Austria (Case C-140/97) [1999] ECR I-3499 .... 822, 823
Recheio-Cash and Carry SA v Fazenda Publica/Registo Nacional de Pessoas Colectivas and Ministerio Publico (Case C-30/02) [2004] ECR I-6051 806
Rechsnungshof v Osterreichischer Rundfunk (Cases C-465/00, 138 and 139/01) [2003] ECR I-4989 .... 485, 505
Regina v Kent Kirk (Case 63/83) [1984] ECR 2689 .... 609, 610
Reina v Landeskreditbank Baden-Württemberg (Case 65/81) [1982] ECR 33 555
Reisdorf v Finanzamt Koln-West (Case C-85/95) [1996] ECR I-6257 290
Reiseburo Broede v Gerd Sandker (Case C-3/95) [1996] ECR I-6511 708
Remia BV and Nutricia BV v Commission (Case 42/84) [1985] ECR 2545 .... 395, 444
Renckens v Commission (Case 27/68) [1969] ECR 274 750
Reti Televisie Italiane SpA (RTI) v Ministero delle Poste e Telecommunicazione (Cases C-320, 328, 329, 337, 338 and 339/94) [1996] ECR I-6471 289

Rewe Zentrale v Bundesmonopolverwaltung für Branntwein (Case 120/78) [1979] ECR 649 690
Rewe-Handelsgesellschaft Nord mbH v Hauptzollamt Kiel (Case 158/80) [1981] ECR 1805 790
Rewe-Zentralfinanz eG and Rewe-Zentral AG v Landwirtschaftskammer für das Saarland (Case 33/76) [1976] ECR 1989 790
Rewe-Zentralfinanz v Landwirtschaftskammer (Case 4/75) [1975] ECR 843 548
Rey Soda v Cassa Conguaglio Zucchero (Case 23/75) [1975] ECR 1279 106
Rica Foods (Free Zone) NV v Commission (Case C-41/03) [2005] ECR I-6875 .... 472, 660
Rinke v Arztekammer Hamburg (Case C-25/02) [2003] ECR I-8349 .... 485, 587
Rinner-Kühn v FWW Spezial-Gebäudereinigung GmbH (Case 171/88) [1989] ECR 2743 .... 592, 699, 700
Roman Angonese v Cassa di Riparmio di Bolzano SpA (Case C-281/98) [2000] ECR I-4139 561
Roquette Frères SA v Directeur General de la Concurrence, de la Consomation et de la Repression des Fraudes and Commission (Case C-94/00) [2002] ECR I-9011 525
Roquette Frères SA v Hauptzollamt Geldern (Case C-228/92) [1994] ECR I-1445 .... 757, 762
Roquette Frères v Commission (Case 20/88) [1989] ECR 1553 787
Roquette Frères v Commission (Case 26/74) [1976] ECR 677 ... 778, 784, 796
Roquette Frères v Council (Case 138/79) [1980] ECR 3333 448
Roquette v Direction des Services Fiscaux du Pas-de-Calais (Case C-88/99) [2000] ECR I-10465 .... 802, 807
Royal Scholten-Honig (Holdings) Ltd v Intervention Board for Agricultural Produce, Tunnel Refineries Ltd v Intervention Board for Agriculture Produce (Cases 103 and 145/77) [1978] ECR 2037 .... 582, 770
Ruckdeschel v Hauptzollamt Hambourg-St Annen (Cases 117/76 and 16/77) [1977] ECR 1753 .... 271, 545, 581
Rudy Grzelczyk v Centre Public D'Aide Sociale d'Ottignes-Louvain-la-Neuve (CPAS) (Case C-184/99) [2001] ECR I-6193 ..... 550, 568, 572, 573, 574, 576, 577, 578
Rummler (Case 237/85) [1986] ECR 2101 590
Rutili v Ministere de l'Intérieur (Case 36/75) [1975] ECR 1219 .... 504, 692

SA Biovilac NV v EEC (Case 59/83) [1984] ECR 4057 ...... 434, 777, 782

SA Roquette Frères v France (Case 145/79) [1980] ECR 2917 762
Sagulo, Brenca and Bakhouche (Case 8/77) [1977] ECR 1495 793
Salgoil v Italian Ministry for Foreign Trade (Case 13/68) [1973] ECR 453 790
Salumi v Amministrazione delle Finanze (Cases 66, 127 and 128/79) [1980] ECR 1237 794
Santex SpA v Unita Socio Sanitaria Locale n.42 di Pavia, Sca Molnlycke SpA, Artsana SpA and Fater SpA (Case C-327/00) [2003] ECR I-1877 .... 803, 805
Sayag v Leduc (Case 9/69) [1969] ECR 329 .... 780, 781
SCAC v Associazione dei Produttori Ortofrutticoli (Case C-56/94) [1995] ECR I-1769 585
Schmidberger Internationale Transporte und Planzuge v Austria (Case C-112/00) [2003] ECR I-5659 ...... 513, 514, 516, 678, 679, 707
Schnitzer (Case C-215/01) [2003] ECR I-14847 694
Scholz v Universitaria di Cagliari (Case C-419/92) [1994] ECR I-505 548
Schrader HS Kraftfutter GmbH & Co KG v Hauptzollamt Gronau (Case 265/87) [1989] ECR 2237 675
Schwarze (Case 16/65) [1965] ECR 877 383
SCK and FNK v Commission (Case C-268/96) [1996] ECR I-4971 ... 751
SEIM-Sociedade de Exportacoa de Materias, Ld v Subdirector-Geral das Alfandegas (Case C-446/93) [1996] ECR I-73 290
Semeraro Casa Uno Srl v Sindaco del Commune di Ebrusco (Cases C-418–421, 460–462, 464/93, 9–11, 14–15, 23–24, and 332/94) [1996] ECR I-2975 713
Serge Briheche v Ministere de l'Interieur, Ministere de l'Education and Ministere de la Justice (Case C-319/03) [2004] ECR I-8807 697
Seymour-Smith and Perez (Case C-167/97) [1999] ECR I-623 592
Sgarlata v Commission (Case 40/64) [1965] ECR 215 484
SGEEM and Etroy v EIB (Case C-370/89) [1992] ECR I-6211 .... 166, 764
Sideradria SpA v Commission (Case 67/84) [1985] ECR 3983 634
Silos e Mangimi Martini SpA v Ministero delle Finanze (Case C-228/99) [2001] ECR I-8401 762
Simon v High Authority (Case 15/60) [1961] ECR 115 626
Sirdar v Army Board (Case C-273/97) [1999] ECR I-7403 .... 595, 696
SNUPAT v High Authority (Cases 42 and 49/59) [1961] ECR 53 ..... 615, 617, 623
Société Bautiaa v Directeur des Services Fiscaux des Landes (Cases C-197 and 252/94) [1996] ECR I-505 795
Société Coopérative 'Providence Agricole de la Champagne' v ONIC (Case 4/79) [1980] ECR 2823 .... 762, 763

Société des Grands Moulins des Antilles v Commission (Case 99/74) [1975] ECR 1531 786
Société Français des Biscuits Delacre v Commission (Cases C-350/88) [1990] ECR I-395 635
Societe La Technique Miniere (LTM) v Maschinenbau Ulm GmbH (Case 56/65) [1966] ECR 235 373
Société pour l'Exploration des Sucres SA v Commission (Case 132/77) [1978] ECR 1061 777
Sociétés de Produits de Maïs v Administration des Douanes (Case 112/83) [1985] ECR 719 762
Sociétés des Fonderies de Pont-á-Mousson v High Authority (Case 14/59) [1959] ECR 215 579
Sofrimport Sàrl v Commission (Case C-152/88) [1990] ECR I-2477 .... 639, 640
Somalfruit SpA and Camar SpA v Ministero delle Finanze and Ministero del Commercio con l'Estero (Case C-369/95) [1997] ECR I-6619 460
Sotgiu v Deutsche Bundespost (Case 152/73) [1974] ECR 153 ... 548, 555
SpA Alois Lageder v Amministrazione delle Finanze dello Stato (Cases C-31–41/91) [1993] ECR I-1761 .... 611, 653
SpA Ferriere San Carlo v Commission (Case 344/85) [1987] ECR 4435 643
Spagl v Hauptzollamt Rosenheim (Case C-189/89) [1990] ECR I-4539 .... 640, 649, 650, 651
Spain and Finland v European Parliament and Council (Cases C-184 and 223/02) [2004] ECR I-7789 677
Spain v Commission (Case C-113/00) [2002] ECR I-7601 460
Spain v Commission (Case C-169/95) [1997] ECR I-135 683
Spain v Commission (Case C-304/01) [2004] ECR I-7655 458
Spain v Commission (Case C-351/98) [2002] ECR I-8031 645
Spain v Commission (Case C-409/00) [2003] ECR I-1487 646
Spain v Commission (Case C-415/96) [1998] ECR I-6993 756
Spain v Council (Case C-342/03) [2005] ECR I-1975 632
Spain v Council (Case C-350/92) [1995] ECR I-1985 408
Spain v Eurojust (Case C-160/03) [2005] ECR I-2077 .... 166, 167, 269
Spitta & Co v Hauptzollamt Frankfurt/Main-Ost (Case 127/78) [1979] ECR 171 632
SPUC v Grogan (Case C-159/90) [1991] ECR I-4685 516
Srl CILFIT and Lanificio di Gavardo SpA v Ministry of Health (Case 283/81) [1982] ECR 3415 .... 284, 285
Stahlwerke Peine-Salzgitter AG v Commission (Case C-220/91) [1993] ECR I-2393 771

State Aid to Bug-Alutechnik GmbH, Commission v Germany, Re (Case C-5/89) [1990] ECR I-3437 812
Stauder v City of Ulm (Case 29/69) [1969] ECR 419 .... 484, 485
Steenhorst-Neerings v Bestuur van de Bedrijfsvereniging voor Detailhandel, Ambachten en Huisvrouwen (Case C-338/91) [1993] ECR I-5475 .... 800, 801, 802, 803
Steymann v Staatsecretaris van Justitie (Case 196/87) [1988] ECR 6159 .... 431, 550
Stichting Sigarettenindustrie v Commission (Cases 240–242, 261–262, 268–269/82) [1985] ECR 3831 395
Stockholm Lindöpark Aktiebolag v Sweden (Case C-150/99) [2001] ECR I-493 824
Stoke-on-Trent CC v B & Q plc (Cases C-306/88, 304/90 and 169/91) [1992] ECr I-6457 713
Stolting v Hauptzollamt Hamburg-Jonas (Case 138/78) [1979] ECR 713 659
Stork v High Authority (Case 1/58) [1959] ECR 17 484
Sucrimex SA and Westzucker GmbH v Commission (Case 133/79) [1980] ECR 1299 786
Sudzucker Mannheim/Ochsenfurt AG v Hauptzollamt Mannheim (Case C-161/96) [1998] ECR I-281 681
Syndicat Français de l'Express International (SFEI) v Commission (Case C-39/93) [1994] ECR I-2681 .... 268, 435

Tariff Preferences Case (Case 45/86) [1987] ECR 1493 .... 408, 409
Telemarsicabruzzo SpA v Circostel, Ministero delle Poste e Telecommunicazione and Ministero della Difesa (Cases C-320–322/90) [1993] ECR I-393 289
Texaco A/S v Havn (Cases C-114–115/95) [1997] ECR I-4263 802
Thyssen AG v Commission (Case 188/82) [1983] ECR 3721 653
ThyssenKrupp GmbH v Commission (Cases C-65 and 73/02) judgment of 14 July 2005 634
Timex Corporation v Council and Commission (Case 264/82) [1985] ECR 849 758
TNT Traco SpA v Post Italiane SpA (Case C-340/99) [2001] ECR I-4109 586
Toepfer v Commission (Cases 106 and 107/63) [1965] ECR 405 785
Torfaen BC v B & Q plc (Case 145/88) [1989] ECR 3851 .... 713, 715
T. Port GmbH & Co KG v Bundesanstalt fur Landwirtschaft und Ernahrung (Case C-68/95) [1996] ECR I-6065 508
Tralli v ECB (Case C-301/02) [2005] ECR I-4071 162
Transocean Marine Paint v Commission (Case 17/74) [1974] ECR 1063 314

Trojani v Centre Public D'Aide Sociale de Bruxelles (CPAS) (Case C-456/02) [2004] ECR I-7573 .... 550, 568, 571, 573, 578

UK v Commission (Case C-180/96) [1998] ECR I-2265 718
UNECTEF v Heylens (Case 222/86) [1987] ECR 4097 794
Unifrex v Commission and Council (Case 281/82) [1984] ECR 1969 .... 584, 787
Union de Pequenos Agricultores v Council (Case C-50/00) [2002] ECR I-6677 .... 331, 335, 336, 337, 339, 340, 341, 342, 343, 346
Union Départment des Syndicats CGT de l'Aisne v SIDEF Conforama (Case C-312/89) [1991] ECR I-997 713
Union Malt v Commission (Cases 44–51/77) [1978] ECR 57 773
Union Royale Belge des Societes de Football Assn ASBL v Bosman (Case C-415/93) [1995] ECR I-4921 .... 426, 561
Unita Socio-Sanitaria Locale No 47 di Biella (USSL) v Instituto Nazionale per l'Assicurazione contro gli Infortuni sul Lavoro (INAIL) (Case C-134/95) [1997] ECR I-195 289
United Kingdom v Commission (Case C-180/96) [1998] ECR I-2265 .... 268, 434
United Kingdom v Council (Case C-84/94) [1996] ECR I-5755 .... 384, 405, 426
United Kingdom v Council (Case C-150/94) [1998] ECR I-7235 472
Upjohn v the Licensing Authority (Case C-120/97) [1999] ECR I-223 .... 794, 815
Ursula Elsen v Bundesversicherungsanstalt (Case C-135/99) [2000] ECR I-10409 569

Van Binsbergen v Bestuur van de Bedrijfsvereniging voor de Metaalnijverheid (Case 33/74) [1974] ECR 1299 .... 560, 693
Van den Bergh en Jurgens and Van Dijk Food Products v Commission (Case 265/85) [1987] ECR 1155 .... 628, 631, 782
Van Duyn v Home Office (Case 41/74) [1974] ECR 1337 .... 285, 708
Van Landewyck SARL v Commission (Cases 209–215, 218/78) [1980] ECR 3125 370
Van Schijndel & Van Veen v Stichting Pensioenfonds voor Fysiotherapeuten (Cases C-430–431/93) [1995] ECR I-4705 .... 799, 804, 805
VBVB and VBBB v Commission (Cases 43, 63/82) [1985] ECR 19 ... 366
Vereinigte Familiapress Zeitungsverlags-und vertriebs GmbH v Heinrich Bauer Verlag (Case C-368/95) [1997] ECR I-368 .... 485, 516, 533, 713, 715
Vereniging voor Energie, Milieu en Water v Directeur van de Dienst uitvoering en toezicht energie (Case C-17/03) [2005] ECR I-4983 636

Verholen v Sociale Verzekeringsbank (Cases C-87–89/90) [1991] ECR I-3757 794
Verli-Wallace v Commission (Case 159/82) [1983] ECR 2711 615
Vinal SpA v Orbat SpA (Case 46/80) [1981] ECR 77 289
Vloeberghs v High Authority (Cases 9 and 12/60) [1961] ECR 197 777
Von Colson and Kamann v Land Nordrhein-Westfalen (Case 14/83) [1984] ECR 1891 .... 793, 797

Wachauf v Germany (Case 5/88) [1989] ECR 2609 ... 485, 502, 503, 504, 512, 514
Wagner v BALM (Case 8/82) [1983] ECR 371 .... 581, 582
Walrave and Koch (Case 36/74) [1974] ECR 1405 561
Walter Rau Lebensmittelwerke v De Smedt, Pvba (Case 261/81) [1982] ECR 3961 .... 289, 689
Weber's Wine World Handels-GmbH v Abgabenberufungskommission Wien (Case C-147/01) [2003] ECR I-11365 811
Weidacher v Bundesminister fur Land-und Forstwirtschaft (Case C-179/00) [2002] ECR I-501 635
Weingut Gustav Decker KG v Hauptzollamt Landau (Case 99/78) [1979] ECR 101 608
Werner (Case C-70/94) [1995] ECR I-3189 711
Westzucker GmbH v Einfuhr-und Vorratsstelle für Zucker (Case 57/72) [1973] ECR 321 .... 433, 439, 440, 441, 444, 445, 446
W. Faust v Commission (Case 52/81) [1982] ECR 3745 635
Wienand Meilicke v ADV/ORGA F.A. Meyer AG (Case C-83/91) [1992] ECR I-4871 289
William Cook plc v Commission (Case C-198/91) [1993] ECR I-2486 377
Williame v Commission (Case 110/63) [1965] ECR 649 783
Willy Gerekens and Association Agricole pour la Promotion de la Commercialisation Laitiere Procola v Luxembourg (Case C-459/02) [2004] ECR I-7315 .... 608, 610
Windpark Groothusen GmbH & Co Betriebs KG v Commission (Case C-48/96) [1998] ECR I-2873 .... 314, 462, 463
Woodcock District Council v Bakers of Nailsea (Case C-27/95) [1997] ECR I-1847 448
Wollast v EEC (Case 18/63) [1964] ECR 85 783
Worms v High Authority (Case 18/60) [1962] ECR 195 764
Wuidart v Laiterie Cooperative Eupenoise Societe Cooperative (Cases 267–285/88) [1990] ECR I-435 584
Württembergische Milchverwertung-Südmilch-AG v Salvatore Ugliola (Case 15/69) [1970] ECR 363 .... 548, 554

Zardi v Consorzio Agrario Provinciale di Ferrara (Case C-8/89) [1990] ECR I-2515 60
Zuckerfabrik Süderdithmarschen AG v Hauptzollamt Itzehoe (Cases C-143/88 and 92/89) [1991] ECR I-415 .... 285, 752, 753
Zunis Holding SA, Finan Srl and Massinvest SA v Commission (Case C-480/93) [1996] ECR I-1 268
Zurstrassen v Administration des Contributions Directes (Case C-87/99) [2000] ECR I-3337 548

EUROPEAN COURT OF HUMAN RIGHTS

Airey v Ireland (1979–1980) 2 EHRR 305 511
Bosphorus Hava Yollari Turizm Ve Ticaret Anonim Sirketi v Ireland, ECHR (2005) No. 450 36/98 525–530
Cantoni v France, ECHR (1996) No.45/95 .... 528, 529, 530
Dangeville v France, ECHR (2002) No.36677/97 528
Lopez Ostra v Spain (1995) 20 EHRR 513 511
Markcx v Belgium (1979–1980) 2 EHRR 330 511
Matthews v United Kingdom, ECHR (1999) No.24833/94 525
Plattform 'Arzte fur das Leben' v Austria (1991) 13 EHRR 204 511
Van de Hurk v Netherlands, ECHR (1994) Series A, No.288 528
X and Y v Netherlands (1986) 8 EHRR 235 511
Young, James and Webster v United Kingdom (1982) 4 EHRR 38 511

NATIONAL COURTS

Canada

Public Service Alliance of Canada v Attorney General of Canada [1991] 1 SCR 614 437
Union des Employes de Service, Local 298 v Bibeault [1988] 2 SCR 1048 437

Germany

Brunner v European Union Treaty [1994] 1 CMLR 57 486
Wunsche Handelsgesellschaft, Re, Dec. of 22 Oct. 1986 [1987] 3 CMLR 225 534

Italy

SpA Fragd v Amminstrazione delle Finance, Dec. 232, 12 April 1989 (1989) 72 RDI 534

SpA Granital v Amminsitazione delle Finanze, Dec. 170, 8 June 1984 534

United Kingdom

B & Q plc v Shrewsbury BC [1990] 3 CMLR 535 713
Nadarajah v Secretary of State for the Home Department [2005] EWCA Civ 1363 651
Payless v Peterborough CC [1990] 2 CMLR 577 713
R v Ministry of Agriculture, Fisheries and Food, ex p Hamble (Offshore) Fisheries Ltd [1995] 2 All ER 714 612
R v Secretary of State for Employment, ex p Equal Opportunities Commission [1995] 1 AC 1 532
R v Secretary of State for Transport, ex p Factortame Ltd (No.2) [1991] 1 AC 603 532
Stoke City Council v B & Q plc [1990] 3 CMLR 31 713
Wellingborough BC v Payless [1990] 1 CMLR 773 713
X (Minors) v Bedfordshire CC [1995] 2 AC 633 774

United States

Bi-Metallic Investment Co v State Board of Equalization of Colorado, 239 US 441 (1915) 319
Bowsher v Synar, 478 US 714 (1986) 136
Chevron USA Inc v NRDC, 467 US 837 (1984) 436
Director, Office of Workers' Compensation Programs, Department of Labor v Greenwich Collieries Director, 114 S.Ct 2251 (1994) 465
Environmental Defense Fund Inc v Ruckelshaus, 439 F.2d 584 (DC Cir 1971) 476
Greater Boston Television Corp v Federal Communications Commission, 444 F.2d 841 (DC Cir 1970), cert. denied 403 US 923 (1971) 476
Immigration and Naturalization Service v Chadha, 462 US 919 (1983) 136
International Harvester Co v Ruckelshaus, 478 F.2d 615 (DC Cir 1973) 138
Mathews v Eldridge, 424 US 319 (1976) 362
Motor Vehicle Manufacturers Assn v State Farm Mutual Automobile Insurance Co, 463 US 29 (1984) 476
National Labour Relations Board v Hearst Publications Inc, 322 US 111 (1944) 437
Portland Cement Assn v Ruckelshaus, 486 F.2d 375 (DC Cir 1973) 138
Professional Air Traffic Controllers Organisation (PATCO) v Federal Labor Relations Authority, 685 F 2d 547 (1982) 372

Steadman v SEC, 450 US 91 (1981) 465
United States v Florida East Coast Railway, 410 US 224 (1973) 137
United States v Mead Corporation, 533 US 218 (2001) 436
Vermont Yankee Nuclear Power Corp v Natural Resources Defence
Council Inc., 435 US 519 (1978) 138

Table of Legislation

EU LEGISLATION

Charters

Charter of Fundamental Rights of the European Union, OJ 2000 C364/1 .... 313, 314, 366, 483, 492, 493, 494, 504, 508, 532, 537, 540, 543, 544, 587, 680, 849
- Art 1 .... 495, 507
- Art 2 495
- Art 3 .... 495, 507
  - (1) 495
- Art 4 495
- Art 5 .... 495, 524
  - (3) 519
- Art 6 495
- Art 7 495
- Art 8 .... 495, 507, 524
- Art 9 .... 495, 524
- Art 10 495
- Art 11 .... 495, 511, 849
  - (2) 517, 519
- Art 12 495
  - (1) 507
- Art 13 495
- Art 14 495
- Art 15 495
  - (3) 517
- Art 16 495
- Art 17 495
- Art 18 .... 495, 507, 517
- Art 19 495
- Art 20 495
- Art 21
  - (1) 495, 507, 518, 587
  - (2) 495, 517
- Art 22 .... 495, 517
- Art 23 .... 495, 498, 517, 519
- Art 24 .... 495, 507
  - (2) 500, 849
- Art 25 495
- Art 26 .... 495, 849
- Art 27 495
- Art 28 .... 495, 511
- Art 29 .... 495, 510
- Art 30 .... 495, 510
- Art 31 .... 495, 510
  - (1)–(2) 519
- Art 32 .... 495, 517, 519
- Art 33 495
  - (2) 849
- Art 34 496
  - (1) 517
- Art 35 .... 496, 517
- Art 36 496
- Art 37 .... 496, 517
- Art 38 .... 496, 509, 517
- Art 39 .... 496, 517, 849
- Art 40 .... 496, 517
- Art 41 .... 346, 385, 386, 496, 520, 522, 849
  - (1) 379, 385, 386, 520, 521, 522
  - (2) 314, 346, 361, 366, 367, 385, 386, 520, 521, 522
  - (3) 385, 521, 522
  - (3)–(4) 521
  - (4) 385, 517, 521
- Art 42 .... 353, 359, 496, 517, 849

Charter of Fundamental Rights of the European Union, OJ 2000 C364/1 (*cont.*):
Art 43 .... 496, 517, 849
Art 44 .... 496, 517
Art 45 496
(1) 517
Art 46 .... 496, 517
Art 47 .... 346, 371, 380, 386, 496, 750
Art 48 496
Art 49 .... 496, 507
Art 50 496
Art 51
(1) 496, 498, 500, 501, 502, 503, 505, 509, 511
(2) 496, 506, 507, 518
Art 52 .... 496, 509, 533
(1) 496, 514, 515, 516, 520, 680
(2) ... 496, 517, 520, 521, 522
(3) 496, 516, 523, 524
Art 53 .... 496, 533, 535
Art 54 496
Ch I 495
Ch II 495
Ch III 495
Ch IV 495
Ch V 496
Ch VI 496
Ch VII 496

Decisions *(chronological order)*

Council Decision 87/373/EEC of 13 July 1987 OJ 1987 L197/33 107
Council Decision 88/591/ECSC of 24 October 1988 OJ 1988 L319/1 284
Council Decision 92/421/EEC of 13 July 1992 OJ 1992 L231/26 6
Council Decision 93/350/ECSC of 8 June 1993 OJ 1993 L144/21 284
Council Decision 93/731/EC of 20 December 1993 OJ 1993 L340/43 .... 352, 672
Art 4(1) 672, 673
Commission Decision 94/90/ECSC of 8 February 1994 OJ 1994 L46/58 352
Council Decision 94/149/ECSC of 7 March 1994 OJ 1994 L66/29 284
Commission Decision 94/442/EC of 1 July 1994 OJ 1994 L182/45 66
Art 1
(1)(b) 66
(2) 66
Art 3 66
Council Decision 94/819/EC of 6 December 1994 OJ 1994 L340/8 9
Decision C(97) 3151 of 15 October 1997 91
Council Decision 99/468/EC of 28 June 1999 OJ 1999 L184/23 110
Art 1 110
Art 2 111
Arts 4–5 110
Art 5(5) 110, 130
Art 5a 111
Art 7 110
(3) 110, 130
Art 8 .... 110, 130
Council Decision 1999/24/EC of 14 December 1998 OJ 1999 L7/28 43
Council Decision 1999/25/Euratom of 14 December 1998 OJ 1999 L7/31 43

Decision 646/2000/EC of the European Parliament and Council of 28 February 2000, OJ 2000 L79/1 ... 43
Decision 647/2000/EC of the European Parliament and Council of 28 February 2000 OJ 2000 L79/6 43
Council Decision 2000/436/EC of 29 June 2000 OJ 2000 L172/26 208
Commission Decision 2000/633/EC of 17 October 2000 OJ 2000 L267/63 .... 280, 398
Decision 2000/649 OJ 2000 L272/41 66
Council Decision 2000/820/JHA of 22 December 2000 OJ 2000 L336/1 151
Decision C(2001) 476 of 2 March 2001 91
Commission Decision 2001/462/EC of 23 May 2001 OJ 2001 L162/21 372
Commission Decision 2001/937/EC of 5 December 2001 OJ 2001 L345/94 353
Decision 50/2002/EC of 7 December 2001 OJ 2002 L10/1 207
Annex 208
Art 2 207
Art 3 208
Art 4 208
Council Decision 2002/187/JHA of 28 February 2002 OJ 2002 L63/1 151
Art 2 173
Art 3 159
Art 4 159
Art 6(a) 151
Arts 6(b)(g) 160
Art 10 173
Art 11 .... 173, 175
Art 29 173
Council Decision 2002/682/EC of 22 July 2002 OJ 2002 L230/7 353
Decision 1786/2002/EC of the European Parliament and Council of 23 September 2002 OJ 2002 L271/1 ... 50
Decision 1230/2003/EC of the European Parliament and Council of 26 June 2003 OJ 2003 L176/29 43
Art 1 48
(1) 48
Arts 1–2 48
Art 2 48
Art 3 49
(1) 45
(2) 45
Art 4 45
(1) 46
(a) 46
(b) 46
(c) 47
(2) 47
Art 5
(1) 45
(2) 46
Art 6 48
Art 7 .... 45, 47
Arts 7–8 49
Art 8 45
Annex 5 49
Council Decision 2003/578/EC of 22 July 2003 OJ 2003 L197/13 204
Decision 2317/2003/EC of the European Parliament and Council of 5 December 2003 OJ 2003 L345/1 49

Decision 2318/2003/EC of the European Parliament and Council of 5 December 2003 OJ 2003 L345/9 .. 48
Commission Decision 2004/20/EC of 23 December 2003 OJ 2004 L5/85 46
Council Decision 2004/100/EC of 26 January 2004 OJ 2004 L30/6 47
Council Decision 2004/407/EC of 26 April 2004 OJ 2004 L132/5 293
Council Decision 2004/752/EC of 2 November 2004 OJ 2004 L333/7 .... 294, 295
Council Decision 2241/2004/EC of 15 December 2004 OJ 2004 L390/6 351
Commission Decision 2004/858/EC of 15 December 2004 OJ 2004 L369/73 49
Commission Decision 2005/56/EC of 14 January 2005 OJ 2005 L24/35 47
Council Decision 2005/600/EEC of 12 July 2005 OJ 2005 L205/21 205
Commission Decison Case IV/M.1016, Price Waterhouse/Coopers & Lybrand, OJ 1999 L50/27 466

Directives *(Chronological order)*

Council Directive 65/65/EEC of 26 January 1965 OJ 1965 L22/369 727
Art 11 .... 727, 728
Council Directive 75/117/EEC of 10 February 1975 OJ 1975 L45/19 .... 589, 590
Art 6 591
Council Directive 76/207/EEC of 9 February 1976 OJ 1976 L39/40 594, 600, 695, 794
Art 2
(1) 594, 695
(2) 594, 595, 695, 696
(3) 594, 697
(6) 595, 696
(8), ex Art 2(4) 594, 596, 597, 598, 599, 697, 698
Arts 3–5 594
Art 3(1) 697
Art 6 .... 795, 796, 799, 800
Arts 6–8 594
Council Directive 76/778/EEC of 27 July 1976 OJ 1976 L262/169 .... 701, 702
Art 6(3) 702, 703
Council Directive 79/7/EEC of 19 December 1978 OJ 1979 L6/24 .... 797, 799
Art 4(1) 800
Art 6 .... 799, 800
Directive 79/32/EEC 823
Council Directive 80/987/EEC of 20 October 1980 OJ 1980 L283/23 ...... 808, 815, 826
Directive 84/5/EEC 824
Directive 90/314/EEC 823
Art 7 823
Directive 90/351/EEC 822
Council Directive 90/364/EEC of 28 June 1990 OJ 1990 L180/26 ...... 571, 573, 574
Directive 90/435/EEC 823
Council Directive 91/271/EEC of 21 May 1991 OJ 1991 L135/40 731
Council Directive 92/43/EEC 21 May 1992 OJ 1992 L206/7 732
Art 6(3) 732, 733

Council Directive 93/36/EEC of 14 June 1993 803
Council Directive 93/96/EEC of 29 October 1993 OJ 1993 L317/59 ..... 573, 574
Art 3 574
Council Directive 96/34/EC of 3 June 1996 OJ 1996 L145/4 .... 239, 245
Council Directive 96/61/EC of 24 September 1996 OJ 1996 L257/26 323
Art 15 323
Art 15a 329
Council Directive 97/80/EC of 15 December 1997 OJ 1997 L14/6 591
Art 2(2) 592
Council Directive 97/81/EC of 15 December 1997 OJ 1998 L14/9 239
Council Directive 99/63/EC of 21 June 1999 OJ 1999 L167/33 240
Council Directive 99/70/EC of 28 June 1999 OJ 1999 L175/43 240
Council Directive 2000/43/EC of 29 June 2000 OJ 2000 L180/22 602
Art 2
(1) 603
(2)(b) 602
(3) 603
Art 3
(1) 603
(2) 603
Art 4 603
Art 5 603
Art 7 603
Art 8 603
Arts 9–13 603
Art 14 603
Art 15 603
Preamble 602
Council Directive 2000/78/EC of 27 November 2000 OJ 2000 L303/16 .... 601, 602, 603
Art 1 603
Preamble 601
Council Directive 2000/79/EC of 27 November 2000 OJ 2000 L302/57 240
Directive 2002/21/EC of 7 March 2002 OJ 2002 L108/33 323
Art 6 323
Directive 2002/73/EC of 23 September 2002 OJ 2002 L269/15 ...... 595, 696, 796
Art 1(2) 696
Art 5 796
(1) 796
Directive 2003/35/EC of 26 May 2003 OJ 2003 L156/17 323
Art 2(2) 323
(a) 323
(b)–(d) 324
Art 4 323
(4) 329
Directive 2004/38/EC of 29 April 2004 OJ 2004 L158/77 .... 552, 575
Art 24 575
(1) 575
(2) 575

Regulations *(Chronological order)*

Council Regulation 17 [1959–62] OJ Spec.Ed 684
Art 17 684

Council Regulation 19/62/EEC of 4 April 1962 OJ 1962 30/933 105
Arts 25–26 105
Council Regulation 172/67/EEC of 27 June 1967 OJ 1968 L122/3 442
Art 1 442
Council Regulation 1009/67/EEC of 18 December 1967 OJ 1967 L308/1 439
Art 9 439
(2) 439, 440
(7) 439
(8) 439
Council Regulation 768/68/EEC of 18 June 1968 OJ 1968 L143/12 .... 439, 440
Council Regulation 802/68/EEC of 17 June 1968 OJ 1968 L148/1 105
Arts 12–14 105
Council Regulation 1612/68/EEC of 15 October 1968 ... 551, 572, 576
Art 1 552
Art 2 .... 552, 576
Art 3 552
Art 4 552
Art 5 .... 552, 576
Art 6 552
Art 7 554
(1) 552
(2) 552, 553, 554, 555
(3) 552
(4) 552
Art 8 552
Art 9 552
Art 10 552
Arts 10–12 552
Art 11 552
Art 12 .... 552, 553
Part I 551
Council Regulation 729/70 OJ 1970 L94/13 61
Art 2 67
Art 3 67
Art 4 64
(1) 61
(2) 61
Art 8 63
(1) 61, 67
(2) 61, 67, 68
Art 9 61
Council Regulation 974/71/EEC of 12 May 1971 441
Art 1 .... 441, 444
(2) 441
Council Regulation 2707/72/EEC of 19 December 1972 OJ 1972 L291/3 639
Art 3 639
Council Regulation 337/75/EEC of 10 February 1975 OJ 1975 L39/1 149
Council Regulation 1365/75/EEC of 26 May 1975 OJ 1975 L139/1 149
Council Regulation 563/76/EEC 769
Financial Regulation of 21 December 1977 OJ 1977 L356/1 .... 26, 35
Art 24 35
Council Regulation 1111/77/EEC of 17 May 1977 OJ 1977 L134/4 770
Commission Regulation 1468/77/EEC of 30 June 1977 OJ 1977 L162/7 770
Council Regulation 1697/79/EEC of 24 July 1979 OJ 1979 L197/1 632
Art 5(2) 632

Council Regulation 170/83 of 25 January 1983 OJ 1983 L24/1 609
Council Regulation 2052/88 of 24 June 1988 OJ 1988 L185/9 72
Arts 1–2 72
Art 3(1) 81
Art 4 .... 73, 81
Art 7(3) 81
Art 8 73
(3) 73
Council Regulation 4253/88 OJ 1988 L374/1 ..... 73, 75, 82
Art 8 73
Art 9 73
(6) 73
Art 21
(1) 83
(2) 83
(3) 83
(3)–(5) 84
Art 23 92
(1) 84, 85, 88
Art 24 .... 90, 91, 92, 93
(1) 93
(2) 83, 92, 93
Council Regulation 4064/89/EEC of 21 December 1989 OJ 1989 L395/1 .... 452, 684
Art 2 455
Art 16 684
Council Regulation 1210/90 of 7 May 1990 OJ 1990 L120/1 .... 40, 149
Arts 1–2 157
Art 18 .... 40, 765
Council Regulation 1360/90 of 7 May 1990 OJ 1990 L131/1 149
Council Regulation 302/93 of 8 February 1993 OJ 1993 L36/1 149
Council Regulation 2081/93 of 20 July 1993 OJ 1993 L193/5 74
Art 1 74
Council Regulation 2082/93 of 20 July 1993 OJ 1993 L193/20 .... 75, 76, 81
Art 1(3) 76
Art 3(2) 77
Art 4(2) 76
(c) 76
Arts 8–14 77
Art 8(1) 76
Art 9(2) 75, 82
Art 11 77
(2) 76
(3) 76
Arts 13–19 76
Art 23 77
(1) 85
Art 25 78
Art 31(4) 78
Art 36 78
Council Regulation 2309/93 of 22 July 1993 OJ 1993 L214/1 149
Art 10 156
Art 28(5) 179
Art 32 156
Art 46 179
Arts 55–56 174
Council Regulation 40/94 of 20 December 1993 OJ 1994 L11/1 ..... 40, 149
Art 61 164
Art 63 .... 40, 164
Council Regulation 1164/94 of 16 May 1994 OJ 1994 L130/1 74
Art 7 74
Art 10(1) 75

Commission Regulation 1681/94 of 11 July 1994 OJ 1994 L178/43 .... 85, 87
Art 5(2) 89
Council Regulation 2062/94 of 18 July 1994 OJ 1994 L216/1 149
Art 2 157
Art 3(1)
(a)–(d) 157
(e) 157
(f) 157, 177
Art 8 171
Art 22 165
Council Regulation 2100/94 of 27 July 1994 OJ 1994 L227/1 149
Council Regulation 2965/94 of 28 November 1994 OJ 1994 L314/1 149
Council Regulation 1287/95 OJ 1995 L125/1 62
Art 1 62
Commission Regulation 1663/95 of 7 July 1995 OJ 1995 L158/6 .... 62, 64
Art 1 62
Art 3 .... 62, 63
Council Regulation 2988/95 of 18 December 1995 OJ 1995 L312/1 89
Art 2(2) 90
Art 5 90
Art 7 90
Council Regulation 2185/96 of 11 November 1996 OJ 1996 L292/2 87
Regulation 258/97 of 27 January 1997 OJ 1997 L43/1 .. 730
Art 12 .... 730, 731, 735
Council Regulation 1035/97 of 2 June 1997 OJ 1997 L151/1 149
Art 4 177
Art 7 177
Art 15(3) 165
Council Regulation 1467/97 of 7 July 1997 OJ 1997 L209/6 196
Art 1 197
Art 2 197
Arts 3–6 198
Art 5 197
Art 6 .... 197, 199
Arts 11–14 198
Protocol No. 20, Art 1 198
Recital 8 196
Commission Regulation 2064/97 of 15 October 1997 OJ 1997 L290/1 85
Art 2 85
Art 7 85
Council Regulation 1638/98/EC of 20 July 1998 OJ 1998 L210/32 335
Council Regulation 659/1999 of 22 March 1999 OJ 1999 L83/1 392
Art 5
(1) 393
(3) 393
Art 6
(1) 392
(2) 392
Art 10 393
Art 20
(2) 392
(3) 393
Art 21 393
Art 22 393
Recital 2 392
Recital 3 392
Regulation 1073/99 of 25 May 1999 OJ 1999 L136/1 666

Council Regulation 1258/1999 of 17 May 1999 OJ 1999 L160/103 .... 62, 67
Art 4 63
Art 7(4) 65
Council Regulation 1260/1999 of 21 June 1999 OJ 1999 L161/1 .... 75, 80
Art 1 75
(2) 75
Art 3(1) 75
Art 4(1) 75
Art 8 .... 80, 81
(1) 82
(3) 85
Art 9
(m) 82
(n) 85
Art 10(1) 82
Art 11
(2) 83
(3) 83
Art 15(6) 82
Art 18
(2) 81
(3) 82
Art 30 88
(4) 88
Art 32
(1) 84
(2) 84
(3) 82, 84
(e) 84
(4) 84
Art 34(1) 85
Art 35 86
Art 36(2)(a) 87
Art 37(2)(b) 87
Art 38
(1) 85, 86, 88
(b) 87
(f) 86
(h) 89
(2) 87
(3) 87
(4) 87
(5) 84
Art 39
(1) 85, 88, 91
(2) 84, 91
(3) 91
(a) 90
(4) 91
Council Regulation 2454/1999 of 15 November 1999 OJ 1999 L299/1 149
Commission Regulation 438/2001 of 2 March 2001 OJ 2001 L63/21 86
Art 2 86
Art 3 86
Art 4 86
Art 5 87
Art 8 88
Arts 10–12 86
Art 15 86
Commission Regulation 448/2001 of 2 March 2001 OJ 2001 L64/13 88
Art 2
(1) 88
(2) 88
Art 4 91
preamble 88
Recital 1 88
Regulation 1049/2001 of 30 May 2001 OJ 2001 L145/43 .... 24, 176, 352, 354, 358, 359
Art 4 356
(1) 356
(2) 357
(2)–(3) 356
(5) 357
Art 9(3) 357

Regulation 1162/2001, OJ 2001 L159/4 339
Regulation 178/2002 of 28 January 2002 OJ 2002 L31/1 .... 149, 743
Art 3
(10) 743
(11) 743
(12) 743
(13) 743
Art 5 .... 743, 744
(3) 744
Art 7 745
(1) 744
(2) 744
Art 9 179
Art 14(4) 745
Art 22(7) 175
Art 25(8) 174
Art 26 172
(2)(b) 174
Art 36 176
Art 38
(1) 176
(2) 176
Recital 1–2 743
Recital 16 743
Recital 17 743
Recital 20 743
Recital 21 744
Regulation 1406/2002 of 27 June 2002 OJ 2002 L208/1 .... 150, 177
Art 2(f) 157
Art 4(2) 176
Art 10(2)(d) 174
Art 11 171
Arts 15–16 172
Regulation 1592/2002 of 15 July 2002 OJ 2002 L240/1 .... 150, 155, 327
Art 11 177
Art 15(2)(a) 177
Art 24(2)(c) 174
Art 25 171
Arts 29–30 172
Art 29(2) 170
Art 30 172
Arts 31–41 164
Art 43 .... 177, 179
Art 46 177
Art 47 176
Regulation 1605/2002 OJ 2002 L248/1 ... 3, 19, 25, 26, 28, 31, 34, 35, 50, 54, 55, 57, 180, 214
Art 2 37
(1) 38
(b) 37
Art 3
(1)–(2) 38
(2) 38
(3) 38
Art 4 38
Art 5 38
Art 6 39
(1) 39
(2)(a)–(c) 39
(3) 39
Art 8 38
Art 9 38
Art 10 38
Art 11 38
Art 18 38
Art 22 .... 41, 42
(1) 41
(5) 41
Art 24(2) 38
Art 53
(1) 26, 33
(2) 26, 33
Art 54 .... 26, 33
(1) 26, 27, 33, 38, 39, 52
(2) 52
(a) 27, 33, 37

(b) 27, 33
(c) 27, 33, 50
Art 55 37
Arts 55–56 39
Art 56(1) 27, 33
Art 57
(1) 27, 34, 52
(2) 27, 34, 52
Art 58 35
Art 59
(1) 35
(2) 36
Art 60
(2) 36
(4) 36
Art 61 35
Arts 64–67 36
Art 75 36
Art 76(1) 36
Art 77(1) 36
Art 78 36
Art 79 36
Art 80 36
Arts 85–86 37
Arts 90–91 53
Art 93 53
Art 94 53
Art 96 53
Art 100 53
Arts 104–106 53
Arts 149–60 27
Arts 151–152 61
Arts 163–171 27
Art 185 180
Art 288(2) 40
Ch 2 .... 26, 33
Title IV 26, 33
Commission Regulation 2342/2002 of 23 December 2002 OJ 2002 L 357/1 34
Art 35 34
Art 38 50
Art 39 50
Art 41 50
Commission Regulation 2343/2002 of 23 December 2002 OJ 2002 L357/72 .... 39, 40, 180
Council Regulation 1/2003 of 16 December 2002 OJ 2003 L1/1 388
Art 7(2) 390
Art 12 391
Art 18 391
(3) 391
Art 20
(3) 391
(4) 391
(6) 391
Arts 20–21 391
Art 22 391
Art 23 391
Art 27
(1) 389
(2) 389
(3) 389
Council Regulation 58/2003 of 19 December 2002 OJ 2003 L11/1 .... 37, 55, 153
Art 11
(3) 40
(4) 40
Arts 12–16 39
Art 14(1) 40
Art 16(2) 40
Art 20 39
Art 21 40
(1) 40, 765
(2) 40
Art 22(2) 41
Recital 5–6 37
Council Regulation 1782/2003 of 29 September 2003 OJ 2003 L270/1 .... 60, 96
Arts 6–7 69

Council Regulation 139/2004 of 20 January 2004 OJ 2004 L24/1 366
Commission Regulation 448/2004 of 10 March 2004 OJ 2004 L72/6 94
Regulation 460/2004 of 10 March 2004 OJ 2004 L77/1 ... 150
Art 2
(1)–(3) 158
(4) 158
Art 3 158
Art 4(j) 179
Art 6 171
Art 7 172
Commission Regulation 773/2004 of 7 April 2004 OJ 2004 L123/18 .... 369, 372
Art 6 390
Art 7(1) 390
Art 10
(1)–(2) 389
(3) 389
Art 12 389
Art 13 389
Art 14(7) 369
Arts 15–16 389
Commission Regulation 794/2004 of 21 April 2004 OJ 2004 L140/1 393
Arts 5–7 393
Commission Regulation 795/2004 of 21 April 2004 OJ 2004 L141/1 60
Commission Regulation 796/2004 of 21 April 2004 OJ 2004 L141/18 60
Regulation 851/2004 of 21 April 2004 OJ 2004 L142/1 150
Arts 5–10 177
Art 14 187
(1) 171
Art 16 172
Art 17 172
Arts 19–20 176
Art 28 165
Regulation 881/2004 of 29 April 2004 OJ 2004 L164/1 150
Art 25(2)(c) 174
Art 32 170
Commission Regulation 1653/2004 of 21 December 2004 OJ 2004 L297/6 40
Art 34 40
Art 36 40
Commission Regulation 1973/2004 of 29 October 2004 OJ 2004 L345/1 60
Council Regulation 2007/2004 of 26 October 2004 OJ 2004 L349/1 152
Commission Regulation 2230/2004 of 23 December 2004 OJ 2004 L379/64 176
Council Regulation 723/2004 of 22 March 2004 OJ 2004 L124/1 .... 7, 25, 369
Arts 3–26 181
Arts 33–34 181
Art 38 181
(5) 181
Art 39 181
Art 41 181
Art 47 181
(3) 181
Arts 60–66 181
Arts 71–73 181
Arts 91–93 181
Art 94 181
Council Regulation 768/2005 of 26 April 2005 OJ 2005 L128/1 150
Art 23(2)(c) 174

Council Regulation 1055/2005 of 27 June 2005 OJ 2005 L174/5 200
Council Regulation 1112/2005 of 24 June 2005 OJ 2005 L184/5 .... 157, 177
Art 1(5) 171
Council Regulation 1290/2005 of 21 June 2005 OJ 2005 L209/1 .... 62, 69, 96
Arts 2–4 68
Art 6 68
Arts 7–8 69
Art 9 69
Art 17 69
Art 27 69
Art 32(4)(a) 69
Art 34(5) 69

Treaties and Conventions
(Alphabetical order)

Constitutional Treaty *see* Treaty Establishing a Constitution for Europe
EC Treaty *see* Treaty of Rome 1957
Euratom Treaty 274
Art 31 274
European Coal and Steel Community Treaty 161, 460, 579, 583, 623, 656
Art 2 647
Art 3 .... 161, 186, 647
(b) 579
Art 4 647
(b) 579
(c) 647
Art 60(1) 579
Art 70(1) 579
Art 95 .... 464, 647
(1) 647
Europol Convention 151
Art 2 159
Art 3 159
Art 4 159
Art 5 159
Arts 6–9 159
Arts 28–29 173
Maastricht Treaty *see* Treaty on European Union
Single European Act 1986 .... 13, 72, 103, 106, 107, 108, 417, 487
Treaty of Amsterdam 110, 203, 204, 236, 269, 272, 351, 352, 405, 410, 426, 487, 488, 835
Protocol No. 30 .... 422, 427
Art 9 423
Treaty Establishing a Constitution for Europe, OJ 2004 C310/1 .... 103, 112, 119, 135, 136, 141, 142, 163, 310, 311, 312, 313, 344, 402, 425, 428, 483, 497, 511, 539, 543
Art I-3(3) 230
Art I-4 421
Art I-6 534
Art I-9
(1) 497, 538
(2) 497, 531
(3) 497
Art I-12 403
(1) 417, 421
Art I-13
(1) 421
(2) 416, 417, 418
(3) 424
Arts I-13–15 270
Art I-15 270
Art I-17 270
Art I-18(1) 409

Treaty Establishing a Constitution for Europe, OJ 2004 C310/1 (*cont.*):
Art I-29 311
(1) 264, 311
(3) 264, 311
Art I-32(1) 125
Art I-33(1) 124, 125, 345
Art I-34(1) 544
Art I-35 125
Art I-36 ...... 125, 127, 128, 130, 131, 132, 133
(1) 125, 128, 132
(2) 125, 127, 129, 130
(3) 126
Art I-37 .... 125, 128
(3) 128
Art I-38
(1) 124
(2) 124
Arts I-39–40 270
Art I-47 324
Art II-11
(1) 403
(2) 403
Art II-61 497
Art II-111
(1) 498
(2) 506
Art II-112 .... 509, 533
(2) 517, 521
(4) 533
(5) 509, 512
(7) 523
Art III-209-212 237
Art III-256(2) 410
Art III-284(2) 410
Art III-308 270
Art III-319(2) 410
Art III-358 312
(3) 311
Art III-359 312
Art III-365 .... 264, 269
(1) 165
(4) 344, 345, 346
(5) 165
Art III-367 264
Art III-369 .... 264, 311, 312
Art III-376 270
Art III-377 270
Art III-396 544
Art III-398 .... 280, 362
Part I 497
Part I, Title III 403
Part II 538
Part III 264, 311, 403, 410
Part III, Title V, Ch II 270
Protocol No. 2 424
Art 2 424
Art 4 424
Art 6 424
Art 7 424
Art 8 424
Treaty Establishing the European Community (Consolidated Version) 13, 102, 147, 155, 206, 484
Art 2 .... 71, 231
Art 3 720
Art 5 .... 401, 402, 419, 420, 424, 425, 427, 656
(2) 420, 421, 422, 423
(3) 422, 426
Art 6 720
Art 7 .... 166, 764
Art 10 .... 67, 278, 341, 506, 703, 793, 811, 816, 841
Art 11a 294
Art 12 .... 264, 486, 559, 560, 562, 563, 564, 565, 566, 567, 568, 569, 570, 571, 572, 573, 574, 576, 577, 585, 601, 604
Art 13 .... 488, 506, 518, 587, 595, 600, 601, 602, 605
(1) 601

(2) 601
Art 17 .... 567, 568, 577
(2) 570
Arts 17–22 587
Art 18 .... 567, 568, 569, 570, 571, 572, 573, 574, 575, 577
(1) 567
(2) 567
(3) 567
Arts 19–22 .... 567, 578
Art 21(1) 834
Art 28 .... 500, 513, 548, 679, 688, 690, 691, 707, 713, 714, 719, 818, 821
Art 29 .... 688, 824
Art 30 .... 688, 689, 690, 691, 706, 711, 719, 734, 824
Art 33 .... 434, 472, 579, 580, 583, 659, 772
(1) 58
Art 34 .... 290, 770
(2) 58, 265, 580, 581, 583
(3) 768
Art 39 .... 547, 549, 550, 551, 555, 556, 557, 559, 561, 562, 576, 578
(2) 576
(3) 688
(4) 555, 556
Art 40 335
Art 43 .... 818, 821
Art 45 556
Art 46 688
Art 49 .... 562, 694
Art 52 809
Art 55 .... 688, 708
Art 58 688
Art 60 535
Arts 61–69 300
Art 68 300
(3) 300
Art 80(2) 414
Art 81 .... 260, 366, 369, 388, 390, 391, 759, 812
(1) 388
(3) 388
Art 82 .... 260, 267, 366, 369, 388, 390, 391
Art 86 .... 363, 364, 379, 380, 586
(1) 363
(3) 380, 381
Art 87 683
(1) 430
(3) 443
(a) 430, 433, 434, 443
(b) 461
(c) 443, 444, 460
Art 88 .... 377, 392, 634
(2) 294, 377
(3) 377
Art 90 265
Art 93 812
Art 94 .... 405, 407
Art 95 .... 274, 405, 407, 409, 426, 428
Art 99 .... 194, 211
(1) 196
(2) 196, 197
(3) 196
(4) 197
Art 104 199
(1) 197
(2) 198
(3) 198
(4) 198
(5) 198
(6) 198
(7) 198
(8) 199
(9) 198, 199
(11) 198
Art 111 411

Treaty Establishing the European Community (Consolidated Version) (*cont.*):
Art 118 .... 406, 407
Art 118a 405, 426
Art 119 .... 591, 592, 593
Art 125 203
Art 126(1) 203
Art 127 203
Art 128 .... 194, 203, 211, 321
(2) 203
Art 129 205
Art 130 .... 204, 321
Art 133 .... 294, 409, 411, 413
(6) 413
Art 136 .... 207, 237, 587
Art 137 .... 238, 239, 265, 405, 587
(1) 237
(2) 207, 237, 238
(a) 237
(b) 237
(3) 238
(4) 237
(5) 587
Art 138 .... 238, 239, 246, 249, 258, 405
(1) 247
(4) 238
Art 139 .... 238, 249, 250, 251, 253, 254, 256, 258, 260, 507
(1) 238
(2) 238, 239, 257
Art 141 .... 265, 487, 498, 561, 586, 588, 589, 590, 594, 600, 605, 698, 699, 700
(4) 598, 599
Art 144 208
Art 145 .... 103, 106, 107, 109, 110
Art 149 103
(3) 411
Art 150 .... 565, 566, 567
(3) 411
Art 151(3) 411
Art 152 402
(1) 720, 730
(3) 411
Art 153 402
(1) 720
(2) 720
Art 155 .... 103, 105, 106, 107
(3) 411
Art 157 402
Art 158 .... 69, 70
Art 159 70
Art 160 70
Art 161 70
Art 162 70
Arts 163–173 402
Art 164 405
Art 170 411
Art 173 .... 274, 275
Art 174 .... 411, 732
(1) 718, 720
(2) 718, 720, 730, 731
Art 177 .... 439, 487
Art 181 411
Art 181a 411
Art 190 394
Art 194 834
Art 195 .... 833, 835, 838, 851, 854
(1) 836, 837
Art 202 .... 106, 110, 127, 294
Art 207(3) 352
Art 208 13
Art 211 .... 103, 449, 725
Art 215 766
(2) 767, 773
Art 220 .... 263, 266, 271, 272, 521
Art 222 300
Art 223 299
Art 224 .... 295, 299

Art 225 312
(1) 293, 294, 295, 296
(2) 294, 296, 297
(3) 297, 298
Art 225a 312
Art 226 .... 88, 285, 288, 293, 295, 414, 711, 735, 811, 835, 837, 841, 842, 853
Art 229 684
Art 230 .... 40, 41, 66, 165, 166, 185, 199, 265, 267, 284, 285, 286, 288, 290, 293, 295, 297, 309, 331, 334, 336, 337, 338, 339, 340, 341, 342, 343, 344, 380, 455, 457, 473, 490, 521, 537, 755, 756, 757, 759, 761, 762, 763, 767, 789, 854
(1) 40, 165, 263, 264, 267, 854
(2) ... 265, 266, 271, 272, 401
(3) 275
(4) .. 332, 333, 334, 335, 339, 340, 344, 345, 347, 380
(5) 268
Art 231 ...... 755, 756, 757, 758, 762, 763
Art 232 ...... 263, 284, 285, 293, 295, 341, 759, 762, 763, 854
(3) 854
Art 233 ...... 755, 758, 759, 760, 761, 762, 763
Art 234 ...... 264, 265, 285, 286, 288, 290, 297, 300, 302, 306, 307, 309, 312, 334, 335, 336, 338, 339, 340, 341, 342, 343, 439, 473, 537, 711, 734, 761, 762, 763, 777, 786, 789
Art 235 .... 293, 784
Art 236 293
Art 238 293
Art 240 .... 783, 784
Art 242 750
Art 243 750
Art 249 .... 239, 267
Art 250 .... 249, 250
Art 251 111, 112, 352, 567, 601
(1) 176
(2) 176
(4) 250
(5) 250
Art 253 ...... 264, 382, 383, 394, 395, 425, 521
Art 255 ...... 264, 265, 352, 359, 673
(1) 352
(2) 352
(3) 352
Art 280 .... 20, 667
Art 281 410
Art 288 ...... 284, 285, 339, 341, 749, 785, 820
(2) 164, 521, 764, 765, 766, 767, 768, 771, 772, 778, 780, 781, 783, 784, 787, 817, 818, 828, 854
Art 291 780
Art 300(1) 411
Art 301 535
Arts 302–304 411
Art 308 .... 42, 150, 151, 280, 402, 405, 407, 408, 409, 410, 428, 486, 491, 535, 594
Art 310 411
Protocol No. 30 656
Title IV 300
Title XI 237
Treaty on European Union 74, 108, 112, 151, 195, 270, 274, 351, 417, 496, 829, 832
Art 1 352

Treaty on European Union (*cont.*):
Art 6
(1) ... 272, 287, 487, 488, 490
(2) ... 487
(3) ... 559
(3) ... 559
Art 7 ... 488
Art 24 ... 410
Art 35 ... 166, 167, 269
(1)–(3) ... 269
(5) ... 269
(6) ... 269
Art 41 ... 166, 835
Art 46 ... 269, 273
(d) ... 487
Art F(2) ... 487
Art K3 ... 151
Protocol on Social Policy ... 236
Title VI ... 166, 542
Treaty of Nice ... 111, 208, 293, 294, 296, 297, 298, 299, 310, 311, 402, 410, 497, 601
Art 7 ... 293

INTERNATIONAL LEGISLATION

Treaties and Conventions

European Convention on Human Rights ... 370, 408, 483, 485, 487, 489, 490, 491, 515, 516, 517, 523, 524, 525, 527, 528, 529, 531, 534, 537, 600, 692
Art 6 .. 370, 371, 387, 528, 530, 750
(1) ... 370, 371
Art 7 ... 528, 529, 530, 609
(1) ... 528
Arts 8–11 ... 514
Art 10 ... 513, 679
Art 11 ... 513, 679
Art 13 ... 387, 750
Protocol No. 1, Art 1 ... 526
New York Convention on the Rights of the Child 1989 ... 507
United Nations Charter ... 535
Ch VII ... 535

NATIONAL LEGISLATION

Canada

Administrative Tribunals Act 2004 ... 437

United Kingdom

Equal Pay Act 1970 ... 807
Human Rights Act 1998 ... 510, 515, 532
ss 2–4 ... 532
s 6(6) ... 510
Merchant Shipping Act 1894 .. 792
Merchant Shipping Act 1988 . 817, 821

United States

Administrative Procedure Act 1946 ... 134, 135, 136, 137, 139, 185, 186, 319, 324, 362, 395, 475, 479, 480
s 556(d) ... 465
s 706(2)(a) ... 475

List of Abbreviations

CAP	Common Agricultural Policy
CdT	Translation Centre for Bodies of the European Union
Cedefop	European Centre for the Development of Vocational Training
CEN	Comité Européen de Normalisation
CENELEC	Comité Européen de Normalisation Electrotechnique
CF	Cohesion Fund
CFCA	Community Fisheries Control Agency
CFI	Court of First Instance
CFSP	Common Foreign and Security Policy
COREPER	Committee of Permanent Representatives
COSAC	Conference of EC and European Affairs committees of national parliaments
CPMP	Committee for Proprietary Medicinal Products
CSF	Community Support Framework
CT	Constitutional Treaty
CPVO	Community Plant Variety Office
DG	Directorate General
EAFRD	European Agricultural Fund for Rural Development
EAGF	European Agricultural Guarantee Fund
EAGGF	European Agricultural Guidance and Guarantee Fund
EAR	European Agency for Reconstruction
EASA	European Aviation Safety Agency
EC	European Community
ECA	European Chemicals Agency
ECB	European Central Bank
ECDC	European Centre for Disease Prevention and Control
ECHO	European Community Humanitarian Office
ECHR	European Convention on Human Rights
ECJ	European Court of Justice
ECOSOC	Economic and Social Committee
ECSC	European Coal and Steel Community Treaty
EDA	European Defence Agency
EEA	European Environment Agency
EEC	European Economic Community
EES	European Employment Strategy
EFSA	European Food Safety Authority
EGs	employment guidelines

EIB	European Investment Bank
EMCDDA	European Monitoring Centre for Drugs and Drug Addiction
EMEA	European Medicines Agency
EMSA	European Maritime Safety Agency
EMU	Economic and Monetary Union
ENISA	European Network and Information Security Agency
EP	European Parliament
EPC	European Political Community
EPSO	European Personnel Selection Office
ERA	European Railway Agency
ERDF	European Regional Development Fund
ESF	European Social Fund
ETF	European Training Foundation
ETUC	European Trade Union Confederation
EU	European Union
EUISS	European Union Institute for Security Studies
EUMC	European Monitoring Centre on Racism and Xenophobia
EU-OSHA	European Agency for Safety and Health at Work
EUROFOUND	European Foundation for the Improvement of Living and Working Conditions
Europol	European Police Office
EUSC	European Union Satellite Centre
FRA	Fundamental Rights Agency
FRONTEX	European Agency for the Management of Operational Cooperation at the External Borders
GATS	General Agreement on Trade in Services
GATT	General Agreement on Tariffs and Trade
GDP	gross domestic product
IGC	Intergovernmental Conference
IPM	Interactive Policy Making
JHA	Justice and Home Affairs
MCA	monetary compensation amount
NAPs	national action plans
NCA	national competition authority
NGO	non-governmental organization
OECD	Organisation for Economic Co-operation and Development
OHIM	Office for Harmonization in the Internal Market
OLAF	European Anti-fraud Office
OMC	Open Method of Coordination
PJCC	Police and Judicial Cooperation in Criminal Matters
SEA	Single European Act
SG/HR	Secretary-General/High Representative
SGP	Stability and Growth Pact

TAO	technical assistance office
TCM	traditional Community method
TEU	Treaty on European Union
TFRA	Task Force for Administrative Reform
ToA	Amsterdam Treaty
UN	United Nations
WTO	World Trade Organization

Part I

Administration and Law

1

Crisis, Reform, and Constitutionalization

1. INTRODUCTION

The resignation of the Santer Commission received front-page attention in the press, proof for those minded to believe it of the malaise which had long existed within that organization. Its downfall was prompted by the First Report of the Committee of Independent Experts. This was followed in quick succession by reforms instituted by Romano Prodi as the new President of the Commission, by the Committee of Independent Experts' Second Report, by the White Paper on reform of the Commission and implementation of these reforms. An understanding of these developments is crucial in order to appreciate the current pattern of Community administration. This chapter will chart these developments leading to administrative reform, including the new Financial Regulation, which established a constitutional framework for Community administration of the kind that had not existed hitherto. Subsequent chapters will analyse in detail the provisions contained therein as they relate to different types of Community administration.

2. THE FALL OF THE SANTER COMMISSION

A. The Committee of Independent Experts, Its Origin and Criteria of Operation

There had been concern in the European Community (EC) for some considerable time about fraud, and mismanagement. Newspaper reports revealed instances of fraud in the Common Agricultural Policy, the Court of Auditors brought to light instances of mismanagement of certain Community policies, and UCLAF (Unité de Coordination de la Lutte Anti-Fraude) investigations showed in greater detail the ways in which Community funds were being misused. The European Parliament repeatedly expressed its dissatisfaction with the management of the Community's financial resources.

This culminated in a resolution of 14 January 1999 which called for a committee of independent experts to be convened under the auspices of the

European Parliament and the Commission with a mandate to detect and deal with fraud, mismanagement, and nepotism. It was for the Committee to decide how far the Commission as a body, or individual Commissioners, had responsibility for such matters. The Committee was also to conduct a fundamental review of the Commission's practices in the award of all financial contracts. The Committee produced its first report within two months, by 15 March 1999. In technical legal terms the Committee was not a Community institution, nor was it a Community agency. It had no formal investigative powers. It derived its authority from the agreement of the Parliament and the Commission, and saw itself as a temporary advisory committee operating by consent.

The Committee began its report by defining its primary terms of reference. Fraud was taken to mean 'intentional acts or omissions tending to harm the financial interests of the Communities', and included misappropriation of funds.[1] Mismanagement was said to be a broader concept and encompassed 'serious or persistent infringements of the principles of sound administration, and, in particular, acts or omissions allowing or encouraging fraud or irregularities to occur or persist'.[2] It would normally be the result of negligence in the exercise of public management functions. Nepotism was 'favouritism shown to relatives or friends, especially in appointments to desirable positions which are not based on merit or justice'.[3] The Committee emphasized that these categories could overlap, and emphasized that they were but examples of a more fundamental idea that public servants should be held to proper standards of behaviour. The core of minimum standards was that public officials should act in the general interest of the Community, with complete independence. Decisions should be made solely in terms of the public interest on the basis of objective criteria.[4]

Exigencies of time meant that the Committee could only investigate a limited number of Community policies. It nonetheless produced a 146-page Report by the stipulated date, and this had an immediate, dramatic effect: the Commission resigned en bloc. The resulting crisis was the dominant headline in newspapers across Europe, being the focus of attention in quality papers and the tabloid press alike. For many Euro-sceptics it was proof of what they had always maintained, empirical vindication of the 'rottenness at the heart of Europe'. The tabloid press in the UK, much of which had lost no opportunity in the past to berate the EC and its officers, vied to devise ever more cutting headlines. Individual sentences plucked from the Committee's Report lent themselves readily to the media sound-bite age. The concluding paragraph of the Committee's Report spoke in terms of it 'becoming difficult

[1] Committee of Independent Experts, *First Report on Allegations regarding Fraud, Mismanagement and Nepotism in the European Commission* (15 March 1999), at 1.4.2.

[2] Ibid. at 1.4.3. [3] Ibid. at 1.4.4. [4] Ibid. at 1.5.4.

to find anyone who has even the slightest sense of responsibility'[5] within the Commission, and there were earlier references to a mismatch between the objectives assigned to the Commission, and the way in which it had chosen to fulfil them.[6]

Whether those who were so ready to dance on the grave of the outgoing Commission had actually read the Report might well be doubted. There is often an inverse correlation between the strength of one's feelings and the depth of one's knowledge. An executive summary is probably as far as most people got. Some might even have read the actual conclusion in the Report itself.

It is, however, only by reading the entire Report that one can really understand precisely what went wrong in the cases investigated by the Committee. And it is only by reading the Report that one is able to form a view about the conclusions reached by the Committee. This is not to deny the existence of matters of real concern which the Committee brought to light. Its Report performed a valuable function in bringing together data on the problems encountered in the running of a number of important Community policies. It is moreover no bad thing in the long term for the Commission to have been publicly criticized in this manner, since there were doubtless those in the Commission who were arrogant, personally and 'institutionally', to others in the Community.

It is nonetheless important to stand back and see what general lessons can be learned from the events that occurred. It is equally important to place these events within the more general context of decision-making by public bodies. It becomes readily apparent that the difficulties encountered were those inherent in contracting-out by a public arm of government: the blurring of the line between policy formation and policy implementation; the difficulty of ensuring proper financial accounting in relation to the activities undertaken by the private contractor; the importance of a proper line of management within the public body; and the fact that the private contractor will normally not be imbued with a public ethos in its decision-making.[7] These lessons must not be forgotten. It should nonetheless be acknowledged that there will often be no viable alternative to contracting out for the effective discharge of many Community policies. This was recognized in the Second Report of the Committee of Independent Experts,[8] and in the White Paper on Reform of the Commission.[9] The objective must be to develop

[5] Ibid. at 9.4.25. [6] Ibid. at 9.4.5.

[7] P. Craig, *Administrative Law* (Sweet & Maxwell, 5th ed., 2003), Chap. 5; Freedland, 'Government by Contract and Private Law' [1994] *PL* 86.

[8] Committee of Independent Experts, *Second Report on Reform of the Commission, Analysis of Current Practice and Proposals for Tackling Mismanagement, Irregularities and Fraud* (10 September 1999).

[9] Reforming the Commission, COM (2000) 200.

techniques to ensure that contracting out functions as an effective and efficient mechanism for the provision of Community public services.

B. The Committee of Independent Experts' Detailed Critique

It is important at the outset to put the Committee's findings into perspective. There was no finding of fraud against any commissioner, and the great majority of the allegations of favouritism against individual commissioners were said to be unfounded.[10] The most serious allegation upheld by the Committee was against Commissioner Cresson who appointed a close friend to a job for which he was not qualified, where the work performed by that person was deficient. The fraud that was found to exist was perpetrated by companies to which work had been contracted out by the Commission, and the mismanagement resided in the Commission's failure to detect this and to act quickly to stop it once it became apparent. This is apparent from the Community policies examined in detail by the Committee.[11]

Tourism can be taken by way of example. Resolutions passed by the Council and European Parliament as early as 1983–1984 prompted the Commission to propose to the Council a programme to highlight the economic significance of tourism in the EC, and to integrate tourism more closely with other Community policies than hitherto. 1990 was designated as European Year of Tourism by the Council,[12] and this was followed in 1992 by the Council's adoption of a three-year action plan to assist tourism.[13] The total sum involved in these projects was ECU 39.3 million. The implementation of the action plan was entrusted to the Commission. DG XXIII took responsibility and a specific unit was set up within Directorate A to implement the Community tourism policy. There were two main problems with the administration of this policy. The Head of the Tourism Unit engaged in unauthorized activities which gave rise to embezzlement, corruption, and favouritism. The Committee of Experts felt that the Commission had been slow in checking whether the accusations levelled against the Head of the Unit were well founded, that the internal inquiries were incomplete, and that the penalty imposed was too lenient.[14] There were also problems with the use

[10] There were, however, previous instances where there had been concern over Commission behaviour, Spence, 'Plus ca change, plus c'est la meme chose? Attempting to reform the European Commission' (2000) 7 *JEPP* 1, at 9–10.

[11] Five of the main policies examined by the Committee of Experts are analysed here. The only policy area not discussed at any length here is the running of the Security Office.

[12] Council Decision 89/46/EEC of 21 December 1988, On an Action Programme for European Tourism Year (1990), OJ 1989 L17/53.

[13] Council Decision 92/421/EEC of 13 July 1992, On a Community Action Plan to Assist Tourism, OJ 1992 L231/26.

[14] Committee of Independent Experts, *First Report, supra* n. 1, at 2.8.1–2.8.3.

of external consultants to whom work had been contracted out. The Committee of Experts criticized the fact that there was no adequate supervision of the consultants with the result that 'those consultants performed managerial duties incumbent on officials and played an important role in the selection and monitoring of projects',[15] and there were unjustified payments made to the firm. Underlying these specific concerns was a more general problem which, as we shall see, was a factor in all of the programmes studied by the Committee of Experts: insufficient staff within the Commission. The tourism project was managed by 11 people subject to Staff Regulations, and an external consultancy. Most of the staff members were on one-year contracts, renewable twice, unless they were appointed to a temporary post. The shortage of human resources undoubtedly contributed to management weaknesses and administrative failures.[16] The Committee of Experts was critical of the College of Commissioners for proposing the tourism initiative without having the resources to do the job, more especially since the action plan involved the management of a large number of undertakings.[17]

Similar problems with contracting out were apparent in relation to the *MED programmes*. These provided for decentralized cooperation with non-member countries of the southern Mediterranean and began in 1992 after the Gulf war with Iraq. The aim was to strengthen political and economic cooperation with these countries in order to counterbalance the aid given to countries in Central and Eastern Europe.[18] A central theme of the programmes was that governmental structures should be avoided and that funds should be channelled to non-governmental organizations, with the object of being close to civil society. The total budget for 1992–1996 was ECU 116.6 million. The management structure for this programme was organized at four levels: DG IB had authority within the Commission; the Agency for Trans-Mediterranean Networks (ARTM), had responsibility for the administration and financial management of the programmes; technical assistance offices (TAOs), of which there was one for each programme, had responsibility for technical supervision; and management of specific projects, of which there were 496 in total. The principal criticism of the MED programmes was that the Commission had illegally delegated its powers to a third party, ARTM, rather than merely signed a service contract. The terms of the contract entrusted ARTM with the implementation of the financing of the programme and gave it broad powers to manage the programme as a whole. The Committee's Report acknowledged that the Commission did not have sufficient manpower to undertake the task in-house,[19] but felt that this did

[15] Ibid. at 2.5.6. [16] Ibid. at 2.7.7. [17] Ibid. at 2.9.1.

[18] There were five such programmes depending on which type of partner institution was involved: MED-Urbs (regional authorities); MED-Campus (universities); MED-Invest (enterprises); MED-Avicenne (research centres); and MED-Media (media professionals).

[19] Committee of Independent Experts, *First Report*, *supra* n. 1, at 3.4.1–3.4.3.

not excuse delegation to the private sector without a sufficient control structure. The Commission's Legal Service, and the Legal Service of the Court of Auditors, had grave reservations as to the legality of this contract. The Committee of Experts was also critical of the fact that the initial contract between ARTM and the Commission was by way of private treaty, without any competitive tendering. There were in addition real conflicts of interest between the Commission and ARTM, and ARTM and TAOs: two of ARTM's founding companies were simultaneously acting as TAOs for the MED programmes. This meant that they were 'able to participate in the process of negotiating contracts concluded with themselves'.[20]

The difficulties of maintaining control when work is contracted out were equally apparent in the context of the *European Community Humanitarian Office* (ECHO). It was established on 1 March 1992 to give the EC a more effective means for providing aid in emergency relief situations. Experience had taught the Commission that 'its usual administrative mechanisms were too slow to provide assistance with the necessary speed, and, incidentally perhaps, they failed to give the Community contribution to disaster relief a visible dimension commensurate with its scale'.[21] During its first six years it disbursed some ECU 3,500 million in aid. It did so largely through partner organizations such as non-governmental organizations (NGOs). ECHO itself was established as a new Directorate. The demands upon it grew exponentially in the years immediately following its establishment, but there was no corresponding increase in the staff available to it; nor were there well-recognized financial or organizational procedures in place to regulate its activities.[22] The Committee of Experts found that budgetary appropriations were used in an irregular manner: money intended to be used for operations was used to finance staffing. Many of those within ECHO regarded this as a mere administrative irregularity, in the sense that the money was being used to cover a shortfall in staffing, and that without such additional staff ECHO could not perform the tasks assigned to it. The Committee of Experts took a different view. It concluded that if the system itself was inadequate, then it invited irregularity. Where, as here, this involved outright fabrication, then it led to a risk of fraud which was too high.[23] It was also critical of the lateness of the Commission's response to the problems with ECHO. The first of the fictitious contracts began in August 1993. Commission intervention only occurred four years later when a whistleblower intervened.[24] It was moreover clear that the Commissioners themselves were aware of the nature of the problem. The Commissioners responsible for ECHO, Marin until 1994 and then Bonino, were aware of the difficult staffing situation in ECHO, and of

[20] Committee of Independent Experts, *First Report*, *supra* n. 1, at 3.5.9.
[21] Ibid. at 4.1.1.
[22] Ibid. at 4.2.2.
[23] Ibid. at 4.2.5.
[24] Ibid. at 4.2.10.

the existence of 'submarine' staff within ECHO who were financed from operating appropriations.[25]

The problems encountered with the running of the *Leonardo da Vinci programme*, launched in 1995, were particularly instructive. The programme was authorized by a Council Decision,[26] and its objective was the implementation of a vocational training policy in support of initiatives conducted by the individual Member States. It was to last for a maximum of five years, from 1995–1999, and had an appropriation of approximately ECU 620 million. The rationale for contracting out was succinctly captured by the Committee.[27]

Normally, such a programme would have been implemented by the Commission's services themselves. However, because of a lack of staff within DG XXII, and since it appeared impossible to re-deploy the necessary staff from other services in the Commission, it was decided to outsource the implementation of the project to a 'technical assistance office' following a public call for tender.

An open tender process was held at the end of 1994 and a firm called Agenor SA was awarded the five-year service contract, which was renewable annually. Agenor therefore constituted the TAO for the Leonardo programme. Its main function was to manage several thousand project proposals per year and involved 'complex processing procedures through a chain of operations leading to the selection of some 750 projects per year by the Commission'.[28] The Committee's report focused on three deficiencies in the way in which this programme was run. The initial criticism related to the performance by Agenor of its role as TAO in the Leonardo programme. Audits revealed that Agenor was in receipt of detailed information about the requirements of the future Leonardo programme prior to publication of its tender; the company was in breach of its contract conditions; it was not in compliance with national tax or social security laws; the company had a poor system of internal control; and there was some evidence that funds had been misappropriated, and evidence also of favouritism. The second criticism focused on the way in which the matter was dealt with by the Commission. While it was clear that the primary wrongdoing was that of Agenor, the TAO, it was also clear that the Commission itself had responsibility to oversee the discharge of the Leonardo programme by Agenor. The Committee questioned whether it could be considered credible that Agenor's deficiencies

[25] The Committee did, however, find that no Member of the Commission knew of the existence of the fictitious contracts until after the UCLAF inquiry had been initiated, ibid. at 4.2.20.

[26] Council Decision 94/819/EC of 6 December 1994, Establishing an Action Programme for the Implementation of a European Community Vocational Training Policy, OJ 1994 L340/8.

[27] Committee of Independent Experts, *First Report*, *supra* n. 1, at 5.2.2.

[28] Ibid. at 5.2.3.

could have occurred and continued without having become known at the highest level of DG XXII.[29] Agenor's contract was finally terminated on 31 January 1999. The final criticism was that the European Parliament was kept in the dark about the problems with the Leonardo programme. This was of particular importance given that in the summer of 1998 the Parliament was working on its report for a proposed Leonardo II programme which would follow on from the Leonardo I programme currently under discussion. It was clear that information regarding the implementation of Leonardo I would have been of central importance when deciding on the possibility of a follow-up programme.

The Committee of Experts was, however, also aware of the need for, and benefits of, contracting out as exemplified by its discussion of *nuclear safety policy*. The Commission had some responsibility in relation to nuclear safety since 1975. The Chernobyl accident in 1986 revealed the dangers of nuclear plants in the Soviet Union that did not conform to state-of-the-art safety requirements. The EC therefore decided to allocate approximately ECU 845 million for nuclear safety programmes. The money was to be used to support domestic safety upgrading programmes and the Community aid constituted approximately 1 per cent of the expenditure required on 65 nuclear stations. The Community resources were delivered under the TACIS and PHARE programmes. DG IA within the Commission managed the programme. The Committee of Experts drew heavily on a Report of the Court of Auditors[30] which had been critical of the way in which Community resources had been delivered. The Court of Auditors' Report expressed concern at the excessive delegation and transfer of responsibilities to third parties. The Committee of Experts put the matter in the following way.[31]

> The DG IA unit in charge of the programmes did not have the necessary manpower at its disposal, in terms of numbers and expertise, to draw up the nuclear safety programmes, follow them up and monitor implementation. For this reason, the Commission delegated some of its responsibilities to the Twinning Programme Engineering Group (TPEG) and to supply agencies to such an extent that the Court of Auditors termed these delegations excessive and likely to jeopardise the institution's independence.

It is, however, clear from reading the Committee of Experts' Report that it did not share all of the criticisms voiced by the Court of Auditors.[32] TPEG was a consortium of EC electricity generators who were responsible for pressurized-water reactors. While the Court of Auditors felt that the Commission had delegated too many of its planning responsibilities to TPEG, the

[29] Committee of Independent Experts, *First Report, supra* n. 1, at 5.4.9.
[30] Special Report No 25/98, OJ 1999 C35/1.
[31] Committee of Independent Experts, *First Report, supra* n. 1, at 7.4.1.
[32] Ibid. at 7.4.9, 7.7.2.

Committee of Experts was more neutral in this respect. It recognized the input of DG IA into planning, and acknowledged the value of the expert assistance provided by all the major electricity generators in the EC. Nor did the Committee of Experts agree with the view taken by the Court of Auditors about the use of supply agencies. Such bodies were used for the implementation of complex, large-scale projects. They verified the neutrality of technical specifications, organized invitations to tender, verified technical reports, drew up contracts with the supplier appointed by the Commission, and ensured payment of invoices in line with the contract. The Court of Auditors had criticized the use of such agencies on the ground that they complicated programme implementation, contributed to delays, and allowed excessive advances to be paid. The Committee of Experts took a different view. It felt that the use of such agencies was both inevitable and beneficial. It was inevitable because the Commission was not in a position to undertake detailed project management itself, since it did not have the necessary expertise. It was beneficial because the alternative to using agencies would have been to entrust the tasks to the electricity generators who were responsible for on-site assistance and this would have given too many powers to such firms. Supply agencies were therefore used by DG IA to assist it in administering the supply contracts. The Committee of Experts while cognizant of the internal staffing problems within the Commission, was nonetheless concerned about the fact that there was little attempt to preserve through archives the expertise of national experts who were on short fixed-term contracts with the Commission. They also expressed doubts as to whether the efforts to co-ordinate the various directorates within the Commission which had an interest in nuclear safety would be successful.[33] The Committee of Experts concluded that there were no grounds for saying that the implementation of the nuclear safety programme gave rise to fraud or serious irregularities.

C. The Committee of Independent Experts' Conclusions

The final section of the Report contained the Committee's conclusions from the detailed studies which it had undertaken. Three general points stand out in this respect.

The first is that, in the Committee's view, the Commissioners did not have sufficient control over their section of the administration. There were no cases found in which Commissioners were directly or personally involved in fraudulent activities, but protestations by the Commissioners that they were unaware of the problems later brought to light were 'tantamount to an admission of a loss of control by the political authorities over the Administration that they are supposedly running'.[34] There were moreover some instances

[33] Ibid. at 7.7.2–7.7.4. [34] Ibid. at 9.2.2.

found where the Commissioners or the Commission as a whole bore some responsibility for instances of fraud, irregularities, or mismanagement in their services.[35]

The second point concerned staffing. One of the common themes in the programmes studied was the need to contract out because of inadequacies in the staffing levels within the Commission. The Committee was not on the whole sympathetic with this rationale for the manner of carrying out Community policies. It was of the view that the Commission should never have taken on policies when it lacked the proper resources to do so. Thus speaking of the MED programmes the Committee stated that the 'Commission as a whole deserves serious criticism (as in other cases under review) for launching a new, politically important and highly expensive programme without having the resources—especially staff—to do so'.[36] Similar sentiments are expressed about the ECHO policy where the Committee stated that the 'Commission as a whole must be held accountable for the fact that a major policy initiative was launched without the service concerned, ECHO, being given the means to implement the policy'.[37] Speaking of the Leonardo programme the Committee concluded by saying that 'the Commission as a whole is again open to criticism for the under-resourcing phenomenon which is at the root of the need to delegate public sector responsibilities to outside consultants'.[38] The Committee also felt that the Commission should have made better use of the staff which it did possess. Thus the Committee spoke of a failure by the Commission to set priorities, that the Commissioners had a collective responsibility to adopt a joint stance on the human resources problem which had been noted by individual Commissioners,[39] and that there were as 'many fiefdoms as there are Commissioners'.[40]

The third point which emerges from the Committee's conclusions is that the control and audit procedures within the Commission were not able to rectify the problems in good time.

3. SERVICE DELIVERY AND ACCOUNTABILITY: REFLECTIONS ON THE COMMITTEE'S REPORT

The Report by the Committee of Independent Experts was important for bringing together and evaluating data on a number of programmes administered by the Commission. The Committee's conclusions deserved to be taken seriously. There were, however, two issues on which there was more to be said both about responsibility for what occurred in the past, and the lessons for the future.

[35] Committee of Independent Experts, *First Report*, *supra* n. 1, at 9.2.3.
[36] Ibid. at 9.2.5. [37] Ibid. at 9.2.6. [38] Ibid. at 9.2.7.
[39] Ibid. at 9.4.3–9.4.4. [40] Ibid. at 9.4.6.

A. Ascription of Responsibility for Taking on Policies Where There Were Staff Shortages

The first issue is as to the ascription of responsibility for taking on policies where there were staff shortages. We have already seen that shortage of staff in-house was one of the major reasons why the Commission contracted-out work connected with these programmes. The Committee was for the most part unsympathetic to the Commission in this respect for three reasons: the Commission should never have proposed and undertaken these programmes without the requisite staff; it should have calculated the aggregate calls on its resources and prioritized between such demands; and the Commission should have asked for budget increases to cover the extra staffing required. All three parts of this critique can be questioned.

The conception of policy formation in the EC which underlies this critique is overly simplistic. The picture of Community decision-making captured in the aphorism 'the Commission proposes, the Council disposes', may well have characterized policy making in the early years of the Community. It no longer captures the more complex reality whereby Community legislation is made now. The European Parliament has, since the Single European Act 1986, had a real input into the content and timing of such legislation. Nor is it meaningful to regard the Council as a mere passive receptor, awaiting legislative proposals which emanate from the Commission. Approximately 40 per cent of the proposals which come from the Commission originate in detailed suggestions made by the Council pursuant to Article 208 EC. Even where the proposal does originate from within the Commission it will be thoroughly reviewed and digested by the Committee of Permanent Representations (COREPER). The quotations mentioned in the previous section all lay the blame for proposing and undertaking policies with inadequate resources on the Commission. It is, however, clear that if blame is to be ascribed in this respect it should not be so readily laid solely at the door of the Commission. The programmes under examination did not emerge simply as a result of a Commission initiative. There were often resolutions and the like passed by the Council and European Parliament, which were then developed by the Commission. This was recognized at certain points in the Committee's Report, albeit not developed in any real detail. Thus the Committee stated that the 'European Parliament and the Council have imposed on the Commission more and more tasks, while at the same time applying rigorous budgetary restrictions'.[41] Later in its Report the Committee talked of the problems encountered in the programmes studied being based on a 'mismatch between the objectives assigned to the Commission, in the context of the new policy laid down by the Council and the Parliament, on a proposal

[41] Ibid. at 5.8.2.

from the Commission, and the resources which the Commission has been able, or has chosen, to employ in the service of that new policy'.[42] To the extent that the Council and Parliament played a real part in the initiation or modification of the proposals which led to these programmes, let alone the fact that they formally voted that the programmes should go ahead, they cannot evade all responsibility for ensuring that the resources were there to do the job. Legislative power within the EC is shared between the Council, European Parliament, and Commission. So too should legislative responsibility. The Commission did of course bear a share of the blame for undertaking policies where it was ill-equipped to do so. The Council and European Parliament cannot, however, be considered blameless in this respect.

The Committee's critique was also that the Commission should have better calculated the overall demands on its resources and that the College of Commissioners should have drawn up a list of priorities. There is force in this point. There should and could have been more macro-level planning by the Commission. The difficulties of undertaking such exercises should not, however, be forgotten. This is particularly so in the context of a decision-making structure such as the EC, where legislative power is shared between a number of important players. A consequence of this is that it might be difficult for the Commission to determine precisely when, or indeed whether, a new programme would come 'on line'. Proposals for a programme might well be included in the legislative agenda for a particular year, but whether they are actually enacted as legislation by the Council and Parliament might be affected by a whole range of factors which could not easily be foreseen ahead of time. Accurate macro-level planning is obviously all the more difficult in such circumstances.

The final element of the Committee's critique concerning resourcing is that the Commission should have pressed for budget increases. The Committee's response to the use of contracting out, auxiliary staff, and the like because of the shortage of staff was that 'the Commission can put forward whatever proposals it sees fit with regard to its Establishment Plan when it submits its preliminary draft budget to the budgetary authority'.[43] It was for that reason that the Committee felt that the 'excuses referring to the shortage of human resources were at odds with the decisions taken by the Commission itself to continue the policy of austerity budgets since 1995'.[44] How much leeway the Commission really had to propose such budget increases may be doubted. The framing and passage of the budget is a complex process in which the Commission, Council, and European Parliament all possess formal legal powers. These powers shape, but do not determine, the actual budget which is approved for any one year, since this will be

[42] Committee of Independent Experts, *First Report, supra* n. 1, at 9.4.5.
[43] Ibid. at 9.4.2. [44] Ibid. at 9.4.2.

dependent upon broader political and economic factors. The Committee recognized that the Council and Parliament were imposing on the Commission an increasing range of tasks, while at the same time maintaining rigorous budget restrictions.[45] In these circumstances the Commission would almost certainly have had to make a political calculation as to whether it was realistic to press for budget increases relating to staff. It could of course be argued that if the Commission did feel thus constrained it could simply have declined to take on new programmes. Yet this too oversimplifies the way in which political institutions operate. It would have been difficult for the Commission to reject important new initiatives pressed by the Council and the European Parliament, since this would have looked like failure on its part whatever the reality was.

B. The Legitimacy of Contracting Out as a Method of Service Delivery

The second issue which is worthy of comment concerns the legitimacy of contracting out as a method of service delivery within the EC. Most of the Community policies implemented in the past had been executed with the help of national bureaucracies. The programmes analysed in the Committee's Report were of a different nature. They were either designed consciously to bypass national bureaucracies, as in the case of the MED programmes; or they entailed the direct evaluation of large numbers of project bids, as in the case of the Tourism and Leonardo initiatives; or the very nature of the programme necessitated working with a range of non-governmental organizations, as in the case of the ECHO. The nature of these programmes therefore required more in the way of direct implementation of policy than had been the case hitherto. In the absence of sufficient staff in-house, it became necessary to contract out much of the work. The Reports of the Court of Auditors, and that of the Committee of Experts, show the need for proper supervision if contracting out is to be acceptable. Indeed the costs of such supervision need to be borne in mind when undertaking the economic calculus about the pros and cons of this strategy. The Committee's more general words about contracting out in the context of the Leonardo programme could be extended to all of the cases studied.[46]

The implementation of Community programmes by private contractors can only be accepted on the basis of a guarantee that the essence of the public function is not abandoned into the hands of the private contractor. Moreover, those private contractors must be subject to contractual provisions imposing strict obligations in the general interest, and the public authorities must effectively supervise this action. It is clear that such supervision has not been exercised with sufficient care in the present

[45] Ibid. at 5.8.2. [46] Ibid. at 5.8.3.

case vis-à-vis the Leonardo/Agenor TAO. It would seem that excessive confidence has been placed in the TAO, and thus excess reliance on outside consultants.

Notwithstanding this extract, the impression created by some parts of the Committee of Experts' Report, is that contracting out was an unfortunate by-product of the Commission's resourcing problem. If this problem had been properly addressed there would have been less need for recourse to contracting out. There is no doubt that if the Commission had possessed more resources in-house there would have been no need for the subterfuges used to staff ECHO, supervision of all the programmes would have been that much easier, and there would have been less likelihood that public sector policy responsibility would have been transferred to the private sector, as was the case in relation to some of the programmes.

It should nonetheless be recognized that contracting out must and should remain an option for the delivery of public services by the EC in the future, as recognized in the Committee's Second Report[47] and the Commission's White Paper.[48] Not only must it remain an option, it will in many instances still be the best option all things considered. The more programmes which are committed to the direct responsibility of the Commission, where implementation is to take place without direct input from national bureaucracies, the more the Commission will need to have recourse to contracting out, as exemplified by nuclear safety where the Committee recognized the necessity to contract out because of the highly complex, technical nature of the work. However, it is readily apparent that some use of contracting out is necessary or desirable in many other areas. Programmes such as Tourism and Leonardo involved the collection of data, the establishment of criteria by which to evaluate projects, and the actual evaluation of particular proposals. Even if the staffing pressures within the Commission were to be alleviated it is by no means clear that it would be desirable, either in terms of efficiency or effectiveness, for this work to be done in-house.[49] The staff would not have any expertise in the relevant areas. Contracting out in such areas, subject to effective oversight by the Commission, will therefore often be the optimal method of delivering Community programmes.

4. THE PRODI COMMISSION AND INSTITUTIONAL REFORM

A. The Initial Prodi Reforms

Romano Prodi, the new President of the Commission, lost no time in introducing reforms designed to restore faith in the Commission. A paper was

[47] *Supra* n. 8. [48] *Supra* n. 9.

[49] See generally, I. Harden, *The Contracting State* (Open University Press, 1992).

produced on the *Formation of the New Commission.*[50] It contained a new Code of Conduct for Commissioners with strict rules about the declaration of interests, and the outside activities which Commissioners are allowed to pursue. The same paper also contained detailed rules about the formation and role of the Commissioners' private offices. A separate paper entitled the *Operation of the Commission*[51] dealt with a number of matters. The Commission's Rules of Procedure were revised. New working groups of Commissioners were established to ensure the better preparation and coordination of the Commission's activities.[52] Increased emphasis was placed on closer internal coordination within the Commission.[53] This was of particular importance. The broad range of activities for which the Commission is responsible, combined with increased decentralization, furthered the need for closer internal coordination to ensure the consistency and effectiveness of the Commission's actions. The paper therefore gave particular emphasis to the setting of priorities, and the need to ensure that the Commission had the resources necessary to meet them.[54] In his first major address to the European Parliament Romano Prodi emphasized these new initiatives.[55] He also made it clear that, although it was not at that time formally dealt with in the Treaty, he would not hesitate to ask for the resignation of an individual commissioner should this prove to be necessary. All of his new team accepted their portfolios on this understanding.

These initial reforms introduced by Romano Prodi were followed by the setting up, on 18 September 1999, of a Task Force for Administrative Reform (TFRA) for which Neil Kinnock was given responsibility. The mission statement of the TFRA[56] listed the following matters which would be considered: human resources; allocation and use of internal and external resources; management of operational activities; internal financial and budgetary controls; audits; interaction between control services and OLAF (the European Anti-Fraud Office); programming; ethics and discipline; and internal communication. The White Paper[57] which emerged as a result of this study will be analysed below. Before doing so it is important to consider the Second Report of the Committee of Independent Experts, since this, as well as the First Report, influenced the recommendations produced in the White Paper.

[50] 12 July 1999. [51] 12 July 1999.

[52] Such groups have been established to deal with the following areas: Growth, Competitiveness and Employment; Equal Opportunities; Reform; Inter-institutional Relations; and External Relations.

[53] The Operation of the Commission, 12 July 1999, at 18–22. [54] Ibid. at 18, 20.

[55] Speech by Romano Prodi, President-designate of the European Commission, to the European Parliament, 21 July 1999.

[56] 20 October 1999. [57] Reforming the Commission, COM (2000) 200.

B. The Second Report of the Committee of Independent Experts

The Second Report of the Committee of Independent Experts was published on 10 September 1999.[58] It was a study of major importance covering two volumes and running to 278 pages. It deserves to be read by all those interested in administrative reform within the Community. The Report received nothing like the attention that had been focused on the earlier document which had led to the downfall of the Santer Commission. In the long term the Second Report was undoubtedly of greater importance for its insights into the workings of the Commission. It is not possible to do full justice to this Report here. The focus will be on the central recommendations made by the Committee in Volume I. The material covered by the Committee in Volume II will be analysed where relevant when considering the Commission's White Paper. Volume I dealt primarily with the different ways in which services are delivered within the Community, the division being between those areas where the Commission has a direct management responsibility, and those instances where this responsibility is shared between the Commission and the Member States.

The discussion of *direct management* was at the same time rich, sophisticated, and blunt. Direct management covers those areas where the Commission itself directly manages a programme without the necessary involvement of national administrations, albeit often with the aid of an outside contractor. The area is of considerable financial importance: appropriations for direct management operations are of the order of €14 billion per annum, or one sixth of the Community budget.[59] The Committee accepted that the 'Commission will in future have a huge number of tasks to perform, the temporary and specialized nature of which requires them to be contracted-out—subcontracting being justified on the grounds of efficiency, expediency and cost'.[60] It noted that recourse to such contracting out had never been challenged by the European Parliament or the Council.[61] While accepting the need for contracting out, the Committee was equally firm in its belief that the existing arrangements were imperfect. Contracting out had been undertaken through the medium of TAOs (technical assistance offices) which were, in the Committee's view, nothing more than Commission contractors.[62] The use of TAOs raised problems as to the dividing line between Commission tasks which could be contracted out without any risk to the public service,

[58] Committee of Independent Experts, *Second Report on Reform of the Commission, Analysis of Current Practice and Proposals for Tackling Mismanagement, Irregularities and Fraud* (10 September 1999).

[59] Ibid. Vol. I, at 2.1.1.

[60] Ibid. Vol. I, at 2.3.1. See also, at 2.0.1, and 2.3.8.

[61] Ibid. Vol. I, at 2.3.1.

[62] Ibid. Vol. I, at 2.3.4, 2.3.14.

and 'those in respect of which the Commission would be abandoning its responsibilities if it were to delegate them to private companies'.[63] The difficulty was to determine what constituted a public service responsibility.[64] This problem was compounded by the fact that it might not be easy in organizational terms to maintain a division between public authority tasks reserved to the Commission, and other tasks which could be legitimately delegated to another body.[65] The way forward favoured by the Committee was to establish a new type of implementing agency. These should not be permanent, nor should they contain Member State representatives.[66] They should exist solely for the duration of the particular project. Such agencies would facilitate the working together of Community officials seconded to the agency, with staff from the private sector who would have responsibility for particular aspects of the Community programme.[67] The Committee's Report contains a number of other valuable recommendations in relation to direct management. There should be better training for Community staff so as to improve their management of contracts.[68] The Financial Regulation, the principal legal provision under which disbursements were made, was in need of thorough overhaul,[69] as were the complex rules concerning public procurement.[70] The position of the authorizing officer should be enhanced, with a correlative increase in the responsibilities attached to the job.[71]

The Committee's discussion of *shared management* served as a timely reminder of the difficulties of executing policies when administration is shared between different levels of government. While the errors identified in the Committee's First Report that led to the downfall of the Commission were all associated with direct management, it has been shared management that has generated most concern in annual reports of the Court of Auditors. Shared management refers to the management of those Community programmes where the 'Commission and the Member States have distinct administrative tasks which are inter-dependent and set down in legislation and where both the Commission and the national administrations need to discharge their respective tasks for the Community policy to be implemented successfully'.[72] The sums involved in shared management programmes are large indeed. The Guarantee section of the European Agricultural Guidance and Guarantee Fund (EAGGF) accounted for 48.5 per cent of the Community's budget in 1999. The Structural Funds[73] are also administered

[63] Ibid. Vol. I, at 2.3.10.
[64] Ibid. Vol. I, at 2.3.19.
[65] Ibid. Vol. I, at 2.3.21.
[66] Ibid. Vol. I, at 2.3.27.
[67] Ibid. Vol. I, at 2.3.27–2.3.31.
[68] Ibid. Vol. I, at 2.0.5.
[69] Ibid. Vol. I, at 2.1.15–2.1.19.
[70] Ibid. Vol. I, at 2.1.17.
[71] Ibid. Vol. I, at 2.2.49–2.2.59.
[72] Ibid. Vol. I, at 3.2.2.
[73] The European Regional Development Fund, the European Social Fund, the European Agricultural Guidance and Guarantee Fund, Guidance Section, and the Financial Instrument for Fisheries Guidance.

jointly by the Community and the Member States, and accounted for 32.8 per cent of the Community budget in 1999. It is clear that the Member States have responsibility to counter fraud.[74] It is clear also that the detailed structure of the relevant regulations often provide a disincentive for them to do so. This is indeed the single most important message which emerges from this chapter of the Committee's Report. It is indicative of the importance which should be paid to the relative ascription of responsibilities when devising regulations in the context of shared administration. We shall return to this issue in the detailed discussion of shared administration below.[75]

The Committee's discussion of both direct and shared management must be seen in the light of its more general recommendations concerning what it termed the *control environment.* It produced a detailed analysis of the shortcomings of internal control and internal audit. Internal or *ex ante* control has traditionally taken the form of the 'visa' system, which was designed to ensure that proposals for expenditure were in conformity with the appropriate rules and procedures. It did not, however, work very effectively, in the sense that many items of expenditure for which a visa had been granted were later found to be irregular or illegal. The system was also criticized by the Committee because it displaced responsibility for financial regularity from the person actually managing the expenditure onto the person approving it, with the consequence that no one was ultimately responsible.[76] The main thrust of the Committee's recommendations were therefore to delegate internal control to the different directorate-generals, to ensure that the authorizing officer therein really did bear responsibility for the proposals which he or she had authorized, and to do away with the need for validation by a separate, central authority of the kind hitherto undertaken by the Financial Controller.[77] The Committee was equally convinced of the need for change in the system of internal audit. The Financial Controller at that time had overall responsibility for both the visa and audit functions. This dual role could cause difficulties in situations where an audit revealed irregularities in relation to payments for which a visa had been issued. The Committee therefore favoured the creation of an independent Internal Audit Service, which should report directly to the President of the Commission.[78]

[74] Art. 280 EC.
[75] See, Chap. 3 below.
[76] Committee of Independent Experts, *Second Report*, Vol. I, at 4.6.2.
[77] Ibid. Vol. I, at 4.7., 4.18.1.
[78] Ibid. Vol. I, at 4.13, 4.18.2.

C. Reforming the Commission: The White Paper

The TFRA produced a consultative document in January 2000,[79] and the White Paper appeared in March of the same year.[80] Part I of the White Paper set out the general principles on which reform of the Commission was to be based, while Part II contained an Action Plan detailing how these general principles were to be achieved. The White Paper acknowledged the contributions made by the Reports of the Committee of Independent Experts,[81] and the DECODE exercise.[82]

The theme which runs through the White Paper was made clear at the outset. The Prodi Commission wished to concentrate more on core functions such as policy conception, political initiative, and enforcing Community law. The fact that almost half of the Commission officials spent their time managing programmes was not regarded as an efficient use of resources.[83] The execution of Community programmes would therefore require the 'building of new forms of partnership between the different levels of governance in Europe',[84] and the identification of those 'activities which could be more usefully and efficiently executed by other bodies, where necessary, under the control of the Commission'.[85] With the Reports of the Committee of Independent Experts firmly in its mind, it was made clear that if the Commission did not have the requisite resources to carry out the tasks which it had reserved for itself, and more resources were not forthcoming, then the Commission would have to discontinue some programmes.[86] The modern Commission should be independent, responsible, accountable, efficient, and transparent.[87] Three more particular themes are explored in the White Paper: priority setting, and the allocation and efficient use of resources; human resources policy; and the overhaul of financial management.

The attention given to *priority setting, and the allocation and efficient use of resources* was to enable the Commission to concentrate on its core activities. Resources had, in the past, not been linked to priorities both because Commission decisions on activities were taken separately from those on the allocation of resources, and because the Council and European Parliament

[79] Consultative Document, Reforming the Commission, CG3 (2000) 1/17, 18 January 2000.

[80] Reforming the Commission, COM (2000) 200.

[81] Ibid. Part I, at 2.

[82] Designing Tomorrow's Commission, A Review of the Commission's Organization and Operation, 7 July 1999. This exercise was begun in 1997 by the Commission and constituted a review of all the activities which it carried out. The principal objective was to determine what work was being done, why it was being done, who did it, and how the work was being carried out.

[83] Reforming the Commission, *supra* n. 80, Part I, at 1.

[84] Ibid. Part I, at 1.

[85] Ibid. Part I, at 2.

[86] Ibid. Part I, at 2.

[87] Ibid. Part I, at 3–4.

gave the Commission new tasks without providing the extra resources needed.[88]

This mismatch was to be addressed in part by the introduction of a system of activity-based management (ABM), the object of which was to ensure that decisions about policy priorities and the corresponding resources were taken together at all levels of the organization.[89] It was also to be addressed by the simplification of working procedures within the Commission, and the introduction of performance-oriented working methods in the Commission.[90]

The desire that the Commission should be able to concentrate on its core activities was the rationale for what was termed an 'externalization policy': the delegation of activities to other bodies. These included Community bodies, decentralization to national public bodies, and contracting out to the private sector.[91] Externalization was only to be pursued where it was the most efficient option; it should not be pursued at the expense of accountability; and there had to be sufficient internal resources to ensure proper control. It should not therefore be used for the administration of ill-defined activities, nor where real discretionary power was involved.[92] It was moreover clear that the type of task which was delegated would depend to some extent on the body to which it was delegated, with outsourcing to private bodies being subject to the strictest limits in this respect.[93] There is much in these strictures on the limits of externalization which harks back to the Reports of the Committee of Independent Experts. Echoes of recommendations made by this Committee are also apparent in the suggestion in the White Paper that there should be a new type of implementing body to be headed by Community staff.[94]

The White Paper proposed a number of detailed changes in relation to *human resources*.[95] These related to management, recruitment, training, career structure, performance appraisal, promotion, and the like. Limits of space preclude any detailed discussion of these matters here. The most interesting point in this part of the White Paper relates to career structure. It was recognized that the current system provided little in the way of incentive to good performance or personal initiative, and that it acted as an artificial constraint on those with particular abilities. The White Paper therefore proposed the development of a new and more linear career structure.[96]

The discussion of *audit, financial management*, and *control* also developed a number of the ideas advocated by the Committee of Independent Experts. The White Paper acknowledged that the centralized system of financial control was no longer capable of dealing with the volume of transactions which

[88] Reforming the Commission, *supra* n. 80, Part I, at 4.
[89] Ibid. Part I, at 5–6.
[90] Ibid. Part I, at 6–7.
[91] Ibid. Part I, at 6.
[92] Ibid. Part I, at 7.
[93] Ibid. Part II, at 17–18.
[94] Committee of Independent Experts, *Second Report*, Vol. I, *supra* n. 58, at 2.3.27–2.3.31; White Paper, *supra* n. 80, Part I, at 7.
[95] White Paper, *supra* n. 80, Part I, at 8–15.
[96] Ibid. Part I, at 10.

the Commission had to process. It recognized that the centralized 'visa' system of control had not worked and that it gave decision-makers a false sense of security. It accepted also that the position of the Financial Controller, being responsible for the ex-ante visa, and the ex-post audit, could give rise to a conflict of interest.[97] The emphasis for the future was to be on decentralization. Directors-General would exercise the powers currently held by the Financial Controller. They would be responsible for adequate controls within their departments.[98] This would be accompanied by allocation of financial responsibility to authorizing officers within departments: 'as far as possible the person taking the operational decision to go ahead with an operation involving expenditure should also be the one authorising the expenditure'.[99] The proposals relating to audit drew heavily on those of the Committee of Experts. There was to be an Internal Audit Service under the authority of the Vice-President for Reform, and each department was to have its own specialized audit capability. There was, in addition, to be an Audit Progress Committee which would monitor the quality of audit work, and the implementation of audit recommendations made by the Court of Auditors.[100]

5. IMPLEMENTATION OF THE REFORMS

An action plan was attached to the White Paper highlighting 98 points on which further measures were required in order to implement the broader objectives of the reform agenda. These have been carried through by an admixture of formal legislation, soft law, and internal administrative reform. The discussion that follows gives a brief overview of progress in the different areas where action was deemed necessary.[101]

A. A Culture Based On Service and Ethical Standards

A number of initiatives were passed in order to effectuate the White Paper actions concerning the creation of a more service-based culture. A Code of Good Administrative Behaviour dealing with relations between the Commission and the public came into effect on 1 November 2000. A Regulation was enacted on access to documents held by Community institutions and

[97] Ibid. Part I, at 17.

[98] Ibid. Part I, at 17. There is, however, to be a Central Financial Service which will provide advice to departments, at 18.

[99] Ibid. Part I, at 16.

[100] Ibid. Part I, at 18.

[101] Communication from the Commission, Progress Review of Reform, COM(2003) 40 final; Communication from the Commission, Completing the Reform Mandate: Progress Report and Measures to be Implemented in 2004, COM(2004) 93 final.

extended to cover other Community bodies, such as agencies.[102] Efforts were made to reduce the time that it took the Commission to pay its bills and to respond to mail from the public.

A number of related initiatives have been concerned with the safeguarding of ethical and professional standards. These include a modified Code of Conduct for Commissioners adopted by the Barroso Commission on 24 November 2004. There have also been changes to the disciplinary procedures applicable to staff where there has been serious wrongdoing, such as corruption or fraud, designed to make the disciplinary measures more efficient. Guidelines have been introduced to deal with under-performance by staff that does not amount to serious wrongdoing, with mechanisms designed to detect professional incompetence at an early stage These modifications have been complemented by procedures that relate to whistle-blowing by staff who believe that they have evidence of fraud, corruption, or other illegal activity.

B. Priority Setting and the Efficient Use of Resources

A number of changes have been made to address the concerns expressed in the White Paper and the Reports of the Committee of Independent Experts about the setting of priorities and the allocation of resources to meet them.

The Commission now operates an annual planning cycle, which begins with the Annual Policy Strategy Decision (APS). This Decision identifies the policy priorities for a particular year and the implications that this has for resource allocation. Thus the 2003 APS identified internal redeployments to match priorities involving around 300 staff, of which approximately 175 were redeployed between services. It also identified the need to recruit further staff in the light of impending enlargement of the European Union (EU). The APS is discussed with the Council and European Parliament (EP) and it will then be used to prepare the Commission Legislative and Work Programme, which is presented to the Council and EP, normally in November. Each Directorate-General establishes Annual Management Plans (AMPs) on the basis of the preceding framework. All Directors-General present an Annual Activity Report (AAR) and sign a declaration on the quality of internal controls. The cycle ends with a Synthesis Report by the Commission of these AARs which, *inter alia*, assesses progress, the way in which resources were used, and proposals for remedying deficiencies revealed in the individual reports from the Directors-General.[103]

[102] Regulation (EC) 1049/2001 of the European Parliament and Council of 30 May 2001, Regarding Public Access to European Parliament, Council and Commission Documents, OJ 2001 L145/43.

[103] Communication from the Commission, Synthesis of Annual Activity Reports 2003 of Directorates-General and Services, COM(2004) 418 final.

The cycle as a whole is conducted through Activity Based Management, (ABM), which means that planning and management are based on 'politically meaningful activities' rather than purely administrative categories. The Commission defines for each of these activities its objectives and the resources allocated to them.

There have also been changes designed to improve policy coordination. There is an ABM Steering Group, which is chaired by the Secretary General, and includes Directors-General and cabinets from central services. It coordinates political and strategic issues related to reform. There is in addition a Directors-General Group, which has responsibility for ensuring consistent implementation of reform and other policies. Two further groups were created in 2002 to facilitate coordination. There is the Group of Resource Directors, which considers detailed operational aspects concerned with the delivery of administrative reform. The Interservice Coordination Group reviews agenda planning in order to identify issues that require particular attention and to oversee the work of ad hoc groups dealing with specific issues.

C. Staff Policy

The White Paper listed numerous action points in relation to human resources policy, 41 to be precise. The centrepiece of the new personnel policy involved significant changes to appraisal and promotion, designed to link merit and career development more closely than had been the case hitherto.

Certain of the modifications concerning staff required amendment to the staff regulations, including matters relating to career structure, mobility, welfare policy, pay and pensions, early retirement, and discipline. Change in this area has not proven easy, with staff representatives threatening to reject significant parts of a draft document and to strike. A mediator was appointed, the draft regulations were amended, and the new staff regulations entered into force on 1 May 2004.[104]

D. Financial Management, Control, and Audit

Not surprisingly in the light of the catalyst for the fall of the Santer Commission, the White Paper listed numerous matters relating to financial management that should be addressed.

Many of these have been dealt with through the new Financial Regulation,

[104] Council Regulation (EC, Euratom) 723/2004 of 22 March 2004, Amending the Staff Regulations of the Officials of the European Communities and the Conditions of Employment of other Servants of the European Communities, OJ 2004 L124/1.

which established a constitutional framework for Community administration of the kind that has not existed hitherto. The term constitutionalization has a plethora of meanings. Its use here signifies, in formal terms, that the principles governing Community administration have been enshrined in a norm that is of constitutional importance. The term constitutionalization signifies, in substantive terms, the emergence of overarching principles that frame the entirety of Community administration.

The previous Financial Regulation was enacted in 1977, and had been amended on many occasions.[105] The new Financial Regulation[106] now provides a legal framework for the structure of Community administration. The detailed provisions of the new Regulation concerning direct and shared management will be considered in the chapters that follow. The present discussion will focus on the structural aspects of the Regulation. The distinction between direct and shared administration was, as we have seen, central to the Second Report of the Committee of Independent Experts, and to the Commission White Paper. It has now been embodied in the Regulation.

Chapter 2 of Title IV, Implementation of the Budget, is concerned with methods of implementation. Article 53(1) of the new Financial Regulation provides that the Commission shall implement the budget either on a centralized basis, or by shared or decentralized management, or by joint management with international organizations. These methods of implementation must be considered separately.

Centralized management covers those instances where the Commission implements the budget directly through its departments, or indirectly.[107] The principles concerning indirect centralized implementation are set out in Article 54. The Commission is not allowed to entrust its executive powers to third parties where they involve a large measure of discretion implying political choices. The implementing tasks delegated must be clearly defined and fully supervised.[108] There may well be problems in deciding whether the task allocated to third parties is *ultra vires*, in the sense that it involves 'a large measure of discretion implying political choices', within the meaning of Article 54(1). Within these limits the Commission can entrust tasks to the new breed of executive agencies, or Community bodies that can receive

[105] Financial Regulation of 21 December 1977 Applicable to the General Budget of the European Communities, OJ 1977 L356/1.

[106] Council Regulation (EC, Euratom) 1605/2002 of 25 June 2002, On the Financial Regulation Applicable to the General Budget of the European Communities, OJ 2002 L248/1. For background, see Proposal for a Council Regulation on the Financial Regulation Applicable to the General Budget of the EC, COM(2000) 461 final; Amended Proposal for a Council Regulation on the Financial Regulation Applicable to the General Budget of the EC, COM (2001) 691.

[107] Reg. 1605/2002, *supra* n. 106, at Art. 53(2).

[108] Ibid. Art. 54(1).

grants.[109] It can also, within the limits of Article 54(1), entrust tasks to national public-sector bodies, or bodies governed by private law with a public service mission guaranteed by the state.[110] These national bodies can only be entrusted with budget implementation if the basic act concerning the programme provides for the possibility of delegation, and lays down the criteria for the selection of such bodies. It is also a condition that the delegation to national bodies is a response to the requirements of sound financial management, and is non-discriminatory. The delegation of executive tasks to these bodies must be transparent, and the procurement procedure must be non-discriminatory and prevent any conflict of interest. There must be an effective internal control system for management operations, proper accounting arrangements, and an external audit.[111] The Commission is not allowed to entrust implementation of funds from the budget, in particular payment and recovery, to external private-sector bodies, other than those which have a public service mission guaranteed by the state.[112] The Commission is, however, empowered to entrust such private-sector entities with tasks involving technical expertise, and administrative, preparatory or ancillary tasks involving neither the exercise of public authority, nor the use of discretionary judgment.[113]

Where aspects of the budget are implemented by *shared management*, tasks are entrusted to the Member States in accordance with specific provisions of the new Financial Regulation concerning the European Agricultural Guidance and Guarantee Fund (EAGGF), Guarantee Section, and the Structural Funds.[114]

Cases of *decentralized management* cover those instances where funds are intended for third country beneficiaries. These funds can be disbursed directly by the Commission, or by the authorities of the beneficiary state.[115] In the latter instance the rules of the new Financial Regulation concerning separation of function between authorizing and accounting officers, internal and external audit, and procurement procedures are applicable. These will be considered in detail below.[116] It is in this area that management may be undertaken jointly with an international organization.

There have been significant organizational changes as a result of the new Financial Regulation. The Central Financial Service operates under the responsibility of the Budget Commissioner and provides assistance, training, and support to departments, more especially to authorizing officers who have the major responsibilities for financial management within the Directorates-General (DGs) under the new Financial Regulation. An Independent Internal

[109] Ibid. Art. 54(2)(a) and (b).
[110] Ibid. Art. 54(2)(c).
[111] Ibid. Art. 56(1).
[112] Ibid. Art. 57(1).
[113] Ibid. Art. 57(2).
[114] Ibid. Arts. 149–60.
[115] Ibid. Arts. 163–171.
[116] See below, Chap. 2.

Audit Service was established in July 2001. There are also specialized audit services within each DG, which report directly to the Director-General or head of department. There is an Audit Progress Committee, with the task of following up reports of the Internal Audit Service to see whether the lessons learned have been implemented.

6. CONCLUSIONS AND ASSESSMENT

There is but little doubt that the forced resignation of the Santer Commission sent shock waves through the Commission bureaucracy. It prompted a wide-ranging inquiry into the methods of administration and service delivery within the EU. There were nonetheless concerns that the lessons learned from the experience, embodied in the reports of the Committee of Independent Experts and in the Commission White Paper, might simply gather dust in the manner redolent of some previous reform initiatives.

This has not happened. The Commission, to its credit, did not seek to deny the need for reform. It followed through on the 'action points' listed in the White Paper. It crafted the new Financial Regulation, which gave formal legal force to many of the more particular suggestions for reform contained in the earlier reports. The Financial Regulation is not a panacea for all ills, real and imagined, that have beset Community administration. Nor, as we shall see in subsequent chapters, does it address all the modes by which the Community delivers policy. It is nonetheless an important initiative that provides a principled foundation for central aspects of Community administration, both direct and shared. The detailed provisions will be discussed in the chapters that follow. The Commission has moreover also undertaken the other reforms adumbrated above, some enshrined in formal legislation, others in codes, and yet others brought about through internal administrative change.

It is, however, important to keep a perspective on what has and what has not been achieved. The Commission documentation on implementation of the reforms reads somewhat in the manner of a checklist, with itemization of the action points that have been met. To be fair, the Commission also recognizes that reform is a 'process of change and discovery'[117] rather than simply an endpoint to be measured in terms of compliance with the 98 issues listed in the White Paper. There is nonetheless still room for disagreement within the Community institutions as to how far the reforms introduced have addressed the relevant problems. This is readily apparent from a reading of the Court of Auditors' Report 2003.[118] Thus the Report stated with reference

[117] Communication from the Commission, Progress Review of Reform, *supra* n. 101, at 1.
[118] Court of Auditors, Annual Report Concerning the Financial Year 2003, OJ 2004 C293/1.

to expenditure through shared management that while progress had been made in relation to financial probity, the 'Court has no reasonable assurance that the supervisory systems and controls of significant areas of the budget are effectively implemented so as to manage the risks concerning the legality and regularity of the underlying operations'.[119] The Court of Auditors' believed that the annual activity reports from the Directors-General could not yet systematically serve as a useful basis for its audit conclusions,[120] and regarded the Commission's assessment that all the action points from the White Paper had been completed or that significant progress had been made as 'very optimistic'.[121] The Commission by way of response acknowledged that certain problems could only be effectively resolved in the medium term. The possible second-order consequences of reforms that have been achieved should also been borne in mind. Thus the emphasis placed on financial regularity can lead to a culture in which the individuals at the front line responsible for authorizing expenditure become overly wary of doing so.

It is equally important to remember that the success of any individual part of the reform strategy is, as the Committee of Independent Experts wisely noted, dependent upon a more general modification in the culture of the Commission. Formal responsibilities can be enshrined in codes of conduct and the like, but this must not be 'confused with respect for substance'.[122] The very idea of responsibility captures a range of ideas including personal integrity, formal procedural safeguards, and institutional accountability.[123]

It should be equally recognized that the successful, fair, and efficient delivery of Community policies is not the responsibility of the Commission alone. The Council and the European Parliament have important roles in the legislative and budgetary process. They cannot shift all responsibility to the Commission when things go wrong. If the Community wishes to take on new tasks, or to develop existing policies, then the Council and the European Parliament must also recognize that this cannot be done without the requisite resources. If the political will is not there to secure these resources then it is better that this is recognized at the outset, so that the Commission is not saddled with the administration of policies which it is unable to deliver.

We should finally be mindful of the different roles played by law in this area. Law, in the form of general Community legislation, establishes the overarching principles to govern Community administration, as exemplified by the new Financial Regulation. Law, in the form of specific Community legislation, encapsulates choices that can markedly affect success or failure, as exemplified by the regulations governing the Common Agricultural Policy

[119] Ibid. at 0.4. [120] Ibid. at 1.70. [121] Ibid. at 1.72.
[122] Committee of Independent Experts, *Second Report, supra* n. 58, Vol. II, at 7.1.4.
[123] Ibid. Vol. II, at 7.1–7.16.

and the Structural Funds.[124] Law is used to legitimate new institutions for policy delivery, such as executive agencies.[125] Law, in the form of judicial review, has a Janus-like focus. The Community courts will control abuse of administrative power. They also use judicial review to read Community legislation in the manner that best conforms to the Community interest. We must also be aware of the limits of law. The bypassing of formal legal norms by key players, and the legal response, is a fascinating part of the story.

[124] See below, Chap. 3.

[125] See below, Chap. 2.

2

Centralized or Direct Community Administration

1. INTRODUCTION

The previous chapter charted the reforms made in the aftermath of the fall of the Santer Commission, including the emergence of a constitutional framework for Community administration embodied in the new Financial Regulation.[1] We have seen that the divide between direct and shared administration was central to the reform initiatives and also to the structure of the new Financial Regulation. This chapter will take the story forward by considering in more detail the emerging regime that governs centralized/direct Community administration.

The discussion begins with a brief overview of the rationale for centralized/direct administration and the problems encountered in the past. This will be followed by detailed analysis of the regime for direct administration found in the new Financial Regulation and related instruments. There will then be an examination of recent initiatives with the use of executive agencies within specific areas of Community policy, with a particular focus on the energy sector. The discussion concludes with reflections on the role of law within direct Community administration.

2. DIRECT/CENTRALIZED MANAGEMENT

A. The Rationale for Direct/Centralized Management

The traditional pattern of Community administration has been shared, with the Commission working directly with national bureaucracies to implement

[1] Council Regulation (EC, Euratom) 1605/2002 of 25 June 2002, On the Financial Regulation Applicable to the General Budget of the European Communities, OJ 2002 L248/1. For background, see Proposal for a Council Regulation on the Financial Regulation Applicable to the General Budget of the EC, COM(2000) 461 final; Amended Proposal for a Council Regulation on the Financial Regulation Applicable to the General Budget of the EC, COM(2001) 691.

policy in areas such as the Common Agricultural Policy and the Structural Funds.

The Commission has, however, increasingly undertaken administration directly, without a systematic relationship with national administrations. This was in part because the Commission was given wider responsibilities, and the enabling provisions did not establish any general pattern of shared management. It was in part because the subject matter did not necessarily lend itself to shared management. It was in part also because the Commission felt that certain policies were best implemented through non-governmental organs. The appropriations for directly managed operations are approximately one sixth of the Community budget. Initiatives in relation to tourism, cooperation with non-member countries of the southern Mediterranean (the MED programmes), emergency aid, vocational training (the Leonardo da Vinci programme), nuclear safety policy, as well as the TACIS and PHARE programmes, have been managed directly by the Commission.

B. Delivery of Direct/Centralized Management and Contracting Out

Direct management captures the idea that the Commission will implement a programme without formal, systematic cooperation with national bureaucracies. It does not mean that the Commission carries out the entirety of the activity itself 'in-house'. It is common in relation to direct management for the Commission to contract out part of the work, as exemplified by the programmes considered above. The motivations for contracting out were eclectic.[2] In some areas, such as nuclear safety, expertise was the key factor. In others, such as the MED programmes, there was a desire to involve civil society in service delivery. The rationale for contracting out in the context of humanitarian assistance was that specialist organizations would be better placed to deliver the aid than the Commission. Shortage of staff within the Commission was another reason for contracting out.

There were, however, as we saw in the previous chapter, problems concerning contracting out. The line between policy formation and policy implementation became blurred. It was difficult to ensure that the private contractor did not breach its contract with or defraud the Commission. The Second Report of the Committee of Independent Experts accepted that the Commission would nonetheless have to contract out tasks,[3] but was equally

[2] See above, Chap. 1.

[3] Committee of Independent Experts, *Second Report on Reform of the Commission, Analysis of Current Practice and Proposals for Tackling Mismanagement, Irregularities and Fraud* (10 September 1999), Vol. I, at 2.3.1. See also, at 2.0.1 and 2.3.8.

firm in its belief that the existing arrangements were imperfect. This was acknowledged also in the Commission's White Paper.[4]

3. THE NEW FINANCIAL REGULATION

A. General Principles

The general principles concerning centralized or direct administration were set out in the previous chapter. It is nonetheless important to rehearse them briefly here, since they frame the subsequent analysis. The principles are found in the new Financial Regulation Title IV, Implementation of the Budget, Chapter 2 of which is concerned with Methods of Implementation. Article 53(1) provides that the Commission shall implement the budget either on a centralized basis, or by shared or decentralized management, or by joint management with international organizations. Centralized management covers those instances where the Commission implements the budget directly through its departments, or indirectly.[5]

The principles concerning indirect centralized implementation are set out in Article 54. The Commission is not allowed to entrust its executive powers to third parties where they involve a large measure of discretion implying political choices. The implementing tasks delegated must be clearly defined and fully supervised.[6] Within these limits the Commission can entrust tasks to the new breed of executive agencies, or Community bodies that can receive grants.[7] It can also, within the limits of Article 54(1), entrust tasks to national public sector bodies, or bodies governed by private law with a public service mission guaranteed by the state.[8] These national bodies can only be entrusted with budget implementation if the basic act concerning the programme provides for the possibility of delegation, and lays down the criteria for the selection of such bodies. It is also a condition that the delegation to national bodies is a response to the requirements of sound financial management, and is non-discriminatory.

The delegation of executive tasks to these bodies must be transparent, and the procurement procedure must be non-discriminatory and prevent any conflict of interest. There must be an effective internal control system for management operations, proper accounting arrangements, and an external audit.[9] Before the Commission entrusts implementation to any of the preceding bodies it must ensure that there are proper control and accounting

[4] Reforming the Commission, COM(2000) 200.
[5] Reg. 1605/2002, *supra* n. 1, Art. 53(2).
[6] Ibid. Art. 54(1).
[7] Ibid. Arts. 54(2)(a) and (b).
[8] Ibid. Art. 54(2)(c).
[9] Ibid. Art. 56(1).

systems in place and proper procedures for the award of contracts and grants.[10]

The Commission is not allowed to entrust implementation of funds from the budget in particular payment and recovery, to external private sector bodies, other than those which have a public service mission guaranteed by the state.[11] The Commission is, however, empowered to entrust such private sector entities with tasks involving technical expertise, and administrative, preparatory, or ancillary tasks involving neither the exercise of public authority, nor the use of discretionary judgment.[12]

B. Five Choices

The new Financial Regulation provides a framework for those activities directly managed by the Commission. Such programmes can be directly managed within the Commission; management tasks can be undertaken by executive agencies; implementation can be entrusted to a Community body or agency; some tasks can be delegated to networks of national agencies; and certain activities can be contracted out.

These modes of direct management interrelate. Thus even where it is decided to use an executive agency, there will still be important aspects of the programme overseen by the Commission, since the management tasks that can be delegated to such agencies are limited. Moreover, the contracting out of certain tasks can be used in conjunction with any of the other modes of direct management. Thus, as will be seen, it is possible for an executive agency to contract out certain of its assigned tasks.

The possibility of implementing Community policy through a Community body or agency, which is not a new-style executive agency, will be considered in detail in a subsequent chapter.[13] The discussion that follows considers the other four ways in which direct/centralized management can be undertaken.

4. MANAGEMENT BY THE COMMISSION: RECASTING RESPONSIBILITY FOR PROJECTS

Public lawyers will be aware of the importance of proper control systems when dealing with contracting out and the like. Such systems are a necessary,

[10] Commission Regulation (EC, Euratom) 2342/2002 of 23 December 2002, Laying Down Detailed Rules for the Implementation of Council Regulation 1605/2002, OJ 2002 L357/1, Art. 35.

[11] Reg. 1605/2002, *supra* n. 1, Art. 57(1).

[12] Ibid. Art. 57(2).

[13] See below, Chap. 5.

albeit not sufficient, element in the accountability of public administration. This is reinforced by the findings of the Committee of Independent Experts. They revealed that many of the problems with direct management were integrally linked to deficiencies in relation to financial controls. The basic provision was the Financial Regulation of 1977.[14] It had been amended many times, but certain fundamentals remained largely unchanged. Two were especially significant.

First, the authorization of expenditure and the collection of revenue were both in the hands of the Financial Controller of each Community institution. It was the Financial Controller that would give the 'visa' authorizing the expenditure, and it was the Financial Controller that would collect the revenue.[15] Secondly, there was a separation of function between the authorizing officer and the accounting officer. The former entered into the financial commitments, subject to the grant of a 'visa' by the Financial Controller, and the latter actually carried out the relevant operation.

The Committee of Independent Experts was critical of this regime.[16] The Financial Controller's responsibility for *ex ante* control, and *ex post* audit, could lead to a conflict of interest. The centralization of *ex ante* control in the Financial Controller through the visa system was ineffective. Control of expenditure should be decentralized to the Directorates-General. The responsibility for authorization of expenditure should be linked to responsibility for the carrying out of the operation.[17] Responsibility should, in this sense, be 'repatriated'[18] through decentralization to those officers authorizing the expenditure.

These ideas were taken up directly into the White Paper on *Reforming the Commission*. The aim was to create 'an administrative culture that encourages officials to take responsibility for activities over which they have control—and gives them control over the activities for which they are responsible'.[19] The system of *ex ante* visas proved inadequate to assess the correctness of financial operations,[20] and led to a culture that denuded officials of responsibility.

The new Financial Regulation gives legal force to these ideas.[21] The duties of the authorizing officer and the accounting officer are separated.[22] The latter is responsible for payments, collection of revenue, keeping the accounts, and the like.[23] It is, however, the authorizing officer that is central to the whole scheme. Each institution 'performs' the duties of authorizing officer.[24] It lays

[14] Financial Regulation of 21 December 1977 Applicable to the General Budget of the European Communities, OJ 1977 L356/1.

[15] Ibid. Art. 24.

[16] Committee of Independent Experts, *Second Report*, *supra* n. 3, at 4.6–4.7.2.

[17] Ibid. at 4.7. [18] Ibid. at 4.7.2.

[19] Reforming the Commission, *supra* n. 4, Part I, at 19. [20] Ibid. at 21.

[21] Reg. 1605/2002, *supra* n. 1. [22] Ibid. Art. 58. [23] Ibid. Art. 61.

[24] Ibid. Art. 59(1).

down rules for the delegation of these duties to staff of an appropriate level, specifies the scope of the powers delegated and the possibility for sub-delegation.[25] The authorizing officer to whom power has been delegated makes the budget and legal commitments, validates expenditure, and authorizes payments.[26] The authorizing officer to whom power has been delegated must establish the organizational structure and internal management and control procedures suited to the performance of his or her duties. Before an operation is authorized, members of staff other than the person who initiated the operation must verify the operational and financial aspects.[27]

The provisions on expenditure reinforce the centrality of the authorizing officer. Every item of expenditure must be committed, validated, authorized, and paid.[28] The budget commitment consists of making the appropriation necessary to cover a legal commitment. The legal commitment is the act whereby the authorizing officer enters an obligation to third parties, which results in expenditure being charged to the budget. The same authorizing officer undertakes the budget and legal commitment,[29] and the former must precede the latter.[30] It is for the authorizing officer, when adopting a budget commitment, to ensure, *inter alia*, that the appropriations are available, that the expenditure conforms to the relevant legal provisions, and that the principles of sound financial management are complied with.[31] It is the authorizing officer that is responsible for validation of expenditure: the creditor's entitlement to payment, and the conditions on which it is due.[32] The onus is also on the authorizing officer to authorize the expenditure through the issuance of a payment order for expenditure that has been validated.[33] These rules are designed to 'give authorizing officers the entire responsibility for the internal controls in their departments and for the financial decisions they take in the exercise of their functions'.[34] There are rules as to the financial liability of authorizing and accounting officers.[35]

The internal auditor is also central to the reform package. The idea was strongly advocated by the Committee of Independent Experts,[36] and endorsed by the Commission White Paper.[37] The central idea was to establish an Internal Audit Service, the auditors of which would advise the institutions about proper budgetary procedures, and the quality of their management and control systems. They are intended to help, *inter alia*, authorizing officers by providing a check on the overall systems adopted. The new

[25] Reg. 1605/2002, *supra* n. 1, Art. 59(2). [26] Ibid. Art. 60(2).
[27] Ibid. Art. 60(4). [28] Ibid. Art. 75.
[29] Ibid. Art. 76(1), subject to limited exceptions. [30] Ibid. Art. 77(1).
[31] Ibid. Art. 78. [32] Ibid. Art. 79. [33] Ibid. Art. 80.
[34] Proposal for a Council Regulation, *supra* n. 1, Explanatory Memorandum, at 17.
[35] Reg. 1605/2002, *supra* n. 1, Arts. 64–67.
[36] Committee of Independent Experts, *Second Report*, *supra* n. 3, at 4.13.
[37] Reforming the Commission, *supra* n. 4, Part I, at 22.

Financial Regulation made provision for internal auditors,[38] and the Internal Audit Service has published a Charter to describe its role.[39]

5. MANAGEMENT BY EXECUTIVE AGENCIES: POLICY AND IMPLEMENTATION, POWER AND RESPONSIBILITY

The origins of executive agencies are to be found in the Committee of Independent Experts' Second Report. The Committee noted that technical assistance offices were nothing more than contractors, who undertook work for the Commission.[40] It was the weak controls over such firms that led to the problems highlighted in the Committee's First Report. The creation of implementing agencies was seen as a way of alleviating these problems.[41] The new Financial Regulation makes provision for such executive agencies.[42] There is also a framework Regulation dealing specifically with these agencies.[43]

It is important to read this Regulation within the broader context of the other institutional reforms. The objective is to foster flexible, accountable, and efficient management of tasks assigned to the Commission. Policy decisions remain with the Commission, implementation is assigned to the agency.[44] The conjunction of power and responsibility, a principal theme of the Financial Regulation, is carried over to this new regime, since the agency director is cast as the authorizing officer. This is apparent from the Regulation on executive agencies.

A. Establishment, Winding-up, Legal Status, and Staffing

It is fitting to begin with the rules relating to the *establishment and winding-up of executive agencies.* The term executive agency covers a legal entity created in accordance with the Regulation, to manage a Community programme.[45]

[38] Reg. 1605/2002, *supra* n. 1, Arts. 85–86.

[39] Charter of the Internal Audit Service of the European Commission, SEC(2000)1801/2.

[40] Committee of Independent Experts, *Second Report, supra* n. 3, at 2.3.4.

[41] Ibid. at 2.3.27.

[42] Reg. 1605/2002, *supra* n. 1, Arts. 54(2)(a), 55.

[43] Council Regulation (EC) 58/2003 of 19 December 2002, Laying Down the Statute for Executive Agencies to be Entrusted with Certain Tasks in the Management of Community Programmes, OJ 2003 L11/1. For background, see Amended Proposal for a Council Regulation laying down the Statute for Executive Agencies to be Entrusted with Certain Tasks in the Management of Community Programmes, COM(2001) 808 final, replacing the earlier version COM(2000) 788 final.

[44] Reg. 58/2003, *supra* n. 43, at recitals 5–6.

[45] Ibid. Art. 2. Community programme covers any activity, set of activities, or other initiative which the relevant basic instrument or budgetary authorization requires the Commission to implement for the benefit of one or more categories of specific beneficiaries, by committing expenditure, Art. 2(b).

The Commission may decide after a cost-benefit analysis to set up such an agency.[46] The cost-benefit analysis must take into account factors such as the justification for outsourcing, the costs of coordination and checks, the impact on human resources, efficiency and flexibility in the implementation of outsourced tasks, possible financial savings, simplification of the procedures used, proximity of the outsourced activities to final beneficiaries, the need to maintain an adequate level of know-how in the Commission, and the visibility of the Community as promoter of the Community programme. A particular agency will not necessarily be permanent. The Commission will determine the lifetime of the agency, which can, within limits, be extended.[47] When the services of the agency are not required, it will be wound up.[48] The creation of a particular agency requires approval under the Comitology regulatory procedure,[49] and a new Comitology Committee is established.[50]

In terms of *legal status*, executive agencies are Community bodies, with a public service role. They are legal entities with the capacity to hold property, be a party to legal proceedings, and the like.[51] The agencies are located in the same place as the Commission and its departments.[52]

The *staffing* arrangements are a blend of the old and the new. The operational head of the agency is the director, who must be a Community official within the Staff Regulations. The Commission makes the appointment, which is for four years renewable.[53] The director is responsible for the agency's tasks, and draws up an annual work programme.[54] The director is assisted by a Steering Committee of five members, who do not have to be Community officials. They are appointed by the Commission for at least two years renewable.[55] The Committee is to meet at least four times a year. Its main tasks are to adopt the agency's annual work programme presented by the director, to adopt the agency's budget, and to report annually to the Commission on the agency's activities.[56] The agency staff are comprised of Community officials, seconded to the agency, and non-Community officials recruited on renewable contracts.[57] This is designed to provide flexibility, facilitating employment of those needed for particular tasks, without the need to incorporate them into the hierarchy of Community officials.

B. Tasks

There are important provisions specifying the agency's tasks. The Commission can entrust the executive agency with any tasks required to implement a Community programme, with the exception of 'tasks requiring discretionary

[46] Reg. 58/2003, *supra* n. 43, Art. 3(1). [47] Ibid. Arts. 3(1)–(2).
[48] Ibid. Art. 3(2). [49] Ibid. Arts. 3(3), 24(2). [50] Ibid. Art. 24(1).
[51] Ibid. Art. 4. [52] Ibid. Art. 5. [53] Ibid. Art. 10.
[54] Ibid. Art. 11. [55] Ibid. Art. 8. [56] Ibid. Art. 9.
[57] Ibid. Art. 18.

powers in translating political choices into action'.[58] The intent is clear. Policy choices remain for the Commission, implementation is for the agency. This is confirmed by the examples of tasks that can be assigned to executive agencies.[59] These are to be defined more fully in the instrument creating a particular executive agency.[60] The tasks include management of projects within a programme, by adopting relevant decisions using powers delegated to the agency by the Commission; adopting the instruments of budget implementation for revenue, expenditure, and the award of contracts on the basis of powers delegated by the Commission; and gathering and analysing data for the implementation of the programme.

While the intent is clear, the actual wording in Article 6 to delimit the agency's power may be problematic. This wording is similar to that found in Article 54(1) of the new Financial Regulation, which precludes delegation of executive powers to executive agencies involving a 'large measure of discretion implying political choices'.[61] There are, however, crucial differences between the two formulations. Article 54(1) of the Financial Regulation prevents delegation of discretionary political choices. Article 6(1) of the Regulation on executive agencies precludes delegation of tasks requiring discretionary power in translating political choices into action. On this formulation the executive agency is not only prevented from making the initial political choices, but also from exercising discretionary power when translating those choices into action. This will, if taken literally, severely limit the tasks that can be given to agencies, since such discretion may exist in relation to the specific functions listed in Article 6(2)(a)–(c). This conclusion might be avoided by reading the phrase 'discretionary powers' more narrowly. On this view, the mere existence of choices as to how to, for example, manage a project, or award a contract, would not be regarded as the exercise of 'discretionary powers', and hence would not be caught by the limit in Article 6(1).

C. Financial Arrangements

The financial arrangements for the new agencies are important. Space precludes a detailed analysis of this issue. Suffice it to say that the principles of the new Financial Regulation concerning financial transparency, internal and external audit, and the like are carried over into the scheme for executive agencies.[62] This is especially so in relation to the fusion of financial power

[58] Reg. 58/2003, *supra* n. 43, Art. 6(1). [59] Ibid. Art. 6(2)(a)–(c).
[60] Ibid. Art. 6(3). [61] Reg. 1605/2002, *supra* n. 1, Art. 54(1).
[62] Reg. 58/2003, *supra* n. 43, Arts. 12–16, 20; Reg. 1605/2002, *supra* n. 1, Arts. 55–56; Commission Regulation (EC, Euratom) 2343/2002 of 23 December 2002, On the Framework Financial Regulation for the Bodies Referred to in Article 185 of Council Regulation (EC, Euratom) 1605/2002 on the Financial Regulation Applicable to the General Budget of the

and responsibility. The director is the authorizing officer for budgetary matters within the agency,[63] and therefore has the general responsibilities laid down in the Financial Regulation. It is the director that is to draw up the provisional statement of revenue and expenditure, and in his capacity as authorizing officer he is to execute the agency's administrative budget.[64]

D. Damages Liability and Review of Legality

The new Regulation specifies rules on agency liability in damages. The law applicable to the contract governs contractual liability.[65] Article 288(2) concerning non-contractual liability has been extended to the executive agency.[66] This follows the legal technique used in relation to 'older' agencies, such as the European Environment Agency.[67] There are also provisions rendering the authorizing officer financially liable for losses caused by serious misconduct and holding the accounting officer to account on certain conditions for losses caused.[68]

The provisions on review of legality have been more controversial. The initial draft Regulation stipulated that the legality of the acts of an executive agency could be reviewed under Article 230 EC on the same conditions as the acts of the Commission itself.[69] It is questionable whether Article 230 could have been used to challenge the legality of actions of executive agencies, since these actions are not included in the list of reviewable acts under Article 230(1). The better view is nonetheless that such agency decisions could, as a matter of principle, be reviewed under Article 230. The Court of Justice has read Article 230 broadly so as to facilitate review of the EP[70] and Court of Auditors,[71] holding that the rule of law demanded that their actions be susceptible to legal control. Moreover, Community legislation has provided for challenge to the legality of decisions made by bodies such as the Office for Harmonization in the Internal Market (OHIM), the OHIM being the defendant in the legality challenge.[72] The EP nonetheless argued that the

European Communities, OJ 2002 L357/72; Commission Regulation (EC) 1653/2004 of 21 December 2004, On a Standard Financial Regulation for the Executive Agencies pursuant to Council Regulation (EC) 58/2003, OJ 2004 L297/6.

63 Reg. 58/2003, *supra* n. 43, Arts. 11(3), 16(2).

64 Ibid. Arts. 11(4), 14(1), 16(2).

65 Ibid. Art. 21(1).

66 Ibid. Art. 21(2).

67 Council Regulation (EEC) 1210/90 of 7 May 1990, On the Establishment of the European Environment Agency and the European Environment Information and Observation Network, OJ 1990 L120/1, Art. 18.

68 Reg. 1653/2004, *supra* n. 62, Arts. 34, 36.

69 COM (2000) 788 final, Art. 21.

70 Case 249/83, *Parti Ecologiste—'Les Verts' v European Parliament* [1986] ECR 1339.

71 Cases 193–4/87, *Maurissen v Commission* [1989] ECR 1045.

72 Council Regulation (EC) 40/94 of 20 December 2003, On the Community Trade Mark, OJ 1994 L11/1, Art. 63.

executive agency was the Commission's responsibility, that the Commission should be legally responsible under Article 230, and that it should 'monitor' the legality of the agency's action.[73] The Commission counter-argued that the executive agency had legal personality, and therefore the Commission should not be liable for the legality of its actions.

The final version of the Regulation is a compromise between these two views: the initial legal responsibility lies with the agency, and the legality of its acts can be reviewed by the Commission, with a further review of the Commission by the European Court of Justice (ECJ) under Article 230 if the Commission rejects the appeal.

Article 22(1) of the Regulation provides for internal review of agency decisions by the Commission. An act of an executive agency that injures a third party can be referred to the Commission by any person directly and individually concerned, or by a Member State, for a review of its legality. Such actions must be brought within one month of the day on which the applicant learnt of the act challenged. The Commission, after hearing arguments, must take a decision within two months. If it does not do so, it means that the action has been implicitly rejected. The Commission is also able, of its own volition, to review an act of the executive agency.[74] The Commission can, pursuant to such internal review, suspend implementation of the measure, or prescribe interim measures; it can, in its final decision, uphold the measure, or decide that the agency must modify it in whole or in part. The executive agency is bound to act as soon as possible on Commission decisions taken under Article 22.

This regime for internal monitoring by the Commission is complemented by recourse to Article 230. Thus Article 22(5) states that an action for annulment of the Commission's explicit or implicit decision to reject an administrative appeal may be brought before the Court of Justice in accordance with Article 230.

The rules on the legality of agency acts raise a number of technical legal issues. The grounds for review are not spelled out, although the implicit assumption is that they will be those used under Article 230. It seems moreover that any act of the executive agency that injures a third party can be reviewed, irrespective of whether it is binding, although the requirement that the act should cause injury may impose an indirect qualification in this respect. There also seems to be an asymmetry as to recourse to the Court of Justice. Article 22(5) is framed in terms of an annulment action where the Commission rejects the administrative appeal. It seems therefore that the

[73] Report of the European Parliament on the Proposal for a Council Regulation laying down the Statute for Executive Agencies, A5-0216/2001, Amendment 12.

[74] Reg. 58/2003, *supra* n. 43, Art. 22(2).

executive agency itself has no such recourse where the Commission upholds the appeal.

The rules on the legality of agency acts also raise important issues of principle. Article 22 has introduced a form of internal review of the legality of executive agency action by the Commission. The procedure in such cases will require careful thought. Executive agencies are only accorded limited implementing powers. Policy formation remains the prerogative of the Commission. This raises two important points of principle. It is, on the one hand, important who hears such cases within the Commission. It is not clear whether they will be heard by the DG to which the executive agency is attached, and if so who within the DG will hold the hearing. If the cases come to the same DG that established the agency, there is a danger of a conflict of interest. It is not easy to keep policy formation and implementation distinct. If an action challenging implementation implicates policy, there could be real objections to the Commission sitting as a 'judge'. There is, on the other hand, an issue of principle arising from the fact that the executive agency seems to have no recourse to the ECJ where the Commission upholds the appeal. This may be especially problematic if the internal hearing is by the same DG as set up the agency. The executive agency may feel that the Commission is using its internal power of review to impose a view concerning detailed matters of implementation that is legitimately within the agency's sphere.

The rules on the legality of executive agency acts also prompt thought about broader issues of 'legal design'. These rules require us to reflect on the optimal structuring of legal liability. It is important at the outset to clear the 'legal ground'. The mere fact that a body has separate legal personality, so that it can hold property, bring actions in its own name etc., does not *a priori* preclude making another body liable for its actions. The principled argument for holding the Commission responsible for the executive agency is that the programme has been assigned to the Commission itself. The Commission may choose to deliver this programme in-house, or through an executive agency. That choice should not affect legal liability, which should remain with the Commission. The argument to the contrary is as follows. Executive agencies are lawful. They have been properly created pursuant to Article 308 EC, and their powers do not infringe the *Meroni* principle.[75] They are Community bodies and have legal personality. Placing liability directly on the executive agencies best serves the broader objectives of the administrative reforms considered above. It reinforces the conjunction of power and responsibility that is central to the new Financial Regulation. This is the approach adopted in relation to damages liability. The rules on review for legality represent a compromise, with the initial and primary responsibility

[75] Case 9/56, *Meroni v High Authority* [1958] ECR 133.

lying on the executive agency, which is subject to review by the Commission, with further review of the Commission's decision by the Court of Justice.

E. The First Executive Agencies

The discussion thus far has focused on the general principles that pertain to executive agencies. This analysis can be usefully complemented by consideration of the first executive agencies to be established. The standard format is to write into the substantive legislation dealing with the particular issue a provision empowering management of the programme through an executive agency, leaving it to the Commission to decide whether and when to bring such an agency on line. The common theme running throughout the areas in which executive agencies have been established or are being considered is that the relevant programme entails multiple grants and/or contracts, which can most effectively be administered through use of this agency option.

(1) The Intelligent Energy Executive Agency

The agency has been established pursuant to the multi-annual programme adopted in 2003 entitled 'Intelligent Energy—Europe'.[76] The EU had previously enacted strategies dealing with various aspects of energy.[77] The objective of the 2003 programme was to draw many of these strategies together, extend them and provide the requisite financial means to enable them to be carried out.

The 2003 Decision originated in proposals made by the Commission.[78] The Commission documentation identified the key features of the proposed programme. There should, said the Commission, be increased attention given to the demand side of energy usage since there was little margin for

[76] Decision 1230/2003/EC of the European Parliament and Council of 26 June 2003, Adopting a Multi-Annual Programme for Action in the Field of Energy: 'Intelligent Energy—Europe', OJ 2003 L176/29.

[77] See, e.g., Council Decision 1999/24/EC of 14 December 1998, Adopting a Multi-Annual Programme of Technological Actions Promoting the Clean and Efficient Use of Solid Fuels (1998 to 2002), OJ 1999 L7/28; Council Decision 1999/25/Euratom of 14 December 1998, Adopting a Multi-Annual Programme (1998–2002) of Actions in the Nuclear Sector Relating to the Safe Transport of Radioactive Materials, OJ 1999 L7/31; Decision 647/2000/EC of the European Parliament and Council of 28 February 2000, Adopting a Multi-Annual Programme for the Promotion of Energy Efficiency (SAVE) (1998–2002), OJ 2000 L79/6; Decision 646/2000/EC of the European Parliament and Council of 28 February 2000, Adopting a Multi-Annual Programme for the Promotion of Renewable Energy Resources in the Community (ALTENER), OJ 2000 L79/1.

[78] Proposal for a Decision of the European Parliament and of the Council, Adopting a Multi-Annual Programme for Action in the Field of Energy: 'Intelligent Energy for Europe' Programme (2003–2006), COM(2002) 162 final.

increasing supply. The demand side of energy use should in particular be concerned with energy saving, energy efficiency, and the use of renewable energy resources. Priority should also be accorded to the combating of global warming and here too the development of new and renewable energy sources was seen as central to achieving this objective. Community involvement with energy efficiency had begun in earnest in 1991 with the SAVE programme, which was followed in 1993 by the ALTENER programme, which was concerned with the promotion of renewable resources. These programmes were complemented by others such as SYNERGY, dealing with international energy cooperation, and SURE dealing with cooperation in the nuclear sector.

It was felt, however, that the EU's involvement in this area would be more efficacious if these various initiatives were brought within one overall programme 'in order to combine Community action to form a coherent, effective whole, both procedurally and in terms of objectives'.[79] It was therefore necessary 'to broaden and strengthen some of the activities and to include them in a single framework'.[80] The new programme was therefore designed to strengthen renewable energy resources and energy efficiency, while adding two further strands to EU energy policy.[81]

> The programme is structured in four specific areas: rational use of energy and demand management (SAVE), new and renewable energy resources (ALTENER), energy aspects of transport (STEER), and promotion at international level in the fields of renewable energy sources and energy efficiency (COOPENER). Six types of action are planned for each area, viz. a) implementation of strategies, development of standards, studies etc.; b) creation of structures and financial and market instruments, including local and regional planning; c) promotion of systems and equipment to ease the transition from demonstration to marketing; d) development of information and education structures and utilisation of the results; e) monitoring, and f) assessment of the impact of the actions.

The Commission also considered in some detail the possible ways in which the programme could be executed. It is here that we see the rationale for the creation of the first executive agency. The Commission acknowledged that the proposed programme would lead to an increase in overall workload, and analysed two options for dealing with this.

One option was to create an executive agency to which certain management tasks could be delegated, thereby enabling the Commission to concentrate its efforts on more strategic issues. The Commission envisaged that the agency could be assigned the following tasks.[82] It could draw up for the Commission recommendations on the execution of the 'Intelligent Energy—Europe' programme, and collect the necessary data to enable the Commission to guide the overall implementation of the programme. The agency

[79] Ibid. at 6. [80] Ibid. at 7. [81] Ibid. at 7. [82] Ibid. at 13.

could manage some or all of the phases in the lifetime of the specific individual projects. It could also manage the budgetary side of specific programmes, including the award of contracts and subsidies. The agency could in addition promote the dissemination of the results of projects at local, regional, and national level. The Commission's preference for the executive agency option was influenced in part by the large number of contracts that would have to be managed. It anticipated that implementation of the programme would lead to some 270 contracts per annum, rising to 330 with the accession of the new Member States. The creation of an executive agency was felt to be the best solution for managing the plethora of contracts required to make the programme a reality. In accord with the idea that executive agencies would contain a mix of seconded Commission staff and those recruited from outside, the Commission estimated that the former would represent about 23 per cent of the total agency staff of 35 people.

The Commission did nonetheless consider another option for managing the programme, which was to have it managed directly by the relevant Commission departments. It was, however, clear that it did not favour this strategy. It was felt that direct management from within the Commission would 'involve major changes to the management of the programme and to its intervention mechanisms'.[83] It would require an increase in Commission staff from 38 to 52; it would result in a substantial reduction in activities relating to promotion and utilization of the results of the projects, thereby limiting the benefits of the programme; and it would in practice lead to the imposition of a minimum threshold for the funding of projects, with the result that there would be a significant reduction in the number of contracts, and the consequential exclusion of important players at local and regional level from the programme's activities.[84]

The 2003 Decision follows much of the Commission's thinking about the substance of EU energy policy. The multi-annual programme is structured around the four specific fields identified by the Commission: energy efficiency (SAVE); use of renewable energy resources (ALTENER); energy aspects of transport (STEER); and support for initiatives concerning renewable energy in developing countries (COOPENER).[85] There can also be 'key actions', which are initiatives combining several of these specific fields.[86] Broad criteria are set out for projects to qualify for Community funding concerning the four specific fields and key actions.[87] It is then for the Commission to establish a work programme, in consultation with the relevant Comitology committee, to effectuate the overall aims of the multi-annual programme.[88] The work programme must set out in detail matters such

[83] Ibid. at 13. [84] Ibid. at 13.
[85] Dec. 1230/2003, *supra* n. 76, Art. 3(1). [86] Ibid. Art. 3(2).
[87] Ibid. Art. 4. [88] Ibid. Arts. 5(1), 7, 8.

as: the guidelines for the specific fields and the suggested key actions; implementation arrangements; selection criteria; timetable for implementation of the programme; rules for coordination with existing Community policies; and if necessary arrangements to encourage the participation of remote regions and small and medium-sized enterprises.[89]

It is unsurprising, given the tenor of the Commission's proposals, that implementation should be entrusted to an executive agency. Formal authority for its establishment came at the end of 2003.[90] The Preamble reiterates the general rationale for the creation of such agencies: they allow the Commission 'to focus on its core activities and functions which cannot be outsourced, without relinquishing control over, or ultimate responsibility for, activities managed by those executive agencies'.[91] This rationale has particular relevance in this area, since management of the energy programme involves 'implementation of technical projects which do not entail political decision-making and requires a high level of technical and financial expertise throughout the project cycle'.[92] It is moreover possible to separate clearly 'between programming, establishing priorities and evaluating the programme, which would be carried out by the Commission, and project implementation, which would be entrusted to the agency'.[93] The Intelligent Energy Executive Agency began life on 1 January 2004, and ends on 31 December 2008. It is managed by a Director and a Steering Committee, in accord with the format laid down in the Regulation on executive agencies.

The tasks of the agency are defined both negatively and positively. They follow closely the thinking in the Commission's proposals set out above. In negative terms it is responsible for implementing the tasks concerning Community aid under the programme, 'except for programme evaluation, monitoring of legislation and strategic studies, or any other action which comes under the exclusive competence of the Commission'.[94] In positive terms the agency is to be responsible for the following tasks. It manages all phases in the lifetime of specific projects and the work programme laid down in Decision 1230/2003 following the advice of the executive committee of the programme, by adopting the relevant decisions where the Commission has empowered it to do so.[95] The agency is responsible for budget implementation and where the Commission has empowered it to do so, all the operations necessary to manage the Community programme, in particular the award of contracts and grants.[96] The agency is also charged with gathering and passing on to the Commission all information needed to guide

[89] Dec. 1230/2003, *supra* n. 76, Art. 5(2).

[90] Commission Decision 2004/20/EC of 23 December 2003, Setting Up an Executive Agency, the 'Intelligent Energy Executive Agency', to Manage Community Action in the Field of Energy in Application of Council Regulation (EC) 58/2003, OJ 2004 L5/85.

[91] Ibid. at para. 4.

[92] Ibid. at para. 5.

[93] Ibid. at para. 6.

[94] Ibid. Art. 4(1).

[95] Ibid. Art. 4(1)(a).

[96] Ibid. Art. 4(1)(b).

the implementation of the Community programme.[97] The Commission Decision allows, subject to approval by the Comitology Committee, the agency to undertake tasks of the same broad type under other Community programmes, provided that they fall within the general area of energy efficiency, renewable energy, and the like.[98] It is made clear in the Commission Decision that the agency is subject to supervision by the Commission and that it must report regularly on its progress in implementing the programmes for which it is responsible.[99]

(2) The Education, Audiovisual and Culture Executive Agency

The need to administer multiple grants and/or contracts, which can most effectively be administered by an executive agency, is apparent once again in relation to the creation of the Education, Audiovisual and Culture Executive Agency.[100]

The Agency was created on 1 January 2005 and will conclude its work on 31 December 2008, unless it is extended. The Agency has responsibility for the management of certain strands of a wide variety of Community programmes concerning education, audiovisual, and culture. These programmes include, *inter alia*, Socrates relating to education, Leonardo da Vinci dealing with vocational training, Culture 2000, Youth Community Action, MEDIA-Training, Erasmus Mundus concerned with enhancement of quality in higher education and the promotion of inter-cultural understanding through cooperation with third countries, integration of information and communication technologies in education and training systems, and Active Citizenship. The Agency is responsible for managing projects entrusted to it in these areas, more specifically in relation to the award of contracts and grants.

We can gain a better idea as to why an executive agency was created by considering more closely the background to three of the areas where the agency has authority, active citizenship, information and communication technologies in education systems, and cooperation in the context of higher education.

The objectives of the active citizenship programme[101] are to promote and disseminate the values and objectives of the EU; to bring citizens closer to the EU and to encourage them to engage more frequently with its institutions; to involve citizens closely in discussion about the EU; to intensify links between citizens by techniques such as the twinning of towns; and to

[97] Ibid. Art. 4(1)(c). [98] Ibid. Art. 4(2). [99] Ibid. Art. 7.

[100] Commission Decision 2005/56/EC of 14 January 2005, Setting up the Education, Audiovisual and Culture Executive Agency for the Management of Community Action in the Fields of Education, Audiovisual and Culture in Application of Council Regulation (EC) 58/2003, OJ 2005 L24/35.

[101] Council Decision 2004/100/EC of 26 January 2004, Establishing a Community Action Programme to Promote Active European Citizenship (Civic Participation), OJ 2004 L30/6.

stimulate initiatives by bodies engaged in the promotion of active and participatory citizenship.[102] It is readily apparent that the list of activities that can be supported is broad and diverse.[103] They include activities of bodies within civil society, NGOs, and the like, as well as initiatives undertaken by municipalities and other official bodies. Financial support is in the form of grants, which can either co-finance expenditure associated with the permanent work programme of the particular body, or co-finance specific action falling within the general objectives outlined above. It is clear that there will be multiple grants to administer under this programme and this was the primary rationale for ensuring that an executive agency could be created. The Decision therefore provided that the Commission could, having undertaken a cost/benefit analysis, decide to entrust all or part of the work of managing the programme to an executive agency and that it might also have recourse to experts, not involving the exercise of public authority, outsourced under ad hoc service contracts.[104] Management of certain strands of the active citizenship programme have now been brought within the purview of the Education, Audiovisual and Culture Executive Agency.

The same features are evident in relation to administration of the programme concerning the integration of information and communication technologies in education and training systems. The Decision establishing the programme was made at the end of 2003.[105] The objectives of the programme are to use e-learning as a means of promoting digital literacy; to exploit the potential of e-learning for enhancing the European dimension in education; and to use e-learning to improve the quality of the learning process.[106] These objectives are to be pursued through strategies designed to promote digital literacy, through virtual campuses, the twinning of schools, and the like.[107] It is for the Commission to ensure that the programme is implemented, with the assistance of a management committee. It is clear, as was the case in relation to the active citizenship programme, that multiple projects will be financed, primarily through subsidies.[108] It was therefore unsurprising that the Decision provided the legal foundation for the creation of an executive agency to manage the programme.[109] The Commission made it clear that it favoured this method of policy implementation. Thus it stated that 'whenever possible and justifiable by a cost/effectiveness analysis, programme administration and other programme execution related tasks

[102] Dec. 2004/100/EC, *supra* n. 101, Art. 1(1). [103] Ibid. Annex Art. 1.
[104] Ibid. Annex Art. 6.
[105] Decision 2318/2003/EC of the European Parliament and Council of 5 December 2003, Adopting a Multi-Annual Programme (2004 to 2006) for the Effective Integration of Information and Communication Technologies (ICT) in Education and Training Systems in Europe (eLearning Programme), OJ 2003 L345/9.
[106] Ibid. Art. 1. [107] Ibid. Art. 2. [108] Ibid. Annex Arts. 1–2.
[109] Ibid. Annex Art. 2.

such as, for example, monitoring and documentation project results, will be entrusted to a future Executive Agency, under study'.[110] The Education, Audiovisual and Culture Executive Agency has now been given authority to manage certain aspects of this programme.

The programme adopted to enhance quality in higher education through cooperation with third countries (Erasmus Mundus) exhibits the same structural characteristics as those considered above.[111] The objectives of the programme include, *inter alia*, improving accessibility to higher education in the EU and encouraging qualified graduates from third countries to obtain qualifications in the EU.[112] These objectives can be pursued through a variety of means, such as scholarship schemes, Masters' courses, partnerships with third-country higher education institutions, and the like. The Commission is, once again, given the primary responsibility for implementing the programme and once again it is to be assisted by a management committee.[113] It is readily apparent that, as with the other programmes examined in this section, there will be many grants or scholarships awarded in furtherance of the programme's objectives. Administration in this area may be especially complex given that specific Masters courses may be established involving a minimum of three educational institutions in different Member States. Provision was therefore made for managing the programme through an executive agency, together with national agencies if this should prove to be appropriate.[114] The Commission was clearly of the view that 'the implementation of the programme, including monitoring, would be largely the responsibility of an executive agency',[115] and the Education, Audiovisual and Culture Executive Agency has been given this authority.

(3) Executive Agency for the Public Health Programme

The third agency in existence at the time of writing is the Executive Agency for Public Health.[116] Space precludes detailed consideration of this area. Suffice it to say for the present that the Agency was established to manage certain aspects of the Community's public health programme, the overall objectives of which are to improve information and knowledge for

[110] COM(2002) 751 final, at 35.

[111] Decision 2317/2003/EC of the European Parliament and Council of 5 December 2003, Establishing a Programme for the Enhancement of Quality in Higher Education and the Promotion of Inter-Cultural Understanding through Co-operation with Third Countries (Erasmus Mundus) (2004 to 2008), OJ 2003 L345/1.

[112] Ibid. Art. 3. [113] Ibid. Arts. 7–8. [114] Ibid. Annex Action 5.

[115] COM(2002) 401 final, at 49.

[116] Commission Decision 2004/858/EC of 15 December 2004, Setting up an Executive Agency, the 'Executive Agency for the Public Health Programme', for the Management of Community Action in the Field of Public Health—pursuant to Council Regulation (EC) 58/2003, OJ 2004 L369/73.

the development of public health, to enhance rapid response to health threats, and to promote health and prevent disease by addressing health determinants across all policies.[117]

6. MANAGEMENT BY NETWORKS OF NATIONAL AGENCIES

It is clear from the Commission's White Paper that externalization could be pursued through devolution of tasks to certain national public bodies.[118] This was confirmed by the new Financial Regulation.[119] Centralized management of Community activities can be undertaken by, *inter alia*, national public sector bodies, or bodies with a public service mission guaranteed by the state.[120] Such bodies must be governed by the law of one of the Member States.[121] They must be chosen in an objective and transparent manner, following a cost-effectiveness analysis, to match the Commission's implementation requirements.[122] Where Community policy is implemented in this way the Commission will conclude agreements with such bodies specifying the tasks assigned, the performance conditions, and reporting rules.[123] The constraints and conditions described above[124] apply to these bodies, just as much as when externalization is pursued through executive agencies.

The Commission's thinking about the use of such bodies is clearer from a Communication devoted to the topic.[125] The idea is to devolve executive responsibilities to national bodies, which are either public or have a public service mission guaranteed by the state. These bodies are collectively referred to as 'national agencies', and this status can be conferred on existing or new entities. The agencies then act as partners in the implementation of Community policies, but the Commission retains overall responsibility for service delivery.[126] The intention is to devolve detailed implementation to national agencies, so that they have no margin of discretion on Community policy. The implementing tasks entrusted to such agencies will 'in no way alter any choices taken by the Commission involving political judgment'.[127] The scale of delegation to national agencies is therefore conceived to be less than to the

[117] Decision 1786/2002/EC of the European Parliament and Council of 23 September 2002, Adopting a Programme of Community Action in the Field of Public Health, OJ 2002 L271/1.

[118] Reforming the Commission, *supra* n. 4, Vol. I, at 10.

[119] Proposal for a Council Regulation, *supra* n. 1, Explanatory Memorandum, at 19.

[120] Reg. 1605/2002, *supra* n. 1, Art. 54(2)(c).

[121] Reg. 2342/2002, *supra* n. 10, Art. 38. [122] Ibid. Art. 39.

[123] Ibid. Art. 41. [124] See above, at 33–34.

[125] Communication from the Commission, Management of Community Programmes by Networks of National Agencies, COM(2001) 648 final.

[126] Ibid. at 3.1. [127] Ibid. at 5.2.

new breed of executive agencies. This is because the Commission will retain a degree of control over executive agencies 'going well beyond what it can exercise over' national agencies.[128] The Commission makes clear that use of national agencies is to be distinguished from shared administration, where the states themselves have responsibility for budget operations.[129]

The Commission perceives a number of advantages in using national agencies.[130] It facilitates *proximity* to the beneficiaries of the policy, as in the case of education and training. It fosters *complementarity*, since there will often be national agencies with experience of a particular policy. National agencies can offer greater *flexibility* than executive agencies, since it is easier to adapt to local circumstance. The Commission has established criteria for when networks of national agencies will be appropriate.[131]

The Commission is also mindful of the need for precautions when using this strategy.[132] These will be necessary to avoid cumbersome procedures, ensure the visibility of the European dimension to the programmes, secure the overall coherence of the programme, and maintain a clear distinction between intermediaries and beneficiaries of the policies.

The Commission was against a general framework regulation for management by networks of national agencies.[133] This was because it would be difficult to draft such a measure that could cover all possible scenarios, while providing sufficiently detailed common rules. The preferred approach was to provide for management by national agencies within the specific regulation governing a particular programme. There will then be a Commission decision laying down the responsibilities of the Commission and the Member States in relation to the national agencies. This will be supplemented by operating agreements, between the Commission and national agencies, which specify the duties and powers of the latter. There will also be an agreement on decentralized measures, which deals with the management of funds transferred to national agencies.

Controls operate *ex ante* and *ex post*. The former include the Commission decision specifying the responsibilities of the Commission and Member States in respect of national agencies, the terms of the operating agreement and of the agreement on decentralized measures. There will be internal audit to consider management and control systems within the national agencies. The latter controls encompass external audit to ensure that expenditure is consistent with the legal provisions, and spot checks through field visits.

[128] Ibid. at 5.2., 7.
[129] Ibid. at 3.2.
[130] Ibid. at 4.1.
[131] Ibid. at 5.1.
[132] Ibid. at 4.2.
[133] Ibid. at 5.3.

7. MANAGEMENT THROUGH CONTRACTING OUT: CONTRACT AWARD, CONTRACT SPECIFICATION, AND THE ALLOCATION OF CONTRACTUAL RISK

Contracts are used to secure the delivery of many of the programmes directly administered by the Commission. Problems surrounding such contracts played a large part in the fall of the Santer Commission, and the Court of Auditors has revealed difficulties in other areas.[134] It is therefore unsurprising that subsequent reforms have been directed towards these contractual relationships. It is necessary to consider separately the type of activities that can be given to another body, the bodies that can perform these tasks, the award of the contract, and the content thereof.

The Financial Regulation contains rules as to the *type of activities that can be entrusted to another body*. The implementing tasks must be clearly defined and supervised, and the Commission is not allowed to entrust its executive powers to third parties where 'they involve a large measure of discretion implying political choices'.[135] Public lawyers will be familiar with the difficulties of divining such expressions, and there could be a legal challenge to 'externalization' for violation of this criterion. Much will depend on how intensively the Community courts decide to review such matters.

The Financial Regulation contains rules as to the *type of bodies to whom such tasks can be assigned*. Within the limits specified in the previous paragraph, the Commission can entrust tasks of public authority, and budget implementation, to the new breed of executive agencies, Community bodies that can receive grants, and national public sector bodies, or bodies with a public service mission guaranteed by the state.[136] The Commission is not allowed to entrust implementation of funds from the budget, in particular payment and recovery, to external private sector bodies, other than those which have a public service mission guaranteed by the state.[137] The Commission is, however, empowered to entrust private sector entities with tasks involving technical expertise, and administrative, preparatory, or ancillary tasks involving neither the exercise of public authority, nor the use of discretionary judgment.[138] The dividing line between technical expertise or administrative tasks, and the exercise of public authority or discretionary judgment, will be difficult to maintain.

[134] Court of Auditors, Special Report 16/2000, On Tendering Procedures for Service Contracts under the Phare and Tacis Programmes, OJ 2000 C350/1; Court of Auditors, Special Report 12/2000, On the Management by the Commission of European Union Support for the Development of Human Rights and Democracy in Third Countries, OJ 2000 C230/1.

[135] Reg. 1605/2002, *supra* n. 1, Art. 54(1).

[136] Ibid. Art. 54(2).

[137] Ibid. Art. 57(1).

[138] Ibid. Art. 57(2).

In relation to the *award of contracts*, the basic strategy of the Financial Regulation is to apply the directives on public procurement to contracts awarded by the Community institutions.[139] There is an obligation to put such contracts out to tender, using the open, restricted, or negotiated procedure, or for there to be a contest.[140] There are safeguards against fraud by contractors. Thus firms are excluded from the tendering process if they are bankrupt, guilty of grave professional misconduct, and the like.[141] A contract cannot be awarded to a firm that has a conflict of interest, or that has been guilty of misrepresentation.[142] The contracting authority is empowered to exclude such firms from contracts financed by the budget for up to five years.[143] The centrality of the authorizing officer to the new Financial Regulation is evident here, since this officer decides to whom the contract is to be awarded.[144]

The *specification of the terms of the contract* is equally important if the mistakes of the past are to be avoided. Fraud and financial irregularities perpetrated by contractors will be prevented in part by the provisions concerning the exclusion of certain firms from the tendering process. This can, however, only be part of the overall strategy. It is also important to ensure the effective discharge of Community policies by those to whom tasks have been contracted out. The specification of the contract terms is all-important. Contracts are bargains, which allocate risks. The Committee of Independent Experts was critical of Commission practice in this respect. It found instances where the contractor's task was poorly defined, where there was insufficient monitoring of contractual performance, and where the Community pre-financed the project by paying a large amount of the contract price 'up front'.[145] There is an integral connection between the specification of the contract terms and the contractual objective. If the objective is set at too high a level of generality, it will be difficult to devise concrete contractual terms that can operate as a meaningful constraint on the other contracting party.

8. CONCLUSIONS AND ASSESSMENT

The shock waves from the fall of the Santer Commission generated a radical rethinking by the Commission of the delivery of programmes for which it has direct management responsibility. The Commission might well have retreated into a defensive shell after the Report of the Committee of Independent Experts. It did not do so. It embraced the majority of the Committee's suggestions. Any assessment of the emerging order must take

[139] Ibid. Arts. 104–106. [140] Ibid. Arts. 90–91. [141] Ibid. Art. 93.
[142] Ibid. Art. 94. [143] Ibid. Art. 96. [144] Ibid. Art. 100.
[145] Committee of Independent Experts, *Second Report, supra* n. 3, at 2.2.4–2.2.14.

account of the legislative and non-legislative initiatives. A number of more general observations on the new administrative order are warranted.

First, the Commission's overall strategy is based on the conjunction of power and responsibility, which are integrally linked, legally and financially, with the authorizing officer being the key figure in this regard. This strategy is to be welcomed. Public lawyers will be aware of the importance of financial responsibility in the overall design of administrative systems. It is a crucial component of administrative accountability. This is recognized in the Financial Regulation. It attempts to address past problems by recasting the regime of financial responsibility and placing this new regime at the heart of the system of direct/centralized management. The Financial Regulation makes an important contribution towards the design of administrative systems so as to maximize accountability by the very centrality accorded to the ideas of power and responsibility, placing these at the forefront of the new system for dealing with direct/centralized Community administration.

Secondly, the divide between policy and implementation is equally central to the new system:[146] policy remains the preserve of the Commission, with implementation devolved to executive agencies, networks of national agencies, or managed through contracting out subject to Commission oversight. It can be accepted that the divide between policy and implementation is difficult to preserve. This does not mean that the overall strategy is misguided. It is inevitable that the Commission will have to externalize the administration of some programmes. The effective delivery of policy is an endemic problem within national polities, so too when programmes are administered at Community level. The Commission cannot administer all policies in-house. It has neither the expertise nor the personnel to do so. Moreover, if implementation were always undertaken in-house, it would divert the Commission from policy formation. The Commission has therefore to 'externalize' the administration of some programmes for which it has direct management responsibility. This cannot be avoided. Given that this is so, it is right that the central policy choices should be made by the Commission, which is given the primary responsibility for implementing a programme. It is right that this basic precept should be enshrined in the new Regulations, even if in some instances an executive agency might 'cross the line' and make some limited discretionary policy choices. The architects of the Financial Regulation were therefore correct in enshrining this principle in formal legal terms.

[146] There are clear analogies to reforms of the administrative landscape within national polities, such as the UK, with the shift to core departments, and Next Steps Agencies. K. Jenkins, K. Caines, and A. Jackson, *Improving Management in Government: The Next Steps* (HMSO, 1988); D. Goldsworthy, *Setting Up Next Steps: A Short Account of the Origins, Launch, and Implementation of the Next Steps Project in the British Civil Service* (HMSO, 1991).

Thirdly, it is equally clear that no single administrative method can serve for the plethora of differing programmes that the Community manages. In some cases the best technique will be to maintain control within the Commission, but to contract out detailed implementation. In other cases executive agencies will be the most appropriate institutional form, and they might use contracts to facilitate fulfilment of their tasks or might liaise with national agencies. In yet other instances existing national agencies will be the most fitting medium and these agencies might use contracts to fulfil their remit. This is recognized in the new regime, and is embodied in the legal and non-legal rules that govern this area. The factors that affect the choice of technique are moreover becoming increasingly clear in the light of more recent programmes in particular areas. It is evident that executive agencies are especially suited to the implementation of programmes involving multiple contracts, grants, or subsidies. This is exemplified by the case of energy where it is clear, extrapolating from existing experience, that upwards of 300 contracts per year may be awarded to effectuate the overall aims of the programme. It is vital that these contracts are properly managed in order that the problems revealed in the First Report of the Committee of Independent Experts are not repeated. Executive agencies, properly staffed with a mix of personnel seconded from the Commission, combined with staff recruited from outside, have the potential to provide an effective method of securing delivery of these programmes. The very fact that these agencies are subject to the general principles of the Financial Regulation, more especially those concerning the financial responsibility of the authorizing officer, serves moreover to enhance accountability and to further the conjunction of power and responsibility that runs throughout the new regime.

Finally, it should be acknowledged that there are several layers to the legal realization of these administrative reforms. This is not excessive legalism. The differing legal norms legitimate the new structures, through the provision of overarching principles applicable to all forms of administration, combined with detailed rules relevant to particular institutional forms. The new Financial Regulation is at the apex. It is of constitutional significance. It contains the budgetary principles, it orders the different forms of Community administration, it establishes principles governing the allocation and exercise of administrative power and it allocates financial power and responsibility. The next level down is the Regulation on Executive Agencies, which draws on the principles in the new Financial Regulation. No such general Regulation is contemplated for networks of national agencies. The use of such networks will nonetheless be legitimated through Community legislation in the specific areas where they are used. There is a further legal level, concerned with the detailed operation of an executive agency, or network of national agencies. Specific Community legislation, combined with operating agreements, defines the tasks of such bodies in particular areas.

3

Shared Management

1. INTRODUCTION

Shared management has been central to the implementation of areas such as the Common Agricultural Policy (CAP) and the Structural Funds. This is all the more significant given that these areas account for a large percentage of Community funds. The new Financial Regulation contains, as we have seen, provisions dealing with shared management, as well as direct/ centralized management.[1] There are nonetheless many issues posed by shared management that are not touched by the new reforms.

These problems will be explored in the context of the CAP and the Structural Funds. There is considerable specialist literature dealing with these areas, but they have received relatively little attention from a more general public law perspective. This is in part because the legal regimes governing agriculture and regional policy are daunting in their complexity. They cannot, however, be ignored by anyone seriously interested in law and administration within the EU, both because expenditure in these areas consumes a large part of the Community budget, and because the regime of shared management poses unique problems and challenges. It may be helpful at the outset to note the definition provided by the Committee of Independent Experts. Shared management connoted,[2]

> [M]anagement of those Community programmes where the Commission and the Member States have distinct administrative tasks which are inter-dependent and set down in legislation and where both the Commission and the national administrations need to discharge their respective tasks for the Community policy to be implemented successfully.

[1] Council Regulation (EC, Euratom) 1605/2002 of 25 June 2002, On the Financial Regulation Applicable to the General Budget of the European Communities, OJ 2002 L248/1, Arts. 149–160.

[2] Committee of Independent Experts, *Second Report on Reform of the Commission, Analysis of Current Practice and Proposals for Tackling Mismanagement, Irregularities and Fraud* (10 September 1999), Vol. I, at para. 3.2.2 (hereafter Second CIE).

2. THE COMMON AGRICULTURAL POLICY

A. Treaty Foundations

The Treaty foundations for the CAP have not altered in substance since the inception of the Community. The objectives of the CAP are laid down in Article 33(1) EC. They are:

(a) to increase agricultural productivity by promoting technical progress and by ensuring the rational development of agricultural production and the optimum utilization of the factors of production, in particular labour;
(b) thus to ensure a fair standard of living for the agricultural community, in particular by increasing the individual earnings of persons engaged in agriculture;
(c) to stabilize markets;
(d) to assure the availability of supplies;
(e) to ensure that supplies reach consumers at reasonable prices.

It is clear that these objectives are set out at a high level of generality, and that they can conflict *inter se.* Decision-making in this area has therefore always necessitated a balancing operation of the factors listed in Article 33(1).

The Treaty does, however, provide further guidance, both positive and negative, as to the attainment of the objectives listed in Article 33(1). In positive terms, Article 34(2) stipulates that the common organization of agricultural markets may, *inter alia,* be directed towards price regulation, production and marketing aids, and storage arrangements to stabilize imports and exports. In negative terms, Article 34(2) provides that there shall be no discrimination between producers or consumers within the Community.

B. From Price Support towards Income Support

The detailed story of the CAP has been told elsewhere.[3] It is, however, necessary to understand the outline of this story in order to comprehend the regime of shared management.

[3] J. Usher, *Legal Aspects of Agriculture in the European Community* (Oxford University Press, 1988); F. Snyder, *New Directions in European Community Law* (Weidenfeld, 1990), Chaps. 4–5; W. Grant, *The Common Agricultural Policy* (MacMillan, 1997); R. Fennell, *The Common Agricultural Policy: Continuity and Change* (Clarendon Press, 1997); N. Nugent, *The Government and Politics of the European Union* (MacMillan, 4th ed., 1999), Chap. 15; J. McMahon, *Law of the Common Agricultural Policy* (Longman, 2000); Rieger, 'The Common Agricultural Policy, Politics against Markets', in H. Wallace and W. Wallace (eds), *Policy-Making in the European Union* (Oxford University Press, 4th ed., 2000), Chap. 7; S. George and I. Bache, *Politics in the European Union* (Oxford University Press, 2001), Chap. 24; M. Cardwell, *The European Model of Agriculture* (Oxford University Press, 2004).

The principal focus of CAP policy has been on *price support.* A rationale for the European Community (EC) has always been that goods should be able to move unhindered by trade barriers, subsidies, and the like. This regime has not applied to agricultural produce. The Council established common prices for most agricultural goods. There was a target price, this being the price that it was hoped farmers would be able to obtain on the open market. There was an intervention price, which was the price at which the Commission would buy up produce from the market. There was also a threshold price, this being the price to which imports were raised when world prices were less than those prevailing in the EC.

The price support system has proven very costly for the EC, consuming the largest share of the Community's budget. Community prices have, on the whole, been higher than those obtainable on the open markets. This has encouraged production, generating surplus goods, which then have to be stored, a further significant cost. If they were exported further cost was incurred, since the CAP regime provided 'restitution' to exporters to ensure that they suffered no loss on such transactions.

The EC adopted a variety of measures to ameliorate the consequences of the CAP price support regime. Quotas and the like were introduced to reduce the impact of the system. The degree of price support for particular agricultural goods was reduced. Farmers were encouraged to set aside certain farmland and hence reduce production. There was a realization that the existing regime could not continue in the light of enlargement. Many of the applicant countries were heavily dependent on agriculture, and hence the financial burden on the Community would increase. Incentives for CAP reform also came from external sources. The EC was under pressure from the USA and other countries to reform its protectionist agricultural policies. These pressures became particularly forceful during the Uruguay round of the General Agreement on Tariffs and Trade (GATT) negotiations in the early 1990s. The Agriculture Commissioner, MacSharry, put together a package of reforms that were accepted after much hard bargaining within the EC, and with the USA. The CAP reforms between 1991 and 1993 were of more long-term significance, since it was acknowledged that support for farmers could be disaggregated from production.

This was the beginning of the shift from price support to *income support.* Fischler, the Agriculture Commissioner in the Santer Commission, continued this trend. Support for farmers began to be seen separately from support for production.[4] This theme was developed in the Commission's *Agenda 2000* document.[5] The Commission proposed large reductions in support prices, coupled with direct compensation to farmers. These

[4] Commission, *The Agricultural Situation in the European Union* (1995).

[5] Commission, *Agenda 2000: For a Stronger and Wider Union* (1997).

proposals were, however, watered down in the Council meeting of the agriculture ministers in March 1999, as a result of French opposition. Further opposition from President Chirac in the Berlin European Council[6] led to a greater dilution of the original proposals. The Commission nonetheless sought to make the 'best' of the outcome of the Berlin European Council, emphasizing those aspects that fitted with its *Agenda 2000* initiative. More detailed plans were also forthcoming to deal with enlargement. The decoupling of support from production was central to this strategy.[7] It was not easy to secure agreement on such changes. However, the pressures of enlargement, and the EU's negotiating position with the World Trade Organization (WTO), were the principal factors leading to an agreement in June 2003, the foundation of which was the disaggregation of financial support from production. The key elements of the reformed CAP are therefore a single farm payment for European Union (EU) farmers, which is with some limited exceptions decoupled from or independent of production, with this payment being linked to respect for standards concerning the environment, food safety, animal and plant health, and animal welfare. The reformed CAP also embodies a strengthened rural development policy.[8] It is clear that the CAP has been 'not only a tool for the technical arrangement for the management of agricultural markets, but also a tool of commercial and humanitarian policy'.[9] This is even more readily apparent in the new CAP regime introduced in 2003.

C. The Framework of Shared Management

The administration of the CAP is 'shared', in the sense that the various forms of price support payments are administered jointly by the Commission and the Member States.[10] This was until recently done through the European Agricultural Guidance and Guarantee Fund (EAGGF). The Guidance

[6] 25 March 1999.

[7] Commission, *Enlargement and Agriculture: An Integration Strategy for the EU's Member States* (2002).

[8] Council Regulation (EC) 1782/2003 of 29 September 2003, Establishing Common Rules for Direct Support Schemes under the Common Agricultural Policy and Establishing Certain Support Schemes for Farmers, OJ 2003 L270/1; Commission Regulation (EC) 1973/2004 of 29 October 2004, Laying Down Detailed Rules for the Application of Council Regulation (EC) 178/2003, OJ 2004 L345/1; Commission Regulation (EC) 795/2004 of 21 April 2004, Laying Down Detailed Rules for the Implementation of the Single Payment Scheme, OJ 2004 L141/1; Commission Regulation (EC) 796/2004 of 21 April 2004, Laying Down Detailed Rules for the Implementation of Cross-Compliance, Modulation and the Integrated Administration and Control System Provided for in Council Regulation (EC) 1782/2003, OJ 2004 L141/18.

[9] Rieger, *supra* n. 3, at 186.

[10] Second CIE, *supra* n. 2, Vol. I, at para. 3.6.3.

section dealt with EC expenditure relating to agricultural structures; the Guarantee section covered payments relating directly to the regulation of agricultural markets, refunds on exports, and intervention payments. It is the latter that is of principal concern here.

The main enabling provision for many years was Regulation 729/70.[11] The Member States designated the bodies within their countries that would make the payments covered by the Guarantee section,[12] and the Commission would make the funds available to the Member States for disbursement by those bodies.[13] The Member States were under an obligation to take the necessary measures to satisfy themselves that the transactions financed by the Fund were actually carried out correctly; to prevent and deal with irregularities; and to recover sums lost as a result of irregularities or negligence.[14] However, in the absence of total recovery, the financial consequences of irregularities or negligence were borne by the Community, with the exception of the consequences of irregularities or negligence attributable to administrative bodies of the Member States.[15] The Member States and the Commission had the power to carry out inspections to ensure the probity of the transactions financed by the Fund.[16]

In addition to the provisions of Regulation 729/70 protection of the Community Budget was to be secured, *inter alia*, through the system of clearance of accounts. This was particularly important since the Commission made payments to national bodies on a monthly basis, and sought to recover thereafter sums that should not have been paid. Prior to 1995 the Commission was required to clear the EAGGF Guarantee accounts by the 31 December of the year following the financial year concerned, that is by 31 December of year n + 1. The Member States were meant to submit the accounts of their paying agencies by the 31 March of the year n + 1. The Commission then examined the accounts. The accounts were, however, rarely closed on time, and it became common for them to be finalized a year late. The Commission could order a correction in relation to a particular irregularity. It could also order flat rate corrections when it discovered a systemic weakness in the procedures of a paying agency, from which it could be concluded that irregular payments had been made.

Three major changes to Regulation 729/70 were made in 1995. It was stipulated that paying agencies had to be *accredited* by the Member States.

[11] Council Regulation 729/70/EEC, On the Financing of the Common Agricultural Policy, OJ 1970 L94/13.

[12] Ibid. Art. 4(1).

[13] Ibid. Art. 4(2). There is evidence of shift to pre-financing by Member States, Reg. 1605/2002, *supra* n. 1, Arts. 151–152.

[14] Reg. 729/70, *supra* n. 11, Art. 8(1).

[15] Ibid. Art. 8(2).

[16] Ibid. Art. 9.

Only such agencies could make payments.[17] Where more than one agency was accredited the Member State had to specify a coordinating body responsible for promoting the harmonized application of Community rules.[18] The accounts of the paying agencies had to be *certified* by a body that was operationally independent of the paying agency.[19] Finally, the timetables and procedures for *accounting* and *compliance* were separated within the system for clearance of accounts.[20] These changes were incorporated in Regulation 1258/99,[21] and have been retained in Regulation 1290/2005[22] that superseded it.

3. THE CAP, SHARED MANAGEMENT, AND LAW

It is interesting to reflect on the role of law within the pattern of shared management that characterizes the CAP. There are, unsurprisingly, a number of dimensions to this inquiry.

A. The Delineation of Legislative Objectives: The Tension between the Collective Interest and the Interests of Individual Member States

It is fitting to begin by considering legislative objectives. It is clear that there is tension between the collective interests of the Member States in the Council, and the interests of individual Member States as recipients of CAP funds. The framers of legislation will approach their task with certain aims. The Member States in their collective capacity have an interest in the allocation of the Community budget, and in the proper use of funds within that allocation. There is, however, a tension between this objective, and the accountability of individual Member States for the correct disbursement of CAP funds. Individual states have sought to minimize their liability for incorrect CAP allocations. This is reflected in the content of the legislation and in the way it is applied.

[17] Commission Regulation (EC) 1663/95 of 7 July 1995, Laying Down Detailed Rules for the Application of Council Regulation (EEC) 729/70 Regarding the Clearance of Accounts of the EAGGF Guarantee Section, OJ 1995 L158/6, Art. 1.

[18] Council Regulation (EC) 1287/95, Amending Regulation (EEC) 729/70 on the Financing of the Common Agricultural Policy, OJ 1995 L125/1, Art. 1.

[19] Reg. 1663/95, *supra* n. 17, Art. 3.

[20] Reg. 1287/95, *supra* n. 18, Art. 1.

[21] Council Regulation (EC) 1258/1999 of 17 May 1999, On the Financing of the Common Agricultural Policy, OJ 1999 L160/103. See also, Proposal for a Council Regulation Amending Regulation 1258/1999, COM(2000) 494 final.

[22] Council Regulation (EC) 1290/2005 of 21 June 2005, On the Financing of the Common Agricultural Policy, OJ 2005 L209/1.

B. Legislative Design and Content: Incentives for Compliance

This leads naturally to the design and content of legislation. Legislation will contain procedural and substantive conditions for eligibility to funds. It will specify rules as to liability if things go wrong. These matters are crucial to the way shared management operates. Law creates incentives or disincentives to certain types of action. The framing of the relevant legal provisions is of central importance to the success of the overall scheme. This can be seen from three examples.

The first concerns the complex system of export refunds. This was intended to bridge the gap between Community prices and those on the world market. The provisions differentiated payments according to product type, and export destination. It has been highly susceptible to fraud and difficult to police. It required careful verification that the goods were of a kind for which the refund was claimed, and that they were destined for a particular country, and not another where the prices were higher, and hence only a lower refund would be payable.[23]

A second example relates to the 1995 legislative reforms that introduced the ideas of accreditation and certification of accounts. The Commission argued that it should be responsible for the accreditation of paying agencies, and for the approval of the national certifying bodies, but these suggestions were rejected by the Council. The Member States were empowered to accredit agencies,[24] and specify the certifying bodies.[25] This has been problematic, with bodies being accredited that did not fulfil the relevant criteria.

The third example of the importance of legislative design is provided by Article 8 of Regulation 729/70.[26] Member States have an obligation to prevent irregularities, and to recover sums lost as a result of irregularities or negligence. However, in the absence of total recovery, the financial consequences of irregularities or negligence are borne by the Community, with the exception of losses attributable to irregularities or negligence by administrative bodies of the Member States. This created, as the Committee of Independent Experts noted, a particular pattern of incentives.[27]

> It is difficult to believe that the administrative authorities . . . in the Member States are always inclined to highlight for the Commission instances of irregularity or negligence on their part which would result in them bearing the resulting financial consequences. It is also difficult to believe that they are never negligent. In other words the arrangements which this basic Regulation established and which still pertain do not provide the immediate disbursers of 48% (at one time as high as 70%)

[23] Second CIE, *supra* n. 2, at 3.13.2–3.13.5.

[24] Reg. 1258/1999, *supra* n. 21, Art. 4.

[25] Reg. 1663/95, *supra* n. 17, Art. 3.

[26] *Supra* n. 11. The provision remained unchanged in Reg. 1258/1999.

[27] Second CIE, *supra* n. 2, at 3.7.5.

of the Community's budget, the EAGGF paying agencies in the Member States, with any immediate incentive for rigour and tight control of what is in effect someone else's, that is the Community's, money.

C. The Undermining of Formal Law: Pressure from the Member States and Acquiescence by the Commission

Formal law, howsoever framed, can only do so much. The history of shared management in this area provides ample testimony to the way in which formal legal norms were undermined in the operation of the CAP. We have already noted the differing incentives of the Member States collectively, and those of individual Member States as recipients of CAP funds. Member States bypassed formal law when it suited their interests.

This can be exemplified by the accreditation of paying agencies. Article 4 of Regulation 729/70[28] was clear: Member States were obliged to submit to the Commission details of the paying agencies, and the accounting conditions for payment. However, prior to 1996 there were 'hundreds of un-notified small de facto agencies making EAGGF Guarantee payments in the Member States without any structured procedures for checking on their activities or accounts'.[29] This illegality was practised by the Member States and tolerated by the Commission. In this context 'shared administration amounted to not much more than shared acceptance that the Regulation could be flouted'.[30]

This point can also be exemplified by the system for clearance of accounts. The time scale for this procedure was rarely adhered to, in part because the Member States were habitually late in submitting the accounts of paying agencies.

D. The Law Attempts to Catch Up: Formal Legal Change and Its Effectiveness

The interplay between formal legal norms and practical reality is readily apparent in the response to the preceding problems. The law attempted to 'catch up' and address the problems caused by shared management. There have been many changes in the CAP regulations. The major changes were motivated by the need to address shortcomings of the previous legal structure. Thus the 1995 Regulations[31] were designed to deal with the weaknesses of the previous legal regime. The accreditation requirements, the stipulation that there must be a coordinating body where there was more than one paying agency, the certification of accounts, and the divide between accounting and compliance were all directed towards this end.

[28] *Supra* n. 11.
[29] Second CIE, *supra* n. 2, at 3.9.6.
[30] Ibid. at 3.9.6.
[31] *Supra* nn. 17, 18.

We must, however, also consider the effectiveness of law reform. The provision of revised legal norms may be a necessary condition for the improvement of the CAP regime. It is not, however, sufficient. The effectiveness of these new norms must be evaluated. The Court of Auditors looked at these issues twice. Its conclusions were that the revised regime was certainly better than before, but that the new system still had deficiencies. Both reports revealed weaknesses in the accreditation system.

The 1995 reforms gave power of accreditation to the Member States. The Court of Auditors found that there were major shortcomings in many paying agencies, which ought to have led the Member States to withdraw accreditation.[32] It also found that the certifying bodies were not always operationally independent of the paying agencies.[33]

Its later Report found that there had been improvements, but that there were still causes for concern. There were still too many paying agencies, some of which failed to meet the criteria for accreditation, but the Member States had not generally withdrawn their accreditation.[34] The independence of certifying bodies had been resolved, but there were shortcomings in the conduct of audits.[35] The Committee of Independent Experts expressed itself more forcefully. It concluded that the 'leeway which the Commission has allowed the Member States on accreditation and certification amounts to a lax implementation of the Regulation'.[36] The Committee was of the view that the 1995 reforms had improved the recovery of money in this area, but that there were insufficient resources devoted to the task and it concluded that the error rate was still too high.[37]

E. The Conciliation Procedure: Bargaining in the Shadow of the Law

The legal regime for the CAP has also been markedly affected by the Conciliation Procedure. There will inevitably be differences of opinion between the Member States, and Commission concerning the clearance procedure. The Commission can exclude expenditure by paying agencies where it is not in compliance with Community rules.[38] Before such a decision is finalized, the

[32] Court of Auditors, Special Report 21/98, Concerning the Accreditation and Certification Procedures as Applied to the 1996 Clearance of Accounts for EAGGF-Guarantee Expenditure, OJ 1998 C389/1, at 2.11.

[33] Ibid. at 3.2.

[34] Court of Auditors, Special Report 22/2000, On Evaluation of the Reformed Clearance of Accounts Procedure, OJ 2000 C69/1, at 13–23.

[35] Ibid. at 31–47.

[36] Second CIE, *supra* n. 2, at 3.9.10.

[37] Ibid. Vol. I, at 3.14.

[38] Reg. 1258/1999, *supra* n. 21, Art. 7(4).

Member State can invoke the Conciliation Procedure, which was introduced in 1994.[39]

The original idea, as advanced by the Belle Group, was for a mandatory mechanism that would obviate settlement out of court, and hence reduce the number of cases brought by Member States under Article 230 EC.[40] What emerged was rather different. The Conciliation Body[41] is instructed to try to reconcile the divergent positions of the Commission and the Member States.[42] This is not, however, binding on the Commission, nor does it preclude a Member State from using Article 230.[43]

Conciliation is in many respects a sensible idea. The effect of the Conciliation Body has, however, been mixed. The number of cases in which it secures agreement is relatively low,[44] and there has not been a marked drop in the cases submitted to the Court of Justice.[45] In more general terms, the Committee of Independent Experts described conciliation as a 'win–win' procedure for the Member States, enabling them to delay recovery of undue payments, while reserving the right to challenge the Commission's final decision before the Court.[46]

F. The Contribution of the ECJ: Teleological Interpretation in Support of the Commission

The discussion of law in CAP shared management would be incomplete if it did not take account of the role of the Court of Justice. There has been a steady stream of cases in which Member States have challenged Commission decisions concerning recovery of payments unduly made by national paying agencies. These have been brought under Article 230. The general reaction of Community lawyers is for the eyes to glaze over concerning annulment actions in relation to EAGGF funding. The Court's contribution to the 'law' that governs the CAP regime is nonetheless important. It has interpreted the legislation in a teleological manner, with important consequences for the allocation of financial responsibilities as between the Community and the Member States.

The Court of Justice has allocated the risk of incorrect interpretation of

[39] Commission Decision 94/442/EC of 1 July 1994, Setting Up a Conciliation Procedure in the Context of the Clearance of Accounts of the EAGGF Guarantee Section, OJ 1994 L182/45.

[40] Doc. VI/216/93.

[41] It is composed of five members appointed by the Commission after consulting the EAGGF Committee. The members must be highly qualified in EAGGF Guarantee Section matters or in the practice of financial audit. Dec. 94/442, *supra* n. 39, Art. 3, as amended by Dec. 2000/649, OJ 2000 L272/41.

[42] Ibid. Art. 1(1)(b). [43] Ibid. Art. 1(2).

[44] Court of Auditors, Special Report 22/2000, *supra* n. 34, at 65–68.

[45] Ibid. at 72. [46] Second CIE, *supra* n. 2, at 3.11.1.

the Community rules to the Member States. The Member States argued that the implication of Article 8(2)[47] of Regulation 729/70 was that losses flowing from an incorrect, but *bona fide*, application of a Community rule by a national authority should be borne by the Community, except where there was negligence at the national level. The Court disagreed. It held that the text of Article 8(2), viewed in the light of the preparatory documents and the language versions, contained 'too many contradictory and ambiguous elements to provide an answer to the question at issue'.[48] The Court decided the case on the basis of Articles 2 and 3 of the same Regulation, from which it concluded that only sums paid in accordance with the relevant rules, correctly interpreted, could be charged to the EAGGF. It was for the Member States to bear the burden of other sums paid.[49] The Court of Justice reasoned that otherwise States might give a broad interpretation to the relevant rules, thereby benefiting their traders as compared to those in other States.

The Court also made it easier for the Commission to impose financial corrections on the Member States in the clearance procedure. Most actions for judicial review involve a challenge to the legality of flat-rate corrections. These are made by the Commission when it discovers a systemic weakness in the procedures of a paying agency, and concludes that a series of irregular payments have been made. Flat-rate corrections can be 2 per cent, 5 per cent, or 10 per cent of the value of the moneys disbursed, depending upon the seriousness of the deficiency, and the degree of probable loss to Community funds.

The Court enunciated the following principles when dealing with these cases. It was for the Member State, in accordance with Article 8(1),[50] to ensure the correct implementation of the CAP, prevent irregularities, and recover sums lost due to irregularity or fraud. This was seen as an application of the general duty of cooperation found in Article 10 EC.[51] It was for the Commission to prove an infringement of the CAP rules, and to give reasons explaining the defect in the national procedures.[52] However, the Commission was not required to demonstrate exhaustively that the checks carried out by national authorities were inadequate, or that there were irregularities in the figures submitted by them, but to adduce evidence of 'serious and reasonable doubt on its part regarding those checks or figures'.[53] The rationale for

[47] Reg. 729/70, *supra* n. 11.

[48] Case 11/76, *Netherlands v Commission* [1979] ECR 245, at para. 6.

[49] Ibid. at para. 8.

[50] Reg. 1258/1999, *supra* n. 21.

[51] Case C-235/97, *France v Commission* [1998] ECR I-7555, at para. 45; Case C-278/98, *Netherlands v Commission* [2001] ECR I-1501, at para. 92.

[52] Case C-253/97, *Italy v Commission* [1999] ECR I-7529, at para. 6; Case C-278/98, *Netherlands v Commission, supra* n. 51, at para. 39.

[53] Case C-54/95, *Germany v Commission* [1999] ECR I-35, at para. 35; Case C-278/98, *Netherlands v Commission, supra* n. 51, at para. 40.

this 'mitigation of the burden of proof' was that it was the Member State that was best placed to verify the data required for the clearance of the EAGGF accounts. Therefore it was for the state to adduce evidence to show that it had carried out the necessary checks, or that its figures were accurate, and that the Commission's assertions were inaccurate.[54]

This judicial reasoning was of real importance for the operation of the clearance procedure. It legitimated the system of flat-rate corrections, without which the compliance aspect of clearance would have been unworkable. It went a considerable way to negate the damaging force of Article 8(2), under which the financial consequences of irregularities or negligence were borne by the Community, unless attributable to irregularities or negligence by the national agencies. The Commission will carry out inspections of national procedures, and might conclude that there is a serious and reasonable doubt as to the soundness of these procedures, or the correctness of the national figures. The 'mitigation' of the burden of proof means that it is for the Member State to adduce evidence to dispel those doubts. It is, in this sense, much easier to *attribute* the irregularities to the Member States, denying them the safe haven of Article 8(2).

G. The Reformed CAP: Looking to the Future

The current reforms to the CAP have been touched on above. The shift to income support that is largely decoupled from production is central to the new regime, as is the condition that such payments are conditional on compliance with standards concerning the environment, food safety, animal and plant health, and animal welfare.

These substantive changes to the CAP regime have been accompanied by reforms relating to the administration and financing of the CAP, most of which take effect from 1 January 2007.[55] Administration of the CAP will henceforth be in the hands of the European Agricultural Guarantee Fund (EAGF) and the European Agricultural Fund for Rural Development (EAFRD). The EAGF will continue the work of the EAGGF, Guarantee section, and will administer, *inter alia*, export refunds to third countries, intervention measures, and direct payments to farmers. The EAFRD will administer the Community's financial contribution to rural development programmes. The rules relating to accreditation of national paying agencies have been reinforced and where more than one such agency exists within a Member State it must specify one of these agencies that will have special responsibilities as the coordinating body.[56] Member States must, as in the past, designate a certification body to verify the accounts of the accredited

[54] Case C-278/98, *Netherlands v Commission, supra* n. 51, at para. 41.
[55] Reg. 1290/2005, *supra* n. 22, Arts. 2–4. [56] Ibid. Art. 6.

paying agency, and both types of body must supply the Commission with a variety of information.[57] Member States are under a duty to adopt all necessary measures to ensure protection of the Community's financial interests, including the prevention of irregularities and the recovery of sums lost through irregularity or negligence.[58] The Commission is empowered to reduce or suspend monthly payments if information supplied by the Member States indicates that funds have not been used in compliance with Community rules.[59] The 2005 Regulation contains important provisions concerning clearance of accounts. They provide in essence that the Member State shall bear the financial costs if it has not initiated all appropriate procedures for recovery within a year of the primary administrative or judicial funding.[60] Moreover if recovery has not taken place within a certain period of time thereafter 50 per cent of the loss is to be borne by the Community and 50 per cent by the Member State.[61]

It is clearly important to see the new substantive provisions on the CAP based on income support and rural development in tandem with the modified rules on administration and financing. There is little doubt that the shift from production subsidies to income support will reduce to some extent the occasion for fraud. It was the very complexity of the previous regime with its multiplicity of rules relating to quotas, subsidies, and the like which varied as between different products that invited the fraud that has been an endemic problem in this area. It should nonetheless be recognized that the new system will not be unproblematic. This is because the criteria for direct farm payments cast in terms of compliance with environmental protection, food safety, animal and plant health, and animal welfare standards might be difficult to evaluate. This is more especially so given that reductions in payments for non-compliance vary depending upon whether this was intentional or negligent.[62]

4. THE STRUCTURAL FUNDS

A. The Treaty Foundations

The principal provisions concerning the Structural Funds have been amended on a number of occasions since they first appeared as a discrete title in the EC Treaty. These developments will be considered below. It is nonetheless helpful to set out the relevant Treaty articles at this juncture. Article 158 EC is the foundational provision.

[57] Ibid. Arts. 7–8. [58] Ibid. Art. 9. [59] Ibid. Arts. 17, 27.
[60] Ibid. Art. 32(4)(a). [61] Ibid. Art. 34(5).
[62] Reg. 1782/2003, *supra* n. 8, Arts. 6–7.

In order to promote its overall harmonious development, the Community shall develop and pursue its actions leading to the strengthening of its economic and social cohesion.

In particular, the Community shall aim at reducing disparities between the levels of development of the various regions and the backwardness of the least favoured regions or islands, including rural areas.

This principle is then fleshed-out by Article 159 EC. Member States are to conduct their economic policies and coordinate them so as to attain the objectives set out in Article 158. Community policy in relation to the internal market must also take into account the objectives specified in Article 158. The EC is to support the attainment of these aims through the Structural Funds: the European Agricultural Guidance and Guarantee Fund, Guidance Section (EAGGF); the European Social Fund (ESF); and the European Regional Development Fund (ERDF). The ERDF is especially important. It is to help to redress the main regional imbalances in the Community through participation in the development and structural adjustment of regions whose development is lagging behind and in the conversion of declining industrial regions.[63] There is also a Cohesion Fund, (CF) to provide a financial contribution to environmental projects and trans-European networks relating to transport infrastructure.[64]

The Council, acting unanimously on a proposal from the Commission, and after obtaining the assent of the EP and consulting with the Economic and Social Council (ECOSOC), defines the tasks, priority objectives, and organization of the Structural Funds. The same procedure is used for the enactment of general rules applicable to the Funds, which are designed to ensure their effectiveness and the coordination between them.[65] The co-decision procedure is, however, used for implementing decisions concerning the ERDF, supplemented by consultation with ECOSOC and the Committee of the Regions.[66] The Commission must report every three years to the Council, EP, ECOSOC, and the Committee of the Regions on progress towards achieving economic and social cohesion and the contribution of the Funds to this end.[67]

B. The Genesis of Structural Fund Policy

The Treaty articles set out above provide the legal framework for Structural Fund policy, but provide little by way of understanding of the forces which

63 Art. 160 EC.
64 Art. 161 EC.
65 Art. 161 EC. This may be changed to co-decision in accord with Art. 161(3) EC.
66 Art. 162 EC.
67 Art. 159 EC.

led to the inclusion of this Title in the Treaty or the ways in which it has developed since its inception.[68]

The original Rome Treaty contained no specific commitment to adjust the imbalance between the regions in Europe. Article 2 did, however, contain within the list of general objectives the promotion throughout the Community of a harmonious development of economic activities and a continuous and balanced expansion, and the Preamble made reference to reducing the differences between the various regions and the backwardness of the less favoured regions.

The initial impetus for a more specific Community role in regional policy came from the Commission and in 1967 a directorate dealing with this area was established. This was followed in 1969 by Commission proposals for the coordination of Member State regional policy and for the creation of Community regional policy, to be carried through by an ERDF. These initial proposals did not fall on fertile ground, and were not well received by major players such as Germany and France.

The fact that a Community regional policy was nonetheless established but three years later was due to a number of factors. Discussion of moves towards economic and monetary union was one such factor, since it was recognized that significant regional disparities would impede this development. Enlargement was another factor, since the then new entrants, Britain, Ireland, and Denmark, each had disadvantaged regions that would benefit from a Community regional policy. The Paris Summit in 1972 decided in principle in favour of a Community regional policy and this was given further impetus by the Thomson Report in 1973 by the EC Regional Policy Commissioner. The Paris Summit in 1974 agreed to the setting up of the ERDF, although the birth was not easy and was accompanied by much

[68] See generally, Marks, 'Structural Policy in the European Community', in A. Sbragia (ed.), *Euro Politics: Institutions and Policymaking in the 'New' European Community* (Brookings Institution, 1992); Marks, 'Structural Policy and Multilevel Government', in A. Cafruny and G. Rosenthal (eds), *The State of the EU, Vol. 2: The Maastricht Debates and beyond* (Longman, 1993), 395; J. Scott, *Development Dilemmas in the European Community: Rethinking Regional Development Policy* (Open University Press, 1995); Pollack, 'Regional Actors in Intergovernmental Play: The Making and Implementation of EC Structural Policy', in C. Rhodes and S. Mazey (eds), *The State of the European Community, Vol. 3: Building a European Polity* (Longman, 1995); L. Hooghe (ed.), *Cohesion Policy and European Integration* (Oxford University Press, 1996); I. Bache, *The Politics of European Union Regional Policy: Multi-Level Governance or Flexible Gatekeeping?* (Sheffield Academic Press, 1998); Christiansen, 'Territorial Politics in the EU' (1999) 6 *JEPP* 349; Scott, 'Regional Policy: An Evolutionary Perspective', in P. Craig and G. de Búrca (eds), *The Evolution of EU Law* (Oxford University Press, 1999), Chap. 17; A. Evans, *The EU Structural Funds* (Oxford University Press, 1999); Wallace and Wallace, *supra* n. 3, at Chap. 9; Sutcliffe, 'The 1999 Reform of the Structural Fund Regulations: Multi-Level Governance or Renationalization?' (2000) 7 *JEPP* 290; George and Bache, *supra* n. 3, at Chap. 27.

brinksmanship by the major state players. These disagreements spilled over into wrangles about the amount available for disbursement, with the result that the 1974 Summit finally agreed on a sum of £540 million. The money was allocated in accord with national quotas, rather than by objective Community criteria as advocated by the Commission.

C. The 1988 Reforms

There were significant reforms to the Structural Funds in 1988. The forces driving the reforms were, as is often the case, eclectic. There was dissatisfaction with the regime established in 1975, both in terms of the meagre amount available for disbursement and because the principles governing the allocation of funds, such as additionality, were often ignored. There were new entrants to the Community, Spain and Portugal, who had incentives to press for a more vibrant Structural Fund policy. Reform of Structural Fund policy was also a consequence of the drive to complete the internal market heralded by the Single European Act 1986 (SEA). This was seen as necessary to ensure the acceptability of the market-based initiatives contained in the SEA. There were fears that it would be the wealthier economies that would benefit from the completion of the single market, with the consequence that the gap between them and the less advantaged economies would widen. Reform of the Structural Funds was seen as one way of alleviating these concerns. The Treaty was amended through the inclusion of new articles under the Title of Economic and Social Cohesion, and there was a commitment to double the funding available for disbursement. This was accompanied by the passage of framework regulations setting out in detail the principles that were to guide the operation of the Funds.

Regulation 2052/88[69] identified the principal objectives and tasks of the Funds. Five such objectives were set out.[70] Objective 1 was the promotion of the development and structural adjustment of the regions whose development was lagging behind, this objective to be pursued by the ERDF, ESF, and EAGGF Guidance Section. Objective 2 was the conversion of regions seriously affected by industrial decline, this to be undertaken by the ERDF and the ESF. Objective 3 was to combat long-term unemployment, with the ESF given responsibility. Objective 4 was to assist in the occupational integration of young people, those under 25, the ESF once again having the responsibility. Objective 5 was concerned with reform of the CAP, through the adjustment of agricultural structures and by promoting development in rural areas,

[69] Council Regulation (EEC) 2052/88 of 24 June 1988, On the Tasks of the Structural Funds and their Effectiveness and on Co-ordination of their Activities between themselves and with the Operations of the European Investment Bank and the other Existing Financial Instruments, OJ 1988 L185/9.

[70] Ibid. Arts. 1–2.

this to be undertaken by the EAGGF Guidance Section, ERDF, and ESF. A small percentage of the budget, approximately 9 per cent, could be used for Community initiatives, programmes designed by the Commission to meet particular regional needs.

A number of principles run through the detailed scheme adopted in 1988. These will be set out here and evaluated more fully below. The new regulations were premised on *concentration*, this connoting the idea that funding should be allocated to the areas in greatest need, as identified through the objectives set out above. The concept of *additionality* was always central to the Commission conception of Structural Fund assistance. Thus Article 9 of Regulation 4253/88[71] stipulated that the Commission and the Member States shall ensure that expenditure from the Funds 'has a genuine additional impact in the regions concerned and results in at least an equivalent increase in the total volume of official or similar (Community and national) structural aid in the Member State concerned, taking into account the macro-economic circumstances in which the funding takes place'. The idea of *partnership* was equally central to the 1988 schema. Article 4 of Regulation 2052/88 provided that Community operations 'shall be established through close consultations between the Commission, the Member State concerned and the competent authorities designated by the latter at national, regional, local or other level with each party acting as a partner in pursuit of a common goal'. The partnership was to cover the preparation, financing, monitoring, and assessment of the operations. This leads naturally on to the fourth guiding principle: *programming*. This had two aspects. In temporal terms, funding would tend to be given for a period of years, in the case of Objective 1 regions this being for five years,[72] for Objective 2 regions the period being three years.[73] In organizational terms, the 1988 regulations established a detailed scheme whereby the different players of the partnership would interrelate. The Community Support Framework was central to the *modus operandi* of the Funds. It can be exemplified in relation to regions claiming assistance under Objective 1.[74] In essence the Member State, having, it was hoped, consulted the relevant parties, would submit to the Commission its regional development plans, setting out its regional development priorities and normally also the operational programmes it wished to pursue in those areas. The Commission reviewed the proposed plans and programmes for conformity with the Regulation. It then established, through the partnership referred to above, and in agreement with the Member State, the Community Support Framework (CSF) for Community structural fund operations. The CSF

[71] Council Regulation (EEC) 4253/88, Laying Down Provisions for Implementing Regulation (EEC) 2052/88, OJ 1988 L374/1, Art. 9.

[72] Reg. 2052/88, *supra* n. 69, Art. 8(3).

[73] Ibid. Art. 9(6).

[74] Ibid. Art. 8. See also, Reg. 4253/88, *supra* n. 71, Art. 8.

specified the priorities adopted for Community assistance, the forms of the assistance, its duration, and the financing plan. There was then more detailed elaboration of the operational programmes that had been given the green light by the CSF.

D. The 1993 Reforms

There was further reform of the Structural Funds in 1993. The reforms were, as on previous occasions, motivated by broader developments in the EU and within the economies of Member States.

The Treaty on European Union, the Maastricht Treaty, contained new provisions concerning economic and monetary union. This created pressures to increase the amount available for regional aid, resulting in agreement that the budget for the Structural Funds should be increased to ECU 27.4 billion by 1999. Pressures from particular Member States, particularly Spain, also led to the creation of the Cohesion Fund, to provide a further compensatory mechanism for the relatively poor Member States. A sum in the order of ECU 16 billion was allocated to the fund for the period between 1993 and 1999. The fund differed from the existing funds because it was targeted at States with a gross domestic product (GDP) of less than 90 per cent of the Community average, rather than aid for specific regions. It allowed moreover a higher percentage of the cost of projects primarily relating to the environment and transport infrastructure to be supported by the Cohesion Fund.[75]

The downturn in the economies of some Member States created, however, countervailing concerns about the effectiveness of Community policies, leading to demands that the regulatory provisions concerning assessment and monitoring of structural fund operations should be strengthened.

The 1993 reforms modified the objectives of structural fund policy.[76] Objectives 1 and 2 remained the same. However, the previous Objectives 3 and 4 were merged to create a new Objective 3 combating long-term unemployment and promoting entry to the labour market. There was a new Objective 4 designed to facilitate the adaptation of workers to industrial change. There were also modifications to Objective 5, most importantly through the creation of a new fund, the Financial Instrument of Fisheries Guidance, which would address problems resulting from the decline in fishing. A new Objective 6 was added allowing funds to be used for the development of sparsely populated Nordic areas.

The principles that had guided the policy in this area, concentration, additionality, partnership, and programming, continued to frame the regime

[75] Council Regulation (EC) 1164/94 of 16 May 1994, Establishing a Cohesion Fund, OJ 1994 L130/1, Art. 7.

[76] Council Regulation (EEC) 2081/93 of 20 July 1993, Amending Regulation 2052/88, OJ 1993 L193/5, Art. 1.

post-1993. There were, however, modifications to the previous position. Thus the very nature of the Cohesion Fund, with its remit being states with a GDP less than 90 per cent of the Community average, reduced the sense in which the aggregate amount of regional aid would be *concentrated* on those areas that were most needy. The definition of *additionality* was altered, weakening its impact. It was now possible to take into account 'a number of specific economic circumstances, namely privatizations, an unusual level of public structural expenditure undertaken in the previous programming period and business cycles in the national economy'.[77] This made it increasingly difficult for the Commission to argue that Community funds were being used instead of national expenditure. The force of additionality was further weakened by the fact that it was not contained in the body of provisions dealing with the Cohesion Fund, although it was mentioned in the preamble. The *partnership* principle remained formally intact in the reformed structural funds, but was largely absent from the Cohesion Fund, which provided that decisions on projects would be made by the Commission in agreement with the beneficiary Member State.[78]

E. The 1999 Reforms

The Structural Funds were reformed once again in 1999, on this occasion in the shadow of enlargement. The shadow cast by the prospective enlargement of the EU was highly significant in budgetary terms, since the extension of the existing regime to the new Member States would mean a radical increase in the overall cost of the regional programme, given that the entirety of the Central and East European countries would qualify for Objective 1 and Cohesion Fund assistance. As it turned out EUR 195 billion was allocated to the funds for the period 2000 to 2006, EUR 18 billion for the Cohesion Fund, and a further EUR 7.28 billion for pre-accession structural assistance.

Regulation 1260/99[79] reduced to three the objectives that could be pursued through the Structural Funds. Objective 1 continued to be concerned with the development and structural adjustment of regions whose development lagged behind, defined as those with a GDP of 75 per cent or less than the EU average over the previous three years.[80] Objective 2 was now cast in terms of supporting the economic and social conversion of areas facing structural difficulties.[81] There was a strong commitment that the aid

[77] Council Regulation (EEC) 2082/93 of 20 July 1993, Amending Regulation 4253/88, OJ 1993 L193/20, Art. 9(2).

[78] Reg. 1164/94, *supra* n. 75, Art. 10(1).

[79] Council Regulation (EC) 1260/1999 of 21 June 1999, Laying Down General Provisions on the Structural Funds, OJ 1999 L161/1, Art. 1.

[80] Ibid. Art. 3(1).

[81] Ibid. Arts. 1(2), 4(1).

would be 'genuinely concentrated on the areas most seriously affected',[82] and the population of these areas was not to exceed 18 per cent of the EU population, subject to a caveat that no Member State's Objective 2 population would be reduced by more than one-third as compared to the status quo ante.[83] Objective 3 was now framed in terms of support for the adaptation and modernization of systems of education, training, and employment.[84]

The principles that had guided policy in this area continued to apply, albeit with some modification. The emphasis on *concentration* was retained. It was made manifest in the reduction of the list of objectives from six to three, in the strictures embodied in the 1999 schema that the criteria for inclusion in these objectives would be strictly applied, and in the reduction of the Community's own initiatives from thirteen to three. The concept of *additionality* was preserved, albeit with the same basic criterion as contained in the 1993 regulations.[85] The 1999 schema did however attempt to put a little more bite into this idea, by providing more specific details as to how additionality would be estimated in relation to the different objectives eligible for funding, and by delineating in more detail three verification points at which the calculus would be undertaken.[86] However, the Member State retained control over the baseline figures for domestic funding. The idea of *partnership* continued to be central to Commission thinking, and the operative provision was modified such that the Member States in designating the relevant bodies within its own state should take account of the need to promote equality between men and women, and sustainable development through the integration of environmental protection and improvement requirements.[87] How far partnership has been a reality will be considered below. *Programming* continued to be integral in the 1999 scheme, being made operational through the Community Support Frameworks.[88] There was, however, a shift towards delegating more responsibility to the Member States for the implementation of and monitoring of particular programmes in the manner described in more detail below.

F. The 2007 Reforms

The Structural Fund regime is set to be reformed once again through Regulations that will cover the period from 2007 to 2013.[89] A sum in the order of EUR 336.1 billion, or one-third of the Community budget, has been allocated. The principal catalysts for reform on this occasion were the fact of

[82] Reg. 1260/1999, *supra* n. 79, Art. 4(2). [83] Ibid. Art. 4(2)(c).
[84] Ibid. Art. 1(3). [85] Ibid. Art. 11(2). [86] Ibid. Arts. 11(2), 11(3).
[87] Ibid. Art. 8(1). [88] Ibid. Arts. 13–19.
[89] Proposal for a Council Regulation Laying Down General Provisions on the European Regional Development Fund, the European Social Fund and the Cohesion Fund, COM(2004) 492 final.

enlargement, coupled with a desire to link the Structural Fund regime more closely with other Community initiatives, the Lisbon and Gothenburg agendas, concerning the knowledge economy and the employment strategy. The proposed new Regulation makes a number of important changes to the pre-existing order and further decentralizes operations in this area.

The objectives have been recast.[90] Objective 1 is now cast in terms of convergence, although it is close to the previous objective of helping those areas that were lagging behind in terms of development. This objective takes up the biggest share of available funds, in the order of 78 per cent of the total. The key test for eligibility is that the region has a per capita gross domestic product that is less than 75 per cent of the average for the enlarged EU, this applying mainly to the new Member States. Funding will also be available through the Cohesion Fund for those Member States whose gross national income is less than 90 per cent of the EU average. Objective 2 has been modified to focus on regional competitiveness and employment, and all regions not covered by the convergence objective will be eligible. Approximately 17 per cent of total funding is available for this objective. Objective 3 is European territorial cooperation and is designed to foster cross-border cooperation in a variety of ways. The remaining 3.9 per cent of funding has been allocated to pursuit of this objective.

The principles that guided structural policy hitherto were preserved,[91] albeit with some modification. There is a clear emphasis on the need to concentrate the resources on the areas that are in the greatest need, as reflected by the fact that the bulk of the funding is devoted to convergence. Programming, partnership, and additionality continue to feature prominently in the new regime. There is, however, a greater and explicit reference to proportionality and subsidiarity, signalling that oversight and management of operational programmes is to be undertaken by the Member States.[92] This is reflected moreover in the provisions on additionality which indicate that this will only be monitored by the Commission in relation to the convergence objective.

The documentation related to programming is significantly altered. Community Support Frameworks, Single Programming Documents, and Programme Complements are replaced by a new scheme. The Council establishes strategic guidelines for Community Structural Fund policy, taking account of the medium-term economic strategy as contained in the Broad Economic Policy Guidelines and the European Strategy for Employment.[93] Each Member State prepares a National Strategic Reference Framework (NSRF), which in effect sets out how the Member State through operational programmes that are consistent with the Council's guidelines intends to use

[90] Ibid. Art. 3(2). [91] Ibid. Arts. 8–14. [92] Ibid. Art. 11.
[93] Ibid. Art. 23.

funding for Objectives 1 and 2 in the period 2007 to 2013.[94] The Member State must submit data justifying an operational programme for Objectives 1 and 2[95] and the Commission can require modification to particular operational programmes if they are not consistent with the Council's strategic guidelines or the NSRF.[96] The intent behind the new scheme is however, that the Commission's 'adoption' of the operational programme takes place at an aggregate level, in the sense that only the most important priorities would be highlighted with further detail being left to the Member States.[97]

G. The Framework of Shared Management

The discussion thus far has focused on the development of Structural Fund policy over time. This is essential in order to understand the subsequent discussion. It is equally important to stand back from the temporal development and appreciate the sense in which this area exemplifies shared management. We should recall here the helpful definition provided by the Committee of Independent Experts. Shared management connoted:[98]

> [M]anagement of those Community programmes where the Commission and the Member States have distinct administrative tasks which are inter-dependent and set down in legislation and where both the Commission and the national administrations need to discharge their respective tasks for the Community policy to be implemented successfully.

Structural Fund policy is especially interesting in this respect, since shared management operates, albeit in different ways, in relation to project and programme selection, and in relation to implementation and monitoring of selected projects and programmes. Shared management applies therefore both with respect to the input stage and the output stage. The role of law in both dimensions will be considered in the section that follows.

5. THE STRUCTURAL FUNDS, SHARED MANAGEMENT, AND LAW

A. The Delineation of Legislative Objectives: The Tension between the Collective Interest and the Interests of Individual Member States

The previous discussion as to the role of law in the context of the CAP revealed a tension between the collective interest and the interests of individual Member States. The same tension is apparent, albeit in different

[94] Ibid. Art. 25. [95] Ibid. Art. 36. [96] Ibid. Art. 31(4).
[97] Ibid. Explanatory Memorandum, at 5.2.
[98] Second CIE, *supra* n. 2, Vol. I, at 3.2.2.

ways, in relation to both the input and output dimensions of the Structural Funds. This tension can be explained generally here and explicated more fully below.

In terms of inputs, the successive regulations on the Structural Funds embodied commitments to concentration, additionality, partnership, and programming as ideals that shaped the collective interest in a rational EU regional policy. It will be seen, however, that the legislation accorded the individual Member States significant discretion concerning the application of these ideals in the context of project selection, or the legislation was amended to weaken the peremptory force of the particular collective commitment.

In terms of output, it is clear that the collective interest favours the proper deployment of EU resources to attain the goals of EU regional policy. This requires machinery to ensure that projects and programmes selected pursuant to a Community Support Framework are properly monitored, that there is effective machinery to detect financial irregularity through audit and the like, and that the rules provide a meaningful regime for compliance by the relevant players. Individual Member States may, however, have an incentive to avoid these consequences in relation to projects conducted on their own territory, more especially where the consequences could be financial penalties imposed on the state itself, or the withholding of further disbursements to particular projects. This issue is all the more significant given that the strategy in the 1999 regulations has been to devolve more responsibility for monitoring and the like on the Member States, since the Commission does not possess the resources to do the job itself. It is then all the more important that the legislative rules casting the Member State as gamekeeper do not allow it to become poacher or to turn a blind eye to poaching by others.

The tensions between the collective interest and that of the Member States came to the fore in the Second Report of the Committee of Independent Experts.[99] The Committee made two kinds of observations concerning the Structural Funds.

It was, on the one hand, critical of certain aspects of the legislative design embodied in the Structural Fund regulations even after 1999. The Committee concluded that the balance of decision-making power had shifted to the Member States, but that a number of factors tended to divest them of responsibility:[100] the criterion for additionality was weak;[101] the shift to programming post-1988 removed the greater part of Commission control over individual projects;[102] and the ceiling of expenditure for each Member State was in effect also a target, with implications for project selection, evaluation,

[99] See above, at 62–64.
[100] Second CIE, *supra* n. 2, Vol. I, at 3.22.
[101] Ibid. Vol. I, at 3.19.
[102] Ibid. Vol. I, at 3.18.

and control,[103] this being exacerbated by Member States' ability to substitute projects for those declared ineligible.[104]

The Committee, on the other hand, expressed concern about the practical effectiveness of the powers possessed by the Commission. Thus while the Committee was mindful of the improvements in the 1999 regulations concerning Member States' obligations to have proper management and control systems, it felt that the resources for control were 'woefully inadequate to ensure proper implementation of the new Regulation'.[105] It expressed similar reservations about the powers relating to on-the-spot checks, and the paucity of claims for recovery in cases of financial irregularity. These provisions were of limited efficacy not because of inadequacies in the legislation per se, but because of inadequate implementation by the Commission combined with resistance by the Member States.[106] The Committee was equally concerned about the gap between what the Commission was appraised of relating to financial irregularity, and the error rate concerning financial transactions revealed by the Court of Auditors.[107]

B. Legislative Design and Input: Project Selection

The tensions between the collective and individual interest, and the way in which they affect the attainment of the ideals underpinning the Structural Fund regulations, can now be explored more fully.

We can begin by focusing on the idea of *partnership*, one of the four guiding ideals in this area. It should be noted at the outset that there is a duality in the very meaning accorded to partnership in the regulatory provisions. In formal legal terms, partnership primarily connotes a relationship between the Member States and the Commission in the application of regional policy. It also captures the idea that when devising a development plan the Member State should involve regional bodies, local authorities, and the like.[108] The relationship between these two senses of partnership lies at the root of the debate among political scientists as to whether this area provides an example of multi-level governance, or whether it is in reality best explained in liberal intergovernmentalist terms.[109] Proponents of multi-level governance point to the Commission's discretion over indicative allocations per Member State and also the involvement of sub-national actors in the drawing up of the development plan, coupled with its implementation.[110]

[103] Second CIE, *supra* n. 2, Vol. I, at 3.15.6.
[104] Ibid. Vol. I, at 3.18.1–3.18.3.
[105] Ibid. Vol. I, at 3.17.3.
[106] Ibid. Vol. I, at 3.17.4–3.17.6.
[107] Ibid. Vol. I, at 3.17.9.
[108] Reg. 1260/1999, *supra* n. 79, Art. 8.
[109] Craig, 'The Nature of the Community: Integration, Democracy and Legitimacy', in P. Craig and G. de Búrca (eds), *The Evolution of EU Law* (Oxford University Press, 1999), Chap. 1 for more general discussion of these views about Community integration.
[110] See, e.g., Marks, *supra* n. 68.

Those who espouse a more liberal intergovernmentalist view respond by pointing to the controls that remain in the hands of the Member States.[111] Thus it is the Member States which designate the other bodies that are to take part in the formulation of the plan.[112] This combined with other provisions enables the Member State to operate as an 'extended gatekeeper', maintaining control over all stages of the policy process, including implementation. On this view, there may well be evidence of multi-level involvement in the implementation of EU regional policy, but less of a case for multi-level governance as such. The duality in the key legal provisions about partnership is central to an understanding of this debate.

The idea of partnership in the first sense, as between the Commission and the Member States, still leaves unresolved the more precise degree of power wielded by each at the input stage. Prior to 1988 each Fund operated in isolation, and assistance was granted largely in the form of individual projects proposed by States and approved by the Commission. In 1988 the Structural Funds moved to coordinated operations on the basis of multi-annual programming in the pursuit of the legislatively defined objectives set out above. The 1988 regulations also confirmed the demise of legislatively set Member State funding eligibility quotas. Instead, it was the Commission's task to establish guideline or indicative allocations per Member State.[113] The move from individual projects to programming and from Member State quotas to indicative ranges determined by the Commission, gave the Commission some significant control over policy formulation and the identification of priorities. The Commission's discretion in this respect was however bounded by specified criteria.[114] It should also be recognized in estimating the balance of power under this partnership that the legislative schema accorded significant powers to the Member States. The development plans were designed by the Member States, and these formed the basis of their operational programmes.[115] The Commission determined whether the operational programmes were consistent with the aims of the Community Support Framework drawn up by the Commission in agreement with the relevant Member State. When a programme was approved and the Community contribution fixed, the 1988 and 1993 regulations made no express provision for the selection of individual projects to implement the programme. This was left to the Member States. In practice, it was reportedly carried out by the monitoring committees.[116] Under the 1999 regulations, Member States must

[111] See, e.g., Pollack, *supra* n. 68. [112] Reg. 1260/1999, *supra* n. 79, Art. 8.

[113] Ibid. Art. 7(3). [114] Ibid. Arts. 3(1), 4, 7(3).

[115] There are informational requirements to be supplied as part of programme applications, which were made more specific in 1999, ibid. Art. 18(2).

[116] Scott, 'Law, Legitimacy and EC Governance' (1998) 36 *JCMS* 175, at 183, 187; Scott, 'Regional Policy', *supra* n. 68, at 634–637.

further submit a 'programme complement'[117] detailing the individual measures to be assisted and the types of final beneficiary, as well as the financing plan for each measure.[118] Compliance was enforced by a bar on interim payments until the complement was supplied.[119] The document was nonetheless only for information,[120] and did not require the Commission's approval. Thus while programmes must be approved by the Commission they are drawn up by the Member States. It is moreover the case that primary control of project selection lies with the Member States, even if the Commission may exercise a de facto veto. This ordering of power as between the Commission and the Member States looks set to continue in the regime for 2007 to 2013.[121]

The idea of partnership in the second sense, capturing the Community's desire formally to involve actors other than the Member States in the decision-making process, has been tempered by the Member States' desire to retain control over who should participate, and the extent of this participation. It is the Member State that designates within the framework of its 'national rules and current practices' the bodies that will participate in drawing up the development plan.[122]

The tension between the collective interest and that of individual Member States is also evident in relation to *additionality*. This idea was always central to the collective interest in the overall regional programme, connoting the idea that Community aid should not be an excuse for the diminution of national programmes. The legal force of this commitment in Article 9 of Regulation 4253/88[123] was, however, qualified by the fact that it allowed account to be taken of the 'macro-economic circumstances in which the funding takes place'. Later amendments further weakened the force of this provision. It became possible to take into account 'a number of specific economic circumstances, namely privatizations, an unusual level of public structural expenditure undertaken in the previous programming period and business cycles in the national economy',[124] thereby making it increasingly difficult for the Commission to argue that Community funds were being used in place of national expenditure. The Court of Auditors attested to the very real difficulties in the application of additionality.[125] It should, however, also be recognized that the practical force of additionality has been strengthened somewhat in the 1999 Regulation by the obligation cast on the Member State to determine the level of expenditure that it will maintain in, for

[117] Reg. 1260/1999, *supra* n. 79, Art. 15(6). [118] Ibid. Art. 18(3).

[119] Ibid. Art 32(3). [120] Ibid. Art. 9(m).

[121] COM(2004) 492, *supra* n. 89, Art. 31.

[122] Reg. 1260/1999, *supra* n. 79, Art. 8(1); COM(2004) 492, *supra* n. 89, Art. 10(1).

[123] *Supra* n. 71. [124] Reg. 2082/93, *supra* n. 77, Art. 9(2).

[125] Court of Auditors, Special Report 6/99, Concerning the Application of the Principle of Additionality, OJ 2000 C68/1.

example, Objective 1 regions, for the programming period of five years and to make this commitment as a pre-condition to the approval of any Community Support Framework.[126] Additionality is verified *ex ante*, at mid-term, and at the end of the six-year period.[127] This approach has been preserved in the 2007 scheme for the convergence objective.[128]

C. Legislative Design and Output: Payment and Incentives for Compliance

The tension between the collective Community interest and that of individual Member States can be particularly prevalent in relation to the output stage. If the regime of shared management is to be effective then proper attention must be given to legislative design in this respect. There must be appropriate rules relating to matters such as payment, monitoring, audit, and the like. This is more especially so given the plethora of projects that will benefit from Community funding at any point in time.

We can begin by considering the regime of payment. Advance payments give the national authorities control over disbursement of the funds, while reimbursements leave that control ultimately with the Commission which can refuse to reimburse ineligible or otherwise irregular expenditure.

Prior to 1999 payments were made according to annual commitments,[129] although they could be suspended where Commission examinations revealed irregularities.[130] Up to 80 per cent of the annual commitments were paid out in the form of two advances.[131] The reality was that the regime enabled national authorities to rely on continuous advance payments to cover their payments to beneficiaries, without too close an inspection of progress. The Commission could suspend payments altogether on account of irregularities, or reduce future commitments because of lack of progress, but these controls largely applied after the fact. Tightening controls on payments was thus rightly on the Commission's agenda for improving financial control.[132]

The legal regime concerning payments changed considerably *post-1999*. The general rule now is for reimbursement of expenditure actually incurred. Commitments and payments were disassociated under the 1999 Regulation. Commitments are still made on an annual basis, but the bulk of payments are now firmly linked to expenditure. An advance is payable, but this cannot be

[126] Reg. 1260/1999, *supra* n. 79, Art. 11(2).

[127] Ibid. Art. 11(3); Twelfth Annual Report on the Structural Funds (2000), COM(2001) 539 final, at 2.1.4.

[128] COM(2004) 492, *supra* n. 89, Art. 13(4).

[129] Reg. 4253/88, *supra* n. 71, Art. 21(1).

[130] Ibid. Art. 24(2).

[131] Ibid. Arts. 21(2) and (3).

[132] S. White, *Protection of the Financial Interests of the European Communities: The Fight against Fraud* (Kluwer Law International, 1998), at 98–99.

more than 7 per cent of the total amount of assistance.[133] After that, all interim and final payments are made solely to reimburse actual and eligible expenditure, which must be certified by the Member State.[134] Interim payments are also subject to the Member State being in full compliance with its obligations both in terms of monitoring and in terms of financial control and corrections. It must provide a programming complement, annual implementation reports, and a mid-term evaluation when due.[135] Payments may be suspended if a request for corrections following the annual consultation on financial controls has not been complied with,[136] or immediately in case of a serious irregularity.[137] They may also be suspended where the Commission finds that a Member State has failed to comply with its obligation to carry out financial corrections or to maintain appropriate systems, or if an operation does not justify the EU contribution.[138] The same general regime operates under the Regulation governing matters for 2007 to 2013.[139]

D. Legislative Design and Output: Control Systems, Reporting, Checks, and Incentives for Compliance

The legislative design of the payment regime is a necessary condition for the effective implementation of shared management. It is not sufficient. There must also be effective control systems over the disbursement of funds at national level, combined with checks to ensure that the rules are being properly applied. The general thrust of Community regulations has been to tighten the applicable provisions. This is apparent both pre- and post-1999. These will be considered in turn.

The regime *prior to 1999* showed a gradual 'ratcheting up' of the relevant provisions. The *1988 schema* required Member States to take the necessary measures to verify that subsidized operations were carried out properly, to prevent and take action against irregularities, and to recover any amount lost through irregularity or negligence.[140] Member States also had to designate appropriate authorities empowered to certify the correctness of the information supplied in payment requests and reports.[141] Certification implied an obligation to carry out some checks, although this was not specified at this stage. The *1993 amendments* went beyond requiring controls as such, by

[133] Reg. 1260/1999, *supra* n. 79, Art. 32(2).

[134] Ibid. Arts. 32(1), (3), and (4).

[135] Ibid. Art. 32(3). It must further have made any adjustments to management and monitoring systems requested following annual implementation reviews, and any corrections to transactions or financial control systems requested following annual consultation on financial controls.

[136] Ibid. Art. 32(3)(e). [137] Ibid. Art. 38(5). [138] Ibid. Art. 39(2).

[139] COM(2004) 492, *supra* n. 89, Arts. 74–91.

[140] Reg. 4253/88, *supra* n. 71, Art. 23(1). [141] Ibid. Arts. 21(3)–(5).

indicating that systems were to be established for this purpose. Member States were required to notify the Commission of the management and control systems it had established.[142] The obligation to maintain control systems was spelt out in greater detail in *1997*.[143] States were required to have management and control systems which were to ensure proper implementation in accordance with sound financial management; to provide satisfactory certification of the validity of payment claims; to provide a sufficient audit trail; to allocate responsibility for controls at the different levels; to facilitate identification of possible weaknesses; and to provide for corrective measures to eliminate weaknesses, risks, or irregularities.[144] In addition to carrying out controls, certifying claims, and establishing systems, Member States had obligations to correct irregularities. The basic obligation to take action against irregularities and to recover amounts lost[145] was made more specific from 1997. Member States were required to ensure investigation and satisfactory treatment of apparent irregularities.[146] 'Satisfactory treatment' meant ensuring that the irregularity was either shown to be non-existent or 'corrected' by the beneficiaries or implementing authorities.

The regime *post-1999* developed and reinforced much of the strategy from the earlier regulations. Member States are expressly declared responsible for the implementation of Structural Funds assistance,[147] for financial control,[148] and for investigating irregularities and making financial corrections.[149] Four more particular aspects of the post-1999 regime should be distinguished.

There is the establishment of *management and control systems*. Member States must designate managing authorities, which may be the Member State itself, and payment authorities, which may be the same as the managing authority.[150] The managing authority is responsible, *inter alia*, for the efficiency and correctness of management, without prejudice to the Member State's responsibility.[151] This includes responsibility for monitoring, as well

[142] Reg. 2082/93, *supra* n. 77, Art. 23(1).

[143] Commission Regulation (EC) 2064/97 of 15 October 1997, Establishing Detailed Arrangements for the Implementation of Council Regulation (EEC) 4253/88 as Regards the Financial Control By Member States of Operations Co-financed by the Structural Funds, OJ 1997 L290/1.

[144] Ibid. Art. 2.

[145] Reg. 4253/88, *supra* n. 71, Art. 23(1); Commission Regulation (EC) 1681/94 of 11 July 1994, Concerning Irregularities and the Recovery of Sums Wrongly Paid in Connection with the Financing of the Structural Policies and the Organization of Information Systems in this Field, OJ 1994 L178/43.

[146] Reg. 2064/97, *supra* n. 143, Art. 7.

[147] Reg. 1260/1999, *supra* n. 79, Art. 8(3).

[148] Ibid. Art. 38(1).

[149] Ibid. Art. 39(1).

[150] Ibid. Art. 9(n).

[151] Ibid. Art. 34(1).

as the obligation to establish management and control systems.[152] The Member State must ensure that these bodies receive adequate guidance on the required control systems,[153] and verify that such systems are being implemented,[154] by carrying out checks on those systems as previously.[155] In the exercise of their responsibility for financial control, Member States continue to have obligations to carry out their own checks on operations. They must take measures to ensure compliance with Community law and rules and sound financial management, and to prevent and detect irregularities.[156] There is also an obligation to establish a monitoring committee to supervise each CSF or single programming document and each operational programme.[157] These are national bodies and a Commission representative participates in an advisory capacity. The tasks of the monitoring committee are, *inter alia*, to consider and approve the criteria for the selection of operations financed under each measure, to review periodically progress made towards achieving the objectives of the assistance, and to consider and approve the annual and final implementation reports before they are sent to the Commission. This overall regime for management and control has been preserved in the Regulation applicable to the period 2007 to 2013.[158] It is, however, clear that under this new scheme the Commission intends to place relatively greater emphasis on the verification of national management and control systems, and once satisfied that these are properly in place the Commission will limit its own on-the-spot checks and audits to exceptional circumstances.[159]

There are obligations concerned with *certification of payment and assurances at the closure of the project.* Member States' obligation to certify payment requests has been retained. Certificates must be provided by an independent person within the paying authority. There is also an obligation to provide statements of assurance at the conclusion of programmes, and this must be provided by a person independent both of the managing authority[160] and intermediate bodies, and of the person or department in the paying authority responsible for certificates.[161]

A third aspect of the post-1999 schema concerns *reporting*. This is

[152] Commission Regulation (EC) 438/2001 of 2 March 2001, Laying Down Detailed Rules for the Implementation of Council Regulation (EC) 1260/99 as Regards the Management and Controls Systems for Assistance Granted under the Structural Funds, OJ 2001 L63/21, Arts. 3 and 4.

[153] Ibid. Art. 2.

[154] Reg. 1260/1999, *supra* n. 79, Art. 38(1).

[155] Reg. 438/2001, *supra* n. 152, Arts. 10–12.

[156] Reg. 1260/1999, *supra* n. 79, Art. 38(1).

[157] Ibid. Art. 35.

[158] COM(2004) 492, *supra* n. 89, Arts. 57–59.

[159] Ibid. Explanatory Memorandum, at 5.3.

[160] Reg. 1260/1999, *supra* n. 79, Art. 38(1)(f).

[161] Reg. 438/2001, *supra* n. 152, Art. 15; COM(2004) 492, *supra* n. 89, Art. 60.

important since it will have a marked impact on the effectiveness of the other regulatory controls discussed above.[162] Earlier regulations had imposed comprehensive reporting requirements,[163] although there were doubts about Member State compliance with these obligations. The 1999 reforms draw on the earlier initiatives. There are requirements: to report on management and control systems set up by the Member State and by its managing and paying authorities;[164] to inform the Commission of the identity and organization of those authorities;[165] to report on checks carried out; and to provide information about the Member State's arrangements for implementation of its financial control obligations. The information required in progress reports has now been specified in detail, and includes information on progress and on results measured against quantified targets.[166]

The final element that is salient to the current discussion is the power to *check*. The Commission has power to carry out on-the-spot checks for operations financed by the Funds and on the management and control systems. It must, however, give the Member State a minimum of one day's notice.[167] The provision for notice assumes cooperation by the Member State. To the extent that such cooperation is not forthcoming, and in particular where a Member State intends to ignore or even conceal irregularities, the notice requirement compromises the Commission's ability to detect irregularities for itself. There is nonetheless provision for annual reviews of the Member State's controls and systems,[168] and such reviews can lead to Commission observations plus requests for action.[169] The Commission therefore has the basic powers required to carry out the checks necessary to hold Member States accountable, subject to the requirement to give notice. However, the practical effectiveness of the checks depends on their coverage. There is no provision requiring a certain level of coverage, so this depends on resources and the Commission's own priorities. This, as we shall see below, is problematic.

The Member States thus have general and detailed responsibility for financial control. There is also a pyramid of responsibility, with more specific responsibilities and obligations being moved down to the managing

[162] 14th Annual Report on the Implementation of the Structural Funds, COM(2003) 646 final, at 3.2.

[163] See, e.g., Reg. 1681/94, *supra* n. 145.

[164] Reg. 1260/1999, *supra* n. 79, Art. 38(1)(b); Reg. 438/2001, *supra* n. 152, Art. 5.

[165] Reg. 438/2001, *supra* n. 152, Art. 5.

[166] Reg. 1260/1999, *supra* n. 79, Arts. 36(2)(a), 37(2)(b).

[167] Ibid. Art. 38(2). See also, Council Regulation (Euratom, EC) 2185/96 of 11 November 1996, Concerning On-the-spot Checks and Inspections Carried out by the Commission in order to Protect the European Communities' Financial Interests against Fraud and other Irregularities, OJ 1996 L292/2.

[168] Ibid. Art. 38(3).

[169] Ibid. Art. 38(4).

authority, without prejudice to the Member State's overarching responsibility. We shall, however, see below some of the difficulties that have beset the practical implementation of this legal regime.

E. Legislative Design and Output: Correction of Irregularities, Sanctions, and Incentives for Compliance

It is essential if the objectives of the legislation are to be achieved that there should be adequate sanctions. It is clear that the general enforcement power under Article 226 EC can be used to enforce Member States' obligations in relation to the Structural Funds. There are in addition a number of other ways in which irregularities can be corrected and sanctions can be imposed. These operate through the Member States and the Commission.

Member States' have an obligation to take measures to correct irregularities and recover amounts lost.[170] This now expressly involves making financial corrections where appropriate, consisting in cancellation of part or all of the Community contribution.[171] While this obligation is expressed to apply where an operation has become ineligible due to substantial unapproved changes,[172] it must have been intended to apply to all types of irregularity. This is confirmed by further provisions for cancellation enquiries for irregularities which refer back to this provision.[173] The further provisions require enquiries in the case of systemic irregularities to cover all the operations liable to be affected, and specify the considerations to be taken into account in determining the amount to be cancelled for any irregularity.[174] Where funding has been cancelled in response to irregularities, the competent service or body must initiate recovery proceedings for any amounts to be recovered.[175] The managing and paying authorities are then charged with ensuring recovery without delay, keeping account of amounts recoverable, and repaying amounts recovered to the Commission.[176] Similar rules apply in the 2007 scheme.[177]

Member States can in certain circumstances be liable for sums unduly paid. There was provision for such liability in the 1988 regulations.[178] We have seen that the equivalent provision in the context of the CAP was criticized by the Committee of Independent Experts as ineffective.[179] The liability clause

[170] Ibid. Art. 38(1). [171] Ibid. Arts. 30(4), 39(1). [172] Ibid. Art. 30.

[173] Commission Regulation (EC) 448/2001 of 2 March 2001, Laying Down Detailed Rules for the Implementation of Council Regulation (EC) 1260/1999 as Regards the Procedure for Making Financial Corrections to Assistance Granted under the Structural Funds, OJ 2001 L64/13, Art. 2(1); see also the preamble, recital (1).

[174] Ibid. Arts. 2(1) and (2). [175] Ibid. Art. 3(1).

[176] Reg. 438/2001, *supra* n. 152, Art. 8.

[177] COM(2004) 492, *supra* n. 89, Arts. 60(f), 69, 99.

[178] Reg. 4253/88, *supra* n. 71, Art. 23(1). [179] See above, at 63–64.

in the Structural Funds' Regulations contained, however, a reverse burden of proof: the Member State was liable unless it provided proof that it was not responsible for the irregularity or negligence that occurred.[180] While the reverse onus provides an incentive to prevent irregularities, it may provide a disincentive to report irregularities that have occurred, since it will thereby place the onus on the Member State to prove its innocence. In any event, the liability clause has remained largely a dead letter.[181] The liability clause in the EAGGF Guarantee section regulation is well utilized as part of the clearance of accounts procedure discussed above.[182] There was no such procedure in the Structural Funds' Regulations and thus no ready setting for applying the liability provision. This seems to have been at least part of the reason why the liability clause was not used. Indeed, several reports expressly stated that the EAGGF Guarantee system of charging amounts to Member States was not available for the Funds.[183] This led the Madrid Council to call for an extension of the clearance of accounts system to other sectors.[184] The lack of use of the liability clause explains its omission from the 1999 regulations.[185] Article 38(1)(h) imposes an obligation on the Member States to recover amounts lost as a result of an irregularity detected, but does not contain a clause imposing liability on the Member States equivalent to that found in the earlier regulations. However, the new Regulation governing the period 2007 to 2013 does contain provision rendering the Member State liable for amounts unduly paid to beneficiaries, unless the Member State can prove that the loss was not caused by its irregularity or negligence.[186]

There are also important provisions empowering the Commission to prevent irregularity. The power to impose penalties is somewhat limited. Regulation 2988/95[187] was passed to provide generally for administrative penalties for financial irregularities across all sectors of Community activity. The Regulation provides that penalties may be imposed for either intentional or

[180] See further, Reg. 1681/94, *supra* n. 145, Art. 5(2).

[181] There is no mention of its operation in the Commission's Annual Reports on the Structural Funds or those on the Protection of the Community's Financial Interests, in the Annual Reports of the Court of Auditors, in the Commission's publications, A Guide to the Reform of the Community's Structural Funds (1989) and Structural Funds and Cohesion Fund 1994–1999: Regulations and Commentary, or in the common provisions of the CSFs.

[182] See above, at 66–68.

[183] 1993 Annual Report on the Protection of the Community's Financial Interests, at 49–51; also 1995 and 1998 reports.

[184] 1996 Annual Report on the Protection of the Community's Financial Interests, at 16.

[185] There was no discussion of this change in the preparatory documentation of the new system: Commission Proposal COM(98)131 final; ESC opinion, OJ 1998 C407; Parliament's opinion, A4–391/98; Court of Auditors' opinion, OJ 1998 C401.

[186] COM(2004) 492, *supra* n. 89, Art. 69(3).

[187] Council Regulation (EC, Euratom) 2988/95 of 18 December 1995, On the Protection of the European Communities' Financial Interests, OJ 1995 L312/1.

negligent irregularities,[188] and that they may be applied either to the perpetrators of the irregularity or to those with a duty to prevent or take responsibility for irregularities.[189] However, the Regulation merely sets out framework rules, to be implemented by further sectoral legislation.[190] The Community has been slow in utilizing the power, and has not done so in the context of the Structural Funds. It is, however, reasonably clear that the principal sanctions are conditional payment and financial correction. Both are important tools at the Commission's disposal, which may be suited to different types of case.

In relation to the former, we have seen that payments have been conditional on certified claims since 1988, and that since 1999, they are almost exclusively by way of reimbursement of certified regular expenditure. Non-reimbursement of expenditure, the regularity of which cannot be assured, potentially represents an effective sanction and incentive to ensure the regularity of expenditure. The 1999 system moreover includes a new power to reduce the payment on account instead of making a financial correction.[191] The 2007 system also contains extensive provisions allowing payment to be interrupted, suspended, or withheld where there are doubts concerning the management and control systems or the regularity of expenditure.[192]

In relation to financial corrections, we should recall that the Structural Funds operate on a multi-annual basis. This provides the foundation for reducing or cancelling the Community contribution to a programme in the event of irregularities. We have already touched on the Member States' obligations to carry out corrections. The focus here is the Commission's power to make corrections. The Commission's practice has been to deduct the amount of any cancelled funding from the following year's funding instalments.[193] The Commission was accorded in the 1988 Regulations a general power to reduce, suspend, or cancel assistance in the event of irregularity.[194] It was, however, willing to allow Member States to reallocate funding which they had earmarked for, or spent on, a project that turned out to be irregular. This was a questionable interpretation of the legal provisions. It led in any event to abusive practices. Some Member States systematically over-declared, that is included more projects than could be funded by the agreed contribution, so as to ensure that the declaration contained sufficient eligible expenditure even if some was disallowed.[195] Some also substituted existing, partially completed projects for ones which had been declared ineligible.[196] The

188 Ibid. Art. 5. 189 Ibid. Art. 7. 190 Ibid. Art. 2(2).

191 Reg. 1260/1999, *supra* n. 79, Art. 39(3)(a).

192 COM(2004) 492, *supra* n. 89, Arts. 89–91.

193 8th to 10th Annual Report on the Structural Funds (1996 to 1998), at 108–111, 125–128 and 122–126 respectively.

194 Reg. 4253/88, *supra* n. 71, Art. 24.

195 Second CIE, *supra* n. 2, at 3.18.2. 196 Ibid. at 3.18.1.

Commission modified its position via soft law, adopting guidelines specifying when it would not allow a Member State the opportunity to reallocate the funds.[197]

The 1999 Regulations introduced more comprehensive provisions for financial corrections. The Commission's power to make financial corrections is now largely a backup power, exercisable where the Member State has failed to carry out corrections or otherwise to comply with its control and management obligations. Where that power needs to be exercised there is no provision for reprogramming.[198] Where corrections are made by the Member State itself then it can re-use the cancelled funding on other eligible projects.[199] Corrections made by the Commission are intended to reverse irregularities, not to operate as penalties, but in the case of systemic irregularities, corrections may be based on extrapolation or a flat rate.[200] Any sum unduly received is to be repaid to the Commission.[201] The net effect of the provisions is that where the Member State has already paid out on the relevant irregular expenditure, cancellation and deduction from the next funding instalment means that the loss due to the irregularity is shifted to the Member State, leaving it out of pocket at the end of the programme unless it can recover from the beneficiaries. This effectively amounts to liability for amounts not recovered. This regime has been carried over into the Regulation covering the Structural Funds 2007 to 2013.[202]

F. The Contribution of the European Court of Justice: Teleological Interpretation in Support of the Commission

The discussion thus far has not addressed the role of the European Court of Justice (ECJ) in adjudicating on disputed claims concerning the Structural Fund Regulations. We saw earlier that the ECJ has played an important role in the context of the CAP. Its role in relation to the Structural Fund Regulations has been less prominent, in part at least because there is no formal system of annual clearance of accounts of the kind that exists in the CAP

[197] Internal guidelines concerning: Net financial Corrections in the context of the application of Article 24 of Regulation (EEC) No 4253/88, Decision C(97) 3151 of 15 October 1997. The guidelines also provided for net corrections greater than the sum relating specifically to the irregularity concerned, where the Commission had good reason to believe that the irregularity reflected a systemic weakness of management, and for flat rate reductions where quantification of loss flowing from the irregularity was difficult.

[198] Reg. 1260/1999, *supra* n. 79, Art. 39(2) and (3).

[199] Ibid. Art. 39(1).

[200] Reg. 448/2001, *supra* n. 173, Art 4. See also, Guidelines on the principles, criteria and indicative scales to be applied by Commission departments in determining financial corrections under Article 39(3) of Regulation (EC) No 1260/1999, Decision C(2001) 476 of 2 March 2001.

[201] Reg. 1260/1999, *supra* n. 79, Art. 39(4).

[202] COM(2004) 492, *supra* n. 89, Art. 100.

regime, and it is this which has provided the vehicle for most of the legal challenges in the agricultural sphere. The Community courts have nonetheless played a significant role in the context of the Structural Funds.

This has been most marked in relation to legal challenges to financial corrections. It will be recalled that the 1988 Regulations allowed the Commission to reduce, suspend, or cancel assistance in the event of an irregularity.[203] The greater part of the case law relates to legal challenges to such financial corrections. The Community courts have interpreted the relevant provisions broadly so as to support the Commission in its endeavour to ensure the probity of the system. This is so both in substantive and procedural terms.

The broad *substantive interpretation* of these provisions is exemplified by *Conserve Italia.*[204] The ECJ accepted that Article 24(2) of Regulation 4253/88 did not in terms allow the cancellation of assistance, even though the Article was entitled reduction, suspension and cancellation of assistance. It concluded nonetheless that Article 24(2) would be deprived of its effectiveness if the Commission could not cancel the entirety of the assistance where this was warranted. This was more especially so since a reduction of assistance directly in proportion to irregularities detected would encourage fraud, since applicants would risk only the loss of the sums unduly paid. In *Valnerina*[205] the Court of First Instance (CFI) held that it was acceptable in principle for a decision granting assistance to specify one of a number of parties involved as the sole person to be financially liable in the event of irregularities, provided that this was made sufficiently clear at the outset. In *COPPI*[206] the ECJ considered whether it was lawful for a Member State to revoke assistance granted to an undertaking from the EAGGF, or whether this power was reserved to the Commission itself. The ECJ acknowledged that Article 23 of the Regulation did not expressly provide for this action by a Member State. It held, however, that the Article would be deprived of useful effect if a Member State could not adopt such measures, more especially because it had the primary responsibility for monitoring the operation of the project.

The Community courts have been equally strident in relation to *procedural aspects* of the enforcement regime. It held in *Sgaravatti Mediterranea*[207] that the Commission could validly comply with its obligation, contained in

[203] Reg. 4253/88, *supra* n. 71, Art. 24.

[204] Case C-500/99 P, *Conserve Italia Soc. Coop arl v Commission* [2002] ECR I-867, at para. 88.

[205] Case T-340/00, *Communita Montana della Valnerina v Commission* [2003] ECR II-811, at paras. 53–54

[206] Case C-271/01, *Ministero delle Politiche Agricole e Forestali v Consorzio Produttori Pompelmo Italiano Soc. Coop arl (COPPI)* [2004] ECR I-1029, at para. 41.

[207] Case T-199/99, *Sgaravatti Mediterranea Srl v Commission* [2002] ECR II-3731, at para. 45.

Article 24(1) of Regulation 4253/88, to conduct an examination prior to ordering reduction of assistance for irregularities by relying on detailed investigations made by the national authorities. In *Conserve Italia*[208] the ECJ held that it was essential for the proper functioning of the system of controls established to ensure the proper use of Community funds that applicants for aid provide the Commission with information which is reliable and which is not apt to mislead it. The same approach is evident in *Thessalonikis.*[209] The CFI confirmed that the Commission had the burden of proof under Article 24 of Regulation 4253/88, but held that if examination revealed irregularities it was then for the beneficiary of the assistance to show that expenditure was properly incurred in relation to the particular project. It was moreover for the beneficiary to provide the Commission with all documentation required to dispel the doubts raised by the Commission. Similar themes are apparent in *Hortiplant,*[210] where the ECJ held that the Commission's power to cancel assistance under Article 24(2) of Regulation 4253/88 would be 'totally deprived of usefulness if, prior to the adoption of a decision, the Commission were obliged to wait for the Member State concerned to submit its observations'.

G. Formal Law and Efficacy

The formal legal regime for the disbursement of Structural Funds has been tightened and strengthened since its inception. The present regime is nonetheless complex and places considerable reliance on effective interaction between the Commission and the Member States. This is especially so given the decentralization of responsibilities to the latter. It is therefore important to assess the effectiveness of this disposition of power and authority. Two reports from the Court of Auditors are valuable in this respect.

The Court of Auditors considered the efficacy of the financial controls introduced in 1994 and 1997.[211] We have seen that these Regulations upgraded the checks required on programmes co-financed from the Structural Funds and introduced a system for communicating information about irregularities that were detected by Member States. The Court found that the new regulatory regime had beneficial effects. It concluded, however, that there were instances where the Member States were not applying the rules correctly, and that this was in part because of inadequate guidance from the

[208] *Supra* n. 204, at para. 100.

[209] Case T-196/01, *Thessalonikis v Commission* [2003] ECR II-3987, at para. 47.

[210] Case C-330/01, *Hortiplant SAT v Commission* [2004] ECR I-1763, at para. 31. See also at para. 32.

[211] Court of Auditors, Special Report 10/2001, Concerning the Financial Control of the Structural Funds, Commission Regulations 2064/97 and 1681/94, together with the Commission's Replies, OJ 2001 C314/26.

Commission. The data on irregularities was moreover incomplete and there was significant room for improvement in the follow up procedures by OLAF and the Commission in relation to these irregularities.

The Court of Auditors has more recently conducted a general audit on the Structural Fund regime for 2000 to 2006.[212] It noted the efforts and achievements of the Commission during this period, but pointed to a number of difficulties that still remained. The Report focused in part on the extent to which funding assistance was actually reaching the intended regions in accord with Objectives 1 and 2 of the 1999 regime, and made recommendations to enhance effectiveness in this respect. It noted moreover the delays and unwieldiness in approving the Structural Fund programmes.[213] The Report also considered the way in which the management and control systems were operating. It found that there were delays in the introduction of such systems within some Member States.[214] It affirmed the centrality of reliable data if devolved management subject to Commission supervision was to work.[215] The Court of Auditors pointed to the danger that when the introduction of new functions was introduced piecemeal into national systems, 'there was an inherent risk as regards the separation of functions and the independence and operational efficiency of the new bodies'.[216] Moreover the allocation of the responsibility for management, payment, and certification to a single national institution, even if different departments therein performed separate functions, could lead to conflicts of interest, unless their operational independence was safeguarded in advance.[217] The Report was in addition critical of imprecision relating to eligibility of expenditure.[218]

H. Soft Law and Reform

The preceding discussion reveals the complexity of the formal legal rules that apply in this area, and how they have changed over time. Legal rules, such as the new provisions on eligibility of expenditure,[219] continue to be made to meet difficulties revealed by, for example, the Court of Auditors.

Soft law has also been used to address difficulties in the functioning of the system, such as the administrative burdens placed on national administrations and the delays attendant on Commission approval. The 1999 system is, as we have seen, based on a balance. The system is premised on

[212] Court of Auditors, Special Report 7/2003, On the Implementation of Assistance Programming for the Period 2000 to 2006 within the Framework of the Structural Funds, together with the Commission's Replies, OJ 2003 C174/1.

[213] Ibid. at paras. 18–24. [214] Ibid. at para. 55. [215] Ibid. at para. 59.

[216] Ibid. at para. 64. [217] Ibid. at para. 66. [218] Ibid. at paras. 68–81.

[219] Commission Regulation (EC) 448/2004 of 10 March 2004, The Eligibility of Expenditure of Operations Co-Financed by the Structural Funds, OJ 2004 L72/66.

decentralization to the Member States of major responsibilities concerning project selection, management, evaluation, and control. The *quid pro quo* is the imposition of stricter controls on the Member States concerning financial management, automatic decommitment of appropriations (the n + 2 rule), and financial corrections; this is coupled with increased power given to the Commission in relation to audit and the like. In 2003 the Commission engaged in discussion with the Member States on ways in which the 1999 regime could be made to work better.[220] The changes proposed largely concerned interpretation of the existing legal rules rather than their modification.

Thus, in relation to controls, there was significant agreement on: comparative analysis of financial and management systems in the Member States, with the aim of revealing best practice in this area; better coordination of the audit activities conducted in the Member States and by the Commission; clarifications as to the nature and incidence of the reporting requirements; fine-tuning the role of the Commission within monitoring committees; and clarification of the application of the n + 2 rule.

The most interesting development to emerge from this discourse concerned what is termed the 'contract of confidence'. It emerged from the Member States' rejection of the Commission proposal to introduce an annual clearance of accounts regime modelled on that in the CAP. We have already seen the importance of this procedure within the CAP,[221] but no Member State was willing to accept these controls with respect to the Structural Funds. The Commission's 'contract of confidence' was thus a fall back position, but interesting nonetheless. It was to be accommodated within the existing framework of legal rules.

The 'contract of confidence' builds on the decentralization that underpins the 1999 regime, and is based on three elements. There must be *assurance that the national financial and control systems* meet the conditions laid down in the Community regulations. There must be a *satisfactory national audit strategy*, which: covers the whole programming period up to closure; provides the framework in which annual audits occur; identifies the bodies responsible for audit work, including their resources; provides assurance of adequate certification of expenditure; mandates regular verification of the management and control systems during the programming period; and is validated by an independent body as required by the Community regulations. The final element is the *submission of reports* through which the effective implementation of the audit strategy and certification of expenditure can be assessed. The operational consequences of a 'contract of confidence' are that

[220] Communication from the Commission, On the Simplification, Clarification, Co-ordination and Flexible Management of the Structural Policies 2000–6, C(2003) 1255.

[221] See above, at 66–68.

the Commission limits its on-the-spot audit to verification of the assurances provided by the contract, and a reduction in the time that it retains supporting documentation on expenditure and checks.

6. CONCLUSIONS AND ASSESSMENT

A number of related conclusions can be drawn concerning the role of law in the administration of the CAP and the Structural Funds

First, sharing the administration of complex activities is difficult. This is a trite statement, but an important one nonetheless. It was natural that the administration of the CAP and the Structural Funds should be shared between the Commission and national bureaucracies. The difficulties of designing and operating such a system should nonetheless be borne firmly in mind. It involves the interrelationship between 12, 15, or 25 different Member States and the Commission. It is important to note the relevance of the words 'different' and 'state' here. The reality is that the Community rules will be administered by states with diverse bureaucratic traditions, more especially so when one gets down to the level of operational detail concerning certification, audit, and the like. It is equally important to remember that the other players are states. This renders the administration of the regimes, and the degree of power possessed by the relevant players, rather different from the paradigm of national administration even where this is undertaken within a federal structure.

Secondly, the interplay between Member States and the Community in the design of the rules governing these two regimes was never going to be straightforward. This is in part because of the very nature of the subject matter covered by the CAP and the Structural Funds. The latter, for example, requires rules to be devised which delineate the objectives of regional policy, and the oversight and management of multiple individual projects across the entire Community. Moves towards the simplification of the CAP legislation are to be welcomed,[222] as are further reforms in the Structural Fund system post-2006.[223] The complexity of relationship between Member States and the Community also exists because of the tension between the collective interest and that of individual Member States adverted to in the previous discussion, and because of the tension between decentralization and effective supervision of regional policy. Thus we have seen that the Structural Funds have been increasingly based on decentralization to the Member States. This

[222] Commission Report on Simplification of Agricultural Legislation, COM(2001) 48 final; Reg. 1782/2003, *supra* n. 8; Reg. 1290/2005, *supra* n. 22.

[223] European Commission, A New Partnership for Cohesion, Convergence, Competitiveness, Co-operation, Third Report on Economic and Social Cohesion (2004); COM(2004) 492, *supra* n. 89.

has been motivated both by subsidiarity and by the realization that the Commission does not possess the resources or personnel to administer the policy in this area itself. It is nonetheless essential that effective supervision over the operation of the Funds be maintained, and this too involves responsibilities shared by the Member States and the Commission in the manner analysed above.

Thirdly, it is clear both in relation to the CAP and the Structural Funds that legislative design is crucial for the successful delivery of these policies. It is certainly a necessary condition in this respect. This is so whether one has regard to the criteria for access to, for example, the Structural Funds, or whether one is concerned with management, oversight, audit, and the correction of irregularity. The rules contained in the Community legislation will embody incentives for compliance, which may be more or less effective depending upon their content. It is equally clear that while legislative design is a necessary condition for successful policy delivery, it is not sufficient. The history of the CAP and the Structural Funds provides important instances where the failings flowed not from inadequate rules, but from inadequacy in their implementation, whether this was due to failures of management systems, insufficient personnel, or personal shortcomings. The 2003 Report of the Court of Auditors bears testimony to the continuing difficulties with ensuring adherence to and proper compliance with the rules applicable to the CAP and the Structural Funds.[224]

Finally, we should be careful about the ascription of blame when things go wrong. The tendency has to been to lay the fault at the door of the Community, and more especially the Commission. This suits the Member States, and anti-European commentators. The Commission has been at fault through, for example, tolerating departures from existing rules, and by allocating insufficient personnel to the EAGGF section. To suggest that the entire malaise of the CAP or that all difficulties with the Structural Funds can be laid at the Commission's door is a gross oversimplification. The Community is not some reified entity that desired the CAP in its present format. The existing regime is largely the result of Member State preferences expressed in the Treaty provisions and in the CAP legislation.[225]

[224] Court of Auditors, Annual Report Concerning the Financial Year 2003, OJ 2004 C293/01, at 4.47–4.49, 5.66–5.69.

[225] Rieger, *supra* n. 3, at 180.

4

Comitology

1. INTRODUCTION

The discussion thus far has focused on direct and shared administration respectively as ways in which Community policy is delivered. This chapter focuses on comitology and the making of secondary norms, which are commonly rules cast in the form of regulations. This cuts across the previous analysis, in the sense that rule-making is a feature of both direct and shared administration. It raises complex issues in its own right, which are addressed in this chapter.

The structure of the discussion is as follows. It begins with an analysis of the nature of the problem presented by rule-making, and the necessity for any polity, including the European Union (EU), to administer an area through secondary norms of a legislative nature. This is followed by an historical overview of rule-making in the EU and the role of comitology therein. The focus then shifts to detailed evaluation of three approaches to rule-making and comitology that are apparent in the relevant literature. The discussion concludes by considering the optimal way of dealing with rule-making from the perspective of principle and practicality, taking full account of the way in which the EU operates.

2. THE NATURE OF THE PROBLEM

The issues raised by this chapter are, as indicated, complex. They will take us into the realms of political science as well as law. We shall need to negotiate the difficult world of comitology. It is all too easy to lose sight of the wood for the trees when traversing this landscape. It is therefore important to be as clear as possible from the outset about the nature of the problem. This is especially so given that it is endemic to all political systems, even if its resolution raises particular issues in the context of the EU.

The problem in essence is how to make and legitimate secondary norms, which are often legislative in nature. The paradigm in democratic statal systems is for legislation to be enacted by the legislature through whichever process the particular state deems to be appropriate for this purpose. It is however commonly the case that such primary legislation is complemented by secondary norms, which flesh out the principles contained in the enabling statute. The reasons for this are well known. The legislature may not be able to foresee all the ramifications of the legislation that it enacts when the initial statute is made. It may well have neither the time nor the expertise to address all the issues in the original legislation. The measures consequential to the original statute may have to be passed expeditiously, which precludes the use of the procedures for primary legislation. These reasons gain added force when viewed in the context of much modern legislation, which is often framed in relatively open-textured terms, thereby necessitating greater specification through subsequent action. The problem of securing the legitimacy of rules is especially significant within the EU, given that it functions in many respects as a regulatory state.[1]

The secondary norms that are enacted will perforce vary depending upon the subject matter of the primary legislation and the nature of the issue that requires elucidation. On some occasions the secondary measure will be an individualized decision, made by the person to whom authority has been delegated by the primary legislation. In other instances the secondary norm will be legislative in nature. It will take the form of a general rule that is intended to apply to all those falling within a certain factual situation. The terminology used to describe such norms varies as between legal systems. Some employ the language of delegated or secondary legislation. Others prefer the appellation rule-making. Yet others use terminology such as directive.

The method by which such measures are made also varies. The premise in some systems is that norms of a legislative nature should so far as possible be legitimated through some degree of oversight from the legislature itself, even if the procedures through which this is done differ from those used for primary legislation. This legitimation from the 'top' via the legislature may then be complemented by legitimation from the 'bottom' through participation in rule-making by affected parties pursuant to a general legal regime providing the framework for such participatory rights. The premise in other regimes is that the executive should have a significant degree of autonomous power to make secondary rules of a legislative nature, the principal check lying with the courts via judicial review.

It is important to be clear about the content of these secondary rules of a legislative nature. It is tempting to think in terms of a simple divide between the primary legislation which captures all points of principle, while secondary norms address insignificant points of detail, with the corollary that the latter

[1] Majone, 'The Rise of the Regulatory State in Europe' (1994) 17 *West European Politics* 77; G. Majone, *Regulating Europe* (Routledge, 1996); Majone, 'Europe's "Democratic Deficit": The Question of Standards' (1998) 4 *ELJ* 5.

can therefore be left to the executive relatively unencumbered by external constraint. This does not represent reality. There is no simple dichotomy between principle and detail. There is no ready equation between detail and absence of political controversy. Secondary norms may deal with uncontroversial detail. They may often address points of principle or involve issues of political choice which are every bit as controversial as those dealt with in the primary legislation. This is self-evidently so in relation to matters such as risk regulation, the detail of which may often be dealt with through secondary norms. It is equally the case, as will be seen below, in relation to secondary norms of a legislative nature fleshing out the Structural Funds' regime to prevent fraud and ensure financial probity.

The extent to which issues of political choice can be delegated to ministers, agencies, and the like will be affected by the extent to which the legal system uses a non-delegation doctrine. The vigorous deployment of such a doctrine, designed to ensure that the essential principles are laid down in the primary statute, will necessarily limit the extent to which there can be delegation of broad rule-making powers to bodies external to the legislature. This does not alter the point being made here. The fact that a legal system takes the non-delegation doctrine seriously simply means that the courts will ensure that there are sufficient principles to guide the framing of the rules to be made by the executive or administration. It does not mean that the rules made pursuant to the primary legislation will thereby be self-executing, politically uncontroversial, or merely technical. The non-delegation doctrine does not therefore serve to ensure that the relationship between the primary legislation and rules made pursuant thereto functions in accord with some idealized transmission belt theory of administrative law.

Everything said thus far is of course standard fare for those familiar with public law. This does not mean that solutions adopted at national level can necessarily be cut and pasted to the EU. Nor does it mean that we should ignore the wealth of experience at national level. We should at the very least be mindful that the problem of ensuring the legitimacy of secondary legislative rules is an endemic one for all systems, and we should be equally mindful that no system has 'cracked' or 'solved' the problem perfectly. It is therefore little wonder that the issue still proves problematic within the EU. Moreover the 'solutions' adopted within national systems necessarily reflect explicitly or implicitly a complex normative and pragmatic calculus. This is as we shall see also the case within the EU. It will, however, become apparent that there are a number of structural factors operating within the EU which have made it especially difficult to devise a satisfactory solution in pragmatic and normative terms to the dilemma of legitimating secondary rules of a legislative nature. This does not mean that the dilemma is incapable of resolution in this context. It does mean that we have to understand the reality of the functioning of the EU in order to make sure that any proposed solutions in this area cohere more generally with its modus operandi. In the EU formal secondary norms of a legislative nature will be cast either as regulations or directives. The omnibus term rule-making will be used to capture both types of secondary norm.

3. RULE-MAKING IN THE EU: A SHORT GUIDE TO A COMPLEX HISTORY

There is a rich literature exploring various facets of rule-making within the EU, and more especially the role of comitology.[2] The present discussion will merely address the most significant staging posts in this historical development, in order to lay the foundations for the analysis developed thereafter.

A. The Ambiguous 'Original Intent'

Most discussions concerning rule-making in the EU naturally begin with the birth of comitology in the early 1960s. This will be considered below. It is, however, important to take a step back to the original Rome Treaty. This is particularly so because, as will be seen, the Commission has articulated a picture of the 'Community method' in which it characterizes itself as the Community executive which should have sole or principal responsibility for the making of such secondary rules.

This vision must, however, be justified, not merely stated. Such justification may be based on first principle, the argument being that this falls within the natural province of the executive, and the Commission is the executive for these purposes. This argument will be assessed below.

The justification could alternatively be grounded in the original Treaty or later amendments thereto. It is this argument that will be considered here. We do not have the *travaux préparatoires* for the EEC Treaty and must therefore base any judgment on an overall reading of the text. A close reading

[2] R. Pedler and G.F. Schaefer (eds), *Shaping European Law and Policy: The Role of Committees and Comitology in the Political Process* (European Institute of Public Administration, 1996); D. Rometsch and W. Wessels (eds), *The European Union and Member States, Towards Institutional Fusion?* (Manchester University Press, 1996); C. Joerges, K-H Ladeur and E. Vos (eds), *Integrating Scientific Expertise into Regulatory Decision-Making: National Traditions and European Innovations* (Nomos, 1997); C. Joerges and E. Vos (eds), *EU Committees: Social Regulation, Law and Politics* (Hart, 1999); *Third Report of the House of Lords' Select Committee on European Legislation: Delegation of Powers to the Commission: Reforming Comitology* (HL 23; 1999); E. Vos, *Institutional Frameworks of Community Health and Safety Legislation: Committees, Agencies and Private Bodies* (Hart, 1999); M. Andenas and A. Turk (eds), *Delegated Legislation and the Role of Committees in the EC* (Kluwer Law International, 2000); C. Bergstrom, *Comitology, Delegation of Powers in the European Union and the Committee System* (Oxford University Press, 2005).

of the original Rome Treaty will, however, reveal that it was ambiguous as to assignment of power over the making of secondary rules.

The disposition of primary legislative power in the Rome Treaty was relatively clear. In most areas the maxim the 'Commission proposes, the Council disposes' held true. Legislative authority was carved up between the Commission, exercising the right of legislative initiative, and the Council that had the right to vote. The Commission's power was increased because unanimity was required for the Council to amend a Commission proposal and because the Commission could alter the original proposal before the Council had acted.[3] The Assembly had a bare right to be consulted, but only where the Treaty so stipulated.

The disposition of power over the making of secondary rules was much less clear. The Treaty itself drew no formal distinction between primary and secondary norms. The same terminology of regulation and directive was applied to both and it was left to the reader to divine that a regulation was made pursuant to an earlier regulation or directive by its title and content. The Commission's claim for power and authority over the making of secondary rules fastened on the wording of Article 155 EC,[4] which provided that in order to ensure the proper functioning and development of the common market the Commission should, *inter alia*, 'exercise the powers conferred on it by the Council for the implementation of the rules laid down by the latter'. This is, however, a decidedly shaky basis for the assertion of authority or autonomy over the making of secondary legislative rules.

This is in part because, as the European Court of Justice (ECJ) pointed out,[5] the provision was optional: it became operative when the Council decided to confer powers on the Commission for the implementation of primary legislation. It is in part because of an ambiguity as to the meaning of 'implementation'. The word could be taken to refer to the 'making' of secondary rules, although this reading still left open the possibility of attaching conditions by the Council to the delegation of such power. It could alternatively refer to the 'execution' of the primary regulation or directive, connoting the need to take measures including individual decisions to ensure that the primary regulation or directive was properly applied.[6] We shall see that ambiguity in this regard persisted in the provisions on the hierarchy of norms contained in the Constitutional Treaty.

The reality was that the Rome Treaty provided little by way of definitive guidance on the making of secondary rules, or the conditions that could be

[3] Art. 149 EEC. [4] Now Art. 211 EC.

[5] Case 25/70, *Einfuhr- und Vorrasstelle fur Getreide und Futermittel v Koster, Berodt & Co* [1970] 2 ECR 1161, at para. 9.

[6] See Case 16/88, *Commission v Council* [1989] ECR 3457, at paras. 11–13, for recognition of this ambiguity in relation to 'implementation' in the revised Art. 145 EC post the SEA.

attached to this process. The early years of the Community's existence should therefore be regarded as a working out of this issue, not as some upsetting of a carefully contrived institutional balance clearly delineated in the original Treaty.

B. The Birth of Comitology

Political reality may well be the mother of legal invention. Comitology was born in the context of the Common Agricultural Policy (CAP).[7] It rapidly became clear that the administration of the CAP would require the deployment of detailed rules in ever-changing market circumstances. Recourse to primary legislation on all such occasions was impracticable. It was equally apparent that the Member States were wary of according the Commission a blank cheque over the making of implementing rules, especially given that power once delegated without encumbrance would generate legally binding rules without further possibility of Council oversight.

This wariness was heightened by the tensions between the Council and the Commission in the mid-1960s leading to the Luxembourg Crisis and subsequent Accords. The relative powers of the Council and Commission were fought out with de Gaulle and Hallstein staking out their visions of the two institutions. It would, however, be mistaken to see the birth of the committee system solely in terms of Council distrust of Commission. The committee system was also conceived as a way of dealing with disagreements between the Member States themselves. It is readily apparent that Member States might agree on the general regulatory principles for a particular area, but disagree on the more detailed ramifications thereof, more especially when the precise nature of the contestable issues might not be apparent when the primary regulation or directive was initially enacted. Involvement in the making of the implementing rules served moreover to facilitate interaction between national administrators who would be responsible for the application of the rules at national level.

The net result was the birth of the management committee procedure, embodied in the early agricultural regulations. The committee composed of national representatives, normally those with expertise or understanding of the relevant area, would be directly involved with the Commission in the deliberations concerning the secondary regulations or directives. The secondary measure would be immediately applicable, subject to the caveat that it could be sent back to the Council if it was not in accord with the committee's

[7] Bertram, 'Decision-Making in the EEC: The Management Committee Procedure' (1967–68) 5 *CMLRev* 246; Schindler, 'The Problems of Decision-Making by Way of the Management Committee Procedure in the EEC' (1971) 8 *CMLRev* 184; Bergstrom, *supra* n. 2, Chap. 2.

opinion. It was then open to the Council to take a different decision by qualified majority within one month.[8]

The committee methodology spread rapidly to other areas, and became a standard feature attached to the delegation of power to the Commission. It was moreover not long before the more restrictive version, known as the regulatory committee procedure, was created in the context of the emerging common commercial policy.[9] On this version of the committee procedure, if the committee failed to deliver an opinion, or if it gave an opinion contrary to the recommended measure, the Commission would have to submit the proposal to the Council, which could then act by qualified majority. There was however a safety net or *filet*, such that if the Council had not acted within three months of the measure being submitted to it, then the proposed provisions could be adopted by the Commission. The desire for greater political control reached its apotheosis in the modified version of the regulatory committee procedure, which embodied what became known as the *contre-filet*: the normal regulatory committee procedure applied, subject to the caveat that the Council could by simple majority prevent the Commission from acting even after the expiry of the prescribed period.

C. Judicial Imprimatur

It is rare for any important institutional development to be unaffected by judicial scrutiny. The legitimacy of the management committee procedure came directly before the ECJ in the *Koster* case.[10] The German court asked through a preliminary reference whether the procedure attached to the delegation of power to the Commission was consistent with the institutional balance established by the Treaty. It is highly likely that the ECJ would have been familiar with the existence and spread of the committee procedure and also with the fact that it was working reasonably well in terms of regulatory output. It was then unsurprising that it crafted its judgment to uphold the legitimacy of the management committee procedure. To have done otherwise would have created a constitutional crisis for EEC decision-making, or if that sounds too dramatic, it would most certainly have led to dire problems.

The ECJ was unequivocal. It reasoned that Article 155 EC accorded the Council discretion to confer on the Commission implementing powers. It followed therefore that the Council could determine the detailed rules to which the Commission was subject when exercising the powers conferred on it, and the management committee procedure constituted just such a detailed

[8] See, e.g., Council Regulation 19/62/EEC of 4 April 1962, On the Progressive Establishment of a Common Organisation of the Market in Cereals, OJ 1962 30/933, Arts. 25–26.

[9] See, e.g., Council Regulation 802/68/EEC of 27 June 1968, On the Common Definition of the Concept of the Origin of Goods, OJ 1968 L148/1, Arts. 12–14.

[10] Case 25/70, *Koster*, *supra* n. 5.

rule. Moreover, because the committee could not take any decision itself, but merely served to send the matter back to the Council in the event of a negative committee opinion, it did not distort the institutional balance within the EEC.[11]

The judicial realization of the centrality of the committees was re-affirmed in *Rey Soda*,[12] where the ECJ opined that the management committee procedure provided a 'mechanism which allows the Council to give the Commission an appreciably wide power of implementation whilst reserving where necessary its own right to intervene'.

Judicial support for the political status quo was evident once again in *Tedeschi*,[13] where the ECJ upheld the legality of the regulatory committee procedure. The ECJ accepted that the committee procedure could have the effect of preventing the Commission from implementing the proposal that had been rejected by the Council, and that this was so even if the latter proffered no alternative solution. The Court concluded that this did not, however, paralyse the Commission, which could issue any other measure it considered appropriate.[14] The relative brevity of the ECJ's reasoning on this point attests to its difficulty: it was clear in reality that any other measure suggested by the Commission would also have to secure the approval of the regulatory committee.

The 'judicial realpolitik' explanation offered by Bergstrom best captures the essence of the Court's reasoning: 'the Commission was obliged to focus its efforts on bringing about reconciliation between the different interests of the Member States'[15] with the corollary that the Commission should normally accept a measure favoured by the qualified majority on the committee.

D. The Single European Act and the First Comitology Decision

Prior to the Single European Act (SEA), comitology was based on an admixture of legislative choice, backed by judicial approval, set against the backdrop of Article 155 EC. It was, as we have seen, the judicial interpretation of Article 155 that formed the cornerstone for the ECJ's reasoning in cases such as *Koster*.[16] The passage of the SEA shifted the Treaty foundation of comitology to the new third indent of Article 145 EC.[17] This stipulated that the Council should confer on the Commission, in the acts adopted by the Council, powers for the implementation of the rules which the Council laid down, and that it could impose certain requirements in respect of the exercise of these powers. These procedures had to be consonant with principles and

[11] Case 25/70, *Koster*, *supra* n. 5, at para. 9.
[12] Case 23/75, *Rey Soda v Cassa Conguaglio Zucchero* [1975] ECR 1279, at para. 13.
[13] Case 5/77, *Carlo Tedeschi v Denkavit Commerciale S.r.l.* [1977] ECR 1555.
[14] Ibid. at para. 55.
[15] Bergstrom, *supra* n. 2, at 149.
[16] *Supra* n. 5.
[17] Now Art. 202 EC.

rules laid down in advance. The revised Article 145 further provided that the Council might also reserve the right, in specific cases, to exercise directly implementing powers itself.

The revised Article 145 certainly had some gains for the Commission, most notably because it embodied the general principle that the Council *should* confer implementing power on the Commission, unless the Council provided reasons as to why it should reserve specific implementing power to itself.[18]

There is, however, equally little doubt that, viewed more generally, Article 145 was a defeat for the more far-reaching Commission ambitions. This is particularly so when it is recognized that the Commission entered the Intergovernmental Conference (IGC) negotiations leading to the SEA with an explicit agenda for the reform of Article 155, the import of which would have been to accord it implementing power without prior authorization from the Council, coupled with a strictly limited number of committee procedures, plus a clear preference against regulatory committees.[19] The result in the SEA, by way of contrast, was no relevant reform of Article 155, Treaty legitimation of comitology, combined with the symbolic impact of placing this within Article 145, thereby emphasizing the centrality of grant of implementing power from Council to Commission.

The Commission, having been thwarted in its vision of Treaty reform, then turned its attention to the formulation of the principles and rules concerning committee procedures demanded by Article 145. There is little doubt that such reform was required, given that there were more than 30 variants of the committee procedures in play at the time of the SEA, and that considerable energy was spent during the legislative process wrangling about the precise procedure to be incorporated in the primary regulation or directive.

The resultant Council Decision[20] was certainly an improvement on the status quo ante, reducing the basic committee procedures to three, advisory, management, and regulatory, with two variants of both the management and regulatory committee procedures, plus safeguard committee procedures. The beneficial impact of the Decision was however qualified by the Council's insistence that it should not be taken to affect the plethora of procedures applicable to existing committees, rejecting thereby the Commission's hope that provision would be made to bring such committees into the new

[18] Case 16/88, *supra* n. 6, at para. 10; Case C-257/01, *Commission v Council* [2005] ECR I-345, at paras. 49–50.

[19] Ehlermann, 'Competences d'Execution Conferees a la Commission—La Nouvelle Decision-Cadre du Conseil' (1988) 316 *RMC* 232, and 'The Internal Market Following the Single European Act' (1987) 24 *CMLRev* 361.

[20] Council Decision 87/373/EEC of 13 July 1987, Laying Down the Procedures for the Exercise of Implementing Powers Conferred on the Commission, OJ 1987 L197/33.

procedural format within a specified period of time. There was also disquiet within the Commission over the continued existence and use of the *contre-filet* version of the regulatory procedure. Moreover, the European Parliament (EP), which had consistently expressed concern over comitology, began to express these reservations more forcefully, for reasons that will now be apparent.

E. The Treaty on European Union, Amsterdam, and the Second Comitology Decision

The EP had expressed disquiet over comitology from the very outset. The strength of its opposition grew commensurately with its increased status in the making of primary regulations and directives. The reason for this is not hard to divine. For nearly the first three decades of the Community's existence the EP had been very much on the side lines of the legislative process, with only a bare right to be consulted and then only where the Treaty so provided. It felt, even at this stage, that the committee procedure limited its capacity to exercise its supervisory powers over the Commission, but it could not readily claim that its legislative powers were compromised by comitology in areas where it had no role in the legislative process.

The SEA began the transformation of the legislative process through the creation of the cooperation procedure, giving the EP a stronger role in the making of regulations and directives, more especially since it applied to important areas such as the passage of harmonization measures to attain the internal market. It is clear that this changed the manner in which primary regulations and directives were enacted. The Commission and Council could no longer ignore the EP or treat its expression of preferences with scant regard. The Treaty on European Union (TEU) took the process a stage further with the creation of the co-decision procedure and this was followed by the expansion of the areas to which the procedure applied, coupled with modification of the procedure so as to further strengthen the role of the EP therein.

The EP's increasingly vocal opposition to comitology, and more especially to the regulatory committee procedure, was readily explicable against this backdrop. From the EP's perspective it had fought long and hard to attain a more co-equal role in the making of primary regulations and directives. The significance of these gains was, however, undermined by its exclusion from the making of secondary regulations and directives, which were still the preserve of the Commission and Council through comitology. The tension was heightened by the 'normality' of comitology: the great majority of important regulations and directives enacted pursuant to co-decision contained a committee procedure, often regulatory, which would then govern the making of implementing regulations. The EP's success in securing the application of co-decision to an ever increased range of primary regulations and directives was therefore tempered by its exclusion from the making of the more detailed secondary rules, which would often entail important issues of principle or political choice.

The EP fought the battle against comitology on the legal and political front.[21] It argued consistently that Article 145 could not be regarded as the basis for comitology in respect of regulations or directives adopted pursuant to co-decision. Article 145 could only be used to legitimate the imposition of committee procedures, so the EP contended, for acts adopted by the Council alone. The Council, not surprisingly, rejected this view.[22] It drew comfort from the ECJ which held, albeit without detailed consideration, that acts of the Council covered acts undertaken jointly with the EP pursuant to co-decision, as well as acts made by the Council alone.[23] The ECJ's jurisprudence moreover served to empower the Council and Commission at the expense of the EP by adopting a broad concept of implementation. It is true that the ECJ continued to insist that the primary regulation or directive should embody the 'essential elements' of the matter to be dealt with. However, it interpreted this relatively loosely, thereby allowing a broad range of implementing measures to be adopted through regulations according to comitology procedures from which the EP was effectively excluded.[24]

The EP continued to contest the application of the committee procedures through the political process,[25] using its powers under co-decision to propose amendment to primary regulations and directives containing comitology and even blocking a measure for this reason. The process of legislative attrition was wearing for all involved and hostilities were temporarily lessened through the conclusion of a *Modus Vivendi* in 1994.[26] This provided that the relevant committee of the EP would be sent general draft implementing acts at the same time as the committee set up by the basic act. Moreover the Council undertook not to adopt a draft general act referred to it in accordance with

[21] Bradley, 'Maintaining the Balance: The Role of the Court of Justice in Defining the Institutional Position of the European Parliament' (1987) 24 *CMLRev* 41; Bradley, 'Comitology and the Law: Through a Glass Darkly' (1992) 29 *CMLRev* 693; Bradley, 'The European Parliament and Comitology: On the Road to Nowhere?' (1997) 3 *ELJ* 230.

[22] Jacqué, 'Implementing Powers and Comitology', in Joerges and Vos (eds), *supra* n. 2, Chap. 4.

[23] Case C-259/95, *European Parliament v Council* [1997] ECR I-5303, at para. 26; Case C-378/00, *Commission v European Parliament and Council* [2003] ECR I-937, at para. 40.

[24] Case C-156/93, *European Parliament v Commission* [1995] ECR I-2019, at paras. 18–22; Case C-417/93, *European Parliament v Council* [1995] ECR I-1185, at para. 30.

[25] R. Corbett, *The European Parliament's Role in Closer EU Integration* (Macmillan, 1998), at 347–348.

[26] *Modus Vivendi* of 20 December 1994 between the European Parliament, the Council and the Commission concerning the implementing measures for acts adopted in accordance with the procedure laid down in Article 189b of the EC Treaty, OJ 1996 C102/1.

the implementing procedure without first informing the EP and obtaining its opinion.

The IGC process leading to the Treaty of Amsterdam was dominated by concerns relating to the legitimacy of the EU and its decision-making processes.[27] Notwithstanding this the Treaty of Amsterdam continued the status quo in relation to the making of secondary rules. Article 145 was not materially altered save for being renumbered Article 202 EC. The Treaty did, however, contain Declaration 31 requiring the Commission to submit a proposal for a revised Comitology Decision by 1998.

The passage of this Decision was difficult to say the least,[28] and was finally adopted in 1999.[29] The management and regulatory committee procedures were simplified to some degree.[30] There were efforts to make the system more accessible to the public.[31] The EP was accorded a greater role in the making of secondary rules than hitherto. It was given power concerning rules made pursuant to the regulatory procedure;[32] and more generally power to indicate by resolution that draft implementing measures, which had been submitted to a committee pursuant to a basic instrument adopted by co-decision, would exceed the implementing powers in that instrument.[33] The EP was also given a right to be informed by the Commission of committee proceedings, receive committee agendas, voting records, and draft measures submitted to the committees for implementation of primary law made under the co-decision procedure.[34] In an agreement made between the EP and the Commission,[35] the latter stated that it would also forward to the EP, at its request, specific draft measures for implementing basic instruments even if they were not adopted under co-decision, where they were of particular importance to the EP. The EP can moreover request access to minutes of committee meetings.[36]

The basic premise of Article 202 EC and Article 1 of the 1999 Comitology Decision is, as seen above, that the Council should grant implementing

[27] Craig, 'Democracy and Rulemaking within the EC: An Empirical and Normative Assessment' (1997) 3 *ELJ* 105.

[28] Bergstrom, *supra* n. 2, at 249–264.

[29] Council Decision 99/468/EC of 28 June 1999, Laying Down the Procedures for the Exercise of Implementing Powers Conferred on the Commission, OJ 1999 L184/23; Lenaerts and Verhoeven, 'Towards a Legal Framework for Executive Rule-Making in the EU? The Contribution of the New Comitology Decision' (2000) 37 *CMLRev* 645.

[30] Dec. 99/468, *supra* n. 29, Arts. 4–5.

[31] Ibid. Art. 7. The public can access certain comitology documents, see <http://europa.eu.int/comm/secretariat_general/regcomito/registre.cfm?CL=en>.

[32] Ibid. Art. 5(5). [33] Ibid. Art. 8. [34] Ibid. Art. 7(3).

[35] Agreement between the European Parliament and the Commission on Procedures for Implementing Council Decision 99/468/EC of 28 June 1999 Laying Down the Procedures for the Exercise of Implementing Powers by the Commission, OJ 2000 L256/19, at para. 2.

[36] Case T-188/97, *Rothmans v Commission* [1999] ECR II-2463.

power to the Commission, subject to the caveat that the Council can reserve implementing power to itself in certain specific cases. The ECJ is willing to review Commission claims that it should have been given implementing power in circumstances where the Council has reserved that power for itself. The Court will review the reasons given by the Council in this respect in the relevant regulations. The Commission nonetheless faces an uphill struggle on this issue. Thus in a recent case the ECJ acknowledged that the reasons given by the Council were 'general and laconic', but notwithstanding this the Court concluded that when they were assessed in their context they showed the rationale for reservation of implementing power to the Council.[37]

The ECJ is also willing to review the choice as between management and regulatory procedures in the 1999 Comitology Decision. It acknowledged that the criteria in Article 2 of this Decision were not formally binding, but held that where the Council and EP sought to depart from those criteria they had to provide reasons for doing so. The ECJ concluded that such reasons had not been given, that the imposition of the regulatory procedure was not therefore justified, and annulled the contested measure in this respect.[38]

F. The Nice Treaty and the Proposed Amendment to the Second Comitology Decision

The complex history of comitology continued after the Nice Treaty. The Commission accepted more formally than hitherto the force of the EP's objection to the existing Comitology Decision in circumstances where co-decision applied. This was the nub of its proposal for amending the Second Comitology Decision.[39] An amended version of the proposal is still being considered, although progress is uncertain.[40]

It is proposed that there should be a new Article 5a of Decision 1999/468, which modifies the regulatory procedure for basic instruments adopted under Article 251 EC of the Treaty. The Commission continues to be assisted by a regulatory committee made up of national representatives, and if the committee delivers a favourable opinion the Commission then adopts a final draft. If the opinion is not favourable or no opinion is delivered then the Commission prepares a modified draft taking account of the committee's view. The final draft is then sent to the EP and the Council. If they do not object it becomes law. If either institution objects the Commission has a number of options: modification of the draft, presentation of a proposal in

[37] Case C-257/01, *supra* n. 18, at para. 53. [38] Case C-378/00, *supra* n. 23.

[39] Proposal for a Council Decision Amending Decision 1999/468/EC Laying Down the Procedures for the Exercise of Implementing Powers Conferred on the Commission, COM(2002) 719 final, at 2.

[40] COM(2004) 324 final.

accord with Article 251, adoption of the original draft, or withdrawal of the draft measure.

The proposed amendment represents a compromise. The Council through its representatives on the regulatory committee is still in the driving seat and can influence the detail of the proposed measure. The EP, as well as the Council, is however accorded a formal right to object to the final draft produced by the Commission and the regulatory committee. The EP, however, objected strongly to the fact that it would still be open to the Commission to adopt the implementing measure, notwithstanding the fact that the EP had opposed it.[41] The Commission's more overall strategy in putting forward this proposal will become apparent in the light of the next section.

G. The Constitutional Treaty

It is very unlikely that the Constitutional Treaty will be ratified, given the negative results of the referenda in France and the Netherlands. The Constitutional Treaty (CT) is nonetheless still part of the 'story' of comitology, more especially because the solution embodied in the CT is one that the Commission still favours. It is likely that the Commission will continue to press for this approach, notwithstanding the fate of the CT, and this could well have significant consequences for the enactment of secondary measures and the role of comitology therein. It is therefore necessary to be cognizant of this approach and its possible implications for comitology.

The Commission has long desired to loosen the constraints imposed by comitology and to have greater autonomy over the passage of secondary rules. The Commission's strategy dating back at least to the IGC leading to the TEU[42] has been to propose a hierarchy of norms for the EU, with a distinction being drawn between primary laws, and secondary acts, the intent being to ensure that the Commission had greater autonomy over the passage of implementing measures. The nub of this strategy has been to accept constraints over secondary acts through the need to specify essential principles within the primary laws, combined with the possibility of recall by the Council or EP if they believe that the secondary act made by the Commission exceeds the powers granted. The Constitutional Treaty embodied a regime of this kind, which will be considered more fully below. It did not in terms say anything about comitology, but the Commission clearly hoped that the comitology constraints over the making of the secondary acts would be abolished or weakened as a result of the new hierarchy of norms.

This is readily apparent from the Commission's White Paper on *European*

[41] Bergstrom, *supra* n. 2, at 326–335. [42] Ibid. at 212–217.

Governance.[43] The key to the White Paper was the Commission's conception of the 'Community method',[44] with the Commission representing the general interest and the Council and the EP as the joint legislature, representing the Member States and national citizens respectively. This was in itself unexceptionable. It was the implications that the Commission drew from it that were contentious. It was, said the Commission, necessary to revitalize the Community method.[45] The Council and the EP should limit their involvement in primary Community legislation to defining the essential elements.[46] This legislation would define the conditions and limits within which the Commission performed its executive role. It would, in the Commission's view, make it possible to do away with the comitology committees, or to retain only advisory committees. There would instead be a simple legal mechanism allowing the Council and EP to control the actions of the Commission against the principles adopted in the legislation.

This general strategy for dealing with delegation was reiterated in a Commission paper in the run up to the Convention on the Future of Europe.[47] It is clear that the proposed amendment to the Second Comitology Decision considered in the previous section was expressly conceived by the Commission as a stopgap until the more far-reaching changes addressed in this section could be attained.[48] The possibility of enhancing the Commission's control over secondary acts by abolishing or amending the comitology procedure was raised again by the Working Group on Simplification.[49] The desirability of this 'solution' will be analysed below.

H. Three Approaches to Comitology

The discussion thus far has provided a brief overview of rule-making and comitology within the EU. The focus now shifts to evaluation. It is possible to view comitology from a variety of perspectives, which relate more broadly to different theories of the EU, realist, federalist, neo-functional, functional, and multi-level governance.[50] The ensuing analysis will not attempt to traverse all such views. It will rather consider three approaches to comitology, which are especially significant for the more general subject matter of this book.

[43] COM(2001) 428 final. The White Paper provoked a variety of critical comment, see the Symposium: Responses to the European Commission's White Paper on Governance, <http://www.jeanmonnetprogram.org/papers/01>.

[44] COM(2001) 428 final, at 8. [45] Ibid. at 29. [46] Ibid. at 20.

[47] Communication of the Commission on the Institutional Architecture, COM(2002) 728 final, at paras. 1.2, 1.3.4

[48] COM(2002) 719 final, *supra* n. 39, at 2.

[49] Final Report of Working Group IX on Simplification, CONV 424/02, Brussels 29 November 2002, at 12.

[50] Wessels, 'Comitology: Fusion in Action. Politico-administrative Trends in the EU System' (1998) 5 *JEPP* 209, at 211–218.

4. DELIBERATIVE SUPRANATIONALISM, RULE-MAKING, AND COMITOLOGY

A. The Thesis

The *modus operandi* of secondary rule-making in the EU and the role of committees therein has been the target of criticism, academically and politically, as will be apparent from the discussion within the following section. The opposing view should however be taken seriously, and will be examined here. This view has been propounded principally by Joerges and Neyer.[51] The essence of the argument is that rule-making subject to comitology is best viewed in terms of deliberative supranationalism, and that this perspective is more accurate than the hitherto prevailing views, which see comitology either in terms of intergovernmentalist bargain, or in terms of supranational administration.

The intergovernmental view of rule-making and comitology is premised on the Member States' awareness of the need to delegate power to the Commission, in order that desired Treaty imperatives can be met, with the equal desire to retain control over the detailed rules that emerge. The variants of committee procedure embodied in the Comitology Decision 1987 reflect, on this view, the capacity of the Member States to impose the degree of control over the details of rule-making that best suit their individual and collective interest. The advisory committee procedure thus places a high premium on getting things done, and a correspondingly low degree of Member State control, while at the other end of the scale the regulatory committee procedure, especially the *contre-filet* version thereof, places prime importance on Member State control even at the ultimate cost of preventing the emergence of an EU rule on the issue. The assumption is that decision-making within the committee system will operate similarly to that in the Council, with a strong emphasis on inter-state bargain, and Member State preferences being regarded as 'givens' in this process.

The supranational view of rule-making and comitology tells a different story. On this view 'it is not the Member States' interests which dominate European politics but rather European institutions which have the capacity to channel and influence Member States' interaction in a way which is compatible with European interests'.[52] This is said to follow from the

[51] See, e.g., Joerges and Neyer, 'From Intergovernmental Bargaining to Deliberative Political Processes: The Constitutionalization of Comitology' (1997) 3 *ELJ* 273; Neyer, 'The Comitology Challenge to Analytical Integration Theory', in Joerges and Vos (eds), *supra* n. 2, Chap. 12; Joerges, 'Good Governance through Comitology?', in Joerges and Vos (eds), *supra* n. 2, Chap. 17.

[52] Neyer, *supra* n. 51, at 222–223.

Commission's control over the flow of information, its setting of committee agendas, its role as chair of committees, and the limited time that national delegations have to respond to Commission proposals.

Joerges and Neyer regard both the intergovernmental and supranational view as too extreme, as 'understating the importance of discourse in facilitating social integration and lack the conceptual space for understanding that supranational preference generation is more than just a process of aggregating individual preferences'.[53] They argue that rule-making pursuant to comitology should be properly perceived as a deliberative discourse. On this view governments might be unaware of their own preferences on the particular detailed issue to be resolved, and the national delegates that take part in the committees will often regard themselves as part of a team dealing with a transnational problem. For advocates of deliberative supranationalism, national representatives shift to becoming representatives of a 'Europeanised interadministrative discourse that is characterized by mutual learning and by an understanding of each others' difficulties in the implementation of specific solutions'.[54]

Comitology is portrayed as a network of European and national actors, with the Commission acting as coordinator.[55] The national participants in the deliberative process are willing to call their own preferences into question in searching for a Community solution,[56] and this deliberative mode is said to be borne out by empirical study concerning the operation of comitology in regulating foodstuffs.[57] This deliberative politics must, for Joerges and Neyer, incorporate objective scientific and technical knowledge,[58] and they argue that ECJ jurisprudence imposes this obligation.[59] They are also willing to accept that the transparency of committee work could be enhanced, especially in the context of standardization, and that there might be some room for development of the duty to give reasons, although they are equivocal about the need for, or desirability of, an Administrative Procedure Act for the EU.

The thesis advanced by Joerges and Neyer is important and clearly articulated. There are nonetheless three aspects of the deliberative supranationalist thesis that are problematic to varying degrees and require more elaboration.

[53] Ibid. at 224. [54] Ibid. at 228. [55] Joerges, *supra* n. 51, at 318.
[56] Ibid. at 315. [57] Ibid. at 318–321. [58] Ibid. at 332–334.
[59] Bradley, 'Institutional Aspects of Comitology: Scenes from the Cutting Room Floor', in Jorges and Vos (eds), *supra* n. 2, at 79–83 was sceptical as to whether Case C-212/91, *Angelopharm v Freie und Hansestadt Hamburg* [1994] ECR I-171, at para. 33, really established the proposition for which Joerges and Neyer argued. The decisions in Case T-13/99, *Pfizer Animal Health SA v Council* [2002] ECR II-3305 and Cases T-74, 76, 83–85, 132, 137 and 141/00, *Artegodan GmbH v Commission* [2002] ECR II-4945 have however reinforced the requirement for scientific evidence, albeit distinguishing between the technical scientific component of a decision and the ultimate political determination, see below, at Chaps. 13, 19.

B. Deliberative Supranationalism and Consensual Deliberation

The first of these issues relates to the consensual nature of the deliberation that is said to characterize comitology deliberations. It is refreshing to see Community rule-making viewed in a positive light. Moreover the central kernel of the deliberative supranationalism thesis should not be readily dismissed. Those who serve on the committees overseeing the making of delegated rule-making may be Member State representatives, but they are also usually bureaucrats or technocrats with some degree of experience in the relevant area. They have not normally spent their lives as politicians. We should not therefore view with surprise or incredulity the claim that they bring to bear a deliberative perspective on the issues to be resolved, nor that they are willing to call their preferences into question. We should not regard it as implausible that the very nature of their individual preferences may be unclear at the outset, nor should we view the socializing impact of regular discourse with others from different national administrations dealing with the same problem as far-fetched.

We should nonetheless be mindful of the constraints on consensual deliberation. It is true that comitology committees rarely exercise their formal powers with the result that it is uncommon for a draft implementing regulation to be sent back to the Council.[60] This, however, tells one relatively little concerning the extent to which state interests constrained the nature and content of the relevant measure, in the same way that the scarcity in use of the Luxembourg veto in the Council tells one only so much about intergovernmental influences on decision-making during the relevant period. Comitology discussion in the shadow of formal powers vested in Member States' representatives can constrain the very nature of the proposal placed on the table and the way in which it is considered,[61] just as Council decision-making could be shaped by the shadow of the veto.

We should moreover, when evaluating the picture of consensual deliberation, not forget that the Commission is minded to weaken the constraints placed by comitology. Its top preference still seems to be that regulatory and management committees should be abolished in their present form and that only advisory committees would remain. The *quid pro quo* for this would be to accord the Council and EP with powers *ex ante* and *ex post* the drafting of the implementing regulation.[62] These suggestions will be considered in detail below. They are nonetheless salient for the present discussion. Such

[60] Wessels, *supra* n. 50, at 224–225; Dehousse, 'Comitology: Who Watches the Watchmen?' (2003) 10 *JEPP* 798, at 800.

[61] Wessels, *supra* n. 50, at 225.

[62] See above at 112–113, below at 124–125. See also, the Commission website at <http://europa.eu.int/comm/governance/governance_eu/comitology_en.htm>.

suggestions do not sit easily with a picture of comitology in which the preferences of national representatives are devoid of some real constraining impact on the content of the draft measures as desired by the Commission. If this were not so the Commission's desire to free itself of the existing institutional structure so that it could exercise its 'full executive autonomy' would not be readily explicable.

C. Deliberative Supranationalism and the European Parliament

A second issue is more problematic and concerns the relationship between rule-making and the EP. Joerges and Neyer are sceptical about the involvement of the EP with the process of delegated rule-making. The scepticism is in part conceptual and in part practical.

The conceptual argument as put by Neyer focuses on the 'no demos' thesis. The limits to the role of the EP in delegated rule-making are rationalized on the assumption that the principal task of the EU is to provide decision-making procedures which enable Member States to cope with problems caused by their economic interdependence by 'means of co-ordinating national policies in a way which is equally effective and respects basic requirements of legitimate governance'.[63] It is not 'about organising the self-governance of a (non-existent) European demos, but about coping with increasing transnational economic interdependence'. Thus 'supranational decision-making is not to be seen as a virtual democratic procedure, but rather as a more or less legitimate way of making collectively binding decisions among governmental actors'.[64]

This argument is not readily sustainable in the terms presented. It is based on the assumption that there is 'no demos' within the EU and it is premised on the assumption that a demos of the kind that exists within Member States is a condition precedent for thinking about the democratic facets of decision-making within the EU. Most important is that the argument proves too much. If it were true it would mean that the claims of the EP to partake in the passage of primary regulations or directives would be undermined: the no demos argument would deny the importance or relevance of the EP in the primary legislative process. Yet it cannot seriously be questioned that the advances made by the EP to a more co-equal role in the primary legislative process through the creation and expansion of co-decision are warranted on democratic grounds. Moreover, the very dividing line as to what is dealt with in primary and delegated regulations will often be fortuitous. It might be argued by way of response that there are practical reasons why the EP's rights cannot be extended to delegated rule-making, but then this ceases to be

[63] Neyer, *supra* n. 51, at 230.
[64] Ibid. at 231.

anything to do with the 'no demos' thesis. It becomes a pragmatic thesis, which must be assessed in these terms.

Joerges articulates the pragmatic argument. He accepts that the EP's claim, that the extension of its rights to partake in the primary legislative process should be mirrored by an extended role in secondary rule-making, may be convincing in principle, but contends that it is not realizable in practice. This is because the EP's committees do not have sufficient resources to engage in continuous supervision of the comitology committees.[65] The EP should instead concentrate its efforts on the procedural domain. It should require those directly involved in rule-making to abide by the deliberative quality of the decision-making process and use its limited resources to investigate particular rules that appear to be problematic.[66]

Joerges is clearly right to point to the practical problems of EP involvement in the making of secondary rules. We should not, however, so readily accept that these are insurmountable or that they serve to confine the EP to the procedural domain adumbrated above. The 'bottom line' is that secondary rules may well entail political choice and controversy every bit as real as in the case of primary legislation. We should therefore hesitate long and hard before concluding that a co-equal partner in the making of the primary legislation should have no substantive input into the making of secondary norms. We should hesitate long and hard before reaching this conclusion when the other co-equal partner in the making of the primary legislation, the Council, is accorded very full substantive involvement in this respect. And we should be equally wary of reaching this conclusion if we seriously wish to sustain the claim that the overall process comports with an ideal of deliberative supranationalism.[67]

We should remember in this respect that the EP makes a sustained and meaningful contribution to many primary regulations, with the relevant EP committee being in the front line. This is readily apparent when one considers the passage of measures through co-decision. It is of course the case that the number of delegated regulations exceeds that of primary norms, and that time can be especially significant in the case of the former. This does not, however, preclude EP involvement, although it will clearly affect its incidence. There are, however, a great many MEPs. It should therefore be within the realms of the possible for EP committees to take on board some measure of substantive scrutiny of delegated norms, if they have the political will to do so. It should also be possible for such committees to make best use of their resources, and cope with the exigencies of time, by concentrating their efforts

[65] Joerges, *supra* n. 51, at 327. [66] Ibid. at 328.

[67] It may of course be argued that comitology committees should be abolished and that therefore neither the Council nor the EP would be involved in the detail of rulemaking of the kind that has existed hitherto. This suggestion will be considered below, at 124–134, 140–142.

on those delegated norms that are more controversial. This would not preclude a call back power of the kind contained in the Constitutional Treaty. The nature of this power will be analysed below. Suffice it to say for the present that meaningful exercise of such a power is itself dependent on an understanding of the delegated measure in question. It is difficult to see how the EP can gain this if the EP committee most involved with the subject matter does not understand the forces and considerations that shaped the measure.

D. Deliberative Supranationalism and Participatory Rights

The other aspect of the thesis that is contentious concerns the relationship between deliberation through committees and participatory rights to be exercised by interested members of the body politic. Joerges is on the whole reluctant to pursue this line. He acknowledges that in areas such as risk regulation where the relevant matter cannot be decided by the legislature *ex ante* 'the opening up of decision-making procedures to representatives of social interests is an obvious response to the perception that there are dimensions to the problem of risk assessment which, in view of their practical normative content, ought not to be delegated to expert bodies no matter how technically competent they may be'.[68] Joerges does not, however, favour this approach, at least not in the context of risk regulation. This is in part because of the 'cognitive content' of such rules, with the consequence that the 'correctness of risk decisions cannot be guaranteed by unmediated recourse to interests or their negotiation'.[69] It is in part because the identification of 'interests' at the European level to whom participation rights would be extended is felt to be inconceivable. And it is in part because it is felt that by virtue of feedback links to the Member States comitology can take all social concerns and interests into account. Attention should therefore be focused on ensuring deliberative decision-making among the established state representatives, rather than extending the range of interests involved.[70] Joerges does, however, appear to favour the extension of participatory rights in the context of technical standardization, as opposed to risk regulation.[71]

This argument is presented forcefully. It is, however, problematic. There is an abundance of literature that attests to the fact that risk regulation is not purely scientific, but involves social and political choice in circumstances

[68] Joerges, *supra* n. 51, at 334.

[69] Ibid. at 334; Joerges, 'Deliberative Supranationalism—Two Defences' (2002) 8 *ELJ* 133, at 145.

[70] Joerges, *supra* n. 51, at 334; Joerges, *supra* n. 69, at 150–1.

[71] Joerges, *supra* n. 51, at 335.

where the scientific evidence may be equivocal.[72] The extension of participatory rights cannot therefore be rejected on the ground that these are matters of pure science. Joerges is ambivalent in this respect. He recognizes that regulatory policy is dependent on expert knowledge that is often 'fragmentary and controversial', and that experts themselves 'must pursue practical and normative discourses and cannot supply the bodies dependent on their advice with objective truths'.[73] Joerges, however, also maintains that the expert's knowledge cannot be substituted or overruled by the preferences of the layman and that expert knowledge should rather be subject to critical scrutiny from experts who hold a different opinion.[74] Those who advocate increased participation rights emphasize, however, the very fact that technical expertise cannot readily be disaggregated from social and political choice. They stress moreover that insofar as it is possible to separate 'pure expertise', comitology is deficient in limiting the provision of that expertise to the national representatives on the relevant committee, providing no ready mechanism whereby other interest groups that may well have considerable expert knowledge can present their arguments. The provision of such expertise is indeed one of the very rationales for the existence of interest groups, which are able through collective organization to muster the skills and resources that are beyond the scope of most individuals.

The argument for such participatory rights is not premised on the assumption that the outcome of risk regulation in a particular instance should be determined by the 'unmediated recourse' to such interests. The issue is whether such interests should be able to have input into the rule-making process, not that they should be determinative in and of themselves. Nor is the argument for such rights premised on the assumption that there are identifiable, in the sense of quasi-official, representatives of European interests 'out there'. It is based rather on the existence of a plurality of interests with a strong concern relating to the subject matter of the regulation and such interests may well have expertise in the relevant area. The idea that these varying concerns can be adequately captured through feedback links to Member States operating via comitology is itself based on an idealized vision of the way in which and degree to which Member State representatives on committees are informed of and represent the plethora of views within their

[72] See, e.g., Jasanoff, 'Science and the Limits of Administrative Rule Making: Lessons from the OSHA Cancer Policy' (1982) 20 *Osgoode Hall LJ* 536; S. Jasanoff, *The Fifth Branch: Science Advisers as Policy Makers* (Harvard University Press, 1990); S. Jasanoff, *Science at the Bar: Law, Science and Technology in America* (Harvard University Press, 1995); U. Beck, *The Risk Society* (Sage, 1992); W. Leiss and C. Chociolko (eds), *Risk and Responsibility* (McGill-Queen's University Press, 1992).

[73] Joerges, *supra* n. 69, at 147.

[74] Ibid. at 145.

home state. It is belied by the very call for increased participation rights in rule-making within national polities.[75]

It is moreover doubtful whether in the long run one can continue to advocate, as Joerges does, increased provision for reason giving, while at the same time resisting extension of participation rights. There is at the very least a tension in this respect, since, as Shapiro has noted, there is a proximate connection between reason giving and the demand for participation and dialogue.[76] This is not to say that the creation of a European APA would be unproblematic, as will be seen below. The point being made here is a narrower one: it is that the arguments advanced against participation rights by Joerges are problematic in their own terms.

The very ideal of deliberative supranationalism which limits or excludes input from either the EP or affected interests must be counted as an attenuated one. The 'distance' between the concept of deliberative supranationalism cast principally in terms of technocratic interaction and the broader meaning accorded to deliberative democracy in the literature has been a more general focus of criticism of the thesis advanced by Joerges and Neyer.[77]

5. TECHNOCRACY, RULE-MAKING, AND COMITOLOGY

Rule-making in the EU and the role of committees therein is, as stated above, a subject on which views differ sharply. There is a vein in the literature that has not looked so kindly as Joerges and Neyer on EU practice. Thus Wessels, while acknowledging that comitology daily routine is based on technical expertise and characterized by camaraderie,[78] highlights concerns with the overall process.[79]

If the European network reflects another and perhaps especially successful attempt of administrations to follow the basic inbuilt instinct of gaining autonomy from their political 'masters', the phenomena we observe would indicate a major move to a new European version of a technocracy, or a *Verwaltungstaat* (administrative state). 'Comrades' in attitudes from 'Bureaus' of several levels use their EU bodies to emancipate themselves as a group from political (in other words democratic) control; this also explains the unsuccessful attempts made by the European Parliament to gain access. The closed clubs with their technical language, their intrinsic procedures and

[75] P. Craig, *Administrative Law* (Sweet & Maxwell, 5th ed., 2003), Chap. 12; T. Ziamou, *Rulemaking, Participation and the Limits of Public Law in the USA and Europe* (Ashgate, 2001).

[76] Shapiro, 'The Giving Reasons Requirement' (1992) *U Chic Legal Forum* 179.

[77] See Joerges, *supra* n. 69, for a response.

[78] Wessels, *supra* n. 50. More generally Wessels sees comitology in terms of the increasing fusion between national and EU administration, at 216–218, 227–228.

[79] Wessels, 'Comitology as a Research Subject: A New Legitimacy Mix?', in Joerges and Vos (eds), *supra* n. 2, at 265.

informal rules are not an example of deliberative democracy, but an immunisation against outside interference; the propensity to transform so called 'political issues' into administrative problems (a major feature of *Verwaltungstaat*) is legitimised both in terms of functional necessity, procedural efficiency and instrumental effectiveness and—in the specific constellation of EU committees—also for the sake of 'Europe' and for guaranteeing positive relations among Member States. In this view the state, especially its features as a 'national' and 'constitutional' entity, is eroded and replaced by a mere bureaucratic set up hidden behind the illusion of ongoing national control. Without realising it, national governments do allow their own administrations to 'usurp' their traditional legitimacy. The counter-bureaucracy established to control . . . the Commission merges with their colleagues from a European level. The intergovernmental strategy of keeping the Member States as 'Masters of the Treaty' backfires by its very procedures.

Similar concerns are apparent in the work of other writers, albeit with varying degrees of force. Thus Harlow comments that committees, in common with agencies and regulators, may acquire a life of their own. This may lead to 'illegitimate policy-making for which they need to be held accountable, or it may involve a form of "agency capture", whereby the committee falls into the hands of an industry or group of experts'.[80] She acknowledges that while steps have been taken to render comitology more accountable, 'these are by no means completed, nor are they adequate'.[81]

Dehousse accepts that comitology should be regarded as a natural development within a system of two-tiered government, more especially when there is decentralized implementation of rules adopted at a central level, and he also acknowledges that serious conflicts are rare.[82] He recognizes that the shift from 'primary' legislative activity towards secondary rulemaking means, however, that a 'growing number of salient political issues are likely to arise in the post-legislative phase, be it in rule-making or in the concrete application of Community rules'.[83] The comitology system through which such rules are made is regarded as problematic in terms of its opacity, and because 'while scientific experts may derive some authority from their technical knowledge, bureaucrats are the focus of widespread mistrust in European countries'.[84] While expert involvement in decision-making may be inevitable, there is a real reluctance to give technocrats *carte blanche*.[85]

Weiler's view is nuanced. He acknowledges the importance of Joerges and Neyer's insights, in particular in regard to the deliberative style of

[80] C. Harlow, *Accountability in the European Union* (Oxford University Press, 2002), at 175.

[81] Ibid. at 175.

[82] Dehousse, 'Towards a Regulation of Transnational Governance? Citizen's Rights and the Reform of Comitology Procedures', in Joerges and Vos (eds), *supra* n. 2, at 111.

[83] Ibid. at 114. [84] Ibid. at 114.

[85] Ibid. at 116. See also, Dehousse, *supra* n. 60.

comitology, and the search for solutions that transcend purely national interests.[86] Weiler is nonetheless troubled by the decisional autonomy of comitology. The Commission and the Council may both regard the committees as their agents, whereas the reality is that the committees 'have long lost their allegiance to their controllers and work very much within their own universe for what they perceive to be their function and task'.[87] Weiler argues that the problem has been exacerbated to some degree by the ECJ's jurisprudence, with its insistence on boundaries in the exercise of power into which committees must be neatly fitted. This serves to privilege the formal actors, viz the Commission and the Council, and to conceal the problems of comitology that flow from unequal access and privileged sectoral influence. Moreover since the Court is forced to believe in the constitutional syntax that it has applied to comitology, to the effect that committees do not exercise discretionary political power, it gives them a 'clear constitutional bill of health',[88] thereby diverting attention from the fact that 'committees *do* exercise considerable political and policy discretion without adequate political accountability'.[89]

Weiler also has concerns relating to the committee system and democracy, notwithstanding his basic agreement with Joerges and Neyer that such committees function in a deliberative manner. Thus Weiler points out that committee members may be unaware of 'the profound political and moral choices involved in their determinations and of their shared biases',[90] and that the shared understandings that prevail between the committee members may mean that 'moral premises are presumed but not discussed'.[91] He points also to a real tension between the deliberative aspects of comitology and democratic precepts.[92]

> Finally there is the issue of equality of access. One cannot, in the analytic mode, explain Comitology as a deliberative network, which inevitably suggests that some interests are included and some are excluded and, in the normative mode, not acknowledge that this is a major problem for democracy. Equally, one cannot affirm that this is a problem for democracy and thus endorse proposals which would ensure transparency, openness and equal access, and not acknowledge that such proposals, if they are to be efficient, would destroy, or at least seriously compromise, the conditions which enable a deliberative process.

The scholars discussed in this section all express disquiet in varying degree with the status quo, but they are not uniform in their view. It follows that their prescriptions as to the desirable path of reform also vary. The ensuing

[86] Weiler, 'Epilogue: "Comitology" as Revolution—Infranationalism, Constitutionalism and Democracy', in Joerges and Vos (eds), *supra* n. 2, at 347.
[87] Ibid. at 342. [88] Ibid. at 345. [89] Ibid. at 345. Italics in the original.
[90] Ibid. at 348. [91] Ibid. at 349. [92] Ibid. at 349.

analysis will not therefore necessarily be in accord with their individual ideas as to reform. The discussion seeks nonetheless to canvass the range of available options. This will be undertaken after we have considered the approach embodied in the Constitutional Treaty.

6. A HIERARCHY OF NORMS, CONTROLS, AND COMITOLOGY

A. A Constitutional Hierarchy of Norms

It is for the reasons given earlier very unlikely that the Constitutional Treaty will enter into force. It is nonetheless clear that the Commission would like to reform comitology. Its preference is for a system in which committees play only an advisory role, with the consequential demise of management and regulatory committees. The *quid pro quo* for this reduction of direct Member State influence over the content of the implementing measures is the creation of *ex ante* and *ex post facto* controls over such measures that can be exercised by the Council and the EP. The Commission hoped that the Council would then be willing to accept the radical downgrading of the committees' role. The Constitutional Treaty gives us an idea of what such a system might look like. It is therefore worth considering this approach to the problem of secondary norms even though the Constitutional Treaty will not come into force, since such an approach still appears to be the Commission's preferred solution and hence may figure in future reforms.

The provisions concerning the hierarchy of norms were set out in Title V of Part I of the Constitution, entitled 'Exercise of Union Competence'. The foundational provision was Article I–33(1). It provided that in exercising the competences conferred on it by the Constitution, the Union should use as legal instruments European laws, European framework laws, European regulations, European decisions, recommendations, and opinions.[93]

The Constitution specified two types of *legislative act*, European laws and European framework laws, Article I–33(1). A European law was a legislative act of general application, which was binding in its entirety and directly applicable in all Member States. This corresponds to a regulation within the present system. A European framework law was a legislative act binding as to the result to be achieved on the Member States to which it was addressed, but

[93] Art. I–38(1) CT stipulated that the choice as between these measures should be in accordance with the principle of proportionality, and Art. I–38(2) CT imposed a duty to give reasons when making any of these Union acts.

left the national authority choice as to the form and means of achieving the result. A European framework law corresponded therefore to a directive in the present system.

Article I–33(1) also provided for what were termed *non-legislative acts*. A European regulation was a non-legislative act of general application for the implementation of legislative acts and certain specific provisions of the Constitution. It could either be binding in its entirety and directly applicable in all Member States, or be binding as regards the result to be achieved, on all the Member States to which it was addressed, but leaving the national authorities the choice of form and methods of achieving that result. The Constitution therefore in effect provided for secondary European laws and secondary European framework laws. Article I–33(1) also specified a category of European decisions, which were non-legislative acts that are binding in their entirety. Where the decision specified those to whom it was addressed it was binding only on them.

The Constitution specified the way in which non-legislative acts were to be made. Article I–35 stipulated that the Council and the Commission should adopt European regulations and decisions in the cases referred to in Articles I–36 and 37 and in cases specifically laid down in the Constitution. Article I–36 was entitled 'Delegated European Regulations'.

It provided, in Article I–36(1), that European laws and framework laws could delegate to the Commission the power to enact delegated regulations to 'supplement or amend certain non-essential elements of the law or framework law'. The objectives, content, scope, and duration of the delegation should be explicitly defined in the European laws and framework laws. The delegation could not cover the essential elements in the area, which had to be reserved for the law or framework law.

Article I–36(2) specified further that the conditions to which the delegation was subject *should* be determined in the law or framework law, and that these *might* consist of the following possibilities: the European Parliament or the Council might decide to revoke the delegation; or the delegated regulation might enter into force only if no objection had been expressed by the European Parliament or the Council within a period set by the law or framework law.

The Constitutional Treaty also made provision in Article I–37 for *implementing acts*. This Article imposed an obligation on Member States to adopt all measures of national law necessary to implement legally binding Union acts. It also empowered the Commission. Implementing acts could take the form of European implementing regulations or European implementing decisions. Where uniform conditions were required for implementing binding Union acts, those acts could confer implementing powers on the Commission, or in specific cases concerned with common foreign and security policy, on the Council. The precise circumstances where such a power would be needed were however by no means clear.[94] European laws should lay down in advance rules and general principles for the mechanisms of control by Member States over implementing acts of the Union.[95]

B. Regulations, Delegated Regulations, and Implementing Acts

This chapter is concerned with secondary or implementing rules and the discussion will therefore concentrate on the impact of the constitutional schema for 'non-legislative' acts. It can be readily accepted that a modern polity should be able to create norms other than primary laws. It can be accepted also that the Constitution did a valuable service in distinguishing between primary laws and secondary norms. There were nonetheless a number of difficulties with these provisions.

(1) Regulations, Delegated Regulations, and Comitology

It should be recognized at the outset that the depiction of European regulations as being non-legislative was misleading. These acts were only non-legislative in the formal sense that they were not primary laws: they were not European laws or European framework laws. This did not mean that they were not legislative in nature. They clearly were, and this conclusion was reinforced by the fact that they were said to be of general application, that they could supplement or amend certain elements of primary law, and because there was a separate provision dealing with administrative decisions. The reality was therefore that a European regulation would often be what would be regarded in domestic legal systems as secondary or delegated legislation. It is interesting to contrast the label attached to European regulations in the Constitution, with the Working Group's more honest depiction of these acts as a category of legislation.[96]

The depiction in the Constitutional Treaty of European regulations as non-legislative acts served, whether intentionally or not, to dispel fears that the Commission would be making legislative choices of its own volition. The combination of greater use of less detailed primary laws, and increased Commission control over delegated norms, would significantly alter the institutional balance of power in the Community by reducing the power of the Council and EP, and increasing that of the Commission.

The category of delegated regulation would so it seemed fill the 'space' presently occupied by regulations made pursuant to the comitology procedure. The Commission hoped that the delegated regulations thus made

[94] Craig, 'The Hierarchy of Norms', in T. Tridimas and P. Nebbia (eds), *European Law for the Twenty-First Century, Rethinking the New Legal Order, Volume 1* (Hart, 2004), Chap. 5.

[95] Art. I–37(3).

[96] Final Report of Working Group IX, *supra* n. 49, at 8.

would be largely freed from the current committee procedures, and that the Council and EP would be content with the framework of controls over delegated regulations set out in Article I–36.

The intention underlying this part of the CT seemed to be that comitology would apply to implementing acts, where, as we shall see, mention was specifically made of mechanisms for Member State control over implementing acts, but not to delegated regulations. It is however open to question whether Article I–36(2) would as a matter of strict law have rendered it impossible to use comitology as presently conceived in relation to delegated regulations.

It could be argued that the only conditions that could be attached to a delegated regulation were those specified, revocation of the delegation and objection to the passage of a particular delegated regulation. It could alternatively be contended that the wording of Article I–36(2), which stated that the 'conditions may be as follows', left open the possibility that other conditions could be imposed. Another way of reaching the same conclusion would be to contend that a comitology committee might be regarded as part of the mechanism through which the Council or EP decided whether to exercise their power to object to a particular delegated regulation, rather than as a free-standing condition independent of those listed in Article I–36(2).

(2) Delegated Regulations, Implementing Acts, and Comitology

The schema concerning the hierarchy of norms in the CT was also confusing because of ambiguities that beset the relationship between delegated regulations and implementing acts.

The ambiguity was most pronounced in relation to the meaning of the word implementation. Implementation can bear the meaning that it has in the current Article 202 EC: delegated rule-making or decision-making subject to comitology conditions. Implementation can also mean the execution of other norms, whether Treaty provisions, primary laws, or delegated regulations: the relevant norm will be applied or executed, but without any supplementation or amendment.

The comitology procedure has hitherto applied to implementation in the first of these senses: it was the condition attached to delegated rule-making or decision-making by the Commission. The discussion in the Convention on the Future of Europe revealed an important shift in thought. The comitology procedures were not mentioned in relation to the making of delegated regulations, even though this was the true analogy with the status quo, the implication being that they would be replaced by the controls in Article I–36(2), although as seen above it is open to question whether that Article would have precluded recourse to comitology-type procedures. The Convention documentation considered the legitimacy of comitology primarily in the context of implementing acts covered by Article I–37, where the emphasis was on implementation in its second sense, as execution or application.

This was apparent in the literature from the Working Group.[97] It was apparent again in the Convention comments on Article I–37(3), which provision allowed for Member State control over implementing acts.[98] The Praesidium stated that several amendments were opposed to the current committee mechanisms, and wished to delete this Article, while other comments proposed confining the control mechanisms to advisory committees alone. The Praesidium considered that this was a matter for secondary legislation and therefore did not amend the Article. The assumption was therefore that in the future comitology would be relevant only in the context of implementing acts, and not in relation to delegated regulations, even though this was in stark contrast to the circumstances where comitology is currently used.

C. The Effectiveness of the Controls over Delegated Regulations

The controls over delegated regulations set out in Article I–36 operated in a number of different ways, two of which can be distinguished for present purposes.

(1) Control Ex Ante

The first species of control was *ex ante.* Article I–36(1) stated that the delegated regulation could only amend or supplement 'certain non-essential elements of the law or framework law', and could not cover the 'essential elements of an area'. These had to be reserved for the European law or framework law, which should also explicitly specify the 'objectives, content, scope and duration of the delegation'.

It would however often be difficult for the Council and the EP to specify with exactitude in the primary law or framework law the criteria that should guide the exercise of delegated power by the Commission. The Council and the EP would often have neither the knowledge, nor the time to delineate in the primary law the precise parameters for the exercise of regulatory choices. The real issues about the assignment of such risks might only be apparent when the matter was examined in detail. It was for these very reasons that the comitology process was first created. It would therefore not be easy for the primary law to define with precision the 'objectives, content, scope and duration' of the delegation.

[97] Final Report of Working Group IX on Simplification, CONV 424/02, Brussels 29 November 2002, at 9.

[98] CONV 724/03, Annex 2, at 94.

If these requirements were to be taken seriously there would have to be oversight by, *inter alia*, the Community courts. They would have to enforce a non-delegation doctrine, striking down delegations where the primary law or framework law was insufficiently precise about the 'essential elements of an area', or about the 'objectives, content, scope and duration' of the delegation. It is uncertain whether the Community courts would be willing to do this with vigour. The indications from the ECJ's previous jurisprudence are not encouraging in this respect. The Court has hitherto generally resisted claims that implementing regulations made pursuant to comitology should be struck down on this ground. It has been willing to define the essential elements that must be specified in the primary law rather loosely, thereby according a broad remit for implementing regulations made thereunder.[99]

The ECJ might of course have chosen to read the requirement that the primary law should specify the 'essential elements' more strictly than hitherto. It is however relatively clear that even if it did so regulatory power would still be delegated to the Commission concerning inherently political matters such as the assignment of risk, or the specification of liability rules as between the Community and the Member States in the context of shared administration. Experience from other legal systems concerning the non-delegation doctrine has been mixed. In the USA it has, for example, provided little by way of control of regulatory choices accorded to agencies,[100] although it, or its equivalent, has however been applied with more rigour in some Continental legal systems.

(2) Control Ex Post

The second type of control was *ex post.* Article I–36(2) stated that the conditions of application to which the delegation was subject 'should' be explicitly determined in the law or framework law. These conditions 'might' entail the possibility of revocation of the delegation by the EP or the Council, or a condition whereby the delegated regulation entered into force only if there was no objection expressed by the EP or the Council within a specified period of time. These controls were important. They should form part of any regime whereby power is delegated to a body such as the Commission. The real issue is how effective they would be. There are two considerations to be borne in mind in this respect.

It should be recognized that these controls were not mandatory in the Constitutional Treaty: the European law or framework law had to specify the

[99] *Supra* n. 24.

[100] A.C. Aman and W.T. Mayton, *Administrative Law* (West, 2nd ed., 2001), Chap. 1; J.M. Rogers, M.P. Healy, and R. J. Krotoszynski, *Administrative Law* (Aspen Publishers, 2003), at 312–345.

conditions attached to the delegation, and these might consist of revocation of the delegation or prevention of entry into force of the delegated regulation. The wording of Article I–36(2) was consciously altered in this regard to make it clear that 'these conditions do not constitute a mandatory element of such a law or framework law'.[101]

The effectiveness of controls such as those embodied in Article I–36(2) would also be dependent upon the willingness of the Council or EP to use them. Revocation of the delegation might be useful as an ultimate weapon, but it is ill-suited by its very nature to fine-tuned control over the content of particular delegated regulations. This can only be achieved by recourse to the other control specified, the prevention of entry into force of a delegated regulation to which the EP or Council objected. The exercise of this power is however crucially dependent on knowledge and understanding of the relevant measure. Neither the Council nor the EP will be in a position to decide whether to object to the measure unless they understand its content and implications. The Member State representatives on the Council clearly have neither the time nor expertise to perform this task unaided. The committees of the EP might develop such expertise, but have not yet done so in a sustained and systematic manner across all areas of EU law. These difficulties would be more pronounced given that the EP and Council would have to raise any such objection within a period specified by the primary law. The period would vary depending on the area, but it would probably have been relatively short.[102] The Council and EP would therefore have to 'get their act together' pretty quickly if either institution sought to prevent the delegated regulation becoming law.

The ghost hovering in the background of this particular discourse is of course comitology, and the informational regime it embodied. The Council has been able to rely on the expertise of these committees in deciding whether to exercise the controls provided by the management and regulatory procedures. The EP has, under the 1999 Comitology Decision, some substantive and procedural rights, enabling it to 'tap into' the committee's expertise.[103] We have, however, seen that the Commission's hope was that the new constitutional regime contained in Article I–36 would result in the dismantling of comitology, or at the least a radical weakening of the existing committee structure. The possibility of this occurring will be considered below, as will its desirability.

Suffice it to say for the present, that comitology provided for generalized

[101] CONV 724/03, Annex 2, at 93.

[102] Thus the proposed amendment to the Second Comitology Decision, *supra* n. 40, specified a period of one month, capable of extension by a further month, in which the Council or EP could object to the final draft of an implementing measure, and this was of course premised on the continued existence of comitology committees.

[103] *Supra* n. 29, Arts. 5(5), 7(3), 8.

and detailed input into the making and content of the delegated norms, with the possibility of formal recourse to the Council, plus some control by the EP. The system embodied in the CT was based on specification of standards in the primary law, combined with the possibility of some control should the draft measure not be to the liking of the EP or Council. Suffice it to say also that if comitology were dismantled, and if no other regime were put in place whereby the Council and the EP could become informed about the complex regulatory choices contained in delegated regulations, then it is difficult to see how they would be able to make an informed choice as to whether to object to any such measure.

It would of course be possible that the Member States might decide quietly to acquiesce in the dismantling of comitology if such a regime as that contained in Article I–36 were introduced, notwithstanding its limitations. They would, on this view, forbear from regularized input into the making of delegated regulations, relying instead on the specification of the essentials in the primary law, combined with the power to revoke the delegation and the power to prevent a particular delegated regulation from entering into force. They might accept this modus operandi, but then again they might not. The Member States have been wedded to the committee system for over 40 years. Committees have continued to be attached to all important primary regulations and directives and it is doubtful whether the Council would readily acquiesce in their removal, or in the downgrading of committees so that they were simply advisory in nature. This is more especially so if there is 'interpretative doubt', as there is in relation to Article I–36, as to whether such committees can be used.

7. RULE-MAKING, DEMOCRACY, AND EFFICIENCY

The need for rule-making/delegated regulation will not disappear. The reasons for the prevalence of such norms that were set out above have continuing force. It is therefore important to stand back and consider what a principled solution might look like that fits the institutional structure and mode of operation of the EU. In searching for such a solution we can draw on ideas from the CT, without the need to embrace them in their entirety.

A. Legislative Mandate and Control: Legitimation from the Top

There is an important role for legitimation from the top via legislative specification of the essential principles that should govern an area. There is equally little doubt that this mode of control can only take one so far for the very reasons highlighted in the preceding discussion. The limits of legislative specification flow from constraints based on knowledge, time, and foresight.

These constraints will be especially problematic in relation to technical issues of risk regulation, but they will be equally present in relation to matters such as the detailed delineation of responsibilities of Commission and Member States for the prevention of fraud in the CAP and Structural Funds. The ECJ has thus far done little to instil substance to the legislative specification of essentials.[104] These difficulties will be exacerbated if the Commission's desire that primary regulations should be more general and less detailed becomes a reality. The more general is the primary regulation, the more abstract will be the essential principles embodied therein.

The previous discussion has also considered the limitations on the methods of control of the kind set out in Article I–36(2). The revocation of the entire delegation is a blunt tool inherently ill-suited to the control over particular delegated regulations. The prevention of entry into force of a particular delegated regulation is a more fine-tuned mode of control, but its use is dependent on knowledge of the area in question and an understanding of the issues raised by the particular measure, especially given that the control will have to be exercised within a limited time frame. These considerations would be all the more pressing if the comitology committees were abolished or radically downgraded, since it would deprive the Council and to some extent the EP of the current informational regime.

B. Legislative Mandate, Control, and Committees: Legitimation from the Top

The controls considered above are therefore important, but are unlikely to suffice. We should therefore consider the possibility of combining a structure such as that laid down in Article I–36 with some form of committee scrutiny. This choice of words is intended: committee scrutiny does not have to replicate the existing regime. There are indeed strong arguments of principle as to why it should not do so. The Council and EP are effectively joint legislators in the many areas where co-decision applies. Given that this is so, it is difficult in terms of principle to see why one constituent part of the legislature, the Council, should continue to have such a predominant role in the making of secondary norms.

This does not, however, mean that all forms of committee scrutiny should be abandoned. This is especially so given the limitations of the controls examined in the previous section. Consider the following two options. There could be substantive scrutiny by the relevant EP committee, and by a committee representing Member State interests. Such committees would inform the EP and Council respectively whether to use their powers to block a particular delegated regulation, but would not play a formal role in the

[104] *Supra* n. 24.

framing of the delegated regulation. It would, alternatively, be possible to conceive of a single committee for the relevant subject matter that would have representatives of Member States and the EP, which committee would function as a comitology committee in the sense that it would play an integral role in the drafting of the delegated regulation. The voting rules could be so devised as to enable the draft measure to be referred back to either the EP or the Council if a stipulated number of the members representing either institution rejected the draft. It is perfectly possible that such a 'joint committee' would operate in the deliberative manner characteristic of comitology committees hitherto. The fact that it would contain politicians does not mean that it would divide along party lines, or that it would resolve matters through bargain based on pre-existing preferences.

It might be argued that such arrangements are wrong in principle, and that the Commission should have the autonomy over the passage of delegated regulations that it has always sought, on the ground that this is part of its 'executive' function. This argument is however tendentious. It provides no explanation as to why the making of detailed political choices in delegated regulations that are legislative in nature should not be subject to the kind of legislative oversight that cannot be provided by the Council or EP acting in their plenary capacities, but can be attained in some degree through committee scrutiny. It furnishes no rationale as to why the making of such political choices should be conceived as part of the executive's autonomous role, more especially when the Commission is largely unelected.

It might equally be maintained that committee scrutiny of the kind envisaged would be impractical. This is by no means self-evident. The reality is that even if comitology in its present form were abolished, and replaced by mechanisms analogous to those in Article I–36 of the Constitutional Treaty, the Council and the EP would have to develop some committee mechanisms if they were to be able to make reasoned exercise of their power to reject a delegated regulation.

In relation to the Council, if the existing committees were abolished then it can be predicted that new ones would spring up to advise the relevant Council formation about the desirability of a delegated regulation. If alternatively the comitology committees were downgraded to become merely advisory in nature then they would likewise operate to guide the Council formation as to whether to object to a delegated regulation. The Commission would perforce have to take the views of such a body seriously if and when it becomes clear that the Council rejects such regulations that the committee regards negatively.

In relation to the EP, there is, as mentioned earlier, no reason why the EP's committees should not exercise substantive scrutiny of delegated regulations in a systematic or even selective manner. They have the numbers to do so. The committees already possess considerable expertise in their respective areas. If the political will is lacking then that is matter for the EP to address: it can scarcely argue about exclusion from the making of secondary norms while at the same time declining to put in the effort necessary for it to have a real role in the area. Moreover, as with the Council, so too with the EP, it will have to deploy committees systematically if it is to make reasoned use of its power of rejection of a delegated regulation.

C. Participation Rights: Legitimation from the Bottom

A common refrain in this area is that participation rights can alleviate to some degree the problems attendant upon comitology. We should be mindful, as Weiler notes, of imagining that an American-style Administrative Procedure Act can readily be transplanted to the EU.[105] We should however be equally wary of dismissing such solutions too readily. The issue should be considered from both a legal and political perspective.

(1) The Legal and Political Status Quo

In legal terms,[106] it is true that the Court has been willing to accord standing in areas such as competition and state aids where the applicant was afforded a role in the initial decision-making of, or complaint to, the Commission.[107] The ECJ's general approach has, however, been to resist a connection between the *fact* of participation in the making of a legislative measure and standing. Such participation does not lead to standing where the relevant Treaty article fails to provide for any intervention *rights* in the making of the original measure.[108] The ECJ has also resisted the grant of any general right to be heard before the adoption of Community legislation. Where a Community act is based on a Treaty article the only obligations to consult are those laid down in that article.[109]

In political terms,[110] the high point for the possible development of participation rights was the European Council's 1993 Inter-institutional Declaration on Democracy, Transparency, and Subsidiarity. This laid the

[105] Weiler, *supra* n. 86, at 347. [106] See below, Chap. 10.

[107] See, e.g., Case 26/76, *Metro-SB-Groβmärkte GmbH & Co KG v Commission* [1977] ECR 1875; Case 169/84, *Compagnie Francaise de l'Azote (COFAZ) SA v Commission* [1986] ECR 391; Case T-37/92, *Bureau Européen des Unions des Consommateurs v Commission* [1994] ECR II-285.

[108] Case T-99/94, *Asociacion Espanalo de Empresas de la Carne (ASOCARNE) v Council* [1994] ECR II-871, upheld on appeal Case C-10/95 P, [1995] ECR I-4149; Case T-135/96, *UEAPME v Council* [1998] ECR II-2335, at para. 63; Case T-585/93, *Stichting Greenpeace Council (Greenpeace International) v Commission* [1995] ECR II-2205.

[109] Case C-104/97 P, *Atlanta AG v European Community* [1999] ECR I-6983, at paras. 31–40.

[110] See below, Chap. 10.

foundation for greater access to Community documentation. It also proposed the creation of a notification procedure, in which the Commission would publish a brief summary of the draft measure in the Official Journal. There would then be a deadline by which interested parties could submit their comments. The implications of this reform could have been far-reaching. There is a clear analogy between this formulation and the United States' Administrative Procedure Act 1946 (APA). The APA established a notice and comment procedure whereby rules have to be published in the Federal Register, and the agency has to allow a period of time for notice and comment. The 1993 Declaration appeared to borrow directly from the American experience. The Commission's response to this aspect of the 1993 Declaration was, however, limited. It did not bring forward any general measure for the European Community (EC) akin to the APA, and the discussion of participation rights in its report for the 1996 IGC was exiguous to say the least.[111] It has broadened consultation through the increasing use of Green and White Papers when important areas of EC policy are being developed. This approach was formalized and generalized in the 2002 Communication from the Commission.[112]

The political situation is nonetheless not promising in relation to participation rights and secondary rule-making. Advances have been made in relation to transparency.[113] The 2002 Commission Communication on Consultation however expressly states that it does not apply to norms made pursuant to comitology.[114] Moreover the Commission's consistent strategy has been to accord itself greater decisional autonomy in the making of such norms. It believed that this could be achieved through the provisions concerning delegated regulations in the CT, which it hoped would lead to the abolition of management and regulatory committees. If it were successful in this respect then having freed itself of controls from the 'top', in the form of the comitology committees, it would be unlikely to accede to controls from the 'bottom' in the form of participation rights. This is more especially so given that the Commission has made it clear that it does not favour any regime of legally enforceable participation rights, even in the areas where the 2002 Communication does apply.[115]

The desirability of developing such participation rights is, as we have seen from the previous discussion, an issue on which commentators are

[111] Craig, *supra* n. 27.

[112] Communication from the Commission, Towards a Reinforced Culture of Consultation and Dialogue—General Principles and Minimum Standards for Consultation of Interested Parties by the Commission, COM(2002) 704 final.

[113] <http://europa.eu.int/comm/secretariat_general/regcomito/registre.cfm?CL=en>.

[114] Communication from the Commission, *supra* n. 112, at 15–16.

[115] Ibid. at 10.

divided.[116] There are three general considerations that should be borne in mind when assessing this issue.

(2) Participation Rights and the Public Law Regime

The need for and desirability of participation rights must be assessed in the overall context of the particular public law regime. Thus the APA procedures of notice and comment in the USA must be viewed in the light of an interpretation of the US Constitution that prevents the legislature from vetoing rule-making by agencies,[117] thereby limiting the legislature's ability to control particular agency rules from 'the top'. It is equally the case that the reluctance of the US courts to give real teeth to the non-delegation doctrine must be viewed against the system as a whole, an essential part being the existence of the notice and comment regime, which allows for participatory input into the content of secondary norms, this being monitored by the courts.[118]

Whether participation rights should be accorded within the EU depends therefore in part on the other controls over secondary rule-making. The regime embodied in the CT placed emphasis on legislative control from the top through the stricture that the primary European law should provide the essential principles to govern the area, coupled with the ability of the Council and the EP to reject a particular rule or the entire delegation. It is moreover highly likely that even if comitology as it has been known hitherto were abolished, the Council and the EP would deploy committees in order to decide whether to exercise their power to object to a particular rule. The EU has therefore more in the way of control from 'the top' than exists in the USA.

It might be argued that legitimation and control from the bottom via participation rights is therefore unnecessary in the EU. This would be too rash a conclusion. The fact that the EU provides more by way of control from 'the top' does not inexorably lead to the conclusion that legitimation from 'the bottom' via participation rights should be rejected. The rationale for such participation is partly instrumental, connoting the idea that the resultant rules may be improved by input from interested parties; it is also partly non-instrumental, in the sense that it allows citizens to partake in the

[116] Compare, e.g., Dehousse, *supra* n. 82; Joerges, *supra* n. 51; Weiler, *supra* n. 86; Bignami, 'The Democratic Deficit in European Community Rulemaking: A Call for Notice and Comment in Comitology' (1999) 40 *Harvard Int LJ* 451; Bignami, 'Three Generations of Participation Rights before the European Commission' (2004) 68 *Law and Contemporary Problems* 61.

[117] *Immigration and Naturalization Service v Chadha* 462 US 919 (1983); *Bowsher v Synar* 478 US 714 (1986); Aman and Mayton, *supra* n. 100, at 587–612, 626–628.

[118] Aman and Mayton, *supra* n. 100, Chaps. 2–4.

business of government.[119] The Commission Communication on Consultation,[120] although not enshrining a right to consultation, was nonetheless premised on the fact that such consultation could be a useful adjunct to legitimation from the top in relation to the passage of primary regulations. The reasons given in the Communication speak to the instrumental and non-instrumental value of such participation. Given that this is so, the issue is whether we should distinguish so dramatically between the role of participation in relation to primary and secondary norms. It is readily apparent that whether a substantive matter is dealt with in one way or the other may be fortuitous, and that secondary norms can deal with matters of political choice. The insights of the Rippon Commission in the UK are telling in this respect.[121]

> The importance of proper consultation on delegated legislation should not be underestimated. For many bodies its importance is equal to—or greater than—the importance of consultation on bills. And from the point of view of those directly affected, it is equally important to get delegated legislation right. Delegated legislation may be of secondary importance to Ministers and those in Parliament . . . but to those to whom the law applies or to the practitioners . . . who have to apply it, the method by which the law is made is of little significance. Primary and delegated legislation are equally the law of the land

(3) Practical Implementation and Cost

A further consideration to be borne in mind when thinking about participation rights concerns the practical implementation of any such regime. These issues are complex and can only be touched on here.

The nature of the participatory process would have to be decided on. The default position in the US Administrative Procedure Act 1946 is for notice and comment. Notice of any proposed rule-making is to be published in the Federal Register, including a statement of the time and place of the rule-making proceedings and the terms or substance of the proposed rule. The agency is to afford interested persons an opportunity to comment on the proposed rule.[122] We have already seen that this idea informed the 1993

[119] D. Galligan, *Due Process and Fair Procedures* (Oxford University Press, 1996), Chap. 4; J. Mashaw, *Due Process in the Administrative State* (Yale University Press, 1985); Resnick, 'Due Process and Procedural Justice', in J. Pennock and J. Chapman (eds), *Due Process* (Nomos, 1977), at 217; Michelman, 'Formal and Associational Aims in Procedural Due Process', in *Due Process, supra*, Chap. 4.

[120] *Supra* n. 112.

[121] Making the Law, The Report of the Hansard Society Commission on the Legislative Process (1993), at 42.

[122] A small number of rules are subject to a full trial-type hearing, which can include the provision of oral testimony and cross-examination, *United States v Florida East Coast Railway* 410 U.S. 224 (1973). Other rules are governed by an intermediate or hybrid process, which

Inter-Institutional Declaration on Democracy, Transparency and Subsidiarity, although it was not pursued with any enthusiasm by the Commission.

It might be felt that any such regime would be problematic in terms of time, cost, and delay. It can be contended by way of reply that such costs are worth bearing, in the sense that a cost of democracy is precisely that of involving more people. Participation may also improve the quality of the resulting rule, thereby reducing the overall costs entailed by implementing a rule that would have been less efficacious if such participation had not occurred. There will in any event be situations where, because of exigencies of time or emergency, participation cannot be afforded. This is, however, recognized in all systems that accord participatory rights.

The claim that participation rights would be unworkable because of time, cost, and the like should also be assessed in the light of the advances made by some EU agencies. Thus the European Aviation Safety Agency (EASA) has developed a highly sophisticated notice and comment mechanism that builds on and improves in certain respects the APA model. It should also be recognized that the EASA affords such participation when making highly detailed draft implementing measures in an area where the subject matter is very technical.[123]

(4) The Courts and Judicial Review

The final consideration to be borne in mind concerns the role of the courts and judicial review. The general precepts of review will be considered in due course.[124] The present discussion focuses on the narrower issue of the role of judicial review in a regime that accords participation rights. Two related issues should be distinguished.

There is, on the one hand, the interrelationship between procedural and substantive review. In a regime that embraces participation rights judicial review will inexorably cross the line between process and substance in the following sense. Experience from the US makes it clear that claimants may argue that they were not accorded the participation rights required by the APA, in effect a process challenge. Such claimants also commonly contend that they were enabled to put their view, but that either this was ignored, insufficiently taken into account, or the resultant rule was based on evidence, scientific findings, and the like that were not sustainable. This necessarily

entails more formality than notice and comment, but less than the trial-type hearing. *International Harvester Co v Ruckelshaus* 478 F. 2d 615 (D.C. Cir. 1973); *Portland Cement Assn v Ruckelshaus* 486 F. 2d 375 (D.C. Cir. 1973). The development in this direction was, however, slowed by *Vermont Yankee Nuclear Power Corp v Natural Resources Defence Council, Inc.* 435 U.S. 519 (1978). See generally, Aman and Mayton, *supra* n. 100, Chaps. 2–4;

[123] See below, at 179–180.

[124] See below, Part II.

brings the substance of the rule before the courts, which are then asked to assess, pursuant to a substantial evidence test or an arbitrary and capricious test, whether the rule should be upheld or not.[125]

There is considerable debate as to the intensity of any such substantive review. There must be enough by way of reasoned justification to ensure that the principles of substantive review can operate meaningfully. Bland statements set at a high level of generality, or justifications rationalized *ex post facto*, do not ensure proper accountability. This is particularly so given that much decision-making will take place within 'bounded rationality'.[126] The courts should, at the same time, be wary of requiring too much by way of reasoned justification. This is because decisions may have to be made in, for example, areas of scientific uncertainty. Public bodies will make decisions about the level of acceptable risk where there is imperfect information about the consequences of a certain substance on the environment or on human physiology. There may well be many instances where 'we do not even know what we do not know', but where regulation is nonetheless warranted.[127] To demand 'perfect' reasoned justification in such instances would stultify important regulatory initiatives. It could also lead to 'paralysis by analysis', whereby those opposed to the regulation seek to use the courts to overturn such initiatives on the grounds that not every piece of data relied on by the agency could be perfectly proven. This can lead to public bodies becoming excessively cautious, or unwilling to suggest a regulation unless they have a veritable mountain of data. It would be for the Community courts to make their own choice as to the intensity of such review.

There is, on the other hand, the equally important issue as to how review should be dealt with in a regime where participation rights for interested parties are accorded in addition to consultation through established committees. The problem does not occur in an acute form in the US, because of the limits of legislative oversight. The focus is therefore on the sufficiency of the participation accorded to interested parties as required by the relevant APA procedures. The situation is more complex in the EU precisely because participation rights afforded to interested parties could be an addition to the input provided by comitology committees.

It would within the context of comitology be possible, as Dehousse suggests, for interested parties to be accorded the right of access to committee agendas and the right to express their view on the proposals contained therein, with the correlative requirement that the committee should explain

[125] Aman and Mayton, *supra* n. 100, Chaps. 2–4.

[126] Lindblom, 'The Science of Muddling Through' (1959) 19 *Pub Adm Rev* 79; D. Braybrooke and C. Lindblom, *A Strategy of Decision, Policy Evaluation as a Social Process* (Free Press, 1963).

[127] See below, Chap. 19.

the considerations that led to their eventual choice.[128] This would still require the Community courts to decide the weight to be given to input from the interested parties where they contested the conclusion reached by the committee.

If comitology as it currently exists were to be abolished, but Council and EP committees took on the role of advising their institutions whether to exercise the power to object to a particular delegated regulation, then the situation would be rather more complex. There would be three sets of players. The Commission would make the delegated regulation. The Council and EP committees would exercise de facto a consultative role by reason of their power to advise their institutions whether to object to the proposed regulation. And there would be the views of the interested parties. The most viable *modus operandi* would be, by way of analogy to Dehousse's suggestions, to require the Commission to publish its proposed delegated regulation, allow interested parties the opportunity to comment thereon, with an obligation on the Commission to explain its eventual choice. In any subsequent legal action it would however be for the Community courts to decide whether the Commission's regulation was defensible in the light of the views proffered by interested parties and those advanced by the Council and EP committee. Thus it may well be that although the contested regulation was not in accord with the preponderance of views proffered by interested parties, it was supported by the views of the relevant committees.

8. CONCLUSION

It is readily apparent that the task of ensuring the legitimacy of secondary rule-making or delegated regulation, consistent with the dictates of practical political life, is an endemic problem for all polities. The nature of the EU's decision-making structure merely serves to render the problem more difficult, not to change its nature. The complexity of the EU system for dealing with delegated regulations should not, however, serve to conceal the most significant issue underlying the entire discourse, which is the nature of the measures enacted as delegated regulations and hence the institutional controls to which they should be subject.

The Commission insists that secondary or delegated regulations are concerned primarily with matters of technical detail, where the primary regulation has established the issues of principle. It has invested significant effort to increase its autonomy over the passage of such measures, which it regards as an inherent part of its 'executive function'. It has fought comitology ever since it was created. It has striven since the early 1990s to find ways of

[128] Dehousse, *supra* n. 82, at 122.

satisfying the Council and EP through a schema of the kind included in the CT, with the hope that regulatory and management committees as presently conceived could be abolished.

The problem is that the premise underpinning the Commission's view accords ill with reality. There are to be sure some secondary regulations that can be properly regarded as purely technical. There are a great many that cannot be characterized in this manner. Community policy evolves across time. The classic mode of development is for there to be a new primary regulation or directive in the relevant area, followed by delegated or implementing regulations. The idea that the implementing regulations can be regarded as purely technical, fleshing out points of detail where all the essentials have been laid down in the primary regulation or directive, is simply fanciful and misrepresents reality. Take any instance where there has been a shift in policy effectuated through a primary regulation, whether in the field of, for example, agriculture, the Structural Funds, the budget, customs, or energy. The implementing regulations that are enacted thereafter will regularly deal with practical and normative issues of real importance, the solution to which may be guided, but rarely determined, by the primary regulation.

This is of course precisely why Member States invented comitology in the first place. If the implementing regulations really just dealt with technical detail then the Member States might have been content to let the Commission get on with it. They realised within a bare five years of the EEC's existence that this was not so. They were unwilling to give the Commission a blank cheque to provide answers to the issues of practical and normative choice left outstanding by the primary regulation, because they did not wish to invest the Commission with that degree of power and because they disagreed amongst themselves as to the desirable answers. Comitology was the response, allowing Member States a real input into the making of implementing measures, thereby exerting some control over the Commission and having an institutionalized forum through which to debate their contending views. The realization that implementing measures will often entail contentious practical and normative issues serves equally to explain the EP's long running battles to secure a greater say in their passage, more especially since the creation and expansion of co-decision.

The Commission's mantra that implementation is a natural part of the executive function over which it should naturally have autonomy is premised ultimately on contentious assumptions about the meaning of those very concepts, implementation and executive function. Its vision of the Community method, as elaborated in the White Paper on Governance, is that pretty much everything after the enactment of the primary regulation or directive should be regarded as implementation, which then falls within the ambit of the executive function residing with the Commission. This vision is given added force by the Commission's explicit desire for the primary regulation or directive to be set at a higher level of generality than hitherto, thereby leaving even more to be done through implementing measures.

This interpretation of implementation and executive function should not however be regarded as self-evident. The idea that the 'executive' should have *prima facie* autonomy over the drafting and content of all delegated norms of a legislative nature that embody practical and normative choices requires justification, not simply assertion as if it were an *a priori* logical proposition. It is true that executives in the Member States have some regulatory power. The precise nature and extent of this power, however, varies considerably from state to state and it must in any event be viewed against the entirety of the constitutional distribution of power that exists within any polity. It is not possible to 'cut and paste' experience in a Member State to the EU, more especially because the Commission does not have a democratic mandate akin to that possessed by some national executives. Nor, to put the reverse side of the same coin, is it self-evident in terms of principle why the Council and EP should not be able to have real input when implementing regulations are enacted. The way in which this input is organized remains open to debate. It is, however, reasonably clear for the reasons given above that a solution of the kind embodied in the CT would shift power over delegated regulations significantly towards the Commission and would do little if anything to alleviate continuing concerns about the legitimacy of decision-making in the EU.

5

Agencies

1. INTRODUCTION

It has become increasingly common for agencies to be deployed in nation states to fulfil certain governmental functions. The same phenomenon has occurred in the European Union (EU), especially since the 1990s. This chapter explores the role played by agencies in the EU.

The discussion begins with consideration of the rationale for agencies in nation states and the EU respectively, followed by examination as to how EU agencies have evolved. The focus then turns to classification of EU agencies in the light of their powers and functions, and explication of the legal limits that constrain the powers that can be given to EU agencies. The remainder of the chapter analyses the legal, political, and financial mechanisms for controlling agencies and rendering them accountable. The chapter concludes with discussion as to whether the powers of agencies ought to be extended.

2. THE RATIONALE FOR AGENCIES IN THE NATION STATE

We have already seen in the preceding chapter that modern democratic polities face a dilemma. The basic tenets of representative democracy tell us that norms of a legislative nature are legitimated through the legislative process. The range of issues over which government now has responsibility means, however, that in practical terms it is not possible for all such matters to be dealt with through primary legislation. This is in part because of time constraints. It is in part because not all eventualities can be foreseen when the primary legislation for a particular area is enacted. It is in part also because the legislature itself may lack the technical competence to fill in the interstices of the legislative scheme. The necessary consequence is to delegate power or to accord some independent legislative capacity to the executive branch of government.

If the delegation option is taken this may mean that, for example, a minister is accorded power to make further rules for the topic in question. These rules will themselves be subject to scrutiny and control. Control may be exercised through the legislative and the judicial process, and there may also be opportunity for participatory input by those who are interested in the subject matter of the proposed rule. This should not disguise the fact that political systems have real problems in legitimating and controlling the passage of such delegated norms.

It may, however, be decided that the optimum strategy is not to deal with such matters 'in house', but rather to create an agency outside of the normal departmental structure. This might be felt to be better for a number of reasons.[1] It facilitates the use of experts who are not part of the normal bureaucratic structure. It frees up the parent department itself so as to enable it to concentrate on strategic policy. It insulates the resolution of technical regulatory issues from the vagaries of day-to-day political change and hence increases the credibility of the choices thus made.[2] It might be felt that certain matters, such as funding for the Arts, should be dealt with outside of the normal departmental structure to safeguard against the possibility of any political bias. It might be thought that an agency is a better option where there are regulatory issues in relation to which the government itself has a stake, such as the licensing of airline routes. The rationale for choosing an agency might be for a mixture of reasons, as exemplified by the regulation of race and gender equality in the UK. The desire to insulate such matters from the day-to-day political process, greater staffing flexibility, the wish to combine rule-making and enforcement capabilities, and the desire on the part of government to immunize itself from any adverse political fallout from day-to-day operations, while still taking the credit for the existence of such regimes, might all incline the government to choose the agency route.

It would be mistaken to think of agencies as a modern creation. They have existed in some states such as the UK for over two centuries.[3] It is nonetheless the case that there has been a considerable increase in the use of agencies over the last two decades. This has been linked with what has become known as

[1] D. Hague, W. Mackenzie, and A. Barker (eds), *Public Policy and Private Interests: The Institutions of Compromise* (MacMillan, 1975), at 362; *Report on Non-Departmental Public Bodies*, Cmnd. 7797 (1980), at paras. 10–16; R. Baldwin and C. McCrudden, *Regulation and Public Law* (Weidenfeld & Nicolson, 1987), Chap. 1; Thatcher and Stone Sweet, 'Theory and Practice of Delegation to Non-Majoritarian Institutions' (2002) 25 *West European Politics* 1.

[2] Majone, 'Temporal Consistency and Policy Credibility: Why Democracies Need Non-Majoritarian Institutions' Working Paper RSC No. 96/57, Florence EUI; Gilardi, 'Policy Credibility and Delegation to Independent Regulatory Agencies: A Comparative Empirical Analysis' (2002) 9 *JEPP* 873.

[3] D. Roberts, *Victorian Origins of the British Welfare State* (Yale University Press, 1960); W. Lubenow, *The Politics of Government Growth* (Archon Books, 1971); Sir N. Chester, *The English Administrative System 1780–1870* (Clarendon Press, 1981); H. Parris, *Constitutional Bureaucracy, The Development of British Central Administration in the Eighteenth Century* (Allen & Unwin, 1969).

the regulatory state hypothesis advanced by Majone.[4] On this view the principal state function in the modern era is the correction of market failure through rule-making. It is argued that in the positive state the main institutions were parliament, government departments, and state-owned industry, with the primary political actors being political parties and civil servants. In the regulatory state, by way of contrast, the main institutions are said to be parliamentary committees and regulatory agencies, with the primary actors being regulators, experts, and courts. Indirect political accountability replaces more traditional direct forms of holding government to account. Thus 'regulatory politics combines a rule-bound legalistic policy style, a pluralist political culture and indirect political accountability'.[5] The regulatory state thesis was undoubtedly fuelled by the changing patterns of government in many European countries over the last two decades, with privatization of previously nationalized industry and the creation of regulatory bodies to oversee the new market structures.[6] Further research on countries in Europe has found much to substantiate the claims about the 'regulatory state', with many instances of privatization, liberalization, and delegation to regulatory agencies and a shift away from state ownership. The research also revealed, however, that several features of the regulatory state were absent or only partially present and that there was some real diversity across countries and across different policy areas.[7]

Where agencies are established, for any of these reasons, political and legal controls are set in place, or developed across time. Political controls may be exercised by the legislature, or the executive, or a combination thereof. There will normally be some degree of judicial review. There may also be rights to participate in the formulation of agency policy. The admixture of these controls will depend on the nature of the agency and the constitutional structure of the particular country.

3. THE RATIONALE FOR AGENCIES IN THE EU

The fact that the EU should be beset by similar problems to those considered in the previous section should not come as a surprise. The way to resolve such

[4] Majone, 'The Rise of the Regulatory State in Europe' (1994) 17 *West European Politics* 77; G. Majone, *Regulating Europe* (Routledge, 1996); Majone, 'From the Positive to the Regulatory State: Causes and Consequences of Changes in the Mode of Governance' (1997) 17 *Jnl of Public Policy* 139.

[5] Thatcher, 'Analysing Regulatory Reform in Europe' (2002) 9 *JEPP* 859, at 867.

[6] J. Vickers and G. Yarrow, *Privatization, An Economic Analysis* (MIT Press, 1988), for a valuable account of these changes in the UK.

[7] Thatcher, *supra* n. 5, at 867–869; Schmidt, 'Europeanization and the Mechanics of Economic Policy Adjustment' (2002) 9 *JEPP* 894.

problems is, however, particularly problematic in the EU because of the very nature of its decision-making process.

We have seen in the previous chapter that the need for the Council to delegate power to the Commission was recognized in the original Rome Treaty. Not all matters could be dealt with through the standard process for the making of Community legislation, particularly when they concerned, for example, the detailed regulation of agriculture, where fast reaction to the exigencies of the market was of the essence. The Council became, however, unwilling to hand over a blank cheque to the Commission. It wished to have some control over the detail of the delegated norms, over and above any control that it could exert through the enabling regulation. This signalled the birth of the management and regulatory committees, an institutionalized mechanism for allowing national, normally technocratic interests, to have a real input into these norms. It was these committees that formed the core of what has become known as comitology.

More recently the institutional structure of the Community has been further developed through the creation of agencies. The initial two were established in 1975 and many others have been created since then. The nature of these agencies will be examined more fully below. Before doing so, we should reflect further on the rationale for their creation. We have seen from the previous discussion that a variety of factors have motivated political systems to choose the agency route, as opposed simply to delegation to a minister or part of the established bureaucracy. It is interesting therefore to ask why we are seeing this route being taken for some matters in the EU.

It is unsurprising that a number of the factors that led to the choice of agencies in nation states have also been of relevance in the EU. Thus the Commission in its Communication on Agencies stated that they 'would make the executive more effective at European level in highly specialized technical areas requiring advanced expertise and continuity, credibility and visibility of public action'.[8] It continued in the following vein, claiming that 'the main advantage of using the agencies is that their decisions are based on purely technical considerations of very high quality and are not influenced by political or contingent considerations'.[9] The Commission also emphasized the value of agencies in enabling the Commission to focus on its core function of policy formation, with the agencies implementing this policy in specific technical areas.[10]

The rationale for the agency option in the EU has also been discussed by academics, and a number of differing views have been proffered. Kreher sees the prime motivation for agency creation as the fostering of administrative

[8] Communication from the Commission, The Operating Framework for the European Regulatory Agencies, COM(2002) 718 final, at 5.

[9] Ibid. at 5. [10] Ibid. at 2.

integration.[11] Shapiro's view is less prosaic.[12] If direct routes to further political integration are presently unacceptable, then best proceed via the creation of small discrete technical units that have the added advantage of not being the Commission, and not being in Brussels. The creation of relatively small agencies, each with a particular remit, is, Shapiro feels, also more likely to lead to the creation of 'Europe-wide epistemic communities' of technocrats 'whose technical truths transcend politics'.[13]

Dehousse sees more general forces at work.[14] He argues that agency creation is a response to conflicting pressures within the Community. There is a sense that legislative harmonization is insufficient to dismantle barriers to trade, and that some greater convergence of administrative practice is required. There is also the growing recognition that further delegation of direct administrative responsibility to the Commission is not politically feasible. Regulation by networks, whereby national and Community administrators come together to try and achieve a uniform response, is said to be the way out of this conundrum. The comitology process is itself a prime example of this form of networking. Many of these committees have developed from bodies whose principal function is to oversee the Commission in the discharge of power delegated to it by the Council, into forums through which national administrators can meet to try and attain a uniform strategy for implementation. The ad hoc nature of these committee meetings is, however, a drawback, and Dehousse therefore sees agencies as a more permanent institutionalized locus through which such networking designed to reach the requisite result can take place.[15]

Majone places the increasing use of agencies within a more general conceptual framework concerning the nature of the EU.[16] He argues convincingly that the framers of the Rome Treaty rejected the option of separating the functional branches of government in favour of a polity in which the Council, Assembly, and Commission, representing respectively the interests of states, the people, and the European interest, were combined, albeit in different ways depending on the particular legislative process. Institutional balance and institutional autonomy were central to this mode of 'mixed government', as they had been in earlier polities in Europe.[17] The division of

[11] Kreher, 'Agencies in the European Community—A Step towards Administrative Integration in Europe' (1997) 4 *JEPP* 225.

[12] Shapiro, 'The Problems of Independent Agencies in the United States and the European Union' (1997) 4 *JEPP* 276.

[13] Ibid. at 282.

[14] Dehousse, 'Regulation by Networks in the European Community: The Role of European Agencies' (1997) 4 *JEPP* 246.

[15] Ibid. at 254–255.

[16] Majone, 'Delegation of Regulatory Powers in a Mixed Polity' (2002) 8 *ELJ* 319.

[17] Ibid. at 320, 323, 325–326.

power among different estates had the objective of balancing different interests, since each could withhold its consent to the proposed measure, and was designed to prevent any single interest or estate from becoming dominant.[18] It is against this model of institutional balance within a mixed polity that Majone advocates increased recourse to agencies. He acknowledges that the debate about delegation of power 'is really a debate about the fundamental political organization of the polity, rather than merely an issue of political and administrative efficiency'.[19] We shall see that delegation of power has been legally constrained in the EU by judicial rulings that any such delegation of discretionary power would upset the institutional balance established by the Treaty. Majone argues, however, that delegation of power to non-majoritarian institutions such as agencies is necessary and can be reconciled with ideals of institutional balance. It is necessary, Majone maintains, because of the credibility problem of traditional Community regulation, as exemplified by the 'mad cow' disease crisis. He argues that there is a 'mismatch between highly complex regulatory tasks and available administrative instruments',[20] exacerbated by the limited administrative, financial, and cognitive resources available to the Commission,[21] with the consequence that 'a growing number of Commission officials and industry representatives feel that the situation can only be improved by creating stronger and more autonomous regulatory institutions at European level'.[22] Majone argues that this institutional change can be regarded as consistent with the idea of institutional balance within a mixed polity by regarding such agencies, and the networks that they form with national, sub-national, and international actors, as a 'regulatory estate' to be added to the other estates that form the EU.

We shall return to some of these matters in due course when we evaluate the agency model. Before doing so it is, however, necessary to understand the basic structure of the existing agencies. It is to this issue that we now turn.

4. EVOLUTION

It would be wrong to imagine that the EU suddenly woke up to the importance or potential of agencies. The reality is rather that agencies have been created at different periods of time.[23]

The agency model was initially used in 1975 when two agencies were established. These were the European Centre for the Development of

[18] For a similar view in this regard, Craig, 'Democracy and Rule-Making within the EC: An Empirical and Normative Assessment' (1997) 3 *ELJ* 105.

[19] Majone, *supra* n. 16, at 322. [20] Ibid. at 329. [21] Ibid. at 330.

[22] Ibid. at 329.

[23] Keleman, 'The Politics of "Eurocratic" Structure and the New European Agencies' (2002) 25 *West European Politics* 93.

Vocational Training (Cedefop)[24] and the European Foundation for the Improvement of Living and Working Conditions (EUROFOUND).[25]

It was, however, to be 15 years before recourse was made to agencies again. This second wave of agencies that occurred in the 1990s saw the creation of 10 further agencies. It began with the setting up of the European Environment Agency (EEA)[26] and the European Training Foundation (ETF).[27] In temporal sequence this decade also saw the establishment of the European Monitoring Centre for Drugs and Drug Addiction[28] (EMCDDA); the European Medicines Agency[29] (EMEA); the Office for Harmonization in the Internal Market[30] (OHIM); the European Agency for Health and Safety at Work[31] (EU-OSHA); the Community Plant Variety Office[32] (CPVO); the Translation Centre for Bodies of the European Union[33] (CdT); the European Monitoring Centre for Racism and Xenophobia[34] (EUMC); and the European Agency for Reconstruction[35] (EAR).

The new millennium has seen further use made of the agency model in what can be regarded as a third wave. A European Food Safety Authority[36]

[24] Council Regulation 337/75/EEC of 10 February 1975, Establishing a European Centre for Vocational Training, OJ 1975 L39/1.

[25] Council Regulation 1365/75/EEC of 26 May 1975, On the Creation of a European Foundation for the Improvement of Living and Working Conditions, OJ 1975 L139/1.

[26] Council Regulation (EEC) 1210/90 of 7 May 1990, On the Establishment of the European Environment Agency and the European Environment Information and Observation Network, OJ 1990 L120/1.

[27] Council Regulation (EEC) 1360/90 of 7 May 1990, Establishing a European Training Foundation, OJ 1990 L131/1.

[28] Council Regulation (EEC) 302/93 of 8 February 1993, On the Establishment of a European Centre for Drugs and Drug Addiction, OJ 1993 L36/1.

[29] Council Regulation (EEC) 2309/93 of 22 July 1993, Laying Down Community Procedures for the Authorization and Supervision of Medicinal Products for Human and Veterinary Use and Establishing a European Agency for the Evaluation of Medicinal Products, OJ 1993 L214/1.

[30] Council Regulation (EC) 40/94 of 20 December 1993, On the Community Trademark, OJ 1994 L11/1.

[31] Council Regulation (EC) 2062/94 of 18 July 1994, Establishing a European Agency for Safety and Health at Work, OJ 1994 L216/1.

[32] Council Regulation (EC) 2100/94 of 27 July 1994, On Community Plant Variety Rights, OJ 1994 L227/1.

[33] Council Regulation (EC) 2965/94 of 28 November 1994, Setting Up a Translation Centre for Bodies of the European Union, OJ 1994 L314/1.

[34] Council Regulation (EC) 1035/97 of 2 June 1997, Establishing a European Monitoring Centre on Racism and Xenophobia, OJ 1997 L151/1.

[35] Council Regulation (EC) 2454/1999 of 15 November 1999, Setting Up of a European Agency for Reconstruction, OJ 1999 L299/1.

[36] Regulation (EC) 178/2002 of the European Parliament and of the Council of 28 January, Laying Down the General Principles and Requirements of Food Law, Establishing the European Food Safety Authority and Laying Down Procedures in Matters of Food Safety, OJ 2002 L31/1.

has been created (EFSA), as has the European Maritime Safety Agency[37] (EMSA) and the European Aviation Safety Agency[38] (EASA). A European Network and Information Security Agency[39] (ENISA) was added to the list of agencies in 2004, as was the European Centre for Disease Prevention and Control[40] (ECDC). The regulation to create a European Railway Agency (ERA)[41] was passed in 2004, and that for a Community Fisheries Control Agency (CFCA)[42] in 2005, and both agencies are currently being established. There is a proposal for a European Chemicals Agency (ECA).[43] The Commission also produced proposals in 2005 for a Regulation establishing a European Union Agency for Fundamental Rights, which will replace the EUMC.[44]

The first and second waves of agencies were with one exception based on Article 308 EC.[45] This practice has now been modified. The Commission signalled that henceforth 'since the regulatory agency is an instrument of implementation of a specific Community policy, it follows that the legal instrument creating it must be based on the provision of the Treaty which constitutes the specific legal basis for that policy'.[46] This has been the approach adopted when setting up the agencies concerned with food safety and transport. Article 308 EC will only be used in the future when that Article is itself the legal basis for the specific action. This change of legal basis for agency creation is more than a mere point of legal nicety. It has substantive implications. This is because the European Parliament (EP) will be likely to have a greater role in the legislative process, through for example

[37] Regulation (EC) 1406/2002 of the European Parliament and of the Council of 27 June 2002, Establishing a European Maritime Safety Agency, OJ 2002 L208/1.

[38] Regulation (EC) 1592/2002 of the European Parliament and of the Council of 15 July 2002, On Common Rules in the Field of Civil Aviation and Establishing a European Aviation Safety Agency, OJ 2002 L240/1.

[39] Regulation (EC) 460/2004 of the European Parliament and of the Council of 10 March 2004, Establishing the European Network and Information Agency, OJ 2004 L77/1.

[40] Regulation (EC) 851/2004 of the European Parliament and of the Council of 21 April 2004, Establishing a European Centre for Disease Prevention and Control, OJ 2004 L142/1.

[41] Regulation (EC) 881/2004 of the European Parliament and of the Council of 29 April 2004, Establishing a European Railway Safety Agency, OJ 2004 L164/1.

[42] Council Regulation (EC) 768/2005 of 26 April 2005, Establishing a Common Fisheries Control Agency and Amending Regulation (EEC) 2847/93 Establishing a Control System Applicable to Common Fisheries Policy, OJ 2005 L128/1.

[43] Proposal for a Regulation of the European Parliament and Council Concerning the Registration, Evaluation, Authorisation and Restriction of Chemicals (REACH), and Establishing a European Chemicals Agency, COM(2003) 644 final.

[44] Commission Proposal, For a Council Regulation Establishing a European Union Agency for Fundamental Rights, COM(2005) 280 final.

[45] Kreher, 'Agencies in the European Community—A Step towards Administrative Integration in Europe' (1997) 4 *JEPP* 225. The exception was the EEA.

[46] Commission Communication, *supra* n. 8, at 7.

co-decision, than it does under Article 308 and it will therefore be in a better position to influence agency design than hitherto.

The discussion thus far has been concerned with agencies set up by Commission initiative. It would, however, be mistaken to think that the agencies listed above constitute the whole picture. This is because a number of agencies owe their origin to action by the Council.[47] There are currently six agencies that fall in this category. Some of these, such as Europol, the European Police Office, are relatively well known. The agreement to set up Europol dates from the Maastricht Treaty. The Europol Convention[48] flowed from a Council act based on what was Article K3 of the Treaty on European Union (TEU). It was ratified by all Member States in October 1998 and Europol became fully operational in July 1999. In 2000 Cepol, a European Police College, came into existence.[49] The European Union Satellite Centre (EUSC) was created in 2001,[50] although it was the direct successor of an earlier organization with the same function. Its mission is to support EU decision-making in the context of the Common Foreign and Security Policy (CFSP), and in particular the European Security and Defence Policy, by enhancing the EU's capability to gather space-related information to help prevent conflicts, support peace-keeping efforts, and provide effective humanitarian aid during man-made disasters. The European Institute for Security Studies (EUISS) dates from 2001 and was also established under the CSFP. Its mandate is to help create a common European security culture, to enrich the strategic debate, and systematically to promote the interests of the EU.[51] Eurojust was established in 2002 to enhance cooperation between the competent authorities responsible for investigation and prosecution of cross-border and organized crime.[52] In 2004 the European Defence Agency[53] (EDA) was added to the list of those created by the Council, its objective being to support the Member States and the Council in their effort to improve European defence capabilities in the field of crisis management and to sustain the European Security and Defence Policy as it stands now and

[47] Curtin, 'Delegation to EU Non-Majoritarian Agencies and Emerging Practices of Public Accountability' forthcoming, at 9–12.

[48] It can be found at <http://www.europol.eu.int/index.asp?page=legalconv>.

[49] Council Decision 2000/820/JHA of 22 December 2000, Establishing a European Police College (Cepol), OJ 2000 L336/1.

[50] Council Joint Action 2001/555/CFSP of 20 July 2001, On the Establishment of a European Union Satellite Centre, OJ 2001 L200/5.

[51] Council Joint Action 2001/554/CFSP of 20 July 2001, On the Establishment of a European Union Institute for Security Studies, OJ 2001 L200/1.

[52] Council Decision 2002/187/JHA of 28 February 2002, Setting up Eurojust with a View to Reinforcing the Fight against Serious Crime, OJ 2002 L 63/1.

[53] Council Joint Action 2004/551/CFSP of 12 July 2004, On the Establishment of the European Defence Agency, OJ 2004 L245/17.

develops in the future. The increased concern about security of external borders is reflected in the creation in 2004 of a Community agency, the European Agency for the Management of Operational Cooperation at the External Borders (FRONTEX).[54] Its principal tasks are to help Member States to apply the EU rules on external border controls and to return non-EU citizens to their country of origin.

This temporal overview reveals increasing recourse to agencies by the Council in the discharge of functions under Pillars 2 and 3 of the EU. If we classify the agencies by function rather than development over time there are three CFSP agencies, EUSC, EUISS, and EDA, and three Justice and Home Affairs/Police and Judicial Cooperation in Criminal Matters (JHA/PJCC) agencies, Europol, Cepol, and Eurojust.

5. CLASSIFICATION

The preceding analysis reveals the variety of agencies established by the EU over time. This has naturally prompted attempts at classification and taxonomy by officials and academics alike. There is, it seems, a natural inclination to see or induce order in the schema of things and classification is the response. Readers will have their own views on whether such exercises are worth the effort. My own feeling is that classification can be of assistance subject to important cautionary notes. We should never lose sight of the fact that taxonomy is of instrumental value, it is there to cast light on substantive differences between different agencies and assist in the appropriate policy response, not to be an end in itself. We should not allow the desire for 'order' to lead to the imposition of a taxonomic Procrustean frame that forces agencies into categories that are ill-fitting. We should moreover remember the tension between generality and specificity. The more general and abstract is any classification then the greater the likelihood that all can be fitted into the category thus fashioned, with the consequential danger that the category loses its utility by grouping together agencies that are significantly different. There are similar dangers in veering too far in the opposite direction, in the sense that categories that are too specific can convey a wilderness of single instances, downplaying commonalities at the expense of differences that may be of little significance to the functioning of the relevant body. With these cautionary notes in mind we can spend a little time reflecting on taxonomy.

[54] Council Regulation (EC) 2007/2004 of 26 October 2004, Establishing a European Agency for the Management of Operational Cooperation at the External Borders of the Member States of the European Union, OJ 2004 L349/1.

A. The Commission View

It is fitting to begin with the official view put forward by the Commission. It is clear that there are both satisfactory and unsatisfactory elements in the Commission's mode of classification.

It is satisfactory in that the Commission distinguishes between executive and regulatory agencies, albeit stressing that some existing agencies do not fall within either category.[55] Executive agencies connote those bodies discussed in detail in a previous chapter[56] that were set up in the aftermath of the fall of the Santer Commission. The reforms that followed led to the creation of a new breed of executive agencies that would be responsible for managing programmes where the Commission had direct administrative responsibility for implementation. These agencies are subject to a specific framework Regulation,[57] they are not intended to be independent and are subject to close supervision by the Commission. The agencies listed in the previous section are not executive agencies. Such agencies are beginning to be established to administer certain specific policies.[58]

The Commission classification becomes unsatisfactory when we move beyond the basic distinction between executive and regulatory agencies and consider the meaning accorded to the term regulatory agency. The latter agencies are 'required to be actively involved in the executive function by enacting instruments which help to regulate a specific sector' and the 'majority of them are intended to make such regulation more consistent and effective by combining and networking at Community level activities which are initially a matter for the Member States'.[59] The Commission properly recognizes that the existing 'regulatory agencies' perform different functions. Some, such as the EMEA and the EFSA, provide technical and scientific assistance that is the basis for a decision made by the Commission; others, such as EMSA, provide inspection reports to enable the Commission to fulfil its role as guardian of Community law; yet others, such as OHIM, CPVO, and EASA, can make individual decisions that are legally binding on third parties.[60] In the light of this the Commission states that a distinction should be drawn within the category of regulatory agencies. The distinction is between decision-making agencies, being those empowered to enact legal instruments binding on third parties, and executive agencies, being those with no independent power of decision in relation to third parties, but which

[55] Commission Communication, *supra* n. 8, at 3–4. [56] See above, Chap. 2.
[57] Council Regulation (EC) 58/2003 of 19 December 2002, Laying Down the Statute for Executive Agencies to be Entrusted with Certain Tasks in the Management of Community Programmes, OJ 2003 L11/1.
[58] See above, at Chap 2. [59] Commission Communication, *supra* n. 8, at 4.
[60] Ibid. at 4.

perform other regulatory tasks.[61] This labelling is confusing in the extreme. We are presented with an initial distinction between executive and regulatory agencies, followed by differentiation within the latter category between decision-making and executive agencies. It is moreover, as Majone forcefully points out, confusing to have a category of regulatory agency and then to delineate within that category a group of bodies that do not have formal regulatory powers, whether of individualized decision-making or rule-making.[62] The instrumental use made of the distinction between decision-making and executive agencies can, as will be seen later, also be questioned, insofar as it informs matters such as the role of the Commission in the choice of agency director.

B. An Alternative View

The academic literature contains various taxonomies to capture the plethora of agencies that have been created under the Community pillar,[63] although there has generally been relatively little consideration accorded to how agencies created under Pillars 2 and 3 might be incorporated into any such classificatory scheme.[64] My own view is as follows.

(1) Regulatory Agencies

The term regulatory agency is normally used to refer to bodies that have decision-making powers, which can be exercised either through individualized adjudication or through the promulgation of rules of a legislative nature that are applicable to those that come within their ambit. This is how the term is used in relation to the classic regulatory agencies in the USA, and many national regulatory agencies conform to this model. Such agencies exercise discretionary power within their designated areas, and the development of agency policy can be through either adjudication or rule-making. Various factors may influence the agency as to whether it uses adjudication or rulemaking as the principal vehicle for the development of policy.

Now it is of course true that terminology at the EU level does not have to

[61] Commission Communication, *supra* n. 8, at 8.

[62] Majone, 'Strategy of Regulatory Reform', in G. Della Cananea (ed), *European Regulatory Agencies* (ISUPE Press, 2004), at 54.

[63] See, e.g., Chiti, 'The Emergence of a Community Administration: The Case of European Agencies' (2000) 37 *CMLRev* 309, at 311–317; Chiti, 'Decentralisation and Integration into the Community Administrations: A New Perspective on European Agencies' (2004) 10 *ELJ* 402, at 431–436; Geradin and Petit, 'The Development of Agencies at EU and National Levels: Conceptual Analysis and Proposals for Reform' Jean Monnet Working Paper 01/04, NYU School of Law, at 43–50.

[64] See however the valuable analysis that includes Council agencies in Curtin, *supra* n. 47.

be tied to that used in nation states. This can be accepted, but does not diminish the force of the point being made here. None of the EU agencies created thus far are regulatory agencies in the way that the term is used in common legal and political parlance,[65] the principal reason being, as will be seen below, that there are legal constraints to the delegation of discretionary power to agencies. It is equally true that agencies might be regarded as having some regulatory input even though they do not exercise discretionary powers through adjudication and rule-making. This too can be acknowledged, but does not thereby lessen the contrast between those bodies that do and do not have formal dispositive powers that can be exercised at their own volition, whether through adjudication or rule-making.

(2) Decision-making Agencies

There are, however, EU decision-making agencies that have the power to make individualized decisions that are binding on third parties. The OHIM, CPVO, and EASA fall within this category. The official rationale for according this type of decisional power is that in these areas a single public interest predominates and the agency is not called on to 'arbitrate on conflicting public interests, exercise any powers of political appraisal or conduct complex economic assessments'.[66] Whether this accords with reality or not the fact that the rationale is framed in these terms, coupled with the repeated injunction that such agencies cannot adopt 'legislative measures of general application', or be 'delegated responsibilities for which the EC Treaty has conferred direct power of decision on the Commission',[67] serves to emphasize the limits of the powers accorded to such agencies and the difference between them and classic regulatory agencies.

(3) Quasi-regulatory Agencies

The EU also has a number of what might be termed quasi-regulatory agencies with strong recommendatory power. This term is admittedly inelegant, but it nonetheless captures reasonably well some of the functions performed by the EASA in the context of air safety. The EASA has actual decisional power in individual cases concerning airworthiness and environmental certification, hence its inclusion in the previous category.[68] Its rule-making role is less well known, but equally important. It is the EASA that in effect drafts the detailed implementing rules passed pursuant to the basic agency Regulation. It has elaborate rule-making procedures, discussed below,[69] the result of

[65] This point is also made by Geradin and Petit, *supra* n. 63, at 48–49.
[66] Commission Communication, *supra* n. 8, at 8. [67] Ibid. at 8.
[68] Reg. 1592/2002, *supra* n. 38, Art. 15. [69] See below, at 179–180.

which will be a draft set out as a Commission implementing regulation. This requires approval from the Commission, which will, however, often have little if any input into these complex rules. The EASA will, in addition, publish codes, as it is empowered to do, that are in effect complex, highly detailed regulatory provisions regarded as binding by the industry, even though they do not have the force of law.[70]

The term quasi-regulatory agency is also apt for bodies such as the EMEA, EFSA, and EMSA. These bodies do not have formal decisional powers. They make recommendations to the Commission, which has the final power of decision. The Commission is not bound by the recommendations thus made, but the views proffered by the relevant agency will nonetheless carry considerable weight, more particularly because they will commonly be concerned with technical and scientific matters. This can be reflected in the language of the Regulation, as in the context of the EMEA.[71]

The importance of such agencies in the decision-making process has been recognized by the Community courts. This story will be told fully below.[72] Suffice it to say for the present that they have held that where the Commission departs from the agency recommendation it will normally have to provide good reasons for doing so, and its decision will be annulled if the reasons do not suffice. The significance of the agencies' work is also evidenced by the courts' willingness to review their reasoning and findings, notwithstanding the fact that they do not have formal decisional powers of their own.

(4) Information and Coordination Agencies

There are also a significant number of agencies whose main tasks are the provision of information and coordination. Most EU agencies, including those considered above, perform some functions of this nature, but for many agencies it is their principal function. The precise tasks performed by these information and coordination agencies vary in nature, but they nonetheless possess common features. Their role will normally be to furnish information and analysis thereof in the relevant area to the Commission, Member States, and related actors whether at the public or private level; to assist the Commission where necessary in the formulation of policy and legislation at the Community level; and to coordinate and interact with a network of other players concerned with the subject matter dealt with by the agency.

We shall see that similar tasks of information provision and coordination are performed by a number of the agencies subject to oversight by the

[70] The two main codes issued by the EASA are 279 and 239 pages respectively.

[71] Reg. 2309/93, *supra* n. 29, Arts. 10, 32. The Commission makes the decision concerning authorization of a drug on the advice of the EMEA, and Arts. 10 and 32 make clear that it will be exceptional for the Commission's draft decision not to be in accord with the EMEA's view.

[72] See below, at 167–168.

Council pursuant to Pillars 2 and 3. What follows are simply some examples of Community agencies that perform information and coordination functions.

The EEA is a prominent example of such an agency. Its principal tasks are the provision of information to enable the Community and the Member States to take the requisite measures to protect the environment, assess the results of such measures, and ensure that the public is properly informed about the state of the environment. In this respect it is charged in particular to consider matters relating to the quality of the environment, pressures on the environment, and its sensitivity.[73]

EU-OSHA is another second generation agency that has similar features. In order to encourage improvements in the safety and health of workers the agency is charged with providing the Community, Member States, the social partners, and those involved in the field with technical, scientific, and economic information on workplace health and safety.[74] The information is intended to identify, *inter alia*, risks and good practices. The agency is also to supply both the Community and Member States with such information as they require to implement judicious and effective policies to protect workers' health and safety, and more particularly to provide such information to the Commission when it is preparing legislation in this area.[75] In order to better attain its goals EU-OSHA is instructed to set up a network comprising the main elements of national information networks, including national social partners' organizations, national focal points, and what are called future topic centres. Member States are obliged to inform the agency of the main components of their national health and safety information networks, including any institution that could contribute to the work of the agency.[76]

The EMSA is a more recent example of an agency performing similar tasks within its field. It was established because there was a need for an expert body to monitor implementation of EU policies on maritime safety and pollution and judge the effectiveness of such policies. To this end the EMSA is the technical body charged with providing the Community and Member States with the necessary means to act effectively to enhance overall maritime safety and prevent pollution by ships, and to assist the Commission in updating and developing Community legislation in these areas. The EMSA is also accorded the more specific task of identifying ships that breach the relevant rules concerning safety and pollution in order that the Commission and the Member States can take appropriate enforcement action.[77]

[73] Reg. 1210/90, *supra* n. 26, Arts. 1–2.

[74] Reg. 2062/94, *supra* n. 31, Arts. 2, 3(1)(a)–(d), as amended by Council Regulation (EC) 1112/2005 of 24 June 2005, Amending Regulation 2062/94 Establishing a European Agency for Safety and Health at Work, OJ 2005 L184/5.

[75] Ibid. Art. 3(1)(e).

[76] Ibid. Arts. 3(1)(f), 4.

[77] Reg. 1406/2002, *supra* n. 37, Art. 2(f).

ENISA is another prominent recent agency whose principal functions concern the provision of information and coordination. It was established because of the increased importance of communication networks and information systems to modern economic and social development. The security of such networks is important, more especially given that this can be jeopardized by accident, attack, and mistake. ENISA is therefore charged with provision of information concerning such risks and analysing ways of dealing with them. As with other agencies that fall within this general category, ENISA is to assist the Commission, when called on, in the preparatory work for developing Community legislation in this area.[78] There are, moreover, numerous internal market measures that entail or require use of communication networks and information systems, and ENISA is intended to provide guidance on these matters. The enabling Regulation repeatedly emphasizes ENISA's role in the provision and analysis of information concerning risks to network security and stresses the need for ENISA to facilitate coordination and cooperation between the Community and Member States in relation to network security and between public and private actors.[79]

The discussion thus far has focused on information and coordination agencies established under the Community Pillar, Pillar 1, normally at the behest of the Commission. It is, however, clear that some of the agencies established by the Council under Pillars 2 and 3 fulfil similar functions within their assigned areas. Take the EDA by way of example. Its tasks include:[80] the development of defence capabilities in the field of crisis management, through, *inter alia*, identifying the EU's future defence capability requirements, promoting and coordinating harmonization of military requirements, and proposing collaborative operational activities; the promotion of European armaments cooperation through coordination of existing programmes in Member States and efficient procurement; the strengthening of the European defence industrial and technological base through harmonization of relevant rules and regulations; and the enhancement of the effectiveness of research and development in the defence area by, *inter alia*, coordinating joint research activities. The same admixture of provision of information, assistance in the promulgation of EU rules, and coordination of relevant action at Member State level, and with other groups and organizations concerned with the same subject matter,[81] is apparent in relation to the EDA in much the same way as with the Community agencies considered in this category.

Europol and Eurojust are the most important agencies established by the Council acting under Pillar 3, JHA/PJCC, and they too can be regarded as

[78] Reg. 460/2004, *supra* n. 39, Art. 2(4).
[79] Ibid. Arts. 2(1)–(3), 3.
[80] Council Joint Action 2004/551/CFSP, *supra* n. 53, Art. 5.
[81] Ibid. Rec. 8.

information and coordination agencies. Thus the objectives of Europol are to enhance effectiveness and cooperation between Member States in dealing with offences that come within Europol's remit.[82] It has important tasks concerning the collection and provision of information:[83] it is to facilitate exchange of information between Member States; obtain, collate, and analyse information and intelligence; notify competent authorities within Member States of information of concern to them; aid investigations in Member States by forwarding relevant information to them; and maintain a computerized information system. Europol can also give advice on investigations, and provide assistance through advice and research in relation to training, crime prevention methods, organization and equipment, and forensic police methods. The centrality of information collation to Europol's tasks is further emphasized by the importance given to the computerized information system that Europol creates and maintains.[84] Coordination and cooperation between Europol and national police forces is also accorded a high prominence and the Europol Convention tries to ensure that this operates as efficiently as possible. Thus each Member State designates a national unit that is to be the sole liaison point between Europol and that country, and information flows are channelled in both directions through this unit.[85] Coordination is further facilitated by the fact that the national unit will second at least one person to Europol to act as a liaison officer.[86]

The same emphasis on information, cooperation, and coordination is apparent in the remit given to Eurojust. It has competence in relation to crimes that fall within Europol's jurisdiction and other crimes specifically listed.[87] Eurojust's objectives are to stimulate and improve coordination between the competent authorities of the Member States concerned with investigation and prosecution of these crimes; to improve cooperation between such authorities by facilitating execution of international mutual legal assistance and implementation of extradition requests; and otherwise to support Member State authorities in order to render their prosecutions and investigations more effective.[88] Eurojust will normally act through its national members, but can also in certain circumstances act as a College. In either eventuality, the twin themes of information provision coupled with cooperation/coordination dominate the more detailed delineation of Eurojust's tasks. Thus when it acts through its national member Eurojust may,[89] *inter alia*, ask the competent national authority to undertake a prosecution; accept that another country may be better placed to do so; or suggest the

[82] Europol Convention, *supra* n. 48, Art. 2.
[83] Ibid. Art. 3.
[84] Ibid. Arts. 6–9.
[85] Ibid. Art. 4.
[86] Ibid. Art. 5.
[87] Dec. 2002/187/JHA, *supra* n. 52, Art. 4.
[88] Ibid. Art. 3.
[89] Ibid. Art. 6(a).

setting up of a joint investigation. In addition Eurojust shall,[90] *inter alia*, give assistance in order to improve cooperation between the national authorities; ensure that the Member State authorities inform each other of investigations and prosecutions of which it has been informed; assist such authorities at their request concerning the best possible coordination of investigations and prosecutions; and cooperate and consult with the European Judicial Network.

6. LIMITS

The preceding discussion will hopefully have cast some light on the types of agencies that have been established by the EU under all three Pillars. The EU does not possess regulatory agencies as that term is commonly used in national parlance, and the principal legal constraint in this regard comes from the jurisprudence of the Community courts, more specifically what has become known as the *Meroni* principle. It will be seen that there are, however, political limits to the types of power that can be accorded to agencies, or that at the very least there are ambiguities and tensions within the political organs, especially the Commission, as to whether the legal limits should be relaxed. Let us begin by making clear the nature of the legal limits.

A. Legal Limits

The *Meroni* case[91] involved a challenge by the applicant company to a decision requiring it to pay the Imported Ferrous Scrap Equalization Fund a sum of money. The applicant argued that the particular decision was vitiated by error because of a failure to state adequate reasons. It further contended that the more general decision underlying the particular decision was unlawful because it entailed a delegation of power that was impermissible under the Treaty. The general decision provided that the operation of the financial arrangements for the ferrous scrap regime should be dealt with by the Joint Bureau of Ferrous Scrap Consumers and the Imported Scrap Equalization Fund, bodies with legal personality under private law. The European Court of Justice (ECJ) decided that the contested decision entailed a true delegation of power and then reasoned as follows.

It held that the delegation was unlawful because *a delegating authority could not confer on another body powers different from those possessed by the delegator under the Treaty*.[92] If the High Authority had exercised the power

[90] Dec. 2002/187/JHA, *supra* n. 52, Art. 6(b)–(g).
[91] Case 9/56, *Meroni & Co, Industrie Metallurgiche SpA v High Authority* [1958] ECR 133.
[92] Ibid. at 149–150.

itself then it would have been subject to Treaty rules concerning a duty to give reasons, publish data, and the like. The contested decision did not make the agencies to which power had been delegated subject to the same constraints, such that in reality those agencies had more extensive power than those held by the High Authority under the Treaty.

The ECJ also held that *it was not possible to delegate power involving a wide margin of discretion.* The Court accepted that it was possible for the High Authority to delegate certain power under the European Coal and Steel Community Treaty (ECSC), but imposed limits in this respect.[93]

> The consequences resulting from a delegation of powers are very different depending on whether it involves clearly defined executive powers the exercise of which can, therefore, be subject to strict review in the light of objective criteria determined by the delegating authority, or whether it involves a discretionary power, implying a wide margin of discretion which may, according to the use which is made of it, make possible the execution of actual economic policy.
>
> A delegation of the first kind cannot appreciably alter the consequences involved in the exercise of the powers concerned, whereas a delegation of the second kind, since it replaces the choices of the delegator by the choices of the delegate, brings about an actual transfer of responsibility.

This rationale for limiting the type of power that could be delegated was reinforced by the concept of institutional balance. It is important to appreciate the ECJ's reasoning on this point.[94] It stated that Article 3 ECSC, which contained eight diverse objectives for the ECSC, not all of which could be simultaneously pursued, was binding not only on the High Authority, but also on the institutions of the Community within the limits of their respective powers. It followed, said the ECJ, from Article 3 that there could be seen in the balance of powers that was characteristic of the institutional structure of the Community a fundamental guarantee granted by the Treaty in particular to the undertakings to which it applied. To delegate a discretionary power, 'by entrusting it to bodies other than those which the Treaty has established to effect and supervise the exercise of such power each within the limits of its own authority, would render that guarantee ineffective'.[95] The ECJ concluded that the power delegated to the agencies in the instant case contained significant discretionary power that was not bounded by objective criteria and hence was not compatible with the Treaty.

The *Meroni* principle has stood for approaching 50 years as a constitutional limit to delegation and continues to be applied in current jurisprudence.[96] It is true that the Community courts have been willing to

[93] Ibid. at 152. [94] Ibid. at 152. [95] Ibid. at 152.

[96] Cases C-154–155/04, *The Queen, on the application of Alliance for Natural Health and Nutri-link Ltd v Secretary of State for Health* [2005] ECR I-6451, at para. 90.

uphold delegations of power when they were felt to be warranted, but they have done so from within the framework of the *Meroni* reasoning, rather than straying outside it. Thus in *Tralli*[97] the ECJ held that a delegation of power within the organs of the ECB to decide on rules as to staff management and contracts was compatible with the *Meroni* principle. More interestingly in *DIR International*[98] the Court of First Instance (CFI) was willing, in the context of the MEDIA programme designed to enhance the European audiovisual industry, to uphold a delegation of power by the Commission to a private body (EFDO) that decided on funding applications, on the ground that the agreement between EFDO and the Commission in effect made EFDO's decisions subject to Commission agreement, hence imputable to the Commission and therefore subject to judicial review.

B. Political Limits

Meroni not only continues to have a pervasive influence over legal doctrine, it has also shaped the political discourse. This is self-evidently so in the formal sense that *Meroni* is the oft-cited reason given for the limited powers that can be accorded to agencies. It should, however, be recognized that in certain political quarters there is a desire to preserve the limits of delegation laid down by the Community courts for reasons that go beyond the formal authority of judicial doctrine.

Consider in this respect the Commission's perspective. It may well be true as Majone relates[99] that there are tensions within the Commission, with certain members wishing to move beyond *Meroni* and create true regulatory agencies. The official Commission view as laid down in its 2002 Communication on Regulatory Agencies is nonetheless still premised on the judicial status quo, complete with the limit on delegation of discretionary power that constitutes the block to the creation of real regulatory agencies. This position has been reiterated in the Commission's 2005 proposal for a Draft Interinstitutional Agreement concerning regulatory agencies.[100] The 2002 document

[97] Case C-301/02 P, *Tralli v ECB* [2005] ECR I-4071, at paras. 42–52.

[98] Cases T-369/94 and 85/95, *DIR International Film Srl and others v Commission* [1998] ECR II-357, at paras. 52–53. The case was reversed on appeal on different grounds, Case C-164/98 P, *DIR International Film Srl and others v Commission* [2000] ECR I-447.

[99] Majone, *supra* n. 16.

[100] Draft Interinstitutional Agreement on the Operating Framework for the European Regulatory Agencies, COM(2005) 59 final. Art. 5(1) stipulates that even where agencies make individual decisions that bind third parties they cannot adopt general regulatory measures; exercise decision-making power in areas where they would be required to arbitrate in conflicts over the public interest; exercise political discretion; or exercise responsibilities where the Treaty confers direct decision-making power on the Commission.

reveals moreover the Commission's rationale for preserving this limit that transcends the dictates of formal law.

The Commission, as we have seen earlier, acknowledged the virtues of independence, credibility, expertise, and the like as reasons for agency creation, combined with the fact that it enabled the Commission to concentrate on its core policy-making functions. This was, however, balanced by repeated references to the need to preserve and reinforce 'the unity and integrity of the executive function' to ensure 'that it continues to be vested in the chief of the Commission if the latter is to have the required responsibility vis-à-vis Europe's citizens, the Member States and the other institutions'.[101] The participation of agencies should therefore be 'organised in a way which is consistent and in balance with the unity and integrity of the executive function and the Commission's ensuing responsibilities'.[102] The same language recurs later in the Communication, when the Commission considers the important issue of the composition of agency boards.[103]

The emphasis placed on the 'unity and integrity of the executive function' and its location in the President of the Commission was not fortuitous given the timing of the Communication. It was issued in 2002 at the same time as the deliberations in the Convention on the Future of Europe. One of the most divisive issues in the Convention deliberations concerned the location of executive power within the Constitutional Treaty and whether this should be said to reside in the Commission, or whether it should be divided between the Commission and European Council. The Commission lost that battle since the Constitutional Treaty in effect embodied a regime of shared executive power.[104]

The Constitutional Treaty may well have passed into history, but the Commission's attachment to the 'unity and integrity of the executive function' with this continuing to be located in the Commission and its President has not. Its conception of the executive function is moreover broad. For the Commission the executive function with which it is vested includes, albeit is not limited to, all that occurs after the passage of primary regulations, directives etc. It is this conception that has informed its opposition to management and regulatory committees, and its desire to replace them with other controls that might satisfy the Council and EP while leaving the Commission more autonomous in the making of legislative norms of a secondary nature.[105]

It is this same conception of the executive function that serves to explain its approach to agencies. It can accept agencies, such as OHIM and CPVO,

[101] Commission Communication, *supra* n. 8, at 1.

[102] Ibid. at 1.

[103] Ibid. at 9.

[104] Craig, 'European Governance: Executive and Administrative Powers under the New Constitutional Settlement' (2005) 3 *I-CON* 407.

[105] See above, Chap. 4.

with individual decision-making power in discrete fields. It can embrace information and coordination agencies, where it continues to have the final say. It is reluctant to create real regulatory agencies exercising discretionary power through adjudication and rule-making, since if such power could be readily delegated then the Commission's sense of the unity and integrity of the executive function vested in it would be undermined. This would be more especially so given that the agencies would have a degree of independence and that Member States would continue to exert considerable influence through membership of the administrative boards.

The *Meroni* principle will be evaluated in detail when we come to consider the possibility of creating real regulatory agencies within the EU. We should first consider the mechanisms for political, legal, and financial accountability that apply to existing agencies.

7. LEGAL ACCOUNTABILITY

A. The Agency Regulation

The natural place to begin with respect to legal accountability is the regulation through which the agency is created. There are not surprisingly points of similarity and points of difference in these regulations.

They are similar in that all agencies are given legal personality. The governing Regulation also makes provision for contractual and non-contractual liability. The former is determined by the law applicable to the contract and the relevant provisions will commonly provide that the ECJ has jurisdiction to give judgment pursuant to an arbitration clause contained in a contract concluded by the agency. In relation to non-contractual liability, the standard format is for the Regulation to replicate Article 288(2) EC within the body of the relevant Regulation: the agency shall, in accordance with the general principles common to the laws of the Member States, make good any damage caused by it or its servants in the performance of their duties.

The differences between the agency regulations are most marked in relation to legality review. There is no standard provision akin to that concerning non-contractual liability. Some Regulations, such as those dealing with OHIM and EASA, contain detailed and explicit provisions on legality review, with a system of internal appeal to a Board of Appeals followed by legality review by the Community courts.[106] Other Regulations, such as that applicable to EUMC, contain no provision for internal appeal, but state that the ECJ shall have jurisdiction in actions brought against the Centre under

[106] Reg. 40/94, *supra* n. 30, Arts. 61, 63; Reg. 1592/2002, *supra* n. 38, Arts. 31–41.

Article 230 EC.[107] The format used in relation to the ECDC is different yet again, enabling a reference to be made to the Commission concerning the legality of the Centre's action, explicitly backed up by the possibility of recourse to the Community courts to annul the Commission decision.[108] The approach taken in the EU-OSHA Regulation is similar, in the sense that it embodies a system of legality review by the Commission, the difference being that there is no explicit reference to further recourse to the ECJ,[109] although the Community courts would have little difficulty in reading this into the Regulation, since the Commission decision on legality would be an act with legal effects and hence reviewable. In some other instances, such as the EMEA, the Regulation contains no mention of legality review, although this is explicable because it is the Commission that makes the final decision and hence it can be reviewed in the normal manner. The regulations in relation to some other agencies, such as EMSA, ENISA, ERA, and CFCA, simply say nothing about legality review.

The provisions pertaining to legal accountability in the agencies established by the Council are similarly diverse. It is common to find provisions concerning contractual liability, less common to find rules about non-contractual liability, and uncommon to find anything that relates to legality review.

B. The Treaty

Given the diversity in the governing regulations pertaining to individual agencies, it is important to consider how far the general Treaty provisions concerning legality review can be used against agencies. Article 230(1) does not contain any explicit mention of agencies or other bodies among the list of those subject to review. If the Constitutional Treaty had been ratified this discussion could have been brief. Article III–365(1) provided explicitly that the Community courts could review the legality of acts of bodies and agencies, albeit providing in Article III–365(5) that the governing provision for an agency could lay down the more detailed procedures for actions brought by private parties.

The fact that the Constitutional Treaty (CT) has not been ratified does not necessarily mean that there is no possibility of recourse to the existing Treaty in respect of legality review. An applicant seeking to review the legality of agency action can reason by analogy from *Les Verts*.[110] The ECJ, as is well known, held that the although the Treaty did not at that time contain

[107] Reg. 1035/97, *supra* n. 34, Art. 15(3).
[108] Reg. 851/2004, *supra* n. 40, Art. 28.
[109] Reg. 2062/94, *supra* n. 31, Art. 22.
[110] Case 294/83, *Parti Ecologiste 'Les Verts' v European Parliament* [1986] ECR 1339.

provision for review of the legality of acts of the EP, it was necessary in a Community based on the rule of law that acts intended to produce legal effects were subject to judicial review. The ECJ has moreover made it clear that this reasoning is not limited to those institutions listed in Article 7 EC, but extends to other Community bodies vested with legal personality.[111] This reasoning could therefore apply to agency actions that produced legal effects.[112]

There are nonetheless difficulties with respect to agencies established by the Council, as evidenced by the *Eurojust* case.[113] Spain sought to review the legality of staff appointment measures contained in advertisements issued by Eurojust on the ground that the language requirements stipulated therein were contrary to the rules contained in the decision setting up Eurojust, to the staff regulations, and to general precepts of non-discrimination. The action was however deemed to be inadmissible by the ECJ. It held that Article 230 EC did not apply to Eurojust, a body established by the Council under the EU. Moreover Article 41 TEU did not render Article 230 EC applicable to the provisions on PJCC in Title VI of the TEU, the jurisdiction of the ECJ being limited in Article 35 TEU to challenges to the legality of the basic decision or framework decision adopted by the Council. The ECJ acknowledged the applicant's argument that in a Community based on the rule of law decisions that produced legal effects must be subject to judicial review, but held that this was met in the instant case because aggrieved candidates for the posts had access to the Community courts under the Staff Regulations.

The ECJ's reasoning stands in marked contrast to that of Advocate General Poiares Maduro. He rejected the applicant's argument that admissibility could be based on Article 230 EC, since the contested measures were not Community measures, and Eurojust had been established under the EU Treaty. He was, however, willing to read Article 35 TEU in the same spirit that the ECJ in *Les Verts* had read Article 230 EC. Thus in a Union based on the rule of law it was essential that Union institutions, as well as those of the EC, should be amenable to review when they produced legal effects vis-à-vis third parties. It should therefore be possible to review the measures taken by Eurojust, in addition to the legality of the decision creating the organization.[114]

It is likely in the light of the above that EC agencies that produce legal effects in relation to third parties will be held amenable to review pursuant to

[111] Case C-15/00, *Commission v EIB* [2003] ECR I-7281, at para. 75; Case C-370/89, *SGEEM and Etroy v EIB* [1992] ECR I-6211, at paras. 15–16.

[112] Lenaerts, 'Regulating the Regulatory Process: "Delegation of Powers" in the European Community' (1993) 18 *ELRev* 23, at 46.

[113] Case C-160/03, *Spain v Eurojust* [2005] ECR I-2077.

[114] Ibid. AG Poiares Maduro, at paras. 15–22.

the reasoning in *Les Verts*. The ECJ in *Eurojust* was unwilling to apply that reasoning to Eurojust primarily because it was an EU rather than an EC agency, although that does not explain why it did not apply the same analysis analogously to the interpretation of Article 35 TEU as the Advocate General had done.

C. Targeting Judicial Review

If judicial review is to be effective it must be capable of being applied to the institution that made the operative decision. This will not normally be a problem, since either the agency or the Commission will be subject to review in the manner considered above.

This can, however, be more problematic in relation to those agencies, such as the EMEA, where the Commission makes the formal decision, but is heavily reliant on the views of the agency, or one of its committees. It might be thought that if the Commission is amenable to review then this will suffice, since it makes the formal decision. The reality is that in most instances the Commission will simply adopt the agency's recommendation, and indeed it is intended that this should be so. If review is to be effective it is necessary for the Community courts to be able to go behind the Commission decision and consider the agency's reasoning. The agency itself must be susceptible to review even though it is not the formal author of the decision.

The CFI took just this step in *Artegodan*, which was concerned with withdrawal of authorization to market medicinal products containing 'amphetamine-like' anorectic agents, used in the treatment of obesity by accelerating the feeling of satiety.[115] The Commission had relied on findings made by the CPMP, the Committee for Proprietary Medicinal Products, one of two committees that undertake the scientific work for the EMEA. While the Commission was not bound by its opinion, the CFI stressed the importance of the mandatory consultation with the CPMP laid down by the relevant Directive. Given that the Commission could not assess for itself the safety or efficacy of the product, consultation with the CPMP was necessary to give the Commission the scientific evidence from which it could make a reasoned decision.[116] The CFI then held that the 'Community judicature may be called on to review, first, the formal legality of the CPMP's scientific opinion and, second, the Commission's exercise of its discretion', in deciding whether to accept that opinion.[117]

While the CFI acknowledged that it could not substitute its view for that

[115] Cases T-74, 76, 83–85, 132, 137 and 141/00, *Artegodan GmbH v Commission* [2002] ECR II-4945.

[116] Ibid. at para. 198.

[117] Ibid. at para. 199.

of the CPMP, it could consider the reasons proffered by it and whether there was an understandable link between the medical evidence relied on by the CPMP and its conclusions. It was moreover incumbent on the CPMP to refer to the main scientific reports on which it had relied and to explain why it disagreed with, for example, divergent scientific opinion presented by the undertakings concerned in the case.[118]

The case will be examined in more detail below, within the general context of judicial review. Suffice it to say for the present that the logic of the CFI's reasoning is unassailable: since the Commission would normally follow the opinion of the scientific committee, and had done so in this case, if judicial review was to be meaningful the CFI should be able to consider the CPMP's reasoning.[119]

D. Applying Judicial Review

The discussion thus far has been concerned with the foundations for legal accountability, whether in the agency regulation or the Treaty, and the targeting of judicial review at the institution or institutions that made the contested decision. This still leaves the all-important issue about the application of the precepts of judicial review to the agencies. The chapters in the second half of this book discuss these matters in detail and reference should be made to those for consideration of the procedural and substantive principles of judicial review that are available to an applicant.

8. POLITICAL CONTROL AND ACCOUNTABILITY

There are, as will be apparent from the subsequent discussion, a number of different aspects to political control and accountability. Part of the rationale for the creation of agencies within the EU was independence based on the agencies' expertise in the relevant area, this independence thereby enhancing the credibility of EU decision-making in the relevant area. There are, however, various political controls, direct and indirect, over agencies, as well as mechanisms designed to ensure their accountability. The extent to which these have an impact on agency independence will become apparent from the analysis that follows.

[118] Ibid. at paras. 199–200.

[119] The CFI's decision was upheld on appeal, but the ECJ did not consider this particular issue, Case C-39/03 P, *Commission v Artegodan GmbH* [2003] ECR I-7885.

A. Agency Tasks, Criteria, and Reporting

It is fitting to begin consideration of political control and accountability by considering how far the enabling regulation specifies the agency's tasks and criteria for their attainment. This is a matter of some significance, although it is often overlooked in discussion of EU agencies. The basic point is, however, simple: the greater the specification of agency objectives and criteria for attainment, the greater the control exercised over agency choices by the legislature. Vague injunctions as to what the agency is intended to do, coupled with criteria set out at a high level of abstraction, will, other things being equal, leave more power to the agency.

This point is especially important where the agency has decision-making power, and even more so where it is accorded discretionary power to make rules and individual decisions. Concerns of this nature have been voiced about grants of power to agencies in the USA, leading some to call for revival of the non-delegation doctrine, compelling Congress to set out more specifically the criteria to be used by the agency when making decisions, although the courts have not generally responded to this call.[120]

Legislative specification of tasks and criteria for their fulfilment are nonetheless relevant for EU agencies, a point emphasized in external evaluation of agency performance.[121] This is particularly so for those that do have decision-making power, but it is also apposite for what were termed quasi-regulatory and information/coordination agencies. The tasks of these agencies include advising the Commission on legislative initiatives and hence the criteria that should inform such advice remain important.

It is impossible within the scope of this chapter to examine all Community and EU agencies to see how they measure up in this regard. That would require a paper in its own right. Suffice it to say for the present that the general pattern is that the basic agency regulation establishes tasks and criteria for their fulfilment with some real specificity. This is so notwithstanding the fact that the subject matter dealt with by some agencies necessarily leaves interpretative power to the agency to determine whether the criteria have been met. The basic regulation will moreover contain provision for implementing regulations to be made to flesh out certain provisions. These regulations will be made by the Commission, subject to comitology procedures. The agency itself will contribute to this process, the degree of this contribution varying from area to area. The more technical the nature of the subject matter, the greater the degree of agency involvement. Thus in the context of aviation safety the two main EASA implementing regulations, which run to

[120] A. Aman and W. Mayton, *Administrative Law* (West, 2nd ed, 2001), at 9–36.

[121] Budget Directorate General, Evaluation Unit, Meta-Evaluation on the Community Agency System (2003).

79 and 165 pages respectively, consisted almost entirely of detailed annexes drafted in large part by the EASA.

The specification of agency tasks and criteria for their fulfilment has an impact *ex ante* on the degree of control exercised by the legislature over agency choices. The obligation to report provides some control *ex post facto*. The general pattern is for the regulation to require the agency to send an annual report to the EP, Council, and Commission, and in some instances to the Member States, the Economic and Social Committee (ECOSOC), and the Committee of the Regions. Some agency regulations contain more far-reaching provisions. Thus, for example, the EASA regulation provides that the EP or Council may invite the director to report on the carrying out of his or her tasks,[122] and the ERA regulation states that the Council and EP can call for a hearing with the agency director at any time.[123]

B. Agency Composition

The extent to which agencies can be controlled and held accountable is dependent in part on their composition. Those familiar with the US system will be aware of changes in agency policy resulting from a new agency head appointed when a President of a different political party takes office. The reality is that no single institution wields this degree of power over agency membership in the EU.

The general structure of *Community agencies* is for there to be an administrative, governing, or management board, an executive director, and in some agencies an advisory forum or a body akin thereto. Control over agency membership is important in any system. The Commission has sought to increase its power in relation to management boards and the director of the agency, but it has been largely unsuccessfully in both areas.

The *administrative, governing, or management board* will normally have the following responsibilities. It will have a role in the appointment of the director of the agency; it adopts the agency's annual work programme, as proposed by the director; it has overall responsibility for ensuring that the agency performs its tasks; it may play a role in defining the agency's strategic orientation; and it adopts the annual report on the agency and its financial rules. The more recent agency regulations place increased emphasis on board members possessing the skills relevant to the area in question. The board meets twice a year, but there is provision for further meetings at the request of the chairman, or some of the board members, the normal requirement being two-thirds. Each member of the board has one vote, and the norm is to require two-thirds majority for management board decisions. The effect is

[122] Reg. 1592/2002, *supra* n. 38, Art. 29(2).
[123] Reg. 881/2004, *supra* n. 41, Art. 32.

that state equality, in formal terms at least, applies within management boards of agencies. It is interesting to speculate on whether there would be pressure for this to change if agencies were accorded discretionary powers coupled with the authority to make binding rules and decisions.

The composition of these boards is important. The paradigm has been for Member State interests to dominate. Thus it was common for agencies created in the 1990s to have one or two representatives from each Member State, somewhere between one and three from the Commission, one or two from the EP, and in some instances representatives from employer and employee organizations.

The Commission expressed dissatisfaction with this practice, stating that it failed to take sufficient account of the Community dimension and hence gave insufficient attention to the importance of preserving the unity and integrity of the executive function at European level. It argued in favour of smaller management boards on which it, the Commission, would have a greater percentage of representatives. It pressed for a fifteen-member management board, where there would be six Council representatives, six from the Commission, plus three representing interested parties who would have no voting rights.[124]

The Commission has not been successful in this regard. The general pattern for agencies created since the Commission's Communication is that the same practice has continued as hitherto, with a representative from each Member State, between one and four from the Commission, and some expert professionals in the relevant area, who commonly do not have the right to vote.[125] The closest that the Commission has come to fulfilling its aspirations has been in relation to amendments to the governing board of EU-OSHA, an older agency. The amended Regulation retains one representative from each Member State, and provides for a representative of employer and employees organizations from each Member State, plus three members from the Commission. However the amended Regulation stipulates that the Member State, employer, and employee representatives should form groups and appoint a coordinator from each group. The coordinator has the right to vote on the governing board, but the other members of the group do not. The net effect is to provide for six voting members, the three coordinators plus the three members of the Commission.[126]

The Commission continues to attach considerable significance to the composition of the administrative board. This is evident in the Draft

[124] Commission Communication, *supra* n. 8, at 9.

[125] See, e.g., Reg. 1406/2002, EMSA, *supra* n. 37, Art. 11; Reg. 1592/2002, EASA, *supra* n. 38, Art. 25; Reg. 460/2004, ENISA, *supra* n. 39, Art. 6; Reg. 851/2004, ECDC, *supra* n. 40, Art. 14(1).

[126] Reg, 1112/2005, *supra* n. 74, Art. 1(5) amending Reg. 2062/94, Art. 8.

Interinstitutional Agreement, which is intended to provide an operating framework for future agencies, albeit with the possibility that existing agencies might be brought into line in the future. The Draft provides for equal representation of Commission and Council on the administrative board.[127]

The *agency director* is central to the running of the organization. The holder of this post has a number of functions including oversight of the day-to-day work of the agency, drawing up the agency work programme, implementing that programme, budgetary responsibility, and the preparation of the annual report of the agency's activities. Appointment is normally either by the management board on a proposal from the Commission, or by the Commission on the basis of candidates put forward by the management board. The Commission argued that the latter should be used in relation to those bodies with formal decision-making powers, since it was especially important in such contexts that the director had the Commission's confidence.[128] The reality is that appointment by the management board on the basis of a list of candidates put forward by the Commission is the norm, and this has continued to be so even in relation to agencies that have decision-making power, such as the EASA.[129]

This method of appointment whereby the Commission provides the list of candidates to the agency still leaves the Commission with power over choice of the agency director. The extent of this power has, however, been qualified by three related developments in the regulations governing more recent agencies. There has been an increased emphasis on the need for the agency director to be independent and to possess the skills relevant to the agency's area.[130] There is provision for the Commission's list of candidates to be produced after an open competition for the post, which must be advertised in the Official Journal and other relevant sites. There is moreover a requirement that the person chosen by the management board as a result of this process must appear before the European Parliament before being formally appointed, make a statement concerning his or her vision for the agency, and answer questions.[131]

The discussion thus far has been concerned with Community agencies established under Pillar 1. Matters are not surprisingly different for *Council agencies* established under Pillars 2 and 3. In relation to agencies created under the CFSP Pillar, EDA, EUISS, and EUSC, the general pattern is for

[127] Draft Interinstitutional Agreement, *supra* n. 100, Art. 11(2).

[128] Commission Communication, *supra* n. 8, at 10.

[129] Reg. 1592/2002, *supra* n. 38, Art. 30.

[130] See, eg, Reg. 1406/2002, EMSA, *supra* n. 37, Arts. 15–16; Reg. 1592/2002, EASA, *supra* n. 38, Arts. 29–30; Reg. 460/2004, ENISA, *supra* n. 39, Art. 7; Reg. 851/2004, ECDC, *supra* n. 40, Art. 16.

[131] See, eg, Reg. 178/2002, EFSA, *supra* n. 36, Art. 26; Reg. 460/2004, ENISA, *supra* n. 39, Art. 7; Reg. 851/2004, ECDC, *supra* n. 40, Art. 17.

the agency to be run by a board and a director.[132] The board is normally chaired by the Secretary-General/High Representative and is composed of a representative from each Member State, plus a member from the Commission. The board's functions tend to be similar to those of the boards in Community agencies, as do their meeting arrangements. A significant difference, however, is that there is weighted voting on the boards of CFSP agencies, by way of contrast to the one member one vote principle that applies to Community agencies. The agency director is appointed by the board from among Member State nationals, and performs similar tasks to the directors of Community agencies. The Member States submit candidates to the Secretary-General/High Representative (SG/HR), who then forwards these to the board, except in the case of the EDA where the SG/HR as head of the agency actually proposes a candidate. A similar organizational structure of board plus director heavily controlled by the Member States is apparent in relation to agencies, such as Europol and Eurojust, which operate under the PJCC Pillar. Thus the management board of Europol has a representative from each Member State, and each representative has one vote. The Commission can be invited to meetings but has no vote. The director is appointed by the Council after obtaining the board's opinion.[133]

C. Agency Work Programme

The rules concerning agency composition are important for the reasons considered above. The extent to which an institution external to the agency is able to exert influence over its work programme is equally significant. Most of the regulatory schemes accord the Commission some input to the agency's work programme over and beyond that flowing from its membership of the management board, although the precise degree varies from agency to agency.

The provisions in relation to the EMSA give the Commission the greatest influence in this respect. The administrative board adopts the agency's work programme for the coming year and forwards it to the Member States, the EP, the Council, and the Commission. Where the Commission expresses within 15 days from the date of adoption of the work programme its disagreement with it, the administrative board must re-examine the programme and adopt it, possibly with amendments, within two months. There must be a two-thirds majority, including the Commission representatives, or unanimity of the Member State representatives on the administrative board for this

[132] Council Joint Action 2004/551/CFSP, EDA, *supra* n. 53, Arts. 8, 10; Council Joint Action 2001/554/CFSP, EUISS, *supra* n. 51, Arts. 5–6; Council Joint Action 2001/555/CFSP, EUSC, *supra* n. 50, Arts. 7–8.

[133] Europol Convention, *supra* n. 48, Arts. 28–29; Council Decision 2002/187/JHA, Eurojust, *supra* n. 52, Arts. 2, 10, 11, 29.

second reading.[134] The same provisions apply to Commission control over the ERA's[135] and the CFCA's[136] work programme.

The EMEA Regulation falls at the other end of the scale. It stipulates that the director prepares the draft programme of work for the coming year, which is then adopted by the management board and forwarded to the Member States, Commission, Council, and EP.[137] There is, however, no explicit provision for any privileged role for the Commission concerning the annual work programme of the kind that exists in the EMSA regulation.

The EFSA Regulation occupies an intermediate position. It is for the management board to adopt the annual work programme. There is no mention at this level of any Commission involvement, over and beyond its membership of the board, albeit there is an injunction that the programme be consistent with the Community's legislative and policy priorities in the area of food safety and this would serve to give the Commission some leverage. The Commission is in any event accorded influence because the director who drafts the annual work programme does so in consultation with the Commission.[138]

The Regulation governing the EASA exemplifies another intermediate position, stipulating that the management board shall adopt the annual work programme after receiving the Commission's opinion, and then forwarding it to the EP, Council, Commission, and Member States.[139] This is perhaps the most common 'format' in use.

There is little doubt that the regulatory provisions concerning the EMSA give the Commission some real leverage over the annual work programme. It is nonetheless difficult to determine in reality how much influence the Commission brings to bear over this programme and equally difficult to assess whether there is any causal relationship between the different legal provisions and the degree of influence wielded by the Commission. My intuition is that if the Commission feels sufficiently strongly about the direction of an annual work programme and has been unable to get it revised through its members on the management board, then it will seek to exert influence from the outside irrespective of the precise provisions of the particular regulation. We should not moreover lose sight of the fact that the Commission is the only institution accorded this extra influence over the annual work programme. This in itself bears testimony to the importance attached by the Commission to the 'unity and integrity' of the executive function.

[134] Reg. 1406/2002, *supra* n. 37, Art. 10(2)(d).
[135] Reg. 881/2004, *supra* n. 41, Art. 25(2)(c).
[136] Reg. 768/2005, *supra* n. 42, Art. 23(2)(c).
[137] Reg. 2309/93, *supra* n. 29, Arts. 55–56.
[138] Reg. 178/2002, *supra* n. 36, Arts. 25(8), 26(2)(b).
[139] Reg. 1592/2002, *supra* n. 38, Art. 24(2)(c).

The situation in relation to Council agencies is different. The norm is that the board will adopt the annual work programme that has been drafted by the director of the agency. There is no formal provision for the Commission to be consulted on this draft by the director or by the board. This is unsurprising given that these agencies are dominated by Member State representatives. While the Commission has a seat on the boards of CFSP agencies, there is no sense that the 'unity and integrity' of the executive function vested in the Commission runs in these areas. To the contrary, the instruments establishing the CFSP agencies emphasize that political supervision is through the Council.[140] The situation is similar in relation to JHA/PJCC agencies. For Europol institutional control is exercised predominantly through the Council. The Commission is afforded a somewhat greater role in the work of Eurojust,[141] but it does not have influence over the annual work programme of the kind that it can exercise in relation to Community agencies.

D. Agency Transparency

Transparency is properly regarded as an important attribute of public decision-making. There is both diversity and some degree of uniformity in relation to agencies and transparency.

There is diversity in the sense that agency regulations differ considerably as to the extent to which they mention transparency. This may be partly explained by the fact that the agencies deal with different subject matter and that transparency may be relatively more or less important in some areas rather than others. This explanation is, however, unconvincing, given that basic precepts of transparency are important in all public decision-making. The EFSA Regulation on food safety is an example of transparency being accorded a high status. The EFSA is instructed to carry out its mission with transparent procedures and methods of operation.[142] It is told more specifically to make public without delay agendas and minutes of the Scientific Committee and Scientific Panels; the opinions of these bodies immediately after adoption, including minority opinions; the information on which its opinions are based; annual declarations of interest by the management board, director, and others; the results of scientific studies; the annual report of its activities; and requests from the EP, Commission, and Member States for scientific opinions that have been refused or modified, together with

[140] Council Joint Action 2004/551/CFSP, EDA, *supra* n. 53, Art. 4; Council Joint Action 2001/554/CFSP, EUISS, *supra* n. 51, Art. 3; Council Joint Action 2001/555/CFSP, EUSC, *supra* n. 50, Art. 3.

[141] Council Decision 2002/187/JHA, *supra* n. 52, Art. 11.

[142] Reg. 178/2002, *supra* n. 36, Art. 22(7).

justification.[143] The Regulation also provides that the management board shall generally meet in public and that it may authorize consumer representatives or other interested parties to observe some of the EFSA's activities.[144] A number of other agency regulations contain provisions about transparency,[145] albeit not in the detail of the EFSA Regulation.

There is, however, uniformity in relation to the aspect of transparency dealing with access to documents, at least as concerns Community agencies. Article 255(1) EC provides a right of access to documents held by the EP, Council, and Commission, subject to conditions and limits to be defined pursuant to Article 255(2) EC. A Regulation was introduced pursuant to Article 255(2) specifying the nature of these conditions and limits.[146] It will be examined in more detail in a later chapter.[147] This Regulation has now been applied to the Community agencies.

E. Agency Networks

A theme that appears repeatedly in the agency regulations is that of network, connoting the idea that the agency should interact in a variety of ways with other key players in the relevant area, whether at national, regional, or international level.

In many of the regulatory schemes the network concept is explicit and formalized, as exemplified by the EFSA and food safety. The original Regulation stipulated that the EFSA should promote the networking of organizations operating in fields that came within the EFSA's mission, in order to facilitate scientific cooperation through coordination of activities, exchange of information, expertise, and the like. Detailed implementation of this idea was to be carried through by a Commission Regulation,[148] which has now been enacted.[149] It established the criteria for organizations that are to take part in the network. They must, for example, have scientific expertise in the relevant area and pursue public interest objectives. It is for the Member States to designate competent organizations from their country. The EFSA will check that they meet the relevant criteria. The EFSA fosters networking with

[143] Ibid. Art. 38(1). [144] Ibid. Art. 38(2).

[145] See, eg, Reg. 1406/2002, EMSA, *supra* n. 37, Art. 4(2); Reg. 460/2004, ENISA, *supra* n. 39, Art. 12; Reg. 851/2004, ECDC, *supra* n. 40, Arts. 19–20; Reg. 1592/2002, EASA, *supra* n. 38, Art. 47.

[146] Regulation (EC) 1049/01 of the European Parliament and of the Council of 30 May 2001, Regarding Public Access to European Parliament, Council and Commission Documents, OJ 2001 L145/43.

[147] See below, Chap. 11. [148] Reg. 178/2002, *supra* n. 36, Art. 36.

[149] Commission Regulation (EC) 2230/2004 of 23 December 2004, Laying Down Detailed Rules for the Implementation of EP and Council Regulation (EC) 178/2002 with regard to the Networking of Organisations Operating in the Fields within the EFSA's Mission, OJ 2004 L379/64.

these organizations with the help of the Advisory Forum. The Regulation specifies tasks that can be entrusted to organizations on the list, including: dissemination of best practices; collecting and analysing specific data with a view to facilitating risk assessment by the EFSA; producing scientific data contributing to risk assessment; preparing the EFSA's scientific opinions; and preparing the harmonization of risk assessment methods.

Networks are accorded an explicit role in relation to many other agencies. The following are simply examples. One of the tasks accorded to EU-OSHA is to establish, in cooperation with the Member States, and coordinate a network of organizations, taking into account the national, Community, and international bodies providing the type of information concerning health and safety at work that falls within EU-OSHA's remit. The agency is enjoined to establish a network comprising principal components of national information frameworks, including social partners' organizations, national focal points, and future topic centres, in order to exchange information and coordinate initiatives.[150] The EASA regulation makes provision for an information network between the agency, the Commission, and national aviation authorities. Networking is evident once again in the fact that the agency can enlist the help of national aviation authorities in the issuing of airworthiness certificates, drawing on their expertise in this area, and can work with such national authorities in relation to investigation and enforcement.[151] Networking is central to the work of the ECDC, in order for it to be aware of and be able to fight disease. The ECDC therefore interacts with and draws information from national bodies, and promotes cooperation between them.[152] The EUMC was enjoined to set up and coordinate a European Racism and Xenophobia Information Network (Raxen), and to cooperate with national, international and non-governmental organizations competent in the field of racism and xenophobia.[153] The remit accorded to the EMSA to provide for maritime safety, maritime security, and the prevention of pollution necessitates significant interaction between the agency and national authorities in relation to a whole range of matters.[154] Networks are also a prominent feature of many of the Council agencies under Pillars 2 and 3.

It is clear that networking makes a good deal of practical sense. It fosters cooperation between national and Community authorities dealing with the same terrain, avoids duplication of effort, and facilitates exchange of information, expertise, and best practice. These benefits are especially significant for those agencies that are primarily concerned with collation of information and coordination. Networking is equally important for agencies such as the EASA

150 Reg. 2062/94, *supra* n. 31, Arts. 3(1)(f), 4, as amended by Reg. 1112/2005, *supra* n. 74.
151 Reg. 1592/2002, *supra* n. 38, Arts. 11, 15(2)(a), 43, 46.
152 Reg. 851/2004, *supra* n. 40, Arts. 5–10.
153 Reg. 1035/97, *supra* n. 34, Arts. 4, 7.
154 Reg. 1406/2002, *supra* n. 37.

and EMSA, which have been established to foster safety and security in their relevant areas. The discharge of these responsibilities not only requires information flows between relevant players at national, Community, and international level. It also necessitates interaction between them when it comes to matters such as criteria for airworthiness, inspection, and enforcement. It is moreover equally clear that the agency model provides a fitting mechanism through which such networking can take place. It enables the EU to establish a body with expertise in the relevant area, and hence the credibility that flows from this, to act as the focal point for the network. Scholars have highlighted the benefits of networking and the way in which it is facilitated by the agency model,[155] although some are more cautious about the utility of the network concept for explicating the nature of the agency administrative regime.[156]

While the benefits of networking can be acknowledged, that still leaves open its relevance for political control and accountability. We need to tread carefully here, since it is easy to elide different concepts. The fact that networking is efficacious does not in and of itself tell one much if anything about its implications for political control and accountability. This is in part because so much depends on the type of networking that operates within a particular agency regime. It is in part also because networking can have countervailing implications for control and accountability.

Thus the existence of the type of network that characterizes Community agencies renders control from and accountability to the top more difficult. The very fact that there are multiple players involved, national, sub-national, international, non-governmental, as well as the Community agency, means that implementation of the agency's agenda will perforce be shaped by these players, who may well come to have an impact on the agenda itself and not merely its implementation. It may moreover, as Shapiro notes, be difficult to differentiate between expert input and policy preference, or to know what the preferences of the other players actually are and how they factor into the practicalities of implementation or shape the policy agenda.[157]

It is, however, also possible to argue that while networks render control from and accountability to the top more difficult, they nonetheless foster other forms of control and accountability. The inclusion of multiple players,

[155] See, e.g., Dehousse, *supra* n. 14; K.-H. Ladeur, *The European Environment Agency and Prospects for a European Network of Environmental Administrations*, EUI Working Paper RSC, No. 96/50, Florence, European University Institute, 1996; T. A. Borzel, *Policy Networks—A New Paradigm for European Governance?*, EUI Working Paper RSC 97/19, Florence, European University Institute, 1997; Borzel, 'Rediscovering Policy Networks as a Form of Modern Governance' (1998) 5 *JEPP* 354.

[156] Chiti, 'Emergence' *supra* n. 63, at 329–331; Chiti, 'Decentralisation', *supra* n. 63, at 425–428.

[157] Shapiro, *supra* n. 12, at 286–287.

in addition to the agency and the formal Community institutions, could be said to facilitate a more pluralist, participatory form of control and accountability. We should not forget the reasons why state, regional, international, and non-governmental parties are included in the networks. They have things to offer, expertise, information; they may be concerned with the same problems themselves and hence duplication of effort can be avoided; and their assistance may be required in order for the agency regime to be operational on the ground. We see here an admixture of instrumental and non-instrumental reasons for the involvement of other parties in the development and application of agency policy. The instrumental rationale is that we hope that a better rule/policy will result if the views of those with expertise, experience, etc. are taken into account. This is complemented by the non-instrumental rationale, that participation of these parties within agency decision-making will enhance their involvement with the polity and render the results more acceptable. This does not mean that the application of this second model of control and accountability is unproblematic in relation to agencies. We shall return to some of these problems in due course. It does mean we should be willing to think of the matter in these terms.

F. Agency Participation

There is a proximate connection between networks and participation in agency decision-making. One purpose of networks is to enable those who are interested and concerned by the agency's work to participate therein. Participation/consultation is nonetheless a topic in its own right, since there may be parties who are not part of any network who wish to have their voice heard on a particular issue.

A number of agency regulations make reference in one way or another to participation/consultation. The EMEA provides that Member States and interested parties should be consulted when it draws up guidance on the form in which applications for authorization should be presented and on the collection and presentation of adverse reaction reports.[158] ENISA is instructed to engage with, *inter alia*, interested parties in the context of risk management.[159] The EFSA Regulation stipulates that there shall be open and transparent public consultation during the preparation, evaluation, and revision of food law, except where urgency precludes this.[160] The EASA is enjoined to consult interested parties and respond to their comments.[161]

It is, however, necessary to press beyond the bare regulations to appreciate the reality of agencies and participation. It is clear, for example, that the

[158] Reg. 2309/93, *supra* n. 29, Arts. 28(5), 46.

[159] Reg. 460/2004, *supra* n. 39, Art. 4(j).

[160] Reg. 178/2002, *supra* n. 36, Art. 9.

[161] Reg. 1592/2002, *supra* n. 38, Art. 43.

EFSA makes frequent use of consultations on an ad hoc basis. It is equally clear that the EASA has by far the best developed practice in this respect. We have touched on the EASA's rule-making programme in the previous discussion.[162] The rulemaking procedures are impressive. The EASA has a rulemaking directorate that publishes an annual rulemaking programme, and any person can propose that an item be included. The terms of reference of a particular rule are then set out, explaining the nature of the problem to be addressed, followed by the draft rule, in relation to which the agency conducts a regulatory impact assessment. Notice of the proposed rule is posted on the website and any person can comment through a standardized form. The comments are then aggregated in a comment response document (CRD), enabling interested parties to gain an overview of comments put forward by others. These comments are then used by the drafting group when finalizing the rule. At this stage the drafting group is reinforced by two additional members, one of whom is drawn from those who dissented from the draft rule. The EASA is also assisted by a Safety Standards Consultative Committee, composed of representatives of organizations directly affected by the regulatory regime, and by the Advisory Group of National Authorities.

The entire rule-making process is easy to access and follow. It could well serve as a model in other related areas. This is especially so given that the instrumental and non-instrumental arguments mentioned in the discussion of networks are salient here too; indeed they were developed to explain the value of participation/consultation in rule-making.

9. FINANCIAL ACCOUNTABILITY

Financial accountability is important for any public institution. The original agency regulations contained provisions about budgets, revenue, and the like. These have now been amended and made more uniform. The catalyst for this change was the enactment of the new Financial Regulation,[163] considered in detail in a previous chapter,[164] Article 185 of which stipulated that a further Regulation should be made applying relevant principles of the Financial Regulation to Community bodies that have legal personality and received grants charged to the budget. This Regulation has now been enacted.[165] It

162 See above, at 155–156.

163 Council Regulation (EC, Euratom) 1605/2002 of 25 June 2002, On the Financial Regulation Applicable to the General Budget of the European Communities, OJ 2002 L248/1.

164 See above, Chap. 2.

165 Commission Regulation (EC, Euratom) 2343/2002 of 23 December 2002, On the Framework Financial Regulation for the Bodies Referred to in Article 185 of Council Regulation (EC, Euratom) 1605/2002 on the Financial Regulation Applicable to the General Budget of the European Communities, OJ 2002 L357/72.

leaves certain choices open to agencies, but nonetheless closely structures and confines their options.

The budgetary principles of unity, annuality equilibrium, universality, specification, sound financial management, and transparency contained in the Financial Regulation are made applicable to Community bodies.[166] So too are the important rules concerning implementation of the budget. The division between authorizing and accounting officer, which was central to the new Financial Regulation, is extended to Community bodies.

The director is presumptively the authorizing officer for the agency, although he can delegate these powers to a staff member who comes within the Staff Regulations.[167] The authorizing officer is responsible for implementing revenue and expenditure commitments in accordance with the principles of sound financial management and for ensuring that requirements of legality and regularity are met.[168] Financial control systems must be put in place. The authorizing officer is the key figure in the financial regime. Every item of expenditure has to be committed, validated, authorized, and paid. Budgetary commitment must precede legal commitment, and it is the authorizing officer who does both. The authorizing officer is responsible for validating the expenditure, which entails verification that the relevant task has been performed and the amount of the claim. The officer then authorizes the expenditure, although the actual payment is made by the accounting officer.[169]

There are numerous checks built into the system. Before any particular operation is authorized it must be verified *ex ante* and *ex post* by a staff member other than the one who initiated the operation.[170] There is provision for a staff member to blow the whistle if the person believes that he or she is being required to agree to something by a superior that is irregular or contrary to principles of sound financial management and this applies *a fortiori* in the event of illegality, corruption, or fraud.[171] There are provisions requiring the authorizing officer to pay compensation if expenditure is authorized that does not comply with the Financial Regulation and the implementing rules.[172] Where power is delegated the director as the original authorizing officer remains responsible for the effectiveness of the internal management and control systems put in place and for the choice of the person to whom the power has been delegated.[173] There is an internal audit regime, and the internal auditor advises the agency on matters such as internal management and control systems.[174] This is complemented by external audit through the Court of Auditors,[175] and the requirement of budgetary discharge exercised

[166] Ibid. Arts. 3–26.
[167] Ibid. Arts. 33–34.
[168] Ibid. Art. 38.
[169] Ibid. Arts. 60–66.
[170] Ibid. Arts. 38(5), 39.
[171] Ibid. Art. 41.
[172] Ibid. Art. 47.
[173] Ibid. Art. 47(3).
[174] Ibid. Arts. 71–73.
[175] Ibid. Arts. 91–93.

by the European Parliament on recommendation from the Council.[176] In addition to these financial controls, it is now common practice to specify that the agency is subject to investigation by OLAF, the European Anti Fraud Office, thereby providing a further check on fraud.

These rules are likely to have an impact on agency decision-making that goes beyond financial accountability *per se*. The authorizing officer is responsible for the budgetary and legal commitment on expenditure; he or she is responsible for validating the expenditure; and it is the authorizing officer that issues the payment order. It means that the agency director as authorizing officer will be acutely aware of agency decision-making that involves any expenditure and mindful of the penalties that can flow if errors are made. The director is, as we have already seen, responsible for the day-to-day running of the agency and the planning of its work agenda. The financial rules locate, subject to any delegation, financial responsibility with the director. This conjunction of responsibilities is likely to be beneficial for the smooth running of agencies, ensuring that policy and financial planning/implementation are closely linked, and that the director maintains control over the agency notwithstanding the networks that feed into it. It also facilitates oversight by the management board, which has the power to adopt the work programme and budget, both of which will have been drafted by the director.

10. THE EXISTING AGENCY REGIME

There is little doubt that agencies have become a settled feature of the EU's institutional landscape. They are subject to a plethora of controls designed to foster accountability from the top and the bottom. These controls are far from perfect, and agencies could learn much from exchange of 'best practices' in relation to matters such as procedures, transparency, and consultation. While there is room for improvement in relation to various aspects of legal and political accountability, the existing controls when viewed in aggregate with the financial provisions secure a reasonable measure of accountability. External evaluation of agency performance has been quite positive, albeit with some recommendations for improving agency efficiency and internal agency management structures.[177]

It should moreover be remembered, as Dehousse forcefully reminds us, that the alternative to agencies is not a genuine political dialogue between Council and Parliament, but regulation through yet another comitology committee with all the problems that this entails.[178] We need to enter a

[176] Ibid. Art. 94. [177] Meta-Evaluation, *supra* n. 121.
[178] Dehousse, *supra* n. 14, at 258.

caveat here, since such committees play a role in relation to agencies, given that agency implementing regulations will be made by the Commission subject to a comitology committee. Notwithstanding this Dehousse's argument still has force: if an agency did not exist it is likely that the entire subject matter would be regulated through a comitology committee and it is difficult to argue that comitology fares better than agencies judged by the accountability criteria considered above.[179]

11. THE FUTURE AGENCY REGIME

The official view is that the future agency regime will continue very much as it has done until now. The Commission's 2005 Draft Interinstitutional Agreement[180] on regulatory agencies is explicitly premised on the continuation of the existing limits to the powers that can be accorded to agencies. The aim of the measure is to secure agreement between the Commission, EP, and Council on agency organization and accountability, assuming that agencies continue to have the types of power they have been given in the past. The Draft Interinstitutional Agreement will only apply to new agencies, although it leaves open the possibility of bringing existing agencies into line over time.

It is important nonetheless to consider whether real regulatory agencies should be created, with discretionary power that could be exercised through formally binding individual decisions and rule-making. The natural starting place is to consider how far the loosening of the *Meroni* constraints would affect the rationale for EU agencies.

A. The Rationale for EU Agencies

The *Meroni* principle has generally had a 'bad press', at least in the modern legal literature.[181] It is seen as the block to the creation of true regulatory agencies that would be beneficial for decision-making in the EU. It is argued that if agencies were accorded real discretionary power then safeguards, such as an Administrative Procedure Act, fiscal oversight, and the like, could be put in place to ensure that the power was used properly. We shall consider the nature of such checks in due course.

It is, however, important to recognize that there is a logically prior issue, which is the rationale for EU agencies if we loosen the *Meroni* constraints. We have seen that EU agencies were justified in terms of their expertise, the

[179] See above, Chap. 4. [180] *Supra* n. 100.

[181] Everson, 'Independent Agencies: Hierarchy Beaters?' (1995) 1 *ELJ* 180; Vos, 'Reforming the European Commission: What Role to Play for EU Agencies?' (2000) 37 *CMLRev* 1113; Majone, *supra* n. 16.

enhanced credibility that they bring to decision-making, their ability to foster networks with other interested parties, and the fact that they enable the Commission to concentrate on its core tasks of policy formation. The granting of real discretionary power to agencies, requiring them to balance competing public interests when making binding formal rules or individual decisions, would require re-evaluation of this rationale.

Justifications cast in terms of expertise become weaker, since the agency accorded such new powers has no special claim to expertise when it comes to balancing broad, competing public interests, or when deciding on, for example, the level of risk that is acceptable within society. Agency technical expertise does not translate into specialist skills in balancing broad public interests. Scientific legitimacy is, as the CFI recognized in *Pfizer*, not the same as democratic legitimacy.[182] The credibility argument captures the idea that by preserving technical regulatory issues from the vagaries of day-to-day political change the credibility of the choices thus made will be increased. If, however, agencies are accorded broad discretionary powers requiring them to balance competing public interests then it is by no means self-evident that such decisions should be insulated from political change expressed by and through the ordinary political process. Nor is it self-evident that EU agencies exercising such enhanced power would be viewed as more credible than majoritarian decision-making institutions.

It follows that if the *Meroni* constraints are to be loosened this must be based on an argument that transcends that made for existing agencies. Majone presents such an argument for enhancing agency power that embraces expertise and credibility, but moves beyond them. There are a number of strands to his thesis.[183] He maintains that it is not really possible in certain areas, such as risk regulation, to distinguish between the technical issues dealt with by an agency, and the policy matters residing in majoritarian institutions. He argues that the complex regulatory tasks faced by the Community cannot be adequately handled by the Commission with its limited administrative, financial, and cognitive resources, and that recourse to stronger and more autonomous regulatory institutions at European level is the best response. Majone argues furthermore that such a development can fit with the idea of institutional balance that characterizes the EU polity, with agencies being regarded as the 'regulatory estate' to be added to the other 'estates' that comprise the EU. The regulatory estate would be subject to controls to ensure accountability and legitimacy.

Some will simply disagree with this line of argument. They may feel that continued attachment to the limits established by *Meroni* is important in the EU and they may be unconvinced by the argument that the creation of real

[182] Case T-13/99, *Pfizer Animal Health SA v Council* [2002] ECR II-3303, at para. 201.
[183] Majone, *supra* nn. 4, 16.

regulatory agencies can be accommodated within the institutional balance that characterizes the EU polity. Others will agree with Majone's general line of argument, provided that adequate checks exist over agencies with such enhanced power. It is therefore interesting to press further and consider more precisely what form these checks would take, remembering that the greater the power accorded to agencies the more important it becomes to ensure that adequate accountability mechanisms exist. The current regime of financial accountability described above would not require any significant modification and therefore the discussion will concentrate on legal and political constraints.

B. Legal Constraints

If agencies were accorded such extended power a necessary condition for legal accountability would be amenability to judicial review. The simplest way to secure this would be through a Treaty revision envisioned by the Constitutional Treaty whereby all agencies and similar bodies were brought within the purview of Article 230 EC.

It is equally clear that legal accountability would demand that we pay due attention to that part of the *Meroni* reasoning requiring that if power is given to agencies it should be subject to the same legal constraints, in terms of reason giving, publication, compliance with fundamental rights, and the like, as if the power were exercised by the primary Community institutions. This was central to the *Meroni* ruling, since the agencies in that case were not subject to duties to give reasons and publication that bound the High Authority. It is all the more important to ensure that this problem is addressed if agencies are to be given discretionary powers and the authority to make binding rules and decisions. In *Meroni* itself the ECJ declined to read these strictures into the grant of power to the agencies,[184] although it would seem, in principle, within the power of the Community courts to do so.

The grant of discretionary power leading to binding individual decisions and rules would also require reforms in agency procedures. The existing agency regulations are diverse in this respect. Those dealing with agencies that have power to make binding individual decisions normally contain classic adjudicatory process rights to hearings and the like, with internal appeal and recourse to the Community courts.

There is greater diversity in the current regulations concerning consultation and participation rights, and much depends, as we saw above, on agency practice. If agencies were accorded discretionary power to make binding rules then greater procedural regularity would be required. This could be achieved through something akin to the US Administrative Procedure

[184] Case 9/56, *Meroni*, *supra* n. 91, at 150.

Act 1946. While doubts have been voiced about the suitability of such legislation in the EU as a means of securing participation in the context of comitology,[185] the EASA experience shows the viability of what is in fact an improved version of the US notice and comment model being deployed by that agency. There would be every reason to extend such a model if agencies were given power to make formally binding rules.

It is, however, important to be mindful of the limits of substantive review if agencies were accorded discretionary powers of the kind under consideration here. There are, as will be seen in the second half of this book, limits to the extent to which the principles of judicial review are able to reach such determinations. Judicial review is designed to control the legality of decisions, rather than their merits. It is true, as will be seen, that the Community courts have extended their conception of legality and consider the reasoning used and result reached by institutions more intensively than hitherto. There are nonetheless limits to the extent to which judicial review can be used to hold the content of discretionary policy choices involving the balancing of public interests accountable.

C. Political Constraints

(1) Agency Tasks and Specification

It would be generally acknowledged that legislative specification of agency tasks and the criteria through which they should be fulfilled would become even more important if the EU were to develop real regulatory agencies. This might be enforced through more vigorous use of a non-delegation doctrine, although there are limits to the extent to which the legislature can specify detailed criteria in certain areas. We should nonetheless remember that the term discretionary power can mean very different things, ranging from the grant of broad open-textured power where there is scant guidance in the enabling legislation as to how it should be exercised, to those instances where the discretion is structured and confined by detailed provisions of the parent legislation. We should be mindful of this when considering the *Meroni* decision itself.[186] Critiques of the case too often ignore the context in which the ECJ made its ruling. It is clear that the ECJ was concerned about the delegation of power to agencies requiring them to balance the eight broad and often conflicting imperatives contained in Article 3 ECSC. The Court's admonitions about the effect of such a delegation on the institutional balance within the Community were made with this expressly in mind.

[185] See above, at Chap. 4.

[186] Case 9/56, *Meroni, supra* n. 91.

(2) Agency Appointments and Reporting

It would also be accepted by most that more recent practice whereby the agency director is appointed after open competition and appears before the EP prior to confirmation should become the norm. The obligation of agencies to report annually to the EP, the Council, and Commission should continue and should include the Member States, ECOSOC, and the Committee of Regions. There would moreover be a strong argument that a director could be called before the EP or one of its committees to explain or justify certain regulatory choices.

(3) Agency Composition

It is when we turn to agency composition and agency planning that matters become more contentious. The general pattern is, as we have seen, for Member States to predominate on agency management boards, with representatives from the Commission and sometimes from the EP making up the balance. The Commission expressed the opinion, in relation to existing agencies, that appointment of MEPs would be inappropriate in view of the agency's regulatory work, combined with the fact that the EP could then feel free to exercise external political supervision over their actions.[187] Political practice continues to differ on this,[188] but the argument itself becomes more contestable if agencies were to be accorded real regulatory powers of the kind being considered here. It is not readily apparent in principle why the EP should be excluded from representation on a body that would make binding rules balancing competing public interests. The same point can be put from a different perspective. The EP has battled for over 40 years to have a greater say in the making of secondary legislative choices via comitology. It would be strange if it were to view with equanimity its exclusion from the making of such secondary legislative choices when they happened to be made by an agency, more especially one on which Member States had significant power.

It might be argued by way of response that even real regulatory agencies would be an integral part of the executive, the unity and integrity of which must still reside in the Commission, hence its privileged status on management boards and in relation to agency planning. This argument reveals a duality in the meaning of executive function that recurs throughout EU law. In a formalistic sense everything that comes after the passage of the primary regulation can be regarded as a matter of execution/implementation of that regulation. It is, however, also readily apparent that execution in this formal

[187] Commission Communication, *supra* n. 8, at 9.

[188] The EP is not represented on the management boards of most recent agencies, with the exception of the ECDC, Reg. 851/2004, *supra* n. 40, Art. 14.

sense can entail anything ranging from simple mechanistic implementation, to the passage of highly complex further regulatory instruments that require a balance of competing public interests. The Commission has, not surprisingly, adhered to the formalistic sense of execution, and it is this that has informed its opposition to comitology, regarding Member State intervention in the passage of implementing regulations through such committees as an unwarranted encumbrance on its executive autonomy. This formalistic reading of execution is, however, flawed. It is incapable of providing a principled rationale as to why in those cases where, for example, execution requires the balancing of competing public interests and results in a rule of a legislative nature the Commission should be autonomous.[189] The formalistic conception therefore provides no ready answer as to why the EP, as well as the Member States, should not be involved in the agency where it makes binding legislative rules balancing competing public interests.

It might alternatively be argued that even if stronger regulatory agencies were created with greater autonomy these would still be primarily concerned with economic integration and that a divide can and should be maintained between the economic and political sphere. There is a vein of such reasoning running through Majone's work.[190] There are, however, real difficulties with this view. Economics and politics are not, and cannot, be kept separate in this manner. Economic regulation raises important normative issues as to the risks which society is willing to accept. These issues should not be excluded from the agenda of majoritarian politics. Nor should we be forced to accept that if formal rule-making powers are accorded to non-majoritarian institutions such as agencies that it is therefore inappropriate for majoritarian influence through the EP to be exercised within the managing body alongside that of the Council and Commission. As Shapiro wisely reminds us, information cannot be equated with technical expertise outside of politics, leading to non-democratic legitimacy in the form of technocracy. Information may often not be technical but political, and technocratic solutions to problems that are inherently political may not be perceived by the public as legitimate.[191]

(4) Agencies and Regulatory Impact Assessment

If agencies were to be accorded real regulatory power then there would be much to be said in favour of extending the emergent regime of regulatory impact assessment to agency rules.

[189] There may be practical reasons as to why involvement by the principal legislative organs has to be limited, but this is another matter.

[190] Majone, 'Europe's "Democracy Deficit": The Question of Standards' (1998) 4 *ELJ* 5.

[191] Shapiro, *supra* n. 12, at 287.

This regime began in earnest in 2003 as part of the more general programme for 'Better Regulation'.[192] It requires the Commission to engage in a regulatory impact assessment for all major initiatives, which are those presented in the Annual Policy Strategy or later in the Commission Work Programme. There is a two stage process, with a preliminary assessment followed by an extended impact assessment where that is deemed to be necessary. The impact assessment is undertaken by the relevant Directorate General (DG) responsible for the area, but the Secretariat General of the Commission has an overall coordinating role and also evaluates the quality of the DG's assessment.

Regulatory impact assessments are already undertaken by some agencies, and the EASA has the most developed policy in this respect. If agencies were to be given formal rule-making power then the requirement to make such assessments should become mandatory, at least so far as major initiatives are concerned.

(5) Agencies and Legislative Veto

The discussion thus far has considered political constraints concerning legislative specification of agency tasks, agency appointments, reporting, composition, work plan, and impact assessments. It is also important to consider the possibility of legislative veto. A schema whereby the Council and EP could exercise a veto over delegated regulations was embodied in the CT. These provisions were directed towards the passage of regulations currently implemented by the Commission subject to the comitology regime. The proposed system was discussed in the previous chapter.[193] There are, as was pointed out in that discussion, limits to the efficacy of this form of legislative veto. There is a real difference between involvement in the framing of the relevant rule and review of that rule after it has been made. This is particularly so where the rule is technically complex. This system of legislative veto was moreover directly linked to provisions stipulating that only matters of technical detail could be fleshed out through delegated regulations.

The possibility of a legislative veto is nonetheless worth considering if real regulatory agencies were to be created with discretionary powers leading to binding rules and decisions. It would provide an opportunity for legislative checks on agency choices. If such a system was established the veto power would reside with the EP and the Council independently, in the sense that a veto by either institution would prevent the agency rule from taking effect. The Community institutional system would demand that the Commission

[192] Communication from the Commission, On Impact Assessment, COM(2002) 276 final.

[193] See above, at 128–131.

should also possess such a veto. Such a system, when combined with other measures considered above, would enhance agency legitimacy. There would be participatory input from the bottom, via notice and comment, combined with legislative control from the top via the veto power. This combination of controls would moreover lessen the concerns underpinning *Meroni* about the impact of delegation of discretionary power on the institutional balance within the EU.

12. CONCLUSION

It is clear that agencies are here to stay as part of the EU's institutional framework. They are increasingly relied on in a wide variety of areas. This chapter has analysed the rationale for EU agencies, their classification, the limits on their powers, and the ways in which the existing agencies are held accountable, legally, politically, and financially. It has also examined the issues involved in the creation of real regulatory agencies within the EU. There is, however, as noted earlier, little evidence of movement in this direction. Commission initiatives are premised on the existing limits of agency power and it shows no inclination to loosen these constraints.[194]

[194] *Supra* n. 100.

6

Open Method of Coordination

1. INTRODUCTION

The preceding chapters have dealt with various methods of policy delivery in the European Union (EU), including direct administration, shared administration, comitology, and agencies. These methods differ, but they all are primarily based on traditional forms of Community law, regulations, directives, and decisions. This chapter deals with a rather different method of policy delivery in the EU, the Open Method of Coordination.

The discussion will begin by reviewing the imprimatur given by the European Council to the Open Method of Coordination, henceforth OMC, at the Lisbon and Nice Summits. This will be followed by a look at the operation of the OMC process in the three key areas of economic policy, employment policy, and social inclusion, which will lay the foundation for the subsequent analysis. There will be consideration of the differences between the OMC and more traditional modes of Community regulation. The focus will then shift to an evaluation of the OMC, looking to see how far it fulfils the aspirations that underpin this mode of policy delivery in the EU.

2. LAUNCH AND RELAUNCH: LISBON, NICE, AND BRUSSELS

The OMC did not 'begin' with the Lisbon Summit in March 2000.[1] Its intellectual origins can be traced to the strategy for dealing with Economic and Monetary Union (EMU) post-Maastricht, and to the European Employment Strategy developed post-Amsterdam, and even earlier to coordination that was part of the original Rome Treaty. The nature of the coordination in these areas will be analysed in the following section. The Lisbon Summit was nonetheless important, since the European Council gave its imprimatur to the OMC as an approach to be used more generally within EU governance.

It is important to be aware of the European Council's reasoning in Lisbon. It began with an assessment of the EU's strengths and weaknesses. Its

[1] Lisbon European Council, Presidency Conclusions, 23–24 March 2000.

strengths were said to be a vibrant macro-economic outlook, the successful introduction of the euro, and major progress towards the completion of the internal market, all of which bode well for growth and job creation.[2] There were, however, weaknesses, most notably in unemployment, both structural and regional. It was therefore necessary to 'undertake economic and social reforms as part of a positive strategy which combines competitiveness and social cohesion'.[3]

The way forward was to be based on a new strategic goal for the coming decade. The EU was 'to become the most competitive and dynamic knowledge-based economy in the world, capable of sustainable economic growth with more and better jobs and greater social cohesion'.[4] The more particular aspects of this plan were in part economic: the enhancement of an information society open to all, encouragement of a European research area, the creation of an environment friendly to the creation of new business, the coordination of macro-economic policy, and a fully operational internal market. The plan also had an overtly social dimension: there was to be education and training for those living and working in the knowledge society, the development of an active employment policy, modernization of social protection, and the promotion of social inclusion.

The implementation of this overall strategy was to be by 'improving the existing processes, introducing a new open method of coordination at all levels, coupled with a stronger guiding and coordinating role for the European Council to ensure more coherent and strategic direction and effective monitoring of progress'.[5] The Lisbon European Council made it clear that the OMC was to be a decentralized process, and hence in accord with subsidiarity, and that the Member States, regional and local government, the social partners, and civil society would be actively involved.[6] The general features of OMC were said to be:[7]

— fixing guidelines for the Union combined with specific timetables for achieving the goals which they set in the short, medium and long terms;
— establishing, where appropriate, quantitative and qualitative indicators and benchmarks against the best in the world and tailored to meet the needs of different Member States and sectors as a means of comparing best practice;
— translating these European guidelines into national and regional policies by setting specific targets and adopting measures, taking into account national and regional differences;
— periodic monitoring, evaluation and peer review organized as mutual learning processes.

The Lisbon approach was developed further at the Nice European Council

[2] Ibid. at para. 3. [3] Ibid. at para. 4. [4] Ibid. at para. 5.
[5] Ibid. at para. 7. [6] Ibid. at para. 38. [7] Ibid. at para. 37.

in December 2000,[8] with particular focus on the European social model. The connection between the economic and the social was evident in Nice as it had been in Lisbon. Thus the European social model was said to be characterized by the 'indissoluble link between economic performance and social progress'.[9] Henceforth the Spring European Council meeting would annually consider progress towards meeting the specified social objectives. The Nice European Council specified in some greater detail the substance of the goals and the methods to be used in attaining them. It stipulated that the employment rate should be increased to 70 per cent and that the proportion of working women should be increased to over 60 per cent by 2010.[10] Social policy should focus on more and better jobs, fighting poverty, all forms of exclusion and discrimination in order to promote integration, modernizing social protection, and the promotion of gender equality.[11] The implementation of the social agenda should make use of 'all existing Community instruments bar none',[12] including the OMC, legislation, the social dialogue, the Structural Funds, the support programmes, the integrated policy approach, analysis, and research. The Commission, sectoral Council formations, and the Member States were instructed or requested to take steps to fulfil these objectives.[13] Thus the Commission was 'requested' to take the OMC forward by developing indicators against which employment policy or social exclusion could be judged, and to present an annual report to the European Council, detailing its initiatives and the contributions of the other actors to attaining the objectives of the social model. The Employment and Social Policy Council was 'instructed' to implement the social agenda, including in this respect the setting of benchmarks and indicators as part the OMC process. The social partners were encouraged to take part in the process. It was for the Member States to translate these objectives into 'national, regional or local policies by setting specific targets and adopting measures which take into account national, regional and local differences'.[14]

Five years on, after suggestions made by the Commission[15] and the Kok Task Force,[16] the Brussels European Council revisited and relaunched the Lisbon strategy in the March 2005 Summit.[17] It acknowledged that results had been mixed and that while progress had been made there were also

[8] Nice European Council, Presidency Conclusions, 7–9 December 2000.
[9] Ibid. at para. 15.
[10] Ibid. at Annex I, para. 2.
[11] Ibid. at Annex I, para. 32.
[12] Ibid. at Annex I, para. 28.
[13] Ibid. at Annex I, para. 32.
[14] Ibid. at Annex I, para. 32.
[15] Communication to the Spring European Council, Working Together for Growth and Jobs, A New Start for the Lisbon Strategy, COM(2005) 24.
[16] Report of the Task Force Chaired by Wim Kok, Jobs, Jobs, Jobs, Creating More Employment in Europe, (November 2003), <http://europa.eu.int/comm/employment_social/employment_strategy/task_en.htm>.
[17] European Council, Presidency Conclusions, 22–23 March 2005.

shortcomings and delays. The European Council said that there was a high price to pay for delayed or incomplete reforms 'as is borne out by the gulf between Europe's growth potential and that of its economic partners'.[18] It was therefore necessary to relaunch the Lisbon strategy without delay and 're-focus priorities on growth and employment'.[19] The European Council then set out the 'vital strands' of the relaunch.

The substantive components of the 'relaunch' are knowledge and innovation; an attractive area in which to invest and work, dealing with completion of the internal market, the removal of impediments to trade, and an improved regulatory environment; and growth and employment making for social cohesion. It is clear from a reading of the European Council's conclusions that these strands are related, with a central theme being improved economic performance, this being perceived as the engine that would drive increased employment.

This interconnectedness is equally apparent in the blue print for 'improving governance' of the Lisbon strategy.[20] The new approach is based on a three-year cycle, the starting point of which is the Commission's synoptic document, the strategic report. This report will be examined in the relevant Council configurations and will then be discussed by the European Council at its Spring Summit, which will establish political guidelines for the economic, social, and environmental strands of the strategy.

On the basis of the European Council's conclusions, the Council, acting in accord with Articles 99 and 128 EC, will then adopt 'integrated guidelines' consisting of the broad economic policy guidelines (BEPGs) and employment guidelines (EGs). The Member States will then, acting on the basis of the integrated guidelines, draw up 'national reform programmes', after consultation with all stakeholders. As a counterpart to these national programmes, the Commission is to present a 'Community Lisbon programme' covering all action to be undertaken at Community level in the interests of growth and employment.

The Member State reports on the follow-up to the Lisbon strategy, including the application of the OMC, are to be grouped in a single document, which distinguishes between different areas of action and sets out the measures taken to implement the national programmes. In the light of these national reports, the Commission reports on the implementation of the strategy each year, with the European Council reviewing progress each Spring and deciding on any adjustments to the integrated guidelines.

There have, as will be seen below, already been developments implementing this revised strategy. It remains to be seen whether these changes of governance for the Lisbon strategy improve its efficacy, and equally importantly whether the regime of integrated guidelines has any substantive impact

[18] Ibid. at para. 4.
[19] Ibid. at para. 5.
[20] Ibid. at paras. 38–41.

on the relative importance attached to different parts of the strategy. The danger of the BEPGs becoming the 'coordination of coordination processes' without proper input from other interested parties has already been noted by the European Parliament (EP).[21]

3. ECONOMIC POLICY, EMPLOYMENT POLICY, AND SOCIAL EXCLUSION

An understanding of the OMC requires us to probe further into its workings in particular areas, more especially because it is clear that the process varies. This is moreover necessary in order to assess the debates about the desirability and efficacy of the OMC that will be considered in detail below. The present section will therefore focus on the rationale for the use of coordination in three key areas and provide an outline structure of this coordination in economic policy, employment policy, and social exclusion.[22] This will provide a foundation for the subsequent discussion concerning the extent to which the OMC promotes deliberation, learning, legitimate difference, and the like.

A. Economic Policy

The coordination of economic policy has been especially important post the Maastricht Treaty, and even more so in the light of monetary union and the single currency.[23] This encapsulates a vision of sound money, sound

[21] Committee on Employment and Social Affairs, On New Proposals for Employment Strategy and Social Policy in the European Union, Rapporteur, Thomas Mann, A5-0062/2003, at para. 4.

[22] For the limits thus far of the OMC in relation to innovation policy and immigration see respectively, Kaiser and Prange, 'Managing Diversity in a System of Multi-Level Governance: The Open Method of Coordination In Innovation Policy' (2004) 11 *JEPP* 249; Caviedes, 'The Open Method of Coordination in Immigration Policy: A Tool for Prying Open Fortress Europe?' (2004) 11 *JEPP* 289.

[23] Harden, 'The Fiscal Constitution of EMU', in P. Beaumont and N. Walker (eds), *The Legal Framework of the Single European Currency* (Hart, 1999), at. 71–93; Hodson and Maher, 'The Open Method as a New Mode of Governance: The Case of Soft Economic Policy Co-ordination' (2001) 39 *JCMS* 719; *Thirteenth Report of the House of Lords' Select Committee on the European Union: The Stability and Growth Pact* (HL 72; 2002–03); Begg, Hodson, and Maher, 'Economic Policy Coordination in the European Union' (2003) 183 *National Institute Economic Review* 66; Amtenbrink and de Haan, 'Economic Governance in the European Union' (2003) 40 *CMLRev* 1075; Begg, 'Hard and Soft Policy Coordination under EMU: Problems, Paradoxes and Prospects' (2004) London School of Economics and Political Science, Centre for European Studies, Working Paper 103; Maher, 'Law and the Open Method of Coordination: Towards a New Flexibility in European Policy-Making?' (2004) 2(2) *Zeitschrift fur Staats- und Europawissenschaften*; Hodson, 'Macroeconomic Co-ordination in

finance.[24] It is clear that the economic health of individual Member State economies can have a marked impact on the valuation of the euro, and hence impact on the economies of all countries that subscribe to the single currency. The sound money, sound finance paradigm therefore made coordination of economic policy essential. Thus as Hodson and Maher state, 'the strong links between monetary policy and economic policies, where monetary policy is uniform and highly centralized, in effect mandated coordination of economic policy while the diversity of national approaches required that coordination remain at the national level so there is adequate room for manoeuvre in response to asymmetric shocks'.[25] The link between monetary union and economic coordination is apparent once again in the regulations establishing the Growth and Stability Pact, which state that for EMU to function properly it is necessary that convergence of economic and budgetary performance of countries with the single currency is stable, and that budgetary discipline is necessary to ensure price stability.[26] This then is the broad rationale for coordination in this area. It is important to understand that the Treaty embodies two forms of coordination.

The *softer version is the multilateral surveillance procedure.* Member States are to regard their economic policies as a matter of common concern, and are to coordinate them in the Council.[27] The Council acting by qualified majority on a recommendation from the Commission formulates a draft for the broad guidelines[28] of the economic policies of the Member States and the Community, and reports this to the European Council. The guidelines are discussed by the European Council, and its conclusion forms the basis for a Council recommendation setting out the broad guidelines.[29] In order to ensure closer coordination of economic policy, it is then for the Council, on the basis of reports from the Commission, to monitor economic developments in the Member States and in the Community. This constitutes the multilateral surveillance.[30] If it becomes apparent that the economic policies

the Euro Area: The Scope and Limits of the Open Method' (2004) 11 *JEPP* 231; Hodson and Maher, 'Soft Law and Sanctions: Economic Policy Coordination and Reform of the Stability and Growth Pact' (2004) 11 *JEPP* 798; Louis, 'The Economic and Monetary Union: Law and Institutions' (2004) 41 *CMLRev* 575; Begg and Schelkle, 'Can Fiscal Policy Co-ordination be Made to Work Effectively?' (2004) 42 *JCMS* 1047.

[24] Dyson, 'EMU as Europeanization: Convergence, Diversity and Contingency' (2000) 38 *JCMS* 645.

[25] Hodson and Maher, 'The Open Method as a New Mode of Governance', *supra* n. 23, at 738.

[26] Council Regulation (EC) 1467/97 of 7 July 1997, On Speeding up and Clarifying the Implementation of the Excessive Deficit Procedure, OJ 1997 L209/6, Rec. 8.

[27] Art. 99(1) EC.

[28] Council Recommendation 95/326/EC of 10 July 1995, On the Broad Guidelines of the Economic Policies of the Member States and of the Community, OJ 1995 L191/24.

[29] Art. 99(2) EC. [30] Art. 99(3) EC.

of the Member States are not consistent with the broad economic guidelines, or that they risk jeopardizing the proper functioning of EMU, the Council may, acting by qualified majority on a recommendation from the Commission, make the necessary recommendations to the Member State concerned.[31] There are provisions requiring the EP to be kept informed.[32]

The Treaty provisions have been complemented by the Stability and Growth Pact (SGP). The foundations are to be found in a Resolution of the European Council in 1997.[33] The Resolution produced guidelines addressed to the Member States, the Commission, and the Council, and were directed to prevention of budget deficit and effective deterrence. The precepts contained in the Resolution formed the basis for two regulations, one of which concerns the multilateral surveillance procedure.[34] The Regulation provides rules covering the content, submission, examination, and monitoring of the stability and convergence programmes so as to prevent at an early stage the occurrence of excessive government deficit, and to promote the surveillance and coordination of economic policies.[35] To this end Member States are required to submit to the Council and Commission information necessary for multilateral surveillance in the form of a stability programme, in order to provide the essential basis for price stability and sustainable economic growth. The stability programme requires the Member States to present information concerning the medium-term objective for a budgetary position of close to balance or in surplus; the main assumptions about expected economic performance; a description of measures to achieve the objectives of the programme; and an analysis of how changes in the principal economic assumptions would affect the budgetary and debt position.[36] It is then for the Council, based on assessments made by the Commission and the Economic and Financial Committee, to decide whether the economic assumptions of the stability programme are realistic, and whether the measures proposed by the Member State will be likely to reach the desired goal.[37] Provision is made for early warnings where there is a danger of excessive deficit.[38]

The *harder version of coordination is embodied in the excessive deficit procedure.* Member States are under an obligation to avoid excessive deficits.[39] The Commission monitors the budgetary situation and government debt in the Member States to identify gross errors. More particularly it examines whether the ratio of the planned or actual government deficit to gross domestic product exceeds a reference value, this being 3 per cent, or whether

[31] Art. 99(4) EC. [32] Arts. 99(2), 99(4) EC.

[33] Resolution of the European Council on the Stability and Growth Pact, 17 June 1997.

[34] Council Regulation (EC) 1466/97 of 7 July 1997, On the Strengthening of the Surveillance of Budgetary Positions and the Surveillance and Coordination of Economic Policies, OJ 1997 L209/1.

[35] Ibid. Art. 1. [36] Ibid. Art. 2. [37] Ibid. Art. 5.

[38] Ibid. Art. 6. [39] Art. 104(1) EC.

the ratio of government debt to gross domestic product exceeds such a reference value, this being 60 per cent.[40] These reference values are specified in the Protocol on the Excessive Deficit Procedure.[41] The Commission must prepare a report where a Member State does not fulfil these criteria, and may do so if it believes that there is a risk of an excessive deficit in a Member State.[42] The Economic and Financial Committee gives an opinion on this report.[43] Where the Commission considers that there is an excessive deficit, or that it may occur, the Commission must address an opinion to the Council.[44] It is then for the Council, acting by qualified majority on the Commission's recommendation, and having considered the views of the relevant Member State, to decide whether the excessive deficit exists.[45] If the Council decides that it does exist it must make recommendations to the Member State to bring the situation to an end.[46] Where the Member State fails to act on these recommendations the Council may decide to give notice to the Member State that it should take certain measures within a specified time to remedy the situation.[47] Where the Member State fails to comply with these measures, the Council may decide to take further measures, such as the imposition of fines, or the requirement that the Member State should deposit a sum with the Community until the excessive deficit has been corrected.[48]

The Treaty provisions on excessive deficit have, like those on surveillance, been complemented by a Regulation concerning excessive deficit,[49] this being the other main limb of the SGP. The Regulation clarifies certain definitional aspects concerning excessive deficit, and contains provisions for speeding up the procedure by imposing time-lines for action on the Council.[50] It also provides greater detail concerning possible sanctions.[51]

The excessive deficit procedure therefore embodies a harder form of coordination than the multilateral surveillance procedure, since the former can ultimately lead to the imposition of sanctions. It should, however, also be recognized that the Treaty provisions are nuanced in this respect. The initial stages of the excessive deficit procedure are couched in mandatory terms: there are obligations cast on the Commission to investigate excessive deficits, the Council must decide whether such a deficit exists, and must then issue recommendations to the Member State. The latter stages of the procedure are cast in more discretionary terms: where the Member State fails to comply with the Council recommendations, the Council may decide to instruct the Member State to take more specific measures, and where these have not

[40] Art. 104(2) EC.
[41] Protocol No. 20 (1992), Art. 1.
[42] Art. 104(3) EC.
[43] Art. 104(4) EC.
[44] Art. 104(5) EC.
[45] Art. 104(6) EC.
[46] Art. 104(7) EC.
[47] Art. 104(9) EC.
[48] Art. 104(11) EC.
[49] Reg. 1467/97, *supra* n. 26.
[50] Ibid. Arts. 3–6.
[51] Ibid. Arts. 11–14.

been complied with, the Council may decide to apply one of the specified sanctions.[52]

While the excessive deficit procedure contains a harder form of coordination there are nonetheless factors limiting its effectiveness. Hodson and Maher point to the procedural softness of the excessive deficit procedure in its latter stages, the inappropriateness of imposing a financial sanction on a state that is in economic difficulty, and the consensus that such a penalty would in any event only be imposed in extreme circumstances. They conclude that the softer form of coordination through multilateral surveillance is in fact the principal method of coordination for fiscal policy.[53]

The frailty of the deficit procedure was brought starkly to light in relation to the deficits run by France, Germany, Portugal, and Italy in 2002–2003. While the states undertook to balance their budget over the medium term, they nonetheless departed from the relevant corrective programme.[54] This led at one and the same time to adjustments to the SGP,[55] and ultimately also to the Commission having recourse to legal action when ECOFIN placed the excessive deficit procedure in abeyance for France and Germany.[56]

The European Court of Justice's (ECJ's) judgment is complex and cannot be examined in detail here.[57] Suffice it to say that the Court held that the Council's decision to place the excessive deficit procedure in abeyance was unlawful, there being no authority for this under the relevant Treaty provisions. In this respect it was a victory for the Commission. The Council could, however, also draw comfort from the case, because the ECJ held inadmissible the other Commission claim, that the Council's failure to adopt the Commission's recommendations pursuant to Article 104(8) and (9) EC was a decision that should be annulled. The ECJ held this to be inadmissible, on the ground that where the requisite majority for the Commission recommendations was not secured in the Council there was no decision taken that could be reviewed under Article 230 EC. The ECJ left open the possibility that the Commission could bring an action for failure to act in such circumstances, although this would not be easy given the wording of Article 104 EC.

[52] It is, however, interesting to note that the Regulation on excessive deficit is framed in mandatory terms even in relation to sanctions. It states that where the relevant conditions apply then the Council shall impose sanctions. It is doubtful in terms of legal principle whether a Regulation can transform a permissive Treaty provision into a mandatory one. Ibid. Art. 6.

[53] Hodson and Maher, 'Soft Law and Sanctions', *supra* n. 23, at 804.

[54] Ibid. at 805–806. [55] Ibid. at 808–810.

[56] 2546th Meeting of the Council of the European Union (Economic and Financial Affairs), Brussels, 25 November 2003.

[57] Case C-27/04, *Commission v Council* [2004] ECR I-6649; Maher, 'Economic Policy Coordination and the European Court: Excessive Deficits and ECOFIN Discretion' (2004) 29 *ELRev* 831.

The shockwaves from the events that placed such a strain on the SGP led to a re-thinking of Community policy. In June 2004 the European Council encouraged the Commission to consider modifications to the SGP. The Commission responded quickly in September 2004, setting out plans for amendment to the SGP Regulations.[58] The essence of the Commission's approach, albeit with some modifications, was endorsed by ECOFIN in March 2005.[59] ECOFIN's report was in turn endorsed by the European Council two days later at the March Summit,[60] and the Commission was invited to bring forward the necessary amending regulations. These have now been enacted with changes being made to both of the SGP Regulations.[61] Space precludes detailed assessment of these changes, but the essence of the amendments can nonetheless be conveyed here.

In relation to multilateral surveillance, the Regulation as amended now provides for greater differentiation as concerns the medium-term budgetary objective that a state should 'be close to balance or in surplus'. The formal rationale for this change was that this was necessary given the economic and budgetary heterogeneity of an enlarged EU. The country-specific medium-term budgetary objective can diverge from the requirement of being close to balance or in surplus, although there is a requirement for a safety margin with respect to the 3 per cent of gross domestic product (GDP) government deficit ratio. There have also been consequential changes as to the criteria that the Commission and Council take into account when reviewing the Member State plans. The net effect of these changes is to soften the surveillance in the sense that, when defining any adjustment that should be made by the Member State to attain the medium-term objective, account should be taken of factors such as expenditure on structural reform that may lead to long-term cost savings, the cost of pension reform, and the fact that only limited efforts to make adjustments to the medium-term objective could be expected in economic bad times.

The excessive deficit procedure has also been softened and made more nuanced. This is because the definition of an excessive deficit that is deemed to be temporary and exceptional has been broadened and because an expanded range of other relevant factors, such as potential growth, prevailing cyclical conditions, the implementation of policies in the context of the

[58] Communication from the Commission to the Council and European Parliament, Strengthening Economic Governance and Clarifying the Implementation of the Stability and Growth Pact, COM(2004) 581 final.

[59] Council of the European Union, ECOFIN, Improving the Implementation of the Stability and Growth Pact, 7423/05, ECOFIN 104, 21 March 2005.

[60] Brussels European Council, 23 March 2005, at 2, and Annex II.

[61] Council Regulation (EC) 1055/2005 of 27 June 2005, Amending Regulation 1466/97, OJ 2005 L174/1; Council Regulation (EC) 1056/2005 of 27 June 2005, Amending Regulation 1467/97, OJ 2005 L174/5.

Lisbon agenda, policies to foster research and development, implementation of pension reform, debt sustainability, and the overall quality of public finances, have to be taken into account when assessing in qualitative terms the excess over the reference value for a particular Member State. The amended Regulation also lengthened the time for decisions to be made by the Council on the existence of an excessive deficit and for Member State compliance with the Council recommendations or decisions.

It is important not to lose sight of the broader tensions that led to these reforms. The difficulties resulting from the excessive deficits run by France and Germany placed the very credibility of the SGP in question. The flouting of the system by these countries brought the SGP into disrepute with the consequence that this non-compliance meant that 'governments that might otherwise have been willing to commit themselves risk opprobrium from their supporters if they are seen to bow to the strictures of a discredited system'.[62] The Commission was in a real sense caught between a rock and a hard place. If reforms were not made then non-compliance or passive resistance to the SGP was likely to continue. If, however, any reform significantly weakened the pre-existing regime then its practical effectiveness for the future would correspondingly diminish.

The Commission put a brave face on the reform exercise. It acknowledged that tensions in the application of the SGP had led to a loss of 'credibility and ownership and institutional uncertainty'.[63] It spoke of the need to strengthen and clarify the SGP, while at the same time recognizing the tension between a rule-based system that was simple and transparent and one that contained a higher degree of discretion.[64] The reality is that the changes made to the multilateral surveillance and excessive deficit procedures make the SGP more discretionary than hitherto. Thus it will in the future be easier, for example, for a Member State to argue that one of the many 'relevant factors' serve to explain and justify any excess over the reference values for the purposes of the excessive deficit procedure, thereby rendering it more unlikely that soft or hard sanctions will be imposed.

B. Employment Policy

The rationale for EU involvement in employment policy and the use of the OMC within this area is interesting.[65] The European Employment Strategy

[62] Begg and Schelkle, *supra* n. 23, at 1051.

[63] Communication from the Commission, *supra* n. 58, at 3.

[64] Ibid. at 3.

[65] Kenner, 'EC Labour Law: The Softly, Softly Approach' (1995) 14 *IJCLLIR* 307; Goetschy, 'The European Employment Strategy: Genesis and Development' (1999) 5 *EJIR* 117; Mosher, 'Open Method of Coordination: Functional and Political Origins' (2000) 13 *ECSA Review* 2; Goetschy, 'The European Employment Strategy from Amsterdam to Stockholm: Has it Reached Cruising Speed Yet?' (2001) 32 *IRJ* 401; de la Porte, 'Is the Open Method of

(EES) emerged as a result of the strains placed on welfare state regimes which became evident in the middle of the 1990s. At this time many Member States 'faced high levels of unemployment and/or low levels of employment participation as well as the need to restructure labour markets and welfare systems to take account of internal changes and external shocks'.[66] There was also during this period a significant re-thinking about social policy in a number of the Member States, more especially the possible impact of high levels of social protection on the overall employment rate. Many of the Member States were nonetheless attached to high levels of social protection and were unwilling to allow the employment problem to be resolved if indeed it could be, by cutting back on the levels of social protection. The imperative to take action at the EU level to combat unemployment was furthered by impending economic and monetary union. It became clear that 'employment measures had to be taken if the European Monetary Union project, or at least the planned timetable, was not to be put at risk'.[67] The need to meet the criteria for monetary union served moreover to place budgetary constraints on states, thereby exacerbating existing problems of unemployment resulting from the slow growth in economies in the mid-1990s. The impetus for EU involvement in employment policy was also in part the result of the very constraints placed by EU law on traditional national mechanisms for combating unemployment. Thus Member States could no longer foster employment through competitive devaluations combined with adjustments to national interest rates because 'EMU entailed an increasingly centralized monetary

Coordination Appropriate for Organising Activities at European Level in Sensitive Policy Areas' (2002) 8 *ELJ* 38; C. de la Porte and P. Pochet, *Building Social Europe through the Open Method of Coordination* (PIE-Peter Lang, 2002); Trubek and Mosher, 'New Governance, Employment Policy and the European Social Model', in J. Zeitlin and D. Trubek (eds), *Governing Work and Welfare in a New Economy* (Oxford University Press, 2003), Chap. 2; Regent, 'The Open Method of Coordination: A New Supranational Form of Governance?' (2003) 9 *ELJ* 190; de la Porte and Nanz, 'The OMC—A Deliberative-Democratic Mode of Governance? The Cases of Employment and Pensions' (2004) 11 *JEPP* 267; Mosher and Trubek, 'Alternative Approaches to Governance in the EU: EU Social Policy and the European Employment Strategy' (2003) 41 *JCMS* 63; Watt, 'Reform of the European Employment Strategy after Five Years: A Change of Course or Merely of Presentation?' (2004) 10 *EJIR* 117; Rhodes, 'Employment Policy: Between Efficacy and Experimentation', in H. Wallace, W. Wallace and M. Pollack (eds), *Policy-Making in the European Union* (Oxford University Press, 2005), Chap. 11; Zeitlin, 'The Open Method of Coordination in Action: Theoretical Promise, Empirical Realities, Reform Strategy', in J. Zeitlin and P. Pochet with L. Magnusson (eds), *The Open Method of Coordination in Action: The European Employment and Social Inclusion Strategies* (PIE-Peter Lang, 2005), Chap. 14; D. Ashiagbor, *The European Employment Strategy: Labour Market Regulation and New Governance* (Oxford University Press, 2005).

[66] Trubek and Mosher, *supra* n. 65, at 34–35.

[67] Goetschy, 'Cruising Speed', *supra* n. 65, at 401.

policy for the EU'.[68] Nor could national governments tackle the problem through public sector job creation, since EMU together with the SGP placed stringent constraints on the size of public deficits.[69]

While there were therefore a plethora of reasons for EU involvement in employment policy, the nature of this involvement and the competence accorded to the EU was shaped by the Member States. There had in the past been a marked reluctance to accord the EU real power over social policy or industrial relations.[70] The 1990s was moreover a period in which there was renewed questioning more generally of the legitimacy and desirability of the EU's involvement in areas previously reserved to Member State competence. The nature of the problems posed by employment were in addition less well suited to traditional methods of Community intervention, in part because they were inherently less susceptible to EU legislation enshrining particular ends, in part because the differing social models extant within the Member States rendered the imposition of such 'uniform solutions' undesirable.

The factors driving EU involvement with employment policy combined with those limiting the nature of that involvement to shape the Employment Chapter placed in the Treaty of Amsterdam. The Member States undertake to work towards a coordinated strategy for employment, and in particular towards a skilled, trained, and adaptable work force,[71] and a high level of employment.[72] The promotion of employment is thus regarded as a matter of common concern, and national action is to be coordinated in accord with the detailed provisions set out below. The Treaty moreover makes it clear that employment policy must be consistent with the broad guidelines on economic policy[73] discussed in the previous section.

Coordination within the EES operates in the following way.[74] The European Council each year considers the employment situation in the Community and adopts conclusions based on the joint report from the Commission and the Council. The conclusions reached by the European Council then form the basis for the Council, acting by qualified majority on a proposal from the Commission, and after consulting the EP, the Economic and Social Committee (ECOSOC), the Committee of the Regions, and the Employment Committee, to draw up guidelines which the Member States

[68] Goetschy, 'The European Employment Strategy, Multi-Level Governance and Policy Coordination: Past, Present and Future', in J. Zeitlin and D. Trubek (eds), *Governing Work and Welfare in a New Economy, European and American Experiments* (Oxford University Press, 2003), Chap. 3.

[69] Ibid. at 60.

[70] Streeck, 'From Market-Making to State-Building: Reflections on the Political Economy of European Social Policy', in S. Leibfried and P. Pierson (eds), *European Social Policy: Between Fragmentation and Integration* (Brookings Institution, 1995), 389–431.

[71] Art. 125 EC. [72] Art. 127 EC. [73] Arts. 126(1), 128(2) EC.

[74] Art. 128 EC.

shall take into account in their employment policies.[75] It is then for each Member State to provide the Council and the Commission with an annual report on the principal measures taken to implement its employment policy in the light of these guidelines. The Council considers these reports and the opinion of the Employment Committee and forms a view on the implementation of the guidelines at national level. It is open to the Council acting on a recommendation from the Commission to decide to make recommendations to a particular Member State. Having completed their examination of the reports from the Member States, the Council and the Commission make their joint report to the European Council on the employment situation in the Community and the implementation of the guidelines for employment. The annual process then begins once again. The Employment Committee, as seen, assists in this process.[76] It is composed of two persons from each Member State, plus two members of the Commission. It acts in an advisory capacity to promote coordination between the Member States on employment and labour market policies and more particularly to monitor the employment situation and policies in the Member States and in the Community, and to formulate opinions to contribute to the preparation of the Council proceedings described above. In fulfilling its mandate the Employment Committee is instructed to consult management and labour.

The Member States did not in fact wait for the Treaty of Amsterdam to be ratified before implementing the strategy laid down in the Employment Chapter. The Luxembourg European Council in 1997[77] began the process by adopting guidelines organized around four pillars. These were employability policies, designed to foster active employment policy and increase the skill levels of the workforce; entrepreneurship and job creation policies aimed to facilitate the creation of new businesses and to render taxation more employment friendly; adaptability policies encouraged employees and businesses to modernize forms of work organization; and equal opportunity policies were directed to gender mainstreaming, re-entry into the labour market, and lessening of the gender gap in employment. The system was modified in 2003, in part by way of response to the suggestions from the Barcelona European Council that the EES should be reinforced and simplified.[78] The four pillars were reduced to three overarching objectives, full employment, improving quality and productivity at work, and strengthening social cohesion and inclusion. Ten guidelines were specified in order to effectuate these objectives.[79] The EES regime has been further modified in the light of the

[75] See, e.g., Council Recommendation 2003/579/EC of 22 July 2003, On the Implementation of Member States' Employment Policies, OJ 2003 L197/22.

[76] Art. 130 EC. [77] Luxembourg European Council, 20–21 November 1997.

[78] Barcelona European Council, 15–16 March 2002, at para. 30.

[79] Council Decision 2003/578/EC of 22 July 2003, On Guidelines for the Employment Policies of the Member States, OJ 2003 L197/13.

relaunching of the Lisbon strategy in March 2005. Revised guidelines for the employment policies of the Member States were adopted.[80] Detailed work has been done on the integrated guidelines encompassing both economic and employment policy.[81] The Commission has also issued its Community Lisbon Programme[82] as mandated by the revisions agreed to in the Lisbon strategy in March 2005.

The provisions concerning employment exemplify the OMC. The emphasis throughout is on a soft law approach fostered through deliberation, learning, and discourse.[83] There are provisions enabling legislation to be made pursuant to the co-decision procedure, but these cannot include harmonization of the laws and regulations of the Member States. The Community's competence is limited to the enactment of measures to encourage cooperation between Member States through exchange of information, best practices, and the like.[84] There are, as Goetschy states, three elements that characterize the Employment Title.[85]

> [I]t is based on the previous experience of the Essen procedure (1994) establishing a multilateral monitoring procedure for national employment policies; the procedural approach of the EES was inspired by the convergence process in the macroeconomic field set up in the Maastricht Treaty; and it is the national level which remains primarily responsible for employment policies and achievements, though employment is considered an issue of common concern for both the national and the Community level. The fact that employment is a 'shared competence' between the Community and national levels is consistent with the principle of subsidiarity and clearly shows that the EES represents an effort to promote greater convergence of national employment policies while at the same time respecting national diversity.

C. Social Exclusion

The application of the OMC to social exclusion dated from the Lisbon and Nice European Councils in 2000, the immediate rationale being, as we have seen, to foster social inclusion as one part of the construction of the European social model.

The deeper rationale for and significance of this strategy has, however,

[80] Council Decision 2005/600/EC of 12 July 2005, On Guidelines for the Employment Policies of the Member States, OJ 2005 L205/21.

[81] Communication from the President, Integrated Guidelines for Growth and Jobs (2005–2008), COM(2005) 141 final.

[82] Communication from the Commission to the Council and European Parliament, Common Actions for Growth and Employment: The Community Lisbon Programme, COM(2005) 330 final.

[83] Communication from the Commission, Taking Stock of Five Years of the European Employment Strategy, COM(2002) 416 final.

[84] Art. 129 EC. [85] Goetschy, *supra* n. 68, at 64.

been articulated by Scharpf.[86] The essence of his argument is that the EU is premised on asymmetrical treatment of the economic and social spheres. The Community economic order has predominated, as evidenced by the content of the Treaty itself, and the primacy accorded to the completion of the single market with the attendant priority placed on market and competitive principles. Scharpf argues that matters need not have developed in this manner, and that it would have been possible when the Rome Treaty was framed to have made harmonization of social protection a pre-condition for market integration, given that the welfare regimes of the original six Member States were relatively rudimentary at that time and closer in substantive terms than they have since become. If the Rome Treaty had been cast in this form then the debates at Community level about the interplay between social protection and the market mechanism would have replicated similar normative discourse at national level. Matters developed very differently. The Treaty focus was heavily on markets with the consequence that there was a decoupling of economic integration and social protection. This led to constitutional asymmetry. Whereas at national level economic and social policy had the same constitutional status, it was economic policy that predominated at Community level. The very predominance afforded to economic policy served moreover to reduce the Member States' ability to influence their own economies or to 'realize self-defined socio-political goals'.[87] Community law doctrines of direct effect and supremacy made these constraints even firmer.

Small wonder then that there came to be increasing pressure for the EU to play a greater role in social policy thereby alleviating the constitutional imbalance between the market-making and market-correcting functions of a polity. Scharpf argues, however, that it was not possible for the EU at the turn of the millennium to adopt the stance towards social policy that it had declined to take when the Rome Treaty was signed. It was not possible to treat social welfare and protection through uniform rules applicable to all, because of the very diversity in systems of welfare that existed within the Member States, embodying differing normative assumptions about seminal issues such as the type and level of assistance to be provided to the unemployed, and the balance between support to be provided by the state and that to be left to private provision.[88] The linkage between this diversity and the OMC emerges clearly in the following extract.[89]

Political parties and unions promoting 'social Europe' are thus confronted by a

[86] Scharpf, 'The European Social Model: Coping with the Challenges of Diversity' (2002) 40 *JCMS* 645 and 'Legitimate Diversity: The New Challenge of European Integration' in T. Borzel and R. Cichowski (eds), *The State of the European Union, Vol. 6: Law, Politics and Society* (Oxford University Press, 2003), Chap. 4.

[87] Scharpf, 'The European Social Model', *supra* n. 86, at 648.

[88] Ibid. at 649–651.

[89] Ibid. at 652.

dilemma: to ensure effectiveness, they need to assert the constitutional equality of social protection and economic integration functions at the European level—which could be achieved either through European social programmes or through the harmonization of national social-protection systems. At the same time, however, the present diversity of national social-protection systems and the political salience of these differences make it practically impossible for them to agree on common European solutions. Faced by this dilemma, the Union opted for a new governing mode, the open method of coordination (OMC), in order to protect and promote social Europe.

We shall consider in due course whether OMC has been capable of delivering social protection while respecting national diversity. For the present the focus will be on the structure of the regime for coordination that applies to social exclusion.[90]

It is important at the outset to recognize that the detailed regime for coordination in relation to social exclusion is not to be found in the Treaty. In this respect it differs from economic and employment policy. The Treaty foundation for Community action is found in Article 136 EC, which provides that the objectives of the Community and Member States in relation to social policy shall include, *inter alia*, the combating of exclusion. Article 137(2) EC specifies that the Council can adopt measures pursuant to the co-decision procedure to encourage cooperation between Member States through initiatives aimed at improving knowledge, developing exchanges of information and best practices, promoting innovative approaches, and evaluating experiences to combat social exclusion.

The EP and Council duly enacted a Decision[91] in 2002 pursuant to Article 137(2). This Decision established a programme to combat social exclusion to run till 2006. The programme is based on the OMC and is designed to give a decisive impetus to combating social exclusion and poverty by setting appropriate objectives at Community level and by the implementation of national action plans (NAPs).[92]

[90] Atkinson and Davoudi, 'The Concept of Social Exclusion in the European Union' (2000) 38 *JCMS* 3; I. Begg, et al., *Social Exclusion and Social Protection in the European Union: Policy Issues and Proposals for the Future Role of the EU* (2001); T. Atkinson, et al., *Indicators for Social Exclusion in the European Union* (Oxford University Press, 2001); de la Porte, *supra* n. 65; Wincott, 'Beyond Social Regulation? New Instruments and/or a New Agenda for Social Policy at Lisbon' (2003) 81 *Pub Adm* 533; Armstrong, 'Tackling Social Exclusion through the OMC: Rebuilding the Boundaries of EU Governance', in T. Boerzel and R. Cichowski (eds), *The State of the European Union: Law, Politics and Society, Vol. 6* (Oxford University Press, 2003), Chap. 8; Atkinson, Marlier, and Nolan, 'Indicators and Targets for Social Inclusion in the European Union' (2004) 42 *JCMS* 47.

[91] Decision 50/2002/EC of the European Parliament and of the Council of 7 December 2001, Establishing a Programme of Community Action to Encourage Cooperation between Member States to Combat Social Exclusion, OJ 2002 L10/1.

[92] Ibid. Art. 2.

Operating within the context of the OMC the programme supports cooperation which enables the Community and the Member States to enhance the effectiveness of policies to combat social exclusion. This is to be done by improving the understanding of social exclusion and poverty, by promoting mutual learning through exchange of policies with the help of comparable indicators, and by developing the capacity of relevant actors to address the problem effectively and to experiment with innovative approaches through networking at the European level and dialogue with those involved at national and regional level.[93] Action can be taken at Community level to implement these objectives.[94] This allows Community funds allocated to the programme to be used in furtherance of these objectives.

Thus, policy strand one, dealing with understanding the causes of social exclusion and poverty, can be fostered by providing support for studies, meetings, the collection of data, development of indicators, research into innovative strategies, and the like. The second policy strand dealing with policy cooperation and the exchange of best practice can be supported by meetings, seminars, the development of benchmarks and indicators, and through NAPs. The third policy strand designed to facilitate participation by interested parties and networking at European level is furthered through the provision of core funding for groups involved in the fight against poverty, and through an annual European Round Table Conference on social exclusion.

Implementation of the programme is entrusted at Community level to the Commission, which is empowered to enact implementing measures pursuant to the management committee procedure. A Social Protection Committee has been established to enhance cooperation between Member States on social protection policies and to provide systematic follow up for action to increase social protection.[95]

D. Streamlining the Procedures

It became clear that the procedures for coordination in the economic and employment spheres were becoming unwieldy. The Commission therefore initiated in 2002 a modified version of the annual policy cycle designed to streamline decision-making.[96] It was hoped that this would enhance the efficiency of policy coordination, improve the coherence between the various policy instruments, foster a wider sense of 'ownership' of the policy process through greater involvement of the EP and national parliaments, and better

[93] Ibid. Art. 3. [94] Art. 4 and Annex.

[95] Council Decision 2000/436/EC of 29 June 2000, Setting up a Social Protection Committee, OJ 2000 L172/26. There is now a Treaty foundation for this committee, Art. 144 EC as modified by the Treaty of Nice.

[96] Communication from the Commission, On Streamlining the Annual Economic and Employment Policy Coordination Cycles, COM(2002) 487 final.

consultation with civil society, and increase the transparency and intelligibility of the policy coordination cycle. It should, however, be emphasized that the proposals were solely concerned with streamlining, with the hope that they would contribute to the other benefits mentioned. We shall consider in more detail below whether these broader aspirations have been fulfilled.[97]

The essence of the new streamlined scheme was that there should be better preparation for the Spring European Council devoted to economic and social policy; that the Commission would present a package of guidelines dealing with the economic and employment sphere; that the focus should shift to the medium term, with major review of the guidelines every three years, and less change during the intermediate period; and that review of Member States' implementation should be concentrated in the latter part of the year.

E. The Open Method of Coordination: Two Sets of Issues

The preceding discussion of the rationale for the use of OMC in economic policy, employment policy and social exclusion, and the structure of coordination in these areas, enables us to press forward and evaluate it as a method for policy delivery in the EU. There are of course various ways in which this might be undertaken. The strategy for the remainder of this chapter is to consider two sets of issues that arise in the literature concerning the OMC. The first is the contrast drawn between the OMC and the more traditional Community method. The second is to evaluate the OMC itself, and to consider more particularly how far it has fostered a deliberative, participative discourse and a learning process that has enabled progress to be made in the relevant areas.

4. THE OPEN METHOD OF COORDINATION AND THE TRADITIONAL COMMUNITY METHOD

There are two dimensions to the contrast between the OMC and the traditional Community method, henceforth TCM.

A. Soft Law v Hard Law

It is clear from the preceding analysis that the OMC operates largely through soft law, by way of contrast to the TCM as epitomized by regulations and directives that result in binding legal norms enforceable through the normal

97 See below, at 215–233.

judicial process.[98] This should not however be held 'against' the OMC as a method for policy delivery in the EU. This is so for a number of reasons.

The *line between hard law and soft law is not that clear cut.*[99] There are of course paradigmatic examples of 'pure hard law', and equally classic instances of 'pure soft law', but any lawyer will know that there is much in between these extremities. Legalization is in that sense a spectrum. The 'hardness' of the law will, other things being equal, be a function of the extent to which it creates legal obligations, the precision of those obligations, and the extent to which interpretation and implementation is delegated to an independent third party such as a court.[100]

It is equally apparent *that there are factors that explain the preference for relatively hard or relatively soft law.*[101] It is important in this respect to focus on their relative capacities to cope with different governance tasks.[102] Thus hard law will tend to be used when the relevant obligations are reciprocal but the performance of those obligations is not. Hard law will increase the credibility of commitments of the relevant parties. It will also be a natural choice when there is high premium on legal certainty, for example to enable business to know precisely what safety requirements it must comply with if a certain product is to be marketed, or to allow governments operating within an international agreement to be clear as to their obligations to admit foreign goods. Hard law may also be the preferred tool when there is doubt about the degree of commitment of other players to comply with the relevant rule. The clarity that comes from hard law, combined with interpretation and implementation by an independent adjudicative body, reduces the likelihood of free riding by a party wishing to take the benefits of the legal regime without accepting the burdens.

There are also instances where soft law or softer law may be the preferred option. This may be so where the parties are unwilling to cast the relevant obligation in legal terms combined with adjudication by an independent third party. This may be especially relevant in the international arena where states may be reluctant to accept external enforcement in sensitive policy

[98] Scott and Trubek, 'Mind the Gap: Law and New Approaches to Governance in the European Union' (2002) 8 *ELJ* 1; Dehousse, 'Conclusion: du bon usage de la methode ouverte de coordination', in R. Dehousse, et al., *L'Europe sans Bruxelles? Une Analyse Ouverte de Coordination* (L'Harmattan, 2004), at 157–180.

[99] Trubek and Trubek, 'The Open Method of Coordination and the Debate over "Hard" and "Soft" Law', in Zeitlin and Pochet with Magnusson (eds), *supra* n. 65, Chap. 3.

[100] Abbott, et al., 'The Concept of Legalization' (2000) 54 *International Organization* 401.

[101] Abbott and Snidal, 'Hard Law and Soft Law in International Governance' (2000) 54 *International Organization* 421; Trubek and Trubek, 'Hard and Soft Law in the Construction of Social Europe: The Role of the Open Method of Co-ordination' (2005) 11 *ELJ* 343; de la Rosa, 'The Open Method of Coordination in the New Member States—the Perspectives for its Use as a Tool of Soft Law' (2005) 11 *ELJ* 618.

[102] Trubek and Trubek, *supra* n. 101, at 344.

areas. They may nonetheless desire some form of regularized cooperation or coordination to deal with a recurrent problem, thereby reducing the transaction costs of ad hoc meetings on the particular topic. The preference for softer law may be because the subject matter is inherently less well suited to being cast in strict legal terms, either because the resultant legal rule will be over- or under-inclusive, or because the problem is polycentric with the result that it is difficult to frame a hard legal rule on the topic at all. Soft law may be the preferred option for the very reason that it facilitates the accommodation of divergent circumstances, or national differences, in a manner that would be difficult if the norm were to be embodied in hard law. A further reason for choosing soft law is that it may be easier to change than hard law and hence more useful as a tool where the factual or economic circumstances may rapidly change, or where the issue to be addressed is a novel one and hence it is felt unwise to embody the rule in hard law. Soft law may also be the chosen option where the law maker believes that it will render compliance more likely than would be the case with harder-edged legal rules.

We should moreover *be careful in the characterization of OMC as being purely soft law or in thinking that it embodies the same kind of soft law as exists in other areas.* It is true that, as we have seen, the outcome of OMC deliberations will sound in the form of recommendations rather than hard edged legal norms. The picture of OMC as being purely soft law is nonetheless flawed. The governing instruments that frame the OMC will normally take the form of hard law. The framework for OMC in economic and employment policy is found in Treaty articles combined with Community legislation. The same is true for the provisions on social exclusion, the difference being that the relevant Treaty article does not embody the OMC regime, this being set out in the form of a binding Community Decision. The picture of OMC as purely soft law also ignores the fact that the Treaty articles combined with the relevant Community legislation will often be couched in mandatory terms in relation to the procedure for coordination, delineating particular tasks that Community institutions and Member States must undertake as part of the coordination process.[103] The picture of OMC as purely soft law must be further qualified even in relation to sanctions or remedies, since the process at least in the context of economic policy can lead to the imposition of formal sanctions. Nor should it be thought that soft law as it operates in the OMC is necessarily the same as the soft law that applies in other areas.[104] Thus traditional soft law in the EU has been made by the Commission and overseen by the ECJ, whereas in the OMC it is the Member States, Commission, Council, and European Council that predominate.

[103] See, e.g., Arts. 99 and 128 EC.

[104] Borras and Jacobsson, 'The Open Method of Coordination and New Governance Patterns in the EU' (2004) 11 *JEPP* 185, at 188–189.

Moreover traditional soft law tends to be ad hoc, whereas in the context of the OMC it is more systematic.

We should be *equally wary of regarding the traditional Community method as being based solely on hard law.* It is of course true that regulations, directives, and decisions are the normal tools of the TCM. It is equally clear that these are often used in conjunction with soft law in areas as diverse as competition law, state aids, and the regulation of the pharmaceutical industry. Guidelines and the like that flesh out the hard law are a standard feature of this regulatory landscape. This can be exemplified by considering the regulatory strategies used in that most quintessential Community sphere, the internal market. The Commission's 2000 Review of the Internal Market[105] identified areas that were of concern for the fulfilment of the single market. These included, *inter alia*, enhancing citizens' health and safety and the promotion of their economic interests, encouraging economic reform in the interests of market efficiency, maximizing the benefits of the digital age, and reducing the regulatory burdens on business. The Commission then set out in detail the legislative and non-legislative initiatives that it was taking to attain the specified goals. The interplay between hard and soft law can be exemplified further by the Commission Recommendation concerning the transposition of directives into national law.[106] Lawyers are of course aware of the problems concerning the transposition of directives into national law. They naturally think of legal redress for this malaise whether in the form of a Commission action against the recalcitrant Member State, or a *Francovich* damages action. Both are classic hard law remedies. Both are important. Neither has cured the problem. The Commission Recommendation acknowledges the legally binding nature of the directive and the repeated calls made for timely transposition, but concludes that 'many such Directives have still not been transposed into national law in all Member States long after the deadline for transposition has passed'.[107] The Commission admits moreover that its 'vigorous legal action against Member States for late or incorrect transposition' has not cured the 'transposition deficits' that continue to persist,[108] that it was therefore necessary for the Commission to take a more proactive role. To this end the Recommendation sets out in detail steps that should be taken by the Member States to alleviate the problem. What is especially interesting in this context is that the methodology employed draws on the OMC. Thus the recitals to the Recommendation talk directly of Member States learning from each other's practice, of identifying best

[105] Communication from the Commission to the European Parliament, the Council ECOSOC and the Committee of the Regions, 2000 Review of the Internal Market Strategy, COM(2000) 257 final.

[106] Recommendation from the Commission, On the Transposition into National Law of Directives Affecting the Internal Market, SEC(2004) 918 final.

[107] Ibid. Rec. 4. [108] Ibid. Rec. 8.

practice, and of choosing the procedures and practices best designed to ensure the timely transposition of directives.[109] It is clear then that an admixture of hard and soft law is to be found even in areas commonly regarded as paradigms of the traditional Community method. We should moreover not forget that policy-making in an area such as employment policy is itself a blend of different regulatory techniques, including the TCM, OMC, and norms generated by the social partners.[110]

B. The Open Method of Coordination v the Traditional Community Method

There is another dimension to the discourse about the OMC that requires separate treatment. The relevant literature contrasts the nature of the OMC with that of the traditional Community method, TCM. The virtues of the OMC are said to be that it fosters deliberation, participation, discourse, mutual learning, and the like while at the same time respecting national differences. There is foundation for these claims, although how fully they are realized will be considered in the next section. The assumption is that these virtues are either absent or exist to a much lesser degree in the context of the TCM. This assumption is contestable. There are of course differences between the OMC mode of governance and the TCM. That is self-evident. To assume that the ideals of deliberation, participation, learning, and the like are absent from the TCM, or even that they exist to a lesser degree, is however not self-evident. Consider this from the following perspectives.

Let us begin with the *passage of regulations and directives*. The relevant players, the Commission, EP, and Council, may of course have veto positions which they are willing to exercise on matters of importance in the particular piece of legislation. There will be elements of bargain between the key institutional players, and within each institutional setting. To regard this as the complete picture is nonetheless to see only half the story and it may well not be the most important half. It leaves out of account the fact that the co-decision procedure embodies a structured deliberative discourse between the key actors.[111] The steps of the process require each of the institutions to assess its own preferences in the light of those voiced by others, and to decide whether to stick to those preferences at the second reading stage, or within the Conciliation Committee. I am not claiming that this works as a perfect model of republican discourse, but nor for that matter does the OMC. I am arguing that the TCM provides the structured forum for such discourse. I am also arguing that this is readily apparent when one follows through particular

[109] Ibid. Recs. 16–18. [110] Rhodes, *supra* n. 65.

[111] See also in this respect European Parliament, Council, and Commission, Institutional Agreement on Better Lawmaking, OJ 2003 C321/1.

pieces of legislation. Yes, there will be institutional intransigence and bargain. But there will also be many instances where the dialogue that occurs in and through co-decision is every bit as deliberative as that which occurs within the OMC, and this is so notwithstanding that TCM measures will normally be legally binding. Furthermore the dialogue includes the EP, which is largely excluded from the OMC.

We need to be *similarly mindful of the capacity for learning within the TCM.* It is clear that the OMC provides considerable opportunities for mutual learning by the relevant players. It is indeed structured with that very idea in mind, and the iterative nature of the OMC operating on an annual basis fosters such learning. We shall look at this in more detail below. It should, however, also be recognized that learning is an important feature of the TCM. Legislative revision will often be the 'didactic result' of the lessons gleaned from the pre-existing legislative regime. Reflect on legal development within particular Community spheres. Take the Structural Funds by way of example.[112] There have been numerous legislative changes over the last 30 years. Some have been prompted by shifts in policy. The catalyst for others has been the lessons learned from the shortcomings of the previous legal regime. The relevant players get a better idea of, for example, the controls that should be imposed on the recipients of funds so as to foster accountability and efficacy. The same capacity for learning through the TCM can be perceived in areas as diverse as the Common Agricultural Policy, State Aids, and the Financial Regulation. Legislative revision within the TCM is a dynamic process designed in part to learn from and improve on the status quo ante.

Similar *caution is warranted in relation to the relative capacities of the OMC and the TCM to foster participation.* A virtue claimed for OMC is that it enables input from interested parties in the deliberative process. The very word 'open' carries this connotation. We shall see that the jury is still out on how far participation is realized within the OMC. This is of course not a zero sum game. It is perfectly possible to favour participation within the OMC and TCM. We should not, however, work on the assumption, implicit or explicit, that the opportunities for such participation are necessarily less within the TCM than the OMC. This is not the place for a general exegesis on the law and practice of consultation and participation as it operates within the TCM. It is by no means perfect, as we saw in the discussion of implementing rules made pursuant to comitology.[113] The topic will be considered in more detail below.[114] The reality is that the opportunities for participation and consultation are greater in relation to primary regulations and directives made pursuant to the TCM than they are in relation to comitology norms.

[112] See above, Chap. 3.
[113] See above, Chap. 4.
[114] See below, Chap. 10.

The Commission has resisted pressures to create a regime of legal rights to participate. It has, however, broadened consultation through increasing use of Green and White Papers when important areas of European Community (EC) policy are being developed. This approach was formalized and generalized in the 2002 Communication from the Commission.[115] The very fact that the TCM will normally lead to discrete pieces of legislation dealing with a specific topic facilitates input from interested parties who can focus on detailed hard-edged aspects of the proposed legislation. The Commission has also initiated Interactive Policy Making (IPM) which is accessible via the web portal 'Your Voice in Europe'.[116] This consists of two internet-based instruments to collect feedback from citizens, consumers, and business. The Commission regards the knowledge thereby gleaned as a way of shaping new policies and improving existing ones. There is a feedback mechanism to collect information from citizens etc. about problems encountered with different EU policies. There is also an online consultation mechanism, operating through structured questionnaires, allowing input on particular policy proposals. The efficacy of these mechanisms will be considered in more detail in the later discussion about access.[117] Suffice it to say at this juncture that this initiative applies in relation to regulations, directives, and decisions enacted pursuant to the TCM. It is designed to foster learning and facilitate participation. It is interesting to note that empirical analysis of the OMC revealed that most interviewees felt that the process was relatively closed not only to the broader public, but also to executive agencies and other interested parties at sub-national level, and that some pointed to the irony of the term 'open' method of coordination, given that it was perceived as less open than the TCM.[118]

5. THE OPEN METHOD OF COORDINATION: AN EVALUATION

The discussion in the previous section has revealed that there is no reason to be dismissive of the OMC because it operates principally through the medium of soft law. It has revealed also that we should be cautious about

[115] Communication from the Commission, Towards a Reinforced Culture of Consultation and Dialogue—General Principles and Minimum Standards for Consultation of Interested Parties by the Commission, COM(2002) 704 final.

[116] <http://www.europa.eu.int/your voice/ipm/index_en.htm>.

[117] See below Chap. 10.

[118] Jacobsson and Vifell, 'Towards Deliberative Supranationalism? Analysing the Role of Committees in Soft Coordination', GOVECOR Final Review Meeting, Brussels, 16–17 February 2004, available at <http://eucenter.wisc.edu/OMC/open12.html#terms>, at 23.

assuming that the virtues of the OMC are necessarily absent from the TCM. The focus within this section shifts to an analysis of the OMC itself, building on what we have learned about it in the key areas of economic policy, employment policy, and social exclusion. We have seen that the virtues of the OMC as a method of governance are that it promotes deliberation, participation, learning, and responsiveness, while at the same time enabling national differences to be respected when addressing solutions to common problems.

Some commentators see these facets of the OMC as an embodiment and exemplification of a broader democratic theory, directly deliberative polyarchy.[119] A central feature of this theory is that centralized decision-making has limits within a modern polity, more especially if it is unconnected with local reality. Politics is seen as a method for dealing with practical problems. In deliberative polyarchy, 'problem solving depends not on harmony and spontaneous collaboration, but on the permanent disequilibrium of incentives and interests imperfectly aligned, and on the collaborative exploration of resulting differences'.[120] Deliberation is to be found 'when collective decisions are founded not on a simple aggregation of interests, but on arguments from and to those governed by the decision, or their representatives'.[121] Democratic deliberative polyarchy requires protection of basic rights, transparency and public participation, coordination across and between the relevant units, mechanisms for accountability that connect deliberative decisions in particular areas with broader public discussion about those topics, and the ability to contest decisions.[122]

It is, however, necessary to assess how far the ideals associated with OMC are realized in practice. This requires us to look more closely at the individual

[119] Cohen and Sabel, 'Directly-deliberative Polyarchy' (1997) 3 *ELJ* 313; Gerstenberg and Sabel, 'Directly-deliberative Polyarchy: An Institutional Ideal for Europe?, in C. Joerges and R. Dehousse (eds), *Good Governance in Europe's Integrated Markets* (Oxford University Press, 2002), at 289–342; Sabel and Zeitlin, 'Active Welfare, Experimental Governance, Pragmatic Constitutionalism: The New Transformation of Europe' (2003) available online at <http://www2.law.columbia.edu/sable/papers.htm>; Zeitlin, 'Social Europe and Experimentalist Governance: Towards a New Constitutional Compromise?', in G. de Burca (ed.), *EU Law and the Welfare State, In Search of Solidarity* (Oxford University Press, 2005), Chap. 7; Eberlein and Kerwer, 'New Governance in the European Union: A Theoretical Perspective' (2004) 42 *JCMS* 121; Smismans, 'Reflexive Law in Support of Directly Deliberative Polyarchy: Reflexive-Deliberative Polyarchy as a Normative Frame for the OMC', in O. De Schutter and S. Deakin (eds), *Social Rights and Market Forces, Is the Open Coordination of Employment and Social Policies the Future of Social Europe?* (Bruylant, 2005), at 99–144; Armstrong, 'Inclusive Governance? Civil Society and the Open Method of Coordination', in S. Smismans (ed.), *Civil Society and Legitimate European Governance* (Edward Elgar, 2006), Chap. 3.

[120] Cohen and Sabel, 'Sovereignty and Solidarity: EU and US', in J. Zeitlin and D. Trubek (eds), *Governing Work and Welfare in a New Economy, European and American Experiments* (Oxford University Press, 2003), at 366.

[121] Ibid. at 366. [122] Ibid. at 369–370.

parts of the overall package, and check the theory against the empirical evidence.

A. Transparency

Transparency is clearly central to the OMC, both in itself and as a pre-condition for fostering participation, debate, and the like. De la Porte and Nanz[123] evaluated transparency in the operation of the employment and pensions OMC. They found that access to information in relation to the EES had improved considerably since 2003 with the creation of a specific website containing the relevant documentation including a description of the OMC strategy, Commission communications, national action plans, indicators, and the like. A similar website exists in relation to social inclusion and documentation is readily accessible and easy to locate.

It is clear, however, that formal access to documentation is only one facet of transparency. Another equally important consideration concerns the transparency or opacity of the decision-making process itself. Consider in this respect the observations of Hodson and Maher on economic policy coordination.[124] They pointed to the difficulties of demarcating responsibilities between the different institutions and committees that operate in this area, with resultant complexity and opacity for the decision-making process as a whole. They noted that transparency is essential for the process, since learning is dependent on information exchange, but that 'the fragmentation of responsibility means that the system lacks transparency beyond the core of elites—national and Community civil servants, and the social partners through the macroeconomic dialogue—who are directly involved in preparing and discussing the national reports, and in framing of the broad guidelines'.[125] Jacobsson and Vifell voiced similar concerns about transparency in relation to the role of committees in the overall decision-making process in the context of economic, employment, and social policy.[126]

This problem was not lost on the Commission. The streamlining introduced in 2002–2003 was motivated in part by just such problems. Thus the Commission noted that as new elements were added to the OMC processes on an *ad hoc* basis 'without necessarily taking the wider picture into account, the present framework has arguably become complex and more difficult to understand and explain'.[127] The streamlining introduced at the Commission's initiative has been beneficial. It has not, however, addressed

[123] De La Porte and Nanz, *supra* n. 65, at 276–277.
[124] Hodson and Maher, 'The Open Method as a New Mode of Governance', *supra* n. 23.
[125] Ibid. at 730.
[126] Jacobsson and Vifell, *supra* n. 118, at 24.
[127] Communication from the Commission, *supra* n. 96, at 2.

the institutional complexity and consequent opacity of decision-making as it operates within particular areas where the OMC is used.

B. Public Debate

The findings in terms of public debate and awareness are less encouraging. Studies indicate that media coverage of the OMC in relation to employment from 1997 to 2002 was principally driven by national initiatives, rather than those taken at European level, and that the learning which takes place through EES is not linked to public debate. The consequence is that there is little pressure placed on governments from such public debate to comply with the recommendations made by the EES.[128]

C. Parliamentary Involvement

It is unsurprising that the media shows little awareness or coverage of OMC procedures, although regrettable nonetheless. The available evidence also indicates that national parliaments have given relatively little attention to OMC processes, and that knowledge of such matters by national parliamentarians is in short supply.

The limited role accorded to the EP within the OMC process is of especial concern. This does not mean that the EP is opposed to use of the OMC. It has, for example, expressed positive support for this method of policy delivery in the context of health care,[129] social exclusion,[130] and as part of more general social policy.[131]

The EP has nonetheless voiced concerns about use of the OMC. The Committee on Employment and Social Affairs stated that leaving aside employment, the areas of governance where the OMC was to be preferred to other executive instruments were not specified by the Treaty, by other regulatory provisions, or by an interinstitutional agreement.[132] The choice of the OMC was 'taken on a case-by-case basis by the Council acting on a proposal from the Commission or on its own initiative'.[133] The Committee noted the

[128] De La Porte and Nanz, *supra* n. 65, at 277.

[129] Committee on Employment and Social Affairs, On Modernising Social Protection and Developing Good Quality Healthcare, Rapporteur, Milan Cabrnoch, A6-0085/2005, at paras. 5, 17, subject to cautionary notes about not overburdening Member States with requests for data.

[130] Committee on Employment and Social Affairs, *supra* n. 21, at para. 10.

[131] Committee on Employment and Social Affairs, On the Social Policy Agenda for the Period 2006–2010, Rapporteur, Ria Oomen-Ruijten, A6-0142/2005, at paras. 35, 47.

[132] Committee on Employment and Social Affairs, Report on Analysis of the Open Coordination Procedure in the Field of Employment Social Affairs and Future Prospects, Rapporteur, Miet Smet, A5-0143/2003.

[133] Ibid. Rec. D.

progressive switch from traditional legislative techniques to the use of new techniques where the traditional approach was felt to be inappropriate. It was of the view that the EP was the only institution which was capable at European level of exercising democratic control over political processes, including the OMC,[134] and that the EP was 'at risk of being marginalized or sidelined by these new political procedures'.[135] The Committee noted that the EP's role in OMC procedures was unspecified, with the exception of the EES, where it had a right to be consulted, but that its role in this area was severely constrained because it had so little time to proffer opinions on the salient issues.[136] It proposed that the OMC procedure should only be used in any policy area after the EP and the Council had given their approval. It argued further that the EP should be consulted and should give an opinion on the guidelines, the summary report, and the recommendations emanating from the OMC process. Moreover each national report should indicate how civil society, including the social partners, local, regional, and national authorities had been consulted. The recommendations resulting from the OMC process should also be accompanied by the EP's report. The Committee exhorted the Council and Commission to take greater account of the EP's views when drawing up guidelines. It also expressed concern that the OMC should not serve as 'fig leaf for a country's failure to take action',[137] and that it should not be used for the purpose of avoiding the binding quality of more traditional Community regulation.

Similar concerns have been voiced by the Committee on Economic and Monetary Affairs. In 2002 it welcomed the Commission's streamlining proposals, but expressed concern that the new timetable for the Guidelines Package would give the EP an even shorter time than before to examine the Commission's proposal.[138] It highlighted the need for greater democratic legitimacy and insisted that the EP should have participation rights with respect to the full coordination policy cycle and the Lisbon process, this to be embodied in an interinstitutional agreement.[139] These points were reiterated in 2003 where the Committee regretted that the EP was not fully included in the development and implementation of the broad economic policy guidelines, and expressed its concern at the time within which it had to deliver an

[134] Ibid. Rec. F. [135] Ibid. Rec. G.

[136] Ibid. Rec. I. The timetable for the EES was modified, in part at least, as a response to this difficulty, Communication from the Commission, *supra* n. 96, at 14.

[137] Ibid. at 9.

[138] Committee on Economic and Monetary Affairs, On the Commission Communication on Streamlining the Annual Economic and Employment Policy Coordination Cycles, Rapporteur, Othmar Karas, A5-0400/2002, at 7.

[139] Ibid. at 7, 10–11.

opinion on the 2003 guidelines.[140] In 2004 the Committee spoke once again about the democratic deficit in relation to economic policy governance, calling for the inclusion of the EP and national parliaments in the Lisbon process, and for greater involvement by the social partners and civil society, in order to 'raise political ownership of the strategy and responsibility for the measures to be undertaken'.[141]

The Committee on Constitutional Affairs has voiced the same view, on this occasion in relation to the new regime of integrated economic and employment guidelines, 'insisting' that the Commission allows proper time for consultation with the EP prior to the Spring European Council Summit.[142]

These concerns should be taken seriously. This is so even if one subscribes to a theory of deliberative-democratic polyarchy. This thesis is premised on the assumption that democratic legitimation should not be felt to rest solely on input from a body such as the EP. Let us for the sake of argument accept this premise. It does not, however, lead to the conclusion that the democratically elected legislature at the European level should be largely excluded from the OMC process. It provides no rationale as to why the EP should not be thought of as a legitimate participant in deciding when the OMC should be used as a mode of policy delivery, and it provides no justification for the exclusion or marginalization of the EP from having input into the content of the OMC process when it is used.

These issues will be of greater importance if the OMC is increasingly used as an adjunct to traditional regulatory techniques. This would see the TCM in the form of regulations, decisions, or directives being complemented by the OMC as method for checking on best practices, benchmarking, iterative learning, and the like in the relevant area. I have no problem with this strategy as such. We have already seen that the admixture of hard and soft law features in many regulatory schemes at both Community and national level. Such a combination may well be the optimal way to deal with a particular issue. The concern is that unless thought is given to the role of the EP in relation to OMC it will be further marginalized by such developments. The emerging pattern will be one in which the EP will have its normal role in

[140] Committee on Economic and Monetary Affairs, On the Broad Guidelines of the Economic Policies of the Member States and the Community for 2003–2005, Rapporteur, Jose Manuel Garcia-Margallo y Marfil, A5-0142/2003. See also, Committee on Economic and Monetary Affairs, On the Annual Assessment of Stability and Convergence Programmes, Rapporteur, Bruno Trentin, A5-0047/2003, at para. 14.

[141] Committee on Economic and Monetary Affairs, On the Situation of the European Economy, Report on the Broad Guidelines for Economic Policies, Rapporteur, Christa Randzio-Plath, A5-0045/2004, at 7, 12.

[142] Committee on Constitutional Affairs, On the Revision of the Framework Agreement between the European Parliament and the Commission, Rapporteur, Jo Leinen, A6-0147/2005, at para. 5.

the passage of the principal regulation or directive, normally through co-decision, but that it may well have little input in deciding whether the OMC should be the chosen mode of implementation, and it will have scant involvement if the OMC is chosen as the method of implementation.

This could well lead to inter-institutional tensions and conflict redolent of those that have dogged the exclusion of the EP from the passage of secondary norms pursuant to the comitology procedures.[143] Indeed there are currents in the literature that draw this analogy, regarding both as instances of deliberative supranationalism to be defended notwithstanding the marginalization or exclusion of the EP. I believe that there are difficulties with this view in relation to comitology.[144] I believe equally that the exclusion or marginalization of the EP from the OMC should not be viewed with equanimity.

It should be emphasized that this does not mean that I am opposed to the OMC. The soft law approach that it embodies with its emphasis on learning, benchmarking, and peer pressure may be a valuable adjunct to normal regulatory techniques. It does mean that we need to think seriously about the role of the EP in this respect. The EP should have a say in the choice of regulatory technique, and if the OMC process is chosen we should then ensure that the EP is able to play a role therein in the manner elaborated by the reports of the EP committees set out above.

This is important in and of itself. It is also important to the broader legitimacy of the OMC. The vision of the OMC as a manifestation of some *democratic* form of deliberative problem-solving assumes that we can locate the input from somewhere, thereby warranting that appellation. If it does not come from the EP or indeed national parliaments then it must be sought through input from the bottom, via participation of affected parties. It is not clear, however, that the empirical evidence of participation can sustain this vision. It is to this issue that we now turn.

D. Participation

Participation is central to the ideal of the OMC. The very word 'open' connotes the idea that the process should be inclusive, not exclusive, and carries the implication that participation should be possible 'throughout the policy chain from agenda-setting to implementation and monitoring—and in all fora: committees subordinate to the Council formations, indicators' working groups, and peer review process'.[145] There seems generally to be some connection between the degree of participation and the degree of

[143] See above, Chap. 4. [144] See above, 114–119.
[145] De la Porte and Nanz, *supra* n. 65, at 272.

politicization, with higher degrees of politicization making it more difficult for actors to participate, although this is not invariably the case.[146]

It is especially important to judge the reality of participation in the different areas where the OMC is used. In the context of the EES de la Porte and Nanz found that the participation of European labour and management organizations had been rather limited, notwithstanding that they were encouraged to contribute.[147] They found that the participation of social partners at the national level had improved, but that 'progress is disappointing overall compared to the incentives taken to improve their participation'.[148] The authors provided valuable data on participation of social partners in the national action plans made under the EES.[149] In all but one instance the NAP was characterized as a governmental rather than joint document, although there were direct contributions made by the social partners to the NAP in seven out of fifteen countries, normally in relation to the adaptability pillar. The study revealed that the quality of social partner participation was vulnerable to domestic political change, and that it had declined in certain countries where right-wing governments were in power. There was, however, a high level of satisfaction with participation in six of the countries, though not surprisingly this correlated with their contribution to the NAP. The Commission also encouraged participation from local actors, even though there is no legal obligation to consult them, basing its initiatives rather on the Lisbon Council remit to foster participation at all levels. There was some evidence that participation by local actors had increased, although this was mainly focused at the level of implementation rather than policy design. There was moreover some involvement of civil society in the EES, notably through interest groups concerned with poverty and the implications of the employment guidelines on poverty. The general conclusion reached by de la Porte and Nanz is that the participation of the social partners in the EES has improved at national level over the last five years, but that the input is still weak, that the impact of other civil society actors has been minimal, and that there is some evidence of involvement of local actors at national level at the implementation stage.[150]

The conclusions reached concerning participation in relation to the EES cannot of course be generalized one way or another to other areas where OMC operates. It is, however, only through studies of this nature that one can discern the reality of participatory involvement. There is some evidence of greater participation in the context of social inclusion,[151] but the extent

[146] De la Porte and Pochet, 'The Participative Dimension of the OMC', paper delivered at the Conference on 'Opening the Open Method of Coordination', EUI Florence, 4 July 2003.

[147] De la Porte and Nanz, *supra* n. 65, at 278–279.

[148] Ibid. at 279. [149] Ibid. at 280. [150] Ibid. at 283.

[151] De la Porte and Pochet, *supra* n. 146, at 10–11.

remains open to question.[152] There is also interesting evidence relating to the willingness and desire of different types of organizations to take part in the OMC, with groups that normally have less power in the political process being more anxious to make use of the opportunities afforded by the OMC, while by way of contrast the social partners have been ambivalent, fearing that too great an involvement in the EES might compromise their bargaining autonomy and being mindful that they have other ways to influence the relevant agenda.[153]

The general picture is not that encouraging, however.[154] Thus in relation to the OMC in pensions there are no mandatory consultative participants, social partners have no formal role to play in the writing of national plans, although there has been some input from civil society groups speaking for the elderly.[155] In the economic sphere it is generally acknowledged that the deliberation takes place among members of a select policy-making community, rather than the broader public.[156] We should also recall the empirical analysis of committees in the OMC, which revealed that most interviewees felt that the process was relatively closed, and that some pointed to the irony of the term 'open method of coordination', given that it was perceived as less open than the TCM.[157]

Participation is key to the vision of the OMC as an exemplar of democratic deliberation. It is central in terms of input to the vision of the OMC as a process that is democratic as well as deliberative. It is integral in terms of output to the learning that is a feature of the OMC. It is therefore unsurprising that weakness in this respect has led to scepticism of the democratic credentials of the process. The EP's Committee on Employment and Social Affairs voiced the opinion that 'as things stand, the open method of coordination is, in many cases, a process conducted between and on behalf of elites, the outcome of intergovernmental negotiation and bargain'.[158] Radaelli acknowledges that the OMC may well embody technocratic deliberation. He argues that there is, however, very little in the current practice of the OMC that resembles democratic governance based on bottom-up learning or directly-deliberative polyarchy, and that the real world of the OMC is weak in terms of participation, transparency, domestic salience of the process, and

[152] Armstrong, 'Tackling Social Exclusion through the OMC', *supra* n. 90; Armstrong, 'How Open is the United Kingdom to the Open Method of Coordination Process on Social Inclusion?', in Zeitlin and Pochet with Magnusson (eds), *supra* n. 65, at Chap. 9.

[153] Zeitlin, 'The Open Method of Coordination in Action', *supra* n. 65.

[154] Zeitlin, 'Opening the Open Method of Coordination', paper delivered at the Committee of the Regions' Conference 'The OMC: Improving European Governance?' 30 September 2002; Zeitlin, 'The Open Method of Coordination in Action', *supra* n. 65.

[155] De la Porte and Nanz, *supra* n. 65, at 281.

[156] Hodson, *supra* n. 23, at 238.

[157] Jacobsson and Vifell, *supra* n. 118, at 23.

[158] Committee on Employment and Social Affairs, *supra* n. 132, at 13.

communicative rationality.[159] Wessels touches a similar chord when remarking that leaving aside the 'usual suspects', members of the executive and bureaucratic elites at national and Community level, the frequency and intensity of participation by other actors has been low, with the result that the process is dominated by closed shops of experts and power is concentrated on the executive.[160] Jacobsson and Vifell note the benefits of the committees that are central to the OMC, but conclude that 'committee deliberation is a type of elite deliberation, or sometimes expert deliberation which hardly fulfils all the requirements of deliberative democratic theory'.[161]

E. Deliberation and Learning

Deliberation and learning are central to the OMC. It is important at the outset to recognize that the deliberative and learning process is dependent on benchmarks and indicators which structure this process. Benchmarking has become a major tool in both the private and the public sphere. It is used frequently by national governments. There is no doubt that it is a valuable device for defining goals and measuring performance. We should be equally mindful of the difficulties associated with it. There are technical problems of defining best practice, of collecting and collating the relevant data, and of deciding on the balance between quantitative and qualitative measures. These difficulties are compounded when there are several potentially conflicting policy goals. Arrowsmith, Sisson, and Marginson capture this point when remarking that 'if companies like Alcan find it difficult to benchmark smelting processes between their different plants, how much more difficult is it to benchmark processes such as skills acquisition, innovation or knowledge transfer across different countries of the Union?'[162]

There is an increasing literature assessing the extent to which the ideals of deliberation and learning are realized in the different areas where the OMC applies.[163] Valuable work has been done on the role of the committees within the OMC.[164] These committees are especially important since they do not fit the paradigm of other committees within the EU. The OMC is not based on a traditional legislative mandate and hence the normal range of

[159] Radaelli, 'The Open Method of Coordination: A New Governance Architecture for the European Union' (2003) 1 *Swedish Institute for European Policy Studies* 1, at 49–50.

[160] Wessels, 'Open Methods of Coordination, New Modes of Governance as a Typical Step in the Evolution of the EU System' (2003), at 20.

[161] Jacobsson and Vifell, *supra* n. 118, at 27.

[162] Arrowsmith, Sisson, and Marginson, 'What can Benchmarking Offer the Open Method of Coordination?' (2004) 11 *JEPP* 311, at 324.

[163] Casey and Gold, 'Peer Review of Labour Market Programmes in the European Union: What Can Countries Really Learn from One Another?' (2005) 12 *JEPP* 23.

[164] Jacobsson and Vifell, *supra* n. 118.

committees and working groups do not generally operate in these areas. The Employment Committee, the Economic Policy Committee, the Economic and Financial Committee, and the Social Protection Committee thus play a crucial role in relation to matters such as the guidelines, indicators, peer review, and the like.[165]

The conclusions reached by the study are interesting. Jacobsson and Vifell found that much turned on the nature of the agenda. The general aim was to reach consensus and common ground. There was real evidence of deliberation and a willingness to learn from the experience of others and in that sense strategic bargaining was not the general mode of committee operation.[166] They also found that negotiation and bargaining did predominate when matters were politically sensitive or where they concerned issues of a more rule-setting character. Thus when 'it comes down to the formulation of recommendations or the exact definition of indicators, the discussion in the committees or in the bilateral consultations with the Commission, takes the form of pure negotiation and bargaining'.[167] It was therefore difficult in sensitive areas to find 'evidence of national standpoints actually being modified during committee interaction'.[168]

Jacobsson and Vifell further concluded that some committees, such as the Employment Committee, operated as surrogate political forums. This was a measure of the committee's importance, in the sense that the relevant Council formation would often adopt the committee's recommendation without modification. Member States would therefore use the committees to place issues on the political agenda, with the consequence that 'discussions have become more negotiations on the basis of national standpoints than open-ended discussions on best practices and exchange of opinions'.[169] The demand for written statements on policy, the weight of the committee agenda, and the limited time frame has furthered the tendency towards negotiation and bargain.

The study revealed that the degree of deliberation may vary as between committees. It was relatively high in relation to the Economic and Finance Committee composed of economists forming an epistemic community, although there was some evidence that the committee was becoming more politicized because of differences concerning the SGP, and the tensions caused by the failure of some states to comply with its dictates. There was moreover some correlation between the degree of deliberation within the committee, and its very lack of openness to other participants, thereby evidencing in this context at least a tension between deliberation and participation.[170] This

165 Ibid. at 8.
166 Ibid. at 20, 22.
167 Ibid. at 20.
168 Ibid. at 22.
169 Ibid. at 21.
170 Ibid. at 16, 22.

tension has been evident more generally in the context of the debates about rule-making and comitology.[171]

In more general terms Zeitlin concluded that the strongest impact of the EES and Social Inclusion strategy was to be seen through indirect or higher-order effects, such as the identification of common European challenges and promising policy options, combined with the impact of the OMC in pressing Member States to think afresh about established approaches. There were, however, relatively few concrete cases at national level of direct learning from other systems as to what worked and what did not. Direct learning, where it did exist, tended moreover to be concentrated on specific topics, such as gender mainstreaming and the shift towards a preventative approach to unemployment. The evidence of reflexive learning from the results of the OMC processes at EU level was also found to be limited.[172] The fullness of the agendas of the OMC committees, combined with the tight timetable for peer review of national action plans, was also found to limit the scope for mutual learning.[173]

There is a further dimension that is relevant to deliberation and learning within the OMC: they are dependent on some measure of agreement on the desired end. In the economic sphere there is general agreement that coordination can be beneficial in circumstances where the autonomous actions of individual actors prove harmful to the welfare of other parties. This is, as we have seen, the general rationale for coordination in this area. There is, however, uncertainty as to the more detailed application of this principle. Thus Hodson notes the 'diagnostic uncertainty over the exact nature of fiscal spillover within the Euro area and hence over the form that macroeconomic coordination should take'.[174] This problem is compounded by 'prescriptive uncertainty over whether macroeconomic coordination is an appropriate cure for the problem of fiscal spillover', and by 'substantive uncertainty over the definition of the medium-term target'.[175] The scope for deliberation within the economic sphere will moreover be 'bounded' by the institutional setting at national level. The deliberative approach has been criticized in this area because 'by assuming that political willingness to coordinate is a sufficient condition for policy coordination, it ignores the role of domestic budgetary institutions and procedures in the formation of Member States' fiscal policy'.[176]

[171] See above, Chap. 4.

[172] Zeitlin, 'The Open Method of Coordination in Action', *supra* n. 65.

[173] See also Watt, *supra* n. 65.

[174] Hodson, *supra* n. 23, at 234.

[175] Ibid. at 234.

[176] Hodson, *supra* n. 23, at 238. See also Kaiser and Prange, *supra* n. 22, at 250–251 in relation to innovation policy.

F. Peer Pressure

The efficacy of the OMC will, as we have seen, depend in part on peer pressure. It can be accepted that national policy change can in principle be driven by mimetic and normative processes, even in the absence of coercive mechanisms and even though there is no lurking shadow of hierarchy.[177] This still leaves open the practical effectiveness of peer pressure and this may well vary as between different areas.

This can be exemplified by coordination in the economic sphere. Hodson notes that macroeconomic policy coordination is an inherently uncertain exercise with costs as well as benefits. The OMC is designed to minimize the costs of coordination, but the delivery of the benefits is doubtful and is dependent on whether 'consensus building and peer pressure can have the desired impact on Member States' budgetary decisions'.[178] The danger is that 'while the ambiguity of soft coordination allows for agreement to be struck in an area that is not suited to harder forms of coordination, it also provides a ready made escape clause for profligate Member States'.[179]

Hodson and Maher elaborated more specific factors affecting the efficacy of peer pressure within the area of economic coordination.[180] The relevant obligations should be defined as specifically as possible, thereby reducing the risk of counterclaim on the part of the censured state; the participants must regard peer rebuke as costly and therefore to be avoided; the body imposing the sanctions must have respect and credibility; the existence of discretion as to whether to impose the sanction can lead to doubts about its imposition and questions about the evenness with which such discretion is exercised.

Hodson, having charted the application of economic coordination in the context of Portugal, remarked that the experience 'reminds us that the impact of peer pressure as a sanction mechanism requires an obligation that is precisely drawn, a credible sanctioning body that is ready, willing and able to perform its functions, and a Member State that has respect for the rule of law'.[181] These sentiments are echoed by Maher who states that national concerns will often trump the guidelines when states fail to meet the multilateral surveillance targets.[182] The very recourse to law by the Commission, unhappy with the way in which the principles of coordination were applied in 2003 to Germany and France, serves to exemplify these issues in a recent

[177] Borras and Jacobsson, *supra* n. 104, at 195–196; Trubek and Trubek, *supra* n. 101, at 356–359.

[178] Hodson, *supra* n. 23, at 233.

[179] Ibid. at 236.

[180] Hodson and Maher, 'Soft Law and Sanctions', *supra* n. 23, at 807; Hodson, *supra* n. 23, at 239–240.

[181] Hodson, *supra* n. 23, at 245.

[182] Maher, *supra* n. 23 above.

high profile case. These concerns have been echoed by the EP's Committee on Economic and Monetary Affairs.[183]

The amendments made to the SGP Regulations have rendered the application of peer pressure in this area even more difficult than hitherto, because the 'impugned' Member State can now point to a broader range of relevant factors that should be taken into account to justify and legitimate its position in circumstances where it is claimed to have an excessive deficit.

G. Substantive and Procedural Impact

The legitimate concern with issues such as transparency, participation, and the like should not lead us to forget the all-important issue concerning the substantive impact of the OMC in the policy areas where it operates. This is a complex issue that cannot be examined in any detail here. Suffice it to say for the present that empirical work combined with official reports suggest that OMC processes have, for example, raised the political salience of employment and social inclusion policies at the national and EU levels, that they have contributed towards the incorporation of EU concepts into national debates, and that they have contributed to changes in some specific national policies.

There are nonetheless difficulties in identifying the precise causal impact of the EES and social inclusion processes on national policy-making, since national attention to such matters often preceded the OMC at EU level, and because the OMC is not truly external to policy formation at national level.[184] The EP's Committee on Employment and Social Affairs called on the Commission to study the effectiveness of the OMC in order to determine, *inter alia*, the 'impact of the open method of coordination on national policies, looking not only at efforts made and results obtained, but also into the causal link between the application of the open method of coordination and the adjustment of national policy'.[185]

There is, however, some positive evidence that the OMC has fostered improvements in national decision-making by encouraging collaboration between independent government departments dealing with employment, social welfare, taxation, and the like, all of which will have some input into national action plans in the areas covered by the OMC.[186]

[183] Committee on Economic and Monetary Affairs, A5-0142/2003, *supra* n. 140, at 6; Committee on Economic and Monetary Affairs, A5-0045/2004, *supra* n. 141, at 12.

[184] Zeitlin, 'The Open Method of Coordination in Action', *supra* n. 65.

[185] Committee on Employment and Social Affairs, A5-0143/2003, *supra* n. 132, at 8.

[186] Ibid.

6. THE OPEN METHOD OF COORDINATION: FUTURE PROSPECTS

The OMC will doubtless remain an important tool for policy delivery within the EU. It is a tool with real potential to promote deliberation, learning, participation, and the like, while respecting national differences in terms of substantive outcomes. This potential has not, however, been fully realized, and there is the danger that the decision-making mechanism will come to be another mode of elite-led technocratic governance. There are however ways to think about the future of the OMC that will diminish this possibility and make it more likely that the reality of the OMC procedure will live up to its expectations.

A. The Relationship between the Economic and Social Order

We should be aware of the underlying normative frame within which OMC procedures operate. There is little doubt that the EU is concerned about employment and social inclusion as issues in their own right. There is equally little doubt that they are pursued within an underlying frame that still accords prominence to market discourse and competition. This is apparent from the process initiated at Lisbon and carried forward at Nice, the rationale for the development of the Employment Chapter, the need to ensure that the employment guidelines and social policies are consistent with the broad economic policy guidelines, and the fact that market integration still remains the dominant 'master discourse' both politically and legally.

The dominance of the market discourse and the constraints that it imposed were clearly represented by Scharpf.[187] De Burca has made the same point forcefully. She points to the clear constitutional hierarchy in terms of available instruments and legal status between the EU's policies concerning market freedoms and those of its social, environmental, and other policies. This was further reinforced by the way in which the ECJ interpreted the relevant provisions. Thus as de Burca states, 'while social, environmental, cultural and other policy concerns were certainly not absent from the EC's or the Court's remit, they have been conceived of and dealt with either as justification-requiring exceptions to market-integration norms, or as politically necessary supplements to market liberalisation goals, but rarely as autonomous policy priorities in their own right'.[188]

[187] Scharpf, *supra* n. 86.
[188] De Búrca, 'The Constitutional Challenge of New Governance in the European Union' (2003) 28 *ELRev* 814, at 818.

It is therefore important to consider the future relationship between the economic and social order. Scharpf argued, as we have seen, that there was a constitutional asymmetry in the sense that economic and social policies have the same constitutional status at national level, but economic policy predominates at Community level. The twin premises behind the OMC are that choices in relation to employment and social policy are still left at the national level, albeit with improvements engendered through benchmarking, peer review, and the like at the EU level, and that the OMC operates through soft law. To alleviate the imbalance between the economic and social order Scharpf proposed a combination of framework directives coupled with the OMC. The rationale for this proposal was that since directives were EU law this would ensure 'constitutional parity' between the rules concerning social policy and economic policy, while the fact that the law took the form of a directive, coupled with the continued use of the OMC, would preserve the freedom of Member State choices in these areas.[189]

It is not clear, however, that this would achieve the constitutional parity that Scharpf desires. Directives, while partaking of the nature of hard law, would have to be relatively open-textured if they were to leave the Member States with the desired freedom of choice. It would moreover be for the Community courts to decide on the relative priorities between directives embodying social norms and those containing economic precepts when there was a clash between the two, and they might well perpetuate the priority of the latter.

Whether they do so turns in part on how the EU's broad objectives are defined. Article I–3(3) of the Constitutional Treaty (CT) makes interesting reading in this respect.[190]

> The Union shall work for the sustainable development of Europe based on balanced economic growth and price stability, a highly competitive social market economy, aiming at full employment and social progress, and a high level of protection and improvement of the quality of the environment. It shall promote scientific and technological advance.
>
> It shall combat social exclusion and discrimination, and shall promote social justice and protection, equality between women and men, solidarity between generations and protection of the rights of the child.
>
> It shall promote economic, social and territorial cohesion, and solidarity among the Member States.
>
> It shall respect its rich cultural and linguistic diversity, and shall ensure that Europe's cultural heritage is safeguarded and enhanced.

It is very doubtful whether the CT will ever see the light of day. If it were to be resurrected then the priority to be accorded to these objectives would

[189] Scharpf, *supra* n. 86, at 662–666.

[190] Treaty Establishing a Constitution for Europe, OJ 2004 C310/1.

necessarily have to be determined through the political and legal process and it would remain to be seen whether this wording, which differs in certain respects from Article 2 EC, would lead to a different balancing as between the economic and social order. It is doubtful whether it would do so, more particularly given the detailed provisions concerning the economic and social orders contained in the CT.

This reflection on what might occur in the future should not, however, blind us to what is already taking place. Kilpatrick has convincingly argued that a significant characteristic of EU employment governance is that it is a self-consciously integrated regime in which the OMC, European Social Fund, and employment law measures each play distinctive and overlapping roles in realizing social justice and competitiveness, with the EES operating as a bridge between employment legislation cast in terms of *imperium* measures and the ESF operating through *dominium* measures.[191] There is moreover already linkage between directives concerned with race and equality and the OMC objectives.

B. Reforming the OMC Process

There is no ready-made or easy fix for the difficulties that beset the OMC considered above. It is necessary to consider each of these in turn to determine the improvements that might be made. It may well be, as Zeitlin observes, that the best way forward to combat deficiencies in the OMC would be to adopt a reflexive reform strategy whereby the key elements of the method, benchmarking, peer review, iterative redesign, and monitoring, are applied to OMC procedures.[192]

In relation to transparency, further steps could be taken to meet the concerns that information about the process is available to the public. This has already been done in part through placing of documentation on the web. This could be taken further by, for example, increasing the transparency of the principal committees used in the OMC processes by making public not only their formal reports, as currently happens, but also agendas of meetings and internal papers. It is more difficult to address the transparency concerns that relate to the opacity and complexity of the decision-making process itself.

In relation to the role of the European Parliament, it would be possible to make headway, along the lines of the proposals made by the EP committees discussed above. If we were to pursue this line then the OMC procedure

[191] Kilpatrick, 'New EU Employment Governance and Constitutionalism', in G. de Burca and J. Scott (eds), *New Governance and Constitutionalism in the EU and the US* (Hart, 2006, forthcoming).

[192] Zeitlin, 'The Open Method of Coordination in Action', *supra* n. 65.

should only be used in any policy area after the EP and the Council had given their approval. It would also be possible to accord the EP a greater role than at present in the operation of the OMC: the EP should be consulted and give an opinion on the relevant guidelines, the summary report, and the recommendations emanating from the OMC process; it should have sufficient time in which to do so; the Council and Commission should take greater account of the EP's views when drawing up guidelines; and the recommendations resulting from the OMC process should be accompanied by the EP's report. Such principles could be enshrined in an interinstitutional agreement as suggested by the EP.[193]

Valuable suggestions have been made to enhance participation. The EP Committee on Employment and Social Affairs suggested that each national report should indicate how civil society, including the social partners, local, regional, and national authorities had been consulted.[194] More far-reaching is the suggestion of Zeitlin and de Burca that there should be an obligation to ensure that the OMC should be conducted as openly as possible in accordance with the principle of transparency, and so as to ensure the fullest possible participation of all relevant bodies and stakeholders.[195] This is a valuable proposal, which could then be fine-tuned in its application to different types of participants. Unfortunately no such provision was incorporated in the CT.[196] It remains to be seen whether the European Council's injunction when relaunching the Lisbon strategy that parliaments, regional and local bodies, social partners, and civil society should be regarded as stakeholders and take an active part in attaining its objectives, will make any difference in this respect.[197]

There is no simple method of increasing the deliberative quality of the discourse within the OMC, and hence of enhancing the learning that is an integral objective of the process. This would, however, be likely to be improved if the process were to become more open in the manner considered above, more especially if this were accompanied by a cognizable obligation to take the views of the participants into account when reaching conclusions. An obligation on Member States to mainstream OMC processes into national decision-making would also be valuable in this respect. So too are initiatives already in play, such as the thematic seminars run by the

[193] EP Resolution B5-282/2003, T5-268/2003.

[194] Committee on Employment and Social Affairs, A5-0143/2003, *supra* n. 132.

[195] De Búrca and Zeitlin, 'Constitutionalising the Open Method of Coordination: What Should the Convention Propose?' (2003) Centre for European Policy Studies Brief No. 31; Zeitlin, 'The Open Method of Coordination in Action', *supra* n. 65.

[196] De Búrca, *supra* n. 188, at 837–838.

[197] European Council, Presidency Conclusions, 22–23 March 2003, at para. 6.

Employment Committee focusing on particular topics such as ageing, which are designed to disseminate best practice and facilitate mutual learning.[198]

The relationship between the OMC and the Charter of Rights is another area in which progress could be made. There are, as de Burca has pointed out, two different ways in which this could occur. The OMC 'could be used as a way of giving concrete contextual meaning to the various rights set out in the Charter'.[199] Thus the OMC could on this view be the vehicle through which general and abstract guarantees in the Charter, such as rights to education, access to healthcare, and the like, were fleshed out in the context of particular policies. The other possibility is that the Charter rights 'could operate as ideal norms in relation to which the outcome of the process would be appraised, and which could be used to stimulate reform or revision of the standards which emerge when the outcomes are considered substantively unsatisfactory'.[200] It would then be open to the Community courts through judicial review to ensure that the rights had been taken into account in the OMC process and to require those involved in the process to explain how this was done.[201]

7. CONCLUSION

The OMC looks set to stay as a mode of policy delivery for the EU for the very reasons considered in this chapter. The areas in which it is used are either ones in which the Member States are unwilling to accord the EU more far-reaching regulatory competence sounding in hard law, or where the imposition of uniform Community solutions would be inherently undesirable, given the normative diversity that exists within the Member States. The OMC technique has considerable potential as a vehicle for promoting deliberation, participation, mutual learning, and the like, while respecting national difference. This potential has not, however, been fully realized. Whether this can be done or whether the OMC will partake more of the character of elite and expert-led dominance is the challenge for the future.

198 <http://www.mutual-learning-employment.net/>.

199 De Búrca, *supra* n. 188, at 834.

200 Ibid. at 834.

201 See also, Bernard, 'A "New Governance" Approach to Economic, Social and Cultural Rights in the EU', in T. Hervey and J. Kenner (eds), *Economic and Social Rights under the EU Charter of Fundamental Rights* (Hart, 2003), Chap. 11; de Schutter, 'The Implementation of Fundamental Rights through the Open Method of Coordination', in de Schutter and Deakin, *supra* n. 119, at 279–342.

7

Social Partners

1. INTRODUCTION

We saw in the previous chapter that the social partners were afforded a role in the Open Method of Coordination (OMC). This chapter considers in detail the ways in which the social partners are involved in the making and delivery of policy within the European Union (EU).[1] The discussion begins with the emergence of the social dialogue. This is followed by analysis of the Treaty articles, with more specific elaboration of the ways in which the social partners can participate in the making of social policy. The focus then turns to the role of the social partners in the making of agreements that can be transformed into formal law, the problems associated with this process, and the justifications offered for this privileged position. The ensuing discussion shifts to consideration of what are now known as autonomous agreements concluded by the social partners, which do not have the formal status of law, but which are important nonetheless. The chapter concludes by looking at less formal texts produced by the social partners through sectoral social committees, and the efforts that have been made to render these more effective than hitherto.

2. THE EMERGENCE OF THE SOCIAL DIALOGUE

The social dialogue is normally regarded as having its origin in the initiative of Jacques Delors in 1985. He invited the European social partners to

[1] Bercusson, 'The Dynamic of European Labour Law after Maastricht' (1994) 23 *ILJ* 1; Bercusson and Van Dijk, 'The Implementation of the Protocol and Agreement on Social Policy of the Treaty on European Union' (1995) 11 *IJCLLIR* 3; Sciarra, 'Social Values and the Multiple Sources of European Social Law' (1995) 1 *ELJ* 60; Brinkmann, 'Lawmaking under the Social Chapter of Maastricht', in P. Craig and C. Harlow (eds), *Lawmaking in the European Union* (Kluwer Law International, 1998), Chap. 12; Cullen and Campbell, 'The Future of Social Policy-Making in the European Union', in Craig and Harlow (eds), *Lawmaking in the European Union*, Chap. 13; Barnard, 'EC "Social" Policy', in P. Craig and G. de Búrca (eds), *The Evolution of EU Law* (Oxford University Press, 1999), Chap. 13; S. Smismans, *Law, Legitimacy and European Governance: Functional Participation in Social Regulation* (Oxford University Press, 2004), Chap. 6.

cooperate with a view to improving growth and employment in the EU. The first step towards a constructive dialogue is traditionally known as the Val Duchesse process. The social partners involved at this stage were CEEP, the European Centre of Enterprises with Public Participation and of Enterprises of General Economic Interest; UNICE, the Union of Industrial and Employers' Confederations of Europe; and ETUC, the European Trade Union Confederation.

The social partners proposed that this process be recognized within the Treaties in 1991. This was achieved in part in the Maastricht Treaty via the Protocol on Social Policy. The Protocol was signed by all Member States and allowed all Member States, with the exception of the UK, which opted-out of the relevant provisions, to make use of Community instruments so as to be able to make social policy on the basis of the Agreement on Social Policy. The Protocol was, however, incorporated into the main body of the Treaty by the Treaty of Amsterdam in 1997, this being facilitated by the change of government in the UK which ended the opt-out from these Articles.

It has become clear that the social dialogue is regarded as being of importance not only as a mechanism for the making of particular pieces of legislation, but also as a way of advancing Community social policy more generally. This is apparent from the Lisbon European Council 2000,[2] the importance of which was considered in the previous chapter.[3] The EU was 'to become the most competitive and dynamic knowledge-based economy in the world, capable of sustainable economic growth with more and better jobs and greater social cohesion'.[4] The focus was in part economic: the enhancement of an information society open to all, encouragement of a European research area, the creation of an environment friendly to the creation of new business, the coordination of macro-economic policy, and a fully operational internal market. The plan also had an overtly social dimension: there was to be education and training for those living and working in the knowledge society, the development of an active employment policy, modernization of social protection, and the promotion of social inclusion. The Lisbon approach was developed further at the Nice European Council in December 2000.[5] The implementation of the social agenda should make use of 'all existing Community instruments bar none',[6] including the OMC, legislation, the social dialogue, the Structural Funds, the support programmes, the integrated policy approach, analysis, and research. The social dialogue was thus regarded as one instrument to help attain the Community's social agenda.

[2] Lisbon European Council, Presidency Conclusions, 23–24 March 2000.
[3] See above, at 191–193.
[4] Lisbon European Council, *supra* n. 2, at para. 5.
[5] Nice European Council, Presidency Conclusions, 7–9 December 2000.
[6] Ibid. at Annex I, para. 28.

3. THE TREATY FRAMEWORK

The principal provisions about the social partners and their role in the legislative process are found in Title XI of the EC Treaty.[7] Article 136 EC provides that the Community and the Member States shall have as their objectives the promotion of employment, improved living and working conditions, proper social protection, dialogue between management and labour, the development of human resources with a view to lasting high employment, and the combating of exclusion. To this end the Community and the Member States shall implement measures which take account of the diverse forms of national practices, in particular in the field of contractual relations, and the need to maintain the competitiveness of the Community economy. In order to achieve these objectives the Community shall support and complement the activities of the Member States in a number of specified fields including, *inter alia*:[8] improvements in the working environment to protect workers' health and safety; working conditions; social security and social protection of workers; protection of workers where the contract is terminated; information and consultation of workers; representation and collective defence of the interests of workers and employers; equality between men and women in the labour market and treatment at work; and the combating of social exclusion.

The Community's legislative competence within these areas is limited. This is apparent from Article 137(2) EC. The Council can adopt measures designed to encourage cooperation between Member States through initiatives to improve knowledge and to develop exchanges of information and best practices, but these measures cannot harmonize the laws of the Member States.[9] The Council can in most of the areas listed[10] adopt directives that set minimum requirements for gradual implementation, having regard to the conditions and technical rules in each Member State.[11] There are further caveats that the provisions adopted shall not affect the right of the Member States to define the fundamental principles of their social security systems and must not affect their financial equilibrium; and such Community provisions shall not prevent any Member State from maintaining or introducing more stringent protective measures compatible with the Treaty.[12]

It is important to disaggregate a number of different ways in which the social partners may be involved with the furthering of social policy.

[7] The key provisions concerning the social partners were preserved in the Constitutional Treaty, Treaty Establishing a Constitution for Europe, OJ 2004 C310/1, Arts. III-209–212.

[8] Art. 137(1) EC. [9] Art. 137(2)(a) EC.

[10] The exceptions being the combating of social exclusion and the modernization of social protection systems.

[11] Art. 137(2)(b) EC. [12] Art. 137(4) EC.

A. The Social Partners and Implementation of Directives: Article 137 EC

It is open to a Member State to entrust management and labour at their joint request with the implementation of Council directives made pursuant to Article 137(2) EC. The Member State must ensure that management and labour have introduced the necessary measures no later than the date when the directive is to be transposed into national law. It is also incumbent on the Member State to take any measures necessary to place it in a position to guarantee the results imposed by the directive.[13]

B. The Social Partners and Consultation: Article 138 EC

There are duties to consult management and labour about social policy.[14] The Commission is charged with the task of promoting consultation of management and labour at Community level and shall take any relevant measure to facilitate that dialogue by ensuring balanced support for the parties. It has a duty to consult management and labour on the *possible direction* of Community action in the social policy field. If after such consultation the Commission considers that Community action is advisable it shall consult management and labour on the *content* of the proposal; it is then for management and labour to send a recommendation or opinion to the Commission.

C. The Social Partners, Agreements, and Law: Article 139 EC

Management and labour may shape the resulting norm and have a role in its promulgation. It is open to them during the consultative process[15] to inform the Commission that they wish to make use of the process contained in Article 139 EC. They can signal that they wish the Community dialogue to lead to contractual relations, including agreements.[16] Thus far cross-industry agreements have been negotiated by ETUC, UNICE, and CEEP, but they may include other organizations in their negotiating team. Such agreements can be implemented in two ways.

The agreement may be implemented in accord with the procedures and practices specific to management and labour and the Member States.[17] The Commission has termed agreements implemented in this manner as autonomous agreements,[18] by way of contrast to those agreements imple-

[13] Art. 137(3) EC. [14] Art. 138 EC. [15] Art. 138(4) EC.
[16] Art. 139(1) EC. [17] Art. 139(2) EC.
[18] Communication from the Commission, Partnership for Change in an Enlarged Europe—Enhancing the Contribution of European Social Dialogue, COM(2004) 557 final, at Annex 2, para. 1.

mented by Council decision. The Commission has also made it clear that it retains a responsibility for agreements implemented in this manner where the agreement was the result of an Article 138 consultation, since the decision to negotiate suspends the normal legislative process at Community level.[19] The Commission will therefore publish such autonomous agreements and inform the Council and the European Parliament (EP). On the expiry of the implementation and monitoring period, while being respectful of the monitoring undertaken by the social partners, the Commission will undertake its own monitoring to assess whether the agreement has contributed to the attainment of the Community's objectives. Where the Commission takes the view that the agreement has not succeeded in meeting these objectives, it may propose a legislative act, and it reserves this power even during the implementation period if it feels that management or labour are delaying the pursuit of Community objectives.

The alternative mode of implementing the agreement is via a Council decision. Where the subject matter falls within Article 137 EC management and labour may request that the agreement be implemented by a Council decision[20] on a proposal from the Commission.[21] The Commission has made it clear that it prefers this mode of implementing an agreement, as opposed to the first mode, where fundamental rights or important political options are at stake, in situations where the rules must be applied in uniform fashion in all Member States, where coverage must be complete, or where there is a modification to a pre-existing directive.[22] The default position is that the Council acts by qualified majority, except where the agreement contains provisions relating to an area where unanimity is required. It is normal for the Council simply to accept the agreement as made between the social partners without amendment, and the Commission has signalled that it would withdraw the draft legislation if the Council sought to amend it. The Council decision will commonly be brief and the agreement made between management and labour will be incorporated as an annex to the decision. If this route is chosen then the decision will be formally binding and cover all workers. It has led to the enactment of intersectoral directives on parental leave,[23] part-time work,[24] and fixed-term

[19] Ibid. at para. 4.4.

[20] The term decision as used here is broader than its usage in Art. 249 EC. It can cover any legally binding act, and it is common for directives to be made pursuant to Art. 139(2) EC.

[21] Art. 139(2) EC.

[22] Communication from the Commission, Partnership for Change, *supra* n. 18, at para. 4.4.

[23] Council Directive 96/34/EC of 3 June 1996, On the Framework Agreement on Parental Leave Concluded by UNICE, CEEP and ETUC, OJ 1996 L145/4.

[24] Council Directive 97/81/EC of 15 December 1997, Concerning the Framework Agreement on Part-time Work Concluded by UNICE, CEEP, and the ETUC—Annex Framework Agreement on Part-Time Work, OJ 1998 L14/9.

work,[25] and to sectoral directives on the organization of working time for seafarers[26] and those in the civil aviation industry.[27] Such directives are referred to as framework agreements, since they will commonly leave room for Member States and/or the social partners to fill out the content.

D. The Social Partners, Process-Oriented Texts, and Joint Opinions

There is a further mode of contribution by the social partners to the development of social policy that warrants separate mention. This is the role of the sectoral social dialogue committees. There were 30 sectoral dialogue committees in 2004, and they cover areas such as agriculture, civil aviation, banking, commerce, personal services, railways, road transport, and construction.[28] The committees have formulated guides, communications, codes of conduct, and recommendations and opinions that are intended to improve practice in the specific industrial sector. More than 300 such texts had been produced by 2004.

The label 'process-oriented texts' was chosen by the Commission to distinguish this aspect of the social dialogue from that considered above.[29]

> This category consists of a variety of joint texts which are implemented in a more incremental and process-oriented way than agreements. In these texts the European social partners make recommendations of various kinds to their membership for follow-up, and they should involve regular evaluation of the progress made towards achieving their objectives in order to ensure they have a real impact. The implementation of some of these texts may require cooperation with national public authorities.

The Commission's taxonomy of the forms of social dialogue distinguished process-oriented texts from 'joint opinions and tools' concerned with the exchange of information.[30]

> This category consists of social partner texts and tools which contribute to exchanging information, either upwards from the social partners to the European

[25] Council Directive 1999/70/EC of 28 June 1999, Concerning the Framework Agreement on Fixed-Time Work Concluded by ETUC, UNICE and CEEP, OJ 1999 L175/43.

[26] Council Directive 1999/63/EC of 21 June 1999, Concerning the Agreement on the Organisation of Working Time of Seafarers Concluded by the ECSA and the FST—Annex: European Agreement on the Organisation of Working Time of Seafarers, OJ 1999 L167/33.

[27] Council Directive 2000/79/EC of 27 November 2000, Concerning the European Agreement on the Organisation of Working Time of Mobile Workers in Civil Aviation Concluded by the AEA, the ETF, the ECA, the ERA and the IACA, OJ 2000 L302/57.

[28] DG for Employment and Social Affairs, The Sectoral Social Dialogue in Europe (2002); Communication from the Commission, Partnership for Change, *supra* n. 18, at Annex 4.

[29] Communication from the Commission, Partnership for Change, *supra* n. 18, at Annex 2, para. II.

[30] Ibid. at Annex 2, para. III.

institutions and/or national public authorities, or downwards, by explaining the implications of EU policies to national members. The instruments in this category do not entail any implementation, monitoring or follow-up provisions.

E. The Social Partners and the Open Method of Coordination

The social partners also contribute to policy development through the Open Method of Coordination, as it applies to economic policy, employment policy, and social policy. This was considered in the previous chapter and reference should be made to that discussion. Suffice it to say for the present that the precise role accorded to the social partners differs in the different areas to which OMC applies. It is, however, generally recognized that the impact of the social partners has been less than many observers might have hoped. The Commission has attempted to reinvigorate this aspect of the OMC process,[31] but there is little evidence as yet to suggest that there has been any significant change.[32]

F. The Tripartite Social Summit for Growth and Employment

It is clear from the discussion thus far that the social partners are involved with social policy in a variety of ways. In their contribution to the Laeken European Council 2001 the social partners pointed out that the existing mechanisms for ensuring coherence and synergy between the various processes in which they were involved were not proving effective. This led the Commission to propose the creation of a Tripartite Social Summit for Growth and Employment,[33] and this has now been established.[34]

The task of the Summit is to ensure that there is 'continuous concertation'[35] between the Council, Commission, and the social partners by enabling the social partners to contribute, in the context of their social dialogue, to the various components of the integrated economic and social strategy. The Summit consists of the Council Presidency, the two subsequent Presidencies, the Commission, and the social partners represented at the highest level. The labour and social affairs ministers from those Presidencies and the Commissioner responsible for these areas also attend, and other ministers can be invited depending on the agenda.

The social partners' representatives consist of two delegations: 10 worker

[31] Communication from the Commission, The European Social Dialogue, a Force for Innovation and Change, COM(2002) 341 final, at paras. 2.2–2.3.

[32] See above, at 221–223.

[33] Communication from the Commission, The European Social Dialogue, *supra* n. 31.

[34] Council Decision 2003/174/EC of 6 March 2003, Establishing a Tripartite Social Summit for Growth and Employment, OJ 2003 L70/31.

[35] Ibid. Art. 2.

representatives, 10 employers' representatives. Each delegation must be made up of representatives of European cross-industry organizations either representing general interests or more specific interests of supervisory and managerial staff and small and medium-sized businesses at European level. The agenda for the Summit is set by the Council Presidency, the Commission, and the workers and cross-industry organizations taking part in the work of the Summit during preparatory meetings. The Summit meets at least once a year and a meeting must be held before the Spring European Council that deals with economic and social matters.

G. The Social Partners and the European Council

The preceding analysis has been concerned with the varying ways in which the social partners contribute to the development of social policy. It would, however, be incomplete if it did not take into account the role of the European Council. This is so even though the European Council has no formal legal power to 'create' new forms of involvement for the social partners. It should be remembered in this respect that the European Council was the principal player in the initiation of the Lisbon strategy for social and economic progress in the EU, with all that this entailed in terms of the OMC and the role of the social partners therein. It was the European Council that drew together the disparate Treaty provisions dealing with these matters, while adding a political overlay that was significant even though not formally binding.

European Council initiatives continue to be of direct relevance for the role of the social partners. This can be exemplified by the Spring Summit 2004,[36] which considered the Lisbon Strategy and the economic, social, and environmental situation in the EU. The European Council specified a number of detailed initiatives that should be undertaken by the Council, the Commission, and the Member States in each of these areas. The conclusions of the European Council then contained a section on 'building partnerships for reform'.[37] The European Council stated that support and advocacy for change must reach beyond governments. It called on Member States to build reform partnerships involving the social partners, civil society, and public authorities in accord with national traditions. The social partners were seen as especially important in this regard, as exemplified by the Tripartite Social Summit, and the European Council advocated further action to boost their role in advancing the Lisbon Strategy. The European Council's initiatives in this regard were partly spurred by the Commission, and led also to the

[36] Council of the European Union, Brussels European Council, 25–26 March 2004, Presidency Conclusions, 9048/04, Brussels 19 May 2004.

[37] Ibid. at paras. 43–45.

subsequent Commission Communication on *Partnership for Change in an Enlarged Europe*,[38] which sought to flesh out in more detail ways in which the social dialogue could be enhanced. The need to relaunch the Lisbon strategy was central to the Spring Summit 2005, and the European Council welcomed the support from the social partners in the Tripartite Summit that preceded the meeting of the European Council.[39]

The following discussion will consider the role of the social partners in the making of agreements that are transformed into formal law, their role in relation to autonomous agreements, and their more diverse contribution to Community social policy through process-oriented texts and joint opinions produced by the sectoral social dialogue committees.

4. THE SOCIAL PARTNERS, AGREEMENTS, AND FORMAL LAW

There is no doubt that the most novel aspect of the Treaty provisions is the ability of the social partners to broker an agreement that can be transformed into Community law. This applies, as we have seen, when the signatory parties request that their agreement should be formalized through a Council decision made pursuant to a Commission proposal.[40] This method of delivering Community policy raises a number of important issues.

A. Rationale and Legitimacy: Representation

It is readily apparent that ensuring adequate representation in the social dialogue leading to an agreement is a necessary if not sufficient condition for its legitimacy and that this is *a fortiori* the case where the agreement is then formalized as binding law. This has been recognized by the Commission, which acknowledged that 'the legitimacy and effectiveness of the social-partner consultation is based on their representativeness'.[41] It should be recalled that the Treaty Articles left this issue open: they are framed in terms of management and labour without any further and better particulars as to which organizations should be able to represent the respective sides of industry.

It was for this reason that the Commission issued a Communication in

[38] Communication from the Commission, Partnership for Change, *supra* n. 18.

[39] Council of the European Union, Brussels European Council, 22–23 March 2005, Presidency Conclusions, 7619/1/05, Brussels 23 March 2005, at paras. 4–9.

[40] Art. 139(2) EC.

[41] Communication from the Commission, The European Social Dialogue, *supra* n. 31, at para. 1.1.

1993, which was re-issued in 1998, that delineated three criteria for inclusion within the social dialogue:[42] the associations must be cross-industry or relate to specific sectors or categories and be organized at European level; they must consist of organizations which are themselves an integral and recognized part of Member State social structures, and have the capacity to negotiate agreements and be representative of all the Member States as far as possible; and they must have effective structures to ensure their effective participation in the consultation process.

The meaning and application of these criteria were considered in a study undertaken at the request of the Commission by the Institute des Sciences du Travail at the Catholic University of Louvain.[43] The IST Report contains a mine of useful information concerning the general characteristics of the organizations studied, data on their representativeness, and the extent to which the organization had been recognized at European level. The study noted, however, that the Commission criteria were ambiguous.

Thus in relation to the first criteria of being cross-industry it was possible for an employers' group representing, for example, various craft workers to claim to fulfil this test 'without in fact representing any significant number in the majority of industrial sectors'.[44] There were also organizations that were cross-industry in that they represented many sectors of economic activity, but which only represented particular categories of workers such as white collar or blue collar. The condition that the association should be organized at European level was equally open to multiple meanings, and if it were interpreted literally then any organization with branches in several Member States, managed by EU nationals, whose statutes declared an intention to operate at the EU level would fulfil this condition.[45]

Similar difficulties beset the interpretation of the second criterion, that the organizations should be an integral and recognized part of Member State social structures, and have the capacity to negotiate agreements and be representative of all the Member States as far as possible. An organization might be cross-industry in vocation and composed of national organizations 'considered as social partners within their countries, but which nevertheless represent only a limited number of sectors of economic activity'.[46] Moreover, the recognition of the legitimacy of an organization to negotiate collective agreements or participate in social policy could be interpreted in different

[42] Commission Communication, Concerning the Application of the Agreement on Social Policy Presented by the Commission to the Council and to the European Parliament, COM(1993) 600 final, at para. 24; Commission Communication, Adapting and Promoting the Social Dialogue at Community Level, COM(1998) 322 final.

[43] Report on the Representativeness of European Social Partner Organisations Part 1 (IST, Universite Catholique de Louvain, 1999).

[44] Ibid. at 3. [45] Ibid. at 5. [46] Ibid. at 5.

ways, including 'the organization's ability to effectively mobilise workers or to quantify thresholds linked to the results of social elections'.[47]

The third condition, that the association must have effective structures to ensure its effective participation in the consultation process, could also be understood in a variety of ways including 'the nature of the organization's internal balance of power, the institutional procedures for taking decisions or deciding on an official position, the process for selecting representatives and delegates etc'.[48]

The IST Report contains, as stated above, valuable data on the representativeness of the different organizations studied. It also revealed that the very idea of representativeness was accorded varying significance by different organizations. Speaking of UNICE, the principal employers' organization, the report noted that the 'question of the representativeness of the employers' organizations has historically been the subject of little debate within industrial relations systems compared with their trade union counterpart'.[49] The report continued in the following vein.[50]

> This no doubt reflects the historically uneven balance of power between capital and work, but also a degree of decentralization among the employers' organizations, the leadership structures of which have never had a strong influence on the lower structures, in contrast to some trade union organizations. Finally, it appears that only when the legitimacy of one or more organizations is called into question is any particular attention paid to representativeness. With a few notable exceptions, the representativeness of employers' organizations has rarely been questioned except with regard to SMEs. The importance of SMEs has sometimes been considerable but, clearly never to the point of justifying precise measurement of their membership of employers' organizations.

The representativeness of employers' organizations did, however, come to the fore in the *UEAPME* case,[51] in which this organization representing small and medium-sized employers challenged the legality of the Parental Leave Directive,[52] arguing that since it had been represented at the 'informal' consultation stage it should have been involved with the formal negotiation leading to the agreement and the directive.[53]

The Court of First Instance (CFI) rejected the claim. It held that the consultation stage had to be distinguished from the negotiation of the agreement: there was no general right for those consulted to partake in the negotiations leading to the agreement, nor was there any individual right to

[47] Ibid. at 5. [48] Ibid. at 6. [49] Ibid. at 43. [50] Ibid. at 43.

[51] Case T-135/96, *Union Européene de l'Artisanat et des Petites et Moyennes Enterprises (UEAPME) v Council* [1998] ECR II-2335.

[52] Dir. 96/34, *supra* n. 23.

[53] Franssen and Jacobs, 'The Question of Representativity in the European Social Dialogue' (1998) 35 *CMLRev* 1295; Betten, 'The Democratic Deficit of Participatory Democracy in Community Social Policy' (1998) 23 *ELRev* 20.

participate in the negotiation of the framework agreement.[54] The CFI qualified this to a certain extent by finding that the Commission had an obligation to consider the representativity of the parties to an agreement proposed for implementation via a Council decision, and that it was for the Council to check that the Commission had done so. Where the required degree of representativity did not exist the Commission and the Council should refuse to implement the agreement at the Community level.[55] The CFI decided that the Commission and Council had fulfilled this obligation in the instant case. The Parental Leave Agreement dealt with the entirety of employment relationships, and the signatories were sufficiently collectively representative to speak for all categories of undertakings and workers, since they were general cross-industry organizations having a general mandate. The CFI also took into account the fact that UNICE represented many small and medium-sized undertakings.

The legal action was not entirely in vain, since it acted as the catalyst for an agreement between UEAPME and UNICE. UEAPME's initial reaction to the judgment was to lodge an appeal to the ECJ. It discontinued the action because it reached a cooperation agreement with UNICE in 1999.[56] Under the agreement UEAPME recognized UNICE as the sole European organization representing business undertakings of all sizes in all sectors of the economy, and acknowledged that many of the businesses represented by UNICE were small and medium-sized. UNICE for its part recognized that UEAPME was the principal cross-industry organization representing the specific interests of small and medium-sized businesses, and that it therefore had a useful role to play in the social dialogue in defending employers' interests. UNICE would therefore consult UEAPME before taking public positions on behalf of employers in negotiations and in the social dialogue. UEAPME would play a full part in the preparatory meetings with the employers' group and in plenary meetings with ETUC.

The Commission for its part is trying to keep the list of social partner organizations consulted up to date. In 2002 it produced a revised list of the social partner organizations consulted under Article 138,[57] and this was revised again in 2004.[58] The list specifies general cross-industry organizations; cross-industry organizations representing certain categories of workers or undertakings; specific organizations; sectoral organizations representing employers; and European trade union organizations. The list will be adapted

[54] Case T-135/96, *UEAPME, supra* n. 51, at para. 82.

[55] Ibid. at para. 90.

[56] IST Report, *supra* n. 43, at 41.

[57] Communication from the Commission, The European Social Dialogue, *supra* n. 31, at Annex 1.

[58] Communication from the Commission, Partnership for Change, *supra* n. 18, at Annex 5.

as new sectoral social dialogue committees are established and in the light of new studies on representativeness.

This is entirely laudable. The problem of ensuring that the social partners that negotiate agreements are properly representative, more especially when the agreements negotiated are transformed into formal law, is nonetheless a continuing one. The problem has moreover been exacerbated by changes in patterns of work and trade union membership. Barnard notes that the decline in trade union membership means that even in traditional labour law areas 'the extent to which trade unions actually represent the "people", especially women is questionable'.[59] The consequential danger is that 'by involving the social partners in an attempt to broaden the legitimacy base of governance in the EU by being more inclusive, the result is greater exclusivity and even competitive elitism'.[60]

B. Rationale and Legitimacy: Better Governance as Social Subsidiarity

Representativeness is a necessary condition for the legitimacy of the social dialogue that leads to agreements which can be transformed into formal law. It is not sufficient. The Commission as the institution with the primary responsibility for organizing the social dialogue[61] sees the justification for this dialogue in terms of better governance.[62] A closer reading of the Commission's reasoning reveals a number of intersecting strands of thought, one of which is social subsidiarity.

The Commission views the scheme embodied in the Treaty as fostering social subsidiarity. The consultation exercise conducted by the Commission may lead to agreements that are then incorporated into Community law. This is seen as a practical application of the principle of social subsidiarity in that 'it is for the social players to make the first move to arrive at appropriate solutions coming within their area of responsibility; the Community institutions intervene, at the Commission's initiative, only where negotiations fail'.[63] The Commission reiterated this idea in 2004. It stated that the social dialogue is a 'pioneering example of improved consultation and the application of subsidiarity in practice and is widely recognized as making an essential contribution to better governance, as result of the proximity of the social partners to the realities of the work place'.[64]

This echoes the earlier Council Resolution on EU Social Policy which

[59] Barnard, 'The Social Partners and the Governance Agenda' (2002) 8 *ELJ* 80, at 93.

[60] Ibid. at 93. [61] Art. 138(1) EC.

[62] Communication from the Commission, The European Social Dialogue, *supra* n. 31, at para. 1.

[63] Ibid. at para. 1.1.

[64] Communication from the Commission, Partnership for Change, *supra* n. 18, at para. 3.1.

welcomed the role of the two sides of industry in the social dialogue as a 'forward-looking result of the Maastricht Treaty and a concrete contribution to the attainment of the subsidiarity principle in social policy'.[65] There are traces of similar ideas within the academic literature. Thus Streeck[66] viewed the social dialogue as functional subsidiarity, in which power is distributed between those operating at the same level, in this instance the Community institutions and the social partners.

We should, however, be mindful of the transfer of terminology and concepts from one context to another. Subsidiarity as traditionally used denotes the division of power on a vertical plane between the Community and the Member States. It provides criteria as to when the *Community should act* and when matters should be left to the Member States. Social subsidiarity as interpreted by the Commission connotes something quite different. The concept is used to justify the privileged status accorded to the social partners when the *Community does act*, the argument being that because the social partners are close to the relevant problems this justifies their role in the making of agreements that can be enshrined in a Community decision. There may be some force in this. The use of subsidiarity should not, however, serve to mask Barnard's important point that the negotiation of European collective agreements is an example of centralized law-making at Community level, at a time when decentralized collective bargaining is on the ascendant in many Member States.[67]

C. Rationale and Legitimacy: Better Governance, Functional Attribution, and Democracy

A prominent strand in the Commission's reasoning about better governance is functional in nature: the 'social partners have a particular role and influence which flow from the very nature of the subjects they cover and the interests they represent in connection with the world of work'.[68] For the Commission it follows that matters such as working conditions, wage standards, training, working time, and the balance between flexibility and security are a 'few examples of specific topics which the social partners, as representatives of employees and employers are entitled to deal with'.[69] Thus the Treaty 'recognizes the social partners' ability to undertake genuine independent

[65] Council Resolution, On Certain Aspects for a European Social Policy: A Contribution to Economic and Social Convergence in the Union, OJ 1994 C368/6.

[66] Streeck, 'Neo-Voluntarism: A New European Social Policy Regime' (1995) 1 *ELJ* 31, at 48–49.

[67] Barnard, *supra* n. 59, at 89.

[68] Communication from the Commission, The European Social Dialogue, *supra* n. 31, at para. 1.

[69] Ibid. at para. 1.

social dialogue, that is to negotiate independently agreements which become law', and it is that 'ability to negotiate agreements which sets the social dialogue apart'.[70]

The Commission's argument is a blend of the descriptive and the normative. The descriptive element is functional in nature and speaks to the nature of the tasks dealt with by the social partners. This is reinforced by the normative argument, to the effect that the social partners are 'entitled' to deal with such matters. This argument is barely developed by the Commission. The 'entitlement' is couched largely in formal terms, in the sense that the social partners are accorded the power by the relevant Treaty articles. It is clear, however, that we must press further if the normative underpinning is to be adequately sustained. This task has been taken up by academic commentators who have explored various ways in which the power accorded to the social partners might be justified.

(1) The Community Democratic Model

It might be argued that the involvement of the social partners can be squared with the normal method for the legitimation of legislation enshrined in the Treaty. An argument of this nature has been advanced by Britz and Schmidt.[71]

They recognize that the role accorded to the social partners is problematic in terms of democratic legitimation. They contend that this can nonetheless be defended in terms of the way in which legislation is classically enacted in the EU. They see sufficient democratic legitimation flowing from the involvement of the Commission and Council through their unlimited right to examine and reject the agreement brokered by management and labour. This is so notwithstanding the fact that Britz and Schmidt maintain that the Council has no legal right to amend the proposed legislation. Their argument in this regard is that the procedure in Articles 138 and 139 EC is costly in terms of time and organization, and that it affords management and labour with a right of autonomous negotiation. It is said that this would be impaired if the Commission and Council were to be authorized to amend agreements. It is argued further that although the Council can amend by unanimity under Article 250 EC, the lack of direct reference indicates that this Article is not applicable to the Article 139 procedure.[72] The exclusion of the EP is seen as regrettable but not fatal in terms of democratic legitimation.[73] They

[70] Ibid. at para. 1.

[71] Britz and Schmidt, 'The Institutionalised Participation of Management and Labour in the Legislative Activities of the European Community: A Challenge to the Principle of Democracy under Community Law' (2000) 6 *ELJ* 45.

[72] Ibid. at 55–56. [73] Ibid. at 54–56, 63–66.

acknowledge, however, that the justification for the role given to the social partners must be sought also in terms of the substantive legitimacy of the law thus produced. Management and labour, while not representative of the entire 'European public' can claim to contribute to the substantive legitimacy of the laws thus enacted where they are at least adequately representative of those affected by such laws.[74]

This is an interesting thesis. It is not, however, unproblematic. It is premised on the assumption that the Commission and Council's right to examine and reject suffices for democratic legitimation even though, in their view, the Commission and Council have no right to amend, and even though the EP is excluded. It can be accepted that the Commission is against any attempt to amend agreements that are being proposed for legislation. The argument that there is no legal right to amend is another matter. The fact that management and labour are given an autonomous right to negotiate the agreement does not mean that the agreement thus concluded could not be amended when enshrined in legislation. Nor is the argument concerning Article 250 EC convincing. This Article applies whenever the Council acts on a proposal from the Commission.[75] There is no requirement that it should be referenced in the specific Article under which the legislation is proposed, in this instance Article 139 EC. Moreover the authors' assumption that amendment is not available significantly weakens the claim that the process as a whole can be regarded as comporting with the requirements of democratic legitimacy. It necessarily renders the Commission and Council's acknowledged right to examine and reject a blunt tool.

This problem is exacerbated by the formal exclusion of the EP, which the authors view as regrettable but not fatal. It is, however, difficult to accept the EP's exclusion from the Article 139 EC procedure. This is so even if one believes that there are sufficiently strong reasons for the privileged position given to the social partners. It would be perfectly possible to preserve this procedure, with the modification that the legislation emanating therefrom should receive the imprimatur of the EP as well as the Council. Or to put the same point the other way round, there has to be some good reason why the EP should have no formal role in the transformation into law of important matters of social policy, or indeed why its role should be any less than that of the Council. No such reason is readily apparent. This issue is especially significant given that there may be interests affected by the legislation that are not represented in the consultation or negotiation process at all. Thus an agreement reached between management and labour may have implications for, *inter alia*, the environment, the unemployed, and those not seeking work, such as adults looking after children. The EP may well have views on

[74] Ibid. at 66–70.

[75] Subject to a specific exception for Art. 251(4) and (5) EC.

such matters and be able to represent the relevant interest, or voice their concerns.

(2) *Participatory Democracy*

Participatory democracy has been suggested as another such model, the argument being as Fredman states, that 'the incorporation of the social partners into the legislative process goes some way towards remedying the democratic deficit at EC level'.[76] Fredman is nonetheless mindful of the difficulties of applying this model to the social partners. She notes that there is a 'continuing risk of fundamental inequality between the two sides of the bargaining process',[77] that the use of bargaining to achieve legislation could well entrench these inequalities which would be more likely to be evened-out through the normal legislative process. She is also concerned by the exclusion of the EP, which although informed about the legislation has no real say in its content and no formal role in the making of legislation under Article 139.

Bernard has similar reservations, stating 'that the relationship between participatory theory and the association of organized interests within civil society to public decision-making is rather tense'.[78] Such interests can serve as schools of democracy, enabling citizens to acquire the skills for civic political involvement; they can function as mediating structures thereby facilitating citizen involvement in decision-making; and they can also help to bring those who are poorly represented into the decision-making process. The downside is that the 'institutionalisation and crystallisation of interests in formal structures can hamper the development of a truly deliberative search for the common good', and 'cosy relationships between public authorities and a small number of strong privileged interest groups can facilitate phenomena of regulatory capture and rent seeking practices'.[79] Bernard concludes in this respect that the 'kind of civil society involvement that would fit best within a participatory logic would be that of relatively small-scale organizations at a fairly localised level, in which individual citizens still have direct or near-direct access' and that the EU model whereby limited peak-level associations enjoy a virtual monopoly position does not readily fit this picture.[80] He also points out the difficulty of applying a model of democracy based on deliberation in search of the common good, to a situation that is

[76] Fredman, 'Social Law in the European Union: The Impact of the Lawmaking Process', in P. Craig and C. Harlow (eds), *Lawmaking in the European Union* (Kluwer Law International, 1998), at 409.

[77] Ibid. at 410.

[78] Bernard, 'Legitimising EU Law: Is the Social Dialogue the Way Forward? Some Reflections on the *UEAPME* Case', in J. Shaw (ed.), *Social Law and Policy in an Evolving European Union* (Hart, 2000), Chap. 14.

[79] Ibid. at 293. [80] Ibid. at 293–294.

still characterized to a considerable degree by bargain, and this tension remains notwithstanding the fact that bargain and deliberation are ideal-types.[81]

(3) *Associative Democracy*

The possibility of seeing the contribution of the social partners through the lens of associative democracy has been considered by Bernard.[82] Conceptions of associative democracy vary,[83] but a core theme is to 'curb faction through a deliberate politics of association while netting such group contribution to egalitarian-democratic governance', by making associations 'less factionalizing and more supportive of the range of egalitarian-democratic norms'.[84] This is to be achieved while maintaining the established organs of governance. It is readily apparent that the Commission makes extensive use of associations and their informational expertise when crafting legislation.

Bernard nonetheless highlights difficulties in the application of this democratic model to the role played by the social partners. He notes the problems of ensuring accountability of the social partners to their members, and the correlative danger of instantiating a regime that allows input from 'oligarchs' within each of the participating organizations, in circumstances where the leaders may be insufficiently responsive to their members.[85] This problem is compounded by the exclusion of certain interests from the decision-making process, whether this is a sub-constituency of a class that is represented, or a class whose voice is not heard in the decision-making process at all.[86] The limited oversight exercised by the established Community institutions exacerbates these problems. Thus as Bernard states, the issue is 'not one of incessant meddling by the Commission into agreements reached by the social partners, but one of keeping sufficient powers to ensure *supervision* of the process'.[87] This harks back to the issue considered earlier about the extent of the Commission and Council's power in relation to agreements reached by the social partners. The established view is that the agreements will be accepted or rejected without amendment, the only check being on the representativity of the social partners and the formal compatibility of the agreement with the precepts of EU law. As Bernard remarks, this hands-off attitude of the Commission may make political sense, but 'it makes the

[81] Ibid. at 294–296. [82] Ibid. at 297–301.

[83] P. Hirst, *Associative Democracy: New Forms of Economic and Social Governance* (Polity Press, 1994).

[84] Cohen and Rogers, 'Secondary Associations and democratic Governance' (1992) 20 *Politics and Society* 393, at 425.

[85] Bernard, *supra* n. 78, at 299. [86] Ibid. at 299–300.

[87] Ibid. at 301. Italics in the original.

Article 139 procedure a rather unattractive proposal from a democratic legitimation point of view'.[88]

(4) Directly-deliberative Polyarchy

Barnard has explored the applicability of a variant democratic theory, directly-deliberative polyarchy,[89] to the role played by the social partners under Article 139 EC.[90] We have already considered this theory in the context of the Open Method of Coordination.[91]

A central feature of the theory is that centralized decision-making has limits within a modern polity, more especially if it is unconnected with local reality. Politics is seen as a method for dealing with practical problems, and there is a premium placed on granting lower-level actors autonomy to experiment with solutions that they have devised for themselves. In deliberative polyarchy, 'problem solving depends not on harmony and spontaneous collaboration, but on the permanent disequilibrium of incentives and interests imperfectly aligned, and on the collaborative exploration of resulting differences'.[92] Deliberation is to be found 'when collective decisions are founded not on a simple aggregation of interests, but on arguments from and to those governed by the decision, or their representatives'.[93] Democratic-deliberative polyarchy requires protection of basic rights, transparency and public participation, coordination across and between the relevant units, mechanisms for accountability that connect deliberative decisions in particular areas with broader public discussion about those topics, and the ability to contest decisions.[94]

Barnard is positive about the application of this democratic model, but is mindful of its limitations in this area. Thus she notes that the social dialogue only applies to those 'already in the loop'.[95] It does not extend to the EU as a whole, 'except insofar as they are members of one of the participating groups'.[96] She also addresses an issue that concerned Bernard, the distinction between deliberation and bargain. Thus Barnard recognizes that the social partners operate primarily through bargain, albeit qualified by the fact that

[88] Ibid. at 301.

[89] Cohen and Sabel, 'Directly-deliberative Polyarchy' (1997) 3 *ELJ* 313; Gerstenberg and Sabel, 'Directly-deliberative Polyarchy: An Institutional Ideal for Europe?', in C. Joerges and R. Dehousse (eds), *Good Governance in Europe's Integrated Markets* (Oxford University Press, 2002), at 289–342.

[90] Barnard, *supra* n. 59, at 96–101. [91] See above, at 216–217.

[92] Cohen and Sabel, 'Sovereignty and Solidarity: EU and US', in J. Zeitlin and D. Trubek (eds), *Governing Work and Welfare in a New Economy, European and American Experiments* (Oxford University Press, 2003), at 366.

[93] Ibid. at 366. [94] Ibid. at 369–370. [95] Barnard, *supra* n. 59, at 100.

[96] Ibid. at 100.

the partners lack the normal means of coercion at national level, leading her to classify the process as one of deliberative bargaining.[97]

(5) Neo-Corporatism, Functional Participation, and Democracy

A rather different view of the social dialogue is taken by Smismans.[98] He is sceptical about the applicability of alternative democratic models to justify the role given to the social partners in Article 139 EC,[99] and argues that their participation should be seen in neo-corporatist terms.

It is necessary to understand the background ideas at play in order to assess their applicability to the social partners in the EU. Pluralist theories depict the political process as one in which a relatively wide range of different groups affect political decision-making. Such groups compete for political influence and no particular group enjoys a monopoly of representational status with the government. In corporatist theory a particular group or groups are accorded a privileged representational status with the government, which 'licences' the group or groups to represent the interests of others within the same area. The privileged status accorded to the dominant group normally carries a 'price', in the sense that it will accept certain constraints on the range of its demands.[100] The rationale for this type of pressure group action stems from the pressures faced by modern states. They must undertake a wide range of activities in order to correct defects in, or problems arising from, the capitalist system. Governments are forced to juggle with goals such as full employment, economic growth, the resolution of labour conflicts, inflation, and the provision of protection for consumers and workers. This requires discussion and collaboration with major interest groups. Such groups help to shape governmental policy and their own objectives are fashioned or constrained by the same process. Major power groups achieve their dominant representational status for a number of reasons. The government perceives benefits in dealing with one bargaining agent. A relationship of trust can be built up, an understanding of the rules of the game, and an assuredness that the organization will promote an agreed policy among the relevant 'constituency'. Industrial concentration and economies of scale further the impetus towards the emergence of a particular interest group, which will bargain and speak for the whole.

Smismans acknowledges that pluralism may best explain interest group access within many areas of the EU, but argues that the role of social partners

[97] Ibid. at 101. [98] Smismans, *supra* n. 1. [99] Ibid. at 329–330.

[100] P. Schmitter and G. Lehmbruch (eds), *Trends Toward Corporatist Intermediation* (Sage, 1979); P. Schmitter and G. Lehmbruch (eds), *Patterns of Corporatist Policymaking* (Sage, 1982); A. Cawson, *Corporatism and Welfare* (Heinemann, 1982); R. Harrison (ed), *Corporatism and the Welfare State* (Allen & Unwin, 1984); P. Birkinshaw, I. Harden and N. Lewis, *Government by Moonlight: The Hybrid Parts of the State* (Unwin Hyman, 1990).

within the social dialogue is nonetheless best viewed as an example of neo-corporatism. This is because the social dialogue creates privileged access for certain groups in policy-making; it creates a separate regulatory space in which management and labour deal with work-related issues; the decision-making process is based on a limited number of organizations; and because it operates as a bargaining forum for the major players involved.[101] He argues that this mode of decision-making can be legitimated.[102] The privileged consultation of a limited number of organizations can be seen as a way to ensure more equal access to certain weaker interests such as labour. It provides an opportunity for management and labour to adjust their respective preferences more readily than in a pluralist setting. The limited number of organizations allowed to take part is said to be justified in terms of governability. He argues that the 'recognition of a self-regulatory space and of horizontal subsidiarity for the social partners can be based on ideas of output-legitimacy, in terms of regulatory efficiency'.[103] The reasoning in the *UEAPME* case[104] that participation of the social partners in the social dialogue assures respect for democracy in the absence of parliamentary participation is used in support of the argument for functional democracy.

Smismans accepts, however, that these legitimating arguments in favour of the social dialogue are premised on the assumptions that the peak organizations are representative and that the output is better than would otherwise obtain. He is doubtful whether these assumptions are met satisfactorily.[105] Thus, he questions the adequacy of representativity of the social partners' organizations in relation to the number of unionized workers, in relation to the entire workforce, and in relation to the general population, and he has doubts about the representativity of the social partners judged in terms of internal accountability within their organizations. Smismans also has reservations about output-legitimacy. He argues that the output from the social dialogue has been modest both in terms of quantity and in terms of the level of social protection provided in the legislation that has been enacted, the root cause being the imbalance between management and labour in the bargaining process.

D. Rationale and Legitimacy: Conclusions

The literature on the social partners and the legitimacy of the role accorded to them by the Treaty is rich and varied. There is a laudable willingness to explore the possible application of differing democratic models. The preceding discussion has nonetheless revealed difficulties with the application of

[101] Smismans, *supra* n. 1, at 330–332. [102] Ibid. at 334–339.
[103] Ibid. at 339. [104] Case T-135/96, *supra* n. 51.
[105] Smismans, *supra* n. 1, at 394–397.

these models to the social dialogue as embodied in Article 139 EC. Their precise relevance varies as between the different theories, but they are present to varying degrees in all the theories examined.

There are problems concerning the procedure, including in this respect who can participate as representatives of workers and management, the relationship between the participants and their members, and the exclusion of other interests that may be legitimately concerned by the resulting agreement/legislation. There are difficulties with the nature of the process, the divide between deliberation and bargain, and the implications that this has for the application of the particular explanatory theory. There are also concerns about the relationship between the agreement brokered between management and labour and the role of the established Community institutions when transforming the agreement into formal law. These concerns relate to the limited role played by the Commission and Council in the legislative process, and to the exclusion of the EP from that process. They must be taken seriously. There may well be good arguments for thinking more broadly and not confining our horizons to traditional notions of representative democracy. This still leaves open the crucial issue about the precise role of the established representative institutions within these differing democratic models. It is, for example, perfectly possible to favour increased participation in the making of legislation by affected interests. The role of the established representative institutions within such a theory is clearly still a live issue. It is indeed the case that most theories of participatory democracy are premised on input from interested parties, with the final decision still residing with traditional legislative bodies or administrative institutions such as agencies. It is, to take another example, perfectly possible to explore the potential of functional participation within decision-making. This still leaves open for debate the precise degree of oversight and input from the traditional institutions that are based on territorial representation.

It might of course be argued that this whole way of thinking about the social dialogue is misconceived and that it should be conceptualized in terms of industrial relations, rather than alternative models of democracy. Bercusson has been the principal exponent of this view,[106] arguing forcefully that the social dialogue is primarily a contractual process of collective bargaining, with agreements at European level playing the role of agreements between the social partners at national level. On this view, the transformation of the collective agreement into formal law functions analogously to mechanisms found in some Member States whereby collective agreements can be accorded an *erga omnes* affect. For Bercusson, the consequence of this conceptualization is that it is misguided to think of the social partners performing a surrogate role equivalent to the EP, or to require of social partners

[106] Bercusson, 'Democratic Legitimacy and European Labour Law' (1999) 28 *ILJ* 153.

procedural norms fashioned against the backdrop of democracy. While there is undoubtedly force in the industrial relations model, there are also difficulties with this way of viewing the social dialogue,[107] which is why the dominant strain within the literature has been to think of it in terms of alternative models of democracy. This is moreover the mode of thought that runs through the CFI's judgment in *UEAPME*.[108]

5. THE SOCIAL PARTNERS, AUTONOMOUS AGREEMENTS, AND THE SHADOW OF THE LAW

The discussion thus far has been concerned with the rationale and legitimacy of the social partners' role in the making of agreements that are transformed into binding law through a Council decision. This is clearly the most controversial aspect of the existing scheme.

There has been less attention given to the other method of implementing agreements set out in Article 139(2), which is in accord with the procedures and practices specific to management and labour and the Member States. This was in part because this method had not been used until recently and in part because the very fact that the agreements were not embodied in formal law made them less controversial. This mode of implementation warrants a closer look now that it is being used, more especially because, as will be seen, it operates in the shadow of the law.

The most prominent example of what the Commission terms an autonomous agreement[109] is the Framework Agreement on Telework,[110] which connotes a form of organizing and performing work using information technology in the context of an employment contract or relationship where work which could be performed at the employer's premises is carried out away from those premises on a regular basis. This is clearly a topic of considerable significance in the high-tech service driven economy. The agreement deals with matters of importance for both employer and employee, including: the extent if any to which an employee might be obliged to undertake Telework; the application of employment conditions to teleworkers; data protection; privacy; equipment; health and safety; organization of work; training; and collective rights. The agreement is to be implemented by the signatories, UNICE/UEAPME, CEEP, and ETUC in accord with the procedures and

[107] Fredman, *supra* n. 76, at 409; Bernard, *supra* n. 78, at 286–287; Barnard, *supra* n. 59, at 96–97.

[108] Case T-135/96, *supra* n. 51.

[109] Communication from the Commission, Partnership for Change, *supra* n. 18, at Annex 2, para. 1.

[110] Framework Agreement on Telework (July, 2002).

practices specific to management and labour in the Member States. Implementation is to be carried out within three years. The member organizations of the signatory parties are to report on implementation to an ad hoc group established by the signatories under the responsibility of the social dialogue committee. The ad hoc group will prepare a report on implementation within four years of signature of the agreement, and the agreement can be reviewed after five years if one of the signatories so requests.

Bercusson has aptly termed the general process under Article 139 EC as bargaining in the shadow of the law, to connote the idea that any deadlock in bargaining may lead to the introduction of legislation by the Commission.[111] This point has been reinforced in the context of autonomous agreements. The Commission, as seen above, has made it clear that it retains a responsibility where the agreement was the result of an Article 138 consultation, since the decision to negotiate suspends the normal legislative process at Community level.[112] The Commission will publish such autonomous agreements and inform the Council and the EP. The shadow of the law is present in a double sense. The Commission will monitor implementation by the social partners and the Member States to determine its efficacy, and on the expiry of the implementation and monitoring period, while being respectful of the monitoring undertaken by the social partners, the Commission will undertake its own monitoring to assess whether the agreement has contributed to the attainment of the Community's objectives. The shadow of the law is also present in that the Commission reserves the right to introduce legislation if the agreement does not meet its objectives and this possibility is applicable even during the implementation period if it feels that management or labour are delaying the pursuit of Community objectives. It will be interesting to see how these powers are used in relation to the Framework Agreement on Telework and other autonomous agreements.

6. THE SOCIAL PARTNERS, PROCESS-ORIENTED TEXTS, JOINT OPINIONS, AND THE SECTORAL SOCIAL DIALOGUE

We have already seen that the social partners contribute to social policy through sectoral social dialogue committees, and formulate guides, communications, codes of conduct, and recommendations and opinions that are intended to improve practice in the specific industrial sector. More than 300 such texts had been produced by 2004. There are two general issues concerning this form of contribution by the social partners.

[111] Bercusson, *supra* n. 1, at 20, 22.

[112] Communication from the Commission, Partnership for Change, *supra* n. 18, at para. 4.4.

The first is the desire to instil some taxonomic order into the plethora of names used to denote the output from these committees. The Commission has made progress in this respect with the distinctions drawn between 'process-oriented texts' and 'joint opinions and tools' described above. The labels may not be particularly elegant, but they do capture significant differences in the texts produced.

The second issue concerns the effectiveness of these contributions. It is obviously difficult to generalize about this, since efficacy may vary significantly between different subject matter areas and between different contributions in the same area. The Commission noted in 2002 that 'in most cases the texts did not include any provision for implementation and monitoring', 'they are not well known and their dissemination at national level has been limited', and 'their effectiveness can thus be called into question'.[113] The way forward for the Commission was to make use of the OMC. It urged the social partners to apply some of their agreements 'by establishing goals or guidelines at European level, through regular national implementation reports and regular, systematic assessment of progress achieved'.[114] It repeated this injunction in 2004, encouraging the 'social partners to make greater use of peer review techniques inspired by the open method of coordination for following up these texts, for example by setting targets (quantitative where feasible) or benchmarks, and regularly reporting on progress towards achieving them'.[115]

There is clearly good sense in this approach. These texts are not formal law. Nor in many cases would it be appropriate or optimal to give them formal legal status. The OMC does therefore provide a way in which implementation can be assessed and monitored. Having said this, the difficulties of this exercise should also be appreciated. The discussion in the previous chapter revealed the difficulties of making a success of the OMC, and that is in a context where the informational resources of the Member States and Community institutions are engaged. It will be all the more difficult where private actors have the responsibility for running the operation, establishing benchmarks, assessing performance, exerting peer pressure, and the like. The factor that might incline in the other direction and make it somewhat easier to agree on benchmarks, performance indicators and so on, is precisely that the Member States are not involved, thus obviating the high-level tensions that have sometimes beset Member State deliberations on these matters.

[113] Communication from the Commission, The European Social Dialogue, *supra* n. 31, at para. 2.4.

[114] Ibid. at para. 2.4.1.

[115] Communication from the Commission, Partnership for Change, *supra* n. 18, at para. 4.3.

7. CONCLUSION

The preceding discussion has analysed the varying ways in which the social partners contribute to the making of social policy in the EU. The most striking is of course the Article 139 EC procedure, allowing agreements concluded between the social partners to be transformed into formal law through a Commission proposal that is voted on by the Council. It is therefore unsurprising that this has been the subject of most comment from scholars who have proffered a range of theories through which to analyse and appraise this process. The Community courts have also been influential, most prominently in the *UEAPME* case,[116] but also in *Albany*[117] where the ECJ effectively exempted agreements made between management and labour from the strictures of the competition rules contained in Articles 81 and 82 EC. While the Article 139 EC procedure is the most prominent instance of involvement of the social partners their influence through autonomous agreements and process-oriented texts should not be ignored.

[116] Case T-135/96, *supra* n. 51.
[117] Case C-67/96, *Albany International v Stichting Bedrijfspensioenfonds Textielindustrie* [1999] ECR I-5751.

Part II

Law and Administration

8

Foundations

1. INTRODUCTION

The discussion thus far has considered the different ways in which the European Union (EU) delivers policy. The focus has been on administration and law. In the second part of the book the focus shifts to law and administration, and an evaluation of the judicial doctrine that is of principal significance for Community administration and for the Member States where the latter act within the scope of European Community (EC) law. It is important to pause and reflect a little more on a number of themes that cut across and are equally pertinent to the analysis of particular aspects of review. This chapter will therefore seek to lay the groundwork for the ensuing discussion.

We begin with the justification for judicial review. This is followed by the sources of EU administrative law and the grounds on which judicial review is available. The focus then turns to the way in which these grounds or categories have been shaped by background principles and the range of acts that are amenable to judicial review. The final section considers whether it would be desirable for there to be a general code of administrative law in the EU.

2. JUSTIFICATION

The justifications proffered for judicial review in national legal systems vary, as does the conceptual foundation for the courts' power. This issue is less problematic in formal terms at least within the EU, given that there is and always has been express Treaty sanction for this species of judicial power.

Its general expression is found in Article 220 EC, which provides that the Court of Justice and the Court of First Instance, each within its jurisdiction, shall ensure that in the interpretation and application of this Treaty the law is observed. The more specific authority for the exercise of review is then located in Article 230(1) EC, which stipulates that the Court of Justice shall review the legality of acts adopted jointly by the European Parliament (EP) and the Council, of acts of the Council, of the Commission, and of the European Central Bank (ECB) other than recommendations and opinions, and acts of the EP intended to produce legal effects *vis-à-vis* third parties.

Provision for failure to act is found in Article 232 EC. The direct action via Article 230(1) EC is complemented by Article 234 EC, which provides the basis for indirect scrutiny of, *inter alia*, the validity and interpretation of acts of the institutions of the Community and of the ECB. This general schema was preserved in the Constitutional Treaty (CT).[1]

These Treaty provisions do not of course resolve all problems concerning the legitimacy and reach of judicial review. They do, however, provide significant formal legitimation for the existence of this species of judicial power.

3. SOURCES

The sources of EU administrative law are eclectic. They are to be found primarily in the Treaty, Community legislation, the case law of the Community courts, and decisions made by the European Ombudsman. The administrative law of the Member States has moreover been influential in shaping the EU regime. The more particular role played by each will become apparent in this chapter and those that follow. It may nonetheless be helpful at this juncture to exemplify their respective contributions.

The Treaty contains certain articles that deal with principles, both procedural and substantive, that are directly relevant for judicial review. The following are simply examples. Thus Article 253 EC establishes a duty to give reasons that applies to regulations, decisions, and directives adopted jointly by the Council and European Parliament, or by the Council or Commission. It is noteworthy that Article 253 imposes a duty to give reasons not only for administrative decisions, but also for legislative norms, such as regulations or directives. Article 255 EC deals with access to information. It provides that any citizen of the Union, and any natural or legal person residing or having their registered office in a Member State, shall have a right of access to EP, Council, and Commission documents, subject to certain principles and conditions. Non-discrimination provides an example of a substantive principle within the Treaty that is of direct relevance for judicial review. Thus Article 12 EC contains a general proscription of discrimination on the grounds of

[1] Treaty Establishing a Constitution for Europe, OJ 2004 C310/1. Art. I-29(1) provided that the Court of Justice, defined for these purposes to mean the European Court of Justice (ECJ), the General Court which was the successor to the Court of First Instance (CFI), and specialized courts, should ensure that in the interpretation and application of the Constitution the law is observed. Art. I-29(3) in effect stated that the Court of Justice should have the specific heads of jurisdiction laid down in Part III of the Constitution. The direct action for judicial review was re-enacted in Art. III-365, with the addition that such review also applied against the European Council, bodies, offices, and agencies of the EU designed to produce legal effects *vis-à-vis* third parties. An analogous amendment was made in relation to failure to act in Art. III-367. The indirect action concerning the validity and interpretation of acts of the EU institutions, bodies, offices, and agencies was contained in Art. III-369.

nationality, and this is also to be found in the specific Treaty articles dealing with free movement of workers, freedom of establishment, and the provision of services. Non-discrimination on the grounds of gender is dealt with by Articles 137 and 141 EC. There are also provisions dealing with non-discrimination as between producers or consumers in the field of agriculture, Article 34(2) EC, and specific provisions such as Article 90 EC prohibiting discriminatory taxation.

Community legislation made pursuant to the Treaty may also deal with the principles of judicial review. This legislation may flesh out a principle contained in a Treaty article. This was the case in relation to the legislation adopted pursuant to Article 255 EC, dealing with access to information. Community legislation may also establish a code of administrative procedure that is to apply in a particular area.

It has, however, been the Community courts that have made the major contribution to the development of administrative law principles. They have read principles such as proportionality, fundamental rights, legal certainty, legitimate expectations, equality, and procedural justice into the Treaty, and used them as the foundation for judicial review under Articles 230 or 234 EC. We need to press further to understand why and how this happened.

4. GROUNDS

It is axiomatic that all systems of administrative law will embody grounds or categories of review that provide the framework within which the courts exercise their powers. These may be developed by the courts. They may be laid down by statute or code. They may be formed from an admixture of the two.

In the case of the EU the Treaty forms the starting point for the elaboration of the grounds of review. Article 230(2) EC stipulates, *inter alia*, that review shall be available for lack of competence, infringement of an essential procedural requirement, infringement of this Treaty or of any rule of law relating to its application, or misuse of powers.

The *travaux préparatoires* for the original Rome Treaty are not available. The influence of French juristic thought is nonetheless, as Schwarze states, clearly imprinted on these grounds of review.[2] The four heads of review, lack of competence, infringement of an essential procedural requirement, infringement of the Treaty, or any rule of law relating to its application and misuse of power, resonate with the French mode of administrative law thought. Having recognized this progeny, it is however important to be

[2] J. Schwarze, *European Administrative Law* (Office for Official Publications of the European Communities/Sweet & Maxwell, 1992), at 40.

mindful of the latitude accorded to the European Court of Justice (ECJ), and later the Court of First Instance (CFI), in fashioning the principles of judicial review.

This judicial discretion stemmed in part from the fact that while French influence might have dominated the choice of grounds for review, these grounds were then applied within a Community of six Member States. Principles of administrative law and modes of thought in Member States other than France naturally exercised an influence on the ECJ's emerging jurisprudence. It was unsurprising that German thought came to exert considerable authority in this respect.

The judicial discretion in developing the grounds of review also stemmed in part from the very fact that they are open-textured. This was especially so with respect to the second and third of the categories. Infringement of an essential procedural requirement could be read in any number of ways and gave ample latitude to the Community judiciary to develop it as they saw fit, as will be seen in later chapters. This was *a fortiori* the case with respect to the third ground of review, infringement of the Treaty or any rule of law relating to its application.

There is, however, a further reason for the existence of judicial discretion in developing the EU heads of judicial review. It is related to that just given, but distinct nonetheless. The heads of review as specified by Article 230(2) EC do not provide any answer to certain key issues that are addressed by all systems of administrative law. They do not on their face tell one anything about the test or standard for review in relation to matters of law, fact, or discretion. Now to be sure the Treaty provides in Article 220 EC, as we have seen, that it is for the ECJ and CFI to ensure that the law is observed in the interpretation and application of the Treaty. To be sure also, there will be certain instances, such as competence strictly conceived, where the courts will naturally incline to strict control and substitution of judgment as to the meaning of the contested Treaty article or provision of secondary legislation. This does not diminish the force of the point being made here, which is that many of the seminal issues concerning the test for review for errors of law, fact, or discretion are not addressed by the Treaty, with the necessary consequence that they have been elaborated by the Community courts. To put the same point in another way, Article 230(2) EC says nothing about, for example, a test of manifest error, or the meaning to be given to this concept when reviewing different types of administrative action in the EU.

5. REVIEWABLE ACTS

The discussion thus far has been concerned with the emergence of the principles of judicial review. We must also consider the range of acts that are subject to judicial review. This is an issue that arises in any system of administrative law, and the EU is no exception in this respect. Article 230(1) EC is the starting point.

The Court of Justice shall review the legality of acts adopted jointly by the European Parliament and the Council, of acts of the Council, of the Commission, and of the ECB other than recommendations and opinions, and acts of the European Parliament intended to produce legal effects vis-à-vis third parties.

It is clear that this allows review of legality of acts other than recommendations and opinions. This covers regulations, decisions, and directives, as listed in Article 249 EC. The ECJ has held that this list is not exhaustive, and that other acts which are *sui generis* can also be reviewed, provided that they have binding force or produce legal effects.[3]

Thus in the well-known *ERTA* case[4] the Member States acting through the Council adopted a Resolution in March 1970, the object of which was to coordinate their approach to the negotiations for a European Road Transport Agreement. The Commission disliked the negotiating procedure established in the Resolution, and sought judicial review. The ECJ held that the proceedings of March 1970 were designed to lay down a course of action binding on both the institutions and the Member States, and destined ultimately to be reflected in the tenor of the regulation. The Council had moreover adopted provisions capable of derogating from the Treaty procedure for negotiations with third countries and the conclusion of agreements. The ECJ concluded therefore that the proceedings in March 1970 were reviewable because they had definite legal effects on relations between the Community and the Member States and on the relationship between institutions.

There may, however, be room for difference of opinion as to whether an act has produced legal effects. This is exemplified by *IBM*.[5] The company sought the annulment of a Commission letter notifying it of the fact that the Commission had initiated competition proceedings against it, in order to determine whether it was in breach of Article 82 EC. The letter was accompanied by a statement of objections, with a request that the company reply to it within a specified time. The Commission objected that the impugned letter was not an act challengeable for the purposes of Article 230 EC. The ECJ accepted that judicial review was available for any measure the legal effects of which were binding on, and capable of affecting the legal interests of an applicant by bringing about a distinct change in its legal position. The

[3] Case C-57/95, *France v Commission (Re Pension Funds Communication)* [1997] ECR I-1627.

[4] Case 22/70, *Commission v Council* [1971] ECR 263

[5] Case 60/81, *International Business Machines Corporation v Commission* [1981] ECR 2639.

applicant nonetheless failed.[6] The letter was merely the initiation of the competition procedure, a preparatory step leading to the real decision at a later stage. The statement of objections did not, in itself, alter the legal position of IBM, although it might indicate, as a matter of fact, that it was in danger of being fined later.[7] This may be contrasted to the *SFEI* case.[8] It was held that in an area, such as competition policy, where the Commission has power to investigate and impose fines pursuant to a complaint from an individual, a letter from the Commission indicating that it did not intend to pursue the matter was reviewable as an act producing legal consequences.[9]

The general principle is that an act which is reviewable will have legal effect until it is set aside by the ECJ or the CFI,[10] and the challenge must be brought within the time limit specified in Article 230(5). The exception is for acts tainted by particularly serious illegality, which are deemed to be 'non-existent'. The normal time limits for challenge do not apply, since such an act can never be cloaked with legality by the passage of time. Such acts do not have any provisional legal effects, and they are not actually susceptible to annulment as such, because there is no 'act' to annul. A judicial finding that an act is non-existent will, however, have the same effect in practice as if it had been annulled. Thus in the *BASF* case[11] the CFI found that a decision of the Commission in competition proceedings against the PVC cartel was non-existent on the grounds that: the Commission could not locate an original copy of the decision which had been duly authenticated in the manner required by the Rules of Procedure; it appeared that the Commissioners had not agreed on the precise text of the decision; and it had been altered after it had been formally adopted. The non-existence of a measure should, said the CFI, be raised by the Court of its own motion at any time during the

[6] See also, Cases C-133 and 150/87, *Nashua Corporation v Commission and Council* [1990] ECR I-719; Case C-282/95 P, *Guérin Automobiles v Commission* [1997] ECR I-1503; Case T-554/93, *Saint v Council* [1997] ECR II-563; Case T-81/97, *Regione Toscana v Commission* [1998] ECR II-2889; Case C-159/96, *Portuguese Republic v Commission* [1998] ECR I-7379; Case C-180/96, *United Kingdom v Commission* [1998] ECR I-2265; Cases T-377, 379, 380/00, 260, and 272/01, *Philip Morris International Inc v Commission* [2003] ECR II-1; Case T-123/03, *Pfizer Ltd v Commission* [2004] ECR II-1631; Case C-240/92, *Portuguese Republic v Commission* [2004] ECR I-10717.

[7] *Cf.* Case 53/85, *AKZO Chemie BV v Commission* [1986] ECR 1965.

[8] Case C-39/93 P, *Syndicat Français de l'Express International (SFEI) v Commission* [1994] ECR I-2681.

[9] See also, Cases T-10–12, 15/92, *SA Cimenteries CBR* [1992] ECR II-2667; Case C-25/92R, *Miethke v European Parliament* [1993] ECR I-473; Case C-480/93, *Zunis Holding SA, Finan Srl and Massinvest SA v Commission* [1996] ECR I-1; Case T-120/96, *Lilly Industries Ltd v Commission* [1998] ECR II-2571.

[10] Case C-137/92 P, *Commission v BASF AG* [1994] ECR I-2555.

[11] Cases T-79, 84–86, 89, 91–92, 94, 96, 98, 102, 104/89, *BASF AG v Commission* [1992] ECR II-315.

proceedings. The matter was appealed from the CFI to the ECJ,[12] which took a different view. It held that the defects were not so serious as to make the act non-existent, but it did find that the decision was tainted by sufficient irregularity for it to be annulled. It is moreover clear from *Solvay* that failure to authenticate an act is an essential procedural requirement, breach of which leads to annulment. The matter can be raised by the Court of its own motion. It is not necessary for the act to be vitiated by some other defect, nor is it necessary to show that the lack of authentication resulted in harm to the person relying on it.[13]

The ECJ does not have power in relation to the CFSP.[14] It has, since the Treaty of Amsterdam, been given limited power, under Article 35 TEU to review the legality of framework decisions and decisions made pursuant to the re-modelled Third Pillar dealing with Police and Judicial Cooperation in Criminal Matters. There is provision for preliminary rulings, provided that the Member State opts in to this regime,[15] and the ECJ held in *Pupino* that the obligation to interpret national law in conformity with EC law is equally applicable in relation to a Framework Decision.[16] Direct actions to review the legality of framework decisions and decisions can be brought by the Commission or a Member State within two months of the publication of the measure.[17] There are, however, limits to this jurisdiction: Article 35(5) TEU prevents the ECJ from reviewing the validity or proportionality of operations by the police or law enforcement agencies, or the exercise of responsibilities of Member States with regard to the maintenance of law and order, and the safeguarding of internal security. It is moreover clear from the *Eurojust* case[18] that there can be difficulties in ensuring review of agencies established by the Council under the Third Pillar, more especially where the measure sought to be reviewed is not a framework decision or a decision.[19]

The CT continued the same general approach towards the reviewability of acts, albeit modified to take account of the new provisions on the hierarchy of norms.[20] The main additional changes were that the European Council was made susceptible to review, a reform that reflected its enhanced role within the CT, and express reference was made to reviewability of the legality

[12] Case C-137/92 P, *supra* n. 10.

[13] Cases 287–288/95 P, *Commission v Solvay SA* [2000] ECR I-2391.

[14] Art. 46 TEU.

[15] Art. 35(1)–(3) TEU.

[16] Case C-105/03, *Criminal Proceedings against Maria Pupino*, judgment of 16 June 2005, not yet published, at paras. 19–48.

[17] Art. 35(6). The ECJ can also review acts made under the TEU where it is claimed that they should have been passed under the EC pillar, Case C-170/96, *Commission v Council (Airport Transit Visas)* [1998] ECR I-2763; Case C-176/03, *Commission v Council* [2005] ECR I-7879, at para. 39.

[18] Case C-160/03, *Spain v Eurojust* [2005] ECR I-2077.

[19] See above, at 166.

[20] Art. III-365 CT.

of acts of bodies, offices, and agencies. The ECJ's general powers applied to the area of freedom, security, and justice, subject to qualifications[21] that mirrored closely those found in the Treaty on European Union (TEU). The CT nonetheless brought judicial cooperation in criminal and policing matters within the same overall framework of judicial control as applied to other areas of EU law, subject to this limited exception. The ECJ's jurisdiction in relation to the Common Foreign and Security Policy (CFSP) remained limited. Article III-376 excluded the ECJ from the CFSP both in relation to Articles I-39–40, and in relation to Chapter II of Title V of Part III.[22]

6. BACKGROUND PRINCIPLES

It was natural given the gaps in the primary Treaty that the ECJ should seek to flesh out the principles that should govern judicial review within EU law. It was moreover natural that in doing so it would resort to certain background principles to inform the more particular rules and principles of judicial review for the emerging Community legal order. A number of such background or meta-principles can be identified.

A. The Rule of Law

The legal systems of the Member States all possess various precepts of administrative law concerning procedural and substantive review. The details vary as between legal systems but there is, not surprisingly, significant overlap, and this is so irrespective of whether the same term or label is used.[23] It is moreover common for the development of these precepts to be justified by recourse to the rule of law. It can be readily accepted that this concept has diverse meanings, both formal and substantive.[24] The idea that administration should be procedurally and substantively accountable before the courts has nonetheless been central to the rule of law.

This core idea had especial force in the emerging Community legal order. This was because even though there might be considerable room for

[21] Art. III-377 CT.

[22] The ECJ was however given jurisdiction under Art. III-308, which was designed to ensure that implementation of the CFSP did not 'affect' the competences listed in Articles I-13–15, and 17. It also provided that the implementation of those policies must not affect the competence over CFSP in Art. I-15. The ECJ was also given jurisdiction under Art. III-376 in relation to the legality of restrictive measures imposed on a natural person by Council decision on the basis of Chapter II of Title V.

[23] Schwarze, *supra* n. 2.

[24] Craig, 'Formal and Substantive Conceptions of the Rule of Law: An Analytical Framework' [1997] *PL* 467.

argumentation as to the detailed rules and principles of judicial review that should follow from this precept, it could hardly be denied that some such rules and principles should exist. This was more especially so given the desire to assure the Member States, national courts, politicians, bureaucrats, and the like, that the rapidly growing Community power over areas such as agriculture would be subject to proper legal scrutiny.

The primary Treaty provisions were, as we have seen, incomplete in this respect. They nonetheless provided fertile ground for the development of a richer set of administrative law principles grounded on the rule of law.

Article 230(2) EC specified, *inter alia*, that review should be available for breach of the Treaty or any rule of law relating to its application. The absence of the *travaux préparatoiries* means that we do not know what the latter part of this phrase was intended to connote. The intent might have been to do nothing more than ensure that Commission decision-making should have to comply not only with the primary Treaty articles, but also regulations, directives, etc. passed pursuant thereto. If this had been the intent it could however have been expressed far more simply and clearly. The intent might alternatively have been to capture not only compliance with secondary legislation, but also with other 'rules of law relating to the application' of the Treaty that might be developed by the courts. In any event, the very ambiguity in the phrase provided the ECJ with a window through which to justify the imposition of administrative law principles as grounds of review.

Article 220 EC was equally important in this respect. It charged the ECJ with the duty of ensuring that in the interpretation and application of the Treaty the law should be observed. This might have been interpreted in a limited manner to connote the idea that, for example, Commission decisions should be made within the limits laid down by the primary Treaty articles and secondary legislation. The word 'law' within this Article was, however, open to a broader interpretation that would serve to legitimate the ECJ fashioning a 'system of legal principles in accordance with which the legality of Community and Member State action must be determined'.[25]

The judicial task of elaborating principles of judicial review was further facilitated by more specific Treaty articles, which made reference to, for example, non-discrimination. It was then open to the ECJ to read these particular Treaty references as indicative of a more general principle of equal treatment and non-discrimination that could be said to underpin the entire Community legal order.[26]

[25] T. Tridimas, *The General Principles of EC Law* (Oxford University Press, 1999), at 11. See also, M. Luisa Fernandez Esteban, *The Rule of Law in the European Constitution* (Kluwer Law International, 1999), at 106–122.

[26] Cases 117/76 and 16/77, *Ruckdeschel v Hauptzollamt Hamburg-St. Annen* [1977] ECR 1753, at para. 7.

The latitude afforded by Articles 220 and 230(2) EC, combined with the reference to concepts such as non-discrimination and proportionality in specific Treaty articles, laid the foundation for the ECJ to read general principles into EU law. A rich body of jurisprudence developed on process rights, fundamental rights, equal treatment and non-discrimination, proportionality, and legal certainty and legitimate expectations. These rights and principles will be examined in detail in the chapters that follow.

In developing these concepts the ECJ and later the CFI drew upon administrative law doctrine from the Member States. They did not systematically trawl through the legal systems of each of the Member States in order to find principles that they had in common, which could then be transferred to the Community context. The approach was, rather, to consider principles found in the major legal systems of the Member States, to use those that were felt to be best developed and to fashion them to suit the Community's own needs. Thus as Advocate General Lagrange stated in an early case, the ECJ does not seek arithmetical common denominators between the national approaches to a particular problem, but rather chooses from 'each of the Member States those solutions which, having regard to the objects of the Treaty, appear to be the best or, if one may use the expression, the most progressive'.[27] German law was perhaps the most influential in this regard. It was German jurisprudence on, for example, proportionality and legitimate expectations that was of principal significance for the development of Community law in these areas.

The Community courts have, as will become apparent from later chapters, used these principles in a number of different ways.[28] They function as interpretative guides in relation to primary Treaty articles and regulations, directives, and decisions enacted pursuant thereto. The general principles also operate as grounds of review. The Community courts cannot invalidate primary Treaty articles. They can, however, annul regulations, directives, decisions, and other Community acts with legal effect. Violation of a general principle of EU law will serve as a ground for annulment. The principles can also be used against national measures that fall within the scope of EU law, although as we shall see the range of measures caught in this manner is not free from doubt. Breach of a general principle may also form the basis for a damages action against the Community. The same should be true with respect to a breach of such a principle by the Member States, subject to fulfilment of the other conditions for this species of liability.

The jurisprudence on general principles informed by the background precept of the rule of law was well developed by the time of the Treaty of Amsterdam. The amendment of the TEU through Article 6(1) was

[27] Case 14/61, *Hoogovens v High Authority* [1962] ECR 253, 283–4, Lagrange AG.
[28] Tridimas, *supra* n. 25, at 17–23.

nonetheless significant. It provides that the Union is founded on the principles of liberty, democracy, respect for human rights and fundamental freedoms, and the rule of law, principles which are common to the Member States. This is supportive of the judicial strategy, and this is so even though the Community courts have no jurisdiction over this provision.[29]

B. Institutional Balance

The rule of law may well be the primary background principle used to develop EU administrative law. It is not, however, the only one. The ECJ has also had recourse to the idea of institutional balance. It is clear that this concept has both a political and legal dimension.[30]

In political terms the idea of balanced government or balanced constitutionalism is, in one sense, self-evident, a proposition on which all people can agree. An attachment to this ideal can be found in many more specific species of constitutional ordering, ranging from that adopted in the United States, to that which exists in certain continental countries. The idea of institutional balance has a rich history. It was an important part of republican discourse in the fifteenth and sixteenth centuries,[31] shaping the desired structure of government in the Italian republics, exerting later influence in England and the United States.[32] Institutional balance was one of the central tenets in the republican conception of government. This was based on the twin precepts that the form of political ordering should encapsulate a balance between different interests, which represented different sections within civil society, and that democratic deliberation should be designed to achieve the public interest rather than narrow sectional desires. The existence of the proper institutional balance would serve to prevent tyranny, in itself an extreme manifestation of sectional self-interest. Such a balance would help to ensure a deliberative democracy within which the differing 'constituencies'

[29] Art. 46 TEU.

[30] Craig, 'Democracy and Rulemaking within the EC: An Empirical and Normative Assessment' (1997) 3 *ELJ* 105; Lenaerts and Verhoeven, 'Institutional Balance as a Guarantee for Democracy in EU Governance', in C. Joerges and R. Dehousse (eds), *Good Governance in Europe's Integrated Market* (Oxford University Press, 2002), Chap. 2; Smismans, 'Institutional Balance as Interest Representation. Some Reflections on Lenaerts and Verhoeven', in *Good Governance in Europe's Integrated Market*, Chap. 3; Jaque, 'The Principle of Institutional Balance' (2004) 41 *CMLRev* 383.

[31] J.G.A. Pocock, *The Machiavellian Moment: Florentine Political Thought and the Atlantic Republican Tradition* (Princeton University Press, 1975) and *Virtue, Commerce and History* (Cambridge University Press, 1985).

[32] Sunstein, 'Interest Groups in American Public Law' 38 *Stan L Rev* 29 (1985) and 'Beyond the Republican Revival' 97 *Yale LJ* 1539 (1988); Michelman, 'Foreword: Traces of Self-Government' 100 *Harv L Rev* 4 (1986); P. Craig, *Public Law and Democracy in the United Kingdom and the United States of America* (Oxford University Press, 1990), Chap. 10.

that made up civil society would be encouraged to treat their preferences not simply as givens, but rather as choices which were open to debate and alteration.

Considerable emphasis has been placed on institutional balance within EU political debates, more especially during Treaty revisions when the major institutional players made explicit reference to it in making recommendations for the desired distribution of power between them.[33] The rationale for the centrality accorded to this idea strikes a direct chord with the historical application of republicanism: the necessity to create a stable form of political ordering for a society within which there are different interests or constituencies. In the present context the interests are primarily those of the Council, EP, and Commission, but we should not forget the national parliaments, regional bodies, and functional interests. This is not the place for detailed exegesis on the political dimension of institutional balance. This brief excursus is, however, important in understanding the more directly legal implications of the concept. This is more especially so given that the relations between the principal EU organs are not *de jure* or *de facto* characterized by any strict separation of powers.

Legal recourse to the concept of institutional balance that is of direct relevance to EU administrative law can be exemplified by the saga concerning the EP's standing to seek judicial review. Prior to the passage of the TEU it was not accorded any formal privileged status in Article 173 EC as it then was. In the *Comitology* case[34] the ECJ rejected the EP's argument that it should have the same unlimited standing as other privileged applicants.

The issue was considered again in the *Chernobyl* case[35] where the ECJ took a different view. The case arose out of a Council Regulation adopted after the Chernobyl incident. The Regulation sought to establish the maximum level of radioactive contamination of food and feeding stuffs. This Regulation was adopted under Article 31 of the Euratom Treaty, but the EP argued that it should be based on Article 100A EC, now Article 95 EC. The rationale for this was that the EP has greater rights under the latter, since the cooperation procedure allowed it more involvement in the legislative process.

In the earlier *Comitology* case the ECJ had denied the EP's claim for standing because Article 173 did not afford the EP a privileged status and because the ECJ felt that there were other remedies through which the EP's prerogatives in the legislative process could be protected. In the *Chernobyl* case the ECJ admitted that these various legal remedies might be ineffective and that it was therefore uncertain whether a measure adopted by the

[33] Craig, *supra* n. 30, at 107–109.
[34] Case 302/87, *European Parliament v Council* [1988] ECR 5615.
[35] Case C-70/88, *European Parliament v Council* [1990] ECR I-2041.

Council or the Commission in disregard of the Parliament's prerogatives would be reviewed. The ECJ then stated that:[36]

Those prerogatives are one of the elements of the institutional balance created by the Treaties. The Treaties set up a system for distributing powers among the different Community institutions, assigning to each institution its own role in the institutional structure of the Community and the accomplishment of the tasks entrusted to the Community.

Observance of the institutional balance means that each institution must exercise its powers with due regard for the powers of the other institutions. It also requires that it should be possible to penalize any breach of that rule which may occur.

The Court, which under the Treaties has the task of ensuring that in the interpretation and application of the Treaties the law is observed, must therefore be able to maintain the institutional balance and, consequently, review the observance of the Parliament's prerogatives when called upon to do so by the Parliament, by means of a legal remedy which is suited to the purpose which the Parliament seeks to achieve.

The ECJ acknowledged that it could not in a literal sense include the EP among the list of privileged institutions under Article 173 EC. It did nonetheless have a duty of ensuring that the provisions of the Treaties concerning the institutional balance were 'fully applied', which meant that there should be an effective legal remedy available to the EP to defend its prerogatives.[37] The absence of any Treaty provision giving the EP the right to bring an action for annulment was conceptualized as a procedural gap, which could not prevail over 'the fundamental interest in the maintenance and observance of the institutional balance laid down in the Treaties establishing the European Communities'.[38] The ECJ therefore concluded that the EP could bring an annulment action to safeguard its prerogatives, which included participation in the drafting of legislative measures, in particular participation in the cooperation procedure laid down in the Treaty.[39]

Formal Treaty amendment followed swiftly after the ECJ's ruling. Article 173 EC was re-drafted in the TEU to reflect the legal position reached by the ECJ. Article 230(3) EC, as it was after the Treaty of Amsterdam renumbering, was further amended by the Treaty of Nice and the EP was added to the list of privileged applicants in Article 230(2). The fact that the formal Treaty 'caught up' with the ECJ's jurisprudence does not diminish the importance of the case as a prime example of the use of background principle to shape the relevant rules of judicial review, in this instance the standing of the EP to seek relief. The Court stepped back from the then prevailing rules

[36] Ibid. at paras. 21–23. [37] Ibid. at para. 25. [38] Ibid. at para. 26.

[39] Weiler, 'Pride and Prejudice—*Parliament v Council*' (1989) 14 *ELRev* 334; Bradley, 'Sense and Sensibility: *Parliament v Council* Continued' (1991) 16 *ELRev* 245; Bebr, 'The Standing of the European Parliament in the Community System of Legal Remedies: A Thorny Jurisprudential Development' (1990) 10 *YBEL* 171.

on standing and considered them in the light of the background principle of institutional balance. It recognized that the EP's role in the legislative process was an essential part of the institutional balance and that the legal remedies were not sufficient to protect the EP in this regard. The ECJ was therefore willing to conceptualize this as a procedural gap, and while recognizing that it could not redress this by making the EP a fully privileged applicant on a par with the Commission, Council, and Member States, it in effect created a quasi-privileged status for the EP, enabling it to bring actions to defend its prerogatives.

A further prominent example of institutional balance shaping the principles of EU administrative law was the *Meroni* decision.[40] The applicant challenged a decision of the High Authority on the ground, *inter alia*, that there had been an improper delegation of power to certain agencies concerning scrap metal. The decision has been considered in greater detail above.[41] Suffice it to say for the present that the case is best known for the eponymous *Meroni* doctrine: delegation of power that involves the exercise of a wide margin of discretion is unlawful. This aspect of the decision must, however, be read in conjunction with the precept that a delegating authority cannot confer power upon another body different from that which it possessed: if the High Authority had exercised the relevant powers itself it would have been subject to a duty to give reasons, a duty to publish an annual report on its activities, a duty to publish data that would have been useful to governments or other concerned parties, and it would have been subject to judicial review. The agency to which power had been delegated was not subject to any of these constraints. The ECJ's conclusion that the delegation would undermine the 'balance of powers which is characteristic of the institutional structure of the Community'[42] was primarily directed at the dangers of granting wide discretion, in the sense that it would accord power over complex discretionary choices to a body not provided for in the Treaty. This argument is, however, reinforced by the other strand of the ECJ's reasoning: the inter-institutional balance of power and that between the High Authority and those subject to it would be undermined if the High Authority could accord power to an agency free from the constraints to which it would have been subject.

The limits to the use of institutional balance were, however, demonstrated in the *FNAB* case.[43] The applicant sought to challenge a measure and failed to meet the restrictive criteria for individual concern. It sought to circumvent

[40] Case 9/56, *Meroni & Co, Industrie Metallurgiche SpA v High Authority* [1957–58] ECR 133.

[41] See above, at 160–162.

[42] Case 9/56, *Meroni, supra* n. 40, at 152.

[43] Case C-345/00 P, *Fédération Nationale d'Agriculture Biologique des Régions de France v Council* [2001] ECR I-3811.

this obstacle by relying on the idea of institutional balance in order to broaden the limited rules on standing. The ECJ rejected the argument. The Court accepted that institutional balance was a fundamental precept of the Community, but held that it could not be interpreted to mean that any individual who considered that a measure had been adopted in breach of that principle could challenge it where the individual was not directly and individually concerned by it.

C. Effectiveness and Cooperation

Administrative law principles have also been shaped by a principle of effectiveness. This background principle has been influential in many areas of EU law. Any regime of administrative law will employ tools of review and compensation in order to hold the administration to account. The interrelationship between the two will be considered in detail in the chapters that follow. The relevance of effectiveness can be exemplified by use made of the principle to lay the foundation for Member States' damages liability in *Francovich*.[44]

The applicants brought proceedings against the Italian state arising out of the government's failure to implement Directive 80/987 on the protection of employees in the event of their employer's insolvency. Both were owed wages from their employers, but since no steps had been taken pursuant to the Directive to guarantee payment of wages, they argued that the state was liable to pay them the sums owed. The ECJ ruled that although the provisions of the Directive lacked sufficient precision to be directly effective, they nevertheless clearly intended to confer rights on the individuals who had been deprived of protection through the state's failure to implement it.

The essence of the ECJ's reasoning was as follows. It reiterated established orthodoxy that Community law created rights for individuals not only where they were expressly granted by the Treaty, but also through obligations which the Treaty imposed in a clearly defined manner on individuals, the Member States, and the Community institutions. It was for national courts when applying Community law in cases within their jurisdiction to ensure that those rules had full effect and protected the rights which they conferred on individuals. The full effectiveness of Community rules would, however, be impaired and the protection of the rights which they granted would be weakened if individuals were unable to obtain compensation when their rights were infringed by a breach of Community law for which a Member State was responsible. This was especially so where the full effectiveness of Community rules was subject to prior action by the state, with the

[44] Cases C-6/90 and C-9/90, *Francovich and Bonifaci v Italy* [1991] ECR I-5357.

consequence that individuals could not, in the absence of such action, enforce the rights granted to them by Community law before the national courts. It followed that the principle of state liability for harm caused to individuals by breaches of Community law for which the state was responsible was inherent in the Treaty. This conclusion was reinforced by Article 10 EC, under which Member States were required to take all appropriate measures, whether general or particular, to ensure fulfilment of their obligations under Community law. The obligations incumbent on Member States flowing from Article 10 EC included the duty to nullify the unlawful consequences of a breach of Community law.[45]

Damages liability will be considered in detail below.[46] It is the ECJ's general mode of reasoning and its implications for administrative law that is of relevance here. The idea of effectiveness was used to reinforce the linkage between rights and remedies, and to legitimate the conclusion that a monetary remedy for breach of Community law by the Member States was inherent in the schema of the Treaty. This conclusion was reinforced by recourse to the Member States' general duty in Article 10 to take all appropriate measures to fulfil their Community obligations. The ECJ's use of this Article was a classic example of the judicial capacity to draw specific obligations from generally worded Treaty provisions.

D. Administrative Efficacy

The discussion of background principles would be incomplete without reference to the background idea of administrative efficacy. We need to tread carefully here and to disaggregate at least two senses of this idea, one of which is well known, the other much less so.

The well-known face of administrative efficacy is that it is a feature in the application of particular principles of administrative law, such as legitimate expectations, proportionality, and the like. The needs of the administration to, for example, respond rapidly to changing market circumstance or alter the direction of Community policy will perforce be considerations that affect the success of any claim for breach of legitimate expectations against the EU. Analogous considerations may affect the outcome of a proportionality claim and will be taken into account when judging the sufficiency of the Community measure to meet the needs for which it was enacted.

There is, however, another less well-known face of administrative efficacy, which is equally important. We have encountered it when examining the

[45] Ross, 'Beyond Francovich' (1993) 56 *MLR* 55; Craig, 'Francovich, Remedies and the Scope of Damages Liability' (1993) 109 *LQR* 595; Dougan, 'The Francovich Right to Reparation: Reshaping the Contours of Community Remedial Competence' (2000) 6 *EPL* 103.

[46] See below, Chaps. 20–21.

different ways in which the Community delivers policy in the earlier chapters. Administrative efficacy is relevant here not directly in relation to the explication of administrative law principles. It is rather of importance in relation to the construction or interpretation of the administrative scheme governing the relevant area, whether that is direct administration, shared administration, comitology, or agencies.

In each of these areas the Community courts have given seminal rulings that affected the legality and effectiveness of that mode of administration.[47] These rulings were given in the context of actions for judicial review, whether direct or indirect. The tendency is to regard such rulings simply as examples where the claimants lost, or as instances of judicial teleological interpretation that are however of no general interest for EU administrative law. This is far too narrow. We should be concerned as administrative lawyers with the overall effectiveness of the administrative systems that exist within the EU. The ECJ's judgments referred to have been of seminal importance in this regard and they were given in the context of judicial review actions, direct and indirect.

This does not of course mean that such decisions should always be accepted with equanimity. Administrative efficacy is no automatic trump that can serve to justify any legal decision given in its name. Nor should we veer in the opposite direction and view such decisions as illegitimate or unwarranted. It is part of the judicial function to effectuate an administrative regime by interpreting the empowering regulations or directives to attain the overall purpose. We should therefore make considered evaluation of the ECJ's case law in this light, and this can only be done with a full appreciation of the particular administrative regime. The discussion in the earlier chapters has addressed this issue as part of the general analysis of particular administrative regimes.[48]

7. A GENERAL CODE OF GOOD ADMINISTRATION

The sources of EU administrative law are, as stated above, eclectic with contributions from Treaty articles, Community legislation, the Community courts, the European Ombudsman, and the Commission. There is, however, no general code, although such codes or something closely proximate thereto exist in certain sectoral areas, such as competition and state aids. The European Ombudsman has been a strong advocate of a general code of good administration and has argued that his existing Code, which elaborates on the meaning of the right to good administration in Article 41 of the Charter,

[47] See above, at 66–68, 91–93, 105–106.

[48] See above, at Chaps. 2–6.

should be transformed into formal law.[49] The discourse on this issue is a delicate admixture of the legal, the political, and the qualitative.

The principal legal issue has been whether there is competence to adopt a general code. Competence to adopt sector-specific codes is based on the Treaty Article governing the relevant substantive area. There have, however, been doubts as to the formal legal basis for a general code. This issue would have been placed beyond doubt if the CT had been ratified, since Article III-398 would have served as the legal foundation. It is nonetheless arguable that a code could be based on Article 308 EC, but the Commission President seems to doubt the existence of competence under the present Treaty.[50]

The legal dimension is overlaid by the political. The Commission has been positive about the idea of a general code, but one gets the feeling that it might not be quite so keen on the idea that it is the European Ombudsman's Code that should be transformed into formal law, more especially given that the Commission has its own Code of Good Administrative Behaviour.[51] If a formal legal code were to become a reality, then it is highly likely that the Commission would wish to have real 'input' into its content and some 'ownership' of the resulting document.

The most important issue is qualitative: the content of any such code and the contribution that it would make to the attainment of good administration. The European Ombudsman's existing Code contains a blend of provisions. Many of these, such as, *inter alia*, those dealing with non-discrimination, proportionality, objectivity, impartiality and independence, legitimate expectations, the right to be heard, the provision of reasons, and fairness, reflect existing law. It should nonetheless be recognized that these principles are formulated at a high level of generality in the Code, and their more specific meaning and application would necessarily continue to depend on the jurisprudence of the Community courts. The Code contains other provisions dealing with matters such as courtesy, which would not naturally

[49] European Ombudsman, The European Code of Good Administrative Behaviour (2005), available at <http://www.euro-ombudsman.eu.int/code/pdf/en/code2005_en.pdf>; Speech by the European Ombudsman, P. Nikiforos Diamandouros, on the Occasion of the Formal Dinner with the EU Institutions, Bodies and Agencies to Mark the 10th Anniversary of the European Ombudsman Institution, available at <http://www.euro-ombudsman.eu.int/10anniversary/en/2005–11–17b.htm>.

[50] Speech by the President of the European Commission, M. Barroso, on the Occasion of the Formal Dinner to Mark the 10th Anniversary of the European Ombudsman, available at <http://www.euro-ombudsman.eu.int/10anniversary/fr/2005–11–17a.htm>. I am grateful to Alexandros Tsadiras for drawing my attention to this.

[51] Commission Decision 2000/633/EC, ECSC, Euratom of 17 October 2000, Amending its Rules of Procedure, OJ 2000 L267/63. The Code of Good Administrative Behaviour for Staff of the European Commission in their Relations with the Public forms the Annex to this Decision.

lend themselves to legal enforcement even if the Code were enshrined in formal law.

It is equally important to be mindful of what the Code does not cover. While the material scope for the Code's application is defined in terms of all relations between the Community institutions, their administrations, and the public, the reality is that the Code's more detailed provisions are primarily targeted at individualized decisions, rather than rule-making. If a general procedural code were to become a legal reality serious thought should therefore be given to its coverage. It would be regrettable for any such code to be premised on a rigid dichotomy between decisions and rules, even if the administrative law precepts might differ as between the two.

9

Courts

1. INTRODUCTION

The preceding chapter considered the foundations of judicial review in the European Union (EU). The discussion now turns to the Community courts. The way in which the principles of review have developed has been affected by the jurisdictional divide between the European Court of Justice (ECJ) and Court of First Instance (CFI), and between these courts and national courts. It will be argued that a necessary condition for an effective regime of judicial control is the existence of a rational judicial architecture, embracing the ECJ, CFI, and national courts.

The discussion will proceed in the following manner. There will be analysis of the central structural and jurisdictional features of the present system, followed by consideration of the case-load problems of the Community courts, and the techniques available to limit the cases that are heard. The focus will then shift to the aims that should underlie reform of the Community's judicial architecture.

The bulk of the chapter will be concerned with the relationship between the ECJ and the CFI, and that between the Community courts and the national courts. The discussion will draw on two important papers concerning the Community's judicial architecture. One was produced by then current members of the ECJ and CFI,[1] and will be referred to hereafter as the Courts' paper. The other was written by a Working Party composed largely of former judges of the ECJ at the behest of the Commission.[2] The Chairman was Ole Due and it will be referred to as the Due Report. The papers generated significant discussion and comment, which will be referred to in the course of the ensuing analysis.[3]

[1] The Future of the Judicial System of the European Union (Proposals and Reflections) (May 1999), available at <http://europa.eu.int/cj/en/instit/txtdocfr/autrestxts/ave.pdf>.

[2] Report by the Working Party on the Future of the European Communities' Court System (January 2000).

[3] Turner and Munoz, 'Revising the Judicial Architecture of the European Union' (1999–2000) 19 *YBEL* 1; Arnull, 'Judicial Architecture or Judicial Folly? The Challenge Facing the European Union' (1999) 24 *ELRev* 516; Rasmussen, 'Remedying the Crumbling EC Judicial System' (2000) 37 *CMLRev* 1071; Craig, 'The Jurisdiction of the Community Courts

2. CENTRAL STRUCTURAL FEATURES

It is clear that there are four types of court adjudicating on Community law, not just three: the ECJ, the CFI, judicial panels *and* national courts. The rationale for inclusion of national courts is that they are enforcers of Community law in their own right, and have been ever since the seminal decisions in *Da Costa*[4] and *CILFIT*.[5] National courts will apply European Community (EC) law to cases which come before them, either where the ECJ/CFI have already decided the point of law in question, or where the matter is *acte clair* in the sense articulated in *CILFIT*. The ECJ in an earlier paper characterized national courts as 'as the courts with general jurisdiction for Community law',[6] and this characterization was repeated in the Courts' later paper.[7]

The division of jurisdictional responsibility between the ECJ and CFI courts has, however, been largely ad hoc. It is well known that the CFI was created to ease the workload of the ECJ. It was therefore natural to assign it certain types of case with a heavy factual quotient, which took up too much time of the ECJ itself. It was for this reason that competition and staff cases were assigned to the CFI.[8] The extension of jurisdictional competence to the CFI over direct actions brought by individuals under Articles 230, 232, and 288 EC, was a further move to ease the ECJ's workload.[9] The same motive, combined with the idea that the CFI had built up expertise in the areas of competition and intellectual property, led to cases concerning the Community

Reconsidered', in G. de Búrca and J. Weiler (eds), *The European Court of Justice* (Oxford University Press, 2001), Chap. 6; Weiler, 'Epilogue: The Judicial Après Nice', *ibid.*, at 215; A. Dashwood and A. Johnston (eds), *The Future of the Judicial System of the European Union* (Hart, 2001); Forwood, 'The Judicial Architecture of the European Union—the Challenges of Change', in M. Hoskins and W. Robinson (eds), *A True European, Essays for Judge David Edward* (Hart, 2003), at 81; Timmermans, 'The European Union's Judicial System' (2004) 41 *CMLRev* 393.

[4] Cases 28–30/62, *Da Costa en Schaake NV, Jacob Meijer NV and Hoechst-Holland NV v Nederlandse Belastingadministratie* [1963] ECR 31.

[5] Case 283/81, *Srl CILFIT and Lanificio di Gavardo SpA v Ministry of Health* [1982] ECR 3415; Case C-495/03, *Intermodal Transports BV v Staatssecretaris van Financien* [2005] ECR I-8151.

[6] Report of the Court of Justice on Certain Aspects of the Application of the Treaty on European Union—Contribution of the Court of First Instance for the Purposes of the 1996 Intergovernmental Conference (May 1995), at para. 15.

[7] The Future of the Judicial System, *supra* n. 1, at 24.

[8] Council Decision 88/591/ECSC, EEC, Euratom of 24 October 1988, Establishing a Court of First Instance of the European Communities, OJ 1988 L319/1.

[9] Council Decision 93/350/ECSC, EEC, Euratom of 8 June 1993, Amending Council Decision 88/591/ECSC, EEC, Euratom Establishing a Court of First Instance of the European Communities, OJ 1993 L144/21; Council Decision 94/149/ECSC, EEC of 7 March 1994, Amending Council Decision 93/350, OJ 1994 L66/29.

trade mark being assigned to the CFI. It will be argued below that a re-thinking of the division of responsibility between the CFI and ECJ, whereby the former becomes a generalized court of first instance, is central to the development of a rational judicial structure.

The division of responsibility between the ECJ/CFI and national courts has been coloured by two primary factors, which are to some extent in tension. The main objective has been to confer a broad power on national courts to enforce Community law, since this enhanced its overall effectiveness. This explains the encouragement given to national courts to apply Community precedent without recourse to the ECJ unless there was need to do so,[10] the ECJ's insistence that any national court must be able to apply EC law in a case which came before it, and its insistence also that national rules should not be able to hinder or impede this.[11] This has been tempered by the desire to preserve the uniformity of application and interpretation of EC law. Thus while national courts can declare EC norms to be valid, and whilst they must treat ECJ decisions that a Community norm is invalid as having *ergo omnes* effect,[12] they cannot themselves declare a Community norm to be invalid,[13] although they can provide interim relief.[14]

3. CENTRAL JURISDICTIONAL FEATURES

The ECJ and CFI possess jurisdictional competence over actions brought before them in a number of different ways, including actions under Articles 226, 230, 232, 234, and 288 EC.

The ECJ's jurisdiction over preliminary rulings under Article 234 is recognized as the jewel in the Crown of the existing regime. Preliminary references have been the procedural vehicle through which key concepts such as direct effect and supremacy have developed.[15] The very existence of this procedure has been part of the justificatory argument for the existence of direct effect itself.[16] Preliminary rulings have been the mechanism through

[10] Cases 28–30/62, *Da Costa*, *supra* n. 4; Case 283/81, *CILFIT*, *supra* n. 5.

[11] Case 106/77, *Amministrazione delle Finanze dello Stato v Simmenthal SpA* [1978] ECR 629.

[12] Case 66/80, *International Chemical Corporation v Amministrazione delle Finanze dello Stato* [1981] ECR 1191.

[13] Case 314/85, *Firma Foto-Frost v Hauptzollamt Lubeck-Ost* [1987] ECR 4199.

[14] Cases C-143/88 and 92/89, *Zuckerfabrik Suderdithmaschen AG v Hauptzollamt Itzehoe* [1991] ECR I-415.

[15] Mancini and Keeling, 'From *CILFIT* to *ERT*: The Constitutional Challenge Facing the European Court' (1991) 11 *YBEL* 1, at 2–3.

[16] Case 26/62, *NV Algemene Transporten Expeditie Onderneming van Gend en Loos v Nederlandse Administratie der Belastingen* [1963] ECR 1; Case 41/74, *Van Duyn v Home Office* [1974] ECR 1337, at para. 12.

which the supremacy doctrine has been 'nationalized', in part because supremacy has been developed through Article 234 cases,[17] in part because the very structure of this procedure means that the case will start and end in the national courts.

It should also be recognized that there is a duality in the types of case that arise under Article 234. A paradigmatic case is the challenge to national action on the ground that it violates a Treaty article, regulation, directive, or other binding norm of Community law. Another prominent type of case concerns the use of Article 234 as a means of indirect challenge to a Community norm on the ground that it is in breach of a Treaty article or a regulation, directive, or decision that is hierarchically superior to the Community norm that is being challenged. Article 234 has been used in this manner, especially by individuals and non-privileged applicants, because of the difficulty of securing standing in a direct action for judicial review under Article 230. In these circumstances Article 234 is often the only practical way for an individual to get the case before the Community courts.

This leads directly to a further jurisdictional feature concerning the Community courts: prior to the Nice Treaty all preliminary references had to go to the ECJ. If all such cases were of real importance then this would not matter. However many requests for preliminary rulings are technical rather than constitutional in nature. Applicants will seek to challenge the validity of Community regulations or decisions under Article 234, which they are unable to contest under Article 230. A common scenario is that a national customs authority, or agricultural intervention board, will apply a Community regulation concerning the details of customs classification, agricultural levies, and the like to a particular producer. The producer feels that the goods have been wrongly classified, or that the levy is discriminatory, and therefore resists payment. The customs authority, or agricultural intervention board, takes legal action and the applicant argues before the national court that the regulation is invalid, and asks that the relevant questions be referred to the ECJ. A glance through the Community law reports for any one year reveals the number of such cases which are heard by the ECJ. It is of course right and proper that such matters are judicially resolved. It is however far less obvious that the ECJ should be spending its time and resources on such matters.

4. CASELOAD

It is clear that the principal rationale driving consideration of reform to the Community's judicial system is workload. The Courts' paper stressed that

[17] Case 6/64, *Costa v ENEL* [1964] ECR 585; Case 106/77, *Simmenthal*, *supra* n. 11.

the organizational and procedural framework 'must be revised to enable the Court of Justice and the Court of First Instance to shorten existing time limits and deal with further increases in the number of cases brought'.[18] If this did not occur then there would be delays on a scale which cannot be reconciled with an acceptable level of judicial protection in the Union. The Courts' paper continued in the following vein.[19]

Furthermore, in the case of the Court of Justice, the extra case-load might well seriously jeopardise the proper accomplishment of its task as a court of last instance which, in addition, has a constitutional role. The Court would then no longer be able to concentrate on its main functions, which are to guarantee respect for the distribution of powers between the Community and its Member States and between the Community institutions, the uniformity and consistency of Community law and to contribute to the harmonious development of the law of the Union. Such a failure on the part of the Court would undermine the rule of law on which, as stated in Article 6(1) EU, the Union is founded.

A. The Rationale for the Caseload Problem

It is important to understand the different factors which have led to the increase in the case-load of the ECJ and CFI. Four such factors can be identified, the most obvious being enlargement of the Community. The expansion of the EC from six to 15 Member States, with the further enlargement to 25, has led to an increase in business for the Community courts.[20] A second reason is that the areas over which the EC has competence have expanded with every major Treaty revision. A further factor placing a strain on Community judicial resources has been the very success of EC harmonization initiatives. Any new piece of EC legislation will always contain important issues which require judicial clarification. This may well lead to a significant increase in the case-load of a court, more especially where the legislation is complex and lengthy, as exemplified by the introduction of the Community trade mark. The final factor that has led to an increase in caseload has been the growing awareness of EC law by lawyers. At the inception of the Community, EC law remained the preserve of a limited number of specialists. Taking an EC point was regarded as rather unusual, and often seen as a matter of last resort. While it is true that countries have specialists in EC law, it is also true that most lawyers will

[18] The Future of the Judicial System, *supra* n. 1, at 8.

[19] Ibid. at 9. See also, Report by the Working Party, *supra* n. 2, at 5–8.

[20] Report by the Working Party, *supra* n. 2, at 9. The number of cases pending before the ECJ continued to rise until 2004. In 2000 there were 748 cases pending, in 2002 the number was 907, and in 2003 it had risen to 948, Proceedings of the Court of Justice, Annual Report 2003, at 9. In 2004 the number of pending cases fell to 804, Proceedings of the Court of Justice, Annual Report 2004, at 12, available at <http://europa.eu.int/cj/en/plan/index.htm>.

naturally now think about whether there is an EC 'angle' to a case which comes before them.

An interesting 'symptom' of the problems facing the Community courts as a result of the increasing case-load is the increasing length of the law reports, coupled with the need to translate decisions into all official languages.[21] This prompted the ECJ to decide not to publish all of its decisions in the law reports, although they will be available on-line. Direct actions and appeals decided by chambers of three judges will *prima facie* not be published in the law reports, nor will those decided by chambers of five judges if, pursuant to Article 20 of the Statute of the Court of Justice, the case is heard without an opinion from an Advocate General. It is, however, open to such chambers to decide in exceptional circumstances to publish the decision in whole or in part. This practice of selective non-publication does not apply to preliminary rulings, which will continue to be published in the law reports.[22]

B. Judicial Mechanisms for Limiting Caseload

It is clear that there are judicial mechanisms for limiting the cases which come before the ECJ/CFI. These juristic devices differ in relation to the main heads of the Community courts' jurisdiction.

In relation to *direct actions contesting the validity of Community norms*, standing requirements are the main control device applicable to actions brought by private parties under Article 230 EC. This topic will be considered in detail in the following chapter. Suffice it to say for the present that the existing rules are very tight and therefore it would not possible to address the workload problem by making them any tighter.

In relation to *enforcement actions brought by the Commission before the ECJ* under Article 226 EC the main control mechanism relevant to caseload is the Commission's discretion as to whether it should take a case or not.[23] The number of cases brought under Article 226 is in any event not that great. Given that the Commission has discretion as to whether to bring a case, and that it uses its scarce resources to fight those cases which it believes to be most significant, then there is no real way of alleviating the workload of the ECJ by reform in this area.

The ECJ has certain mechanisms whereby it can limit the number of requests for a *preliminary ruling under Article 234 EC*. The procedure under Article 234 is based on co-operation between the national court and the

[21] Jacobs, 'Recent and Ongoing Measures to Improve the Efficiency of the European Court of Justice' (2004) 29 *ELRev* 823, at 827–828.

[22] Proceedings of the Court of Justice, Annual Report 2004, *supra* n. 20, at 11–12.

[23] Rawlings, 'Citizen Action and Institutional Attitudes in Commission Enforcement' (2000) 6 *ELJ* 4.

ECJ. The early case law indicated that the ECJ would rarely if ever question the factual basis of, or reasons for, a referral.[24] However in the seminal *Foglia* jurisprudence[25] the ECJ made it clear that it would make the ultimate decision as to the scope of its own jurisdiction. The ECJ was not simply to be a passive receptor, forced to adjudicate on whatever was placed before it. It asserted control over the suitability of the reference. The principle in *Foglia* lay dormant for some time, and attempts to invoke it did not prove markedly successful.[26] However from the early 1990s the ECJ used the *Foglia* principle to decline to give rulings in cases which were hypothetical, where the questions raised were not relevant to the resolution of the substantive action in the national court,[27] where the questions were not articulated clearly enough for the ECJ to be able to give any meaningful legal response, and where the facts were insufficiently clear for the Court to be able to apply the relevant legal rules.[28] The ECJ incorporated some of the results of this case law in a memorandum providing information and guidance for national courts.[29] Paragraph 22 states that the order for reference should contain a statement of reasons which is succinct but sufficiently complete to give the Court a clear understanding of the factual and legal context of the main action. It should include a statement of the essential facts; the relevant national law; the provisions of Community law felt to be applicable to the case; the reasons why the national court referred the matter; and a summary of the parties' arguments where appropriate. While the ECJ has therefore exerted greater control over

[24] P. Craig and G. de Burca, *EU Law, Text, Cases and Materials* (Oxford University Press, 3rd ed., 2003), at 457–460.

[25] Case 104/79, *Pasquale Foglia v Mariella Novella* [1980] ECR 745; Case 244/80, *Pasquale Foglia v Mariella Novello (No. 2)* [1981] ECR 3045.

[26] Case 261/81, *Walter Rau Lebensmittelwerke v De Smedt PvbA* [1982] ECR 3961; Case 46/80, *Vinal SpA v Orbat SpA* [1981] ECR 77; Case C-150/88, *Eau de Cologne and Parfumerie-Fabrik Glockengasse No 4711 KG v Provide Srl* [1989] ECR 3891.

[27] Case C-83/91, *Wienand Meilicke v ADV/ORGA F.A. Meyer AG* [1992] ECR I-4871; Case C-18/93, *Corsica Ferries Italia Srl v Corpo dei Piloti del Porto di Genova* [1994] ECR I-1783; Case C-428/93, *Monin Automobiles-Maison du Deux-Roues* [1994] ECR I-1707; Case C-134/95, *Unita Socio-Sanitaria Locale No 47 di Biella (USSL) v Istituto Nazionale per l'Assicurazione contro gli Infortuni sul Lavoro (INAIL)* [1997] ECR I-195; Cases C-320, 328, 329, 337, 338, and 339/94, *Reti Televisive Italiane SpA (RTI) v Ministero delle Poste e Telecommunicazione* [1996] ECR I-6471.

[28] Cases C-320–322/90, *Telemarsicabruzzo SpA v Circostel, Ministero delle Poste e Telecommunicazioni and Ministerio della Difesa* [1993] ECR I-393; Case C-157/92, *Banchero* [1993] ECR I-1085; Case C-386/92, *Monin Automobiles v France* [1993] ECR I-2049; Case C-458/93, *Criminal Proceedings against Saddik* [1995] ECR I-511; Case C-167/94R, *Grau Gomis* [1995] ECR I-1023; Case C-2/96, *Criminal Proceedings against Sunino and Data* [1996] ECR I-1543; Case C-257/95, *Bresle v Prefet de la Region Auvergne and Prefet du Puy-de-Dome* [1996] ECR I-233.

[29] Information Note on References from National Courts for a Preliminary Ruling, OJ 2005 C143/1.

the admissibility of references than hitherto, the Court has also continued to make it clear that it will only decline to give a ruling if the issue of EC law on which an interpretation is sought is manifestly inapplicable to the dispute before the national court, or bears no relation to the subject matter of that action.[30]

The ECJ also has a *more indirect way of limiting case load under Article 234, by limiting the intensity of judicial oversight.* This is the classic technique used by the ECJ when reviewing cases brought to it under Article 234 to contest the validity of Community acts which cannot be challenged directly through Article 230 because of the limited standing rules. Applicants who wish to challenge the validity of Community action will often have to do so through national courts. The national court will send the case to the ECJ for a preliminary ruling as to whether, for example, an agricultural measure was disproportionate and hence in breach of Article 34 EC. The ECJ has made it clear that it will not readily find that the challenged Community norm was invalid, more especially in an area where the Commission and Council have broad discretionary power.[31] The applicant may well have to prove that the measure was manifestly disproportionate, or very obviously discriminatory.[32] In one sense this is not a method of control over caseload since the ECJ will have to hear the relevant dispute, even if at the end of the day it decides that the measure is valid. However, in another sense low intensity review can operate as a tool for controlling caseload. Those who are thinking of challenging the validity of a measure will come to realize that they have to prove something quite extreme before they can succeed. They will therefore desist from bringing the action where the chance of proving this is remote.

These techniques for limiting the caseload under Article 234 have not, however, stemmed the tide of references coming to the ECJ. The *Foglia* principle only excludes a limited number of references. Moreover, national courts will learn to frame their references better and in that sense there will over time be fewer cases which can be excluded on this ground. References for a preliminary ruling have increased by 85 per cent since 1990, and constitute half of the new cases brought before the ECJ.[33]

[30] Case C-85/95, *Reisdorf v Finanzamt Koln-West* [1996] ECR I-6257; Case C-118/94, *Associazione Italiana per il World Wildlife Fund v Regione Veneto* [1996] ECR I-1223; Case C-129/94, *Criminal Proceedings against Bernaldez* [1996] ECR I-1829; Case C-446/93, *SEIM—Sociedade de Exportacoa de Materias, Ld v Subdirector-Geral das Alfandegas* [1996] ECR I-73.

[31] Craig, 'Judicial Review, Intensity and Deference in EU Law', in D. Dyzenhaus (ed), *The Unity of Public Law* (Hart, 2004), Chap. 13.

[32] Craig and de Burca, *supra* n. 24, at 537–540.

[33] The Future of the Judicial System, *supra* n. 1, at 5.

5. REFORM OBJECTIVES

The discussion thus far has identified central structural and jurisdictional features of the Community judicial system, and the problems relating to caseload. We are now in a position to consider how the system could best be reformed. The answer to this inquiry depends, explicitly or implicitly, on certain assumptions about the principal objectives of a reformed regime. Thus the Courts' paper and the Due Report posited three fundamental requirements that should be taken into account when thinking about the future of the Community's judicial system:[34] the need to secure the unity of Community law by means of a supreme court; the need to ensure that the judicial system is transparent, comprehensible, and accessible to the public; and the need to dispense justice without unacceptable delay.

These issues are important, but do not exhaust the considerations that are pertinent to reform of the Community's judicial system. We can more generally disaggregate three key aspects of judicial architecture that should be addressed, even though they are perforce related.

There are issues concerning *input/access*. This is exemplified by the need to ensure that the judicial system is transparent, comprehensible, and accessible to the public, and that Community justice is available without excessive delay. It is scant comfort to litigants to be presented with an impressive array of judicial protection if the time to secure relief renders such protection chimerical. We should be equally mindful of cost implications. If the system is structured such that litigants find it necessary to fight their way through multiple courts before reaching a forum that is capable of resolving the matter at hand then it is likely to dissuade many who do not have the resources for such a 'journey'.

There are equally important matters relating to the *distribution of jurisdictional competence* as between the ECJ and CFI, and as between the Community courts and national courts. It is axiomatic that the division of judicial power between the ECJ and CFI should be as coherent and symmetrical as possible, while accepting that there can be legitimate differences of view as to what this entails. It is also self-evident that the system should be structured to ensure that the most important points of law are decided by the ECJ, and that it is, so far as possible, not troubled by less important cases. The principles that should guide the division of authority between the Community courts and the national courts are more contentious. Thus, as will be seen, there is debate as to whether it would be desirable to move from the present reference system, to one which is more appellate in nature. There is equally

[34] The Future of the Judicial System, *supra* n. 1, at 18; Report by the Working Party, *supra* n. 2, at 10.

vibrant discourse about whether national courts should be accorded more latitude by, for example, loosening the criteria of the *acte clair* doctrine, and/or according them competence to pronounce on the validity of Community norms.

There are finally issues concerning *output*. The success or otherwise of the Community judicial architecture should be judged in part by whether it secures the effective enforcement of Community law. We should moreover be willing to think openly about whether certain assumptions about output should continue to be treated as 'givens'. Thus the need to ensure the unity and uniformity of Community law has shaped key aspects of judicial doctrine and has had ramifications for the Community judicial system. Whether such a high premium should continue to be placed on this 'output objective' has, as will be seen, been questioned.

The following discussion will focus on the relationship between the ECJ and the CFI, and that between the Community courts and the national courts. This is central for a rational judicial system and has implications for input/access and for output.

A cautionary note should be added before proceeding further. The principled discussion about reform of the Community judicial system must be tempered by political reality. The ultimate decision concerning judicial reform lies with the EU's political organs. This should not be forgotten. It will be seen moreover that the 'agenda' of the main political players, the European Council, Council, the European Parliament (EP), and Commission, is not uniform. It is therefore necessary to acknowledge not only the existence of political pressures, but also that they might pull in different directions.

6. THE RELATIONSHIP BETWEEN THE ECJ AND CFI

The jurisdiction of the CFI has, as seen above, grown in an ad hoc manner. Heads of jurisdiction have been given to it primarily to relieve the workload of the ECJ, hence the assignment of staff cases and competition cases to the CFI. The transfer of all direct actions brought by non-privileged applicants was fuelled by similar concerns. The future role and jurisdiction of the CFI is of central importance to the overall judicial architecture of the Community. An objective of reform must be a system which is as coherent as possible. A significant step in this direction would be for the CFI to become a general court of first instance for all actions, with limited rights of appeal to the ECJ. This will be considered both for direct actions and for preliminary rulings.

A. Direct Actions

The possibility that the CFI might become a court of first instance for all direct actions was considered by both of the reports that preceded the Nice Treaty. The Courts' paper was, however, hesitant about the possible transfer of further competence to the CFI to hear direct actions. It stated that there were no grounds at that time for proposing the transfer of any heads of jurisdiction over and above those whose transfer had already been proposed by the ECJ, while leaving open the possibility that 'it may become necessary, if the volume of cases continues to grow, to review the basis on which jurisdiction is allocated between the two Community courts and to transfer further heads of jurisdiction to the Court of First Instance'.[35]

The Due Report was more forthcoming in this respect.[36] Its starting point was that the CFI should, as a matter of principle, be the first judicial forum for direct actions, including review for legality and compensation. The CFI's jurisdiction would include actions brought by a Member State or Community institution. This principle was then qualified in the Report such that direct actions involving matters of urgency and importance would be assigned to the ECJ.[37] Only those cases where a rapid judgment was essential to avoid serious problems in the proper functioning of the Community institutions would fall into this category.[38]

The changes made by the Nice Treaty moved matters in the direction suggested by the Due Report. The position hitherto had been that the CFI would be accorded jurisdiction over certain classes of case as a result of a determination made by the Council, albeit at the request of the ECJ, subject to the Treaty limitation that the CFI could not hear preliminary rulings. The Nice Treaty modified Article 225(1) by providing that the CFI could hear actions covered by Articles 230, 232, 235, 236, and 238, with the exception of those cases assigned to a judicial panel and those reserved in the Statute of the Court of Justice for the ECJ.[39]

Article 51 of the Statute of the Court Justice had reserved jurisdiction to the ECJ in all actions brought by Member States, the Community institutions, and the ECB. This Article has now been amended so as to give the CFI some increased jurisdiction over direct actions.[40] Article 51 continues to

[35] The Future of the Judicial System, *supra* n. 1, at 21.

[36] Report by the Working Party, *supra* n. 2, at 23–29.

[37] Ibid. at 24–25.

[38] Ibid. at 25. The Report makes it clear that actions under Art. 226 EC would fall within this category.

[39] Art. 7 of the Nice Treaty repealed the previous Protocol on the Statute of the Court of Justice and replaced it with a Protocol on the Statute of the Court of Justice annexed to the Nice Treaty, OJ 2001 C80/1.

[40] Council Decision 2004/407/EC, Euratom of 26 April 2004, Amending Articles 51 and 54 of the Protocol of the Statute of the Court of Justice, OJ 2004 L132/5.

reserve jurisdiction for the ECJ in relation to direct actions brought by a Community institution against another Community institution, including the ECB. Jurisdiction also remains with the ECJ where a Member State seeks to challenge an act or failure to act by the EP or Council, or where these institutions act jointly. This is, however, now subject to limited exceptions. An action by a Member State can be heard by the CFI where it relates to a Council decision under paragraph three of Article 88(2) EC concerning state aids; where it concerns measures to protect trade pursuant to Article 133 EC; and most significantly in relation to acts of the Council where the Council exercises implementing powers in accord with the third indent of Article 202 EC. This last exception covers Council acts either where the Council has reserved the right to exercise implementing power to itself, or where it has regained the right to exercise such power as a result of comitology procedures. The CFI has moreover been given jurisdiction in actions brought by Member States against the Commission, except in the area covered by Article 11a EC dealing with enhanced cooperation.

Article 225(1) stipulates further that the Statute may provide for the CFI to have jurisdiction for other classes of case, thereby obviating the need for Treaty amendment. The decisions of judicial panels created pursuant to the Nice Treaty can be appealed to the CFI, subject to a limited right of review by the ECJ in exceptional instances where there is a serious risk of the unity or consistency of Community law being affected.[41] A European Union Civil Service Tribunal has now been created to adjudicate on staff cases.[42]

The thrust of the Due Report's proposal is to be welcomed, as are the steps in that direction taken by the Nice Treaty. There is a strong case for rationalizing the present regime and making it more coherent by transforming the CFI into a general first instance court in direct actions. This would be a rational working through of Declaration 12 attached to the Nice Treaty, which stipulated that the ECJ and the Commission should, as soon as possible, present proposals for the division of jurisdiction between the ECJ and the CFI, particularly in the area of direct actions. We should move away from the idea that the CFI is a court primarily for technical or factually complex cases. We should not accept that the jurisdiction of the CFI is destined forever to remain eclectic and ad hoc. The changes made to Article 51 of the Statute, which have increased the CFI's jurisdiction over direct actions, while welcome for that reason, also serve by their very patchwork nature to complicate the jurisdictional divide between the ECJ and the CFI. It is moreover

[41] Art. 225(2) EC; Draft Council Decision, Amending the Protocol on the Statute of the Court of Justice of the European Communities, specifies in greater detail this review function of the ECJ, available at <http://europa.eu.int/cj/en/plan/index.htm>.

[42] Council Decision 2004/752/EC, Euratom of 2 November 2004, Establishing the European Union Civil Service Tribunal, OJ 2004 L333/7.

difficult to sustain a principled argument as to why the CFI should be accorded jurisdiction in these areas and not others. The CFI is already the first instance court for direct actions involving non-privileged applicants who seek to challenge the validity of Community norms. Its jurisdiction should be extended to enable it to hear all direct actions under Articles 230 or 232, even where the case is brought by a privileged applicant such as the Council, Commission, or a Member State, or by a quasi-privileged applicant such as the European Central Bank. It would also be desirable if the CFI could operate as a first instance court in enforcement actions brought under Article 226.[43] The Member States are, however, likely to be particularly resistant to a change which would mean that they could be sued before the CFI for non-compliance with Community obligations, rather than before the ECJ itself. This should not dissuade us from making the CFI a general court of first instance in direct actions under Articles 230 and 232, with the possibility of appeal to the ECJ.[44] CFI decisions made pursuant to Article 225(1) are in any event subject to appeal to the ECJ on a point of law, under the conditions laid down by the Statute.

The vision of the CFI as general first instance court in direct actions does moreover fit well with other developments in the general regime of Community adjudication. To an increasing extent cases which come before the Community courts will already have been the subject of some form of adjudication. This has always been the case in the context of competition and state aids where the Commission will have given a formal, legally binding decision on the matter which the parties can challenge before the CFI. The development of a specialist agency in the context of trade marks is a further move in the same direction. Staff cases are now to be dealt with through the new Civil Service Tribunal,[45] subject to appeal to the CFI, and further review by the ECJ where there is a serious risk of the unity or consistency of Community law being affected, and consideration is being given to the creation of a panel to deal with patents.

If we put together these ideas then a rational division of jurisdiction begins to emerge. The CFI should become the general court of first instance in direct actions irrespective of the nature of the applicant. If this requires more judges in the CFI this can be done within the limits of Article 224, which specifies that the CFI should have at least one judge per Member State, leaving open the possibility of more, although Article 48 of the Statute does currently specify 25 judges for the CFI. The CFI works in Chambers and this

[43] Forwood, *supra* n. 3, at 87.

[44] A filter for appeals from the CFI to the ECJ was part of the proposals made in the Due Report, Report by the Working Party, *supra* n. 2, at 28.

[45] Council Decision 2004/752, *supra* n. 42. The idea was mooted in The Future of the Judicial System, *supra* n. 1, at 17; Report by the Working Party, *supra* n. 2, at 30–31.

can be used to accommodate the need for subject matter specialization. Article 225(1) limits appeal to the ECJ to points of law, and the details of such appeals are specified further by Articles 56 to 62 of the Statute. It is doubtful whether, as suggested by the Due Report, the criterion should be more limited, by requiring that there must be a point of law of major importance either for the development of Community law, or for the protection of individual rights.[46] In circumstances where the CFI has determined an appeal from a judicial panel then the approach in the Nice Treaty, whereby there is the possibility of review by the ECJ where there is serious risk to the unity or consistency of Community law, is sound.

B. Preliminary Rulings

The discussion thus far has concentrated on the role of the CFI as generalized court of first instance in direct actions. This still leaves open the issue of preliminary rulings. Possible reform of the preliminary ruling procedure raises, as will be seen below, important issues concerning the nature of the relationship between the national courts and the Community courts. It also, however, has implications for the relationship between the ECJ and the CFI.

Prior to the Nice Treaty all requests for a preliminary ruling were heard by the ECJ. Article 225(1) stated that the CFI was not competent to hear such actions. We have seen, however, that the ECJ's workload problem arose in part from the increasing burden of preliminary rulings. The reports prior to the Nice Treaty therefore considered whether this problem could be alleviated by allowing the CFI to give preliminary rulings. This possibility was canvassed positively, albeit cautiously, in the Courts' paper.[47] The Due Report however, was opposed to this change, except in a limited number of special areas. Such rulings should, said the Report, be given by the ECJ because this was the most important task for the development of Community law. The Due Report was also influenced in reaching this conclusion by the fact that preliminary rulings take the form of a reference of a question from a national court to the ECJ, while the substance of the case remains for resolution within the national court. It was felt that the consequence must be a 'one stop shop', in the sense that the questions referred by the national court should go to only one Community court, because of the time delays thereby involved, and thus there would be difficulties in providing for an appeal to the ECJ from the CFI's rulings.[48]

[46] Report by the Working Party, *supra* n. 2, at 28–29.

[47] Ibid. at 27.

[48] Report by the Working Party, *supra* n. 2, at 22. Compare however the discussion in the Courts' paper, which explicitly considered the possibility of two adjudications on preliminary rulings in the context of its discussion of decentralized judicial bodies, The Future of the Judicial System, *supra* n. 1, at 28–29.

The Nice Treaty did, however, accord the CFI power for the first time to hear preliminary rulings. Article 225(3) provides that the CFI has jurisdiction to determine preliminary rulings in specific areas laid down by the Statute of the Court of Justice. Where the CFI believes that the case requires a decision of principle which is likely to affect the unity or consistency of Community law, it may refer the case to the ECJ. Preliminary rulings given by the CFI can, exceptionally, be subject to review by the ECJ, under the conditions laid down in the Statute, where there is a serious risk to the unity or consistency of Community law being affected.[49] A Draft Council Decision has specified in greater detail the nature of the ECJ's review procedure that operates under Article 225(2) and (3).[50]

There is much to be said for the idea that the CFI should be able to give preliminary rulings. We have already seen that one major category of preliminary ruling involves indirect challenges to the validity of Community norms through Article 234 where the non-privileged applicants cannot satisfy the standing criteria under Article 230. The perverse institutional consequence of the restrictive standing rules limiting access under Article 230 has therefore been to compel such applicants to use Article 234, thereby further overburdening the ECJ. The substance of such cases is concerned with just the kind of issues that would be heard by the CFI in a direct action under Article 230 if the standing criteria were less restrictive. It cannot therefore be argued that the CFI is ill-equipped to hear such actions if they emerge indirectly via national courts as requests for preliminary rulings. Moreover many of these cases involve no general point of importance for Community law. The paradigm is normally a technical issue concerning the meaning of a provision in a Community norm, which requires judicial resolution, but not the scarce resources of the ECJ.

Nor should we be wedded to the idea that the other paradigm category of preliminary ruling, challenge to Member State action for violation of EU law, must necessarily be heard by the ECJ. It is mistaken to think that all such cases are of significance either for the development of Community law, or for the Member State concerned. Many such cases involve technical issues as to whether, for example, a Member State provision is compatible with EC rules on VAT and the like. There is no reason why preliminary rulings should not go initially to the CFI, with the possibility of further recourse to the ECJ in accord with Article 225(3). It should be noted that this provides two mechanisms for getting a case from the CFI to the ECJ: either the CFI refers it on to the ECJ because the CFI considers that the case raises an issue of principle likely to affect the unity or consistency of EU law, or the CFI's decision can be subject to review by the ECJ where there is a serious risk that the unity or

[49] See Art. 62 of the Statute of the Court of Justice.
[50] Draft Council Decision, *supra* n. 41.

consistency of EU law will be affected. The CFI could, on this view, subject to the caveat just mentioned, be the general first instance court for preliminary rulings as well as direct actions.

This conclusion can be reinforced by considering the plausibility of the strategy in the Nice Treaty that the CFI has jurisdiction to give preliminary rulings only in specific areas. There has been no progress thus far in delineating these 'areas'.[51] This is not fortuitous. A moment's reflection will reveal the difficulty in applying this precept. The phrase 'specific areas' indicates that the criterion is to be subject matter: the CFI would be afforded competence to give preliminary rulings in relation to energy or agriculture, transport, or customs. This is, however, problematic. This is in part because cases do not always fit neatly into such pigeon holes, and hence there would inevitably be boundary problems leading to uncertainty for national courts and costly procedural litigation. The strategy is flawed more importantly because there is no correlation between subject matter area and the importance of the point of Community law raised by the case. We know full well from existing jurisprudence that, for example, preliminary rulings in agricultural and customs cases have generated some of the most important points of Community law principle, even where the sums at stake in the instant case were small; we know equally well that there are many cases in these areas that entail no issue of general Community law principle at all. There is therefore no ready method of choosing particular areas in which the CFI should be competent to give preliminary rulings. The only way to avoid this conclusion is to limit the CFI's competence to very specialist areas, such as judicial cooperation in civil matters, which give rise to specific issues of private international law.[52] This would, however, have little impact on the overall work problem of the ECJ. Nor would it furnish any reason as to why the CFI should be precluded from acting as the first instance court for preliminary rulings in other areas. Judge Forwood took the view that the mere fact that an area is important or central to the Community legal order should not necessarily preclude a transfer to the CFI, although he argued that the relative maturity of the case law should be taken into account.[53]

The principled and pragmatic solution would therefore be to accord the CFI with a general competence to hear preliminary rulings, with the possibility of further recourse to the ECJ where necessary.[54] Article 225(3) already embodies sound criteria in this respect: the CFI can refer the matter on to the ECJ where the case requires a decision of principle likely to affect the unity and consistency of Community law, and the ECJ can review the decisions made by the CFI where there is a serious risk of the unity or consistency of

[51] Jacobs, *supra* n. 21, at 826.

[52] Report by the Working Party, *supra* n. 2.

[53] Forwood, *supra* n. 3, at 86.

[54] See also, Rasmussen, *supra* n. 3, at 1098–1103; Weiler, *supra* n. 3, at 222–223.

Community law being affected. These criteria could then be more liberally interpreted in areas where recourse to the ECJ might be more desirable because the case law is not yet well developed.

7. THE RELATIONSHIP BETWEEN THE COMMUNITY COURTS AND NATIONAL COURTS

The workload problems of the Community courts were considered above. There is little doubt that the steep rise in the number of references for preliminary rulings has been a major factor in this respect: 85 per cent since 1990, with an increase of 10 per cent in 1998 as compared with the previous year.[55] The Courts' paper carries a stark warning of the need for reform.[56]

> The constant growth in the number of references for preliminary rulings emanating from courts and tribunals of the Member States carries with it a serious risk that the Court of Justice will be overwhelmed by its case-load. If current trends continue without any reform of the machinery for dealing with cases, not only will proceedings become more protracted, to the detriment of the proper working of the preliminary ruling system, but the Court of Justice will also be obliged to conduct its deliberations with such dispatch that it will no longer be able to apply to cases the thorough consideration necessary for it to give a useful reply to the questions referred.
>
> It is highly likely that the impact of its decisions will diminish as their number increases and as they deal more frequently with questions of secondary importance or of interest only in the context of the case concerned.

The Rules of Procedure have been modified to alleviate these difficulties,[57] and these Rules can now be adopted by qualified majority in the Council, unanimity no longer being required.[58] Thus there have been changes allowing expedited procedure in cases of urgency, Article 62a of the Statute. There have also been changes to the procedures applicable in cases of preliminary rulings. For example, where the request is identical to a point dealt with by existing case law, or where the answer can clearly be deduced from existing cases, or where the answer admits of no reasonable doubt, then the ECJ can give its decision by reasoned order in which it refers, where relevant, to the prior case law, Article 104(3) of the Rules of Procedure.[59] The Nice Treaty

[55] The Future of the Judicial System, *supra* n. 1, at 5. [56] Ibid. at 22.

[57] The Rules of Procedure of the Court of Justice of the European Communities of 19 June 1991, OJ [1991] L176/7, as amended, available at <http://europa.eu.int/cj/en/plan/index.htm>.

[58] Arts. 223, 224 EC.

[59] Jacobs, *supra* n. 21, at 825. This power was used on 11 occasions in 2003, Proceedings of the Court of Justice, Annual Report 2003, *supra* n. 20, at 10, and on 22 occasions in 2004, Proceedings of the Court of Justice, Annual Report 2004, *supra* n. 22, at 13.

also enabled a case to be decided without an Opinion from the Advocate General,[60] and this power was used in approximately 30 per cent of cases in 2004.[61]

The length of time to process a preliminary ruling rose in 2003,[62] but fell slightly in 2004.[63] This slight reduction in the length of time to deal with preliminary rulings may, however, not last. It was achieved in part at least because of the increase in the number of judges on the ECJ as the result of enlargement, enabling a faster 'throughput' of cases. There is inevitably a time lag between new states joining the EU and cases coming from their courts to the ECJ. When individuals in such countries realize the potential of EU law there is likely to be a further increase in the number of requests coming to the ECJ.

The discussion in the previous section is clearly of relevance in this regard, since the grant of competence over preliminary rulings to the CFI would alleviate the problems of the ECJ. However even if this occurred it would still be possible to reconfigure the relationship between the ECJ/CFI and the national courts under Article 234. The Nice Treaty made no changes to the nature of this relationship, but the matter was addressed by the Courts' paper and the Due Report.

A. Limitation of the National Courts Empowered to Make a Reference

There is clearly a precedent for such reform in Articles 61 to 69, Title IV of the EC Treaty dealing with 'Visas, Asylum, Immigration and Other Policies Related to Free Movement of Persons'. These matters were, prior to the Treaty of Amsterdam, dealt with in Pillar 3, concerning Justice and Home Affairs. The Article 234 procedure was modified in relation to Title IV. Article 68 stipulates that a preliminary ruling can only be sought by a national court or tribunal against whose decisions there is no judicial remedy in national law, as opposed to the normal position under Article 234 whereby any such court or tribunal has discretion to seek a reference.[64]

The Courts' paper and the Due Report nonetheless came down firmly

[60] Art. 222 EC; Art. 20 Statute of the Court of Justice, *supra* n. 39.

[61] Proceedings of the Court of Justice, Annual Report 2004, *supra* n. 22, at 13.

[62] References for preliminary rulings took on average 25 months in 2003 as compared to 24 months in 2002, while appeals took 28 months as compared to 19 months in 2002, Proceedings of the Court of Justice, Annual Report 2003, *supra* n. 20, at 9.

[63] References for preliminary rulings took on average 23 months, direct actions 20 months, and appeals 21 months, Proceedings of the Court of Justice, Annual Report 2004, *supra* n. 22, at 12.

[64] Art. 68(3) EC also provides that the Council, Commission or a Member State can request the ECJ to give a ruling on a question of interpretation arising under Title IV, or acts of the institutions based on this Title. Such rulings do not apply to judgments of national courts etc. which have become *res judicata*.

against this as a method of limiting preliminary rulings.[65] Nor is this surprising. The ability of any national court or tribunal to refer a question to the ECJ has been central to the development of Community law in both practical and conceptual terms.[66]

In practical terms, it has been common for cases raising important points of EC law to be referred by lower level national courts. To limit the ability to refer to a court of last resort would result in cases being fought to the apex of national judicial systems merely to seek a referral to the ECJ. To reduce the burden on the ECJ by increasing that of the national courts is undesirable. While this might lead to a shorter time for the giving of preliminary rulings, this would be scant comfort to litigants for whom the overall length of proceedings would increase, since they would have to fight their case to the top national court, and bear the cost of doing so, which many might find impossible. Furthermore, the 'uniform application of Community law frequently depends on the answer to a question of interpretation raised before a national court not having to await the outcome of appeal proceedings but being given by the Court of Justice at the outset, so that the case law can become established at an early stage in the Member States of the Union'.[67]

In conceptual terms, the ability of any national court or tribunal to refer has been important in emphasizing the penetration of EC law throughout the national legal system. It is of course true that even if references were limited to courts of last resort, lower courts would still have the ability to apply existing precedent of the Community courts. The fact that any national court or tribunal can refer serves, however, to emphasize that individuals can rely on their directly effective Community rights at any point in the national legal system. If the lower level national court is unsure about the interpretation of a point of EC law it can make a reference on that issue without the need for approval from any higher national court. It should moreover not be forgotten that preserving the ability of any national court to refer acts as an important safeguard against the possibility that the court of final resort might be 'conservative or recalcitrant' and hence reluctant to refer even where this is warranted.

B. The Introduction of a Filtering Mechanism

Another way to reduce the volume of preliminary rulings would be to introduce a filtering mechanism based on the novelty, complexity, or importance of the question raised.

[65] The Future of the Judicial System, *supra* n. 1, at 23–24; Report by the Working Party, *supra* n. 2, at 12–13.

[66] *Cf.* Rasmussen, *supra* n. 3, 1104–1107.

[67] The Future of the Judicial System, *supra* n. 1, at 24.

The Courts' paper pointed to two advantages of such a filtering mechanism. From the national perspective 'such a filtering system would prompt national courts and tribunals to exercise selectivity in choosing which questions to refer, and would thus encourage them to exercise yet more fully their functions as Community courts of general jurisdiction'.[68] From the EC's perspective 'the existence of a filtering mechanism would enable the Court of Justice to concentrate wholly upon questions which are fundamental from the point of view of the uniformity and development of Community law'.[69]

The Due Report advocated constraints of this kind. National courts should, it said, be encouraged to be bolder in applying Community law themselves.[70] The Report recommended amendment to Article 234 to make it clear that, subject to the power to refer, national courts should be regarded as having general jurisdiction over matters of EC law. It suggested that lower national courts should consider both the importance of the question in terms of Community law, and whether there was reasonable doubt about the answer, before referring. National courts of final resort should moreover only be obliged to refer on questions which are 'sufficiently important for Community law', and where there is still 'reasonable doubt' after examination by lower courts. The Report was, however, equivocal as to whether such factors should merely be taken into account by national courts in deciding when to refer, or whether they should operate as a substantive bar on the cases which could be referred, the application of this bar being decided by the ECJ. The Report appeared to incline towards the former,[71] but it is doubtful whether this position is sustainable. If Article 234 were reformulated as suggested in the Due Report[72] then the 'importance issue' and the 'reasonable doubt issue' would be factors to be taken into account by a national court in deciding whether to refer. The interpretation of these factors would, however, be a matter of Community law, to be decided on ultimately by the ECJ.[73]

Such a filtering mechanism would necessarily alter the relationship between national courts and the ECJ. The ECJ has traditionally answered the questions referred to it. It is true that the ECJ has, through the *Foglia* ruling, and the cases decided thereafter, made it clear that it will not be forced to accept any reference from national courts. This, however, only provides the foundation for declining to hear a case where it is hypothetical, where the

[68] Ibid. at 24. [69] Ibid. at 25.

[70] Report by the Working Party, *supra* n. 2, at 14–15.

[71] This reading is reinforced by the fact that the Report at a later stage came out explicitly against giving the ECJ the power to select those questions which it considered were sufficiently important for Community law, *ibid.* at 21.

[72] Ibid. at 53–54.

[73] This does seem to be recognized, since the Report stated it would be for the ECJ to determine the precise scope which should be given to the 'importance' or 'significance' issue, *ibid.* at 15.

facts are insufficiently clear, or where the question of law does not arise on the facts of the case. Under the filtering mechanism being considered here questions which were clear, well-framed, of current relevance, and backed-up by adequate factual findings could be rejected on the ground that the question posed was not sufficiently important to warrant the time of the ECJ. In the Courts' paper there was concern that 'national courts and tribunals might well refrain from referring questions to the Court of Justice, in order to avoid the risk of their references being rejected for lack of interest'[74] and that this could jeopardize the machinery for ensuring that Community law should be interpreted uniformly throughout the Member States.

The application of the filtering mechanism within the context of a referral, as opposed to an appellate, system would also be problematic. It is true that filters are common in appellate legal systems such as that in the USA: the Supreme Court will decide which cases it is willing to hear, and uses this power to control the size and content of its docket. It is, however, mistaken to believe that this can be directly copied in the EC. The US is an appellate system, and the EC is a referral system. In the USA if the Supreme Court declines to hear a case there will be a decision on the point of law and its application to the facts given by a lower court.[75] The situation in the EC is markedly different. The national court has not decided the case. It has referred a question for resolution by the ECJ. If the ECJ declines to answer the question because it is not sufficiently important or novel then there is no decision by a Community court on the question.

There would then be two options open to the national court.[76] It could attempt to decide the matter of EC law for itself. If this were regarded as acceptable it would mean that the role of national courts as Community courts of general jurisdiction would have been expanded. We would be accepting that national courts could apply EC law in three situations: where there is a Community law precedent, where the matter is *acte clair*, or where the ECJ declined to take the case. The national court could alternatively decline to decide the EC point one way or the other. The effect on the substantive outcome of the case would be that the party who sought to rely on the point of EC law would be unable to do so, and the case would be decided on the assumption that this point was unproven.

It would be incumbent on the ECJ to give guidance to the national courts

[74] Ibid. at 25.

[75] This will commonly be given by a lower tier federal court, either a federal court of appeals or a federal district court, or by a state supreme court.

[76] The national court should of course apply existing Community law precedent where that exists, and decide the matter for itself if the question can be regarded as *acte clair* within the confines of that doctrine. The premise behind the filtering idea is, however, that the ECJ may decline to take a reference where there is no existing precedent, and where the matter is not *acte clair*.

as between these two options. The former risks undermining the uniformity of application of EC law. The latter has the de facto consequence that EC law is ignored in such instances. The former is therefore to be preferred. It is better that EC law be applied, albeit with the possibility that the national courts might err or differ, than that it should be ignored. The lack of uniformity would moreover be less significant, because the filtering mechanism is designed, as the Courts' paper makes clear, 'to weed out at a preliminary stage cases of lesser importance from the point of view of the uniformity and development of Community law'.[77] If differences of view between national courts on a matter which the ECJ had initially declined to hear were problematic, then a reference in a later case could always be possible. The ECJ would be inclined to accept such a reference.[78]

C. The National Court Proposes an Answer to the Question

A further suggestion for easing the ECJ's caseload would be for the national court to include in its reference a proposed reply to the question referred. The advantages of such a system are said in the Courts' paper to be that it would 'lessen the adverse effect of the filtering mechanism on the co-operation between the national court and the Court of Justice, while the proposed reply could at the same time serve as the basis for deciding which questions need to be answered by the Court of Justice and which can be answered in the terms indicated'.[79] A similar proposal was advanced in the Due Report, which stated that national courts should be encouraged, though not obliged, to include in the preliminary questions reasoned grounds for the answers that the national court considered to be most appropriate. Where the ECJ concurred with the national court it could reply, specifying its reasoning by reference to the reasons given by the national court.[80]

Neither the Courts' paper, nor the Due Report, gives further consideration to this option. Most national courts and tribunals are not specialists in EC law. It is one thing for the national court or tribunal to identify a question which is necessary for the resolution of the case. It is another thing for it to be able to provide an answer to that question. The latter will at the very least require an expenditure of time and resources at the national level by courts and tribunals, some of which may be ill-equipped for the task demanded of them. It is true that higher level national courts might be able to furnish an answer to the question posed. It should nonetheless be recognized that the proposal would transform the task faced by such courts.

[77] The Future of the Judicial System, *supra* n. 1, at 24.
[78] Report by the Working Party, *supra* n. 2, at 16.
[79] The Future of the Judicial System, *supra* n. 1, at 25–26.
[80] Report by the Working Party, *supra* n. 2, at 18.

It is moreover unclear how far this would alleviate the work load of the ECJ. Even if national courts were required to provide an answer to the question, the ECJ would still have to give the matter some detailed consideration. This would be necessary in order to decide whether the question really could be answered in the terms indicated by the national court, or whether it needed to be considered afresh by the ECJ.

The status of the resulting ECJ decision is a further matter that would have to be thought through if a proposal of this kind were to be carried forward. The existing preliminary reference mechanism allows argumentation by, for example, other privileged parties before the ECJ, and they frequently make use of this power. If a national court proposes an answer to the question posed and if this is used to expedite the resolution of the case by curtailing the opportunity for input by other parties before the ECJ then this would raise difficult issues concerning the status of such decisions as compared with those where the standard preliminary reference procedures apply.

A *via media* would be that national courts should not be required to provide a possible answer to the question posed, but they should have the power to do so if they so wish, thereby building on the idea of discourse that is central to the preliminary ruling procedure.[81] This possibility is in fact already included in the information provided for national courts concerning the preliminary reference mechanism, which states that the referring court may, if it considers itself to be in a position to do so, briefly state its view on the answer to be given to the questions referred for a preliminary ruling.[82]

D. The National Court Gives Judgment

A more radical option was considered in the Courts' paper, which would have the effect of transforming the present system from one which is reference-based, to one which is more appellate in nature.[83]

A more radical variant of the system would be to alter the preliminary ruling procedure so that national courts which are not bound to refer questions to the Court of Justice would be required, before making any reference, first to give judgment in cases raising questions concerning the interpretation of Community law. It would then be open to any party to the proceedings to request the national court to forward its judgment to the Court of Justice and to make a reference for a ruling on those points of Community law in respect of which that party contests the validity of the judgment given. This would give the Court of Justice the opportunity of assessing, at the filtering stage, whether it needed to give its own ruling on the interpretation of Community law arrived at in the contested judgment.

Such a procedure, resembling an appeal in cassation, would facilitate the task of

[81] Weiler, *supra* n. 3, at 226. [82] Information Note, *supra* n. 29, at para. 23.
[83] The Future of the Judicial System, *supra* n. 1, at 26.

the Court of Justice. It would enable the Court to give its ruling on the reference in full knowledge of the national context, both factual and legal, in which the points of Community law raised in the case in question fall to be interpreted.

This proposal is interesting and has far-reaching implications. The Due Report was, however, strongly opposed to the change, stating that it 'would debase the entire system of cooperation established by the Treaties between national courts and the Court of Justice'.[84]

It is nonetheless worth dwelling on the pros and cons of such a change. The argument in favour is that an appellate system is more characteristic of a developed federal or confederal legal system than is a reference system. In an appellate regime the court gives a decision on the case that is binding on the parties, subject to appeal, which lies in the hands of the litigants, although it may be necessary to secure the leave of the court to undertake the appeal. In a reference system as presently conceived the national court gives no decision on the case or the question of EC law raised therein prior to making the reference to the ECJ. A question is referred to the ECJ and the final decision in the case will only be given by the national court once the answer to that question is forthcoming from the ECJ. The decision whether to refer will lie with the national court. The proposal under consideration would in effect change the regime from a reference system to an appellate one. It could be argued that the EC is ready for such a change. National courts have become more familiar with EC law over the years and it may be time to move towards an appellate regime in which the national court gives judgment on the case, subject to appeal to the ECJ or CFI.

There are also a number of difficulties attendant upon this change. The proposal would require Treaty amendment,[85] although this is not in itself an objection. To require national courts or tribunals to decide the point of EC law in issue would be to impose a burden that many lower tier courts or tribunals would find difficult to discharge. It would be unlikely to limit the caseload of the ECJ, since there would, as acknowledged in the Courts' paper,[86] always be an incentive on the losing party before the national court to seek a reference to the ECJ, if only to defer enforcement of the judgment. It would also seem to involve overruling *Foto-Frost*.[87] Many requests for preliminary rulings seek to challenge the validity of Community norms. It

[84] Report by the Working Party, *supra* n. 2, at 13.

[85] Art. 234 EC is framed in terms of a national court requesting a ruling from the ECJ where the national court considers that a decision on the question is necessary to enable it to give judgment. Under the proposal set out above this criterion would, by definition, not be met. The national court would already have given its judgment, including on the points of EC law. Reference to the ECJ would happen thereafter at the behest of the parties. The very language of preliminary ruling would be inappropriate under this new regime.

[86] The Future of the Judicial System, *supra* n. 1, at 26.

[87] Case 314/85, *supra* n. 13.

would seem to follow from this proposal that the national court could give judgment that the Community norm was invalid, which could then be contested before the ECJ. There is moreover a crucial ambiguity in the proposal in the Courts' paper. The extract quoted above is framed in terms of a party to the proceedings 'requesting' the national court to refer its judgment to the ECJ, in order that the latter can rule on those points of Community law when the correctness of the national court's judgment is contested. Later the Courts' paper talks in terms of the parties to an action being able to 'require' the national court to make a reference.[88] This latter formulation appears to capture the essence of this proposal. The language of a 'reference' would no longer be suitable in such a regime. The transformation of Article 234 entailed by this proposal was acknowledged in the Courts' paper.[89]

> [S]uch a procedure would involve a fundamental change in the way in which the preliminary ruling system currently operates. Judicial co-operation between the national courts and the Court of Justice would be transformed into a hierarchical system, in which it would be for the parties to an action to decide whether to require the national court to make a reference to the Court of Justice, and in which the national court would be bound, depending on the circumstances, to revise its earlier judgment so as to bring it into line with a ruling by the Court of Justice. From the point of view of national procedural law this aspect of the system would doubtless raise problems which could not easily be resolved.

E. The Creation of Decentralized Judicial Bodies

Another option for easing the ECJ's burden would be to create in each Member State a judicial body responsible for dealing with preliminary rulings from courts within their territorial jurisdiction. The creation of some form of regional courts to supplement the existing judicial architecture of the Community has been advocated in the past.[90] The Courts' paper left open the issue as to whether they should have the status of a Community or a national court.[91] The discussion in the Due Report was, however, premised on the assumption that they would be national courts.[92] This regime of decentralized courts was said to have the benefit of alleviating translation costs, since it was assumed that the parties to the case would be from that country. A decentralized regime would also bring legal redress physically closer to citizens. The Courts' paper and the Due Report were, however,

[88] The Future of the Judicial System, *supra* n. 1, at 26.
[89] Ibid. at 26.
[90] Jacque and Weiler, 'On the Road to European Union—A New Judicial Architecture: An Agenda for the Intergovernmental Conference' (1990) 27 *CMLRev* 185.
[91] The Future of the Judicial System, *supra* n. 1, at 28.
[92] Report by the Working Party, *supra* n. 2, at 20–21.

concerned that decentralized courts would jeopardize the uniformity of Community law.[93]

> Any reorganisation of the preliminary ruling procedure on a national or regional basis, regardless of whether jurisdiction is conferred on national or Community courts, involves a serious risk of shattering the unity of Community law, which constitutes one of the cornerstones of the Union and which will become still more vital and vulnerable as a result of the enlargement of the Union. Jurisdiction to determine the final and binding interpretation of a Community rule, as well as the validity of that rule, should therefore be vested in a single court covering the whole of the Union.

The Due Report was against the creation of such bodies largely for this reason.[94] The CFI had, in earlier reports, been strongly opposed to the establishment of decentralized courts, arguing that such a development would be of no relevance or interest to the Community and would be costly.[95]

The Courts' paper, however, gave greater consideration to this institutional development. It suggested that there should be the possibility of a case going to the ECJ from one of the decentralized judicial bodies in order to meet the concern set out above. The proposal appeared to involve a mix of reference and appeal. Thus, the decentralized judicial body should have the power to refer a matter to the ECJ where the legal issue was of more general relevance for the unity or development of Community law. There should also be provision for 'the possibility of appealing to the Court of Justice "on a point of general legal interest", in accordance with detailed procedures to be laid down, against preliminary rulings given by those bodies'.[96] Any conclusion as to the desirability or not of such decentralized bodies is dependent upon a number of issues which must be discussed separately.

It is important to decide whether such bodies would be part of the national judiciary or whether they would be Community courts operating at a national or regional level. This issue was left open in the Courts' paper. It is surely better that they should be Community courts. The principal argument for their being regarded as national courts is that the financial cost might then fall on the Member States rather than the EC. This consideration must be outweighed by other factors. Such courts should be regarded as Community courts since this best fits with the idea of building a developed

[93] The Future of the Judicial System, *supra* n. 1, at 28; Report by the Working Party, *supra* n. 2, at 21. See also, The Role and Future of the European Court of Justice, A Report of the EC Advisory Board of the British Institute of International and Comparative Law, chaired by the Rt. Hon. The Lord Slynn of Hadley (1996), at 101–104.

[94] Report by the Working Party, *supra* n. 2, at 21–22.

[95] Report of the Court of Justice on Certain Aspects of the Application of the Treaty on European Union—Contribution of the Court of First Instance for the Purposes of the 1996 Intergovernmental Conference, (May 1995).

[96] The Future of the Judicial System, *supra* n. 1, at 28–29.

Community judicial system below the ECJ, of the kind which exists within other countries such as the USA. It would be detrimental to begin this process of building a Community judicial hierarchy by placing these new courts within the national legal system, and this is so notwithstanding the fact that the national courts themselves are, as we have seen, Community courts in their own right in certain respects.

Closely allied to this matter is the issue of whether the decentralized bodies should operate on a national or regional level. The Courts' paper was ambiguous in this respect. The primary impression was that such courts would operate within each Member State,[97] but there were also references to reorganization on a national or regional basis. A regional form of organization would be preferable. In practical terms, it would almost certainly be more efficient, since a number of Member States would be too small to warrant such a court of their own.[98] In normative terms, a regional regime would be preferable since it would obviate the danger that differences of view between such courts would be cast as the 'German v French view', or the 'UK v Italian' etc. This danger would be exacerbated if such courts were to be regarded as national rather than Community courts. This hazard would be much reduced if the courts were organized regionally rather than nationally.[99]

A further issue would be the relationship between such bodies and the CFI. This is a complex issue, since the nature of the relationship would depend on what other changes to the Community judicial architecture were put in place. Thus if the CFI became a general court of first instance, with jurisdiction over direct actions under Article 230, and indirect actions under Article 234, it would be difficult to find a place for regional or decentralized courts, since the CFI would be taking indirect actions as well as direct actions. It would be possible in theory to think of decentralized judicial bodies being vested with jurisdiction over direct and indirect actions and hence replacing the CFI. It must, however, be recognized that there is little prospect of this occurring in practical terms. The CFI is well-established and would fight vigorously for its survival. It would also be possible in theory to conceive of a Community judicial architecture with both the CFI and

[97] This impression is reinforced by the desire to save on translation costs, the assumption being that if the courts were organized on a national basis then the proceedings could be in the national language.

[98] Translation costs would not be that high since many cases would still arise between litigants who were from the same Member State. It should nonetheless be recognized that there would still be translation costs irrespective of whether such courts were organized on a regional or national basis since the litigants would not always be from the same country.

[99] In the USA, where a regional organization exists, there may be differences of view between the different circuits. These are, however, cast in just such terms: the 5th Circuit may, for example, be regarded as less liberal than the 2nd Circuit on a certain issue.

decentralized judicial bodies. The CFI might, for example, become the general first instance court for all direct actions, while decentralized judicial bodies would hear preliminary rulings, with the prospect of further recourse to the ECJ. There are, however, problems with this approach. Thus if indirect actions go to the decentralized bodies then they will often be dealing with cases concerned with the validity of Community norms brought by non-privileged parties who are unable to bring a direct action because of the restrictive standing rules. It is desirable that the CFI should hear such cases, more particularly if it is regarded as the general first instance court for the Community in the context of direct actions.

8. THE CONSTITUTIONAL TREATY

The Constitutional Treaty (CT) made significant changes in a number of areas. Unfortunately this did not include the Community judicial architecture. It is all the more regrettable that the Convention on the Future of Europe gave scant consideration to the role of the Community courts. The Convention would have been the obvious locus for a thorough debate on the Community judicial system of a kind lacking hitherto. This is so independently of the substantive conclusions that might have been reached from such a discourse. The debate never happened, there was no discourse, and the CT simply took over, with minor modifications, the regime embodied in the Nice Treaty.

The reason for this lies in the more general modus operandi of the Convention.[100] Working groups were established to consider many of the main issues prior to discussion in the plenary sessions. It was felt, however, that institutional reform could only be dealt with in the plenary, because particular issues such as the role of the European Council, and the composition of the Commission, were important and controversial. These deliberations did not begin until January 2003. They were divisive with strongly held divergent views being proffered. It also became apparent that the Convention was subject to a tight deadline for the production of a Draft Constitutional Treaty and that the Intergovernmental Conference (IGC) was unwilling to extend this. The net effect was that Spring 2003 was principally taken up with fights about the main institutional issues, plus the drafting of provisions on topics that had been dealt with by working groups and on which consensus had been reached. There had, at this point, been no discussion about the Community courts at all, and the Praesidium hurriedly convened a

[100] Craig, 'Constitutional Reform and Process in the EU: Nice, Laeken, the Convention and the IGC' (2004) 10 *EPL* 653.

'Discussion Circle' to consider judicial matters.[101] The group was, however, subject to severe time constraints. There was no general overview of the Community judicial architecture, and no discussion as to how this might need to be modified in the light of the more general precepts of the Constitutional Treaty. The group's limited time was spent rather on a number of specific issues, such as reform of the standing requirements for direct actions. These are important. This can be accepted. It does not alter the fact that the Convention was a major missed opportunity. It should have been the locus for a wide-ranging discussion about the Community judicial system, including the allocation of power between the ECJ and CFI, and the relationship between Community courts and national courts. These are the key issues that affect the Community judicial architecture, and that architecture is central to the reform project that the CT embodies. My own views as to the desirable outcome of such discussion have been set out above. Others may of course differ. The Convention would have been the natural forum for such a discourse. It did not happen.

The provisions of the CT[102] replicated, with minor modifications, the schema from the Nice Treaty. Article I–29(1) provided, somewhat confusingly,[103] that the Court of Justice shall *include* the ECJ, the General Court, which was the new name for the CFI, and specialized courts, the new name for judicial panels. Article I–29(3) stipulated in essence that the Court of Justice, remembering that this included the ECJ, General Court, and specialized courts, should rule on actions provided for in the Constitution. The detailed division of jurisdiction between the Community courts was dealt with by Part III of the Constitutional Treaty. This preserved the Nice Treaty

[101] Discussion Circle on the Court of Justice, CONV 543/03, Brussels 7 February 2003.

[102] Treaty Establishing a Constitution for Europe, OJ 2004 C310/1. The Constitutional Treaty was accepted by the Member States in the IGC in June 2004, Council of the European Union, Brussels European Council, Presidency Conclusions 10679/04, ADD 1, CONCL 2, Brussels 18 June 2004. The text agreed to by the European Council was based on the version produced by the Convention on the Future of Europe as modified by the group of legal experts and as modified by the IGC itself. The version modified by the legal experts is contained in Conference of the Representatives of the Governments of the Member States, 2003 IGC—Draft Treaty Establishing a Constitution for Europe (following editorial and legal adjustments by the Working Party of IGC Legal Experts), CIG 50/03, Brussels 25 November 2003. The modifications agreed to by the IGC are to be found in: Conference of the Representatives of the Governments of the Member States, IGC 2003—Meeting of Heads of State or Government, Brussels, 17–18 June 2004 CIG 85/04, PRESID 27, Brussels 18 June 2004, and in Conference of the Representatives of the Governments of the Member States, IGC 2003—Meeting of Heads of State or Government, Brussels, 17–18 June 2004, CIG 81/04, PRESID 23, Brussels 16 June 2004.

[103] See Art. III–369 CT, which by using the word Court of Justice rather than ECJ gave the impression that the General Court could hear all preliminary rulings given the definition of Court of Justice in Art. I–29. This of course could not be so given the wording of Art. III–358(3).

strategy. Articles III–358 and III–359 repeated the previous Articles 225 and 225a EC, and Article III–369 left Article 234 EC largely unchanged.

9. CONCLUSION

It is very doubtful whether the CT will ever be revived in the light of the negative votes in the French and Dutch referenda. It is also doubtful whether the existing judicial architecture can be preserved. The strains posed by enlargement are likely to exacerbate the ECJ's existing case law burdens. It remains moreover to be seen whether having a judge from each Member State on the ECJ will lead to problems of it becoming a deliberative assembly rather than a court.[104]

The provisions of the Nice Treaty certainly allow for reform in the 'right direction'. Thus significant use could be made of the power to delegate preliminary rulings in certain areas to the CFI. Further judicial panels could be created to deal with certain topics, thereby relieving some of the burden on the CFI.

It should nonetheless be recognized that the current provisions place constraints on the scope of any such reform. More imaginative changes in the relationship between the Community courts and national courts would require amendment to Article 234. It should also be recognized that the existing provisions fail to provide a clear, principled structure for the Community judicial system overall. This could be done, as suggested above, with the CFI being acknowledged as the general court of first instance for all actions, direct or indirect, irrespective of the nature of the claimant, with recourse to the ECJ in the manner set out earlier. It would be regrettable if this principled solution, or something akin thereto, were only to be introduced because of an impending crisis in the workings of the Community judiciary.

[104] Report of the Court of Justice on Certain Aspects of the Application of the Treaty on European Union—Contribution of the Court of First Instance for the Purposes of the 1996 Intergovernmental Conference (May 1995), at point 16.

10

Access

1. INTRODUCTION

The previous chapters were concerned with the foundations of judicial review and judicial architecture. The focus now turns to principles of administrative law that are of direct relevance for the way in which policy is delivered by the European Union (EU).

This chapter is concerned with access. It is the natural starting point for consideration of administrative law doctrine. Any system of administrative law will have access points or gateways, which determine who can get into the system. There are two crucial access points in any legal regime. There will be procedural rules determining who is entitled to be heard or intervene before the initial decision is made, or who is entitled to be consulted before a legislative-type norm is enacted. There will also be rules of standing that determine who should be able to complain to the court that the initial decision-maker overstepped its powers. The judicial and legislative stance on these matters is crucial, and it is clear that the Community courts make real connections concerning the ambit of these two access points, as do courts in other legal systems.[1] A legal system may have very sophisticated tools for substantive judicial review, but if the access points or gateways are drawn too narrowly the opportunity for an individual to utilize such tools will perforce be limited.

The discussion will begin with the jurisprudence of the European Court of Justice (ECJ) and Court of First Instance (CFI) concerning the right to take part in the initial determination, and it will be seen that the courts have distinguished sharply between the right to be heard in relation to individualized decisions and consultation and participation in relation to norms of a legislative nature. This will be followed by consideration of political initiatives to foster consultation in the Community legislative process. The remainder of the chapter will be concerned with the other main access point, standing to seek judicial review. There will be a critical evaluation of the case law, discussion of the possible impact of the Charter of Rights, and consideration of the reform that would have been made by the Constitutional Treaty (CT).

[1] Stewart, 'The Reformation of American Administrative Law' (1975) 88 *Harv LR* 1667.

2. ACCESS, THE INITIAL DETERMINATION, AND THE COURTS

The access point or gateway that is most immediately relevant concerns the ability to be heard or participate in the making of the initial determination by the Community authorities. The Community courts have distinguished sharply in their approach to access with regard to individualized determinations and norms of a legislative nature.

A. Access, Individual Decisions, and the Right to be Heard

The right to be heard before an individual measure is taken that would affect the person adversely is now included within the Charter of Fundamental Rights.[2] This reflects the pre-existing legal position. The Community courts have been activist in protecting access in relation to individual decisions, and imposed a right to be heard as a general rule of Community law, irrespective of whether this requirement was found in the relevant Treaty article, regulation, directive, or decision.[3]

In *Transocean Marine Paint*[4] the ECJ held that there was a general rule that a person whose interests were perceptibly affected by a decision taken by a public authority must be given the opportunity to make his point of view known. The rules about hearings in the competition regulations were therefore statutory manifestations of this more general principle. The principle was reiterated in *Hoffmann-La Roche*, albeit with the more restrictive condition that the right to be heard was a fundamental principle of Community law in cases where sanctions might be imposed.[5] The general trend of the case law has, however, been to require a hearing even where no sanction is imposed, provided that there is some adverse impact, or some

[2] Charter of Fundamental Rights of the European Union, Art. 41(2), OJ 2000 C364/1.

[3] Curtin, 'Constitutionalism in the European Community: The Right to Fair Procedures in Administrative Law', in J. O'Reilly (ed.), *Human Rights and Constitutional Law, essays in Honour of Brian Walsh* (1992), at 293; Schwarze, 'Developing Principles of European Administrative Law' [1993] *PL* 229; Nolte, 'General Principles of German and European Administrative Law—A Comparison in Historical Perspective' (1994) 57 *MLR* 191; Schwarze, 'Towards a Common European Public Law' (1995) 1 *EPL* 227; Lenaerts and Vanhamme, 'Procedural Rights of Private Parties in the Community Administrative Process' (1997) 34 *CMLRev* 531; H. Nehl, *Principles of Administrative Procedure in EC Law* (1999), at 70–99.

[4] Case 17/74, *Transocean Marine Paint v Commission* [1974] ECR 1063, at para. 15.

[5] Case 85/76, *Hoffmann-La Roche v Commission* [1979] ECR 461, at para. 9; Case C-48/96 P, *Windpark Groothusen GmbH & Co Betriebs KG v Commission* [1998] ECR I-2873.

significant affect on the applicant's interests.[6] The right to be heard was regarded as part of the fundamental rights jurisprudence and extended to anti-dumping proceedings in *Al-Jubail*.[7] The ECJ held that it must be observed not only where it might lead to penalties, but also where the investigative proceedings prior to the adoption of the duty might directly and adversely affect the undertakings and entail adverse consequences for them. It held further that the provisions concerning hearings contained in the relevant regulation on dumping did not provide all the procedural guarantees that existed in national legal systems and therefore could be complemented by recourse to the fundamental right itself.[8] These themes were taken up in *Air Inter*,[9] where the CFI stated that the fundamental principle of the rights of the defence could not be excluded or restricted by any legislative provision. Respect for the principle must therefore be ensured both where there was no specific legislation and where legislation did exist, but did not take account of the principle. It is also significant that observance of the right to be heard can be raised by the Court of its own motion.[10]

The precise application of the right to be heard can be difficult where the administration of the particular scheme is divided or shared between the Community and the Member States, as in the context of customs or the Structural Funds. In such instances it can be problematic locating the right to be heard at national or Community level or an admixture of the two. Notwithstanding this the ECJ concluded in *Technische Universitat Munchen* that the right to be heard in such an administrative procedure in the customs context required that the person concerned should be able during the procedure before the Commission to put his case and make his views known.[11] A similar approach was taken in *Lisrestal*[12] in the context of the European Social Fund. The administration of such Funds is, as we have

[6] Case T-450/93, *Lisrestal v Commission* [1994] ECR II-1177; Case C-32/95 P, *Commission v Lisrestal* [1996] ECR I-5373; Case T-50/96, *Primex Produkte Import-Export GmbH & Co. KG v Commission* [1998] ECR II-3773, at para. 59; Case C-462/98 P, *MedioCurso-Etabelecimento de Ensino Particular Ld v Commission* [2000] ECR I-7183, at para. 36; Case C-395/00, *Distillerie Fratelli Cipriani SpA v Ministero delle Finanze* [2002] ECR I-11877, at para. 51; Case T-102/00, *Vlaams Fonds voor de Sociale Integratie van Personen met een Handicap v Commission* [2003] ECR II-2433, at para. 59.

[7] Case C-49/88, *Al-Jubail Fertilizer v Council* [1991] ECR I-3187, at para. 15. See also, Cases T-33–34/98, *Petrotub and Republica SA v Council* [1999] ECR II-3837; Case C-458/98 P, *Industrie des Poudres Sphériques v Council and Commission* [2000] ECR I-8147, at para. 99.

[8] Ibid. at para. 16.

[9] Case T-260/94, *Air Inter SA v Commission* [1997] ECR II-997, at para. 60.

[10] Case C-291/89, *Interhotel v Commission* [1991] ECR I-2257, at para. 14; Case C-367/95 P, *Commission v Sytraval and Brink's France* [1998] ECR I-1719, at para. 67.

[11] Case C-269/90, *Hauptzollamt München-Mitte v Technische Universität München* [1991] ECR I-5469, at para. 25; Case T-50/96, *Primex Produkte, supra* n. 6. *Cf* Case T-346/94, *France-Aviation v Commission* [1995] ECR II-2843.

[12] Case T-450/93, *Lisrestal*, affirmed in Case C-32/95 P, *supra* n. 6.

seen,[13] shared. The Commission issued a decision to the Portuguese ministry requiring the repayment of funding to Lisrestal on the grounds that it had mismanaged the funds. The relevant regulation gave no opportunity for the firm to comment before the decision was made, although this was given to the national ministry. The CFI held that the right to be heard as an aspect of the right of defence was applicable in all proceedings initiated against a person liable to culminate in a measure adverse to him. It was a fundamental principle of Community law that applied even in the absence of specific rules concerning the proceedings in question.[14] The ECJ, confirming the CFI's decision, stated that the right to be heard would apply because the measure would significantly affect the applicant's interests, in this instance the loss of funding.[15] The CFI in *Air Inter* stated that it must be determined whether the right to be heard had been observed either directly through the applicant's dealings with the Commission, or indirectly through the national authorities, or through a combination of the two.[16] Moreover in *Primex Produkte*[17] the CFI emphasized that in the context of customs procedures administered in part at national level and in part at Community level it was especially important to safeguard the right to be heard, given that the Commission had discretion whether to accept the initial evaluation of the matter made by the national authorities.

B. Access, Legislative Norms, Consultation, and Participation

The stance of the Community courts is markedly different when it comes to access to the making of Community norms of a more legislative nature, or where the applicant is not the party directly affected by the relevant measure. The applicant's claim in such instances will normally be couched in terms of a right to participate, be consulted, or intervene in the making of the provision. The Community courts have consistently resisted such claims. They have denied consultation rights unless they are expressly provided by the relevant Treaty article, or by a regulation, directive, or decision governing the area in question.

The *Atlanta* case is the leading authority.[18] The applicant sought compensation for damage caused by a Community regulation concerning the

[13] See above, Chap. 3.

[14] Case T-450/93, *Lisrestal*, *supra* n. 6, at para. 42. See also, Cases C-48 and 60/90, *Netherlands v Commission* [1992] ECR I-565, at para. 44; Case C-135/92, *Fiskano v Commission* [1994] ECR I-2885, at para. 39; Case T-50/96, *Primex Produkte*, *supra* n. 6, at para. 59.

[15] Case C-32/95 P, *supra* n. 6, at para. 33; Case T-102/00, *Vlaams Fonds voor de Sociale Integratie*, *supra* n. 6, at para. 60.

[16] Case T-260/94, *Air Inter*, *supra* n. 9, at para. 65.

[17] Case T-50/96, *Primex Produkte*, *supra* n. 6, at para. 60.

[18] Case C-104/97 P, *Atlanta AG v Commission* [1999] ECR I-6983.

bananas market. It argued, *inter alia*, that the CFI had erred in finding that the right to be heard in an administrative procedure affecting a specific person could not be transposed to the process leading to a regulation, more especially because it was irrelevant to the individual concerned whether his legal situation was affected as a result of an administrative or a legislative procedure. The applicant sought to rely on *Al-Jubail* to show that the absence of a Treaty provision requiring consultation in relation to a legislative procedure did not allow a hearing to be dispensed with.[19] The ECJ rejected the argument. It held that the case law according a right to be heard related only to acts of direct and individual concern to the applicant. It could not be extended to the procedure culminating in legislation involving a choice of economic policy and applying to the generality of traders concerned. The only obligations of consultation incumbent on the Community legislature were those laid down by the Treaty article in question.[20] This approach has been reaffirmed by later authority. Thus in *Bactria*[21] the ECJ held that the fact that a regulation dealing with biocidal products provided that a list of existing substances was to be drawn up with the help of information from producers did not mean that the Commission was required to hear producers such as the applicant when adopting the regulation. In *Jégo-Quéré*,[22] discussed in detail below, the ECJ concluded that there was no provision of Community law requiring the Commission when adopting the contested regulation to follow a procedure under which the applicant would be entitled to the right to be heard. The *Atlanta* principle was forcefully applied in *Pfizer*[23] where the CFI held that the right to be heard when decisions were taken against a specific person could not be transposed to a legislative procedure leading to the adoption of a regulation, and that this was so notwithstanding the fact that the applicant was directly and individually concerned by the contested measure. The same approach is evident in the CFI's interpretation of the Agreement on Social Policy. In *UEAPME*[24] the CFI rejected a challenge to the framework Directive on parental leave brought by the applicant association representing small and medium-sized undertakings. In the course of its judgment the CFI held that the applicant did not have a right to participate in the negotiation stage of the Agreement on Social Policy, nor did it have a right to participate in the negotiation of the framework agreement. The mere fact that the applicant contacted the Commission on several occasions asking to participate in the negotiations between other

[19] Ibid. at paras. 31–32. [20] Ibid. at paras. 35–39.

[21] Case C-258/02 P, *Bactria Industriehygiene-Service Verwaltungs GMbH v Commission* [2003] ECR I-15105, at para. 43.

[22] Case C-263/02 P, *Commission v Jégo-Quéré & Cie SA* [2004] ECR I-3425, at para. 47.

[23] Case T-13/99, *Pfizer Animal Health SA v Council* [2002] ECR II-3305, at para. 487; Case T-70/99, *Alpharma Inc v Council* [2002] ECR II-3495, at para. 388.

[24] Case T-135/96, *UEAPME v Council* [1998] ECR II-2335, at paras. 69–80.

representatives of management and labour did not change matters, since it was those representatives and not the Commission which were in charge of the negotiation stage.

The Community courts have been similarly unwilling to draw any legal consequences from the fact of participation in the making of the legislative measure. Thus in *Asocarne*[25] the ECJ held that the fact that a body set up for the defence of a collective interest had taken part in the preparation of a directive in circumstances where the relevant Treaty article accorded no right to participate in the preparation of the measure did not serve to give it any preferential treatment with regard to challenging the measure. The applicant lacked standing and the fact of its participation in the making of the measure made no difference.[26] The same approach is evident in other cases. In *Jégo-Quéré*[27] the fact that the applicant was the only fishing company to make proposals to the Commission when the regulation was being adopted did not make it individually concerned for the purposes of standing to challenge the measure. In *Greenpeace*[28] the CFI, in deciding that the applicants lacked standing, stated that the fact that some applicants had submitted a complaint to the Commission concerning the Community funding of the power station did not give them standing, since the relevant Structural Funds' regulations made no provision for individuals to be associated with the grant or implementation of such decisions. In *Merck* the CFI was similarly unequivocal:[29] the fact that a person participated in the process leading to the adoption of a Community act did not distinguish that person individually in terms of standing to challenge the act, unless the relevant Community legislation laid down specific procedural guarantees for such a person.

C. Legal Access, Principle, and Policy

There are a number of points that might be made concerning the Community courts' jurisprudence on access.

The most obvious is that the *jurisprudence embodies a normative choice.*

25 Case C-10/95 P, *Asociasion Espanola de Empresas de la Carne (Asocarne) v Council* [1995] ECR I-4149, at para. 39.

26 The Community courts have been willing to accord standing where the applicant was given rights to complain in the making of the initial decision, Case 26/76, *Metro-SB-Großmärkte GmbH & Co KG v Commission* [1977] ECR 1875; Case 169/84, *Compagnie Francaise de l'Azote (COFAZ) SA v Commission* [1986] ECR 391; Case T-435/93, *ASPEC v Commission* [1995] ECR II-1281; Case T-380/94, *AIUFFASS v Commission* [1996] ECR II-2169.

27 Case C-263/02 P, *Jégo-Quéré*, *supra* n. 22, at para. 48.

28 Case T-583/93, *Stichting Greenpeace Council (Greenpeace International) v Commission* [1995] ECR II-2205, at para. 56.

29 Case T-60/96, *Merck & Co Inc, NV Organon and Glaxo Wellcome plc v Commission* [1997] ECR II-849, at para. 73.

The right to be heard in relation to individual determinations is regarded as fundamental; it is not dependent on a foundation in a Treaty article, regulation, or directive; Community norms will be read subject to the right; and the courts can raise the right of their own motion. The courts' stance in relation to participation or consultation in relation to norms of a legislative nature is markedly different. Such rights will only exist where there is foundation in a Treaty article, regulation, directive, or decision; the courts will not lightly interpret these norms as giving rise to such rights; and the fact of participation in their making will not increase the applicant's chance of being accorded standing to seek judicial review.

This *distinction is reinforced by the reasoning used to differentiate between individual determinations and those of a legislative nature.* The Community courts have in effect 'reasoned back' from their jurisprudence on standing to seek judicial review to determine whether a norm should be recognized as individualized and hence subject to the fundamental right to be heard in the making of the initial decision. The right to be heard before the decision is made will only be held to be applicable when the decision is of direct and individual concern to the applicant. The difficulty of proving individual concern in relation to standing is well known and will be discussed below. The narrow definition of individual concern therefore reinforces the difficulty of arguing that rights to be heard in the form of consultation or participation should apply in the making of legislative norms, where those norms would not be regarded as being of individual concern to the applicant as judged by the criteria used in relation to standing.

The *normative choice embodied in the jurisprudence can be defended.* The premise underlying the case law is that there is a real distinction between provisions that impact on a person in the form of an individualized determination, and those that impact through rules of a more generalized character. This dichotomy is accepted in many legal systems. It should be noted in this respect that even in the USA the foundation for procedural rights in rule-making is a statute, the Administrative Procedure Act 1946. It is not the Constitution, the courts having held that constitutional due process does not apply to rule-making as opposed to adjudication.[30]

It should however also *be recognized that the distinction is contestable.* It may be entirely fortuitous whether a person is affected through an individualized determination, or through a rule. The individualized determination may in any event have precedential impact and establish a rule or principle for a category of cases that impact on a broad range of people: policy can be developed by ad hoc adjudication as well as through rules. Furthermore, the background principles that serve to justify procedural rights in individual adjudications are equally applicable in the context of rule-making. The twin

[30] *Bi-Metallic Investment Co v State Board of Equalization of Colorado* 239 US 441 (1915).

rationales are instrumental and non-instrumental or dignitarian.[31] The former justifies process rights because they will render it more likely that a correct outcome will be reached on the substance of the case.[32] The latter sees the justification as being a part of what it means to treat a person as a human being, with the corollary that it is right to accord a hearing before taking action that can deleteriously affect an individual.[33] It is perfectly possible to support both, albeit in varying degrees. These rationales are also applicable in the context of rule-making. The argument for participation is based in part on instrumental grounds, the assumption being that the resultant rule will better achieve its end if the considered views of interested parties are admitted; it is based in part on dignitarian grounds, the argument being that it affords a way in which people can take part in the process of governance to which they are subject, thereby enhancing legitimacy.[34] This is of particular importance in the EU given the general concerns about legitimacy.[35] There is, moreover, as Shapiro correctly notes, a connection between transparency and participation: 'full transparency can only be achieved through participation or through dialogue as a form of participation'.[36]

It should also be recognized that *according hearing rights in adjudication does not make up for the absence of participation rights when a norm of a legislative nature is made.* It might be argued by way of response to the preceding discussion that the unwillingness of the Community courts to require participatory rights when norms of a legislative nature are made does not matter since an individual will be accorded a hearing when the relevant regulation is applied in an individual case. This will not withstand examination. Some regulations can take effect without any individualized determination. Thus a regulation may specify fishing nets of a certain mesh. There will be no decision applying the measure to a particular person, unless he violates the stipulated rule. The argument is, however, defective even where the regulation is applied through individual determinations. The fact that a

[31] J. Mashaw, *Due Process in the Administrative State* (Yale University Press, 1985); D. Galligan, *Due Process and Fair Procedures* (Oxford University Press, 1996), at 75–82.

[32] Resnick, 'Due Process and Procedural Justice', in J. Pennock and J. Chapman (eds), *Due Process* (Nomos, 1977), at 217.

[33] H.L.A. Hart, *Concept of Law* (Clarendon, 1961), at 156, 202; J. Rawls, *A Theory of Justice* (Oxford University Press, 1973), at 235; Michelman, 'Formal and Associational Aims in Procedural Due Process', in *Due Process, supra* n. 32, at Chap. 4; Mashaw, *supra* n. 31, at Chaps. 4–7.

[34] C. Pateman, *Participation and Democratic Theory* (Cambridge University Press, 1970); J. Cohen, *Constitution, Democracy and State Power: The Institutions of Justice* (Edward Elgar, 1996).

[35] Craig, 'Democracy and Rulemaking within the EC: An Empirical and Normative Assessment' (1997) 3 *ELJ* 105; de Burca, 'The Quest for Legitimacy in the European Union' (1996) 59 *MLR* 349.

[36] Shapiro, 'The Giving Reasons Requirement' (1992) *U Chic Legal Forum* 179, at 205.

person might get a right to be heard concerning the application of the regulation to his individual case does not make up for the absence of the right to participate when the regulation was initially made. The object of according participation rights is to enable interested parties to have an input into the content of the proposed measure with the instrumental objective that it might be improved and with the non-instrumental objective of allowing those affected to take part in the process of governance to which they are subject. The inability to participate is not made good by affording a hearing when the measure is applied in a particular case. This ensures that a person is heard before the regulation is applied, whatsoever its content might be. It does not function as a surrogate method for influencing the content or merits of the regulation, nor does it address the non-instrumental value of participation. It should moreover be recognized that there will be many instances where the merits of the regulation made in the absence of participation will remain unchallengeable through doctrines of substantive review such as proportionality, equality, and the like, since the courts will be reluctant to interfere with the discretionary policy choice embodied in the regulation. It is input into the content of this discretionary policy choice that interested parties hope to secure through participation in rule-making, subject of course to procedural rules designed to regulate the fairness of this process.

The preceding discussion reveals *that advancement in participation rights is unlikely to come through the Community courts.* This is of course relevant to the discussion in earlier chapters, concerning Comitology, agencies, and the open method of coordination.[37] The Community courts have made it clear that such rights must be found in the Treaty or a provision made pursuant thereto. The parent regulations or directives pursuant to which implementing rules are made by the comitology procedure normally contain no provision for participation by those other than in the comitology committees, nor do the comitology procedures themselves normally provide for wider consultation. There is a similar picture in relation to the Open Method of Coordination (OMC). It is true that there is much talk in the Lisbon process of involving broad sections of society. The Treaty articles and Community legislation that deal with the OMC in specific areas are less prescriptive. Thus in the employment context the Treaty specifies that the European Parliament (EP), the Economic and Social Committee (ECOSOC), the Committee of the Regions, and the Employment Committee should be consulted by the Council when it draws up the employment guidelines on a proposal from the Commission.[38] Consultation of the social partners is felt to be desirable, but the Treaty merely provides that the Employment Committee in fulfilling its mandate shall consult management and labour,[39] and even this provision would probably not suffice under the Court's jurisprudence to give any

[37] See above, Chaps. 4, 5, 6. [38] Art. 128 EC. [39] Art. 130 EC.

particular management or labour organization a right to be consulted. It is of course true that participation and consultation can occur even if it is not backed by a legal right. We shall consider this in detail below. The background of what the law requires or does not require is nonetheless important. It signals to the citizenry what they can and cannot expect from the law if they feel that the consultation in a particular instance was ineffective or non-existent. It signals to the Community institutions that they can provide de facto consultation secure in the knowledge that if this is not legally required in accord with the Courts' jurisprudence it will not afford any legal rights to those taking part.

3. ACCESS, THE INITIAL DETERMINATION, AND THE POLITICAL PROCESS

The interrelationship between what the courts mandate in relation to access and the making of the initial determination, and what the political process provides is interesting and instructive.

A. Rights to be Heard Accorded by Community Legislation

It is clear that so far as individualized determinations are concerned the Community legislature has responded to the Court's strictures concerning the right to be heard, at least in some areas. Thus it is common to find that the principal regulation or directive governing an area will make provision for hearing rights. Having said this it is also not uncommon to find, especially in areas where administration is shared between the Member State and the Community that the relevant legislation lags behind the demands imposed by the Community courts, making no express provision for contact between the individual and the Commission. The political system when it responds in such instances will do so largely through formal legislation enshrining the process right.

B. Rights to Participate or be Consulted Accorded by Community Legislation

We have seen from the preceding discussion that the Community courts have not been willing to impose requirements to participate in the making of norms of a legislative nature. They have held that such rights only exist where they can be founded on a Treaty article or derived from a specific regulation or directive. Regulations or directives have granted such rights in a number of important areas. It should, however, also be recognized that many of the most prominent instances where this has occurred have entailed the imposition of rights to participate in relation to national regulatory bodies, rather than the Commission.

This is exemplified by the regime applicable to telecommunications. Article 6 of the Framework Directive[40] provides, subject to limited exceptions, that where national regulatory authorities intend to take measures in accordance with the Framework Directive or specific Directives which have a significant impact on the market they must give interested parties the opportunity to comment on the draft measure within a reasonable period. The national regulatory authorities must publish their national consultation procedures and establish a single information point through which all current consultations can be accessed. The results of the consultation must be made publicly available, subject to exceptions for confidentiality.

The Directive on Integrated Pollution Prevention and Control[41] stipulated that the public should be given access to information concerning a permit application in order to be able to comment thereon before a decision was reached.[42] It provided further that where a Member State was aware that an installation was likely to have significant effects on the environment of another Member State, or where that other state so requested, the Member State in whose territory the application for a permit was made should forward the information required for a permit to the neighbouring state and this served as the basis for consultation between the two states. The Member States also had the obligation to make this information available to the public in their respective countries and allow them to comment before a final decision was reached.

This Directive was amended and strengthened by a more general Directive concerned with public participation and the environment.[43] In addition to this amendment the Directive makes provision for public participation in a number of areas. Member States have an obligation to ensure that the public is given early and effective opportunities to participate in the preparation and modification or review of plans or programmes in a wide variety of areas concerned with the environment, including water, hazardous waste, packaging and packaging waste, and air quality.[44] The Member State must ensure

[40] Directive of the European Parliament and of the Council 2002/21/EC of 7 March 2002, On a Common Regulatory Framework for Electronic Communications Networks and Services (Framework Directive), OJ 2002 L108/33.

[41] Council Directive 96/61/EC of 24 September, Concerning Integrated Pollution Prevention and Control, OJ 1996 L257/26.

[42] Ibid. Art. 15.

[43] Directive 2003/35/EC of the European Parliament and of the Council of 26 May 2003, Providing for Public Participation in respect of the Drawing Up of Certain Plans and Programmes Relating to the Environment and Amending with regard to Public Participation and Access to Justice Council Directives 85/337/EEC and 96/61/EC, OJ 2003 L156/17, Art. 4.

[44] Ibid. Art. 2(2).

that the public is informed about proposals, their right to participate, and the body to whom comments should be sent.[45] The Directive emphasizes that the public must have this opportunity to comment while all options are open and before decisions on the plans are made; that the resultant decision should take account of the comments received; and that reasons should be given for the decision reached.[46] It is for the Member State to identify the public entitled to participate for these purposes and the detailed arrangements for the participation.

C. Participation, Consultation, Soft Law, and the Commission

Formal law does therefore provide for participation rights in certain areas, especially those where Member States make plans or the like pursuant to Community legislation. The Commission has, however, been reluctant to accord legally enforceable participation rights in relation to its own legislative or policy proposals, and the demise of the CT means that we are never likely to know whether the provisions contained therein on participatory democracy would have made any difference in this respect.[47] The Commission has proceeded mainly through measures that are not legally binding, but which have nonetheless become more effective over time. The story is an interesting one.

The European Council's 1993 Inter-institutional Declaration on Democracy, Transparency, and Subsidiarity[48] laid the foundation for greater access to Community documentation. It also seemed to herald a new approach to participation in the making of Community legislation. It proposed the creation of a notification procedure, in which the Commission would publish a brief summary of the draft measure in the Official Journal. There would then be a deadline by which interested parties could submit their comments. The implications of this reform could have been far-reaching. There is a clear analogy with the United States' Administrative Procedure Act 1946 (APA). The APA established a notice and comment procedure whereby rules have to be published in the Federal Register, and the agency has to allow a period of time for notice and comment. The 1993 Declaration appeared to have borrowed directly from the American experience. The Commission's response to this aspect of the 1993 Declaration was, however, limited. It did not bring forward any general measure for the European Community (EC) akin to the APA, and the discussion of participation rights in its report for the 1996 Intergovernmental Conference (IGC) was exiguous to say the least.[49] The

[45] Ibid. Art. 2(2)(a). [46] Ibid. Arts. 2(2)(b)–(d).

[47] Treaty Establishing a Constitution for Europe, OJ 2004 C310/1, Art. I-47.

[48] It was adopted by the Commission, Council, and EP on the margins of the 1993 Brussels European Council, M. Westlake, *The Commission and the Parliament, Partners and Rivals in the European Policy-Making Process* (Butterworths, 1994), at 159–161.

[49] Craig, *supra* n. 35.

Commission was clearly not minded to go down the road of legally binding participation or consultation rights.

The Commission has, however, broadened consultation de facto. It made increasing use of Green and White Papers when important areas of EC policy were being developed, inviting comments on an ad hoc basis to particular legislative initiatives. The Commission generalized this approach in its 2002 Communication on Consultation.[50] The Communication acknowledged the instrumental and non-instrumental rationales for consultation, stating that 'good consultation serves a dual purpose by helping to improve the quality of the policy outcome and at the same time enhancing the involvement of interested parties and the public at large'.[51] It set out a number of general principles that should inform the consultation process: participation, openness and accountability, effectiveness, and coherence.[52] It laid down minimum standards for consultation. The content of the consultation should be clear and concise, including all necessary information to facilitate responses; it should be public, be available on the internet and announced through a single access point; there should be adequate time for participation, the default position being that this should not be less than six weeks; there should be acknowledgement of contributions, the results should be displayed on the internet, and there should be an explanation as to how the results were taken into account in the proposal; and where consultations were more focused care should be taken to ensure adequate coverage of those affected by the policy, those involved in its implementation, and bodies that have a direct interest in the policy.[53]

The Communication is an important step in fostering consultation within the EU. Its limitations should also be noted. Consultations tend to be used only for the more major policy initiatives,[54] with the consequence that other provisions that can have a marked impact on the individual will not be subject to consultation.[55] The principles and minimum standards are specifically stated not to be legally binding.[56] They only apply

[50] Communication from the Commission, Towards a Reinforced Culture of Consultation and Dialogue—General Principles and Minimum Standards for Consultation of Interested Parties by the Commission, COM(2002) 704 final.

[51] Ibid. at 5. [52] Ibid. at 15–18 [53] Ibid. at 19–22.

[54] Ibid. at 15–16.

[55] Thus to take an example: at the time of writing there was only one open consultation in relation to Fisheries and that was concerned with gleaning information about the problems posed by excessive regulation in general rather than anything specific about fisheries. There were two consultations that had closed, dating from 2001 and 2003 respectively. A quick glance at the Eur-lex site for the Common Fisheries Policy will reveal the large amount of legislation enacted for this area. The very great majority of the 'primary regulations' will not therefore have been through the IPM exercise; and what is equally important the many delegated regulations applicable to this area are not covered by the exercise.

[56] Communication from the Commission, *supra* n. 50, at 10, 15.

to consultations 'through which the Commission wishes to trigger input from interested parties to its policy-making prior to a decision by the Commission'.[57] This serves to exclude: specific consultation frameworks provided for in the Treaties or in other Community legislation, such as the institutionalized advisory bodies and the social dialogue, thereby also excluding, *inter alia*, policy-making pursuant to the OMC;[58] consultation under international agreements; and rule-making subject to comitology procedures.[59]

The Commission sought to give more practical force to the aims of the 2002 Communication through Interactive Policy Making (IPM),[60] which is a principal component of 'Your Voice in Europe'.[61] This consists of two internet-based instruments to collect feedback from citizens, consumers, and business. The Commission regards the knowledge thereby gleaned as a way of shaping new policies and improving existing ones. There is a feedback mechanism to collect information from citizens, etc. about problems encountered with different EU policies. There is also an online consultation mechanism, operating through structured questionnaires allowing input on particular policy proposals. This technique for consultation is designed to make it easier for individuals to contribute, and to facilitate the Commission's task of analysing the resulting data. The system can handle structured questions in an unlimited range of languages and deliver the output in the desired language, which expedites the process.

The system is easy to use, and the website is well designed. The site provides examples of consultations that are currently open, with topics ranging from strengthening the EU–US Economic Partnership to reform of the directive dealing with pressure machinery, and from review of the sustainable development strategy to an action plan for electronic public procurement. These are just examples. The website contains links to consultations that are currently ongoing in all areas of Community activity. Thus the link to the Internal Market site reveals that there are consultations about defence procurement, financial services, electronic procurement, EU legislation on copyright, and shareholder's rights. The IPM site also allows access to consultation exercises that have recently closed, with information about the results gleaned from the consultation and the follow-up to be undertaken.

57 Ibid. at 15–16.

58 It is significant that the consultations listed for Employment and Social Affairs deal with important legislative matters, but do not touch the OMC process as it relates to the European Employment Strategy or social inclusion. Economic and Financial Affairs, which deals with coordination of economic policy, has, at the time of writing, no open consultation and none foreseen. The areas in which the OMC operates are regarded as self-contained, even though the ability to participate in policy-making therein is far from perfect, see above, at 221–224.

59 Communication from the Commission, *supra* n. 50, at 16.

60 Ibid. at 6–7.

61 <http://europa.eu.int/yourvoice/consultations/index_en.htm>.

Information about consultations that have closed can be obtained more generally from the particular subject-matter websites, as exemplified by the Internal Market site that contained reports from 15 consultations that had closed within the last nine months. The websites on consultations that have closed will contain the results from the consultation exercise, including the questions posed and the responses received. Many sites did not, however, contain any Commission synthesis of the results, although some did as exemplified by the Commission synthesis of the consultation exercise carried out on the role of independent, non-executive directors.[62]

It is more difficult to generalize about the impact of the consultation on the ultimate policy proposal. Thus in relation to the consultation about the role of independent directors, the Commission synthesis concluded by stating that the suggestions made would be borne in mind when it worked on a future recommendation.[63] The impact of the consultation exercise on the resultant policy is even more difficult to determine when the subject matter is very broad, such as the efficacy of cohesion policy, the importance of nanotechnology for the EU, or the design of cultural cooperation for the EU post 2006.

D. Participation, Consultation, and Agencies

The previous section has concentrated on the provision of consultation and participation by the Commission. We should also be aware of agency practice. The regulations governing agencies differ in the extent to which they impose any legal requirement to consult or allow participation.[64] Procedures to foster participation have, however, been adopted by some agencies even in the absence of a legal obligation. The European Aviation Safety Agency, the EASA, has the most interesting and innovative practice in this regard.[65]

The EASA has a rule-making directorate that publishes an annual rule-making programme, and any person can propose that an item be included. The terms of reference of a particular rule are then set out, explaining the nature of the problem to be addressed, followed by the draft rule, in relation to which the agency conducts a regulatory impact assessment. Notice of the proposed rule is posted on the website and any person can comment through a standardized form. The comments are then aggregated in a comment response document (CRD), enabling interested parties to gain an overview of

[62] DG Internal Market, Synthesis of the Comments on the Consultation Document of the Services of the Internal Market Directorate-General, 'Recommendations on the Role of (Independent) Non-Executive or Supervisory Directors', September 2004.

[63] Ibid. at 9. [64] See above, Chap. 5.

[65] Regulation (EC) 1592/2002 of the European Parliament and of the Council of 15 July 2002, On Common Rules in the Field of Civil Aviation and Establishing a European Aviation Safety Agency, OJ 2002 L240/1.

comments put forward by others. These comments are then used by the drafting group when finalizing the rule. At this stage the drafting group is reinforced by two additional members, one of whom is drawn from those who dissented from the draft rule. The EASA is also assisted by a Safety Standards Consultative Committee, composed of representatives of organizations directly affected by the regulatory regime, and by the Advisory Group of National Authorities.

E. Access and the Political Process: Politics, Law, and Participation

Some might be tempted in the light of the above to conclude that the courts' unwillingness to impose a legal obligation to consult or allow participation does not matter, since this has in any event been introduced through the political process. Others might incline towards the opposite position, and conclude that the present initiatives are no substitute for cognizable legal rights enforceable through the courts. We should avoid both such extremes. There are not surprisingly pros and cons of the present situation.

There are advantages to the present regime whereby participation and consultation are secured through the political process. The system provides well-structured opportunities for the giving of views. It demonstrates the trite but important proposition that the absence of a legal obligation to do something does not mean that it will not be done. It can moreover avoid the excessive legalism attendant upon a legal regime to protect participatory rights. The dangers of such a regime are well known. It can lead to lengthy challenges to regulatory norms as groups that dislike the content of the norm seek to use the law to prevent its enactment, by arguing, *inter alia*, that their views were not sufficiently taken into account when the rule was made. On the worst case scenario this can lead to 'paralysis by analysis', whereby important regulatory provisions are held up in the courts for an inordinate time as the lawyers and judges pore over the provision to determine whether it is, for example, sustainable in the light of the available scientific evidence.

There are however also disadvantages of the current system. It is reliant on the grace and favour of the Commission. It is the Commission that will decide which particular proposals should be put out for consultation. It is the Commission that will determine which types of rule should be subject to the consultative regime, the exclusion of delegated rule-making pursuant to comitology being a prominent example. The practical reality is that many primary regulations and all delegated regulations are not touched by the IPM process. Where IPM is used it is the Commission that will assess the results and decide on the best way forward. There is no legal mechanism for challenging the Commission's conclusions, no opportunity to argue before the courts that the conclusions did not reflect the preponderance of evidence placed before the Commission, or that they were weighted towards a particular interest group or lobby. This is because the Community courts have made it clear that consultation or participation rights only exist when enshrined in positive law, whether this is a Treaty article, regulation, directive, or decision. The fact of having engaged in participation does not as we have seen give the individual any privileged status to challenge the resulting rule.

The reluctance to enshrine legally enforceable participation rights as against the Commission stands in marked contrast to the Commission's willingness to impose such a regime on Member States. The asymmetry in this regard is exemplified by changes to the participatory requirements imposed on Member States in the context of pollution prevention and control. This regime was strengthened in 2003 by a provision entitled 'access to justice', which required Member States to provide access to a review procedure before a court of law or other independent and impartial body to enable challenge to the substantive or procedural legality of decisions that were subject to the public participation provisions of the Directive.[66] This reinforcement of participation rights against the Member States may well be laudable. The Commission, however, shows no inclination to apply analogous precepts of 'access to justice' to itself. This is readily apparent from its response to comments received on the draft of its Communication about consultation, which comments had suggested that the consultation standards should be included in a legally binding document. The Commission's response was peremptory.[67]

> [A] situation must be avoided in which a Commission proposal could be challenged in the Court on the grounds of alleged lack of consultation of interested parties. Such an overly-legalistic approach would be incompatible with the need for timely delivery of policy, and with the expectations of the citizens that the European Institutions should deliver on substance rather than concentrating on procedures.

It can, however, be argued that the disadvantages of participation rights mentioned above are not the inevitable consequence of a legal regime for protecting process, but flow more from the courts' attitude towards substantive review. The dangers adverted to tend to occur when the courts demand, for example, a degree of scientific support for a proposed rule which may not be available in the current state of scientific knowledge. The regulatory authorities may nonetheless justifiably conclude that measures are required now, since to wait until there is more perfect knowledge of the effects of a particular substance on the environment or health could be too late. It is perfectly possible for the courts to safeguard the participatory process while

[66] Dir. 2003/35, *supra* n. 43, Art. 4(4), inserting a new Art. 15a to Dir. 96/61, *supra* n. 41.
[67] Communication from the Commission, *supra* n. 50, at 10.

being cognizant of the limits that can reasonably be expected by way of evidential support for the measure.

A *via media* is possible. The Community courts could continue to maintain their general proposition that consultation and participation rights must be sought from the political arm of government in a Treaty article, regulation, directive, or decision. They could continue to decline to impose participatory rights in the way that they impose a right to be heard in an individualized decision, which is applicable irrespective of whether there is foundation in positive law. The courts could nonetheless modify their stance, by holding that if the political arm of government has chosen to afford consultation, even if not obliged to, then the courts will monitor the fairness of the procedure. Some might feel that this does not go far enough, and that there should be parity between the right to be heard in individualized decisions and a right to be consulted in relation to legislative norms. There is, as we have seen, force in this argument. It is, however, unlikely to be accepted by the Community courts. Others might argue that if the proposed change were to occur then the Commission would simply pull back from its present consultation initiatives. This is possible. Few legal initiatives are risk free. It would not however be an easy thing for the Commission to do. The Commission has made much of its 'Your Voice in Europe' strategy, and justifiably so. To cut this programme or to reduce its incidence if the courts were to signal a willingness to monitor the fairness of the consultation procedure would be difficult in the extreme. The Commission would be doubly vulnerable to criticism, on the grounds that it had cut a programme designed to give citizens more input into decision-making thereby enhancing the EU's legitimacy, and that it had done so in order to avoid a modicum of legal accountability.

It must also be acknowledged that even if this suggestion were to be accepted it would only resolve the problem to a limited extent. This is because there is so much 'primary' legislative activity that is not touched by the IPM initiative, while 'delegated' rule-making and the OMC do not even come within its purview. It is not fortuitous that legal challenges concerning participation and consultation have tended to arise in relation to regulations, whether primary or delegated, that have a real impact on traders in a particular area. These will normally not have been subject to the IPM at all. It might be felt that practical problems preclude extension of process rights in this way. We should, however, pause before reaching this conclusion. It did not appear to be a self-evident objection to the European Council when it proposed the notice and comment scheme in 1993. The analogy drawn with notice and written comment serves moreover to confirm that participatory process rights do not have to take the form of trial-type oral hearings. The consultation process does not therefore need to be as detailed and elaborate as that commonly used where IPM does operate.

4. ACCESS TO JUDICIAL REVIEW: STANDING

The discussion thus far has been concerned with access to the original decision-making process, both in relation to individualized determinations and norms of a legislative nature. The focus now shifts to access to judicial review where a party seeks to challenge such norms.

There is an extensive case law and literature[68] on standing to seek judicial review in EU law, especially in relation to non-privileged applicants. The discussion will begin with a brief overview of the case law, and will then focus on the more recent jurisprudence in *UPA*[69] and *Jégo-Quéré*.[70] This will provide the foundation for a normative assessment of the present law and for consideration of how far modified provisions on standing of the kind included in the Constitutional Treaty would alleviate existing problems.

A. *Locus Standi*: The Background

The complex case law on standing to contest the legality of Community norms is well known. A brief outline will be given here in order to set the scene for the later discussion of more recent jurisprudence.

Article 230 EC provides for direct review of legality. Member States, the EP, Council, and Commission are regarded as privileged applicants and therefore have standing to challenge the legality of any acts. The Court

[68] Barav, 'Direct and Individual Concern: An Almost Insurmountable Barrier to the Admissibility of Individual Appeal to the EEC Court' (1974) 11 *CMLRev* 191; Harding, 'The Private Interest in Challenging Community Action' (1980) 5 *ELRev* 354; Rasmussen, 'Why is Article 173 Interpreted against Private Plaintiffs?' (1980) 5 *ELRev* 112; Greaves, '*Locus Standi* under Article 173 EEC when Seeking Annulment of a Regulation' (1986) 11 *ELRev* 119; Weiler, 'Pride and Prejudice—*Parliament v Council*' (1989) 14 *ELRev* 334; Bebr, 'The Standing of the European Parliament in the Community System of Legal Remedies: A Thorny Jurisprudential Development' (1990) 10 *YBEL* 170; Bradley, 'Sense and Sensibility: *Parliament v Council* Continued' (1991) 16 *ELRev* 245; Arnull, 'Challenging EC Anti-Dumping Regulations: The Problem of Admissibility' [1992] *ECLR* 73; Harlow, 'Towards a Theory of Access for the European Court of Justice' (1992) 12 *YBEL* 213; Craig, 'Legality, Standing and Substantive Review in Community Law' (1994) 14 *OJLS* 507; Arnull, 'Private Applicants and the Action for Annulment under Article 173 of the EC Treaty' (1995) 32 *CMLRev* 7; Hedemann-Robinson, 'Article 173 EC, General Community Measures and *Locus Standi* for Private Persons: Still a Cause for Individual Concern?' (1996) 2 *EPL* 127; Neuwahl, 'Article 173 Paragraph 4 EC: Past, Present and Possible Future' (1996) 21 *ELRev* 17; Cooke, '*Locus Standi* of Private Parties under Article 173(4)' (1997) *Irish Jnl of European Law* 4; A. Ward, *Judicial Review and the Rights of Private Parties in EC Law* (Oxford University Press, 2000), Chap. 6; Arnull, 'Private Applicants and the Action for Annulment since *Codorniu*' (2001) 38 *CMLRev* 7; P. Craig and G. de Burca, *EU Law, Text, Cases and Materials* (Oxford University Press, 3rd ed., 2002), Chap. 12; Craig, 'Standing, Rights and the Structure of Legal Argument' (2003) 9 *EPL* 493.

[69] Case C-50/00 P, *Unión de Pequenos Agricultores v Council* [2002] ECR I-6677.

[70] Case C-263/02 P, *Jégo-Quéré, supra* n. 22.

of Auditors and the ECB can bring actions to protect their prerogatives. Non-privileged applicants must satisfy Article 230(4), which provides that,

> Any natural or legal person may, under the same conditions, institute proceedings against a decision addressed to that person or against a decision which, although in the form of a regulation or decision addressed to another person, is of direct and individual concern to the former.

Direct challenge to the legality of Community norms by non-privileged applicants has proven extremely difficult. The *Plaumann* test[71] has remained authoritative ever since the early 1960s. Persons other than those to whom a decision was addressed could only claim to be individually concerned if the decision affected them by reason of certain attributes peculiar to them, or by reason of circumstances in which they were differentiated from all other persons and by virtue of these factors distinguished them individually just as in the case of the person addressed. The applicant in the instant case failed because it practised a commercial activity that could be carried on by any person at any time. This made little sense pragmatically, since the existing range of firms is established by the ordinary principles of supply and demand: if there are two or three firms in the industry they can satisfy the current market demand. The number is unlikely to alter significantly if at all. The ECJ's reasoning also rendered it impossible for an applicant to succeed, except in a very limited category of retrospective cases. The applicant failed because the activity of clementine-importing could be carried out by anyone at any time. It was, however, always open to the Court to contend that others could enter the industry, and hence to deny standing to existing firms.

The *difficulty of directly challenging Community norms in the form of regulations was equally marked.* The *Calpak* test[72] required the non-privileged applicant to show that the measure in question was not a real regulation, but that it was in reality a decision that was of individual concern to him. This was not easy, because of the abstract terminology test set out by the ECJ. It held that a real regulation was a measure that applied to objectively determined situations and produced legal effects with regard to categories of persons described in a generalized and abstract manner. The nature of the measure as a regulation was not called in question by the mere fact that it was possible to determine the number or even identity of those affected. The Court recognized that the purpose of allowing such challenge was to prevent the Community institutions from immunizing matters from attack by the form of their classification. If regulations were never open to challenge

[71] Case 25/62, *Plaumann & Co v Commission* [1963] ECR 95.

[72] Cases 789 and 790/79, *Calpak SpA and Societa Emiliana Lavorazione Fruita SpA v Commission* [1980] ECR 1949; Case C-10/95 P, *Asocarne, supra* n. 25, at paras. 28, 30.

the institutions could classify matters in this way, secure that private individuals could never contest them. Article 230(4) sought to prevent this by permitting a challenge when the regulation was in reality a decision, which was of direct and individual concern to the applicant. This required, as acknowledged in *Calpak*, the Court to look behind the form of the measure, in order to determine whether in substance it really was a regulation or not. The problem with the abstract terminology test was that rather than looking behind form to substance, it came very close to looking behind form to form. This was because it was always possible to draft norms in the manner specified by the abstract terminology test, and thus to immunize them from attack. This was especially so since the Court made it clear that knowledge of the number or identity of those affected would not prevent the norm from being regarded as a true regulation.

The *Codorniu* case[73] *raised hopes that the standing rules for direct challenge were being liberalized, but the decision proved to have a limited impact.* In that case the ECJ affirmed the abstract terminology test as the criterion for whether a regulation was a real regulation, rather than a decision. It held, however, that this did not prevent the regulation from being of individual concern to some applicants. The test for whether an applicant was individually concerned was that laid down in *Plaumann*.[74] It was for the applicant to show that the contested provision affected him by reason of certain attributes which were peculiar to him, or by reason of circumstances in which he was differentiated from all other persons. The hope raised by *Codorniu* was dashed by the realization that in most instances the *Plaumann* test of individual concern would be interpreted in the same manner as in *Plaumann* itself. The fact that the applicant operated a trade, which could be engaged in by any other person, served to deny individual concern.[75] The fact that the applicant was the only firm affected by the contested measure did not suffice to afford standing.[76] Nor did the Community courts appear to be willing to apply the more liberal case law developed in areas such as state aids, dumping, and competition to challenges outside those areas.[77] If the Community courts felt that an applicant should be regarded as individually concerned by a true regulation it required complex legal reasoning to square this with existing orthodoxy.[78]

Indirect challenge to contest the legality of Community norms was an imperfect substitute for more liberal standing rules for direct challenge. The narrow rules for standing in cases of direct challenge were often justified judicially by the

[73] Case C-309/89, *Codorniu v Council* [1994] ECR I-1853.
[74] Case 25/62, *Plaumann, supra* n. 71.
[75] Craig and de Burca, *supra* n. 68, at 496–500.
[76] Case T-13/99, *Pfizer, supra* n. 23, at para. 89.
[77] Craig and de Burca, *supra* n. 68, at 503–509.
[78] Case T-13/99, *Pfizer, supra* n. 23, at paras. 81–106.

existence of indirect challenge via Article 234 EC, since the individual could get to the ECJ via the national courts. Advocate General Jacobs in *Extramet* pointed out, however, the limits of indirect challenge.[79] He noted that Article 230 contained no suggestion that the availability of annulment depended on the absence of an alternative means of redress in the national courts. Such a result would, in any event, have been far from satisfactory, since the existence and scope of any domestic remedy would depend on national law. Advocate General Jacobs held furthermore that the indirect method of challenge had serious disadvantages by comparison with the direct action under Article 230. National courts lacked expertise in the subject and did not have the benefit of participation of the Council and Commission. They were not therefore the most appropriate forum for dealing with challenges to, for example, anti-dumping regulations. The proceedings in national courts, combined with a reference under Article 234, could moreover involve substantial delays and extra costs. The national courts had no jurisdiction to declare Community regulations invalid, and this made it likely that interim measures would be necessary in some cases, even though the national courts might not be the appropriate forum for granting such measures. There were moreover procedural difficulties attendant upon indirect challenge. This was because a reference from a national court on the validity of regulation did not always give the Court as full an opportunity to investigate the matter as would a direct action against the adopting institution. Where complex issues of law and fact were raised the Advocate General felt that only a full exchange of pleadings as in a direct action was likely to be adequate for proper consideration of the issues. Furthermore, it was only in a direct action that all the concerned parties would be able to participate. The ECJ's general strategy has, however, been to ignore the applicants' difficulties in using indirect challenge. Thus in *Asocarne*[80] the applicants argued that widespread structural delays in the Spanish judicial system should be taken into account when assessing standing for direct actions. The ECJ's response, subsequently cited in many cases, was unequivocal: such circumstances could not alter the system of remedies provided by the Treaties, and could not justify a direct action where the standing conditions in Article 230(4) were not satisfied.

The courts *have also limited the possibility for intervention in direct and indirect actions.* Intervention rights are governed by Article 40 of the Statute of the Court of Justice: Member States and Community institutions can intervene as of right; private parties can do so only in cases between private parties and only where they can establish an interest. Intervention rights clearly cannot be a substitute for standing: someone must be granted standing

[79] Case C-358/89, *Extramet Industrie SA v Council* [1991] ECR I-2501, AG Jacobs.
[80] Case C-10/95 P, *Asocarne, supra* n. 25, at para. 26.

before others can intervene. There is much to be said for using such rights to enable interest groups to make their views known when a case does come before the Court. It obviates the need for separate action on the same point; facilitates class actions; and makes it easier for interest groups to proffer their opinions. Intervention rights in judicial review actions can therefore be important as a means of facilitating public-interest litigation before the ECJ.[81] The ECJ's interpretation of Article 40 has, however, limited this potential. Those seeking to intervene must show that they are directly affected by the contested act, and must establish an interest in the result of the case. The intervener must also establish a direct, existing interest in the grant by the Court of the order sought, and not just an interest in the legal pleas advanced. The interest must therefore relate not merely to abstract legal arguments, but to the actual form of order sought by the party to the main action.[82]

B. *UPA*: The Advocate General's Opinion

In the *UPA* case[83] an association of farmers, UPA, sought the annulment of Regulation 1638/98, which substantially amended the common organization of the olive oil market. The CFI dismissed the application because the members of the association were not individually concerned by the Regulation under Article 230(4). UPA argued, *inter alia*, that it was denied effective judicial protection because it could not readily challenge the measure via Article 234.

Advocate General Jacobs made an extensive analysis of the law relating to standing. He began with the right to effective judicial protection, which framed the entirety of the analysis. The ability of an individual to contest the legality of a Community norm, indirectly or directly, was tested against this background right.

The Advocate General considered whether this basic right could be adequately protected by indirect challenge via Article 234. He was unequivocal in this regard: there were serious difficulties in regarding the preliminary reference as providing full and effective judicial protection against general measures.[84] This was so for a number of reasons.[85] The applicant had no right under the preliminary ruling procedure to decide whether a reference was made, which measures were referred for review, or what grounds of

[81] Harlow, *supra* n. 68.
[82] Cases C-151 and 157/97 P(I), *National Power plc and PowerGen plc v British Coal Corporation and Commission* [1997] ECR I-3491; Case T-138/98, *Armement Coopératif Artisanal Vendéen (ACAV) v Council* [1999] ECR II-1797.
[83] Case C-50/00 P, *supra* n. 69.
[84] Case C-50/00 P, *supra* n. 69, AG Jacobs, at para. 102(1).
[85] Ibid. AG Jacobs, at para. 102(1).

invalidity were raised and thus had no right of access to the Court of Justice. The national court could not itself grant the desired remedy of declaring the measure invalid, because of the rule preventing national courts annulling Community norms.[86] There could be cases where it was difficult or impossible for an applicant to challenge a general measure indirectly, for example where there were no challengeable implementing measures, or where the applicant would have to break the law in order to be able to challenge ensuing sanctions. Considerations of legal certainty were in favour of allowing a general measure to be reviewed as soon as possible and not only after implementing measures had been adopted. There were moreover procedural disadvantages for applicants who brought indirect challenges via Article 234.

Advocate General Jacobs gave consideration as to whether the problem could be overcome by expanding direct actions only where the particular legal system made the indirect action especially difficult. This 'solution' was rejected for a number of reasons. It had no basis in Treaty, it would require the Community courts to interpret and apply rules of national law, a task for which they were not well prepared or competent, and would lead to inequality between operators from different Member States, with a consequential loss of legal certainty.[87]

He also discussed whether a 'solution' could be found through an obligation for national legal orders to ensure that references on the validity of general Community measures were available in their legal systems. He rejected such an approach, since it would 'leave unresolved most of the problems of the current situation such as the absence of remedy as a matter of right, unnecessary delays and costs for the applicant or the award of interim measures'.[88] It would also be difficult to monitor and enforce, and would entail 'far-reaching interference with national procedural autonomy'.[89]

It was for these reasons that Advocate General Jacobs concluded that the only way to secure the effective right of judicial protection was to have a test for direct challenge based on substantial adverse impact. This would accord applicants 'a true right of direct access to a court which can grant a remedy'.[90] It would remove the anomaly under the current case law that the greater the number of persons affected, the less likely it was that there would be effective judicial review. This solution was not, said Advocate General Jacobs, precluded by the wording of Article 230, nor by the fear of overloading the ECJ. The fact that the prior case law had stood for a long time should not be seen as an obstacle. The case law was not stable and had become increasingly complex and unpredictable. It was out of line with more liberal developments

[86] Case 314/85, *Firma Foto-Frost v Hauptzollamt Lübeck-Ost* [1987] ECR 4199.
[87] Case C-50/00 P, *supra* n. 69, AG Jacobs, at para. 102(2).
[88] Ibid. at para. 102(3). [89] Ibid. at para. 102(3).
[90] Ibid. at para. 102(4).

in the Member States. Moreover, the 'Court's case-law on the principle of effective judicial protection in the national courts makes it increasingly difficult to justify narrow restrictions on standing before the Community Courts'.[91]

The Opinion is a classic example of the use of background rights as a mechanism for the re-assessment of existing doctrine. The reality is that the right to effective judicial protection, although part of Community jurisprudence, had not featured significantly in the case law on *locus standi.* It had more commonly been part of the reasoning in cases concerned with the effectiveness of national remedial protection.[92] The very fact that the right to effective judicial protection had not featured prominently in the case law on challenges to Community acts was one of the reasons why that case law had continued to develop in the illiberal fashion. It is clear that placing the right to effective judicial protection at the centre of the analysis exerted a powerful force in the demand for re-evaluation of the case law.

C. *UPA*: The ECJ's Reasoning

The role afforded to the right to effective judicial protection in the Advocate General's Opinion stands in sharp relief to the place of that right in the ECJ's reasoning.

The major premise of the ECJ's reasoning was that the applicants had not fulfilled the standard requirements for *locus standi* under Article 230. They had not shown they were affected by the regulation by reason of certain attributes peculiar to them, or by reason of factual circumstances in which they were differentiated from all others, as required by the *Plaumann* test.[93] The ECJ acknowledged that a measure of general application, such as a regulation, could be of individual concern to particular persons, but only where they were differentiated in the manner set out in the *Plaumann* test. The ECJ emphasized this major premise by stating that if the *Plaumann* condition were not fulfilled then a natural or legal person would not have standing to seek the annulment of a regulation 'under any circumstances'.[94]

The right to effective judicial protection entered the ECJ's reasoning against the backdrop that the applicants had failed to meet the normal rules for *locus standi.* The ECJ held that it was necessary to see whether, 'in those circumstances', the applicant could 'nonetheless' have standing on the ground that the absence of a remedy before the national courts meant that there must, in the light of the right to effective judicial protection, be a direct action.[95] The ECJ acknowledged that the right to effective judicial protection

[91] Ibid. at para. 102(6).
[92] Craig and de Burca, *supra* n. 68, Chap. 6.
[93] Case C-50/00 P, *supra* n. 69, at paras. 32, 34–36.
[94] Ibid. at para. 37.
[95] Ibid. at para. 33.

was a fundamental right, which was part of the Community legal order based on the rule of law. It read the existing *locus standi* rules against this fundamental right to see if those rules required amendment.[96]

The ECJ decided that no such amendment was warranted. It held that the Treaty established a complete system of legal remedies for challenging the legality of Community action.[97] In relation to indirect challenges, it was for the Member States to ensure that they had in place a system of legal remedies that ensured respect for the right to effective judicial protection. The national legal orders should therefore interpret and apply their national legal rules so far as possible to enable applicants to plead the invalidity of a Community act in an action before the national court.[98] In relation to direct challenge, the ECJ refused to extend standing under Article 230 where the rules of the particular national legal order meant that indirect challenge under Article 234 would not be possible. The Court felt, as did the Advocate General, that this would require the ECJ to examine national procedural law on a case by case basis. It was ill-equipped to do this, and it would entail too great an intrusion into national procedural autonomy.[99]

The ECJ concluded its judgment by reaffirming its major premise and the secondary, limited role accorded to the right to effective judicial protection. The Court declined to follow the lead of the Advocate General. It concluded its judgment in the same vein that it had begun.[100] The applicants had failed to satisfy the legal requirements for standing in Article 230. While the meaning of individual concern must be interpreted in the light of the right of effective judicial protection this could only be in the context of defining the circumstances that could distinguish an applicant individually. An interpretation of individual concern in the light of the right to effective judicial protection could not have the effect of setting aside that condition, which was expressly laid down in the Treaty. This would be to go beyond the jurisdiction of the Community courts, and would require an amendment of the Treaty.

The contrast between the ECJ's judgment and the Advocate General's Opinion is marked. The ECJ paid heed to the right to effective judicial protection, but its role in the Court's judgment was minimal. The Court began and ended its judgment with the *Plaumann* formula, and the fact that the applicants had been unable to meet this test. The right to effective judicial protection was accorded a secondary role, to determine whether some extension of standing was required or warranted. This secondary role was moreover interpretative in a minimalist sense. The right to effective judicial protection might influence the meaning of individual concern only in the limited sense of helping to define the circumstances that could

[96] Ibid. at paras. 33, 38–39.
[97] Ibid. at para. 40.
[98] Ibid. at paras. 41–42.
[99] Ibid. at para. 43.
[100] Ibid. at paras. 44–45.

distinguish an applicant individually, as exemplified by *Codorniu.*[101] It could not have any greater impact, since this would, in the view of the Court, entail the setting aside of a Treaty condition.

D. *Jégo-Quéré*

The issue of standing for non-privileged applicants came before the Community courts once again in *Jégo-Quéré.*[102] The applicant was a French fishing company that sought the annulment of provisions in Regulation 1162/01.[103] The Regulation was designed to protect the fishing stock of hake and to this end proscribed net sizes of less than 100mm. The applicant sought to challenge the measure by a direct action under Article 230, and argued that it could not have recourse to Article 234, because the Regulation did not provide for any implementing measures. There was therefore nothing that it could challenge at national level, and the only way that it could raise the matter indirectly was if it violated the law and raised the invalidity of the regulation by way of defence. It argued that its right to an effective remedy would be denied if it could not have recourse to the direct action under Article 230.

Its claim succeeded before the CFI.[104] This decision was given after the Advocate General had delivered his Opinion in the *UPA* case, but before the ECJ gave its judgment in that case. The CFI was clearly influenced by the Advocate General's Opinion. The CFI held that the right to an effective remedy could not be secured in a case such as this either through Article 234 or Article 288. It held further that there was no compelling reason why the requirement of individual concern within Article 230(4) had to mean that an individual must be differentiated from all others in the same way as the addressee. The CFI concluded that the only way to ensure effective judicial protection was to allow a direct action, stating that individual concern should be satisfied where the measure in question affects a person's legal position in a manner which is both definite and immediate, by restricting his rights or by imposing obligations on him, the number of persons likewise affected being of no relevance in this regard.[105]

The Commission unsurprisingly appealed to the ECJ, which by this time had given its judgment in *UPA*. The Advocate General in *Jégo-Quéré* was once again Francis Jacobs. He felt compelled to conclude in the light of the ECJ's decision in *UPA* that the CFI's judgment in *Jégo-Quéré* could not stand, although he made it patently clear that he stood by his own reasoning as

[101] Case C-309/89, *Codorniu, supra* n. 73.
[102] Case C-263/02 P, *supra* n. 22.
[103] OJ 2001 L159/4.
[104] Case T-177/01, *Jégo-Quéré v Commission* [2002] ECR II-2365, at paras. 44–52.
[105] Ibid. at para. 51.

Advocate General in the *UPA* case and continued to have grave reservations about the test for individual concern as re-affirmed by the ECJ in *UPA*.[106]

The ECJ in *Jégo-Quéré* nonetheless endorsed and followed its decision in *UPA*, and the reasoning in that case.[107] It acknowledged the right to effective judicial protection, but held once again that the Treaty established a complete system of legal protection through the combination of Articles 230 and 234. It was for the Member States to ensure that individuals should be able to challenge Community measures at national level, even where no implementing measures were involved. But the criteria for standing under Article 230(4) would not be relaxed even where it was apparent that the national rules did not allow the individual to contest the validity of the measure without having contravened it. The right to effective judicial protection could not moreover have the affect of setting aside a condition expressly laid down by the Treaty, and the ECJ therefore roundly rejected the alternative test proposed by the CFI.

E. A Complete System of Legal Protection: Indirect Challenge?

The ECJ framed its analysis in *UPA* and *Jégo-Quéré* on the premise that the Treaty provided for a complete regime of legal protection in terms of access to court, via Articles 234 and 230.[108] There are, however, three major difficulties with the indirect challenge aspect of the regime of legal protection.

First, the ECJ simply ignored the Advocate General's analysis of the difficulties faced by individuals who seek to use Article 234. These difficulties are varied in nature. They are in part procedural: proceeding via the national court can have implications for the participation of the institutions that adopted the contested measure, delays, costs, the award of interim measures, and the possibility of third party intervention. They are in part inherent in the very nature of Article 234: it is a reference and not an appellate system. The applicant must therefore convince the national court that a reference is required, and may have to fight its way through more than one national court to achieve this result. The national court is moreover precluded from pronouncing the measure invalid, and hence the applicant will necessarily have to proceed to the ECJ, if the national court is willing to make the reference. The difficulties entailed by indirect challenge are also in part substantive: an individual may not be able to challenge the illegality of the measure in the national court without placing itself in contravention of the measure in question. The individual is therefore forced to act illegally and raise the invalidity of the measure by way of defence.

[106] Case C-263/02 P, *supra* n. 22, AG Jacobs, at paras. 42–47.
[107] Case C-263/02 P, *supra* n. 22, at paras. 29–39.
[108] Case C-50/00 P, *supra* n. 69, at para. 40.

Secondly, the ECJ, while not responding to these difficulties, sought to circumvent them by exhorting national courts, in accordance with Article 10 EC, to interpret national procedural rules governing the right of action in such a way so as to enable applicants to challenge Community norms of general application before the national courts. This strategy is, however, of limited utility. It cannot resolve the procedural difficulties adverted to above. It cannot overcome, although it might alleviate, the difficulties flowing from the discretionary nature of the Article 234 system, which has the consequence that the applicant may be forced to fight its way through successive national courts. It provides no answer to the critique that it is wrong for an applicant to have to place itself in breach of a Community norm in order to challenge its validity. The ECJ's reliance on Article 10 is moreover open to the objection, voiced clearly by the Advocate General, that it would be difficult to monitor and enforce, and would require far-reaching interference with national procedural autonomy.[109]

Thirdly, it should also be recognized that the Article 234 mode of indirect challenge has had undesirable consequences for the institutional division of competence between the ECJ and the CFI. The division of jurisdictional responsibility between the two courts has been largely ad hoc. The CFI was created to ease the workload of the ECJ. It was therefore natural to assign it certain types of case, which by their very nature, had a heavy factual quotient. It was for this reason that competition and staff cases were assigned to the CFI. The extension of jurisdictional competence to the CFI over direct actions brought by individuals under Articles 230, 232, and 288 was a further move to ease the workload of the ECJ. The continuing problems of workload, more especially in the light of enlargement, led to consideration of reform of the Community judicial system.[110] The relevance of this for the issue presently under discussion is, however, marked, and can be stated succinctly. Preliminary rulings have traditionally been the preserve of the ECJ, although this monopoly has been modified by the Nice Treaty. The consequence is that indirect challenges to the validity of Community norms that arise via Article 234 have gone to the ECJ, where the very same issues would have been adjudicated on by the CFI if they had arisen via a direct challenge under Article 230. This has had the effect of increasing the workload of the ECJ. It has meant that the ECJ's scarce resources have been diverted to answering such preliminary rulings, which will often not involve any point of general importance of Community law. Challenges to the legality of Community norms will often be concerned with technical points relating to the compatibility of a Community regulation with another, more general regulation on that subject, or its compatibility with a Treaty article or a general

[109] Case C-50/00 P, *supra* n. 69, AG Jacobs, at para. 102(3).

[110] See above, Chapter 9.

principle of Community law, such as proportionality. These legal issues must of course be answered. They do not, however, have to be addressed by the ECJ, the top court of the Community legal system. The very restrictive reading given to direct challenge under Article 230, and the consequential pushing of cases through indirect challenge under Article 234, has meant that these cases have ended up on the ECJ's case docket. This has exacerbated the caseload of the ECJ, and forced it to spend time addressing issues that could perfectly well be dealt with by the CFI. Thus even if Article 234 were not problematic from the perspective of the applicant, it would nonetheless be institutionally undesirable from the perspective of a rational allocation of function between the ECJ and the CFI.

F. A Complete System of Legal Protection: Direct Challenge?

The prospect of reforming the case law on direct challenge via Article 230 raises two issues, legitimacy and practicality. These will be considered in turn.

The ECJ in *UPA* and *Jégo-Quéré* believed that the boundaries of legitimate Treaty interpretation constrained any modification to the traditional case law on direct challenge. It held, as we have seen, that the right of effective judicial protection could influence the application of individual concern, 'by taking account of the various circumstances that may distinguish an applicant individually'.[111] It could not, however, have the effect of 'setting aside the condition in question, expressly laid down in the Treaty, without going beyond the jurisdiction conferred by the Treaty on the Community Courts'.[112] More far-reaching reform would require a Treaty amendment.[113]

This argument is unconvincing. The ECJ has, as is well known, often stretched the meaning of Treaty articles, and the provisions of Community legislation, through teleological interpretation, in order to attain Community goals. It is moreover not readily apparent that a reading of individual concern of the kind proposed by Advocate General Jacobs or the CFI would involve any transgression of the bounds of normal Treaty interpretation, let alone that it would be akin to Treaty amendment through judicial fiat. The Treaty requires and has always required the applicant to prove individual concern. It is the meaning to be given to that phrase that is the question in issue. The meaning accorded in *Plaumann* is certainly linguistically possible, even though the result has been to limit very significantly the possibility of direct challenge. The fact that the *Plaumann* test is a possible reading of the text does not mean that any other interpretation would stray beyond the bounds of legitimate judicial interpretation. The ECJ in *UPA* gave no explanation as to why it felt that the Advocate General's test would be incompatible with

[111] Case C-50/00 P, *supra* n. 69, at para. 44. [112] Ibid. at para. 44.
[113] Ibid. at para. 45.

the wording of Article 230. There is in reality no reason why a test framed in terms of substantial adverse impact, or in the terms suggested by the CFI, cannot be a legitimate reading of the requirement of individual concern.

It is therefore fitting to consider practicality. While the ECJ in *UPA* said nothing about the practical consequences of a more liberal test one is left with the feeling that the ECJ was concerned with the workload problems that would follow from embracing a more liberal test. The practical consequences of such a change are a legitimate cause for concern. They should not, however, preclude a shift to a test of substantial adverse impact or something similar thereto. This is so for four reasons.

Firstly, the Community prides itself on being a legal order based on the rule of law. It is axiomatic to such an order that there should be proper mechanisms for the control of legality. A legal system may possess an impressive range of procedural and substantive principles for the review of governmental action, but these will be of scant comfort to those who cannot access the system because the standing rules are unduly narrow. It is right and proper in normative terms that those who have suffered some substantial adverse impact should have access to judicial review. This is more especially so given that such a test is no more liberal than that which prevails in most domestic legal orders. Insofar as such a test would increase caseload by allowing actions to be brought that cannot be brought at present that is a proper consequence for a legal system that regards itself as being based on the rule of law.

Secondly, there is in fact no reason why such a change should necessarily involve any dramatic net increase in the overall number of challenges to legality brought by non-privileged applicants. It should be remembered that at present the very fact that Article 230 is so restrictive forces applicants to use Article 234. Indeed this possibility was a central aspect of the ECJ's defence of the status quo. The ECJ has, however, almost no control over the range of applicants that can challenge via Article 234, or the type of norm that can be challenged. The consequence of a more liberal interpretation of standing under Article 230 would be to shift some of these cases back to the realm of direct challenge, and away from indirect challenge. It would indeed give the Community courts more scope for control through the determination of whether there was a substantial adverse impact.

Thirdly, the implicit assumption seems to be that there would be numerous challenges to any individual regulation by applicants, each of whom claimed to have suffered substantial adverse impact. This does not accord with legal or practical reality. This is in part because there is the possibility of cases being joined. It is in part because once the ECJ or CFI had pronounced on the legality of the contested measure in relation to a claim brought by an applicant who was deemed to have a substantial adverse impact that would be the end of the matter. The decision would resolve the issue in relation to any other possible claimant, unless they could raise some new legal argument that had not been addressed in the earlier case.

Finally, it must also be recognized that the Community courts can influence the number of actions that are brought through the standards of procedural and substantive review that they apply. The concern over the potential flood of case law has been felt in particular in relation to norms promulgated under the Common Agricultural Policy and the like, where there will often be winners and losers from any regime of agricultural regulation. The Community courts have, however, already signalled that they will not lightly find that such norms are disproportionate or discriminatory. The fact that applicants will have a relatively high hurdle to surmount in order to win on the substance of the case will have an impact on the number of actions brought, since applicants will calculate their chances of success before embarking on the expense of litigation.

G. The Constitutional Treaty and the Charter

The ECJ expressly placed the onus for reform on to the political agenda. The Convention on the Future of Europe established an ad hoc working group to consider issues relating to the Community Courts,[114] including the possible modification of Article 230. The Discussion Circle was divided on the matter:[115] one group felt that the current position was satisfactory taking account of indirect challenge, and therefore it was not necessary to change Article 230(4); another group felt that the current interpretation of Article 230(4) was too restrictive and should be broadened. The Chairman, Antonio Vitorino, proposed a compromise, which was incorporated in Article III-365(4) of the CT.[116]

> Any natural or legal person may, under the same conditions, institute proceedings against an act addressed to that person or which is of direct and individual concern to him or her, and against a regulatory act which is of direct concern to him or her and does not entail implementing measures.

The CT is very unlikely to become a reality in the light of the no votes in the French and Dutch referenda. It is nonetheless worth considering how far a provision of this kind would alleviate the problems adverted to above. The novelty of the provision is that individual concern would not have to be shown for regulatory acts which were of direct concern to a person and which did not entail implementing measures. Liberalization of this kind is to be welcomed, and goes some way to meet the difficulties exemplified by the

[114] Discussion Circle on the Court of Justice, CONV 543/03, Brussels 7 February 2003.

[115] Discussion Circle on the Court of Justice, CIRCLE I, Working Document 08, Brussels 11 March 2003.

[116] Treaty Establishing a Constitution for Europe, OJ 2004 C310/1.

existing case law. There are nonetheless reasons to believe that this particular cup would still be 'half empty rather than half full' even if such a reform were to be introduced through later Treaty amendment.

If the CT had been ratified the liberalization would only have applied in the case of regulatory acts as defined in the provisions on the hierarchy of norms. Article I-33(1) of the CT established the legal acts of the Union: European laws, European framework laws, European regulations, European decisions, recommendations, and opinions. European laws and European framework laws were regarded as legislative acts corresponding to old-style regulations and directives respectively. A European regulation was said to be a non-legislative act of general application for the implementation of legislative acts and certain specific provisions of the Constitution. It could either be binding in its entirety and directly applicable in all Member States, or be binding as regards the result to be achieved, on all the Member States to which it was addressed, but leaving the national authorities free to choose the form and means of achieving that result. This provision therefore embraced secondary European laws and secondary European framework laws. The liberalization contained in Article III-365(4) would therefore only have operated in relation to regulatory acts, secondary norms, and would not have applied in relation to EU laws, framework laws, decisions, or implementing acts. Thus where there was a European law that did not require implementing measures, it would still have been necessary for the individual to show direct and individual concern.[117]

There are also some dangers in recasting Article 230(4) in the manner suggested in the CT. There is nothing in Article III-365(4) equivalent to the provision in Article 230(4) EC that provides that an act in the form of a regulation may in reality be a decision that is of direct and individual concern to the applicant. There is therefore no invitation to look behind the form of the measure to its substance. There is moreover nothing to suggest any alteration of the *Plaumann* test as to the meaning of individual concern. Thus if an applicant challenges an act in the form of a decision which is addressed to a third party, but which the applicant claims is of individual concern to him or her, it would still be necessary to satisfy the *Plaumann* test with all its difficulties.

[117] The only way to avoid this conclusion would have been to read the phrase 'regulatory act' to mean something broader than the term European Regulation within Art. I-33(1). This might have been possible, but it would have been difficult both textually and historically. The formulation proposed by Commissioner Vitorino to the Discussion Circle had left open the type of act to which the new liberalization should apply: the draft had suggested that it might apply either to regulatory acts or to an act of general application. The CT embodied the former, not the latter. The significance of this choice should now be apparent. If the latter criterion had been adopted it could have been applicable to primary European laws, and not just secondary norms.

It should also be recognized that reform along the lines set out above does not address the more general difficulties with indirect challenge, which were set out by Advocate General Jacobs in the *UPA* case.[118] If the standing provisions for direct actions were changed in the above manner this would meet the problem of contesting a Community norm at national level where there were no implementing measures, but the more general difficulties of indirect challenge would not be touched by such a change.

It remains to be seen what impact if any the Community Charter of Fundamental Rights[119] might have, more especially if it is accorded binding legal status. Article 41 enshrines a right to good administration, which is said to inhere in every person. Article 41(2) sets out certain more specific rights that are included in this right. Article 47 provides that everyone whose rights and freedoms guaranteed by EU law are violated has the right to an effective remedy before a tribunal in compliance with the conditions laid down in this Article. Standing rules are not explicitly mentioned in either article. It would be open to the Community courts, if they wished to do so, to regard these provisions as the basis for expanding the existing standing rules. They are, however, unlikely to do so given their approach to standing hitherto. This is especially so given that the explanatory memorandum stated in relation to Article 47 that there was no intent for this provision to make any change to the rules on standing other than those embodied in the revised III-365(4).[120]

It should nonetheless be recognized that there is an uneasy tension between the Charter rights and the standing rules for direct actions. The Charter accords *individual rights*, yet the application of the standing rules means that a person who claims that his rights have been infringed by Community law would normally not be able to meet the requirements of *individual concern*. There is something decidedly odd about the infringement of an individual right not counting as a matter of individual concern. The ECJ touched on this in *Bactria*,[121] where the applicant argued that it should be regarded as individually concerned by the Regulation because it affected its property and data protection rights. The ECJ briefly concluded that the alleged infringement of the applicant's property right was insufficient to distinguish it individually for the purposes of standing. This conclusion is sustainable in formalistic terms, since the Regulation could equally affect the property rights of other operators in the area. This merely serves to demonstrate the limits of the formalistic reasoning. The fact that a Regulation might affect equally a number of traders does not alter the fact that the effect in the instant case is on the individual right that each possesses. In this sense *Bactria*

[118] Case C-50/00 P, *supra* n. 69.

[119] OJ 2000 C364/01.

[120] Charte 4473/00, Convent 49, 11 October 2000, at 41; CONV 828/03, Updated Explanations Relating to the Text of the Charter of Fundamental Rights, 9 July 2003, at 41.

[121] Case C-258/02 P, *Bactria, supra* n. 21, at paras. 48–51.

fails to resolve or recognize the tension between individual rights and individual concern.

5. CONCLUSION

It is clear that the scope of those entitled to take part in the making of the initial determination, and those entitled to challenge that determination before the courts, remains contentious.

The former has been shaped principally by the courts, but has been influenced also by the political branch, more especially the Commission. There has been relatively little difficulty in relation to process rights and individual decisions, although the application of the right to be heard in circumstances where administration is shared between the Community and the Member States has been problematic in certain instances. There continues to be greater difficulty in relation to process rights and norms of a legislative nature. It is by no means clear that the admixture of legal doctrine and political initiative has resolved this issue in a satisfactory manner, more especially given the broader concerns about legitimacy that are raised by consultation in rule-making.

The rules relating to standing remain problematic. This is the other main access point for those seeking to use administrative law doctrine. There continues to be a steady flow of cases where applicants seek to challenge Community norms directly through Article 230(4), the great majority of which are turned back at the gate. The Community courts continue to insist that we have a complete system of legal protection through the combination of the direct and the indirect action. This conclusion is difficult to sustain from the perspective of the individuals concerned. It has also led to undesirable institutional consequences, since insistence on recourse to indirect actions that are then heard by the ECJ has exacerbated its workload and many such challenges to the validity of Community action do not warrant the time of the Community's top court. The limited rules on standing may, moreover, lead to difficulties with the European Convention on Human Rights.[122]

[122] See below, at 523–531.

11

Process

1. INTRODUCTION

This chapter is concerned with process rights, and should be read in conjunction with the previous chapter on access. The sources of process rights are, as will become clear from the subsequent discussion, eclectic. Treaty articles, Community legislation, the Community courts, the European Ombudsman, and the Commission have all contributed towards the enumeration and interpretation of such process rights, drawing inspiration from provisions in national legal systems. The discussion that follows takes a broad view of process and addresses the topic from three perspectives.

The initial perspective is concerned with discrete process rights and the way that they have been developed by the Community courts and by Community legislation. The discussion begins with transparency. This will be followed by examination of the right to be heard. There will be a brief recapitulation of the criteria for the applicability of this right, before considering its content. The focus then shifts to the obligation of diligent and impartial examination, and thereafter to the duty to give reasons.

It is important to be clear at the outset about the relationship between these rights, since otherwise confusion will result: the 'trigger' for rendering these process rights applicable varies. It will be seen that, depending on the situation, the applicant might be entitled to all of these process rights, transparency, hearing, diligent examination, and reasons, albeit with the qualification that the content of these rights might vary with the specificities of the particular case. It will, however, also be apparent that an applicant might have a right to a diligent examination of the case, and a reasoned decision, but that there might be no right to a hearing. The appropriate visual metaphor is therefore one of overlapping circles, where each of the circles represents a particular process right, with the consequence that if a fact pattern falls within a certain area the applicant will be entitled to the process rights accorded by the circles that overlap at that point. This part of the discussion will conclude with some observations about the possible impact of the right to good administration contained in the Charter of Fundamental Rights.

The second perspective is concerned with process rights and sector-specific legislation. This helps us to understand how particular process rights fit together within a specific context. It sheds light on the interrelationship between process rights as developed by the Community courts and the Community legislature. It also reveals the interaction between process rights accorded to the individual and procedural rights and powers given to the administration, thereby serving as a counterweight to the asymmetry that characterizes much thought about process.

The final perspective considers the way in which the meaning accorded to process rights has broader implications for the more general aims and objectives of judicial review. There will be discussion of the extent to which the jurisprudence on reasons, access to the file, and the duty of diligent examination may evince movement, directly or indirectly, towards a dialogue between the individual and the decision-maker, requiring the latter to respond to arguments advanced by the former. There will also be analysis of the relationship between process rights, especially the duty to give reasons, and the intensity of substantive review, which serves as a fitting link between this chapter and subsequent discussion.

2. PROCESS AND TRANSPARENCY

A. The Values Served by Transparency

Transparency is rightly regarded as central to a democratic polity.[1] Access to the relevant documentation is crucial for understanding the reasons behind governmental action. It facilitates construction of a reasoned argument by those opposed to a measure. Access to documentation is moreover of the essence of democracy. Government should be accountable for its action, and this is difficult if it has a 'monopoly' over the available information. Individual citizens should be able to know the information held about them in order to check its correctness and the uses to which it is put. It is hoped furthermore that public disclosure of information will improve decision-making.

It should moreover be recognized that there is an additional value served by transparency in the context of the European Union (EU). Transparency serves not only to foster the preceding values as between citizen and the EU, but also functions as a valuable method of ensuring that Member States adhere to their EU obligations. Thus it is common to find obligations placed on Member States to be transparent about, for example, their regulatory

[1] P. Birkinshaw, *Freedom of Information, The Law, the Practice and the Ideal* (Butterworths, 3rd ed., 2001); P. Birkinshaw, *Government and Information: The Law Relating to Access, Disclosure and Their Regulation* (Tottel, 3rd ed., 2005).

choices in order to facilitate evaluation of whether those choices comply with EU law.[2]

The notion of transparency encompasses a number of different features, such as the holding of meetings in public, the provision of information and the right of access to documents. This latter right forms the most developed legal dimension of transparency and will be the principal focus of the subsequent discussion. It is clear therefore that transparency is connected with process more broadly than in relation to litigation, since it operates as an important safeguard for democracy and can foster critical evaluation of the decision-making process. While transparency is therefore of significance for 'process writ large' it should also be acknowledged that it can be of relevance for 'process writ small'. It is clear that transparency viewed in terms of access to documents can provide information that will then form the basis for a legal challenge to a Community measure.

B. Transparency and the EU Treaty

Transparency is a value that has become of increased importance within EU law since the Maastricht Treaty.[3] The early years of the European Economic Community (EEC) were weak in terms of democracy, accountability, and accessibility to public scrutiny. Meetings of the Council were secretive and minutes were not published. The Commission was perceived as a distant and remote bureaucracy and the Community processes as labyrinthine and opaque, populated by a bewildering number of committees.

There was a greater focus on transparency in the 1990s, not least as a result of the near failure to have the Treaty on European Union (TEU) ratified in Denmark and France. This was particularly apparent during the Intergovernmental Conference (IGC) preceding the Amsterdam Treaty where there was much discussion of the need to improve the openness and transparency of the Union and its institutions, in order to make them more accessible to the public.[4] Moreover, a number of Member States, such as the Netherlands, Denmark, and Sweden, increasingly objected to the secrecy

[2] For a recent example, see, Decision 2241/2004/EC of the European Parliament and of the Council of 15 December 2004, On a Single Community Framework for the Transparency of Qualifications (Europass), OJ 2004 L390/6. For more general discussion, see, Weatherill, 'New Strategies for Managing the EC's Internal Market' (2000) 53 *CLP* 595, at 608–617.

[3] Peers, 'From Maastricht to Laeken: The Political Agenda of Openness and Transparency in the EU', in V. Deckmyn (ed), *Increasing Transparency in the European Union* (Maastricht EIPA, 2002); Tomkins, 'Transparency and the Emergence of a European Administrative Law' (1999–2000) 19 *YBEL* 217.

[4] Lodge, 'Transparency and Democratic Legitimacy' (1994) 32 *JCMS* 343; de Búrca, 'The Quest for Legitimacy in the European Union' (1996) 59 *MLR* 359.

surrounding the Council of Ministers, and were dissatisfied with the steps which the Council had taken.[5]

The Council and Commission adopted a joint Code of Conduct in 1993,[6] and each implemented it into their rules of procedure by decision.[7] The 1993 Inter-institutional Declaration on Democracy, Transparency, and Subsidiarity provided further impetus for reform, since it expressed at the highest possible level the EU's commitment towards, *inter alia*, greater transparency.[8]

The Treaty of Amsterdam enshrined access to documents as a Treaty right. Article 1 of the TEU, as amended by the Treaty of Amsterdam, states that decisions shall be taken as openly and as closely as possible to the citizen, and Article 255(1) EC provides:[9]

> Any citizen of the Union, and any natural or legal person residing or having its registered office in a Member State, shall have a right of access to European Parliament, Council and Commission documents, subject to the principles and the conditions to be defined in accordance with paragraphs 2 and 3.

Article 255(2) stipulated that the general principles concerning such access and the limits thereto should be determined by the Council, acting in accord with the Article 251 EC procedure, within two years of the entry into force of the Treaty of Amsterdam. Article 255(3) instructed each institution to adopt Rules of Procedure regarding access to documents. This point was reinforced in relation to the Council by Article 207(3), specifying that access to documents, explanations and results of votes, and statements of minutes are particularly important when the Council is acting in its legislative capacity.

The legislation required by Article 255 EC was adopted in the form of a Regulation in 2001,[10] following a number of earlier more specific decisions. Regulation 1049/2001 improved the position governing access to documents

[5] Curtin, 'Betwixt and Between: Democracy and Transparency in the Governance of the European Union', in J. Winter *et al.* (eds), *Reforming the Treaty on European Union: The Legal Debate* (Kluwer, 1996), at 95; Curtin, 'Citizens' Fundamental Right of Access to EU Information: An Evolving Digital Passepartout?' (2000) 37 *CMLRev* 7.

[6] Code of Conduct Concerning Access to Council and Commission Documents, OJ 1993 L340/41.

[7] Council Decision 93/731/EC of 20 December, On Public Access to Council Documents, OJ 1993 L340/43; Commission Decision 94/90/ECSC, EC, Euratom of 8 February 1994, On Public Access to Commission Documents, OJ 1994 L46/58; M. Westlake, *The Council of the European Union* (Cartermill, 1995), at 144–162.

[8] It was adopted by the Commission, Council and EP on the margins of the 1993 Brussels European Council, M. Westlake, *The Commission and the Parliament, Partners and Rivals in the European Policy-Making Process* (Butterworths, 1994), at 159–161.

[9] Art. 255 EC was held to lack direct effect in Case T-191/99, *Petrie v Commission* [2001] ECR II-3677.

[10] Regulation (EC) 1049/2001 of the European Parliament and of the Council of 30 May 2001, Regarding Public Access to European Parliament, Council and Commission Documents, OJ 2001 L145/43.

in several respects, by, for example, abolishing the authorship rule, softening the nature of some of the exceptions, and requiring a register of documents to be kept.[11] The new legislation was implemented by the three EU institutions into their own rules of procedure,[12] and has been applied to EU agencies.[13] The right of access to documents is moreover now enshrined in Article 42 of the Charter of Fundamental Rights of the European Union.[14]

The European Ombudsman has been central to the development of openness and transparency as broader principles of law. He undertook an own-initiative inquiry into public access to documents addressed to 15 Community institutions other than the Council and Commission.[15] The Ombudsman concluded that failure to adopt rules governing public access to documents and to make those rules easily available to the public constituted maladministration. The consequence was that most other important EU bodies including the Court of Auditors, the European Central Bank (ECB), and agencies adopted rules governing access to documents.

C. Transparency and the Community Courts

The Community courts were generally supportive of transparency, even before the reforms brought in by the Treaty of Amsterdam, but they refrained from far-reaching statements of principle that would enshrine a general right of transparency or access to information.

The Court of First Instance (CFI) stressed in *Carvel*[16] that when the Council exercised its discretion whether to release documents it must genuinely balance the interests of citizens in gaining access to documents with the need to maintain confidentiality of its deliberations. It could not simply adopt a general blanket denial of access to a class of documents. The CFI held, however, that transparency did not require the adoption of secondary

[11] Peers, *supra* n. 3; Peers, 'The New Regulation on Access to Documents: A Critical Analysis' (2002) 21 *YBEL* 385; Broberg, 'Access to Documents: A General Principle of Community Law' (2002) 27 *ELRev* 194; de Leeuw, 'The Regulation on Public Access to European Parliament, Council and Commission Documents in the European Union: Are Citizens Better Off?' (2003) 28 *ELRev* 324; Bjurluf and Elgström, 'Negotiating Transparency' (2004) 42 *JCMS* 249. For discussion of the applicability of the transparency rules to the second and third pillars of the EU, see Peers, 'Access to Information on EU External Relations and Justice and Home Affairs', in Deckmyn, *supra* n. 3.

[12] Council Decision 2002/682/EC, Euratom of 22 July 2002, Adopting the Council's Rules of Procedure, OJ 2002 L230/7; Commission Decision 2001/937/EC, ECSC, Euratom of 5 December 2001, Amending its Rules of Procedure, OJ 2001 L345/94.

[13] See above, at 175–176; Lenaerts, ' "In the Union we Trust": Trust Enhancing Principles of Community Law' (2004) 41 *CMLRev* 317, at 321.

[14] OJ 2000 C364/1. [15] (616/PUBAC/F/IJH), OJ 1998 C44/9.

[16] Case T-194/94, *Carvel and Guardian Newspapers Ltd v Council* [1995] ECR II-2765; Case T-105/95, *WWF UK (World Wide Fund for Nature) v Commission* [1997] ECR II-313.

legislation by the Council, declaring instead that Council decisions on access to documents could properly be based on its Rules of Procedure.

In *Netherlands v Council*[17] the Dutch government argued that the principle of openness of the legislative process was an essential requirement of democracy, and that the right of access to information was an internationally recognized fundamental human right. The European Court of Justice (ECJ) confirmed the importance of the right of public access to information, and its relationship to the democratic nature of the institutions, but rejected the argument that such a fundamental right should not be dealt with purely as a matter of the Council's internal Rules of Procedure.

In *Hautala*, the ECJ upheld the CFI's decision to annul the Council's refusal to consider granting partial access to politically sensitive documents, but the ECJ declared that it was not necessary for it to pronounce on whether or not EC law recognized a general 'principle of the right to information'.[18]

Nonetheless, despite the failure to articulate a general principle of transparency or a general right of access to information, the Community courts played a significant role in elaborating the nature and content of the right of access to information contained in the procedural rules and legislative decisions of the institutions. Thus the CFI and the ECJ annulled a number of decisions of the Council and Commission refusing access to their documents, not on the ground that the institutions had breached a 'general principle of transparency', but on other grounds such as the automatic application of non-mandatory exceptions, the inappropriate use of the authorship rule, the refusal to consider partial access, or the inadequacy of the reasons given for refusal.[19]

D. Transparency, Regulation 1049/2001, and the Community Courts

The present regime for access to documentation is governed by Regulation 1049/2001. It is therefore important to focus more closely on this Regulation and its interpretation by the Community courts. Any regime of access to information will contain provisions defining the institutions covered, the meaning of the term document, the beneficiaries of the scheme, and the exceptions that limit or preclude access. Regulation 1049/2001 follows this general pattern. Judicial interpretation of this Regulation has been 'mixed', with some good decisions, and others that are more contestable. This can be exemplified by focusing on key issues that have arisen in the courts' jurisprudence.

[17] Case C-58/94, *Netherlands v Council* [1996] ECR I-2169, at paras. 31–36.

[18] Case C-353/99 P, *Hautala v Council* [2001] ECR I-9565, at para. 31.

[19] See, e.g., Case T-105/95, *WWF, supra* n. 16; Case T-188/97, *Rothmans International v Commission* [1999] ECR II-2463; Case T-174/95, *Svenska Journalistförbundet v Council* [1998] ECR II-2289; Case C-353/99 P, *Kuijer v Council* [2001] ECR I-9565; Case T-211/00, *Kuijer v Council* [2002] ECR II-485.

(1) *Protecting the Reality of Access*

The Community courts have been willing to protect the reality of access. This is evident from *Hautala*[20] where the ECJ held that the right of access to documents included access to information contained in the document, not just the document itself. The ECJ held further that proportionality required the Council to consider partial access to a document that contained information the disclosure of which could endanger international relations, and that derogation from the right of access should be limited to what was appropriate and necessary for achieving the aim in view. The aim pursued by the Council in refusing access to the contested report could be achieved if the Council removed, after examination, the passages that might harm international relations.

The CFI adopted the same approach in *Verein für Konsumenteninformation*,[21] notwithstanding the volume of documentation involved. The applicant, VKI, was an Austrian consumer organization with legal capacity under Austrian law to bring actions on behalf of consumers where they had assigned rights to VKI. The VKI sought access to documents held by the Commission concerning a cartel found to exist in the banking sector, in order to enable it to pursue legal actions in Austria for customers that might have been charged excessive rates of interest. The file was large and the Commission denied VKI's request in its entirety, stating *inter alia* that the documents were covered by exceptions to the Regulation governing access, and that partial access was not possible since a detailed examination of each document would entail an excessive amount of work. The CFI held that the Regulation required the Commission in principle to carry out a concrete individual assessment of the content of the documents contained in the request, except where it was manifestly clear that access should be refused or granted. The refusal to undertake any concrete assessment was therefore in principle manifestly disproportionate.[22] There could, said the CFI, be cases where because of the number of documents requested the Commission must retain the right to balance the interest in public access against the burden of work in order to safeguard the interests of good administration. This possibility was, however, only applicable in exceptional cases. The right of access, coupled with concrete individual examination, was the norm.[23] The CFI acknowledged that the relevant file was large, but nonetheless annulled the Commission's decision.

[20] Case C-353/99 P, *Hautala, supra* n. 18. See also, Case C-41/00 P, *Interporc Im- und Export GmbH v Commission* [2003] ECR I-2125, at paras. 42–44; Case C-353/01 P, *Mattila v Commission* [2004] ECR I-1073, at paras. 30–32.

[21] Case T-2/03, *Verein für Konsumenteninformation v Commission,* judgment of 13 April 2005, not yet published.

[22] Ibid. at para. 100.

[23] Ibid. at paras. 101–115.

(2) Interpretation of the Exceptions

It is readily apparent that the effectiveness of any regime for access to information will be crucially affected by the exceptions contained in the legislation and the way in which these are interpreted by the courts. The exceptions in Regulation 1049/2001 are listed in Article 4. They vary in nature. Most are qualified by provisions allowing access even if the document relates to a protected interest where there is an overriding public interest in disclosure.[24] There are, however, some exceptions that are mandatory, in the sense that access is prohibited where disclosure would undermine the relevant interest with no provision allowing access on grounds of public interest.[25]

There are a number of juridical techniques open to courts when construing such provisions. They can review the facts to determine whether the institution properly invoked the exception; they can decide on the legal meaning of an exception; and they can pass judgment on whether the public interest warrants disclosure. The Community courts state repeatedly that exceptions to the right of access to documents should be interpreted narrowly. There are, however, a number of contestable decisions, where the Community courts have used the juridical techniques at their disposal sparingly to say the least.

The *Sison* case[26] reveals the judicial approach to the determination of whether an exception was properly invoked. The applicant's assets were frozen pursuant to a Community Regulation enacted to combat terrorism and he sought access to documentation that had served to place him on the relevant list. The CFI reiterated the principle that exceptions to access should be construed narrowly,[27] and that it was for the institution to show that the documents to which access was sought fell within one of the listed exceptions.[28]

The CFI, however, also held that the Council had a wide discretion in deciding whether access should be refused on the ground that it might harm the public interest, and hence judicial review was limited to deciding whether procedural rules including the duty to give reasons had been complied with, and whether there had been a manifest error or misuse of power.[29] The scope of review was further qualified because the CFI held that it might be impossible to give reasons justifying the need for confidentiality in respect of individual documents without disclosing the document and thereby depriving the exception of its purpose.[30] This argument can, however, be met, since the court could consider such reasons in private, which would enable it to take an

[24] Reg. 1049/2001, *supra* n. 10, Art. 4(2)–(3). [25] Ibid. Art. 4(1).

[26] Cases T-110, 150, 405/03, *Sison v Council*, judgment of 25 April 2005, not yet published.

[27] Ibid. at para. 45. [28] Ibid. at para. 60. [29] Ibid. at paras. 46–47.

[30] Ibid. at paras. 60, 63.

informed view as to whether invocation of the exception really was warranted in relation to the relevant documents. The CFI nonetheless rejected the plea relating to the provision of reasons, notwithstanding the court's acknowledgement that the reasons given were 'formulaic' and 'brief'.[31] This rendered it virtually impossible for the applicant to challenge the legality of his inclusion on the list of those whose assets should be frozen.

In the *IFAW* case[32] it was the legal meaning of an exception to Regulation 1049/2001 that came before the CFI. It held that Article 4(5) of Regulation 1049/2001, which provides that a Member State may request the Community institution not to disclose a document originating from that Member State without its prior agreement, constituted an instruction from the Member State to the Community institution not to disclose the relevant document. This was so notwithstanding the wording of Article 4(5), which was not framed in mandatory terms and did not naturally suggest that the Member State possessed a veto in this regard. If the Community legislature had intended the Member States to have a veto power this could have been simply and clearly expressed in terms comparable to Article 9(3) of the Regulation, which states that sensitive documents shall be released only with the consent of the originator.

In the *Turco* case[33] the legal meaning of a different exception came before the CFI. The applicant sought documents relating to a proposed Council Directive on minimum standards for reception of asylum seekers in Member States. The Council refused access to the opinion of its legal service, relying on the exception for legal advice contained in Regulation 1049/2001.[34] The CFI held that the exception for legal advice could in principle apply to advice given during the legislative as well as the judicial process, but that the mere fact that the document was a legal opinion did not in itself justify invocation of the exception.[35] The Council justified its refusal to disclose by arguing that it could give rise to uncertainty as regards the legality of legislative acts adopted following such advice, and that disclosure would be premature since it might reveal the position taken by particular delegations and hence reduce their ability to reconsider their positions.

The CFI acknowledged that these arguments could apply to all legal advice relating to legislative acts, and not just the specific legal opinion at issue here. It nonetheless held that the Council's reasoning was justified, since if any further information were given it would deprive the exception of its

[31] Ibid. at paras. 63, 65.

[32] Case 168/02, *IFAW Internationaler Tierschutz-Fonds GmbH v Commission*, judgment of 30 November 2004, not yet published. See also, Case T-187/03, *Scippacercola v Commission*, judgment of 17 March 2005, not yet published.

[33] Case T-84/03, *Turco v Council*, judgment of 23 November 2004, not yet published.

[34] Reg. 1049/2001, *supra* n. 10, Art. 4(2).

[35] Case T-84/03, *Turco, supra* n. 33, at paras. 56, 71.

effect;[36] it could give rise to 'lingering doubts as to the lawfulness of the legislative act in question';[37] and it might expose the Council's legal service to improper external influence.[38]

It can be accepted that it might well be necessary to protect advice proffered by the legal services in relation to particular legislative acts, but the effect of the judgment is that such advice relating to legislative acts will generally be *prima facie* immune from disclosure. The rationale proffered is unconvincing. The fact that the legal service might express doubt as to the legality of a legislative act or part thereof is surely not a good reason to deny access to its opinion, more especially if the Council chooses to press ahead with the measure notwithstanding those doubts. If there are qualms concerning the legality of a measure expressed by expert legal insiders, EU citizens should be able to know this. The relevant legislative act, once duly enacted, would still be lawful and binding on those affected unless and until legally challenged. If challenged it may well be that a court would reject the doubts expressed by the legal service, and the measure would remain valid. If the court agreed with the concerns voiced by the legal service then the measure would be annulled as it should be. The idea that the legal service might be subject to improper external influence seems fanciful. It is perfectly robust enough to rebuff any such pressure and in any event it would be possible to devise rules to prevent this. The related idea that the legal service might be less candid if it knew that its opinion might be disclosed is equally suspect. The 'diminishing candour' argument has been used time and again by public organs seeking to resist freedom of information legislation. The fact that disclosure might in some way undermine the smooth running of institutional business should not suffice to justify refusal of access.[39]

The *Turco* case also casts light on how the Community courts will use the third juridical option at their disposal, the balancing test. The exception for legal advice is one that can be overridden where disclosure would be in the public interest. The applicant argued that this was so in the instant case, because of principles of transparency, openness, and participation of the citizen in the decision-making process. The CFI rejected the argument. It held that those principles were implemented through Regulation 1049/2001 as a whole and that therefore the applicant should present arguments for an overriding public interest that were distinct from these principles, or at the very least show why those principles were especially pressing in the particular case.[40]

The reasoning reveals the difficulties of applying the balancing test. While

[36] Ibid. at para. 74. [37] Ibid. at para. 78. [38] Ibid. at para. 79.

[39] Case T-111/00, *British American Tobacco International (Investments) Ltd v Commission* [2001] ECR II-2997, at para. 52.

[40] Case T-84/03, *Turco, supra* n. 33, at paras. 82–83.

the CFI is surely right to point out that principles of openness, transparency, and the like permeate Regulation 1049/2001 as a whole, it is for this very reason that they are likely to inform or underpin the applicant's argument that the exception should be overridden because of the public interest in disclosure. The difficulty faced by the applicant in fashioning this argument should moreover be recognized, since he or she will often be in a 'Catch 22' situation. The applicant is required to proffer convincing reasons why the public interest necessitates overriding the exception in circumstances where the information that might sustain this argument is contained in documents that are protected and hence unseen. It is true that this is an endemic problem where freedom of information legislation contains qualified exceptions of the kind in issue here. The problem should nonetheless be borne firmly in mind since otherwise the hurdle faced by an applicant in proving an overriding public interest will always prove too high.

E. Conclusion

There is no doubt that the EU has taken important steps towards greater transparency. Developments such as Article 255 EC, Regulation 1049/2001, and Article 42 of the Charter of Fundamental Rights, led Judge Lenaerts, writing extra-judicially, to conclude that 'it can at present hardly be denied that the principle of transparency has evolved into a general principle of Community law'.[41] This view is reinforced by the ECJ's greater willingness to read Community legislation as subject to transparency, even where there is no explicit mention of this principle in the relevant articles of the legislation.[42]

It is, however, equally important to be mindful of the fact that even if transparency is regarded as a general principle of Community law, the impact of this on citizens will be crucially dependent on the meaning accorded to the principle in specific cases. The courts' jurisprudence when interpreting Regulation 1049/2001 is a timely reminder that we should look beyond general judicial statements of the need to afford real protection for the right of access to documents, in order to consider how the judiciary interpret and apply the detailed provisions of the legislation in concrete cases.

We should moreover be aware of the practical operation of Regulation 1049/2001. Thus the Commission in its review of this Regulation noted that those who had benefited were mainly specialists and that increased efforts should be made to bring the Regulation to the attention of the general

[41] Lenaerts, ' "In the Union we Trust" ', *supra* n. 13, at 321.

[42] Cases 154 and 155/04, *The Queen, on the application of Alliance for Natural Health and Nutri-Link Ltd v Secretary of State for Health* [2005] ECR I-6451, at paras. 81–82.

public.[43] The review contained interesting data on success rates, with more than two out of every three applications receiving a positive response.[44] It is clear that only a few of the exceptions are regularly invoked[45] and the Commission, while generally satisfied with the exceptions, felt that they did not, however, take adequate account of the inter-institutional nature of decision-making in the EC.[46] It also expressed concern about the impact of unreasonable or repetitive applications.[47]

There are other recent developments of note concerning transparency. There has been some extension of access to the public in relation to Council proceedings.[48] The Commission announced a Transparency Initiative, the details of which are to be set out in a Green Paper, and it is designed to improve transparency in relation to matters such as the use of Community funds, the role played by lobby groups, and consultation with civil society.[49]

3. PROCESS AND HEARING

Any legal system will have to determine the applicability of the right to a hearing and the content of that right if a hearing is accorded. The previous chapter considered in detail the criteria for the applicability of hearing rights and the distinction drawn in this respect between individualized determinations and norms of a legislative nature.[50] There will therefore be a very brief summary of applicability of hearing rights in individualized determinations, followed by more detailed treatment of the content of hearing rights.

A. Applicability

It is important not to lose sight of the background principles that serve to justify procedural rights in individual adjudications. The twin rationales are instrumental and non-instrumental or dignitarian.[51] The former justifies process rights because they will render it more likely that a correct outcome will be reached on the substance of the case.[52] The latter sees the justification

[43] Report from the Commission, On the Implementation of the Principles in EC Regulation 1049/2001 Regarding Public Access to European Parliament, Council and Commission Documents, COM(2004) 45 final, at 2.5.

[44] Ibid. at 3.11.

[45] Ibid. at 6.3.

[46] Ibid. at 3.4.4.

[47] Ibid. at 4.10.

[48] Shaw, 'Transparency and the Council of Ministers' (2006) *Federal Trust Newsletter* 3.

[49] <http://europa.eu.int/comm/commission_barroso/kallas/transparency_en.htm>.

[50] See above, at 314–322.

[51] J. Mashaw, *Due Process in the Administrative State* (Yale University Press, 1985); D. Galligan, *Due Process and Fair Procedures* (Oxford University Press, 1996), at 75–82.

[52] Resnick, 'Due Process and Procedural Justice', in J. Pennock and J. Chapman (eds), *Due Process* (Nomos, 1977), at 217.

as being a broader part of what it means to treat a person as a human being, with the corollary that a hearing should be accorded before taking action that can deleteriously affect an individual.[53] It is perfectly possible to support both, albeit in varying degrees.

The Community courts have been activist in protecting process in relation to individualized decisions. They have imposed a right to be heard as a general rule of Community law, irrespective of whether this requirement was found in the relevant Treaty article, regulation, directive, or decision. The general trend of the case law has been to require a hearing even where no sanction is imposed, provided that there is some adverse impact, or some significant affect on the applicant's interests,[54] and the Community courts have applied and adapted this criterion to the many instances where administration is shared between the Community and the Member States.

The right to be heard has been held to be part of the fundamental rights jurisprudence.[55] It cannot be excluded or restricted by any legislative provision, and the principle must be protected both where there is no specific Community legislation and also where legislation exists, but does not take sufficient account of the principle.[56] Observance of the right to be heard can be raised by the Court of its own motion.[57] The right to be heard before an individual measure is taken that would affect a person adversely is included within the Charter of Fundamental Rights.[58]

B. Content: General Approach

All legal systems necessarily have to determine the content of the right to be heard. This will include matters such as the right to notice of the relevant decision; whether there is a right to an oral hearing or only a paper hearing;

[53] H.L.A. Hart, *Concept of Law* (Clarendon Press, 1961), at 156, 202; J. Rawls, *A Theory of Justice* (Oxford University Press, 1973), at 235; Michelman, 'Formal and Associational Aims in Procedural Due Process', in *Due Process, supra* n. 52, Chap. 4; Mashaw, *supra* n. 51, Chaps. 4–7.

[54] Case T-450/93, *Lisrestal v Commission* [1994] ECR II-1177; Case C-32/95 P, *Commission v Lisrestal* [1996] ECR I-5373; Case T-50/96, *Primex Produkte Import-Export GmbH & Co. KG v Commission* [1998] ECR II-3773, at para. 59; Case C-462/98 P, *MedioCurso-Etabelecimento de Ensino Particular Ld v Commission* [2000] ECR I-7183, at para. 36; Case C-395/00, *Distillerie Fratelli Cipriani SpA v Ministero delle Finanze* [2002] ECR I-11877, at para. 51; Case T-102/00, *Vlaams Fonds voor de Sociale Integratie van Personen met een Handicap v Commission* [2003] ECR II-2433, at para. 59.

[55] Case C-49/88, *Al-Jubail Fertilizer v Council* [1991] ECR I-3187, at para. 15; Cases T-33–34/98, *Petrotub and Republica SA v Council* [1999] ECR II-3837; Case C-458/98 P, *Industrie des Poudres Sphériques v Council and Commission* [2000] ECR I-8147, at para. 99.

[56] Case T-260/94, *Air Inter SA v Commission* [1997] ECR II-997, at para. 60.

[57] Case C-291/89, *Interhotel v Commission* [1991] ECR I-2257, at para. 14; Case C-367/95 P, *Commission v Sytraval and Brink's France* [1998] ECR I-1719, at para. 67.

[58] *Charter of Fundamental Rights of the European Union*, OJ 2000 C364/1, Art. 41(2).

whether the hearing must precede the relevant decision or whether it can be given thereafter; whether there should be any right to discovery of documents or any right to cross-examination; whether the evidential rules applied in a normal trial should be modified or relaxed in their application to administrative decision-making; whether there can be any contact between the administration and one of the parties prior to the decision being made; whether causation should matter, in the sense that the reviewing court should consider if the hearing would have made a difference to the final outcome; whether there is a right to be represented by a lawyer; whether reasons should be given for the decision; and the meaning to be given to impartiality.

Any legal system will also have to decide how to go about deciding these issues. There are a number of options.[59] At one end of the spectrum is the all-embracing procedural code, which addresses such matters in detail. At the other end of the spectrum are *ad hoc* judicial decisions, with the courts deciding the issues on a case by case basis. There are various options in between. The courts may develop a general formula through which to determine the content of process rights.[60] Legislation may stipulate the content of process rights for hearings of a certain type, for example those that are more formal in nature.[61] The content of hearing rights can alternatively be determined by a mixture of *ad hoc* case law, combined with sector-specific legislation that applies the courts' precepts and fleshes them out.

The last of these most accurately captures the position in the EU. There is no general, detailed procedural code. This is in part because it was not felt to be desirable, given the diversity of situation to which it would have to apply, and in part because there were doubts as to whether the EU had competence to enact such a measure, although the Constitutional Treaty (CT), if ratified, had addressed the latter problem.[62] There is no explicit balancing formula of the kind embodied in the *Mathews* case in the USA,[63] although there may well be evidence of implicit balancing. There is no legislative stipulation of a set formula of process rights that must be applied to, for example, all formal adjudications. The reality is that the courts have developed the content of process rights on a case by case basis. The precepts laid down by the courts have then been taken up into sector-specific legislation and moulded in a detailed manner to fit the needs of the area.

[59] Harlow, 'Codification of EC Administrative Procedures? Fitting the Foot to the Shoe or the Shoe to the Foot' (1996) 2 *ELJ* 3; Shapiro, 'Codification of Administrative Law: The US and the Union' (1996) 2 *ELJ* 26; della Cananea, 'Beyond the State: The Europeanization and Globalization of Procedural Administrative Law' (2003) 9 *EPL* 563.

[60] See, e.g., the approach adopted in relation to the content of constitutional due process in the USA, *Mathews v Eldridge* 424 US 319 (1976).

[61] This is the methodology for formal adjudication and formal rulemaking under the Administrative Procedure Act 1946 in the USA.

[62] Art. III-398 CT. [63] *Supra* n. 60.

The development of the content of the right to a hearing by the Community courts, and the way in which this is then filled out by sector-specific legislation, is especially interesting in the EU, given the fact that some national administrative law systems are grounded in the common law, others within the civil law tradition. This does not necessarily mean that there will be differences in concrete doctrine as between such regimes, nor does it mean that the EU will simply 'cut and paste' from such systems when developing EU administrative law. We should nonetheless be mindful of the fact that certain aspects of national administrative law doctrine will be grounded in assumptions derived from common law or civil law modes of thought, and these assumptions will not always cohere. The Community courts will therefore necessarily have to choose which mode of thought to prioritise when fashioning the detailed rules concerning the content of the right to be heard. With this cautionary note in mind, we can now examine certain of the key aspects of the right to a hearing. The principle of care in the discharge of Community administration and the duty to give reasons will be subject to separate analysis.

C. Content: Notice and the Right to Respond

The Community courts have been assiduous in their insistence that notice should be given of the nature of the case and that the individual should have a right to respond to it.

This is exemplified by *Netherlands v Commission*.[64] The ECJ annulled a Commission decision finding that a Dutch law regulating postal services was in breach of Article 86(1) EC. The Commission, before making the decision, had sent a telex to the Dutch government informing it that it believed the law to be in violation of Article 86 EC and the government responded. The ECJ held that the rights of the defence had been infringed because the telex had been cast in general terms, without setting out in detail the features of the national law that were felt to place it in breach of Community law. The Court stated that the Member State must receive 'an exact and complete statement of the objections which the Commission intended to raise against it',[65] and that the Member State must be 'placed in a position in which it may effectively make known its views on the observations submitted by interested third parties',[66] in this case private messenger service organizations.

It is clear moreover from *Vlaamse Televisie Maatschappij*[67] that while the

[64] Cases C-48 and 66/90, *Netherlands and Koninklijke PTT Nederland NV and PTT Post v Commission* [1992] ECR 565.

[65] Ibid. at para. 45.

[66] Ibid. at para. 46; Case C-301/87, *France v Commission* [1990] ECR I-307, at para. 30.

[67] Case T-266/97, *Vlaamse Televisie Maatschappij NV v Commission* [1999] ECR II-2329, at paras. 32–37.

direct beneficiary of a state measure named in the law contested under Article 86 EC is not in the same position as the state itself, and must be regarded as a third party in this respect, it must nonetheless have a right to be heard where it is directly affected in economic terms by the Commission decision. The Commission was required to communicate formally with such an undertaking, informing it of the objections to the state measure and allowing it the opportunity to respond, although it did not have to afford the undertaking the opportunity to comment on the views of the Member State or third parties.

The importance of notice and the right to respond is equally apparent from *Fiskano*.[68] The applicant fishing company was penalized for fishing in Community waters without the requisite licence on the relevant dates, with the consequence that it would not be considered for a fishing licence for a further period of twelve months. The ECJ annulled the Commission decision on the ground that the right to be heard requires that any person 'on whom a penalty may be imposed must be placed in a position in which he can effectively make known his view of the matters' concerning the basis on which the Commission imposed the penalty.[69]

The nature of the right to respond was explicated in more detail in *MDF*,[70] where the ECJ stated in the context of a competition violation that during the administrative procedure the undertaking must be afforded the opportunity to make known its views on the truth and relevance of the facts and the circumstances alleged and on the documents used by the Commission to show an infringement of the Treaty.

The Community courts have also protected the right to notice and the right to respond in cases where administration is shared between the Commission and Member States. We have already seen that the Community courts have protected the right to be heard in cases of shared administration.[71] The content of the right in such cases is exemplified by *Eyckeler*.[72] The case concerned remission of import duties. The regulatory scheme provided for an initial assessment by the national authority, which could reject the application of its own volition. If it believed the remission should be granted the national authority had to submit the matter to the Commission, which

[68] Case C-135/92, *Fiskano AB v Commission* [1994] ECR I-2885.

[69] Ibid. at para. 40.

[70] Cases 100–103/80, *Musique Diffusion Française v Commission* [1983] ECR 1825, at para. 10; Cases C-204–205, 211, 213, 217, 219/00 P, *Aalborg Portland v Commission* [2004] ECR I-123, at para. 66.

[71] See above, at 315–316.

[72] Case T-42/96, *Eyckeler & Malt AG v Commission* [1998] ECR II-401; Case T-346/94, *France-Aviation v Commission* [1995] ECR II-2841; Case T-50/96, *Primex Produkte, supra* n. 54, at paras. 57–70; Cases T-186, 187, 190, 192, 210, 211, 216–218, 279–280, 293/97 and 147/99, *Kaufring AG v Commission* [2001] ECR II-1337, at paras. 151–162.

made the final decision. The regulatory scheme provided for contact between the individual concerned and the national administration, and between the national administration and the Commission, but there was no provision for a right to be heard by the applicant before the Commission. The CFI nonetheless held that the rights of defence, including the right to be heard, were fundamental whenever the contested measure could have an adverse impact on the individual, with the consequence that the applicant should be placed in a position from which he could effectively make his views known, at least as regards the matters taken into account by the Commission as the basis for its decision.[73]

The right to be heard will not necessarily require an oral hearing.[74] The ECJ will normally leave it to the Commission to make the initial determination as to whether the hearing should be oral, or whether the opportunity to make written observations should suffice. It is, however, in principle open to the Community courts to decide that the right to be heard requires, in the particular circumstances of the case, an oral hearing. Moreover, sector-specific legislation may stipulate that oral hearings should be required for some part of the decision-making process, as is the case in the context of competition.[75]

D. Content: Access to the File

An important component of the right to be heard is access to the file. The nature and significance of this right should be made clear at the outset. Access to the file may be of relevance before the decision is made by the administration, or after it has been made when an applicant seeks to challenge the decision by way of judicial review. Access facilitates understanding of the evidentiary basis on which the decision is to be made or has been made, and of the reasoning underlying it, thereby placing the individual in a better position from which to be able to proffer counter-arguments when exercising the right to be heard or challenging the decision by way of judicial review.

It will be seen that EU law, after some initial hesitation and subject to some reservations, accords access to the file as part of the rights of the defence. This is by way of contrast to, for example, the situation in the UK, where there is no such right of access to the file prior to the initial decision being taken. Nor is there any such right when seeking judicial review: the individual must apply for discovery/disclosure of documentation from the public body, and the UK courts have placed strict limitations as to when this

[73] Case T-42/96, *Eyckeler, supra* n. 72, at paras. 76–78.

[74] J. Schwarze, *European Administrative Law* (Sweet & Maxwell, 1992), at 1363–1364.

[75] See below, at 387–393.

will be ordered.[76] A right of access to the file is, however, accorded in a number of Member States.[77]

The fact that EU law has sanctioned access when the initial decision is being made is therefore to be welcomed as a valuable process right, as is the inclusion of this right as one component of the right to good administration in the Charter of Fundamental Rights.[78] The initial jurisprudence was developed in relation to competition law, but has been extended to other areas. The application of the principle of access is not especially difficult where the decision affects only one party or a small number of parties. It can, however, be problematic when the administrative decision affects a multiplicity of parties, even more so where the litigation is complex and generates a large amount of documentation, as exemplified by some cases on horizontal cartels. The Community courts have placed certain limitations on access in such instances, and these should be critically appraised. It should also be recognized that such limits have only been necessary because of the breadth of the initial principle concerning access to the file.

The early jurisprudence on access arose in competition proceedings.[79] The ECJ initially held in *VBVB*[80] that there was no legal obligation to disclose the complete file, only those documents on which the Commission had based its decision. The Commission chose not to stick to the legal letter of this judgment, and permitted access, except where, for example, information covered by professional secrecy was involved. The CFI in *Hercules*[81] gave legal force to this administrative practice. The Commission is obliged to make available all documents obtained in the course of the investigation, save where they involve business secrets of other undertakings, confidential information, or internal Commission documents.[82] This was regarded as part of a wider principle of equality of arms, allowing addressees of a decision to examine the

[76] P. Craig, *Administrative Law* (Sweet & Maxwell, 5th ed., 2003), Chap. 23.

[77] Case C-310/93 P, *BPB Industries and British Gypsum v Commission* [1995] ECR I-865, at 890–893, AG Leger.

[78] Art. 41(2), OJ 2000 C364/1.

[79] Schwarze, *supra* n. 74, at 1341–1357; Levitt, 'Access to the File: the Commission's Administrative Procedures in Cases under Articles 85 and 86' (1997) 34 *CMLRev* 1413; Ehlermann and Drijber, 'Legal Protection of Enterprises: Administrative Procedure, in particular Access to Files and Confidentiality' [1996] *ECLRev* 375; H. Nehl, *Principles of Administrative Procedure in EC Law* (Hart, 1999), Chap. 5.

[80] Cases 43, 63/82, *VBVB and VBBB v Commission* [1985] ECR 19, at para. 25.

[81] Case T-7/89, *SA Hercules Chemicals NV v Commission* [1991] ECR II-1711, at paras. 53–54; Case T-65/89, *BPB Industries plc and British Gypsum Ltd. v Commission* [1993] ECR II-389.

[82] Commission Notice, On Internal Rules of Procedure for Access to the File, OJ 1997 C23/3, now overtaken by Commission Notice, On the Rules for Access to the Commission File in Cases Pursuant to Articles 81 and 82 EC, Articles 53, 54, and 57 of the EEA Agreement and Council Regulation 139/2004, OJ 2005 C325/7.

file so that they could effectively proffer their views on the evidentiary basis of the Commission decision.[83] It was made clear that it was not for the Commission alone to decide which documents were useful to the undertakings, which should have the opportunity to examine them in order to determine their probative value for the applicants' defence. The Community courts might, however, decide not to annul for failure to grant access unless this adversely affected the right to a hearing. In any event, a right to access to the file is now included in the regulations governing competition.[84]

It was originally thought that the right of access to the file was confined to competition proceedings. It is clear that this is no longer the case. The Community courts have applied the reasoning from the competition cases in other contexts. Thus in *Eyckeler* the CFI reasoned by analogy from the competition cases and held that access to the file was equally important in challenging customs' decisions. It stated that if the right to be heard was to be exercised effectively there must be access to the non-confidential documentation relied on by the Commission when it made the contested decision.[85] It was not open to the Commission to exclude documents that it did not consider relevant, since these might well be of interest to the applicant. It would moreover be a serious breach of the rights of the defence if the Commission could unilaterally exclude from the administrative procedure documents which might be detrimental to it.[86]

The ease with which the CFI reasoned by analogy from competition to customs signifies the generalization of access to the file as an aspect of the right to be heard, irrespective of the subject-matter area in question, and this is in accord with the formulation in the Charter of Fundamental Rights.[87] At the very least it renders it all the easier for applicants contesting decisions in other areas to argue that the right should be equally applicable, and places the onus on the Commission, if it is so minded, to show why this should not be so.

The precise boundaries of the principle were tested in complex litigation in

[83] Cases T-30–32/91, *Solvay SA v Commission* [1995] ECR II-1775; Case T-36–37/91, *ICI v Commission* [1995] ECR II-1847, at para. 93; Case C-51/92 P, *Hercules Chemicals NV v Commission* [1999] ECR I-4235; Case T-175/95, *BASF Lacke & Farben AG v Commission* [1999] ECR II-1581; Cases C-238, 244–245, 247, 250, 252 and 254/99 P, *Limburgse Vinyl Maatschappij v Commission* [2002] ECR I-8375; Case T-5/02, *Tetra Laval BV v Commission* [2002] ECR II-4381, at paras. 89–91.

[84] See below, at 389.

[85] Case T-42/96, *Eyckeler, supra* n. 72, at paras. 79–80.

[86] Ibid. at para. 81. See also, Case T-50/96, *Primex Produkte, supra* n. 54, at paras. 57–70; Cases T-186–187/97, *Kaufring, supra* n. 72, at para. 185; Case T-205/99, *Hyper Srl v Commission* [2002] ECR II-3141; Case T-53/02, *Ricosmos BV v Commission*, judgment of 13 September 2005, not yet published, at paras. 71–74.

[87] Art. 41(2), which provides that the right to good administration includes 'the right of every person to have access to his or her file, while respecting the legitimate interests of confidentiality and of professional and business secrecy', OJ 2000 C364/1.

Aalborg Portland.[88] The case concerned a long-running Commission investigation into agreements and concerted practices engaged in by a number of European cement producers. The documentation supporting the alleged practices was very large. The Commission therefore did not append to the statement of objections the documents supporting its conclusions. It prepared a box of documents that was made available for each addressee relating to the statement of objections addressed to that firm. The Commission refused access to the chapters of the statement of objections which they had not received and refused to grant access to all documents in the investigation file. The ECJ reiterated the right of access to the file, which meant that 'the Commission must give the undertaking concerned the opportunity to examine all the documents in the investigation which may be relevant for its defence',[89] including incriminating and exculpatory evidence.

This general principle was subject to a number of limitations. There was no access to business secrets and confidential information. There was no general principle that the parties must receive copies of all documents taken into account in the case of other persons.[90] There was no right for access to documentation that was irrelevant and bore no relation to the allegations of fact or law in the statement of objections.[91] It was for the applicant to show that the result would have been different if incriminating evidence not communicated to the applicant had been relied on by the Commission in reaching its decision,[92] although where the document not communicated was exculpatory it was only necessary to show that its non-disclosure was able to influence disadvantageously the Commission decision.[93]

It was for the CFI to make these determinations in the light of a provisional examination of certain evidence to see whether the documents 'could have had a significance which ought not to have been disregarded'.[94] The CFI in performing this task had used an 'objective link' criterion: there had to be some objective link between the document not disclosed and the finding against the relevant undertaking. The ECJ upheld this test.[95]

The application of the access principle to complex litigation of this kind is undoubtedly problematic. There are, as the applicants claimed in argument,[96] difficulties in the CFI applying the objective link criterion, since it will not have the same knowledge and understanding of the situation as the Commission. There is also a sense in which the ECJ's approach limits the force of the right of access to the file, given that the Commission's failure to respect the right will only lead to annulment if the undertakings can

[88] Cases C-204–205, 211, 213, 217, and 219/00 P, *Aalborg Portland, supra* n. 70.
[89] Ibid. at para. 68.
[90] Ibid. at para. 70.
[91] Ibid. at para. 126.
[92] Ibid. at para. 73.
[93] Ibid. at paras. 74–75.
[94] Ibid. at paras. 76, 77, 101.
[95] Ibid. at para. 129.
[96] Ibid. at para. 115.

discharge the burden of proof of showing that the documentation to which they were denied access would have made a difference. The ECJ's approach is nonetheless explicable. It is reluctant to allow what may well be years of Commission investigation into a complex cartel to be overturned through annulment whenever the undertaking can point to something in the mass of documents that it did not have access to.

E. Content: Cross-Examination

The Community courts developed access to the file into an important component of the right to be heard, and this is so even when the right of access is read subject to the limits mentioned above. It should, however, be recognized that access to the file does not necessarily entail cross-examination on its content, the two issues being conceptually distinct. Thus in *Aalborg Portland* the ECJ held that the undertakings had no right to cross-examine a particular witness in relation to documents in the file at the investigative stage of the competition proceedings, since this was a purely administrative procedure.[97] Cross-examination may, however, be afforded either directly or indirectly.

The ability to cross-examine, or at least the ability to ask questions, may be granted directly by sectoral-specific legislation. Thus in the context of competition the Regulation provides that the hearing shall be conducted by a hearing officer, who may allow the parties to whom a statement of objections has been addressed, the complainants, other persons invited to the hearing, the Commission, and the Member States to ask questions during the hearing.[98] It should be noted that even this provision is framed in discretionary terms: the hearing officer may allow such parties to ask questions. It is clearly open to the Community courts to infer a right to cross-examine from the provisions applicable in a particular area. Thus in *de Compte*[99] the ECJ held that where a Disciplinary Board established under the Staff Regulations was empowered to order an inquiry in which each side could submit its case and reply to the case put by the other side, this meant that if the Board decided to hear witnesses the official that was charged or his representative had to be given the opportunity to be present at the hearing and to put questions to those witnesses. It was not sufficient merely to give the official a transcript of the hearing plus the ability to submit his views thereon.

Access to the file may indirectly serve the same ends to some limited degree. The applicant who gains access to the file will learn the evidentiary

[97] Ibid. at paras. 197–200.

[98] Commission Regulation (EC) 773/2004 of 7 April 2004, Relating to the Conduct of Proceedings by the Commission Pursuant to Articles 81 and 82 of the EC Treaty, OJ 2004 L123/18, Art. 14(7).

[99] Case 141/84, *Henri de Compte v European Parliament* [1985] ECR 1951.

basis of the decision reached. Where the applicant believes that there are flaws or errors in the evidence it will use its right to respond to highlight these defects. It will then be for the Commission to provide a convincing counter-response and if it does not do so the court may conclude that there was a manifest error in the Commission's reasoning.[100]

F. Content: Separation of Functions

It is clear from the previous chapters of this book that the decision-maker will often be the Commission. This has prompted claims that the position of the Commission as prosecutor and judge is contrary to Article 6(1) of the European Convention on Human Rights (ECHR). The ECJ has rejected such arguments, although its reasoning has been terse.

In *Van Landewyck*[101] the Commission responded to this argument by stating that it could not be regarded as a tribunal for the purposes of Article 6(1) ECHR, since one of the criteria for the existence of a tribunal laid down by the European Court of Human Rights was that such a body should be independent of the executive, and given that the Commission was the repository of executive power within the EU it could not therefore be a tribunal for the purposes of Article 6(1). The ECJ appeared to accept this reasoning, but said little. It merely stated that the applicant's argument was irrelevant, and that while the Commission was subject to procedural obligations it was not a tribunal within the meaning of Article 6(1) ECHR.

The ECJ maintained this position in the *MDF* case,[102] where the applicant argued that the contested competition decision was unlawful because the Commission combined the functions of prosecutor and judge, contrary to Article 6(1) of the ECHR. The ECJ rejected the argument in peremptory fashion, stating that the Commission was not a 'tribunal' within the meaning of Article 6, while softening the conclusion by noting that during the administrative procedure before the Commission, it was bound to observe the procedural safeguards provided for by Community law. These safeguards included the right to a fair hearing, and the opportunity afforded to the undertaking during the administrative procedure to make known its views on the truth and relevance of the facts and circumstances alleged and on the documents used by the Commission to support its claim that there has been an infringement of the Treaty.

The brevity of the ECJ's reasoning is indicative of the sensitivity of the

[100] Cases C-204–205, 211, 213, 217, and 219/00 P, *Aalborg Portland, supra* n. 70, at para. 79.

[101] Cases 209–215, 218/78, *Van Landewyck SARL v Commission* [1980] ECR 3125, at paras. 79–81.

[102] Cases 100–103/80, *Musique Diffusion Française, supra* n. 70.

issue. There is a tendency for courts to dismiss arguments with the briefest of reasons where they feel that they are on shaky ground. The terse dismissal therefore represents, to borrow from Falstaff, 'discretion being the better part of valour', the message being say little lest if you say more it can get you into deeper difficulty.

The problem with the ECJ's reasoning is readily apparent when one considers the wording of Article 6(1) ECHR. This mandates that in the determination of civil rights or obligations or any criminal charge, everyone is entitled to a fair and public hearing within a reasonable time by an independent and impartial tribunal established by law. The Commission's reasoning in *Van Landewyck*, accepted by the ECJ, in effect put 'the legal cart before the horse'. It was no answer to say that the Commission was not a tribunal independent of the executive, because Article 6(1) stipulates that where civil rights and obligations, etc. are in issue they must be decided by a tribunal that is independent.

The ECJ might have avoided this conclusion by finding that application of the competition rules did not entail 'civil rights or obligations' for the purposes of Article 6(1). It is however doubtful whether this would have been consonant with the broad interpretation of this phrase in the Strasbourg jurisprudence,[103] and in any event the ECJ has not imported the requirement to prove breach of a civil right or obligation, nor is it a condition for Article 47 of the Charter of Fundamental Rights.

The ECJ might, more promisingly, have fastened on the Strasbourg jurisprudence that has accepted determinations of civil rights and obligations by administrative authorities that are not independent, provided that there is adequate appeal or judicial review to a tribunal or court that does conform to Article 6(1).[104] This was in effect the reasoning adopted by the CFI in *Enso Espanola*.[105] It reiterated the 'orthodoxy' that the Commission could not be regarded as a tribunal for the purposes of Article 6 ECHR. It held, however, that not only was the Commission bound to comply with the procedural guarantees under Community law, but that the CFI exercised full powers of judicial review over the Commission and the CFI was an independent and impartial court for the purposes of Article 6.

The Community administration and legislature have in any event responded to the concerns voiced by the applicants in the previous cases. Since 1982 the Commission has appointed a Hearing Officer to preside over the hearing and to ensure that the rights of the defence are properly protected. The Commission later made a decision that strengthened the role of

[103] P. van Dijk and G van Hoof, *Theory and Practice of the European Convention of Human Rights* (Kluwer Law International, 3rd ed., 1998), Chap. 7, Part 6.

[104] Craig, 'The Human Rights Act, Article 6 and Procedural Rights' [2003] *PL* 753.

[105] Case T-348/94, *Enso Espanola SA v Commission* [1998] ECR II-1875, at paras. 60–65.

the hearing officer in the competition proceedings.[106] It acknowledged the importance of entrusting the proceedings to an independent person experienced in competition matters. This precept has been included in the new regime that came into effect post-2003, with the oral hearings being conducted by an independent Hearing Officer.[107]

While it has therefore been the Community administration and legislature that responded to the specific concerns raised by the applicants in the preceding cases, part of the Community courts' motivation for developing access to the file and the duty of diligent examination may well have been to foster process rights that would act as a counterweight to the power of the Commission, and more particularly to the combination of investigative, prosecutorial, and adjudicatory powers that it possesses in certain areas.[108] This is more especially so, given that the recognition of these process rights for the individual means that the Community courts can then monitor Commission compliance through judicial review.

G. Content: Causation

All legal systems have to decide on the consequence of the failure to observe process rights. The normal outcome is that the decision will be annulled, but courts may choose to qualify this conclusion, and can employ various juridical tools to do so. Thus it might be held that failure to comply with a particular process right renders the decision voidable and not void, such that it will only be set aside where the consequences of the breach are especially serious.[109] The distinction between mandatory and directory provisions is also used, such that breach of the former will necessarily lead to the decision being overturned, whereas annulment will not follow automatically in relation to breach of the latter.[110]

A different juridical technique is to use causation and inquire whether the failure to accord the process right would have made a difference to the outcome of the case, and decline to annul if this is not proven to the satisfaction of the reviewing court. The Community courts use causation with some

[106] Commission Decision 2001/462/EC, ECSC of 23 May 2001, On the Terms of Reference of Hearing Officers in Certain Competition Proceedings, OJ 2001 L162/21.

[107] Reg. 773/2004, *supra* n. 98, Art. 14.

[108] For recognition of this as a factor in the intensity of substantive review by the CFI of Commission competition decisions, see, Judge B. Vesterdorf, 'Certain Reflections on Recent Judgments Reviewing Commission Merger Control Decisions', in M. Hoskins and W. Robinson (eds), *A True European, Essays for Judge David Edward* (Hart, 2004), Chap. 10.

[109] *Professional Air Traffic Controllers Organisation (PATCO) v Federal Labor Relations Authority* 685 F.2d 547 (1982).

[110] De Smith, Woolf and Jowell, *Judicial Review of Administrative Action* (Sweet & Maxwell, 5th ed., 1995), at 267–271.

frequency.[111] It tends to be employed as a control device where breach of the process right might have far-reaching consequences. Thus causation has been used in cases concerned with access to the file, so as to justify not annulling a decision merely because an undertaking has not been given access to a particular document.

There are undoubtedly dangers in the use of causation. The reviewing court may not be well placed to determine whether the decision would have been different if the procedural error had not occurred. The causation argument serves moreover to emphasize the instrumental rationale for process rights at the expense of the non-instrumental rationale. The assumption is that process rights are accorded in order to ensure the correctness of the substantive outcome, hence if the outcome would have been the same there is no need for annulment, thereby down-playing the importance of the non-instrumental or dignitarian value underlying process.

We should therefore be cautious about too-ready a resort to causation. Where courts are nonetheless minded to use it the dangers can be alleviated by paying close attention to the specifics of the causation test employed by the reviewing court. It is especially important that the test is not set too high: it should be sufficient for the applicant to show that the process right denied might have made some difference to the outcome, and any uncertainties should be resolved in favour of the applicant.

4. PROCESS AND THE DUTY OF CARE/DILIGENT AND IMPARTIAL EXAMINATION

A. Recognition of the Principle

The ECJ developed early in its jurisprudence an obligation that care should be exercised in particular when discretionary determinations were made in relation to individual cases,[112] and this jurisprudence was applied especially in the context of competition[113] and state aids.[114] The principle of care 'establishes a duty on the administration carefully to examine the relevant

[111] See, e.g., Case C-142/87, *Belgium v Commission (Tubemeuse)* [1990] ECR I-959; Case T-7/89, *Hercules Chemicals NV v Commission* [1991] ECR II-1711; Cases T-30–32/91, *Solvay, supra* n. 83; Case T-290/97, *Mehibas Dordtselaan BV v Commission* [2000] ECR II-15; Cases C-204–205/00 P, *Aalborg Portland, supra* n. 70.

[112] Cases 16–18/59, *Geitling, Mausegatt and Prasident v High Authority* [1960] ECR 17, at 20; Case 14/61, *Koninklijke Nederlandsche Hoogovens en Staalfabrieken NV v High Authority* [1962] ECR 253; Schwarze, *supra* n. 74, at 1223–1238; Nehl, *supra* n. 79, Chaps. 8–9.

[113] Case 56/65, *Société La Technique Minière (LTM) v Maschinenbau Ulm GmbH* [1966] ECR 235, at 248; Cases 56 & 58/64, *Consten & Grundig v Commission* [1966] 299, at 374.

[114] Case 120/73, *Gebrüder Lorenz GmbH v Germany* [1973] ECR 1471, at 1481.

factual and legal aspects of the individual case'.[115] While there are antecedents for this duty going back to the ECJ's early jurisprudence it has been developed more fully in the case law of the CFI and the ECJ. The case law will be examined here and its broader implications will be considered below.[116]

In *Nolle*[117] the applicant was an independent importer of goods on which an anti-dumping duty had been imposed and had actively taken part in the investigation leading to the imposition of the duty. The applicant contended that the normal value of the product should have been based on considerations pertaining in Taiwan rather than Sri Lanka. Advocate General van Gerven stated that the Community institutions should be subject to a principle of care when applying broad discretionary powers to individual cases, and that this required the Commission to give serious consideration to the suggestion made by the applicant.[118] The ECJ followed the Advocate General's line of reasoning. It questioned whether the 'information contained in the documents in the case was considered with all the due care required',[119] and concluded that the applicant had produced sufficient facts to raise doubts as to whether the choice of Sri Lanka as a reference country was really appropriate.[120]

The development of the principle of due care was given further impetus by the decision in *Technische Universität München*,[121] the importance of which has already been addressed in relation to the right to a hearing where authority is shared between the EU and a Member State.[122] It will be remembered that the Technical University of Munich sought to import an electron microscope from Japan. Its application for exemption from customs duties was rejected on the ground that apparatus of equivalent scientific value was manufactured in the EU, this decision having been reached after having consulted experts in the area. The Bundesfinanzhof sought a preliminary ruling and made it clear that the ECJ's deferential approach to the review of discretion involving the exercise of complex technical matters did not sit easily with the approach of the German courts.[123] The ECJ held that where the Community institutions have a power of appraisal then respect for the rights guaranteed by the Community legal order was especially important. The rights guaranteed included the right of the person to make his views

[115] Nehl, *supra* n. 79, at 107. [116] See below, at 393–396.

[117] Case C-16/90, *Nölle v Hauptzollamt Bremen-Freihafen* [1991] ECR I-5163.

[118] Ibid. at 5175, AG van Gerven. [119] Ibid. at para. 29.

[120] Ibid. at para. 30. See also Case T-167/94, *Nölle v Council* [1995] ECR II-2589.

[121] Case C-269/90, *Hauptzollamt München-Mitte v Technische Universität München* [1991] ECR I-5469.

[122] See above, at 315–316.

[123] Schwarze, 'Developing Principles of European Administrative Law' [1993] *PL* 229; Nolte, 'General Principles of German and European Administrative Law—A Comparison in Historical Perspective' (1994) 57 *MLR* 191.

known, the right to have an adequately reasoned decision, and the duty of the competent institution to examine carefully and impartially all the relevant aspects of the individual case. It was only in this way that the courts could 'verify whether the factual and legal elements upon which the exercise of the power of appraisal depends were present'.[124] The ECJ annulled the contested decision on the ground, *inter alia*, that there was a breach of the duty of care by the Commission through its reliance on experts who did not possess the requisite technical knowledge in the relevant area.[125]

Subsequent decisions, such as the *British Airways* case,[126] further stressed the proximate connection between the duty to examine carefully and impartially all aspects of the case, and the obligation to give reasons, since the latter is a prerequisite to ensure that the former has been properly complied with.

B. Application of the Principle to Competition

The application of the principle of care has been taken up and developed by the CFI, especially in relation to competition and state aids. In the context of competition the principle of care operates both with respect to whether to pursue an investigation and as to the conduct of the investigation if it is pursued.

The Commission is under a duty to consider a complaint submitted to it.[127] The Commission has limited resources with which to pursue competition violations, the corollary being that it will pick and choose which possible infringements are worthy of its attention. It was made clear in *Automec*[128] that the Commission cannot be compelled to conduct an investigation, and that the power to set priorities was an inherent part of the work of administration. The Commission was however obliged 'to examine carefully the factual and legal aspects of which it is notified by the complainant'[129] in order to decide whether they indicated behaviour likely to distort competition, and the ECJ would verify whether this had been done. Where

124 Case C-269/90, *supra* n. 121, at para. 14.

125 Ibid. at para. 135. See also, Case T-241/00, *Azienda Agricola 'Le Canne' Srl v Commission* [2002] ECR II-1251, at paras. 53–54.

126 Cases T-371 and 394/94, *British Airways plc and British Midland Airways Ltd v Commission* [1998] ECR II-2405, at para. 95.

127 Case 210/81, *Demo-Studio Schmidt v Commission* [1983] ECR 3045.

128 Case T-24/90, *Automec Srl v Commission* [1992] ECR II-2223; Case T-144/92, *Bureau Européen des Médias de l'Industrie Musicale (BEMIM) v Commission* [1995] ECR II-147; Case T-37/92, *Bureau Européen des Unions Consommateurs and National Consumer Council v Commission* [1994] ECR II-285; Cases C-359 and 379/95 P, *Commission and France v Ladbroke Racing Ltd.* [1999] ECR I-6265; Cases T-185, 189, 190/96, *Riviera Auto Service Etablissements Dalmasso SA v Commission* [1999] ECR II-93; Case 449/98 P, *International Express Carriers Conference (IECC) v Commission, La Poste, UK and the Post Office* [2001] ECR I-3875.

129 Case T-24/90, *Automec, supra* n. 128, at para. 79.

the Commission decided not to pursue a complaint then it should inform the complainant of its reasons.[130] These had to be sufficient to enable the Court to review the lawfulness of the decision and make clear to the parties concerned the circumstances in which the Commission applied the Treaty.

Where the Commission decided to conduct an investigation the principle of care applied once again, as was made clear in *Asia Motor France II*: the Commission must investigate with the degree of care that would enable it to assess the factual and legal considerations submitted by the complainant.[131] To similar effect was the statement in *Metropole* that while the Commission was not obliged to investigate each of the complaints lodged with it, it must in the absence of a duly substantiated statement of reasons conduct the investigation with 'the requisite care, seriousness and diligence so as to be able to assess with full knowledge of the case the factual and legal particulars submitted for its appraisal by the complainants'.[132] It is clear moreover from cases such as *Volkswagen*[133] that the relevant duty is one of care and impartiality in the conduct of the investigation.

The Community courts have, however, emphasized limits of the requirement to give reasons in this context. They have held that in stating the reasons for the decisions it has to take to ensure that the competition rules are applied the Commission is not obliged to adopt a position on all the arguments relied on by the parties. It is sufficient if it sets out the facts and legal considerations having decisive importance for the decision.[134]

C. Application of the Principle to State Aids

A two-stage investigative procedure operates in state aids and the Community courts have used the principle of care to foster procedural justice in this area as they have done in the context of competition.

[130] Case T-77/95 RV, *Union Francaise de l'Express (Ufex), DHL International, Service CRIE and May Courier v Commission* [2000] ECR II-2167, at para. 42.

[131] Case T-7/92, *Asia Motor France SA v Commission* [1993] ECR II-669, at para. 36; Case T-154/98, *Asia Motor France SA v Commission* [2000] ECR II-3453, at paras. 53–56; Case T-31/99, *ABB Asea Brown Boveri Ltd v Commission* [2002] ECR II-1881, at para. 99; Cases T-191, 212, 214/98, *Atlantic Container Line AB v Commission* [2003] ECR II-3275, at para. 404.

[132] Case T-206/99, *Métropole Télévision SA v Commission* [2001] ECR II-1057, at para. 59.

[133] Case T-62/98, *Volkswagen AG v Commission* [2000] ECR II-2707, at para. 269.

[134] Case T-7/92, *Asia Motor, supra* n. 131, at para. 31; Case T-459/93, *Siemens v Commission* [1995] ECR II-1675, at para. 31; Case T-387/94, *Asia Motor France SA v Commission* [1996] ECR II-961, at para. 104; Case T-5/97, *Industrie des Poudres Sphériques SA v Commission* [2000] ECR II-3755, at para. 199; Case 187/99, *Agrana Zucker und Stark AG v Commission* [2001] ECR II-1587, at para. 84; Case T-206/99, *Métropole, supra* n. 132, at para. 44; Cases T-228 and 233/99, *Westdeutsche Landesbank Girozentrale and Land Nordrhein-Westfalen v Commission* [2003] ECR II-435, at para. 280.

For monitoring of state aids to be effective, it is essential for the Commission to be notified of the existence of any aid proposal. It is for this reason that Article 88 EC establishes a two-stage procedure for state aids. Stage one concerns prior notification of any plan to grant aid and preliminary investigation by the Commission.[135] The Commission must come to some preliminary view within two months.[136] If there are serious difficulties in reaching a decision within this time then the Commission should proceed to the more complete review.[137] This is important since other parties are entitled to be consulted under the formal investigation, but have no such rights in relation to the preliminary assessment.[138]

This can be problematic if the Commission finds that an aid is compatible with the Common Market under the preliminary assessment, but an interested party disagrees and believes that the more thorough investigation should have been initiated. In *William Cook*[139] the Court held that the procedural guarantees applicable to the more detailed investigation under Article 88(2) EC could, in such a situation, only be properly safeguarded if such parties were able to challenge a Commission decision concerning the preliminary investigation before the Court.[140] Advocate General Tesauro framed his Opinion against the more general procedural precepts laid down in the *Technische Universität München* case,[141] including the principle of care, although this aspect of the case was less fully developed by the ECJ.

The judgment of the CFI in *Sytraval*[142] represented a high-point in the application of the principle of care. The applicant sought the annulment of a decision rejecting a complaint about a state aid. The CFI considered in detail the arguments advanced by the applicant in the light of the available evidence and compared this to the findings made by the Commission. It held that the Commission was under a duty to give a reasoned answer to each of the objections raised in the complaint.[143] The CFI held further that when the Commission had obtained the information from its inquiries that it would use to decide whether to proceed to the second, more detailed investigation, the Commission came under an 'automatic obligation to examine the

[135] Art. 88(3) EC. [136] Case 84/82, *Germany v Commission, supra* n. 138.

[137] Art. 88(2) EC.

[138] Case 120/73, *Gebrüder Lorenz GmbH v Germany* [1973] ECR 1471; Case 84/82, *Germany v Commission* [1984] ECR 1451. The Commission must also be notified of any amendment to the aid proposal: Cases 91 and 127/83, *Heineken Brouwerijen BV v Inspecteur der Vennootschapsbelasting* [1984] ECR 3435.

[139] Case C-198/91, *William Cook plc v Commission* [1993] ECR I-2486; Case C-367/95 P, *Commission v Sytraval and Brink's France SARL* [1998] ECR I-1719, at paras. 40–41.

[140] Hancher, 'State Aids and Judicial Control in the European Communities' [1994] *ECLRev* 134.

[141] Case C-269/90, *supra* n. 121.

[142] Case T-95/94, *Sytraval and Brink's France v Commission* [1995] ECR II-2651.

[143] Ibid. at para. 62.

objections which the complainant would certainly have raised if it had been given the opportunity of taking cognizance of that information'.[144] Moreover, the Commission's duty to give reasons for its decision might in certain circumstances require an exchange of views and arguments with the complainant, since the Commission needed to ascertain the view taken by the complainant of the information gathered by the Commission in the course of its inquiry, this being regarded as a corollary of the Commission's obligation to deal diligently and impartially with the inquiry by eliciting all necessary views.[145]

The ECJ was far more circumspect when the *Sytraval* case was appealed.[146] It held that the Commission was not under an obligation to conduct an exchange of views with the complainant: such an obligation could not be based on the duty to give reasons; the Commission was not obliged to give the complainant an opportunity to state its view during the preliminary inquiry; and the Commission's duty in relation to the more formal investigation was limited to giving notice to such persons in order that they could submit their comments,[147] there being no right to engage in an adversarial debate with the Commission.[148] The ECJ also rejected the CFI's decision insofar as the latter imposed an obligation on the Commission to examine of its own motion objections which the complainant would have raised had it been given the opportunity to take cognizance of the information obtained by the Commission in the course of its preliminary inquiry.[149] Notwithstanding this finding, the ECJ concluded that the Commission might be obliged where necessary to extend its investigation of a complaint beyond mere examination of the facts and law brought to its attention by the complainant. The Commission could be required in the interests of sound administration of the rules on state aid to 'conduct a diligent and impartial examination of the complaint, which may make it necessary for it to examine matters not expressly raised by the complainant'.[150]

D. Development and Limitation of the Principle

The CFI has not sought to expand the principle of care or diligent and impartial administration in the way that it had in the *Sytraval* case. It took heed of the more restrictive reading given to the principle by the ECJ in that case. The CFI accepted that in the context of state aid interested parties other than the Member State responsible cannot claim a right to debate the issues

[144] Ibid. at para. 66. [145] Ibid. at para. 78.
[146] Case C-367/95 P, *Sytraval, supra* n. 139.
[147] Ibid. at paras. 58–59.
[148] Cases C-74 and 75/00, *Falck SpA and Accialierie di Bolzano SpA v Commission* [2002] ECR I-7869, at para. 82.
[149] Case C-367/95 P, *Sytraval, supra* n. 139, at para. 60. [150] Ibid. at para. 62.

with the Commission, and that this limitation applies even to the recipient of the aid.[151]

The CFI nonetheless developed the principle in a rather different fashion in the *max.mobil* case.[152] The essence of the applicant's complaint was that it was adversely affected by an Austrian state measure which enabled Mobilkom, a company to which Austria had granted a monopoly, to abuse its dominant position on the relevant mobile telephony market, in breach of Article 86 EC. The Commission accepted part of the applicant's complaint, but rejected it in part and the applicant sought the annulment of the Commission's decision in this respect. The CFI conceptualized the principle of diligent and impartial treatment as but part of the broader right to sound administration recognized by the Charter of Rights.[153]

> Since the present action is directed against a measure rejecting a complaint, it must be emphasized at the outset that the diligent and impartial treatment of a complaint is associated with the right to sound administration which is one of the general principles that are observed in a State governed by the rule of law and are common to the constitutional traditions of the Member States. Article 41(1) of the Charter of Fundamental Rights of the European Union proclaimed at Nice on 7 December 2000 confirms that '[e]very person has the right to have his or her affairs handled impartially, fairly and within a reasonable time by the institutions and bodies of the Union'.

The Commission argued that the duty of diligent and impartial examination recognized by the earlier jurisprudence on competition was dependent on provisions of the Treaty or secondary legislation that accorded procedural rights to complainants, and that no such rights were formally granted to them in the context of Article 86 EC. The CFI held that the duty was nonetheless applicable. It stated that Article 86 EC should be read in conjunction with other Treaty articles on competition that granted procedural rights to complainants.[154] This was reinforced by reliance on the general duty of supervision to which the Commission was subject,[155] from which the CFI concluded that the 'Commission's general duty of supervision and its corollary, the obligation to undertake a diligent and impartial examination of complaints submitted to it, must apply as a matter of principle, without distinction'[156] in the context of all the Treaty articles concerned with com-

[151] Case T-198/01, *Technische Glaswerke Ilmenau GmbH v Commission* [2004] ECR II-2717, at paras. 192–199, relying on Case C-367/95 P, *Sytraval, supra* n. 139, and Cases 74 and 75/00, *Falck SpA, supra* n. 148.

[152] Case T-54/99, *max.mobil Telekommunikation Service GmbH v Commission* [2002] ECR II-313; See also, Case T-211/02, *Tideland Signal Ltd v Commission* [2002] ECR II-3781, at para. 37.

[153] Ibid. at para. 48. See also, Cases T-228 and 233/99, *Westdeutsche Landesbank, supra* n. 134, at para. 167.

[154] Ibid. at para. 51.

[155] Ibid. at para. 52.

[156] Ibid. at para. 53.

petition.[157] Compliance with this duty should moreover be amenable to judicial review and an individual should be able to obtain an effective remedy as 'confirmed' by Article 47 of the Charter of Fundamental Rights.[158]

The CFI clearly pushed the boundaries of the duty of diligent examination further than hitherto.[159] The duty was viewed as a corollary of a more general duty of supervision; it could be implied from the wording of a Treaty article or from the schema of the relevant part of the Treaty; and the duty once established had remedial consequences, providing the foundation for judicial review to vindicate the duty.

It is equally clear that the ECJ was unwilling to read the duty as extensively as the CFI. This is apparent from the ECJ's decision on appeal,[160] which set aside the CFI's judgment. The ECJ reached this conclusion by focusing more narrowly on the duties incumbent on the Commission under Article 86 EC. The ECJ acknowledged in line with earlier authority that individuals could in certain circumstances seek the annulment of a Commission decision addressed to a Member State under Article 86(3) EC if the conditions for standing under Article 230(4) were satisfied. It held, however, that the wording and place of Article 86(3) in the schema of the Treaty meant that the Commission was not obliged to bring proceedings against a Member State under that Article. The fact that the applicant had a direct and individual interest in the Commission's decision by which it refused to act did not confer any right of action on the applicant, and the Commission's letter by which it informed the applicant that it would not bring proceedings against Austria was in any event not regarded as an act producing legal effects and thus was not challengeable under Article 230. The ECJ stated that its conclusion was not at variance with the principle of sound administration or any other principle of Community law. There was, said the ECJ, no general principle of Community law that required an undertaking to be given standing to challenge a refusal by the Commission to take action under Article 86(3).

157 A further strand of the CFI's reasoning was based on the wording of Art. 86(3) EC, which provides that the Commission shall ensure the application of Art. 86 and shall where necessary address appropriate directives or decisions to Member States. The CFI held that the fact that the Commission had to decide whether intervention was 'necessary' implied a duty to conduct a diligent and impartial examination of complaints, Ibid. at para. 54.

158 Ibid. paras. 56–57.

159 The CFI did, however, make it clear that the precise manner in which the obligation was discharged could vary depending on the specific area to which the duty was applied and that the procedural rights accorded by the Treaties or secondary legislation were an important factor in this respect, Ibid. at para. 53. This was equally clear from the CFI's approach in *Technische Glaswerke* to the application of the duty in the context of state aids, where it accepted that the limits to the duty were set by the relevant Treaty articles, Case T-198/01, *Technische Glaswerke Ilmenau, supra* n. 151, at paras. 191–199.

160 Case C-141/02 P, *Commission v T-Mobile Austria GmbH* [2005] ECR I-1283, at paras. 68–75.

The precise impact of the case on the scope and incidence of the duty of diligent and impartial examination is debatable. The ECJ did not call into question any of the previous authority concerning this duty, nor did it directly contradict the CFI's general statements linking the duty with the right to sound administration and the Charter of Rights. The ECJ's judgment could therefore be viewed simply as a decision that turned on the interpretation of Article 86(3), combined with orthodox narrow construction of standing criteria. It should, however, be recognized that the ECJ's judgment was informed by an unwillingness to take an expansive view of the duty of diligent examination of the kind that had been apparent in the CFI's decision. The ECJ was therefore unwilling, by way of contrast to the CFI, to interpret particular Treaty articles against the backdrop of the duty of diligent examination. The ECJ and Advocate General Maduro[161] were also disinclined to allow such a duty to circumvent the traditional remedial regime, more especially the limited rules on standing.

It is clear in any event that the CFI remains willing to apply the duty of care in other areas, in order to enhance the accountability of the Community administration. This is apparent from the *Pfizer* case,[162] which will be examined in detail below.[163] Suffice it to say for the present that it involved a challenge to the withdrawal of authorization for an additive used in feeding stuffs for animals. The authorization had been withdrawn because of fears concerning the additive's effect on resistance to bacteria by humans. The CFI held that the contested Regulation could be justified on the basis of the precautionary principle. It emphasized, however, that procedural guarantees were especially important in this context, including the duty of the competent institution to examine carefully and impartially all aspects of the individual case. It followed, said the CFI, that 'a scientific risk assessment carried out as thoroughly as possible on the basis of scientific advice founded on the principles of excellence, transparency and independence is an important procedural guarantee whose purpose is to ensure the scientific objectivity of the measures adopted and preclude arbitrary measures'.[164]

5. PROCESS AND REASONS

As stated at the outset, process rights within the EU owe their origin to Treaty articles, Community legislation, and the jurisprudence of the Community

[161] Ibid. at paras. 56–57, AG Maduro.

[162] Case T-13/99, *Pfizer Animal Health SA v Council* [2002] ECR II-3305, at paras. 170–172.

[163] See below, at 447–452.

[164] Case T-13/99, *Pfizer, supra* n. 162, at para. 172.

courts. The precise blend varies with the process right in question. A prime example of an important process right that was encapsulated in the original Treaty is the duty to provide reasons, which was originally found in Article 190 EEC and is now Article 253 EC.

> Regulations, directives and decisions adopted jointly by the European Parliament and the Council, and such acts adopted by the Council or the Commission, shall state the reasons on which they are based and shall refer to any proposals or opinions which were required to be obtained pursuant to this Treaty.

There are a number of policy rationales for the duty to provide reasons. From the perspective of affected parties, it makes the decision-making process more transparent, so that they can know why a measure has been adopted. From the perspective of the decision-maker itself, an obligation to give reasons will help to ensure that the rationale for the action has been thought through; having to explain oneself, and defend the rationality of one's choice, is always a salutary exercise. From the perspective of the ECJ, the existence of reasons facilitates judicial review, by, for example, enabling the Court to determine whether a decision was disproportionate.

These policy arguments are reflected in the oft-repeated judicial statements that reasons inform the addressee of the decision of the factual and legal grounds on which it is based, thereby enabling the person to decide whether to seek judicial review and facilitate the exercise of that review by the Community courts. Thus as the ECJ stated early in its jurisprudence:[165]

> In imposing upon the Commission the obligation to state reasons for its decisions, Article 190 is not taking mere formal considerations into account but seeks to give an opportunity to the parties defending their rights, to the court of exercising its supervisory functions and to Member States and to all interested nationals of ascertaining the circumstances in which the Commission has applied the Treaty.

The scope of Article 253 EC is broad: it applies to regulations, decisions, and directives adopted either jointly by the Council and European Parliament, or by the Council or by the Commission. This is noteworthy. The duty to give reasons varies in the domestic law of the Member States, but in most countries it is narrower than that in Article 253, which imposes a duty to give reasons not only for administrative decisions, but also for legislative norms, such as regulations or directives. Many national legal systems do not impose an obligation to furnish reasons for legislative norms, or do so only in limited circumstances.

[165] Case 24/62, *Germany v Commission* [1963] ECR 63, at 69; Case T-7/92, *Asia Motor France, supra* n. 131, at para. 30; Case T-387/94, *Asia Motor France, supra* n. 134, at para. 103; Case 187/99, *Agrana Zucker, supra* n. 134, at para. 83; Case T-241/00, *Azienda Agricola, supra* n. 125, at para. 54; Case T-206/99, *Metropole, supra* n. 132, at para. 44.

The most common general formulation of the scope of the duty to give reasons can be taken from the *Sytraval* case.[166]

[I]t is settled case law that the statement of reasons required by Article 190[[167]] of the Treaty must be appropriate to the act at issue and must disclose in a clear and unequivocal fashion the reasoning followed by the institution which adopted the measure in question in such a way as to enable the persons concerned to ascertain the reasons for the measure and to enable the competent Community court to exercise its powers of review. The requirements to be satisfied by the statement of reasons depend on the circumstances of each case, in particular the content of the measure in question, the nature of the reasons given and the interest which the addressees of the measure, or other parties to whom it is of direct and individual concern, may have in obtaining explanations. It is not necessary for the reasoning to go into all the relevant facts and points of law, since the question whether the statement of reasons meets the requirements of Article 190 of the Treaty must be assessed with regard not only to its wording but also to its context and to all the legal rules governing the matter in question.

The obligation to give reasons will normally require specification of the Treaty article on which the measure was based; the factual background to the measure; and the purposes behind it. This is exemplified by the *Tariff Preferences* case,[168] where the ECJ annulled a Council measure in part because the legal basis of the measure had not been specified. In *Germany v Commission*[169] the Court held that it was sufficient to set out in a concise, clear, and relevant manner the principal issues of law and fact upon which the action was based, such that the reasoning which led the Commission to its decision could be understood. Where a decision established a new principle, or applied it in a novel fashion, there would have to be sufficient reasons in the decision itself,[170] but on some occasions the Court will sanction the incorporation of reasons from another instrument.[171]

The content of the duty will also be affected by the very scope of Article 253, applying as it does both to general legislative norms, and to

[166] Case C-367/95 P, *Sytraval, supra* n. 139, at para. 63; Cases 296 and 318/82, *Netherlands and Leeuwarder Papierwarenfabriek v Commission* [1985] ECR 809, at para. 19; Case C-316/97 P, *European Parliament v Gaspari* [1998] ECR I-7597, at para. 26; Case C-301/96, *Germany v Commission* [2003] ECR I-9919, at para. 87; Case C-76/00 P, *Petrotub SA and Republica SA v Council* [2003] ECR I-79, at para. 81; Case T-198/01, *Technische Glaswerke Ilmenau, supra* n. 151, at para. 59.

[167] Now Art. 253 EC.

[168] Case 45/86, *Commission v Council* [1987] ECR 1493.

[169] Case 24/62, *supra* n. 165.

[170] See e.g. Case 73/74, *Papiers Peints de Belgique v Commission* [1975] ECR 1491.

[171] This will occur not infrequently in areas such as the CAP, where the Commission may have to make numerous decisions or pass many regulations within a short space of time. Where this is so the Court has accepted that the Commission can refer back to a previous decision or regulation setting out the considerations which shaped the Commission's action: see, e.g. Case 16/65, *Schwarze* [1965] ECR 877.

individualized decisions. The degree of specificity will, therefore, depend upon the nature of the contested measure. In *Beus*[172] the ECJ explicitly recognized that the extent of the requirement to state the reasons on which a measure was based would depend on the nature of the measure in question. In the case of a regulation it might well, therefore, suffice for the preamble to indicate the situation which led to its adoption, and the general objectives which it was intended to achieve. It was not necessary for the regulation to set out the factual basis of the measure, which was often complex, nor was it necessary for the relevant measure to provide a complete evaluation of those facts. Where a measure was of a general legislative nature it was necessary for the Community authority to show the reasoning which led to its adoption, but it was not necessary for it to go into every point of fact and law. Where the essential objective of the measure had been clearly disclosed there was no need for a specific statement of the reasons for each of the technical choices that had been made.[173]

The Court may well demand greater particularity where the measure being challenged is of an individual, rather than legislative nature. Thus in *Germany v Commission*[174] Germany produced an alcoholic drink called Brenwein, which was made from wine much of which was imported from outside the Community. The establishment of the common external tariff resulted in significant cost increases, and therefore the German Government asked the Commission for permission to import 450,000 hectolitres of this wine at the old, lower rate of duty. The Commission acceded to this request in principle, but only for 100,000 hectolitres. The Commission justified this decision on the grounds that there was ample production of wine in the EC, and that the grant of the requested quota would lead to serious disturbances on the relevant product market. The ECJ found the Commission's reasoning to be insufficiently specific concerning the size of any Community surplus, and that it was unclear why there would be serious disturbances in the market.

The context in which individual decisions are taken will, however, be of importance in determining the extent of the duty to give reasons. Thus as we have seen in relation to competition, the Community courts have held that in stating the reasons for the decisions it takes in this area the Commission is not obliged to adopt a position on all the arguments relied on by the parties. It is sufficient if it sets out the facts and legal considerations having decisive importance for the decision.[175]

[172] Case 5/67, *Beus* [1968] ECR 83, at 95; Case C-205/94, *Binder GmbH v Hauptzollamt Stuttgart-West* [1996] ECR I-2871.

[173] Case C-122/94, *Commission v Council* [1996] ECR I-881, at para. 29; Case C-84/94, *United Kingdom v Council* [1996] ECR I-5755, at paras. 74, 79.

[174] Case 24/62, *Commission v Germany, supra* n. 165; Case T-5/93, *Tremblay v Commission* [1995] ECR II-185.

[175] See cases cited *supra* n. 134.

6. PROCESS AND THE CHARTER OF FUNDAMENTAL RIGHTS

We have touched in the preceding discussion on the right to good administration contained in Article 41 of the Charter of Fundamental Rights.[176] It is important to reflect further on its possible significance for the development of process rights within EU law.[177] Article 41 states that:

(1) Every person has the right to have his or her affairs handled impartially, fairly and within a reasonable time by the institutions and bodies of the Union.
(2) This right includes:
— the right of every person to be heard, before any individual measure which would affect him or her adversely is taken;
— the right of every person to have access to his or her file, while respecting the legitimate interests of confidentiality and of professional and business secrecy;
— the obligation of the administration to give reasons for its decisions.
(3) Every person has the right to have the Community make good any damage caused by its institutions or by its servants in the performance of their duties, in accordance with the general principles common to the laws of the Member States.
(4) Every person may write to the institutions of the Union in one of the languages of the Treaties and must have an answer in the same language.

The Charter is intended to be declaratory of existing EU law rather than creative of new obligations, although as we shall see in later discussion the extent to which this is so is debatable.[178]

The very fact that the right to good administration is contained in the Charter of Rights is significant. It emphasizes the importance of this right as one component of citizens' rights within a democratic polity, and reinforces the legitimacy of judicial imposition of procedural obligations on the Community administration.

Article 41(1) operates as an 'umbrella principle', with some of the detailed facets being spelled out through Article 41(2). The particular matters listed in Article 41(2) are not exhaustive and it will be open to the Community courts to reason from the general principle of Article 41(1) and develop more detailed aspects of process rights not mentioned in Article 41(2). Article 41 of the Charter should moreover be read in conjunction with the European Ombudsman's Code of Good Administrative Behaviour.[179] The Code is

[176] OJ 2000 C364/1.

[177] Kanska, 'Towards Administrative Human Rights in the EU. Impact of the Charter of Fundamental Rights' (2004) 10 *ELJ* 296; Ward, 'Access to Justice', in S. Peers and A. Ward (eds), *The EU Charter of Fundamental Rights, Politics, Law and Policy* (Hart, 2004), Chap. 5.

[178] See below, Chap. 14.

[179] European Ombudsman, The European Code of Good Administrative Behaviour (2005), available at <http://www.euro-ombudsman.eu.int/code/pdf/en/code2005_en.pdf>.

designed to elaborate the more specific administrative obligations that should flow from the right to good administration. These include, *inter alia*, non-discrimination, proportionality, objectivity, impartiality and independence, legitimate expectations, the right to be heard, the provision of reasons and fairness.

It is important to be clear about the juridical impact of Article 41. The right to good administration can function as an interpretative device, such that ambiguity in Treaty articles or Community legislation will be resolved in favour of the interpretation that best accords with that right. This interpretive function of the Charter will clearly be applicable if the Charter is made binding, but there is nothing to prevent the Community courts from drawing on Charter articles as interpretive guides even if the Charter is not made formally binding, more especially so given that it is said to be declaratory of existing law. An applicant may also argue that Community legislation that does not accord with the right to good administration should be annulled. This will clearly be possible if the Charter is made formally binding. It is, however, also possible now, insofar as an applicant argues that a particular right included within Article 41 is already well-established within the existing jurisprudence of the Community courts.

The principal responsibility for the detailed elaboration of process rights will remain with the Community courts, but the judiciary will necessarily be influenced in their interpretation by the wording of Article 41. The judiciary may well use the generalized formulation in Article 41(1) as part of the justification for extending a particular process right. This is exemplified by the reasoning in *max.mobil*,[180] where the CFI used Article 41(1) to help justify application of the principle of care, and this was so notwithstanding the fact that the principle is not specifically listed in Article 41(2), the CFI fastening on the concepts of impartiality and fairness within Article 41(1). Having said this it should also be recognized that the Community courts have considerable room for manoeuvre in deciding how broadly or narrowly to interpret Article 41.

Another Charter provision that is relevant for process is Article 47, which is concerned with the right to an effective remedy and to a fair trial. It provides,

> Everyone whose rights and freedoms guaranteed by the law of the Union are violated has the right to an effective remedy before a tribunal in compliance with the conditions laid down in this Article.
>
> Everyone is entitled to a fair and public hearing within a reasonable time by an independent and impartial tribunal previously established by law. Everyone shall have the possibility of being advised, defended and represented.
>
> Legal aid shall be made available to those who lack sufficient resources in so far as such aid is necessary to ensure effective access to justice.

[180] Case T-54/99, *max.mobil, supra* n. 152; Case T-211/02, *Tideland Signal, supra* n. 152.

The explanatory memorandum[181] stated that the first paragraph was based in part on Article 13 ECHR, and in part on the case law of the Community courts. It was considered in the context of access.[182] The second paragraph is based on Article 6 of the ECHR, but is drawn more broadly because it does not require the existence of a civil right or obligation before the right to a fair hearing is triggered. This broadening of Article 6 is to be welcomed given the difficulties that have beset the interpretation and application of the phrase 'civil rights and obligations'.[183] The third paragraph is drawn from the case law of the Strasbourg court.

7. PROCESS AND SECTOR-SPECIFIC LEGISLATION

The discussion thus far has been concerned with particular process rights, such as the right to be heard, the right to reasons, and the like. It is, however, important to consider process rights from a rather different perspective, which is that of sector-specific legislation.

This helps us to understand how the particular rights analysed above fit together within a specific context and the interrelationship between process rights as developed by the Community courts and the Community legislature. It also reveals the interaction between process rights accorded to the individual and procedural rights and powers given to the administration, thereby serving as a counterweight to the asymmetry that characterizes much thought about process.

We tend automatically to conceptualize process in terms of rights given to the individual and this is reflected in the nomenclature, 'the rights of the defence'. It can be readily accepted that this is the paradigmatic application of process rights. It can be accepted also that the classic process rights given to the individual generally have a higher status than the procedural rights and powers possessed by the administration. The individuals' process rights are, as we have seen, not dependent on positive grant by the Community legislature, and Community legislation will be read so as to conform to these fundamental procedural rights. The procedural powers and rights possessed by the administration are almost always the product of Community legislation and they must be compatible with the Treaty and other fundamental rights, including the process rights of the individual.

This can be acknowledged. It should not, however, prevent us from recognizing the importance of procedural rights and powers possessed by the

[181] Charte 4473/00, Convent 49, 11 October 2000, at 40–41; CONV 828/03, Updated Explanations Relating to the Text of the Charter of Fundamental Rights, 9 July 2003, at 41–42.
[182] See above, at 346–347. [183] Craig, *supra* n. 104.

administration together with the consequential obligations that may be placed on either individuals or Member States when Community policy is administered. Community legislation is often the ideal vehicle for the working-out of these detailed rights. This can be exemplified by the legislation dealing with competition and state aids.

A. Competition

There were until recently two foundations to the enforcement of EC Competition law. Agreements had, subject to certain exceptions, to be notified to the Commission, and the Commission had a monopoly over the application of Article 81(3) EC. The system was, in this sense, a centralized one, but there were nonetheless decentralized aspects. Articles 81 and 82 EC had direct effect. National courts could therefore apply Article 81(1) in cases that came before them, but could not grant an individual exemption under Article 81(3). The traditional approach came under increasing strain. The Commission did not have the resources to deal with all the agreements notified to it within a reasonable time, nor did it have the resources to adjudicate on anything but a handful of individual exemptions. The Commission therefore encouraged national courts to apply Articles 81 and 82. However, in the *White Paper on Modernization*[184] it proposed a thorough overhaul of the enforcement regime. The new approach is based on more radical decentralization. Notification is abolished, as is the Commission's monopoly over Article 81(3) EC. National courts and national competition authorities (NCAs) are empowered to apply Article 81 in its entirety, and the Commission will concentrate its resources on novel problems, or egregious breaches of competition rules. The new regime was put in place through a Regulation in 2003.[185]

[184] White Paper on Modernization of the Rules Implementing Articles 85 and 86 of the EC Treaty, Commission Programme 99/27, 28 April 1999. There is a voluminous literature on the White Paper, see, e.g., Wesseling, 'The Commission White Paper on Modernisation of EC Antitrust Law: Unspoken Consequences and Incomplete Treatment of Alternative Options' [1999] *ECLR* 420; Ehlermann, 'The Modernization of EC Antitrust Policy: A Legal and Cultural Revolution' (2000) 37 *CMLRev* 537; Schaub, 'Modernisation of EC Competition Law: Reform of Regulation No. 17', in B. Hawk (ed), *Fordham Corporate Law Institute* (Fordham, 2000), Chap. 10; Forrester, 'Modernisation of EC Competition Law', Ibid., Chap. 12; Whish, and Sufrin, 'Community Competition Law: Notification and Exemption—Goodbye to All That', in D. Hayton (ed), *Law's Future(s): British Legal Developments in the 21st Century* (Hart, 2000), Chap. 8; Gerber, 'Modernising European Competition Law: A Developmental Perspective' [2001] *ECLR* 122.

[185] Council Regulation 1/2003/EC of 16 December 2002, On the Implementation of the Rules on Competition Laid Down in Articles 81 and 82 of the Treaty, OJ 2003 L1/1.

(1) *Individual Process Rights*

The classic elements of individual process rights are included in the new regulatory regime, as they were in the old. There is a right to a hearing for the undertakings concerned by the proceedings before the Commission takes a decision and the Commission must base its decision only on objections on which the parties have been able to comment.[186] The statement of objections must be notified to each of the parties and the Commission must set a time limit within which the parties may inform it in writing of their views.[187] It is then open to the parties in their written submissions to set out all facts known to them which are relevant to their defence and to submit relevant documentation.[188] The Commission must give parties to whom it has addressed a statement of objections the opportunity to develop their arguments at an oral hearing if they so request in their written submissions.[189] Complainants must be closely associated with the proceedings. If the Commission or NCAs consider it necessary, they may also hear other natural and legal persons. Applications to be heard by such persons shall be granted where they show sufficient interest.[190] The Commission may, where appropriate, invite such persons to develop their arguments at the oral hearing of the parties to whom the statement of objections has been addressed, and the Commission may moreover invite any other person to express its views in writing and attend the oral hearing and may invite them to express their views at the oral hearing.[191]

The rights of defence of the parties concerned must be fully respected in the proceedings.[192] They are entitled to access to the file, subject to the legitimate interest of undertakings in the protection of their business secrets.[193] The right of access to the file does not extend to confidential information and internal documents of the Commission or NCAs. These provisions accord with the jurisprudence of the Community courts.[194] The Commission decision must contain reasons for the conclusion reached.[195]

The discussion thus far has been primarily concerned with the process rights of those undertakings alleged to have infringed the competition rules, although we have seen that other parties may also take part to varying degrees

[186] Ibid. Art. 27(1).
[187] Reg. 773/2004, *supra* n. 98, Art. 10(1)–(2).
[188] Ibid. Art. 10(3).
[189] Ibid. Art. 12.
[190] Reg. 1/2003, *supra* n. 185, Art. 27(3).
[191] Reg. 773/2004, *supra* n. 98, Art. 13.
[192] Reg. 1/2003, *supra* n. 185, Art. 27(2).
[193] Reg. 773/2004, *supra* n. 98, Arts. 15–16; Commission Notice, On the Rules for Access, *supra* n. 82.
[194] See above, at 365–369.
[195] Cases T-374, 375, 384, and 388/94, *European Night Services v Commission* [1998] ECR II-3141.

in the decision-making process. The procedural rights of the complainant have been addressed more fully through a Regulation and a Commission Notice. The Commission has made it clear that a complainant has a number of options:[196] an action can be pursued in the national courts; a formal complaint can be lodged with the Commission; or the person may simply provide market information indicating competition infringements that can be logged on a Commission website. There are various process rights for persons with a legitimate interest[197] who seek to lodge a formal complaint with the Commission pursuant to Article 7(2) of Regulation 1/2003. The Commission Notice unsurprisingly supports existing orthodoxy that the Commission does not have an obligation to take up all such complaints, given the limited nature of its resources and the relative importance of a complaint for the Community interest.[198] The Commission, however, fully acknowledges the obligation derived from the jurisprudence[199] that it must consider carefully the factual and legal issues brought to its attention by the complainant.[200] The Commission will therefore carefully examine the complaint and may collect further information and have an informal exchange of views with the complainant. If it decides not to pursue the complaint it will give reasons to the complainant and allow comment thereon.[201] Where the Commission decides to take the matter forward the complainant is provided with a copy of the non-confidential version of the statement of objections. The complainant is allowed to comment in writing and may be afforded the opportunity to express views at the oral hearing.[202] The Commission has, however, emphasized pre-existing orthodoxy that proceedings of the Commission in competition cases are not adversarial as between the complainant and the companies under investigation, and hence 'the procedural rights of the complainants are less far-reaching than the right to a fair hearing of the companies which are the subject of an infringement procedure'.[203]

(2) Procedural Rights and Powers Accorded to the Commission

The new regulatory regime also exemplifies the significance of procedural rights and powers accorded to the administration. The rationale underlying these rights and powers is not surprisingly instrumental, enabling the substantive goals of Community competition policy to be attained.

[196] Commission Notice, On the Handling of Complaints by the Commission under Articles 81 and 82 of the EC Treaty, OJ 2004 C101/65, at paras. 3–4.

[197] Ibid. at paras. 33–40.

[198] Ibid. at paras. 41–45.

[199] See *supra* n. 128–133.

[200] Commission Notice, On the Handling of Complaints, *supra* n. 196, at paras. 42, 53.

[201] Ibid. at para. 56; Reg. 773/2004, *supra* n. 98, Art. 7(1).

[202] Reg. 773/2004, *supra* n. 98, Art. 6.

[203] Commission Notice, On the Handling of Complaints, *supra* n. 196, at para. 59.

It is axiomatic that the Commission must know of the existence of a competition infringement in order to take appropriate action. The Commission is empowered to request information from undertakings, competent authorities of Member States, and governments,[204] and there are penalties for non-compliance.[205]

The Commission has power to inspect. The officials authorized by the Commission to conduct an inspection are empowered to enter any premises of the concerned undertakings. This includes the homes of directors, managers, and other staff members, in so far as it is suspected that business records are being kept there. The officials can examine company books and business records, and take copies of, or extracts from, the documents. They can seal any premises or business records during the inspection. They can moreover ask any staff member questions relating to the subject matter and purpose of the inspection.[206] Inspections can be either voluntary or mandatory. Voluntary inspections require the Commission officials to produce a written authorization, which specifies the subject matter and purpose of the investigation, and also the possible penalties.[207] Mandatory inspections are based on a decision ordering the investigation. The decision must state the subject matter and purpose of the investigation, the susceptibility to penalties, and the right to have the decision reviewed by the ECJ.[208] The authorities of the Member State must afford the necessary assistance to the Commission in the event that the firm in question proves intractable. This can include police assistance.[209]

There are moreover significant procedural powers and obligations that flow from the fact that Regulation 1/2003 introduced a system of parallel competence by empowering NCAs and national courts to apply Articles 81 and 82 EC in their entirety.[210] This is exemplified by the power granted to the Commission and NCAs to provide one another with any matter of fact or law, including confidential information, which can then be used in evidence,[211] and the provisions facilitating assistance in investigations by NCAs in different Member States, coupled with the power given to the Commission to use a particular NCA in effect as its agent for the carrying out of inspections.[212]

[204] Reg. 1/2003, *supra* n. 185, Art. 18. [205] Ibid. Arts. 18(3), 23.
[206] Ibid. Arts. 20–21. [207] Ibid. Art. 20(3).
[208] Ibid. Art. 20(4). [209] Ibid. Art. 20(6).
[210] Commission Notice, On the Co-operation between the Commission and the Courts of the EU Member States in the Application of Articles 81 and 82 EC, OJ 2004 C101/54; Commission Notice, On Co-operation within the Network of Competition Authorities, OJ 2004 C101/43.
[211] Reg. 1/2003, *supra* n. 185, Art. 12. [212] Ibid. Art. 22.

B. State Aids

The preceding discussion showed that the administration of Community policy on state aids generated a significant body of case law dealing with procedure. This should now be read within the more general context of the legislative scheme established for the administration of this policy.

The principal Regulation dates from 1999,[213] the preamble of which states that the purpose of the Regulation is codify Commission practice that developed in the light of the jurisprudence from the Community courts and thereby enhance transparency and legal certainty in relation to the procedures applied in relation to state aids.[214] We have seen from the earlier discussion that Article 88 EC established a two-stage procedure for state aids: stage one is preliminary investigation by the Commission; stage two is the more complete review that applies if there are serious difficulties in reaching a preliminary decision within two months.

(1) Individual Process Rights

The Regulation establishes a number of process rights for the benefit of the Member State and other interested parties. These relate to the initiation of the state aid rules, their application, and knowledge of the outcome. The process rights reflect the jurisprudence of the Community courts and develop it in more specific detail.

Thus it is open to any interested party to inform the Commission of any alleged unlawful aid or misuse of aid.[215] The Commission must inform the party where it believes that there is insufficient material on which it can form a view, and when it takes a decision on the case concerning the subject matter of the information it must send a copy of the decision to the interested party. There are notice requirements for the formal investigative procedure.[216] The decision to initiate this procedure must summarize the relevant issues of fact and law and include a preliminary assessment by the Commission as to why the Member State's action constitutes aid and the Commission's doubts as to its compatibility with the common market.

The Member State and other interested parties are allowed to submit comments within a prescribed period, normally not longer than one month. The Member State granting the contested aid is allowed to see the comments and given the opportunity to respond to them.[217] An interested party that has submitted comments and the beneficiary of the aid are sent a copy of the

[213] Council Regulation (EC) 659/1999 of 22 March 1999, Laying Down Detailed Rules for the Application of Article 93 of the EC Treaty, OJ 1999 L83/1.

[214] Ibid. Recs. (2) and (3).

[215] Ibid. Art. 20(2).

[216] Ibid. Art. 6(1).

[217] Ibid. Art. 6(2).

Commission's decision where the Commission decides to close the formal procedure, and any interested party is entitled to a copy of other decisions made pursuant to the Regulation when it requests one.[218]

(2) Procedural Rights and Powers Accorded to the Commission

It would, however, be mistaken to think of the Regulation solely from the perspective of process rights for the individual. It also accords significant process rights to the Commission, which lead to obligations for the Member State or private parties. The rights granted to the Commission serve largely instrumental goals, in that they facilitate the attainment of the substantive ends of state aid policy. They operate in differing ways in relation to the initiation of the state aid investigations, the way in which aid is used, and the uncovering of unlawful aid.

Thus the Commission has the right to request information where it believes that the information provided by the Member State is incomplete, with the consequence that the Commission cannot properly undertake its preliminary review.[219] The Member State's duty to provide the information is given added teeth by stipulating in effect that if the information requested is not provided notification of the aid will be deemed withdrawn,[220] leading to the strong likelihood that the aid will be illegal.

Process rights and obligations during the currency of a state aid scheme are mainly directed towards ensuring that aid is used for its authorized purpose. Member States are obliged to submit annual reports on all aid schemes,[221] and the Commission is empowered to monitor on site, including in this respect entering premises, examining records, and asking oral questions on the spot.[222]

Process rights play an equally important role in discovering unlawful aid. Where the Commission has information from whatever source indicative of unlawful aid, it shall if necessary request information from the Member State concerned which is obliged to provide it.[223]

8. PROCESS, CARE, REASONS, AND DIALOGUE

The discussion thus far has been concerned with various process rights provided by EU law. It is clear, as stated at the outset, that an applicant might have the benefit of all such rights, but that this might not be so if, for

[218] Ibid. Art. 20(3). [219] Ibid. Art. 5(1). [220] Ibid. Art. 5(3).

[221] Ibid. Art. 21. See also, Commission Regulation (EC) 794/2004 of 21 April 2004, Implementing Council Regulation (EC) 659/1999, OJ 2004 L140/1, Arts. 5–7.

[222] Reg. 659/1999, *supra* n. 213, Art. 22. [223] Ibid. Art. 10.

example, the person does not satisfy the criteria for a hearing. It is for this very reason that the process rights must be considered separately. It is, however, perfectly consistent with this precept to recognize that the process rights can interrelate.

The discussion within this section will deal with one important facet of this interrelationship, that between transparency, the duty of diligent and impartial examination, and the provision of reasons. Shapiro has explained the nature of the relationship and the tensions that can be engendered in this regard.[224]

> The basic reason that the parties push and the ECJ resists dialogue lies in the difference between transparency and participation. Courts are likely to be initially hostile to demands for dialogue. Such requests are the last resort of regulated parties who have no substantive arguments left. Moreover, if dialogue claims are judicially accepted, they lead to a more and more cumbersome administrative process because the regulated parties will be encouraged to raise more and more arguments to which the agency will have to respond. If the only instrumental value for giving reasons is transparency, the courts will resist dialogue demands. One can discover an agency's actions and purposes without the agency rebutting every opposing argument.
>
> . . .
>
> If the ECJ sticks closely to transparency as the sole goal of Article 190, the ECJ is unlikely to move towards a dialogue requirement. Yet participation in government by interests affected by government decisions presents an increasingly compelling value in contemporary society, particularly where environmental matters are involved. The ECJ has already, however unintentionally, opened one avenue for linking participation to Article 190 by stating that the Council need not give full reasons to the Member States where they have participated in the decisions. To be sure, these ECJ opinions are transparency-based. They require that those Member States already know what was going on because they were there. Nevertheless they create an opening for counter-arguments from complainants who were not present and claim that, therefore, they need the Commission to be responsive. In short, full transparency can only be achieved through participation or through dialogue as a form of participation.

The key issue is therefore the extent to which the jurisprudence on process rights considered above might be moving, directly or indirectly, towards a dialogue between the individual and the decision-maker, requiring the latter to respond to arguments advanced by the former. This is a theme developed interestingly by Nehl in his study of administrative procedure in EU law, who, at the time of his writing, perceived movement in this direction.[225] There is, however, rather less evidence for this proposition now.

This is in part because the case law has taken a step back from the tentative

[224] Shapiro, 'The Giving Reasons Requirement' (1992) *U Chic Legal Forum* 179, at 203–204. References to Art. 190 EC should now be read as referring to Art. 253 EC.

[225] Nehl, *supra* n. 79, at 155–165.

moves in this direction. The ECJ's initial approach was cautious. In the *Sigarettenindustrie* case[226] the Court held that, although Article 253 required the Commission to state its reasons, it was not required to discuss all issues of fact and law raised by every party during the administrative proceedings. It therefore dismissed the claim that the Commission had ignored the applicants' arguments, none of which had featured in the decision. We have seen that 'dents' appeared in this orthodoxy, especially in the CFI's case law and it was moreover the CFI that was literally at the front line in hearing direct actions brought by individuals seeking judicial review. The high point of this case law was the CFI's decision in *Sytraval*,[227] which if it had been upheld by the ECJ and if it had been extended to other areas of EU law, would have established a dialogue requirement.

The reality is that neither happened. The ECJ reined in the CFI, and rejected the more far-reaching aspects of dialogue that the latter had advanced, even within the context of state aids. This was confirmed by later judgments that stressed that the process was not one of dialogic or adversarial debate,[228] and emphasized that the courts would not allow it to be turned into one through an expansive reading of the duty of diligent administration. Nor would they allow this to occur through expansive interpretation of the duty to give reasons. Thus, as we have seen in relation to competition, the Community courts have held that in stating the reasons for the decisions it takes the Commission is not obliged to adopt a position on all the arguments relied on by the parties. It is sufficient if it sets out the facts and legal considerations having decisive importance in the context of the decision.[229] If there is a countervailing tendency it is an indirect by-product of the jurisprudence on access to the file, which places the individual in a better position to know the arguments that should be advanced at the hearing, thereby leading to some obligation on the Commission to respond.

There is, however, another reason for being cautious about the extent to which the Community courts might be willing to foster a dialogue requirement. This concerns the distinction between rule-making and individualized determinations. The idea of dialogue in the USA is primarily a feature of rule-making. It emerged in part at least as a by-product or corollary of the notice and comment provisions of the Administrative Procedure Act 1946, with the courts requiring the agency to respond to important comments

[226] Cases 240–242, 261–262, 268–269/82, *Stichting Sigarettenindustrie v Commission* [1985] ECR 3831, at para. 88; Case 42/84, *Remia BV and Nutricia BV v Commission* [1985] ECR 2545.

[227] Case T-95/94, *Sytraval, supra* n. 142.

[228] Cases C-74 and 75/00, *Falck, supra* n. 148; Case T-198/01, *Technische Glaswerke Ilmenau, supra* n. 151.

[229] See cases cited *supra* n. 134.

made by the parties before finalizing the draft rule.[230] It is important not to lose sight of the fact that insofar as the Community courts have moved towards dialogue, the case law has, by way of contrast, been exclusively concerned with individualized discretionary determinations. It is moreover not fortuitous that the cases in which the Community courts have been tempted to move furthest in this direction have been concerned with especially problematic decisions of this nature.

Thus it is questionable whether the CFI in *Sytraval*[231] ever intended its reasoning to apply outside of the specific circumstances of state aids, with its two-stage procedure and the disadvantages that could ensue for the individual if a complaint was dismissed at the preliminary stage at which the complainant could not participate. There is a strong vein running through the CFI's judgment that seeks to develop the duty of diligent administration as a way of meeting this particular problem, and the ECJ curbed the more far-reaching aspects of this reasoning.

The apposite point for present purposes is that neither the ECJ nor the CFI has shown any inclination to develop a dialogue requirement in relation to rule-making. To the contrary, as we have seen in the previous chapter,[232] they have drawn a sharp distinction between rule-making and individualized determinations, and have been very reluctant to develop process rights in relation to rule-making, even in the form of bare consultation or participation, let alone in an extended form so as to foster dialogue.

9. PROCESS AND SUBSTANTIVE REVIEW

It is clear not only that process rights can interrelate, but also that there is an interrelationship between procedural and substantive review. It is fitting to touch on this issue at the conclusion of this chapter, since it is a theme that will be explored again in the chapters that follow, which deal with substantive review. The inter-connection between procedural and substantive review can operate on a number of levels, two of which are especially significant.

A. Process Rights Facilitating Substantive Review

It is readily acknowledged that process rights can facilitate substantive review. This is exemplified by the application of the duty of careful examination in *Pfizer*, where the procedural duty served to justify the requirement of scien-

[230] A. Aman and W. Mayton, *Administrative Law* (West Group, 2nd ed., 2001), Chap. 2; Shapiro, 'APA: Past, Present and Future' 72 *Va L Rev* 447 (1986).

[231] Case T-95/94, *Sytraval, supra* n. 142.

[232] See above, at 316–318.

tific advice with the aim of ensuring that the resultant regulation was not substantively arbitrary.[233]

The connection between process and substance is apparent once again in relation to reasons. Thus the rationale for the obligation to give reasons is in part that it will enable the courts to determine whether the administration acted for improper purposes, or took irrelevant considerations into account when reaching its decision. The CFI has emphasized that the reasons given must be sufficient to enable it to exercise its judicial review function, and it has scrutinized the Commission's reasoning, annulling the decision if it did not withstand examination.[234] There is in this sense a proximate connection between expansion of the duty to give reasons and closer judicial scrutiny of the administration's reasoning process in order to discover a substantive error. This is neatly exemplified by *Artegodan*[235] where the CFI held that it could review not only the relevant Commission determination, but also the opinion of the scientific committee on which the Commission's determination was based.[236] It could in this regard consider the reasons given by the committee, whether there was an understandable link between the medical evidence on which it relied and its conclusions and whether the committee had adequately explained its rejection of scientific evidence that was contrary to its own view.[237]

The nature of this connection must nonetheless be delineated with care. It is perfectly possible in principle for the courts to demand more by way of reasons, but still to engage in low intensity substantive review, requiring some manifest error before annulling the decision. The reality is however that expansion of the process rights will at the least encourage the courts to engage in more intensive substantive review, because they have more to work with and therefore feel more confident about asserting judicial control. It is common, as will be seen in later chapters, for courts to retain their original criterion of substantive review, such as manifest error, but to apply this more exactingly.

B. Process Rights as a Means to Consider the Substance of the Case

The expansion of procedural review may alternatively encourage courts to set aside the contested decision on procedural grounds, in circumstances where the process rights have enabled the court to have a look at the substance of

233 Case T-13/99, *Pfizer, supra* n. 162, at paras. 171–172.

234 See e. g. Case T-44/90, *La Cinq SA v Commission* [1992] ECR II-1; Case T-7/92, *Asia Motor, supra* n. 131; Nehl, *supra* n. 79, at 142–146.

235 Cases T-74, 76, 83–85, 132, 137 and 141/00, *Artegodan GmbH v Commission* [2002] ECR II-4945.

236 Ibid. at para. 199.

237 Ibid. at paras. 199–200.

the case. Nehl brings this out clearly in relation to the court's use of access to the file.[238] Thus, if the administration has not accorded full rights of access to the file, the CFI or ECJ may, as we have seen, consider whether the document was relevant for the individual's case and whether its disclosure might have made a difference to the decision reached. This will require the court to consider the Commission's reasoning process in relation to the merits of the case.[239] If the court has doubts about the substantive reasoning it may then choose to uphold the applicant's procedural claim that it was denied proper access to the file.

10. CONCLUSION

The law on process has developed significantly since the inception of the EEC. It has been a development to which all the major players have contributed. The framers included certain process rights in the original EEC Treaty such as the duty to give reasons, and have added more since then. The Community legislature has made a significant contribution both in terms of sector-specific legislation, and through more generally applicable provisions concerning matters such as access to documentation. The CFI and the ECJ have been at the forefront of this development, drawing on principles from common law and civil law systems alike and fashioning them to the needs of the EU. The European Ombudsman[240] and the Commission[241] have contributed by formulating codes of good administrative behaviour.

The different players have moreover worked symbiotically in developing the law on process. The paradigm may well be the articulation of principles by the CFI and ECJ, which are then taken up and developed in more detail through sector-specific regulations or directives. There are, however, also instances in which the legislature has gone further than demanded by the jurisprudence of the Community courts, and aspects of procedure where the courts have been reticent in the absence of more specific imprimatur expressed through Treaty amendment or Community regulation.

It should cause little surprise that the content of the process rights can be controversial. It is axiomatic that process rights are premised on certain underlying substantive values, and that people may well disagree as to the

[238] Nehl, *supra* n. 79, at 53–54.

[239] See, e.g., Cases C-204–205, 211, 213, 217, 219/00 P, *Aalborg Portland, supra* n. 70.

[240] *Supra* n. 179.

[241] Commission Decision 2000/633/EC, ECSC, Euratom of 17 October 2000, Amending its Rules of Procedure, OJ 2000 L267/63. The Code of Good Administrative Behaviour for Staff of the European Commission in their Relations with the Public forms the Annex to this Decision.

weight or blend of values that inform a particular process right. It is part of the function of academic discourse to reveal these values and engage in reasoned debate about them. The possible impact of a formally binding code of administrative behaviour was considered above and reference should be made to that discussion.[242]

[242] See above, at 279–281.

12

Competence and Subsidiarity

1. INTRODUCTION

The previous chapters were concerned with access and process. We now turn to consideration of substantive review and it is natural for this discussion to begin with competence and subsidiarity. The European Union (EU) is based on attributed power. It only has competence when it can point to a power contained in the Treaties. This is reflected in Article 230(2) EC, which provides that the European Court of Justice (ECJ) can review the legality of acts on a number of grounds, including lack of competence. This chapter will examine the way in which issues of competence have been interpreted by the Community courts. The analysis will begin by considering the difficulties of delineating internal and external competence. The focus then shifts to subsidiarity and the judicial approach to actions based on non-compliance with this principle.

2. INTERNAL COMPETENCE

The requirement that legislation must be properly based upon a Treaty article is not normally problematic: the particular regulation, directive, or decision will stipulate the Treaty article on which it is based. The boundaries of the EU's competence can nonetheless be difficult to divine for a number of reasons.

A. Competence, Shared Competence, and Uncertainty

The existing Treaties are unclear as to the precise delimitation of competence between the EU and the Member States. Thus while Article 5 EC mentions the concept of exclusive competence, this is nowhere defined in the Treaty.

The reality is that competence is commonly divided between the European Community (EC) and the Member States, and the great majority of powers are shared rather than exclusive. However, it is mostly in relation to the newer competences granted to the EC that the non-exclusive nature of these powers is made express.

It is equally important to recognize that the precise division of competence between the EC and the Member States varies in different subject-matter areas,[1] and that it is often drawn in imprecise terms. It may therefore be contestable whether a measure falls within the sphere allocated to the Community or to the Member States, and normally this question will be decided ultimately by the European Court of Justice (ECJ).

The division of competence between the Member States and the EU was one of the topics listed in the Nice Treaty for further consideration at what would have been the Intergovernmental Conference (IGC) in 2004. The idea of separate consideration of discrete issues was, however, overtaken by the establishment of the Convention on the Future of Europe, which drafted the Constitutional Treaty (CT).[2] It is, as we have seen, unlikely that the Constitution will enter into force. It is nonetheless worth dwelling briefly on the relevant provisions, since the issue of competence will remain of importance to both the Member States and the EU.

A predominant concern was that the subsidiarity principle contained in Article 5 EC provided scant protection for state rights, and scant safeguards against an ever-increasing shift of power from the states to the EU, notwithstanding the strictures about subsidiarity and proportionality contained in the second paragraph of Article 5. This was the rationale for the inclusion of competence as one of the issues to be addressed post the Nice Treaty.

This view of the 'competence problem' is, however, based on implicit assumptions as to how the EU acquires competence over certain areas. The inarticulate premise is that the shift in power upward towards the EU was the result primarily of an unwarranted arrogation of power by the EU institutions to the detriment of states' rights, which Article 5 EC has been powerless to prevent. This is an over-simplistic view of how and why the EU acquired its current range of power.

The reality is that the EU's power has been expanded by a broad interpretation accorded to existing Treaty provisions, either legislatively or judicially, by a teleological view of Article 308 EC, and by the attribution of new competences to the EU through successive Treaty amendments. Commentators may disagree as to the relative importance of these factors.

It is nonetheless important not to lose sight of the fact that the conscious decisions by the Member States to grant the EU competence in areas such as the environment, culture, health, consumer protection, employment, and vocational training were reached after extensive discussion within IGCs

[1] Compare, for example, the different formulations in Art. 152 EC (health), Art. 153 EC (consumer protection), Art. 157 EC (industry), Arts. 163–173 EC (research and technological development).

[2] Treaty Establishing a Constitution for Europe, OJ 2004 C310/1.

leading to Treaty revisions. The fact that the EU wields competence in such areas can scarcely be regarded as illegitimate given that the Member States consciously consented to these grants of power.[3]

Four principal forces drove the reform process in the Convention on the Future of Europe that led to the provisions concerning competence: clarity, conferral, containment, and consideration.[4] The desire for clarity reflected the sense that the existing Treaty provisions on competences were unclear, jumbled, and unprincipled, and that it was unclear what the EU could do. Conferral captured not only the idea that the EU should act within the limits of the powers attributed to it, but also the more positive connotation that the EU should be accorded the powers necessary to fulfil the tasks assigned to it by the Treaties. The desire for containment reflected the concern, voiced by the German Lander as well as some Member States, that the EU had too much power, and that it should be substantively limited.[5] The final factor was consideration of whether the EU should continue to have the powers that it had been given in the past, and a re-thinking of the areas in which the EU should be able to act.

The provisions on competence were contained in Title III of Part I of the Constitution, which retained the central principle that the EU operates on the basis of attributed competence. This is made clear by Article I-11(1), which stipulated that Union competences were based on conferral and that their exercise was governed by subsidiarity and proportionality. This was reinforced by Article I-11(2), which stated that the Union must act within the limits of the competences conferred on it by the Member States, and that competences not conferred on the Union remained with the Member States.

Different categories of competence were set out in Article I-12 and the divide between them was the subject of intense debate within the Convention: the EU could have exclusive competence, it could share competence with the Member States, the EU could be limited to taking supporting/coordinating action, and there were special categories for EU action in the sphere of economic and employment policy, and Common Foreign and Security Policy (CFSP). The Constitution ascribed particular subject-matter areas to each of the heads of competence. The constitutional strategy was also premised on attaching concrete consequences in terms of EU and state power in relation to each head of competence. The categories therefore mattered,

[3] It is of course possible to accept this, and to argue also that the legislative and judicial interpretation accorded to these heads of EU competence has, on occasion, been too expansive. See further, Weatherill, 'Better Competence Monitoring' (2005) 30 *ELRev* 23.

[4] Craig, 'Competence: Clarity, Conferral, Containment and Consideration' (2004) 29 *ELRev* 323.

[5] We have however already seen that a significant factor in the distribution of competence has been the decision of the Member States to grant new spheres of competence to the EU.

since the categorization had consequences, in terms of the possession and retention of legislative power.

This is not the place for detailed exegesis on these constitutional provisions. Suffice it to say for the present that there were some real difficulties with these provisions.[6] It should nonetheless be recognized that the division of power between different levels of government is an endemic problem within any non-unitary polity. So too is the problem of ensuring that central power remains within bounds.[7] Experience from elsewhere is helpful. We should nonetheless be mindful of the distinctive features of the EU. The divide between EU and Member State power in the Constitution was not based on a general constitutional provision, such as an inter-state commerce clause, to be policed by the courts. The EU Constitution scheme was premised on categories of competence in Part I, coupled with detailed provisions in Part III, which elaborated the more specific nature and bounds of EU action in the areas that comprise EU substantive law. German law was the closest inspiration. The competence issue is likely to remain high-profile notwithstanding the fate of the CT and the competence provisions from that document may yet find their way into some future, more limited Treaty reform.

B. Treaty Articles, Interpretation, and Disagreement

The preceding discussion focused on the general issues concerning division of competence between the EU and the Member States. Such issues can arise more specifically when interpreting particular Treaty articles. These may be drafted relatively specifically, or they may be framed in more broad open-textured terms. In either case it is always possible for there to be disagreement about the ambit, scope, or interpretation of the relevant Treaty article, more especially so when it is cast in broad terms. Disagreements of this nature are an endemic feature of adjudication. It is not uncommon for the applicant to argue that the Community legislation could not be validly based on the Treaty article expressed as the basis for that legislation. The strength and plausibility of such claims will necessarily differ from case to case, and there may well be scope for legitimate differences of view as to the ambit or interpretation of a particular Treaty article.

It should also be recognized that while on some occasions the applicant will contend that the EU lacked any competence to enact the contested measure, on other occasions the stakes are rather different, and the applicant is effectively claiming that it should have been based on a different Treaty article, which has different voting rules.

[6] Craig, *supra* n. 4.

[7] Young, 'Protecting Member State Autonomy in the European Union: Some Cautionary Tales from American Federalism' (2002) 77 *NYULRev* 1612.

This is exemplified by the *Working Time Directive* case.[8] The UK sought the annulment of a Directive concerned with the organization of working time. The Directive had been adopted by qualified majority pursuant to what was Article 118a of the Treaty,[9] concerned with health and safety. The UK argued that the measure should have been made under Article 100 or Article 235 EC, now Articles 94 and 308 EC, which required unanimity in the Council. Article 118a was, the UK contended, not suitable for measures of broad social policy, and provisions concerning working time were insufficiently related to health and safety. The ECJ, save for one small point, rejected the argument and concluded that Article 118a was a sound legal basis for the measure.

The ECJ has, in the past, been disinclined to place limits on broadly worded Treaty articles. It can, however, do so. In the *Tobacco Advertising* case[10] the ECJ held that a Directive relating to tobacco advertising could not be based on Article 100a, now Article 95 EC.[11] Germany sought the annulment of a Directive designed to harmonize the law relating to the advertising and sponsorship of tobacco. The Directive had been based on, *inter alia*, Article 100a, which allows the adoption of harmonization measures for the functioning of the internal market.

The ECJ annulled the measure.[12] It held that the measures referred to in Article 100a(1) must be intended to improve the conditions for the establishment and functioning of the internal market. That Article could not be construed as vesting the Community legislature with a general power to regulate the internal market since that would be incompatible with the principle that the powers of the Community were limited to those specifically conferred on it. If a mere finding of disparities between national rules and an abstract risk of obstacles to the exercise of fundamental freedoms, or of distortions of competition liable to result therefrom, were sufficient to justify Article 100a as a legal base, judicial review of compliance with the proper legal basis might be nugatory. The Court would then be prevented from discharging its function under Article 164 EC of ensuring that the law is observed in the interpretation and application of the Treaty.

The subsequent history of legislation and adjudication on measures

[8] Case C-84/94, *United Kingdom v Council* [1996] ECR I-5755. For a similar argument in the context of Art. 47, see Case C-233/94, *Germany v European Parliament and Council* [1997] ECR I-2405. See also, Case C-377/98, *Netherlands v Parliament and Council* [2001] ECR I-7079.

[9] The Treaty of Amsterdam substantially amended this and related Arts. of the EC Treaty: see Arts. 137 and 138 EC.

[10] Case C-376/98, *Germany v European Parliament and Council* [2000] ECR I-8419.

[11] Hervey, 'Up in Smoke? Community (Anti)-Tobacco Law and Policy' (2001) 26 *ELRev* 101.

[12] Case C-376/98, *supra* n. 10, at paras. 83–84.

designed to curb smoking and tobacco advertising shows, however, that the Community courts are still likely to read broadly framed Treaty articles as providing a valid basis for Community action and have distinguished the *Tobacco Advertising* case.[13]

C. Power, Implied Power, and the Scope of Implication

The issue of competence may also arise where the Community institutions claim that a Treaty article contains an implied power to make the particular measure. The notion of implied powers is well known in both domestic and international legal systems. The precise meaning of the phrase 'implied power' is more contestable. It can, as Hartley notes, be given a narrow or a wide formulation:[14]

> According to the narrow formulation, the existence of a given power implies also the existence of any other power which is reasonably necessary for the exercise of the former; according to the wide formulation, the existence of a given *objective* or *function* implies the existence of any power reasonably necessary to attain it.

The narrow sense of implied power has been long accepted within the Community.[15] The ECJ has also been willing to embrace the wider formulation. This is exemplified by *Germany v Commission.*[16]

The Commission, acting under what was Article 118 EC, made a decision that established a prior communication and consultation process in relation to migration policies affecting workers from non-EC countries. The Member States were to inform the Commission and other Member States of their draft measures concerning entry, residence, equality of treatment, and the integration of such workers into the social and cultural life of the country. There would then be consultation with the Commission and other Member States. It was argued that the measure was *ultra vires*, since Article 118, which concerned collaboration in the social field, did not cover migration policy in relation to non-Member States and because it did not expressly give the Commission power to make binding decisions.

The ECJ disagreed. It held that the employment situation and improvement of working conditions within the Community were liable to be affected by policies pursued by the Member States with regard to workers from non-Member countries and therefore did not fall entirely outside

[13] Case C-377/98, *Netherlands v Council, supra* n. 8, at paras. 27–28; Case C-491/01, *The Queen v Secretary of State for Health, ex p. British American Tobacco (Investments) Ltd and Imperial Tobacco Ltd* [2002] ECR I-11453.

[14] T. C. Hartley, *The Foundations of European Community Law* (Oxford University Press 4th edn., 1998), at 102. Italics in the original.

[15] Case 8/55, *Fédération Charbonnière de Belgique v High Authority* [1956] ECR 245, at 280.

[16] Cases 281, 283–285, 287/85, *Germany v Commission* [1987] ECR 3203.

Article 118, although the decision was held to be partly *ultra vires* in relation to cultural matters. The ECJ also concluded that Article 118, which provided that the Commission was to act, *inter alia*, by arranging consultations, gave it the power to adopt a binding decision with a view to the arrangement of such consultations. It reasoned that where a Treaty Article 'confers a specific task on the Commission it must be accepted, if that provision is not to be rendered wholly ineffective, that it confers on the Commission necessarily and *per se* the powers which are indispensable in order to carry out that task'.[17] Thus Article 118 should be interpreted as conferring on the Commission all the necessary powers to arrange the consultations. This included empowering the Commission to require the Member States to notify the essential information and to require them to take part in the consultation.

D. Power, Community Objectives, and Necessity

The delineation of Community competence has also been rendered more difficult because of Article 308 EC. Most Treaty articles relate to a specific subject-matter area, such as workers or goods. The Treaty also contains broader legislative provisions, such as Articles 94 and 95 EC, concerning harmonization of laws. Article 308 EC is broader still. It provides that:

> If action by the Community should prove necessary to attain, in the course of the operation of the common market, one of the objectives of the Community and this Treaty has not provided the necessary powers, the Council shall, acting unanimously on a proposal from the Commission and after consulting the European Parliament, take the appropriate measures.

Article 308 was a valuable legislative power for the EC, particularly when it did not possess more specific legislative authority in certain areas. Thus the Article was used to legitimate legislation on areas such as the environment and regional policy, before these matters were dealt with through later Treaty amendments. This threw into sharp relief the limits of Article 308. Weiler captured this well, noting that in a variety of fields the Community made use of Article 308 in a manner that 'was simply not consistent with the narrow interpretation of the Article as a codification of implied powers doctrine in its instrumental sense'.[18] The broader reading of the Article meant however that it became virtually impossible to find an activity which could not be brought within the objectives of the Treaty.[19]

There have, to be sure, been certain instances in which the ECJ found that

[17] Ibid. at para. 28.

[18] Weiler, 'The Transformation of Europe' (1991) 100 *Yale LJ* 2403, at 2445.

[19] Ibid. at 2445–2446.

Article 308 could not be used. Thus in *Opinion 2/94*,[20] which was concerned with the legality of the EC's possible accession to the European Convention on Human Rights (ECHR), the ECJ held that Article 308 could not be used to widen the scope of Community powers beyond the framework created by the EC Treaty taken as a whole. Nor could it be used as the foundation for the adoption of provisions which would, in substance, amend the Treaty without following the necessary amendment procedures. The ECJ was, however, probably content to reach this conclusion, thereby avoiding subjecting itself to the ultimate authority of the European Court of Human Rights.

The most problematic aspect of Article 308 is the condition that the Treaty has not 'provided the necessary powers'. The mere fact that another, more specific, Treaty provision has given a power to make recommendations will not preclude the use of Article 308 to enact binding measures.[21] Nor, it seems, will Article 308 be excluded by the fact that the particular Treaty provisions could be interpreted broadly by using the implied-powers doctrine discussed above.[22]

Whether the Treaty has provided necessary powers elsewhere can, however, be of particular significance where specific Treaty Articles provide for more extensive involvement of the European Parliament than does Article 308. This Article only requires the Council to consult the Parliament, whereas other Treaty Articles give the Parliament greater rights in the legislative process. If the Council is able to proceed via Article 308, there is a danger that this will diminish the European Parliament's role. The ECJ has, therefore, stressed that Article 308 can only be used where no other provision of the Treaty gives the Community institutions the necessary power to adopt the relevant measure. The Court will closely scrutinize the use of Article 308 where it is argued that another more specific Treaty Article would afford the European Parliament a greater role in the legislative process.[23] The other situation in which the choice between Article 308 and a more specific Treaty article can be of significance is where there are differences in the Council voting rules under the respective articles. Article 308 requires unanimity in the Council, whereas many other Treaty provisions demand only a qualified majority.

Cases involving the appropriate boundaries of Article 308 have not infrequently been litigated before the ECJ. Thus in the *Tariff Preferences*

[20] Opinion 2/94, *Re the Accession of the Community to the European Human Rights Convention* [1996] ECR I-1759.

[21] Case 8/73, *Hauptzollamt Bremerhaven v Massey-Ferguson* [1973] ECR 897.

[22] Ibid. at para. 4.

[23] Case 45/86, *Commission v Council* [1987] ECR 1493; Case C-350/92, *Spain v Council* [1995] ECR I-1985; Case C-271/94, *European Parliament v Council: Re the Edicom Decision* [1996] ECR I-1689.

case[24] the Commission sought the annulment of Regulations concerning tariff preferences for goods from developing countries. The Council argued that, since the purpose of the measures was in reality development aid, they could only be adopted by using Article 308. The Commission contended that Article 113 EC, now Article 133 EC, which concerned the common commercial policy, could be used, and that this only required qualified majority voting. In fact the Council did not specify any particular Treaty article in the contested measure. The ECJ annulled the Regulations because of failure to state the legal basis of the measures, and because they could have been adopted under Article 113. In the *Biotechnology Directive* case, the ECJ ruled that a Directive concerning patent protection for such inventions was properly adopted under Article 95 EC and did not require Article 308 as an additional legal basis.[25] By contrast, in a case concerning a Regulation on mutual assistance between national administrative authorities to deal with EC agricultural and customs fraud, the Court upheld the use of Article 308, ruling that Article 95 would be inappropriate in this context.[26]

Article 308 has long been viewed with suspicion by those calling for a clearer delimitation of Community competences and in particular by the German Lander. Various calls for reform were made before and during recent IGCs.[27] This question was placed explicitly on the post-Nice and post-Laeken agenda for future reform of the Union. The Laeken Declaration, adopted by the Member States in December 2001, expressly asked whether Article 308 ought to be reviewed, in light of the twin challenges of preventing the 'creeping expansion of competences' from encroaching on national and regional powers, and yet allowing the EU to 'continue to be able to react to fresh challenges and developments and . . . to explore new policy areas'.[28] In the Convention on the Future of Europe the Working Group on Complementary Competences recognized the concerns about the use of Article 308. The Group nonetheless recommended the retention of the Article in order that it could provide for flexibility in limited instances.[29]

The flexibility clause was retained in Article I-18(1) of the CT. It provided that if action by the Union should prove necessary in the framework of the

[24] Case 45/86, [1987] ECR 1493. See also, Case 165/87, *Commission v Council* [1988] ECR 5545; Case C-295/90, *European Parliament v Council* [1992] ECR I-4193.

[25] Case C-377/98, *Netherlands v European Parliament Council* [2001] ECR I-7079.

[26] Case C-209/97, *Commission v Council* [1999] ECR I-8067.

[27] Von Bogdandy and Bast, 'The Union's Powers: A Question of Competence. The Vertical Order of Competences and Proposals for its Reform' (2002) 38 *CMLRev* 227; de Búrca 'Setting Limits to EU Competences' Francisco Lucas Pires Working paper 2001/02, <http://www.fd.unl.pt/je/wpflp02a.doc>.

[28] European Council, 14–15 December 2001, SN 300/1/01 REV 1, at 22.

[29] CONV 375/1/02, Final Report of Working Group V on Complementary Competencies, Brussels 4 November 2002, at 14–18.

policies defined in Part III to attain one of the Constitution's objectives, and the Constitution had not provided the necessary powers, the Council, acting unanimously on a proposal from the Commission, and after obtaining the consent of the European Parliament, should adopt the appropriate measures. There was an additional requirement that the attention of national parliaments should be drawn to such proposals. It was moreover made clear that Article I-18 could not be used to achieve harmonization in cases where this was precluded by the Constitution. If the CT had been ratified the need to use this power would have diminished, since the Constitution created a legal basis for action in many areas where recourse was previously had to Article 308.[30]

The CT was not ratified, but recourse to Article 308 EC will in any event be more difficult in an enlarged EU, since it will be harder to secure unanimity than hitherto.

3. EXTERNAL COMPETENCE

The discussion thus far has been concerned with difficulties of drawing the boundaries of the EU's internal competence. There are equal if not greater problems in delineating the sphere of the EU's external competence. This is a complex subject in its own right[31] and the discussion that follows is not intended in any sense to cover the entirety of this area. The object is rather to highlight some of the principal points in the jurisprudence in order that the problems of drawing the boundaries of the EU's competence in this area can be better understood.

A. The Early Case Law, Express Power, and Judicial Implication

The EC has always had legal personality.[32] The EU was not expressly given legal personality when it was created, but the effect of Article 24 TEU, which was added by the Treaty of Amsterdam, and modified by the Nice Treaty, was to confer upon it the capacity to enter international agreements.[33] This

[30] See, e.g., Energy, Art. III-256(2); Civil Protection, Art. III-284(2); Economic Aid to Third Countries, Art. III-319(2).

[31] I. Macleod, I. Hendry, and S. Hyett, *The External Relations of the European Communities: A Manual of Law and Practice* (Oxford University Press, 1996); D. McGoldrick, *International Relations Law of the European Union* (Longman, 1997); M. Koskenniemi (ed), *International Law Aspects of the European Union* (Kluwer, 1998); A. Dashwood and C. Hillion (eds), *The General Law of EC External Relations* (Sweet & Maxwell, 2000); P. Eeckhout, *External Relations of the European Union: Legal and Constitutional Foundations* (Oxford University Press, 2004).

[32] Art. 281 EC.

[33] P. Craig and G. de Búrca, *EU Law, Text, Cases and Materials* (Oxford University Press, 3rd ed., 2002), Chap. 1.

applies to agreements made under the Common Foreign and Security Policy (CFSP) Pillar, and also to those under the Police and Judicial Cooperation in Criminal Matters (PJCC) Pillar.[34]

The Treaty lays down the procedure for the negotiation and conclusion of international agreements.[35] In essence the Commission is the principal negotiator, and the Council concludes the agreement on the basis of the proposal put forward by the Commission, after having consulted the European Parliament (EP). The voting rules in the Council and the extent of the EP's involvement may vary depending on the subject matter of the agreement.

The choice of the legal basis for a measure adopting an international agreement must be based on objective factors that are amenable to judicial review. If the agreement pursues a twofold purpose, one of which is predominant, then the measure must be founded on a single legal basis, namely that required by the predominant purpose. Where exceptionally there are several objectives pursued simultaneously, none of which predominates, then the measure can be founded on the corresponding legal bases.[36]

The EC has *express external competence* in areas stipulated by the Treaty. The number of such areas has expanded with successive Treaty amendments and now includes commercial policy;[37] association agreements;[38] the maintenance of relations between the Community and international organizations such as the United Nations (UN), the General Agreement on Tariffs and Trade (GATT), the Council of Europe, and the Organisation for Economic Co-operation and Development (OECD);[39] development policy;[40] environmental policy;[41] research and technology;[42] monetary and foreign exchange policy;[43] and economic, financial and technical cooperation with third countries.[44] There are also Treaty provisions on the fostering of cooperation with third countries and international organizations concerning matters such as education, vocational training, culture, health, and trans-European networks.[45] The existence of express Community competence is, however, logically distinct from the issue of whether the Community's competence in these areas is exclusive and the answer can vary from area to area.

It is, however, clear that even if there is no express grant of competence the Community can have *implied external competence* in accord with the ECJ's jurisprudence. It held in a series of cases that when Community law created powers within its internal system for the purpose of attaining a specific

[34] Art. 38 TEU. [35] Art. 300(1) EC.

[36] Opinion 2/00, *Opinion Pursuant to Article 300(6) EC, Cartegena Protocol* [2001] ECR I-9713, at paras. 22–23.

[37] Art. 133 EC. Eeckhout and Tridimas, 'The External Competence of the Community and the Case-Law of the Court of Justice: Principle Versus Pragmatism' (1994) 14 *YBEL* 143.

[38] Art. 310 EC. [39] Arts. 302–304 EC. [40] Art. 181 EC.

[41] Art. 174 EC. [42] Art. 170 EC. [43] Art. 111 EC.

[44] Art. 181a EC. [45] Arts 149(3), 150(3), 151(3), 152(3), 155(3) EC.

objective, the Community was empowered to enter into the international commitments necessary for attainment of that objective even in the absence of an express provision to that effect.[46]

The issue of whether external power is exclusive is, as stated above, distinct from the existence of such power. While it is clear that the EC's implied external competence can be shared with the Member States, the ECJ also held that in certain circumstances the EC's implied external power would be exclusive. The precise circumstances where this would be so were, however, not entirely clear,[47] although the formulations used by the ECJ as to when exclusivity would arise were far reaching.

Thus in *ERTA* the ECJ held that when the Community acted to implement a common policy pursuant to the Treaty, the Member States no longer had the right to take external action where this would affect the rules thus established or distort their scope.[48] This position was modified in *Kramer*.[49] The ECJ held that the EC could possess implied external powers even though it had not taken internal measures to implement the relevant policy, but that until the EC duly exercised its internal power the Member States retained competence to act provided that their action was compatible with Community objectives. The scope of exclusivity was thrown into doubt because of the *Inland Waterways* case,[50] where the ECJ held that the EC could have exclusive external competence even though it had not exercised its internal powers, if Member State action could place in jeopardy the Community objective sought to be attained.

B. The WTO Case, External Competence, and the Limits of Exclusive Competence

The ECJ, however, pulled back from the very broad reading of exclusivity contained in the *Inland Waterways* case. In *Opinion 1/94 on the WTO Agreement*[51] the ECJ ruled that certain issues covered by the General Agreement on Trade in Services (GATS) and the Agreement on Trade-related Intellectual

[46] Case 22/70, *Commission v Council* [1971] ECR 263; Cases 3, 4, and 6/76, *Kramer* [1976] ECR 1279; Opinion 1/76, *On the Draft Agreement Establishing a Laying-up Fund for Inland Waterway Vessels* [1977] ECR 741; Opinion 2/91, *Re the ILO Convention 170 on Chemicals at Work* [1993] ECR I-1061; Opinion 2/94, *supra* n. 20.

[47] Cremona, 'External Relations and External Competence: the Emergence of an Integrated Policy', in P. Craig and G. de Búrca (eds), *The Evolution of EU Law* (Oxford University Press, 1999), 137; Dashwood and Heliskoski, 'The Classic Authorities Revisited', in A. Dashwood and C. Hillion (eds), *The General Law of EC External Relations* (Sweet & Maxwell, 2000), 3.

[48] Case 22/70, *Commission v Council*, *supra* n. 46.

[49] Cases 3, 4, and 6/76, *Kramer*, *supra* n. 46.

[50] Opinion 1/76, *supra* n. 46.

[51] Opinion 1/94, *Competence of the Community to Conclude International Agreements Concerning Services and the Protection of Intellectual Property, WTO* [1994] ECR I-5267.

Property Rights (TRIPS) were not in the scope of the Common Commercial Policy.[52]

The Commission argued in the alternative that exclusive external competence resided with the EC to conclude GATS and TRIPS either because it flowed implicitly from Treaty provisions concerning internal competence, or from legislative acts of the EC giving effect to that competence, or from the need to make an international agreement in order to attain an internal EC objective.[53] The ECJ rejected this contention.

It held in relation to GATS that exclusive external competence was in general dependent on actual exercise of internal powers and not their mere existence.[54] The *Inland Waterways* case was distinguished on the ground that the EC's very internal objective could not be attained without the making of an international agreement and internal EC rules could not realistically be made prior to the conclusion of such an agreement.[55] This rationale did not apply to the subject matter covered by GATS, since attainment of the Community objective did not necessitate agreement with non-Member States.[56] In relation to TRIPS, the ECJ also concluded that the EC did not have exclusive competence. This was because the international action envisaged was not necessary to attain an internal Community objective, and because the EC, although competent to enact harmonization measures, had not done so to any significant extent.[57]

C. The Open Skies Cases, the *ERTA* Ruling, and Exclusive External Competence

The *WTO* case limited the instances where the ECJ would be willing to conclude that the EC possessed exclusive external competence: it restricted the *Inland Waterways* ruling in the manner set out above, and reasoned from the premise that exclusive external competence was normally dependent on the actual exercise of the EC's internal power, and not merely its existence. This reasoning has been followed in later decisions.[58] Subsequent jurisprudence has nonetheless revealed that where the EC has exercised its powers

[52] Ibid. at paras. 53, 71. Art. 133 was amended by the Treaty of Amsterdam after Opinion 1/94 to empower the Council expressly to bring agreements on services and intellectual property within the scope of the Art. It was amended again by the Treaty of Nice. In most areas covered by Art. 133 the EC will have exclusive external competence, but there are exceptions where competence is shared, Art. 133(6).

[53] Ibid. at para. 72.

[54] Ibid. at paras. 77, 88–89.

[55] Ibid. at paras. 85–86.

[56] Ibid. at para. 86. The ECJ reached the same conclusion in relation to TRIPS, ibid. at para. 100.

[57] Ibid. at paras. 99–105.

[58] See, e.g., Opinion 2/92, *Competence of the Community or one of its Institutions to Participate in the Third Revised Decision of the OECD on National Treatment* [1995] ECR I-521.

internally, the ECJ is prepared to interpret broadly the circumstances in which this gives rise to exclusive external competence for the EC.

This is apparent from the 'open skies' litigation, involving Commission actions against a number of Member States.[59] The ruling in *Commission v Germany*[60] can be taken by way of example. The Commission brought an action against Germany under what is now Article 226 EC, alleging that it had infringed the Treaty by concluding bilateral 'open skies' agreements with the USA, on the ground that the EC had exclusive external competence in this area.

The Commission argued that this exclusive competence flowed from the principle laid down in the *Inland Waterways* case as interpreted by the *WTO* judgment. The ECJ disagreed. It accepted that an implied external competence could exist not only where the internal competence had been exercised through enactment of measures to implement the common policy, but also where the Community measures were adopted only when the international agreement was concluded. This was, however, subject to the limits articulated in the *WTO* case: the principle applied where the internal competence could only be exercised at the same time as the external competence on the ground that conclusion of an international agreement was necessary to attain the Community objective, and internal rules could not be adopted prior to such an agreement. The ECJ found that this rationale for exclusive external competence was inapplicable to the instant case.[61]

The ECJ then considered the alternative argument advanced by the Commission, to the effect that the EC had exclusive external competence in line with the *ERTA* ruling, because it had exercised its internal competence to some degree within the relevant area. Article 80(2) EC empowered the Council to decide whether and to what extent provision should be made for air transport and the Council had adopted a 'package of legislation' based on this Article. The ECJ held that the *ERTA* ruling could apply to internal power exercised in this manner and therefore the EC had an implied external competence. It followed that when the EC made common rules pursuant to this power, the Member States no longer had the right, acting individually or collectively, to undertake obligations towards non-Member States, which affected those rules or distorted their scope.[62]

The importance of the judgment lies in its confirmation of the broad reading given to the phrase 'affected those rules or distorted their scope',

[59] Case C-466/98, *Commission v United Kingdom* [2002] ECR I-9427; Case C-467/98, *Commission v Denmark* [2002] ECR I-9519; Case C-468/98, *Commission v Sweden* [2002] ECR I-9575; Case C-469/98, *Commission v Finland* [2002] ECR I-9627; Case C-471/98, *Commission v Belgium* [2002] ECR I-9681; Case C-472/98, *Commission v Luxembourg* [2002] ECR I-9741; Case C-475/98, *Commission v Austria* [2002] ECR I-9797.

[60] Case C-467/98, *Commission v Germany* [2002] ECR I-9855.

[61] Ibid. at paras. 80–90.

[62] Ibid. at paras. 101–105.

since it is this that transforms external competence into exclusive external competence.[63] The ECJ, in accord with prior case law, held that this would be so where the international agreement fell within the scope of the common rules, or within an area that was already largely covered by such rules, and this was so in the latter case even if there was no contradiction between the international commitments and the internal rules. EC legislative provisions relating to the treatment of non-Member State nationals, or expressly conferring power to negotiate with non-Member States, gave the EC exclusive external competence. This was so even in the absence of express provision authorizing the EC to negotiate with non-Member States in areas where the EC had achieved complete harmonization, since if Member States were able to conclude international agreements individually it would affect the common rules thus made. Distortion in the flow of services in the internal market that might arise as a result of the bilateral agreement did not, by way of contrast, affect the common rules adopted in the area.

D. Shared Competence, Mixed Agreements, and Cooperation

Notwithstanding the relatively broad reading given to exclusive external competence, the reality is that many external powers continue to be shared between the Member States and the EC. There are a number of reasons why this is so. It may be because the conditions set out above for the Community's exclusive external competence are not satisfied, where, for example, the EC has not adopted sufficient internal measures to accord it exclusive external competence.[64] External competence may also be shared because the EC Treaty does not confer sufficient competence on the EC to ratify the agreement in its entirety, thereby requiring allocation as between the EC and the Member States of the power to conclude the agreement with non-Member States,[65] or where the EC's has some competence over the relevant area, but this is limited to laying down minimum requirements, thereby leaving Member States free to apply the rules flowing from the international agreement over and beyond this.[66] A further rationale for shared competence is where the appropriate legal basis for the measure concluding the agreement lays down a legislative procedure different from that which has in fact been followed by the Community institutions.[67]

The fact that external competence is shared requires close cooperation between the Member States and EC when the agreement is negotiated. The

[63] Ibid. at paras. 107–113.

[64] Opinion 1/94, *supra* n. 51, at paras. 99–105; Opinion 2/00, *supra* n. 36, at paras. 45–46.

[65] Opinion 2/00, *supra* n. 36, at para. 5.

[66] Opinion 2/91, *supra* n. 46, at paras. 16–21.

[67] Opinion 2/00, *supra* n. 36, at para. 5.

fact that participation of the Member States and the EC as parties to the international agreement may give rise to problems of coordination when the agreement is interpreted or implemented, cannot be used to deny their respective legal rights to partake in the agreement.[68] The Member States and EC do, however, have a duty to cooperate in the negotiation, conclusion, and implementation of the agreement.[69]

It is possible for an agreement in an area of shared competence to be signed only by the Member States,[70] or only by the Community.[71] An international agreement made where there is shared competence and where the EC and Member States are parties is known as a 'mixed agreement'.[72] A mixed agreement will be mandatory in those areas of shared competence where the EC and Member States have different obligations.

E. The Constitutional Treaty, External Competence, and Exclusivity

The complexity of the law relating to the EU's external competence is readily apparent even from the preceding brief discussion. Article I-13(2) of the CT bears further testimony to the difficulties that beset this area. This is so notwithstanding the fact that the Constitution has not been ratified, since the Article reveals the real problems of drafting a provision that accurately encapsulates existing doctrine and/or makes sense in its own terms. Article I-13(2) provided that 'the Union shall have exclusive competence for the conclusion of an international agreement when its conclusion is provided for in a legislative act of the Union, or is necessary to enable the Union to exercise its internal competence, or insofar as its conclusion may affect common rules or alter their scope'.[73]

The first of these situations, where the conclusion of such an agreement is stipulated by a legislative act of the Union, may seem unproblematic. This is not however so. Article I-13(2) did not state that the Union should have exclusive external competence where a Union legislative act said that this should be so. Nor did it state that the EU should have such exclusive external competence only in the areas in which it had an exclusive internal

[68] Opinion 2/91, *supra* n. 46, at paras. 19–20; Opinion 1/94, *supra* n. 51, at para. 107; Opinion 2/00, *supra* n. 36, at para. 41.

[69] Opinion 2/91, *supra* n. 46, at paras. 36–37; Opinion 1/94, *supra* n. 51, at paras. 108–109; Opinion 2/00, *supra* n. 36, at para. 18.

[70] Opinion 2/91, *supra* n. 46, at para. 5.

[71] Case C-268/94, *Portugal v Council* [1996] ECR I-6177, at paras. 68–77.

[72] D. O'Keeffe and H. Schermers (eds), *Mixed Agreements* (Martinus Nijhoff, 1983); Cremona, 'The Doctrine of Exclusivity and the Position of Mixed Agreements in the External Relations of the European Community' (1982) 2 *OJLS* 393.

[73] The content of Art. I-13(2) CT was in marked contrast to the more cautious recommendations of Working Group VII on External Action, CONV 459/02, Final Report of Working Group VII on External Action, Brussels 16 December 2002, at 4, 16.

competence. It stated that where the conclusion of an international agreement was provided for in a legislative act, the Union would have exclusive external competence.[74] The consequence was that express external empowerment to conclude an international agreement was taken to mean exclusive external competence, with the corollary that Member States were pre-empted from adopting any legally binding act.[75]

This is problematic in terms of past practice and principle. A number of the Treaty articles adding express external powers in, for example, the Single European Act (SEA) and the Treaty of European Union (TEU) were cast in non-exclusive terms.[76] This possibility must apply *a fortiori* to legislation granting the EC power to conclude an international agreement, such that the Member States could specify, expressly or impliedly, in the legislation that they retain their competence in that area.[77] This reasoning is further reinforced when one reflects on the relationship between the provisions on external competence and the other heads of competence in the CT. Thus, to take an example, it might well be decided that it would be useful if the Union were to have the power to make an international agreement in one of the areas where it could take coordinating or supporting action. A legislative act is passed giving it this power. The legislation would, it seems, in accord with Article I-13(2), mean that the Union had exclusive external competence in this regard. It is, however, extremely doubtful whether the Member States would have intended to deprive themselves of shared external competence, more especially because to accord exclusive external competence to the Union could run wholly counter to the objective of coordinating action between Member States, non-Member States, and the EU in the relevant area.

The same elision of external power and exclusive external power was evident in the second of the situations listed in Article I-13(2) where the Union has exclusive external competence, this being where it is necessary to enable the Union to exercise its internal competence. The best reading of this provision is that it was intended to cover the *Inland Waterways* principle as construed in the *WTO Opinion.* This is where the Union's internal objective could not be attained without the making of an international agreement and internal EC rules could not realistically be made prior to the conclusion of

[74] The same reasoning would seem to apply *a fortiori* where an article of the Constitution, as opposed to a legislative act, accorded the Union power to conclude an international agreement, but there was no mention of this in Art. I-13(2).

[75] Art. I-12(1) CT.

[76] Cremona, *supra* n. 47, at 158–161.

[77] There are statements to the effect that an express conferment of power to negotiate with non-Member States confers exclusive external competence on the EC, Opinion 1/94, *supra* n. 51, at para. 95, Case C-467/98, *Commission v Germany*, *supra* n. 60, at para. 109, but there is no indication that the ECJ intended these statements to be as broad as the formulation in Art. I-13(2).

such an agreement. The 'fit' between this and the other provisions on competence could nonetheless still be problematic. Taken literally it meant that exclusive external competence to conclude an international agreement resided with the Union, where this was necessary to enable the Union to exercise its internal competence, even where the internal competence was only shared, or even where the EU could only take supporting or co-ordinating action. This result might be limited by fastening on the word 'necessary'. It might also be restricted by arguing that any EU external competence to make an international agreement must be bounded by the nature of its internal competence in the relevant area, with the consequence that the EU could not have exclusive competence to make such an agreement if its content were to take the EU beyond supporting or coordinating action in an area where its internal competence was thus limited.

The third situation mentioned in Article I-13(2) was that the EU should have exclusive competence to conclude an international agreement 'insofar as its conclusion may affect common rules or alter their scope'. The best interpretation of this part of the Article is that it was intended to reflect the ECJ's jurisprudence on exclusive external competence in those circumstances where the internal power had been exercised. We have seen that this case law accords implied external competence where internal power has been exercised and that the external competence is exclusive insofar as it precludes independent Member State action that might affect common rules or distort their scope.[78] While there is therefore foundation for this provision, this should not mask the difficulties with this test. An international agreement might 'affect common rules' directly or indirectly, and the impact on the Union act might be significant or tangential. The difficulties in this respect are compounded by the fact that the application of the test, 'affect common rules or alter their scope', will depend significantly on the precise scope and content of the rules made by the EC, as juxtaposed and compared with the provisions of the international agreement. The 'open skies' litigation exemplifies these problems, as the ECJ struggled to apply the principles that it had enunciated to the facts of the case.[79]

The interpretative problems with Article I-13(2) revealed the difficulties of committing to paper an intelligible set of propositions as to when the EU should have exclusive external competence. It is moreover readily apparent that the Article did little to facilitate clarity *ex ante* as to when exclusive external competence resided with the Union, because the very nature of the criteria meant that their application would be contestable and hence require judicial resolution.

[78] *Supra* n. 46.

[79] Case C-467/98, *Commission v Germany*, *supra* n. 60, at paras. 114–137.

4. SUBSIDIARITY

The discussion thus far has been concerned with problems relating to the existence of Community competence. We turn now to the principle of subsidiarity, which is intended to regulate the exercise of Community competence, although, as will be seen, the issues of existence and exercise can interrelate. The centrality of subsidiarity to the Maastricht negotiations is well known. For those who feared further movement to a 'federalist Community' the concept of subsidiarity was the panacea designed to halt such centralizing initiatives.[80] The circumstances when subsidiarity should apply are contestable,[81] but we can at least be clear about the wording of Article 5 EC:

> The Community shall act within the limits of the powers conferred upon it by this Treaty and of the objectives assigned to it therein.
>
> In areas which do not fall within its exclusive competence, the Community shall take action, in accordance with the principle of subsidiarity, only if and in so far as the objectives of the proposed action cannot be sufficiently achieved by the Member States and can therefore, by reason of the scale or effects of the proposed action, be better achieved by the Community.
>
> Any action by the Community shall not go beyond what is necessary to achieve the objectives of this Treaty.

The requirement in the first paragraph of the Article merely affirms existing principle. It has always been recognized that the Community must act within the limits of its powers and that it only has competence within the

[80] A. Estella, *The EU Principle of Subsidiarity and its Critique* (Oxford University Press, 2002), at 82–89.

[81] Constantinesco, 'Who's Afraid of Subsidiarity? (1991) 11 *YBEL* 33; Toth, 'The Principle of Subsidiarity in the Maastricht Treaty' (1992) 29 *CMLRev* 1079; Emiliou, 'Subsidiarity: An Effective Barrier against the "Enterprises of Ambition"?' (1992) 17 *ELRev* 383; Dehousse, 'Does Subsidiarity Really Matter?', *EUI Working Paper in Law 92/32*; Toth, 'A Legal Analysis of Subsidiarity', in D. O'Keeffe and P. M. Twomey (eds), *Legal Issues of the Maastricht Treaty* (Chancery, 1994), Chap. 3; Steiner, 'Subsidiarity under the Maastricht Treaty', in O'Keeffe and Twomey (eds), ibid., Chap. 4; Emiliou, 'Subsidiarity: Panacea or Fig Leaf?', in O'Keeffe and Twomey (eds), ibid., Chap. 5; Lenaerts, 'The Principle of Subsidiarity and the Environment in the European Union: Keeping the Balance of Federalism' (1994) 17 *Fordham ILJ* 846; Lenaerts and Ypersele, 'Le Principe de Subsidiarité et Son Contexte: Etude de L'Article 3B du Traité CE' (1994) 30 *CDE* 3; Bermann, 'Taking Subsidiarity Seriously: Federalism in the EC and in the USA' (1994) 94 *Columbia Law Rev* 331; Harrison, 'Subsidiarity in Article 3b of the EC Treaty: Gobbledegook or Justiciable Principle?' (1996) 45 *ICLQ* 431; de Búrca, 'Reappraising Subsidiarity's Significance after Amsterdam' Jean Monnet Working Paper 7/1999, <http://www.jeanmonnetprogram.org/>; de Witte and de Burca, 'The Delimitation of Powers between the European Union and its Member States', in A. Arnull and D. Wincott (eds), *Accountability and Legitimacy in the European Union* (Oxford University Press, 2002), Chap. 12; Estella, *supra* n. 80.

areas where power has been conferred on it. The difficulties of determining the limits of Community competence were considered above. The heart of subsidiarity is contained in the remainder of Article 5.

A. The Meaning of Exclusive Competence

It is clear from Article 5, paragraph 2, that subsidiarity only has to be considered in areas that do not fall within the EC's exclusive competence. If an area is within the EC's exclusive competence there is no legal obligation to apply subsidiarity, although it is in fact taken into account.

There is, however, as noted earlier, no simple criterion for determining the scope of the Community's exclusive competence. The Commission took the view that this included areas where the Treaties imposed on the Community a duty to act, in the sense that it had sole responsibility for the performance of a particular task.[82] It argued that there was a 'block' of exclusive powers which were joined by the thread of the internal market, including: free movement of goods, persons, services, and capital; the Common Commercial Policy; competition; the Common Agricultural Policy (CAP); the conservation of fisheries; and transport policy.

Commentators differed considerably on the issue. Toth[83] took a broad view, arguing that exclusive competence existed in those areas where the Member States transferred power to the Community, irrespective of whether the Community had actually exercised the power. He concluded that subsidiarity did not apply to any matter covered by the original EEC Treaty, including: the free movement of goods, services, persons, and capital; the Common Commercial Policy; competition; the CAP; Transport Policy; and the common organization of the fisheries. Toth accepted that the Community did not have exclusive competence within many of the newer areas in which it had been given power, such as the environment, economic and social cohesion, education and vocational training, consumer protection, and social policy, because the relevant Treaty articles empowering the Community were framed in more limited terms. If, however, Community legislation on the environment or health facilitated completion of the internal market then Toth maintained that this would take such matters outside the formal remit of subsidiarity.[84]

Steiner took a narrower view.[85] She argued that the EC was concerned to share rather than divide competence between the Community and the Member States and that in most areas competence was concurrent. Steiner accepted that when the EC exercised its powers to regulate a particular matter

[82] Bull. EC 10–1992, 116; 1st Report of Commission on Subsidiarity, COM(94) 533.
[83] Toth, 'Legal Analysis', *supra* n. 81, at 39–40. [84] Ibid. at 41.
[85] Steiner, *supra* n. 81, at 57–58.

within a certain area Member States were not free to enact measures which conflicted with those rules, but she contended that the only areas in which the Community had exclusive competence for the purposes of Article 5 were therefore those in which it had already legislated. The competence of Member States ended not where the competence of the Community began, but where its powers had been exercised: 'to allow whole areas of activity to escape scrutiny under paragraph 2, simply because the Community has potential competence in these areas, would surely undermine the very purpose for which this provision was intended'.[86] There is force in this view, although it should be recognized that Community power can be exercised judicially as well as through legislation. The principles relating to free movement have, for example, been implemented in part by Community legislation, and in part by Court decisions, and they often interact.

Given the uncertainties concerning the meaning of exclusive competence under the existing Treaty, it is interesting to reflect briefly on the meaning accorded to that term under the CT, when the drafters were compelled to be specific in this respect because of the different categories of competence delineated in the Constitution.

It is worthy of note that Article I-13(1) did not accord with the broad view of exclusive competence espoused by the Commission and Toth. The EU was said to have exclusive competence only in the following areas: customs union; the establishing of the competition rules necessary for the functioning of the common market; monetary policy, for the Member States that adopted the euro; the conservation of marine biological resources under the common fisheries policy; and common commercial policy.

It is equally noteworthy that the final version of the Constitution differed from earlier drafts by removing the four freedoms from the sphere of exclusive competence, and re-assigning them to the category of shared competence. The reason given for this change was the creation of a specific provision dealing directly with the four freedoms, Article I-4, which was said to make their legal and political importance more visible than hitherto, and to underline the fact that they are directly applicable. While it might have been felt desirable to emphasize the centrality of the four freedoms, the argument based on direct applicability was odd, given that many other Treaty provisions have this quality. The real reason for the excision of the four freedoms from Article I-13(1) was almost certainly different. If they had remained within the category of exclusive competence Member States would have had no legislative capacity in these areas, nor could they have adopted any legally binding non-legislative act, unless so empowered by the Union or for the implementation of Union acts.[87] Taken literally, this would have

[86] Ibid. at 58.

[87] Art. I-12(1) CT.

meant that a Member State would have been prevented from enacting legislation that, for example, liberalized trade in postal services, unless it had first secured the agreement of the Union. Thus, Member State action which was 'ahead' of EU action would have not have been permitted, even though it might have been in accord with the overall aims of the EU, and even though it might well have been the catalyst for EU action in such areas.

B. The Subsidiarity Calculus

It seems clear that the drafting of Article 5 was influenced by the German experience concerning the relationship of the Federal authorities and the Lander.[88] Article 5, paragraph 2, provides that the Community is to take action 'only if and in so far as the objectives of the proposed action cannot be sufficiently achieved by the Member States and can therefore by reason of the scale or effects of the proposed action, be better achieved by the Community'. Article 5, paragraph 3, adds the further condition that 'any action by the Community shall not go beyond what is necessary to achieve the objectives of this Treaty'.

Subsidiarity therefore embraces three separate, albeit related, ideas. The Community is to take action only if the objectives of that action cannot be sufficiently achieved by the Member States; the Community can better achieve the action, because of its scale or effects; if the Community does take action then this should not go beyond what is necessary to achieve the Treaty objectives. The first two parts of this formulation entail what the Commission has termed a test of comparative efficiency:[89] is it better for the action to be taken by the Community or the Member States? The third part of the formulation brings in a proportionality test.

The 1993 Inter-institutional Agreement on Procedures for Implementing the Principle of Subsidiarity required all three institutions to have regard to the principle when devising Community legislation. This was re-confirmed by the Protocol on the Application of the Principles of Subsidiarity and Proportionality attached to the Treaty of Amsterdam.[90] The Commission must provide in its explanatory memorandum concerning proposed legislation a justification for the measure in terms of the subsidiarity principle, and it must furnish reasons why an objective can be better achieved at Community level that are supported by qualitative and wherever possible quantitative indicators.[91] Amendments by the Council or the EP must likewise be accompanied by a justification in terms of subsidiarity, if they entail more

[88] Emiliou, 'Subsidiarity: An Effective Barrier', *supra* n. 81.

[89] Commission Communication to the Council and the European Parliament, Bull. EC 10–1992, 116.

[90] Protocol No. 30. [91] Ibid. at para. 4.

extensive Community intervention.[92] The Protocol established guidelines to be considered when applying Article 5, paragraph 2:[93] the issue under consideration has transnational aspects that cannot be satisfactorily regulated by Member States; action by Member States or lack of Community action would conflict with the requirements of the Treaty, such as the need to correct distortions of competition or avoid disguised restrictions on trade; and action at Community level would produce clear benefits by reason of its scale or effects compared with action at the level of Member States. The form of the Community legislation should be as simple as possible, with a preference for framework directives over regulations.[94] The Protocol nonetheless confirmed that subsidiarity only applied where the Community did not have exclusive competence, and that the subsidiarity principle did not call into question the powers conferred on the EC, as interpreted by the ECJ.[95] The Commission must submit an annual report to the European Council, Council, and EP on the application of Article 5.[96]

The impact of subsidiarity has been less than hoped for by its proponents. This is so for a number of reasons. It is clear that there will be many areas in which the comparative efficiency calculus comes out in favour of Community action. The idea that matters should be dealt with at the level closest to those affected is fine in principle. The very *raison d'être* of the Community will, however, often demand Community action to ensure the uniformity of general approach which is of central importance to the realization of a common market. This is confirmed by the Commission's reports made pursuant to Article 9 of the Protocol.[97] It should also be recognized that business interests will often favour one regulatory approach, thereby reducing transaction costs, and they will press for the matter to be regulated by the EU rather than by Member States. It will often be impossible to provide meaningful quantitative indicators that action is better taken at Community rather than national level, with the result that 'softer' qualitative indicators will be used instead.[98] There are moreover difficulties with the general approach embodied in the Protocol. Thus as Estella states:[99]

> The truth of the matter is that attempting to define *ex ante* criteria of a general and abstract character for the purpose of limiting central intervention stands little hope of success. The reasons for this limitation are functional and can be found in the nature of modern regulatory problems. The functional interconnection between regulatory areas. . . makes the task of establishing clear dividing lines difficult. Even in those areas in which there seem to be clear reasons in favour of national, or even

[92] Ibid. at para. 11. [93] Ibid. at para. 5. [94] Ibid. at para. 6.
[95] Ibid. at para. 3. [96] Ibid. at para. 9.
[97] Commission Report to the European Council, Better Lawmaking 1999, COM(1999) 562 final, at 2.
[98] Estella, *supra* n. 80, at 124–131. [99] Ibid. at 113–114.

regional or local, regulation . . . it will always be possible to argue that due to the close relationship between these areas and the development of the single market, some Community intervention will always be necessary.

It should nonetheless be acknowledged that the very existence of Article 5 EC can have an impact on the existence and form of Community action. The Commission will consider whether action really is required at Community level, and its reasoning will be found in the recitals, or explanatory memorandum.[100] If Community action is required, the Commission is encouraged to proceed through directives rather than regulations. There will be a greater use of guidelines and codes of conduct. The idea that there should be Community control with a 'lighter touch' fits with changes that pre-date subsidiarity, such as the new approach to harmonization, and directives that lay down minimum rather than total harmonization.

It is worth dwelling briefly on the changes to subsidiarity that would have been made by the CT.[101] The subsidiarity principle was reiterated in Article I-11(3). The principal innovation was the Protocol on Subsidiarity attached to the Constitution.[102] This built on the earlier Protocols, the most important change made by the Protocol attached to the CT being the enhanced role accorded to national parliaments. The Commission was obliged to send legislative proposals to the national parliaments at the same time as to the Union institutions.[103] It was then open to a national parliament, within six weeks, to send the Presidents of the Commission, EP, and Council a reasoned opinion as to why it considered that the proposal did not comply with subsidiarity,[104] which the EP, Council, and Commission had to take into account.[105] Where non-compliance with subsidiarity was expressed by national parliaments that represented one third of all the votes allocated to such Parliaments, there was a duty to review the proposal.[106] It was, however, open to the Commission or other relevant institution, after such review, to decide to maintain, amend, or withdraw the proposal, giving reasons for the decision.[107] A legal challenge for non-compliance with subsidiarity could be brought by the Member State, or 'notified by them in accordance with their legal order on behalf of their national Parliament or a chamber of it'.[108]

[100] Commission Report to the European Council, Better Lawmaking 2000, COM(2000) 772 final, at 4–8, 15–21.

[101] Craig, *supra* n. 4, at 342–344; Bermann, 'Competences of the Union', in T. Tridimas and P. Nebbia (eds), *European Union Law for the Twenty-First Century, Rethinking the New Legal Order, Vol. I* (Hart, 2004), at 70–72; Tridimas, 'The European Court of Justice and the Draft Constitution: A Supreme Court for the Union?', ibid., at 132–135; Cygan, 'The Role of National Parliaments in the EU's New Constitutional Order', ibid., at 162–168.

[102] CT, Protocol No 2, On the Application of the Principles of Subsidiarity and Proportionality, Art. 2.

[103] Ibid. Art. 4. [104] Ibid. Art. 6. [105] Ibid. Art. 7.

[106] Ibid. Art. 7. [107] Ibid. Art. 7. [108] Ibid. Art. 8.

It is unlikely, given the fate of the CT, that we will ever know how effective such provisions would have been. While the role accorded to national parliaments was a significant innovation, the limits in this regard should also be borne in mind. The national parliament could not simply have expressed its dislike for the measure. It would have had to submit a reasoned opinion as to why it believed that the measure infringed subsidiarity, and this would have required it to contest the Commission's comparative efficiency calculus. It would have been even more difficult for the requisite number of national parliaments to present reasoned opinions within the stipulated time limits in relation to the same Union measure so as to compel the Commission to review the proposal. Having said this, the Commission would have been likely to take seriously any such reasoned opinion, particularly if it emanated from the parliament of a larger Member State.

The desire for there to be some further check on subsidiarity that was evident in the CT resonated with other suggestions made in recent years. Thus the UK Prime Minister Tony Blair, amongst others, called for the establishment of a non-judicial forum to consider the compatibility of proposed Community action with the subsidiarity principle. Other proposals ranged from a specially constituted 'subsidiarity committee' to a second chamber of the European Parliament, to the COSAC (conference of EC and European Affairs committees of national parliaments). These calls have been fuelled by the limited role played by the ECJ when reviewing for compliance with subsidiarity, and it is to this issue that we now turn.

C. The Role of the Court

It is clear that questions concerning the interpretation of Article 5 can be adjudicated by the ECJ. The real issue has always been the intensity of the judicial review. We shall see that the Court reviews Community action with varying degrees of intensity.[109] Much therefore depends upon the intensity with which it reviews, for example, a Commission assertion that, on grounds of comparative efficiency, Community action was required in a particular area. The indications are that the ECJ will not lightly overturn Community action for non-compliance with Article 5 EC.

This is apparent in *procedural* terms from *Germany v European Parliament and Council.*[110] The ECJ held that the duty to give reasons now contained in Article 253 EC did not require that Community measures contain an express reference to the subsidiarity principle. It was sufficient that the recitals to the measure made it clear why the Community institutions believed that the aims of the measure could best be attained by Community action.

The difficulty of overturning a measure because of subsidiarity is equally

[109] See below, Chaps. 14, 17, 18.

[110] Case C-233/94, *supra* n. 8, at paras. 26–28.

apparent in *substantive* terms from the *Working Time Directive* case.[111] The UK argued that the contested Directive infringed the principle of subsidiarity, since it had not been shown that action at Community level would provide clear benefits compared with action at national level. The ECJ disposed of the argument briskly. It was, said the Court, the responsibility of the Council under what was Article 118a EC to adopt minimum requirements so as to contribute to the improvement of health and safety. Once the Council found it necessary to improve the existing level of protection and to harmonize the law in this area, while maintaining the improvements already made, achievement of that objective necessarily presupposed Community-wide action. A similarly 'light' judicial approach to subsidiarity review is evident in other cases. Thus in *Alliance for Natural Health*[112] the applicant challenged a Directive regulating food supplements on grounds of subsidiarity, arguing that in a sensitive area of health policy Member States were better placed to determine on their territory the rules that should apply to food supplements. The ECJ disagreed. The Directive was based on Article 95 EC, and there would be obstacles to trade if Member States regulated trade in food supplements that did not comply with the Directive.[113]

The burden faced by an applicant seeking to challenge on grounds of subsidiarity must also take account of an important interpretative constraint placed on Article 5, paragraph 3, which deals with *proportionality*. In *Bosman*[114] the ECJ held that the principle that Community intervention must be limited to what is strictly necessary would not be interpreted so as to mean that private associations could adopt rules that restricted rights conferred on individuals by the Treaty.

The leading judicial decisions[115] were given before the Protocol attached to the Treaty of Amsterdam came into force. The judgments since then do not, however, reveal any shift in judicial approach. The ECJ is clearly not inclined to use intensive judicial review to test for compliance with subsidiarity and the judgments commonly deal with this aspect of the case within a few paragraphs.

It should be acknowledged that the ECJ is faced with difficulties in this regard. If it takes a detailed look at the evidence underlying the

[111] Case C-84/94, *supra* n. 8, at paras. 46–47, 55

[112] Cases C-154–155/04, *The Queen, on the application of Alliance for Natural Health and Nutri-Link Ltd. v Secretary of State for Health* [2005] ECR I-6451, at paras. 99–108

[113] See also, Case C-377/98, *Netherlands v Council, supra* n. 8, at paras. 30–33; Case C-491/01, *British American Tobacco, supra* n. 13, at paras. 177–185; Case C-103/01, *Commission v Germany* [2003] ECR I-5369, at paras. 46–47.

[114] Case C-415/93, *Union Royale Belge des Sociétés de Football Assn ASBL v Bosman* [1995] ECR I-4921, at para. 81.

[115] Case C-233/94 and Case C-84/94, *supra* n. 8.

Commission's claim it will have to adjudicate on what may be a complex socio-economic calculus concerning the most effective level of government for different regulatory tasks. If, by way of contrast, the ECJ reviews less intensively, and only intervenes if there is some manifest error, it is open to the critique from Member States that it is effectively denuding the obligation in Article 5 of all content.

This 'dilemma' can, however, be viewed somewhat differently. The Community courts have the power and duty to review for compliance with subsidiarity. It is readily apparent in principle and from judicial practice in other areas that there is a proximate connection between process and substance.[116] The difficulty of adjudicating on the substantive issue of comparative efficiency would be alleviated if the Community courts were to require more from the Commission in procedural terms. The obligation to give reasons could be used to require the Commission to disclose the qualitative and quantitative data that is meant to inform its reasoning pursuant to the Protocol attached to the Treaty of Amsterdam. The provision of such reasons and data would not be a panacea that would cure all problems of substantive review. It would nonetheless provide the Community courts with significantly more to go on as compared to their present reliance on the exiguous reasoning contained in the Preamble to the contested measure. The procedural obligation may also reveal that the Commission has done little by way of analysis to determine that the matter is best regulated at Community rather than national level, thereby furnishing the rationale for overturning the measure on procedural grounds.

5. CONCLUSION

The delineation of competence between different levels of government is difficult in any system. The relevant constitutional provisions will perforce be interpreted by courts, with the result that the distribution of power may well come to be very different over the years from that envisaged by those who framed the Constitution. This is more especially so when the criteria for dividing power between tiers of government are cast in rather general, open-textured terms.

The position in the EU is problematic for somewhat different reasons. The powers attributed to the EU and EC have grown over the years with successive Treaty revisions. Each new head of competence has been cast in terms specific to the relevant subject matter and the precise content of the attributed power has reflected the contending play of political forces in the IGC that led to the particular Treaty revision. The heads of competence did not,

[116] See above, Chap. 11.

in general, come with any label attached to signify whether the EU or EC had exclusive power, shared power, or some lesser form of competence. The consequence was, as we have seen, that it was contestable in which areas the EC had exclusive internal competence. It meant also, and this is equally significant, that even where it was clear that power was shared, the manner of this sharing could vary very significantly as between different areas. This pattern of attributed competence was always open to charges of 'competence creep'.[117] There was until the CT no attempt to bring 'order' into this schema through the elaboration of different categories of competence.

The uncertainty as to the delineation of competence in the Treaty has meant that much has been left to the ECJ. It has been the ECJ that elaborated the implied powers doctrine and the limits thereto. It has been the ECJ that adjudicated on the boundaries of broadly framed Treaty provisions such as Articles 95 and 308 EC. It has moreover been the ECJ that crafted the law on external competence, fashioning the doctrines of implied external competence and establishing the criteria for exclusive external competence. The choices open to the judiciary are evident from the preceding discussion. Commentators may agree or disagree with, for example, the broad reading given to external competence and exclusive external competence, and there is room for similar difference of opinion concerning the relative lack of intensity of review for compliance with subsidiarity. What cannot be denied is that the doctrinal positions taken by the ECJ on these and other competence issues reflect important normative choices concerning the scope of EU and EC power. This jurisprudence exemplifies moreover the Janus-like quality of judicial review mentioned earlier.[118] Judicial review is certainly a method for controlling excess of power, but the reverse side of this coin is judicial elaboration of the powers that should properly be accorded to the administration under the relevant Treaty article and the latter has featured prominently in the case law in this area.

[117] Weatherill, *supra* n. 3; Pollack, 'Creeping Competence: The Expanding Agenda of the European Community' (1994) 14 *Journal of Public Policy* 95.

[118] See above, at 278–279.

13

Law, Fact, and Discretion

1. INTRODUCTION

The discussion in the earlier chapters revealed the link between procedural and substantive judicial review. This chapter focuses on some of the central precepts of substantive review. There is an extensive literature on certain aspects of substantive review, such as proportionality, which will be discussed as a separate topic in its own right. There is, however, considerably less by way of detailed explication of the basic principles of judicial review pertaining to law, fact, and discretion.[1] It is these issues that will be analysed in this chapter.

The discussion begins with the meaning accorded to the concepts of law, fact, and discretion in EU law. This will be followed by examination of the test for review for questions of law. The focus then shifts to review of fact and discretion. The test for review and the meaning accorded to it in the early case law will be explicated. This will be followed by examination of the more recent jurisprudence, and it will be seen that the Community courts have been using the tests for review more intensively than hitherto. The final two sections of this chapter contain broader reflections on the standard of review emerging from the case law in relation to fact and discretion respectively.

2. LAW, FACT, AND DISCRETION

A. Introduction

Substantive judicial review applies in relation to law, fact, and discretion. It is common for the test for review to differ depending upon which of these is in issue before the court in any particular case. This necessarily requires distinctions to be drawn between law, fact, and discretion in order that

[1] See, however, the valuable analyses in relation to competition law, Bailey, 'Standard of Proof in EC Merger Proceedings: A Common Law Perspective' (2003) 40 *CMLRev* 845; Bailey, 'Scope of Judicial Review under Article 81 EC' (2004) 41 *CMLRev* 1327.

the test for review deemed to be appropriate by the legal system can be applied.

The demarcation between law, fact, and discretion can, however, be problematic as any scholar or practitioner of administrative law will attest. This is in part because there can be disagreement in analytical terms as to where the line should be drawn, and in part because it is not uncommon for courts to demarcate on functional grounds, in the sense that the labels, law, fact or discretion will be chosen to reflect judicial preconceptions as to how far the court wishes to intervene in a particular case. While recognizing that this is so, it is nonetheless necessary to start with the analytical distinction, while being mindful that this will not always be determinative. It is sensible to begin in each instance with the paradigm instance of law, fact, and discretion, and then work outwards to the more problematic boundaries.

The delineation of the boundaries between law, fact, and discretion is facilitated by having a clear conceptual idea of the way in which power is granted to administrative bodies. All such grants of power will take the form 'if X you may or shall do Y'. It is common for there to be multiple X conditions, so that the grant of power states that if X^1, X^2, X^3, X^4 exists you may or shall do Y. The X conditions may in principle entail matters of law, fact, or discretion, in the manner that will become clear in the course of the ensuing discussion.

Thus to take an example, Article 87(1) EC is the foundational provision on state aids. It provides in effect that if aid is granted by a Member State or through state resources in any form whatsoever and the aid distorts or threatens to distort competition by favouring certain undertakings or the production of certain goods, then the aid shall be incompatible with the common market. The obligation to prohibit state aid therefore only becomes applicable if a number of X conditions are fulfilled. There must be aid granted by the state, it must distort or threaten to distort competition, this distortion must take the form of favouring certain undertakings over others, and it must affect trade between Member States. Where these conditions are present then the Commission must do Y, in this instance prohibit the state aid, unless one of the exceptions listed in the Treaty is applicable.

The application of these exceptions, however, also follows the 'if X, you may or shall do Y' format. Thus Article 87(3)(a) EC states that if aid promotes the economic development of areas where the standard of living is abnormally low or where there is serious underemployment, the Commission may consider it to be compatible with the common market. There are therefore once again X conditions that must be fulfilled, the aid must promote economic development, it must do so where the standard of living is abnormally low, or where there is serious underemployment. Where these conditions are met, the Commission may do Y, in this instance find the aid to be compatible with the common market.

B. Law

A paradigm of a question of law that arises in the context of judicial review concerns the meaning to be ascribed to a term in the enabling Treaty provisions, regulations, directives, or decisions. The term will commonly be one of the X conditions, although it is of course possible for such terms to appear at the Y level. Courts will normally treat the meaning of terms such as state aid, worker, services, goods, capital, agreement, and a thousand other such provisions that appear in the Treaty or rules made pursuant thereto as questions of law.

The meaning of such terms cannot readily be regarded as a question of pure fact.[2] The facts may tell one that a particular person undertook work in a community where no pay was received, but where there was a sharing of the benefits and burdens of running that community.[3] Those facts do not, however, determine the answer as to whether the person should be regarded as a worker for the purposes of free movement of workers. The facts may tell one that a retailer sold goods at a loss, but they do not resolve the issue of whether this should be treated as a measure equivalent to a quantitative restriction for the purposes of the free movement of goods.[4]

The meaning to be ascribed to worker or measure equivalent to a quantitative restriction will properly be treated as an issue of law, where a decision will have to be made in the light of existing case law, legal principle, and the perceived purposes of the provision in question. It is of course true that the legal meaning of the disputed term will be made in the light of facts. This is, however, to say no more than that courts decide such issues on the basis of concrete cases that come before them.

C. Fact

Let us now turn to the meaning of fact. There is a tendency to treat fact as a 'residual unitary category' embracing cases where there is no issue of law or discretion. The paradigm is of a mistake relating to a primary fact, or direct inference therefrom, in the sense of an error pertaining to the existence of something said, done, or perceived. Closer examination reveals a more complex spectrum of situations covered by the terms fact or factual error.[5]

[2] For discussion in the UK context, see Wilson, 'A Note on Fact and Law' (1963) 26 *MLR* 609 and 'Questions of Degree' (1969) 32 *MLR* 361; Mureinik, 'The Application of Rules; Law or Fact?' (1982) 98 *LQR* 587; Beatson, 'The Scope of Judicial Review for Error of Law' (1984) 4 *OJLS* 22; Endicott, 'Questions of Law' (1998) 114 *LQR* 292.

[3] Case 196/87, *Steymann v Staatsecretaris van Justitie* [1988] ECR 6159.

[4] Cases C-267 and 268/91, *Criminal Proceedings against Keck and Mithouard* [1993] ECR I-6097.

[5] Craig, 'Judicial Review, Appeal and Factual Error' [2004] *PL* 788, at 793–796.

The paradigm is where a simple factual finding made by the decision-maker is challenged as being incorrect. This covers the case where the initial decision was premised on the existence of certain relatively simple or straightforward primary facts, such as whether a person was in a certain place at a certain time, or whether two firms met and exchanged information about future prices. There can, however, be cases involving more complex factual findings, which require a greater degree of evaluative judgment. This is exemplified by many of the cases in competition law where the facts are multifaceted and difficult, and where there can be real differences of view as to the possible consequences flowing from them. There can also be yet other cases where the primary decision-maker factually misinterpreted or misunderstood evidence presented at the hearing. A type of case that is related but distinct is where the initial decision-maker made a mistake of fact by failing to take account of crucial evidence when it reached its initial decision, or where the decision was made on certain factual assumptions and the applicant seeks to show, sometimes through the admission of fresh evidence, that these were mistaken.

We should also be mindful of the interrelationship between issues of fact and questions of law concerning the meaning of a term in a Treaty article, regulation, directive, or decision. The interpretation of the term worker or concerted practice should for the reasons given above normally be regarded as an issue of law. There will, however, also be instances where the essence of the claim is that the initial decision-maker made a factual error relating to the application of that term to the instant case. Thus the applicant may well accept the legal meaning of the term worker or concerted practice articulated by the courts, and may also accept that the primary decision-maker attempted to apply that meaning to the facts of the case. The applicant may nonetheless maintain that the primary decision-maker made a factual error when applying the given legal meaning of the relevant term.

Thus it might be accepted by all parties to the case that the term worker can cover a person who is doing part-time work, subject to a *de minimis* qualification concerning the amount of work involved. A Member State might nonetheless argue that the claimant does not qualify under this definition because it believes that the claimant really is only giving one cello lesson a week and therefore does not qualify as a part-time worker because of the *de minimis* qualification. The claimant then wishes to show that she has in fact been giving ten lessons per week and also working as a trainee chef. Or to take another example, the legal concept of the private investor test might be accepted by all sides in the context of determining whether there is state aid, but the applicant might then dispute the application of this legal concept to the facts of the particular case.[6]

[6] Case T-152/99, *Hijos de Andres Molina SA (HAMSA) v Commission* [2002] ECR II-3049, at paras. 125–127; Case T-36/99, *Lenzing AG v Commission*, judgment of 21 October 2004,

D. Discretion

Discretion is a complex concept, on which there is a considerable philosophical literature. The administrative law systems of the Member States have developed their own conceptions of discretion, as exemplified by the distinction drawn in French law between discretionary power and tied power. The discussion that follows will, however, not attempt to unravel the jurisprudential intricacies of discretion. Nor will it survey the diverse meanings accorded to the concept of discretion in the different legal systems of the Member States.

The approach adopted here is to begin with the case law of the Community courts and to identify the different senses in which discretion is employed within this jurisprudence. This has the advantage of focusing on the positive law of the EU that is most directly pertinent, while at the same time leaving room for more considered reflection about the use of the term discretion within that jurisprudence. It is clear that the Community courts have used the term discretion to cover a number of different situations. The relevant case law will be explored more fully below, but the different types of situation can be identified at this juncture.

The first type of case can for convenience be termed classic discretion. This is where the relevant Treaty article, regulation directive, or decision states that where certain conditions exist the Commission *may* take certain action. Put in terms of the conceptual schema set out above this is a case where the Treaty article or regulation, etc. states that if X^1, X^2, X^3, X^4 exists you may do Y. Thus in *Westzucker*[7] examined in detail below the regulation provided that when certain conditions were present denaturing premiums might be granted, but did not have to be. The European Court of Justice (ECJ) readily characterized this as giving rise to discretion on the part of the Commission in the grant of such premiums.

It is, however, also clear that the Community courts have used the term discretion in a second type of case in relation to situations where there are broadly-framed conditions that have to be established before the power or duty can be exercised at all. The phrase jurisdictional discretion can be used to capture this type of situation. This is exemplified by *Philip Morris Holland*.[8] The case will be considered fully below. Suffice it to say for the present that the issue before the ECJ concerned the meaning to be attributed to the phrases 'abnormally low', and 'serious under employment' within Article 87(3)(a) EC. The ECJ held that the Commission had a discretion,

not yet published; See also, Case T-137/02, *Pollmeier Malchow GmbH & Co KG v Commission*, judgment of 14 October 2004, not yet published, at para. 51 for a different example of the same point.

[7] Case 57/72, *Westzucker GmbH v Einfuhr-und Vorratsstelle für Zucker* [1973] ECR 321.

[8] Case 730/79, *Philip Morris Holland BV v Commission* [1980] ECR 2671.

the exercise of which involved economic and social assessments that had to be made in a Community context. Put in terms of the conceptual schema identified above, if X^1, X^2, X^3, X^4 exists you may or shall do Y, the discretion recognized in *Philip Morris Holland* resided in one of the X conditions. Article 87(3)(a) provides, as seen above, that if aid promotes the economic development of areas where the standard of living is abnormally low or where there is serious underemployment, the Commission may consider it to be compatible with the common market. The dispute concerned the meaning to be given to 'abnormally low', and 'serious under employment', these being conditions that had to be met before the Commission's power to declare such aid compatible with the common market became applicable. The ECJ was willing to characterize these conditions as involving discretion, which then had an impact on the standard of review applied.

There is also a third type of situation where discretion can exist, even where the enabling Treaty article, regulation, directive, or decision is cast in mandatory terms. There will of course be many instances where this is not so. Where the relevant legislation provides 'if X, you shall do Y' and Y entails a specific measure there will be no room for any meaningful discretion once the conditions have been met. There are, however, other instances where the content of Y, the mandatory obligation, is cast in more general terms, thereby leaving some measure of discretion as to how it should be fulfilled. This is exemplified by the Common Agricultural Policy (CAP). Article 34 EC states that a common organization of agricultural markets shall be established, and in that sense imposes a mandatory duty. Article 34 EC further provides that the common organization is designed to attain the objectives set out in Article 33 EC. These objectives include an increase in agricultural productivity, a fair standard of living for the agricultural community, stable markets, availability of supplies, and fair prices for consumers. The many detailed rules made pursuant to the CAP are designed to attain these objectives within different agricultural sectors. It is, however, clear that the objectives in Article 33 that serve to guide the implementation of the common organization of markets are set out at a high level of generality and that there can be tensions between, for example, a fair standard of living for farmers and reasonable prices for consumers. What we have is an obligation to establish a common organization of agricultural markets, coupled with a broad range of objectives that are to inform the way in which this is done. It is therefore unsurprising that the Community courts have repeatedly held that the Commission and Council have discretion in balancing and determining the priority between these objectives when making rules under the CAP,[9] and in determining the best way that the overall objectives can be achieved.[10]

[9] See, e.g., Case 59/83, *SA Biovilac NV v EEC* [1984] ECR 4057.
[10] See, e.g., Case C-180/96, *UK v Commission* [1998] ECR I-2265, at para. 60.

3. REVIEW OF LEGAL ISSUES

A. The General Approach: Substitution of Judgment

The discussion in the previous section has laid some foundations for the meaning ascribed to law, fact, and discretion. It does not tell us what the test or standard of review should be in each of these categories. For this we need to press further.

There is little overt discussion in the EU jurisprudence about the test for review of issues of law. This is so even though questions of law will frequently arise in the course of judicial review. The initial decision-maker, normally the Commission, will be accorded power to do certain things on certain conditions. The conditional grant of power may be contained in a Treaty article, or in Community legislation, but this makes no difference for the point at issue. A claimant will contend that the Commission has committed an error in the interpretation of the conditions that establish its power over the relevant topic. It will be argued, for example, that the financial assistance given by a Member State does not constitute state aid and therefore that the EU rules on the matter are inapplicable; it will be contended that the Commission erred in the meaning given to the term concerted practice for the purpose of competition law; or disputes will arise over the construction of the term monetary measure, the argument being whether this can also include an economic measure. It will be for the Community courts to decide on the existence of such errors, and it will be for the Community courts to decide on the appropriate test for review to be employed in such circumstances.

The general approach of the EU courts is simply to substitute judgment on these questions of law. The ECJ or Court of First Instance (CFI) will lay down the meaning of the disputed term, and if the Commission interpretation is at variance with this then it will be annulled. Thus the entire jurisprudence on, for example, the meaning of state aid, concerted practice, or a hundred and one other such issues is premised on the Community courts substituting their judgment and providing the legal meaning that the term should bear.[11]

[11] See, e.g., in relation to the meaning of 'state aid', Case C-387/92, *Banco de Credito Industrial SA (Banco Exterior de Espana SA) v Ayuntamiento de Valencia* [1994] ECR I-877; Case C-39/94, *Syndicat Français de l'Express International (SFEI) v La Poste* [1996] ECR I-3547; Case T-106/95, *Fédération Française des Sociétés d'Assurances (FFSA) v Commission* [1997] ECR II-229; Case C-75/97, *Belgium v Commission* [1999] ECR I-3671; Case C-53/00, *Ferring SA v Agence Centrale des Organismes de Sécurité Sociale (ACOSS)* [2001] ECR II-9067; Cases T-127, 129, and 148/99, *Territorio Historico de Alava—Diputacion Foral de Alava v Commission* [2002] ECR II-1275; Case T-152/99, *HAMSA, supra* n. 6, at para. 159. See, e.g., out of the many cases concerning competition law, Case T-41/96, *Bayer AG v Commission* [2000] ECR II-3383.

We should nonetheless pause to note that there are a range of possibilities concerning the test for review. Courts may apply a correctness test, whereby they substitute judgment on the meaning of the contested term. This is generally the approach adopted in civil law systems, and in some common law systems such as the UK. It is therefore unsurprising that the Community courts have adopted this mode of thought. On this view it is simply regarded as axiomatic that courts decide issues of law, in the sense of substituting judgment on the meaning of the contested term for that of the primary decision-maker, and it would be seen as constitutional heresy to suggest otherwise. It should moreover be made clear that the Community courts have taken this approach even where the disputed term relates to a topic, such as state aids, competition, or agriculture where the Commission has responsibility for the application of the regime and has developed considerable expertise over the relevant subject matter.

It should nonetheless be recognized that there are in principle other options open to courts when choosing the test for review of issues of law. They might choose to apply a more nuanced test exemplified by the approach of the US courts.[12] The leading decision is *Chevron*[13] where the Supreme Court drew the following distinction. If a court reviewing an agency's construction of a statute decided that Congress had a specific intention on the precise question in issue then that intention should be given effect to. The court will substitute judgment for that of the agency and impose the meaning of the term Congress had intended. If, however, the reviewing court decided that Congress had not directly addressed the point of statutory construction, the court did not simply impose its own construction on the statute. Rather, if the statute was silent or ambiguous with respect to the specific issue, the question for the court was whether the agency's answer was based on a permissible construction of the statute. In answering this question the reviewing court might uphold the agency finding even though it was not the interpretation which the court itself would have adopted, and even though it was only one of a range of permissible such findings that could be made.[14] Moreover, the Supreme Court also held that the delegation to an agency of the determination of a particular issue might well be implicit rather than explicit, and that in such instances 'a court may not substitute its own construction of a statutory provision for a reasonable interpretation made by the administrator of an agency'.[15]

The Canadian courts have also taken a more nuanced approach to review of issues of law, which is somewhat different from that of the US courts. The

[12] A. Aman and W. Mayton, *Administrative Law* (West, 2nd ed., 2001), at 471–505.

[13] *Chevron USA Inc v NRDC* 467 US 837 (1984).

[14] Ibid. at 842–843.

[15] Ibid. at 844. The sphere of application of the *Chevron* test has, however, been thrown into question by *United States v Mead Corporation* 533 US 218 (2001).

case law is rich and complex.[16] The courts will on some occasions use a correctness test, while on others they will employ a reasonableness or rational basis test. They will take account of functional considerations, such as the expertise of the tribunal, the rationale for its existence, and the nature of the contested issue in deciding between the two,[17] rather than employing the criteria used in the US case law. It is clear that the approach of the Canadian courts has ebbed and flowed and that while some judges favour a test based on correctness, others prefer one which allows greater latitude for agency interpretation, as expressed through some form of reasonableness test.[18] The legislature has also intervened in some provinces, setting out in statutory form the relative capacities of courts and tribunals.[19]

It is clear that each approach is premised on different assumptions that should be revealed. The premise underlying substitution of judgment for questions of law concerning the meaning of terms contained in the Treaty or provisions made thereunder is that courts should be the arbiters of all legal meaning; that primary decision-makers should be controlled; and that substitution of judgment on questions of law is therefore the proper standard of review. The premise underlying the approach in some other systems is that the courts must exercise control over interpretations of questions of law made by the initial decision-maker; that this may sometimes be through substitution of judgment; but that this does not have to be the test in all instances, since adequate control can be maintained through some lesser standard of review cast in terms of rationality and the like. The rationale for this greater flexibility in the standard of review is the belief that the agency making the initial determination may well have significant knowledge, expertise, and understanding of the relevant legal issue. Thus if a generalist court is faced with the meaning of the term 'employee' in labour law legislation there may be good reason to accord respect to the interpretation of that term by the agency charged with applying the legislation, and subject it to review for rationality rather than substitution of judgment.[20]

This brief discussion is, as stated above, merely intended to illustrate the choices open to courts when faced with questions of this nature. The virtue

[16] D. Brown and J. Evans, *Judicial Review of Administrative Action in Canada* (1998), Chap. 14; D. Mullan, *Administrative Law* (Irwin Law, 2001), Chaps. 3–5.

[17] Brown and Evans, *Judicial Review*, *supra* n. 16, Chap. 14: 2531; *Union des Employes de Service, Local 298 v Bibeault* [1988] 2 SCR 1048; *Public Service Alliance of Canada v Attorney General of Canada* [1991] 1 SCR 614.

[18] Madame Justice L'Heureux-Dubé, 'The "Ebb" and "Flow" of Administrative Law on the "General Question of Law" ', in M. Taggart (ed), *The Province of Administrative Law* (Hart, 1997), Chap. 14.

[19] See, e.g., in relation to British Columbia, *Administrative Tribunals Act*, SBC 2004, c. 45. I am grateful to Geoffrey Gomery for bringing this to my attention.

[20] *National Labour Relations Board v Hearst Publications, Inc* 322 US 111 (1944).

of comparative law resides in part in the way that it can reveal different modes of dealing with the same issue and challenge preconceptions that might previously have been taken as 'given'. It does not, however, mean that the established orthodoxy in any particular system will or should change as a result of the comparative insight, more especially because that orthodoxy might well be based on constitutional assumptions that are different from those prevailing in another system.

B. The General Approach: Qualifications

Substitution of judgment on questions of law remains a cornerstone of judicial review in the EU. It would, however, be mistaken to think that this approach is unqualified. The Community courts have tempered the force of this proposition in ways that would be readily recognized by scholars and practitioners of administrative law.

The Community courts have been willing to characterize certain X conditions contained in the relevant Treaty article, regulation, decision, or directive as involving discretion rather than pure questions of law. This was, as we have seen, the approach taken in *Philip Morris Holland*.[21] This technique will tend to be used in circumstances where there are complex economic and social assessments to be made that lie within the particular expertise of the Commission. The consequence is that review is cast in terms of manifest error rather than correctness, although as we shall see below, the meaning ascribed to this test has altered over time.

It is also open to the Community courts to characterize the contested issue in a case as pertaining wholly or in part to the factual application of a legal concept to the circumstances of an individual case. Where this is so the focus will be on the factual foundation and evidentiary basis for the finding made by the Commission, and it will be accorded some margin of discretion when determining whether the facts justify the application of the relevant legal concept. Thus in *Pfizer*[22] examined in detail below the CFI was faced with a challenge to a Regulation that removed an additive from the list of substances that could be used in animal feeds. The CFI held, *inter alia*, that where a Community authority was required to make complex assessments in the performance of its duties, its discretion also applied to some extent to the establishment of the factual basis of its action, and that where the Community institutions were required to undertake a scientific risk assessment and evaluate complex scientific facts judicial review must be limited. The court should not substitute its assessment of the facts for that of the

[21] Case 730/79, *Philip Morris Holland BV*, *supra* n. 8 above.

[22] Case T-13/99, *Pfizer Animal Health SA v Council* [2002] ECR II-3303. See also Case T-70/99, *Alpharma Inc v Council* [2002] ECR II-3495.

Community institution, but should confine its review to manifest error, misuse of power, or clear excess in the bounds of discretion.[23] It will, however, be seen that the intensity of review in such types of case has nonetheless increased in the more recent jurisprudence.

4. REVIEW OF FACT AND DISCRETION: THE EARLY CASE LAW

We have already considered different senses of the term discretion. It is now time to look more closely at the test for judicial review of discretionary determinations. The discussion within this section will focus on the early case law, the type of discretionary determination in issue, the legal test used by the ECJ, and the way in which it was applied.

A. Classic Discretion

The *Westzucker* case[24] dates from 1973 and has been oft-quoted since then. It was an indirect action for judicial review brought under Article 177 EEC, now Article 234 EC. The applicant challenged a Commission Regulation that set the denaturing premium for sugar at zero. This in effect suspended the premium, which the applicant was not surprisingly unhappy about. It is necessary to understand the bare framework of the regulatory regime in order to appreciate the ECJ's reasoning.

Council Regulation 1009/67[25] was the basic Regulation for the common organization of the sugar market. Article 9(2) stated that intervention agencies might grant denaturing premiums for sugar rendered unfit for human consumption; Article 9(7) authorized the Council to enact further rules for the application of, *inter alia*, this scheme; and Article 9(8) provided that the Commission should lay down the detailed rules for the application of Article 9. The Council duly enacted more detailed rules pursuant to Article 9(7),[26] and the Commission in turn exercised its power under Article 9(8) to lay down more specific rules, taking into account the criteria contained in the Council's later enactment. It was this Commission Regulation that was challenged by the applicant.

The case raised judicial review of discretionary power in its paradigmatic

[23] Case T-13/99, *Pfizer*, *supra* n. 22, at para. 169.

[24] Case 57/72, *Westzucker*, *supra* n. 7.

[25] Council Regulation 1009/67EEC of 18 December 1967, On the Common Organisation of the Market in Sugar, OJ 1967 L308/1.

[26] Council Regulation 768/68/EEC of 18 June 1968, Establishing the General Rules for the Denaturation of Sugar used for Animal Feed, OJ 1968 L143/12.

form. Discretion was apparent at two levels in the regulatory scheme subject to review, both of which were recognized by the ECJ. There was a primary discretion because Article 9(2) stated that intervention agencies *may* grant denaturing premiums. The Commission Regulation was therefore not susceptible to challenge merely because it reduced the premium to zero, since there was no obligation to grant any premium at all.[27]

There was also a secondary discretion, in the form of criteria indicating how the primary discretion should be exercised. These criteria were laid down by the Council when enacting further rules for the application of the denaturing scheme,[28] and the Commission took these into account when passing the Regulation subject to challenge. The criteria were, however, broad and open-textured, including matters such as the level of intervention prices, the foreseeable market prices for animal feeding stuffs that would compete with denatured sugar, the costs of denaturing, the nutritional value of competing animal feeding stuffs, and the whole of the sugar surplus available for denaturing in the Community. The applicant's challenge was to the way in which the Commission had exercised this discretion by setting the denaturing premium at zero.

The ECJ was, however, clear that the Commission's significant freedom of evaluation meant that it was not for the courts to substitute their judgment for that of the Commission. Judicial review was limited to deciding whether there was a patent error or misuse of power.[29]

It is also important in the light of later case law to appreciate how the ECJ applied the test of patent error. The ECJ was brief in this respect, devoting but one paragraph of its judgment to the issue.[30] It contented itself with stating that the applicant's allegations revealed no indication of such an error or misuse of power. The applicant had argued that the sugar market was not being reorganized at the relevant time and that there was a continuing surplus of sugar requiring the maintenance of the denaturing premiums. The ECJ accepted that the existence of a surplus had been proven, but held that that this did not affect the Commission's freedom of evaluation to decide how best to eliminate it. The patent error test was therefore applied with a light touch.

B. Jurisdictional Discretion

The early jurisprudence also provides prominent examples of the ECJ being faced with broadly-framed conditions that had to be established before the relevant power could be exercised. The phrase jurisdictional discretion is simply designed to capture this type of situation.

[27] Case 57/72, *Westzucker, supra* n. 7, at para. 6.

[28] Reg. 768/68, *supra* n. 26, Art. 2.

[29] Case 57/72, *Westzucker, supra* n. 7, at para. 14.

[30] Ibid. at para. 15.

The matter arose frequently in the context of the CAP and is exemplified by the decision in *Racke*.[31] It was an indirect challenge coming from the German courts to the validity of certain regulations concerning monetary compensation amounts (MCAs). The MCA system was introduced to cope with the consequences of exchange-rate movements over and beyond their normal parities.[32] Such movements could lead to serious difficulties for the functioning of the common market, because there could be a difference between the value of the national currency as affected by the exchange rate movements and the intervention prices laid down by the Community on the basis of the official parity. This would then affect the operation of the intervention regime in that state, and the MCA system was designed to forestall such difficulties by allowing the state concerned to apply MCAs in trade with other Member States and third countries. Article 1 of Regulation 974/71[33] provided in effect that if for the purposes of commercial transactions a Member State allows the exchange rate of its currency to fluctuate by a margin wider than that permitted by international rules, and if such monetary measures lead to disturbances in trade in agricultural products, it *shall* be authorized to charge or grant MCAs on certain types of products.

The applicant challenged certain Commission Regulations applying the MCA regime to wine. The foundation for the claim was that the Commission failed to observe the condition in the basic Regulation that the authorization to charge or grant MCAs could only be exercised when changes in the exchange rates of currencies would bring about disturbance in trade in agricultural products.[34]

The ECJ rejected the argument. It held that it was for the Commission, assisted by the management committee, to decide on the existence of the risk of disturbance. This involved evaluation of a complex economic situation and therefore the Commission plus management committee had a wide measure of discretion. The ECJ would only intervene if there was a manifest error, a misuse of power, or some other clear excess in the bounds of its discretion.[35]

The application of this test for review was, as in the *Westzucker* case, brief. Once again the ECJ devoted but one paragraph to the matter in which it noted that the Commission had provided the facts justifying the contested measure, and that the Commission had specified factors leading it to conclude that there was a serious risk of disturbance to the wine

[31] Case 98/78, *Firma A. Racke v Hauptzollamt Mainz* [1979] ECR 69.

[32] Council Regulation 974/71/EEC of 12 May 1971, On Certain Measures of Conjunctural Policy to be Taken in Agriculture Following the Temporary Widening of the Margins of Fluctuation for the Currencies of Certain Member States, OJ 1971 L106/1.

[33] Reg. 974/71, *supra* n. 32. [34] Ibid. Art. 1(2).

[35] Case 98/78, *Racke, supra* n. 31, at paras. 4–5.

market.[36] Judicial review based on manifest error was done with a light touch, the ECJ concluding that it did not appear that the Commission had committed a manifest error or that it had exceeded the bounds of its discretion under the relevant rules.

The same approach is apparent in other agricultural cases where there was discretion in the conditions that had to be established before the power or duty could or should be exercised. Thus in *CNTA*[37] the applicant complained of the withdrawal of MCAs. The Court held that the Commission possessed a large degree of discretion in determining whether alterations in monetary values as a result of exchange-rate movements might lead to such disturbances in trade and therefore whether MCAs were warranted. The same reasoning is to be found in the *Deuka* case.[38] The applicant sought to test the legality of a particular Regulation under which premiums payable on wheat were modified. It was argued that this was illegal, on the ground that the basic Regulation on these matters only permitted adjustments 'where the balance of the market in cereals is likely to be disturbed'.[39] The Court rejected the claim. It stated that the Commission had a 'significant freedom of evaluation' in deciding on both the existence of a disturbance, and the method of dealing with it. The ECJ would only intervene if there were a patent error or a misuse of power, and the Court quickly reached the conclusion that no such error existed.[40]

C. Jurisdictional Discretion Plus Classic Discretion

In the cases considered in the previous category the relevant Community regulations set out broadly-framed conditions that had to be established before the power could be exercised, but then mandated that the power should be exercised when those conditions were met. Thus the MCA regime provided that Member States *shall* be authorized to charge MCAs where the conditions specified in the basic Regulation existed.

There are also instances where the Treaty provisions or regulations set out broadly-framed conditions that had to be established before the power could be exercised, but then provided that the Commission *might* authorize certain action but did not make this mandatory. In such instances we have a

[36] Ibid. at para. 6.

[37] Case 74/74, *Comptoir National Technique Agricole (CNTA) SA v Commission* [1975] ECR 533, at para. 21.

[38] Case 78/74, *Deuka, Deutsche Kraftfutter GmbH, B. J. Stolp v Einfuhr-und Vorratsstelle für Getreide und Futtermittel* [1975] ECR 421, at 432.

[39] Council Regulation 172/67/EEC of 27 June 1967, On General Rules Governing the Denaturing of Wheat and Rye of Bread Making Quality, OJ 1967 130/2602, as amended by Regulation 644/68, OJ 1968 L122/3, Art. 1.

[40] Case 78/74 *Deuka, supra* n. 38, at paras. 8–9.

combination of what was termed jurisdictional discretion combined with classic discretion.

This is exemplified by the legal provisions concerning state aids. The basic principle is that state aid is contrary to EU law, since it distorts the ideal of a level playing field between competitors in different Member States. The Commission is, however, afforded power to authorize state aid in certain circumstances specified in the Treaty. Thus Article 87(3)(a) EC provides that 'aid to promote the economic development of areas where the standard of living is abnormally low or where there is serious under-employment' may be considered to be compatible with the common market. Proof that the aid will have this effect is therefore a condition precedent for the Commission to exercise its discretion as to whether to authorize the aid.

The meaning of this provision came before the ECJ in *Philip Morris Holland*.[41] The Dutch Government gave aid to a tobacco manufacturer. The Commission found that the aid did not come within Article 87(3)(a), and this was challenged by the applicant. It argued, *inter alia*, that the Commission was wrong to hold that the standard of living in the relevant area was not 'abnormally low', and was wrong to conclude that the area did not suffer serious 'under employment' within the meaning of Article 87(3)(a). The ECJ rejected the argument. It held that the Commission had a discretion, the exercise of which involved economic and social assessments that had to be made in a Community context.[42] The Commission had advanced good reasons for assessing the standard of living and serious under-employment in the relevant area, not with reference to the national average in the Netherlands but in relation to the Community level.

This approach is evident in other decisions concerning state aids, made pursuant to Article 87(3)(c) EC. This provides that 'aid to facilitate the development of certain economic activities or of certain economic areas, where such aid does not adversely affect trading conditions to an extent contrary to the common interest' may be compatible with the common market. This Article is the provision through which a State can seek to justify aid to a particular depressed region as judged by national criteria. This nationally based criterion is not, however, unqualified. It is still necessary to consider the impact of the aid on inter-Community trade, and its sectoral repercussions at Community level. The Article was considered in the *Glaverbel* case.[43] The Belgian Government gave aid to certain glass producers. The Commission found that the aid did not come within Article 87(3).

[41] Case 730/79 *Philip Morris Holland*, *supra* n. 8.

[42] Ibid., at para. 24; Case 310/85, *Deufil Gmbh & Co KG v Commission* [1987] ECR 901, at para. 18.

[43] Cases 62 and 72/87, *Executif Régional Wallon and Glaverbel SA v Commission* [1988] ECR 1573.

This was because the aid, which was for periodic plant renovation, did not satisfy the requirement that there must be economic development of the relevant sector, without this adversely affecting trading conditions to an extent contrary to the common interest. The applicant argued that the Commission had misinterpreted the Treaty Article. The ECJ rejected the claim. It held that the Commission's reasoning was comprehensible, and that the Commission should be accorded a power of appraisal when applying the criteria in Article 87(3)(c). The applicant had not shown that the Commission had misused its powers or committed a manifest error, and hence the claim was dismissed.[44]

D. Contrast and Similarity

The test for review applied in the preceding cases was the same, but this should not mask the fact that in analytical terms the discretion operated at different levels in the three types of case. This does not mean that the ECJ was wrong to apply the same test in the three situations. It does mean that we should be aware that it did so.

In *Westzucker* we had the paradigm instance of primary discretion, denaturing premiums *may* be granted, coupled with secondary discretion as to a complex array of factors that should be taken into account in deciding whether the primary discretion should be exercised or not.

In *Racke* the evaluative discretion existed within the conditions that triggered the application of the MCA regime, and where these conditions were met the application of that regime was mandatory. This is clear from Article 1 of Regulation 974/71 set out above.[45] The charge or grant of MCAs was therefore conditioned on proof of the existence of disturbance in trade in agricultural products. This was acknowledged by the ECJ in *Racke,*[46] and in *CNTA* where the ECJ held that 'the option for Member States to apply compensatory amounts may only be exercised where the monetary measures in question would lead to disturbances to trade in agricultural products'.[47]

In the *Philip Morris Holland* type of case the evaluative discretion existed once again within the conditions that triggered the application of the rules allowing state aids, but even where the particular condition was met the Commission still possessed a discretion as to whether to authorize the aid or not.[48]

[44] Ibid. at paras. 21, 31–34.

[45] Reg. 974/71, *supra* n. 32.

[46] Case 98/78, *Racke, supra* n. 31, at para. 3.

[47] Case 74/74, *CNTA, supra* n. 37, at para. 19.

[48] See also in the context of competition law, Cases 56 and 58/64, *Etablissements Consten SaRL and Grundig-Verkaufs-GmbH v Commission* [1966] ECR 299, at 347; Case 42/84, *Remia BV v Commission* [1985] ECR 2545, at para. 34; Cases 142 and 156/84, *BAT and Reynolds v Commission* [1987] ECR 4487, at para. 62.

E. Discretion: Positive and Normative Reflections

The word discretion undoubtedly has somewhat different connotations in different national legal systems. This is matched by diversity of academic opinion as to the 'correct' meaning and application of this legal concept. There will therefore doubtless be those who disagree with the use of the word discretion to cover the different types of situation analysed above. A pause for reflection may nonetheless be warranted for both positive and normative reasons.

In positive legal terms it is clear that the ECJ used the word discretion to cover all three types of case discussed thus far. It did so in *Westzucker* to capture the fact that denaturing premiums might, but did not have to be given, and to capture also the complex range of variables to be taken into account by the Commission when deciding whether to give such a premium and at what level.[49] It employed the language of discretion in *Racke* in the context of an open-textured condition that had to be satisfied before the power could be authorized: the need to find a disturbance in trade in agricultural products entailed the evaluation of a complex economic situation that gave the Commission a 'wide measure of discretion' and that in reviewing the 'legality of the exercise of such discretion' the courts should use the test of manifest error.[50] In *Philip Morris Holland* the ECJ was faced with an open-textured condition that had to be met as a condition precedent to possible approval for aid. It framed its judgment in terms of the Commission having a discretion the exercise of which involved economic and social assessment.[51]

In normative terms, the paradigm of discretion may well be what was termed the classic case, as exemplified by *Westzucker*: the enabling legislation states that a particular benefit *may* be given. This is the legislature according the initial decision-maker a choice as to whether to exercise the power or not. Now to be sure all legal systems will then build in constraints as to how the discretion should be exercised, whether cast in terms of rationality or proportionality, respect for fundamental rights, and the like. This does not, however, alter the fundamental precept that a choice has been given as to whether to exercise the relevant power and if so how.

It should of course be recognized that the discretion that was the subject matter of litigation in the other types of case was different. Analytical clarity is important in this respect and the preceding discussion has been designed with this in mind. These cases concerned the interpretation of open-textured terms in the enabling legislation that were conditions precedent before the

[49] Case 57/72, *Westzucker, supra* n. 7, at paras. 6, 13–14.
[50] Case 98/78, *Racke, supra* n. 31, at para. 5.
[51] Case 730/79, *Philip Morris Holland, supra* n. 8, at para. 24.

power could be exercised at all. The issue in *Racke* and other such cases was whether this particular condition was satisfied or not. The ECJ was willing to characterize the condition as discretionary because it entailed complex economic evaluation that the Commission plus management committee was best suited to determine, subject to light review through the test for manifest error.

The Court could have undertaken an extensive re-evaluation of the factual and legal issues, in order to determine whether such circumstances existed. This would, however, have been time-consuming. It would have encouraged applicants to ask the Court to second-guess evaluations made by the Community institutions. It would moreover have involved intensive review of measures that were often adopted under severe time constraints or in situations where there was an urgent need for measures to combat a temporary problem in the market.[52]

It is scarcely surprising that the ECJ was unwilling to engage in such searching exercises during the early years of the EEC, more especially when it was the only judicial body that could determine the validity of Community regulations. The ECJ's readiness to conceptualize open-textured terms in the enabling legislation that were conditions precedent before the power could be exercised as discretionary and to accord the Commission the authority to appraise and evaluate whether there was, for example, a risk of disturbance to the market, is therefore readily explicable.

5. REVIEW OF FACT AND DISCRETION: CONSTANCY AND CHANGE IN THE MODERN JURISPRUDENCE

A cursory glance at the modern case law on review of fact and discretion might lead the observer to conclude that little if anything had changed. Cases such as *Westzucker* and *Racke* continue to be cited. The criteria for review are formally the same. Manifest error, misuse of power, or a clear excess of the bounds of discretion remain the grounds of review, with the corollary that the Community courts do not substitute judgment. A closer look at the judicial reasoning reveals a rather different picture. It is clear that while retaining the established grounds of review the Community courts, and more especially the CFI, have been applying these with greater intensity than hitherto. This is, as will be seen later in the discussion, a common phenomenon in national legal systems. The reasons for this will be considered in due course, as will the policy implications of this development. It is nonetheless important to understand the nature of the shift in judicial reasoning that has occurred before venturing hypotheses as to its cause.

[52] Lord Mackenzie Stuart, *The European Communities and the Rule of Law* (Stevens, 1977), at 91, 96.

The Community courts have in particular used the concept of manifest error more rigorously than hitherto. The nature of the change might be indicated through brief mention of many cases. This would not, however, convey the reality of the shift in judicial review. The discussion in this section will therefore focus in some depth on prominent examples of the more modern approach. This is so even though the applicant lost in the first of these cases; it nonetheless demonstrates the nature of the modern approach. The in-depth analysis of particular cases will be followed by briefer mention of cases from other areas where fact and discretion feature prominently. We shall then be in a position to consider the current state of the positive law and reflect on its practical and normative implications.

A. Manifest Error: *Pfizer*

The *Pfizer* case[53] concerned a challenge by the applicant company to a Regulation that withdrew authorization for an additive to animal feeding stuffs. The additive in question, virginiamycin, was an antibiotic that was added in very small quantities to animal feed in order to promote growth. The rationale for the withdrawal of the authorization was the fear that such additives could reduce the animals' resistance to antibiotics, and that this lessening of resistance could be transmitted to humans. This would then reduce the effectiveness not only of that particular antibiotic, but might also limit the efficacy of antibiotics of the same class. Pfizer not surprisingly disputed this scenario, and argued forcefully that it could not be proven in the light of the scientific evidence. The CFI held that the Council and Commission could proceed through the precautionary principle, even if the scientific evidence could not be said to prove unequivocally the dangers in the use of the additives. There is much in the judgment that is of interest concerning the meaning and application of the precautionary principle, some of which will be touched on below. There will be more detailed treatment of the precautionary principle as a separate topic below.[54]

It is, however, the general test for judicial review and the way in which it was applied that is of prime concern here. The CFI proceeded in line with orthodoxy. It cited the well-established case law that in matters concerning the CAP the Community institutions had a broad discretion regarding the objectives to be pursued and the means of doing so. Judicial review should therefore be confined to examining whether the exercise of the discretion was vitiated by a manifest error, misuse of power, or clear excess in the bounds of

[53] Case T-13/99, *Pfizer*, *supra* n. 22. See also Case T-70/99, *Alpharma Inc v Council* [2002] ECR II-3495.

[54] See below, Chap. 19.

discretion.[55] The CFI also referred[56] to settled case law to the effect that where a Community authority was required to make complex assessments in the performance of its duties, its discretion also applied to some extent to the establishment of the factual basis of its action.[57] It followed, said the CFI, that in a case such as the present where the Community institutions were required to undertake a scientific risk assessment and evaluate complex scientific facts, judicial review must be limited. The court should not substitute its assessment of the facts for that of the Community institution, but should confine its review once again to manifest error, misuse of power, or clear excess in the bounds of discretion.[58]

The CFI reasoned in line with established orthodoxy, and the applicant lost on the facts. The case nonetheless exemplifies a shift in the approach to judicial review as compared to the early jurisprudence of the ECJ. This becomes apparent when we look more closely at the CFI's method when dealing with the applicant's arguments concerning factual error and manifest error, which occupied the greater part of the judgment.

(1) Pfizer *and Factual Error*

Pfizer made numerous allegations of factual error against the Community institutions. It might be thought in the light of the test set out above that the CFI would deal with such matters very swiftly, given that the applicant had to prove some form of manifest error, etc. in order to succeed. This intuition would be reinforced by the early jurisprudence referred to in the previous section where the ECJ would normally take no more than one or two paragraphs to conclude that there was no error of sufficient magnitude to warrant annulment of the contested measure. The contrast with the CFI's judgment is marked: it devoted 39 pages to this issue, or if you prefer it in this way, 125 paragraphs of its judgment.

The CFI began by considering the applicant's argument that the contested Regulation was unlawful because of the inadequate nature of the scientific data provided by the Danish authorities, since it was these authorities that sounded the initial alarm bells concerning the additive. The CFI rejected this claim primarily because the risk assessment undertaken by the Community authorities was independent of that done by Denmark, and only the

[55] Case T-13/99, *Pfizer, supra* n. 22, at para. 166. [56] Ibid. at para. 168.

[57] Case 138/79, *Roquette Frères v Council* [1980] ECR 3333, at para. 25; Cases 197, 200, 243, 245, 247/80, *Ludwigshafener Walzmühle Erling KG v Council and Commission* [1981] ECR 3211, at para. 37; Case C-27/95, *Woodcock District Council v Bakers of Nailsea* [1997] ECR I-1847, at para. 32; Case C-4/96, *Northern Ireland Fish Producers' Association (NIFPO) and Northern Ireland Fishermen's Federation v Department of Agriculture for Northern Ireland* [1998] ECR I-681, at paras. 41–42.

[58] Case T-13/99, *Pfizer, supra* n. 22, at para. 169.

lawfulness of the Community-level risk assessment was subject to judicial review by the CFI. It followed that even if the Danish action was unlawful because of the inadequacy of the scientific data, this would not prove that the contested Regulation was unlawful.[59]

The CFI then turned to the applicant's principal argument, which was that the Regulation was tainted by various factual errors. The most important aspect of this argument was that the Commission and Council had disregarded and distorted the findings of the Scientific Committee for Animal Nutrition (SCAN) which was established to assist the Commission at the latter's request on all scientific questions relating to the use of additives in animal nutrition. SCAN had, at the Commission's request, looked into the possible harmful effects of virginiamycin, and analysed the Danish claims in this respect. It concluded that there was no new evidence to substantiate the transfer of resistance to antibiotics from animals to humans; that while the development of bacterial resistance to antibiotics was a cause for concern, the data provided by the Danish authorities did not justify the action taken by Denmark to preserve streptogramins as therapeutic agents of last resort in humans; and that the use of virginiamycin as a growth promoter did not constitute an immediate risk to public health in Denmark.

The CFI rejected the argument. It found that the Commission and Council had not ignored SCAN's findings, even though it had not accepted its final conclusions. It held further that the Commission was not bound under the relevant legislation to adopt SCAN's conclusions. Where the Commission chose not to accept its conclusions, however, it had to provide reasons, which had to be at a scientific level commensurate with that of the opinion in question.[60] The fact that the Commission did not have to accept SCAN's conclusions was, said the CFI, justified by the Commission's political responsibility and democratic legitimacy, secured respectively through Article 211 EC and political control by the European Parliament (EP). This was by way of contrast to SCAN. It had scientific legitimacy but 'this was not a sufficient basis for the exercise of public authority'.[61] The CFI decided that the Council, when ratifying the Commission's opinion, did give reasons for not accepting the SCAN conclusions, drawing in part on SCAN's own reasoning and in part on reports from other specialist national, international, and Community bodies.[62] The CFI also rejected the argument that the Commission and Council had distorted the SCAN opinion. The arguments and counter-arguments on this issue were lengthy. They cannot be analysed in detail here. Suffice it to say that the CFI considered each of the allegations of distortion in turn, devoting 34 paragraphs of its judgment to the issue.

[59] Ibid. at paras. 177–185.
[60] Ibid. at para. 199.
[61] Ibid. at para. 201.
[62] Ibid. at para. 204.

The CFI subsequently focused on another allegation of factual error, this being that the contested Regulation was influenced by a new study produced by the Danish authorities after the SCAN opinion and that the Council and Commission should have sought a further opinion from SCAN on this matter. The CFI held against the applicants on this point. It held that there was no obligation to undertake a second consultation. The CFI distinguished previous cases[63] on the ground that the relevant legislation was ambiguous as to whether consultation was mandatory or not. The judicial conclusion that the consultation should be deemed to be mandatory in all circumstances was a purposive interpretation of ambiguous legislation, which was inapplicable to the instant case where it was clear that consultation with SCAN was discretionary.[64] This finding was, however, qualified, the CFI holding that it would only be in exceptional circumstances where there were sufficient guarantees of scientific objectivity that the Community institutions might, when assessing complex scientific facts, proceed without obtaining an opinion from the relevant Community committee on the new scientific material. The CFI moreover rejected the Council and Commission's argument that consultation with a different committee, the Standing Committee, sufficed in this respect, since it was a regulatory comitology committee and hence should be regarded as 'a political body representative of the Member States and not as an independent scientific body'.[65] The CFI nonetheless concluded that the Council and Commission were aware of the limitations of the new study when taking it into account and the study was in any event only regarded as part of the evidence in favour of the contested regulation.[66]

The implications of the CFI's approach to review of fact will be considered in due course. It is equally important to be mindful of its reasoning in relation to manifest error and discretion. It is to this that we now turn.

(2) Pfizer *and Discretion*

The CFI spent, as we have seen, considerable time reviewing the allegations of factual error advanced by the applicant. This still left a further important issue: it was necessary for the CFI to decide whether 'the Community institutions made a manifest error of assessment when they concluded, on the basis of those facts, that the use of virginiamycin as a growth promoter constituted a risk to human health'.[67] In other words, even though the applicant company had failed to establish factual error, it could still argue that the Community

[63] Case C-212/91, *Angelopharm GmbH v Freie Hansestadt Hamburg* [1994] ECR I-171, at paras. 31–41.
[64] Case T-13/99, *Pfizer, supra* n. 22, at paras. 262–266.
[65] Ibid. at para. 283.
[66] Ibid. at para. 298.
[67] Ibid. at para. 311.

institutions manifestly erred when deciding on the basis of those facts that there was sufficient ground to ban use of the additive.

The CFI emphasized once again that in assessing whether the scientific evidence enabled the Community institutions to conclude that there was a risk associated with the use of virginiamycin as a growth promoter, the role of the court was limited: it was not to substitute judgment; it was limited to finding a manifest error, misuse of power, or clear excess of discretion; and any determination of such errors must be made on the basis of the material available to the Community institutions when the contested Regulation was made.[68] The CFI nonetheless considered in detail the argument proffered by the applicant company. To put matters in perspective, the CFI devoted 28 pages or 92 paragraphs of the judgment to this matter, which contrasts markedly with the one or two paragraphs to be found in the earlier jurisprudence.

The applicant company maintained that human resistance to antibiotics of the streptogramin class did not have any adverse effect on human health. The CFI was unconvinced for a number of reasons. The SCAN findings were related to Denmark, rather than the problem at Community level. It was moreover clear from studies at national, Community, and international level that resistance to antibiotics was perceived as a major problem in human medicine. It was therefore proper for the Community institutions to develop a cautious approach designed to preserve the effectiveness of certain antibiotics used in human medicine, even though when the contested Regulation was made they were relatively little used in that sphere.[69]

The applicant company also argued that the Community institutions were not entitled, on the basis of the available scientific data, to find a link between use of virginiamycin as an additive in feeding stuffs and the development of antibiotic resistance in humans. The argument and counter-argument was complex. Suffice it to say that the CFI examined these claims in some detail, and concluded that the Community institutions had a scientific basis on which to find the linkage.[70] The CFI also gave close consideration to the company's argument that the scientific data was not sufficient to warrant the challenged Regulation. It concluded against the company, holding that the precautionary principle justified the measure, even though there was no scientific certainty, more especially given that a full risk assessment would not have been possible in the time available.[71]

The implications of the reasoning in *Pfizer* will be considered below, in the light of the discussion of judgments in prominent competition cases in which the Community courts annulled Commission merger decisions for manifest error.

[68] Ibid. at paras. 322–324. [69] Ibid. at para. 341. [70] Ibid. at para. 369.
[71] Ibid. at paras. 381–384, 389, 393, 401.

The year 2002 will almost certainly go down as an *annus horribilis* as far as the Commission is concerned. It suffered a number of setbacks in the Community courts and some of its major merger decisions were annulled for manifest error, two of which will be examined here.

B. Manifest Error: *Airtours*

The CFI's judgment in *Airtours*[72] was especially harsh. The Commission had prohibited a merger between Airtours and First Choice on the ground that it would create a collective dominant position in the UK market for short-haul foreign package holidays, as a result of which competition within the common market would be significantly impeded. Airtours was successful in having the decision annulled.

The judgment was long, over 100 pages, and involved complex issues of competition law. It would not be possible to analyse the arguments in detail. Nor would this be directly relevant for the purposes of the present discussion, which is concerned with EU administrative law rather than competition law. The focus of the ensuing analysis will therefore be on the meaning ascribed to the concept of manifest error in the CFI's reasoning. It will, however, be necessary to explicate some of the competition issues in order that the CFI's judgment and the use made of manifest error can be understood.

The applicant argued that the Commission had erred in the definition of the relevant product market, but the CFI found against it on this point. The principal focus of the CFI's judgment was on the applicant's other claim, which was that the Commission had erred in applying the idea of collective dominance to the instant case. The CFI set out the criteria for the existence of collective dominance and emphasized that it was for the Commission to adduce convincing evidence thereof, including evidence of whether a situation of collective dominance existed and the weakness of competition by other actual and potential players in the market.[73] The CFI acknowledged that the provisions of the Merger Regulation[74] conferred on the Commission 'a certain discretion especially with respect to assessments of an economic nature, and, consequently, when the exercise of that discretion, which is essential for defining the rules on concentrations is under review, the Community judicature must take account of the discretionary margin implicit in the provisions of an economic nature which form part of the rules on concentrations'.[75]

[72] Case T-342/99, *Airtours plc v Commission* [2002] ECR II-2585.

[73] Ibid. at para. 63.

[74] Council Regulation 4064/89/EEC of 21 December 1989, On the Control of Concentrations between Undertakings, OJ 1989 L395/1.

[75] Case T-342/99, *Airtours*, *supra* n. 72, at para. 64.

The CFI, notwithstanding the acknowledgement of this margin of discretion, found against the Commission. It identified what it regarded as a number of significant errors concerning collective dominance. Thus the CFI concluded that the Commission was mistaken in finding that there was a tendency towards collective dominance in the relevant market,[76] and that it had not taken into account the volatility in market shares, this being evidence of the competitive nature of the market.[77] Nor was the CFI convinced by the Commission assumption that the market was characterized by low growth, which if true would have been a factor conducive to collective dominance.[78] This error combined with mistakes concerning market transparency were said to be of direct relevance to whether the remaining tour operators would have an incentive to cease competing with each other after the merger.[79] The CFI also held that the Commission had erred in finding that there would be sufficient incentives to deter a member of the dominant oligopoly from departing from the common policy,[80] and that mistakes marred the Commission's findings concerning the possible reactions of smaller competitors and new entrants to the market.[81] The CFI concluded in trenchant tone.[82]

In the light of all of the foregoing, the Court concludes that the decision far from basing its prospective analysis on cogent evidence, is vitiated by a series of errors of assessment as to factors fundamental to any assessment of whether a collective dominant position might be created. It follows that the Commission prohibited the transaction without having proved to the requisite legal standard that the concentration would give rise to a collective dominant position of the three major tour operators, of such a kind as significantly to impede effective competition in the relevant market.

C. Manifest Error: *Tetra Laval*

(1) Tetra Laval: *The CFI*

The tone of the CFI's judgment in *Tetra Laval*[83] was less trenchant, but the result was the same, annulment of a major Commission merger decision. The Commission prohibited a conglomerate merger[84] between Tetra Laval, a leading manufacturer of cartons for liquid food, and Sidel, a company that designed and made production and packaging equipment systems, particularly those used for a certain type of plastic bottle. The rationale for the

[76] Ibid. at para. 108.
[77] Ibid. at para. 120.
[78] Ibid. at para. 134.
[79] Ibid. at para. 182.
[80] Ibid. at para. 207.
[81] Ibid. at para. 277.
[82] Ibid. at para. 294.
[83] Case T-5/02, *Tetra Laval BV v Commission* [2002] ECR II-4381.
[84] This is a merger between two firms normally operating at the same level, for example manufacturing or retailing, but where the firms operate in different markets.

prohibition was that the merger could strengthen Tetra's dominant position in the market for certain carton packaging machines and for aseptic cartons, and that it could create a dominant position in the market for particular packaging equipment. The merged entity's future dominant position in two closely related markets would be likely to reinforce its position in both, raise barriers to entry, and minimize the significance of existing competitors, thereby leading to a monopolistic structure for the market as a whole.

The *Tetra Laval* decision was, like that in *Airtours*, long and complex, the judgment coming close to 140 pages. The CFI reiterated the Commission's discretionary margin in assessments of an economic nature,[85] but emphasized also that it was for the Commission to show that the merger created or strengthened a dominant position and that if it could not do so the merger must be approved.[86] The CFI found that it had not discharged this burden and the bulk of its judgment is devoted to explaining why it felt that the Commission had not proved that the merger would strengthen or create a dominant position.

The CFI's reasoning and language is interesting in this respect. On some occasions it identified what it regarded as a flaw in the Commission's reasoning, for example concerning the possible horizontal and vertical effect of the merger on the creation of a dominant position, and then characterized this as a manifest error of assessment.[87] On most occasions the CFI's conclusions were framed in terms of the Commission decision not being proven to the 'requisite legal standard', in the sense that the evidence proffered by the Commission was insufficient as a matter of law to show that a dominant position would emerge.[88] On yet other occasions, the CFI combined the previous modes of reasoning, holding that the contested decision did not prove the possible creation of a dominant position to the requisite legal standard, and that therefore it followed that there had been a manifest error. Thus the CFI stated by way of conclusion that:[89]

It follows from all of the foregoing that the contested decision does not establish to the requisite legal standard that the modified merger would give rise to significant anti-competitive conglomerate effects. In particular, it does not establish to the requisite legal standard that any dominant position would be created on one of the various relevant PET packaging equipment markets, and that Tetra's current position on the aseptic carton market would be strengthened. It must therefore be concluded that the Commission committed a manifest error of assessment in prohibiting the modified merger on the basis of the evidence relied on in the contested decision relating to the foreseen conglomerate effect.

The significance of these different modes of reasoning will become apparent

[85] Case T-5/02, *Tetra Laval*, *supra* n. 83, at para. 119. [86] Ibid. at para. 120.
[87] Ibid. at paras. 140–141. [88] Ibid. at paras. 214, 235, 251, 254–256, 333.
[89] Ibid. at para. 336.

when we reflect on the impact of the more recent jurisprudence on the test for manifest error.

(2) The Commission: The Limits of Review

The Commission was not surprisingly 'stung' by the CFI's decisions considered above, and appealed the *Tetra Laval* case to the ECJ. A measure of the 'heat' generated by this issue is apparent from the Commission's ground of appeal, which stated, *inter alia*, that the CFI had distorted the content of the contested decision.

The Commission's argument focused directly on the appropriate standard of judicial review.[90] It contended that the CFI erred by invoking a standard of review that was self-contradictory and inconsistent with Article 230 EC and with Article 2 of the Merger Regulation, by purporting to apply review based on manifest error while in reality applying a different standard. The Commission argued further that the actual standard of review applied by the CFI exceeded the role of the Community courts in reviewing the Commission, by substituting the CFI's view for that of the Commission on a number of central points. The meaning accorded to manifest error of assessment had, said the Commission, significantly raised the level of proof required for a conglomerate merger and went beyond what could be regarded as review for legality. This was especially so given the CFI's emphasis on the need for the Commission to 'convince' the Court, rather than the necessity for the applicant to show a manifest error, and this new approach had led the CFI to substitute its assessment for that of the Commission.

(3) Vesterdorf: The Defence of the CFI

A measure of the significance attached by both sides to the standard of review is that Judge Vesterdorf, President of the CFI, wrote extra-judicially to explain and defend the CFI's judgments, albeit making clear that he was writing in his personal capacity.[91]

Judge Vesterdorf rejected the charge that the CFI had adopted a new approach to the review of Commission merger decisions, stating that it had rather 'adjusted the normal approach to reviewing competition decisions so as to take account of the peculiarities of the merger cases'.[92] Such cases

[90] Case 12/03P, Appeal brought by the Commission against the judgment delivered by the CFI in Case T-5/02, OJ 2003 C70/7.

[91] Judge Vesterdorf, 'Certain Reflections on Recent Judgments Reviewing Commission Merger Control Decisions', in M. Hoskins and W. Robinson (eds), *A True European, Essays for Judge David Edward* (Hart, 2003), Chap. 10.

[92] Ibid. at 137.

required a prospective analysis of the relevant markets and this involved two stages.

The merger had to be assessed on existing material facts, including the present position of the relevant undertakings and of competing undertakings. The CFI should, said Judge Vesterdorf, 'examine closely and without constraint whether the Commission has got the material facts right',[93] and this included 'direct factual inferences drawn therefrom'.[94]

The second stage of the inquiry required the Commission to evaluate the likely effects of the merger on the competitive situation in the relevant markets. It was for the Commission to show, as mandated by the Merger Regulation, that the merger would create or strengthen a dominant position, and that it would have significant negative effects on competition. Vesterdorf acknowledged that the Commission had a margin of discretion in this respect, pointing to the acceptance of this in the case law. The margin of appreciation was nonetheless a 'function of the degree of discretion involved':[95] a greater margin would be accorded to pure economic assessments, rather less to inferences drawn from primary facts concerning the likely creation or strengthening of a dominant position.

It is clear moreover that Judge Vesterdorf characterized the CFI's intervention in cases such as *Airtours* and *Tetra Laval* as justified because the Court was reviewing primary facts and inferences therefrom. Thus he stated that when the CFI in those cases referred to the Commission not having proved a claim to a sufficient legal standard or the absence of convincing evidence this meant that 'having regard to primary facts and the direct inferences made therefrom, the particular prospective positive or negative analysis of the Commission decision at issue is so uncertain as to amount to, or form part of what amounts overall to, a manifest error of appreciation'.[96]

It is equally clear from the President of the CFI's analysis that his motivation for more searching review was based in part on the need to allay past criticism from academics and practitioners about individual Commission decisions and about the role of the Commission as investigator, prosecutor, and judge in such cases.[97] Judge Vesterdorf's summation of the proper scope of review will however afford scant comfort to the Commission.[98]

> [I]f the Commission presents a case for or against a merger . . . in a contested decision in which, for example, it has clearly overlooked, underestimated or exaggerated relevant economic data, drawn unconvincing, in the sense of implausible, direct inferences from primary material facts or adopted an erroneous approach to assessing material facts, such failings may, depending on their cumulative effect in the context of the circumstances of the case viewed as a whole, suffice to constitute, for the purpose of the CFI's review of the relevant overall economic analysis, a manifest error

93 Ibid. at 138.
94 Ibid. at 139.
95 Ibid. at 140.
96 Ibid. at 140.
97 Ibid. at 118, 143.
98 Ibid. at 143.

of assessment. On the other hand, if no such or very few or insignificant such errors are found, then the CFI, even if it would not have subscribed to the Commission's economic assessment of the foreseeable effects of the merger and/or the adequacy of the commitments offered, should uphold the Commission's findings.

(4) Tetra Laval: *The ECJ*

The ECJ's judgment in *Tetra Laval*[99] rejected the great majority of the Commission's arguments and upheld the CFI's decision. Many of the Commission's claims were dismissed on the ground that the issues concerned assessment of evidence and the like by the CFI, which the ECJ held did not raise any issue of law and were therefore not susceptible to appeal.[100] Reference will be made to this in the subsequent discussion. The essence of the ECJ's reasoning concerning review of fact is, however, contained in the following paragraph.[101]

> Whilst the Court recognises that the Commission has a margin of discretion with regard to economic matters, that does not mean that the Community courts must refrain from reviewing the Commission's interpretation of information of an economic nature. Not only must the Community courts, *inter alia*, establish whether the evidence relied on is factually accurate, reliable and consistent but also whether that evidence contains all the information which must be taken into account in order to assess a complex situation and whether it is capable of substantiating the conclusions drawn from it. Such a review is all the more necessary in the case of a prospective analysis required when examining a planned merger with conglomerate effect.

The ECJ concluded that the CFI had conducted its review in the manner required of it as measured against the role of the Community courts set out in the preceding paragraph. The CFI had, said the ECJ, explained and set out reasons why the Commission's conclusions 'seemed to it to be inaccurate in that they were based on insufficient, incomplete, insignificant and inconsistent evidence'.[102] In reaching this conclusion the ECJ held that the CFI 'observed the criteria to be applied in exercising the Community courts' power of judicial review and, accordingly, complied with Article 230 EC'.[103]

D. Manifest Error: Common Policies, State Aid, and Structural Funds

The discussion thus far has focused in-depth on particular high profile cases concerning review of fact and discretion, since this enables us to appreciate

[99] Case C-12/03 P, *Commission v Tetra Laval BV* [2005] ECR I-987.
[100] Ibid. at paras. 104, 131–132, 145. [101] Ibid. at para. 39.
[102] Ibid. at para. 48. [103] Ibid. at para. 49.

the intensity with which review was applied in the instant cases. It is, however, necessary to complement this analysis by considering, albeit more briefly, other cases in this area. It is only by doing so that one can tell whether the case law considered above merely exemplifies a wider judicial practice, or whether it signals more intensive review for fact and discretion over and beyond that to be found in other cases. If the latter is true it then raises the issue of the broader implications of cases such as *Tetra Laval*.

It may be helpful to summarize the conclusion now: the general pattern that emerges from the wider case law is that review is more searching than in the early jurisprudence, but less intensive than in the cases considered in depth above. This can be exemplified through consideration of cases in important areas that require analysis of fact and exercise of discretion.

(1) Common Policies

There have been numerous cases dealing with review of fact and discretion in relation to common Community policies, agriculture, fisheries, and transport. Thus in *Italy v Council*[104] the Italian government sought the annulment of a Council Regulation made pursuant to the common fisheries policy limiting total allowable catch for blue fin tuna. It argued, *inter alia*, that the criteria for allocating percentages of total allowable catch were manifestly inappropriate because they were based on information about catches for one year, and not even the most recent year, rather than figures for catches over several years. The ECJ found that there was no rule requiring that catch quotas should be based on more than one year of fishing, and that in any event it found that the Council had used figures for two years. It then referred to the settled case law that the Community legislature has considerable discretion when evaluating a complex economic situation, as was so in the Common Agricultural Policy and the Common Fisheries Policy. This discretion 'is not limited solely to the nature and scope of the measures to be taken, but also, to some extent, to the finding of basic facts'.[105] Review should therefore be confined to manifest error, misuse of power, or a clear excess in the bounds of discretion. The ECJ concluded in two paragraphs that the Italian government had not shown that the Council acted in a manifestly inappropriate way when it exercised its discretion.[106]

[104] Case C-120/99, *Italy v Council* [2001] ECR I-7997. See also, Case C-390/95 P, *Antillean Rice Mills NV and others v Commission* [1999] ECR I-769, at para. 48; Case C-289/97, *Eridania SpA v Azienda Agricola San Luca di Rumagnoli Viannj* [2000] ECR I-5409, at paras. 48–49.

[105] Ibid. at para. 44.

[106] See also, Case C-304/01, *Spain v Commission* [2004] ECR I-7655, at paras. 23–25.

In *Omega Air*[107] the claimant sought the annulment of part of a Community Regulation setting the by-pass ratio for certain types of plane. The by-pass ratio affected the noise levels of the aircraft. The ECJ held that it was not for the Community courts to substitute their judgment for that of the legislature in relation to the Common Transport Policy. Review must therefore be confined to the trilogy of manifest error, misuse of power, or clear excess in the bounds of discretion. Such review should moreover take full account of the discretion possessed by the Community legislature when assessing a complex economic situation, which was relevant not only in relation to the scope and nature of the provisions to be adopted but also to a certain extent to the findings as to basic facts, 'especially in the sense that it is free to base its assessment, if necessary on findings of a general nature'.[108] The ECJ then reviewed the by-pass ratio in accord with these strictures, and concluded that the Council had sound reasons for choosing the by-pass ratio, which was simpler and hence more workable than other tests.

The approach taken to fisheries and transport has, not surprisingly, been replicated in relation to agriculture. In *Niemann*[109] the claimant company challenged a Commission Regulation laying down detailed rules for the application of a parent Regulation concerned with the grant of aid for skimmed milk and skimmed milk powder intended for use in animal feed. It argued, *inter alia*, that the Commission Regulation infringed certain limits established in the earlier Regulation. The ECJ prefaced its inquiry into this *vires* issue with more general comments about the CAP.[110] It noted that the Commission must be in a position to act quickly under the CAP and therefore it was legitimate for the Council to confer wide discretion on the Commission, the limits of which should be determined by the general aims of this form of market organization. The ECJ noted also that the Community institutions have a wide discretion in relation to the CAP, the corollary being that review should be limited to manifest error, misuse of power, and clear excess of discretion. It was accepted by the ECJ that the contested Regulation, which required in effect that skimmed milk had to be incorporated into feeding stuffs or made into powder before qualifying for aid, was restrictive. It found nonetheless within a few paragraphs that there was no manifest error on the ground, *inter alia*, that the contested Regulation made it easier to ensure that the product was in fact used for

[107] Cases C-27 and 122/00, *R v Secretary of State for the Environment, Transport and the Regions, ex p Omega Air Ltd* [2002] ECR I-2569.

[108] Ibid. at para. 65.

[109] Case C-14/01, *Molkerei Wagenfeld Karl Niemann GmbH & Co KG v Bezirksregierung Hannover* [2003] ECR I-2279.

[110] Ibid. at paras. 38–39.

animal feeds, thereby diminishing abuse of the overall objectives of the scheme.[111]

(2) State Aids

The early case law contained numerous applications for review of fact and discretion in the context of state aids. It is therefore interesting to see the approach taken by the Community courts to such challenges in more recent jurisprudence. The Community courts have continued to limit judicial review in this area. The cases nonetheless reveal more searching scrutiny of the facts and the discretionary determinations than was apparent in the early case law in this area, although falling considerably short of the intensity of review found in the competition cases.

There have been frequent attempts to review what was termed above, 'classic discretion': the decision made by the Commission as to whether to authorize aid under the Treaty provisions according it a discretion provided that certain conditions are met. In *Salzgitter*[112] the applicant sought the annulment of a Commission decision concerning aid to the steel industry. It had refused to authorize the aid in part because Germany had produced no plan for any reduction in production capacity in the Salzgitter group. The CFI held that the Commission had discretion to determine whether the aid was necessary to achieve the objectives of the Coal and Steel Treaty. Legality review was therefore limited to determining whether there was clear excess of discretion, manifest error of assessment of the facts, misuse of power, or abuse of process. It was for the applicant to adduce evidence that would suffice to make the Commission's factual assessments implausible. It had not done so, and nor did the Commission's conclusion about production capacity amount to a manifest error.[113]

The CFI will nonetheless examine more closely than hitherto whether there has been a manifest error of assessment. Thus in *Graphischer*[114] the applicant contested a Commission decision reducing the amount of state aid that could be given to it under Article 87(3)(c) EC on the ground that since some of the relevant restructuring work had been started before the aid had

[111] Ibid. at paras. 40–45. See also, Case C-369/95, *Somalfruit SpA and Camar SpA v Ministero delle Finanze and Ministero del Commercio con l'Estero* [1997] ECR I-6619, at para. 50; Case C-99/99, *Italy v Commission* [2000] ECR I-11535, at para. 26; Case C-87/00, *Nicoli v Eridania SpA* [2004] ECR I-9357, at paras. 37–40.

[112] Case T-308/00, *Salzgitter AG v Commission* [2004] ECR II-1933.

[113] Ibid. at paras. 136–145. See also, Case T-288/97, *Regione Autonoma Friuli-Venezia Giulia v Commission* [2001] ECR II-1169, at para. 74; Case C-113/00, *Spain v Commission* [2002] ECR I-7601, at para. 67.

[114] Case T-126/99, *Graphischer Maschinenbau GmbH v Commission* [2002] ECR II-2427.

been authorized by the Commission the aid could not therefore be said to have induced the applicant to attain the objectives in that Treaty Article. The CFI repeated the normal precepts about limited judicial review of the complex economic assessments involved in state aid.[115] It held, however, that while a firm could not be certain of state aid until it was authorized by the Commission, the mere fact that part of the work had been undertaken prior to that authorization did not preclude a finding that inducement for the work flowed from a promise of aid by the national authorities. It was therefore necessary to decide whether such an inducement existed in the present case, and the Commission should have taken account of the precise form and nature of communications emanating from the national authorities, combined with the urgency of the applicant's situation. The CFI examined the facts in some detail against this criterion, found that there had been a manifest error of assessment by the Commission, and concluded also that the error had a decisive effect on the outcome of the case.

There have also been a number of challenges to what was termed above 'jurisdictional discretion', capturing the situation where one of the X conditions for the exercise of power is framed in terms that are held to accord a discretion to the Commission. In *Freistaat Sachsen*[116] the ECJ considered a challenge to a Commission decision concerning aid to Volkswagen for investment in the new German Lander post reunification. The applicants challenged the decision, *inter alia*, on the ground that the Commission had misapplied Article 87(3)(b) EC, which provides that aid may be considered compatible with the common market if it is to remedy a serious disturbance in the economy of a Member State. The ECJ rejected the argument in part because the question of whether German reunification caused a serious disturbance in the economy of Germany involved complex assessments of an economic and social nature 'which fall within the exercise of the wide discretion which the Commission enjoys under' the Article.[117] It was not for the Community courts to substitute their assessment for that of the Commission: review was therefore confined to ensuring that the facts were materially accurate, that there was no manifest error, and no misuse of power.[118] The applicants had moreover not put forward concrete evidence capable of establishing that the Commission had made a manifest error when it reached the conclusion that German reunification did not in itself constitute a ground for applying Article 87(3)(b). The need for the applicant to adduce evidence to counter the factual and discretionary assessments

[115] Ibid. at para. 32.
[116] Cases C-57 and 61/00 P, *Freistaat Sachsen and Volkswagen Ag and Volkswagen Sachsen GmbH v Commission* [2003] ECR I-9975.
[117] Ibid. at para. 169. [118] Ibid. at para. 169.

made by the Commission has been emphasized by the Court on a number of occasions.[119]

(3) Structural Funds

The pattern identified thus far of review going beyond that found in the early cases, but falling short of that in the recent competition cases is also apparent in the context of the Structural Funds.

In *Associacao Comercial de Aveiro*[120] the applicant challenged a Commission decision reducing the amount of assistance granted to it for vocational training. The reduction had been made because a national audit had revealed that the applicant had charged for certain expenditure that was ineligible. The operative Regulation provided that where European Social Fund assistance had not been used in accordance with the conditions stipulated, the Commission had discretion to suspend, reduce, or withdraw the assistance. The CFI held that this required the Commission to undertake an evaluation of complex facts and accounts, which gave it a considerable measure of discretion, the corollary being that review should be confined to manifest error in assessing the relevant information. It concluded that no such manifest error existed, but it was nonetheless willing to examine in some detail the criteria used by the Commission when determining the amount of eligible expenses.[121]

E. Misuse of Power

Little mention thus far has been made of judicial review for misuse of power. This is an acknowledged head of review for discretionary power and is pleaded frequently by claimants before the Community courts, although it is rarely successful.

The meaning ascribed to this concept has remained largely constant over time. The ECJ has consistently held that there is a misuse of power if it appears, on the basis of objective, relevant, and consistent factors that an institution adopted a measure with the exclusive or main purpose of achieving an end other than that stated, or evading a procedure specifically provided by the Treaty for dealing with the circumstances of the case.[122] This

[119] Case C-456/00, *France v Commission* [2002] ECR I-11949, at para. 47; Case T-199/99, *Sgaravatti Mediterranea Srl v Commission* [2002] ECR II-3731, at para. 69; Case T-198/01, *Technische Glaswerke Ilmenau GmbH v Commission* [2004] ECR II-2717, at paras. 168, 171; Case C-91/01, *Italy v Commission* [2004] ECR I-4355, at para. 55.

[120] Case T-81/00, *Associacao Comercial de Aveiro v Commission* [2002] ECR II-2509.

[121] Ibid. at paras. 51–68.

[122] Cases T-244 and 486/93, *TWD Textilwerke Deggendorf GmbH v Commission* [1995] ECR II-2265, at para. 61; Case C-48/96 P, *Windpark Groothusen Gmbh & Co Betriebs KG v*

head of review is therefore primarily directed towards the purpose of the challenged measure rather than its content.[123]

It is for the applicant to adduce objective evidence that the Community institution has misused its power in this manner. Thus the claim that a Commission decision in the context of state aid constituted misuse of power because the real purpose was to attain tax harmonization was rejected since the applicant failed to present objective evidence to back up the allegation.[124] The CFI similarly rejected a claim for misuse of power in relation to Commission action in the sugar sector, stating that the applicant had failed to proffer evidence that the contested regulation was not adopted to deal with deterioration in that sector.[125] The applicant failed to convince the CFI that the Commission had misused its power by allegedly neglecting the interests of competition and favouring public postal services over express mail services operated by private undertakings.[126] Nor was the applicant in a staff case able to convince the court that a report on his work efficiency and effectiveness that graded him lower than previous reports was a misuse of power. The CFI was not persuaded by the argument that bad relations with his superiors had influenced their evaluation and hence was a misuse of power.[127]

The determination as to whether there has been a misuse of power will necessarily require evaluation of the scope and purpose of the relevant Treaty article, or piece of Community legislation on which the contested measure was based. This will then provide the foundation for deciding whether the contested measure was adopted to attain some other end than that stated or to evade a procedure laid down by the Treaty. This is exemplified by *Wirtschaftsvereinigung Stahl*.[128] The applicants argued in effect that the Commission had authorized aid to a steel firm in breach of the criteria set out in

Commission [1998] ECR I-2873, at para. 52; Case T-182/96, *Partex-Companhia Portuguesa de Servicos SA v Commission* [1999] ECR II-2673, at para. 202; Case T-30/99, *Bocchi Food Trade International GmbH v Commission* [2001] ECR II-943, at para. 58; Case C-301/97, *Netherlands v Council* [2001] ECR I-8853, at para. 153; Cases T-344–345/00, *CEVA Sante Animale SA and Pharmacia Enterprises SA v Commission* [2003] ECR II-229, at paras. 71–73; Case C-452/00, *Netherlands v Commission* [2005] ECR I-6645 at para. 114;

[123] Case T-52/99, *T. Port & Co. KG v Commission* [2001] ECR II-981, at para. 56.

[124] Cases C-186 and 188/02 P, *Ramondin SA and others v Commission* [2004] ECR I-10653, at paras. 42–48.

[125] Case T-332 and 350/00, *Rica Foods (Free Zone) NV and Free Trade Foods NV v Commission* [2002] ECR II-4755, at para. 203.

[126] Cases T-133 and 204/95, *International Express Carriers Conference v Commission* [1998] ECR II-3645, at paras. 179–196.

[127] Case T-23/91, *Maurissen v Court of Auditors* [1992] ECR II-2377, at paras. 28–34.

[128] Case T-244/94, *Wirtschaftsvereinigung Stahl and others v Commission* [1997] ECR II-1963, at paras. 31–47.

the Aid Code for the steel industry adopted under the European Coal and Steel Community Treaty (ECSC). They contended that the Commission had thereby misused its power by favouring that firm in a manner not allowed by the Code and that it had covertly modified the Code. The CFI rejected the argument. It held that the Aid Code was not designed to cover the type of case in issue and that aid could be validly given pursuant to Article 95 ECSC. There was no evidence that in authorizing the aid the Commission had sought to evade the Aid Code. In *Compagnie Maritime Belge*[129] the CFI rejected a claim alleging misuse of power by the Commission when it fixed the fine for a competition violation taking into account the amount of the fine imposed on another undertaking in the same sector. The CFI stated that this was necessary and legitimate to secure consistency in the application of EC competition law.

Successful claims for misuse of power are rare, but a claimant will have more chance of succeeding if something akin to *détournement de pouvoir* can be shown on the facts of the case, as in *Giuffrida*.[130] The applicant sought the annulment of a decision appointing Martino to a higher grade in the Community service, pursuant to a competition in which he and Martino were the two contestants for the post. He claimed that the competition was in reality an exercise to appoint Martino to the job, the rationale being that Martino had already been performing the duties associated with the higher grade. The Court quashed the appointment, stating that the pursuit of such a specific objective was contrary to the aims of the recruitment procedure, and was, therefore, a misuse of power. Internal promotions should be based on selecting the best person for the job, rather than pre-selecting a particular candidate to whom the job would be given.

6. FACT, STANDARD OF PROOF, AND STANDARD OF REVIEW

The recent case law analysed above has thrown into sharp relief judicial review of fact and discretion. The former will be considered in this section, the latter in the section that follows.

The proper scope of judicial review of fact is an issue that arises in any system of administrative law. The answer will be dependent on both normative and practical considerations. Some will applaud the recent jurisprudence of the Community courts in the merger cases, seeing it as an application of the rule of law in the EU, and a fitting counterweight to the power of the Commission. Others might deprecate the test embodied in the case law,

[129] Cases 24–26 and 28/93, *Compagnie Maritime Belge Transports SA and others v Commission* [1996] ECR II-1201, at para. 238.

[130] Case 105/75, *Giuffrida v Council* [1976] ECR 1395.

viewing it as crossing the line between review for legality and substitution of judgment.

A properly reasoned reaction to the jurisprudence requires us to press further and enhance our understanding of two issues that arise in relation to review of fact that should be distinguished. There is the standard of proof to be required of the initial or primary decision-maker before it makes the decision. There is the standard of judicial review applied by the reviewing court in deciding whether the primary decision-maker has met the standard of proof required of it. It will be seen that failure to distinguish between these issues can cause confusion.

A. The Standard of Proof Required of the Primary Decision-maker

It is axiomatic that the existence or not of a factual error will be affected by the standard of proof demanded in relation to the facts before the primary or initial decision-maker makes the contested decision. There are a range of standards from which to choose, including high degree of probability, probability, possibility, sufficiency, a requirement that the evidence should be convincing, or that there should be a preponderance of evidence to sustain the action taken.[131] It is common for legal systems to require different standards of proof depending on the nature of the issue, as exemplified most obviously by the higher standards demanded in criminal as opposed to civil actions. There may be dispute or disagreement as to what the standard of proof ought to be in any particular case. It is nonetheless right and proper for the reviewing court to determine the standard of proof required for the establishment of facts by the primary decision-maker.

This is exemplified by the competition cases. In *Airtours* the CFI elaborated the standard of proof that should be required in the instant case. It will be remembered that it was concerned with the possible creation or strengthening of a collective dominant position as the result of a merger. The CFI reiterated the legal test for collective dominance.[132] It then focused on the standard of proof required to meet this legal test. The CFI drew on the decision in *Kali & Salz*,[133] where the ECJ held that when determining whether a concentration would lead to collective dominance there should be close examination of the circumstances relevant for determining the effect of the concentration on the competition in the reference market. The ECJ

[131] The Administrative Procedure Act 1946, s. 556(d) has been interpreted as establishing preponderance of evidence as the general standard of proof, *Steadman v SEC* 450 US 91 (1981). See also, *Director, Office of Workers' Compensation Programs, Department of Labor v Greenwich Collieries Director* 114 S. Ct. 2251 (1994).

[132] Case T-342/99, *Airtours, supra* n. 72, at para. 62.

[133] Cases C-68/94 and 30/95, *France, SCPA and EMC v Commission* [1998] ECR I-1375, at para. 222.

did not, however, specify exactly what the standard of proof should be. The CFI nonetheless used the ECJ's decision as the foundation for a test based on the need for the Commission to show convincing evidence that a merger would create or strengthen a situation of collective dominance.[134] The CFI reinforced this conclusion by making reference to a Commission decision in a different merger case, where the Commission had interpreted *Kali & Salz* to require a test framed in terms of convincing evidence.[135]

The CFI in *Tetra Laval* endorsed and applied the convincing evidence test.[136] When the case was appealed to the ECJ the Commission argued that the convincing evidence test was a misreading of *Kali & Salz*, and the Commission pressed instead for a standard of proof framed in terms of the need to show cogent and consistent evidence.[137] The ECJ held, however, that the CFI had not erred in law when it 'specified the quality of the evidence which the Commission was required to produce'[138] for this type of case, and specifically endorsed the convincing evidence test.[139]

This aptly demonstrates the disagreement that can arise as to what the standard of proof ought to be in any particular case.[140] It is nonetheless right and proper for the reviewing court to determine the standard of proof required for the establishment of facts and hence the making of the decision by the primary decision-maker. This right entails a correlative judicial duty, in the sense that the court should lay down clearly the standard of proof required. This is essential to ensure legal certainty for both applicants and the Commission alike.

B. The Standard of Judicial Review applied by the Court

There is, however, a further aspect to the inquiry. This is the role that should be played by the reviewing court in deciding whether the standard of proof has been met or not. To put the same point in another way, *the standard of proof tells us the degree of likelihood that must be established in relation to factual findings in order for the primary decision-maker to make its initial decision.* It does not tell us the *standard of judicial review applied by the court in deciding whether the primary decision-maker has met the standard of proof required of it.* It is the latter that tells us how far the reviewing court should reassess findings of fact made by the primary decision-maker to decide whether the standard

[134] Case T-342/99, *Airtours, supra* n. 72, at para. 63.

[135] Case IV/M.1016, *Price Waterhouse/Coopers & Lybrand*, OJ 1999 L50/27, at paras. 104–106.

[136] Case T-5/02, *Tetra Laval, supra* n. 83, at para. 155.

[137] Case C-12/03 P, *Commission v Tetra Laval, supra* n. 99, at paras. 26–27.

[138] Ibid. at para. 45.

[139] Ibid. at para. 41.

[140] For detailed consideration of what the standard of proof should be in merger cases, see Bailey, 'Standard of Proof', *supra* n. 1.

of proof for the initial decision has been attained or not. The distinction between the standard of proof required of the initial decision-maker and the standard of judicial review when assessing whether the former has been met is important conceptually in legal systems.[141]

The standard of proof required of the primary decision-maker will frame the test for review applied by the court, but the latter is nonetheless distinct from the former. Thus it might be decided that the standard of proof for certain Commission action should be probability, such that a chemical could only be prohibited if it was probable that it would cause harm. This would still leave open the standard to be applied by the reviewing court when determining whether the facts and evidence before the Commission sufficed to establish the requisite probability. It might be felt that the test for review should, for example, be cast in terms of substantial evidence: the court would then consider whether the primary decision-maker had substantial evidence to justify the conclusion that there was a probability of the chemical causing harm such as to warrant Commission intervention.[142]

It is moreover important that review does not collapse into substitution of judgment. Consider once again the preceding example, where the standard of proof demanded of the primary decision-maker is that there should be a probability that a chemical might cause harm before it could be banned. It is not for the reviewing court to decide whether, if it had been the primary decision-maker, it would have concluded that such a probability existed. This would be substitution of judgment by the reviewing court for the view taken by the primary decision-maker. The reviewing court must instead develop a standard of review that will allow it to assess whether the person making the initial decision had enough evidence to warrant its conclusion that the chemical would probably be harmful. The test for such review might be that the evidence used by the decision-maker to justify the finding of probability was, for example, substantial or sufficient, even if the reviewing court might not itself have reached that conclusion had it been charged with the initial decision. This is especially so given that the existence of facts and evidence might be contestable, more particularly when the contested decision is a complex one.

C. The Standard of Judicial Review applied by the Court: The Meaning of Manifest Error

The reader might well accept the reasoning thus far, but feel that the answer as to the standard of review is obvious: it is manifest error. That was the test

[141] For clear recognition of this distinction in US law, see Aman and Mayton, *supra* n. 12, at 234–236; *Steadman, supra* n. 131.

[142] Aman and Mayton, *supra* n. 12, at 453–471.

used in the competition cases and in many other areas. It is undeniable that manifest error is the standard of review generally applied by the Community courts to cases of this kind. We must, however, press further and consider how the test was applied.

In *Tetra Laval*[143] the CFI held that the contested decision did not establish to the requisite legal standard that the modified merger would give rise to significant anti-competitive conglomerate effects, and that 'it must therefore be concluded that the Commission committed a manifest error of assessment in prohibiting the modified merger on the basis of the evidence relied on in the contested decision relating to the foreseen conglomerate effect'.[144] It is clear that the requisite legal standard of proof demanded of the initial decision-maker was the convincing evidence test.[145] The CFI's decision was therefore that because the Commission had not established to the requisite legal standard, the convincing evidence test, that the merger would give rise to significant anti-competitive conglomerate effects, it should therefore be concluded that the Commission had committed a manifest error of assessment in prohibiting the merger.

The same reasoning is evident in Judge Vesterdorf's analysis: where the Commission made factual errors by, for example, overlooking or exaggerating relevant economic data, or by adopting an erroneous approach to assessing material facts, such failings may, 'depending on their cumulative effect in the context of the circumstances of the case viewed as a whole, suffice to constitute, for the purpose of the CFI's review of the relevant overall economic analysis, a manifest error of assessment.'[146]

This, however, comes close to eliding the standard of proof required of the Commission for the making of its merger decision with the standard of review applied by the court in assessing its legality. The latter performs merely a conclusory role, expressive of the CFI's view that the evidence advanced by the Commission was not convincing: the convincing evidence test was the standard of proof required of the Commission when it made its initial determination, and the CFI held that because this test was not met, *therefore* there was a manifest error of assessment. This does not tell us *what test* the CFI was bringing to bear in deciding that the evidence was unconvincing. It should be recalled that it is not for the reviewing court to decide whether, if it had been the primary decision-maker, it would have concluded that the evidence was convincing, since this would be substitution of judgment.

To put the same point the other way round, the conclusory finding of manifest error is dependent upon some criterion for assessing whether the Commission evidence was convincing or not. In the absence of some articulated criterion the conclusory label manifest error could be used to

[143] Case T-5/02, *Tetra Laval, supra* n. 83.
[144] Ibid. at para. 336.
[145] Ibid. at para. 155.
[146] Vesterdorf, *supra* n. 91, at 143.

justify intervention in almost any circumstances. It would be open to a reviewing court to substitute judgment for that of the Commission, decide that in *the court's view* the evidence was unconvincing, and then conclude that because *it* found that the evidence was unconvincing there had *therefore* been a manifest error of assessment.

It is, however, generally accepted that courts should not, when reviewing legality, substitute judgment about the relevant factual matter for that of the initial fact-finder. The court is not well-equipped or well-placed to undertake *de novo* review. The finding and evaluation of facts is quintessentially a matter accorded to the initial decision-maker, who will normally have dealt with many such cases and hence have developed an understanding and expertise in the relevant area that a generalist court cannot match. It would moreover be inappropriate for the courts to exercise *de novo* judgment in circumstances where the initial decision-maker has conducted an oral hearing, and evaluated the cogency of witnesses, which process the reviewing court will rarely wish or be able to replicate. If it did so with any degree of frequency and proceeded to make a *de novo* judgment in cases where the factual issues were complex then this would moreover seriously overburden the courts. This is acknowledged by the Community courts, which have repeatedly stated that their role is not to substitute judgment on facts.[147]

This still leaves open the issue of what test the Community courts were bringing to bear in deciding that the evidence was unconvincing in a case such as *Tetra Laval*. The CFI and ECJ would undoubtedly deny that they were substituting judgment for that of the Commission, as to whether there was convincing evidence that the merger would create or strengthen a dominant position. They would point to the recognition in *Airtours* that the Merger Regulation conferred on the Commission 'a certain discretion especially with respect to assessments of an economic nature, and, consequently, when the exercise of that discretion, which is essential for defining the rules on concentrations is under review, the Community judicature must take account of the discretionary margin implicit in the provisions of an economic nature which form part of the rules on concentrations'.[148]

This was endorsed by the ECJ in *Tetra Laval*, but it was also heavily qualified. It held that the Community courts should not refrain from reviewing matters of an economic nature, but must rather *establish* whether the evidence relied on was factually accurate, reliable, and consistent, and also whether that evidence contained all the information which must be taken into account in order to assess a complex situation and whether it was capable of substantiating the conclusions drawn from it.[149]

[147] See, e.g., Case T-13/99, *Pfizer*, *supra* n. 22, at para. 168.
[148] Case T-342/99, *Airtours*, *supra* n. 72, at para. 64.
[149] Case C-12/03 P, *Commission v Tetra Laval*, *supra* n. 99, at para. 39.

It is, however, evident that the primary facts and inferences drawn from cases of this kind involve complex assessments requiring evaluative judgment of economic and factual matters. The determination of whether the evidence is factually accurate, reliable, and consistent requires evaluation, not simply observation. This is *a fortiori* so in relation to issues such as whether the evidence contains all the information that must be taken into account in order to assess a complex situation and whether the evidence is capable of substantiating the conclusions drawn from it. The need for complex assessment is equally present when deciding on the 'various chains of cause and effect with a view to ascertaining which of them are the most likely'.[150] It is, however, precisely in relation to these more complex findings, where the facts are multifaceted and difficult, requiring a greater degree of evaluative judgment, that there can be real differences of view as to the facts and the possible consequences flowing from them.[151]

It is not clear how much real margin of appreciation is accorded to the Commission in relation to such matters. The President of the CFI, writing extra-judicially, opined that there was a margin of discretion, but that this was a 'function of the degree of discretion involved',[152] such that a greater margin would be accorded to pure economic assessments, rather less to inferences drawn from primary facts concerning the likely creation or strengthening of a dominant position. It is, however, clear that in reality the CFI in *Tetra Laval* gave not just 'rather less', but very little margin of appreciation to the Commission in relation to such matters. The ECJ's judgment contains little guidance in this respect.

D. The Standard of Judicial Review for Fact: Future Prospects

Judicial review of fact and evidence in EU law continues to evolve. There is but little doubt that the recent jurisprudence will generate more case law testing the application of the precepts laid down. Four points can be made in this regard.

(1) Standard of Proof

The Community courts should be as clear as possible as to the standard of proof that is required of the initial decision-maker when making the contested decision. It is, for the reasons given above, right that this matter should

[150] Ibid. at para. 43.

[151] It is open to the Community courts to commission an expert report as done in e.g. Cases C-89, 104, 114, 116, 117, 125–9/85, *Ahlström Osakeyhitiö v Commission* [1993] ECR I-1307, but this does not alter the force of the point being made.

[152] Vesterdorf, *supra* n. 91, at 140.

be determined by the Community courts, but this carries a judicial obligation to specify as clearly as possible what the requisite legal standard actually is within any particular area. Legal certainty for applicants and the Commission demands this.

(2) Standard of Judicial Review

Any conclusion as to whether the Community courts were right to annul the Commission in a case such as *Tetra Laval* is dependent on a view, explicit or implicit, as to the standard of review that should be brought to bear in such cases. It might well be that the Community courts' decision would be warranted under, for example, a test for review cast in terms of substantiality or sufficiency of evidence, the argument being that the Commission decision could not survive review on this criterion.

There is in any event a pressing need for clarity as to the standard of review that is currently being applied. The repeated articulation of manifest error conceals more than it reveals. It is clear that the test as applied by the Community courts has evolved a long way from the early jurisprudence. It captures far more than the decision that is facially or self-evidently wrong. The test as currently used in relation to facts allows the court to decide either that a single factual mistake is serious enough to be characterized as a manifest error, or that a series of less important such errors should when aggregated be regarded as giving rise to a manifest error. It is clear that the test is used in cases where the error only becomes evident after searching inquiry by the judiciary. It is equally apparent that it is used in a conclusory manner in the sense articulated above.

(3) A Differential Standard of Judicial Review

It will be interesting to see whether review of fact and evidence developed in *Tetra Laval* is applied with such rigour in other areas of Community law. Courts reason by analogy, the corollary being that they distinguish cases where they believe that there are cogent reasons for differential treatment. We have already seen that judicial review of fact in recent cases concerned with common policies, state aids, and Structural Funds may be more far-reaching than in the early jurisprudence, but it is still significantly less intensive than in the risk regulation and merger cases.

It will be for the Community courts to decide whether to 'cut and paste' the key passage from the ECJ's judgment in *Tetra Laval*[153] to other areas, or to find some principled way of distinguishing between them. It would certainly be possible to do the former and apply the precepts about factual

[153] Case C-12/03 P, *Tetra Laval, supra* n. 99, at para. 39.

review in *Tetra Laval* to assess in more depth the factual and evidentiary basis of, for example, a CAP decision or regulation. It is, however, likely that the ECJ and CFI would find the implications of this to be startling. It will then be necessary for the Community courts to find some principled basis for distinguishing the areas where they are willing to engage in more intensive factual scrutiny from those where they are not.

It might, for example, be argued that factual scrutiny in the context of common policies should continue to be less intensive because the facts have been found by the legislature, because they are more complex being based on micro- or macro-economic projections, because the facts are less easily separable from the discretionary policy choices as to the objectives that should be pursued under the CAP, or for a conjunction of all these reasons. Related considerations might be thought to distinguish state aid. The determination of whether there is, for example, a serious disturbance in the economy of a Member State necessarily requires factual estimation and evaluation of complex micro- and macro-economic data.

Considerations of this nature have indeed been taken into account by the Community courts. In a series of cases concerned with common policies the ECJ and CFI have moved beyond saying merely that limited review is warranted because of the broad discretion accorded to the Community institutions in these areas. They have in addition articulated a rationale for limited review that is more explicitly normative in nature, stating that review must be limited where the Community institutions 'have to reconcile divergent interests and thus select options within the context of the policy choices which are their own responsibility'.[154] This is an especially salient concern in the context of policies such as the CAP, where Article 33 EC sets out a number of general objectives for the policy that can clearly clash *inter se* such that there will often be winners and losers in relative terms at least. The tensions that this can produce became evident in the 'banana litigation'. The ECJ forcefully pointed out that the Council had to reconcile, *inter alia*, the conflicting interests of Member States that produced bananas and therefore favoured policies enabling their agricultural populace to dispose of their produce to avoid economic hardship and consequent social unrest, and other Member States that did not produce the fruit and simply sought on behalf of their consumers unlimited access to third country production at the best available price.[155]

[154] Case C-41/03 P, *Rica Foods (Free Zone) NV v Commission* [2005] ECR I-6875, at para. 54. The same formulation can be found in earlier cases, see, e.g., Case C-280/93, *Germany v Council* [1994] ECR I-4973, at paras. 90–91; Case C-150/94, *UK v Council* [1998] ECR I-7235, at para. 87; Case C-17/98, *Emesa Sugar (Free Zone) NV v Aruba* [2000] ECR I-675, at para. 53; Case C-301/97, *Netherlands v Council, supra* n. 122, at paras. 74–75.

[155] Case C-280/93, *Germany v Council, supra* n. 154, at para. 92.

It is reasonably clear by way of contrast that the most searching application of manifest error review has been in the context of competition and risk regulation. The considerations that have shaped the more intensive review in these areas are eclectic. In the context of competition it has been driven in part by the criticisms voiced about the role of the Commission as prosecutor, judge, and jury, and thus more intensive review for manifest error is seen as a counterweight in this respect. In the context of risk regulation the Community judiciary doubtless recognize the controversy surrounding the precautionary principle that informs much of Community policy in this area, and intensive review of risk assessment and the like is designed to allay fears that the precautionary principle will be used as a disguised mode of arbitrary trade restriction.[156]

(4) Judicial Review and Institutional Capacity

The obligations placed on Community courts by the ECJ in *Tetra Laval* in relation to findings of fact are far-reaching. The burden on the judiciary of examining cases in this detail will be significant. Yet if they fail to do so then the very legitimacy of judicial intervention over such matters will be called in question. Thus if the Community courts take seriously the injunction placed on them by the ECJ to review facts in complex cases, but then attempt to do so too briefly, their credibility will be undermined, more especially if the judgments lead to the annulment of Commission decisions.

We should moreover be aware of the relative burden borne by the CFI and ECJ respectively. Judgments of the length of those considered in detail above will become more frequent. The task of engaging in such scrutiny falls principally on the CFI. It is the CFI that hears annulment actions brought by individuals. It is clear that when cases are taken on appeal the ECJ will only review for questions of law, and that this excludes, as seen in *Tetra Laval*, any re-opening of the way in which the CFI assessed the factual evidence. So far so good. The CFI bears the burden of factual scrutiny, it has the greater institutional capacity to do so, and more experience with such matters, although one may wonder as to how far even the CFI has the institutional capacity to produce judgments in this detail.

Indirect challenges to the validity of Community norms are, however, only heard by the ECJ. It is already overburdened with work, and would not view with equanimity the task of producing on a regular basis 100 to 200 page judgments investigating the factual correctness of a Community norm. Yet it would be odd to say the least if the ECJ because of its workload were to engage in less intensive review under Article 234 EC than that undertaken by the CFI under Article 230 EC where the substance of the case is the same.

[156] For more detailed discussion, see below, Chap. 19.

The intensity of review would become dependent on the fortuity of whether the matter was heard via a direct or indirect challenge, thereby further undermining the claim that the barriers to direct actions do not prejudice claimants. It might be argued that this problem is apparent rather than real since detailed factual review in indirect actions should be undertaken by the national court making the reference. It is, however, doubtful whether a generalist national court would have the expertise or capacity for this type of in-depth factual scrutiny.

7. DISCRETION, MANIFEST ERROR, AND HARD LOOK

A. Substantive Review and Judicial Choice: Two Techniques

The discussion in the previous section focused on judicial review for factual error. We should now turn our attention to review of discretion. The courts have repeatedly stated that they do not substitute judgment on the exercise of discretion for that of the initial decision-maker, and that their role is limited to finding a manifest error, misuse of power, or clear excess in the bounds of discretion. This standard formula must, however, be treated with some caution. This is in part because substantive review of discretionary determinations will often take place within the context of proportionality review, which will be considered in a later chapter.[157] The reason for caution with respect to the standard formula resides also in the interpretation accorded to manifest error itself. Many cases will not be pleaded or decided on the basis of proportionality, but will turn on the Community courts' assessment as to whether there has been a manifest error in the way that the discretion has been exercised. The meaning accorded to manifest error is therefore crucial in such instances, and the discussion that follows will deal with this aspect of substantive review.

It might well be helpful in this regard to take a step back before moving forward. It is axiomatic that if the courts operating in any system of administrative law wish to expand the scope of substantive review they can do so in one of two ways. They might choose to add new heads of substantive review to those currently available within that system, a classic example being the recognition and generalization of proportionality review. They might also expand the reach of substantive review by taking existing heads of review and giving them a more expansive interpretation than hitherto. Both techniques might be used in tandem.

The latter does, however, have 'attractions' for the judiciary. It is, other things being equal, easier for courts minded to expand substantive review

[157] See below, Chaps. 17–18.

to preserve the impression of continuity with existing doctrine if they continue to use well-recognized labels or heads of review, while at the same time imbuing them with greater force than hitherto. This approach obviates the need for the type of judicial self-inquiry that normally attends the decision as to whether to introduce a new head of review to the existing armoury. It will, moreover, often be the case that investing existing heads of review with more vigour will only become apparent when the task has been judicially accomplished. Reflection on the new status quo, whether by academics or courts, will therefore take place against the backdrop of an already developed jurisprudence that embodies the new or modified meaning given to the 'classic' head of review. It is in that sense *ex post facto*, as compared with the judicial and scholarly discourse that will attend the decision as to whether to introduce a new head of review, which will normally be *ex ante*.

B. Substantive Review and Judicial Choice: US Law

The point made above can be neatly exemplified by a brief glance at US law. Under the Administrative Procedure Act 1946, agency findings can be set aside if they are 'arbitrary, capricious or an abuse of discretion'.[158] The arbitrary and capricious test was therefore a principal tool for substantive review of discretion. Judicial interpretation often matched the facial language of the test. Plaintiffs faced an uphill task to convince a reviewing court that an agency decision really was arbitrary and capricious, The criterion tended to be narrowly interpreted, it being sufficient for the agency to show some minimal connection between the statutory goal and the discretionary choice made by it;[159] or to put the matter conversely, the plaintiff would have to demonstrate some manifest irrationality before the court would intervene. Thus as Shapiro states, 'in fact in the 1940s and '50s, rules almost never failed the arbitrary and capricious test',[160] with New Deal judges being very reluctant to say that New Deal bureaucrats had failed 'the APA sanity test, that is had done something arbitrary and capricious'.[161]

The label 'hard look' developed because the courts began to desire more control than allowed by this limited reading of the arbitrary and capricious

[158] Administrative Procedure Act 1946, s. 706(2)(a).

[159] Aman and Mayton, *supra* n. 12, at 519–529; S. Breyer, *et al.*, *Administrative Law and Regulatory Policy* (Aspen Law & Business, 5th ed., 2002), at 415.

[160] Shapiro, 'Codification of Administrative Law: The US and the Union' (1996) 2 *ELJ* 26, at 28.

[161] Ibid. at 33.

test.[162] In *State Farm*[163] the Supreme Court founded its intervention on the arbitrary and capricious test, but then gave a broader reading to that phrase than that provided in earlier cases. The court accepted that it should not substitute its judgment for that of the agency. It could, however, intervene if any of the following defects were present: if the agency relied on factors which Congress had not intended it to consider; failed to consider an important aspect of the problem; offered an explanation which ran counter to the evidence before the agency; was so implausible that it could not be sustained; failed to provide a record which substantiated its findings; or where the connection between the choice made by the agency and the facts found was not rational.

The hard look doctrine therefore represented a shift from a previously more minimal substantive review, where judicial intervention would occur only if there was serious irrationality, to one where the courts would interfere where the broader list of defects set out above are present. Controversial issues touching on the merits can, not surprisingly, arise. Deciding whether a particular consideration is relevant can often be difficult in complex cases.[164] Moreover, insofar as the factors which make up the hard look doctrine look to process it is equally clear that complex substantive judgments underlie the determination of many ostensibly process-related issues. Whose views should be taken into account, and what type of process rights an individual should be given both entail substantive judgments of considerable complexity.[165] The hard look test proved to be a powerful tool, because of the insistence on the provision of reasons, the demand for a more developed record, and a judicial willingness to assess the cogency of the reasoning process used by the agency when it made its initial determination. This is not to say that the test was unproblematic. There have been problems resulting from an excessive

[162] See, *Greater Boston Television Corp. v Federal Communications Commission* 444 F.2d 841, at 850–853 (DC Cir 1970), cert. denied 403 US 923 (1971); *Environmental Defense Fund Inc v Ruckelshaus* 439 F2d 584 (DC Cir 1971); Leventhal, 'Environmental Decision Making and the Role of the Courts' 122 *U Pa L Rev* 509 (1974); Stewart, 'The Reformation of American Administrative Law' 88 *Harv L Rev* 1667 (1975); Stewart, 'The Development of Administrative and Quasi-Constitutional Law in Judicial Review of Environmental Decision Making; Lessons From the Clean Air Act' 62 *Iowa L Rev* 713 (1977); Aman, 'Administrative Law in a Global Era: Progress, Deregulatory Change & The Rise of the Administrative Presidency' 73 *Corn L Rev* 1101 (1988).

[163] *Motor Vehicle Manufacturers Assn v State Farm Mutual Automobile Insurance Co.* 463 US 29, at 42–43 (1983). The case was concerned with the adequacy of an agency's explanation for rescinding a regulation concerned with passive restraints in motor vehicles.

[164] See, Breyer, 'Vermont Yankee and the Courts' Role in the Nuclear Energy Controversy' 91 *Harv L Rev* 1833 (1978); Skelly Wright, 'The Courts and the Rulemaking Process: The Limits of Judicial Review' 59 *Cornell L Rev* 375 (1974).

[165] E.g. Tribe, 'The Puzzling Persistence of Process Based Constitutional Theories' 89 *Yale LJ* 1063 (1980); Brest, 'The Substance of Process' 42 *Ohio St. LJ* 131 (1981); Dworkin, 'The Forum of Principle' 56 *NYUL Rev* 469 (1981).

demand for information and justification by the courts, which led some to coin the phrase 'paralysis by analysis'.

This brief excursus into US law reveals the judicial creativity and choice in giving meaning to the controlling head of substantive review, transforming the arbitrary and capricious test from a relatively minimal long stop to catch clear arbitrariness into a more potent tool for substantive control over discretion. This still leaves open the reasons why the US courts were minded to transform substantive review in this manner. The reasons were eclectic. There was, as Shapiro notes, an increasing distrust of technical expertise combined with a greater willingness to engage in more serious review of technocratic decision-making.[166] This was combined with increasing emphasis placed on the importance of transparency and participation in the making of the initial decision or rule.[167] This served to place before a reviewing court a wider range of arguments about the content of the contested norm, thereby facilitating closer review of the cogency of the reasoning used by the agency. Shapiro captures well the resulting transformation.[168]

> American judges deferred to administrators in the 1950s. By the 1970s they deferred to no one. In the 1950s they openly said, who are we, as laymen to overturn expert administrative judgments. By the 1970s judges were saying, we are partners with administrators in administrative rule-making and indeed the senior partners with the final say. It was not the APA that had changed. Nor did the review provisions of new statutes significantly alter APA doctrine. What had changed was the judges' belief in the relative capacity of administrators and judges to make the right decisions. This change in judicial beliefs runs too startlingly parallel to broad changes in political alignments and general world view to deny the connection between the two.

C. Substantive Review and Judicial Choice: Manifest Error

It is interesting to reflect on the development of manifest error in EU law in the light of the preceding discussion. The label manifest error, like that of arbitrary and capricious, is suggestive of review that will only be employed as a long stop to catch extreme and obvious forms of substantive error. This was the way in which the concept was commonly used in the early years of the Community, with the courts being very reluctant to set aside decisions on this ground. It was, as we have seen, common for the ECJ to give scant attention to the reasoning used by the Commission when reviewing the contested decision, and the Court would normally content itself with a brief one or two paragraphs before finding that the pleadings revealed no evidence of manifest error.

[166] Shapiro, *supra* n. 160, at 33–36.
[167] Stewart, 'The Reformation of American Administrative Law', *supra* n. 162.
[168] Shapiro, *supra* n. 160, at 36.

The modern jurisprudence reveals a different picture. The Community courts continue to repeat the classic formulation to the effect that they do not substitute judgment, and that review of discretion must be limited to a finding of manifest error, misuse of power, and clear excess of discretion. There is little doubt that review of discretion in areas such as the common policies, agriculture, fisheries, and transport, has become more rigorous than in the early years of the Community's existence, although it is equally clear that an applicant will still face an uphill struggle to convince a Community court to overturn a CAP regulation for manifest error in the way that the discretion was exercised. This must, however, be seen against the backdrop of the Treaty Articles that frame these areas, characterized as they are by objectives set at a high level of generality which can conflict *inter se*,[169] coupled with the need for frequent Community intervention under extreme exigencies in time.

In other areas, such as risk regulation and competition, the transformation of manifest error has been more marked and the Community courts undertake significantly more intensive review of the reasoning used by the Commission when assessing whether the contested provision can survive judicial scrutiny. This change is reflected also in the way in which the CFI has asserted control over the reasoning process used by the scientific committees that feed into the regulatory process. It will be common for the Commission to rely heavily on such committees when making regulations or decisions. In one such case the CFI held that the 'Community judicature may be called on to review, first, the formal legality of the Committee for Proprietary Medicinal Products (CPMP) scientific opinion and, second, the Commission's exercise of its discretion'.[170] While the CFI acknowledged that it could not substitute its view for that of the CPMP, it could consider the reasons proffered by the CPMP and whether there was an understandable link between the medical evidence relied on by the CPMP and its conclusions. It was, moreover, incumbent on the CPMP to refer to the main scientific reports on which it had relied and to explain why it disagreed with, for example, divergent scientific opinion presented by the undertakings concerned in the case.[171] Given that the Commission would normally accept the opinion of the scientific committee, and had done so in the instant case, it followed that if judicial review was to be meaningful the CFI should be able to consider the reasoning used by the CPMP.[172]

[169] See cases cited *supra* n. 154.

[170] Cases T-74, 76, 83–85, 132, 137, and 141/00, *Artegodan GmbH v Commission* [2002] ECR II-4945, at para. 199. The case was upheld on appeal, but the ECJ did not consider this issue, Case C-39/03 P, *Commission v Artegodan GmbH* [2003] ECR I-7885.

[171] Ibid. at paras. 199–200.

[172] The CFI did not state how this fitted with the standard requirement that for an act to be reviewable it must be binding on and capable of affecting the legal interests of the applicant. It could, however, have argued that the mandatory consultation of the CPMP rendered its

The tools used to transform review for manifest error in the EU bear some analogy to those used in the US, subject to the caveats discussed below. Thus the Community courts will look closely at the discrete parts of the Commission reasoning process in order to see whether they make sense, they will consider the evidentiary foundations for the Commission's argument, and will assess the cogency of the Commission's overall conclusions in the light of this judicial scrutiny. Process rights are therefore used to facilitate substantive review.

This is exemplified by the application of the duty of careful examination in *Pfizer*, where the procedural duty served to justify the requirement of scientific advice with the aim of ensuring that the resultant regulation was not substantively arbitrary.[173] The connection between process and substance is apparent once again in relation to reasons. Thus the rationale for the obligation to give reasons is in part that it will enable the courts to determine whether the administration acted for improper purposes, or took irrelevant considerations into account when reaching its decision. The CFI has emphasized that the reasons given must be sufficient to enable it to exercise its judicial review function, and it has scrutinized the Commission's reasoning, annulling the decision if it did not withstand examination.[174] There is therefore a proximate connection between expansion of the duty to give reasons and closer judicial scrutiny of the administration's reasoning process in order to discover a substantive error. While it is perfectly possible in principle for the courts to demand more by way of reasons, but still to engage in low intensity review of the reasoning process in the context of substantive review, the reality is that expansion of process rights will at the least encourage the courts to engage in more intensive substantive review, because they have more to work with and therefore feel more confident about asserting judicial control.

There is, however, an important difference between the modern application of manifest error in the EU and the hard look version of the arbitrary and capricious test in the US. We saw that the latter was fuelled in part by the protection afforded to participation when rules of a legislative nature are made by agencies. The Administrative Procedure Act 1946 (APA) provided the foundation for the requirement that the agency should respond to comments made by the parties before finalizing the draft rule. This then furnished the

opinion, which was then adopted by the Commission, an integral part of the legally binding decision made by the Commission, and was therefore reviewable. This was in effect the approach taken in Case T-326/99, *Olivieri v Commission and EMEA* [2003] ECR II-6053, at para. 55.

[173] Case T-13/99, *Pfizer, supra* n. 22, at paras. 171–172.

[174] See e.g. Case T-44/90, *La Cinq SA v Commission* [1992] ECR II-1; Case T-7/92, *Asia Motor France SA v Commission* [1993] ECR II-669; Cases T-374, 375, 384, and 388/94, *European Night Services v Commission* [1998] ECR II-3141.

courts with contrasting views on the cogency of the rule and a significant dossier of evidence when it was challenged by way of judicial review. The courts therefore had ready-made material on which hard look review could bite. The contrast with EU law in this respect is marked. The EU does not have an APA and the Community courts have resisted attempts to develop participation rights in relation to the making of the initial rule in the absence of a specific obligation to consult being contained in a Treaty article or in Community legislation.[175] This has a two-fold impact on manifest error.

It means that there is less material readily available from the making of the initial rule on which to test its cogency in the reviewing court. The applicant can of course present such arguments at the review stage, but this does not undermine the contrast, since in an APA-type regime there will be a wealth of material available not only from the particular applicant who chooses to press for review, but also from others who have lodged comments when the rule was being drafted.

The difference also means that part of the very rationale for harder look review in the US falls away in the EU. In the US the harder look has been justified in part by the very desire to protect participation rights embodied in the APA, the argument being that such rights will be undermined if the agency could simply go through the motions of listening to people while not really taking their views into account when making the final rule. The hard look interpretation of the arbitrary and capricious test was designed therefore to allow the reviewing court to evaluate the agency's reasoning process to make sure that the comments that flowed from participatory rights were taken seriously. This incentive for a more intensive reading of manifest error in the EU may be present when consultation rights are mandated in a particular instance. It will, subject to the qualification below, be absent in other cases precisely because there will not be participatory rights to be protected in this manner.

This naturally leads to reflection as to the reasons why the Community courts have, subject to the preceding caveats, developed the test of manifest error to be a more searching tool for review than it was in the early years of the Community's existence. This must necessarily be a matter for speculation, but a number of arguments can nonetheless be posited.

The application of manifest error with a light touch in the early years was likely influenced by the ECJ's reticence in overturning norms in the new Community order, more especially when they were brokered through hard fought battles in the legislative arena. The EU is now firmly established and the Community courts may well justifiably feel that it can withstand annulment of some of its initiatives without thereby sending shock waves through the system as a whole.

[175] See above, Chap. 10.

More intensive deployment of manifest error in relation to discretion and fact may also be explicable in terms of legitimacy. There has, as is well known, been a growing discourse on the legitimacy of the EU and on accountability of the decisions made therein. Imbuing the manifest error test with greater force and thereby bolstering substantive review is one way in which to enhance the accountability of those who made the initial decision and hence to increase the legitimacy of the resulting norms. Indeed it might, for example, be contended, contrary to what was said above, that the very fact that the Community courts have refused to recognize participation rights in the making of the original decision or rule, unless such rights have granted by a Treaty article or Community legislation, provides a reason why the courts are willing to engage in more searching scrutiny by way of judicial review. On this reading, review would enhance the legitimacy of the contested provision by enabling claimants to challenge its precepts in circumstances where they were unable to have input into the making of the original provision.

The creation of the CFI is also undoubtedly of importance in this respect. It was established to ease the burden on the ECJ. Its initial jurisdiction was for complex cases with a heavy factual quotient, which required in-depth scrutiny of facts and attention to the reasoning of the primary decision-maker. These skills could be carried over when its jurisdiction was expanded to cover all direct actions brought by non-privileged applicants. The CFI was therefore well placed to put more intensive substantive review into practice. This is reflected in the view expressed by Advocate General Vesterdorf that the creation of the CFI as a court of both first and last instance for the examination of facts in the cases brought before it was 'an invitation to undertake an intensive review in order to ascertain whether the evidence on which the Commission relies in adopting a contested decision is sound'.[176]

8. CONCLUSION

The meaning accorded to the concepts of law, fact, and discretion is central to judicial review in any regime of administrative law. It should therefore come as no surprise that this is equally so for the EU. Nor should we be surprised to find that the meaning given to central concepts in substantive review such as manifest error has evolved over time. This too is common within national legal systems. The relationship that does and should prevail between reviewing court and initial decision-maker in relation to law, fact, and discretion may be contested in any administrative law system, and the EU is no exception in this respect, as evidenced by the recent jurisprudence.

[176] Case T-7/89, *Hercules v Commission* [1991] ECR II-867, I.B.1. See also, Case C-344/98, *Masterfoods Ltd v HB Ice Cream Ltd* [2000] ECR I-11369, AG Cosmas, at para. 54.

14

Rights

1. INTRODUCTION

The emergence and status of rights-based protections against governmental action is important in any polity. This chapter will focus on this issue in relation to the EU, and will consider the relevance of rights for judicial review. This is of significance in practical terms, given the sphere over which the EU has competence. It is interesting in political terms, given the respective input from the Community courts and the political institutions. It is also central in normative terms, since the existence of rights-based protections within the EU raises a plethora of interesting issues concerning the relationship between these rights and those found within the European Convention on Human Rights (ECHR), national law, and international law.

The discussion will begin with the evolution of Community rights, revealing the input from the European Court of Justice (ECJ), the Court of First Instance (CFI), and the Community political organs. This will be followed by an overview of the concerns voiced about the protection of rights within the Community prior to the Charter of Fundamental Rights of the European Union. The focus will then shift to the Charter of Fundamental Rights, its genesis, and content. The Charter is not, at the time of writing, formally binding. It would have been accorded this status if the Constitutional Treaty (CT) had been ratified. Discussion of rights and judicial review within the EU without detailed analysis of the Charter would, however, be odd to say the very least, more especially because the document has an impact on judicial reasoning and because there is a reasonable likelihood that it will be made binding in a future Treaty revision. There will therefore be an analysis of central features of the Charter, more especially those relevant for judicial review. The discussion will conclude by examining the broader relevance of human rights within the EU.

2. THE EVOLUTION OF FUNDAMENTAL RIGHTS

A. The Judicial Contribution

The evolution of the Community's right's jurisprudence is well known[1] and therefore only the bare outlines need be related here.[2]

The original Treaties contained no express provisions concerning the protection of human rights. This may have been a reaction to the failure of the ambitious attempts to found a European Political Community (EPC) in the mid-1950s. The failure of the EPC convinced advocates of closer integration to scale down their plans. The EEC Treaty focused on economic integration and contained no mention of human rights. The absence of human rights may also have been because the framers did not realize that the EEC Treaty, with its economic focus, could encroach on traditionally protected fundamental human rights. This was belied by subsequent events. It quickly became apparent that Community action could affect social and political, as well as economic, issues. The expansion of Community competences attendant upon successive Treaty amendments reinforced this.

It was the ECJ that developed what amounts to an unwritten charter of rights. The ECJ's early approach was unreceptive to rights-based claims.[3] In *Stauder* there were nonetheless indications that fundamental rights would be

[1] A. Cassese, A. Clapham, and J. Weiler (eds), *European Union: The Human Rights Challenge* (Nomos, 1991); N. Neuwahl and A. Rosas (eds), *The European Union and Human Rights* (Kluwer, 1995); P. Alston, with M. Bustelo and J. Heenan (eds), *The EU and Human Rights* (Oxford University Press, 1999); Dauses, 'The Protection of Fundamental Rights in the Community Legal Order' (1985) 10 *ELRev* 398; Clapham, 'A Human Rights Policy for the European Community' (1990) 10 *YBEL* 309; Lenaerts, 'Fundamental Rights to be Included in a Community Catalogue' (1991) 16 *ELRev* 367; Weiler, 'Thou Shalt not Oppress a Stranger: On the Judicial Protection of the Human Rights of Non-Community Nationals—a Critique' (1992) 3 *EJIL* 65; Coppel and O'Neill, 'The European Court of Justice: Taking Rights Seriously?' (1992) 12 *Legal Studies* 227; Phelan, 'Right to Life of the Unborn v Promotion of Trade in Services: The European Court of Justice and the Normative Shaping of the European Union' (1992) 55 *MLR* 670; de Búrca, 'Fundamental Human Rights and the Reach of EC Law' (1993) 13 *OJLS* 283; Twomey, 'The European Union: Three Pillars without a Human Rights Foundation', in D. O'Keeffe and P. Twomey (eds), *Legal Issues of the Maastricht Treaty* (Wiley, 1994), at 121; Weiler and Lockhart, ' "Taking Rights Seriously" Seriously: The European Court and its Fundamental Rights Jurisprudence' (1995) 32 *CMLRev* 51, 579; O'Leary, 'The Relationship between Community Citizenship and the Protection of Fundamental Rights in Community Law' (1995) 32 *CMLRev* 519.

[2] De Witte, 'The Past and Future Role of the European Court of Justice in the Protection of Human Rights, *The EU and Human Rights*, *supra* n. 1, Chap. 27.

[3] Case 1/58, *Stork v High Authority* [1959] ECR 17; Cases 36, 37, 38, and 40/59, *Geitling v High Authority* [1960] ECR 423; Case 40/64, *Sgarlata and others v Commission* [1965] ECR 215.

protected in the Community order by the ECJ.[4] It was however *Internationale Handelsgesselschaft* which secured fundamental rights within the Community legal order.[5] The applicant, a German import–export company, argued that a Community Regulation, which required forfeiture of a deposit if goods were not exported within a specified time, was contrary to principles of German constitutional law. The ECJ's response was a mixture of stick and carrot. It forcefully denied that the validity of a Community measure could be judged against principles of national constitutional law. It then held that respect for fundamental rights formed an integral part of the general principles of Community law protected by the ECJ. The ECJ would therefore decide whether the deposit system infringed these fundamental rights. In subsequent case law the ECJ emphasized that it would draw inspiration from the constitutional traditions of the Member States, from international human rights Treaties,[6] and especially from the European Convention on Human Rights (ECHR).[7]

The early case law was concerned with the compatibility of Community norms with fundamental rights. The ECJ also later confirmed that these rights could be binding on the Member States when they acted within the sphere of Community law. This covered situations where Member States were applying provisions of Community law which were based on protection for human rights.[8] It applied to the many important areas where a Member State acted as agent for the Community in the application of EC law within its own country, as exemplified by *Wachauf*.[9] The ECJ held further in *ERT* that Member States which sought to derogate from EC law on free movement, by relying on public policy, public health, and the like, would be subject to the requirements of fundamental rights when deciding whether the derogation was lawful.[10] The requirement to respect

[4] Case 29/69, *Stauder v City of Ulm* [1969] ECR 419, at para. 7.

[5] Case 11/70, *Internationale Handelsgesellschaft v Einfuhr- und Vorratstelle für Getreide und Futtermittel* [1970] ECR 1125.

[6] Case 149/77, *Defrenne v Sabena* [1978] ECR 1365.

[7] See, e.g., Case 4/73, *Nold v Commission* [1974] ECR 491; Case 44/79, *Hauer v Land Rheinland-Pfalz* [1979] ECR 3727; Case C-235/99, *The Queen v Secretary of State for the Home Department, ex p Kondova* [2001] ECR I-6427; Case C-25/02, *Rinke v Arztekammer Hamburg* [2003] ECR I-8349; Cases C-465/00, 138 and 139/01, *Rechsnungshof v Österreichischer Rundfunk and others* [2003] ECR I-4989.

[8] Case 222/84, *Johnston v Chief Constable of the Royal Ulster Constabulary* [1986] ECR 1651.

[9] Case 5/88, *Wachauf v Germany* [1989] ECR 2609; Cases C-74/95 and 129/95, *Criminal Proceedings against X* [1996] ECR I-6609.

[10] Case C-260/89, *Elliniki Radiophonia Tileorassi AE v Dimotiki Etairia Pliroforissis and Sotirios Kouvelas* [1991] ECR I-2925, at para. 43; Case C-368/95, *Vereinigte Familiapress Zeitungsverlags- und vertriebs GmbH v Heinrich Bauer Verlag* [1997] ECR I-368, at para. 24; Case C-60/00, *Carpenter v Secretary of State for the Home Department* [2002] ECR I-6279, at paras. 40–41; Cases C-482 and 493/01, *Orfanopoulos v Land Baden-Wurttemberg* [2004] ECR I-5257, at paras. 97–98.

fundamental rights is also applicable when a national court interprets a Framework Decision adopted under Pillar 3.[11] The ECJ will not, however, allow fundamental rights to be pleaded against a Member State where there is no real connection with European Community (EC) law.[12]

While the ECJ stated repeatedly that it gave particular attention to the ECHR, it held in *Opinion 2/94* that the Community lacked competence under the EC Treaty to accede to the ECHR.[13] The ECJ acknowledged that the Community might have an implied as well as an express international treaty-making competence: an express internal power could generate an implied external power. However there was, said the ECJ, no such express internal power in the field of human rights. Nor could Article 308 EC be used to fill the gap. That Article could not widen the scope of Community powers beyond the general framework created by the provisions of the Treaty as a whole. It could not be used as a basis for the 'adoption of provisions whose effect would, in substance, be to amend the Treaty without following the procedure which it provides for that purpose'.[14] The ECJ accepted that respect for human rights was a condition for the lawfulness of Community acts. The Court held, however, that accession to the Convention would entail a substantial change in the existing Community system. The Community would thereby be entering a distinct international institutional system, the provisions of which would have to be integrated into the Community legal order. This could not be done through Article 308, but only through a Treaty amendment.

B. The Political and Legislative Contribution

It would be mistaken to think that the ECJ made the sole contribution to the evolution of human rights within the Community. The Treaty itself contained certain provisions that would find a place in any modern Bill of Rights. Non-discrimination on the grounds of nationality was secured by Article 12 EC, and also more specifically in the Treaty provisions on free

[11] Case C-105/03, *Criminal Proceedings against Maria Pupino* [2005] ECR I-5285.

[12] Case C-144/95, *Maurin* [1996] ECR I-2909; Case C-299/95, *Kremzow v Austria* [1997] ECR I-2629; Case C-309/96, *Annibaldi v Sindaco del Commune di Guidonia and Presidente Regione Lazio* [1997] ECR I-7493; Case C-328/04, *Criminal Proceedings against Attila Vajnai* [2005] ECR I-8577.

[13] Opinion 2/94, *On Accession by the Community to the ECHR* [1996] ECR I-1759. For comment, see, G. Gaja, (1996) 33 *CMLRev* 973; A. Toth, (1997) 34 *CMLRev* 491; N. Burrows, (1997) 22 *ELRev* 594; S. O' Leary, (1997) *EHRLR* 362; P. Allott, [1996] *CLJ* 409, C. Vedder, *Europarecht* (1996) 309. Cf Case C-268/94 *Portuguese Republic v Council* [1996] ECR I-6177.

[14] Opinion 2/94, *supra* n. 13, at para. 30. Cf. *Brunner v European Union Treaty* [1994] 1 CMLR 57, at para. 99.

movement. Gender equality was protected by Article 141 EC and the legislation made thereunder.[15]

The ECJ's approach to fundamental rights was cloaked with legitimacy in a declaration of the three major Community institutions on 5 April 1977.[16] They emphasized the prime importance of fundamental rights, as derived in particular from the constitutions of the Member States and the ECHR, and stated that they would respect them in the exercise of their powers. This was followed by several other non-binding political initiatives. These included a Joint Declaration of the three institutions in 1986; various declarations and resolutions on racism and xenophobia by the European Council;[17] a Declaration of Fundamental Rights and Freedoms by the European Parliament in 1989;[18] a Community Charter of Fundamental Social Rights, signed by 11 of the then 12 Member States in 1989;[19] as well as references in the preamble to the Single European Act (SEA) to the ECHR, the European Social Charter, and to 'equality and social justice'.

The 'soft law' approach manifested in the preceding declarations was given added 'hard law' force by the Treaty on European Union (TEU). Article 177 EC provided that Community policy in relation to development cooperation 'shall contribute to the general objective of developing and consolidating democracy and the rule of law, and to that of respecting human rights and fundamental freedoms'. Article F(2) of the TEU, which was not at that stage justiciable, provided that the Union would respect the fundamental rights guaranteed by the ECHR and by national constitutional traditions. Respect for human rights and fundamental freedom was also mentioned in the two other pillars of the TEU.

The Amsterdam Treaty (ToA) made further changes. Article 6(1) TEU was strengthened. It had previously stated that the Union would respect fundamental rights etc. The amended provision declared that the Union 'is founded on' the principles of liberty, democracy, and respect for human rights and fundamental freedoms. Article 6(2), which stipulated that the Union should respect fundamental rights as guaranteed by the ECHR and as they result from the constitutional traditions of the Member States as general principles of law, was made justiciable by Article 46(d) TEU. The ECJ was given jurisdiction not only under the EC Treaty, but under any provision of the other two pillars over which it had been given jurisdiction (which was primarily pillar three), to review the conduct of the European institutions for

[15] Barnard, 'Gender Equality in the EU: A Balance Sheet', in Alston, *The EU and Human Rights, supra* n. 1, Chap. 8.

[16] OJ 1977 C103/1. See generally, Bradley, 'Reflections on the Human Rights Role of the European Parliament', in *The EU and Human Rights, supra* n. 1, Chap. 26.

[17] See e.g. OJ 1986 C158/1, Bull. EC 5–1990, 1.2.247, Bull. EC 6–1991, I.45, and Bull. EC 12–1991, I.19.

[18] OJ 1989 C120/51.

[19] COM(89) 471 Final. See Bull. EC 12–1989, 2.1.104.

compliance with these principles. Article 7 TEU as modified enabled the Council to suspend certain Member State rights' under the TEU, where it committed serious and persistent breach of the principles set out in Article 6(1) TEU. Following the ToA, respect for these fundamental principles has also been made a condition of application for membership of the European Union. The ToA also added an important new head of legislative competence. Article 13 EC provides that the Community legislature may, within the limits of the Community's powers, take 'appropriate action to combat discrimination based on sex, racial or ethnic origin, religion or belief, disability, age or sexual orientation'.[20] This enables the Community to adopt measures to combat such discrimination within the scope of the policies and powers otherwise granted in the Treaty.[21]

3. CONCERNS PRIOR TO THE CHARTER OF FUNDAMENTAL RIGHTS

Limits of space preclude detailed analysis of the concerns about the Community's protection of rights prior to the adoption of the Charter. Some discussion is nonetheless necessary in order to understand and place in perspective the emergence of the Charter itself.

A. Community Rights and National Differences

One such concern related to the difficulty of fashioning Community rights given the political, cultural, and ideological divergences between the Member States. The Member States might have different views as to what should be regarded as fundamental rights, and they might well differ on how those rights should be protected.[22] Thus while all states might agree that freedom of expression should be protected, they could have rather different views on how this should be done in a particular context.

The national legal systems vary, for example, in the degree to which they

[20] Flynn, 'The Implications of Article 13—After Amsterdam Will Some Forms of Discrimination be More Equal than Others?' (1999) 36 *CMLRev* 1127.

[21] De Búrca, 'The Role of Equality in European Community Law', in S. O'Leary and A. Dashwood, (eds), *The Principle of Equal Treatment in EC Law* (Sweet & Maxwell, 1997), 13–34.

[22] M. Cappelletti, *The Judicial Process in Comparative Perspective* (Clarendon Press, 1989), at 175, 381; de Búrca, 'The Language of Rights and European Integration', in J. Shaw and G. More, (eds), *New Legal Dynamics of the European Union* (Oxford University Press, 1995), at 29–54; O' Higgins, 'The Constitution and the Communities—Scope for Stress?', in J. O'Reilly (ed), *Human Rights and Constitutional Law* (Round Hall Press, 1992), at 227, 237–40.

regulate the nature and content of broadcasting.[23] Rights may well be divisive as well as cohesive. This is particularly so in relation to matters such as abortion, blasphemy, surrogacy, and the like, although the existence of a 'margin of appreciation' can serve to blunt these tensions, just as it does under the ECHR.[24] The very fact that legal systems may have differing conceptions of human rights, combined with the fact that these rights will normally be afforded constitutional status, led some to argue that the ECJ would have to adopt the maximum standard on offer from the Member States.[25] This view was, however, controversial.[26]

B. Taking Rights Seriously

A second concern was that the ECJ did not 'take rights seriously'. It was argued that the Court manipulated the language of rights while in reality advancing the commercial goals of the EC, that it was biased towards 'market rights' instead of protecting values which are genuinely fundamental to the human condition.[27] This view was vigorously contested.[28] It is true that claimants found it difficult to succeed when challenging the legality of Community norms for violation of fundamental rights. Many such claims were, however, factually weak and it is doubtful whether they would have been any more successful if brought before a national court. It was challenges to Member State action that provoked the most ire from those critical of the ECJ.

The argument that the Court favoured market rights over more traditional human values requires, however, more careful analysis than that accorded by the critics. The fact that the ECJ might balance some species of market right with a more traditional human value does not mean that the former will outweigh the latter. It is, moreover, mistaken to think of Treaty rights concerning free movement and the like attaching to individuals simply as factors of production. Community freedoms derived initially from a Treaty primarily concerned with economic integration can also have moral and social importance beyond their economic significance.[29] In any event the majority of these cases were concerned with Member State restriction of free movement rights on grounds of public policy or health. It was this restriction that had an adverse impact on an individual's civil right such as free speech.

[23] See R. Craufurd-Smith, *Broadcasting Law and Fundamental Rights* (Oxford University Press, 1997).

[24] Clapham, 'A Human Rights Policy for the European Community', *supra* n. 1, at 309, 311.

[25] Besselink, 'Entrapped by the Maximum Standard: On Fundamental Rights, Pluralism and Subsidiarity in the European Union' (1998) 35 *CMLRev* 629.

[26] Weiler, 'Fundamental Rights and Fundamental Boundaries', in Neuwahl and Rosas, *The European Union and Human Rights*, *supra* n. 1, at 51.

[27] Coppel and O'Neill, *supra* n. 1; Phelan, *supra* n. 1.

[28] Weiler and Lockhart, *supra* n. 1.

[29] De Búrca, *supra* n. 1.

C. Rights and General Principles

A further critique was a variant on the argument that the ECJ did not take rights seriously. It was argued that the ECJ conceived of fundamental rights in terms of general principles, and that it thereby accorded them less force than if they had been conceptualized specifically as rights, as they are within Member States.[30]

This critique is largely misconceived. It elides the conceptual basis through which the ECJ read fundamental rights into the Community legal order, with the interpretation of those rights within that order. The window through which fundamental rights were brought into EC law was as general principles of law. This was in accord with Article 6(1) TEU and Article 230 EC, the latter laying down the grounds for judicial review, which include breach of the Treaty or any rule of law relating to its application. Fundamental rights were regarded as one such rule of law, as were principles such as proportionality, legitimate expectations, and the like. However once they were read into the Treaty the fundamental rights were interpreted in the same general manner as they are in domestic legal orders.

The claim that there is some major difference between a 'specific requirements approach' and 'a general formula' is equally suspect. Under the former approach, each provision protecting a particular right will lay down specific requirements in order for the infringement of the right to be legal. Under the latter approach, a court will determine in general terms the weight to be given to the right in the light of other competing principles and in accord with proportionality. It has been shown that the specific requirements approach has proven to be impracticable within some national legal orders, and that in reality the courts adopt a general formula.[31]

D. The Relationship between the EC and the ECHR

The relationship between the EC and the ECHR in the sphere of human rights was another fertile source of comment. A number of different, albeit connected, points were made about this relationship. There was concern about the possibility of overlap and potential conflict between the pronouncements of the two courts. This happened on occasion,[32]

[30] Besselink, *supra* n. 25, at 633–638.

[31] Von Bogdandy, 'The European Union as a Human Rights Organization? Human Rights and the Core of the European Union' (2000) 37 *CMLRev* 1307, at 1330–1332.

[32] P. Craig and G de Búrca, *EU Law, Text, Cases and Materials* (Oxford University Press, 3rd ed., 2003), Chap. 8; Spielmann, 'Human Rights Case Law in the Strasbourg and Luxembourg Courts: Conflicts, Inconsistencies and Complementarities', in *The EU and Human Rights, supra* n. 1, Chap. 23.

although commentators differed as to how seriously they regarded this problem.[33]

There was the oft-voiced critique that the Community should be subject to the ECHR system. The ECJ's decision[34] denying that the EC had competence to accede without a Treaty amendment was subject to critical scrutiny. What appeared to place accession to the ECHR beyond the scope of Community competence, in the ECJ's view, was not the fact that it would entail concluding an agreement for the protection of fundamental rights. It was rather that the agreement would bring fundamental institutional and constitutional changes which would require a Treaty amendment, rather than Community legislation under Article 308 EC.[35] Analogous arguments did not, however, serve to prevent the ECJ holding that the EC could sign up to the WTO.[36] For many the real nub of the issue in relation to the ECHR was that the ECJ did not wish to be subject to a superior court in the form of the European Court of Human Rights. We shall return to the relationship between the EC and the ECHR in the following discussion.

E. The Need for a Coherent Human Rights Policy

The most far-reaching concern voiced prior to the Charter was the need for the Community to develop a more general, coherent human rights policy. In an important article[37] Alston and Weiler cast their net broadly in their overview of the achievements and shortcomings of Community policy on human rights. A dominant theme was the need to think beyond the judicial focus. They argued that excessive reliance had been placed on the power of

[33] Jacobs and White, *The European Convention on Human Rights* (Oxford University Press, 3rd ed., C. Ovey and R. White, 2002), at 442–447; P. Van Dijk and G. Van Hoof, *Theory and Practice of the European Convention on Human Rights* (Kluwer Law International, 3rd ed., 1998), at 18–21, 117; Clapham, 'A Human Rights Policy for the Community', *supra* n. 1, at 338.

[34] *Opinion 2/94, supra* n. 13.

[35] *The Human Rights Opinion of the ECJ and its Constitutional Implications* (Cambridge University CELS, Occasional Paper No.1, 1996).

[36] Weiler and Fries, 'A Human Rights Policy for the European Community and Union: The Question of Competences', in *The EU and Human Rights, supra* n. 1, Chap. 5.

[37] Alston and Weiler, 'An "Ever Closer Union" in Need of a Human Rights Policy: The European Union and Human Rights', in *The EU and Human Rights, supra* n. 1, Chap. 1. See also, von Bogdandy, 'The European Union as a Human Rights Organization: Human Rights and the Core of the European Union' (2000) 37 *CMLRev* 1307; de Búrca, 'Convergence and Divergence in European Public Law', in P. Beaumont, C. Lyons, and N. Walker (eds), *Convergence and Divergence in European Public Law* (Hart, 2002), Chap. 8; Beaumont, 'Human Rights: Some Recent Developments and Their Impact on Convergence and Divergence of Law In Europe', in *Convergence and Divergence, supra* n. 37, Chap. 9; Nic Shuibhne, 'The European Union and Fundamental Rights: Well in Spirit but Considerably Rumpled in Body?', in *Convergence and Divergence, supra* n. 37, Chap. 10.

legal prohibition and judicial enforcement. Their own focus was more institutional in nature.

They argued, *inter alia*, for the establishment of a Directorate General within the Commission with special responsibility for human rights; a monitoring agency; a specialist human rights unit for the Common Foreign and Security Policy (CFSP); that the European Parliament (EP) should have a Committee responsible for human rights; and that there should be improved access to the ECJ. The Community should, in their view, accede to the ECHR, and proper protection should be afforded to social rights, as well as traditional civil and political rights.

It is readily apparent that many of these specific points will continue to be of relevance whatever happens in terms of the legal status of the Community Charter. We shall therefore return to them in the course of the ensuing discussion.[38]

4. THE CHARTER OF FUNDAMENTAL RIGHTS OF THE EUROPEAN UNION: GENESIS

Whatever one might feel about the concerns raised in the preceding section, it was undeniable that protection of rights was fragmented and piecemeal, thereby making it more difficult for the citizenry to understand the legal status quo.[39] Moreover, the very fact that the scope of Community power had increased considerably made the promulgation of some form of Community bill of rights more pressing. It is a basic tenet of liberal democratic regimes that a *quid pro quo* for the power wielded by government is that there should be rights-based constraints on the exercise of that power. This fundamental idea is just as applicable to the EC as to traditional nation states. Thus even if the ECJ had not been 'pressed' into recognizing fundamental rights by the threat of revolt from the German and Italian courts, it would, in all likelihood, have realized the necessity for such limits on governmental power of its own accord.

While the ECJ laid the groundwork for rights-based protection, the framing of a Community Charter had a number of advantages. In substantive terms, it enabled considered thought to be given to the range of rights which should be recognized. In procedural terms, it enabled a spectrum of views to be taken into account, both governmental and non-governmental, thereby enhancing the legitimacy of the resulting document.[40]

[38] See below, at 539–543.

[39] A. Vitorino, *The Charter of Fundamental Rights as a Foundation for the Area of Freedom, Justice and Security* (Centre for European Legal Studies, Exeter Paper in European Law, No. 4, 2001), at 12–14.

[40] See, however, Weiler, 'Editorial: Does the European Union Truly Need a Charter of Rights?' (2000) 6 *ELJ* 95.

The immediate catalyst for the Charter of Fundamental Rights came from the European Council. In June 1999 the Cologne European Council[41] decided that there should be a European Union Charter of Fundamental Rights to consolidate the fundamental rights applicable at Union level and to make their overriding importance and relevance more visible to the citizens of the Union.[42] The Charter was to contain fundamental rights and freedoms, as well as the basic procedural rights guaranteed by the ECHR. It was to embrace the rights derived from the constitutional traditions common to the Member States that had been recognized as general principles of Community law. It was also made clear that the document should include economic and social rights.

The institutional structure for the discussions about the Charter was laid down in the Tampere European Council in October 1999.[43] It was decided to establish a body called the Convention. It consisted of representatives of the Member States, a member of the Commission, members of the EP, and representatives from national parliaments. The first meeting took place in December 1999. The Convention was instructed to conclude its work in time for the Nice European Council in December 2000. The discussion in the Convention was therefore conducted in parallel with the Intergovernmental Conference (IGC) concerning the institutional consequences of enlargement that led to the Nice Treaty.

The draft Charter was submitted by the Chairman of the Convention, Roman Herzog, to President Chirac, who held the Presidency of the European Council, on 5 October 2000.[44] It was considered at an informal meeting of the European Council at Biarritz on 14 October 2000.[45] The Charter was accepted, and this was reinforced at the Nice European Council. The Charter was drafted so as to be capable of being legally binding. The precise legal status of the Charter was, however, left undecided in Nice, a matter to be resolved at the next IGC in 2004. It is important, at this juncture, to stress two things about the Charter.

In substantive terms, the catalyst was the heads of state meeting in the European Council. Some of the press coverage painted the Charter as but yet another example of expansionism by some reified entity called the EU, with

[41] 3–4 June 1999.

[42] de Búrca, 'The Drafting of the European Charter of Fundamental Rights' (2001) 26 *ELRev* 126; Maduro, 'The Double Constitutional Life of the Charter of Fundamental Rights of the European Union', in T. Hervey and J. Kenner (eds), *Economic and Social Rights under the EU Charter of Fundamental Rights: A Legal Perspective* (Hart, 2003), at 272–276; de Búrca and Beatrix Aschenbrenner, 'European Constitutionalism and the Charter', in S. Peers and A. Ward (eds), *The EU Charter of Fundamental Rights, Politics, Law and Policy* (Hart, 2004), Chap. 1; J. Schonlau, *Drafting the EU Charter, Rights, Legitimacy and Process* (Palgrave, 2005).

[43] 15–16 October 1999.

[44] Charte 4960/00, Convent 55, 26 October 2000.

[45] Charte 4955/00, Convent 51, 17 October 2000.

the Commission playing a Machiavellian role in the process. This is wrong. The Commission was in favour of the initiative, but it was launched by the Member States. It was the Member States meeting in the European Council that set the broad terms for the Charter, more particularly the fact that it should include social and economic, as well as traditional civil rights, although it should also be acknowledged that this broad remit had been recommended by an independent group of experts in February 1999. Indeed given that the development of fundamental rights had hitherto been in the hands of the Community courts there is force in Maduro's observation that the drafting of the Charter represented 'the political process taking back into its own hands the definition of the system and catalogue of fundamental rights in the EU'.[46]

In procedural terms, the deliberations of the Convention were transparent with discussion papers readily available on the website. There were public meetings in which individuals, NGOs, and the like were invited to submit their views. It is moreover worth noting how much was achieved within such a short time. The Convention had to submit a document to the Nice European Council in December 2000. This meant that it had but one year in which to forge a far-reaching document that would be acceptable to the 15 Member States. In reality the period in which it had to complete its work was even shorter than this. The members of the Convention recognized that the Charter would have to be ready by autumn 2000, in order that it could be presented to the heads of state prior to the Nice European Council. The framing of the Charter has therefore much to commend it as an exercise in efficient and inclusive governance. This is so even though it can be accepted that the process was not perfect with regard to, for example, the inclusion of civil society or the power wielded by the Praesidium and Secretariat.[47]

5. THE CHARTER OF FUNDAMENTAL RIGHTS OF THE EUROPEAN UNION: CONTENT

There was, as might be imagined, considerable debate as to issues concerning the content of the Charter. Certain of these key issues will be considered in due course. It will, however, be easier to understand these points against the backdrop of the finished document.[48] A bare outline of the structure of the

[46] Maduro, *supra* n. 42, at 276.

[47] De Búrca, *supra* n. 42; de Búrca and Aschenbrenner, *supra* n. 42; de Schutter, 'Europe in Search of its Civil Society' (2002) 8 *ELJ* 198.

[48] Charter of Fundamental Rights of the European Union [2000] OJ C364/1.

Charter will be given here.[49] There will be more detailed discussion of selected issues below.[50]

Chapter I of the Charter has the title Dignity, and contains five articles. Article 1 states that human dignity is inviolable and that it must be respected and protected. Article 2 protects the right to life and outlaws the death penalty. The right to the integrity of the person is enshrined in Article 3. This covers physical and mental integrity, Article 3(1). It also deals with medical practices, forbidding, *inter alia*, cloning and eugenics. Torture and inhuman and degrading treatment or punishment is prohibited in Article 4. Article 5 prohibits slavery, forced labour, and the trafficking in human beings.

Chapter II of the Charter covers Freedoms, and contains 14 articles. The right to liberty and security of the person is guaranteed in Article 6; respect for private and family life in Article 7; protection of personal data, Article 8; the right to marry and found a family, Article 9; freedom of thought, conscience, and religion, Article 10; freedom of expression and information, Article 11; freedom of assembly and association, Article 12; freedom of the arts and sciences, Article 13; the right to education, Article 14; freedom to choose an occupation and the right to engage in work, Article 15; freedom to conduct a business, Article 16; the right to property, Article 17; the right to asylum, Article 18; and protection in the event of removal, expulsion, or extradition, Article 19.

Chapter III is entitled Equality. There are seven articles within this chapter. Equality before the law is covered by Article 20. Article 21(1) prohibits discrimination based on a variety of grounds such as sex, race, colour, and sexual orientation, while Article 21(2) prohibits discrimination on the ground of nationality. Respect for cultural, religious and linguistic diversity is dealt with in Article 22; gender equality in Article 23; children's rights, Article 24; the rights of the elderly, Article 25; and the integration of those with disabilities Article 26.

Chapter IV is concerned with Solidarity and contains 12 articles. Article 27 covers workers' right to information and consultation; Article 28 the right of collective bargaining; Article 29 right of access to placement services; Article 30 protection against unjustified dismissal; and Article 31 fair and just working conditions. Article 32 prohibits child labour and deals with protection of young people at work. Article 33 is concerned with the protection of

[49] Heringa and Verhey, 'The EU Charter: Text and Structure' (2001) 8 *MJ* 11; McCrudden, 'The Future of the EU Charter of Fundamental Rights' (Harvard Jean Monnet Working Paper No. 10/01); Lord Goldsmith, 'A Charter of Rights, Freedoms and Principles' (2001) 38 *CMLRev* 1201; Craig, 'The Community, Rights and the Charter' (2002) 14 *ERPL* 195.

[50] E. Eriksen, J. Fossum and A. Menéndez (eds), *The Chartering of Europe* (Arena Report No. 8/2001); K. Feus (ed), *An EU Charter of Fundamental Rights: Text and Commentaries* (Federal Trust, 2000); Hervey and Kenner, *supra* n. 42; Peers and Ward, *supra* n. 42.

family life and the reconciliation of work with the family. Article 34 deals with social security; Article 35 with health care; Article 36 with access to services of general economic interest; Article 37 with environmental protection; and Article 38 with consumer protection.

Chapter V is entitled Citizens' Rights, and has eight articles. The right of Union citizens to vote and stand for election to the EP is covered by Article 39, and the corresponding right to stand for municipal elections in Article 40. The right to good administration is enshrined in Article 41; access to documents in Article 42; the right to refer maladministration to the Ombudsman, Article 43; the right to petition the EP, Article 44; freedom of movement and residence, Article 45; and diplomatic protection, Article 46.

Chapter VI deals with aspects of Justice. There are four articles. The right to an effective remedy and fair trial is provided in Article 47, and the presumption of innocence in Article 48. The proscription of retrospective criminal penalties is dealt with in Article 49, and the right not to be punished twice for the same offence is found in Article 50.

Chapter VII contains four General Provisions which pertain to the Charter as a whole. Article 51(1) defines the scope of application of the Charter. It is addressed to the institutions and bodies of the Union with due regard to the principle of subsidiarity, and to Member States only when they are implementing Union law. Article 51(2) states that the Charter does not establish any new power or task for the Community or the Union, or modify powers and tasks defined by the Treaties.

The scope of the guaranteed rights is covered by Article 52. Article 52(1) contains the general limitation clause for the Charter. It stipulates that any limits on Charter rights must be provided by law, and respect the essence of the right or freedom. Subject to the principle of proportionality, limitations can only be made if they are necessary and genuinely meet objectives of general interest recognized by the Union or the need to protect the rights and freedoms of others. Article 52(2) states that Charter rights which are based on the Community Treaties or the EU Treaty shall be exercised under the same conditions and within the limits defined by those Treaties. The relationship with the ECHR is dealt with in Article 52(3). It provides that the meaning and scope of Charter rights which correspond to ECHR rights shall be the same as the ECHR rights. This is subject to the caveat that Union law can provide more extensive protection.

Article 53 addresses the 'level of protection' for rights, and is concerned with the relation between the Charter, national law, international law, and international agreements. It will be considered in detail below. The final provision of the Charter, Article 54, contains a prohibition on abuse of rights.

This chapter will not seek to consider the detailed interpretation of all rights contained in the Charter. That would require a book in itself, and such a book would be directly about human rights law. The principal focus of the discussion will rather be on the implications of the Charter for EU judicial review. This will be followed by consideration of ways in which human rights might be mainstreamed so as to be of more general relevance outside the litigation process.

6. THE CHARTER AND THE CONSTITUTIONAL TREATY

We have seen that the precise legal status of the Charter was left hanging by the Nice Treaty, the expectation being that it would be resolved at the next IGC. The issue was, however, addressed by the Convention on the Future of Europe that drafted the Constitutional Treaty (CT).[51]

Article I-9(1) of the CT stated that the Union shall recognize the rights, freedoms, and principles contained in the Charter. The intent was that the Union should be bound by the Charter, although the choice of the word 'recognize' was not the best suited to convey this. Article I-9(2) provided that the EU should accede to the ECHR, but that this should not affect the EU's competences as defined by the Constitution. Article I-9(3) conceptualized the fundamental rights derived from the ECHR and the constitutional traditions of the Member States as general principles of EU law. The substance of the Charter was incorporated as Part II of the Constitution.[52]

The Convention on the Future of Europe and subsequent IGC made some changes to the provisions of the Charter, most notably in relation to what is now termed Title VII dealing with general provisions. The relevant changes will be considered in the subsequent discussion.

The Member States agreed to the CT in 2004, but its entry into force was dependent on ratification in accord with the constitutional requirements of the Member States. The failure of the referenda in France and the Netherlands means that it is now very unlikely that the CT will come into effect, more especially because the ratification process in other countries was placed 'on hold' as a result of the two negative votes. The present legal status of the Charter of Fundamental Rights will be considered in more detail below.[53]

[51] Treaty Establishing a Constitution for Europe, OJ 2004 C310/1.

[52] The numbering of the Charter Articles was different from that given above, since it ran on directly from the numbering in Part I of the Constitution. Thus the first article of the Charter dealing with dignity became Article II-61 of the Constitution, with the other Charter articles being numbered seriatim.

[53] See below, at 538–539.

7. THE REACH OF THE CHARTER: UNION INSTITUTIONS, VERTICALITY, AND HORIZONTALITY

A. The Distinction

Charter rights seem only to have a vertical impact. Article 51(1) stipulates that the provisions of the Charter are addressed to the institutions and bodies of the Union with due regard for the principle of subsidiarity and to the Member States only when they are implementing Union law. Article II-111(1) of the Constitutional Treaty modified this formulation to make it clear that the Charter provisions applied to the institutions, bodies, offices, and agencies of the Union with due regard for subsidiarity and to Member States only when they are implementing Union law.

Treaty articles can, by way of contrast, have direct effect, which can be horizontal, binding private parties, as well as vertical, binding the state. The same is true for regulations and decisions. Directives, by way of contrast, can lead to vertical but not horizontal direct effect, although doctrines such as indirect effect and the like can produce similar results.[54]

The importance of this difference can be exemplified in the context of equality. Article 23 of the Charter stipulates that equality between men and women must be ensured in all areas, including employment, work, and pay. It will in accord with Article 51(1) of the Charter have a vertical impact and bind the Union institutions and the Member States when they are implementing Union law. It will not be binding on private parties such as employers. The most closely proximate Treaty provision is Article 141 EC, which has both vertical and horizontal direct effect, with the consequence that it can be relied on against the state and private parties.[55]

While the Charter appears to have only a vertical dimension we should pause to consider a more radical reading of Article 51(1). It provides that Charter rights are addressed to, *inter alia*, Union institutions, which must respect the rights, observe the principles, and promote the application thereof. The paradigm that comes to mind is of course Community legislation or executive action that infringes a right, with a subsequent annulment action brought by the aggrieved individual. This is the classic vertical application of constitutional rights to protect private autonomy.

It should, however, be noted that the Community courts are Union institutions and are bound to 'respect the rights, observe the principles and promote the application thereof in accordance with their respective powers'.

[54] Craig and de Búrca, *supra* n. 32, Chap. 5.

[55] There are differences in the wording between Art. 141 EC and Art. 23 of the Charter, but they do not alter the point being made in the text.

There is nothing that expressly limits this obligation to cases brought against public authorities, whether at Union or national level. It might therefore be argued that this obligation is equally applicable where an individual seeks to rely on a Charter right against another private individual, provided of course that the subject matter falls within EU law. If this were the case then the Charter would have direct horizontal effect or something pretty close thereto.

This reading might, however, seem too radical. It could be argued that if this were the intent then the Article could have been drafted explicitly to make this clear. There is nothing in the explanatory memorandum to give the impression of direct horizontal effect.[56] The analysis presented above might, however, be accepted in a somewhat weaker form as the justification for indirect horizontal effect, in the manner discussed below.

B. The Normative Argument

Any legal system that protects fundamental rights will have to decide how far those protections are to apply. The view that protections for rights should only apply vertically is premised, as Hunt has argued, on a 'rigid distinction between the public and private sphere and presupposes that the purpose of fundamental rights protection is to preserve the integrity of the private sphere against coercive intrusion by the state'.[57] Legal relations between individuals are, by way of contrast, seen as part of private autonomy, with the consequence that the choices individuals make about how to live their lives and deal with each other should not be dictated by the state.

The view that rights-based protections should apply even as between private parties is premised ultimately on the hypothesis that all legal relations are constituted by the state, in the sense that the law itself is constructed and supported by the state.[58] Viewed from this perspective, choices are constantly being made and expressed through legal rules as to the limits on private freedom of action. Legal rules frequently impose limits on private choice whether in the sphere of contract, tort, property, or restitution.

When the matter is viewed in this light the formal divide between the public and private sphere begins to crumble. The issue becomes which types of restraint on private action are felt to be normatively warranted. It becomes more difficult to argue that rights-based protections should have no application in the private sphere, more especially since power which is nominally

[56] Charte 4473/00, Convent 49, 11 October 2000, at 46; CONV 828/03, Updated Explanations Relating to the Text of the Charter of Fundamental Rights, 9 July 2003, at 45–46.

[57] Hunt, 'The "Horizontal Effect" of the Human Rights Act' [1998] *PL* 423, at 424.

[58] A. Clapham, *Human Rights in the Private Sphere* (Oxford University Press, 1993); P. Alston (ed), *Non-State Actors and Human Rights* (Oxford University Press, 2005).

private may be just as potent as power which is formally public. Even if constitutional rights are applied horizontally this does not mean that there would be no difference in the way in which they would be interpreted in public and private contexts.

The Charter embodies a choice in this respect and the choice seems to be to accord the rights only a vertical dimension, subject to the possible more radical reading considered above. This is readily explicable in 'political' terms. There is little doubt that agreement on the Charter would have been considerably more difficult if its scope or field of application had been horizontal as well as vertical. This is especially so given the broad range of rights included in the Charter. The 'solution' embodied in Article 51(1) does, however, give rise to a number of tensions if it is read as being restricted to the vertical dimension.

There is an uneasy tension in normative terms between the solely vertical scope of the Charter rights, when compared to the vertical and horizontal scope of some Treaty articles.[59] The very fact that the comparable Treaty article is thought suited to a horizontal as well as a vertical application makes it seem odd that the analogous Charter right is limited to a vertical impact. It could be argued by way of response that the distinction is justified since Treaty articles will only have horizontal direct effect if they satisfy the requirements of that doctrine, which include clarity as to the obligation imposed on the private party. There are, however, many Charter rights that would satisfy this criterion and it could in any event be made a condition for horizontal application of Charter rights.

There is furthermore a strain between those Charter rights that do have some readily identifiable provision in other parts of the Treaty, and those that do not. Where there is some comparable provision with horizontal direct effect the individual can at least rely on it in an action against another private party. This is perforce not possible where there is no readily identifiable provision in the Treaty that deals with the same subject matter as the Charter right.

There is moreover an uneasy practical tension between the vertical scope of the Charter and the wording of some of the rights contained therein. Thus Article 24(2) provides that 'in all actions relating to children, whether taken by public authorities or private institutions, the child's best interests must be a primary consideration'. The Article imposes a substantive obligation on, *inter alia*, private institutions, even though the general field of application of the Charter is limited to Union institutions and Member States when implementing Union law. This tension might

[59] There may be reasons why certain Treaty articles do not have horizontal direct effect flowing from the nature of those articles and their interrelationship with other Treaty articles, as exemplified by Art. 28 EC dealing with free movement of goods.

be reconciled by allowing an action to compel a public body to ensure that the private institution complies with the obligation contained in this Article. The issue might be addressed more generally by considering ways in which Charter rights might have an impact on private parties, notwithstanding the limits imposed by Article 51(1). It is to this issue that we now turn.

C. The Distinction Qualified

It is clear that a legal system may decline to afford 'direct horizontal effect' to rights contained in a constitutional document, but may be willing nonetheless to give them some limited 'indirect horizontal effect'. Canadian and German jurisprudence both indicate that the values and principles enshrined in the protection of rights may have an influence on the rules applicable as between private parties.[60] There are signs of similar development in the UK where such rights can be used to help shape the development of, for example, the rules in a particular area of private law.[61]

It would therefore be possible in principle for courts to use Charter rights as interpretative guides when construing the rules applicable as between private parties. It should be noted that Article 51(1) states that the Charter provisions are addressed to, *inter alia*, Union institutions, which must 'respect the rights, observe the principles and promote the application thereof'. The Community courts are clearly Union institutions and are therefore bound by this precept. There is moreover nothing to suggest that this precept is only relevant when a case involves a public authority. It could be argued that giving Charter rights a degree of indirect horizontal effect fits with the injunction that Charter rights should be respected, observed, and promoted. A similar argument could be made in relation to national courts. Member States are bound by the Charter when implementing Union law. This includes national courts, which would therefore also be subject to the injunction to respect, observe, and promote the application of Charter rights, irrespective of whether the case involves a public authority or not.

[60] Hunt, *supra* n. 57; Markesinis, 'Privacy, Freedom of Expression and the Horizontal Effect of the Human Rights Bill: Lessons from Germany' (1998) 114 *LQR* 47.

[61] Young, 'Remedial and Substantive Horizontality: The Common Law and *Douglas v Hello! Ltd*' [2002] *PL* 232; Phillipson, 'The Human Rights Act, "Horizontal Effect" and the Common Law: A Bang or a Whimper' (1999) 62 *MLR* 824.

8. THE REACH OF THE CHARTER: MEMBER STATES, VERTICALITY, AND HORIZONTALITY

A. The Meaning of Implementation

The discussion in the previous section touched on the reach of the Charter in relation to the Member States. This issue must now be examined in more detail. Article 51(1) states that the Charter provisions are addressed to the Member States only when they are implementing Union law. Various formulations of the circumstances in which Member States would be bound by Charter provisions were put forward in the Convention that drafted the Charter.[62] The meaning of the word 'implementing' is crucial in the current formulation.

The narrow interpretation would be that Member States are only bound by the Charter when they are acting as agents in the application of EU law in the classic *Wachauf* type of case.[63] On this view the Charter provisions would only bite on the Member States in circumstances of shared administration of the kind discussed in detail above.[64] The Charter would not be applicable in other instances where the Community courts had held that the fundamental rights' jurisprudence bound the Member States. There is some support for a narrow interpretation in the literature, although commentators differ as to how narrow it should be.[65]

This interpretation would, however, be regrettable in normative terms. It would lead to formalistic distinctions between situations where Member States act as agents for the Union, where they would be bound by the Charter, and situations where the Member States apply Union law in the absence of such an agency relationship, where they would not be bound. This makes little sense in terms of principle.

It is clear, moreover, that the narrow interpretation is not necessitated by the wording of Article 51(1). The explanation attached to Article 51(1) made it evident that the wording was intended to reflect the existing corpus of ECJ jurisprudence. Thus the explanatory memorandum stated that 'as regards the Member States, it follows unambiguously from the case law of the Court of Justice that the requirement to respect fundamental rights defined in a Union context is only binding on the Member States when they act in the *context of*

[62] De Búrca, *supra* n. 42, at 136–138.

[63] Case 5/88, *Wachauf*, *supra* n. 9.

[64] See above, Chap. 3.

[65] Besselink, 'The Member States, the National Constitutions and the Scope of the Charter' (2001) 8 *MJ* 68; Thym, 'Charter of Fundamental Rights: Competition or Consistency of Human Rights Protection in Europe?' [2002] *Finnish Yearbook of International Law* 11; Arnull, 'From Charter to Constitution and Beyond: Fundamental Rights in the New European Union' [2003] *PL* 774, at 780–781.

Community law'.[66] This reading is reinforced by the updated explanatory memorandum on the Charter of Rights produced by the Convention on the Future of Europe when drafting the CT.[67] This memorandum stated in relation to Article 51 that 'it follows unambiguously from the case law of the Court of Justice that the requirement to respect fundamental rights defined in a Union context is only binding on the Member States when they act *in the scope of Union law*.'[68] The memorandum cited *Wachauf*,[69] *ERT*,[70] and *Annibaldi*[71] for this proposition, and then continued by stating that the ECJ 'confirmed' this case law in *Karlsson*[72] when it held that the protection of fundamental rights was also binding on the Member States when they implemented Community rules. The message from these explanatory memoranda is therefore that Member States are bound by fundamental rights when they act in the scope of Union law, and that the phrase 'implementing Union law' is intended to capture the various senses in which Member States could be said to be acting in the scope of Union law.

This must surely be right in terms of existing law and in terms of principle. On this view the Member States are bound by the Charter when they act in the scope of Union law, and the phrase in Article 51(1) of the Charter should be interpreted accordingly. It signals that Member States are bound to observe the Charter rights only when EU law is applicable to the instant case. This fits with the fact that the ECJ tends to use the phrase 'implementing Community rules' as synonymous with Member State rules that fall within the scope of Community law,[73] and with the views of a number of academic commentators.[74] It means that Member States should be bound to respect Charter rights whenever they act in the scope of EU law.

[66] Charte 4473/00, Convent 49, 11 October 2000, at 46. Emphasis added. The EP is of the same view, <http://www.europarl.eu.int/comparl/libe/elsj/charter/art51/default_en.htm>.

[67] CONV 828/03, Updated Explanations Relating to the Text of the Charter of Fundamental Rights, 9 July 2003, at 46–47.

[68] Ibid. at 45. Emphasis added.

[69] Case 5/88, *Wachauf*, *supra* n. 9.

[70] Case C-260/89, *ERT*, *supra* n. 10.

[71] Case C-309/96, *Annibaldi v Sindaco del Commune di Guidonia and Presidente Regione Lazio* [1997] ECR I-7493.

[72] Case C-292/97, *Kjell Karlsson* [2000] ECR I-2737.

[73] Case C-442/00, *Caballero v Fondo de Garantia Salarial (Fogasa)* [2002] ECR I-11915, at paras. 29–30.

[74] Schwarze, 'A German View on the European Charter of Fundamental Rights: Effect on the *Bundesverfassungsgericht*' (2001) 3 *CYELS* 407, 410; Alonso Garcia, 'The General Provisions of the Charter of Fundamental Rights' (2002) 8 *ELJ* 492, at 495–496; Maduro, *supra* n. 42, at 290–291; Eeckhout, 'The EU Charter of Fundamental Rights and the Federal Question' (2002) 39 *CMLRev* 945.

B. Scope of Application

If we accept that Member States are bound to respect Charter rights when they act in the scope of EU law this still leaves open the more specific types of case covered by this general precept.

The Charter will be applicable when the Member States act as agents for the EU in the context of shared administration in the classic *Wachauf* type of case.[75] It will also apply when the Member States seek to take advantage of a derogation from EU law, as exemplified by *ERT*.[76]

The Charter should in principle also apply to Member States when their action falls within the bounds of a Treaty article, regulation, or decision. This might or might not sound startling depending on the reader's perspective. It is, however, based on sound principle: if a Member State's attempt to derogate from a Treaty article is subject to Charter precepts, then *a fortiori* so too should Member State compliance with the primary Treaty article, regulation, or decision itself. Thus if a Member State acting in the area of free movement of goods has national provisions that arguably infringe, for example, the right to protection for personal data then this Charter right should be capable of being raised by the affected individual. Similarly, where Member State action is covered by free movement of persons then it should be open to the affected individual to argue that, for example, the national provisions violate respect for private and family life. The proposition argued for here is perfectly consistent with cases such as *Kremzow*[77] and *Annibaldi*:[78] the claimant would still have to show a sufficient connection between the Charter right allegedly infringed and a particular area of EU law in order to justify the conclusion that the Member State action fell within the scope of Union law.

The Charter should also be applicable when a Member State implements a directive. We need to tread carefully here. The ECJ held in the past that duties imposed by a directive on Member States should be read in the light of general principles of Community law, although it had stopped short of saying that they are binding as such on the Member States when adopting measures to transpose a directive.[79] It is of course true that a directive will leave the manner and form of implementation to the Member States. It is nonetheless clear that the Member States have an obligation to implement directives, and thus if the choice of form and methods are felt to violate a Charter right then this should be capable of being raised in the national or Community courts. This reading is reinforced by the fact that the Community courts will oversee the choice of form and methods so as to ensure that they achieve the

[75] Case 5/88, *Wachauf, supra* n. 9. [76] Case C-260/89, *ERT, supra* n. 10.

[77] Case C-299/95, *Kremzow v Austrian State* [1997] ECR I-2629.

[78] Case C-309/96, *Annibaldi, supra* n. 71.

[79] Case 36/75, *Rutili* [1975] ECR 1219; Case 222/84, *Johnston, supra* n. 8.

substantive ends stipulated by the directive. It is, as de Witte states,[80] difficult to argue that the choice of form and methods of implementation should include the choice of whether to violate a fundamental right, and natural by way of contrast to argue that respect for fundamental rights should be regarded as an implicit part of the result to be achieved under the directive.

The ECJ has now taken this step in *Caballero.*[81] It held in essence that where a directive left the definition of 'pay' to a Member State, the meaning accorded to that term had to comply with the requirements of Community law, and these requirements included fundamental rights. The Member States were therefore bound by Community fundamental rights when they implemented Community law, in this instance through a directive, the ECJ reasoning by analogy from the *ERT* case. This paradigmatic case must be distinguished from the situation where the directive seeks merely to impose minimum standards, and does not prevent Member States from imposing more stringent standards. In this situation the Member State when imposing more stringent standards is not operating in the context of EU law and hence would not be bound by Charter rights.

C. Verticality and Horizontality

It should also be recognized that the preceding discussion about verticality and horizontality is relevant in relation to Member States as well as Union institutions. It is clear in principle that the obligation on Member States in Article 51(1) applies to central authorities, regional and local bodies, and the explanatory memorandum is cast in these terms.[82] The obligation must also be incumbent on national courts, which would have the duty to 'respect the rights, observe the principles and promote the application thereof in accordance with their respective powers'.

It would then be open to an individual to raise a Charter right in an action against a national public body on the ground that it had, for example, breached a Charter right in the way that it had chosen to implement a directive. Whether a Charter right could be invoked in an action against another individual before a national court in circumstances where EU law was applicable raises the same issue about horizontality considered above. The 'radical reading' of Article 51(1) would countenance this, but the objections to this reading given above would be equally pertinent here. The argument in favour of some measure of indirect horizontal effect would, however, be equally applicable.

[80] De Witte, *supra* n. 2, at 873.

[81] Case C-442/00, *Caballero, supra* n. 73, at paras. 29–32. See also, Cases C-465/00, 138 and 139/01, *Rechsnungshof, supra* n. 7.

[82] Charte 4473/00, Convent 49, 11 October 2000, at 46.

9. THE REACH OF THE CHARTER: EXISTING EU LAW AND COMPETENCE

There was concern during the negotiations that led to the Charter that it might broaden the scope of EU competence or power. The concern was addressed by Article 51(2), which stipulated that the Charter does not establish any new power or task for the Community or Union, or modify powers and tasks defined by the Treaties. This was reaffirmed by Working Group II at the Convention on the Future of Europe, which proposed to make this clearer through an amendment to Article 51(2).[83] Article II–111(2), the corresponding provision in the CT, stated that this 'Charter does not extend the field of application of Union law beyond the powers of the Union or establish any new power or task for the Union, or modify powers and tasks defined in the other Parts of the Constitution'. The 'fit' between these provisions and the substantive provisions of the Charter may be questioned.[84] Much turns on the precise meaning accorded to the key words 'power or task'.

These words could be interpreted to mean a new head of *legislative competence*. If viewed in this way Article 51(2) prohibits construction of the Charter such as to afford new or modified legislative competence to the Union.[85] The application of this precept will itself be problematic given the uncertainties concerning competence under the existing Treaties.[86] It is, however, important to note that the denial of new heads of legislative competence would not preclude, for example, claims to new social entitlements from the EU 'on the basis of fundamental social rights so long as those claims can be satisfied through the exercise of an existing competence'.[87]

It is moreover clear that the Charter *will add to the matters that can be taken into account when determining the legality of Community action*. It can be accepted that the fact that the Charter, for example, protects religious freedom in Article 10 will not of itself accord the EU any new legislative competence in this area, although it may exercise such competence as it has under existing provisions such as Article 13 EC. The recognition of freedom of religion in Article 10 will nonetheless be relevant in assessing the legality of Community legislation where that legislation does not seek to regulate religion as such, but may be felt to impinge directly or indirectly on the

[83] CONV 354/02, Final Report of Working Group II, 22 October 2002, at 5.

[84] Maduro, *supra* n. 42, at 277.

[85] See Charte 4423/00, Convent 46, 31 July 2000, at 35; Charte 4473/00, Convent 49, 11 October 2000, at 46–47.

[86] For discussion of difficulties of the competence provisions in the CT see, Craig, 'Competence: Clarity, Conferral, Containment and Consideration' (2004) 29 *ELRev* 323.

[87] Maduro, *supra* n. 42, at 286 and 289.

protected right. This is equally true of all Charter rights. The point is especially significant in relation to those rights that were wholly or partly based on international conventions and the like rather than primarily on existing Treaty provisions.[88] Thus Article 24, concerned with the protection of children, was said to be based on the New York Convention on the Rights of the Child 1989, which had been ratified by the Member States. It seems that the provision within the Article that children may express their views freely could affect the legality of Community or state action. It is, however, doubtful whether there would be a ground for such reasoning under existing EU law. The same point can be made about other Charter provisions, such as the proscription of eugenics and cloning contained in Article 3.[89] These rights could affect the interpretation and validity of Union acts that are alleged to infringe them.

The *Charter might also have a validating rather than potentially invalidating impact on the legality of Community action.* Thus Article 51(2) would make it difficult for the EU to adopt legislation specifically requiring the social partners or Comité Européen de Normalisation (CEN) and Comité Européen de Normalisation Electrotechnique CENELEC to observe fundamental rights, but it would not necessarily preclude attaching human rights considerations based on the Charter to action founded on other competences. It would, as Bernard states, be possible for the Council in deciding whether to adopt a Community act to implement an agreement between the social partners under Article 139 EC 'to consider whether the agreement complies with the Charter', and when mandating CEN or CENELEC to adopt standards to implement directives 'it would be appropriate to include human rights clauses in the contract, where relevant'.[90]

It is moreover clear that the line between *prohibition* and *positive action* can be a fine one. The ECHR jurisprudence contains several instances where a basic prohibition is held to generate a duty of positive action on the part of the relevant state authorities.[91] The relevant right might not generate legislative competence, but it might well require some positive action by Union and/or Member State authorities to safeguard the right in question. There is some recognition of a positive duty to act on the EU institutions to protect fundamental rights, but this was in the context of a Community scheme that gave a discretionary power to act, the ECJ taking

[88] See, eg, Arts. 1, 3, 8, 18, 12(1), 21(1), 24, 49.

[89] Charte 4473/00, at 5, where the source of this provision is said to be the Convention on Human Rights and Biomedicine. However as of January 2001 only ten Member States had signed the Convention and only three had ratified it.

[90] Bernard, 'A "New Governance" Approach to Economic, Social and Cultural Rights in the EU', in Hervey and Kenner, *supra* n. 42, at 260.

[91] See *infra* n. 101, 102, 103.

the view that this power should be triggered where fundamental rights were at stake.[92]

10. CHARTER INTERPRETATION: RIGHTS AND PRINCIPLES

A. The Rationale for the Divide

The classic form of rights-based action is for an individual to rely on a provision in the Charter in order to challenge the legality of a legislative, executive, or administrative norm, and to do so via judicial review either directly or indirectly. This will be the paradigm for many cases where reliance is placed on the Charter. Certain Charter provisions may, however, be held to embody principles rather than rights, and this may have consequences for judicial review.

The catalyst for discussion of the rights–principles dichotomy was the broad range of rights, political, social, and economic, enshrined in the Charter, in accord with the remit given to the Convention established to draft the Charter by the European Council in Cologne and Tampere. There was, not surprisingly, much discussion within the Convention about the structure of the Charter as a whole,[93] and the particular place of social and economic rights therein.[94]

The issue was addressed directly by Commissioner Vitorino, the Commission representative to the Convention that drafted the Charter.[95] He distinguished between rights enforceable in the courts and principles that could be relied on against official authorities, and said that this was the basis for a consensus in the Convention, particularly as regards social rights. The Commissioner argued that rights could be pleaded directly in the courts. Principles, by way of contrast, were mandatory in relation to the authorities which had to comply with them when exercising their powers, and could be used as a basis for censuring their acts. Private individuals would not, however, be able to bring a legal action to enforce them.

Vitorino admitted that the Charter did not state explicitly what was to be regarded as a right and a principle. He concluded, however, that there is 'a right where the holder is clearly designated and that there is a principle where the Union is referred to as having to respect or recognize a specific value such

[92] Case C-68/95, *T. Port GmbH & Co KG v Bundesanstalt für Landwirtschaft und Ernahrung* [1996] ECR I-6065, at paras. 37–41.

[93] See, e.g., Charte 4428/00, Contrib 282, 20 July 2000; Charte 4423/00, Convent 46, 31 July 2000; Charte 4470/00, Convent 47, 14 September 2000.

[94] See, e.g., Charte 4383/00, Convent 41, 3 July 2000; Charte 4401, Contrib 258, 4 July 2000.

[95] Vitorino, *supra* n. 39, at 25–26.

as a healthy environment or protection of consumers'.[96] Future practice and case law would, he said, refine this dichotomy. This same issue was addressed, albeit indirectly, by the Convention in two explanatory memorandums.[97] Thus health care and access to services of general economic interest were, for example, said to be principles and not rights.

This issue was addressed again in Working Group II of the Convention on the Future of Europe, which considered the issue of rights. It recommended a modification to the effect that provisions of the Charter that contained principles might be implemented by legislative and executive acts taken by the EU institutions, and by acts of the Member States when implementing EU law. They were, however, to be judicially cognizable only in the interpretation of such acts when ruling on their legality.[98] It would be for the ECJ to decide as to which articles fell into the categories of rights and principles.

The suggestions of Commissioner Vitorino and the Working Group were taken up in the final version of the CT. Article 52 of the Charter, renumbered as Article II–112 of the CT, was amended by the addition of Article II–112(5), which stated:

> The provisions of this Charter which contain principles may be implemented by legislative and executive acts taken by institutions, bodies, offices and agencies of the Union, and by acts of Member States when they are implementing Union law, in the exercise of their respective powers. They shall be judicially cognisable only in the interpretation of such acts and in the ruling on their legality.

It is, as noted earlier, very unlikely that the CT will enter into force. The modifications made to the Charter may, however, be incorporated in a revised version, which is then made binding. Even if this does not occur it is possible that the Community courts will employ some form of distinction between rights and principles when interpreting the Charter, more especially because it is mentioned in Article 51(1). It is therefore worth pressing further to explore the nature and impact of this distinction.

B. The Nature of the Divide

There are Charter provisions, such as that concerned with consumer protection, which by its wording is indicative of a principle and not a right, since Article 38 merely states that the Union shall ensure a high level of consumer protection. We must, however, resist falling into two common errors when thinking about the divide between rights and principles.

[96] Ibid. at 26.

[97] Charte 4423/00, Convent 46, 31 July 2000, at 24; Charte 4473/00, Convent 49, 11 October 2000, at 31–32.

[98] CONV 354/02, Final Report of Working Group II, 22 October 2002, at 8.

It is tempting to think that there is an equation between rights and the civil and political Charter provisions, and principles and the social/economic provisions of the Charter. This would be mistaken. The matter is more complex.[99] A great many of the Charter provisions dealing with social matters can properly be thought of as rights, capable of individual legal enforcement. The following are merely examples. The injunction in Article 29 that everyone has the right to a free placement service provides one such example. There is no reason why an individual should not be able to bring a legal rights-based claim against a state that sought to charge for such services. The same is true for the right to working conditions which respect the health, safety, and dignity of the worker, Article 31. This is amenable to an individual rights-based legal claim by a particular worker that, for example, the conditions of his employment by the Community were unsafe. The injunction against unfair dismissal in Article 30 provides a further example. This provision, like a number of others, stipulates that this protection operates in accordance with 'Union law and national law and practices'. This is, however, simply a recognition that there is a shared competence between the Community and the Member State on this issue. It does not preclude interpretation of the relevant Article as an enforceable right. Thus if a state agency was implementing Community law and dismissed a worker in breach of relevant Union law or national law, it would violate the Article. There is no reason why this should not be cognizable by a court as a legal right.

It is equally tempting to think in terms of an equation between rights and prohibition, and principles and positive action. This too would be mistaken. It is true that the classic response to an individual rights claim is to prohibit the state or Community from intruding on the protected sphere of private autonomy defined by the right. It is equally true that there are principles that require positive action, by the legislative or executive branch of government, such that failure to take the requisite action is a cause for censure, but not the basis for a legal action. It is nonetheless clear that a right can be infringed by inaction as well as action,[100] and that protection of a right can require positive action on the part of the state or other public body. The ECHR jurisprudence provides ample examples of the derivation of positive obligations from the Convention rights.[101] The positive obligation imposed on the state

[99] Alston, 'The Contribution of the EU Fundamental Rights Agency to the Realization of Economic and Social Rights', in P. Alston and O. de Schutter (eds), *Monitoring Fundamental Rights in the EU, The Contribution of the Fundamental Rights Agency* (Hart, 2005), at 161–165.

[100] See, e.g. Human Rights Act 1998, s. 6(6).

[101] Van Dijk and van Hoof, *supra* n. 33, at 494, 500–502, 508–509, 517, 534–536; A. Mowbray, *The Development of Positive Obligations under the European Convention on Human Rights by the European Court of Human Rights* (Hart, 2004).

may be designed to ensure the effective exercise of the right.[102] It may require the state to act so as to prevent a third party from interfering with the right.[103] The Strasbourg case law has been mainly concerned with positive obligations in the context of civil or political rights, since that is the principal remit of the ECHR. The same arguments could readily be made in relation to the civil rights in the Charter, and there is no reason why positive obligations could not attach to Charter social rights. The argument would, of course, have to be considered on its merits in relation to the particular social right in question, but there is no reason in principle why it should not be accepted. If, for example, an employer were to dismiss employees for seeking to conclude a collective agreement, the state could, pursuant to Article 28, have a positive obligation to secure this right against the actions of the private party.[104]

The Community courts will undoubtedly have to decide which of the provisions contained in the Charter are enforceable as individual rights, and which merely enshrine principles directed to the political institutions. Such decisions will have to be made in relation to each provision of the Charter. We should, however, dispel any notion that a general divide can be made between civil/political rights, and social/economic rights.

C. The Consequences of the Divide

It is equally important to be clear about the consequences of the distinction between rights and principles for the purposes of judicial review. It is likely that the Community courts will read the rights–principles distinction into the Charter even though the CT is very unlikely to be ratified. There is foundation for doing so in terms of the wording of Article 51(1), which mentions principles as well as rights. We must however be careful when elaborating the consequence of the distinction.

Charter provisions that are deemed to be rights will be judicially enforceable by individuals in the classic form set out above. They will be able to challenge EU norms on the basis that they have, for example, violated the right to free speech, conscience, or assembly.

[102] See, e.g., *Airey v Ireland* (1979–1980) 2 EHRR 305; *Markcx v Belgium* (1979–1980) 2 EHRR 330.

[103] See, e.g., *X and Y v Netherlands* (1986) 8 EHRR 235; *Lopez Ostra v Spain* (1995) 20 EHRR 513; *Plattform 'Arzte fur das Leben' v Austria* (1991) 13 EHRR 204; *Young, James and Webster v United Kingdom* (1982) 4 EHRR 38.

[104] The converse argument succeeded before the Strasbourg Court in *Young, James and Webster, supra* n. 103, where the Court accepted that the state could be required, under Article 11, to take action to prevent an employer from dismissing employees who did not wish to join a union.

Charter provisions characterized as principles, such as consumer protection, guide legislative and executive action at Union level, and by Member States when implementing Union law. They are judicially cognizable only when the Community courts interpret such acts and rule on their legality.[105]

This divide may, however, be less clear cut than might initially be thought. In both instances individuals will commonly be seeking to challenge Community norms, whether of a legislative or executive nature. Where such a norm is felt to violate a Charter right this will constitute the individual's cause of action in the judicial review claim. Where a Charter norm is characterized as a principle the individual will still be able to argue that the legislative or executive norm should be interpreted in the way best designed to enhance, for example, consumer protection.

It would, moreover, be open to a court so minded to 'interpret' a Community norm that it felt gave insufficient attention to consumer protection in such a way as to enhance that protection even where there was little in the way of ambiguity in the challenged measure. The same result might be achieved indirectly. If the substance and tenor of Article II–112(5) of the CT is incorporated in a revised version of the Charter or if it is read into the Charter through judicial interpretation then principles will be judicially cognizable in the interpretation of legislative and executive acts, *and* in the ruling on their legality. It might then be possible for a claimant who felt that the measure gave insufficient consumer protection to contest its legality on the basis of proportionality, even where it was not ambiguous.

11. CHARTER INTERPRETATION: THE GENERAL LIMITATION CLAUSE

It should be acknowledged at the outset that the precise test for limitation of rights currently applied by the Community courts is not absolutely clear. The relevant case law will be analysed in detail in the context of the discussion of proportionality and rights in a later chapter.[106] Suffice it to say for the present that the general test applied by the ECJ is that such a limitation is allowed provided that it corresponds to objectives of general interest pursued by the Community and does not constitute, with regard to the aim pursued, a disproportionate and unreasonable interference that undermines the very substance of the right.[107] Having said this, it is clear that the ECJ has on

[105] CONV 828/03, Updated Explanations, *supra* n. 67, at 51.

[106] See below, Chap. 17.

[107] Case 5/88, *Wachauf, supra* n. 9, at para. 18; Case C-292/97, *Kjell Karlsson, supra* n. 72, at para. 45.

occasion sometimes applied the Community test for limitation of rights, while on others it has employed a test closer to that used by the ECHR.[108]

A high profile example of the ECJ's approach to the limitation of rights is provided by *Schmidberger*.[109] The Austrian government gave implicit permission for a demonstration by an environmental group on the Brenner motorway, the effect of which was to close it for 30 hours. Schmidberger ran a transport firm and argued that the closure of the motorway was in breach of EU law on free movement of goods. The issue before the ECJ was the relation between Article 28 EC on free movement, and freedom of expression and assembly as protected by Articles 10 and 11 of the ECHR and the Austrian Constitution.

The ECJ reaffirmed that Article 28 EC required the state to refrain from imposing obstacles to free movement of goods itself, and also to take all necessary action to ensure that free movement was not impeded by the acts of private parties.[110] The failure by the Austrian government to ban the demonstration was therefore *prima facie* a breach of Article 28 EC, unless it could be objectively justified.[111] The justification proffered by the government was respect for the right to freedom of expression and assembly guaranteed by the ECHR and the Austrian Constitution.

The ECJ accepted this justification. It held that Member States and the Community were both required to respect fundamental rights, and that therefore those rights could justify a restriction of other Community obligations, even a fundamental freedom such as free movement of goods.[112] The ECJ noted, however, that Articles 10 and 11 of the ECHR protecting freedom of expression and assembly were not absolute. They could be limited, provided that the restrictions corresponded to objectives of general interest and did not constitute disproportionate and unacceptable interference that impaired the very substance of the right.[113] It was therefore necessary to decide whether the restrictions placed on Community trade were proportionate in the light of the relevant fundamental rights. The ECJ held that they were: the disruption of Community trade was for a limited time on a limited route; it was in pursuit of a genuine environmental aim; it was not designed to keep foreign goods out of a particular state; efforts had been made to limit the disruption caused by the demonstration; and a ban on the demonstration would have been an unacceptable limit on the right to peaceful demonstration.[114]

[108] Peers, 'Taking Rights Away? Limitations and Derogations', in Peers and Ward, *supra* n. 42, at 142–149.

[109] Case C-112/00, *Schmidberger Internationale Transporte und Planzuge v Austria* [2003] ECR I-5659.

[110] Ibid. at para. 59, reaffirming Case C-265/95, *Commission v France* [1997] ECR I-6959.

[111] Ibid. at para. 64.

[112] Ibid. at para. 74.

[113] Ibid. at para. 80.

[114] Ibid. at paras. 83–94.

The criterion for limitation of rights is set out in Article 52(1), which specifies the conditions on which a Charter right can be limited.

Any limitation on the exercise of the rights and freedoms recognized by this Charter must be provided for by law and respect the essence of those rights and freedoms. Subject to the principle of proportionality, limitations may be made only if they are necessary and genuinely meet objectives of general interest recognized by the Union or the need to protect the rights and freedoms of others.

This formulation combines criteria some of which, such as proportionality, are similar to those used by the Strasbourg court, others of which owe their origin to German law, such as the requirement that the essence of the right should be protected.[115] These criteria are found in the ECJ's existing case law,[116] to which the explanatory memorandum makes explicit reference.[117] There are a number of important issues concerning the interpretation of this Article.

The Charter enshrines a *general limitation clause*, whereas the ECHR's limitations are attached to certain rights, others of which are not capable of derogation. Peers has, however, correctly pointed out that the Article does not actually state that any Charter right can be limited, but rather that if such rights are limited the conditions laid down in the Article apply.[118] It would therefore be open to the Community courts to conclude that certain Charter rights are not open to limitation or derogation at all. The ECJ recognized in *Schmidberger*[119] that the ECHR rights to life and freedom from torture were non-derogable. The ECJ stopped short of expressly stating that EU law would preclude derogation from such rights, but this is a reasonable inference.

A further worrying difference between the Charter test and that found in the ECHR is that the former allows a limitation *if necessary to meet 'objectives of general interest recognized by the Union or the need to protect the rights and freedoms of others'*, as compared with the more discrete justifications found in Articles 8 to 11 of the ECHR. The breadth of the possible justifications allowed by the Charter test is exemplified by the explanatory memorandum, which construed reference to 'general interest' to cover any of the Union objectives in Article 3 of the CT, as well as other interests protected by specific provisions dealing with free movement.[120]

115 De Witte, *supra* n. 2, at 880.

116 Case 5/88, *Wachauf, supra* n. 9, at para. 18; Case C-292/97, *Kjell Karlsson, supra* n. 72, at para. 45.

117 Charte 4473/00, Convent 49, 11 October 2000, at 48; CONV 828/03, Updated Explanations, *supra* n. 67, at 48.

118 Peers, *supra* n. 108, at 163.

119 Case C-112/00, *Schmidberger, supra* n. 109, at para. 80.

120 Charte 4473/00, Convent 49, 11 October 2000, at 48; CONV 828/03, Updated Explanations, *supra* n. 67, at 48.

We should also pay close attention to the meaning accorded to the phrase *respect the essence of the rights and freedoms.* This formulation is derived from German law.[121] It captures the important idea that a restriction should not be deemed lawful if it undermines the essence of the guaranteed right. This is part of the Community test for limitation of rights currently applied by the ECJ. However, the way in which it is applied by the Community courts is often subtly different from that of their German counterparts. The Community jurisprudence commonly provides that a restriction will be deemed to be lawful provided that it does not infringe the essence of that right.[122] This gives the relevant phrase a very different role from that accorded to it by the German courts. The interpretation of this phrase within the context of the Charter is therefore especially important. It should be interpreted in accord with its German origins, and the structure of Article 52(1) facilitates this. The Article makes it clear that any limitation must respect the essence of the right, and that even if it does it will still only be lawful if proportionate, necessary, and in the general interest.

The Charter formulation *makes no reference to the needs of a democratic society,* although given that the EU is founded on respect for democracy, human rights, and the rule of law, it is therefore, as Peers argues, 'hard to see how limitations on human rights can be justified without taking account of the element of democracy'.[123]

A further interpretative issue that arises concerning the Charter general limitation clause is *whether the margin of appreciation is applicable in this context.* The rationale for its use in the ECHR is that it enables the Strasbourg court to take cognizance of the different views on morality and the like prevalent in the diverse countries that are signatories to the Convention. This argument as such would be inapplicable in relation to rights-based review of the Union institutions. It would nonetheless be open to the Community courts to develop an autonomous concept of deference to Union institutions when assessing rights-based arguments, as exemplified by the approach of the UK courts under the Human Rights Act 1998.[124] While this would be possible, it should also be acknowledged that such deference is not a common feature in constitutional adjudication by the courts of most Member States, and would therefore be unlikely to be adopted by the Community courts when reviewing acts of the Union institutions for compatibility with Charter rights.

It is *more contestable whether a margin of appreciation would apply in relation to application of the Charter to Member States.* It has been argued that a

[121] de Witte, *supra* n. 2, at 880.

[122] See below, Chap. 17.

[123] Peers, *supra* n. 108, at 168.

[124] P. Craig, *Administrative Law* (Sweet & Maxwell, 5th ed., 2003), Chap. 17.

margin of appreciation is not warranted even here, principally on the ground that there are already a number of ways in which national diversity can be taken into account.[125] There is some force in this argument, but the contrary view is preferable. The rationale for according Member States a margin of appreciation in the ECHR jurisprudence is similarly applicable when Member States are, for example, derogating from EU law. It enables the strength of national preferences on issues as diverse as abortion[126] or pluralism of the press to be given due weight.[127] This is particularly so given that cases on derogations may entail a balance between a fundamental right, such as freedom of the press or assembly, and a Community freedom, such as free movement of goods.[128] The ECJ has been willing to accord Member States a margin of appreciation in assessing derogations from the four freedoms,[129] and there is no reason why it should cease to do so under the Charter. This argument is reinforced by Article 52(3): Charter rights that correspond to those in the ECHR must be given the same meaning and scope. The margin of appreciation in effect has an impact on the meaning accorded to a particular right. It would, moreover, be odd for the margin of appreciation to apply in relation to some Charter rights, those that correspond to the rights in the ECHR, but not to other rights contained in the Charter.

It is also necessary to *clarify the relationship between Article 52(1) and Article 52(3) insofar as limitations of rights are concerned.* The injunction that the 'meaning and scope' of Charter rights that correspond to ECHR rights should be the same should include the rules on limitations. This is supported by the explanatory memorandum,[130] such that for rights falling in this category the Community legislator, when laying down limitations, must comply with the ECHR rules on limitations. The EU is, however, permitted by Article 52(3) to provide more extensive protection. It would therefore be possible for the limitation conditions laid down in Article 52(1) to apply in addition to those of the ECHR for Charter rights that correspond to ECHR rights, assuming that the Charter limitation was read as granting

[125] Peers, *supra* n. 108, at 168.

[126] Case C-159/90, *SPUC v Grogan* [1991] ECR I-4685.

[127] Case C-368/95, *Familiapress, supra* n. 10.

[128] In Case C-112/00, *Schmidberger, supra* n. 109, at paras. 82, 89, the ECJ spoke of the wide margin of discretion of the Austrian government in balancing freedom of assembly and freedom of trade, albeit the ECJ then undertook a reasonably searching proportionality analysis of its own; the margin of appreciation was expressly referred to in Case C-274/99 P, *Connolly v Commission* [2001] ECR I-1611, although it was not applied to the facts.

[129] Case C-124/97, *Laara, Cotswold Microsystems Ltd and Oy Transatlantic Software Ltd v Finland* [1999] ECR I-6067; Case C-36/02, *Omega Spielhallen- und Automatenaufstellungs-GmbH v Oberbürgermeisterin der Bundesstadt Bonn* [2004] ECR I-9609.

[130] Charte 4473/00, Convent 49, 11 October 2000, at 48; CONV 828/03, Updated Explanations, *supra* n. 67, at 49.

more extensive protection than application of the ECHR rules on limitations in the instant case.[131]

12. CHARTER INTERPRETATION: EXISTING EU LAW AND CONSISTENT INTERPRETATION

Interpretation and application of rights-based provisions is often complex and difficult because of contestability as to the meaning of the particular rights and as to their application in concrete circumstances. These difficulties are exacerbated in the EU because the Charter subsists alongside a lengthy Treaty, many of the provisions of which touch on the same subject matter as rights contained in the Charter.[132]

This issue was addressed by Article 52(2) of the Charter: 'rights recognized by this Charter which are based on the Community Treaties or the Treaty on European Union shall be exercised under the conditions and within the limits defined by those Treaties'. The corresponding provision of the CT, Article II–112(2), was slightly different: 'rights recognized by this Charter for which provision is made in other Parts of the Constitution shall be exercised under the conditions and within the limits defined by these relevant Parts'.

The application of Article 52(2) will be problematic. The key words are 'rights recognized by the Charter which are based on' the Community or Union Treaties. It is unclear whether the formulation in the CT, 'rights recognized by this Charter for which provision is made in other Parts of the Constitution', was intended to be wider. The explanatory memorandum is not especially helpful about the reach of this Article. The explanation attached to Article 52(2) gives no list of Charter rights that are based on existing Treaties. The matter is addressed in relation to explanations of particular Charter rights, but somewhat inconsistently. Thus comments on some Charter articles state expressly that they are based on a Treaty provision and that Article 52(2) applies;[133] the comments on other Charter rights state that they are based wholly or partly on a Treaty provision, but make no reference to Article 52(2).[134] Three types of problems will therefore arise in deciding on the reach of this provision.

[131] Lenaerts and de Smijter, 'A "Bill of Rights" for the European Union' (2001) 28 *CMLRev* 273, at 292–293.

[132] De Búrca, 'Fundamental Rights and Citizenship', in B. de Witte (ed), *Ten Reflections on the Constitutional Treaty for Europe* (Robert Schumann Centre for Advanced Studies, 2003), at 29–44.

[133] Arts. 15(3), 39, 40, 41(4), 42, 43, 44, 45(1), and 46; Peers, *supra* n. 108, at 155.

[134] Arts. 11(2), 18, 21(2), 22, 23, 32, 34(1), 35, 37 and 38; Peers, *supra* n. 108, at 155–156.

A. Charter Rights and Treaty Rights

The initial difficulty will be to decide which Charter rights are based on Treaty provisions. This will not be easy. Lenaerts and de Smijter[135] considered the difficulties posed by Article 52(2) in relation to discrimination.

The Charter deals with this in Article 21(1), which prohibits discrimination on grounds such as: sex, race, colour, ethnic or social origin, genetic features, language, religion or belief, political or other opinion, membership of a national minority, property, birth, disability, age, or sexual orientation. This is broader than Article 13 EC in a number of ways. The list in Article 21(1) is more extensive; it applies to all three pillars and to Member State action when implementing Community law; and it actually prohibits discrimination on the listed grounds, whereas Article 13 EC merely empowers Community action to tackle discrimination. Whether Charter Article 21(1) can be read as imposing a stronger protection than Article 13 EC depends upon whether the former is based on the latter. If it is then Article 52(2) applies with the consequence that Article 21(1) of the Charter would have to be exercised within the limits laid down by the EC Treaty.

The answer proposed by Lenaerts and de Smijter is complex, but persuasive, and reveals the difficulties posed by Article 52(2). They argue,[136] in essence, that the grounds listed in Article 21(1) which are not to be found in Article 13 EC are not based on the latter, and therefore Article 52(2) is inapplicable. They contend that this is probably also true for the listed grounds common to both provisions where the Council has not yet taken any measures. When the Council has exercised its power under Article 13 EC the Community act will serve as a basis for construing the scope of the corresponding right recognized by Article 21(1).

B. Charter Rights and Community Legislation

There is a further difficulty concerning the relationship between Charter rights and Community regulations, directives etc. Article 52(2) specifies that Charter rights based on the Treaty must be exercised under the conditions and limits defined by those Treaties. It is, however, common for a Treaty provision to be set in general terms and for the more specific conditions for its exercise to be laid down in Community legislation. The issue is therefore whether Article 52(2) is applicable in such instances. Would the conditions and limits contained in a regulation or directive impose constraints on the interpretation of an analogous Charter right? Could the Charter right be said to be based on the Community Treaty in such instances? The question is

[135] Lenaerts and de Smijter, *supra* n. 131, at 283–289.
[136] Ibid. at 284–285.

further sharpened by the fact that certain Charter rights are said in the explanatory memorandum to be based wholly or partly on Community legislation.[137]

It is clear as a matter of principle that the Community legislation must be *intra vires* the Treaty article on which it is based. If conditions are imposed on the Treaty article which are inconsistent with it then the legality of the Community legislation could be contested on that ground. It might be argued in the light of this that in the converse case where the regulation or directive is not open to challenge on this ground that therefore any conditions to the right could be said to be defined by the Treaties and hence the Charter right would have to be interpreted subject to those limits.

This is a possible view. It is, however, unconvincing and would be regrettable. In addressing this issue we should not lose sight of the fact that at present the fundamental rights doctrine as developed by the Community courts is used to challenge the legality of Community regulations, directives, and the like. This is premised on a normative hierarchy in which fundamental rights are superior to Community legislation and hence operate as a ground of judicial review. Thus under the fundamental rights regime that preceded the Charter the meaning given to those rights was not bounded by conditions laid down in Community legislation. To the contrary, the legality of the Community legislation and any conditions laid down therein was tested for conformity with fundamental rights as developed by the Community courts. This is exemplified by the jurisprudence on the right to be heard where the Community courts held that provisions concerning hearings contained in a regulation could be complemented by recourse to the fundamental right itself.[138] The fundamental principle of the rights of the defence could not be excluded or restricted by any legislative provision and respect for the right to be heard should be ensured both where there was no specific legislation and where legislation existed, but did not take sufficient account of the right.[139]

It would therefore be a retrograde step to interpret the Charter as in effect reversing this normative hierarchy, such that conditions laid down by Community legislation defined the boundaries of Charter rights. It follows that it should be open to the Community courts to read any conditions or limits to a Treaty article laid down in Community legislation made pursuant thereto in the light of the Charter right when assessing the legality of those

137 Arts. 5(3), 11(2), 23, 31(1)–(2), and 32.

138 Case C-49/88, *Al-Jubail Fertilizer v Council* [1991] ECR I-3187, at para. 15. See also, Cases T-33–34/98, *Petrotub and Republica SA v Council* [1999] ECR II-3837; Case C-458/98 P, *Industrie des Poudres Sphèriques v Council and Commission* [2000] ECR I-8147, at para. 99.

139 Case T-260/94, *Air Inter SA v Commission* [1997] ECR II-997, at para. 60.

conditions.[140] This is more especially so where the Treaty article is open-textured, and does not in terms specify particular limits or conditions for its exercise. The interpretation of the Charter right should not be subject to Article 52(2) and should not be formally bounded by the conditions laid down in the Community legislation. The extension of Article 52(2) to the latter would diminish the sense of Charter rights as constitutional rights and risk ossifying their interpretation by the conditions attached to Community legislation.

It can, however, also be maintained, consistently with the preceding argument, that where the Community legislature has given considered thought to the more particular meaning to be accorded to a right laid down in a Treaty article and expressed this through Community legislation, the Community courts should treat this with respect and should not lightly find this to be inconsistent with the Charter right.

C. Charter Rights, Treaty Rights, and the Courts' Jurisprudence

A further difficulty with the application of Article 52(2) is whether it applies to the courts' jurisprudence. We need to tread carefully here.

There will of course be many instances where the meaning and hence the conditions and limits of a particular Treaty article will only become apparent in the light of case law from the Community courts. Thus the meaning of state aid, competition, agreement, and many other prominent terms in Treaty provisions that serve to define their scope or the conditions in which they apply will only become apparent by and through judicial interpretation. In such instances it is perfectly natural to think of Article 52(2) applying, subject of course to the condition that the Charter right is based on the relevant Treaty article. Where this is met then the definition of the conditions and limits for application of the relevant Treaty article should include the courts' jurisprudence defining those conditions and limits.

There are, however, other instances where the right or principle is in reality created by the courts and where it is based on an open-textured or generally worded Treaty article. Consider in this respect the possible relation between Article 52(2) and Article 41 of the Charter, concerned with the right to good administration. Article 41(1) imposes an obligation on the Community and Union institutions to be impartial in the handling of the affairs of every person, and to deal with them in a reasonable time. Article 41(2) then provides that the right in Article 41(1) shall be taken to *include* the 'right of every person to be heard, before any individual measure which would affect

[140] It is moreover the case that the requirements of the general limitation clause in Article 52(1) of the Charter would be applicable in such a situation. Thus it would, for example, be necessary to show that such limitations respected the essence of the relevant right.

him or her adversely is taken'. It also includes the right of access to the person's file, subject to exceptions for confidentiality, and the obligation to give reasons. Article 41(3) covers damages actions against the Community in language that replicates Articles 288(2) EC. The right to communicate to the Union institutions in a person's own language is guaranteed in Article 41(4). The explanatory documents produced by the Convention[141] make it clear that the rights contained within Articles 41(1) and most of Article 41(2)[142] are derived from the courts' case law. The memorandum also states that the rights contained in Articles 41(3)–(4) are, in accordance with Article 52(2), to be applied under the conditions and within the limits defined by the Treaties.[143]

This leaves open the issue of principle as to whether Article 52(2) can or should apply to such Charter rights based on the courts' jurisprudence. The wording of the Article, framed in terms of rights that are *based on* the Treaties, is ambiguous in this respect. This could be read to include rights derived from case law that is conceptually based on Articles 220 and 230 EC.[144] The wording of Article 52(2) states, however, that Charter rights based on the Treaties must be exercised *under the conditions and within the limits defined by those Treaties.*[145] The Treaties do not define the conditions and limits to rights fashioned by the ECJ, except in the attenuated sense that all of the ECJ's jurisprudence will constitute an interpretation of some Treaty provision. Where, however, the Community courts have read extensive principles into vaguely framed Treaty articles it is strained to say that the Treaty article itself establishes the conditions and limits to the exercise of that right.

We should not, moreover, when addressing this issue lose sight of the underlying point of principle. Thus even if one subscribes to the thesis that in formal terms the Community jurisprudence is premised on some Treaty article, the salient issue here is whether conditions and limits placed on principles or rights derived by the Community judiciary from broadly framed Treaty articles should necessarily constrain the interpretation of the analogous Charter right. It is one thing to say that Charter rights must

[141] See Charte 4423/00, Convent 46, 31 July 2000, at 27; Charte 4473/00, Convent 49, 11 October 2000, at 36–37.

[142] The obligation to give reasons, the third indent of Article 41(2), is based on Article 253 EC.

[143] Charte 4473/00, Convent 49, 11 October 2000, at 37; CONV 828/03, *Updated Explanations, supra* n. 67, at 37.

[144] Article 220 EC is the foundational provision in relation to the ECJ and provides that the Court of Justice shall ensure that in the interpretation and application of this Treaty the law is observed. Article 230 EC sets out the grounds for judicial review, which include breach of the Treaty or any rule of law relating to its application, and it was this that served as the window for the ECJ to read into the EC Treaty many of the principles of good administration.

[145] The same point applies to the wording of Art. II–112(2) of the CT, which states that the rights recognized by the Charter for which provision is made in other Parts of the Constitution shall be exercised under *the conditions and within the limits defined by these relevant Parts.*

respect the conditions and limits defined by the Member States when they ratified the Treaty. It is another thing altogether to say that where Charter rights owe their origin to Community jurisprudence, the interpretation of the Charter right must forever be constrained by the limits and conditions of that initial jurisprudence.

It should also be acknowledged that even if it was felt that Charter rights based on Community jurisprudence should be constrained by the limits and conditions laid down by that case law, this would not impede a creative court minded to develop the law in the relevant area. Such a court could if it so wished simply develop its traditional case law under the Treaties so as to make it conform to the interpretation that it would like to give to the relevant Charter right.

The actual coverage of Article 41 raises further questions about the relationship between it and Article 52(2). Article 41(1) is the *lex generalis*, and Article 41(2) the *lex specialis* which sets out three specific rights which are said to be *included* in Article 41(1). It seems therefore that the rights listed in Article 41(2), which all relate to the hearing by the initial decision-maker, are not exhaustive. There is nothing explicitly within Article 41 that is directed towards judicial review, either the rules on standing, or the grounds thereof. It might be contended that this is because the Article as a whole is directed towards obligations imposed on the initial decision-maker. This will not withstand examination, since Article 41(3), concerning damages actions against the Community, directly addresses the individuals' remedial rights when an error in the original decision has been made. It is axiomatic that judicial review, leading to annulment, and damages actions leading to compensation, are both methods of recourse when an error in the initial decision has occurred. It will, therefore, be interesting to see whether there are attempts made to base claims concerning judicial review on Article 41(1).[146] An individual might argue that the restrictive rules on standing to seek judicial review violated the right to have one's affairs handled fairly by the institutions of the Union. It would of course be open to the ECJ to respond either by raising Article 52(2), or by interpreting Article 41(1) so as not to require more extensive standing requirements than currently exist. It would also be open to the ECJ if so minded to use Article 41(1) as the *raison d'être* for broadening the existing restrictive rules.

D. To Replicate or Not

It might be felt in the light of the above that it would have been more sensible to avoid replication in the Charter of provisions found elsewhere in the

[146] See above, at 346–347.

Treaties. There is certainly force in this argument.[147] The avoidance of replication would, however, have required the identification of rights found in the Charter that already exist in the Treaties and the removal thereof. This would not have been easy, as the preceding discussion revealed. It would moreover be very odd for a Charter of Fundamental Rights not to include, for example, important provisions concerning equality on the ground that the existing Treaties covered the issue. This point is reinforced by the possibility that over time the Charter rights may come to have a higher status de jure or de facto than other Treaty provisions.

13. CHARTER INTERPRETATION: THE RELATIONSHIP WITH THE ECHR

A. Charter Rights that Correspond to ECHR Rights

The relation between the Charter and the ECHR was an issue that occupied much time in the drafting process.[148] The result is encapsulated in Article 52(3), which provides that Charter rights that correspond to rights guaranteed by the ECHR shall have the same scope and meaning as those in the ECHR. This is subject to the caveat that Union law can provide more extensive protection.[149]

Article 52(3) requires the identification of those rights which *correspond* to those guaranteed by the ECHR. The task is facilitated by guidance from the drafting process, and was addressed by an explanatory memorandum. The memorandum is not legally binding but it is a useful guide.[150] The memorandum concluded that the right to life, the prohibition of torture, the prohibition on slavery and forced labour, the right to liberty and security, respect for private and family life, freedom of thought, conscience, and religion, freedom of expression and information, freedom of assembly and association, right to property, protection in the event of removal, expulsion, or extradition, and the presumption of innocence and right of defence, had the same meaning and scope as the corresponding Articles of the ECHR.[151]

[147] Arnull, *supra* n. 65, at 778–779.

[148] See, e.g., SN 3340/00, 29 June 2000; Charte 4423/00, Convent 46, 31 July 2000; Charte 4961/00, Contrib 356, 13 November 2000; Lemmens, 'The Relationship between the Charter of Fundamental Rights of the EU and the ECHR: Substantive Aspects' (2001) 8 *MJ* 49.

[149] This was reconfirmed by CONV 354/02, Final Report of Working Group II, 22 October 2002, at 7.

[150] The CT added a provision to the Charter that explanations drawn up to provide guidance in the interpretation of the Charter should be given due regard by the Union courts and those of the Member States, Art. II–112(7) CT.

[151] Charte 4473/00, Convent 49, 11 October 2000, at 49.

It should nonetheless be recognized that there are a number of Charter articles where the relationship with the ECHR rights is more complex,[152] albeit for different reasons. Some Charter rights, such as Article 5 dealing with slavery and forced labour, are based on an ECHR right *in part*, but go beyond it, by expressly prohibiting trafficking in human beings. Other rights, such as Article 8 dealing with personal data, are based on *more than one source*, in this instance an EC Treaty article plus directive, as well as an ECHR right. Yet other Charter rights *modify* the analogous ECHR right. This is exemplified by Article 9, which countenances the possibility of marriage by those of the same sex, where this is permitted by the relevant national law. There are also instances where the Charter article is based *on more than one source, and modifies* the relevant ECHR right. This is so for the right to education, and for the important right to equality.

B. Charter Rights To Be Given the Same Meaning and Scope

The other major injunction in Article 52(3) is that the meaning and scope of Charter rights that correspond to ECHR rights should be the same as those laid down in the ECHR.

It should be noted that earlier versions of the Charter were crucially different in this respect, requiring only that the meaning and scope of such Charter rights were *similar* to the corresponding ECHR right.[153] This would have given rise to significant problems of interpretation. While the present formulation does not refer expressly to the case law of the Strasbourg court this must be implicit in the injunction that the meaning and scope of Charter rights corresponding to rights contained in the ECHR should be the same.

It should, however, be recognized that the present formula, requiring the interpretation of corresponding rights to be the same, may still be problematic. This will especially be so in areas where the ECHR jurisprudence on the point is unclear, or where the point is a novel one, as emphasized by comments from the Council of Europe observers' on the drafting of the Charter.[154] They expressed concern that the Charter would generate a large increase in the number of preliminary references, and that this would raise the risk that ECJ decisions would be at variance with those of the Strasbourg Court. This in turn would lead to courts of Member States being under mutually inconsistent Treaty obligations. Harmony between the Charter and the ECHR could, they said, only be secured if the EU acceded to the ECHR.[155]

[152] Ibid. at 49–50.

[153] Charte 4423/00, Convent 46, 31 July 2000, at 36.

[154] Charte 4961/00, Contrib 356, 13 November 2000, at 3.

[155] Ibid. at 3–4. This view was echoed by the Committee on Legal Affairs and Human Rights of the Parliamentary Assembly of the Council of Europe, Charte 4499/00, Contrib 349, 4 October 2000.

This raises the issue of the relationship between the EU and the ECHR in the absence of accession and the nature of that relationship if the EU did accede. These will be considered in turn.

C. Relationship between the EU and the ECHR in the Absence of Accession

The relationship between the EU and the ECHR in the absence of accession must be considered from the perspective of both the ECJ and the European Court of Human Rights.

(1) The ECJ's Perspective

The relationship between the EU and the ECHR as perceived by the ECJ is well known and can be stated briefly. While the EU is not bound by the ECHR, and while the ECJ has made it clear that a Treaty amendment would be required for accession to the Convention, the ECJ nonetheless regards the ECHR as a very important source of inspiration for its own decisions in the field of fundamental rights. It is therefore a standard feature of fundamental rights' adjudication in the EU for the Community courts to have detailed recourse to Convention jurisprudence on the relevant matter. The Community courts will moreover strive for an interpretation in the instant case that is compatible with that reached in the Strasbourg jurisprudence, and the ECJ has been willing to revise some previous judgments in order to bring them into line with subsequent Strasbourg case law.[156]

(2) The ECHR's Perspective: The General Approach

The relationship between the EU and the ECHR is also dependent on how the European Court of Human Rights views the nature of that relationship.[157] Cases such as *Matthews* had shown that a Member State of the EU could be held in violation of the Convention even where the cause of the breach was an act of the EU.[158] The leading decision on the relationship

[156] Case C-94/00, *Roquette Fréres SA v Directeur Général de la Concurrence, de la Consommation et de la Représsion des Fraudes and Commission* [2002] ECR I-9011, at para. 29; Cases C-238, 244, 245, 247, 250–252, and 254/99 P, *Limburgse Vinyl Maatschappij (LVM) and Others v Commission* [2002] ECR I-8375, at paras. 273–275.

[157] Canor, '*Primus Inter Pares:* Who is the Ultimate Guardian of Fundamental Rights in Europe?' (2000) 25 *ELRev* 3; Costello, 'The *Bosphorus* Ruling of the European Court of Human Rights: Fundamental Rights and Blurred Boundaries in Europe' [2006] *Human Rights Law Rev* 1.

[158] *Matthews v United Kingdom*, ECHR (1999) No. 24833/94.

between fundamental rights protection afforded by the EU and the ECHR is now the *Bosphorus* case.[159]

The applicant had leased two planes from the Yugoslav Airlines, JAT, and one of these planes was impounded in Ireland. The plane was impounded pursuant to an EC Regulation and this Regulation had been enacted in furtherance of UN sanctions against the former Federal Republic of Yugoslavia. The applicant argued, *inter alia*, that the seizure infringed its property rights under the Convention. This issue was considered by the ECJ, which found against the applicant, the essence of its decision being that the Regulation implementing the UN sanctions policy was proportionate.[160] The applicant then brought an action against Ireland before the European Court of Human Rights arguing that the impounding of the plane violated Article 1 of Protocol No 1, which protects property rights.

The Strasbourg Court considered the relationship between the EU and the ECHR since Ireland had taken the aircraft pursuant to a Community Regulation.[161] The Court accepted that it was legitimate for contracting parties to the ECHR to transfer power to an international organization such as the EU, even if the organization was not itself a contracting party under the ECHR. The state contracting party, however, remained responsible for all acts and omissions of its organs, irrespective of whether they were the result of domestic law or the need to comply with an international obligation flowing from membership of an international organization. If this were not so then the state's obligations under the ECHR could be evaded when power was transferred to an international organization.

State action taken in compliance with such international obligations could nonetheless be justified as long as the relevant international organization was considered to protect fundamental rights 'as regards both the substantive guarantees offered and the mechanisms controlling their observance, in a manner which can be considered at least equivalent to that for which the Convention provides'.[162] The Strasbourg Court made it clear that 'equivalent' meant comparable, not identical, and that the finding of equivalence might alter if there was a relevant change in fundamental rights' protection

[159] *Bosphorus Hava Yollari Turizm Ve Ticaret Anonim Sirketi v Ireland*, ECHR (2005) No. 45036/98.

[160] Case C-84/95, *Bosphorus Hava Yollari Turizm Ve Ticaret AS v Minister for Transport, Energy and Communications and others* [1996] ECR I-3953. The case received much critical comment, Canor, ' "Can Two Walk Together, Except they be Agreed?" The Relationship between International Law and European Law: The Incorporation of United Nations Sanctions against Yugoslavia into European Community law through the Perspective of the European Court of Justice' (1998) 35 *CMLRev* 137; Burrows, 'Caught in the Cross-Fire' (1997) 22 *ELRev* 170.

[161] *Bosphorus Hava Yollari*, *supra* n. 159, at paras. 152–158.

[162] Ibid. at para. 155.

by the international organization.[163] Where equivalent protection was provided by the international organization, there was a presumption that a state had not departed from the ECHR when it did no more than implement legal obligations flowing from its membership of that international organization. This presumption could be rebutted if it could be shown in the circumstances of a particular case that the protection of Convention rights was manifestly deficient.[164]

The Strasbourg Court found that the protection afforded to fundamental rights by the EU was equivalent in the preceding sense, thereby raising the presumption that Ireland had not departed from the ECHR by complying with the EC Regulation. It found also that the protection afforded in this instance was not manifestly deficient and hence that the presumption was not rebutted.[165]

The reasoning and result reached by the Strasbourg Court render it unlikely that a ruling of the ECJ would be held to violate the ECHR, given that the EU was held to have met the test for equivalence thereby raising the presumption of compliance with Convention standards which could only be rebutted by showing that the result in a particular case was manifestly deficient. This may well be so, but this 'conclusion' needs to be qualified in two ways.

(3) The ECHR's Perspective: Qualification to the General Approach

Lawyers, academics, and practitioners alike, are properly mindful of exceptions or qualifications to 'general rules'. The need for caution in this respect is exemplified by the *Bosphorus* judgment. The Strasbourg Court having set out its general approach based on equivalence leading to a presumption of compliance with the Convention that could only be rebutted by showing manifest deficiency in the instant case, then immediately qualified this. It emphasized that a 'State would be fully responsible under the Convention for all acts falling outside its strict international legal obligations',[166] that numerous Convention cases had confirmed this, and that such cases concerned review by the Strasbourg Court 'of the exercise of State discretion for which EC law provided'.[167]

It is clear from the majority's judgment that it did not regard the *Bosphorus* case on its facts as raising such an issue, since the impugned act concerned solely compliance by Ireland with an EC obligation flowing from a directly applicable Regulation that left no discretion to the Irish authorities.[168]

It is, however, less clear what the Strasbourg Court meant when it said that

[163] Ibid. at para. 155.
[164] Ibid. at para. 156.
[165] Ibid. at paras. 165–166.
[166] Ibid. at para. 157.
[167] Ibid. at para. 157.
[168] Ibid. at paras. 148, 158.

the state would remain fully responsible under the Convention for all acts falling outside its strict international legal obligations, and that this enabled the Strasbourg Court to review the exercise of state discretion for which EC law provided. The case law cited by the Court provides some guidance in this respect.

There are some cases where the review of 'state discretion for which EC law provided' is uncontroversial in terms of principle and entails no real conflict or tension between the EU and the ECHR. This includes cases where the Strasbourg Court considered whether the state had complied with Article 6 of the Convention when applying EC agricultural regulations,[169] or whether a state that failed to implement a Directive within the assigned time, with the consequence that it levied taxes that it should not have done if the Directive had been properly implemented, was thereby in breach of Article 1 of Protocol No 1.[170]

There are, however, other cases that raise more problematic issues concerning the relationship between the EU and the ECHR. It is significant that the case singled out for special mention[171] as being one in which the Strasbourg Court would review the exercise of discretion for which EC law provided was *Cantoni*, a judgment of the Grand Chamber.[172] The applicant was prosecuted for unlawfully selling pharmaceutical products in supermarkets contrary to French law. The applicant argued by way of defence that the products in question were not medicinal products within the meaning of the French law and that the definition of such products was not sufficiently clear to satisfy the requirements of Article 7(1) of the Convention. The French approach allowed a product to be defined as medicinal by virtue of its function, presentation, or composition. It followed in this respect the meaning given by the ECJ to medicinal product in the relevant Community Directive. This Directive was primarily concerned with the authorization for placing medicinal products on the market and the application of the test for medicinal product was often left to national authorities, subject to review by the ECJ. The ECJ held, moreover, that in principle a Member State could reserve to pharmacists the sale of medicinal products, since this would safeguard public health, subject to a proportionality test designed to check whether such a monopoly was really required for products the use of which would not involve any serious danger to public health.[173] The Strasbourg Court concluded that the French definition of medicinal product was not in breach of Article 7 of the ECHR.

[169] *Van de Hurk v Netherlands*, ECHR (1994) Series A, No. 288.

[170] *Dangeville v France*, ECHR (2002) No. 36677/97.

[171] *Bosphorus Hava Yollari*, *supra* n. 159, at para. 157.

[172] *Cantoni v France*, ECHR (1996) No. 45/95.

[173] Case C-60/89, *Criminal Proceedings against Jean Monteil and Daniel Sammani* [1991] ECR I-1547.

The judgment throws into sharp relief the relationship between the general principle propounded by the majority in *Bosphorus* with their endorsement of the principle flowing from *Cantoni*. The position appears to be that where the state is simply applying a legal obligation pursuant to a Community Regulation, as in *Bosphorus*, then the Strasbourg Court will consider whether the EU provides equivalent protection for fundamental rights, and if it does so it will then only intervene if it feels that this was manifestly deficient in the instant case. The *Cantoni* decision and its endorsement in *Bosphorus* means, however, that the Strasbourg Court will continue to hold the state 'fully responsible' for acts done 'outside its strict international legal obligations' and that this includes review by the Strasbourg Court of the 'exercise of state discretion for which EC law provided'.[174] The Strasbourg Court will exercise its normal review in such cases as exemplified by *Cantoni* itself, and this is clearly more extensive than review bounded by the ideas of equivalence and manifest deficiency. There are at least two kinds of situation in which *Cantoni* as interpreted in *Bosphorus* can apply, both of which can give rise to problems, especially the latter.

The first type of situation is where the Strasbourg Court reviews the way in which a state implemented a Directive, and the way in which it applied the Directive to particular cases. The assumption underlying the *Cantoni* judgment is that the Strasbourg Court can and will review such matters and this reading is reinforced by the *Bosphorus* judgment, which held that *Cantoni* exemplified 'review by this Court of the exercise of state discretion for which EC law provided'.[175] There is, however, potential for tension between Strasbourg and Luxembourg because the ECJ already exercises review over such matters.

The second type of case is more problematic. It is important to recognize that in *Cantoni* the Strasbourg Court was indirectly assessing whether the definition given to a term in Community legislation, which was then applied by a Member State, was compatible with the ECHR. This was the actual legal issue posed by *Cantoni*. It was the definition of medicinal product adopted by the ECJ and then applied in French law that was said by the applicant to be contrary to Article 7. Thus the Strasbourg Court held that the fact that the French law was based almost word for word on the ambit of the Community Directive did not remove it from the ambit of Article 7 of the Convention.[176]

The difficulty with this is immediately apparent once it is recognized that in *Cantoni* France did not have, nor was it exercising, discretion for which EC law provided. The case was not concerned with the way in which a state chose to implement a Community Directive. The essence of the applicant's

[174] *Bosphorus Hava Yollari*, *supra* n. 159, at para. 157.
[175] Ibid. at para. 157. [176] *Cantoni*, *supra* n. 172, at para. 30.

claim was not simply that the French authorities had misapplied the definition, but that the very definition itself was contrary to Article 7. That was how the case was pleaded, reasoned, and decided. The salient issue was therefore whether the meaning accorded to a certain term in a Community Directive by the ECJ, which was then applied in French law, was compatible with Convention rights. On this issue the French authorities had no discretion provided by EC law. They could not have adopted a definition of medicinal product that differed in substance from that laid down by the Community courts.

The precise dividing line between the limited review provided for by *Bosphorus* and the fuller scrutiny exemplified by *Cantoni* remains unclear. The reasoning in the latter would appear to allow the Strasbourg Court indirect review over the definition of terms in a Community Directive through the claimant's ability to argue that its application by a state was contrary to the Convention, even where the state had no discretion as to whether to apply that definition. If this is so then the '*Cantoni* exception' could well overshadow the '*Bosphorus* rule'. It is moreover difficult in terms of logic to see why the *Cantoni* reasoning should not apply to Regulations as well as Directives. If Strasbourg is willing indirectly to engage in fuller review as to whether the meaning of a term in a Community Directive is compatible with the Convention, why should it not do so when the disputed meaning relates to a term in a Regulation? The state against whom the action is brought has no discretion in the relevant sense in either such instance.

(4) The ECHR's Perspective: The Concurring Opinion by Judge Ress

Lawyers interpreting judicial opinions will not only be mindful of exceptions to the general rule laid down by the majority, but also of concurring opinions that imbue terms used by the majority with a different meaning.

This is exemplified by Judge Ress's concurring opinion, which was more nuanced both about equivalence and about the meaning of manifest deficiency. Thus while Judge Ress was willing to accept the majority's findings that the EU met the test of equivalence judged generally in terms of substantive guarantees of rights, he was a good deal more equivocal as to whether the EU's method of protection for those rights, with its limited standing rules, was really in accord with Article 6 of the ECHR, and he was also less willing to conclude that the presumption of Convention compliance could be said to exist in relation to all Convention rights.[177]

Judge Ress also in effect transformed the concept of manifest deficiency into a far more potent tool of review. He was willing to find such a deficiency where there was no adequate review because the ECJ lacked competence,

[177] *Bosphorus Hava Yollari*, *supra* n. 159, Judge Ress concurring opinion at para. 2.

where the ECJ had been too restrictive in its interpretation of individual access, where there had been an obvious misinterpretation or misapplication by the ECJ of a Convention right, where the ECJ departed from well-established Strasbourg case law or where the result of the ECJ's judgment was that the level of protection was not the same as that which would be afforded under the ECHR.[178]

This was, it should not be forgotten, an individual concurring opinion. It shows nonetheless that there are diverse strands of opinion within the Strasbourg Court as to the proper relationship between it and Luxembourg. The reality is that under the guise of manifest deficiency Judge Ress would in effect assure the Strasbourg Court dominance over Luxembourg.

D. Relationship between the EU and the ECHR if the EU Accedes

We should now consider the relationship between the EU and the ECHR if the EU accedes to the Convention. This was always open to the EU if the necessary Treaty amendment was made.[179] Many commentators advocated the step,[180] as did Working Group II of the Convention on the Future of Europe.[181] This issue was addressed by the CT, Article I–9(2) of which provided that the EU should accede to the ECHR, although no precise time line for this was stipulated. The fate of the Constitutional Treaty means that this obligation to accede is unlikely to become a legal reality. This does not of course preclude the EU from deciding on some other occasion to accede to the ECHR, although it is very likely that this would still require a Treaty amendment.

The effect of any future accession is, however, more complex than is often imagined. Decisions would have to be made as to whether, for example, to build in a preliminary reference relationship between the Luxembourg and Strasbourg courts.[182] Accession would not, moreover, as is sometimes claimed, obviate the need for the EU to have its own Charter. This is so for both substantive and jurisdictional reasons.

In substantive terms, a political entity with the power of the EU should, as a matter of principle, be subject to rights-based constraints on the exercise of that power. The absence of such constraints was the source of the initial revolt by the German and Italian courts, which served as the catalyst for the

[178] Ibid. at para. 3. [179] Opinion 2/94, *supra* n. 13.

[180] See, e.g., Vitorino, *supra* n. 39; Assembly of the Council of Europe, *supra* n. 155; House of Lords' Select Committee on European Union, Eighth Report, *EU Charter of Fundamental Rights* (2000; HL 67); Fredman, McCrudden, and Freedland, 'The EU Charter of Fundamental Rights' [2000] *PL* 178, at 180; Lenaerts and de Smijter, 'The Charter and the Role of the European Courts' (2001) 8 *MJ* 90, at 99–101; Arnull, *supra* n. 65, at 785–787.

[181] CONV 354/02, Final Report of Working Group II, 22 October 2002, at 11.

[182] Arnull, *supra* n. 65, at 788–789.

introduction of the ECJ's fundamental rights jurisprudence. The Charter has enhanced the political legitimacy of the EU by furnishing its citizens with a comprehensive, transparent document that includes a broad range of rights. The Charter was premised on the political choice made by the heads of state in the European Council that it should cover social and economic, as well as more traditional civil and political rights. The ECHR covers only some of the rights included in the Charter, and for that reason accession would not obviate the need for the EU's own document enshrining the rights that it believes are worthy of protection. Moreover, as we have already seen, the Charter protection accorded to certain civil rights differs from that in the ECHR. This is exemplified by the broader remit of the Charter protection for equality.

In jurisdictional terms accession to the ECHR would not render moot the choices open to citizens as to how they protect their human rights. This point would hold true even if the EU's human rights document had been an exact copy of the ECHR. This is because of the differing impact of the EU and ECHR Treaties in at least some states, as exemplified by the UK. The supremacy doctrine is a central principle of EU law. The UK courts have held that even primary legislation that is inconsistent with EU law can be declared inapplicable to the instant case. Such legislation will be 'disapplied' by the national court.[183] The status of the ECHR is different. Under the Human Rights Act 1998, where primary legislation is incompatible with Convention rights, the court can issue a declaration of incompatibility.[184] This declaration does not, however, affect the validity of the legislation. It serves to send the legislation back to the political forum, with the expectation that Parliament will remove the offending provision. There is therefore an incentive for those minded to challenge primary legislation to do so through EU rights where that is possible.

14. CHARTER INTERPRETATION: THE RELATIONSHIP WITH NATIONAL CONSTITUTIONS

We have already considered the extent to which Member States are bound by the Charter. There are, however, further provisions that serve to define the relationship between the Charter and fundamental rights at national level.

[183] *R v Secretary of State for Transport, ex p Factortame Ltd (No.2)* [1991] 1 AC 603; *R v Secretary of State for Employment, ex p Equal Opportunities Commission* [1995] 1 AC 1.

[184] Human Rights Act 1998, ss. 2–4.

A. The Interpretative Obligation

Working Group II of the Convention on the Future of Europe recommended a new provision,[185] which was added to the Charter by the CT. Article II–112(4) states that 'insofar as this Charter recognizes fundamental rights as they result from the constitutional traditions common to the Member States, those rights shall be interpreted in harmony with those traditions'. It imposes an interpretative obligation on courts and legislature alike. The obligation is one which the institutions would in any event be minded to comply with, at least as a starting point. Article II–112 is the renumbered Article 52 of the Charter. Although the CT is unlikely to become a legal reality it is open to the Member States to retain this new clause if and when they choose to make the Charter legally binding. It is therefore worth dwelling on it a little further, more especially because its precise impact is not entirely clear.

The interpretative duty is triggered when the Charter recognizes fundamental rights as they result from the constitutional traditions common to the Member States, and the duty is one of harmonious interpretation, rather than identity of result. However, as we have seen, there is a stricter duty in relation to Charter rights that correspond to those contained in the ECHR, and many of these rights will also be found in national constitutions.

There is, moreover, the fact that the particular conception or meaning accorded to a right can vary as between Member States. This does not present an insuperable problem because the obligation is one of harmonious interpretation rather than identity of result. There will nonetheless be cases where the construction of a Charter right might arise in a case concerning Member State implementation of EC law, where, as in *ERT*[186] or *Familiapress*,[187] another Member State's laws are directly implicated in the action. It is perfectly possible for an interpretation of the Charter right to affect adversely the constitutional right protected by one Member State, while the contrary construction would be regarded as constitutionally objectionable by the other state. In these circumstances the ECJ will necessarily have to make difficult choices.

B. The Substantive Obligation

Article 53 is entitled 'Level of Protection'. It deals with the interrelationship of the Charter and other bodies of law. The aim of this provision was said to be to maintain the level of protection 'currently afforded within their respective scope by Union law, national law and international law'.[188] Special

[185] CONV 354/02, Final Report of Working Group II, 22 October 2002, at 7–8.
[186] Case C-260/89, *supra* n. 10. [187] Case C-368/95, *supra* n. 10.
[188] Charte 4473/00, Convent 49, 11 October 2000, at 50.

mention was made of the ECHR because of its importance, and it was held to constitute a minimum standard in all cases.

Nothing in this Charter shall be interpreted as restricting or adversely affecting human rights and fundamental freedoms as recognized, in their respective fields of application, by Union law and international law and by international agreements to which the Union, the Community or all the Member States are party, including the European Convention for the Protection of Human Rights and Fundamental Freedoms, and by the Member States' constitutions.

The present discussion will concentrate on the relation between the Charter and Member States' constitutions. It should be noted at the outset that there is an ambiguity as to the meaning of the phrase 'in their respective spheres of application'. It appears to mean that nothing in the Charter should be interpreted as restricting or adversely affecting human rights recognized in the respective areas to which public international law, international agreements, and Member State constitutions apply. It therefore delineates the spheres of application of human rights norms derived from these other areas.

This raised concerns that the supremacy of EU law might be jeopardized.[189] This was in part because of the absence of a supremacy clause in the Charter. It was in part because the jurisprudence from German and Italian courts had not in the past been premised on the assumption that their human rights norms only applied within a limited field, being that to which Community rules did not apply. It had been premised rather on the assumption that such national constitutional protection continued to be generally applicable, but that national courts might choose not to exercise their jurisdiction if satisfied that the protection of rights within the Community legal order was sufficient.[190]

These concerns are, however, probably unwarranted.[191] The CT did contain a supremacy clause, although it should be acknowledged that it was ambiguous as to whether it accorded supremacy to EU law in the event of a clash with a national constitution.[192] It is equally significant that the approach of, for example, the German courts has softened in the last decade.

[189] Liisberg, 'Does the Charter of Fundamental Rights Threaten the Supremacy of Community Law?' (2001) 38 *CMLRev* 1171.

[190] *Re Wunsche Handelsgesellschaft*, Dec. of 22 Oct. 1986 [1987] 3 CMLR 225; Frowein 'Solange II' (1988) 25 *CMLRev* 201; Roth, 'The Application of Community Law in West Germany: 1980–1990' (1991) 28 *CMLRev* 137; *SpA Granital v Amminsitazione delle Finanze*, Dec. 170, 8 June 1984; *SpA Fragd v Amminstrazione delle Finanze*, Dec. 232, 21 April 1989, (1989) 72 RDI; Pettricione, 'Italy: Supremacy of Community Law over National Law' (1986) 11 *ELRev* 320; Gaja, 'New Developments in a Continuing Story: The Relationship between EEC Law and Italian Law' (1990) 27 *CMLRev* 83; Craig, 'National Courts and Community Law', in J. Hayward and A. Menon (eds), *Governing Europe* (Oxford University Press, 2003), Chap. 2.

[191] Maduro, *supra* n. 42, at 296–297.

[192] Art. I–6 CT.

The *Bundesverfassungsgericht* emphasized that the level of protection provided by the ECJ could differ from that of the German courts in individual cases and that it was only if the overall level of protection generally fell below a minimum acceptable level would the German courts reassert their control function.[193] It is therefore the case that from the perspective of German constitutional law there is less of a problem than hitherto about the delineation of the respective spheres of application of EU law and national law in relation to fundamental rights.

15. CHARTER INTERPRETATION: THE RELATIONSHIP WITH INTERNATIONAL LAW

We have seen that Article 53 addresses the relationship between the Charter and fundamental rights as recognized and protected by, *inter alia*, international law.

The difficulties concerning the nature of this relationship were thrown into sharp relief by the *Kadi* case.[194] The applicant challenged a Community Regulation that froze the funds of those suspected of supporting Al-Qaeda. The Regulation was passed pursuant to Security Council Resolutions, which established a Sanctions Committee to designate those who should be subject to such freezing orders. This Committee obtained its information from states and regional organizations, and the names placed on the list were reviewed after 12 months. The applicant's name was included on the list and his assets in the EU were frozen in accord with the Community Regulation. He argued that he was never involved in the provision of financial support for terrorism and that his fundamental rights were infringed by the Regulation. The CFI held that the contested Regulation could be based on Articles 60, 301, and 308 EC and then considered the argument concerning fundamental rights.

The CFI reasoned that Member States were bound by Resolutions adopted by the Security Council under Chapter VII of the UN Charter, and so too was the EU, even though it was not a member of the UN, because when they created the EEC the Member States could not transfer to it more powers than they possessed.[195] The Community could not therefore infringe the obligations imposed on its Member States by the UN Charter, and in exercising its powers the Community was bound to adopt all measures necessary to enable it to fulfil those obligations.[196] It was, however, by virtue of the

[193] Thym, *supra* n. 65, at 15–16; Schwarze, *supra* n. 74, at 411–417; Hoffmeister, 'Case Note' (2001) 38 *CMLRev* 791.

[194] Case T-315/01, *Yassin Abdullah Kadi v Council and Commission*, judgment of 21 September 2005, not yet published.

[195] Ibid. at para. 195.

[196] Ibid. at para. 204.

EC Treaty, rather than general international law, that the EC was required to give effect to Security Council Resolutions.[197]

The CFI declined to exercise generalized review of the contested Community Regulation for compliance with fundamental rights as protected by the Community legal order, since this would entail indirect review of the Security Council Resolutions for compliance with those rights.[198] The CFI held that it could, however, review the Security Council Resolutions for compliance with *jus cogens*, since this was a body of higher rules of international law binding on all, including the United Nations.[199]

The exercise of this review did not, however, avail the applicant. The CFI concluded that there had been no infringement of the right to property, since the temporary freezing of funds was not arbitrary and did not affect the substance of the relevant right. The applicant's claim with respect to the right to be heard was undoubtedly stronger, since there was no right to be heard by the Sanctions Committee, the Community had no power to check the basis on which the Sanctions Committee placed the applicant on their list, and re-examination of the list was dependent on a petition from the individual's state, which lay within the state's discretion. The CFI held that there was nonetheless no violation of the *jus cogens* in this regard. Its reasoning in this respect was however strained. It held that adaptation of the right to be heard was necessary in this type of case, that the freezing order was only temporary, and that the applicant had no right that the evidence against him should be communicated to him.[200] Nor did the applicant succeed in convincing the CFI that his right to judicial review had been violated. The CFI acknowledged that it could not review the correctness of the findings made by the Sanctions Committee, and that in this sense there was no judicial remedy available to the applicant. The CFI found, however, that this did not constitute a breach of *jus cogens*, since the right of access to courts was not absolute and the limitation of that right in the instant case was justified by the nature of the decisions taken by the Security Council and the legitimate objective pursued.[201]

Kadi would be regarded as a 'hard case' in all senses of that term. It would have been very difficult, perhaps impossible, for the CFI to review the evidential basis on which the Sanctions Committee placed the applicant on the list. It could, however, have struck down the Community Regulation for violation of *jus cogens*, on the ground that there was no effective review of this issue, either at UN or Community level. This was the real essence of the applicant's complaint. The CFI nonetheless chose not to do so, and rejected pleas couched in terms of the right to be heard and access to court. Its

[197] Ibid. at para. 207.
[198] Ibid. at paras. 215–225.
[199] Ibid. at paras. 226, 230.
[200] Ibid. at paras. 267–274.
[201] Ibid. at paras. 284–290.

reasoning on both issues was strained. The case highlights the pressing need for administrative law safeguards at the international level.[202] In the absence of these safeguards the reality is that those targeted by 'smart sanctions' such as those in issue here will be deprived of meaningful opportunity to contest the substance of the case against them.

16. THE CHARTER, RIGHTS, AND REMEDIES

Rights demand remedies. This is an obvious proposition, but important nonetheless. It is axiomatic, as van Gerven states, that 'fundamental rights are only truly respected when the legal order concerned makes them enforceable against those who have breached them'.[203] An individual may seek redress for a violation of fundamental rights through a national legal system, the ECHR, or EU law, and van Gerven provides a comprehensive overview of the possibilities open to the aggrieved individual. The present discussion will focus on remedies available under EU law. The principal remedies are review of legality leading to annulment of the offending measure, and damages liability.

Review of legality can be direct through Article 230 EC, or indirect through Article 234 EC. The main obstacle for direct actions is the narrow criterion for standing. This issue has been considered in detail in an earlier chapter, and reference should be made to that discussion. It included analysis of the possible impact of the revised rules on standing contained in the CT and of the rights to good administration and an effective remedy in the Charter of Rights.[204] The discussion also focused on the interrelationship between direct and indirect actions and the difficulties that still persist with the latter. This analysis should moreover be read in conjunction with that concerning the courts,[205] since it is clear that the restrictive rules on direct access have resulted in part from the caseload pressures that beset the Community courts, especially the ECJ.

It would be possible to make special provision for rights-based actions by drawing on the *Verfassungsbeschwerde* in German law, or the *recurso de amparo* in Spanish law. They are subsidiary procedures in the sense that a direct complaint to the Constitutional Court is only possible where it can be shown that the ordinary courts have failed to uphold the applicant's constitutional rights. The applicant will moreover have to show personal, direct, and present affect from the contested measure, but this criterion has not prevented

[202] Kingsbury, Krisch, and Stewart, 'The Emergence of Global Administrative Law' (2005) 68 *LCP* 15.

[203] van Gerven, 'Remedies for Infringements of Fundamental Rights' (2004) 10 *EPL* 261.

[204] See above, at 344–347.

[205] See above, Chap. 9.

thousands of such complaints each year to the German and Spanish Constitutional Courts.[206] However, as de Witte has shown, if the criterion for standing were broadened there would be no need for such a mechanism in relation to challenge to Community acts.[207] It would by way of contrast have a marked impact on judicial review of Member State action for violation of fundamental rights, since it would allow the aggrieved individual to bring an action before the Community courts without the need for a preliminary reference by a national court.[208] De Witte nonetheless concludes against the creation of a European *amparo.*

Liability in damages is the other main remedy that might be sought for violation of fundamental rights. This issue will be considered in detail in a later chapter.[209] Suffice it to say for the present that the general principles that govern Community liability under Article 288 EC and Member State liability under the *Francovich* principle[210] will apply here. Thus provided that the applicant can show that the provision was intended to confer rights on individuals, breach, causation, and damage then liability will ensue. It may well be necessary to show a sufficiently serious breach where the contested measure entailed the exercise of meaningful discretion. Damages will not readily be available in relation to Charter provisions judged to be principles rather than rights, since such provisions are intended to guide legislative and executive action rather than confer rights on individuals.

17. THE LEGAL STATUS OF THE CHARTER

The legal status of the Charter was left unresolved at the Nice European Council, and placed on the agenda for the next IGC. The Commission[211] and the EP[212] favoured giving legal force to the Charter. Working Group II of the Convention on the Future of Europe recommended that the Charter should be incorporated in a form that would make the Charter legally binding and give it a constitutional status.[213] This was done by the CT in Article I–9(1), although the wording of the Article, the Union shall 'recognize' the rights etc. contained in the Charter, could have been improved. The main body of the Charter was, we have seen, included in Part II of the CT, with the specific provisions being renumbered to follow on from those in

[206] De Witte, *supra* n. 2, at 894. [207] Ibid. at 895.
[208] Ibid. at 895–896. [209] See below, Chaps. 20–21.
[210] Cases C-6 and 9/90, *Francovich and Bonifaci v Italy* [1991] ECR I-5357.
[211] Communication from the Commission, On the Legal Nature of the Charter of Fundamental Rights of the European Union, COM(2000) 644 final, at para. 11.
[212] Resolution A5–0064/2000, 16 March 2000; Resolution B5–767/2000, 3 October 2000.
[213] CONV 354/02, Final Report of Working Group II, 22 October 2002, at 2.

Part I. If the CT had been ratified the legal status of the Charter would therefore have been clear.

The failure to secure ratification of the CT means that the Charter is not at present formally legally binding. It is nonetheless clear that the Charter has already had and will continue to have an impact on the Community institutions.[214] The Commission has announced that it will engage in a form of *ex ante* review, to test the compatibility of new legislative instruments with the Charter.[215] The Charter has also featured in the Opinions of the Advocate General when construing Community legislation, and has been referred to by the CFI.[216] The Charter would in this regard operate as an interpretative guide as to the scope and content of Community fundamental rights. The explanatory documents produced during the drafting of the Charter were certainly at pains to locate the Charter rights within the *acquis communautaire*,[217] and this would enhance the legitimacy of the Community courts drawing on the Charter. The ECJ has, however, been reticent on this precise issue. Thus it did not comment on an argument adduced by the applicant that the fact that the Charter did not have the force of law did not preclude reliance on it, since it merely confirmed the fundamental rights of the EU.[218]

18. HUMAN RIGHTS POLICY FOR THE EUROPEAN UNION

We saw earlier that one of the causes for disquiet concerning fundamental rights in the EU related to the absence of a broader internal human rights policy for the EU,[219] particularly when seen in contrast to the EU's external policy in this regard.[220]

[214] de Witte, 'The Legal Status of the Charter: Vital Question or Non-Issue?' (2001) 8 *MJ* 81.

[215] SEC(2001) 380/3; Peers and Ward, *supra* n. 42, at App. I.

[216] Jose Menendez, 'Chartering Europe: Legal Status and Policy Implications of the Charter of Fundamental Rights of the European Union' (2002) 40 *JCMS* 471, at 473–476; Peers and Ward, *supra* n. 42, at App. I.

[217] Charte 4423/00, Convent 46, 31 July 2000; Charte 4473/00, Convent 49, 11 October 2000.

[218] Case C-141/02 P, *Commission v T-Mobile Austria GmbH* [2005] ECR I-1283, at para. 65.

[219] *Supra* n. 37.

[220] Simma, Beatrix Aschenbrenner, and Schulze, 'Human Rights Considerations in Development Co-operation', Alston, *The EU and Human Rights, supra* n. 1, Chap. 18; Clapham, 'Where is the EU's Human Rights Common Foreign Policy, and How is it Manifested in Multilateral Fora?', in *The EU and Human Rights*, ibid., *supra* n. 1, Chap. 19; Williams, 'Enlargement of the Union and Human Rights Conditionality: A Policy of Distinction?' (2000) 25 *ELRev* 601; de Witte and Toggenburg, 'Human Rights and Membership of the EU', in *The EU Charter of Fundamental Rights, supra* n. 42, Chap. 3; L. Bartels, *Human Rights Conditionality in the EU's International Agreements* (Oxford University Press, 2005).

Space precludes detailed examination of the general human rights policy for the EU, since it raises a plethora of more particular concerns relating to diverse areas where the EU operates and proper discussion of these matters would require a book in itself. Suffice it to say for the present that the debate about a human rights policy for the EU raises three general issues that cut across particular subject matter areas: competence, content, and desirability. The issues are perforce related. Whether the EU has competence to enact a human rights policy depends in part at least on what specific types of measures one has in mind. In this sense the issue of competence resonates with that of content. So too does the issue of content relate to that of desirability, since it is only by considering proposals in detail that one can come to a view about, for example, the desirability of the EU exercising greater control over human rights within Member States.

It should moreover be recognized that this interconnection between competence, content, and desirability is just as salient post the Charter as it was before. It is true, as we have seen, that the Charter is not to establish any new power or task for the Community or Union or modify the powers and tasks defined by the Treaties. This still, however, leaves open the scope of the existing competence in relation to human rights and the debate in the academic literature attests to the controversy that surrounds this issue.[221] Moreover, as we have seen, the Charter denial of new heads of legislative competence would not preclude, for example, claims to new social entitlements from the EU derived from fundamental social rights provided that those claims could be satisfied through the exercise of an existing competence.

While a general foray into the debate about human rights policy for the EU involves considerations beyond those that can be dealt with here, it is nonetheless important to be mindful of recent developments that are directly relevant to the subject matter of this book.

An EU Network of Independent Experts on Fundamental Rights was created in 2002.[222] The Network consists of one expert per Member State and its objective is to ensure a high degree of expertise in relation to each Member State and the EU as a whole. The Network produces an annual report on how fundamental rights are safeguarded in practice.[223] It

221 Compare, Weiler and Fries, *supra* n. 36, with Beaumont, *supra* n. 37.

222 <http://www.europa.eu.int/comm/justice_home/cfr_cdf/index_en.htm>.

223 See, e.g., EU Network of Independent Experts on Fundamental Rights, Report on the Situation of Fundamental Rights in the European Union in 2004, January 2005, CFR-CDF.rep.EU.en.2004; EU Network of Independent Experts on Fundamental Rights, Synthesis Report, Conclusions and Recommendations on the Situation of Fundamental Rights in the European Union and the Member States, April 2005, CFR-CDF.Conclusions.2004.en. The Reports of the Network are available at <http://www.europa.eu.int/comm/justice_home/cfr_cdf/index_en.htm>.

can in addition give opinions on specific questions at the request of the Commission and can provide assistance to the Commission and EP in developing EU human rights policy. The Network's annual reports also address a particular theme selected by the Commission and the EP, the theme for 2004 being the protection of minorities in the EU. The Reports produced by the Network contain a great deal of valuable information and insightful analysis.

There are also firm proposals for the creation of a Fundamental Rights Agency. In 2003 the European Council agreed to build on the existing European Monitoring Centre on Racism and Xenophobia and extend its mandate so that it could become a Human Rights Agency.[224] This decision came as something of a surprise,[225] more particularly because the Commission had previously been opposed to suggestions for the creation of a human rights agency.[226] The Commission, duly converted to the cause, published a consultation document in 2004 concerning the possible establishment of the Fundamental Rights Agency (FRA)[227] developing the idea that the existing European Monitoring Centre on Racism and Xenophobia would be converted into the FRA. The FRA according to the Commission proposal would be primarily concerned with data collection and monitoring fundamental rights. It would not on the Commission's model have decision-making powers. Nor would it deal with human rights and third countries, which would continue to be dealt with separately. This still left a host of issues to be resolved, as the Commission consultation document recognized. These included the geographical reach of the Agency, and the subject matter that it should deal with.

The initial reaction to the consultation was on the whole positive, although there were reservations and differences of view about particular aspects of the FRA, including matters such as its relation with other bodies at national, regional, or international level, the legal basis on which the FRA could be established, and doubts about having an EU Gender Institute separate from the FRA.[228] It was, however, encouraging that some of those consulted saw the role of the FRA not only in terms of monitoring and data collection, but more proactively in terms of encouraging best practice. This picks up a theme developed in the academic literature, advocating use of the

[224] Brussels European Council, 12–13 December 2003, at 27.

[225] de Búrca, 'New Modes of Governance and the Protection of Human Rights', in Alston and de Schutter, *supra* n. 99, at 33–34.

[226] The suggestion was made by a number of commentators including Alston and Weiler, *supra* n. 37.

[227] Communication from the Commission, The Fundamental Rights Agency, Public Consultation Document, COM(2004) 693 final.

[228] The views of those who responded to the consultation can be found on the Commission website: <http://europa.eu.int/comm/justice_home/news/consulting_public/fundamental_rights_agency/news_contributions_fund_rights_agency_en.htm>.

Open Method of Coordination (OMC) as a helpful way of advancing the protection of human rights.[229]

The Commission produced legislative proposals, drafted in the light of the consultation exercise, for a Regulation establishing a European Union Agency for Fundamental Rights and a Council Decision empowering the Agency to pursue its activities in areas covered by Pillar 3, Title VI of the TEU.[230] The aim is that the Agency will become operational by 1 January 2007. According to these proposals the basic objective of the FRA is to provide Community institutions, agencies and bodies, and Member States when implementing Community law, with assistance and expertise relating to fundamental rights in order to support them when they take measures or formulate courses of action within their respective spheres of competence to respect fully fundamental rights.

The FRA is to have a number of tasks including collection, recording, and dissemination of data. The FRA is in addition to carry out, cooperate, or encourage scientific research at the request of the EP, Council, or Commission; formulate conclusions or opinions on subjects for the Union institutions and Member States when implementing Community law, either on its own initiative or at the request of the EP, Council, or Commission; make its technical expertise available in the context of proceedings under Article 7 TEU; publish an annual report on the situation of fundamental rights, highlighting examples of good practice; publish thematic reports based on its analysis and research; publish an annual report on its activities; enhance cooperation with civil society; organize conferences, campaigns, and the like to disseminate its work; and develop a strategy for raising public awareness about human rights.

The Commission acting with a comitology committee is to adopt a Multiannual Framework for five years, which specifies the thematic areas of the Agency's activity, subject to the caveat that this is always to include the fight against racism and xenophobia. The Framework is to be in line with the Union's priorities as defined by the Commission's strategic objectives and is to be designed to avoid overlap with the remit of other Community bodies and agencies. The FRA will, however, still be able to respond to requests from the EP, Council, or Commission outside these areas, provided its resources permit. The draft Regulation contains provisions for cooperation between the FRA and other organizations concerned with fundamental

[229] de Búrca, 'The Constitutional Challenge of New Governance in the European Union' (2003) 28 *ELRev* 814; Bernard, *supra* n. 90, at 263–268; de Schutter, 'The Implementation of Fundamental Rights through the Open Method of Coordination', in O. De Schutter and S. Deakin (eds), *Is the Open Coordination of Employment and Social Policies the Future of Social Europe?* (Bruylant, 2005), at 279–342.

[230] Commission Proposal, For a Council Regulation Establishing a European Union Agency for Fundamental Rights, COM(2005) 280 final.

rights at Member State and European level, with specific mention made of cooperation with the Council of Europe.

The FRA will, if established, provide a valuable additional component in human rights protection in the EU.[231] The traditional mechanisms of judicial review necessarily focus on specific cases and are by their nature *ex post facto* in their orientation, although they may well lay down certain precepts that have a more generalized *ex ante* impact. The functions performed by the FRA will complement these legal mechanisms by furnishing *ex ante* information that can be used to identify problems and possible solutions.[232]

The limits of the powers accorded to the FRA should, however, also be borne in mind. The FRA's agenda will be controlled and structured through the Multiannual Framework, and a recital to the Regulation emphasizes that the FRA should not set its own political agenda.[233] It is clear, moreover, that it does not have decision-making power and this limitation is further reinforced by a provision in the draft Regulation that precludes the FRA, when making reports or presenting opinions, from raising issues concerning the legality of Community or Member State action.[234] It is therefore readily apparent that while the Community institutions want the FRA, they do not want it to 'cramp' their freedom of action by issuing opinions on legality cast in terms of the compatibility of specific Community measures with fundamental rights.

19. CONCLUSION

If the CT had been ratified the Charter would have become formally binding and it is likely that we would have seen an upsurge in claims contesting the legality of EU and Member State action on rights-based grounds. The failure of the CT means that the Community courts will doubtless continue to develop their fundamental rights jurisprudence and the Charter will be used as an interpretative guide. The fate of the CT will not, however, signal the end of Treaty revision in the EU. It is likely that future Treaty reform will be more modest, but such change could well include making the Charter formally binding. We should by way of conclusion be cognizant of certain more general themes that are at play in this area.

There is, on the one hand, a duality in the Charter project, which will not disappear whatever the outcome of future Treaty reform. Maduro captures this duality well.[235]

[231] For detailed consideration of the contribution that such an agency could make, see, Alston and de Schutter, *supra* n. 99.

[232] Alston and Weiler, *supra* n. 37.

[233] COM(2005) 280 final, *supra* n. 230, at rec. 9.

[234] Ibid. Art. 4(2).

[235] Maduro, *supra* n. 42, at 269.

[T]he Charter of Fundamental Rights of the European Union represents a constitutional paradox. It reflects an emerging trend to agree on the use of the language of constitutionalism in European integration without agreeing on the conception of constitutionalism underlying such language. For some, the Charter is the foundation upon which to build a true constitutional project for the European Union. It will promote the construction of a European political identity and mobilise European citizens around it. For others, the Charter is simply a constitutional guarantee that the European Union will not threaten the values of the Member States. It is a constitutional limit to the process of European integration. The Charter reflects this tension between its conception as a constitutional instrument for polity building and its conception as a simple consolidation of the previous fundamental rights *acquis* aimed at guaranteeing regime legitimacy. These two conceptions confronted each other in the drafting of the Charter and are reflected in many of its provisions.

It should, on the other hand, be recognized that if the Charter becomes binding the Community courts are likely to be faced with an increasing number of complex challenges based on infringement of Charter rights, because of the very breadth of the Charter provisions and because such rights would be formally binding. It is true that the Charter rights are meant to be declaratory. It is nonetheless predictable that their formal embodiment in the Treaty would lead to a significant increase in the number of applicants seeking to use such rights as part of a judicial review claim. This would place the ECJ ever more squarely in the role of a constitutional court, with the power to invalidate regulations and the like for breach of these constraints on governmental power.

It would then be interesting to see whether this generated concerns about the legitimacy of constitutional review. Such concerns are a regular feature of debates in common law systems, albeit considerably less so in civil law regimes. These concerns have in any event been deflected hitherto in the EU. Judicial power was based on the twin assumptions that it was justified because what was being reviewed was not primary legislation and because there were democratic deficiencies in the way that such regulations, etc. were made. The counter-majoritarian difficulties attendant on constitutional review could therefore be side-stepped. The CT, if it had been ratified, would have altered this picture to a certain degree. It would have instantiated a hierarchy of norms, with primary legislation made by the co-decision procedure, which was deemed to be the ordinary legislative procedure for Union acts.[236] The justification for constitutional review would then fall more squarely on the precept that it is right and proper for there to be rights-based constraints on the scope of governmental action including primary legislation in a democratic polity.

[236] Ibid. Art. I–34(1), III–396.

15

Equality

1. INTRODUCTION

The previous chapter analysed the role played by rights in the Community legal order and their impact on judicial review. This chapter is concerned with equality and the way in which it has been shaped by Community legislation and the Courts' jurisprudence. The principle of equality and the prohibition of discrimination are found expressly within a number of Treaty articles,[1] but the European Court of Justice (ECJ) held at an early stage that these were merely specific enunciations of the general principle of equality as one of the fundamental principles of Community law,[2] which must be observed by any court.[3]

It is important at the outset to recognize that there are a number of more particular conceptions of equality. Thus formal equality or equality as consistency dictates that like should be treated alike and that different cases should be treated differently. This important precept is integral to equality law in most legal systems, including the European Community (EC). It does not, however, dictate any particular substantive result, and can be met whether people are treated equally badly or equally well.[4] Equality of results, by way of contrast, 'goes beyond a demand for consistent treatment of likes, and requires instead that the result be equal', thereby recognizing that 'apparently identical treatment can in practice reinforce inequality because of past or on-going discrimination'.[5] There are, however, as Fredman notes, ambiguities in the meaning accorded to results for these purposes. The focus might be on the particular individual, it might be on the group to which the individual belongs, or it might be on equality of outcome designed to overcome under-representation of a particular group within certain types of employment.[6] Equality of opportunity constitutes a third conception of equality, and is a *via media* between formal equality and equality of result.

[1] Lenaerts, 'L'Égalité de Traitement en Droit Communautaire' (1991) 27 *CDE* 3.

[2] Cases 117/76 and 16/77, *Ruckdeschel v Hauptzollamt Hamburg-St. Annen* [1977] ECR 1753, at para. 7.

[3] Case 8/78, *Milac GmbH v Hauptzollamt Freiburg* [1978] ECR 1721, at para.18.

[4] S. Fredman, *Discrimination Law* (Oxford University Press, 2002), at 7–11.

[5] Ibid. at 11. [6] Ibid. at 11–14.

Using the metaphor of a race, equality of opportunity is premised on the assumption that real equality cannot be achieved if individuals begin this race from different starting points. There are once again difficulties with the more precise meaning of this conception of equality, with some emphasizing its procedural dimension, and others placing greater emphasis on substance so as to ensure that 'persons from all sections of society have a genuinely equal chance of satisfying the criteria for access to a particular social good'.[7]

We shall return to these ideas in the course of the discussion. This chapter is not intended to provide exhaustive treatment of equality in all areas of Community law. That would require a book in itself. The object is rather to consider five major areas where equality is of particular importance, to analyse the interplay between the social and economic rationales for equality, to reveal the more particular conception of equality that prevails in the areas studied, and to consider the implications that this has for the standard of judicial review and the relationship between adjudication and legislation as methods for attaining equality.

2. THE FOUR FREEDOMS, NATIONALITY, AND EQUAL TREATMENT

A. Economic and Social Rationales

The interplay between the economic and the social rationale for equality is readily apparent in the four freedoms. These have always been central to the EC and non-discrimination on grounds of nationality lies at the core of these provisions. It is of course true that the ambit of these Articles has extended beyond discrimination and much comment has been devoted to discerning their outer limits.[8] This should not, however, mask the fact that non-discrimination on grounds of nationality remains of central importance for the four freedoms. It is equally important to recognize at the outset the economic and social rationales that underlay these provisions.

The basic economic object is to ensure the optimal allocation of resources within the Community, by enabling factors of production to move to the area where they are most valued. Thus, for example, labour is one of the factors of production. It may be that this factor of production is valued more highly in some areas than in others. This would be so if there were an excess of supply over demand for labour in southern Italy, and an excess of demand

[7] Ibid. at 15.

[8] P. Craig and G. de Búrca, *EU Law, Text, Cases and Materials* (Oxford University Press, 3rd ed., 2003), Chaps. 13–18; C. Barnard, *The Substantive Law of the EU, The Four Freedoms* (Oxford University Press, 2004).

over supply in certain parts of Germany. In this situation labour is worth more in Germany than it is in Italy. The value of labour within the Community as a whole is, therefore, maximized if workers are free to move within the Community to the area where they are most valued and such movement is not impeded by discrimination on grounds of nationality. The same idea is applicable to freedom of establishment. If a firm established in Italy believes that it could capture part of the German market, if it were allowed to set up in business there, then it should not be prevented from so doing by rules of German law that discriminate on grounds of nationality.

There has, however, always been a social as well as an economic rationale underlying the proscription of discrimination on grounds of nationality within the four freedoms. This is at its most fundamental the idea that it should be regarded as natural and something to be encouraged that, for example, workers should be employed or firms should carry on business in Member States other than their home state, and that when they did so they could not be treated in a disadvantageous manner as compared with nationals of that state. This was integral to the very idea of a 'community'. There are of course barriers to the realization of this ideal, some practical, others cultural in nature, which provisions embodied in a Treaty cannot in themselves dispel. This can be accepted, while at the same time recognizing that the four freedoms are designed to facilitate this integration.

The subsequent discussion will reveal the interplay between the economic and social rationales for free movement and equal treatment cast in terms of non-discrimination on grounds of nationality.

B. Discrimination and Equal Treatment

It may be helpful at this stage to recall briefly the strident approach taken by the Community courts to nationality discrimination. The jurisprudence in relation to workers and goods attests to the judicial approach.

Thus the ECJ has been especially keen to stamp out direct discrimination in relation to workers and held that provisions of the French Maritime Code, which required a certain proportion of the crew of a ship to be of French nationality, were contrary to what is now Article 39 EC. The ECJ stated that the Article was directly applicable in the legal system of every Member State and rendered inapplicable all contrary national law.[9] The ECJ also stressed the importance of equal treatment through an expansive reading of indirect discrimination on grounds of nationality, holding that a condition of eligibility for a benefit which is more easily satisfied by national than by non-national workers is likely to fall foul of the Treaty. Proof of indirect

9 Case 167/73, *Commission v French Republic* [1974] ECR 359; Case C-185/96, *Commission v Hellenic Republic* [1998] ECR I-6601.

discrimination does not require the applicant to prove that a national measure in practice affected a higher proportion of foreign workers, but merely that the measure was 'intrinsically liable' to affect migrant workers more than nationals.[10] This will be so where benefits are made conditional, in law or fact, on residency or place of origin requirements that can more easily be satisfied by nationals as opposed to non-nationals.[11] Language requirements for certain posts may also be indirectly discriminatory, since it is likely that a far higher proportion of non-nationals than nationals will be affected by them, although such requirements can be imposed where warranted by the nature of the post to be filled.[12]

The same strident approach to nationality discrimination, direct and indirect, is apparent in the case law on free movement of goods. The ECJ has been particularly harsh on discriminatory rules in the form of import or export restrictions, holding that import or export licences are caught by Article 28 EC,[13] as are provisions which subject imported goods to requirements that are not imposed on domestic products.[14] Article 28 has also been held to prohibit action by a State that promotes or favours domestic products to the detriment of competing imports. This may occur where the Member State engages in a campaign to promote the purchase of domestic as opposed to imported goods;[15] where a Member State has rules on the origin-marking of certain goods thereby allowing consumers to manifest prejudice against foreign products;[16] where public procurement rules are structured so as to favour domestic producers;[17] or where the discrimination in favour of

[10] Case C-237/94, *O'Flynn v Adjudication Officer* [1996] ECR I-2617; Case C-278/94, *Commission v Belgium* [1996] ECR I-4307.

[11] Case 15/69, *Württembergische Milchverwertung-Südmilch-AG v Salvatore Ugliola* [1970] ECR 363; Case 152/73, *Sotgiu v Deutsche Bundespost* [1974] ECR 153; Case C-419/92, *Scholz v Universitaria di Cagliari* [1994] ECR I-505; Case C-15/96, *Kalliope Schöning-Kougebetopoulou v Freie und Hansestadt Hamburg* [1998] ECR I-47; Case C-187/96, *Commission v Hellenic Republic* [1998] ECR I-1095; Case 35/97, *Commission v Belgium* [1998] ECR I-5325; Case C-355/98, *Commission v Belgium* [2000] ECR I-1221; Case C-87/99, *Zurstrassen v Administration des Contributions Directes* [2000] ECR I-3337.

[12] Case 379/87, *Groener v Minister for Education* [1989] ECR 3967.

[13] Cases 51–54/71, *International Fruit Company v Produktschap voor Groenten en Fruit (No 2)* [1971] ECR 1107; Case 68/76, *Commission v French Republic* [1977] ECR 515.

[14] Case 154/85, *Commission v Italy* [1987] ECR 2717; Case 4/75, *Rewe-Zentralfinanz v Landwirtschaftskammer* [1975] ECR 843; Case 53/76, *Procureur de la République Besançon v Bouhelier* [1977] ECR 197.

[15] Case 249/81, *Commission v Ireland* [1982] ECR 4005.

[16] Case 207/83, *Commission v United Kingdom* [1985] ECR 1201. See also, Case 12/74, *Commission v Germany* [1975] ECR 181; Case 113/80, *Commission v Ireland* [1981] ECR 1625.

[17] Case 72/83, *Campus Oil Ltd. v Minister for Industry and Energy* [1984] ECR 2727; Case C-21/88, *Du Pont de Nemours Italiana SpA v Unita Sanitaria Locale No. 2 Di Carrara* [1990] ECR I-889; Case 45/87, *Commission v Ireland* [1988] ECR 4929.

domestic goods is evident in administrative practice, as opposed to formal rules.[18]

C. Equal Treatment and the Interplay between the Economic and Social Rationale

The strident approach taken by the ECJ towards nationality discrimination, whether direct or indirect, is well known. It is nonetheless interesting to reflect further on the way in which the economic and social rationales for equal treatment irrespective of nationality play out in certain areas. Space precludes exhaustive treatment of this issue in all areas of free movement. The interplay can nonetheless be exemplified by focusing in more detail on the meaning accorded to the term worker, the benefits afforded to workers within the host state, and the interpretation given to the public service exception in the context of the free movement of workers.

(1) The Definition of Worker

The ECJ emphasized from the outset that the term worker was to be given an autonomous Community definition, and was not dependent on characterization by national law.[19] It has since then given an expansive reading to the Community concept of worker.

Thus in *Antonissen*[20] the ECJ gave a teleological interpretation to what is now Article 39, so as to include those seeking work. It acknowledged that the Article was worded so as to give Community nationals the right to move freely when accepting offers of employment actually made, and that the right to stay in the territory of a Member State was stated to be for the purpose of employment. It held nonetheless that the Article should not be interpreted so as to exclude the right to move freely in order to look for work, since this strict interpretation 'would jeopardize the actual chances that a national of a Member State who is seeking employment will find it in another Member State, and would, as a result, make that provision ineffective'.[21] The ECJ concluded that the rights enumerated in the Article were not exhaustive and that they included the right to move freely in order to seek employment, although it should be noted that the status of an EC national searching for work is not exactly the same as that of such a person who is actually employed, although the law in this area is developing.[22]

[18] Case 21/84, *Commission v France* [1985] ECR 1356.

[19] Case 75/63, *Hoekstra (née Unger) v Bestuur der Bedrijfsvereniging voor Detailhandel en Ambachten* [1964] ECR 177.

[20] Case C-292/89, *R. v Immigration Appeal Tribunal, ex p Antonissen* [1991] ECR I-745.

[21] Ibid. at para. 12.

[22] Case C-138/02, *Collins v Secretary of State for Work and Pensions* [2004] ECR I-2703.

In *Levin*[23] the ECJ affirmed that part-time work could come within what is now Article 39 EC, even where the sum earned did not equal the minimum wage prevailing in the Netherlands, subject to the caveat that the employment activity had to be genuine and excluded activities on such a small scale as to be regarded as purely marginal and ancillary. The ECJ held that the freedom to take up employment was important, not just as a means towards the creation of a single market for the benefit of the Member State economies, but as a right for the worker to raise her standard of living, even if the worker did not reach the minimum level of subsistence in a particular state.[24] Advocate General Slynn noted the increasing dependence on part-time work, especially in times of unemployment. He emphasized that the exclusion of part-time work from the protection of Article 39 would exclude not only women, the elderly, and disabled who, for personal reasons might wish only to work part-time, but also women and men who would prefer to work full-time, but were obliged to accept part-time work.

The ECJ persisted with this broad interpretation of the term worker in later cases concerning part-time work and in cases where the worker was remunerated in kind,[25] although it is clear that there are limits in this respect.[26] The general rule is, moreover, that the purpose for which the employment is undertaken will not be relevant in determining whether a person is a worker. Provided that the employment is genuine and not marginal it will benefit from Article 39.[27] The interplay between the economic and social rationales for equal treatment and non-discrimination on nationality grounds can be seen in this case law.

In economic terms, the ruling in *Antonissen*[28] broadened the ambit of Article 39, since if nationals could move to another Member State only when they already had an offer of employment, the number of people who could move would be relatively small, and many workers who could well seek and

[23] Case 53/81, *Levin v Staatssecretaris van Justitie* [1982] ECR 1035.

[24] Ibid. at para. 15.

[25] Case 139/85, *Kempf v Staatssecretaris van Justitie* [1986] ECR 1741; Case 66/85, *Lawrie-Blum v Land Baden-Württemberg* [1986] ECR 2121; Case 196/87, *Steymann v Staatssecretaris van Justitie* [1988] ECR 6159; Case C-357/89, *Raulin v Minister van Onderwijs en Wetenschappen* [1992] ECR I-1027; Case C-456/02, *Trojani v Centre Public D'Aide Sociale de Bruxelles (CPAS)* [2004] ECR I-7573.

[26] Case C-138/02, *Collins, supra* n. 22, at paras. 26–33.

[27] There are some cases where some account has been taken of the purpose of the employment, Case 344/87, *Bettray v Staatssecretaris van Justitie* [1989] ECR 1621, although this decision was interpreted narrowly in Case C-456/02, *Trojani, supra* n. 25, at paras. 18–22. The purpose of the employment was also of some relevance in Case 197/86, *Brown v Secretary of State for Scotland* [1988] ECR 3205, which should, however, be read in the light of Case C-184/99, *Rudy Grzelczyk v Centre Public D'Aide Sociale d'Ottignes-Louvain-la-Neuve (CPAS)* [2001] ECR I-6193, at paras. 34–35.

[28] Case C-292/89, *supra* n. 20.

find employment on arrival in a Member State would be prevented from so doing. In *Levin*[29] and the subsequent jurisprudence there is the recognition that the nature of the employment relationship is changing, with a shift towards part-time work. To exclude such work from the ambit of Article 39 would therefore seriously limit its reach, more especially because a worker might justifiably hope to move from part-time work to full-time employment. The optimal allocation of employment resources within the EC as a whole should not, therefore, exclude the relative demand and supply of part-time workers as between different Member States.

The judgments also evince concern with the social dimension of free movement of workers and equal treatment. The right to move to look for work served to diminish the differential impact of Article 39 on different categories of workers, since, other things being equal, it would normally be those in higher paid or professional employment who would have a job offer before moving to another Member State, by way of contrast to unskilled or semi-skilled workers who might be more likely to secure employment after arrival in the host Member State. The social dimension is also apparent in the right for the worker to raise her standard of living, even if she did not reach the minimum level of subsistence in a particular state. It is evident in the recognition that to exclude part-time work from the reach of Article 39 would in effect indirectly discriminate against women who were more likely to work part-time, and against others who chose for a variety of reasons to limit the number of hours which they worked. The emphasis throughout the jurisprudence that the level of remuneration did not matter, subject to the condition that the employment was genuine and above a *de minimis* level, served to emphasize moreover that a person should be free to move within the Community as a worker, notwithstanding the fact that the pay had to be supplemented by other monetary resources.

(2) The Benefits Given to Workers

The discussion thus far has focused on the way in which the interpretation accorded to the term worker reflected the economic and social rationales underlying non-discrimination on grounds of nationality. The benefits afforded to workers provide further interesting evidence of the same theme. The content of these benefits has been determined by an admixture of Community legislation and judicial interpretation.

The principal secondary legislation was until recently Regulation 1612/68,[30] Part I of which required Member States to ensure that Community

[29] Case 53/81, *supra* n. 23.

[30] Council Regulation 1612/68/EEC of 15 October 1968, On Freedom of Movement for Workers within the Community, OJ 1968 L257/2, OJ 1968 Spec. Ed. 475. Arts. 10 and 11

workers were given a considerable range of the benefits available to nationals. Article 1 set out the right of Member State nationals to take up employment in another Member State under the same conditions as its nationals, while Article 2 prohibited discrimination against such workers in relation to the conclusion and performance of contracts of employment. A range of discriminatory practices, such as quotas for foreign workers, special recruitment procedures, measures limiting advertising of vacancies, and special registration procedures were prohibited by Articles 3 and 4, subject to an exception for genuine linguistic requirements. A national of another Member State who sought employment was entitled to the same assistance from employment offices as that given to their own nationals seeking work, Article 5. Discriminatory vocational or medical criteria for recruitment and appointment were proscribed by Article 6.

Article 7(1) provided that a worker from another Member State could not be treated differently from national workers in relation to conditions of employment, such as remuneration, dismissal, or reinstatement; Article 7(2) stipulated that such workers should enjoy the same social and tax advantages as nationals; Article 7(3) required equal access to vocational training; and Article 7(4) rendered void any discriminatory provisions of collective or individual employment agreements. Equality in relation to trade union rights with nationals was guaranteed by Article 8, and equality in relation to rights and benefits concerning housing was established by Article 9.

The rights of family members were dealt with in Articles 10 to 12. Article 10 stated that the worker's spouse and their descendants, who are either under 21 or dependent, and dependent relatives in the ascending line of the worker and spouse, have the right, irrespective of their nationality, to install themselves with a worker who is employed in another Member State, so long as the worker has adequate housing available. Member States were also required to 'facilitate the admission' of other family members who were either dependent on the worker, or living under the worker's roof in the Member State of origin. Article 11 made it clear that the spouse and children mentioned in Article 10 could take up activity as employed persons in the host Member State, while Article 12 provided for equal access for the children of a resident worker to the state's educational courses.

The economic rationale for Regulation 1612/68 is readily apparent. The economic objective of free movement to facilitate the optimal allocation of employment resources in the Community as a whole would have had little

were replaced by provisions of the Citizenship Dir.: Directive 2004/38/EC of the European Parliament and of the Council of 29 April 2004, On the Right of the Citizens of the Union and their Families to Move and Reside Freely within the Territory of the Member States, Amending Regulation 1612/68, and Repealing Directives 64/221, 68/360, 72/194, 73/148, 75/34, 75/35, 90/364, 90/365, and 93/96, OJ 2004 L158/77.

impact if Member States had been able to discriminate about the matters proscribed by the Regulation. The imposition of quotas or discriminatory provisions concerning employment would have denuded the right to free movement of substance. The same is true in relation to provisions about matters such as access to vocational training and the like. The Articles dealing with workers' families were equally important in this respect, since it is clear that many workers would have been dissuaded from seeking employment in another Member State if they could not be accompanied by their immediate family, or if those family members could be treated disadvantageously in relation to matters such as education.

There were, however, also prominent social objectives underlying Regulation 1612/68. This is evident from particular Articles, such as those dealing with workers' families, which were framed so as to foster the stability and cohesiveness that comes when people move as a family unit, thereby alleviating the social problems that can occur when families are divided for considerable periods of time.

A more general social objective can also be discerned running throughout the provisions of the Regulation. At its most fundamental this is that once a person fulfils the conditions for being a worker there should as a matter of principle be equality of treatment within the society where the person is working. There should be no sense in which the worker from another Member State should be treated or regarded as 'second class' by way of contrast to nationals of that State. This is reflected in the wording of the preamble to the Regulation, which speaks of the need for equality of treatment in fact and law in order that freedom of movement can be exercised in freedom and dignity. This imperative has influenced the interpretation of different provisions of the Regulation.

This is exemplified by *Michel S*[31] in the context of Article 12. The disabled son of an Italian employee who had worked in Belgium until he died sought benefits that were available under Belgian legislation to enable disabled Belgian nationals recover their ability to work. The ECJ held that the claim could not be based on Article 7(2) of Regulation 1612/68, holding that this only covered benefits connected with employment. It held, however, that the claim could be based on Article 12. The ECJ drew inspiration from the reference to freedom and dignity in the preamble to conclude that the list of educational arrangements for workers' children in Article 12 was not exhaustive, and that it could also cover the Belgian disability benefit.

The social objective of not treating workers from other Member States as second class has also informed the ECJ's activist jurisprudence when

[31] Case 76/72, *Michel S v Fonds National de Reclassement Handicapés* [1973] ECR 457. See also, Case 9/74, *Casagrande v Landeshauptstadt München* [1974] ECR 773; Case C-7/94, *Landesamt für Ausbildungsförderung Nordrhein-Westfalen v Lubor Gaal* [1996] ECR I-1031.

interpreting 'social and tax advantage' in Article 7(2) of Regulation 1612/68. The very generality of this provision enabled applicants to use it to challenge the discriminatory application of certain benefits by Member States that were not dealt with by other specific provisions of the Regulation. In the seminal *Cristini* case[32] the ECJ made it clear, contrary to its earlier ruling in *Michel S*, that Article 7(2) was not limited to benefits connected with employment. The Italian widow of an Italian worker in France was refused a reduction card for rail fares for large families on the ground of her nationality. The defendant contended that the benefits in Article 7 were restricted to those connected with the contract of employment. The ECJ held to the contrary, stating that the term 'social advantages' in Article 7(2) should not be interpreted in this limited manner. Given the equality of treatment which the provision sought to achieve, 'the substantive area of application must be delineated so as to include all social and tax advantages, whether or not attached to the contract of employment, such as reductions in fares for large families'.[33] Similarly in *Inzirillo*,[34] the ECJ held that an allowance for a handicapped adult, which a Member State awarded to its own nationals, would be a social advantage to a non-national worker.

There are of course limits to Article 7(2). The social advantage must be of some direct or indirect benefit to the worker, and not just to a family member.[35] It must also be an advantage which, whether or not linked to a contract of employment, is generally granted to a national worker primarily *qua* worker and does not cover national benefits granted for wartime service.[36]

This does not serve to undermine the fact that Article 7(2) covers all social and tax advantages, not just those that are linked to employment, and even when they are of indirect rather than of direct benefit to the worker. The basic imperative is that once a person is deemed to be a worker for the purposes of Community law then he or she must be placed on an equal footing in terms of social advantages with nationals from that Member State. The social advantages that are accorded to workers may remain a matter of national policy, but when that policy decision is made the benefit will accrue to all those working in that State, including nationals from other Member States. The ECJ will be resistant to claims that the benefit or advantage

[32] Case 32/75, *Fiorini (neé Cristini) v Société Nationale des Chemins de Fer Français* [1975] ECR 1085.

[33] Ibid. at para. 13.

[34] Case 63/76, *Inzirillo v Caisse d'Allocations Familiales de l'Arrondissement de Lyon* [1976] ECR 2057. See also, Case 94/84, *Office National de l'Emploi v Joszef Deak* [1985] ECR 1873.

[35] Case 316/85, *Centre public d'aide sociale de Courcelles v Lebon* [1987] ECR 2811, at para. 12.

[36] Case 207/78, *Ministère Public v Even and ONPTS* [1979] ECR 2019. See also, Case C-315/94, *De Vos v Bielefeld* [1996] ECR I-1417. Compare however, Case 15/69, *Württembergische Milchverwertung-Südmilch-AG v Salvatore Ugliola* [1970] ECR 363.

should be reserved for nationals of the host State. Thus in *Reina* Germany granted an interest-free 'childbirth loan' to German nationals to stimulate the birth rate of the population. This was held to be a social advantage within Article 7(2), with the consequence that an Italian couple in Germany, one of whom was a worker, were eligible for the loan.[37] The defendant argued that the refusal to grant a loan did not hinder mobility of workers within the Community, and that since it was a matter of demographic policy it could be limited to those of German nationality. The ECJ rejected the argument and held that the loan was a social advantage since its main aim was to alleviate the financial burden on low-income families and the fact that there were also demographic objectives did not preclude the application of Community law.

(3) The Public Service Exception

The interrelationship between the economic and social rationales for equal treatment and non-discrimination on grounds of nationality is also apparent in the interpretation accorded to Article 39(4) EC, which stipulates that Article 39 shall not apply to 'employment in the public service'.

In *Sotgiu*[38] the ECJ echoed its stance in relation to the definition of worker by making it clear that it would define the meaning and ambit of the public service exception. It would not be bound by national definitions of public service since 'these legal designations can be varied at the whim of national legislatures and cannot therefore provide a criterion for interpretation appropriate to the requirements of Community law'.[39] The Member States could not therefore deem a particular post to be 'in the public service' by the name or designation given to that post, or by the mere fact that its terms were regulated by public law.

The Member States were not, however, minded to concede lightly that the ECJ had an interpretative monopoly over the meaning of public service, nor were they willing to accept that national conceptions of public service should not control or strongly influence the interpretation of Article 39(4).

They returned to the attack in *Commission v Belgium*.[40] Possession of Belgian nationality was required as a condition of entry for posts with Belgian local authorities and public undertakings, regardless of the nature of the duties to be performed, including unskilled railway workers, hospital nurses, and night-watchmen. Belgium, supported by the UK, German, and French governments, argued that what is now Article 39(4), by way of contrast to

[37] Case 65/81, *Reina v Landeskreditbank Baden-Württemberg* [1982] ECR 33. See also Case C-111/91, *Commission v Luxembourg* [1993] ECR I-817; Case C-237/94, *O'Flynn v Adjudication Officer* [1996] ECR I-2617; Case C-185/96, *Commission v Greece* [1998] ECR I-6601.

[38] Case 152/73, *Sotgiu v Deutsche Bundespost* [1974] ECR 153, at para. 5.

[39] Ibid. at para. 5.

[40] Case 149/79, *Commission v Belgium* [1980] ECR 3881.

Article 45 EC, embodied an institutional test, such that the key criterion for application of the exception was the institution within which the worker was employed, rather than the nature of the work itself. Belgium argued moreover that when the Treaties were drafted there was no Community concept of the objectives and scope of public authorities and that the Member States' governments had wished the conditions of entry to public office to remain their preserve.

The ECJ was unmoved by this argument. The fact that nationality was a necessary condition for entry to any post in the public service of a Member State and that this condition had constitutional status in certain states was not determinative. The need for the 'unity and efficacy' of Community law meant that the interpretation of concepts such as employment in the public service could not be left to the discretion of Member States, even if the state's rules were of a constitutional nature.[41]

The ECJ held rather that the exception removed from the ambit of Article 39 a series of posts which involved direct or indirect participation in the exercise of powers conferred by public law and duties designed to safeguard the general interests of the State or of other public authorities. These posts 'presume on the part of those occupying them the existence of a special relationship of allegiance to the State and reciprocity of rights and duties which form the foundation of the bond of nationality'.[42] The scope of the derogation made by Article 39(4) had therefore to be determined in the light of this objective. This could, however, be difficult where Member State authorities, acting under public law, assumed responsibilities of an economic and social nature or were involved in activities that were not readily identifiable with typical public service functions. To extend the public service exception to such posts which, although undertaken by the State or an organization governed by public law, did not involve any association with tasks belonging to the public service properly so called, 'would be to remove a considerable number of posts from the ambit of the principles set out in the Treaty and to create inequalities between Member States according to the different ways in which the State and certain sectors of economic life are organized'.[43]

It was not therefore open to a Member State to bring activities of an economic or social nature within the exception simply by including them in the scope of the public law of the state, and taking responsibility for their performance. The ECJ's key criterion was that the exception would apply to posts which required a specific bond of allegiance and mutuality of rights and duties between state and employee. Such posts had to involve participation in

[41] Ibid. at paras. 18–19. See also, Case C-473/93, *Commission v Luxembourg* [1996] ECR I-3207, at para. 38.

[42] Ibid. at para. 10.

[43] Ibid. at para. 11.

the exercise of powers conferred by public law, and should entail duties designed to safeguard the general interests of the state.[44] These requirements are best regarded as cumulative.[45] In a subsequent ruling the ECJ found that the majority of the posts did not satisfy these criteria.[46] The Court has reaffirmed its approach in later cases.[47] It has in particular emphasized the need for the Member State seeking to rely on the exception to proffer specific arguments as to why the task undertaken relates to the exercise of powers conferred by public law and is concerned with safeguarding the general interests of the state.

The interplay between the economic and social objectives underlying equality in relation to free movement is evident in this case law. The economic rationale for the restrictive interpretation of the exception is not hard to divine. The broader the reach of the exception, the narrower is the ambit of the basic principle enshrined in Article 39. If the exception were to be liberally interpreted then there would be a significant diminution in the range and type of employment relationships where workers could rely on equality free from differential treatment on nationality. This was of particular concern, given the breadth of the conception of public service traditionally applied within some Member States. Deference to national conceptions of public service would moreover necessarily lead to inequalities between Member States. These twin concerns were reflected in the case law, where the ECJ voiced concern that an institutional reading of the exception that was tied to national conceptions of public service would remove a considerable number of posts from the ambit of the Treaty and create inequalities between Member States depending on the different ways in which the state and economic life were organized.[48]

The strength of feeling generated by the case law in this area attests to the social dimension of the public service exception. The institutional test advocated by certain Member States, whereby the criterion for application of the public service exception was the institution within which the worker was employed, rather than the nature of the work itself, embodied a view as to when it was legitimate for the Member States to require nationality as a

[44] See also the Commission's view on the type of posts that would qualify for the public service exception, [1988] OJ C72/2.

[45] Case 66/85, *Lawrie-Blum*, *supra* n. 25, at para. 27; Case C-473/93, *Commission v Luxembourg* [1996] ECR I-3207, at para. 18, Léger AG. There are however formulations that cast the conditions in the alternative, Case 225/85, *Commission v Italy* [1987] ECR 2625, at para. 10.

[46] Case 149/79, *Commission v Belgium II* [1982] ECR 1845.

[47] Case 225/85, *Commission v Italy*, *supra* n. 45; Case 66/85, *Lawrie-Blum*, *supra* n. 25, at para. 28; Case 33/88, *Allué and Coonan v Università degli Studi di Venezia* [1989] ECR 1591; Case C-213/90, *ASTI v Chambre des Employés Privés* [1991] ECR I-3507; Case C-4/91, *Bleis v Ministère de l'Education Nationale* [1991] ECR I-5627.

[48] Case 149/79, *Commission v Belgium*, *supra* n. 40, at para. 11.

condition for employment. It was underpinned by the idea that 'the legitimate interests of the State can best be served and protected by the recruitment of the State's own nationals to perform certain tasks on its behalf'.[49] It reflected a deep-rooted conviction 'that the public service is an area in which the State should exercise full sovereignty'.[50] The ECJ's rejection of the institutional test and its adherence to a functional criterion challenged the prevalent Member State view. The challenge was based not merely on the undesirable economic consequences for the Community that would follow if the Member State view were to be accepted. The ECJ's juridical stance also embodied a social view as to when it was legitimate for nationality to be regarded as a condition of employment. The functional test was premised on the assumption that this would only be so where the character of the post required the reciprocal bond of allegiance which is said to be characteristic of nationality. This test denied by its very nature that all posts in the public service as traditionally conceived by Member States should necessarily be reserved to nationals of that State. It required Member States to think the unthinkable, that in a Community it might well be the case that, for example, the best qualified applicant for a job as an economist in the public service might be a national from another Member State and that where the post did not require the reciprocal bond of allegiance that characterized nationality the applicant should be able to put forward her credentials for the job on an equal footing with nationals from the state in which she sought employment. The struggles over the ambit of the public service exception therefore cast into sharp relief the extent to which Community conceptions of equal treatment would force Member States to reconsider the reserved domain where nationality could still be a condition for employment. Advocate General Mancini captured this in typically strident tone, when he remarked that while an extremist disciple of Hegel might truly think that access to posts like nursing should be denied to foreigners, 'anyone who does not regard the State as "the march of God in the world" must of necessity take the contrary view'.[51]

The limits of the preceding argument should of course be recognized. The ECJ's jurisprudence did not stop Member States from seeking to advance their broader conception of the public service exception, as attested to by the steady flow of cases arising for adjudication on this issue.[52] It is

[49] O'Keeffe, 'Judicial Interpretation of the Public Service Exception to the Free Movement of Workers', in D. Curtin and D. O'Keeffe (eds), *Constitutional Adjudication in European Community and National Law* (Butterworths, 1992), at 105.

[50] Case 307/84, *Commission v France* [1986] ECR 1725, at 1727, Mancini AG.

[51] Ibid. at 1733. See also, Mancini, 'The Free Movement of Workers in the Case-Law of the European Court of Justice', in Curtin and O'Keeffe (eds), *supra* n. 49, at 67.

[52] Case C-473/93, *Commission v Luxembourg* [1996] ECR I-3207; Case C-173/94, *Commission v Belgium* [1996] ECR I-3265; Case C-290/94, *Commission v Greece* [1996] ECR

moreover doubtful whether that jurisprudence in and of itself produced a major psychological readjustment by national bureaucracies, in terms of positive willingness to consider foreign applicants for public service jobs. The national culture in certain Member States, whereby public servants are commonly recruited from those who have followed a certain pattern of education within that system, constitutes a further de facto barrier for those competing from outside. This can be acknowledged and serves to show the constraints on change that can be effectuated through law, and more particularly through adjudication.

The importance of the economic and social dimension to the ECJ's case law should nonetheless also be recognized. A quantitatively large sector of employment would have been immune from the demands of equal treatment if the Member States' view of the public service exception had been accepted, and this would have been detrimental given the economic objective of equal treatment in Article 39. Acceptance of the institutional reading of the public service exception would moreover have perpetuated a view as to when it was legitimate for nationality to be a condition of employment that would have been detrimental to the social objectives underlying free movement. The preservation of national identity may well be a legitimate national aim, as made clear by Article 6(3) TEU, but that interest could be safeguarded by other means and did not justify the general exclusion of foreign nationals from the public service.[53]

3. ARTICLE 12 EC, NATIONALITY AND EQUAL TREATMENT

A. Economic and Social Rationales

The preceding discussion has been concerned with nationality and equal treatment in the context of the four freedoms. It is, however, clear that the general prohibition on discrimination laid down in Article 12 EC is important for the protection of equal treatment in its own right. Article 12 is cast in the following terms.

Within the scope of application of this Treaty, and without prejudice to any special provisions contained therein, any discrimination on grounds of nationality shall be prohibited.

The Council, acting in accordance with the procedure referred to in Article 251, may adopt rules designed to prohibit such discrimination.

I-3285; Case C-405/01, *Colegio de Oficiales de la Marina Mercante Espanola v Administración del Estado* [2003] ECR I-10391; Case C-47/02, *Anker, Ras and Snoek v Germany* [2003] ECR I-10447.

[53] Case C-473/93, *supra* n. 52, at para. 35.

The economic and social rationales for non-discrimination on grounds of nationality that were identified when discussing the four freedoms are also central to the general proscription of nationality discrimination in Article 12. The relationship between these rationales is brought out clearly by Advocate General Jacobs in the *Phil Collins* case.[54]

> The fundamental purpose of the Treaty is to achieve an integrated economy in which the factors of production, as well as the fruits of production, may move freely and without distortion, this bringing about a more efficient allocation of resources and a more perfect division of labour. The greatest obstacle to the realization of that objective was the host of discriminatory rules and practices whereby the national governments traditionally protected their own producers and workers from foreign competition. Although the abolition of discriminatory rules and practices may not be sufficient in itself to achieve the high level of economic integration envisaged by the Treaty, it is clearly an essential prerequisite.
>
> The prohibition of discrimination on grounds of nationality is also of great symbolic importance, inasmuch as it demonstrates that the Community is not just a commercial arrangement between the governments of the Member States but is a common enterprise in which all the citizens of Europe are able to participate as individuals ... No other aspect of Community law touches the individual more directly or does more to foster that sense of common identity without which the 'ever closer union among the peoples of Europe', proclaimed in the preamble to the Treaty, would be an empty slogan.

While it is therefore clear that there are economic and social rationales underlying Article 12, the scope of its application is problematic as will be apparent from the subsequent discussion. We can nonetheless identify a number of different types of case where Article 12 has been used and by doing so build up a more general picture of the contribution made by Article 12 to equal treatment within the EC. It is helpful in this respect to begin with the most obvious instances where the Article has been deployed and move outward from there to more difficult cases.

B. Article 12 EC as an Interpretative Device in Relation to the Four Freedoms

There are a number of cases where Article 12 has been used as an interpretative tool when considering the reach of the four freedoms. It was recognized early in the ECJ's jurisprudence that the principle of equal treatment on grounds of nationality underpinned and united the four freedoms.[55] The Court has drawn on Article 12 when deciding upon a range of particular

[54] Case C-92/92, *Phil Collins v Imtrat Handelsgesellschaft mbH* [1993] ECR I-5145, at 5163.

[55] Case 33/74, *Van Binsbergen v Bestuur van de Bedrijfsvereniging voor de Metaalnijverheid* [1974] ECR 1299.

issues concerning the four freedoms. Space precludes detailed treatment of this issue, but the judicial approach can nonetheless be discerned from some prominent examples.

Thus in *Angonese*[56] the ECJ drew on Article 12 to reinforce the conclusion that Article 39 EC had horizontal direct effect. Angonese was an Italian national whose mother tongue was German. He was resident in Bolzano in Italy, but studied in Austria between 1993 and 1997. He applied to take part in a competition for a post with a private bank in Bolzano, the Cassa di Riparmio. A condition for entry to the competition imposed by the bank was a certificate of bilingualism (in Italian and German). The bank was allowed to impose requirements of this type by a collective agreement with national savings banks in Italy, but an individual bank was free as to whether to impose such conditions at all. The certificate was issued by the public authorities in Bolzano after an examination held only in that province. The national court found that Angonese was bilingual, and that there could be practical difficulties for non-residents of Bolzano to obtain the certificate in good time. Angonese did not obtain the certificate and the bank refused to admit him to the competition for the post. Angonese argued that the Bank's requirement for an applicant to have the certificate was contrary to what is now Article 39.

The ECJ held that the principle of non-discrimination in relation to workers was drafted in general terms and was not specifically addressed to the Member States. It pointed to case law showing that the prohibition of discrimination based on nationality applied not only to the actions of public authorities, but also to other rules aimed at regulating gainful employment and the provision of services in a collective manner, since obstacles to freedom of movement would be compromised if the abolition of State barriers could be neutralized by obstacles resulting from the exercise of powers by associations not governed by public law.[57] Since working conditions in different Member States were sometimes governed by formal law and sometimes by agreements between private parties, it could create inequality in the application of Article 39 if it were limited to discriminatory acts of public authorities. The ECJ reinforced this conclusion by adverting to other provisions of the Treaty, such as Article 141, which, while formally addressed to Member States, had been held applicable to all agreements intended to regulate paid labour collectively, as well as to contracts between individuals.[58] The Court concluded that such considerations must, *a fortiori*, be applicable

[56] Case C-281/98, *Roman Angonese v Cassa di Riparmio di Bolzano SpA* [2000] ECR I-4139.

[57] Case 36/74, *Walrave and Koch* [1974] ECR 1405; Case C-415/93, *Union Royale Belge des Sociétés de Football Association and others v Bosman* [1995] ECR I-4921.

[58] Case 43/75, *Defrenne v Société Anonyme Belge de Navigation Aérienne* [1976] ECR 455.

to what is now Article 39, which laid down a fundamental freedom and constituted a specific application of the general prohibition of discrimination contained in Article 12.

The use of Article 12 to reinforce the desired reading of a more specific Treaty Article concerning free movement is apparent once again in *Cowan*.[59] A British tourist in France was refused state compensation for victims of violent crime, which was available to nationals and to residents. The ECJ referred to the general prohibition on discrimination 'within the scope of application of this Treaty' in Article 12, and to its earlier ruling that tourists were covered by Article 49 as recipients of services.[60] It held in the light of this that when Community law guaranteed a natural person the freedom to go to another Member State, the corollary was that the person was protected from harm in that state on the same basis as that of nationals and persons residing there. It followed that the prohibition of discrimination was applicable to recipients of services as regards protection against the risk of assault and the right to obtain financial compensation provided for by national law when that risk materialized.[61]

C. Article 12 EC as Protector of the Objectives Underlying the Four Freedoms

There is another series of case that is related to that considered above, but nonetheless constitutes a distinct category. The distinguishing feature in this second group is that Article 12 is used as the principal mechanism for attacking national measures that are discriminatory on grounds of nationality, where the contested measures could undermine the objectives of the provisions concerning free movement. The case law on security for costs provides a good example of this use of Article 12.

In *Kronenberger*[62] the applicants were an English partnership and sought payment for goods supplied to a German company that had gone into liquidation. The applicants were required to furnish security for costs under the German rules of civil procedure. This obligation was imposed on foreign nationals who brought proceedings before the German courts, when such a request was made by the defendant. There were certain exceptions to this obligation, but they were not applicable in the instant case.

The case was decided by using Article 12. The ECJ acknowledged that the proscription of discrimination on grounds of nationality within Article 12

[59] Case 186/87, *Cowan v Le Trésor Public* [1989] ECR 195.

[60] Cases 286/82 and 26/83, *Luisi and Carbone v Ministero del Tesoro* [1984] ECR 377.

[61] Case 186/87, *supra* n. 59, at para. 17. See also, Case C-45/93, *Commission v Spain* [1994] ECR I-911.

[62] Case C-323/95, *Hayes and Hayes v Kronenberger GmbH* [1997] ECR I-1711. See also, Case C-43/95, *Data Delecta Aktiebolag and Forsberg v MSL Dynamics Ltd* [1996] ECR I-4661.

only applied 'within the scope of application of this Treaty'. It was therefore necessary to decide whether the German rule about security for costs that applied to foreign nationals bringing actions in Germany came within the scope of application of the Treaty. The Court accepted that Member States could, in the absence of Community legislation, lay down rules of civil procedure for the bringing of actions, but held that Community law nonetheless imposed limits on Member State competence. Such legislative provisions 'may not discriminate against persons to whom Community law gives the right to equal treatment or restrict the fundamental freedoms guaranteed by Community law'.[63]

The ECJ's reasoning thus far did not furnish any specific ground for finding that the discrimination fell within the scope of application of the Treaty. The Court filled this gap by making clear the connection between the contested rule of civil procedure and the four freedoms.[64]

> It must be held that a national procedural rule, such as the one described above, is liable to affect the economic activity of traders from other Member States on the market of the State in question. Although it is, as such, not intended to regulate an activity of a commercial nature, it has the effect of placing such traders in a less advantageous position than nationals of that State as regards access to its courts. Since Community law guarantees such traders free movement of goods and services in the common market, it is a corollary of those freedoms that they must be able, in order to resolve any disputes arising from their economic activities, to bring actions in the courts of the Member State in the same way as nationals of that State.

The ECJ further reinforced its ruling by holding that national legislative provisions that fell within the scope of application of the Treaty were, by reason of their impact on intra-Community trade in goods and services, 'necessarily subject to the general principle of non-discrimination' contained in Article 12 'without there being any need to connect them with the specific provisions' concerning free movement of goods and services.[65] It was sufficient in this regard if the impact on trade in goods and services was indirect.[66] The prohibition on discrimination contained in Article 12 required, moreover, that persons governed by Community law and nationals of the Member State concerned should be treated 'absolutely equally'.[67] The defendant unsuccessfully argued that the German rule was justified, at least in circumstances where orders for judicial costs could not be enforced in the plaintiff's domicile, since it thereby prevented a plaintiff from bringing an action without running any risk if he should lose the case. The ECJ rejected the argument for a number of reasons, including the fact that the German rule was disproportionate to the objective pursued.

[63] Ibid. at para. 13.
[64] Ibid. at para. 14.
[65] Ibid. at para. 16.
[66] Ibid. at para. 17.
[67] Ibid. at para. 18.

The use of Article 12 EC to protect the objectives underlying the provisions concerned with free movement is also the best explanation of the *Phil Collins* case.[68] The applicant was the singer who sought to prevent the sale in Germany of a bootleg recording of his concert in the United States. Under German law German nationals would have been afforded relief in such circumstances, but this was not available for non-Germans. The ECJ held that this was discrimination on grounds of nationality and constituted a breach of what is now Article 12. This Article was directly effective and could be relied on by the applicant in the national courts. The ECJ reasoned that copyright and related rights fell within the ambit of the Treaty because they could distort competition and hinder trade and that this brought the subject matter of the action within the scope of Article 12.[69]

D. Article 12 EC and the Implementation of Community Legislation

Article 12 is also of importance in relation to the implementation of Community legislation. The requirement that for Article 12 to apply the discrimination must operate within the scope of application of the Treaty is generally not problematic in this area, since the very fact that the Community has legislated and that the Member State is implementing the legislation will mean that Article 12 will be applicable, assuming of course that the Community legislation is itself made within the EC's competence.

The *Pastoors* case furnishes a good example of the application of Article 12 in this context. The EC adopted Regulations designed to improve working conditions and road safety in the road transport sector. The Member States were required to adopt the laws or administrative provisions needed to implement the Community measures in relation to, *inter alia*, the penalties to be imposed for breach of the Regulations. Belgium implemented the Regulations by providing that the offender could either pay 10,000 Belgian francs per breach immediately, which would normally extinguish the prosecution, or the offender could submit to criminal proceedings. This latter option was, however, subject to the condition that where the offender had no official or permanent residence in Belgium he was required to lodge a deposit of 15,000 Belgian francs per breach to cover the amount of any fine plus legal costs, in default of which the vehicle was impounded at his risk and expense.

The ECJ held that the Belgian rule was in breach of Article 12. Although it was not framed in terms of nationality, but rather in terms of residence, it was nonetheless indirectly discriminatory, since far more foreign nationals would be caught by it. It would only ever catch Belgian nationals if they did not live or have an official residence in Belgium.

[68] Case C-92/92, *Phil Collins*, *supra* n. 54.

[69] Ibid. at paras. 22–28.

The ECJ rejected the Belgian government's claim that the rule was objectively justified on the grounds that greater costs were involved in actions against non-residents and it was more difficult to enforce decisions. The Court accepted that some differential treatment based on these factors might be justified, since it would prevent non-resident offenders from opting for continuation of ordinary criminal proceedings, with no intention of taking part or of complying with the findings. However the Belgian rule was excessive, since the deposit demanded was 50 per cent higher than the penalty levied when the immediate payment option was chosen, and because the security demanded of non-residents was levied for each breach, even though all such breaches would normally be dealt with in the same criminal proceedings.[70]

E. Article 12 EC, Gravier and the 'Scope of Application' of the Treaty

The cases considered thus far have shown how the ECJ has used Article 12 in a number of ways, primarily to reinforce the four freedoms and to ensure that Community legislation is applied in an equal manner. It should, however, be acknowledged that the condition for the application of Article 12, that the discrimination should be within the 'scope of application' of the Treaty, is open to differing interpretations, since much depends upon the extent to which the subject matter of the action falls within the Treaty and on the nature of the contested national measure.

This is evident from the reasoning and result in the *Gravier* case.[71] Gravier was a French art student who was charged an enrolment fee, *minerval*, for a course in strip-cartoon art in Liège in Belgium, which Belgian nationals were not required to pay. She claimed exemption from the *minerval*, and argued that it was inconsistent with what is now Article 12. The EC had competence under Article 150 EC in relation to vocational training, but this was limited to supporting and supplementing Member State action. It was clear that the treatment accorded to Gravier was unequal and that the discrimination was based on nationality. The key issue was whether the subject matter fell within the scope of application of the Treaty.

The ECJ held that it did. The Court accepted that although educational organization and policy were not entrusted to the Community institutions, access to and participation in courses of instruction and apprenticeship, in particular vocational training, were not unconnected with Community law. It pointed to Community provisions concerning access to vocational training by workers and children of workers, but these did not avail Graver since she was not a worker or a child of a worker. The ECJ therefore focused more directly on Article 150 EC, which concerns Community involvement with

[70] Ibid. at para. 25.

[71] Case 293/83, *Gravier v City of Liège* [1985] ECR 593.

vocational training, and noted that it empowered the Council to lay down general principles for implementing a common vocational training policy capable of contributing to the harmonious development of the national economies and of the common market. It concluded that the common vocational training policy referred to in Article 150 was 'gradually being established',[72] and that it 'constituted an indispensable element of the activities of the Community, whose objectives include *inter alia* the free movement of persons, the mobility of labour, and the improvement of the living standards of workers'.[73] Access to vocational training promoted free movement of persons in the EC by enabling them to obtain a qualification in the Member State where they intended to work and by allowing them to complete their training in the Member State whose training programmes included the desired subject of study. It followed, said the Court, that the conditions of access to vocational training fell within the scope of the Treaty, and hence that the imposition of a *minerval* on non-national students as a condition of access to such training was contrary to Article 12.

The ruling in *Gravier* was undoubtedly contentious. The Danish and UK governments intervened in the case and argued that Article 12 should not be read so as to prevent a Member State from treating its own nationals more favourably in the area of education, particularly as regards access to education, scholarships and grants, and other social facilities provided for students, since on these issues each Member State had special responsibilities towards its own nationals. The ECJ rejected such arguments, at least with regard to payment of the *minerval*. However in *Lair*[74] and *Brown*[75] the Court ruled that while the conditions for access to vocational training, including university studies, fell within the scope of the Treaty for the purpose of Article 12, assistance given by Member States to its nationals when they undertook such studies nonetheless fell outside the Treaty, at the stage of development of Community law then prevailing, except to the extent to which such assistance was intended to cover charges relating specifically to access to vocational training, such as registration and tuition fees. The ECJ has, as will be seen below, departed from its rulings in *Lair* and *Brown* through reliance on Community provisions concerning citizenship.

The present discussion is not directly concerned with the scope of Community involvement with educational policy. The salient point for our purposes is rather the way in which the case law in this area reveals the latitude afforded to the ECJ in the interpretation of Article 12 and more especially the meaning given to the key phrase 'scope of application of the

[72] Ibid. at para. 23. [73] Ibid. at para. 23.
[74] Case 39/86, *Lair* [1988] ECR 3161.
[75] Case 197/86, *Brown v Secretary of State for Scotland* [1988] ECR 3205.

Treaty'.[76] The *Gravier* decision showed the Court's willingness to construe this phrase broadly in order that the principle of non-discrimination on grounds of nationality could apply, notwithstanding the fact that the scope of Community competence in the area was limited to taking action that was supportive of and supplementary to that of the Member States, and notwithstanding the fact that even within these confines Community vocational policy was only gradually being established.

F. Article 12 EC, Citizenship and the 'Scope of Application' of the Treaty

The expansive reading given to the 'scope of application' of the Treaty evident in *Gravier* has been developed in later cases. The driving force in this case law has been the provisions on citizenship, more especially Articles 17 and 18 EC. It is the interpretation accorded to these Articles and the symbiotic relationship between them and Article 12 that has served to expand the principle of equal treatment on grounds of nationality.[77]

Article 17 establishes citizenship of the Union. It provides that every person who is a national of a Member State shall be a citizen of the Union and that Union citizenship shall complement and not replace national citizenship. Citizens of the Union enjoy the rights conferred by the Treaty and are subject to the duties that it imposes. Articles 19 to 22 set out certain specific rights that flow from Union citizenship. Article 18 is of particular significance for present purposes and it is therefore important to set it out in full.

1. Every citizen of the Union shall have the right to move and reside freely within the territory of the Member States, subject to the limitations and conditions laid down in this Treaty and by the measures adopted to give it effect.
2. If action by the Community should prove necessary to attain this objective and this Treaty has not provided the necessary powers, the Council may adopt provisions with a view to facilitating the exercise of the rights referred to in paragraph 1. The Council shall act in accordance with the procedure referred to in Article 251.
3. Paragraph 2 shall not apply to provisions on passports, identity cards, residence

[76] See also, Case C-357/89, *Raulin v Minister van Onderwijs en Wetenschappen* [1992] ECR I-1027, where the ECJ held that the principle of non-discrimination deriving from what is now Art. 12 combined with Art. 150 EC meant that an EC national, admitted to a vocational training course in another Member State, must have a right of residence in that state for the duration of the course. That right, which was derived from the Treaty, was independent of the possession of a residence permit, but the Member States could legitimately impose conditions 'such as the covering of maintenance costs and health insurance'.

[77] O'Leary, 'Nationality Law and Community Citizenship: A Tale of Two Uneasy Bedfellows' (1992) 12 *YBEL* 353; O' Leary, 'Putting Flesh on the Bones of European Union Citizenship' (1999) 24 *ELRev* 68; White, 'Free Movement, Equal Treatment and Citizenship of the Union' (2005) 54 *ICLQ* 885.

permits or any other such document or to provisions on social security or social protection.

The cases to be discussed within this section are complex and it is therefore important to stand back from the detail and understand at the outset the reason for this complexity. We have already seen that the 'trigger' for the application of Article 12 is that the discrimination must occur within the 'scope of application of the Treaty'. The interpretation of this condition can, as seen from the preceding discussion, be difficult in and of itself. That difficulty is exacerbated when the linkage with the Treaty is based on citizenship and Article 18, since the right to reside and move freely in this Article is 'subject to such limits and conditions as are laid down in the Treaty and by the measures adopted to give it effect'.

The ECJ has nonetheless used three juridical techniques, sometimes independently, sometimes in tandem, to expand the reach of the citizenship provisions and the sphere to which Article 12 will apply.

First, it has been willing to apply Union citizenship to situations where the citizen is lawfully resident within the Member State in accord with that Member State's law. Thus even where the applicant does not satisfy the conditions laid down by other Treaty Articles or Community legislation, and cannot therefore rely on Article 18, he or she will be held to be within Article 17 and benefit from Article 12, provided that the applicant is lawfully resident in the particular Member State, and provided that the subject matter of the action comes within the scope of the Treaty *rationae personae* and *ratione materiae.* This juridical technique is exemplified by the rulings in *Martinez Sala*[78] and *Trojani.*[79]

Secondly, the ECJ has given an expansive interpretation to the right to move and reside within Article 18 and has interpreted the qualification to this right, that it is subject to limits and conditions laid down in the Treaty and in Community legislation, narrowly, thereby enabling applicants to benefit from Article 18 and Article 12. This juridical technique is evident in *Grzelczyk*[80] and *Bidar.*[81]

Thirdly, the Court has used the introduction of the citizenship provisions into the Treaty as a reason for rethinking and expanding the interpretation given to other Treaty Articles or Community legislation, thereby expanding the scope of equal treatment and Article 12. The ruling in *Collins*[82] provides a clear example of this, as does that in *Bidar.*

[78] Case C-85/96, *Maria Martinez Sala v Freistaat Bayern* [1998] ECR I-2691.

[79] Case C-456/02, *Trojani, supra* n. 25.

[80] Case C-184/99, *Grzelczyk, supra* n. 27.

[81] Case C-209/03, *The Queen (on the application of Bidar) v London Borough of Ealing and Secretary of State for Education* [2005] ECR I-2119.

[82] Case C-138/02, *Collins, supra* n. 22.

These juridical approaches can, as stated above, be used separately or in tandem, depending on the nature of the case and the preference of the Court. Subject to this caveat it is nonetheless helpful in terms of analytic clarity to consider the cases in terms of the juridical technique that predominated in the particular case.

(1) The First Juridical Technique: Martinez Sala *and* Trojani

The original approach to citizenship was cautious. The ECJ made clear in *Uecker*[83] that citizenship was not intended to extend the scope *ratione materiae* of the Treaty to cover internal situations with no link with Community law. However in *d'Hoop* the ECJ held that the applicant could rely on Article 18 to contest national legislation that granted the right to a tideover allowance only to its nationals who completed their secondary education in Belgium, since this could dissuade such a person from availing herself of educational opportunities in other Member States.[84] The willingness to make use of Article 18 in conjunction with Article 12 is also evident in *Bickel & Franz.*[85] The case was concerned with German and Austrian nationals subject to criminal proceedings in Italy. They requested use of German in the proceedings, in accord with the rights granted to German-speaking Italians resident in that Italian province. The ECJ ruled that Article 12 applied, and stressed that the accused were not only potential recipients of services, but also that they were exercising their right to free movement as European citizens based on Article 18.

It was, however, *Martinez Sala*[86] that showed the real potential for the conjunction between Articles 12 and 17. The applicant was a Spanish national who had lived in Germany since 1968. She had undertaken work at various times, but since 1989 she had received social assistance. Until 1984 she had obtained residence permits from the German authorities, but thereafter she merely had documents saying that the extension of her permit had been applied for. She was issued with a residence permit in 1994. In 1993, when she did not possess a permit, she applied for a child-raising allowance. Her application was rejected because she did not have German nationality, a residence entitlement, or a residence permit.

[83] Cases C-64/96 and 65/96, *Land Nordrhein-Westfalen v Uecker and Jacquet v Land Nordrhein-Westfalen* [1997] ECR I-3171.

[84] Case C-224/98, *D'Hoop v Office National de L'Emploi* [2002] ECR I-6191. See also, Case C-148/02, *Carlos Garcia Avello v Belgium* [2003] ECR I-11613.

[85] Case C-274/96, *Criminal Proceedings against Bickel and Franz* [1998] ECR I-7637, at para. 15.

[86] Case C-85/96, *supra* n. 78. See also, Case C-411/98, *Angelo Ferlini v Centre Hospitalier de Luxembourg* [2000] ECR I-8081; Case C-135/99, *Ursula Elsen v Bundesversicherungsanstalt* [2000] ECR I-10409, at para. 34.

The ECJ considered whether Community law precluded a Member State from requiring nationals of other Member States to have a residence permit in order to receive a child allowance. It was clear that this requirement was discriminatory on grounds of nationality,[87] provided that the subject matter of the case fell within the scope of application of the Treaty. The German government denied that this condition was fulfilled. The Court held that a child-raising allowance was within the scope *ratione materiae* of the Treaty, and that if she were found to be a worker or an employed person she would be within the Treaty *ratione personae.*[88] The Commission argued that, even if she was not a worker, she could come within the personal scope of the Treaty as a citizen because of Article 18.

The ECJ held, however, that in the instant case it was not necessary to decide whether the applicant could rely on Article 18 in order to obtain a 'new right' to reside in Germany, since it was accepted that she had been authorized to reside there, although she had been refused a residence permit.[89] The very fact that she was a national of a Member State lawfully residing in the territory of another Member State brought the applicant within the scope *ratione personae* of the citizenship provisions of the Treaty,[90] with the consequence that Article 17(2) applied, and she had the rights and duties of a citizen laid down by the Treaty, including the right in Article 12 not to suffer discrimination on grounds of nationality within the scope *ratione materiae* of the Treaty.[91] It followed that the requirement of a formal residence permit imposed on non-German nationals was contrary to Article 12.

The essence of the Court's reasoning was therefore as follows. The applicant's right to reside was based not on Article 18, but on the fact that Germany had authorized her residence. This brought her within the citizenship provisions of the Treaty, and entitled her in accordance with Article 17(2) to the rights and duties of citizenship, including the right not to be discriminated against on grounds of nationality within the scope *ratione materiae* of the Treaty. The fact that her right to reside was not based on Article 18 meant that the Court did not have to confront the limiting conditions therein. Under the relevant Regulations, child allowances were given to workers or employed persons. The ECJ was willing to find that such an allowance fell within the scope *ratione materiae* of the Treaty, disaggregating the condition that under the relevant Regulations non-discrimination in relation to such benefits applied to workers or employed persons, and concluding that the duty not to discriminate in relation to such benefits attached also to citizenship.

The potency of the juridical technique used in *Martinez Sala* is clear from

87 Ibid. at para. 54.
88 Ibid. at paras. 57–58.
89 Ibid. at para. 60.
90 Ibid. at para. 61.
91 Ibid. at para. 62.

the reasoning and result in *Trojani*.[92] The applicant was a French national who lived in Belgium in a Salvation Army hostel, where he did various jobs in return for board and lodging and some pocket money. He applied for the minimex, the minimum subsistence allowance, but was refused on the ground that he was not a Belgian national and did not qualify as a worker for the purposes of Community law. The ECJ discussed whether he could be regarded as a worker, but the case is of interest here because the ECJ also considered the applicant's claim on the basis of citizenship.

The ECJ held that the applicant had a *prima facie* right to reside in Belgium as a Union citizen based on Article 18. It acknowledged, however, that this was not unconditional and that the right to reside was subject to limitations laid down by the Treaty or Community legislation. Those limits included the conditions in Directive 90/364:[93] Member State nationals wishing to reside in the host state had to have sickness insurance and sufficient resources to avoid becoming a burden on the social assistance system of that state. The ECJ accepted that it was precisely the lack of such resources that had led the applicant to claim the minimex. Given that this was so, the applicant did not derive a right to reside in Belgium based on Article 18, since he lacked the resources that were a condition for exercise of this right.[94]

It proved, however, premature for Belgium to signal victory in the case since the ECJ proceeded to find in favour of the applicant, notwithstanding what it had said thus far. It reached this conclusion by focusing, as in *Martinez Sala*, on the fact that the applicant was lawfully resident in Belgium as attested by the residence permit given to him by the Belgian municipal authorities.[95] This lawful residence made Article 12 applicable. This was so despite the fact that a Member State might make the existence of sufficient resources a condition of lawful residence, and that it might decide that the lack of such resources meant that a person no longer fulfilled the conditions of that right to reside. Article 12 was nonetheless applicable while the applicant was lawfully resident in accord with national law. The provision of the minimex fell within the scope of the Treaty *ratione materiae*, the applicant was discriminated against on grounds of nationality, and hence the Belgian rule was contrary to Article 12.

This reasoning, however, is problematic. The reality, both legal and political, is almost certainly that the applicant was regarded as lawfully resident by the Belgian authorities because of Directive 90/364 and subject to the

[92] Case C-456/02, *Trojani, supra* n. 25.

[93] Council Directive 90/364/EEC of 28 June 1990, On the Right of Residence, OJ 1990 L180/26.

[94] Case C-456/02, *Trojani, supra* n. 25, at para. 36.

[95] Ibid. at paras. 37–46.

conditions laid down therein. The effect of the judgment is that failure to fulfil the financial conditions in the Directive meant that the applicant could not take advantage of Article 18 combined with Article 12. This same failure did not, however, serve to prevent the applicant using Article 12 on the assumption that he was lawfully resident in Belgium, notwithstanding the fact that his lawful residence in Belgium flowed from the Directive. The ECJ accepted that Belgium could decide that the applicant no longer fulfilled the conditions for lawful residence because of lack of resources. The effect of the judgment was nonetheless to disaggregate the right to reside granted by Belgium because of the Directive, from the financial conditions attached thereto and allow the applicant to claim the very type of financial resources that the Directive made a pre-condition for the right to reside.

(2) The Second Juridical Technique: Grzelczyk *and* Bidar

The judgment in *Grzelczyk*[96] also made reference, as will be seen, to the fact that the applicant was lawfully resident in Belgian, but the decision is of particular interest for the way in which it 'read down' conditions in other Community legislation that could limit the force of Article 18. The applicant was a French national studying in Belgium. He worked part-time during his initial three years of study, but in his fourth year he applied to the CPAS (Centre Public d'Aide Sociale) for payment of the minimex, the non-contributory minimum subsistence allowance. The CPAS granted this, but then withdrew it after the Belgian minister decided that Grzelczyk was not entitled to it since he was not a Belgian national. The minimex had been held to be a social advantage for workers within the context of Regulation 1612/68, but the ECJ approached the case on the assumption that the applicant was not a worker.

The ECJ nonetheless decided that the action of the Belgian government was contrary to EC law. It reasoned as follows. A Belgian student, even though not a worker, who was in the same situation as the applicant would get the minimex, and hence the case clearly involved discrimination on grounds of nationality and would come within Article 12, provided that it came within the scope of application of the Treaty. It was therefore necessary to read Article 12 in conjunction with the provisions of the Treaty concerning citizenship of the Union in order to determine its sphere of application.

The Court made clear its approach to those provisions when it stated that 'Union citizenship is destined to be the fundamental status of nationals of the Member States, enabling those who find themselves in the same situation to enjoy the same treatment in law irrespective of their nationality, subject to

[96] Case C-184/99, *Grzelczyk, supra* n. 27.

such exceptions as are expressly provided for'.[97] It drew on *Martinez Sala* for the proposition that a citizen of the Union, lawfully resident in the territory of a host Member State, could rely on Article 12 in all situations that fell within the scope *ratione materiae* of Community law. Those situations included the exercise of the fundamental freedoms guaranteed by the Treaty and the exercise of the right to move and reside freely in another Member State, as conferred by Article 18.

The ECJ then confronted the fact that the right to reside and move conferred by Article 18 was subject to limits and conditions laid down by the Treaty and measures adopted to give it effect. This was relevant in the instant case, since Directive 93/96[98] required that students who were nationals of a different Member State had to show, *inter alia*, that they had sufficient resources to avoid becoming a burden on the social assistance system of the host Member State during their period of residence. This would seem to be a condition that would limit the application of Article 18 in this case, but the ECJ avoided this conclusion by reading the Directive narrowly.[99] It held that the Directive did not require resources of a specific amount, nor that those resources should be evidenced by particular documents.[100] The ECJ concluded that while a Member State might take the view that a student who had recourse to social assistance no longer fulfilled the conditions for a lawful right to reside established by the Directive, it could not take this view automatically in every case, more especially because there were no provisions in the Directive that prevented a student from receiving social security benefits. The applicant's right to reside under Article 18 was not therefore limited by other Community legislation and hence the discriminatory Belgian provision was caught by Article 12.

It should, however, also be recognized that the juridical technique exemplified by *Grzelczyk* can place real strains on the normal canons of statutory interpretation, even when judged by the interpretive methodology commonly used by the Community courts. This is evident from the subsequent decision in *Bidar*.[101] The ECJ's judgment is a blend of the second and third of the juridical techniques set out above, but it is the use made of the former that was controversial. The applicant was a French national who had been resident in the UK since 1998 in order to accompany his mother who was

[97] Ibid. at para. 31.

[98] Council Directive 93/96/EEC of 29 October 1993, On the Right of Residence for Students, OJ 1993 L317/59.

[99] Case C-184/99, *Grzelczyk*, *supra* n. 27, at paras. 38–46.

[100] The ECJ distinguished in this respect Dir. 93/96, from Dir. 90/364, saying that the latter did indicate the minimum level of income that persons must have to avail themselves of the Dir., ibid. at para. 41. This explains in part why the ECJ in Case C-456/02, *Trojani*, *supra* n. 25, did not feel able to decide the case on the basis of Art. 18 EC.

[101] Case C-209/03, *Bidar*, *supra* n. 81.

undergoing medical treatment. Bidar began a University course, received assistance with tuition fees from the UK government, but was refused a student loan because he was not settled in the UK as required by the UK rules. He claimed that this refusal was contrary to Article 12. The key issue was whether any discrimination fell within the scope of application of the Treaty for the purposes of Article 12.

The ECJ stated that the scope of application of the Treaty for the purposes of Article 12 had to be assessed in conjunction with the Treaty provisions on citizenship, and repeated the '*Grzelczyk* principle' that citizenship was destined to be the fundamental status of Member State nationals. A citizen of the EU who was lawfully resident in the host state could rely on Article 12 in all situations that fell within the scope *ratione materiae* of Community law. Those situations included the exercise of the fundamental freedoms guaranteed by the Treaty, and the exercise of the right to move and reside conferred by Article 18. The prior case law that had held maintenance grants and the like to be outside the scope of the Treaty[102] was said to have been overtaken by subsequent Treaty developments, notably the introduction of the citizenship provisions and those dealing with education and vocational training.

The ECJ however, provided little by way of detailed justification as to why these developments should be taken to have undermined the prior case law. The mere fact that the EU has some limited competence in the field of education tells one little if anything about whether the provision of maintenance grants falls within the scope of application of the Treaty. This is more especially so, given that the prevailing Community legislation and that about to come into effect excluded the provision of such assistance. The way in which the Court dealt with both of these reveals the strains that its teleology placed on normal canons of statutory construction.

The current rules were embodied in Directive 93/96, Article 3 of which specifically stated that the Directive did not establish any right for a student to receive a maintenance grant from the host state. The defendant, supported by other intervening states and the Commission, not unnaturally argued that this constituted a limitation on the consequences of the right to reside for the purposes of Article 18, with the corollary that such grants were still outside the scope of the Treaty.

The ECJ's response was brief and unconvincing.[103] It held that while a student could not base any right to maintenance on Directive 93/96, this did not preclude a student who, by virtue of Article 18 combined with Directive 90/364, was lawfully resident in a Member State from relying on Article 12.

This 'circumvention' of the limitation in Directive 93/96 does not readily withstand examination. It was this Directive that clearly regulated the position

[102] Case 39/86, *Lair, supra* n. 74; Case 197/86, *Brown, supra* n. 75.
[103] Case C-209/03, *Bidar, supra* n. 81, at paras. 45–46.

of a person *qua* student who was residing in another Member State and defined the rules about grants. It expressly stated that such residence gave rise to no right to maintenance payment. On any normal reading, this constituted a limitation of the consequences of the right to reside for the purposes of Article 18.

The rules about maintenance grants for the future are embodied in the Citizenship Directive,[104] which came into effect in April 2006. Article 24(1) enshrines a general right to equal treatment for Union citizens residing on the basis of the Directive, subject to such specific provisions as might be found in the Treaty and secondary law. Article 24(2) is an express derogation from Article 24(1) and states, *inter alia*, that the host state is not obliged, prior to acquisition of the right of permanent residence to grant maintenance aid for studies, including vocational training, consisting of student grants or loans to persons other than workers, the self-employed, persons who retain such status, and members of their families.

Notwithstanding this wording, the ECJ read this provision as reinforcing its conclusion that Treaty developments in relation to education and citizenship justified its finding that maintenance grants and loans were within the scope of application of the Treaty. It said that Article 24(2) defined the content of Article 24(1) in more detail and that by so doing the Community legislature had taken the view that the grant of such aid was within the scope of the Treaty.[105]

This is, with respect, not in accord with the overall language and meaning of Article 24. The natural reading of Article 24 taken as a whole is that equal treatment does not extend to student grants and loans, prior to acquisition of the right of permanent residence, unless the person is a worker, self-employed, or a family member of such a person. Article 24(2) is explicitly cast in terms of a derogation from Article 24(1). It shows that the grant of such assistance is only within the scope of application of the Treaty for those listed, viz, those who have a right of permanent residence, workers, and the like.[106]

(3) The Third Juridical Technique: Collins

The third of the juridical techniques in the case law on Article 12 and citizenship is exemplified by *Collins*.[107] The applicant, an Irish national

[104] Dir. 2004/38, *supra* n. 30.

[105] Case C-209/03, *Bidar*, *supra* n. 81, at para. 43.

[106] The ECJ accepted that it was legitimate for a Member State to make assistance for maintenance costs dependent on the student showing a certain degree of integration with the host state, but found that the UK rules prevented a student such as the applicant from showing such integration, ibid. at paras. 54–63.

[107] Case C-138/02, *Collins*, *supra* n. 22.

looking for work in the UK, contended, *inter alia*, that the requirement in UK legislation that a person claiming a jobseeker's allowance must be habitually resident in the UK was contrary to the principle of equal treatment.

It was clear from existing case law that those seeking work came within Article 39 EC, and were entitled to equal treatment in relation to access to employment, albeit not in relation to social and tax advantages, but the provisions dealing with access to employment in Regulation 1612/68[108] said nothing expressly about financial benefits. The ECJ stated that these provisions must, however, be read in the light of Article 12 and the Treaty Articles on citizenship and it reiterated the foundational principle from *Grzelczyk* about citizenship of the Union becoming the fundamental status of Union citizens, with the correlative proscription of discrimination on grounds of nationality.[109]

When construed in this light, the ECJ concluded that it was no longer possible to exclude from the scope of Articles 12 and 39(2) a financial benefit that was intended to facilitate access to employment in the labour market. The UK legislation, although based on residence, was indirectly discriminatory, but the Court accepted that it could in principle be objectively justified, provided that it did not go beyond what was necessary to attain the underlying objective.

G. Conclusion

The jurisprudence on Article 12 and more especially that concerning this Article and the citizenship provisions throws into sharp relief the ECJ's role in the interpretation of broadly-framed Treaty provisions and the interplay between the Community courts and Community legislature in the development of this area of the law. It is helpful when drawing conclusions to stand back from the detail to see the broader contours of this part of Community law.

It is clear that Article 12 in conjunction with the citizenship provisions has been used to break down the pre-existing dichotomy between free movement *qua* worker and free movement *qua* citizen. The necessary corollary of this development has been that greater emphasis has been placed on the social as opposed to the economic rationale for free movement. This is not controversial in and of itself. It is indeed the very *raison d'être* of the citizenship provisions in the Treaty and also underlies the Citizenship Directive.

It is, however, equally clear that the Treaty provisions, while according greater rights to citizens *qua* citizens, are explicitly premised on the

[108] Council Regulation 1612/68, *supra* n. 30, Arts. 2, 5.
[109] Case C-138/02, *Collins*, *supra* n. 22, at para. 61.

assumption the citizens' right to move and reside are subject to limits and conditions derived from the Treaty and Community legislation. The real area of controversy centres on the issue of how far rules that distinguish between the position of nationals of the host state and other Member State nationals who are not workers should be allowed to persist in relation to matters such as the payment of benefits, grants, and the like.

The contentious nature of the issue in this case is readily apparent from the observations submitted to the Court. Thus, for example, in *Grzelczyk*[110] the Belgian, French, Danish, and UK governments all submitted arguments that were strongly opposed to the conclusion reached by the ECJ. While the details of their arguments differed, the common thread was that the discrimination fell outside the scope of the Treaty and hence Article 12 was inapplicable, that Article 12 read together with Articles 17 and 18 should not be interpreted such as to accord Union citizens greater rights than those conferred in more specific Treaty articles and Community legislation made pursuant thereto, and that the citizenship provisions should not be used to sidestep limits on rights contained in Community legislation. Similar arguments were made in all of the other cases considered in the previous section.

The ECJ's willingness to persist in the face of this opposition bears testimony to the importance that it attaches to the idea that Union citizenship should be the fundamental status of Member State nationals, with the consequence that those who are in the same situation enjoy the same treatment in law irrespective of their nationality, subject to such exceptions as are expressly provided for. This telos underpinned and drove the more detailed legal analysis, and it is clear that the Court was not inclined to find that an exception existed. The juridical techniques discussed above were the tools used to achieve this underlying objective.

There is clearly room for differing views on the ECJ's contribution. Some might feel that the case law running from *Martinez Sala* to *Bidar* is warranted either as a justifiable reading of the Treaty text, or because of the telos underlying this jurisprudence, or from an admixture of both arguments. On this view, any difficulties in the ECJ's reasoning when judged from a textual perspective might be regarded as warranted given the importance of the outcome sought by the Court.

A more cautious view is, however, possible. The content of the desired telos must be determined in part at least from the relevant Treaty articles, more especially those on citizenship. These tell us that the Member States were certainly willing to accord greater rights to citizens *qua* citizens, but they make it equally clear that this is subject to limits and conditions to be found elsewhere in the Treaty or Community legislation. These limits and

[110] Case C-184/99, *Grzelczyk, supra* n. 27.

conditions speak to the degree of 'social solidarity' that the Member States have been willing to accept as between their own nationals and other Community nationals who are not workers. It should, moreover, be recognized that while the Citizenship Directive improved the rights accorded to citizens *qua* citizens, it retained distinctions between the position of citizens and workers and reiterated a number of the limits on benefits obtainable by citizens that existed in previous Community legislation.

The net effect of the Court's jurisprudence is, however, that it is increasingly difficult for Member States to rely on any such limits or conditions. The Court may employ the juridical technique from *Martinez Sala/Trojani* and conclude that since the applicant is lawfully resident under Member State law there is therefore no need to rely on Article 18 and hence any limits and conditions derived from other Treaty articles or Community legislation are irrelevant. It may choose instead to deploy the juridical technique used in *Grzelczyk/Bidar* and read down any limits to the Article 18 right to move and reside. The ECJ may, as in *Collins*, reinterpret the consequences that flow from, for example, Article 39, in the light of the citizenship provisions and hold that they should now be read so as to cover the type of benefit claimed by the applicant. These juridical techniques may, as seen above, be used separately or in tandem.

It has been common to criticize the citizenship provisions of the Treaty on the grounds that the particular rights attached to Union citizenship, although important, were limited in nature and scope. The ECJ's repeated invocation of the principle that Union citizenship should be the fundamental status of Member State nationals, with the consequence of equal treatment, is indicative of its desire to address this critique. Its jurisprudence complements the rights granted to Union citizens in Articles 19 to 22, by demanding that benefits given by the host state should in principle be available to other Community nationals. This may be unexceptionable in and of itself, but the legitimacy of the Court's case law depends ultimately on one's view of the way in which it has treated exceptions and limits provided elsewhere in the Treaty or Community legislation.

4. COMMON POLICIES, EQUAL TREATMENT, AND CONSTRAINTS ON REGULATION

A. The Regulatory Role of Equal Treatment

The discussion thus far has been concerned with equal treatment and nationality. We have seen that non-discrimination in relation to nationality is central to the economic ideal of a common market in which there is a level playing field allowing the free interplay of market forces with the aim of moving closer to the optimum allocation of resources for the Community. It also serves broader social goals relating to the creation of a community among the Member States of the Union, this being evident both in relation to the case law and legislation on workers and even more so in the jurisprudence on citizenship.

There are, however, areas where the normal market mechanisms do not apply or are heavily qualified. The principle of non-discrimination performs what More[111] aptly terms a regulatory role in these areas, in that it constrains the regulatory choices that can be made by the administration.

This was particularly evident in the context of the European Coal and Steel Community Treaty (ECSC), where the governing institutions set or influenced many of the decisions relating to pricing and output. These decisions were subject to the principle of non-discrimination, which featured at various points in the Treaty.[112] The ECJ made clear in its early jurisprudence that it adhered to the basic Aristotelian concept of discrimination, holding that discrimination could exist where either comparable situations were treated differently or where dissimilar situations received comparable treatment.[113]

The most prominent examples of interventionist economic policy in the EC are the common policies, most notably the Common Agricultural Policy (CAP) where prices and output have been set or strongly influenced by Community regulations.[114] It is important to view the proscription of discrimination against the more general Treaty Articles concerning the CAP, since it is only by doing so that its role can be adequately understood.

Article 33 EC is the foundational provision of the CAP. It is of a broad discretionary nature and sets out a range of general objectives to be served by the CAP. They include increase in agricultural productivity, with the object, *inter alia*, of ensuring a fair standard of living for the agricultural community; the stabilization of markets; assuring the availability of supplies; and reasonable prices for consumers. It is readily apparent that these objectives can clash with each other.[115] The Commission and Council therefore have to make difficult discretionary choices. Whether the resultant choices discriminate

[111] More, 'The Principle of Equal Treatment: From Market Unifier to Fundamental Right', in P. Craig and G. de Búrca (eds), *The Evolution of EU Law* (Oxford University Press, 1999), at 530–535.

[112] Arts. 3 (b), 4(b), 60(1) and 70(1) ECSC.

[113] Case 14/59, *Sociétés des Fonderies de Pont-á-Mousson v High Authority* [1959] ECR 215; Cases 7 & 9/54, *Groupement des Industries Sidérurgiques Luxembourgeoises v High Authority* [1955–56] ECR 53; Cases 8/55, *Fédération Charbonnière de Belgique v High Authority* [1954–56] ECR 292.

[114] See above, Chap. 3 for discussion of the regime of shared administration that pertains in this area.

[115] See e.g. Case 34/62, *Germany v Commission* [1963] ECR 131; Case 5/67, *Beus v Hauptzollamt München* [1968] ECR 83.

between producers may be contentious. The ECJ has, not surprisingly, accepted that the Community institutions have a considerable degree of choice as to how to balance the objectives which are to be pursued.[116] The principle of non-discrimination must therefore be viewed against this background. Article 34(2) EC provides that:

The common organisation established in accordance with paragraph 1 may include all measures required to attain the objectives set out in Article 33, in particular regulation of prices, aids for the production and marketing of the various products, storage and carryover arrangements and common machinery for stabilising imports or exports.

The common organisation shall be limited to the pursuit of the objectives set out in Article 33 and shall exclude any discrimination between producers or consumers within the Community.

Any common price policy shall be based on common criteria and uniform methods of calculation.

A necessary condition for an applicant to be able to rely successfully on non-discrimination in Article 34(2) is therefore that it is in a comparable situation to that of another producer or consumer and is being treated differently, or that it is in a different situation and is being treated in the same manner. Comparability is a necessary condition for successful invocation of Article 34(2). It is not, however, sufficient. The applicant will also have to rebut arguments advanced by the defendant concerning objective justification. Thus the defendant, normally the Commission and/or the Council, may argue that the differential treatment was objectively justified in order to attain one of the objectives in Article 33. We should, however, bear in mind Schwarze's cautionary note in this respect:[117]

Thus in some decisions the starting point has been a purely formal consideration of the relationship between the objects being compared, in order to test, on the basis of objective criteria, whether the objects in question are 'like' or 'unlike'. Other decisions, in contrast, have not initially considered the compared objects themselves at all, but have immediately looked at the question whether the equal or unequal treatment complained of is 'objectively justified'.

[116] See e.g. Cases 197–200, 243, 245, 247/80, *Ludwigshafener Walzmühle Erling KG v Council* [1981] ECR 3211; Case 8/82, *KG in der Firma Hans-Otto Wagner GmbH Agrarhandel v Bundesanstalt für Landwirtschaftliche Marktordnung* [1983] ECR 371; Case 283/83, *Firma A. Racke v Hauptzollamt Mainz* [1984] ECR 3791.

[117] J. Schwarze, *European Administrative Law* (Office for Official Publications of the European Communities and Sweet & Maxwell, 1992), at 563–564.

B. Comparability and Objective Justification: *Ruckdeschel* and *Royal Scholten-Honig*

The interplay between comparability and objective justification can be seen in leading cases that arose for determination early in the ECJ's jurisprudence.[118]

In *Ruckdeschel*[119] the applicants contested Community Regulations concerning production refunds for the manufacture of products derived from maize. They argued that the Regulations should be annulled because they did not grant the same refund when maize was used for the manufacture of quellmehl as they did when it was used to make starch. The production refund for quellmehl had been abolished, while that for starch had been maintained, and the applicants claimed that this constituted discrimination contrary to what is now Article 34(2). The original rationale for granting refunds for both was that quellmehl and starch were interchangeable. The premise underlying the Regulation that withdrew the refund for quellmehl was that the possibility of substituting the former for the latter was felt to be 'economically slight, if not non-existent'.[120]

The ECJ noted that the wording of Article 34(2) undoubtedly prohibited discrimination between producers of the same product, but did not specifically address the relationship between different industrial or trade sectors in the sphere of processed agricultural products. It nonetheless held that the prohibition of discrimination in this Article was 'merely a specific enunciation of the general principle of equality which is one of the fundamental principles of Community law'.[121] This required that 'similar situations shall not be treated differently unless differentiation is objectively justified'.[122]

The ECJ then considered whether the products could be regarded as comparable and held in favour of the applicants, because the Council and Commission had produced no new technical or economic data to substantiate their view that the products should no longer be regarded as interchangeable, given that previous Regulations had been premised on the assumption that they were substitutes. It therefore fell to the ECJ to decide whether the contested Regulations could be objectively justified. The defendants argued that the abolition of the refund was justified because quellmehl was no longer used for human consumption, but rather for animal feed. The ECJ rejected this defence, stating that the Council and Commission had produced no evidence for this and that even if such evidence existed it would

[118] See also, Case 13/63, *Italian Republic v Commission* [1963] ECR 165; Case 79/77, *Firma Kühlhaus Zentrum AG v Hauptzollamt Hamburg-Harburg* [1978] ECR 611; Case 230/78, *Eridania Zuccherifici Nazionali v Ministre de l'Agriculture et des Forêts* [1979] ECR 2749; Case 8/82, *Wagner v BALM* [1983] ECR 371; Case C-150/95, *Portugal v Commission* [1997] ECR I-5863.

[119] Cases 117/76 and 16/77, *Ruckdeschel, supra* n. 2.

[120] Ibid. at para. 6.

[121] Ibid. at para. 7.

[122] Ibid. at para. 7.

only have justified removal of the refund in respect of the quantities of quellmehl put to such use. The Regulations therefore breached the principle of non-discrimination.

The interplay between comparability and objective justification is apparent once again in *Royal Scholten-Honig*.[123] The applicants were producers of isoglucose, which was a sweetener produced from starch, and contested the legality of Regulations imposing a production levy on them. The rationale for the levy was that isoglucose was regarded as a substitute for sugar, at least in liquid form, and sugar producers were subject to a production levy in order to try and reduce the sugar surplus on the Community market.

The ECJ accepted that isoglucose and sugar were comparable in liquid form, and that it would be wrong for the former to have a competitive advantage over the latter. It noted, however, that the production levy imposed on manufacturers of isoglucose affected their entire production, whereas the levy on sugar manufacturers was calculated on only part of their production. It was therefore *prima facie* discriminatory. The Council and Commission contended that there was objective justification for the difference, because isoglucose was not subject to the same production constraints as sugar and because the charges borne by isoglucose manufacturers were comparable to those of sugar producers. The ECJ rejected this defence because the reality was that 60 per cent of the production levy was in fact borne by sugar beet growers, not the manufacturers, and because it was open to sugar manufacturers to reduce the incidence of the levy by reducing production, whereas this was not so readily open to isoglucose producers, given the way in which their levy was calculated.

C. Comparability, Objective Justification, and Arbitrariness

It is common when reading the case law in this area to find reference to arbitrariness. Schwarze[124] rightly points out that the concept is used both in relation to the initial determination of comparability and in relation to the requirement of objective justification. It should, however, also be recognized that the role played by the concept in these areas differs.

The ECJ's reference to arbitrariness when discussing comparability is principally designed to reinforce the requirement that comparability be determined objectively. The ECJ has repeatedly emphasized[125] the need for there to be objective differences between producers or consumers in order to

[123] Cases 103 and 145/77, *Royal Scholten-Honig v Intervention Board for Agricultural Produce* [1978] ECR 2037.

[124] Schwarze, *supra* n. 117, at 574–575.

[125] See, e.g., Case 16/61, *Acciaieriere Ferriere e Fonerie di Modena v High Authority* [1962] ECR 289, at 306; Case 230/78, *Eridania*, *supra* n. 118, at para. 18; Case 8/82, *Wagner*, *supra* n. 118, at paras. 19–21.

warrant differential treatment, and it has on occasion reinforced this precept by stating that a decision would be arbitrary if there were no such objective differences. Thus in an early case dealing with the ECSC,[126] the ECJ stated that equality of treatment concerning economic rules did not prevent different prices being fixed in accord with the particular situation of categories of consumers, provided that the difference in treatment corresponded to a difference in the situation of such persons. If there was no objectively established basis for the distinction, it would be 'arbitrary, discriminatory and illegal'.[127] It did not, however, follow that economic rules were discriminatory or unfair, where the differential treatment followed from the different operating conditions of those affected. Moreover the fact that the relevant rules gave the undertakings some discretion did not mean that the criterion for distinguishing between them lost its objective nature and hence was arbitrary, since the resulting factual differences stemmed from their dissimilar operating conditions, and not from any legal inequality inherent in the contested decision.[128]

The concept of arbitrariness when used in relation to objective justification will often function in a conclusory fashion, denoting the Court's finding that there is no such justification for a measure that is *prima facie* discriminatory.[129] In similar vein, the Court will conclude that where there is such justification the measure will not be arbitrary and hence will be upheld.

Denkavit[130] exemplifies this usage of arbitrariness. The German government revalued the German mark, which led to losses of income for German agriculture. A Council Regulation, passed in the light of this revaluation, provided that aid up to a certain amount would be compatible with the common market, and Germany enacted a law whereby compensation was given to agricultural undertakings through a reduction in the turnover tax that would otherwise have been payable. The applicant argued, *inter alia*, that the term agricultural producer within the Council Regulation should include industrial breeders of livestock as defined by German tax law, as well as agricultural livestock breeders, and that any differential treatment between the two groups was discriminatory.

The ECJ held that Article 33 did not exclude the possibility of differential treatment between various agricultural sectors, provided that they were based on objective criteria and were not arbitrary. It followed that although Article 34(2) prohibited discrimination between producers, differential treatment constituted discrimination only if it was arbitrary. This was not so in

[126] Case 8/57, *Groupement des Hauts Fourneaux et Acieries Belges v High Authority* [1957–8] ECR 245.

[127] Ibid. at 256. [128] Ibid. at 257.

[129] See, e.g., Case 106/81, *Julius Kind AG v EEC* [1982] ECR 2885, at para. 22.

[130] Case 139/77, *Denkavit Futtermittel GmbH v Finanzamt Warendorf* [1978] ECR 1317.

the instant case because there was an objective justification for the differential treatment, since agricultural livestock breeders used their own fodder and were therefore subject to the risks inherent in working the land. This was not the case for industrial livestock breeders, who bought their animal feed on national or international markets. They could therefore, when the currency was revalued, obtain such feed from abroad at advantageous prices.[131]

There are, however, cases where arbitrariness plays a more meaningful, substantive role in its own right. In these cases it is indicative of the intensity of review that will be applied to CAP measures, more especially when they are adopted in situations where time is of the essence. We have already seen from earlier discussion that the Community courts tend to apply relatively low intensity review to discretionary determinations made under the CAP.[132] This is reflected in the approach to claims based on discrimination, and judicial use of the term arbitrary betokens the type of error that the applicant must prove in order to succeed.

Thus in *Merkur*[133] the applicant alleged discrimination because monetary compensation amounts (MCAs) had not been fixed for its products. These MCAs were designed to compensate for exchange rate movements, but only where such movements would lead to disturbances in trade in agricultural products. The ECJ held that the differential treatment of which the applicant complained would not violate the principle of non-discrimination unless it was arbitrary.[134] It was clearly influenced in reaching this conclusion by the fact that the regime for MCAs was designed to cope with an emergency situation and that it had to be applied to a broad range of products within tight time limits. The fact that some decisions might appear in hindsight to be debatable in economic terms did not suffice to prove discrimination and the Court would intervene only if the determination was manifestly erroneous.[135]

The same approach is evident in other cases, such as *Wuidart*,[136] where the ECJ held that judicial review for compliance with the principle of non-discrimination must take account of the fact that in matters concerning the CAP, the Community legislature had a broad discretion imposed on it by the relevant Treaty articles, and that where it was obliged to assess the future effect of rules the effects of which could not be accurately foreseen, its assessment would only be open to criticism if it was manifestly incorrect in the light of the information available when the rules were adopted.

131 Ibid. at paras. 16–17. 132 See above, Chap. 13.

133 Case 43/72, *Merkur GmbH & Co KG v Commission* [1973] ECR 1055. See also, Case 49/79, *Pool v Council* [1980] ECR 569; Case 281/82, *Unifrex v Commission and Council* [1984] ECR 1969.

134 Ibid. at para. 22. 135 Ibid. at para. 24.

136 Cases 267–285/88, *Wuidart v Laiterie Coopérative Eupenoise Société Coopérative* [1990] ECR I-435.

D. Conclusion

The reality is that it is not easy for the applicant to win in this area. Claims often fail either because the Community courts find that there is no comparability between the applicant and another party, or because the differential treatment is objectively justified. The difficulties faced by applicants are exacerbated by the low intensity review and by the fact that attainment of an integrated market may well require differential treatment of previously compartmentalized markets.[137] Thus, as Barents states, 'the overriding objective of market integration and common management allows for a considerable difference in treatment of operators'.[138] This necessarily limits the regulatory role played by equality within this area. It will nonetheless be interesting to see whether the changing nature of the CAP, with the shift away from price support to income support, leads to modification in the judicial approach.

5. ARTICLE 141, SEX DISCRIMINATION AND EQUAL TREATMENT

A. Economic and Social Rationales

The discussion thus far has been concerned with discrimination on grounds of nationality within the four freedoms and in the context of Article 12 EC, and with the role played by equal treatment in the context of common policies. The focus now turns to sex discrimination. This is a complex topic in its own right and it is not possible within the confines of this chapter to give more than an overview of some of the central issues within this area. Sex discrimination is part of social policy. The scope of the EC's competence over such policy has evolved over time,[139] and the extent to which it should have competence remains contested. The principal issue in this respect is how far EC involvement in social policy, including sex discrimination, should be rationalized in market-oriented terms and how far it should be perceived as having a social dimension independent thereof. Thus as Bell states:[140]

[137] Case 153/73, *Holtz & Willemsen v Council* [1974] ECR 675; Case 2/77, *Hoffman's Stärkefabriken v Hauptzollamt Bielefeld* [1977] ECR 1375; Case C-280/93, *Germany v Council* [1994] ECR I-5039, at para. 74; Case C-56/94, *SCAC v Associazione dei Produttori Ortofrutticoli* [1995] ECR I-1769; Case C-150/95, *Portugal v Commission* [1997] ECR I-5863.

[138] Barents, 'Recent Developments in Community Case Law in the field of Agriculture' (1997) 34 *CMLRev* 811, at 842.

[139] Barnard, 'EC "Social" Policy', in Craig and de Búrca, *supra* n. 111, Chap. 13.

[140] M. Bell, *Anti-discrimination Law and the European Union* (Oxford University Press, 2002), at 6–7. Italics in the original.

Two theoretical models of European social policy may be identified. First, there is the *market integration model* which prescribes a limited social policy for the European Union. This is predicated on the assumption that the primary goal of the Union is to achieve economic integration. Therefore the EU only intervenes in the social sphere when this is required to support and sustain the smooth functioning of the common market. Essentially this is a model for a social policy dependent on the economics of European integration. Alternatively, there is a model of social policy as an independent policy objective for the EU, foreseeing a social policy as vibrant and autonomous as the Union's activities in the economic sphere. This is centred around a role for the Union as a guarantor of fundamental social rights and may be described as the *social citizenship model*. It is within these policy frameworks that EU anti-discrimination law has developed.

The market-integration model is exemplified by the rationale for what is now Article 141 EC. It is generally accepted that this Article was included in the original Treaty primarily to meet French fears that its goods would be disadvantaged as compared to those produced in other Member States, since France had more stringent rules on equal pay for men and women and felt that this might make its goods more expensive and hence less competitive if other Member States were not subject to the same constraints.[141] The original rationale for Article 141 was therefore primarily market-oriented, although as we shall see below the ECJ has emphasized the social dimension of this Article in its jurisprudence. The market-integration model was driven more generally by fears of social dumping, whereby those economies with low social standards would gain an unfair competitive advantage. The reality of this fear might well be questioned,[142] but perception of social dumping as giving some economies an illegitimate competitive advantage has nonetheless been a recurring one within the EC. The market-integration model also served as the foundation for the Court's jurisprudence under Article 86, limiting the Member States' ability to maintain state monopolies in areas such as employment placement services and the supply of labour,[143] although in later case law the Court has been more willing to accept that there is a defensible reason for the special rights accorded to the state entity.[144]

[141] Barnard, *supra* n. 139, at 481–482.

[142] Deakin and Wilkinson, 'Rights vs Efficiency? The Economic Case for Transnational Labour Standards' (1994) 23 *ILJ* 289.

[143] Case C-179/90, *Merci Convenzionali Porto di Genova SpA v Siderurgica Gabrielli SpA* [1991] ECR I-5889; Case C-41/90, *Höfner and Elser v Macrotron GmbH* [1991] ECR I-1979; Case C-55/96, *Job Centre coop. arl.* [1997] ECR I-7119; Case C-258/98, *Criminal Proceedings against Carra* [2000] ECR I-4217.

[144] Case C-67/96, *Albany International BV v Stichting Bedrijfspensioenfonds Textielindustrie* [1999] ECR I-5751; Cases 147–148/97, *Deutsche Post AG v Gesellschaft für Zahlungssyteme mbH and Citicorp Kartenservice GmbH* [2000] ECR I-825; Case C-340/99, *TNT Traco SpA v Poste Italiane SpA* [2001] ECR I-4109; Case C-475/99, *Ambulanz Glöckner v Landkreis Südwestpfalz* [2001] ECR I-8089.

The social citizenship model, by way of contrast, denies that social policy should be seen simply as supplementing economic integration, and 'prescribes for the EU a role as the guarantor of fundamental human and social rights'.[145] While there is disagreement as to the precise content of these rights, the core idea is that social policy should not be perceived as necessarily linked to the 'market citizen'.[146] The aspirations of advocates of the social citizenship model have been fuelled by developments such as the recognition by the ECJ that the right not to be discriminated against on grounds of sex was a fundamental human right, the observance of which it would ensure;[147] the Social Charter 1989; the expansion of competence in the area of social policy;[148] the citizenship provisions analyzed above;[149] the addition of Article 13 EC empowering the EC to take action to combat discrimination on a wide variety of grounds; and provisions in the Charter of Fundamental Rights of the European Union.[150] There are, however, limits to the foregoing provisions, some of which contain important exceptions,[151] others of which, such as the Charter of Rights, are not yet legally binding. It is for this reason that Bell remarks that 'whilst the social citizenship model has evolved as a theoretical alternative to the market integration model, in practice it remains more an aspiration than a reality'.[152] We should also be mindful of the relationship between the social citizenship model and precepts of equality and discrimination. A broad reading of discrimination of the kind contained in Article 13 EC and Article 21(1) of the Charter would generally be supported by advocates of this model. The social citizenship model is, however, capable of embracing social rights in the field of, for example, labour law that are not concerned with equality as such.

It will be clear from the subsequent analysis that the development of equality in the context of social policy has come from an admixture of judicial and legislative intervention, and that elements of the market-integration and social-citizenship models can be seen in case law and legislation.

[145] Bell, *supra* n. 140, at 12.

[146] Everson, 'The Legacy of the Market Citizen', in J. Shaw and G. More (eds), *New Legal Dynamics of the European Union* (Oxford University Press, 1995), at 73–90.

[147] Case 149/77, *Defrenne v Société Anonyme Belge de Navigation Aérienne (No. 3)* [1978] ECR 1365, at paras. 26–27; Cases 75 and 117/82, *Razzouk and Beydoun v Commission* [1984] ECR 1509, at para. 16; Case C-13/94, *P v S and Cornwall County Council* [1996] ECR I-2143, at para. 19; Case C-25/02, *Rinke v Arztekammer Hamburg* [2003] ECR I-8349, at paras. 25–26.

[148] Arts. 136, 137 EC.

[149] Arts. 17–22 EC.

[150] OJ 2000 C364/1.

[151] Art. 137(5) EC.

[152] Bell, *supra* n. 140, at 15–16.

B. Equal Pay

It was the courts that gave the initial impetus to gender discrimination and pay,[153] and their decisions exemplify the interplay between the economic and social rationales underlying this area of the law.

In *Defrenne*[154] the applicant, who was an air hostess, brought an action for discrimination against her employer Sabena, because she was paid less than male colleagues who did the same job. The principal issue was whether Article 119 EEC, now Article 141 EC, should have direct effect.

This question should, said the ECJ, be considered in the light of the 'nature of the principle of equal pay, the aim of this provision and its place in the scheme of the Treaty'.[155] The ECJ held that there were two aims underlying this Article. The market-integration objective was designed 'to avoid a situation in which undertakings established in States which have actually implemented the principle of equal pay suffer a competitive disadvantage in intra-Community competition as compared with undertakings established in States which have not yet eliminated discrimination against women workers as regards pay'.[156] The second aim was social in nature: Article 119 'forms part of the social objectives of the Community, which is not merely an economic union, but is at the same time intended, by common action, to ensure social progress and seek the constant improvement of the living and working conditions of their peoples, as is emphasized by the Preamble to the Treaty'.[157]

This double aim, economic and social, was indicative of the foundational role played by the principle of equal pay within the EC.[158] This conclusion reinforced the Court's resolve that Article 119 should have direct effect, notwithstanding the fact that it was couched in general terms and required further elaboration through Community legislation. The ECJ therefore drew a distinction between direct discrimination, which could be identified solely through the criteria of equal work and equal pay referred to by Article 119, and indirect discrimination which could only be identified through more detailed implementing provisions. The Court's willingness to identify the principle embodied in the Article and to hold that direct discrimination that violated this principle could give rise to direct effect, bears testimony to

[153] S. Prechal and N. Burrows, *Gender Discrimination Law of the European Community* (Dartmouth, 1990); T. Hervey and D. O'Keefe, *Sex Equality in the European Union* (Wiley, 1996); C. Hoskyns, *Integrating Gender—Women, Law and Politics in the European Union* (Verso, 1996); A. Dashwood and S. O'Leary, *The Principle of Equal Treatment in European Community Law* (Sweet & Maxwell, 1997); Bell, *supra* n. 140; E. Ellis, *EU Anti-Discrimination Law* (Oxford University Press, 2005).

[154] Case 43/75, *Defrenne v Société Anonyme Belge de Navigation Aérienne* [1976] ECR 455.

[155] Ibid. at para. 7. [156] Ibid. at para. 9. [157] Ibid. at para. 10.

[158] Ibid. at para. 12.

the importance it attached to the social as well as the economic aims of gender equality in the context of pay, more especially given that Community legislation to elaborate on this basic precept was slow in coming given the malaise that beset the legislative process at that time.

In *Schröder*[159] the ECJ went further, holding that the social objective underlying Article 141 took precedence over the economic. The case was concerned with entitlement to membership of an occupational pension scheme by part-time workers, the great majority of whom were women. If the social aim were accorded priority, then it would be permissible for German law to apply the equal pay principle retroactively so as to permit part-time workers access to such a scheme. However, if the economic aim were to take priority the opposite result might be reached, since it was argued that by allowing retroactive membership of the scheme German firms would be placed at a competitive disadvantage as compared with those in other Member States.

The ECJ reiterated the twin objectives of Article 141 that had been elaborated in *Defrenne.* It then pointed to subsequent decisions where it had held that the right not to be discriminated against on grounds of sex was a fundamental human right, whose observance the Court had a duty to ensure.[160] The ECJ concluded in the light of this case law that the economic aim pursued by Article 141, namely the elimination of distortions of competition between undertakings established in different Member States, 'is secondary to the social aim pursued by the same provision, which constitutes the expression of a fundamental human right'.[161]

The law concerning gender discrimination and pay also exemplifies the interrelationship between judicial and legislative initiatives in developing this area of equality law. The principles concerning equal pay were further elaborated through Directive 75/117.[162] It required the elimination of sex discrimination in pay in cases involving the same work or work of equal value, and required job classification schemes to be free from discrimination. Member States were required to abolish discrimination in legislative or administrative provisions. They were also obliged to take the necessary measures to ensure that provisions contained in collective agreements or contracts that were in breach of the principle of equal pay should be rendered void or amended. The Directive in addition imposed a more positive obligation on Member States to take effective measures to ensure that the equal pay

[159] Case C-50/96, *Deutsche Telekom v Schröder* [2000] ECR I-743.

[160] Ibid. at para. 56, citing Case 149/77, *Defrenne III* [1978] ECR 1365, at paras. 26–27, Cases 75 and 117/82, *Razzouk and Beydoun v Commission* [1984] ECR 1509, at para. 16, and Case C-13/94, *P. v S. and Cornwall County Council* [1996] ECR I-2143, at para. 19.

[161] Ibid. at para. 57.

[162] Council Directive 75/117/EEC of 10 February 1975, On the Approximation of the Laws of the Member States Relating to the Application of the Principle of Equal Pay for Men and Women, OJ 1975 L45/19.

principle was observed. A duty was imposed on Member States to introduce measures enabling employees who considered themselves wronged to be able to pursue their claims by judicial process, and to ensure that complainants were protected against dismissal.

Directive 75/117 was designed to flesh out the more detailed meaning of what was Article 119. The fact that the Directive expressly included 'work of equal value' did not, however, mean that this was outside the Treaty Article. On the contrary, the foundational right to equal pay has always been held to flow directly from the Treaty.[163] Thus although Article 141 was amended to include reference to work of equal value, it was possible to invoke the horizontal direct effect of this Article in such cases even prior to this amendment. The Directive was nonetheless important in setting out in more detail the obligations that flowed from the principle of equal pay.

It naturally fell to the ECJ to interpret the Treaty and the provisions of the Directive. There were not surprisingly controversial rulings.[164] The general stance of the ECJ was to interpret the Treaty and the accompanying Directive procedurally and substantively so as to ensure that their objectives were fulfilled.

The decision in *Commission v UK*[165] exemplifies the procedural dimension of the Court's approach. The Commission argued that the UK had failed to ensure an adequate job-classification system for assessing work of equal value. The ECJ ruled that if there was disagreement concerning application of the equal-pay principle, a worker should have a right of access to an appropriate authority which could give a binding ruling on whether or not his or her work had the same value as other work.

The *Danfoss* ruling[166] provides a further important example of the way in which judicial interpretation concerning matters of procedure can reinforce the practical efficacy of the Directive. The employer in this case paid the same basic wage to employees in the same wage group, but also awarded individual pay supplements, which were calculated on the basis of mobility, training, and seniority. Two female employees worked in different wage groups, and within these two groups it was shown that a man's average wage was higher than that of a woman.

[163] Case C-381/99, *Brunnhofer v Bank der Österreichischen Postsparkasse* [2001] ECR I-4961, at para. 29; Case C-309/97, *Angestelltenbetriebsrat der Wiener Gebietskrankenkasse* [1999] ECR I-2865.

[164] See, eg, Case 237/85, *Rummler* [1986] ECR 2101 and the criticism by Fredman, 'EC Discrimination Law: A Critique' (1992) 21 *ILJ* 119, at 123.

[165] Case 61/81, *Commission v UK* [1982] ECR 2601, at para. 9.

[166] Case 109/88, *Handels-og Kontorfunktionærernes Forbund i Danmark v Dansk Arbejdsgiverforening, acting on behalf of Danfoss* [1989] ECR 3199; Shaw, 'The Burden of Proof and the Legality of Supplementary Payments in Equal Pay Cases' (1990) 15 *ELRev* 260. See also, Case 318/86, *Commission v France* [1988] ECR 3559.

The ECJ found that the individual pay supplements were applied in such a way that it was impossible for a woman to identify the reasons for a difference between her pay and that of a man doing the same work. The employees did not know the criteria used in relation to pay supplements and were therefore unable to compare the various components of their pay with those of their colleagues' pay in the same wage group. The pay system was in this respect 'totally lacking in transparency',[167] with the consequence that female employees could establish differences from male employees only in relation to their average pay. The principle of equal pay would therefore be deprived of effectiveness 'if the effect of adducing such evidence was not to impose upon the employer the burden of proving that his practice in the matter of wages is not in fact discriminatory'.[168] It was for the Member States, in accord with Article 6 of Directive 75/117, to make the necessary adjustments to national rules on the burden of proof where these were necessary for the effective implementation of the principle of equality.[169] The ECJ thus reversed the normal burden of proof in order to safeguard the efficacy of the principle of equal pay. It did so notwithstanding the fact that a Commission proposal from 1988 for a Directive on reversing the burden of proof in sex-discrimination cases had been blocked in the Council.[170] It was to take nearly another decade before a Directive was successfully enacted.[171]

The ECJ has also interpreted the substantive reach of the Treaty and Directive in order to ensure that the underlying objectives are secured. Space precludes detailed treatment of this issue. Suffice it to say for the present that it is evident in, for example, the expansive interpretation accorded to the concept of pay. It is apparent also in the jurisprudence on indirect discrimination, the outlines of which can be examined here. Such discrimination can occur where the challenged rule has the effect of disadvantaging a much larger percentage of one sex, even though it is not framed in terms of gender.

After earlier doubts, the ECJ made it clear in *Jenkins*[172] that indirect discrimination could fall within what was Article 119. The applicant was a part-time female employee of Kingsgate, and was paid a lower hourly rate than her full-time male colleagues performing the same work. The category of part-time workers was exclusively or predominantly comprised of women, but the defendant argued that the differential rates of pay were the result of distinguishing factors other than gender. The ECJ ruled that differential rates

[167] Case 109/88, *supra* n. 166. at para. 11. [168] Ibid. at para. 13.

[169] Ibid. at para. 14. [170] OJ 1988 C176/5.

[171] Council Directive 97/80/EC of 15 December 1997, On the Burden of Proof in Cases of Discrimination Based on Sex, OJ 1998 L14/6.

[172] Case 96/80, *Jenkins v Kingsgate (Clothing Productions) Ltd* [1981] ECR 911.

of pay did not *per se* violate Article 119, provided that those rates were applied to workers belonging to either category without distinction based on sex. There would therefore be no breach of Article 119 if the pay differences were attributable to factors that were objectively justified and did not relate to discrimination based on sex.[173] This would be the case if the pay differences were intended to encourage full-time work irrespective of the sex of the worker. However the Court acknowledged that women might find it difficult to work the minimum hours required for full-time work, and ruled that in such circumstances Article 119 could bite if the employer's pay policy could not be explained by factors other than discrimination based on sex.[174] The determination of this issue was left to the national court. Subsequent Community legislation affirmed the concept of indirect discrimination.[175] In a case such as *Jenkins* the same task was undertaken by part-time and full-time workers. It is more difficult to sustain a claim of indirect discrimination where the work done by women and men is different and the essence of the claim is that the task performed predominantly by women is undervalued in comparison to that done by men.[176]

It is clear from the ECJ's decision in *Jenkins* and from the relevant Community legislation that indirect discrimination is capable of objective justification. The issue of objective justification is often left to the national court, but the ECJ has nonetheless provided guidance on the matter. The Court's case law shows that purported justifications cast in abstract, general terms are unlikely to succeed, more especially when they are not backed up by any meaningful empirical evidence.[177] Its jurisprudence also reveals something close to a proportionality analysis, as exemplified by *Bilka*.[178] The ECJ ruled that exclusion of part-time workers from membership of an occupational pension scheme would be contrary to Article 119 where the great

[173] Ibid. at para. 11. [174] Ibid. at para. 13.

[175] Dir. 97/80, *supra* n. 171, Art. 2(2) provides that: 'indirect discrimination shall exist where an apparently neutral provision, criterion or practice disadvantages a substantially higher proportion of the members of one sex unless that provision, criterion or practice is appropriate and necessary and can be justified by objective factors unrelated to sex'.

[176] Case 127/92, *Enderby v Frenchay Health Authority and the Secretary of State for Health* [1993] ECR 5535; Case C-236/98, *JämställdhetsOmbudsmannen v Örebro läns landsting* [2000] ECR I-2189.

[177] Case 171/88, *Rinner-Kühn v FWW Spezial-Gebäudereinigung GmbH* [1989] ECR 2743; Case 184/89, *Nimz v Freie und Hansestadt Hamburg* [1991] ECR 297; Case C-243/95, *Hill and Stapleton v Revenue Commissioners* [1998] ECR I-3739; Case C-167/97, *Seymour-Smith and Perez* [1999] ECR I-623, at paras. 71–76.

[178] Case 170/84, *Bilka-Kaufhaus GmbH v Karin Weber von Hartz* [1986] ECR 1607. See also, Case 171/88, *Rinner-Kühn*, *supra* n. 177; Case 33/89, *Kowalska v Freie und Hansestadt Hamburg* [1990] ECR 2591; Case C-360/90, *Arbeiterwohlfahrt der Stadt Berlin v Bötel* [1992] ECR I-3589; Case C-457/93, *Kuratorium für Dialyse und Nierentransplantation v Lewark* [1996] ECR I-243; Case C-278/93, *Freers and Speckmann v Deutsche Bundespost* [1996] ECR I-1165; Case C-236/98, *JämO* [2000] ECR I-2189, at paras. 61–62.

majority of such workers were women, who would have real difficulties working full-time, and where the exclusion could not be explained by factors that excluded discrimination on grounds of sex. This would not be so if there were some objective justification based on factors unrelated to gender. The employer sought to justify the measure on the ground that it was intended to discourage part-time work, since such workers often refused to work in the late afternoon and on Saturdays. The object was therefore to make full-time employment more attractive in order to ensure an adequate workforce during those periods, hence allowing such workers to take part in the pension scheme. The ECJ left it to the national court to determine the plausibility of this explanation, but gave guidance as to how the national court should go about its task. It was for the national court to consider whether the measures chosen by the employer corresponded to a real need on its part, whether they were appropriate with a view to achieving the objectives pursued, and were necessary to attain that end.[179] If this inquiry produced an affirmative answer, the fact that the measures affected more women than men was not sufficient to show infringement of Article 119.

It should, however, also be acknowledged that while the onus of proving objective justification rests on the defendant, it may be difficult for the claimant to rebut the argument advanced, more especially when the justification is cast in terms of the market. Thus the ECJ has ruled that the needs of the market might constitute adequate justification, where the increase in pay was attributable to the need to attract suitable candidates to the less popular job.[180] Commentators have been justly critical of the way in which the concept of objective justification has been used to defeat claims to indirect discrimination in some cases.[181] The ECJ has, however, been willing to look closely at the objective justifications proffered by Member States and employers for practices that are indirectly discriminatory. It has been increasingly less willing to accept purported justifications cast in abstract, general terms, and it has subjected justifications that are *prima facie* plausible to closer scrutiny in terms of the suitability and necessity of the contested measure.[182]

C. Equal Treatment

The interrelationship between case law and Community legislation that we saw in the context of equal pay is evident once again in relation to equal

[179] Case 170/84, *Bilka-Kaufhaus, supra* n. 178, at para. 36.

[180] Case 127/92, *Enderby, supra* n. 176.

[181] Fredman, *supra* n. 164, at 125; Szyszczak, 'L'Espace Social Européenne: Reality, Dreams or Nightmares?' [1990] *German Yearbook of International Law* 284, at 296.

[182] See cases, *supra* n. 177.

treatment. Article 141 specified from its inception equality in pay as between men and women, but it did not, until amendments made by the Treaty of Amsterdam, refer expressly to equal treatment in terms other than pay. The ECJ in *Defrenne II*[183] was, as seen above, willing to interpret Article 141 broadly so as to give it direct effect in relation to pay, and it highlighted the economic and social aims underlying this Article. There were, however, limits to judicial activism. Thus in *Defrenne III*[184] the applicant argued that the discriminatory compulsory termination of her employment at the age of 40 was contrary to Article 141, but the Court ruled that it was not possible at that stage to extend the Article to aspects of employment other than pay.

This gap was filled by Directive 76/207 on equal treatment,[185] and the fact that it was enacted pursuant to Article 308 EC is indicative of uncertainty as to whether it could have been made under any more specific Treaty article. The Directive, as its title indicated, was designed to ensure equal treatment between men and women in relation to access to employment and promotion, vocational training, and working conditions. The principle of equal treatment was defined to mean that there should be no discrimination 'on grounds of sex either directly or indirectly by reference in particular to marital or family status'.[186] The subsequent provisions of the Directive applied this principle in more detail to access to employment, vocational training, and working conditions.[187] Other provisions mirrored those of the Equal Pay Directive, by stipulating for access to a legal remedy, the protection of complainants and dissemination of information about the rights guaranteed by the Directive.[188]

The Directive also contained exceptions to the principle of equal treatment. The occupational qualification exception allowed Member States to exclude the principle from those occupational activities, including the training leading thereto, where 'by reason of their nature or the context in which they are carried out, the sex of the worker constitutes a determining factor'.[189] There was an exception for provisions concerning the protection of women, particularly as regards pregnancy and maternity.[190] The Directive was also said to be without prejudice to measures to promote equal opportunity for men and women, 'in particular by removing existing inequalities which affect women's opportunities'[191] in the areas covered by the Directive.

The Equal Treatment Directive was amended in 2002, and the amended

[183] Case 43/75, *Defrenne, supra* n. 154.
[184] Case 149/77, *Defrenne III, supra* n. 147.
[185] Council Directive 76/207/EEC of 9 February 1976, On the Implementation of the Principle of Equal Treatment for Men and Women as regards Access to Employment, Vocational Training and Promotion, and Working Conditions, OJ 1976 L39/40.
[186] Ibid. Art. 2(1).
[187] Ibid. Arts. 3–5.
[188] Ibid. Arts. 6–8.
[189] Ibid. Art. 2(2).
[190] Ibid. Art. 2(3).
[191] Ibid. Art. 2(4).

provisions had to be implemented by the Member States by 5 October 2005.[192] The amendments reflect some of the ECJ's case law, and are designed to ensure consistency with the Directives adopted under Article 13 EC on race and employment, as exemplified by the definition of indirect discrimination.[193] The changes also provide for stronger remedial provisions and for bodies at national level to support equal treatment.

This is not the place for detailed exegesis on the judicial interpretation of the Directive and the exceptions contained therein.[194] The remainder of this section will rather focus on two high-profile issues that demonstrate the contested boundaries of the principle of equal treatment.

(1) The Limits of Equal Treatment: Affirmative Action

The protection of equality inevitably raises the contentious issue of whether there can be affirmative action in order to remove previous inequalities. There is a rich theoretical literature on the legitimacy of affirmative action. Those opposed argue that equality must be symmetrical, that past wrongs to a group cannot be remedied via measures that disadvantage individuals and that there is a moral equivalence between laws designed to subjugate a race or gender and those that distribute benefits on the basis of race or gender. This critique of affirmative action is, as Fredman notes, based on a particular conception of equality and rests on three basic propositions:[195]

> First, it assumes that justice is defined *a priori* and applies in all societies regardless of the particular distribution of benefits, historical or social context . . . If discrimination on grounds of gender or race is unjust, it must be unjust whether it creates extra burdens on a group already disadvantaged, or whether it redistributes those burdens to a previously privileged group. Equality must therefore be symmetrical. Secondly, this critique of affirmative action assumes the primacy of the individual. Group characteristics such as sex or race must, on this view, always be disregarded in distributing benefits such as jobs or promotion; instead, individuals must be rewarded only on the basis of individual merit. Conversely, burdens should only be allocated on the basis of individual responsibility. Thus individuals may only be treated as responsible

[192] Directive 2002/73/EC of the European Parliament and of the Council of 23 September 2002, Amending Council Directive 76/207/EEC on the Implementation of the Principle of Equal Treatment for Men and Women as Regards Access to Employment, Vocational Training and Promotion and Working Conditions, OJ 2002 L269/15.

[193] Dir. 76/207, *supra* n. 185, as amended by Dir 2002/73, Art. 2(2).

[194] On the scope of Art. 2(2), see, eg, Case 165/82, *Commission v UK* [1983] ECR 3431; Case 318/86, *Commission v France* [1988] ECR 3559; Case 222/84, *Johnston v Chief Constable of the RUC* [1986] ECR 1651; Case C-273/97, *Sirdar v Army Board* [1999] ECR I-7403; Case C-285/98, *Kreil v Bundesrepublik Deutschland* [2000] ECR I-69. The amended version of this provision is Council Dir. 76/207, Art. 2(6)

[195] Fredman, 'Affirmative Action and the Court of Justice: A Critical Analysis', in J. Shaw (ed), *Social Law and Policy in an Evolving European Union* (Hart, 2000), at 172–173.

for their own actions; they should not be held accountable for more general societal wrongs . . . Finally, this conception of equality asserts that the state should be neutral as between citizens, favouring no-one above any other. Thus official policies giving preferential treatment to women or blacks are evidence of an impermissible partiality on the part of the state.

The assumptions underlying this symmetrical, individualist view of equality are, as Fredman makes clear, highly contestable, and have been opposed by those who advance a substantive, non-individualistic conception of justice and by those who argue from the premise of equal opportunity.[196]

It will commonly fall to courts to decide on the permissible limits of affirmative action. They may or may not be assisted in their deliberations by legislative measures, but even where such measures exist the courts will necessarily have to adjudicate on the more particular meaning of such provisions. Thus in the EU the Community legislature addressed the issue of affirmative action in the Equal Treatment Directive, by stipulating that it was without prejudice to measures to promote equal opportunity for men and women, 'in particular by removing existing inequalities which affect women's opportunities' in the areas covered by the Directive.[197] It fell to the Community courts to decide on the scope of this exception and the decisions have proven controversial.

This was especially so in relation to the ruling in *Kalanke*.[198] The case concerned a German regional law that contained the weakest form of affirmative action, the 'tie-break', such that where candidates of different sexes short-listed for promotion were equally qualified, priority should be given to women in sectors where they constituted less than half of the staff. The ECJ's conclusion was shaped by the fact that it viewed Article 2(4) of the Directive as 'derogating' from the right to equal treatment, the consequence being that it should be strictly interpreted. This tendentious premise coloured the remainder of its reasoning. Thus the Court held that national rules that guaranteed women absolute and unconditional priority for appointment or promotion went beyond the exception in Article 2(4). This exception only allowed for equality of opportunity, and did not sanction measures such as the German regional law that were designed to attain equality of result.[199] The *Kalanke* judgment provoked fierce academic comment and proved an embarrassment to the Commission, which had been supportive of affirmative action.

The ECJ took the opportunity offered by the *Marschall* case[200] to limit the force of *Kalanke*. *Marschall* concerned a German regional law which provided

[196] Ibid. at 173–176.
[197] Dir. 76/207, *supra* n. 185, Art. 2(4).
[198] Case C-450/93, *Kalanke v Freie Hansestadt Bremen* [1995] ECR I-3051.
[199] Ibid. at paras. 22–23.
[200] Case C-409/95, *Hellmut Marschall v Land Nordrhein Westfalen* [1997] ECR I-6363.

that where there were fewer women than men in a higher grade post in a career bracket, women were to be given priority for promotion in the event of equal suitability, competence, and professional performance, unless reasons specific to an individual male candidate tilted the balance in his favour. The ECJ confirmed that a rule guaranteeing 'absolute and unconditional priority' for women was impermissible,[201] but held that the rule in the instant case that allowed for individual consideration of circumstances could come within Article 2(4).[202] The Court was influenced in reaching this conclusion by its recognition that even where male and female candidates were equally qualified, the former tended to be promoted in preference to the latter 'because of prejudices and stereotypes concerning the role and capacities of women in working life and the fear, for example, that women will interrupt their careers more frequently, that owing to household and family duties they will be less flexible in their working hours, or that they will be absent from work more frequently because of pregnancy, childbirth, and breastfeeding'.[203] The mere fact that a male candidate and a female candidate were equally qualified did not therefore mean that they had the same chances,[204] and a national rule such as that in issue in the instant case could 'thus reduce actual instances of inequality which may exist in the real world'.[205] The very fact that the Court in *Marschall* was willing to limit the force of *Kalanke* was to be welcomed. It is, however, difficult, as Fredman notes,[206] to see what difference the savings clause would make in practice. By definition the male applicant could not claim to be more meritorious, since the German law in *Marschall* was premised on the assumption of equal merit. Other distinguishing features that might be proffered by the male candidate to tilt the balance in his favour, such as age or status as breadwinner, could well be regarded as indirectly discriminatory to women, and the Court in *Marschall* expressly cautioned against allowing this to happen.[207]

The ECJ persisted with the formulaic approach developed in *Marschall* in the later case of *Badeck*.[208] The affirmative action programme in this case was more far-reaching and sophisticated than that in the earlier cases. The ECJ nonetheless found that it was compatible with the Equal Treatment Directive, because it did not automatically and unconditionally give priority to women who were equally qualified with men applying for the same posts and because the candidates were subject to an objective assessment that took into account their specific personal situations.[209]

201 Ibid. at para. 32.
202 Ibid. at para. 33.
203 Ibid. at para. 29.
204 Ibid. at para. 30.
205 Ibid. at para. 31.
206 Fredman, *supra* n. 195, at 179.
207 Case C-409/95, *Hellmut Marschall*, *supra* n. 200, at para. 33.
208 Case C-158/97, *Badeck* [2000] ECR I-1875.
209 Ibid. at para. 23.

The Court was not, however, willing to accept the more far-reaching affirmative action programme that came before it in *Abrahamsson*.[210] The issue as framed by the referring court was whether legislation was compatible with Article 2(4) of the Directive under which a candidate for a public post who belonged to the under-represented sex and possessed sufficient qualifications for that post must be chosen in preference to a candidate of the opposite sex who would otherwise have been appointed, where this was necessary to secure the appointment of a candidate of the under-represented sex and the difference between the respective merits of the candidates was not so great as to give rise to a breach of the requirement of objectivity in making appointments.

The ECJ, following *Badeck*, accepted that it was legitimate for the purposes of assessment to take account of criteria for appointments which generally favoured women, where the objective was to achieve substantive, rather than formal, equality by reducing *de facto* inequalities in society and thereby prevent or compensate for disadvantages in the professional career of persons belonging to the under-represented sex, provided that these criteria were transparent and amenable to review. The ECJ felt that this was not, however, the case here, since a candidate for a public post belonging to the under-represented sex and possessing sufficient qualifications for that post had to be chosen in preference to a candidate of the opposite sex who would otherwise have been appointed, where that was necessary for a candidate belonging to the under-represented sex to be appointed. This amounted, said the Court, to granting an automatic preference to candidates belonging to the under-represented sex, provided that they were sufficiently qualified, subject only to the proviso that the difference between the merits of the candidates of each sex was not so great as to result in a breach of the requirement of objectivity in making appointments. It held that the scope and effect of that condition could not be precisely determined, and that the appointment system did not contain provision for an objective assessment that took account of the specific personal situations of all the candidates. The Swedish legislation could not, therefore, come within Article 2(4) of the Directive.

The cases considered above were concerned primarily with the scope of Article 2(4) of the Equal Treatment Directive. The relationship between this provision and Article 141(4) EC is uncertain. The latter was introduced by the Treaty of Amsterdam. It provides that with a view to ensuring full equality in practice, the principle of equal treatment should not prevent a Member State from maintaining or adopting measures to give advantages in order to make it easier for the under-represented sex to pursue a vocational activity or to prevent or compensate for disadvantages in professional careers. In *Abrahamsson* the ECJ ruled that this could not save the Swedish legislation because the selection method was disproportionate to the

[210] Case C-407/98, *Abrahamsson v Fogelqvist* [2000] ECR I-5539.

aim pursued.[211] The ECJ reached the same conclusion in *Briheche.* It left open the possibility that Article 141(4) might allow affirmative action that would not be allowed under Article 2(4) of the Directive, but held that it did not sanction action that was disproportionate to the aim pursued.[212]

The key criteria that emerge from the case law are therefore that measures intended to give priority to women will take the benefit of Article 2(4) of the Directive and be regarded as compatible with Community law if they do not automatically and unconditionally give priority to women when women and men are equally qualified and the applicants are subject to objective assessment which takes account of the specific personal circumstances of all candidates.[213] It seems from *Badeck* and *Abrahamsson* that this formula may, in principle, also be applicable where the criteria for appointment are not based on the applicants being equally qualified. This will, however, only be so if the Court is satisfied that the conditions under which the less-qualified female applicant can be appointed are capable of objective and precise assessment, and the Court is moreover likely to look more closely in such cases at the extent to which the system allows the personal circumstances of all applicants to be taken into account.

The amendments made to the Equal Treatment Directive in 2002 altered the wording of Article 2(4). The provision, which is now Article 2(8), states that 'Member States may maintain or adopt measures within the meaning of Article 141(4) of the Treaty with a view to ensuring full equality in practice between men and women'. It remains to be seen whether this leads to any change in the interpretation of Article 2(8). The new wording, however, renders it less likely for there to be cases that fail under the Directive, but succeed under the Treaty, since the revised wording expressly links the two more closely than hitherto.

(2) The Limits of Equal Treatment: Sex and Sexual Orientation

The limits of the equal treatment regime were tested in a rather different manner in a series of cases dealing with gender reassignment and sexual orientation.

In *P v S*[214] the applicant was dismissed from his employment after undergoing gender reassignment. The ECJ held that this was covered by the Equal Treatment Directive. It reasoned that sex equality was a fundamental human right and that it could not therefore be restricted to discrimination based on the fact that the applicant was a person of one sex or the other. If a person was

211 Ibid. at para. 55.

212 Case 319/03, *Briheche v Ministre de l'Intérieur, Ministre de L'Éducation and Ministre de la Justice* [2004] ECR I-8807, at para. 31.

213 See also, Case 319/03, *Briheche, ibid*, at para. 23.

214 Case C-13/94, *P v S, supra* n. 147.

dismissed on the ground of gender reassignment he or she was in effect being treated less favourably by comparison with persons of the sex to which he or she belonged prior to the reassignment. To allow such discrimination would fail to respect the dignity and freedom to which he or she was entitled, which the Court had the duty to safeguard.[215] The Court was influenced in its conclusion by the Opinion of Advocate General Tesauro, who drew analogies between traditional sex discrimination and the unfavourable treatment accorded to transsexuals.[216]

The ECJ nonetheless placed limits on the ambit of the Equal Treatment Directive in *Grant*, where it ruled, contrary to the Opinion of the Advocate General, that the prohibition on discrimination on grounds of sex within Article 141 did not cover discrimination on grounds of sexual orientation.[217] The applicant was a female employee who claimed discrimination because she was refused travel concessions for her same-sex partner, where such concessions had been granted to her predecessor and his partner of the opposite sex. The ECJ held that there was no direct discrimination, since a male employee cohabiting with a same-sex partner would also have been refused the concessions. It then considered whether those living in stable relationships with a person of the same sex were in the same situation as those who were in stable relationships with a person of the opposite sex. The ECJ looked at Member State laws and the European Convention on Human Rights (ECHR), and took account of the fact that the EC had not adopted rules on the issue. It concluded that in the present state of EC law stable relationships between those of the same sex were not regarded as equivalent to those between persons of opposite sex. The ECJ was content to pass responsibility in this area back to the political branch of the EC to take action under the new Article 13 EC.[218]

6. ARTICLE 13 EC, THE RACE AND FRAMEWORK DIRECTIVES AND EQUAL TREATMENT

A. Economic and Social Rationales

The judicial reticence to confront issues of sexual orientation, and the ECJ's desire that such matters should be dealt with in the political forum, is more

[215] Ibid. at paras. 20–22; Barnard, '*P v S*: Kite Flying or a New Constitutional Approach', in Dashwood and O' Leary, *supra* n. 153, at 59–79.

[216] See also, Case C-117/01, *KB v National Health Service Pensions Agency and Secretary of State for Health* [2004] ECR I-541.

[217] Case C-249/96, *Grant v South-West Trains Ltd* [1998] ECR I-621.

[218] Ibid. at paras. 47–48. See also, Cases C-122 and 125/99 P, *D and Sweden v Council* [2001] ECR I-4319.

readily explicable since the recently introduced Article 13 EC gave the Community competence to legislate in this and other areas. Article 13 provides:

1. Without prejudice to the other provisions of this Treaty and within the limits of the powers conferred by it upon the Community, the Council, acting unanimously on a proposal from the Commission and after consulting the European Parliament, may take appropriate action to combat discrimination based on sex, racial or ethnic origin, religion or belief, disability, age or sexual orientation.
2. By way of derogation from paragraph 1, when the Council adopts Community incentive measures, excluding any harmonization of the laws and regulations of the Member States, to support action taken by the Member States in order to contribute to the achievement of the objectives referred to in paragraph 1, it shall act in accordance with the procedure referred to in Article 251.

It is generally accepted that Article 13 EC, couched as it is in terms of empowering action, does not have direct effect.[219] While Article 13(1) requires unanimity in the Council, and only accords the European Parliament (EP) a right to be consulted, Article 13(2), introduced by the Nice Treaty, provides for qualified majority voting in the Council and use of the co-decision procedure for incentive measures that do not entail harmonization. Article 13 can, however, only be used 'within the limits of the powers' conferred on the Community by the Treaty. There has been considerable academic debate about the meaning of this phrase,[220] but the better view is that the term 'powers' in the English version signifies 'competences', which is the wording used in a number of other language versions of the Treaty.[221] This of course still leaves open the thorny issue of the scope of Community competence.[222] Experience with the judicial interpretation of the 'scope of application' of the Treaty for the purposes of Article 12 EC indicates that the Community courts are unlikely to strike down legislation enacted pursuant to Article 13 on the ground that it exceeds the bounds of Community competence. They are likely to fasten on the existence of some direct Community competence over the relevant area, even if it is attenuated, and conclude that this suffices for the purposes of legislation enacted under Article 13. An alternative juridical option is to emphasize the linkage between the content of the Article 13 measure and the fulfilment of the internal market.[223]

[219] Flynn, 'The Implications of Article 13 EC—After Amsterdam will some Forms of Discrimination be More Equal than Others?' (1999) 36 *CMLRev* 1127; Waddington, 'Testing the Limits of the EC Treaty Article on Non-Discrimination' (1999) 28 *ILJ* 133; Bell, *supra* n. 140, at 125.

[220] Flynn, *supra* n. 219, at 1135; Waddington, *supra* n. 219, at 136; Bell, *supra* n. 140, at 131–134.

[221] Bell, *supra* n. 140, at 134

[222] See above, Chap. 12.

[223] Council Directive 2000/78/EC of 27 November 2000, Establishing a General Framework for Equal Treatment in Employment and Occupation, OJ 2000 L303/16, Preamble, at

The economic and social rationales underlying Community equality law in other areas are apparent here also. The economic focus is highlighted by the fact that the Framework Directive[224] enacted pursuant to Article 13 is concerned with combating discrimination in employment and occupation. The scope of the Race Directive[225] is however broader, covering not only employment and working conditions, but also social protection, including social security and healthcare, social advantages, education, and access to and supply of goods and services available to the public, including housing. It should also be recognized that even where the Directives address employment issues, they will in practice commonly have little connection with inter-state trade or movement of workers, and will avail workers within their own state. Thus, as Bell states, 'whilst the Directives do not contradict the objectives of market integration, they are not central to this project'.[226] The social dimension underlying Article 13 and the Directives enacted pursuant thereto is therefore just as important, perhaps more so, than any economic imperative. The Directives are not perfect and we should therefore be cautious about regarding them as heralding a new era based on fundamental human rights. This can be accepted, while recognizing also the rights-based foundations of this legislation.

B. The Race and Framework Directives

The structure of the Race Directive and the Framework Directive is similar and there is also much commonality in terms of content. There are, however, differences between the two, some of which flow from differences in subject matter, others of which are the result of legislative choice about the remit of the respective provisions.

The purpose of the Race Directive is to advance equal treatment by combating discrimination on grounds of race or ethnic origin. Discrimination may be direct, where a person is treated less favourably than another in a comparable situation on grounds of race or ethnic origin. Indirect discrimination is also proscribed, and is defined to cover cases where an apparently neutral provision, criterion, or practice would put persons of a racial or ethnic origin at a particular disadvantage compared with other persons, unless it is objectively justified by a legitimate aim and the means of achieving the aim are appropriate and necessary.[227] Harassment that is related to racial

para. 11; Council Directive 2000/43/EC of 29 June 2000, Implementing the Principle of Equal Treatment between Persons Irrespective of Racial or Ethnic Origin, OJ 2000 L180/22, Preamble, at para. 9. See however Bell, *supra* n. 140, at 136–143, for possible competence problems with the Directives passed under Art. 13

[224] Council Dir. 2000/78, *supra* n. 223.
[225] Council Dir. 2000/43, *supra* n. 223.
[226] Bell, *supra* n. 140, at 193.
[227] Dir. 2000/43, *supra* n. 223, Art. 2(2)(b).

or ethnic origin is deemed to constitute discrimination.[228] Member States must take the necessary measures to ensure that laws, regulations, etc. contrary to the Directive are abolished, and that provisions in individual or collective agreements and the like that are inconsistent with the Directive are declared void or amended.[229] There must be sanctions for breach of the Directive, and these must be effective, proportionate, and dissuasive.[230]

The Directive applies to all persons within the public and private sectors, although there are qualifications for third-country nationals,[231] and, as we saw above, covers discrimination relating to employment and a broad range of other matters.[232] There are exceptions similar in nature to those found in the Equal Treatment Directive. Thus differences of treatment based on genuine occupational requirements are allowed,[233] and there is provision for positive action to prevent or compensate for disadvantages linked to racial or ethnic origin.[234] Member States are obliged to provide judicial and/or administrative procedures for enforcement of the Directive,[235] and must take the necessary measures to put in place a system where the normal burden of proof is reversed once the applicant has shown facts from which it could be presumed that discrimination had occurred.[236] There are provisions to prevent victimization of complainants, to provide for dissemination of information, to promote social dialogue, and mandate the designation of a body or bodies to promote equal treatment irrespective of race or ethnic origin.[237]

The Framework Directive is designed to combat discrimination in relation to religion or belief, disability, age, or sexual orientation.[238] Many of its provisions are the same as those in the Race Directive. The scope of the Framework Directive is, however, as noted above, narrower. It is confined to access to employment, access to vocational training, employment and working conditions, and membership of organizations concerned with the workplace or a profession.[239] Payments made by social security schemes and the like are expressly excluded.[240]

7. CONCLUSION

It is interesting to reflect more generally on the conception of equality used by the Community courts, and the implications that this has for the standard of judicial review and the interrelationship of legislation and adjudication.

[228] Ibid. Art. 2(3). [229] Ibid. Art. 14. [230] Ibid. Art. 15.
[231] Ibid. Art. 3(2). [232] Ibid. Art. 3(1). [233] Ibid. Art. 4.
[234] Ibid. Art. 5. [235] Ibid. Art. 7. [236] Ibid. Art. 8.
[237] Ibid. Arts. 9–13. [238] Dir. 2000/78, *supra* n. 223, Art. 1.
[239] Ibid. Art. 2(1). [240] Ibid. Art. 2(3).

The ECJ has been most strident in relation to nationality discrimination, both in the context of the four freedoms and in the interpretation accorded to Article 12 EC. This is unsurprising given the centrality of non-discrimination on grounds of nationality to the Community legal and political order. While the Courts' jurisprudence certainly covers formal equality, it has in reality transcended this conception. The Community courts are not indifferent as to whether individuals are treated equally well or equally badly so far as nationality is concerned. Their jurisprudence has moved beyond this towards equality of result or outcome, at least so far as the particular individual is concerned. The immediate objectives have been the removal of impediments to movement based directly or indirectly on nationality, and the provision of benefits afforded by the host state irrespective of nationality. These are, however, instrumental to the more fundamental aim of ensuring that nationals living and working in another Member State can truly function as equals in familial, social, and economic terms with nationals of the host state. The ECJ has to this end given an expansive reading to direct and indirect discrimination when adjudicating on the four freedoms. It has been similarly strident in its jurisprudence on Article 12, more especially that entailing citizenship.[241] The corollary of this approach has been intensive judicial review, which would in legal systems that use the language be cast in terms of strict scrutiny. The judicial stance taken towards nationality discrimination has also had implications for the relationship between legislation and adjudication. The ECJ has given an expansive reading to Community legislation, in order to ensure that nationals from other Member States really are placed, so far as possible, in the same position as nationals of the host state, as exemplified by the expansive case law on social advantage. It has also been willing to break down barriers of nationality discrimination, even where Community legislation indicated limits to the extent to which the Member States were willing to embrace 'social solidarity' and accord benefits to those from other Member States, as exemplified by case law on Article 12 and citizenship.

This approach is in marked contrast to the conception of equality that prevails where equality operates as a constraint on Community regulatory initiatives, in particular those within the common policies such as the CAP. The prevailing concept of equality is that of formal equality or equality as consistency. This conception of equality is dependent on threshold determinations as to whether two individuals are relevantly alike, and on the need to find a comparator who has been treated more favourably than the

[241] Barnard, 'EU Citizenship and the Principle of Solidarity', in M. Dougan and E. Spaventa (eds), *Social Welfare and EU Law* (Hart, 2005), Chap. 8; Dougan and Spaventa, '"Wish You Weren't Here . . ." New Models of Social Solidarity in the European Union', ibid. Chap. 9.

applicant.[242] These problems are vividly revealed by the case law, and the applicant company will not uncommonly fail because the ECJ decides that it was not similarly situated to that of the alleged comparator. The application of formal equality is, moreover, significantly affected by low intensity judicial review, as evidenced by the need to show that the criterion in the challenged legislation was arbitrary, and the use made of objective justification to rescue regulatory norms that are *prima facie* discriminatory. This low intensity review in turn reflects judicial perceptions about the relationship between legislation and adjudication in relation to common policies, with the ECJ aware of the difficult regulatory choices made by the Community legislature and hence unwilling lightly to overturn such policies.

The conception of equality that is prevalent in the context of sex discrimination and Article 13 EC is somewhat different again. It is also rather more complex. It clearly embraces formal equality, but it is similarly evident from the jurisprudence on the limits of affirmative action that it does not encompass equality of result.[243] The Community courts have, however, endorsed equality of opportunity in relation to gender discrimination, at least so far as that signifies the removal of some obstacles to the advancement of women, and Community legislation, as exemplified by the amended Equal Treatment Directive and the Race Directive, makes provision for bodies at national level to promote and support equal treatment. The ECJ's approach to judicial review and the relationship more generally between adjudication and legislation has been nuanced. Where it felt on secure ground, in terms of the primary Treaty Article or Community legislation, it applied the principles contained therein vigorously and closely scrutinized Member State action. Where, however, it was less secure in this respect, it awaited legislative intervention, more especially if it believed that there were complex practical or moral issues that were best resolved through legislation. Thus by way of example the ECJ engaged in intensive review in cases concerning equal pay, while being unwilling to read Article 141 as covering equal treatment, and it spoke of gender equality as a fundamental right, while leaving the development of the law concerning sexual orientation to the legislature.

[242] Fredman, *supra* n. 4, at 7–9.
[243] Case C-450/93, *Kalanke*, *supra* n. 198, at paras. 22–23.

16

Legal Certainty and Legitimate Expectations

1. INTRODUCTION

The connected concepts of legal certainty and legitimate expectations are to be found in many legal systems, although their precise legal content may vary from one system to another.[1] These concepts are used in a number of different ways and it is important to distinguish them in order to avoid confusion.

The discussion begins with the constraints placed on Community norms that have an actual retroactive effect. This is followed by differentiation of the other types of case where legal certainty and legitimate expectations are utilized and the rationale for affording legal protection. The remainder of the chapter analyses in detail the law and policy applicable in these differing areas, including revocation of lawful and unlawful decisions; individual representations; representations and changes of policy; departure from existing policy; and unlawful representations.

2. LEGAL CERTAINTY AND ACTUAL RETROACTIVITY: PROCEDURAL AND SUBSTANTIVE CONSTRAINTS

The most obvious application of legal certainty is in the context of rules with an 'actual retroactive' effect. This covers the situation where a rule is introduced and applied to events which have already been concluded.[2] Retroactivity of this nature may occur either where the date of entry into force precedes the date of publication, or where the regulation applies to circumstances which have actually been concluded before the entry into force of the measure.

The arguments against allowing such measures to have legal effect are simple and compelling. A basic tenet of the rule of law is that people ought to

[1] S. Schonberg, *Legitimate Expectations in Administrative Law* (Oxford University Press, 2000); J. Schwarze, *European Administrative Law* (Sweet & Maxwell, 1992), Chap. 6; T. Tridimas, *The General Principles of EC Law* (Oxford University Press, 1999), Chap. 5; Sharpston, 'Legitimate Expectations and Economic Reality' (1990) 15 *ELRev* 103.

[2] Schwarze, *supra* n. 1, at 1120.

be able to plan their lives, secure in the knowledge of the legal consequences of their actions. This central aspect of the rule of law is violated by the application of measures that were not in force when the actual events took place. These concerns about retrospective norms are particularly marked in the context of criminal penalties, where the effect of the norm may be to criminalize activity that was lawful when it was undertaken. The application of retrospective rules may also be extremely damaging in commercial circumstances, upsetting the presuppositions on which important transactions were based. It is therefore unsurprising that national legal systems take a very dim view of attempts to apply rules in this manner.

The Community is no different in this respect. The basic principle was enunciated in *Racke*.[3] The Commission had introduced monetary compensatory amounts for a certain product by a Regulation, and then in two further Regulations altered the amounts. Each of the relevant Regulations provided that they would apply 14 days before they were published. The Court held that it was a fundamental principle of the Community legal order that a measure should not be applicable to those concerned before they had the opportunity to make themselves acquainted with it.[4] The Court then drew out the implications for retroactive measures.[5]

> Although in general the principle of legal certainty precludes a Community measure from taking effect from a point in time before its publication, it may exceptionally be otherwise where the purpose to be achieved so demands and where the legitimate expectations of those concerned are duly respected.

The Court has, in accordance with this proviso, upheld the validity of retroactive measures, particularly in the agricultural sphere where they were necessary to ensure market stability, or where the retroactivity placed the individual in a more favourable position.[6] The normal presumption is, however, against the validity of retroactive measures. This manifests itself in both procedural and substantive terms.

In procedural terms, the Court has made it clear that it will interpret norms as having retroactive effect only if this clearly follows from their terms, or from the objectives of the general scheme of which they are a part. The general principle of construction is, therefore, against giving rules any

[3] Case 98/78, *Firma A. Racke v Hauptzollamt Mainz* [1979] ECR 69. See also Case 99/78, *Weingut Gustav Decker KG v Hauptzollamt Landau* [1979] ECR 101; Case C-34/92, *GruSa Fleisch GmbH & Co KG v Hauptzollamt Hamburg-Jonas* [1993] ECR I-4147; Case T-115/94, *Opel Austria GmbH v Council* [1997] ECR II-2739; Cases C-74 and 75/00 P, *Falck SpA and Acciaierie di Bolzano SpA v Commission* [2002] ECR I-7869; Case C-459/02, *Willy Gerekens and Assocation Agricole pour la Promotion de la Commercialisation Laitière Procola v Luxembourg* [2004] ECR I-7315.

[4] Case 98/78, *Racke*, *supra* n. 3, at para. 15.

[5] Ibid. at para.20.

[6] Case T-7/99, *Medici Grimm KG v Council* [2000] ECR II-2671.

retroactive impact. Thus in *Salumi*[7] the European Court of Justice (ECJ) held that the general rule of construction for substantive provisions was that they should only be interpreted as applying to situations existing before their entry into force in so far as this clearly followed from the terms of the relevant provision or from the general scheme of which they were a part. This interpretation ensured respect for the principles of legal certainty and the protection of legitimate expectations, 'by virtue of which the effect of Community legislation must be clear and predictable for those who are subject to it'.[8]

In substantive terms, the Court will strike down measures that have a retroactive effect where there is no pressing Community objective which demands this temporal dimension, or where the legitimate expectations of those affected by the measure cannot be duly respected. Thus in *Meiko-Konservenfabrik*[9] the ECJ struck down a Regulation that retroactively subjected the payment of aid to the forwarding to the national intervention agency of the contract made between producer and processor of the relevant goods, since the date fixed for the forwarding of the contracts could not reasonably have been anticipated by the parties. This substantive control is even more marked where the retroactivity leads to the imposition of criminal penalties, as in the case of *Kent Kirk.*[10] Criminal proceedings were brought in the UK for infringement of fisheries legislation. During the course of these proceedings the question arose whether Council Regulation 170/83 of 25 January 1983, by which, with retroactive effect from 1 January 1983, national measures contravening Community law prohibitions on discrimination were approved by way of transitional arrangements, could retroactively validate national penal provisions. The ECJ held that even leaving aside the general legality of the retroactivity of the Council Regulation, such retroactivity could not validate *ex post facto* national penal measures which imposed penalties for an act which was not punishable at the time at which it was committed. The principle that penal provisions could not have retroactive effect was common to the legal orders of the Member States and was enshrined in Article 7 of the European Convention on Human Rights (ECHR).[11]

[7] Cases 212–217/80, *Amministrazione delle Finanze dello Stato v Srl Meridionale Industria Salumi* [1981] ECR 2735.

[8] Ibid. at para. 10. See also, Case C-400/98, *Finanzamt Goslar v Brigitte Breitsohl* [2000] ECR I-4321; Case C-396/98, *Grundstückgemeinschaft SchoIBstraBe GbR v Finanzamt Paderborn* [2000] ECR I-4279; Case C-110/03, *Belgium v Commission* [2005] ECR I-2801, at para. 73.

[9] Case 224/82, *Meiko-Konservenfabrik v Federal Republic of Germany* [1983] ECR 2539.

[10] Case 63/83, *Regina v Kent Kirk* [1984] ECR 2689.

[11] Ibid. at paras. 21–22. See also, Cases C-189, 202, 205, 208, and 213/02 P, *Dansk Rorindustri A/S and others v Commission* [2005] ECR I-5425, at para. 202.

Where there is a pressing Community objective and where the legitimate expectations of those concerned are duly respected, then retroactivity may, *exceptionally*, be accepted by the Court in the non-criminal context. This is exemplified by *Fedesa*.[12] The applicants argued that the challenged Directive was in breach of the principle of non-retroactivity, since it was adopted on 7 March 1988, and stipulated that it was to be implemented by 1 January 1988 at the latest. The ECJ drew a distinction between the retroactive effect of penal provisions and retroactive effect outside the criminal sphere. The ECJ re-affirmed *Kent Kirk* concerning the retroactive effect of penal provisions, but held that the Directive in *Fedesa* did not impose criminal liability. The ECJ ruled further that the Directive did not contravene the principle of non-retroactivity. It had been adopted to replace an earlier Directive that had been annulled. The time frame of the challenged Directive was necessary in order to avoid a temporary legal vacuum where there would be no Community legislation to back up the Member States' existing implementing provisions. It was for this reason that the Council had maintained the date of the earlier Directive when it passed the later Directive. The ECJ concluded that there was no infringement of legitimate expectations, since the earlier Directive was only annulled because of a procedural defect. Those affected by the national implementing legislation could not expect the Council to change its attitude on the substance of the matter in the Directive during the short time between the annulment of the first Directive and the notification of the second Directive.[13]

It is clear moreover from *Gerekens*[14] that this exception, whereby rules can exceptionally take effect from a point in time before publication when the purpose to be attained so demands provided that the legitimate expectations of those concerned are duly respected, can apply to national rules that are implementing Community law.

3. LEGAL CERTAINTY, LEGITIMATE EXPECTATIONS, AND APPARENT RETROACTIVITY: TYPES OF CASE AND RATIONALE FOR PROTECTION

It is important to recognize that problems of legal certainty and legitimate expectations can arise in a variety of circumstances over and beyond the classic case where legislation has an actual retroactive effect. In some of these other situations there is what is termed apparent retroactivity. This covers the

[12] Case C-331/88, *R v Minister for Agriculture, Fisheries and Food, ex p Fedesa* [1990] ECR 4023

[13] Ibid. at para. 47.

[14] Case C-459/02, *Willy Gerekens, supra* n. 3, at paras. 21–34.

scenario where the legal act takes effect for the future. It nonetheless has an impact on events that occurred in the past, but which were not yet definitively concluded.[15] It will be seen that some of the cases where legal certainty and legitimate expectations apply involve apparent retroactivity, although this is not so in all instances. The Member States are also bound to comply with legal certainty and legitimate expectations when they are implementing EU law.[16] It is in any event important to distinguish between the different types of case that raise issues concerning legal certainty and legitimate expectations.

(i) A public authority makes a formal decision concerning a person or a limited group of persons and then seeks to revoke that decision.
(ii) A representation is relied on by a person or a group, and the administration later makes a decision that is inconsistent with the representation.
(iii) A general norm or policy choice, which an individual or group has relied on, is replaced by a different policy choice.
(iv) A general norm or policy choice is departed from in the circumstances of a particular case.

These different types of case may well raise somewhat different considerations. Thus, for example, in cases of the second type we have an unequivocal representation made to a person and this carries a particular moral force. Moreover, holding the public body to such a representation is less likely to have serious consequences for the administration as a whole. Cases falling into the third category are, by way of contrast, generally regarded as more problematic for reasons to be discussed below. Different principles of judicial review may therefore be appropriate in this type of case. The fact that principles of review will have to be tailored to meet the different needs of these types of case should not mask the fact that they raise similar underlying problems.

This leads naturally to consideration of the rationale for affording legal protection. The moral arguments against allowing laws to have actual retroactive effect are powerful and straightforward. Other cases, including those raising issues of apparent retroactivity, are more problematic because the

[15] It can, however, be difficult to distinguish cases of actual and apparent retroactivity, Case C-162/00, *Land Nordrehein-Westfalen v Beata Pokrzeptowicz-Meyer* [2002] ECR I-1049; Cases C-189, 202, 205, 208, and 213/02 P, *Dansk Rorindustri, supra* n. 11, at paras. 198–232.

[16] Cases C-31–44/91, *SpA Alois Lageder v Amministrazione delle Finanze dello Stato* [1993] ECR I-1761, at para. 33; Case C-107/97, *Criminal Proceedings against Max Rombi* [2000] ECR I-3367, at paras. 65, 67, 73; Cases C-80–82/99, *Flemmer v Council and Commission* [2001] ECR I-7211, at paras. 59–60; Case C-62/00, *Marks & Spencer plc v Commissioners of Customs & Excise* [2002] ECR I-6325, at para. 44; Case C-495/00, *Azienda Agricola Giorgio v AIMA* [2004] ECR I-2993, at para. 40.

administration must have the power to alter its policy for the future, even though this may have implications for the conduct of private parties which has been planned on the basis of the pre-existing legal regime. There are nonetheless a variety of arguments for protecting individuals in such cases.[17]

There is the argument based on *fairness in public administration.* The essence of the argument is captured by Sedley J in a UK case concerning substantive legitimate expectations.[18]

> [T]he real question is one of fairness in public administration. It is difficult to see why it is any less unfair to frustrate a legitimate expectation that something will or will not be done by the decision-maker than it is to frustrate a legitimate expectation that the applicant will be listened to before the decision-maker decides whether to take a particular step. Such a doctrine does not risk fettering a public body in the discharge of public duties because no individual can legitimately expect the discharge of public duties to stand still or be distorted because of that individual's peculiar position.

It may also be argued that the law should provide protection for legitimate expectations because of *reliance.* Schonberg puts the argument as follows.[19]

> [A] public authority's freedom to take action in the public interest is limited to the extent that it causes harm to particular individuals. If a public authority has induced a person to rely upon its representations or conduct, realising that such reliance was a real possibility, it is under a prima facie duty to act in such a way that the reliance will not be detrimental to the representee. The authority must honour the expectations created by its representation or, at least, compensate the person affected for his reliance loss.

Reliance may well be part of the rationale for protecting legitimate expectations. It cannot, however, be the only reason for according protection. This is because there may be circumstances where it is felt that legal protection should be given even though there was no actual reliance by the claimant. This is particularly so in relation to the fourth category of case mentioned above. The administration may well be prevented from departing from its existing policy in relation to a particular individual even though there was no actual reliance, for reasons of equality and because of the principle that like cases should be treated alike. It may, moreover, be fortuitous whether there was any reliance causing actual detriment short of the moral harm that flows from having one's expectations disappointed. While there are therefore limits to reliance as the principled foundation for legitimate expectations, the existence of loss caused by detrimental reliance induced by the public authority is

[17] Schonberg, *supra* n. 1, Chap. 1.

[18] *R v Ministry of Agriculture, Fisheries and Food, ex p Hamble (Offshore) Fisheries Ltd* [1995] 2 All ER 714, 724.

[19] Schonberg, *supra* n. 1, at 10.

nonetheless still a good reason why the law should afford protection in cases where such justified reliance exists.

The rationale for affording protection can also be supported by *rule of law considerations.* The concept of legal certainty, which underlies much of continental and European Community (EC) thinking in this area,[20] is connected to mainstream thinking about the formal conception of the rule of law, with its concern for autonomy and the ability to plan one's life. There is one aspect of the rule of law that is of particular relevance to the present analysis. It is concerned with the importance within adjudication of considering matters across time. This idea is to be found in Raz's work.[21] Thus Raz stresses the 'principled faithful application of the law',[22] in which the courts, while faithful to legislation, act in a principled manner so as to 'facilitate the integration of particular pieces of legislation with the underlying doctrines of the legal system'.[23] This is justified in part to mix 'the fruits of long-established traditions with the urgencies of short-term exigencies'.[24] It is precisely because the legislature or the executive can be susceptible to short-term influences, whether generated by elections or the need to respond quickly to public pressure, that the courts should have a role as the guardians of longer-term tradition. This argument is of importance where the applicant possesses an expectation which is normatively justified.

A further rationale for the protection of legitimate expectations is that it *fosters good administration and trust in government.* The discussion thus far has considered various arguments for the protection of legitimate expectations that focus on the individual. It is nonetheless important to recognize that such protection can also benefit the public authority. Thus as Schonberg states:[25]

> [A]dministrative power is more likely to be perceived as legitimate authority if exercised in a way which respects legitimate expectations. Perceived legitimate authority is more efficacious because it encourages individuals to participate in decision-making processes, to co-operate with administrative initiatives, and to comply with administrative regulations. Greater compliance will in turn improve the administration's ability to solve co-ordination problems, and that may actually make its exercise of authority more legitimate. The acceptance of principles of administrative law, which require authorities to respect legitimate expectations, is therefore not merely in the interest of individuals. It is, very much, in the interest of the administration itself.

There are therefore powerful arguments for the protection of legitimate expectations. It should be stressed at this juncture that the protection afforded to legitimate expectations does not mean that the government's

[20] Schwarze, *supra* n.1, Chap. 6.
[21] J. Raz, *Ethics in the Public Domain* (Oxford University Press, 1994), Chap. 17.
[22] Ibid. at 373. [23] Ibid. at 375. [24] Ibid. at 376.
[25] Schonberg, *supra* n. 1, at 25.

ability to alter policy will be unduly fettered. There are three reasons why this fear is misplaced.

Firstly, the recognition of a doctrine of legitimate expectations still requires an applicant to prove the existence of the requisite expectation on the facts of the case. This is, as will be seen below, not easy. The mere fact that there has been some change of policy does not mean that those who in some way operated under the old policy would be able to prove the existence of such an expectation.

Secondly, even if the applicant is able to prove the existence of the substantive legitimate expectation on the facts of the case, this does not mean that she wins. The proof of the expectation is but the first step in the analysis. There is a second legal step, in which the courts inquire whether the public body had sufficient reasons to depart from the expectation. The precise nature of the test that should apply at this level will be examined in more detail below.

Thirdly, even if the applicant does win this does not necessarily mean that the development of policy is fettered or ossified. This is because the applicant's claim will often have a temporal limit or dimension: the issue will be when the new policy should take effect not whether it should take affect at all. It should moreover be recognized that the government may acknowledge the problems created by change in policy, as shown by the existence of transitional or pipeline provisions when a new policy is adopted. Given that this is so, and given also that such provisions themselves constitute administrative choices, the courts should be able to review their existence and adequacy.

4. REVOCATION OF LAWFUL DECISIONS

A. The General Principle: Favourable Decisions Bind

All legal systems have to face the issue of the legal effect to ascribe to formal decisions made by the administration. To what extent will the decisions be regarded as binding on the administration and to what extent will the administration be able to revoke the decision thus made?

The issue arose early in the courts' jurisprudence in the *Algera* case.[26] The applicant was a temporary employee with the Common Assembly who was then appointed to a permanent position by a decision of the board that dealt with employment matters. The Assembly, seven months later, then changed its mind, largely because of an industrial dispute in which the applicant had been involved. It sought to dismiss her, which entailed a revocation of the

[26] Cases 7/56 and 3–7/57, *Algera v Common Assembly* [1957] ECR 39.

employment decision with prospective effect. The ECJ began its legal assessment by wisely noting a 'vicious circle' that should be avoided. This consisted of asserting a vested right and then inferring that the right could not be revoked. This reasoning was, the ECJ noted, circular, since if the right conferred by the administrative measure could be unilaterally revoked it would not therefore constitute a vested right. The ECJ addressed the matter more directly, holding that if the appointment decisions were legal and valid in law they constituted individual administrative measures that gave rise to individual rights. It then considered whether such measures could be withdrawn. The ECJ drew on principles from French and German law and held that:[27]

It emerges from a comparative study of this problem of law that in the six Member States an administrative measure conferring individual rights on the person concerned cannot in principle be withdrawn, if it is a lawful measure; in that case since the individual right is vested, the need to safeguard confidence in the stability of the situation thus created prevails over the interests of an administration of reversing its decision. This is true in particular of the appointment of an official.

The Community courts have used different linguistic formulations to capture the criterion that triggers this legal protection against revocation. Some decisions use the formula that a legal measure that confers rights or similar benefits cannot be revoked. We find this linguistic formula in cases such as *Verli-Wallace*,[28] where the ECJ held that an applicant who had been allowed to sit for a competitive staff examination had a personal right to take part and this could not be withdrawn by a subsequent decision that she was not entitled to take part, the retroactive withdrawal of a legal measure that conferred rights or similar benefits being contrary to Community law.[29] This same formulation is evident in more recent cases. Thus in *Lagardère and Canal*[30] the applicants challenged a Commission decision revoking an earlier decision holding that a concentration was compatible with the common market. The Court of First Instance (CFI) stated that the earlier decision granted the applicants subjective rights and that the case therefore fell within the principle that retroactive withdrawal of a legal measure that conferred individual rights or similar benefits was contrary to general principles of Community law.[31]

In other cases the court has used the language of favourable administrative act, as in *de Compte*.[32] The applicant who had been employed by

[27] Ibid. at 55. See also, Cases 42 and 49/59, *SNUPAT v High Authority* [1961] ECR 53, 78; Case 111/63, *Lemmerz-Werke v High Authority* [1965] ECR 677.

[28] Case 159/82, *Verli-Wallace v Commission* [1983] ECR 2711.

[29] See also, Case T-123/89, *Chomel v Commission* [1990] ECR II-131, at para. 34.

[30] Case T-251/00, *Lagardère SCA and Canal+ SA v Commission* [2002] ECR II-4825.

[31] Ibid. at paras. 139, 142.

[32] Case C-90/95 P, *Henri de Compte v EP* [1997] ECR I-1999.

the European Parliament (EP) suffered from mental illness. A medical committee decided that this was work-related in accord with the relevant staff rules. Acting on this report, the appointing committee then decided in January 1991 that the applicant should receive certain compensation. Three months later in April 1991 the appointing authority revoked this decision on the ground that it had been based on an erroneous interpretation of occupational injury. It argued that it was therefore entitled to revoke the earlier decision with retroactive affect. The ECJ held that retroactive withdrawal of a favourable administrative act was generally subject to very strict conditions. There was nothing to suggest that de Compte had provoked the earlier decision through false information. It followed that legitimate expectations as to the legality of a favourable administrative act, once acquired, could not subsequently be undermined and there was no public-policy interest that overrode the beneficiary's interest in the maintenance of a situation which he was entitled to regard as stable.[33]

There is no indication that the Community courts intend any substantive differences to flow from these alternative formulations. The very fact that the triggering criterion cast in terms of rights also includes 'other similar benefits' indicates that the courts are not intending to limit the applicability of the legal protection to rights *stricto sensu*. It is clear, moreover, that the Community courts take a relatively broad view of what constitutes a favourable decision or a benefit similar to a right. Thus a decision reducing the size of a quota as compared to that given by an earlier decision fell within the principle since the initial decision had conferred a benefit.[34]

The decision will not, however, be irrevocable until it is communicated to the person concerned. It is this rather than the date when the initial decision was adopted that is controlling, since the addressee will not have any legitimate expectation until he or she knows of the decision.[35]

It is equally clear that the binding effect of formal decisions and hence the prohibition on retroactive revocation applies only in relation to later unfavourable decisions. The principle of legitimate expectations does not therefore preclude the Commission from reassessing a decision imposing a fine on a member of a cartel.[36]

[33] Ibid. at paras. 35–40.

[34] Case 14/81, *Alpha Steel v Commission* [1982] ECR 749.

[35] Case C-90/95 P, *Henri de Compte*, *supra* n. 32, at para. 36.

[36] Case T-227/95, *Assidoman Kraft Products AB v Commission* [1997] ECR II-1185, at paras. 90–92.

B. Qualifications to the General Principle: Consent and Fraud

The general principle that formal decisions cannot be revoked retroactively is subject to a number of qualifications.

It is clear that the parties can consent to the revocation of the initial decision. This is, as Schonberg states, 'unsurprising, since the protection of legal certainty and legitimate expectations, which underpin the principle of irrevocability, does not require decisions to be upheld against the wishes of those affected'.[37]

The position is similarly clear in relation to those cases where the initial decision was obtained by fraud or deception. There is no moral rationale for allowing a person to claim a 'legitimate' expectation based on an initial decision that was obtained by fraud or deception. On the contrary, there is every reason to allow the administration to take another decision correcting the mistake induced by the individual's fraud.

The Community courts have taken a broad view of this exception, allowing revocation not only where there has been fraud, but also where the decision rests on wrong or incomplete information from the persons concerned.[38] Thus in *Euroagri*[39] the CFI stated in relation to aid granted under the Structural Funds that information provided by the applicant was important in assessing the validity of the project for funding. If it was subsequently proved that 'the information did not correspond to the facts, the award decision is vitiated by an error of fact and must therefore be considered to be unlawful'.[40] The CFI said that this illegality could then justify retroactive withdrawal of the aid.

There is, however, a danger in pressing the equation between fraud and misrepresentation too far. There is a real difference between fraud and innocent misrepresentation, and that is so even though the line between the two may be difficult to divine on the facts of particular cases. There may well, therefore, be reasons for limiting powers of revocation if the misinformation was innocent.[41] This should at the very least be a significant factor that is taken into account in the balancing process applied when deciding whether retroactive withdrawal of an illegal benefit should be allowed.[42]

[37] Schonberg, *supra* n. 1, at 79.
[38] Cases 42 and 49/59, *SNUPAT*, *supra* n. 27.
[39] Case T-180/01, *Euroagri Srl v Commission* [2004] ECR II-369, at para. 87.
[40] Ibid. at para. 87.
[41] Schonberg, *supra* n. 1, at 80.
[42] See below, at 649–652 for a discussion of this balancing process.

C. Qualifications to the General Principle: Conditional Decisions

A further situation in which the initial decision may be capable of being revoked is where it was granted subject to certain conditions. If these conditions were never met, but the failure to meet the conditions did not render the initial decision unlawful, then the case would fall within the fraud/deception exception on the assumption that it was the applicant that misled the administration. If the conditions were never met and there was no such wrongdoing by the applicant then, assuming that non-fulfilment of those conditions rendered the initial decision unlawful, the case would fall within the category of unlawful decisions, considered below.

There can, however, be cases where the initial decision was conditional, where the facts satisfied those conditions when the initial decision was made, but where they no longer do so because of subsequent events. Prospective revocation of the decision is clearly an option in these circumstances. This was the result achieved in *Herpels*,[43] albeit indirectly. The applicant received a separation allowance because he lived in Brussels and worked in Luxembourg. He was transferred back to Brussels in 1968, but continued to receive the allowance until the mistake was revealed in 1976. The ECJ held that while retroactive revocation of an erroneous decision was subject to strict conditions, such a decision could always be revoked for the future.[44]

There can also be cases where it is clear that the initial decision was subject to certain conditions that had to be met, and where the determination of whether those conditions had been met could not be unequivocally decided until a later date. Where it is found at the later date that the conditions have not been fulfilled there is no breach of legitimate expectations when the Commission enforces such conditions strictly. This is exemplified by *Interhotel-Sociedade*.[45] The applicant had been given a grant from the European Social Fund (ESF) for vocational training. The scheme under the ESF was for the Commission, when it approved an application, to give an advance, with the remainder of the payment given on completion of the assignment, subject to approval by national authorities and in certain circumstances by the Commission, that the task had been completed in accord with the terms of the award initially given. The Commission refused to pay the full amount to the applicant on completion of the assignment on the grounds, *inter alia*, that certain expenditure had not been mentioned in the initial application and other expenditure had not been properly documented. The CFI held that the Commission could reduce the final payment on both grounds without thereby infringing the principle of legitimate expectations.

[43] Case 54/77, *Herpels v Commission* [1978] ECR 585.

[44] Ibid. at para. 38.

[45] Case T-81/95, *Interhotel-Sociedade Internacional de Hotéis SARL v Commission* [1997] ECR II-1265.

The rules in force governing the ESF scheme clearly provided for the possibility of financial assistance being recovered where the conditions for payment had not been fulfilled, and by parity of reasoning the applicant acquired no definitive right to full payment if the conditions were not met.[46]

It is, however, equally clear from the *Interhotel-Sociedade* case that the applicant must be able to know the conditions attached to the assistance granted. Thus the CFI also considered the legality of a reduction of the final payment to the applicant on the ground that certain expenses had not been allowed in the approval decision. The CFI found for the applicant on this point. It held that the approval decision communicated to the applicant indicated only the total amount granted and the number of persons approved. The Commission's assessment concerning the eligibility of the proposed expenses was not brought to the applicant's notice before completion of the project. In these circumstances, notwithstanding the fact that the rules did not require such details to be communicated to the applicant, the CFI held that it would breach legitimate expectations and legal certainty to reduce the final payment on this ground, since the beneficiary of the aid was not in a position to identify the detail of the items approved.[47]

D. Qualifications to the General Principle: Change of Policy

The issue of whether the original decision is revocable can also arise when there has been a general change in policy, which has a marked impact on the decision initially made. Academic opinion tends to be against the ability to revoke the initial decision in such circumstances.[48] This is a sound conclusion in terms of principle: if a decision was lawful at the time that it was made it should not in general be capable of being revoked either retroactively or prospectively merely because of a change of policy.

This statement of principle assumes that the initial decision was not subject to conditions, express or implied. Where such conditions are expressly attached to the original decision and the conditions are undermined by the change of policy then the benefit in question may in principle be subject to prospective revocation. The same would be true if the conditions to which

[46] Ibid. at paras. 42, 46–47, 61–62. See also, Case T-126/97, *Sonasa-Sociedade de Seguranca Ld v Commission* [1999] ECR II-2793, at paras. 47, 59; Cases T-46 and 151/98, *CEMR v Commission* [2000] ECR II-167, at paras. 68–70; Cases 141–142, 150–151/99, *Vela Srl and Tecnagrind SL v Commission* [2002] ECR II-4547, at paras. 224, 317, 391; Case T-137/01, *Stadtsportverband Neuss eV v Commission* [2003] ECR II-3103, at paras. 46, 82, 84, 86; Case T-180/01, *supra* n. 39.

[47] Case T-81/95, *Interhotel-Sociedade*, *supra* n. 45, at paras. 49–59; Cases T-46 and 151/98, *CEMR*, *supra* n. 46, at para. 72.

[48] Schonberg, *supra* n. 1, at 81, 88; Schwarze, *supra* n. 1, at 1023–1024.

the initial decision was subject flowed from a statutory provision in force when that decision was made.

These qualifications do not, however, affect the force of the general proposition that a favourable, unconditional decision that has been duly notified to the applicant should not be able to be revoked merely because the decision-maker would, in the light of subsequent change in policy, have assessed the facts differently when making the original decision. If there were a later statutory provision that specifically allowed revocation in such circumstances it should in principle be open to challenge for breach of legitimate expectations.

Having said this, it is not easy to find specific case law authority for the general principle set out above. The principle can, however, be supported inferentially by case law from three related areas.

Firstly, it coheres with the reasoning concerning the revocation of decisions in the seminal *Algera* case,[49] which laid the foundations for the courts' jurisprudence in this area. It is also consistent with more recent case law, such as the *Interhotel-Sociedade* case,[50] and *CEMR*,[51] where the CFI affirmed the binding nature of matters approved in the original decision. While this case law is therefore consistent with the general principle propounded above, it was not specifically concerned with the situation in which the Commission sought to justify revocation of the original decision on grounds of a shift in policy.

Secondly, support for the general principle can, however, also be found in the case law concerned with retroactivity considered above.[52] It is clear from this jurisprudence that the Community courts are opposed to legislation and the like that has an actual retroactive effect. This is so even in a non-criminal context, and retroactivity will only exceptionally be permitted when there is a pressing Community objective and where the legitimate expectations of those concerned are duly respected. There are, as we have seen, qualifications to this proposition, but the general presumption is nonetheless against the legality of such measures. The paradigmatic situation to which this presumption applies is one where activity which was generally lawful at the time that it was undertaken is rendered retrospectively unlawful by a later Community measure. That presumption should apply *a fortiori* when there is a formal decision that is sought to be revoked retroactively on account of a change in policy embodied in later legislation.

Thirdly, the general principle adumbrated above can also be supported by the case law concerning changes of policy in the context of representations.

[49] Cases 7/56 and 3–7/57, *Algera, supra* n. 26.
[50] Case T-81/95, *Interhotel-Sociedade, supra* n. 45.
[51] Cases T-46 and 151/98, *CEMR, supra* n. 46, at para. 72.
[52] See above, at 607–610.

This jurisprudence will be examined in detail below.[53] Suffice it to say for the present that the Community courts have emphasized the mutability of policy, and thus it is not easy for an applicant who has relied on a policy embodied in an earlier general legislative norm to claim a legitimate expectation when it is replaced by a later legislative norm. It is, however, evident that the Community courts are also willing to recognize exceptional cases where legitimate expectations arise from the earlier provision, and have been willing to do so even where the expectation was based on something falling short of a formal decision. The normative argument for recognizing such a legitimate expectation is all the stronger when it is based on a formal decision.

The general principle should therefore be that a favourable, unconditional decision that has been duly notified to the applicant should not be able to be revoked merely because the decision-maker would, in the light of subsequent change in policy, have assessed the facts differently when making the original decision. Retroactive revocation should normally be unlawful, and there would have to be very exceptional circumstances to warrant this. The onus should also be firmly on the defendant to justify any prospective revocation in the light of the change in policy. It should be for the defendant to show that the original decision is inconsistent with the new policy adopted. It would be for the courts to decide whether this argument was *prima facie* sustainable, and assuming an affirmative answer, it would then be for the courts to balance the harm to the applicant's legitimate expectation flowing from the original decision with the public interest embodied in the new policy initiative. The nature of this balancing exercise will be considered in more detail below.[54]

5. REVOCATION OF UNLAWFUL DECISIONS

A. The Nature of the Problem: Legality v Justice

The discussion thus far has been concerned with the extent to which lawful decisions are revocable. We must now consider the position where the initial decision is unlawful. This is an endemic problem faced by all legal systems. The nature of the tension between legality and individual justice is readily apparent.

There is clearly a public interest in ensuring that the administration does not make decisions that are unlawful. The legal limits to the exercise of power are laid down in Treaty articles, regulations, and the like. If the administration makes a decision that is unlawful it is therefore overstepping these limits,

[53] See below, at 635–641. [54] See below, at 649–652.

and there is in that sense a public interest in ensuring that such decisions can be overturned. This is more especially the case where the illegality that afflicts the decision can have a marked impact on third parties.

It is, however, equally apparent that if unlawful decisions are always deemed to have no legal effect and can be retroactively revoked this can lead to serious consequences for the person who relied on the tainted decision. The legal rules that are applied to individuals will often be complex. The precise boundaries to the lawful exercise of power may not be evident even to the most assiduous of individuals dealing with government. Indeed it will not infrequently be the case that even legal experts may differ as to the dividing line between lawful and unlawful exercise of power. The matter may only be resolved when it is adjudicated before the courts. There may well be differences of view even as between judges or courts as to whether a particular measure falls on the lawful or the unlawful side of the divide.

It is precisely because of the contending interests that are at play in this area, legality and individual justice, that there is a need for an approach that seeks to balance them in the circumstances of particular cases. This is in fact the general approach adopted by the Community courts, as will be seen below.

B. The Divide between Illegality and Legality

The consequences of holding that the original measure is illegal are significant, since if the measure is deemed to be illegal the case law on revocation of illegal decisions will be applicable, as opposed to that considered above concerning the revocation of lawful decisions.

It is now clear that the burden of proving that the initial measure was illegal rests with the defendant that is seeking to withdraw it. In *Lagardere and Canal*[55] the CFI found that a Commission decision in June 2000 declaring that a concentration was compatible with the common market gave the applicants subjective rights, more especially because the Commission approved certain ancillary restrictions notified to it as being necessary for the implementation of the concentration. The Commission then made a decision in July 2000 to the effect that the earlier decision was incorrect, and that the later decision was more consistent with the Commission's past decisions and case law on the meaning of ancillary restrictions. The CFI held that 'the institution responsible for the act has the burden of proving the illegality of the withdrawn act', and that it is 'for that institution to prove that the other conditions for retrospective withdrawal are fulfilled'.[56] The Commission had not shown that the earlier decision was illegal and it should not therefore have withdrawn it retrospectively.

[55] Case T-251/00, *Lagardère SCA and Canal+ SA*, *supra* n. 30.
[56] Ibid. at para. 141.

C. Retroactive Revocation: Balancing

The Community's case law on the revocability of illegal decisions developed early, and was derived from decisions concerning the functioning of the European Coal and Steel Community Treaty (ECSC).[57] In *Algera*[58] the ECJ, having considered German, French, and Italian law, concluded that an illegal administrative measure could be revoked retroactively, provided that this occurred within a reasonable period of time.

It was, however, the *SNUPAT* case[59] that developed this area of the law most fully. The scrap metal scheme in existence at that time imposed a levy on such metal, subject to an exception for scrap that resulted from a company's own production. A competitor of SNUPAT, Hoogovens, received scrap from a company in its business group and it was decided that this benefited from the exemption for scrap coming from one's own production. SNUPAT failed to receive a similar exemption for scrap coming from its business group, and therefore asked the administration to revoke retroactively the exemption granted to Hoogovens. This did not happen and therefore SNUPAT sought judicial review. The ECJ decided that the exemption granted to Hoogovens was unlawful and then considered whether it should be retroactively revoked. The Court stated that neither the principle of legal certainty, nor that of legality could be applied in an absolute manner. Consideration should be given to both principles. Which of the principles prevailed in a particular case would depend on 'a comparison of the public interest with the private interests in question'.[60] In the instant case the relevant interests were:[61]

> On the one hand, the interest of the beneficiaries and especially the fact that they might assume in good faith that they did not have to pay contributions on the ferrous scrap in question, and might arrange their affairs in reliance on the continuance of this position.
>
> On the other hand, the interest of the Community in ensuring the proper working of the equalization scheme, which depends on the joint liability of all undertakings consuming ferrous scrap; this interest makes it necessary to ensure that other contributors do not permanently suffer the financial consequences of an exemption illegally granted to their competitors.

The ECJ referred the decision on this balance of interests back to the High Authority, although its decision in this respect would itself be subject to judicial review. It is, however, clear from later cases that the Community courts are willing to undertake this balancing themselves. They will take into

[57] Schwarze, *supra* n. 1, at 991–1025.

[58] Cases 7/56 and 3–7/57, *Algera, supra* n. 26, at 55.

[59] Cases 42 and 49/59, *SNUPAT, supra* n. 27.

[60] Ibid. at 87.

[61] Ibid. at 87. See also, Case 14/61, *Hoogovens v High Authority* [1962] ECR 253.

account the nature of the illegality, whether the illegal decision gave rise to any legitimate expectations for the person concerned, the impact that retroactive withdrawal of the decision would have on the individual, the effect on third parties, and the time that has elapsed between the initial decision and the attempt to revoke it. It is not easy for the individual to succeed in this balancing exercise, but there are instances where this has occurred.

In *Consorzio Cooperative d'Abruzzo*[62] the applicant sought the annulment of a Commission decision that reduced by approximately one billion lire the amount of assistance granted from the European Agricultural Guarantee and Guidance Fund (EAGGF). The decision reducing the amount of assistance occurred two years after the earlier decision granting the applicant the higher amount. The Commission argued that retroactive revocation was justified because the earlier decision had been legally erroneous. The ECJ disagreed. It held that withdrawal of an unlawful measure was only permissible provided that the withdrawal occurred within a reasonable time and provided that the Commission gave sufficient regard to how far the applicant might have been led to rely on the lawfulness of the measure.[63] Retroactive revocation failed on both counts in this case. Two years had elapsed between the initial decision and the later decision reducing the aid. This was not a reasonable period of time, since the Commission could have discovered and corrected its error far sooner. Moreover, the applicant was justified in relying on the legality of the initial decision, since the irregularities that were said to beset it were not discernible.

The ECJ also found that the balancing favoured the applicant in *de Compte*.[64] The facts of the case have been set out above. It will be recalled that the defendant in the action sought to justify the retroactive withdrawal of an earlier decision on the ground that it was illegal, being based on an erroneous interpretation of occupational injury. The ECJ rejected the defence. It held that an illegal measure could be retroactively withdrawn within a reasonable period of time, but that the right to withdraw was restricted by the need to respect the legitimate expectations of the beneficiary of the measure who had been led to rely on its lawfulness. In this instance the applicant was entitled to have confidence in the apparent legality of the measure that the defendant now sought to revoke. There was nothing to suggest that the applicant had 'provoked' the earlier decision through false or incomplete information. Nor was there any public-policy interest in overriding the beneficiary's justifiable belief in the maintenance of a situation that he was entitled to regard as stable.

Confidence in the apparent legality of the measure was an important factor

[62] Case 15/85, *Consorzio Cooperative d'Abruzzo v Commission* [1987] ECR 1005.

[63] Ibid. at para. 12.

[64] Case C-90/95 P, *Henri de Compte, supra* n. 32.

in the more recent case of *Lagardère and Canal*.[65] The CFI held, as we have seen above, that the initial decision was not in fact unlawful and could not therefore be withdrawn retrospectively. It held moreover that even if the original decision had been tainted with illegality concerning the meaning of ancillary restriction, this would still not have justified retroactive withdrawal. Any inconsistency in the meaning of ancillary restrictions was not so manifest as to raise doubts for the applicants when they received the original decision, which seemed untainted by any error. There was nothing to give rise to doubts as to its legality in the minds of the applicants as careful business undertakings. Retroactive withdrawal would therefore be contrary to the applicant's legitimate expectations.[66]

By way of contrast, an applicant will fail in the balancing test where it is unable to demonstrate any legitimate expectation flowing from the original measure. It is clear that an applicant will be unable to demonstrate a legitimate expectation to trigger the balancing test where it is has been guilty of illegality, as in *Conserve Italia*.[67] The applicant had been granted assistance from the EAGGF. It was discovered that the applicant had broken the rules by, *inter alia*, purchasing equipment prior to the approval of the aid. The Commission cancelled the assistance and this was held to be within its powers under the relevant Structural Fund regulations. The ECJ firmly rejected the applicant's argument concerning legitimate expectations. It reiterated the principle that an illegal act advantageous to an individual could be withdrawn retroactively, provided that it did not infringe legal certainty or legitimate expectations. The ECJ then noted that given that this was possible where the beneficiary of the aid did not contribute to its illegality, the possibility of retroactive withdrawal applied *a fortiori* where the illegality was attributable to the applicant.[68]

An applicant will also find it difficult to succeed where, for example, the illegality that besets the measure is obvious, thereby undermining any legitimate expectation in its continuance. Thus in *Cargill*[69] the ECJ reiterated the principle that the right to withdraw an illegal measure retroactively was qualified by the need to fulfil the legitimate expectations of the beneficiary of the measure who had been led to rely on its lawfulness. It found, however, that the measure in question was revoked within three months of the defect becoming apparent. Moreover, the defect in the measure was so obvious that several traders had contacted the Commission when it was published in order to bring the error to its attention and ascertain the steps the Commission

[65] Case T-251/00, *Lagardère SCA and Canal + SA*, *supra* n. 30.

[66] Ibid. at paras. 146–150.

[67] Case C-500/99 P, *Conserve Italia Soc. Coop. arl v Commission* [2002] ECR I-867.

[68] Ibid. at para. 90.

[69] Case C-365/89, *Cargill BV v Produktschap voor Margarine, Vetten en Olien* [1991] ECR I-3045, at para. 18; Case C-248/89, *Cargill BV v Commission* [1991] ECR I-2987, at para. 20.

intended to take. The prudent trader could not therefore have been led to rely on the lawfulness of a measure containing such an error.

The applicant's chances of success will be further diminished where it is unable to show any reliance on the lawfulness of the measure later found to be illegal, more especially if it cannot show any adverse effect by the lapse of time between the original measure and its later rectification. *Alpha Steel*[70] exemplifies this point. The applicant company was granted a steel quota for a certain period, which it challenged as being unlawful. When these proceedings had begun the Commission replaced the contested decision with another decision, on the ground that the former had been made erroneously. The later decision nonetheless fixed the quota at a lower level than the earlier decision. The applicant argued that the Commission could not withdraw a decision that was the subject of a legal action and replace it with one that was even more detrimental to it. The ECJ disagreed. It applied the principle from *Algera*,[71] to the effect that withdrawal of an unlawful measure was permissible if it occurred in a reasonable time, and provided that regard was had as to how far the applicant might have been led to rely on the lawfulness of the measure. Applying that principle to the instant case, the ECJ found that the applicant had not relied on the lawfulness of the earlier decision. To the contrary, it had challenged its legality and was aware also of the Commission's misgivings about the original decision. Nor had the applicant shown that it was affected adversely by the time that had elapsed before the later decision, which had in any event been made reasonably promptly given that the Commission had to process data concerning a large number of undertakings.[72]

D. Prospective Revocation: Balancing?

The discussion thus far has been concerned with retroactive revocation of unlawful measures and the balancing test that the Community courts undertake. It is now necessary to consider the position with respect to prospective revocation of unlawful measures.

The positive law is not entirely clear. There are some judicial statements that indicate that prospective revocation is always possible, simply as a matter of principle.[73] There are other judgments that are more nuanced or ambiguous. Thus the formulation in *Herpels* was that while retroactive revocation of a wrongful or erroneous decision was subject to strict conditions, revocation of such a decision for the future was always possible.[74] This could mean that prospective revocation would always be possible, and that it would not be

[70] Case 14/81, *Alpha Steel, supra* n. 34.

[71] Cases 7/56 and 3–7/57, *Algera, supra* n. 26.

[72] Case 14/81, *Alpha Steel, supra* n. 34, at paras. 11–12.

[73] Case 15/60, *Simon v High Authority* [1961] ECR 115, 123.

[74] Case 54/77, *Herpels, supra* n. 43, at para. 38.

subject to conditions at all. It could alternatively mean that prospective revocation would always be possible, subject to less strict conditions than those applicable for retroactive revocation.

The latter interpretation is preferable in terms of principle. It is of course the case that prospective revocation will, other things being equal, be less dramatic for the applicant than retroactive revocation. It is, however, readily apparent that prospective revocation might cause considerable hardship to the individual. Take the *de Compte*[75] case by way of example. The applicant might well have changed his circumstance in reliance on the representation that he could receive benefits for occupational stress, such that it would no longer be possible for him to return to work in the EP or in any similar occupation. If this were so it would be little comfort for him to be told that while his benefits for occupational stress could not be revoked retroactively they could nonetheless be withdrawn prospectively. There may of course be cases where the facts are different and where the payment of a benefit that turns out to be unwarranted can be withdrawn prospectively without undue hardship for the recipient. A balancing test for cases of prospective revocation would, however, allow such matters to be determined in individual cases.

It should, moreover, be recognized that to allow prospective revocation without any consideration for the position of the applicant could undermine the rules about retroactive revocation considered above. Thus it would be scant comfort for the applicants in a case such as *Lagardère and Canal*[76] to be told that while the decision authorizing their concentration could not be withdrawn retroactively, it could be withdrawn prospectively.

There is therefore no reason why the same type of balancing exercise that applies to retroactive revocation should not be applicable here. This means that the courts should be equally willing to weigh the legality interest against the justice interest so far as it relates to the individual. They should take account of whether the original measure gave rise to legitimate expectations and whether the prospective revocation occurred within a reasonable time. The nature of the test should therefore be the same as that applicable to retroactive revocation. This would still leave it open to the courts to apply the test somewhat less strictly by reason of the fact that the case was concerned with prospective as opposed to retrospective revocation.

6. DEPARTURE FROM INDIVIDUAL REPRESENTATIONS

The discussion thus far has been concerned with revocation of formal decisions. We now turn to the type of case where an individual claims

[75] Case C-90/95 P, *Henri de Compte, supra* n. 32.

[76] Case T-251/00, *Lagardère SCA and Canal + SA, supra* n. 30.

a legitimate expectation flowing from a specific representation made to that person or group. It is clear from the jurisprudence that a number of conditions have to be satisfied before a claim of this kind can succeed.

A. The Nature of the Representation: Precise and Specific Assurance

The general principle is that protection of legitimate expectations extends to any individual who is in a situation from which it is clear that, in giving precise and specific assurances,[77] the Community institutions caused that person to entertain justified hopes.[78]

There are no strict rules as to the form of the representation.[79] It can arise from letters,[80] faxes,[81] reports,[82] communications,[83] administrative practice,[84] codes of conduct,[85] and the like.[86] A legitimate expectation cannot, however, arise from the unilateral action of the person seeking to plead the expectation.[87] The crucial issue from the perspective of the applicant is, however, to show that the representation, in whatever form it was issued, was sufficiently precise and specific to give rise to a legitimate expectation that it would be adhered to. It is this hurdle that applicants have found difficult to surmount, since the Community courts will not readily find that this criterion has been met.[88] This is apparent from consideration of cases arising in a variety of different areas.

In *Innova Privat-Akademie*[89] the applicant sought damages for loss caused

[77] Case T-72/99, *Meyer v Commission* [2000] ECR II-2521; Case T-290/97, *Mehibas Dordtselaan BV v Commission* [2000] ECR II-15.

[78] Case T-489/93, *Unifruit Hellas EPE v Commission* [1994] ECR II-1201; Case T-534/93, *Grynberg and Hall v Commission* [1994] ECR II-595; Case T-456/93, *Consorzio Gruppo di Azioni Locale Murgia Messapica v Commission* [1994] ECR II-361.

[79] Schonberg, *supra* n. 1, at 120–122.

[80] Case 144/82, *Detti v ECJ* [1983] ECR 2421.

[81] Cases T-46 and 151/98, *CEMR, supra* n. 46, at paras. 79–80.

[82] Case 265/85, *Van den Bergh en Jurgens and Van Dijk Food Products v Commission* [1987] ECR 1155.

[83] Case T-7/89, *Hercules v Commission* [1991] ECR II-1711, at paras. 53–55.

[84] Case T-310/00, *MCI, Inc v Commission,* judgment of 28 September 2004, not yet published, at para. 112, provided that the administrative practice is not contrary to legislation in force and does not involve the exercise of discretion.

[85] Case C-313/90, *CIRFS v Commission* [1993] ECR I-1125.

[86] Cases 424–425/85, *Frico v VIV* [1987] ECR 2755, at paras. 32–33.

[87] Case T-107/02, *GE Betz, Inc, formerly BetzDearborn Inc v OHIM* [2004] ECR II-1845, at para. 87.

[88] See, e.g., Case T-65/98, *Van den Bergh Foods Ltd v Commission* [2003] ECR II-4653, at para. 186; Case T-223/00, *Kyowa Hakko Kogyo Co Ltd and Kyowa Hakko Europe GmbH v Commission* [2003] ECR II-2553, at paras. 38–54; Case T-283/02, *EnBW Kernkraft GmbH v Commission,* judgment of 16 March 2005, not yet published.

[89] Case T-273/01, *Innova Privat-Akademie GmbH v Commission* [2003] ECR II-1093.

by the Commission's decision not to award a grant to finance a feasibility study for the setting up of a joint venture for professional training in India. Such grants could be given pursuant to a Community scheme designed to promote investment by Community operators in areas such as Asia and Latin America. The applicant claimed that the Commission's decision was unlawful because it violated legitimate expectations that the Commission would approve the grant, this expectation being said to flow from faxes sent by the Commission. The CFI reiterated the principle that the protection of legitimate expectations extended to any individual in a situation where the Community authorities had given precise and unconditional assurances that caused the applicant to entertain the legitimate expectation. It denied, however, that this test was met in the instant case. The relevant faxes did not, said the CFI, contain a precise assurance that the grant would be given. They merely indicated a provisional conclusion and contained an explicit statement that the formal decision would follow thereafter.

In *Alpharma*[90] the applicant challenged the withdrawal of authorization for certain additives in feeding stuffs and argued, *inter alia*, that the withdrawal was in breach of legitimate expectations. The applicant acknowledged that it could not have a legitimate expectation that the Community would never exercise their discretionary power to withdraw the authorization of this particular feeding stuff if it were in the interest of public health to do so. It claimed nonetheless that the fact that the relevant Directive established a surveillance programme to assess possible problems about resistance to antibiotics induced by additives in animal feed created a situation in which it could reasonably expect that no decision banning its additive would be taken before the results of the programme were known. The applicant argued that these expectations were encouraged by a Commission letter sent to it and by statements made by the Agriculture Commissioner. The CFI found to the contrary. It held that neither the Directive, nor the surveillance programme set up by the Commission, gave any indication that a decision to withdraw the authorization for additives would be conditional on completion of the research. The Court held that there was sufficient evidence for the Community institutions to conclude that the additive constituted a risk to health that warranted the taking of protective measures. This justified according priority to human health over the conclusion of research in progress, even though the research had been initiated by the Community and led to considerable expense for the industry.[91] The CFI also rejected the argument for legitimate expectations based on the Commission's letter and statements by the Commissioner for Agriculture

[90] Case T-70/99, *Alpharma Inc v Council* [2002] ECR II-3495.
[91] Ibid. at paras. 375–377.

on the ground that neither gave the precise and specific assurance claimed by the applicant.[92]

In *Martinez*[93] a number of MEPs formed a group called TDI, Technical Group of Independent Members. Its declared purpose was to ensure that all MEPs were able to exercise their parliamentary mandates in full, but the members of TDI retained their political independence from each other. The EP decided that TDI did not fulfil the requirements for a political grouping as laid down by the EP's rules of procedure, because the TDI's members did not share any political affiliation. In a subsequent legal challenge the members of TDI argued, *inter alia*, that other 'technical' groups had been established in the EP over the past 20 years and that therefore there was a legitimate expectation that TDI should be regarded as a political group within the EP. The CFI rejected the argument based on past practice, on the ground that the other groups that had been established differed from TDI, since they did not reject the notion of shared political affinity. This past practice could not therefore give rise to any specific assurance in the minds of the founders of TDI that it would be accepted as a group within the EP.

The great majority of claims for breach of legitimate expectation fail because the applicant, as in the preceding cases, cannot establish to the satisfaction of the Community courts the requisite precise and specific assurance. There are, however, instances where this aspect of the claim has been held to be met.

Thus in *Embassy Limousines*[94] it was held that there could be a breach of legitimate expectations where a company submitting a tender was encouraged to make irreversible investments in advance of the contract being awarded, and thereby to go beyond the risks inherent in making a bid. In *CEMR*[95] the CFI held that the Commission could not, without infringing the principle of legitimate expectations, reduce the budgetary allocation for a project financed from the Structural Funds where the relevant work had been included in the original budget that had been accepted by the Commission.

A legitimate expectation was also sustained in the *MCI* case, where the CFI held that parties to a merger had a legitimate expectation that a letter they had written indicating that they would not proceed with the merger in its current form would result in closure of the file, in accord with the Commission's prior administrative practice that had been made public and in the absence of indications to the contrary.[96] A further example is apparent from

[92] Ibid. at paras. 378–379.

[93] Cases T-222, 327, and 329/99, *Jean-Claude Martinez, Charles de Gaulle, Front National and Emma Bonino v EP* [2001] ECR II-2823.

[94] Case T-203/96, *Embassy Limousines & Services v European Parliament* [1998] ECR II-4239.

[95] Cases T-46 and 151/98, *CEMR, supra* n. 46.

[96] Case T-310/00, *MCI, supra* n. 84.

state aids. In *ARAP*[97] the ECJ held that when the Commission had before it a specific grant of aid alleged to have been made pursuant to a previously authorized scheme, it could not at the outset examine it directly in relation to the Treaty. It should rather examine whether the aid was covered by the general scheme. If it did not do so, the Commission could, whenever it examined an individual aid measure, go back on its decision approving the general aid scheme, which had already been examined in the light of the primary Treaty articles. This would jeopardize the principles of legitimate expectations and legal certainty. It is moreover clear that in exceptional circumstances delay by the Commission in seeking the recovery of aid that has been granted in breach of the Treaty provisions may give rise to a legitimate expectation in the recipient of the aid so as to prevent the Commission seeking to recover it.[98]

B. The Conduct of the Representee: The Prudent Trader

It is clear from the jurisprudence of the Community courts that an applicant's claim for breach of legitimate expectations will fail if the conduct complained of could have been foreseen by a prudent, discriminating, and well-informed trader. To put the same point in a different way, the representee will not be held to have an expectation that is legitimate insofar as the conduct complained of could have been foreseen by the prudent, etc. trader.

Thus in *Van den Bergh*[99] the applicants were producers of edible fats who claimed to have suffered loss as a result of the implementation of a Christmas butter scheme, which was designed to reduce excess stocks of butter in the Community by reducing prices. The applicants claimed, *inter alia*, that the introduction of this scheme was in breach of the principle of legitimate expectations. They argued that the Commission had stated publicly on a number of occasions that such schemes were not capable of attaining the desired aim of leading to a durable reduction in the stocks available, and therefore that they had no reason to expect, in the light of such statements, that the Commission would introduce such a scheme again. The ECJ found that the Commission had not given an undertaking that such schemes would never be used again, and had at the most indicated that they would be used in moderation. Christmas butter schemes had been used over a number of years and there had also been other measures to encourage disposal of butter at reduced prices. In such circumstances 'the possibility could not be excluded

[97] Case C-321/99 P, *Associacao dos Refinadores de Acucar Portugueses (ARAP) v Commission* [2002] ECR I-4287, at para. 83.

[98] Cases C-74 and 75/00 P, *Falck, supra* n. 3, at para. 140; Case C-298/00 P, *Italy v Commission* [2004] ECR I-4087, at para. 90.

[99] Case 265/85, *Van den Bergh en Jurgens, supra* n. 82.

that a further Christmas butter scheme would be operated and a prudent and discriminating trader ought to have taken that possibility into account'.[100] The plea of breach of legitimate expectations therefore failed.

The demands placed on the trader to be prudent, discriminating, and well-informed have led to the failure of many claims for legitimate expectations, more especially in the areas where common policies operate, such as agriculture, fisheries, and transport. The rules in these areas are frequently changed to cope with internal and external factors that affect the relevant markets. It is therefore especially difficult to sustain a claim for legitimate expectations, since the Community courts will expect the prudent trader to factor the possibility of such change into their own market calculations.[101]

It is clear, moreover, that the trader must be legally as well as factually well-informed, even though this can be very demanding. Thus in *Behn*[102] the applicant had imported paper from non-Member States and had paid customs duties of 3 per cent and 7.5 per cent in reliance on the rates for such duties laid down in the customs tariff manual published by the German Finance Ministry. The rates that should have been paid were however 3.2 per cent and 8 per cent, and the German customs office sought payment of the difference. The applicant resisted and argued that he could not reasonably have detected the error made in the German manual and therefore that he should not have to pay the extra amount. The relevant Community customs legislation provided a defence to claims for payment couched in these terms.[103] The referring court was clearly sympathetic to the applicant and questioned whether the vigilance demanded of the individual might be excessive, insofar as he would be expected to be better informed than the German Finance Ministry and Customs Office as to the applicable rates. The ECJ did not share this sympathy: the 'applicable Community tariff provisions constituted the sole relevant positive law as from the date of their publication in the Official Journal of the European Communities, and everyone was deemed to

[100] Ibid. at para. 45.

[101] Case 78/77, *Luhrs v Hauptzollamt Hamburg-Jonas* [1978] ECR 169; Case 127/78, *Spitta & Co v Hauptzollamt Frankfurt/Main-Ost* [1979] ECR 171; Case C-350/88, *Delacre v Commission* [1990] ECR I-395; Case T-489/93, *Unifruit Hellas EPE v Commission* [1994] ECR II-1201; Case T-336/94, *Efisol SA v Commission* [1996] ECR II-1343; Cases T-466, 469, 473, 474, and 477/93, *O'Dwyer v Council* [1996] ECR II-2071; Cases T-142 and 283/01, *Organización de Productores de Túnidos Congelados (OPTUC) v Commission* [2004] ECR II-329; Case C-342/03, *Spain v Council* [2005] ECR I-1975, at para. 48.

[102] Case C-80/89, *Behn Verpackungsbedarf GmbH v Hauptzollamt Itzehoe* [1990] ECR I-2659.

[103] Council Regulation 1697/79/EEC of 24 July 1979, On the Post-Clearance Recovery of Import Duties or Export Duties which have not been Required of the Person Liable for Payment of Goods Entered for a Customs Procedure Involving the Obligation to Pay such Duties, OJ 1979 L197/1, Art. 5(2).

know that law'.[104] It was therefore for the trader to read the Official Journal and acquaint himself with the relevant rules.

While the obligation for a trader to be prudent and well-informed will be of particular significance in cases concerned with common policies, it is clear that it can also be a difficult hurdle to overcome in other types of case. This is evident from *Alpharma*.[105] We have already seen that the applicant failed to convince the CFI that there had been any precise and specific undertaking. The CFI reinforced its rejection of the legitimate expectation claim by finding that Alpharma could have foreseen the possibility that the authorization of its product as an additive would be withdrawn. It held that Alpharma as a prudent and discriminating operator in the pharmaceutical sector knew or should have known that where authorization was granted under the relevant Directive it could be withdrawn where there was a risk to human health. This possibility was, said the CFI, made all the greater by reports from international, Community, and national bodies, and from scientific publications, all of which should have put the company on notice as to the possibility of Community action removing the authorization.

It is clear from the jurisprudence that the Community courts take a strict view of what traders and indeed Community employees[106] should foresee. Schonberg has rightly questioned the strictness of this approach.[107]

> While this view may be suitable for the largest and most well-informed economic operators, many smaller and less experienced operators are, as a result of increasing European integration, involved in cross-border trade. There is arguably room for a more flexible and liberal approach towards such operators and private individuals who rely upon statements from the Community administration.

C. The Conduct of the Representee: The Legitimacy of the Claim

The conduct of the applicant claiming that there is a legitimate expectation will also be relevant. There are three types of factor that should be distinguished in this respect.

Firstly, the Community courts will assess the legitimacy of the expectation against the general framework of the applicable Community rules in the relevant area. Thus it was held in *Regione Autonoma della Sardegna*[108] that

[104] Case C-80/89, *Behn, supra* n. 102, at para. 13.

[105] Case T-70/99, *Alpharma, supra* n. 90, at para. 380. See also in a different context, Cases C-13–16/92, *Driessen en Zonen v Minister van Verkeer en Waterstaat* [1993] ECR I-4751, at paras. 33–35.

[106] Case 3/83, *Abrias v Commission* [1985] ECR 1995, at paras. 23–27; Cases T-576–582, *Browet v Commission* [1994] ECR II-677, at para. 46.

[107] Schonberg, *supra* n. 1, at 128.

[108] Case T-171/02, *Regione Autonoma della Sardegna v Commission*, judgment of 15 June 2005, not yet published, at paras. 64–69.

since the impact of Article 88 EC was to suspend the grant of state aid pending a Community decision, an applicant could not legitimately expect that aid would be approved until a formal, positive decision had been made to this effect under the relevant Regulation. Similarly in *Daewoo Electronics*[109] the ECJ held that given the mandatory nature of the review of state aid under Article 88 EC, undertakings to which aid had been granted could not entertain a legitimate expectation that the aid was lawful unless it had been granted in accord with the procedure in that Article, and that a diligent businessman should normally be able to determine whether that procedure had been followed.

Secondly, it is clear that wrongdoing by the applicant will defeat the claim.[110] This includes the case where the alleged expectation is based on fraud or deception. Thus in *Kol*[111] the ECJ held that employment under a residence permit obtained by fraudulent conduct could not give rise to any legitimate expectation on the part of the person concerned. It is clear that wrongdoing can preclude the claim even where there is no fraud. In *Sideradria*[112] the ECJ tersely rejected the applicant's claim based on legitimate expectations on the ground that since the company had manifestly broken the rules on quotas for steel production it could not take advantage of this principle of Community law. Similarly in *Oliveira*[113] the CFI stated unequivocally that the grant of assistance from the European Social Fund (ESF) was conditional on compliance by the beneficiary with the conditions set out in the decision of approval. It was therefore not possible for the beneficiary to invoke the principle of legitimate expectations where the conditions attached to the award had been broken, since that principle could not be relied on by an undertaking that had committed a manifest infringement of the relevant rules.

Thirdly, the Community courts have also rejected claims even where there is no actual wrongdoing by the applicant, but where it is felt nonetheless that the expectation was not legitimate. This has been so where, for example, the challenged Community activity was designed to close a legal gap in order to prevent traders from making a speculative profit. Thus in

[109] Cases C-183 and 187/02 P, *Daewoo Electronics Manufacturing Espana SA (Demesa) and another v Commission* [2004] ECR I-10609, at paras. 44–48. See also, Case C-278/00, *Greece v Commission* [2004] ECR I-3997, at para. 104.

[110] Cases C-65 and 73/02 P, *ThyssenKrupp Stainless GmbH and another v Commission*, judgment of 14 July 2005, not yet published, at paras. 40–41.

[111] Case C-285/95, *Kol v Land Berlin* [1997] ECR I-3069, at para. 28.

[112] Case 67/84, *Sideradria SpA v Commission* [1985] ECR 3983, at para. 21.

[113] Case T-73/95, *Estabelecimentos Isidore M. Oliveira SA v Commission* [1997] ECR II-381; Case T-126/97, *Sonasa-Sociedade Nacional de Seguranca Ld v Commission* [1999] ECR II-2793; Case T-199/99, *Sgaravatti Mediterranea Srl v Commission* [2002] ECR II-3731; Case T-347/03, *Eugénio Branco Ld v Commission*, judgment of 30 June 2005, not yet published, at paras. 102–109.

Mackprang[114] the ECJ rejected a challenge to a Commission decision made under the Common Agricultural Policy (CAP). The decision was made to prevent traders making a speculative profit in a manner that undermined the overall purpose of the Community regime. The decision could not, therefore, be attacked for breach of legitimate expectations. The same principle is evident in *Weidacher*,[115] where the ECJ, in rejecting the claim based on legitimate expectations, stated that the Community institutions had not given any indication that they would not take measures to prevent the accumulation of speculative profits as a result of enlargement.

7. REPRESENTATIONS AND CHANGES IN POLICY

The discussion thus far has been concerned with representations of an individual nature. We should now turn to those situations where a general norm or policy choice, which an individual or group has relied on, is replaced by a different policy choice. This type of case is especially difficult because of the obvious need for government to alter policy.

A. The General Principle: Mutability and No Legitimate Expectation

It is clear that the mere fact that a trader is disadvantaged by a change in the law will not, in and of itself, give any cause for complaint based upon disappointment of legitimate expectations. A trader will not be held to have a legitimate expectation that an existing situation, which is capable of being altered by decisions taken by the institutions within the limits of their discretionary powers, will be maintained.[116] This is particularly so in the

[114] Case 2/75, *Einfuhr-und Vorratsstelle für Getreide und Futtermittel v Firma C. Mackprang* [1975] ECR 607.

[115] Case C-179/00, *Weidacher v Bundesminister für Land- und Forstwirtschaft* [2002] ECR I-501, at paras. 30–35.

[116] Case 52/81, *W. Faust v Commission* [1982] ECR 3745, 3762; Case 245/81, *Edeka v Federal Republic of Germany* [1982] ECR 2745, 2758; Case C-350/88, *Société Français des Biscuits Delacre v Commission* [1990] ECR I-395; Cases C-133, 300 and 362/93, *Crispoltoni v Fattoria Autonoma Tabachi and Donatab* [1994] ECR I-4863; Case C-63/93, *Duff v Minister for Agriculture and Food Ireland and the Attorney General* [1996] ECR I-569; Case C-22/94, *Irish Farmers Association v Minister for Agriculture, Food and Forestry (Ireland) and the Attorney General* [1997] ECR I-1809; Case C-372/96, *Pontillo v Donatab* [1998] ECR I-5091; Case C-104/97 P, *Atlanta AG v Commission and Council* [1999] ECR I-6983; Case C-402/98, *ATB v Ministero per le Politiche Agricole* [2000] ECR I-5501; Case C-110/97, *Netherlands v Council* [2001] ECR I-8763; Case T-18/99, *Cordis Obst und Gemüse GrossHandel GmbH v Commission* [2001] ECR II-913; Case T-52/99, *T. Port GmbH & Co KG v Commission* [2001] ECR II-981; Case T-43/98, *Emesa Sugar (Free Zone) NV v Council* [2001] ECR II-3519; Case T-196/99, *Area Cova SA v Council* [2001] ECR II-3597; Case C-340/98, *Italy v Council* [2002] ECR I-2663; Cases C-37 and 38/02, *Di Leonardo Adriano Srl and Dilexport Srl v*

context of the CAP, where constant adjustments to meet new market circumstances are required. It is also so in other areas, such as competition policy, where the Community courts have emphasized the Commission's discretion to alter the level of fines within the limits allowed by the relevant empowering Regulations.[117]

This point is exemplified by the *ATB* case.[118] The case was concerned with the common organization of the tobacco market. The primary Regulation dating from 1992 provided for a system whereby tobacco producers were paid premiums by processing undertakings when they delivered the tobacco. It was, however, made clear in this Regulation that this regime would be transitional and that subsequent measures would be taken to ensure that the quotas were allocated to producers directly. The processing quota system was duly replaced by a production quota system through a Regulation enacted in 1995. The applicants challenged the 1995 Regulation, and measures enacted pursuant thereto, on the ground that the new Regulation came into effect in early April 1995, by which time planting decisions for tobacco for that harvest year had already been taken. They argued that the 1995 Regulation should therefore be annulled on the ground that it infringed their legitimate expectations, since they had suffered losses amounting to the difference between the production quota and the processing quota. The ECJ dismissed the claim.[119]

> [W]hilst the protection of legitimate expectations is one of the fundamental principles of the Community, economic operators cannot have a legitimate expectation that an existing situation which is capable of being altered by the Community institutions in the exercise of their discretion will be maintained; this is particularly true in an area such as the common organisation of the markets, the object of which entails constant adjustments to meet changes in the economic situation. It follows that economic operators cannot claim a vested right to the maintenance of an advantage which they derive from the establishment of the common organisation of the markets and which they enjoyed at a given time.

The ECJ found that there was no infringement of legitimate expectations on the facts of the case, given that the 1992 Regulation provided that the production quota regime should be introduced by all Member States by 1995 at the latest. The producers had therefore known that the new system

Ministero del Commercio con l'Estero [2004] ECR I-6911; Cases T-64–65/01, *Afrikanische Frucht-Compagnie GmbH and another v Commission* [2004] ECR II-521, at paras. 83–84; Case C-17/03, *Vereniging voor Energie, Milieu en Water and others v Directeur van de Dienst uitvoering en toezicht energie* [2005] ECR I-4983, at paras. 73–87.

[117] Case T-31/99, *ABB Asea Brown Boveri Ltd v Commission* [2002] ECR II-1881; Case T-23/99, *LR AF 1998 A/S v Commission* [2002] ECR II-1705; Cases C-189, 202, 205, 208, and 213/02 P, *Dansk Rorindustri, supra* n. 11, at paras. 171–173.

[118] Case C-402/98, *ATB, supra* n. 116.

[119] Ibid. at para. 37.

would be introduced and the 1995 Regulation that was contested merely confirmed this.

It is clear that the principle contained in the preceding quotation will apply even if there is nothing in the earlier regulation indicating that it is transitional. It is the very nature of the constant adjustment to meet changes in economic situation that serves to preclude a legitimate expectations claim based on the earlier regulation.

Thus in *Cordis*[120] the applicant challenged the reference period by which licences for import of bananas was determined. The reference period in the earlier 1993 Regulation was changed by a Regulation enacted in 1998. The applicant argued that this change infringed its legitimate expectations. The CFI disagreed. It reiterated the principle that the Community institutions have a margin of discretion in the choice of means to achieve their policy, with the consequence that operators cannot claim a legitimate expectation that an existing situation that is capable of being altered by decisions taken within the limits of their discretionary power will be maintained. This was especially so in an area such as the common organization of markets, which involved constant adjustments to meet changes in the economic situation. The applicant could not, therefore, have a legitimate expectation that the relative timing of the reference period for the issuing of import licences as provided in the 1993 Regulation would be maintained.[121]

The same point is apparent in *Italy v Council.*[122] In rejecting a challenge to rules concerning the sugar market, the ECJ held that since the 1981 Regulation governing the issue required the Council and Commission each year to determine intervention prices, minimum prices, and increased prices afresh on the basis of the pattern of production and consumption, economic operators could not therefore have a legitimate expectation that the prices fixed for previous marketing years would be maintained.

B. The Exceptions: Bargain, Assurance, and Legitimate Expectation

It is clear, therefore, that it will be difficult for an applicant to show that there is a legitimate expectation where a general policy choice embodied in an earlier regulation or directive is replaced by a later regulation or directive that modifies the policy. There are, however, instances where the Community courts have been willing to find the existence of a legitimate expectation. The applicant must be able to point either to a bargain of some form between the individual and the authorities, or to a course of conduct or assurance on the part of the authorities which can be said to generate the legitimate expectation.

[120] Case T-18/99, *Cordis, supra* n. 116.

[121] Ibid. at paras. 74–76.

[122] Case C-340/98, *Italy v Council, supra* n. 116.

The *Mulder* case[123] illustrates the first of these situations. The Community had an excess of milk. In order to reduce this excess it passed a Regulation under which producers could cease milk production for a certain period in exchange for a premium for non-marketing of the milk. The applicant made such an arrangement in 1979 for five years. In 1984 he began to plan a resumption of production and applied to the relevant Dutch authorities for a reference quantity of milk which he would be allowed to produce without incurring the payment of any additional levy. He was refused on the ground that he could not prove milk production during the relevant reference year, which was 1983. This was of course impossible for Mulder since he did not produce at all during that period, because of the bargain struck in 1979. He challenged the 1984 Regulation, which was the basis of the Dutch authorities' denial of his quota, arguing, *inter alia*, that it infringed his legitimate expectations.

The ECJ found in his favour. It held that a producer who voluntarily ceased production for a certain period could not legitimately expect to be able to resume production under the same conditions as those which previously applied and not to be subject to any rules of market or structural policy adopted in the interim period. However where a producer was encouraged by a Community measure to suspend marketing for a limited period in the general interest and against payment of a premium he could legitimately expect not to be subject, upon the expiry of his undertaking, to restrictions which specifically affected him precisely because he availed himself of the possibilities offered by the Community provisions.[124] This was, said the ECJ, what had occurred here. The Regulations on the additional levy on milk gave rise to such restrictions for producers who, pursuant to the undertaking entered into under the 1977 Regulation, did not deliver milk during the reference year. Those producers could therefore be denied a reference quantity under the new system precisely because of that undertaking if they did not fulfil the specific conditions laid down in the 1984 Regulation or if the Member States had no reference quantity available. There was, said the ECJ, nothing in the provisions of the 1977 Regulation to show that the non-marketing undertaking entered into under that Regulation might, when it expired, entail a bar to resumption of the activity in question. Such an effect therefore frustrated those producers' legitimate expectations that the effect of the system to which they had rendered themselves would be limited.[125]

The following cases illustrate the second type of situation, where the legitimacy of the applicant's expectation is based upon some course of conduct

[123] Case 120/86, *Mulder v Minister van Landbouw en Visserij* [1988] ECR 2321.
[124] Ibid. at para. 24. [125] Ibid. at para. 26.

by the administration, or an assurance it has given. In *Sofrimport*[126] the applicant sought to import apples from Chile into the Community. A licence was required in accordance with the relevant Regulation. By a later Regulation the Commission took protective measures and suspended all such licences for Chilean apples. The parent Regulation, 2707/72,[127] which gave the Commission power to adopt protective measures, specifically stated in Article 3 that account should be taken of the special position of goods in transit, for the obvious reason that such measures could have a particularly harmful effect on traders. The applicant's goods were already in transit when the Regulation suspending licences for the import of Chilean apples was introduced, but they were refused entry to the Community. In an action for annulment the Court held that the failure of the Commission to make any special provision for goods in transit as required by the parent Regulation was an infringement of the applicant's legitimate expectations.[128] A similar theme is apparent in *CNTA*.[129] The case centred on monetary compensation amounts (MCAs), which were payments designed to compensate for fluctuations in exchange rates. The applicant was a firm which had made export contracts on the supposition that MCAs would be payable. After these contracts had been made, but before they were to be performed, the Commission passed a Regulation abolishing MCAs in that sector. The applicant suffered loss, since it had made the contracts on the assumption that the MCAs would be payable. The Court held that, while MCAs could not be said to insulate exporters from all fluctuations in exchange rates, they did have the effect of shielding them from such risks, with the consequence that even a prudent exporter might choose not to cover against it. The Court then stated:[130]

> In these circumstances, a trader might legitimately expect that for transactions irrevocably undertaken by him because he has obtained, subject to a deposit, export licences fixing the amount of the refund in advance, no unforeseeable alteration will occur which could have the effect of causing him inevitable loss, by re-exposing him to the exchange risk.

C. Overriding Public Interest: The Balancing Exercise

If a legitimate expectation has been found to exist then the Community courts will ensure that it is protected either through annulment of the offending provision or through the instrumentality of a damages action, provided of

[126] Case C-152/88, *Sofrimport Sàrl v Commission* [1990] ECR I-2477. Cf. Case T-336/94, *Efisol SA v Commission* [1997] ECR II-1343.

[127] Council Regulation 2707/72/EEC of 19 December 1972, Laying Down the Conditions for Applying Protective Measures for Fruit and Vegetables, OJ 1972 L291/3.

[128] Cf. Case C-110/97, *supra* n. 116.

[129] Case 74/74, *CNTA SA v Commission* [1975] ECR 533.

[130] Ibid. at para. 42.

course that the other requirements of damages liability are present. It is, however, clear that a *prima facie* legitimate expectation may be trumped by an overriding public interest. The Court has, therefore, sought to balance the need of the Community to alter its policy for the future, with the impact that such alteration might have on traders who based their commercial bargains on pre-existing norms.

Thus in the *CNTA* case the ECJ held that the Community would be liable in damages if, in the absence of an overriding public interest, the Commission abolished the MCAs without adopting transitional measures that would have enabled the traders either to have avoided the loss suffered in the performance of the export contracts or to be compensated for such loss.[131] Similarly in *Sofrimport*[132] the ECJ concluded that the adoption by the Commission, without any overriding public interest, of protective measures that affected traders importing fruit and vegetables from third countries without taking account of the interests of those who had goods in transit constituted a breach of their legitimate expectations such as to amount to a sufficiently serious breach for the purposes of damages liability.

The same approach is evident in the second *Mulder* case,[133] in which those who had been denied a milk quota sought damages for loss suffered. The ECJ found that a damages action could lie in relation to the Regulation that denied the farmers any quota at all. This Regulation constituted a breach of the farmers' legitimate expectations, and there was no countervailing, higher public interest justifying this action.[134] With reference to a later Regulation imposing a 60 per cent quota on those farmers that had made the bargain judged by the year before the bargain was entered into, the ECJ reached the opposite conclusion. The Court accepted that this, too, infringed the legitimate expectations of the applicants, but this illegality was not sufficiently serious. It was not sufficiently serious because there was a higher public interest at stake here. The 60 per cent quota was a choice of economic policy made by the Council, seeking to balance the need to avoid excess production in this area with the interest of the farmers who had entered the earlier scheme.

There may, however, be cases where there is an overriding public interest to protect consumers, which means that transitional measures should *not* be adopted. This is exemplified by *Dieckmann*.[135] The Commission made a Decision that fishery products coming from Kazakhstan should no longer be permitted into the EC. It made this Decision in the light of a report by

[131] Ibid. at para. 43. [132] Case C-152/88, *Sofrimport, supra* n. 126.

[133] Cases C-104/89 & 37/90, *Mulder and Heinemann v Council and Commission* [1992] ECR I-3061; Case C-189/89, *Spagl v Hauptzollamt Rosenheim* [1990] ECR I-4539.

[134] See also, Case C-152/88, *Sofrimport Sàrl v Commission* [1990] ECR I-2477.

[135] Case T-155/99, *Dieckmann & Hansen GmbH v Commission* [2001] ECR II-3143.

experts who had inspected operations within the country and concluded that there were systemic deficiencies with the general regime of health supervision. The experts did not report on difficulties with specific production sites. The applicant had concluded a contract to import caviar from a particular company in Kazakhstan. The ECJ held, however, that the absence of any transitional measures in the Decision to preclude import from that country did not violate the applicant's legitimate expectations, since there was an overriding public interest to protect the health of consumers in the EC. This was so even though the Commission had not undertaken inspections of particular facilities in the country producing caviar. The ECJ accepted that more detailed information of this nature would have enabled the Commission to assess the health risk from caviar more accurately. However, the ECJ concluded that the general deficiencies in the regime of health supervision were sufficient to justify the Decision that was taken.[136] The fact that health considerations can trump any possible legitimate expectations is also evident in *Affish*.[137] The Commission made a Decision prohibiting the import of fishery products from Japan following the finding by a group of experts that there were serious defects as regards hygiene with respect to production and storage. At the time when the contested Decision was adopted certain consignments of fish products had already been dispatched to the EC, and it was argued that provision should have been made for transitional measures in that Decision. The ECJ rejected the argument. It held that even if the Community had created a situation giving rise to a legitimate expectation, which was doubtful, there was an overriding public interest in terms of consumer health that overrode any such expectation.[138]

8. DEPARTURE FROM EXISTING POLICY/GUIDELINES

A. The General Principle: Guidelines Bind

It is axiomatic that a public body must follow formal legal rules that are applicable to the case. Problems of legitimate expectations can, however, arise where the public authority seeks to depart from an existing policy in relation to a particular person, where the policy is not enshrined in formal law. It is common in all legal systems for public authorities to develop guidelines, notices, communications, and the like. These norms are designed to imbue formal legal rules with greater specificity, and/or to

[136] Ibid. at paras. 80–81.

[137] Case C-183/95, *Affish BV v Rijksdienst voor de keuring van Vee en Vlees* [1997] ECR I-4315.

[138] Ibid. at para. 57.

structure the way in which discretionary power contained in formal law is to be exercised. They can also be used where there are no detailed formal rules yet existing on the particular topic.[139] The Community legal system is no different in this respect and increasing use has been made of such devices.[140]

An applicant may raise the issue of legitimate expectations where the public authority seeks not to apply the policy to that particular person, while not altering the policy itself. Such cases are somewhat less difficult than those considered above, where there is a general change of policy for the future. This is because it will normally be less drastic for a court to compel the administration to apply an existing policy to a particular applicant. It is also because considerations of equality as well as legitimate expectations will be relevant here. It can indeed be convincingly argued that even if the applicant is unable to prove a legitimate expectation, considerations of equality should, in and of themselves, suffice as the basis of the claim, unless the administration can show convincing reasons for departure from the policy in this instance. This has been the stance adopted by the Community courts from the early days of the Community's existence.

In *Louwage*[141] the applicant sought the annulment of a Commission Decision concerning entitlement to expenses in relation to moving, relying on an internal Commission directive dealing with the matter. The ECJ concluded that although an internal directive did not have the character of a rule of law that the administration was always bound to observe, it did nonetheless set out a rule of conduct indicating the practice to be followed. The administration could not depart from this without giving the reasons that led it to do so, 'since otherwise the principles of equality of treatment would be infringed'.[142]

Guidelines, notices, and the like are especially important in areas where the Commission is dealing with a large number of cases, such as in the context of state aids[143] and competition.[144] It has made extensive use of soft law devices in this area, and the Community courts have made it clear that the Commission cannot readily depart from such general statements in individual cases.

[139] Case C-58/94, *Netherlands v Council* [1996] ECR I-2169.

[140] L. Senden, *Soft Law in European Community Law* (Hart, 2004).

[141] Case 148/73, *Louwage v Commission* [1974] ECR 81.

[142] Ibid. at para. 12. See also, Case 282/81, *Ragusa v Commission* [1983] ECR 1245; Case T-33/91, *Williams v Court of Auditors* [1992] ECR II-2499. Compare, Case T-134/96, *Smets v Commission* [1997] ECR II-2333.

[143] della Cananea, 'Administration by Guidelines: The Policy Guidelines of the Commission in the Field of State Aids', in I. Harden (ed), *State Aid: Community Law and Policy* (Bundesanzeiger, 1993), at 68.

[144] Cases C-189, 202, 205, 208, and 213/02 P, *Dansk Rorindustri, supra* n. 11.

Thus in *CIRFS*[145] the ECJ annulled a Commission Decision approving state aid granted by France. The approval was contrary to a detailed Commission communication known as the discipline, which sought to curtail aid to the synthetic fibre industry because there was over-capacity. The communication embodying the 'discipline' did not have a formal basis in the Treaty, but the ECJ held nonetheless that it was a measure of general application that could not be impliedly amended by an individual decision.[146]

In *Vlaamse Gewest*[147] the CFI held that it was for the Commission to select the criteria that would be used to determine whether aid was compatible with the common market, provided that they were relevant having regard to the Treaty articles. It was open to the Commission to set out such criteria in guidelines, the adoption of which should be seen as a way in which the Commission chose to exercise its discretion. The guidelines should, however, be applied in accord with the principle of equal treatment, with the implication that like cases, as defined in the guidelines, had to be treated alike.[148]

The paradigm case of departure from an existing policy is where, as in the preceding cases, the policy is embodied in a guideline, code, notice, or some equivalent document. It is, however, possible, albeit more difficult, to sustain such a claim where there is departure from policy established through practice, even where it is not formalized through inclusion in a guideline or similar document. In *Ferriere San Carlo*[149] the applicant sought the annulment of a fine imposed for exceeding its production quota for steel. It argued that the sale was carried out in accordance with the general practice adopted by the Commission, which allowed the disposal of certain stocks in addition to the delivery quota. The ECJ found that there had been no decision terminating the previous practice, nor was the applicant firm individually warned that the practice had been terminated. The applicant was therefore entitled to assume that the practice had not been discontinued and it was incumbent on the Commission, before imposing the fine, to verify that the excess complained of could not be attributed to that practice. The Commission had, however, refused to carry out that check and the imposition of the fine in those circumstances was in breach of the applicant's legitimate expectations.

The ECJ in *Dansk Rorindustri* has, however, more recently refused to apply

[145] Case C-313/90, *CIRFS, supra* n. 85, at paras. 34–36. See also, Cases T-369/94 & 84/95, *DIR International Film Srl v Commission* [1998] ECR II-357, at para. 82.

[146] Ibid. at para. 44.

[147] Case T-214/95, *Vlaamse Gewest v Commission* [1998] ECR II-717; Case C-311/94, *Ijssel-Vliet Combinatie BV v Minister van Economische Zaken* [1996] ECR I-5023.

[148] Cases C-189, 202, 205, 208, and 213/02 P, *Dansk Rorindustri, supra* n. 11, at paras. 211–213.

[149] Case 344/85, *SpA Ferriere San Carlo v Commission* [1987] ECR 4435.

the reasoning in *Ferriere San Carlo* in the context of competition law. It held that alleged past practice in relation to the setting of the level of fines did not create any legitimate expectation that the level of fine would not be altered without warning, more especially because a change of the kind that occurred was felt to be foreseeable.[150]

B. Application of the General Principle: Judicial Construction of Guidelines

A corollary of the principle that guidelines are binding and generate a legitimate expectation that they will not be departed from in a particular case is that the Community courts will construe them to ensure that they are properly applied to the instant case. This can be seen in the case law on guidelines in the context of state aid.

The *Pollmeier Malchow* case[151] was concerned with the interpretation of the guidelines relating to small and medium-sized enterprises (SMEs) for the purposes of state aid. Germany had granted aid for the construction of a sawmill to the applicant, and the aid amounted to 48.18 per cent of the costs involved. The rules on state aid, however, only allowed aid up to 50 per cent for SMEs, the ceiling for other enterprises being 35 per cent. The Commission declared the aid above 35 per cent to be illegal on the ground that the applicant did not come within the definition of a SME as laid down in Commission guidelines. It found that the applicant, immediately prior to receipt of aid from the German government, had holdings in a number of other companies that constituted an economic unit, and that the applicant had only altered the pattern of ownership in order to come within the definition of a SME. The rules and guidelines on state aid stipulated that a company could only acquire the status of a SME if it met the relevant thresholds for two consecutive years. The Commission said that this criterion was not met here since the applicant was above the threshold prior to the change of the pattern of ownership. The applicant argued that the Commission had erred in its application of the criteria as to the meaning of SME.

The CFI disagreed. It acknowledged that the Commission was bound by the guidelines and notices that it issued in this area where they did not depart from the rules in the Treaty and were accepted by the Member States.[152] The guidelines set out three criteria for an enterprise to qualify as a SME: the number of persons employed, a financial test, and an independence test.

[150] Cases C-189, 202, 205, 208, and 213/02 P, *Dansk Rorindustri, supra* n. 11, at paras. 174–175, 196, 227–231.

[151] Case T-137/02, *Pollmeier Malchow & Co KG v Commission*, judgment of 14 October 2004, not yet published.

[152] Ibid. at para. 54.

The applicant argued that the Commission had misconstrued the independence test and that it had used a test that differed from that laid down in the guidelines and an accompanying recommendation. The independence test provided that an independent enterprise was one in relation to which no other enterprise falling outside the definition of SME had more than 25 per cent holding, the obvious rationale being to prevent large enterprises taking advantage of the rules on SMEs by taking stakes in smaller companies. The CFI held that the 25 per cent rule should be interpreted in the light of this rationale. It was therefore open to the Commission to find that there was an economic unit that exceeded the thresholds for a SME, even where an enterprise was owned as to less than 25 per cent by another enterprise belonging to the same economic unit.[153]

The decision in *Spain v Commission*[154] provides a further example of judicial construction of the guidelines, and in this instance the ECJ found for the applicant. Spain initiated an aid plan, the purpose being to facilitate the replacement of commercial vehicles. The Commission decided that certain aspects of this scheme violated Community principles on state aid and that they could not benefit from the *de minimis* rule that exempted small amounts of aid from the reach of the Treaty. This was because the *de minimis* rule did not apply to the transport sector and the Commission construed this to include transport undertaken by non-transport companies on their own account, the rationale being that this transport was interchangeable with that provided by specialist companies.

The ECJ found for the Spanish government and against the Commission. It held that the Commission was wrong to treat professional transport companies and companies that carried out transport only to meet their own needs in the same way. It followed that it was wrong for the Commission not to consider the possible application of the *de minimis* notice to companies falling within the latter category. The notice was binding on the principle that such guidelines and notices bound the Commission provided that they did not depart from the Treaty and were accepted by the Member States. The Commission could not therefore refuse to apply the *de minimis* notice to aid granted in sectors which the applicable provisions of the notice, properly construed, did not exclude from its application.[155]

The ECJ also held that the Commission's Decision was tainted with error in relation to professional transport companies, because of its incompatibility with the guidelines on environmental aid. The Spanish government argued that the entire aid package could be regarded as legitimate on environmental grounds, and was in line with the Commission's environmental guidelines,

[153] Ibid. at paras. 56–65. See also, Case C-91/01, *Italy v Commission* [2004] ECR I-4355.
[154] Case C-351/98, *Spain v Commission* [2002] ECR I-8031.
[155] Ibid. at paras. 48–53.

on the ground that new vehicles would be cleaner than those replaced. The environmental guidelines drew a sharp distinction between investment and operating aid, the former being far more likely to be approved than the latter. The ECJ found that it was not clear from the Commission's Decision whether it considered the aid to be for investment or operating aid, notwithstanding the centrality of this distinction. Because of the uncertainty in this respect, the Spanish government was not in a position to defend itself and the challenged Decision was therefore set aside for this reason.[156]

The *Ferriere Nord* case[157] provides a useful third example of the judicial role in this area, more especially because it shows the interrelationship between procedural and substantive legitimate expectations. Ferriere Nord was granted aid by an Italian region towards the cost of a new steel plant. The aid was ostensibly granted for environmental reasons, but the Commission declared the aid to be incompatible with the common market because its primary purpose was economic, the replacement of old plant and improvement of competitiveness, rather than environmental protection, and because even assuming that the environmental purpose was predominant it was not possible to distinguish within the total cost of the investment the part relating to environmental protection, as required by the guidelines.

The applicant argued, *inter alia*, that its procedural legitimate expectations had been violated because the Commission had not asked the Italian government for documentation relating to the environmental purpose of the investment. The CFI accepted that the Commission should take account of the legitimate expectation which a party might entertain as a result of what was said in the Decision opening the procedure in a case of state aids. It found, however, that there was no breach of this principle on the facts of the case, since the Commission had from the very inception of the procedure stated its doubts about the environmental credentials of the contested aid. The Italian government was therefore fully apprised of the need to proffer all relevant evidence showing that the investment did have an environmental objective.[158]

The applicant argued further that the aid granted to it did pursue an environmental objective within the meaning of the environmental guidelines. The CFI reiterated orthodoxy, that the Commission is bound by the guidelines and notices in the area of state aids where they do not depart from the Treaty and are accepted by the Member States. The consequence was that the parties concerned are 'entitled to rely on those guidelines

[156] Ibid. at paras. 74–84. See also, Case C-409/00, *Spain v Commission* [2003] ECR I-1487.

[157] Case T-176/01, *Ferriere Nord SpA v Commission*, judgment of 18 November 2004, not yet published.

[158] Ibid. at paras. 86–91.

and the Court will ascertain whether the Commission complied with the rules it has itself laid down when it adopted the contested decision'.[159] It held, however, that the Commission had not departed from or misconstrued the environmental guidelines. The guidelines were clear that only investment aid linked to environmental protection was eligible for aid; it was only investment, the very object of which was to improve environmental performance, that qualified for aid. The Commission was perfectly entitled to find that this criterion was not met. The fact that the applicant maintained that the investment brought some advantages in terms of environmental protection was not therefore determinative, since it had not shown that the investment was undertaken in order to bring about such improvements.[160]

C. Qualification to the General Principle: The Scope of the Guidelines

The assumption in the case law considered above was that the guideline or notice generated an expectation, such that the applicant could argue that departure from its terms constituted a breach of legitimate expectations. Whether the guideline or notice does generate any expectation will, however, depend on its wording and place within the overall scheme of policy in that area. It may be concluded that there is in fact no tension between the guidelines and the individual case alleged to be a departure from them because they are dealing with different situations.

This is exemplified by the *British Steel* case.[161] British Steel sought the annulment of aid approved by the Commission that had been given to certain steel producers in Spain and Italy. Article 4(c) ECSC prohibited state aid in the steel sector as being incompatible with the ECSC Treaty. Article 95(1) ECSC provided that where a decision or recommendation was necessary to attain one of the objectives set out in Articles 2, 3, and 4 of the Treaty, the decision could be taken or the recommendation could be made with the unanimous assent of the Council after the Consultative Committee had been consulted. The Commission relied on Article 95 for a Community scheme whereby aid could be authorized in limited circumstances. These schemes took the form of aid codes, which were amended over time. The fifth steel aid code provided that aid could be compatible with the ECSC where it was for research and development, where it was designed to enhance environmental protection, where it facilitated closures, and in the context of certain regional aid schemes. The contested Decision authorizing aid for restructuring of steel plants in Spain and Italy was, however, taken outside the confines of the aid code, albeit pursuant to Article 95 ECSC. British Steel argued that it was not

[159] Ibid. at para. 134. [160] Ibid. at paras. 146–156.
[161] Case C-1/98 P, *British Steel plc v Commission* [2000] ECR I-10349.

competent for the Commission to adopt such a Decision and moreover that it breached its legitimate expectation.

The ECJ disagreed. The code established certain categories of aid that could be regarded as compatible with the Treaty, and it would not generally be open to the Commission to authorize aid through an individual decision that conflicted with the rules laid down in the code. The steel aid code was, however, only binding for matters that fell within its remit. It followed that aid that did not fall within the provisions of the code could be authorized through an individual decision, provided of course that such aid was necessary to attain one of the Treaty objectives. The applicant could not claim that its legitimate expectations had been violated, since adjustment to changes in the economic situation meant that undertakings could not claim any vested right to the maintenance of a legal situation existing at a given time: the code could not therefore give rise to any legitimate expectation that there would not be derogation from it in exceptional cases through individual decision.

D. Qualification to the General Principle: Discretion Inherent In or Left By the Guidelines

A claim based on legitimate expectations for unwarranted departure from guidelines may also fail where the particular guideline is relatively open-textured, thereby giving the Commission discretion as to its meaning and application.

This can be seen in the case law on guidelines for fines in competition law, as exemplified by *JFE Engineering*.[162] The case was concerned with a complex cartel in the market for seamless steel tubes and pipes. The applicants contested, *inter alia*, the level of fines imposed. The CFI reiterated the principle derived from earlier case law, to the effect that the Commission could not depart from rules that it had set for itself, and that it must therefore take account of the guidelines when determining fines, in particular the elements that are mandatory under the guidelines.[163] The CFI held, however, that the wording of particular provisions in the guidelines left discretion to the Commission to take account of the size of the undertaking as a factor in determining the level of fine.[164]

Similarly in *Kyowa Hakko*[165] the CFI held in the context of a challenge to the fines in relation to a lysine cartel that while the guidelines did not provide that fines were to be calculated in relation to total turnover or turnover in the

[162] Cases T-67, 68, 71, and 78/00, *JFE Engineering Corp v Commission* [2004] ECR II-2501. See also, Cases T-191, 212–214/98, *Atlantic Container Line AB v Commission* [2003] ECR II-3275.

[163] Ibid. at para. 537. [164] Ibid. at para. 553.

[165] Case T-223/00, *Kyowa Hakko Kogyo, supra* n. 88, at para. 67.

relevant market, they did not preclude the Commission taking these criteria into account when determining the amount of the fine.

9. REPRESENTATIONS, THE BALANCING EXERCISE, AND THE LEGAL TEST

The preceding discussion has considered the jurisprudence of the Community courts in relation to individual representations, changes of policy, and departure from existing policy. It is readily apparent that even if the applicant is able to prove a *prima facie* legitimate expectation this may be defeated if there is an overriding public interest that trumps the expectation. We have touched on case law dealing with this aspect of the problem in the context of changes of policy.[166] We should, however, consider this important issue in more detail, since the nature of the legal test applied by the courts is not entirely clear, nor is its application to the different types of case in which legitimate expectations can arise. These issues will be considered in turn.

A. The Nature of the Legal Test

Let us begin with the nature of the legal test. It is clear from the case law on changes of policy that if there is a *prima facie* legitimate expectation it is for the defendant Community institution to show some overriding public interest if it is to avoid legal censure for not respecting the expectation.[167] This does not, however, tell us the standard of review that the Community courts will apply when judging whether there was an overriding public interest sufficient to defeat the expectation. To put the same point in another way, the defendant Community institution may plead that there was an overriding public interest that justified, for example, the absence of transitional measures when a policy was altered, but this still leaves open the extent to which the Community court will inquire whether the interest was overriding and it also leaves open whether they will balance the public interest against that of the individual claiming the legitimate expectation.

It is clear that the Community courts will inquire whether the public interest was overriding. The *Spagl* case[168] provides a good example. The case arose from the milk levy saga. We have seen that the ECJ in *Mulder*[169] had declared a Regulation invalid on the ground that it infringed the legitimate expectations of those who had made agreements pursuant to a Community scheme not to produce milk for a particular period and were then unable because of new provisions in force to secure a milk reference quantity when

[166] See above, at 639–641.
[167] See above, at 639–640.
[168] Case C-189/89, *Spagl, supra* n. 133.
[169] Case 120/86, *Mulder, supra* n. 123.

they sought to return to the market. In *Spagl* the applicant challenged the amended Regulation put in place to comply with the earlier judgment. His challenge was based, *inter alia*, on the ground that the amended scheme only gave those who returned to the market a reference quantity for milk equivalent to 60 per cent of the amount produced in the year before the non-marketing undertaking.

The ECJ accepted that some reduction in the reference quantity would be acceptable, since other milk suppliers who had not ceased trading also had their quantities reduced, this being part of the overall rationale of the scheme. It held, however, that the principle of legitimate expectations precluded a rate of reduction for those who had taken the non-marketing undertaking being fixed at such a high level that it penalized such producers by reason of their taking such undertakings. The ECJ requested from the Commission the comparable figures for producers who had continued trading, and it became clear that their reference quantities were only being reduced by approximately 17.5 per cent. The Commission and Council sought to defend this differential reduction of 40 per cent and 17.5 per cent respectively on the ground that it was not possible to give a reference quantity of more than 60 per cent to those who had taken the non-marketing undertakings without undermining the objective of the whole scheme, which was to reduce the milk surplus. The ECJ rejected this argument, stating that even if the objective of the scheme demanded limits on the additional quantity of milk placed on the market 'it would have been sufficient to reduce the reference quantities of the other producers proportionally by a corresponding amount, so as to be able to allocate larger reference quantities to the producers who gave an undertaking'[170] under the earlier Regulation. The 60 per cent rule was therefore declared void for breach of legitimate expectations.

The fact that the Community courts will inquire into the public interest defence advanced by the defendant does not, however, tell us precisely what legal test is being used. The ECJ and CFI have been rather reluctant to assign a discrete legal label to this exercise. It has therefore been left to commentators to divine the legal test from the courts' reasoning. Schonberg has argued that the test that emerges is one of significant imbalance. On this view the Community courts 'will restrict the application of a policy change if there is a *significant imbalance* between the interests of those affected and the policy considerations in favour of the change'.[171] There is force in this view. It coheres with the reasoning used in a case such as *Spagl*,[172] and with the judicial approach in other cases where the Community courts have considered a defence couched in terms of the overriding public

[170] Case C-189/89, *Spagl, supra* n. 133, at para. 28.
[171] Schonberg, *supra* n. 1, at 150. Italics in the original.
[172] Case C-189/89, *Spagl, supra* n. 133.

interest, including cases such as *Dieckmann*[173] and *Affish*[174] in which the applicant lost.

This view does, however, leave open the question of the precise difference between a test of significant imbalance and a test of proportionality. The latter is of course a general head of review in Community law. It is not clear why it should not be used here. It is true that proportionality involves the classic three-stage inquiry, and it might be felt that this is somewhat cumbersome in this context. However, the test framed in terms of significant imbalance entails consideration of similar issues, notwithstanding the fact that they are not separated as discretely as within a proportionality test. This is readily apparent from *Spagl*.[175] The essence of the ECJ's reasoning was in many ways classic proportionality. It found a *prima facie* legitimate expectation; it found that the modified Regulation imposed a significant burden on the applicant; it examined the public interest justification for the differential reduction in the reference quantities for milk; and it decided that this differential impact was not necessary to achieve the overall purposes of the scheme. If the ECJ had formally concluded its judgment by stating that the purported overriding public interest justification for the amended Regulation imposed a disproportionate burden on the applicant and was hence invalid, this would have been accepted by the legal community with equanimity.

A test framed in terms of proportionality would also cohere with principle. It is a general test for review of the legality of Community action. It is used in cases where rights are infringed, to contest the size of penalties, and to determine the legality of other forms of discretionary action. The situation being addressed here also entails consideration of the legality of the Community action, viz, whether there is an overriding public interest that justifies the trumping of the expectation. Given that proportionality will readily be used to test whether the infringement of a right can be justified, it is not clear why it should not also be used to determine whether the trumping of an expectation is warranted. This is especially so given that the three-part proportionality test provides a structured analysis which facilitates review and forces the defendant to give a reasoned justification for its course of action.[176]

B. The Application of the Test

Irrespective of whether the test is cast in terms of significant imbalance or proportionality, the application of the test is likely to depend on the nature of the case. This variability can, however, be accommodated within either test.

[173] Case T-155/99, *Dieckmann, supra* n. 135.

[174] Case C-183/95, *Affish, supra* n. 137.

[175] Case C-189/89, *Spagl, supra* n. 133.

[176] The UK courts have recently developed a test for review when the public body seeks to resile from a legitimate expectation that is framed in terms of proportionality, *Nadarajah v Secretary of State for the Home Department* [2005] EWCA Civ 1363, at para. 68.

The courts will be more reluctant to interfere with general changes of policy embodied in the shift from one regulatory scheme to another, than with cases where a specific representation is made to a discrete group.

The courts should, however, be very reluctant to admit that departure from an existing policy in relation to a particular individual was warranted by some overriding public interest. This is so irrespective of whether there has been any detrimental reliance leading to cognizable loss, since the very departure will offend the principle of equality that like cases should be treated alike. If the alleged public interest justifying departure from an existing policy is ephemeral then it weakens the argument that it should be regarded as overriding. If, by way of contrast, the alleged public interest is not ephemeral then the appropriate response should be to alter the policy, rather than to depart from it in relation to a particular individual.

10. UNLAWFUL REPRESENTATIONS

A. Positive Law

The discussion thus far has been conducted on the assumption that the representation was lawful. The preceding analysis concerning revocation of unlawful decisions revealed that the Community courts have adopted a balancing approach, such that the illegality of the initial decision will not always justify its retroactive revocation.[177] The situation with respect to unlawful representations seems to be more draconian: such representations are said not to give rise to any legitimate expectation.

In the *CIRFS* case,[178] considered above,[179] the ECJ held that a policy document known as the discipline, which was concerned with limiting aid to certain types of industry, was binding. The Commission argued, *inter alia*, that the discipline had been amended by a decision that it had made that served to sharpen its scope. The ECJ rejected the argument stating that a measure of general application could not be impliedly amended by an individual decision. It then went on to say that the principle of legitimate expectations could not be 'relied on in order to justify repetition of an incorrect interpretation of a measure'.[180] The same reasoning was applied in *Air France*,[181] where the CFI held that a Community institution could not be forced by virtue of the principle of legitimate expectations to apply Community rules *contra legem*.

[177] See above, at 621–626.
[178] Case C-313/90, *CIRFS, supra* n. 85.
[179] See above, at 643.
[180] Case C-313/90, *CIRFS, supra* n. 85, at para. 45.
[181] Case T-2/93, *Air France v Commission* [1994] ECR II-323, at paras. 101–102.

Analogous reasoning is to be found in *Thyssen*,[182] where the applicant was fined for exceeding its steel quota. It argued, *inter alia*, that the fine should be annulled because of a promise that had been made by Commission officials that it would not be fined if it exceeded its quota solely with a view to supplying a specific undertaking. The ECJ rejected the argument, stating that no official could give a valid undertaking not to apply Community law, and therefore no legitimate expectation could be aroused by such a promise, assuming that one had been made.[183]

The Community courts have not surprisingly applied the same reasoning where the conduct of a Member State has been in issue, as is apparent from *Lageder*.[184] The applicants exported wine in 1973, and were told by an Italian public authority that they did not have to pay monetary compensation amounts on the exports because the wine was quality wine and hence exempt from payment under the relevant Community Regulation. In 1977 a different Italian public body found that the wines could not be designated as quality wines for the purpose of the Community Regulation and therefore demanded post-clearance payment of the monetary compensation amounts. The applicants resisted the demand, arguing that it infringed legitimate expectations, more especially given the effluxion of time. The ECJ accepted that the Italian authorities were bound by the principle of legitimate expectations when acting within the sphere of Community law.[185] The practice of a Member State that did not conform to Community law could, however, never give rise to a legitimate expectation on the part of the trader who had benefited from the situation thus created.[186]

> It follows that the principle of the protection of legitimate expectations cannot be relied upon against an unambiguous provision of Community law; nor can the conduct of a national authority responsible for applying Community law, which acts in breach of that law, give rise to a legitimate expectation on the part of the trader of beneficial treatment contrary to Community law.

B. Normative Considerations

The positive law on this issue is clear. It is, however, unsatisfactory in normative terms. The conflicting policy considerations that are in play here are the same as those considered above when discussing the revocation of unlawful decisions. There is the legality interest in ensuring that Community rules are properly applied; there is the interest of the individual who may be caused

[182] Case 188/82, *Thyssen AG v Commission* [1983] ECR 3721, at para. 11.

[183] See also, Cases 303 and 312/81, *Klöckner v Commission* [1983] ECR 1507; Case 228/84, *Pauvert v Court of Auditors* [1985] ECR 1973.

[184] Cases C-31–44/91, *SpA Alois Lageder, supra* n. 16.

[185] Ibid. at para. 33.

[186] Ibid. at para. 34.

harm by reliance on a representation that turns out to be unlawful in circumstances where he would have no particular reason to doubt the legality of what was said to him.

We have seen that the Community courts are willing to balance these interests when deciding whether an unlawful decision can be revoked retroactively. They are, however, unwilling to do so when the illegality resides in a representation rather than a decision. Nor does the case law on representations make any reference to that concerning revocation of unlawful decisions. This makes little sense in normative terms, more especially so given that the dividing line between a decision and a representation may be a fine one.

It might be argued that the distinction is warranted because of the greater formality inherent in a decision, the argument being that there is therefore more justification for the individual deriving legitimate expectations from it than is the case with a representation. This argument is unconvincing. If balancing were to be countenanced in the context of unlawful representations, a necessary precondition for this exercise would be that the individual could show that the representation did contain a specific assurance such as to give rise to a legitimate expectation. It is moreover clear from the case law on revocation of unlawful decisions that the balancing exercise allows full account to be taken of the legality interest. This would be equally so if this exercise were applied in the context of unlawful representations.

11. CONCLUSION

The development of the principles of legal certainty and legitimate expectations as part of Community administrative law doctrine has been a significant achievement of the Community courts. They began very early in the Community's existence by drawing on principles to be found in the legal systems of the original six Member States, placing particular reliance on French and German law, and then fashioned these principles to the needs of the Community legal system. It is not surprising that with the passage of time the Community courts have relied less on national law and more on their own developing body of precedent. This does not of course mean that the case law of the Community courts is unproblematic. There are, as we have seen, aspects of the courts' jurisprudence that are certainly open to question and criticism. These should be altered and such changes would serve to strengthen this body of administrative law doctrine.

17

Proportionality I

1. INTRODUCTION

Proportionality is an important principle of EU administrative law.[1] It can be used to challenge Community action, and also the legality of Member State action which falls within the sphere of application of Community law. Different considerations tend to apply in these two spheres, and therefore this chapter will focus on proportionality as a ground of challenge to Community action, while the following chapter will consider the way in which the principle is used to contest the legality of Member State action.

The discussion will begin with analysis of the meaning of proportionality as it has been elaborated by the Community courts. The focus thereafter will be on the way in which proportionality has been applied and the intensity of review. It will become apparent that three broad types of case can be distinguished in this respect. There are cases involving discretionary policy choices, whether social, political, or economic in nature. There are cases where the applicant alleges that the Community measure infringes a right recognized by EU law. There are finally those cases where the essence of the claim is that a penalty or financial burden that has been imposed is disproportionate.

2. THE MEANING OF PROPORTIONALITY

The Treaties do not, as we have seen, contain an explicit, detailed set of principles against which to test the legality of Community or state action within the sphere covered by Community law. It has therefore largely fallen to the European Court of Justice (ECJ) and the Court of First Instance (CFI)

[1] J. Schwarze, *European Administrative Law* (Sweet & Maxwell, 1992), Chap. 5; de Búrca, 'The Principle of Proportionality and its Application in EC Law' (1993) 13 *YBEL* 105; N. Emiliou, *The Principle of Proportionality in European Law* (Kluwer, 1996); G. Gerapetritis, *Proportionality in Administrative Law* (Sakkoulas, 1997); E. Ellis, (ed), *The Principle of Proportionality in the Laws of Europe* (Hart, 1999); T. Tridimas, *The General Principles of EC Law* (Oxford University Press, 1999), Chap. 3; U. Bernitz and J. Nergelius, *General Principles of European Community Law* (Kluwer, 2000).

to fashion principles of administrative legality. In undertaking this task they have reasoned partly from specific Treaty provisions, which justify Community action only where it is 'necessary' or 'required' in order to reach a certain end. They have also inevitably drawn upon principles from the legal systems of the Member States and, as in many other contexts, they have then fashioned these principles to suit the needs of the Community itself.

The concept of proportionality is most fully developed within German law. It appeared initially in the context of policing, as a ground for challenging measures on the basis that they were excessive or unnecessary in relation to the objective being pursued.[2] In its modern German formulation the consensus appears to be that proportionality involves three factors. The courts will consider whether the measure was suitable for the attainment of the desired objective. They will examine whether the disputed measure was necessary, in the sense that the agency had no other option at its disposal which was less restrictive of the individual's freedom. The final stage of the inquiry is whether the measure was disproportionate to the restrictions thereby involved.[3]

Proportionality is now well established as a general principle of Community law. There was early reference to the idea of proportionality in the case law concerning the European Coal and Steel Community Treaty, ECSC.[4] The principle, however, began to be developed more fully after the decision in *Internationale Handeslgesellschaft*,[5] where proportionality was used as the ground for challenging the system of deposits accompanying import and export licences. While the action failed on the facts the judgment nonetheless established proportionality as a ground of review. A version of the principle is now also enshrined in Article 5 EC as part of subsidiarity. It provides that where Community action is warranted pursuant to subsidiarity, it shall not go beyond what is necessary to achieve the objectives of the Treaty, and these requirements are further fleshed out in a protocol to the Treaty.[6]

The meaning of proportionality has, however, been primarily determined by the Community courts. In any proportionality inquiry the relevant interests must be identified, and there will be some ascription of weight or value to those interests, since this is a condition precedent to any balancing operation. It is clear from this jurisprudence that the courts will inquire whether the measure was suitable or appropriate to achieve the desired end. They will also examine whether it was necessary to achieve that objective, or whether this could have been attained by a less onerous method. The first two

[2] Schwarze, *supra* n. 1, at 685–686. [3] Ibid. at 687.

[4] Case 8/55, *Fédération Charbonnière Belgique v High Authority* [1954–6] ECR 292, 299; Case 19/61, *Mannesmann AG v High Authority* [1962] ECR 357, at 370–1.

[5] Case 11/70, *Internationale Handeslgesellschaft mbH v Einfhur- und Vorratsstelle für Getreide und Futtermittel* [1970] ECR 1125.

[6] Protocol No 30 On the Application of the Principles of Subsidiarity and Proportionality.

elements of the classic German formulation are therefore also to be found in Community law.

There has been greater uncertainty as to whether the third element, often referred to as proportionality *stricto sensu*, is also part of the Community test. Thus even skilled observers such as van Gerven admit that the case law is uncertain in this regard.[7] This is a point of some importance, since the existence or not of the third limb changes the nature of the test. If proportionality comprises merely suitability and necessity then once these hurdles are surmounted the measure would be regarded as legal, even if the burden thereby imposed on the individual might be felt to be disproportionate to the desired objective. The addition of the third limb requires the court to undertake this further inquiry. The answer as to whether proportionality *stricto sensu* is part of the test or not is best determined when the case law has been examined. Suffice it to say for the present that although the Community courts do not always make reference to this aspect of the proportionality inquiry, they will generally do so when the applicant presents arguments directed specifically to it. This of course still leaves open the way in which the Community courts apply the balancing inherent in proportionality *stricto sensu*, an issue analysed in the light of the relevant case law below.

There is, moreover, a further issue that has a marked impact on the application of proportionality. This is the intensity with which the concept is applied. In any system of administrative law the courts will have to decide not only which tests to apply to determine the legality of administrative action, but also the rigour or intensity with which to apply them. In some legal systems this is worked out to a high degree, but the issue is pertinent for all systems. The relative intensity of judicial review is just as much a live question in relation to proportionality in the EU. Thus as de Búrca states:[8]

> It becomes apparent that in reaching decisions, the Court of Justice is influenced not only by what it considers to be the nature and the importance of the interest or right claimed by the applicant, and the nature and importance of the objective alleged to be served by the measure, but by the relative expertise, position and overall competence of the Court as against the decision-making authority in assessing those factors. It becomes apparent that the way the proportionality principle is applied by the Court of Justice covers a spectrum ranging from a very deferential approach, to quite a rigorous and searching examination of the justification for a measure which has been challenged.

We can distinguish three broad types of case where challenges are commonly made on grounds of proportionality. These are cases involving

[7] Van Gerven, 'The Effect of Proportionality on the Actions of Member States of the European Community: National Viewpoints from Continental Europe', in Ellis (ed), *The Principle of Proportionality*, *supra* n. 1, at 37–38.

[8] De Búrca, *supra* n. 1, at 111.

discretionary policy choices, rights, and penalties or financial burdens. It will become clear that the intensity of review may well differ in these types of case.

3. PROPORTIONALITY AND DISCRETIONARY POLICY CHOICES

The most common case is where proportionality is used to challenge a discretionary policy choice made by the administration. The applicant will commonly argue that the very policy choice made by the administration was disproportionate, because, for example, the costs were excessive in relation to the benefits, or because the measure was not suitable or necessary to achieve the end in view. The judiciary is likely to be cautious in this type of case. The reasons are not hard to find. The administrative/political arm of government makes policy choices, and it is generally recognized that the courts should not overturn these merely because they believe that a different way of doing things would have been better. They should not substitute their judgment for that of the administration.

This does not mean that proportionality is ruled out in such instances. It does mean that the courts are likely to apply the concept less intensively than in the other two categories of case, and will only overturn the policy choice if it is clearly or manifestly disproportionate. This is more especially so where the policy choice made by the administration or the political arm of government required the weighing of a number of complex variables when the contested decision was made.

There are, as will become apparent, a number of areas in which the Community courts apply proportionality with relatively low intensity because of the discretionary nature of the policy choices involved. The guiding principle is, as stated in *British American Tobacco*,[9] that this measure of review will be deemed appropriate whenever the Community legislature exercises a broad discretion involving political, economic, or social choices requiring it to make complex assessments. The particular categories set out below should therefore be regarded as exempliflying this general principle.

A. Common Policies: Agriculture and Fisheries

Many proportionality challenges have arisen from measures adopted under the Common Agricultural Policy (CAP). It is important to appreciate

[9] Case C-491/01, *R v Secretary of State for Health, ex p British American Tobacco (Investments) Ltd and Imperial Tobacco Ltd* [2002] ECR I-11453, at para. 123; Case C-210/03, *The Queen, on the application of Swedish Match AB and Swedish Match UK Ltd v Secretary of State for Health* [2004] ECR I-11893, at para. 48.

that the objectives of the CAP are set out at a high level of generality. Article 33 EC lists the CAP's objectives as being to increase agricultural productivity by promoting technical progress, the rational development of agricultural production, and the optimum utilization of factors of production; thus to ensure a fair standard of living for the agricultural community; to stabilize markets; to assure the availability of supplies; and to ensure that supplies reach consumers at reasonable prices. It is clear that these objectives can clash *inter se*, with the result that the Commission and Council have to make difficult discretionary choices, often under fairly extreme exigencies of time, in order to decide how best to balance and attain these aims.

The Court has frequently emphasized that the Community institutions possess a wide discretion in the operation of the CAP, and that review will not therefore be intensive.[10] This more deferential approach has carried across to challenges based on proportionality, as exemplified by *Fedesa*.[11] In 1988 the Council adopted a Directive prohibiting the use of certain hormones in livestock farming. The Directive sought, *inter alia*, to remove barriers to trade and distortions of competition flowing from differences in Member State legislation concerning the administration of substances having a hormonal action. An earlier identical Directive from 1985 had been declared void by the ECJ on procedural grounds. The applicants were manufacturers and distributors of veterinary medicine who challenged the validity of the national legislative measure implementing the 1988 Directive, on the ground that the Directive itself was invalid. They argued that the Directive infringed, *inter alia*, proportionality.

The applicants claimed that the Directive was not suitable to attain the declared objectives, since it was impossible to apply in practice and led to the creation of a dangerous black market in hormones. They argued also that outright prohibition was not necessary, because consumer anxieties could be allayed simply by the dissemination of information and advice. The applicants maintained, moreover, that the prohibition imposed excessive burdens on them in the form of considerable financial losses, in relation to the alleged benefits accruing to the public interest.

The ECJ acknowledged that proportionality was a general principle of Community law. The lawfulness of the Directive was therefore subject to the condition that it was appropriate and necessary to achieve the objectives legitimately pursued by the legislation. When there was a choice between several appropriate measures recourse should be had to the least onerous, and

[10] See e.g. Case 138/78, *Stölting v Hauptzollamt Hamburg-Jonas* [1979] ECR 713; Case 265/87, *Schräder v Hauptzollamt Gronau* [1989] ECR 2237.

[11] Case C-331/88, *R v Minister for Agriculture, Fisheries and Food, ex p Fedesa* [1990] ECR I-4023.

the disadvantages caused should not be disproportionate to the aims pursued. The ECJ then continued as follows.[12]

However, with regard to judicial review of compliance with those conditions it must be stated that in matters concerning the common agricultural policy the Community legislature has a discretionary power which corresponds to the political responsibilities given to it by . . . the Treaty. Consequently, the legality of a measure adopted in that sphere can be affected only if the measure is manifestly inappropriate having regard to the objective which the competent institution is seeking to pursue.

The applicants had to show that the measure was manifestly inappropriate and the Court concluded that they had not discharged this burden. The ECJ felt that the measure was suited for its intended aim, and that any system of partial authorization would require costly control measures. It held that the measure passed the necessity test in that the Council was entitled to take the view that having regard to requirements of health protection, the removal of trade barriers and distortions of competition could not be achieved through less onerous means such as dissemination of information to consumers and labelling. The ECJ's response to the argument that the Directive had serious financial consequences for the applicants was terse: it simply stated that the importance of the objectives pursued justified even substantial negative financial consequences for certain traders.

The reasoning in *Fedesa* has been applied in many other cases. It is clear that applicants will find it difficult to convince the ECJ that a measure is manifestly disproportionate.[13] It is nonetheless easy to form a mistaken impression of the way in which proportionality applies in this type of case. It is true that low intensity review prevails in this area. The ECJ will nonetheless check in some detail within the proportionality inquiry to see whether the foundations for the challenged decision are sound. This is equally true of the CFI.[14]

[12] Ibid. at para. 14.

[13] Case C-8/89, *Zardi v Consorzio Agrario Provinciale di Ferrara* [1990] ECR I-2515; Cases C-133, 300, and 362/93, *Crispoltoni v Fattoria Autonoma Tabacchi* [1994] ECR I-4863; Case C-4/96, *Northern Ireland Fish Producers' Federation and Northern Ireland Fishermen's Federation v Department of Agriculture for Northern Ireland* [1998] ECR I-681; Case T-30/99, *Bocchi Food Trade International GmbH v Commission* [2001] ECR II-943, at para. 92; Case C-434/02, *Arnold André GmbH & Co KG v Landrat des Kreises Herford* [2004] ECR I-11825, at paras. 46–56; Case C-171/03, *Maatschap Toeters and M. C. Verberk v Productschap Vee en Vlees* [2004] ECR I-10945, at para. 52; Case C-452/00, *Netherlands v Commission* [2005] ECR I-6645, at paras. 101–102; Case C-41/03 P, *Rica Foods (Free Zone) NV v Commission* [2005] ECR I-6875, at paras. 85–86; Case T-158/03, *Industrias Quimicas del Vallés, SA v Commission,* judgment of 28 June 2005, not yet published, at para. 136.

[14] Cases 125 and 152/96, *Boehringer Ingelheim Vetmedica GmbH and CH Boehringer Sohn v Council and Commission* [1999] ECR II-3427.

Affish[15] provides a fitting example. The applicant imported fish from Japan and sought the annulment of a Commission Decision banning Japanese fish products from the EU. The Decision had been made pursuant to a Community Directive allowing protective measures to be taken when there were fears about the health risks from such imports. The Decision imposed a total ban on Japanese fish and was based on a report from Commission experts who had visited a number of fish plants in Japan and found that there were serious concerns as to hygiene. The plant from which the applicant imported fish had not, however, been investigated by the experts and there was no evidence that its fish posed a health risk. The applicant argued that the total ban was therefore disproportionate. The ECJ disagreed and found that the contested Decision was warranted and proportionate. In reaching this conclusion the ECJ did, however, consider in some detail the defensibility of a total ban flowing from selective investigation. It found this to be defensible for a number of reasons. It would not have been practical to investigate all Japanese fish plants; the firms investigated were chosen by the Japanese government and could thus be considered reasonably representative; it was reasonable to extrapolate from the firms investigated to others in the industry; and the hygiene risks meant that protective measures should be put in place expeditiously.

The same linkage between the *Fedesa* principle and scrutiny of the underlying foundations of the contested measure is evident in *Jippes*.[16] The applicant contested the legality of a Community Directive that adopted a policy to combat foot and mouth disease of non-vaccination for animals, subject to limited exceptions. She argued, *inter alia*, that the Directive and the emphasis that it placed on animal slaughter as the optimal method of disease control was disproportionate. The ECJ reiterated the *Fedesa* principle that measures of this kind would only be struck down if they were manifestly disproportionate. It emphasized that 'the criterion to be applied is not whether the measure adopted by the legislature was the only one or the best one possible but whether it was manifestly inappropriate'.[17] It stressed that this criterion was not to be applied retrospectively: where the Community legislature was obliged to assess the future effects of rules to be adopted and those effects could not be accurately foreseen, the assessment embodied in the legislation could only be challenged if it appeared to be manifestly incorrect in the light of the available information when it was adopted.[18] One might expect in the light of this vigorous re-affirmation of *Fedesa* that the ECJ would rapidly

[15] Case C-183/95, *Affish BV v Rijksdienst voor de keuring van Vee en Vlees* [1997] ECR I-4315.

[16] Case C-189/01, *Jippes v Minister van Landbouw, Natuurbeheer en Visserij* [2001] ECR I-5689.

[17] Ibid. at para. 83.

[18] Ibid. at para. 84.

dispose of the case. It is true that the ECJ found against the applicant. But not before it examined in some detail the policy foundation for the contested measure.[19] The ECJ emphasized that the no vaccination policy had been adopted after a scientific study undertaken by the Commission. The Court then examined the rationale for this policy: preventive vaccination did not ensure eradication of the disease from a herd since vaccinated animals could still carry the virus and contaminate healthy animals; it was impossible, even where no outbreaks of foot and mouth had occurred, to ensure that the virus was absent from a vaccinated herd; preventive vaccination for all animals in the Community would involve greater expense and more drawbacks than a non-vaccination policy; a vaccination policy would have significant repercussions on exports; and it had not been shown that a vaccination policy would reduce the incidence of foot and mouth or the need for sanitary slaughter if an outbreak occurred. It was only after having examined such factors that the Court concluded that the Directive was proportionate to the aims pursued.

Risk regulation is a theme common to a number of the cases concerning proportionality and agriculture discussed thus far. It was central to the disputes in *Pfizer*[20] and *Alpharma*.[21] The cases provide further insight on the theme considered within this section: the conjunction between low intensity proportionality review and judicial willingness nonetheless to examine in detail the contested measure.

Pfizer can be taken by way of example. It concerned a challenge by the applicant company to a Regulation that withdrew authorization for an additive to animal feeding stuffs. The additive in question, virginiamycin, was an antibiotic that was added in very small quantities to animal feed in order to promote growth. The rationale for the withdrawal of the authorization was the fear that such additives could reduce the animals' resistance to antibiotics, and that this lessening of resistance could be transmitted to humans. This would then reduce the effectiveness not only of that particular antibiotic, but might also limit the efficacy of antibiotics of the same class. The case was considered in detail in a previous chapter, in the context of discussion of manifest error.[22] The applicant also attacked the measure on grounds of proportionality.

The CFI reiterated the *Fedesa* principle, to the effect that proportionality required that Community measures should not exceed the limits of what was necessary and appropriate to attain the desired ends; that where there was a choice between several appropriate measures recourse must be had to the least onerous; and that the disadvantages caused must not be disproportionate to

[19] Ibid. at paras. 87–101.
[20] Case T-13/99, *Pfizer Animal Health SA v Council* [2002] ECR II-3305.
[21] Case T-70/99, *Alpharma Inc v Council* [2002] ECR II-3495.
[22] See above, Chap. 13.

the aims pursued. The CFI also emphasized, in line with *Fedesa*, that the discretionary power accorded to the Community institutions meant that it had to be shown that the measure was manifestly inappropriate before it could be found to be unlawful.[23] The Court held moreover that a cost/benefit analysis was a particular expression of proportionality in cases involving risk management.[24]

The CFI found against the applicant, but not before it had examined its arguments in some detail. It devoted 70 paragraphs/20 pages of its judgment to the issue. This is to be sure a purely 'formal' guide to the degree of scrutiny involved, but it does nonetheless serve to place low intensity review in perspective. It would be wrong to regard this form of proportionality review as the court merely going through the motions. This is more especially so given that proportionality was merely one ground of challenge considered in a judgment that stretched to nearly 200 pages. Space precludes examination of the full detail of the proportionality analysis. The essence of the contending arguments can nonetheless be conveyed.

The CFI examined whether the withdrawal of the authorization was manifestly inappropriate to the objective pursued. Pfizer argued that this was so because the principal cause of antibiotic resistance in humans was excessive use of such substances in human medicine. The CFI held that even assuming that the Community institutions had the power and duty to adopt other measures to prevent excessive use of antibiotics this could not affect the validity of the ban on additives in feedingstuffs.[25] It also considered Pfizer's argument that the additives improved animal health, that a ban would lead to an increase in antibiotics for therapeutic use, and that this could not realistically be avoided by improvements in animal husbandry. The CFI was doubtful that the ban would lead to any significant rise in antibiotics for therapeutic use, and pointed to evidence that low-level, long-term exposure to antibiotics could have more effect on the development of resistance than short-term larger doses for therapeutic use.[26]

The CFI then turned to the claim that the ban was not necessary since other less onerous measures could have been taken. The applicant argued that studies were being undertaken to test for any correlation between the additives and resistance to antibiotics in humans and that no ban should therefore have been introduced pending the outcome of these studies. The CFI disagreed. It pointed to studies by the institutions that showed an increase in antibiotic resistance in the years preceding the ban. There was therefore some scientific data on which the Community institutions could act. It was for those institutions to exercise their political responsibility

[23] Case T-13/99, *Pfizer, supra* n. 20, at paras. 411–412. [24] Ibid. at para. 410.
[25] Ibid. at paras. 414–419. [26] Ibid. at paras. 420–429.

and discretion in the face of a complex situation. Their choice of provisionally banning the additive to prevent the risk from becoming a reality, while continuing with the studies, was in accord with the precautionary principle.[27]

In the final part of the proportionality analysis the CFI examined the claim that the disadvantages of the ban were disproportionate to the objectives pursued and entailed a breach of the right to property. This was in effect the third part of the proportionality calculus, what is often referred to as proportionality *stricto sensu*. The CFI's reasoning in this respect will be examined in detail below when we consider how far the Community courts make use of this third limb of the proportionality inquiry. Suffice it to say for the present that the Court rejected the argument on the facts of the case.

B. Common Policies: Transport

The decision in *Omega Air*[28] provides further evidence of how the ECJ scrutinizes the suitability and necessity of a contested measure even within the confines of low intensity proportionality review of transport policy.

The applicant challenged the legality of a Community Regulation which stipulated that re-engined planes with engines of a by-pass ratio of three or more were not subject to prohibitions imposed by the Regulation, whereas planes with a by-pass ratio of less than three were subject to such prohibitions. The objective of the Regulation was to prevent environmental damage through noise, fuel burn, and emissions. The applicant had re-fitted certain planes with engines that had a by-pass ratio of less than three. It argued that the Regulation was disproportionate because the by-pass ratio was an inadequate criterion for noise reduction, and because the objectives of the Regulation could have been achieved by measures that were less damaging to the applicant. It would, said the applicant, have been less restrictive if separate thresholds had been set for noise, fuel burn, and gaseous emissions.

The ECJ reiterated its previous holdings that review was limited where the legislature had wide discretionary powers, as was the case with the common transport policy, emphasizing that the Court should not substitute its view for that of the Community legislature.[29] It rejected the applicant's claim, but, as in the cases discussed in the previous section, it engaged with the arguments notwithstanding the low intensity review. Thus the ECJ concluded, after studying data produced by the Commission, that the by-pass ratio was a suitable criterion for attaining the objectives of the Regulation. The

[27] Ibid. at paras. 441–448.

[28] Case C-27/00, *R (on the application of Omega Air Ltd) v Secretary of State for the Environment, Transport and the Regions* [2002] ECR I-2569.

[29] Ibid. at paras. 62–64.

argument that the objectives could be attained through less restrictive means, viz, separate thresholds for noise, fuel burn, and emissions, was rejected on the ground that the application of separate criteria would be complex and uncertain, and was not warranted by the limited number of planes re-engined by the applicant.

C. Anti-Dumping

The Community courts have signalled that low intensity proportionality review applies in the context of anti-dumping, but it is also evident that they are willing, as in the cases considered in the previous section, to consider seriously the argument advanced by the applicant.

Both of these features are apparent in *International Potash*.[30] The applicant was an exporter of potash from Russia and Belarus into the EU. It challenged a modified anti-dumping Regulation imposed on it by the Council, claiming *inter alia* that it was disproportionate because it imposed a fixed duty in addition to a variable duty. The CFI accepted that proportionality was applicable. The measure must therefore be suited to attain the objective, it must be necessary to achieve the desired goal, and the least onerous method must be adopted. The objective of anti-dumping regulations was to eliminate the dumping margin so far as that harmed Community industry. However, given that the basic Regulation governing anti-dumping left the Community institutions a wide discretion to determine the appropriate duty, judicial review was limited to ascertaining whether the measures adopted by the legislature were manifestly inappropriate to the objective pursued.[31]

Having made clear that review was confined to showing that the measure was manifestly inappropriate, the CFI nonetheless examined in some detail the nature of the applicant's complaint.[32] The CFI began by noting that a variable duty was generally more favourable to exporters and importers than a fixed duty, since the former was easier to evade. The efficacy of a variable duty was therefore dependent on a relationship of trust between the Community institutions and the undertaking, as manifested through accurate declarations of the export price. It had, however, become clear that the variable duty was being circumvented and this led to the imposition of the fixed duty. The retention of the variable duty as an alternative to the newly imposed fixed duty was moreover necessary to guard against economic circumstances where the latter would be ineffective to prevent dumping. The

[30] Case T-87/98, *International Potash Company v Council* [2000] ECR II-3179. See also, Case 255/84, *Nachi Fujikoshi Corporation v Council* [1987] ECR 1861, at paras. 21–22; Case T-162/94, *NMB France SARL v Commission* [1996] ECR II-427, at paras. 72–73; Cases T-33–34/98, *Petrotub SA and Republica SA v Council* [1999] ECR II-3837, at para. 89.

[31] Case T-87/98, *International Potash, supra* n. 30, at paras. 39–40.

[32] Ibid. at paras. 41–60.

CFI considered and rejected the applicant's claim that there were other means of combating customs fraud. It was for the Community institutions to determine the most appropriate type of anti-dumping duty after weighing the various interests, which included not only the undertakings concerned, but also Community industry, users, and consumers. It was for the legislature to balance these interests and to make the Regulation that best eliminated the dumping and was least open to risk of circumvention.

D. Inter-institutional Controls

The discussion thus far has been concerned with the interpretation of proportionality as it applies to EU substantive law in areas where the Community institutions have a broad discretion. The ECJ has, however, adopted a similar approach when asked to review the proportionality of inter-institutional controls established by the Community legislature. That this is so is apparent from the *EIB*[33] and *ECB*[34] cases, in which the European Central Bank (ECB) and the European Investment Bank (EIB) contested the legality of a Regulation[35] making the two institutions subject to the European Anti-Fraud Office, OLAF.

The *ECB* case can be taken by way of example, since the ECJ's reasoning in the two cases was very similar. The ECB challenged the legality of the Regulation on a number of grounds, including proportionality. It argued that the application to it of the investigative powers possessed by OLAF was unnecessary, since there were various other mechanisms for detecting and preventing fraud within the ECB, including independent external auditors, the Court of Auditors, and two other committees established by the ECB's Governing Council. The ECB also claimed that investigations by OLAF would not be a suitable or appropriate way to prevent fraud, given that many ECB documents were confidential and would therefore have to be excluded from any OLAF inquiry, with the consequence that its role could only be marginal. Given, moreover, that OLAF's powers would only be applied to the ECB, and given that the ECB operated in a decentralized way through national central banks, OLAF could not effectively combat fraud.

The ECJ disagreed. It held that with regard to judicial review of suitability and necessity 'the Community legislature must be allowed a broad discretion in an area such as that involved in the present case, so that the legality of a measure adopted in that sphere can be affected only if the measure is

33 Case C-15/00, *Commission v European Investment Bank* [2003] ECR I-7281.

34 Case C-11/00, *Commission v European Central Bank* [2003] ECR I-7147.

35 Regulation (EC) 1073/1999 of the European Parliament and of the Council of 25 May 1999, Concerning Investigations Conducted by the European Anti-Fraud Office (OLAF), OJ 1999 L136/1.

manifestly inappropriate having regard to the objective which the competent institution is seeking to pursue'.[36]

The ECJ considered the arguments advanced by the ECB based on proportionality. It rejected the ECB's claim concerning the necessity of OLAF's involvement. It was, said the ECJ, open to the legislature to decide that, notwithstanding the existence of bodies attached to specific institutions whose mandate was to fight fraud, it was nonetheless necessary to strengthen this fight by creating a 'control mechanism which is simultaneously centralized within one particular organ, specialized and operated independently and uniformly with respect to those institutions, bodies, offices and agencies'[37] of the Community. This was more especially so given that OLAF's tasks were not the same as bodies such as the Court of Auditors, or the bodies set up by the ECB itself.

The Court was equally unconvinced by the ECB's arguments concerning the suitability of the Regulation for attaining the desired goal. The ECJ acknowledged the need for confidentiality in the sensitive tasks performed by the ECB. However, it was for the ECB to show and not merely assert that restrictions on access to information were necessary. There were, moreover, provisions, both within the Regulation and in other parts of Community law, which served to ensure that any information revealed in OLAF investigations would be subject to professional secrecy. It was accepted that the fact that OLAF could not investigate the activities of national central banks would limit its operations, but it would not, said the ECJ, render ineffective OLAF investigations within the ECB or the communication of information from the ECB to OLAF in accord with the requirements of the Regulation.

It is interesting to reflect a little further on the rationale for the relatively low intensity proportionality review applied in this case. It should be noted that the contested Regulation was adopted pursuant to Article 280 EC, which provides that the Community and the Member States shall counter fraud and other illegal activities affecting the financial interests of the Community through measures adopted pursuant to this Article.

The ECJ confined itself to saying that the Community legislature must be allowed a broad discretion in an area such as that involved in the present case,[38] the implication being that the limited review was seen to flow from the type of power given by Article 280 EC, which accorded the Community institutions discretion as to the measures to be taken to fight fraud. This reading is reinforced by the fact that the ECJ referred[39] to the *British American Tobacco* case,[40] where it had said that proportionality review should require a

[36] Case C-11/00, *Commission v European Central Bank*, *supra* n. 34, at para. 157.

[37] Ibid. at para. 158. [38] Ibid. at para. 157. [39] Ibid. at para. 157.

[40] Case C-491/01, *R v Secretary of State for Health, ex p. British American Tobacco*, *supra* n. 9, at para. 123.

finding that the measure was manifestly inappropriate where the Community legislature had a broad discretion involving matters of social, economic, or political choice requiring it to make complex assessments.

Advocate General Jacobs gave a rather more general rationalization for the same conclusion. He stated that it was not for the Court of Justice to substitute its judgment for that of the Community legislature when reviewing the lawfulness of general measures. The issue in the instant case was therefore not whether the internal and external controls on the ECB were adequate, but whether by establishing a general regime of external and independent control the legislature clearly exceeded what was necessary to combat fraud.[41]

It is not clear whether the difference in formulation as between the Advocate General and the ECJ was intended to signal a real difference in substance. The Advocate General's Opinion was framed in terms of low intensity review when considering the lawfulness of general measures. The ECJ's criterion was the existence of social, economic, or political choice requiring the making of complex assessments. Notwithstanding this difference in formulation it is doubtful whether it signified any real difference in substance. It is unlikely that Advocate General Jacobs would regard low intensity review as being appropriate where the relevant Treaty article left no meaningful discretion requiring the making of complex choices of the kind adverted to by the Court.

If this is correct, it should nonetheless be recognized that low intensity review will apply whenever the Community legislature is faced with not only complex assessments that are primarily economic in nature, but also where the discretion and attendant complexity is social or political in nature. Given that a great many Treaty articles will be of this nature, low intensity review will be the norm.

E. Evaluation: Suitability, Necessity, and Manifest Disproportionality

It is important to stand back from the case law and assess more generally the judicial approach to the suitability and necessity limbs of the proportionality test. The pertinent issue is the criterion of manifest disproportionality and the way in which it is applied by the courts.

Let us begin by reflecting on the concept of manifest disproportionality. The rationale for this reading of proportionality is an admixture of concerns relating to legitimacy and expertise. The root idea is that where the Treaties explicitly or implicitly accord a broad discretion to the legislative institutions or the administration, the courts should be wary of substituting their

[41] Case C-11/00, *Commission v European Central Bank, supra* n. 34, AG Jacobs, at para. 183.

judgment for that of the primary decision-maker under the guise of proportionality. This is a valid concern. There are, as we have seen, numerous factors that have to be balanced by the Community legislature in the context of, for example, the Common Agricultural Policy (CAP). It is not for the Community courts to intervene merely because they would, if they had been making the primary decision, have come to a different balance from that decided by the Community legislature or administration. This is more especially so in areas where decisions as to the suitability or necessity of measures involve issues of expertise. While these twin considerations of legitimacy and expertise are especially prevalent in relation to discretionary economic choices, they are equally present in the context of discretionary social and political choices, as exemplified by the *ECB* case.[42]

Now it might be argued that while such considerations are valid they should not lead to a test framed in terms of 'manifest disproportionality'. On this view the concerns relating to legitimacy and expertise can be properly taken into account through a proportionality test couched in less extreme terms. There is force in this view. We should, however, also factor in the way in which the Community courts actually apply the manifest disproportionality test. We have seen that this criterion has not precluded the Community courts from looking hard at the facts and arguments adduced by the parties in order to determine whether the measure should be regarded as manifestly disproportionate. This is not to say that no cases would be decided differently if the test were revised in the manner considered in the previous paragraph. It is, however, unlikely that many cases would fall into this category. It is true that detailed investigation of the facts and arguments is not inconsistent with review framed in terms of manifest disproportionality. Such investigation may simply be required to determine whether the measure meets or fails to meet this criterion. It should nonetheless also be acknowledged that this detailed scrutiny is not mandated by the test currently applied by the Community courts.

It would, in other words, have been perfectly possible for the courts to operate with a test of manifest disproportionality and apply it in a very cursory fashion, in a similar manner to the early case law on manifest error where the courts' review of the contested measure was perfunctory.[43] The very fact that the courts, while operating within a manifest disproportionality test, do commonly assess the contending arguments in some depth means that they are more likely to find an error warranting annulment.[44] It also means that the 'gap' between the test as currently formulated and a test

[42] Case C-11/00, *Commission v European Central Bank*, *supra* n. 34.

[43] See above, at 439–446.

[44] See, e.g., Cases C-177 and 181/99, *Ampafrance SA v Directeur des Services Fiscaux de Maine-et-Loire* [2000] ECR I-7013.

framed in more moderate terms is likely to be less significant in reality than might otherwise have been thought.

F. Evaluation: *Stricto Sensu* Proportionality, the Third Limb of the Test

We saw from the earlier discussion that there was uncertainty in the literature as to whether the Community courts used a two or three part proportionality test. I expressed the view that there was evidence for a three part test, but postponed further discussion pending analysis of the case law. It is now time to examine this issue in more detail and to substantiate the preliminary view that I adumbrated above. To reiterate for the sake of clarity, the third limb of the test is relevant where the court has found that the measure was both suited and necessary to achieve the desired end, but the applicant argues that the burden placed on it by the measure should nonetheless be regarded as disproportionate to the benefits secured.

The position from the case law may be summarized as follows. The normal judicial formulation of proportionality is cast in terms of suitability and necessity. Moreover, the Community courts will not always address what is generally known as the *stricto sensu* proportionality inquiry. There are many cases where the judicial analysis begins and ends with consideration of suitability and necessity. It is for this very reason that there is uncertainty as to whether this is an integral part of proportionality as applied in the EU. There is, it should be acknowledged, little evidence that the ECJ and CFI will raise the third limb of proportionality of their own volition. All this would seem to point towards the conclusion that it is a two part test.

The reason for resisting this conclusion is that the courts will, however, address the third part of the test when the applicant contesting the legality of the measure puts arguments couched in those terms. The Community courts, do in other words, accept that this can be regarded as a proper part of the proportionality analysis, but the onus is on the applicant to raise arguments that place the matter before them. This is what occurred in a number of the cases discussed above.[45]

The fact that the Community courts are willing to consider the *stricto sensu* proportionality inquiry does not, however, tell one how they undertake this balancing exercise. This is of course of real importance. It is clear from a consideration of the case law that the depth of the Court's inquiry in this respect differs markedly.

There are some cases such as *Fedesa*[46] where the ECJ addressed the issue, but only in the briefest manner. It will be remembered that the applicants

[45] Case C-331/88, *Fedesa, supra* n. 11; Case C-183/95, *Affish, supra* n. 15; Case T-13/99, *Pfizer, supra* n. 20; Case C-426/93, *Germany v Commission* [1995] ECR I-3723.

[46] Case C-331/88, *Fedesa, supra* n. 11.

argued that the ban on hormones was neither appropriate nor necessary to attain the desired effect and that the prohibition entailed excessive disadvantages in the form of financial losses as compared to the alleged benefits accruing to the general interest.[47] The ECJ's response may have been correct on the facts, but it was terse in the extreme. Its response was simply that 'the importance of the objectives pursued is such as to justify even substantial negative financial consequences for certain traders'.[48]

There are other cases such as *Affish*[49] where there is a little more by way of judicial reasoning. The applicant argued, *inter alia*, that the ban on import of fish products from Japan was an excessive restriction of its business activity and was likely to endanger its viability since a significant part of its revenue came from such imports.[50] The ECJ responded by stating that the contested measure should be regarded as proportionate because it fulfilled the requirements of a Directive applicable in the area, which was designed to ensure that due attention was paid to the interests of traders and because the protection of public health, which the contested Decision intended to secure, must take precedence over economic considerations.[51]

There are yet others cases such as *Pfizer*,[52] where the CFI gave rather more detailed consideration to the third part of the proportionality test. The CFI decided, as we have seen, that the contested measure withdrawing the authorization for the use of certain additives in feedingstuffs was appropriate and necessary for attaining the desired end. It then turned its attention to the applicant's claim that the measure entailed disadvantages that were disproportionate to the objectives pursued. Pfizer claimed that withdrawal of authorization could only be proportionate where there was a serious risk causing great uncertainty and where there was evidence that the source against which the action was taken was the most likely explanation for the risk. It argued, moreover, that it was the only producer in the world of the additive and that the ban would lead to significant financial losses and job cuts. An immediate ban was therefore disproportionate. The CFI rejected the argument for a number of reasons. It reiterated the reasoning in *Fedesa* and *Affish* that public health must take precedence over economic considerations and that the importance of the public health objective could justify even substantial financial adverse consequences for traders.[53] The CFI emphasized moreover that the Community institutions had not erred in their assessment of the risk posed by the additive, and that the withdrawal of authorization

[47] Ibid. at para. 12. [48] Ibid. at para. 17.

[49] Case C-183/95, *Affish*, *supra* n. 15. [50] Ibid. at para. 41.

[51] Ibid. at para. 43.

[52] Case T-13/99, *Pfizer*, *supra* n. 20. See also, Cases T-125 and 152/96, *Boehringer Ingelheim Vetmedica*, *supra* n. 14, at paras. 102–109.

[53] Ibid. at para. 456.

was a provisional measure, which the Commission and Council had a duty to re-examine.

It is clear from the case law that applicants face an uphill battle convincing the Community courts that a measure should be struck down as being *stricto sensu* disproportionate. The ECJ or CFI will in such cases already have decided that the contested measure withstands scrutiny under the suitability and necessity limbs of the test. The arguments adduced by the applicant at the third stage of the analysis will commonly focus on the financial losses suffered as a result of the measure. These will be placed in the balance against the objective sought by the Community and where, as in many of the cases, this involves protection of public health, the ECJ and CFI will be unlikely to find that the balance tilts in favour of the applicant. Some may be tempted to conclude that the third stage of the proportionality inquiry is therefore stacked against the applicant to a degree that is unwarranted. We should nonetheless hesitate before reaching this conclusion. Balancing of this kind is inherently contestable. It is moreover doubtful whether the results in such cases would be different if the issue arose for adjudication before national courts.

4. PROPORTIONALITY AND RIGHTS

The discussion thus far has been concerned with the 'paradigm case' where proportionality is used to challenge a discretionary policy choice made by the Community legislature or administration. The focus now shifts to consideration of cases involving proportionality and rights.

A. Rights Enshrined in the Treaty or Community Legislation

Some claims will be made on the basis of rights enshrined in the Treaties or Community legislation. The ECJ will tend to construe limits to such rights strictly, with the consequence that there will be a searching inquiry into the suitability and necessity elements of proportionality, as exemplified by *Hautala*.[54]

Ms Hautala, an MEP, sought access to a Council document concerning arms exports. The Council refused to grant access, on the ground that this could be harmful to the EU's relations with third countries, and sought to justify this under Article 4(1) of Decision 93/731,[55] governing access

[54] Case C-353/99 P, *Council v Hautala* [2001] ECR I-9565. See also, Case C-353/01 P, *Olli Mattila v Council and Commission* [2004] ECR I-1073.

[55] Council Decision 93/731/EC of 20 December 1993, On Public Access to Council Documents, OJ 1993 L340/43.

to Council documentation. The ECJ held that the right of access to documents[56] was to be broadly construed so as to include access to information contained in the document, not just the document itself. The principle of proportionality required the Council to consider partial access to a document that contained information the disclosure of which could endanger one of the interests protected by Article 4(1). Proportionality also required that derogation from the right of access be limited to what was appropriate and necessary for achieving the aim in view.[57] The aim pursued by the Council in refusing access to the contested report could be achieved if the Council removed, after examination, the passages that might harm international relations.

The same approach is evident in *Verein fur Konsumenteninformation.*[58] The applicant, VKI, was an Austrian consumer organization, which had legal capacity under Austrian law to bring actions on behalf of consumers where they had assigned such rights to VKI. The VKI sought access to documents held by the Commission concerning a cartel that had been found to exist in the banking sector, in order to enable it to pursue legal actions in Austria for customers that might have been charged excessive rates of interest. The file containing the documentation was large and the Commission denied VKI's request in its entirety, stating *inter alia* that the documents were covered by exceptions to the Regulation governing access, and that partial access was not possible in this case since a detailed examination of each document would entail an excessive and disproportionate amount of work. The CFI held that the Regulation required the Commission in principle to carry out a concrete individual assessment of the content of the documents contained in the request, except where it was manifestly clear that access should be refused or granted. The refusal to undertake any concrete assessment was therefore in principle manifestly disproportionate.[59] There could, said the CFI, be cases where because of the number of documents requested the Commission must retain the right to balance the interest in public access against the burden of work in order to safeguard the interests of good administration. This possibility was, however, only applicable in exceptional cases. The right of access, coupled with concrete individual examination, was the norm.[60] The CFI acknowledged that the relevant file was large, but nonetheless annulled the Commission's decision.

[56] Art. 255 EC.

[57] Cases T-222, 327 and 329/99, *Martinez, de Gaulle and Bonino v European Parliament* [2001] ECR II-2823 reveal how proportionality might be used to challenge internal rules as to the organization of political parties within the EP, although the challenge failed on the facts.

[58] Case T-2/03, *Verein für Konsumenteninformation v Commission*, judgment of 13 April 2005, not yet published.

[59] Ibid. at para. 100.

[60] Ibid. at paras. 101–115.

B. Discretionary Policies, Fundamental Rights, and Proportionality

The most common type of case raising issues of proportionality and rights is, however, different from that discussed immediately above. It is where a measure is passed pursuant to a Community common policy, and one of the grounds of challenge is that it infringes fundamental rights recognized by the Community legal order. The crucial issue is how far the assertion of such a fundamental right changes the nature of the proportionality inquiry undertaken by the Community courts. The answer is rather more complex than might be initially thought, because of two considerations.

There are, on the one hand, principled arguments for more vigorous scrutiny in cases concerned with rights. Society might well accept that such rights cannot be regarded as absolute, but the very denomination of certain interests as Community rights means that any interference should be kept to a minimum. In this sense proportionality is a natural and necessary adjunct to the recognition of such rights. Moreover, courts regard it as a natural and proper part of their legitimate function to adjudicate on the boundary lines between state action and individual rights, even though this line may be controversial.

There is, on the other hand, the fact that cases concerned with proportionality and rights do not comprise a discrete, self-contained category. We might imagine that such cases arise in circumstances different from those discussed in the previous section, such that there are no complications about the fact that the case is concerned with discretionary policy choices. Some cases fit this picture. Most do not. The reality is that rights-based challenges arise most frequently as one part of a proportionality action directed against a measure where the Community is exercising discretionary power. It is therefore necessary to 'unpack' the judicial analysis and to disaggregate the test which the Community courts generally bring to bear in relation to discretionary policy from the way in which they treat the specific allegations about proportionality and rights.

The judicial approach can be summarized as follows. The Community courts will continue to apply the test of manifest disproportionality to non-rights based claims that the discretionary policy measure was unsuited or unnecessary to achieve the desired aim. The most common rights-based claims raised by applicants who seek to challenge such Community measures are property rights or the right to pursue a profession, trade, or occupation. The Community courts have acknowledged such rights within the Community legal order, but have made it clear that they are not absolute and must be viewed in relation to their social function. The ECJ and CFI will therefore consider whether the restrictions imposed by the measure correspond to objectives of general interest pursued by the Community and whether they constitute a disproportionate and intolerable interference, which impairs the very substance of the rights guaranteed.[61]

This interconnection between common policies, proportionality, and rights is apparent in the early *Hauer* case.[62] The applicant challenged a Community Regulation that placed limitations on the planting of new vines. The Court found that this did not, in itself, constitute an invalid restriction on property rights. It then proceeded to determine whether the planting restrictions were disproportionate, 'impinging upon the very substance of the right to property'.[63] The Court found that they were not, but in reaching this conclusion it carefully examined the purpose of the general scheme in which the contested Regulation fell. The objects of this scheme were to attain a balanced wine market, with fair prices for consumers and a fair return for producers; the eradication of surpluses; and an improvement in the quality of wine. The disputed Regulation, which prohibited new plantings, was part of this overall plan. It was not disproportionate in the light of the legitimate, general Community policy for this area. This policy was designed to deal with an immediate problem of surpluses, while at the same time laying the foundation for more permanent measures to facilitate a balanced wine market.

The *British American Tobacco* case[64] provides a more recent example of the connection between common policies, proportionality, and rights. The applicants challenged a 2001 Directive made pursuant to Articles 95 and 133 EC, which was designed to approximate the laws of the Member States concerning the manufacture, presentation, and sale of tobacco products. An earlier tobacco advertising Directive had been struck down by the ECJ[65] and the applicants in the present case claimed that the 2001 Directive should fare no better. They argued that neither Articles 95 nor 133 EC furnished a proper legal basis for the measure, but the ECJ found to the contrary and held that since the measure genuinely aimed to improve the functioning of the internal market it could be made under Article 95 EC. The applicants also maintained that the Directive was disproportionate in a number of respects. This was so in particular with regard to provisions of the Directive

[61] Case 265/87, *Schräder HS Kraftfutter GmbH & Co KG v Hauptzollamt Gronau* [1989] ECR 2237, at para. 15; Case C-280/93, *Germany v Council* [1994] ECR I-4973, at para. 78; Case C-200/96, *Musik Metronome GmbH v Music Point Hokamp GmbH* [1998] ECR I-1953, at para. 21; Case T-113/96, *Dubois et Fils SA v Council and Commission* [1998] ECR II-125, at paras. 74–75; Cases T-125 and 152/96, *Boehringer Ingelheim Vetmedica, supra* n. 14, at paras. 102–103; Case C-293/97, *R v Secretary of State for the Environment and Ministry of Agriculture, Fisheries and Food, ex p Standley* [1999] ECR I-2603, at para. 54; Case T-13/99, *Pfizer, supra* n. 20, at paras. 456–457.

[62] Case 44/79, *Hauer v Land Rheinland-Pfalz* [1979] ECR 3727.

[63] Ibid. at para. 23.

[64] Case C-491/01, *R v Secretary of State for Health, ex p British American Tobacco, supra* n. 9.

[65] Case C-367/98, *Germany v Parliament and Council* [2000] ECR I-8419.

that prohibited statements on tobacco products to the effect that the product was less harmful than some other product because of low tar yields and the like, and because the Directive applied to export to non-Member countries. The applicants claimed further that the Directive infringed their fundamental right to property.

The ECJ accepted that proportionality required that the measure be suited to achieve the intended aim and that it should not go beyond what was necessary to do so. Where, however, the measure entailed political, social, and economic choice, involving complex assessments, the Community legislature must be allowed a broad discretion, the consequence being that the legality of the measure could only be affected if it was manifestly inappropriate with regard to the objective being pursued.[66] The ECJ found the Directive to be proportionate judged by these criteria. It held that the contested provision prohibiting the use of terms such as 'mild' or 'low tar' could be justified, given that they might mislead consumers into thinking that such products really were less harmful than others. The provisions rendering the Directive applicable to exports to non-Member countries were seen as warranted given the need to prevent evasion of the Community rules through illicit reimport of tobacco products that did not meet the requirements of those produced for use in the Community.

The ECJ then turned its attention to the argument based on infringement of property rights. The applicants maintained that the requirements for very large health warnings infringed their intellectual property rights. The Court was, not surprisingly, unconvinced. It held that while property was a right recognized by Community law, it was not an absolute right. Exercise of the right could be restricted provided that the restrictions corresponded to objectives of general interest pursued by the Community and did not constitute a 'disproportionate and intolerable interference, impairing the very substance of the rights guaranteed'.[67] Judged by this criterion the Directive was held to be proportionate. The provisions of the Directive limited the space on the packet on which the manufacturer could display its trade mark, but this was a proportionate restriction designed to allow the remainder of the space to be used for display of health warnings. Moreover the fact that the Directive prohibited certain descriptors on the packet did not prevent the manufacturer from using other distinctive signs to distinguish its product.[68]

The same approach is evident in other cases. Thus in *Booker Aquacultur*[69]

[66] Case C-491/01, *R v Secretary of State for Health, ex p British American Tobacco, supra* n. 9, paras, 122–123.

[67] Ibid. at para. 149.

[68] Ibid. at paras. 150–152.

[69] Cases C-20 and 64/00, *Booker Aquacultur Ltd and Hydro Seafood GSP Ltd v Scottish Ministers* [2003] ECR I-7411.

the applicants claimed that the failure of the UK government to provide compensation for fish destroyed pursuant to Community policy contained in a Directive infringed their right to property. The ECJ rejected the claim. It held that the Directive clearly pursued a legitimate Community objective, the safeguarding of health from diseased fish stock. The destruction of such stock was necessary to attain this aim. The absence of compensation did not constitute a disproportionate and intolerable interference impairing the very substance of the right to property. Fish farming carried certain commercial risks, of which the applicants were fully aware, and the Community measures were designed to facilitate the clearance of diseased stock, thereby enabling restocking as quickly as possible.

Similar reasoning is evident in *Spain and Finland v European Parliament and Council*[70] where the two governments contested the legality of a Directive making provision for working time in the road transport sector. They argued, *inter alia*, that the inclusion of self-employed drivers infringed the freedom to conduct a business and to pursue an occupation. The ECJ accepted that these freedoms were general principles of Community law.[71] However in accord with previous case law, the Court stated that those freedoms were not absolute. Restrictions could therefore be imposed provided that they corresponded to objectives of general interest and that in the light of the aim pursued they did not constitute a disproportionate and intolerable interference, which impaired the very substance of the right. The contested measure was intended to improve road safety, which was an objective of general interest. It did not affect the existence of the freedom to be a self-employed driver, but merely regulated the way in which this was pursued. The mode of regulation was proportionate given in particular that the Directive distinguished between the activities of the self-employed drivers directly linked to driving, to which the Directive was applicable, and administrative activities, which were not touched by the provision.

The CFI applied proportionality in a similar manner in the *Kadi* case.[72] The case was considered in the more general discussion of rights.[73] It will be recalled that the applicant sought the annulment of a Community Regulation freezing the applicant's assets, pursuant to a Security Council resolution made in the context of the policy to curb Al-Qaeda. The CFI decided that the Community courts could only indirectly review this Resolution if it infringed *jus cogens*. Hence insofar as respect for the right to property could be regarded as part of the mandatory rules of general international law, it was

[70] Cases C-184 and 223/02, *Spain and Finland v European Parliament and Council* [2004] ECR I-7789.

[71] Ibid. at para. 51.

[72] Case T-315/01, *Yassin Abdullah Kadi v Council and Commission*, judgment of 21 September 2005, not yet published.

[73] See above, at 535–537.

only an arbitrary deprivation of that right that could be regarded as contrary to *jus cogens.* The CFI held that the freezing of assets did not amount to an arbitrary and disproportionate interference with the applicant's property, because it was part of a legitimate international policy designed to preserve international peace and fight terrorism; the applicant's funds were frozen, not confiscated, and this affected the use of the funds but not the substance of the property right; and because the Security Council Resolution provided some albeit indirect mechanism for review of those whose funds were frozen.[74]

C. Evaluation

It is important to step back and evaluate the Courts' jurisprudence. The fact that fundamental rights are not regarded as absolute is not in itself problematic in normative terms. Legal systems generally recognize that the right to property, freedom to pursue a trade or an occupation can be subject to restrictions. This is equally true of rights such as free speech or association, which can be limited in certain instances as recognized by the European Convention on Human Rights (ECHR) and national legal systems. There may be rights that can be regarded as absolute, in the sense that they do not admit of limitation. The right not to be tortured is an obvious example. The ECJ's judgments were not, however, issued with such rights in mind, and it would be very likely to modify its position if faced with such a situation.[75]

The fact that any restrictions on the right must be justified by some objective of general interest pursued by the Community is, as seen above, a necessary condition for the legality of the measure. It is, however, difficult to regard this as a significant hurdle. The very fact that this condition is cast in such general terms, as opposed to the more discrete list of justified grounds for restrictions found in other rights-based documents, means that it will be rare for a measure not to surmount this hurdle. To put the same point another way, Community measures that limit rights will almost always be designed to attain some general interest pursued by the Community.

This brings us to the actual test used in the preceding cases. Assuming that there is a general interest pursued by the Community, restrictions will be upheld unless they constitute a disproportionate and intolerable interference, which impairs the very substance of the rights guaranteed. There are a number of issues concerning this test that should be disaggregated.

[74] Case T-315/01, *Kadi, supra* n. 72, at paras. 242–251.

[75] In Case C-112/00, *Schmidberger, Internationale Transporte und Planzüge v Austria* [2003] ECR I-5659, at para. 80 the ECJ noted that certain rights contained in the ECHR admitted of no limitation. The ECJ did not explicitly state that EU law would preclude derogations from such rights, but that is a reasonable implication from the judgment, given that the ECJ gave no hint of wishing to differ from the Convention jurisprudence in this respect.

It is fitting to begin with its scope of application. We noted earlier that the test was developed and applied principally in cases where the applicant claimed that the right to property or the freedom to pursue a trade, profession, or business had been infringed by a Community discretionary measure. This begs the question of whether the test will also be used in relation to other rights. The case law provides no certain answer to this.[76] In *Connolly*[77] the ECJ considered whether the removal of a Community official from his post because he had published without permission a book that was highly critical of EU monetary policy was unlawful on the ground that it infringed the applicant's freedom of speech. The details of the judgment do not concern us here. What is apposite is that the ECJ, in reaching its conclusions about limitations of rights, followed the ECHR jurisprudence with its emphasis on the necessity for the limitation, the existence of a pressing social need, and strict scrutiny of the rationale for the restriction. In *Schmidberger*[78] the approach was rather different. The Austrian government gave implicit permission for a demonstration by an environmental group on the Brenner motorway, the effect of which was to close it for 30 hours. Schmidberger ran a transport firm and argued that the closure of the motorway was in breach of EU law on free movement of goods. The issue before the ECJ was the relation between Article 28 EC on free movement, and freedom of expression and assembly as protected by Articles 10 and 11 of the ECHR and the Austrian Constitution. Once again it is not the detail of the judgment that concerns us here.[79] What is relevant for present purposes is that the test applied by the ECJ was identical to that used in the property/freedom to trade cases. Thus the ECJ stated that freedom of expression and assembly were part of Community law; that they were not absolute, but must be viewed in relation to their social purpose; and that restrictions could be justified if they corresponded to objectives of general interest and did not constitute disproportionate and unacceptable interference, which impaired the very substance of the right.[80]

This leads naturally onto the meaning of the EU test and the extent to which it differs from that applied by the Strasbourg courts. It might be argued that there is no tension since the two tests do not in reality differ. On this view the criterion developed by the ECJ in relation to property/freedom to trade and applied to speech in *Schmidberger* is no different from that used in Strasbourg and applied in *Connolly*. We should hesitate before endorsing this conclusion. A test premised on a finding of some general Community

[76] See more generally on this point, Peers, 'Taking Rights Away? Limitations and Derogations', in S. Peers and A. Ward (eds), *The EU Charter of Fundamental Rights, Politics, Law and Policy* (Hart, 2004), at 142–149.

[77] Case C-274/99 P, *Connolly v Commission* [2001] ECR I-1611.

[78] Case C-112/00, *Schmidberger, supra* n. 75.

[79] See above, at 513–514.

[80] Case C-112/00, *Schmidberger, supra* n. 75, at para. 80.

interest, coupled with the requirement that the restrictions do not constitute disproportionate and intolerable/unacceptable interference, which impairs the very substance of the right, is not self-evidently the same as one framed in terms of specific grounds for limiting rights, coupled with strict scrutiny as to whether the restriction is necessary to meet a pressing social need and proportionate to that end. This is so notwithstanding the fact that the application of the two tests might lead to the same result in a particular case.

Hesitation is warranted moreover by the very ambiguity latent in the test commonly applied by the ECJ. Consider in this respect the meaning of the key phrase, a 'disproportionate and intolerable interference, which impairs the very substance of the rights guaranteed'. The inclusion of the latter part of this formulation, to the effect that the restriction should not impair the very substance of the right, is derived from German law.[81] It captures the idea that a restriction should not be deemed lawful if it undermines the essence of the guaranteed right. It can, however, also have a rather different connotation, to the effect that a restriction will be deemed to be lawful provided that it does not infringe the essence of that right. Whether intended or not, the wording of the ECJ's formulation that restrictions will be lawful provided that they do not constitute a disproportionate and intolerable interference that impairs the substance of the right, carries the latter connotation rather than the former.

The significance of the criterion for limitation is further reinforced by contrasting the ECJ's test with that found in the Charter of Rights.[82] Article 52(1) provides:

> Any limitation on the exercise of the rights and freedoms recognized by this Charter must be provided for by law and respect the essence of those rights and freedoms. Subject to the principle of proportionality, limitations may be made only if they are necessary and genuinely meet objectives of general interest recognized by the Union or the need to protect the rights and freedoms of others.

The framing of the Article as a whole, coupled with the shift in language from impairing the substance of the right to respecting its essence, gives the limitation clause a different feel from the test currently used by the ECJ. Article 52(1) makes it clear that any limitation must respect the essence of the right, and that even if it does it will only be lawful if proportionate, necessary, and in the general interest.

In striving to understand the uncertainties and difficulties that inhere in the existing test we should not, however, lose sight of the practical dimension. We should reflect on whether that test has led to 'bad' decisions, or decisions

[81] de Witte, 'The Past and Future Role of the European Court of Justice in the Protection of Human Rights', in P. Alston (ed), with M. Bustelo and J. Heenan, *The EU and Human Rights* (Oxford University Press, 1999), at 880.

[82] Charter of Fundamental Rights of the European Union, OJ 2000 C364/1.

that we feel should have gone the other way and would have done so if a different test had been employed. This is of course a difficult question on which commentators can legitimately differ. There is no doubt that some cases have caused disquiet, with claimants feeling that the ECJ has given less weight to a right than it should have done.[83] If, however, one reflects on the leading cases discussed above where applicants have argued that the discretionary measure infringes a right to property or freedom to pursue a trade it is difficult to avoid the conclusion that most such claims were rather weak on the facts. This does not obviate the need for critical scrutiny as to whether the test used by the Community courts is framed in the right way. But it does indicate that the test is not in general leading to unjust outcomes.

5. PROPORTIONALITY, PENALTIES, AND FINANCIAL BURDEN

A. The General Approach

Proportionality has regularly been used by applicants claiming that a penalty or other financial burden is excessive. The Community courts have less reason for reticence in this type of case, primarily because a penalty or financial burden can be struck down without thereby undermining the entirety of the administrative or legislative policy with which it is connected. They have made it clear that where Community rules impose a primary and a secondary obligation, the penalty for failure to fulfil the latter obligation should generally be less onerous than that imposed for failure to comply with the primary duty.[84]

There has been a regular stream of such cases, in which the essence of the proportionality argument is that a penalty was excessive in relation to the aim of the measure. In *Man (Sugar)*[85] the applicant was required to give a security deposit to the Board when seeking a licence to export sugar outside the Community. The applicant was then late, but only by four hours, in completing the relevant paperwork. The Board, acting pursuant to a Community Regulation, declared the entire deposit of £1,670,370 to be forfeit. Not surprisingly the company was aggrieved. The Court held that the automatic forfeiture of the entire deposit in the event of any failure to fulfil the time requirement was too drastic, given the function performed by the system of

[83] de Witte, *supra* n. 81, at 878–882.

[84] Case 122/78, *Buitoni v Forma* [1979] ECR 677; Case C-104/94, *Cereol Italia v Azienda Agricola Castello* [1995] ECR I-2983; Case C-161/96, *Südzucker Mannheim/Ochsenfurt AG v Hauptzollamt Mannheim* [1998] ECR I-281.

[85] Case 181/84, *R. v Intervention Board, ex p E. D. & F. Man (Sugar) Ltd* [1985] ECR 2889.

export licences.[86] The same reasoning underlies the decision in *Atalanta*,[87] where the ECJ held that provisions of a Community Regulation concerned with storage aid for pig meat, which stipulated that the security would be forfeited if the obligations imposed by the storage contract were not fulfilled were disproportionate, because they did not enable the penalty to be made commensurate with the seriousness of the contractual breach.

In addition to cases dealing with penalties *stricto sensu* the Court has applied proportionality in the field of economic regulation, scrutinizing the level of charges imposed by the Community institutions. Thus in *Bela-Mühle*[88] the Court held that a scheme whereby producers of animal feed were forced to use skimmed milk, rather than soya, in their product, in order to reduce a milk surplus, was unlawful. Skimmed milk was three times more expensive than soya: the obligation to purchase the milk, therefore, imposed a disproportionate burden on the animal feed producers.

There have been other, more recent, cases in which the essence of the argument was that the burden imposed by a Community norm was excessive. 'Mad cow' disease, and the Community response thereto, generated a number of such cases. Thus in *Portugal v Commission*[89] Portugal argued that an export ban on meat products, imposed in response to mad cow disease, was disproportionate. This was because Portugal was not a significant meat exporter, and it was therefore easier to regulate low-volume exports as compared to the large volume exports from the UK. The ECJ rejected the argument. Beef exports from the UK had not been allowed until the UK had put in place export arrangements of a kind advocated by a certain health code. This had not been done at the time when the ban was imposed on Portugal.

B. Proportionality, Penalties, and Legislative Objectives

While the Community courts will review the proportionality of penalties with some rigour, it is also clear that they apply the principle so as to effectuate the aims of the relevant Treaty provisions or legislation. This explains the

[86] Case 181/84, [1985] ECR 2889 at para. 29; Case 240/78, *Atalanta Amsterdam BV v Produktschap voor Vee en Vlees* [1979] ECR 2137; Case 122/78, *Buitoni SA v Fonds d'Orientation et de Régularisation des Marchés Agricoles* [1979] ECR 677.

[87] Case 240/78, *Atalanta Amsterdam BV v Produktschap voor Vee en Vlees* [1979] ECR 2137. See also, Case 21/85, *Maas & Co NV v Bundesanstalt für landwirtschaftliche Marktordnung* [1986] ECR 3537.

[88] Case 114/76, *Bela-Mühle Josef Bergman KG v Grows-Farm GmbH & Co. KG* [1977] ECR 1211; Case 116/76, *Granaria BV v Hoofdprodukschap voor Akkerbouwprodukten* [1977] ECR 1247; Cases 119 and 120/76, *Ölmühle Hambourg AG v Hauptzollamt Hamburg-Waltershof* [1977] ECR 1269. See also, Case C-295/94, *Hupeden & Co KG v Hauptzollamt Hamburg-Jonas* [1996] ECR I-3375; Case C-296/94, *Pietsch v Hauptzollamt Hamburg-Waltershof* [1996] ECR I-3409.

[89] Case C-365/99, [2001] ECR I-5645.

oft-repeated statements that the obligation to recover unlawful state aid with interest cannot be regarded as disproportionate, given that the objective of Article 87 EC is to eliminate illegal state aid.[90] The same theme is to be found in the jurisprudence on proportionality and the Structural Funds. The legal framework that governs this area was considered in detail in a previous chapter.[91] Applicants have not infrequently challenged decisions reducing or cancelling the aid given under the Structural Funds, arguing that this was a disproportionate response to the breach of the condition attached to the funding. The application of proportionality in this context is clearly shaped by the desire to ensure that the aims of this funding system are attained.

This is exemplified by *Conserve Italia*.[92] The ECJ held that it was essential for the proper functioning of the system of controls set up to ensure proper use of Community funds that applicants for aid provided the Commission with information that was reliable and not apt to mislead. The fact that the beneficiary of the assistance had failed to fulfil its obligation not to start work on the project before receipt by the Commission of the aid application, and that it forwarded inaccurate information about the contract of sale for a machine referred to in the project, constituted serious breaches of fundamental obligations under the scheme. The ECJ concluded that 'only the possibility that an irregularity may be penalized not by reduction of the aid by the amount corresponding to the irregularity, but by complete cancellation of the aid can produce the deterrent effect required to ensure the proper management of the resources of the EAGGF'.[93]

The Community courts will nonetheless treat claims concerning the proportionality of a reduction or discontinuance in funding seriously. Thus in *Astipeca*[94] the CFI decided that a reduction in fisheries assistance on the ground that a vessel had breached the conditions by fishing in the wrong waters was proportionate, but only after it had considered the facts and arguments of the applicant in considerable detail.[95] And in one of the many

[90] Case C-142/87, *Belgium v Commission* [1990] ECR I-959, at para. 66; Case C-169/95, *Spain v Commission* [1997] ECR I-135, at para. 47; Case T-55/99, *CETM v Commission* [2000] ECR II-3207, at paras. 160–164; Case T-288/97, *Regione Fiuli Venezia Giulia v Commission* [2001] ECR II-1169, at para. 105; Case 372/97, *Italy v Commission* [2004] ECR I-3679, at para. 103; Case C-278/00, *Greece v Commission* [2004] ECR I-3997, at para. 103.

[91] See above, Chap. 3.

[92] Case C-500/99 P, *Conserve Italia Soc. Coop arl v Commission* [2002] ECR I-867.

[93] Ibid. at para. 101. See also, Case T-199/99, *Sgaravatti Mediterranea Srl v Commission* [2002] ECR II-3731, at paras. 134–138; Case T-186/00, *Conserve Italia Soc. Coop rl v Commission* [2003] ECR II-719, at paras. 83–89; Case T-305/00, *Conserve Italia Soc. Coop rl v Commission* [2003] ECR II-5659, at paras. 110–120; Cases T-61 and 62/00, *APOL and AIPO v Commission* [2003] ECR II-635, at para. 119; Case T-340/00, *Communita Montana della Valnerina v Commission* [2003] ECR II-811.

[94] Case T-180/00, *Astipeca SL v Commission* [2002] ECR II-3985.

[95] Ibid. at paras. 77–114.

Conserve Italia cases[96] the CFI held that a Commission reduction in funding by an amount approximately 20 times greater than the breaches complained of was disproportionate, since it bore no relationship to the relative lack of seriousness of the infringement and the applicant had no fraudulent intent.

C. Penalties and Unlimited Jurisdiction

The cases considered thus far involve review of penalties by the Community courts for compliance with proportionality. There are, however, areas where they have unlimited jurisdiction in relation to penalties. Article 229 EC states that regulations adopted by the European Parliament (EP) and Council or by the Council alone may give the Court of Justice unlimited jurisdiction with regard to the penalties provided for in those regulations. The Council and EP have conferred such power on the ECJ.[97] This is especially important since fines are regularly challenged in competition cases, a fact that is unsurprising given the very large sums of money involved.[98] Proportionality may still of course figure in the argument in these cases, since this is used to support the applicant's claim that the fine should be reduced.[99] This does not alter the fact that the Community courts have unlimited jurisdiction and can alter the fine irrespective of whether any proportionality argument can be sustained.

D. Evaluation

The courts' jurisprudence in relation to proportionality, penalties, and financial burdens is relatively uncontroversial. The judicial starting point is close scrutiny of the contested measure, an approach influenced by the fact that such cases will commonly involve annulment either of a single administrative act or a particular article of a regulation, without calling into question the

[96] Case T-306/00, *Conserve Italia Soc. Coop. rl v Commission* [2003] ECR II-5705, at paras. 127–150.

[97] See, e.g., Council Regulation 17 [1959–62] OJ Eng. Spec. Ed at 87, Art. 17; Council Regulation 4064/89/EEC of 21 December 1989, On the Control of Concentrations between Undertakings, OJ 1990 L257/13, Art. 16.

[98] For some recent examples, see, Cases C-238, 244, 245, 247, 250, 252, and 254/99 P, *Limburgse Vinyl Maatschappij NV v Commission* [2002] ECR I-8375; Case T-224/00, *Archer Daniels Midland Company and Archer Daniels Midland Ingredients Ltd v Commission* [2003] ECR II-2597; Case T-223/00, *Kyowa Hakko Kogyo Co Ltd and Kyowa Hakko Europe GmbH v Commission* [2003] ECR II-2553; Case T-219/99, *British Airways plc v Commission* [2003] ECR II-5917; Case C-359/01 P, *British Sugar plc v Commission* [2004] ECR I-4933; Cases C-204–5, 211, 213, 217, 219/00 P, *Aalborg Portland A/s and others v Commission* [2004] ECR I-123.

[99] See, e.g., Case T-59/99, *Ventouris Group Enterprises SA v Commission* [2003] ECR II-5257.

more general legislative schema.[100] The considerations that operate to limit proportionality review of discretionary policy choices are largely absent here. It is, moreover, not surprising that the ECJ and CFI should take account of the objectives of the relevant Treaty provisions or legislative scheme when deciding on how to deal with proportionality claims in areas such as state aids and the Structural Funds. The appropriateness and necessity of a penalty or financial burden can best be determined in the light of the legislative objectives pertaining to the particular area.

6. CONCLUSION

The centrality of proportionality to EU administrative law is readily apparent from the preceding analysis. We should be aware in this respect of the need for careful identification of the positive law and of the normative foundations on which it is based. We should also be mindful of the connections between proportionality and other related grounds of review. Proportionality will often be but one of the grounds of challenge in a case. The link between this principle and review for manifest error is especially important, all the more so given the increased force with which the latter has been imbued through recent developments in the case law.[101]

[100] See also, Case T-211/02, *Tideland Signal Ltd v Commission* [2002] ECR II-3781, at paras. 39–44.

[101] See above, at Chap. 13.

18

Proportionality II

1. INTRODUCTION

The discussion in the previous chapter was concerned with challenge to Community action on the ground of proportionality. This head of review has, however, also been frequently used to contest the legality of Member State action. It is to this issue that we now turn.[1]

The discussion begins with positive law and analysis of the principal areas in which proportionality is used to contest the legality of Member State action. The application of proportionality in the context of the four freedoms will be considered, to be followed by examination of the case law on proportionality and equality, with the focus then shifting to the way in which proportionality constrains the way in which Member States implement and apply Community legislation.

The remainder of the chapter is normative in orientation. We shall look more closely at the intensity of review and the justification for the close scrutiny that the Community courts bring to bear when applying proportionality to Member State action. It will also become apparent that the European Court of Justice (ECJ) is nonetheless willing to apply proportionality in a way that is tolerant of differences in Member State values. The chapter concludes by considering the allocation of responsibility as between the ECJ and the national courts when deciding on the application of proportionality.

2. POSITIVE LAW: THE FOUR FREEDOMS

It is important at the outset to be aware of the paradigm case in which

[1] J. Schwarze, *European Administrative Law* (Sweet & Maxwell, 1992), Chap. 5; de Búrca, 'The Principle of Proportionality and its Application in EC Law' (1993) 13 *YBEL* 105; N. Emiliou, *The Principle of Proportionality in European Law* (Kluwer, 1996); G. Gerapetritis, *Proportionality in Administrative Law* (Sakkoulas, 1997); E. Ellis, (ed), *The Principle of Proportionality in the Laws of Europe* (Hart, 1999); T. Tridimas, *The General Principles of EC Law* (Oxford University Press, 1999), Chap. 4; U. Bernitz and J. Nergelius, *General Principles of European Community Law* (Kluwer, 2000).

proportionality is used to contest the legality of Member State action. This is where the Community courts have found a *prima facie* infringement of one of the four freedoms concerning goods, workers, freedom of establishment and the provision of services, and free movement of capital. The defendant Member State then seeks to rely on a defence allowed by the Treaty, to the effect that the infringement of the freedom was justified on one of the specified grounds laid down in the relevant Treaty article. Thus to take an example, Article 30 EC states that:

> The provisions of Articles 28 and 29 EC shall not preclude prohibitions or restrictions on imports, exports or goods in transit justified on grounds of public morality, public policy or public security; the protection of health and life of humans, animals or plants; the protection of national treasures possessing artistic, historic or archaeological value; or the protection of industrial and commercial property. Such prohibitions or restrictions shall not, however, constitute a means of arbitrary discrimination or a disguised restriction on trade between Member States.

Similar provisions exist in relation to the other freedoms.[2] The Community courts have construed such provisions strictly. The challenged rule must come within one of the listed categories, and the burden of proof will rest with the Member State seeking to rely on the exception.[3] The Member State action must also pass a test of proportionality. This is not an explicit condition for the application of the Treaty provisions allowing limitations to be placed on the four freedoms, but the ECJ has nonetheless demanded that the challenged measure must be the least restrictive possible to attain the end in view.

The proportionality requirement was read in as an underlying requirement flowing from the last sentence of Article 30. The requirement that a restriction of free movement justified on grounds of, for example, public health should not constitute a means of arbitrary discrimination or a disguised restriction on trade between Member States was taken by the Community courts to warrant the application of proportionality, thereby enabling them to check whether such a measure went beyond that which was necessary in all the circumstances. Analogous reasoning has, as will be seen, been used to justify the application of proportionality when a Member State seeks to take advantage of one of the mandatory requirements in the context of indistinctly applicable rules.[4] Member States must in addition comply

[2] Arts. 39(3), 46, 55, 58 EC.

[3] Case C-17/93, *Openbaar Ministerie v Van der Veldt* [1994] ECR I-3537; Case C-358/95, *Morellato v Unita Sanitaria Locale (USL) n. 11 di Pordenone* [1997] ECR I-1431, at para. 14; Case C-14/02, *ATRAL SA v Belgium* [2003] ECR I-4431, at para. 67.

[4] P. Craig and G. de Búrca, *EU Law, Text, Cases and Materials* (Oxford University Press, 3rd ed., 2003), at 636–658.

with proportionality when adopting measures to implement Community legislation.[5]

The Community courts tend to engage in fairly intensive review in order to determine whether the restriction which the Member State has imposed on an important right granted by the Treaties really is necessary or warranted. This same theme can be seen throughout the Court's case law when dealing with free movement, whether of goods, persons, establishment and the provision of services or capital.[6]

A. Goods

There are numerous examples of proportionality in the context of free movement of goods.[7] The judicial approach is exemplified by *Sandoz*.[8] Holland refused to allow the sale of muesli bars that contained added vitamins, on the ground that the vitamins were dangerous to public health, notwithstanding the fact that the muesli bars were readily available in Germany and Belgium. It was accepted that vitamins could be beneficial to health, but it was acknowledged that excessive consumption could be harmful. Scientific evidence was not certain as regards the point at which consumption of vitamins became excessive, particularly because vitamins consumed in one source of food might be added to those eaten from a different food source. The ECJ accepted that in so far as there were uncertainties in the scientific research it was for the Member States, in the absence of harmonization, to decide what degree of protection to afford to human health. National rules prohibiting the marketing of foodstuffs with added vitamins could therefore be justified in principle. This was, however, subject to proportionality, which underlay the last sentence of Article 30 EC, thereby requiring that limits on imports should be restricted to what was necessary to attain public health. Proportionality required that the Member State should authorize marketing when the addition of vitamins to foodstuffs met a real need, especially a technical or nutritional one.[9]

[5] Case C-313/99, *Mulligan and others v Minister for Agriculture and Food, Northern Ireland* [2002] ECR I-5719, at paras. 35–36; Cases C-480–2, 484, 489, 490–1, 497–9/00, *Azienda Agricole Ettore Ribaldi v AIMA* [2004] ECR I-2943, at para. 43.

[6] Space precludes specific treatment of proportionality and capital; for a recent example, see, Case C-334/02, *Commission v France* [2004] ECR I-2229.

[7] See, e.g., Case 104/75, *de Peijper* [1976] ECR 613; Case 261/81, *Walter Rau Lebensmittelwerke v De Smedt, Pvba* [1982] ECR 3961; Case 124/81, *Commission v UK* [1983] ECR 203; Case 72/83, *Campus Oil Ltd v Minister for Industry and Energy* [1984] ECR 2727; Case C-62/90, *Commission v Germany* [1992] ECR I-2575; Case C-124/95, *R, ex p Centro-Com v HM Treasury and Bank of England* [1997] ECR I-81.

[8] Case 174/82, *Officier van Justitie v Sandoz BV* [1983] ECR 2445

[9] See also, Case 53/80, *Officier van Justitie v Koniklijke Kassfabriek Eyssen BV* [1981] ECR 409; Case 94/83, *Albert Heijin BV* [1984] ECR 3263; Case 178/84, *Commission v Germany*

We can see the same approach at work in the famous *Cassis de Dijon* case.[10] The Court decided that a German rule which prescribed the minimum alcohol content for a certain alcoholic beverage could constitute an impediment to the free movement of goods. The Court then considered whether the rule was necessary in order to protect consumers from being misled. It rejected the defence, because the interests of consumers could be safeguarded in other, less restrictive ways, by displaying the alcohol content on the packaging of the drinks.[11]

It is moreover clear from the case law that when assessing proportionality the Community courts will pay special attention to the factual basis on which the defence is based. It is not enough for a Member State simply to assert that a measure is warranted on grounds of public health. It will also need to produce evidence or data to substantiate this claim. This is exemplified by *Commission v Italy*.[12] The Commission challenged an Italian law that required prior authorization and payment of administrative costs in relation to the manufacture and import of food products for sportsmen. The ECJ in accord with established case law held that the Italian law constituted a measure having equivalent effect to a quantitative restriction and was therefore caught by Article 28 EC. The Italian government argued by way of defence that the measure could be justified on grounds of public health, either within Article 30 EC or within the mandatory requirements laid down by the *Cassis* ruling. The ECJ was unconvinced. It held that it was for the Italian authorities to show that their law came within Article 30 or the mandatory requirements, and that it was proportionate.[13]

> Despite the requests of the Commission, the Italian government has not shown any alleged risk to public health which the products in question are likely to pose. It failed to explain on what scientific data or medical reports the guidelines which it enclosed were based and has not given general information on those alleged risks. Furthermore, it has not made clear the link between the procedure in question and the alleged risk to public health, nor explained the reasons why such protection is more effective than other forms of control and thus proportionate to the objective pursued.

The ECJ was also unimpressed with the claim that the Italian law might be

[1987] ECR 1227; Case 304/84, *Ministère Public v Muller* [1986] ECR 1511; Case C-62/90, *Commission v Germany* [1992] ECR I-2575; Case C-239/02, *Douwe Egberts NV v Westrom Pharma NV* [2004] ECR I-7007.

[10] Case 120/78, *Rewe Zentrale v Bundesmonopolverwaltung für Branntwein* [1979] ECR 649.

[11] See also, Case C-217/99, *Commission v Belgium* [2000] ECR I-10251; Case C-473/98, *Kemikalieinspektionen v Toolex Alpha AB* [2000] ECR I-5681; Case C-20/03, *Criminal Proceedings against Burmanjer, Van der Linden and de Jong* [2005] ECR I-4133.

[12] Case 270/02, *Commission v Italy* [2004] ECR I-1559.

[13] Ibid. at para. 24.

justified as protective of consumers. It had not been shown how the prior authorization procedure was necessary and proportionate to that objective. There were moreover less restrictive measures that could be devised to prevent consumers from being misled, such as obligations relating to the accuracy of the labelling and the veracity of the factual data presented on the label.[14]

The Community courts will insist on some factual evidence to substantiate the claim even where there may be some scientific uncertainty about the matter in issue. This is evident from *Commission v Netherlands*.[15] The Commission brought proceedings against a Dutch law and administrative practice based thereon whereby foodstuffs for every day consumption that were fortified with certain vitamins and minerals, which had been lawfully marketed in another Member State, could be marketed in the Netherlands only if the enrichment provided by the vitamins and minerals met a nutritional need in the Netherlands population. This was unsurprisingly found to be in breach of Article 28 EC, and the focus then shifted to a public health justification under Article 30. The ECJ accepted that it might be lawful for a Member State in accord with the precautionary principle to require prior authorization before foodstuffs could be marketed with nutrients other than those whose addition was lawful under the national legislation. The Member State must, however, comply with proportionality: the means chosen must be confined to what was necessary to safeguard public health and must be proportional to the objective pursued, which could not be attained by less restrictive measures. Since Article 30 was an exception to Article 28 it should be interpreted strictly.[16]

A decision to prohibit the marketing of a fortified foodstuff, which indeed constitutes the most restrictive obstacle to trade in products lawfully manufactured in other Member States, can be adopted only if the real risk for public health alleged appears sufficiently established on the basis of the latest scientific data available at the date of the adoption of such decision. In such a context, the object of the risk assessment to be carried out by the Member State is to appraise the degree of probability of harmful effects on human health from the addition of certain nutrients to foodstuffs and the seriousness of those potential effects.

The ECJ acknowledged that there could be uncertainties in this assessment and accepted that these could affect the scope of the Member State's discretion and the way in which the precautionary principle was applied. A Member State could therefore in accord with the precautionary principle take protective measures without having to wait until the existence and gravity of the risks became fully apparent. Notwithstanding this latitude afforded to the

[14] Ibid. at para. 25.
[15] Case C-41/02, *Commission v Netherlands* [2004] ECR I-11375.
[16] Ibid. at para. 49.

Member State, the ECJ concluded that the Netherlands government had not produced scientific studies showing that any intake of the nutrients in question over and above the recommended daily allowance entailed a risk for public health.[17]

B. Workers and Persons

The juridical technique considered above is also evident in relation to workers, where the ECJ has insisted that derogation from the principle of free movement can only be sanctioned in cases which pose a genuine and serious threat to public policy, and even then the measure must be the least restrictive possible in the circumstances.

Thus in *Rutili*[18] the ECJ considered the legality of a measure taken by France limiting the area in which the applicant, an Italian national, could reside and move. It held that free movement of workers was fundamental to the Treaty and that therefore any measure limiting that right had to be strictly construed. Restrictions on freedom of movement within a state could only be imposed to meet a genuine and serious threat posed by the particular worker. This conclusion was reinforced by reference to the European Convention on Human Rights (ECHR), and to the reasoning drawn from a number of Convention articles, to the effect that restrictions could only be justified if they were necessary in a democratic society.

It is clear, moreover, from cases such as *Commission v Austria*[19] that the Member State must adduce evidence to support its claim that the measure it has adopted is appropriate for the problem addressed and that it is the least restrictive possible and hence proportionate.

C. Establishment and the Provision of Services

The same principle is apparent in cases on freedom of establishment[20] and the provision of services. *Commission v Greece*[21] provides a clear example in relation to establishment. The ECJ found that a Greek law that prohibited a

[17] Ibid. at paras. 52–67. See also, Case C-192/01, *Commission v Denmark* [2003] ECR I-9693; Case C-24/00, *Commission v France* [2004] ECR I-1277; Case C-212/03, *Commission v France* [2005] ECR I-4213, at paras. 40–44.

[18] Case 36/75, *Rutili v Ministre de l'Intérieur* [1975] ECR 1219. See also, Case 30/77, *R v Bouchereau* [1977] ECR 1999; Case C-413/99, *Baumbast and R v Secretary of State for the Home Department* [2002] ECR I-7091, at para. 94; Cases C-482 and 493/01, *Georgios Orfanopoulos and others v Land Baden-Württemberg* [2004] ECR I-5257, at para. 99.

[19] Case C-147/03, *Commission v Austria* [2005] ECR I-5969, at para. 63.

[20] Case C-299/02, *Commission v Netherlands* [2004] ECR I-9761.

[21] Case C-140/03, *Commission v Greece* [2005] ECR I-3177.

qualified optician from operating more than one optician's shop constituted a restriction on freedom of establishment, notwithstanding the alleged absence of any discrimination on grounds of nationality. Greece argued that the prohibition was justified to protect public health, more specifically to safeguard the personal relationship of trust within the optician's shop, and to ensure the liability of the optician who owned the shop. The Greek government also maintained that these objectives could not be attained by less restrictive measures. The ECJ disagreed. In a brief judgment, the Court held that the protection of public health could be attained by less restrictive measures 'for example by requiring the presence of qualified, salaried opticians or associates in each optician's shop, rules concerning civil liability for the actions of others, and rules requiring professional indemnity insurance'.[22]

The approach is, not surprisingly, consistent in the context of services.[23] In *Van Binsbergen*[24] the ECJ considered the legality of a provision of Dutch law requiring those who acted as legal representatives before certain courts and tribunals to be established within the Netherlands. The lawyer in question was a Dutch national, but had moved to Belgium, and sought to rely on the Community law provisions concerning freedom to provide services. The ECJ accepted that the particular nature of the service to be provided could justify the imposition of special requirements where their purpose was justified by some common good, such as the application of rules relating to professional ethics, supervision, and liability, more especially if those rules could be evaded if the person provided the service from another Member State. The requirement that those concerned with the administration of justice must be permanently established for professional purposes within the jurisdiction of certain courts or tribunals was not therefore incompatible with the Treaty provisions on freedom to provide services, where the requirement was objectively justified on the preceding grounds. This was subject to the qualification that the objective could not be secured by less restrictive measures. Applied here, the objectives pursued by the Dutch measure could be attained by less restrictive means. An address for service within the jurisdiction could be demanded, without stipulating that the lawyer should actually reside in the Netherlands.

This judicial reasoning was reiterated and developed in later cases. Thus in *Corsten*[25] the ECJ decided that the requirement that an undertaking in one

[22] Ibid. at para. 35. See also, Case C-193/94, *Criminal Proceedings against Sofia Skanavi and Konstantin Chryssanthakopoulos* [1996] ECR I-929; Case C-167/01, *Kamer van Koophandel en Fabrieken voor Amsterdam v Inspire Art Ltd* [2003] ECR I-10155.

[23] Case C-60/00, *Carpenter v Secretary of State for the Home Department* [2002] ECR I-6279, at paras. 40–4; Case C-445/03, *Commission v Luxemburg* [2004] ECR I-10191.

[24] Case 33/74, *Van Binsbergen v Bestuur van de Bedrijfsvereniging Metaalnijverheid* [1974] ECR 1299; Case 39/75, *Coenen v Social Economische Raad* [1975] ECR 1547.

[25] Case C-58/98, *Corsten* [2000] ECR I-7919.

Member State should have to be entered on the trade register of the Member State in which it was to provide the service was a restriction within the meaning of Article 49 EC. While such a restriction could be justified on public interest grounds, such as the objective of guaranteeing the quality of the skilled work and the protection of those who commissioned it, the national rules should not go beyond what was necessary to attain the objective. The authorization procedure could not delay or complicate exercise of the Community right, where the conditions for engaging in that type of work had already been examined in the home Member State. The ECJ held in addition that the authorization procedure in the host Member State could not lead to administrative expense for the service provider, nor could it result in an obligation to pay subscriptions to the chamber of trades.[26]

The legality of prior authorization was at issue once again in *Canal*.[27] The applicant challenged national legislation that rendered the marketing of certain television satellite services subject to prior authorization and registration of the details of their equipment in a national register. The ECJ found that this restricted both free movement of goods and freedom to provide services. It could therefore only be justified if it pursued a public interest objective recognized by Community law. It should also comply with proportionality, in the sense of being appropriate to achieve the aim pursued and not go beyond what was necessary to achieve it. Compliance with proportionality required in this instance that the prior administrative authorization scheme should be based on objective, non-discriminatory criteria that were known in advance.[28] The ECJ held, moreover, that such a measure could not satisfy the necessity requirement of the proportionality test if the registration requirement duplicated controls that had already been carried out, either in the same state or in another Member State.[29] Nor could it be regarded as necessary if subsequent as opposed to prior authorization could achieve the objective sought by the national provision, or where the duration and disproportionate costs of complying with the national measures deterred the operators from pursuing their business plans.[30]

[26] See also, Case C-493/99, *Commission v Germany* [2001] ECR I-8163; Case C-215/01, *Schnitzer* [2003] ECR I-14847.

[27] Case C-390/99, *Canal Satélite Digital SL v Administación General del Estado and Distribuidora de Television Digital SA (DTS)* [2002] ECR I-607.

[28] Ibid. at para. 35. See also, Cases C-358 and 416/93, *Criminal Proceedings against Bordessa, Mellado and Maestre* [1995] ECR I-361, at para. 25; Case C-157/99, *BSM Geraets-Smits v Stichting Ziekenfonds VGZ* [2001] ECR I-5473, at para. 90; Case C-205/99, *Analir v Administración General del Estado* [2001] ECR I-1271, at para. 38.

[29] Ibid. at para. 38.

[30] Ibid. at paras. 39–42.

3. POSITIVE LAW: EQUALITY AND DISCRIMINATION

The discussion thus far has been concerned with the application of proportionality in the context of litigation about the four freedoms. Proportionality has also featured in the case law on equality and discrimination. This is a complex topic.[31] It is nonetheless important to convey the way in which proportionality is applied in some of the areas that comprise EU equality law.

A. Equal Treatment

The jurisprudence on equal treatment can be taken by way of example. The aim of Directive 76/207[32] was to secure equal treatment between men and women in three broad, employment-related areas: access to employment and promotion, vocational training, and working conditions. Article 2(1) defined the equal-treatment principle to prohibit any discrimination 'on grounds of sex either directly or indirectly by reference in particular to marital or family status.' This was qualified by Article 2(2), which allowed a Member State to exclude from the field of application of the Directive those occupational activities, and where appropriate the training leading thereto, in respect of which 'by reason of their nature or the context in which they are carried out' the sex of the worker constitutes a determining factor.

Article 2(2) was considered in *Johnston*,[33] in which the Royal Ulster Constabulary (RUC) sought to justify its decision not to employ women as full-time members of the RUC Reserve. It was argued that if women were permitted to carry and use firearms, they would be at greater risk of becoming targets for assassination. It was argued by the Commission that the occupational activity of an armed police officer could not be considered as an activity for which the sex of the officer was a determining factor, and moreover that if an exception were to be made in relation to specific duties, the principle of proportionality would have to be observed. The ECJ accepted the UK's argument that the carrying of firearms by policewomen might create additional risks of assassination. It did not inquire whether women might not be trained to use firearms just as safely and effectively as men. The ECJ therefore accepted that the sex of police officers

[31] Craig and de Búrca, *supra* n. 4, at Chap. 20; Ellis, 'The Concept of Proportionality in European Community Sex Discrimination Law', in Ellis (ed), *The Principle of Proportionality*, *supra* n. 1, at 165–181. See above, Chap. 15.

[32] Council Directive 76/207/EEC of 9 February 1976, On the Implementation of the Principle of Equal Treatment of Men and Women as regards Access to Employment, Vocational Training and Promotion, and Working Conditions, OJ 1976 L39/40.

[33] Case 222/84, *Johnston v Chief Constable of the RUC* [1986] ECR 1651.

could constitute a 'determining factor' for carrying out certain policing activities. The issue of proportionality was left to the national court, which should consider whether 'the refusal to renew Mrs Johnston's contract could not have been avoided by allocating to women duties which, without jeopardizing the aims pursued, can be performed without firearms'.[34]

The ECJ has, however, been more willing in some other cases to make the determination of proportionality itself and to intervene. In *Kreil*[35] the applicant challenged a prohibition under German law that barred women from military posts involving the use of arms, and allowed them access only to the medical and military-music services. The ECJ found that the Directive was applicable, notwithstanding the fact that the contested sphere of activity related to the military. The Court ruled that 'in determining the scope of any derogation from a fundamental right such as the equal treatment of men and women, the principle of proportionality, one of the general principles of Community law' must be observed.[36] It acknowledged that Member States have a certain degree of discretion when adopting measures considered necessary to guarantee public security, but affirmed that judicial review could still be used to assess whether the measures taken did really have that purpose and whether they were appropriate and necessary to achieve that aim.[37] The ECJ ruled that since the Article 2(2) derogation was intended to apply only to specific activities, the scope and breadth of this prohibition exceeded the discretion given to Member States when adopting measures they considered necessary to guarantee public security.[38] The challenged rule that excluded women from all military posts involving the use of arms was also held to be disproportionately broad, given the fact that basic training in the use of arms was already provided to women in the services of the Bundeswehr which remained accessible to them.[39]

Article 2(2) was amended and tightened in 2002,[40] although the Member States were given until October 2005 to comply with its provisions. The formulation contained in Article 2(6) of the amended Directive stipulates that Member States may provide, as regards access to employment and training leading thereto, that a difference of treatment based on characteristics relating to sex shall not constitute discrimination where, by reason of the nature of the particular occupational activities concerned or of the context in

[34] [1986] ECR 1651, at para. 39. See also, Case C-273/97, *Sirdar v Army Board* [1999] ECR I-7403; Case 318/86, *Commission v France* [1988] ECR 3559.

[35] Case C-285/98 *Kreil v Bundesrepublik Deutschland* [2000] ECR I-69.

[36] Ibid. at para. 23.

[37] Ibid. at paras. 24–25.

[38] Ibid. at para. 27.

[39] Ibid. at paras. 28–29.

[40] Directive 2002/73/EC of the European Parliament and of the Council of 23 September 2002, Amending Council Directive 76/207/EEC on the Implementation of the Principle of Equal Treatment for Men and Women as Regards Access to Employment, Vocational Training and Promotion, and Working Conditions, OJ 2002 L269/15, Art. 1(2).

which they are carried out, such a characteristic constitutes a genuine and determining occupational requirement, provided that the objective is legitimate and the requirement is proportionate. The emphasis placed on the relationship between gender and the particular occupational activities, the genuineness of the occupational requirement, and the explicit reference to proportionality is intended to limit the scope of this exception to equality of treatment.[41]

The Community courts have also assessed proportionality in relation to claims concerning other Articles of Directive 76/207. In *Commission v Austria*[42] the ECJ was concerned with the compatibility of an Austrian law that prohibited women from working in underground mining, subject to a limited number of exceptions. Article 3(1) of Directive 76/207 provided that there shall be no discrimination whatsoever on grounds of sex in the conditions, including the selection criteria, for access to all jobs or posts, whatever the sector or branch of activity, and to all levels of the occupational hierarchy. The Austrian government sought to defend its law by relying on Article 2(3) of the Directive, which stated that the Directive shall be without prejudice to provisions concerning the protection of women, particularly as regards pregnancy and maternity. The ECJ rejected the argument. It held that Article 2(3) does not allow women to be excluded from employment solely on the ground that they ought to be given greater protection than men against risks which affect men and women in the same way and which are distinct from protections specific to the needs of women. The prohibition contained in the Austrian law was very broad and excluded women even from work that was not physically strenuous and that posed no danger to a women's capacity to become pregnant. The exceptions provided for in the Austrian law were moreover very limited. The ECJ therefore concluded that the legislation went beyond what was necessary to ensure that women were protected within the meaning of Article 2(3).

In *Lommers*[43] it was Article 2(4) of Directive 76/207 that was in issue. This Article stated that the Directive shall be without prejudice to measures to promote equal opportunity for men and women, in particular by removing existing inequalities which affect women's opportunities in the areas covered by the Directive. The Dutch court asked the ECJ whether a ministerial circular made pursuant to a Dutch law that allocated subsidized nursery places only to female employees, subject to an emergency exception for male employees, was compatible with Community law. The ECJ decided that the

[41] Ibid. Preamble at para. 11.

[42] Case C-203/03, *Commission v Austria* [2005] ECR I-935.

[43] Case C-476/99, *Lommers v Minister van Landbouw, Natuurbeheer en Visserij* [2002] ECR I-2891. See also, Case C-319/03, *Serge Briheche v Ministre de l'Intérieur, Ministre de l'Éducation and Ministre de la Justice* [2004] ECR I-8807.

circular was unequal in its treatment for men and women. It concluded, however, that the circular could be justified within Article 2(4), because women were significantly under-represented in the Dutch Ministry of Agriculture, the public body running the subsidized nursery scheme. The applicability of Article 2(4) was, however, subject to proportionality. The ECJ acknowledged that proportionality would normally be a matter for the national court. It held, however, in accordance with prior case law that it could 'provide the national court with an interpretation of Community law on all such points as may enable that court to assess the compatibility of a national measure with Community law for the purposes of the judgment to be given in the case before it'.[44] The ECJ accordingly considered the proportionality of the scheme embodied in the circular. It concluded that it was proportionate: the number of places was limited such that even female workers at the Ministry had no guarantee of a place; men could still obtain a nursery place on the general market for such services; and the circular should be read such as to allow single fathers access to the scheme on the same condition as mothers.

B. Equal Pay

The Community courts have also had occasion to consider proportionality in the context of equal pay claims. The right to equal pay enshrined in Article 141 EC can be infringed where there is direct or indirect discrimination in the remuneration granted to men and women. Indirect discrimination, once established, is prohibited unless the defendant can show some objective justification. Exactly what can constitute objective justification is not entirely clear and the ECJ has often left the matter for the national court to decide.

The ECJ has, however, provided guidance on the notion of objective justification and the test that has been formulated is very similar to that of proportionality as used in the case law on the four freedoms. This is apparent from *Bilka-Kaufhaus*,[45] which was concerned with the eligibility of part-time workers for an occupational pension scheme. The Court held that if it should be found that a much lower proportion of women than men worked full time, the exclusion of part-time workers from the occupational pension scheme would be contrary to what is now Article 141 EC where, taking into account the difficulties encountered by women workers in working full-time, that measure could not be explained by factors which excluded any discrimination on grounds of sex. There would, however, be no such breach if the undertaking could show that its pay practice could be explained by

[44] Ibid. at para. 40.
[45] Case 170/84, *Bilka-Kaufhaus GmbH v Karin Weber von Hartz* [1986] ECR 1607.

objectively justified factors unrelated to any discrimination on grounds of sex. Bilka argued that the exclusion of part-time workers from the occupational pension scheme was intended solely to discourage part-time work, since in general part-time workers refused to work in the late afternoon and on Saturdays. Thus, in order to ensure the presence of an adequate workforce during those periods it was therefore necessary to make full-time work more attractive than part-time work, by making the occupational pension scheme open only to full-time workers. The ECJ decided that it was for the national court to determine whether and to what extent the employer's argument could be objectively justified. It then provided guidance for the national court in this respect.[46]

If the national court finds that the measures chosen by the employer correspond to a real need on the part of the undertaking, are appropriate with a view to achieving the objectives pursued and are necessary to that end, the fact that the measures affect a far greater number of women than men is not sufficient to show that they constitute an infringement of Article 119.

The guidance provided for the national court is in substance a proportionality inquiry. Thus an indirectly discriminatory measure could be justified if it addressed a 'real need' of the employer, if the measure was 'appropriate' to achieve its objective and if it was 'necessary' to achieve that end.

In *Brunnhofer*[47] the ECJ repeated the holding from *Bilka-Kaufhaus* that it was for the defendant employer in that case to justify the inequality by showing that it corresponded to a real need of the undertaking, that it was appropriate to achieve the objectives pursued, and that it was necessary to that end. It held moreover that the objectively justified reasons unrelated to discrimination on grounds of sex must comply with the principle of proportionality.

This approach was developed and applied in later cases. In *Rinner-Kühn*[48] the Court considered national legislation that excluded part-time workers from sick-pay provision. The ECJ held that although the legislative provision was in principle contrary to the aim of Article 141 EC, it was capable of objective justification, but found that the justification proffered by the government was inadequate. The German Government sought to justify the legislation on the ground that workers who worked for less than 10 hours a week or 45 hours a month were not as integrated in, or as dependent on, the undertaking employing them as other workers. The

[46] Ibid. at para. 36. See also, Case C-256/01, *Allonby v Accrington & Rossendale College, Education Lecturing Services, Trading as Protocol Professional and Secretary of State for Education and Employment* [2004] ECR I-873.

[47] Case C-381/99, *Brunnhofer v Bank der Österreichischen Postsparkasse AG* [2001] ECR I-4961, at paras. 67–68.

[48] Case 171/88, *Rinner-Kühn v FWW Spezial-Gebäudereinigung GmbH* [1989] ECR 2743

ECJ was unconvinced by this argument. It responded by stating that such considerations were only generalizations about certain categories of workers, and therefore did not enable criteria which were objective and unrelated to any discrimination on grounds of sex to be identified. If, however, the Member State could show that the means chosen met a necessary aim of social policy and that they were suitable and requisite for attaining that aim, the mere fact that the provision affected a much greater number of female workers than male workers would not infringe what is now Article 141 EC. While the proportionality test was phrased slightly differently in *Rinner-Kühn*, where discrimination by the State rather than an employer was in issue, the essence of the test remained unchanged. It was for the defendant to show that any discrimination was suited to achieving a legitimate purpose and went no further than was necessary to achieve that purpose.[49]

The reasoning in *Rinner-Kühn* was echoed in *Nimz*,[50] where the issue before the ECJ was whether an indirectly discriminatory term in a collective agreement, whereby only half of the period of service of certain part-time workers was taken into account in calculating their salary grade, could be justified. The City of Hamburg argued that full-time employees or those who worked for three-quarters of normal working time acquired the abilities and skills relating to their particular job more quickly than others. The ECJ responded by stating that such considerations, 'in so far as they are no more than generalizations about certain categories of workers, do not make it possible to identify criteria which are both objective and unrelated to any discrimination on grounds of sex.'[51] While experience went hand in hand with length of service, and experience in principle enabled the worker to improve performance of the allotted tasks, the objectivity of such a criterion depended on all the circumstances in a particular case, more especially the relationship between the nature of the work performed and the experience gained from the performance of that work upon completion of a certain number of working hours. The ECJ held that it was, however, for the national court to determine whether and to what extent a provision in a collective agreement such as that in issue was based on objectively justified factors unrelated to any discrimination on grounds of sex. Although the ECJ left the matter for the national court, the ECJ's ruling makes it clear that general assumptions or assertions about the attributes of part-time workers

[49] See also, Case 33/89, *Kowalska v Freie und Hansestadt Hamburg* [1990] ECR 2591; Case C-360/90, *Arbeiterwohlfahrt der Stadt Berlin v Bötel* [1992] ECR I-3589; Case C-457/93, *Kuratorium für Dialyse und Nierentransplantation v Lewark* [1996] ECR I-243; Case C-278/93, *Freers and Speckmann v Deutsche Bundespost* [1996] ECR I-1165; Case C-187/00, *Kutz-Bauer v Freie und Hansestadt Hamburg* [2003] ECR I-2741.

[50] Case 184/89, *Nimz v Freie und Hansestadt Hamburg* [1991] ECR 297.

[51] Ibid. at para. 14.

are unlikely to constitute adequate grounds for justifying a measure which has a disproportionately adverse impact on one sex.

4. POSITIVE LAW: APPLICATION OF COMMUNITY LEGISLATION

It is clear from the preceding analysis that proportionality can be of relevance in the interpretation of Community directives adopted in the sphere of equality. It should also be recognized that proportionality operates more generally as a constraint on Member State options when applying Community norms such as regulations[52] and directives, irrespective of the particular sphere of Community action that is in issue, and that they must comply with proportionality when taking measures to implement Community legislation.[53] Two examples from very different areas serve to demonstrate this.[54]

The litigation in *Garage Molenheide*[55] was concerned with the Sixth VAT Directive. The claimant argued in essence that provisions of Belgian law that allowed the domestic authorities to refuse to refund a VAT credit for a specific period or to carry it forward to a later period, but rather to retain it for as long as it had a claim against the taxpayer for a previous tax period even though that demand was contested, was contrary to certain provisions of the Sixth VAT Directive. The ECJ found that the Belgian withholding measure was not precluded by the Directive. It held, however, that 'in accordance with the principle of proportionality, the Member State must employ means which, whilst enabling them effectively to attain the objective pursued by their domestic laws, are the least detrimental to the objectives and the principles laid down by the relevant Community legislation'.[56] Thus while it was legitimate for Belgium to preserve the rights of its Treasury as effectively as possible, the measures adopted must not go further than necessary for that purpose, nor could they be used such as to undermine the right to deduct VAT, this being a fundamental principle established by the Community legislation.

The ECJ acknowledged that the specific application of proportionality would commonly be for the national court, but in line with many rulings the ECJ nonetheless proceeded to provide detailed guidance as to the application

[52] Case C-29/95, *Pastoors and Trans-Cap GmbH v Belgian State* [1997] ECR I-285.

[53] *Supra* n. 5.

[54] See also, Case C-200/02, *Kunqian Catherine Zhu and Man Lavette Chen v Secretary of State for the Home Department* [2004] ECR I-9925, at paras. 32–33; Case C-25/03, *Finanzamt Bergisch Gladbach v HE* [2005] ECR I-3123, at para. 82.

[55] Cases C-286/94, 340 and 401/95, and 47/96, *Garage Molenheide BVBA v Belgische Staat* [1997] ECR I-7281.

[56] Ibid. at para. 46.

of the principle in the instant case. It found that the retention system embodied in the Belgian law was disproportionate because it was based on an irrebuttable presumption, in the sense that it was not open to the claimant to argue that the retention was unnecessary or to put forward arguments concerning urgency. The ECJ held that the availability of judicial review was important in determining whether the retention regime was proportionate, and that national provisions preventing the national judge from lifting the retention were therefore disproportionate. So too were rules that prevented the taxpayer from requesting a national court to adopt a different measure that would be equally effective in protecting the interests of the Treasury in place of the retention of the VAT credit.

The relevance of proportionality in a very different context can be seen in *Unilever*.[57] The applicant challenged the marketing of toothpaste by a rival company, which had made claims about its curative effects, the prevention of plaque, dental cavities, and the like. The applicant argued that these claims were likely to mislead consumers because the toothpaste did not contain substances capable of having this effect, judged in the light of a list drawn up pursuant to an Austrian law concerning consumer protection. The defendant company argued that the Austrian law was inconsistent with Community law, more particularly Article 6(3) of a Directive,[58] which provided that Member States should take all necessary steps to ensure that in the labelling and advertising of such products, text, names, pictures, and the like were not used to imply that the products had characteristics that they did not possess. The ECJ held that the measures which the Member States were required to take to implement this provision must be in accordance with the principle of proportionality. It concluded that the Austrian law did not meet this test. It was, said the ECJ, possible to ensure the protection of consumers, public health, and fair trade by measures that were less restrictive of the free movement of goods than the automatic exclusion of advertising substances not expressly listed in the Austrian law, more especially because the list contained in that law of substances that could prevent dental decay, etc. was not complete.

The same reasoning is evident in *Linhart and Biffl*.[59] The case arose out of a criminal prosecution of the applicants for marketing certain cosmetic products. The applicants were prosecuted for infringing an Austrian law concerned with trade in, *inter alia*, cosmetics, because their products contained the statement that they were 'dermatologically tested' and this was

[57] Case C-77/97, *Österreichische Unilever GmbH v SmithKline Beecham Markenartikel GmbH* [1999] ECR I-431.

[58] Council Directive 76/778/EEC of 27 July 1976, On the Approximation of the Laws of the Member States relating to Cosmetic Products, OJ 1976 L262/169.

[59] Case C-99/01, *Criminal Proceedings against Linhart and Biffl* [2002] ECR I-9375.

held by the Austrian authorities to engender in the mind of consumers erroneous ideas as to the characteristics of the products due to lack of information as to the content and outcome of such opinions. The applicants argued that the prosecution was precluded by the same Community Directive as that in issue in *Unilever.* The ECJ reiterated that the measures that the Member State were required to take to implement Article 6(3) must observe the principle of proportionality. The Court considered, therefore, whether the statement on the packaging 'dermatologically tested' would lead consumers to believe that the product had curative properties that it did not in fact possess. It applied the test of the average consumer who is reasonably well informed and observant, and concluded that such a person would not form any misleading impression from the wording on the package, with the consequence that the Austrian law was prohibited by Article 6(3) of the Directive read in the light of the proportionality principle.

5. POSITIVE LAW: THE IMPACT OF ARTICLE 10 EC

The discussion thus far has been concerned with the application of proportionality as a control mechanism over Member State action in various areas of Community law. It is, however, clear from *Commission v Greece*[60] that proportionality can also be of relevance in relation to Member State action to take measures to ensure the effectiveness of Community law.

The ECJ held that the duty of cooperation under Article 10 EC meant that where Community legislation did not provide a remedy for infringement of its provisions it was for national law to take all necessary measures to ensure the effectiveness of Community law. For that purpose, while the choice of remedy remained within the discretion of the Member State, it had to ensure not only that the remedy was similar to that applicable for infringements of a similar nature under national law, but also that the penalty was effective, proportionate, and dissuasive. The same principle applies where the Community legislation lays down particular penalties, but does not exhaustively prescribe the penalties that a Member State can impose.[61]

[60] Case 68/88, *Commission v Greece* [1989] ECR 2965; Case C-383/92, *Commission v UK* [1994] ECR I-2479; Case C-354/99, *Commission v Ireland* [2001] ECR I-7657, at para. 46; Cases C-387, 391 and 403/02, *Criminal Proceedings against Silvio Berlusconi and others* [2005] ECR I-3565, at para. 53.

[61] Case C-186/98, *Criminal Proceedings against Nunes and de Matos* [1999] ECR I-4883.

6. NORMATIVE CONSIDERATIONS: THE INTENSITY OF REVIEW

A. Justification for Strict Proportionality Scrutiny

The analysis thus far has been on positive law, with a survey of the principal areas of Member State action to which the proportionality principle has been applied. The remainder of this chapter will be more normative in orientation. This analysis begins by considering more closely the intensity with which the proportionality principle is applied to Member State action. This is a matter of some importance, more especially because there is suspicion in some quarters that the Community courts have applied the principle more intensively where Member State action is in issue as compared with the lighter touch review associated with proportionality and Community action. Whether this is in fact so is undoubtedly a matter on which commentators might well differ. I shall nonetheless attempt to approach the matter as objectively as possible.

The most fitting starting point is to recognize that the Community courts, primarily the ECJ in this context, have made it apparent in numerous cases that the proportionality inquiry is indeed a strict or searching one, insofar as it relates to many of the areas considered above. The rationale for this is readily explicable. The paradigm application of proportionality in relation to the four freedoms entails the case where a *prima facie* breach of one of the freedoms has been found to exist, and the Member State then seeks to raise a defence based on the relevant Treaty article. The four freedoms are central to the very idea of market integration that lies at the economic heart of the EU. They also embody non-economic values. Thus the legislation and case law on, for example, free movement of workers is infused with social as well as economic objectives. It is therefore unsurprising that the ECJ has monitored defences to free movement closely, including in this respect proportionality.

The Member State must, as we have seen, show that the defence falls within one of the grounds listed in the relevant Treaty article. Proportionality then requires that the defence couched in terms of public health, public security, etc. is the least restrictive in all the circumstances. This serves a twofold aim. It is designed to ensure that the scope of the defence really was warranted, by testing whether the objective could be attained in a less restrictive manner. It is designed also to ensure that the defence raised does not operate as arbitrary discrimination or a disguised restriction on trade between Member States. When perceived in this manner it is fitting that proportionality scrutiny should be strict or intensive, given the very centrality of the four freedoms to the schema of the Treaty and given that a *prima facie* breach of these provisions has been found to exist before we ever get to proportionality.

There is a further reason for the close judicial scrutiny of proportionality, which relates to more general developments in the law of free movement. Proportionality has become of greater importance because of the way in which the Community courts have defined the circumstances in which a Member State may be said to have breached these freedoms. This is a point of some complexity, but its essence can be explained quite simply. The Community courts have a choice as to how to interpret the four freedoms. They might decide to limit their application to cases where there is some form of discrimination, direct or indirect. In such cases equality provides the primary mechanism for judicial control, although proportionality will still be of relevance especially in relation to cases of indirect discrimination. They have, however, decided that the Treaty articles also catch impediments to market access, even where the national law does not discriminate directly or indirectly on grounds of nationality. In such cases there will by definition be no control through equality, since the measure is not discriminatory. The principal tools for judicial control are objective justification and proportionality. This serves to explain why the Community judiciary wish to satisfy themselves that the contested measure really is the least restrictive possible in the circumstances. This point is captured well by Tridimas.[62]

> If it is accepted that free movement is exhausted in the obligation of Member States to treat imported products or services on an equal footing with domestic ones, discrimination is the touchstone of integration. But if it is accepted that free movement goes beyond equal treatment and requires freedom of access to the market, then any obstacle to free access becomes an unlawful impediment unless objectively justified. Under the second model, proportionality is elevated to the principal criterion for determining the dividing line between lawful and unlawful barriers to trade. It may be said then that equality and proportionality are in an inverse relationship: the less one relies on the first, the more it has to rely on the latter to determine what is a permissible restriction on trade.

There are also powerful reasons for close scrutiny via proportionality in the context of equality and discrimination. The paradigm here is that state action has been found to discriminate indirectly, and the defendant then seeks to provide an objective justification for the discrimination. Proportionality is of relevance in determining whether the action that the Member State seeks to justify is really suitable to attain the end in question, whether it is necessary, and whether the desired end could be achieved by less restrictive measures. Strict proportionality scrutiny is warranted here given the *prima facie* breach of equality already proven and the centrality of equality as a principle within the Treaty. There are therefore sound reasons for the general approach of the Community courts to proportionality and Member State action, while

[62] Tridimas, *supra* n. 1, at 127.

accepting that the application of the principle in particular cases can still be criticized.

The intensity of review in any particular case will naturally be affected by the nature of the subject matter. Where a Member State raises genuine concerns relating to public health, and there is scientific uncertainty about the effects of certain foodstuffs, the Court has been more willing to accept that limitations on free movement are warranted.[63] However, one should be cautious about characterizing such cases as involving less intensive review.[64] They may equally well be regarded as instances where the Court, having surveyed the evidence, believed that the Member State's action was warranted. There are, moreover, examples of public health claims where the Court, while accepting that there was some scientific uncertainty, none the less concluded that there was a less restrictive way of achieving the Member State's aim.[65]

The intensity of the Court's review will also be influenced by how seriously it takes the Member State's argument that measures really were necessary in order to protect, for example, public health. If the Court feels that these measures were really a 'front' for a national protective policy, designed to insulate its own producers from foreign competition, then it will be inclined to subject the Member State's argument to close scrutiny. This is exemplified by *Commission v United Kingdom*.[66] The Court considered a claim by the UK government that a ban on the import of poultry could be justified on grounds of public health under what is now Article 30 EC. A reading of the Court's judgment leaves one in little doubt that it was suspicious, to say the least, of the motives for the UK action. The Court felt that the measures were, in reality, aimed at protecting UK poultry producers from the effects of French imports in the run up to Christmas. The Court accordingly rejected the UK's defence.

B. Proportionality and Sensitivity to National Values

The Member State does not always lose. This is a trite proposition, but important nonetheless. It is easy to take away the impression that the Member State will be found to have infringed proportionality each time that the issue arises for adjudication. A cursory glance at the prominent cases might seem to confirm this impression. This is unsurprisingly not so. The ECJ has

[63] Case 174/82, *Sandoz*, *supra* n. 8; Case 97/83, *Melkunie* [1984] ECR 2367.

[64] Compare, Schwarze, *supra* n. 1, at 790 and Lord Slynn, 'The Concept of Free Movement of Goods and the Reservation for National Action under Art. 36 EEC', in J. Schwarze (ed), *Discretionary Powers of the Member States in the Field of Economic Policies and their Limits under the EEC Treaty* (Nomos 1988).

[65] Case 178/84, *Commission v Germany* [1987] ECR 1227.

[66] Case 40/82, *Commission v United Kingdom* [1982] ECR 2793.

found in favour of the Member States and has shown sensitivity to national values.

This is exemplified by *Schmidberger*,[67] considered in detail in an earlier chapter.[68] It will be remembered that the Austrian government gave implicit permission for a demonstration by an environmental group on the Brenner motorway, the effect being to close it for 30 hours. Schmidberger ran a transport firm and argued that the closure was in breach of free movement of goods. The ECJ held that the failure by the Austrian government to ban the demonstration was *prima facie* a breach of Article 28 EC, unless it could be objectively justified.[69] The justification proffered by the government was respect for the right to freedom of expression and assembly guaranteed by the ECHR and the Austrian Constitution. This was accepted in principle, and the Court decided that the restrictions on Community trade were proportionate in the light of these fundamental rights.[70]

A similar message emerges from *Commission v France*.[71] The Commission brought an action against France alleging infringement of freedom to provide services. France enacted Loi Evin in 1991, which restricted advertising for smoking and alcohol on television. A Code of Conduct was drawn up pursuant to this law that applied to the transmission or retransmission of sporting events in which advertising for alcohol was visible on hoardings or sports shirts. This Code in effect provided that in relation to 'bi-national' sporting events, being those that were specially aimed at a French audience, the broadcaster should take all measures possible to prevent the appearance on their channels of brand-named alcoholic products. The ECJ had little difficulty in deciding that this constituted an infringement of the freedom to provide services. It then focused on justification and proportionality. The justification hurdle was swiftly met, given that the French measure clearly had the object of protecting public health. The ECJ spent some time addressing proportionality, rejected the Commission's argument, and upheld that of the French government. Thus the Court rejected the argument that the French measure was inconsistent on the ground that it only applied to alcohol above a certain strength, replying that the degree of protection to be afforded to public health fell within France's discretion. It found that there was no way of securing the end in view that was less restrictive than the contested measure, given the nature of the sport's broadcast. It was equally dismissive of the argument that the measure should be regarded as disproportionate because

[67] Case C-112/00, *Schmidberger Internationale Transporte und Planzuge v Austria* [2003] ECR I-5659.

[68] See above, at 513–514.

[69] Case C-112/00, *Schmidberger*, *supra* n. 67, at para. 64.

[70] Ibid. at paras. 83–94. See also, Case C-71/02, *Karner Industrie-Auktionen GmbH v Troostwijk GmbH* [2004] ECR I-3025.

[71] Case C-262/02, *Commission v France* [2004] ECR I-6569.

such advertising was allowed in some Member States, since the fact that one Member State imposed less strict rules than another did not mean that the latter's rules were disproportionate.

The ECJ has, by way of contrast, become rather stricter in its scrutiny of cases where the Member State seeks to prevent or impede free movement by imposing on nationals of other Member States rules that are said to be justified on grounds of public policy, where such policy concerns are, however, not thought sufficiently pressing to impose on their own citizens. The Court has tended to be more intensive in its review of such cases as time has gone on. Cases which have come before the Court involving similar facts or raising similar principles have been subject to more rigorous scrutiny, with the result that Member State action that was regarded as lawful in the earlier case has been held not to be so in a later action.[72]

C. Proportionality and Sensitivity to Differences in National Values

The ECJ is, moreover, willing to interpret concepts of objective justification and proportionality in the light of the particular values applicable within that Member State, notwithstanding that those values, or the importance attached to them, differ from that accorded by other Member States.[73]

This is exemplified by *Omega*.[74] The Bonn police issued an order forbidding the applicant company from allowing laser games in which the participants engaged in simulated killing of opponents, on the ground that this infringed the right to human dignity contained in the German Constitution. The Court found that the order *prima facie* constituted a limit on the freedom to provide services. It then considered whether it could be justified on grounds of public policy under Article 55 EC. The ECJ held that the concept of public policy as a derogation from a fundamental freedom must be interpreted strictly, and could only be relied on if there was a genuine and sufficiently serious threat to a fundamental interest of society.[75] The public policy measure must be necessary for the attainment of the specified aim and would be lawful only insofar as it could not be achieved by less restrictive measures.[76] The Court accepted, however, that the specific circumstances that could justify recourse to public policy could vary from country to coun-

[72] Compare e.g. Case 41/74, *Van Duyn v Home Office* [1974] ECR 1337, with Cases 115 and 116/81, *Adoui and Cornuaille v Belgian State* [1982] ECR 1665. Compare Case 34/79, *R v Henn and Darby* [1979] ECR 3795, with Case 121/85, *Conegate v Customs and Excise Commissioners* [1986] ECR 1007.

[73] Case C-384/93, *Alpine Investments BV v Minister van Financien* [1995] ECR I-1141, at para. 51; Case C-3/95, *Reisebüro Broede v Gerd Sandker* [1996] ECR I-6511.

[74] Case C-36/02, *Omega Spielhallen- und Automatenaufstellungs-GmbH v Oberbürgermeisterin der Bundesstadt Bonn* [2004] ECR I-9609.

[75] Ibid. at para. 30. [76] Ibid. at para. 36.

try, and that the national authorities must be accorded a margin of discretion within the limits imposed by the Treaty.[77] Nor was it vital for the restrictive measure to be such that it would be chosen by all Member States to protect the relevant public policy interest.[78] Thus the need for and proportionality of a measure was not excluded merely because a Member State had chosen a method of protection different from that of other states.[79] Viewed in this way the ECJ found that the public policy justification for the action of the Bonn police was proportionate.

The same willingness to interpret proportionality so as to afford latitude to the values and policies of the particular Member State is evident in *Läärä*.[80] National legislation granting an exclusive right to a public body to operate slot machines infringed the freedom to provide services. The ECJ accepted that this could be justified on grounds of consumer protection and maintenance of public order. It was, said the Court, for the national authorities to determine whether these aims could be met by prohibiting the activity or limiting it. Likewise it was for the national authorities to decide whether to grant an exclusive right to a public body or to impose a code of conduct on private operators. The mere fact that a Member State opted for a system of protection different from that adopted by another Member State did not affect the assessment of the need for, and proportionality of, the relevant provisions, which had to be assessed solely by reference to the objectives pursued by the particular Member State and the level of protection they were intended to provide. The ECJ held that the Finnish legislation was proportionate, and it has made it clear more generally that the mere fact that Member State X has adopted a less restrictive approach to gambling than Member State Y will not affect the assessment of whether the latter is proportionate and hence lawful.[81]

The ECJ has adopted the same approach of according respect to national policy choices when assessing proportionality where the defence is cast in terms of public health. In *Mac Quen*[82] the applicant and others worked in Belgium for a subsidiary of a UK company. They were subject to criminal charges for providing certain optical services that under a judicial interpretation of Belgian law could only be provided by a fully trained ophthalmologist. This issue was not regulated by any directive and the ECJ held that while the Member State was therefore free to regulate such matters, they must nonetheless respect the basic freedoms guaranteed by the Treaty. National

[77] Ibid. at para. 31. [78] Ibid. at para. 37. [79] Ibid. at para. 38.

[80] Case C-124/97, *Läärä, Cotswold Microsystems Ltd and Oy Transatlantic Software Ltd v Finland* [1999] ECR I-6067. See also, Case C-67/98, *Questore di Verona v Zenatti* [1999] ECR I-7289, at paras. 33–34; Case C-277/02, *EU-Wood-Trading GmbH v Sonderabfall-Management-Gesellschaft Rheinland-Pfalz mbh* [2004] ECR I-11957, at para. 51.

[81] Case C-6/01, *Anomar v Estado Portugues* [2003] ECR I-8621, at paras. 80–81.

[82] Case C-108/96, *Criminal Proceedings against MacQuen* [2001] ECR I-837.

measures liable to hinder or render less attractive the exercise of the freedom could be justified subject to four conditions: they were not discriminatory, they were justified by an overriding public interest, they were suited to attaining the objective sought, and did not go beyond what was necessary to achieve that objective. The Belgian law was not discriminatory and was designed to secure public health. The applicants argued that the legislation was disproportionate and that the objective sought could be achieved by less restrictive measures. The ECJ disagreed. It made it clear that the fact that one Member State imposed less strict rules than another did not mean that the rules of the latter were disproportionate; the mere fact that a Member State had chosen a system of protection different from that adopted by another could not affect the appraisal as to the need for and proportionality of such provisions.[83] The ECJ noted, however, that the criminal prosecution was based on an interpretation of Belgian law, and that assessment of such matters might change over time as a result of technical and scientific progress. The ECJ therefore remitted the matter to the national court to determine whether its interpretation of national law remained a valid basis for the prosecutions in the instant case.

The reasoning in *MacQuen* was applied and developed in *Gräbner*.[84] Grabner, an Austrian national, had taken a course to become a lay medical practitioner offered by a German company. He refused to pay for the course and in the subsequent contract action he relied on the fact that Austrian law prohibited lay medical practitioners. The ECJ found that the activity was not governed by any Community directive. It was clear that the Austrian law impeded freedom of establishment and the provision of services, and the ECJ therefore applied the four conditions mentioned above. The Austrian law, which was not discriminatory, was based on the protection of health, and the restriction of medical diagnoses to those who were medically qualified, was held to be a suitable method to achieve this aim. The ECJ's findings on proportionality echoed directly those in the preceding case: the fact that one Member State imposed less strict rules than another did not mean that the latter's rules were disproportionate.[85] It was therefore open to Austria to ban the practice of lay medical practitioner. It was, said the ECJ, also open to Austria to prohibit the organization of training for such a practice, at least insofar as this might undermine the efficacy of the national prohibition in Austria. It was, by way of contrast, not possible for the Austrian government to ban advertising for training as a lay medical practitioner where the training was to take place in a different Member State and where the advert made it clear that such an activity could not be pursued in Austria.

[83] Ibid. at paras. 33–34.

[84] Case C-294/00, *Deutsche Paracelsus Schulen für Naturheilverhafen GmbH v Gräbner* [2002] ECR I-6515.

[85] Ibid. at paras. 46–47.

7. NORMATIVE CONSIDERATIONS: THE ROLE OF THE NATIONAL COURTS AND THE COMPLEXITY OF THE PROPORTIONALITY INQUIRY

Cases concerning proportionality traditionally come before the ECJ via one of two routes. Some take the form of enforcement actions brought by the Commission pursuant to Article 226 EC. In such cases the ECJ will resolve the entirety of the case itself, including the proportionality inquiry.

Many other cases are decided via preliminary rulings under Article 234 EC, which gives the ECJ power to interpret the Treaty, but does not specifically empower it to apply the Treaty to the facts of a particular case. Indeed the very distinction between interpretation and application is meant to be one of the characteristic features of the division of authority between the ECJ and national courts: the former interprets the Treaty, while the latter apply that interpretation to the facts of a particular case. Theory and reality have not, however, always marched hand in hand. The dividing line between interpretation and application can be perilously thin. The more detailed the interpretation provided by the ECJ, the closer it approximates to application.[86] It is, moreover, clear that the ECJ will be particularly motivated to provide 'the answer' or to give 'detailed guidance' to national courts where it wishes to maintain maximum control over the development of an area of the law, as exemplified by cases concerning damages liability of Member States.[87]

The interrelationship between the ECJ and national courts under Article 234 EC in the context of proportionality is especially interesting in this respect. The ECJ's 'standard' starting point is to reiterate orthodoxy, to the effect that it is for the national court to judge the proportionality of the Member State's action in a specific case. The nature of the case may well mean that the proportionality inquiry must be assessed in detail by the national courts. This will be so where, for example, there are a number of factors to be weighed in deciding whether Member State action was proportionate in the particular case, which can only be done by the national courts. Thus in *Richardt*[88] the ECJ held that what is now Article 30 EC authorized Member States to impose restrictions on the transit of goods

[86] See, e.g., Case 32/75, *Cristini v SNCF* [1975] ECR 1085; Case C-106/89, *Marleasing SA v La Comercial Internacional de Alimentacion SA* [1990] ECR I-4135.

[87] Cases C-46 and 48/93, *Brasserie du Pêcheur SA v Germany, R v Secretary of State for Transport, ex p Factortame Ltd* [1996] ECR I-1029; Case C-392/93, *R v HM Treasury, ex p British Telecommunications plc* [1996] ECR I-1631.

[88] Case C-367/89, *Criminal Proceedings against Richardt and Les Accessoires Scientifiques SNC* [1991] ECR I-4621. See also, Case C-70/94, *Werner* [1995] ECR I-3189; Case C-83/94, *Leifer* [1995] ECR I-3231.

on grounds of public security and that this covered internal and external security. It was therefore *prima facie* legitimate for the Member State to require special authorization for the transit of goods that were of strategic importance, irrespective of the existence of a Community transit document issued by another Member State. However, the measures adopted by the Member State for failure to comply with its requirements had to be proportionate. Penalties such as seizure of the goods for failure to comply with the obligation to obtain authorization might be disproportionate where return of the goods to the Member State of origin would suffice. It was for the national court to determine whether the system established complied with proportionality, taking account of all the elements of each case, such as the nature of the goods capable of endangering the security of the state, the circumstances in which the breach was committed, and whether or not the trader making the transit was acting in good faith. It is clear that even in this case the ECJ laid down the specific considerations that the national court should take into account when deciding whether the Member State action was proportionate in a particular case.

It is, however, readily apparent from the case law considered throughout this chapter that the ECJ will often displace the 'default position' whereby the application of proportionality is decided by the national court and will instead provide detailed guidance for the Member State on the proportionality issue, such that the national court may have little to do other than 'execute' the ECJ's judgment. This approach is motivated by two principal considerations that are related, albeit distinct.

There is the ECJ's desire to retain control over the development of important facets of EU law, which would be lost if it handed the entirety of the proportionality inquiry to the national courts. This is exemplified by the guidance it provided in the case law concerning diversity of national values and how this should impact on the proportionality inquiry. It is clear that the ECJ wished to ensure that its view of this important matter of principle should prevail and this required it to give detailed guidance to the national courts. The same holds true in relation to the specific interpretation of proportionality given by the ECJ in some of the case law on equality.

The other factor driving the ECJ towards the retention of greater aspects of the proportionality inquiry is the difficulty faced by national courts when applying proportionality in circumstances where the factors to be balanced are complex. The complexity might be essentially quantitative in nature, flowing from uncertainties as to the relevant data that was integral to the proportionality analysis. It might also be qualitative in nature, stemming from the fact that the national court would be asked to balance values that were not readily commensurable.

The Sunday trading case law is the best known example of this, the problem being especially pressing because it entailed both quantitative and qualitative complexity. In *Torfaen*[89] the ECJ held that national rules preventing Sunday trading were *prima facie* incompatible with Article 28 EC, unless the national objective was justified with regard to Community law, and unless any obstacle to Community trade thereby created did not exceed what was necessary in order to ensure the attainment of the objective in view. The Court found that the objectives of such rules, which reflected certain national choices about the balance between work and non-working hours, were justified. The ECJ then turned its attention to proportionality to determine whether the effects of such national rules exceeded what was necessary to achieve this aim. The issue was whether the restrictive effect of such measures on the free movement of goods exceeded the effects intrinsic to trade rules. This was, said the ECJ, a matter to be determined by the national court. It rapidly became clear that national courts in the UK had great difficulty in applying the proportionality inquiry, and this difficulty was exacerbated by the fact that the issue would often come before a relatively low level national court. Such courts were in effect being asked to balance the social good inherent in Sunday trading rules, with the limits on trade produced by such rules, in circumstances where the precise impact was often difficult to measure. It was unsurprising that some courts found that the Sunday trading laws were compatible with Article 28, while others reached the opposite conclusion.[90] The confusion created by leaving the proportionality inquiry to national courts caused the ECJ to rethink the matter and take back much of the proportionality calculus into its own hands, making it clear that Sunday trading rules were proportionate.[91] The decision in *Keck*[92] meant that selling rules of the kind present in *Torfaen* would not come within Article 28 EC, thereby obviating the need for discussion of proportionality.

The problem about the allocation of responsibility for the proportionality inquiry is, however, an enduring one, as evidenced by *Familiapress*.[93] Familiapress was an Austrian newspaper publisher, which sought to restrain a

[89] Case 145/88, *Torfaen BC v B & Q plc* [1989] ECR 3851.

[90] *Stoke City Council v B & Q plc* [1990] 3 CMLR 31; *Wellingborough BC v Payless* [1990] 1 CMLR 773; *B & Q plc v Shrewsbury BC* [1990] 3 CMLR 535; *Payless v Peterborough CC* [1990] 2 CMLR 577; Arnull, 'What Shall We Do On Sunday?' (1991) 16 *ELRev* 112; Lord Hoffmann, 'The Influence of the European Principle of Proportionality upon UK Law', in Ellis (ed), *The Principle of Proportionality, supra* n. 1, at 107–116.

[91] Case C-312/89, *Union Département des Syndicats CGT de l'Aisne v SIDEF Conforama* [1991] ECR I-997; Case C-332/89, *Ministère Public v Marchandise* [1991] ECR I-1027; Cases C-306/88, 304/90, and 169/91, *Stoke-on-Trent CC v B & Q plc* [1992] ECR I-6457, at 6493, 6635; Cases C-418–421, 460–462, and 464/93, 9–11, 14–15, 23–24, and 332/94, *Semeraro Casa Uno Srl v Sindaco del Commune di Erbusco* [1996] ECR I-2975.

[92] Cases C-267 and 268/91, *Criminal Proceedings against Keck and Mithouard* [1993] ECR I-6097.

[93] Case C-368/95, *Vereinigte Familiapress Zeitungsverlags-und Vertreibs GmbH v Heinrich Bauer Verlag* [1997] ECR I-368.

German publisher from publishing in Austria a magazine containing crossword puzzles for which the winning readers would receive prizes. Austrian legislation prohibited publishers from including such prize competitions in their papers. Austria argued that its legislation was not caught by what is now Article 28 EC, since the national law related to a method of sales promotion, and was therefore, according to *Keck*, outside Article 28. The ECJ disagreed and held that the Austrian law concerned the nature of the product and not a selling arrangement. It was therefore caught by Article 28. The ECJ nonetheless recognized the value of pluralism of the press and held that this might legitimate the national legislation, since the offering of prizes for games in magazines could drive out smaller papers which could not afford to make such offers. It was then for the national court to decide whether the national ban could be saved on the ground that it was a proportionate method of preserving press diversity, and whether that objective could be achieved by less restrictive means. The inquiry demanded of the national court was rendered even more complex because it was required to balance press diversity not only against free movement of goods, but also against the principle of freedom of expression. The national court was, moreover, required to decide on the degree of competition between papers offering prizes, and those small newspapers that could not afford to do so. It was then to estimate the extent to which sales of the latter would decline, if the former could be offered for sale. It should be remembered in this context that a reference can be made to the ECJ by any national court. The questions posed in this case would be daunting for any national court, let alone for those at the lower level. This is captured well by Van Gerven.[94]

> [T]he judgment imposes on the national courts a far-reaching balancing test, in that not only the means employed to achieve a (legitimate) objective of national law are to be weighed but also the national aim so pursued against the Community law objective of free movement of goods and freedom of expression, as enshrined in Article 10 of the ECHR. To the extent that such a complex balancing test is not wholly beyond the possibilities of a court of law, it will at least compel the court to carry out its investigation in a distant way.

While there will be cases where it is necessary or wise to leave the proportionality issue to the national court, it may, as Advocate General Jacobs stated, be preferable for the ECJ to decide the matter, where it is in possession of the relevant facts and has the requisite technical expertise.[95] This is more

[94] van Gerven, 'The Effect of Proportionality on the Actions of Member States of the European Community: National Viewpoints from Continental Europe', in Ellis (ed), *The Principle of Proportionality, supra* n. 1, at 42.

[95] Jacobs, 'Recent Developments in the Principle of Proportionality in European Community Law', in Ellis (ed.), *The Principle of Proportionality, supra* n. 1, at 19–20.

especially so where the factors involved in the proportionality inquiry are complex in the manner exemplified by *Familiapress.*

8. CONCLUSION

In the previous chapter we considered some of the more general difficulties about the structure of the proportionality analysis, and the problems attendant on weighing the value of the interests involved. These problems are present to a certain degree when it is Member State action that is being reviewed. The nature of the cases in which proportionality is in issue in relation to Member State action does, however, obviate certain difficulties.

This is because the proportionality inquiry will normally occur in circumstances where there is a clear enunciation in the Treaty of the importance of the interests involved. The paradigm case of proportionality and free movement is premised on the assumption that there has been a *prima facie* breach of an explicit Treaty provision, which is central to the realization of the EU's objectives. Those who framed the Treaties have therefore accorded the relevant interest a high status. It is then for the Member State to defend its action by showing that it comes within one of the recognized exceptions, and that it was proportionate. Judicial review in terms of proportionality is strict, but the ECJ has shown that it is willing to accept diversity of national values.

The importance accorded by the Treaty framers to the relevant Community interest frames the subsequent proportionality inquiry. It does not mean that difficult value judgments can be avoided in such cases. These are inherent in the proportionality inquiry. They are thrown into sharp relief by the complexity of the inquiries in cases such as *Torfaen*[96] and *Familiapress,*[97] which are challenging to say the least for any court, whether it be the ECJ or the national court. The outcome in such cases is perforce bound to be somewhat impressionistic, in the sense that the factors involved are too broad and multi-faceted to be susceptible to any more 'scientific' analysis. The recourse to such value judgments within adjudication is, however, not exceptional or confined to this area, more especially when the adjudication has a constitutional dimension.

[96] Case 145/88, *Torfaen BC, supra* n. 89.
[97] Case C-368/95, *Vereinigte Familiapress, supra* n. 93.

19

The Precautionary Principle

1. INTRODUCTION

Many of the principles of administrative law discussed in the previous chapters will be familiar to scholars of the subject from their domestic jurisprudence. The subject matter of this chapter, the precautionary principle, differs in this respect. While it is found in some legal systems, such as Germany, it is nonetheless relatively novel as a precept of administrative law. It is, however, clear that it has become of increased importance in EU law.

The chapter begins by examining the development of the precautionary principle and its transformation into a general principle of EU law. This is followed by analysis of the use of the principle for review of Community and Member State action. The focus then shifts to consideration of the political status of the principle and the way in which it informs decision-making. The chapter concludes by assessing the principle from a more normative dimension. There is considerable controversy over the meaning of the precautionary principle and its application.[1] The nature of this controversy will be explicated, and the political and legal interpretation of the principle will be evaluated in the light of this critical literature.

[1] There is a very large literature on the precautionary principle. The following are some of the most directly relevant for present purposes. R. Harding and E. Fisher (eds), *Perspectives on the Precautionary Principle* (Federation Press, 1999); Fisher, 'Is the Precautionary Principle Justiciable?' (2001) 13 *Jnl of Environmental Law* 315; Scott and Vos, 'The Juridification of Uncertainty: Observations on the Ambivalence of the Precautionary Principle within the EU and the WTO', in C. Joerges and R. Dehousse (eds), *Good Governance in Europe's Integrated Market* (Oxford University Press, 2002), Chap. 9; Fisher, 'Precaution, Precaution Everywhere: Developing a "Common Understanding" of the Precautionary Principle in the European Community' (2002) 9 *MJECL* 7; Cass Sunstein, *Risk and Reason, Safety, Law, and the Environment* (Cambridge University Press, 2002); Majone, 'What Price Safety? The Precautionary Principle and its Policy Implications' (2002) 40 *JCMS* 89; Sunstein, 'Beyond the Precautionary Principle' (2003) 151 *University of Pennsylvania Law Rev* 1003; Forrester, 'The Dangers of too much Precaution', in M. Hoskins and W. Robinson (eds), *A True European, Essays for Judge David Edward* (Hart, 2003), Chap. 16; Jose Luis da Cruz Vilaca, 'The Precautionary Principle in EC Law' (2004) 10 *EPL* 369; G. Marchant and K. Mossman, *Arbitrary and Capricious: The Precautionary Principle in the European Union Courts* (AEI Press, 2004); Arcuri, 'The Case for a Procedural Version of the Precautionary Principle Erring on the Side of Environmental Preservation', NYU School of Law, Global Law Working Paper 9/04; M. Lee,

2. A NEW GENERAL PRINCIPLE OF EU LAW

A. Foundations

We shall consider in the next section the way in which the Court of First Instance (CFI) developed the precautionary principle into a general principle of EU law. This transformation would, however, not have been possible if the CFI had not been able to draw on cases where the European Court of Justice (ECJ) had made implicit use of the precautionary principle. Recognition of the need for regulation when the scientific evidence was uncertain is apparent in the ECJ's jurisprudence at two levels: challenges to and interpretations of Community legislation, and actions brought against Member States. These will be considered in turn.

It is scarcely surprising that the ECJ should refer to the precautionary principle when interpreting Community legislation made under Article 174 EC, which makes the principle applicable in the environmental field.[2] The ECJ was also willing to use the principle as an interpretative tool when construing a Community directive that had an impact on the environment.[3] More significant for present purposes was the ECJ's acceptance of the need for intervention in the *BSE* case.[4] The UK challenged the legality of a Commission decision banning export of beef and beef products from the UK in the wake of mad cow disease. The UK argued, *inter alia*, that the decision was disproportionate, being neither appropriate nor necessary to achieve the desired end. The ECJ, having reiterated that proportionality was a general principle of Community law, stated that at the time when the contested decision was adopted there was great uncertainty as to the risks posed by live animals, bovine meat, and derived products. It then held that 'where there is uncertainty as to the existence or extent of risks to human health, the institutions may take protective measures without having to wait until the reality and seriousness of those risks become apparent'.[5] That approach was, said the ECJ, 'borne out' by Article 174(1) EC, requiring Community policy on the environment to pursue the objective, *inter alia*, of public health, and by Article 174(2) EC, which incorporated the precautionary principle into

EU Environmental Law, Challenges, Change and Decision-Making (Hart, 2005), Chap. 4; Fisher, 'The Precautionary Principle, Administrative Constitutionalism and European Integration', in E. Fisher, *Risk Regulation and Administrative Constitutionalism* (Hart, forthcoming 2007).

[2] See, e.g., Cases 175 and 178/98, *Criminal Proceedings against Paolo Lirussi and Francesca Bizzaro* [1999] ECR I-6881, at paras. 51–52.

[3] Case C-6/99, *Association Greenpeace France v Ministère de l'Agriculture and de la Pêche* [2000] ECR I-1651, at para. 44.

[4] Case C-180/96, *UK v Commission* [1998] ECR I-2265.

[5] Ibid. at para. 99.

environmental decision-making.[6] This reasoning was repeated in the *NFU* case,[7] where the National Farmers' Union (NFU) challenged the legality of Community measures to combat mad cow disease. In neither case did the ECJ mention the precautionary principle explicitly, but it was clearly implicit in the legitimation of protective measures when there was scientific uncertainty.

Scientific uncertainty was also of relevance in actions brought against Member States. The paradigm case involves a *prima facie* infringement of Article 28 EC on the free movement of goods. The Member State then seeks to defend its action on the ground of public health under Article 30 EC, arguing that its action is warranted because of the uncertain health risks associated with the product in question. The ECJ did not make specific reference to the precautionary principle, but it accepted, subject to certain conditions, the legitimacy of state action to protect health when the scientific effects of the particular substance or product were difficult to estimate.[8] Thus in *Toolex*[9] the ECJ found that a national ban on the use of a substance called trichloroethylene infringed Article 28 EC. It then held that 'taking account of the latest medical research on the subject, and also the difficulty in establishing the threshold above which exposure to trichloroethylene poses a serious risk to humans, given the present state of research, there is no evidence in this case to justify a conclusion by the Court that national legislation such as that at issue in the main proceedings goes beyond what is necessary to achieve the objectives in view'.[10]

B. Development

Legal reasoning is eternally interesting. It is one of the rationales for academic engagement with law. The way in which courts justify the formulation of a new principle is especially significant in this respect, all the more so when it is the CFI that takes the leading role. The previous discussion revealed the precautionary principle at work in the ECJ's judgments, even though it was not explicitly 'named'.

It was, however, the CFI that decided to render explicit what had been implicit in the ECJ's jurisprudence and to elevate the precautionary principle to the status of a new general principle of EU law. *Pfizer*[11] and

[6] Ibid. at para. 100.

[7] Case C-157/96, *The Queen v Ministry of Agriculture, Fisheries and Food, Commissioners of Customs & Excise, ex p National Farmers' Union* [1998] ECR I-2211, at paras. 62–64.

[8] Case C-174/82, *Officier van Justitie v Sandoz BV* [1983] ECR 2445; Case 247/84, *Criminal Proceedings against Leon Motte* [1985] ECR 3887; Case 54/85, *Ministère Public against Xavier Mirepoix* [1986] ECR 1067.

[9] Case C-473/98, *Kemikalieinspektionen v Toolex Alpha AB* [2000] ECR I-5681, at para. 45.

[10] Ibid. at para. 45.

[11] Case T-13/99, *Pfizer Animal Health SA v Council* [2002] ECR II-3305.

Artegodan[12] are the seminal judgments in this respect. The application of the precautionary principle in both of these cases will be considered in detail below. For now we are concerned with the reasoning used to justify precaution as a general principle of EU law. There are many similarities in the reasoning in the two cases, even though they were decided by different chambers.[13] The judicial building blocks for the new general principle were drawn in part from Treaty articles and in part from prior case law.

The obvious starting point in terms of Treaty foundations was the express mention of the precautionary principle in Article 174(2) EC concerning environmental policy. A single mention in relation to a specific area of Community action is scarcely sufficient to ground a new general principle. The CFI therefore looked further for Treaty legitimation. It placed reliance on Article 6 EC, which stipulates that environmental protection must be integrated into the definition and implementation of other Community policies listed in Article 3 EC. Given this injunction, it must follow, said the CFI, that the precautionary principle being a part of environmental protection should also be a factor in other Community policies.[14] This conclusion was reinforced through interpretation of other more specific Treaty articles. Thus the CFI held in *Artegodan*[15] that Article 174(1) EC provided that an objective of environmental protection was public health; that Article 152(1) EC stated that a high level of human health protection should be secured in the definition and implementation of all Community policies; that a similar injunction to ensure a high level of consumer protection and to integrate such protection into the definition and implementation of other Community policies was to be found in Article 153(1) and (2) EC; and that the precautionary principle was to be applied in these areas in order to ensure this requisite level of protection.

The CFI buttressed the argument from the Treaty by drawing on prior case law. It was unsurprising that it placed reliance on the *BSE* and *NFU* decisions for the proposition that the precautionary principle applies where the Community takes measures in the context of the CAP in order to safeguard health.[16] The CFI also followed well-established techniques of reasoning by analogy, alluding to other cases where the existence of the precautionary principle 'has in essence and at the very least implicitly been recognized by the Court of Justice'.[17]

[12] Cases T-74, 76, 83–85, 132, 137 and 141/00, *Artegodan GmbH v Commission* [2002] ECR II-4945.

[13] Case T-13/99, *Pfizer, supra* n. 11, at paras. 113–115; Cases T-74, 76, 83–85, 132, 137 and 141/00, *Artegodan, supra* n. 12, at paras. 181–186.

[14] Case T-13/99, *Pfizer, supra* n. 11, at para. 114; Cases T-74, 76, 83–85, 132, 137, and 141/00, *Artegodan, supra* n. 12, at para. 183.

[15] Cases T-74, 76, 83–85, 132, 137, and 141/00, *Artegodan, supra* n. 12, at para. 183.

[16] See, e.g., Case T-13/99, *Pfizer, supra* n. 11, at para. 114.

[17] Ibid. at para. 115.

The Treaty articles combined with prior case law provided the foundations for the recognition of a new general principle of Community law. The CFI in *Artegodan* expressed its conclusion in the following terms.[18]

It follows that the precautionary principle can be defined as a general principle of Community law requiring the competent authorities to take appropriate measures to prevent specific potential risks to public health, safety and the environment, by giving precedence to the requirements related to the protection of those interests over economic interests. Since the Community institutions are responsible, in all their spheres of activity, for the protection of public health, safety and the environment, the precautionary principle can be regarded as an autonomous principle stemming from the abovementioned Treaty provisions.

There is much in common in the reasoning of the different chambers of the CFI in *Pfizer* and *Artegodan* in establishing the precautionary principle as a general principle of EU law. There were, however, some differences of nuance, although it is difficult to determine whether these were intended or not. Thus in *Artegodan* the CFI framed its conclusion in obligatory terms: the precautionary principle is a general principle of Community law *requiring* the competent authorities to take appropriate measures to prevent specific potential risks to health, safety, and the environment, and it was this formulation that was adopted in the later *Solvay* decision.[19] This seems to go further than *Pfizer*, where the emphasis is on the EU having *discretion* to adopt protective measures in accord with the precautionary principle.

Now to be sure there may be instances where a specific Treaty article, regulation, or directive could be said to give rise to an obligation to take protective measures in furtherance of the precautionary principle, and it may be that this was all that the CFI had in mind in *Artegodan*. This is, however, different from positing a general obligation requiring that such measures be adopted pursuant to the precautionary principle throughout the relevant spheres of EU law.[20] A little later in its judgment in *Artegodan* the CFI appeared to accept that the competent authorities had discretion as to whether to apply the precautionary principle, but nonetheless qualified this by stating that the discretionary choice must comply with the principle that protection of health, safety, and the environment take precedence over economic interests, and with the principles of proportionality and non-discrimination.[21]

[18] Cases T-74, 76, 83–85, 132, 137, and 141/00, *Artegodan, supra* n. 12, at para. 184; Case T-147/00, *Les Laboratoires Servier v Commission* [2003] ECR II-85, at para. 52.

[19] Case T-392/02, *Solvay Pharmaceuticals BV v Council* [2003] ECR II-4555, at para. 121.

[20] Cruz Vilaca, *supra* n. 1, at 400–401.

[21] Cases T-74, 76, 83–85, 132, 137, and 141/00, *Artegodan, supra* n. 12, at paras. 185–186; Case T-392/02, *Solvay, supra* n. 19, at para. 122.

3. THE PRECAUTIONARY PRINCIPLE AND REVIEW OF COMMUNITY ACTION

It is clear that the precautionary principle is used when reviewing the legality of Community action.[22] The more particular meaning ascribed to the concept can, however, only be determined by paying close regard to the leading cases in which it was applied. Clarity concerning the positive law is moreover necessary before evaluating in normative terms the role played by the principle within EU law.

A. *Pfizer*

We have considered the *Pfizer* case[23] on a number of previous occasions, most notably when discussing the general principles of judicial review as they apply to discretionary determinations.[24] The present inquiry focuses more specifically on the way in which the precautionary principle was interpreted and applied by the CFI.

(1) Interpretation of the Precautionary Principle

It will be remembered that the case concerned a challenge by the applicant company to a Regulation that withdrew authorization for an additive to animal feeding stuffs. The additive in question, virginiamycin, was an antibiotic that was added in very small quantities to animal feed in order to promote growth. The rationale for the withdrawal of the authorization was the fear that such additives could reduce the animals' resistance to antibiotics, and that this lessening of resistance could be transmitted to humans. This would then reduce the effectiveness not only of that particular antibiotic, but might also limit the efficacy of antibiotics of the same class. Pfizer argued forcefully that this could not be proven in the light of the scientific evidence.

The CFI analysed, as we saw in the previous section, the place of the precautionary principle in the schema of the Treaty and in the light of the prior case law. It held that the Council and Commission could therefore proceed through the precautionary principle, even though because of scientific uncertainty, the reality and seriousness of the risks associated with the additives were not fully apparent.[25] The remainder of this part of the

[22] Case T-177/02, *Malagutti-Vezinhet SA v Commission* [2004] ECR II-827, at para. 54.

[23] Case T-13/99, *Pfizer*, *supra* n. 11. See also Case T-70/99, *Alpharma Inc v Council* [2002] ECR II-3495.

[24] See above, Chap. 13.

[25] Case T-13/99, *Pfizer*, *supra* n. 11, at paras. 139–141.

CFI's judgment casts important light on the more specific meaning of the precautionary principle in EU law.

The CFI *identified the risk assessed when the precautionary principle was applied*.[26] It steered a middle course in this respect. It was not necessary for the risk assessment to prove conclusive scientific evidence of the reality of the risk and the seriousness of the adverse consequences were that risk to become a reality. Nor, however, could a preventive measure be based on a purely hypothetical approach to the risk without any scientific verification. A preventive measure could only be introduced 'if the risk, although the reality and extent thereof have not been "fully" demonstrated by conclusive scientific evidence, appears nevertheless to be adequately backed up by the scientific data available at the time when the measure was taken'.[27] Risk was a function of the probability that the relevant product would adversely affect interests protected by the Community legal order, combined with assessment of the seriousness of those affects.[28]

There were, said the CFI, *two complementary components of this risk assessment*.[29] It was for the Community institutions to determine the level of protection which they deemed appropriate for society. This was an essentially political determination. While the Community institutions could not operate on zero-risk assumptions, they could legitimately decide to ensure a high level of human health protection. The second component of the risk assessment involved the estimation as to whether the level of risk determined by the political organs was present in a particular case. This required a scientific risk assessment to be carried out by experts before preventive measures could be adopted. The scientific advice should be based on principles of excellence, independence, and transparency. The very fact of scientific uncertainty, combined with the need to take preventive measures at short notice, meant that a full assessment might not always be possible. However, the competent public authority must nonetheless be given sufficiently reliable and cogent information by the scientific experts to enable it to decide on the appropriate response.[30]

> Consequently, if it is not to adopt arbitrary measures, which cannot in any circumstances be rendered legitimate by the precautionary principle, the competent public authority must ensure that any measures that it takes, even preventive measures, are based on as thorough a scientific risk assessment as possible . . . Notwithstanding the scientific uncertainty, the scientific risk assessment must enable the competent public authority to ascertain, on the basis of the best available data and the most recent results of international research, whether matters have gone beyond the level of risk that it deems acceptable for society.

[26] Ibid. at paras. 142–148.
[27] Ibid. at para. 144.
[28] Ibid. at paras. 147–148.
[29] Ibid. at paras. 149–163.
[30] Ibid. at para. 162.

The *apportionment of the burden of proof followed from the preceding analysis.* It was for the Community institutions to show that the contested regulation was adopted following from as thorough a scientific risk assessment as possible, and that they had as a result of that assessment sufficient scientific indications to conclude on an objective scientific basis that the use of virginiamycin as a growth promoter constituted a risk to health.[31]

The *success of any challenge would, however, be affected by the general principles of judicial review applicable to this type of case.*[32] In this respect the CFI repeated the well-established principle that the scope of review was limited where the Community institutions had a broad discretion relating to the level of risk deemed acceptable for society, and where they were required to make complex assessments when applying such discretion to the facts of particular cases. It was not for the Community courts to substitute their assessment of the facts for that of the Community institutions. The courts were confined to determining whether the exercise of discretion was vitiated by a manifest error, misuse of power, or whether the institutions clearly exceeded the bounds of their discretion. The very fact that the scientific assessment must be carried out thoroughly and in accord with the principles of excellence, independence, and transparency was, however, an important procedural guarantee against arbitrariness, and should be seen as an application of the procedural duty to take care incumbent on Community institutions.[33]

(2) Application of the Precautionary Principle

The CFI then applied the principles set out above to the instant case. It is important to understand that the CFI's judgment responded to a number of different allegations of error advanced by the applicant.

The CFI began by considering the claim that the *contested Regulation was tainted by factual errors.* The applicant argued that the Commission and Council had disregarded and distorted the findings of the Scientific Committee for Animal Nutrition (SCAN), which was established to assist the Commission at the latter's request on all scientific questions relating to the use of additives in animal nutrition. SCAN had, at the Commission's request, looked into the possible harmful effects of virginiamycin, and analysed the Danish claims in this respect. It concluded that there was no new evidence to substantiate the transfer of resistance to antibiotics from animals to humans; that while the development of bacterial resistance to antibiotics was a cause for concern, the data provided by the Danish authorities did not justify the action taken by Denmark to preserve streptogramins as therapeutic agents of last resort in humans; and that the use of virginiamycin as a

[31] Ibid. at para. 165.
[32] Ibid. at paras. 164–170.
[33] Ibid. at paras. 171–172.

growth promoter did not constitute an immediate risk to public health in Denmark.

The CFI rejected the argument. It found that the Commission and Council had not ignored SCAN's findings, even though they had not accepted its final conclusions. It held further that the Commission was not bound under the relevant legislation to adopt SCAN's conclusions. Where the Commission chose not to accept its conclusions it had, however, to provide reasons, which had to be at a scientific level commensurate with that of the opinion in question.[34] The fact that the Commission did not have to accept SCAN's conclusions was, said the CFI, justified by the Commission's political responsibility and democratic legitimacy, secured through Article 211 EC and political control by the European Parliament (EP). This was by way of contrast to SCAN. It had scientific legitimacy but 'this was not a sufficient basis for the exercise of public authority'.[35] The CFI decided that the Council, when ratifying the Commission's opinion, gave reasons for not accepting SCAN's conclusions, drawing in part on SCAN's own reasoning and in part on reports from other specialist national, international, and Community bodies.[36] The CFI also rejected the argument that the Commission and Council had distorted the SCAN opinion.

The CFI subsequently focused on the allegation that the contested Regulation was influenced by a new study produced by the Danish authorities after the SCAN opinion and that the Council and Commission should have sought a further opinion from SCAN on this matter. The CFI rejected the argument. It held that there was no obligation to undertake a second consultation. The CFI distinguished previous cases[37] on the ground that the relevant legislation was ambiguous as to whether consultation was mandatory or not. The judicial conclusion that the consultation should be deemed to be mandatory in all circumstances was a purposive interpretation of ambiguous legislation, which was inapplicable to the instant case where it was clear that consultation with SCAN was discretionary.[38] This finding was, however, qualified, the CFI holding that it would only be in exceptional circumstances where there were sufficient guarantees of scientific objectivity that the Community institutions might, when assessing complex scientific facts, proceed without obtaining an opinion from the relevant Community committee on the new scientific material.[39] The CFI, moreover, rejected the Council and Commission's argument that consultation with a different committee, the Standing Committee, sufficed in this respect, since it was a regulatory comitology committee and hence should be regarded as 'a political body

[34] Ibid. at para. 199. [35] Ibid. at para. 201. [36] Ibid. at para. 204.

[37] Case C-212/91, *Angelopharm GmbH v Freie Hansestadt Hamburg* [1994] ECR I-171, at paras. 31–41.

[38] Case T-13/99, *Pfizer*, *supra* n. 11, at paras. 262–266. [39] Ibid. at para. 270.

representative of the Member States and not as an independent scientific body'.[40] The CFI nonetheless concluded that the Council and Commission were aware of the limitations of the new study when taking it into account, and the study was in any event only regarded as part of the evidence in favour of the contested Regulation.[41]

The CFI, having rejected the arguments based on factual error, then considered a separate albeit related claim of *manifest error of assessment.* This was whether 'the Community institutions made a manifest error of assessment when they concluded, on the basis of those facts, that the use of virginiamycin as a growth promoter constituted a risk to human health'.[42] The CFI re-emphasized that in assessing whether the scientific evidence enabled the Community institutions to conclude that there was a risk associated with the use of virginiamycin as a growth promoter, the role of the court was limited: it was not to substitute judgment; it was limited to finding a manifest error, misuse of power, or clear excess of discretion; and any determination of such errors must be made on the basis of the material available to the Community institutions when the contested Regulation was made.[43] The CFI nonetheless considered in detail the applicant's argument. The applicant maintained that human resistance to antibiotics of the streptogramin class did not have any adverse effect on human health. The CFI was unconvinced. The SCAN findings were related to Denmark, rather than the problem at Community level. It was moreover clear from studies at national, Community, and international level that resistance to antibiotics was perceived as a major problem in human medicine. It was therefore proper for the Community institutions to develop a cautious approach designed to preserve the effectiveness of certain antibiotics used in human medicine, even though when the contested Regulation was made they were relatively little used in that sphere.[44]

The applicant argued further that the Community institutions were not entitled, on the basis of the available scientific data, to find a link between use of virginiamycin as an additive in feeding stuffs and the development of antibiotic resistance in humans. The argument and counter-argument was complex. Suffice it to say that the CFI examined these claims in some detail, and concluded that the Community institutions had a scientific basis on which to find the linkage.[45] The CFI also gave close consideration to the company's argument that the scientific data was not sufficient to warrant the challenged Regulation. It concluded against the company, holding that the precautionary principle justified the measure, even though there was no scientific certainty, more especially given that a full risk assessment would not have been possible in the time available.[46]

40 Ibid. at para. 283.
41 Ibid. at para. 298.
42 Ibid. at para. 311.
43 Ibid. at paras. 322–324.
44 Ibid. at para. 341.
45 Ibid. at para. 369.
46 Ibid. at paras. 381–384, 389, 393, 401.

The CFI then analysed the applicant's argument cast in terms of *proportionality*. We looked at this aspect of the CFI's reasoning when discussing proportionality.[47] Suffice it to say for the present that the court rejected the arguments that the withdrawal of the authorization was manifestly inappropriate to the objective pursued, and that the ban was not necessary since other less onerous measures could have been taken. It also found that the disadvantages of the ban were not disproportionate to the objectives pursued, nor did they entail a breach of the right to property.

B. *Artegodan*

(1) Interpretation of the Precautionary Principle

Artegodan was concerned with withdrawal of authorization to market medicinal products containing 'amphetamine-like' anorectic agents, used in the treatment of obesity by accelerating the feeling of satiety. The CFI annulled the Commission decisions withdrawing the authorization, principally because under the relevant Community legislation the Commission did not have the competence to make the contested decisions. The ECJ upheld the CFI in this respect.[48] The CFI also held that even if the Commission had been competent to make the decisions they were nonetheless flawed because of infringement of the Directive applicable in the area. It was in this context that the CFI discussed the precautionary principle, although the ECJ did not do so.

The rationale for consideration of the precautionary principle was that Article 11 of Directive 65/65[49] stipulated that the competent authorities should suspend or revoke the marketing authorization of a medicinal product where it proves to be harmful in the normal conditions of use, or where its therapeutic efficacy is lacking or where its quantitative or qualitative composition was not as declared. The CFI stated that these conditions for withdrawal of an authorization must be interpreted in accord with the general principle identified in the case law to the effect that public health should take precedence over economic considerations.[50] In the context of withdrawal of marketing authorization, three considerations flowed from this principle.[51]

The general principle that public health take priority over economic considerations was, said the CFI, reinforced in this context by the provisions

[47] See above, Chap. 17.

[48] Case C-39/03 P, *Commission v Artegodan GmbH* [2003] ECR I-7885.

[49] Council Directive 65/65/EEC of 26 January 1965, On the Approximation of Provisions Laid Down by Law, Regulation or Administrative Action Relating to Proprietary Medicinal Products, OJ 1965 L22/369.

[50] Cases T-74, 76, 83–85, 132, 137, and 141/00, *Artegodan, supra* n. 12, at para. 173.

[51] Ibid. at para. 174.

of Directive 65/65, which meant that when authorizing and withdrawing authorization of medicinal products account should be taken exclusively of considerations relating to health protection.[52]

A further consequence of the general principle of priority for public health meant in this context that there should be a re-evaluation of the benefit/risk balance where new data gave rise to concerns about efficacy. The CFI recognized, however, that the degree of harmfulness which the competent authority might regard as acceptable depended on the benefits the medicinal product were thought to provide. The concepts of harmfulness and therapeutic efficacy could therefore only be examined relative to one another and depended on the progress of scientific knowledge.[53]

The priority accorded to public health meant, moreover, that in cases of scientific uncertainty the competent authority should assess the medicinal product in the light of the precautionary principle.[54] The CFI provided important guidance as to how the rules of evidence should be interpreted in the light of the precautionary principle.[55] Where initial authorization to market a medicinal product was sought it was for the producer to prove its efficacy and safety. Where, however, the Commission sought to withdraw authorization it had the burden of proving that one of the conditions for withdrawal laid down in Article 11 of Directive 65/65 was met. The precautionary principle was relevant in discharging this burden of proof. The suspension or withdrawal of authorization was warranted in accord with the precautionary principle where new data gave rise to serious doubts as to the safety or efficacy of the product, even if there was still a measure of scientific uncertainty as to the reality of these doubts. The CFI nonetheless emphasized that withdrawal of authorization was only allowed where a potential risk or lack of efficacy could be substantiated by 'new, objective, scientific and/or medical data or information'.[56]

(2) Application of the Precautionary Principle

The CFI concluded that the contested decisions were flawed in the light of the principles set out above. Its decision is significant in two respects.

The CFI emphasized the *importance of consultation with the relevant scientific committee.* The Commission had relied on findings made by the CPMP, the Committee for Proprietary Medicinal Products. The Commission was not bound by its opinion, but the CFI stressed nonetheless the importance of the mandatory consultation with the CPMP laid down by the relevant Directive: given that the Commission could not assess for itself the safety or efficacy of the product, consultation with the CPMP was necessary to give

[52] Ibid. at paras. 175–177.
[53] Ibid. at para. 178.
[54] Ibid. at para. 181.
[55] Ibid. at paras. 187–195.
[56] Ibid. at para. 194.

the Commission the scientific evidence from which it could make a reasoned decision.[57]

The *CFI also asserted control over the reasoning process used by the scientific committee.* It held that, for the purposes of reviewing the Commission's decision under the Community Directive, the 'Community judicature may be called on to review, first, the formal legality of the CPMP's scientific opinion and, second, the Commission's exercise of its discretion'.[58] While the CFI acknowledged that it could not substitute its view for that of the CPMP, it could consider the reasons proffered by the CPMP and whether there was an understandable link between the medical evidence relied on by the CPMP and its conclusions. It was moreover incumbent on the CPMP to refer to the main scientific reports on which it had relied and to explain why it disagreed with, for example, divergent scientific opinion presented by the undertakings concerned in the case.[59]

The 'practical logic' of the CFI's reasoning is in many ways unassailable. The CFI had already stressed the importance of consultation with the CPMP, since the Commission did not have the requisite expertise to make the scientific evaluation. Given that the Commission would normally accept the opinion of the scientific committee, and had done so in this case, it followed that if judicial review was to be meaningful the CFI should be able to consider the reasoning used by the CPMP. The CFI did not, however, trouble to reconcile this 'practical logic' with the standard requirement that for an act to be reviewable it must be binding on and capable of affecting the legal interests of the applicant. It is nonetheless possible to conjecture what the response of the court could have been. It could have argued that the mandatory consultation of the CPMP rendered its opinion, which was then adopted by the Commission, an integral part of the legally binding decision made by the Commission, and was therefore reviewable.[60] The very fact that the CFI expressly affirmed its power to review the reasoning used by the CPMP bears ample testimony to its desire that review should 'bite' where the 'real decision' was made. Nor was this mere formal window dressing, since the CFI looked in detail at the CPMP's reasoning.

In terms of review of the Commission decision made in reliance on the CPMP's opinion, the CFI reiterated orthodoxy, to the effect that where the Commission exercised broad discretionary power the court's role was limited to assessing whether the decision was vitiated by manifest error or misuse of power and to ensuring that the competent authority did not clearly exceed the bounds of its discretion.[61]

[57] Ibid. at para. 198. [58] Ibid. at para. 199. [59] Ibid. at paras. 199–200.

[60] This was in effect the approach taken in Case T-326/99, *Olivieri v Commission and EMEA* [2003] ECR II-6053, at para. 55.

[61] Cases T-74, 76, 83–85, 132, 137, and 141/00, *Artegodan, supra* n. 12, at para. 201.

Notwithstanding the fact that the Commission had relied on the CPMP's opinion, and notwithstanding the CFI's statements as to the limits of judicial review, it nonetheless held that the decisions withdrawing authorization were flawed. This was because neither the CPMP, nor the Commission, had pointed to any new scientific data relating to safety or efficacy since the authorization had originally been granted. Change in what was felt to be good clinical practice was not sufficient in this respect.

C. *Monsanto*

The previous cases were concerned with the precautionary principle as a 'shield': it was used as a defence by the Community institutions to justify the Community provision being attacked. It is, however, clear that the principle can also be used as a 'sword' by an applicant who is challenging the legality of a Community norm.

The *Monsanto* case provides a good example.[62] Regulation 258/97[63] laid down a regulatory regime for the placing on the market of novel foods and novel food ingredients, which were essentially foods consisting of or containing ingredients produced from genetically modified organisms. A simplified procedure for authorization applied in relation to such foods that were substantially equivalent to existing foods. This procedure was relied on by the applicants concerning certain strains of genetically modified maize. The Italian Ministry of Health maintained that this procedure was not warranted, and that the fuller procedure under the Regulation should have been used instead. The Italian Ministry therefore had recourse to the safeguard clause in Article 12 of the Regulation, which allowed a Member State to restrict temporarily or suspend the trade in the use of such foods where, as a result of new information or re-assessment of existing information, it has detailed grounds for considering that the use of foods complying with the Regulation endangers human health or the environment.

The national court asked, *inter alia*, whether the simplified procedure, which did not require a comprehensive risk assessment, was coupled with detailed rules sufficient to ensure a high level of protection for health and the environment within the meaning of Articles 152(1) EC and 174(2) EC and whether it guaranteed compliance with the precautionary principle and proportionality.

[62] Case C-236/01, *Monsanto Agricultura Italia SpA v Presidenza del Consiglio dei Ministri* [2003] ECR I-8105. See also, Case C-6/99, *Association Greenpeace France v Ministère de l'Agriculture et de la Pêche* [2000] ECR I-1651, at paras. 40–44. The precautionary principle was also relied on to challenge Community action in Case C-393/01, *France v Commission* [2003] ECR I-5405, but the case was decided on other grounds.

[63] Regulation (EC) 258/97 of the European Parliament and of the Council of 27 January 1997, Concerning Novel Food and Novel Food Ingredients, OJ 1997 L43/1.

The ECJ held that the simplified procedure could be justified according to these criteria. The procedure only applied where there was substantial equivalence with existing foods. If dangers were identifiable the more comprehensive risk assessment under the normal procedure was required.[64] The obvious response to this is that it begs the question in issue, since the dangers might only be identifiable if the comprehensive risk assessment is carried out. The ECJ sought to address this by pointing out that the simplified procedure was but the first stage in a series of assessments that could be made under the Regulation, including the use of the safeguard clause in Article 12. This clause was seen as giving specific expression to the precautionary principle and the principle should also be taken into account under the normal procedure in order to decide whether, in the light of conclusions flowing from the risk assessment, the food could be placed on the market without danger for the consumer.[65] The simplified procedure was moreover seen to be compatible with proportionality.[66]

4. THE PRECAUTIONARY PRINCIPLE AND REVIEW OF MEMBER STATE ACTION

The discussion thus far has been concerned with the way in which the precautionary principle is used when reviewing the legality of Community action. It is, however, clear that the principle is also of relevance for the review of Member State action. The cases can be broken down into a number of different categories.

A. Member State Compliance with Environmental Directives

We have already seen that the most explicit reference to the precautionary principle is to be found in Article 174(2) EC concerned with environmental policy. It is therefore not surprising that the principle should be of relevance in cases concerned with Member State compliance with environmental directives.

This is exemplified by *Commission v France*[67] where the issue was whether France had properly applied a Directive on urban waste water treatment.[68] The Directive stipulated that discharge of waste water in 'sensitive areas' should be subject to more stringent treatment than for less sensitive areas,

[64] Case C-236/01, *Monsanto, supra* n. 62, at para. 129. [65] Ibid. at para. 133.

[66] Ibid. at paras. 134–136.

[67] Case C-280/02, *Commission v France* [2004] ECR I-8573.

[68] Council Directive 91/271/EEC of 21 May 1991, Concerning Urban Waste-Water Treatment, OJ 1991 L135/40.

this being to prevent the growth of algae that could damage the organic balance in the water where the discharge occurred. The Commission argued that France was in breach of these provisions in a number of areas. The French government denied that the areas were sensitive for the purposes of the Directive, and challenged the scientific evidence relied on by the Commission. The ECJ held that environmental policy was based on the precautionary principle and that the available scientific and technical data provided sufficient evidence of a causal link between discharge of waste water and growth of algae in the Seine bay.[69]

Similar reasoning is evident in *ARCO*.[70] The ECJ held in accord with established principle that in the absence of harmonization Member States were free to choose the modes of proof of the various matters defined in directives which they transposed, provided that the effectiveness of Community law was not undermined. The effectiveness of Article 174 EC would, however, be undermined if the national legislature used modes of proof restricting the scope of the Directive, with the result that it did not cover substances that corresponded to the meaning of waste within the Directive. This was particularly important since the inclusion of the precautionary principle in Article 174 meant that the concept of waste should not be interpreted restrictively.[71]

The precise demands imposed on Member States by environmental directives may also be influenced by the precautionary principle, as is evident from the *Waddenzee* case.[72] The National Association for the Protection of the Waddenzee and the Netherlands Association for the Protection of Birds challenged the grant of licences by the Dutch Secretary of State for Agriculture for cockle fishing in the special protection area of the Waddenzee, arguing that the licences infringed certain provisions of the Habitats Directive.[73] Article 6(3) of the Directive provided that any plan or project not directly connected with or necessary to the management of the site but likely to have a significant effect thereon, either individually or in combination with other plans or projects, should be subject to an appropriate assessment of its implications in view of the site's conservation objectives.

The ECJ held that the requirement for an appropriate assessment of the implications of the plan or project was conditional on its being likely to have

[69] Case C-280/02, *Commission v France supra* n. 67, at para. 34.

[70] Cases C-418–419/97, *ARCO Chemie Nederland Ltd v Minister van Volkshuisvesting, Ruimtelijke Ordening en Milieubeheer* [2000] ECR I-4475.

[71] Ibid. at para. 40.

[72] Case C-127/02, *Landelijke Vereniging tot Behoud van de Waddenzee and Nederlandse Vereniging tot Bescherming van Vogels v Staatssecretaris van Landbouw, Natuurbeheeer en Visserij* [2004] ECR I-7405.

[73] Council Directive 92/43/EEC of 21 May 1992, On the Conservation of Natural Habitats and of Wild Fauna and Flora, OJ 1992 L206/7.

a significant effect on the site. It was not, however, necessary to show that these consequences were definite. It was sufficient to trigger the protections of Article 6(3) if there was some probability or risk of such an effect following from the plan or project. This interpretation was reinforced in the light of the precautionary principle, by reference to which the Habitats Directive had to be interpreted. Construed in this manner 'such a risk exists if it cannot be excluded on the basis of objective information that the plan or project will have significant effects on the site concerned'.[74] In such circumstances an assessment in accord with Article 6(3) had to be undertaken.

The precautionary principle was used once again in answering the national court's question as to the meaning of 'appropriate assessment' for the purposes of Article 6(3). The second sentence of Article 6(3) stated in effect that in the light of the conclusions of the assessment the national authorities should agree to the plan or project only after having ascertained that it would not adversely affect the integrity of the site and if appropriate after having obtained the opinion of the general public. The ECJ held that this meant that if there were remaining doubts as to the absence of adverse effects on the integrity of the site, then the authorization would have to be refused. It was clear, said the ECJ, that the authorization criterion in Article 6(3) 'integrates the precautionary principle'.[75] The competent national authorities could therefore only authorize activity 'if they have made certain that it will not adversely affect the integrity of the site', that being so 'where no reasonable scientific doubt remains as to the absence of such effects'.[76]

B. Member States and the Four Freedoms

We saw from the preceding analysis on the development of the precautionary principle that the Community courts acknowledged scientific uncertainty in the context of actions against Member States for breach of the four freedoms. They took account of this uncertainty when assessing defences to, for example, free movement of goods framed in terms of protection of public health. This theme has persisted in more recent case law, the main difference being that there has been more explicit reference to the precautionary principle.

This can be seen in the case law on vitamins and nutrients. There have been a number of cases in which the ECJ has adjudicated on the legality of Member State legislation restricting the sale of goods containing vitamins

[74] Case C-127/02, *Landelijke Vereniging tot Behoud van de Waddenzee, supra* n. 72, at para. 44. See also, Case C-6/04, *Commission v UK* [2005] ECR I-9017, at para. 54.

[75] Case C-127/02, *Landelijke Vereniging tot Behoud van de Waddenzee, supra* n. 72, at para. 58.

[76] Ibid. at para. 59.

and food supplements.[77] The ECJ's reasoning is exemplified by *Greenham and Abel*.[78] The ECJ held that national rules whereby a Member State prohibited the marketing without prior authorization of foodstuffs lawfully manufactured and marketed in another Member State, where nutrients such as vitamins and minerals had been added, could be justified under Article 30 EC, provided that certain conditions were met.

If there was an authorization procedure it must be readily accessible and be capable of being completed within a reasonable time. If authorization was refused that decision must be open to legal challenge.

An application for inclusion on the national list of authorized substances could only be refused by the national authorities if such substances posed a genuine risk for public health. It was for the Member States in the absence of harmonization and to the extent that there was scientific uncertainty to decide on the level of protection for human health. The broad discretion possessed by the Member States was, however, qualified by the principle of proportionality, so that the measures chosen must be limited to what was necessary to safeguard health.

The requirement of showing that there was a real risk to health meant that the Member State had to undertake a detailed assessment of the risk posed by the food additive. Prohibition of the marketing of foodstuffs with such additives could only be justified on the basis of the latest scientific data available when the decision was adopted, designed to show the probability and seriousness of harm. This risk assessment might well reveal that scientific uncertainty persisted as to the existence or extent of risk to health. It must be accepted, said the ECJ, that in such circumstances 'a Member State may, in accordance with the precautionary principle, take protective measures without having to wait until the existence and gravity of those risks are fully demonstrated',[79] although this risk assessment could not be based on purely hypothetical considerations.

In an action based on Article 234 EC it will normally be for the national court to decide whether the conditions mentioned in the ECJ's judgment were met. Thus it will be for the referring court to determine whether scientific data was taken into account when the national legislation was adopted, whether that data showed a real risk, and whether in the event of scientific uncertainty the precautionary principle justified the state action. The ECJ may well, however, give guidance or indeed answers to some of these matters

[77] Case C-192/01, *Commission v Denmark* [2003] ECR I-9693; Case C-24/00, *Commission v France* [2004] ECR I-1277; Case C-41/02, *Commission v Netherlands* [2004] ECR I-11375; Cases C-154–155/04, *The Queen on the Application of Alliance for Natural Health and Nutri-Link Ltd v Secretary of State for Health* [2005] ECR I-6451.

[78] Case C-95/01, *Criminal Proceedings against John Greenham and Leonard Abel* [2004] ECR I-1333.

[79] Ibid. at para. 43. See also, at para. 48.

in a preliminary ruling if it wishes to do so. Where the action is based on Article 226 EC it will be for the ECJ to make these assessments.[80]

C. Member States and the Interpretation of Community Legislation

The most obvious situations where the precautionary principle will be of relevance in actions against Member States are those considered above. It is, however, clear that the principle can also be apposite when interpreting Community legislation in other circumstances.[81]

The *Monsanto* case provides a good example.[82] We have already considered the case in relation to challenge to Community legislation. It also entailed review of Member State action, since the applicant argued that recourse to the safeguard clause by the Italian government was not warranted. The ECJ held that the twofold objective of Regulation 258/97 was to ensure the functioning of the internal market in novel foods and to protect against the public health risks to which such foods might give rise.

In the light of this assessment of legislative objectives, the ECJ laid down criteria for reliance on the safeguard clause that were very similar to those developed in the case law on free movement. The safeguard clause in Article 12 was 'understood as giving specific expression to the precautionary principle'[83], and it therefore followed that protective measures could be taken without having to wait until the reality and seriousness of those risks became apparent.[84] It was not, however, sufficient for such measures to be based on a purely hypothetical approach to risk. The risk assessments must be as complete as possible and must indicate that the foods constitute a danger to the consumer in accord with the requirements of the Regulation.[85]

5. THE PRECAUTIONARY PRINCIPLE, POLITICS, AND THE COMMISSION COMMUNICATION

The preceding analysis has considered the interpretation accorded to the precautionary principle by the Community courts. The Commission has, however, also contributed to the debate about the role of the principle in EU law. It is therefore important to analyse its Communication.[86] We will then

[80] See, e.g., Case C-24/00, *Commission v France, supra* n. 77.

[81] Case T-147/00, *Les Laboratoires Servier, supra* n. 18; Case C-286/02, *Bellio F. IIi Srl v Prefettura di Treviso* [2004] ECR I-3465.

[82] Case C-236/01, *Monsanto Agricultura, supra* n. 62. See also, Case C-132/03, *Ministero della Salute v Codacons* [2005] ECR I-4167.

[83] Ibid. at para. 110. [84] Ibid. at para. 111. [85] Ibid. at paras. 106–109.

[86] Communication from the Commission, On the Precautionary Principle, COM(2000) 1 final.

be in a better position to assess the wider debate about the desirability or not of the precautionary principle.

In April 1999 the Council asked the Commission to be in the future more guided by the precautionary principle in preparing legislative proposals and in its other consumer-related activities, and requested it to develop as a matter of priority clear and effective guidelines for the application of the principle.

The Commission responded to this request by publishing in 2000 its Communication, which was designed 'to establish a common understanding of the factors leading to recourse to the precautionary principle and its place in decision-making, and to establish guidelines for its application based on reasoned and coherent principles'.[87] It was also intended to allay fears that recourse to the principle could 'serve as a justification for disguised protectionism',[88] or that it was inconsistent with the EU's obligations under the World Trade Organization (WTO).

The Commission examined the place of the precautionary principle in the schema of the Treaty and the existing case law and concluded, much as the Community courts were to do a few years later, that although the principle was only explicitly mentioned in the environmental field, its scope was nonetheless far wider. It covered those circumstances where scientific evidence was insufficient, inconclusive, or uncertain, but where preliminary scientific evaluation indicated that there were reasonable grounds for concern that the potentially dangerous effects on the environment, human, animal, or plant health might be inconsistent with the chosen level of protection.[89]

Having assessed the place of the precautionary principle in international law, the Commission then turned its attention to the constituent parts of the principle. It distinguished between the political decision to act or not to act, which was said to be linked to the factors triggering recourse to the precautionary principle, from the decision how to act, connoting the measures resulting from application of the principle.[90]

There were various factors that triggered recourse to the precautionary principle, which informed the political decision whether to act or not.[91] The potentially negative effects of a phenomenon should be identified through scientific data. This should be followed by scientific evaluation of the potential adverse effects, in particular the probability and seriousness of the harm that might occur, although it might not be possible in certain instances to complete a comprehensive risk assessment. The concept of risk assessment consisted of hazard identification, hazard characterization, appraisal of exposure, and risk characterization. Scientific uncertainty could exist in relation to each of these components of risk assessment. This uncertainty could

87 Ibid. at 8. 88 Ibid. at 8. 89 Ibid. at 9–10. 90 Ibid. at 12.
91 Ibid. at 13–14.

result from the variable chosen, the measurements made, the samples drawn, the models used, the causal relationship employed, and from controversy about existing data. These triggering factors taken as a whole would inform the decision whether to act or not, this being 'an eminently political decision, a function of the risk level that is "acceptable" to the society on which the risk is imposed'.[92]

The Commission then laid down guidelines for those situations where action was deemed necessary based on the precautionary principle in order to manage risk.[93] The guidelines contain substantive, procedural, and evidentiary precepts. There should be a cost/benefit analysis to compare the likely positive and negative consequences of the envisaged action and inaction, and this should include non-economic considerations. All interested parties should be involved to the fullest extent possible in the study of various risk management options that might be envisaged once the results of the scientific evaluation or risk assessment become available. The procedure should be as transparent as possible. Risk management in accord with the precautionary principle should moreover be consistent with and take account of certain other principles. It should be proportionate, in the sense that measures based on the precautionary principle should not be disproportionate to the desired level of protection and must not aim at zero risk, since this rarely if ever exists. In some instances a total ban might not be a proportional response to a potential risk, in others it might be the only possible response. Measures taken in pursuance of the precautionary principle should not be discriminatory, and should be consistent with measures already adopted in similar circumstances. The guidelines also addressed the temporal dimension of measures made pursuant to the precautionary principle. Such measures, although provisional, should be maintained as long as the scientific data remained 'incomplete, imprecise or inconclusive and as long as the risk is considered too high to be imposed on society'.[94] These measures should, however, be re-examined and modified if necessary depending on results of scientific research.

The Commission addressed by way of conclusion the delicate and important issue of the burden of proof. This will necessarily be a matter for the Community courts to decide, but it is nonetheless interesting to see the Commission's thinking in this respect.[95] There were, said the Commission, some instances where the Community legislator might reverse the burden of proof. Substances that were deemed to be *a priori* hazardous might therefore have to be approved before they could be marketed. It would then be for the manufacturer to show that the substances were not hazardous and to carry out the scientific work necessary to evaluate the risk. These cases were to be

[92] Ibid. at 15. [93] Ibid. at 16–21. [94] Ibid. at 20.
[95] Ibid. at 20–21.

contrasted to those where there was no prior approval procedure, so that it would be for citizens or public authorities to demonstrate the nature of the danger and the level of risk posed. Even in this type of case the burden of proof might be partially reversed, in the sense that once a certain level of danger had been revealed it would then be for the manufacturer to counter these arguments.

The Commission's Communication was generally welcomed by the EP, which stressed the desirability of widespread public involvement in the policy choices involving the precautionary principle, and the need to see the principle as but one part of a broader strategy for risk management.[96]

6. THE PRECAUTIONARY PRINCIPLE, ACADEMIC DISCOURSE, AND THE EU

A. The Academic Discourse

There may well be a measure of disagreement with the EU's principles of administrative law and the way in which they have been applied in particular cases. That is natural when reflecting on any regime of administrative law. There is nonetheless little doubt that the degree of controversy that surrounds the precautionary principle is significantly greater. Thus Scott and Vos began their discussion by remarking:[97]

> Few legal concepts have achieved the notoriety of the precautionary principle. Praised by some, disparaged by others, the principle is deeply ambivalent and apparently infinitely malleable.

The tensions generated by the precautionary principle have been evident in sharp academic exchanges and political clashes that have spilled over into the dispute resolution mechanisms of the WTO. The nature of the contending arguments is captured well by Fisher.[98]

> Those who promote the precautionary principle argue that regulatory regimes that place too much faith in scientific method and crude understandings of acceptable risk are inadequate to deal with the analytical and deliberative challenges created by scientific uncertainty. Those that are critical of the precautionary principle argue that the principle threatens to be a mandate for arbitrary administrative decision-making because it represents an abandonment of objective, and thus accountable,

[96] European Parliament Report, On the Commission Communication on the Precautionary Principle, A5-0352/2000. See also, Opinion of the Economic and Social Committee, Use of the Precautionary Principle, OJ 2000 C268/04.

[97] Scott and Vos, *supra* n. 1, at 253.

[98] Fisher, 'The Precautionary Principle, Administrative Constitutionalism and European Integration', *supra* n. 1, at 1.

administrative decision-making. The model of good administration that is legitimate to one group is illegitimate to the other and vice versa.

It would certainly not be possible to 'resolve' these disagreements within the confines of this chapter. Nor is that the aim. It would, however, be inappropriate to ignore the intense debate that surrounds the precautionary principle. The present objective is therefore to convey an understanding of the arguments advanced by those who are opposed to the principle, and then to reflect on the way in which the principle has been used by the Community both politically and legally in the light of these arguments.

Majone has been one of the main critics of the precautionary principle. He argued that the 'precautionary approach is deeply ambiguous' and that 'this ambiguity is abetted by a lack of clear definitions and sound logical foundations'.[99] Majone noted that the similarity of different statements of the principle was often more apparent than real, and pointed out that in Germany where the principle originated 11 different meanings of the principle had been distinguished. He argued that the Commission Communication was beset by a deep-rooted ambiguity, caused by the desire to prevent use of the precautionary principle by Member States to extend their own regulatory autonomy, while at the same time maximizing the EU's regulatory discretion at the international level.[100]

Majone's principal criticism of the principle related, however, to the logic of decision-making. He maintained that the Commission Communication failed to consider the opportunity cost of precautionary measures, such that 'the attempt to control poorly understood, low-level risks necessarily uses up resources that in many cases could be directed more effectively towards the reduction of well-known, large-scale risks'.[101] This was especially important given that resources were limited so that it was impossible to control all actual and potential risks.

Majone argued moreover that the precautionary principle was seriously flawed as an aid to decision-making under uncertainty. The essence of the argument was that risk is a compound or product of the probability of harm and its severity. The optimal decision was to choose the course of action that minimized the expected loss, this being the sum of the product of the losses taking account of the corresponding probabilities.[102] The precautionary principle by way of contrast 'tends to focus the attention of regulators on some particular events and corresponding losses, rather than the entire range of possibilities'.[103] The preceding difficulties were compounded, said Majone, by the artificial distinction between those situations where scientific information was sufficient for formal risk assessment, and those where it was inconclusive or uncertain. These were in reality 'two points

[99] Majone, *supra* n. 1, at 90. [100] Ibid. at 98–99. [101] Ibid. at 101.
[102] Ibid. at 102. [103] Ibid. at 103.

on a knowledge-ignorance continuum rather than two qualitatively distinct situations'.[104]

Sunstein has been an equally strident critic of the precautionary principle.[105] Precisely because this is so, it is important to be clear as to his target. Sunstein acknowledged that there were different versions of the precautionary principle. He followed Stewart[106] in distinguishing between four such versions.[107] There was the *non-preclusion precautionary principle*, which connoted the idea that regulation should not be precluded by the absence of scientific certainty about activities that posed a risk of substantial harm. A second version was termed the *margin of safety precautionary principle*, meaning that regulation should include a margin of safety, limiting activities below the level at which adverse effects had not been found or predicted. A third interpretation was labelled the *best available technology precautionary principle*, requiring that best technology requirements 'should be imposed on activities that pose an uncertain potential to create substantial harm, unless those in favour of those activities can show that they present no appreciable risk'.[108] There was finally the *prohibitory precautionary principle*, which stipulated that prohibitions should be imposed where the activities have 'an uncertain potential to impose substantial harm, unless those in favour of the activities can show that they present no appreciable risk'.[109]

Sunstein accepted that weak versions of the precautionary principle were 'unobjectionable and important',[110] and was reasonably positive about the approach taken to the precautionary principle in the Commission's Communication.[111] He argued that there should be some correlation between the level of risk and the type of regulatory response, and few if any would disagree with this.

The focus of his attack was on strong versions of the principle, which 'suggest that regulation is required whenever there is a possible risk to health, safety, or the environment, even if the supporting evidence is speculative and even if the economic costs of regulation are high'.[112] On this view, once there was some relatively minimal threshold of risk there was a presumption in favour of stringent regulatory controls.

The core of Sunstein's challenge to the strong version of the precautionary principle was that it was paralysing, forbidding all courses of action, including inaction. The need to be selective as to what we take precautions about was seen as not merely an empirical fact, but a conceptual inevitability,

[104] Ibid. at 104. [105] Sunstein, 'Beyond the Precautionary Principle', *supra* n. 1.

[106] Stewart, 'Environmental Regulatory Decision Making under Uncertainty', in T. Swanson (ed), *20 Research in Law and Economics* 71, at 76.

[107] Sunstein, 'Beyond the Precautionary Principle', *supra* n. 1, at 1014.

[108] Ibid. at 1014. [109] Ibid. at 1014. [110] Ibid. at 1016, 1029, 1031.

[111] Ibid. at 1017–1018, 1029. [112] Ibid. at 1018.

since 'no society can be highly precautionary with respect to all risks'.[113] The precautionary principle could therefore only offer guidance if 'those who apply it wear blinders',[114] in the sense of focusing on certain aspects of the regulatory situation and disregarding others. The belief that the principle required, for example, restrictions on genetically modified foods meant ignoring the potential health benefits that could accompany such products.[115]

Sunstein articulated a number of behavioural factors that might cause people to wear such blinders, such as loss aversion, probability neglect, and neglect of the impact of one-off interventions, which served to explain the readiness to focus on a particular subset of the hazards involved.[116] It was precisely because there were risks involved in all regulatory choices that it was vital to have a 'wider view screen'. The strong version of the precautionary principle was, however, said to provide no guidance in choosing between the broader risks thus identified.[117]

B. The Precautionary Principle and Political Decision-Making in the EU: An Evaluative Strategy

The preceding discussion has revealed the concerns of those opposed to the precautionary principle. A response might simply be to deny the force of these arguments in their entirety. It would then be necessary for those of this persuasion to show why arguments of the kind advanced by Majone and Sunstein are flawed. That is not the approach adopted here. It will become clear that I have some reservations about their analyses, but I also think that they proffer arguments that should be taken seriously. So the alternative is to consider how far the precautionary principle as actually used in political decision-making in the EU is susceptible to the critique set out above. This is not an easy question to answer for reasons that will become apparent below. It is nonetheless the important question. Let me at least suggest a strategy as to how to approach the question.

We should begin by *identifying what are regarded as the central problems with the precautionary principle.* This is a necessary step in order to decide whether these deficiencies are present in the EU version of the principle. The principal difficulties articulated by Majone and Sunstein with the stronger versions of the principle are threefold. There is the propensity to impose 'blinders' on decision-making, such that only certain aspects of a regulatory situation are taken into account, these characteristically being the risks associated with the activity and not its attendant benefits; there is the related idea that the principle offends decision-making logic by focusing on

[113] Ibid. at 1029, 1054.
[114] Ibid. at 1035.
[115] Ibid. at 1035–1036.
[116] Ibid. at 1035–1054.
[117] Ibid. at 1054, 1057–1058.

possible losses with insufficient attention being paid to the probability that they will occur; and there is the concern that regulatory constraints will be imposed where the evidence of possible harm is very speculative and the costs of regulation high. It is not fortuitous that Majone and Sunstein stress respectively the need to consider the 'entire range of possibilities' and the 'wide screen' view. For these authors, the very broadening of the inquiry renders the stronger version of the precautionary principle of little assistance in deciding whether a particular risk should be subject to regulation or not.

The *issue is therefore whether these problems are apparent in the EU version of the precautionary principle.* The Commission Communication provides only limited guidance. This is in part because it is ambiguous in certain respects, a point that has been noted by a number of commentators. This is reflected by the fact that Sunstein, with some reservations, generally regards it as an acceptable weak version of the principle, while Majone is more critical and believes that it embodies a defective decision-making logic. It should moreover be recognized that the Commission Communication is just that, a document setting out its general approach to use of the principle.

We can therefore *only properly assess whether the difficulties with the principle are prevalent in EU law by analysing particular areas where it has been applied.* This must surely be the central inquiry. Now some might argue that the very fact that the EU regulates, for example, possible defects in foods on the basis, *inter alia*, of the precautionary principle somehow 'proves' that the difficulties associated with the principle set out above are prevalent in EU law. Put in this form the argument does not withstand examination. The existence of such a regulatory instrument in the EU does not in itself tell one anything as to whether the version of the precautionary principle that informed it was subject to the criticisms voiced above. The same point can be put in another way. It is clear that the US chooses to regulate certain risks more stringently than the EU and vice versa.[118] In relation to the former, the fact that the US regulatory authorities might be more precautionary about certain risks does not tell one whether the version of the principle used was weak or strong, or whether it was open to the central critique adumbrated above. It is only through close analysis of the particular regulatory provision and the role played by the precautionary principle therein that the argument can be taken forward. This can be briefly exemplified by considering an important area where the regulatory strategy has been informed by the precautionary principle.

[118] Ibid. at 1015–1016.

C. The Precautionary Principle and Political Decision-Making in the EU: Food Safety

The BSE crisis was one of the catalysts for the EU to become more closely involved with food safety and led to the passage of Regulation 178/2002.[119] We have already touched on this regulatory regime in the context of the earlier discussion of agencies.[120] The analysis undertaken here focuses more specifically on the role of risk and the precautionary principle in the design of this legislation in order to cast light on the issues set out in the previous section.

It is important to recognize at the outset the twin objectives of Regulation 178/2002. It was designed to foster a high level of health in the EU and to facilitate free movement of food, the latter requiring that food safety requirements should not differ significantly as between the Member States.[121] This duality of health promotion and removal of national regulatory barriers based on food safety runs throughout the entire Regulation. It is linked to risk analysis predicated on scientific evidence, which is also central to the legislative schema. Thus the recitals make clear that the purpose of risk analysis of measures introduced by Member States as well as the Community is to prevent the creation of unjustified barriers to trade.[122]

Risk analysis is said to be composed more specifically of risk assessment, risk management, and risk communication.[123] Risk assessment is a scientific process entailing the four stages mentioned in the earlier Commission Communication: hazard identification, hazard characterization, exposure assessment, and risk characterization.[124] Risk management 'means the process, distinct from risk assessment, of weighing policy alternatives in consultation with interested parties, considering risk assessment and other legitimate factors, and, if need be, selecting appropriate prevention and control options'.[125] The third component of risk analysis, risk communication, is as the name would suggest about exchange of information at all stages of risk analysis between all interested parties, including not only those involved directly in the process, but also consumers, the food industry and the academic community.[126]

The precautionary principle features as part of this risk analysis. Thus the recitals state that 'where a risk to life or health exists but scientific uncertainty

[119] Regulation (EC) 178/2002 of the European Parliament and of the Council of 28 January 2002, Laying Down the General Principles and Requirements of Food Law, Establishing the European Food Safety Authority and Laying Down Procedures in Matters of Food Safety, OJ 2002 L31/1.

[120] See above, Chap. 5.

[121] Reg. 178/2002, *supra* n. 119, Rec. 1–2, 20, Art. 5.

[122] Ibid. Rec. 16.

[123] Ibid. Rec. 17, Art. 3(10).

[124] Ibid. Art. 3(11).

[125] Ibid. Art. 3(12).

[126] Ibid. Art. 3(13).

persists, the precautionary principle provides a mechanism for determining risk management measures or other actions in order to ensure the high level of health protection chosen in the Community'.[127] This theme is carried through to the main body of the Regulation. In order to ensure a high level of health protection, food law is, in general, to be based on scientific risk analysis. The risk assessment is to be based on the available scientific evidence, and is to be independent, transparent, and objective.[128] Risk management, in the sense defined above, is to take account of the risk assessment undertaken by scientific panels of the European Food Safety Authority and, *inter alia*, in certain circumstances the precautionary principle.[129]

The precautionary principle is deemed to be relevant where, following the assessment of available information, the possibility of harmful effects on health is identified but scientific uncertainty persists. In such circumstances 'provisional risk management measures to ensure the high level of health protection chosen in the Community may be adopted, pending further scientific information for a more comprehensive risk assessment'.[130] The measures adopted on this basis must be proportionate and no more restrictive of trade than required to achieve the high level of protection, regard being had to technical and economic feasibility and other relevant factors. The measures are also to be reviewed within a reasonable period of time, depending on the nature of the risk and the type of scientific information needed to clarify the scientific uncertainty and conduct a more comprehensive risk assessment.[131]

It is interesting to reflect on this legislative scheme and the role of the precautionary principle therein in the light of the critique of the principle considered above. There is much to be said for regarding the legislative scheme as an example of a weaker version of the precautionary principle. The Regulation repeatedly emphasizes scientific risk analysis, which is undertaken in an objective and transparent manner by an independent body. The legislative definitions of the risk analysis stress the need to consider alternative policy choices, after wide consultation, and with an awareness of the range of control options. The decision-makers are in this sense enjoined to consider the 'wider screen' view. The Regulation could therefore be said to embody a non-preclusion version of the precautionary principle: it allows measures to be made where possible harmful effects have been identified but scientific uncertainty persists. The measures made in this manner are then subject to the conditions and constraints mentioned above, relating to the temporal dimension of the measure, proportionality, and the like. The risk analysis, with the attendant role of the precautionary principle, should not moreover be viewed in isolation in the overall regulatory regime. This analysis is

[127] Ibid. Rec. 21. [128] Ibid. Art. 5. [129] Ibid. Art. 5(3).
[130] Ibid. Art. 7(1). [131] Ibid. Art. 7(2).

undertaken in order to show whether the product is injurious to health, and the Regulation specifies in this respect that regard shall be had to the *probable* short or long-term effects on the person consuming it and the probable cumulative toxic effects.[132]

It is, however, possible to take a different view of the legislative scheme. Much depends on which parts of the regime that one chooses to highlight. The opposing view would emphasize the broad discretion inherent in Article 7 of the Regulation, which embodies the precautionary principle. Proponents of this view might argue that a degree of scientific uncertainty will commonly exist in relation to certain foods and that provisional risk management measures can be triggered provided that there is a possibility of identified harmful effects occurring. They would point moreover to the fact that the provisional nature of the measure thus adopted is a weak constraint, judged both in the light of the wording of Article 7, which makes provisionality dependent on the state of scientific knowledge, and judged also against the views expressed on this issue in the Commission Communication.

It is undeniable that there is discretion in the interpretation of Article 7. I do not, however, think that it serves to make this a strong version of the precautionary principle in the sense considered above, nor do I think that it proves that the criticisms voiced against the strong version of the principle are applicable here. The very fact that scientific uncertainty is prevalent to varying degrees in relation to many matters means that a regime for food safety will perforce have to make provision for the enactment of safety measures notwithstanding that uncertainty. The issue then becomes one of drafting the criteria that allow such measures to be made given this uncertainty. It is true that the test framed in terms of possibility might be regarded as too weak by the WTO, which appears to demand some estimation of likelihood or probability.[133] The criterion of possibility would, however, fall to be applied by the Community courts, which demand adequate evidence to substantiate this finding, and this would naturally lead to consideration of likelihood. They would moreover read Article 7 as a whole, with its requirement that the measure should be proportionate. Nor should we assume that the regulatory authorities charged with applying the existing regime will seek to use the precautionary principle as currently defined in a protectionist or arbitrary manner. Such a claim could only be sustained after careful empirical examination of the use made of the principle by the scientific panels of the Food Safety Authority.

There are doubtless those who will not agree with my evaluation of the version of the precautionary principle found in Regulation 178/2002. That is to be expected. Such disagreement should not, however, blind one to the purpose of this inquiry. It is only possible to evaluate whether the criticism of

[132] Ibid. Art. 14(4). [133] Lee, *supra* n. 1, at 107–108.

the principle is warranted by looking closely at the particular regulatory regime and the role played by the principle therein. This is the key inquiry irrespective of the fact that differing answers might be forthcoming.

D. The Precautionary Principle and Legal Decision-Making in the EU

It is also important to stand back and consider the role of the courts in relation to the precautionary principle. We should for the sake of clarity distinguish between different issues when undertaking this normative assessment.

It should be acknowledged that the *Community courts have made a normative choice in elevating the precautionary principle into a general principle of EU law.* This was a creative decision informed by the reasoning set out earlier in the chapter.[134] There was nothing inevitable about this juridical choice, but the analogical reasoning that drew on specific mention of the precautionary principle is familiar to lawyers. Some might question the legitimacy of the judicial elevation of the precautionary principle into a general principle of EU law. Whether one agrees with this line of criticism must ultimately depend on one's view about what courts can and should do when they adjudicate. The theory of adjudication that should inform judicial reasoning cannot be examined here. Suffice it to say for present purposes that I do not believe that the Community courts overstepped the legitimate boundaries of their adjudicatory responsibilities in this regard.

There is *room for disagreement as to which version of the precautionary principle was adopted by the Community courts judged in terms of the Stewart/Sunstein taxonomy.* The basic judicial formulation is that where there is uncertainty as to the existence or extent of risks, the institutions may take precautionary measures without having to wait until the reality and seriousness of the risks become fully apparent. This does not in terms incorporate a requirement of substantial harm, but is otherwise akin to the weaker non-preclusion version of the precautionary principle. The seriousness of the harm is in any event a factor taken into account in the more particular conditions stipulated by the Community courts when recourse is had to the precautionary principle. The CFI's judgments in cases such as *Pfizer*,[135] *Alpharma*,[136] *Artegodan*[137] and *Solvay*[138] established legal precepts relating to the nature of the risk assessment that must be undertaken to justify a protective measure premised on the precautionary principle and the role of scientific committees in this process.[139] The courts held that protective measures could not be based on a hypothetical approach to risk, rejected as unrealistic the

[134] See above, at 718–721.
[135] Case T-13/99, *Pfizer, supra* n. 11.
[136] Case T-70/99, *Alpharma, supra* n. 23.
[137] Cases T-74, 76, 83–85, 132, 137, and 141/00, *Artegodan, supra* n. 12.
[138] Case T-392/02, *Solvay, supra* n. 19.
[139] See above, at 722–731.

search for zero risk, and stipulated that the measure must be adequately backed up by the available scientific data.[140] They made it clear that risk was a function of the probability that the relevant product would adversely affect interests protected by the Community legal order, combined with assessment of the seriousness of those affects.[141] The Community courts emphasized the need to ensure that regard is had to the benefits as well as the potential harm that flow from the regulated product.[142] Indeed, the explicit recognition of the precautionary principle within EU law has led, as Fisher astutely notes, to increased judicial emphasis on scientific method as a means of ensuring non-arbitrary decision-making.[143]

It might be argued that *some leading cases are open to criticism because they did not, on the facts, accord sufficient weight to the expert scientific opinion.* This is the essence of the criticism[144] voiced of the judgment in, for example, *Pfizer.*[145] The CFI's reasoning in this respect has been considered in detail above,[146] and will not be repeated here. There is clearly room for difference of opinion on this issue. The line between the political responsibility of the institutional decision-makers and the scientific tasks of the expert committee can be difficult to maintain.[147] It may be equally contestable as to whether the political institutions have sufficient alternative material to base their judgment on when they choose not to follow the committee's opinion. These tensions are inherent in a scheme where the political decision must be premised on scientific evidence.

It might also be claimed that *judicial review does not allow sufficient scrutiny of decisions premised on the precautionary principle.* On this view the classic tools of review for manifest error, proportionality and the like do not provide review that is sufficiently searching to prevent arbitrary decisions. This view ignores the transformation in judicial review apparent in the courts' jurisprudence. The way in which review for manifest error has been developed and transformed was discussed in detail in an earlier chapter.[148] It no longer merely captures decisions that are facially arbitrary. It has become far more intensive and the courts are looking ever more closely at the detailed reasoning process that led to the contested decision. The CFI has announced its willingness to review the reasoning process of the scientific committee as

[140] See above, at 723–724.

[141] Case T-13/99, *Pfizer, supra* n. 11, at paras. 147–148.

[142] See, e.g., Cases T-74, 76, 83–85, 132, 137, and 141/00, *Artegodan, supra* n. 12, at paras. 178–180.

[143] Fisher, 'The Precautionary Principle, Administrative Constitutionalism and European Integration', *supra* n. 1, at 2.

[144] See, e.g., Forrester, *supra* n. 1.

[145] Case T-13/99, *Pfizer, supra* n. 11.

[146] See above, at 722–727.

[147] Lee, *supra* n. 1, at 81–82.

[148] See above, Chap. 13.

well as the Commission decision based on the committee's opinion.[149] It is moreover apparent from a case such as *Artegodan*[150] that the CFI is willing to annul the contested decision even where the scientific committee and the Commission are in agreement, if the court feels that the reasoning does not accord with the dictates of the empowering legislation.

7. CONCLUSION

The political and legal debate about the precautionary principle is intense. It affects areas such as international trade law that fall outside the remit of this book. Commentators disagree about the meaning of the precautionary principle and even more so about its desirability. This chapter has sought to explicate how it has been elevated into a general principle of EU law and the way in which it is applied in the review of Community and Member State action. We have seen the role accorded to the precautionary principle by the Commission's Communication and evaluated some of the critical literature. There is no doubt that the debate will continue. If there is a message about this aspect of the inquiry, it is that only by paying close attention to the particular legislative scheme is it possible to assess which version of the precautionary principle is being used and hence whether the critique of the principle is warranted.

[149] Cases T-74, 76, 83–85, 132, 137, and 141/00, *Artegodan, supra* n. 12, at paras. 199–200.
[150] Ibid. at para. 220.

20

Remedies I: The Community

1. INTRODUCTION

The discussion in the previous chapters has focused on the various procedural and substantive principles of judicial review applied by the Community courts. Remedies are an equally important part of administrative law in any legal system and this is equally true for the EU. This chapter and that which follows will consider the remedies available against the Community and the Member States respectively.

The two principal remedies available against the Community are annulment and compensation, which are also the main remedial mechanisms for holding public bodies to account in domestic legal systems. Annulment embodies the fundamental precept that where the action that has been taken is invalid or illegal then it should *prima facie* be held to be void and of no effect. Compensation is equally significant as a remedy for losses caused to those who have suffered financially as a result of public action that is unlawful, although as we shall see in the discussion that follows the precise criterion for recovery depends upon whether the loss flows from the exercise of a discretionary or non-discretionary power.

The discussion begins with consideration of the principles governing the grant of interim relief pending the final decision on the substance of the case and the way in which those principles are applied in relation to both direct and indirect actions. This is followed by analysis of the consequences of finding that the contested measure is illegal or invalid, the extent to which the Community courts modify the basic precept that a measure found to be invalid or illegal idea is void *ab initio*, and the relationship between the finding that the measure is void and the obligations placed on the Community institutions to redress the wrong. The focus then turns to compensation, the criteria for recovery under Article 288 EC, and the way in which the tests have evolved over time.

2. INTERIM MEASURES

A. Direct Actions

The judicial resolution of any action takes time and this applies just as much to challenges to the legality of Community action as it does to other kinds of legal action. The interests of one of the parties to the litigation may, however, be seriously harmed pending the final outcome of the case. All legal systems therefore make some provision for interim measures to protect the parties before the court reaches its decision on the substance of the case.[1]

The issue of interim relief is addressed expressly in the EC Treaty. Article 242 EC provides that the Court may, if it considers that the circumstances so require, order that the application of the contested measure be suspended. This is complemented by Article 243 EC, which states that it may prescribe interim measures. The provision of interim relief is conceptualized as part of a right to effective judicial protection. Thus the European Court of Justice (ECJ) stated that 'the right to full and effective judicial protection means that individuals must be granted interim protection if this is necessary to ensure the full effectiveness of the subsequent definitive judgment, in order to prevent a lacuna in the legal protection afforded by the Court'.[2] It has also been said that effective interim legal protection is a general principle of Community law that underlies the constitutional traditions common to the Member States and that the principle is to be found in Articles 6 and 13 of the European Convention on Human Rights (ECHR) and Article 47 of the Charter of Fundamental Rights of the EU.[3]

The criteria for the award of interim relief will normally require some showing by the applicant that the contested measure is likely to be invalid and some showing of urgency combined with resulting harm. These elements are present in the test applied by the Community courts.[4] The judge hearing the application can order suspension of the measure or other interim

[1] De la Sierra, 'Provisional Court Protection in Administrative Disputes in Europe: The Constitutional Status of Interim Measures Deriving from the Right to Effective Court Protection. A Comparative Approach' (2004) 10 *ELJ* 42.

[2] Case 27/68 R, *Renckens v Commission* [1969] ECR 274, 276; Case C-399/65 R, *Germany v Commission* [1996] ECR I-2441, at para. 46; Case C-445/00 R, *Austria v Council* [2001] ECR I-1461, at para.111; Case T-306/01 R, *Aden v Council and Commission* [2002] ECR II-2387, at para. 45; Case T-78/04, *Sumitomo Chemical (UK) plc v Commission* [2004] ECR II-2049, at para. 44.

[3] Case T-198/01 R, *Technische Glaswerke Illmenau GmbH v Commission* [2002] ECR II-2153, at paras. 50, 113–115.

[4] Case C-149/95 P(R), *Commission v Atlantic Container Line AB* [1995] ECR I-2165; Case C-377/98 R, *Netherlands v Council* [2000] ECR I-6229, at para. 41; Case C-445/00 R, *Austria, supra* n. 2, at para. 73.

measures if it is established that such an order is *prima facie* justified in fact and law and that it is urgent in so far as, in order to avoid irreparable harm to the applicant's interests, it must be made and take effect before a decision is reached in the main action. Where appropriate, the judge hearing the application must weigh the respective interests involved. The conditions in the test are cumulative and therefore if the applicant fails to prove any one of them the claim fails.[5] It is for the applicant to prove the requisite elements in the test. Thus the applicant must prove that the matter is urgent and that he cannot wait for the outcome of the proceedings without suffering irreparable damage.[6] It is for the applicant to show with a sufficient degree of probability that serious and irreparable damage is likely to occur.[7] Pecuniary damage is not generally regarded as irreparable since it can be the subject of financial compensation. Such damage will only qualify in this respect if the applicant can show that unless the measure is suspended its very existence would be threatened or its market shares would be altered irretrievably.[8]

An application to suspend the operation of any measure can only be made if the applicant is challenging the measure before the Community courts.[9] An application for interim measures can generally be made where there is a sufficiently close link between the interim measure sought and the subject matter of the main action. Where, however, the application for interim measures is seeking to achieve the same end as an application for suspension then it will only be admissible if the applicant is challenging the measure before the Community courts.[10] It is, moreover, for the applicant to specify the interim measures that are sought, with the consequence that vague and imprecise applications will be rejected.[11] The applicant will have to show some interest in obtaining the interim measures sought,[12] and the application will be rejected where it could not have the effect of changing the applicant's

[5] Case C-268/96 R, *SCK and FNK v Commission* [1996] ECR I-4971, at para. 30; Case C-7/04 P(R), *Commission v Akzo Nobel Chemicals Ltd and Akcros Chemicals Ltd* [2004] ECR I-8739, at paras. 28–29; Case T-163/02 R, *Montan Gesellschaft Voss mbH Stahlhandel and others v Commission* [2002] ECR II-3219, at para. 17.

[6] Case T-163/02 R, *Montan Gesellschaft, supra* n. 5, at para. 28.

[7] Ibid. at para. 29.

[8] Case C-213/91 R, *Abertal and others v Commission* [1991] ECR I-5109, at para. 24; Case T-168/95 R, *Eridania and others v Council* [1995] ECR II-2817, at para. 42; Case T-163/02 R, *Montan Gesellschaft, supra* n. 5, at paras. 30–31; Case T-198/01 R, *Technische Glaswerke Illmenau, supra* n. 3, at paras. 96, 99.

[9] Case T-78/04, *Sumitomo, supra* n. 2, at paras. 42–43.

[10] Ibid. at para. 43; Case T-395/94 R II, *Atlantic Container Line v Commission* [1995] ECR II-2893, at para. 39.

[11] Ibid. at paras. 49–50.

[12] Case C-107/89 R, *Caturla-Poch v Parliament* [1989] ECR 1357; Case T-164/96 R, *Moccia Irme v Commission* [1996] ECR II-2261, at para. 26; Case T-78/04, *Sumitomo, supra* n. 2, at para. 52.

position and therefore could not be of any practical use to the applicant.[13] In principle the admissibility of the main action will not generally be examined in an application for interim measures so as not to prejudge the substance of the case. However, where it appears that the main action is manifestly inadmissible it may be necessary for the Court to examine this issue when interim measures are sought.[14]

B. Indirect Actions

The same considerations that require powers of suspension and interim relief apply in relation to indirect actions that raise the validity of Community action.[15] This is particularly important given that national courts do not have the power to find a Community regulation to be invalid,[16] and given also that many challenges to the validity of Community norms will be indirect via the national courts since the standing rules for direct actions brought by individuals are so limited.[17]

The Treaty contains no formal provisions concerning suspension or the grant of interim relief by national courts, but the ECJ held that such powers existed and defined the circumstances in which they could be exercised. The leading cases are *Zuckerfabrik Süderdithmarschen*[18] and *Atlanta*[19] and they established the following principles.

The powers that reside in the Community courts to order suspension or interim relief when the legality of a Community act is challenged directly must also reside with national courts when such a challenge arises indirectly. This was necessary to ensure the coherence of the system of interim legal protection.

These powers can apply where the applicant seeks the suspension of a national act on the ground that the Community regulation on which it was based is invalid. Thus in *Zuckerfabrik* the applicant challenged a national decision imposing a levy on sugar, where the national decision implemented

[13] Case C-89/97 P(R), *Moccia Irme v Commission* [1997] ECR I-2327, at para. 45; Case T-369/03, *Arizona Chemical and others v Commission* [2004] ECR II-205, at para. 62; Case T-78/04, *Sumitomo, supra* n. 2, at para. 52.

[14] Case T-219/95 R, *Danielsson v Commission* [1995] ECR II-3051, at para. 58; Case T-13/99 R, *Pfizer Animal Health v Council* [1999] ECR II-1961, at para. 121; Case T-219/95 R, *Montan, supra* n. 5, at para. 21.

[15] Sharpston, 'Interim Relief in National Courts', in J. Lonbay and A. Biondi (eds), *Remedies for Breach of EC Law* (Wiley, 1997), Chap. 5.

[16] Case 314/85, *Foto-Frost v Hauptzollamt Lübeck-Ost* [1987] ECR 4199.

[17] See above, Chap. 10.

[18] Cases C-143/88 and 92/89, *Zuckerfabrik Süderdithmarschen AG v Hauptzollamt Itzehoe* [1991] ECR I-415.

[19] Case C-465/93, *Atlanta Fruchthandelgesellschaft mbH v Bundesamt für Ernährung und Forstwirtschaft* [1995] ECR I-3761.

a Community regulation. The applicant sought suspension of the national decision pending the ruling on the legality of the Community regulation. The national court also has power where the applicant seeks a positive interim measure pending determination of the legality of the Community regulation. Thus in *Atlanta* the applicant challenged via the national courts a Community regulation that imposed a quota on bananas from third countries and raised the import levy on bananas from what it had been hitherto. The interim measure sought from the national court entailed the grant of additional import licences at the lower rate pending the ECJ's ruling on the validity of the regulation. In that sense the applicant sought a positive order from the national court temporarily disapplying the Community regulation. The ECJ made it clear that the same principles must also govern applications for interim relief where the compatibility of a national measure with Community law was raised in the national courts, as in *Factortame*.[20]

The conditions that had to be satisfied before suspension or interim relief could be granted were established in *Zuckerfabrik* and *Atlanta*, subject to some further refinement in *Krüger*.[21] There has to be serious doubts as to the validity of the Community regulation, the corollary being that when the national court makes the reference it must set out the reasons why it considers that the ECJ should find the regulation invalid. The national court should take account in this respect of the discretion accorded to the Community institutions in the sectors concerned. The grant of relief by the national court must retain the character of an interim measure. The interim measures cannot be maintained when the ECJ has ruled pursuant to the preliminary reference that the Community regulation is valid.

The ECJ stressed the parity between interim relief given by national courts in indirect actions and that given by the Community courts in direct challenges for annulment. The same conditions must apply to both. Interim measures could therefore only be ordered where they were urgent, that is where they were necessary before the decision on the substance of the case, in order to avoid serious and irreparable damage. Purely financial damage is not in principle regarded as irreparable, but it is for the national court to consider the circumstances of the instant case and consider whether immediate enforcement will be likely to result in irreversible damage to the applicant that cannot be made good if the Community act is declared invalid.

It is moreover incumbent on the national court to ensure that full effect is given to Community law and hence when there is doubt about the validity of

[20] Case C-213/89, *R v Secretary of State for Transport, ex p Factortame Ltd* [1990] ECR I-2433.

[21] Case C-334/95, *Krüger GmbH & Co KG v Hauptzollamt Hamburg-Jonas* [1997] ECR I-4517.

Community regulations account must be taken of the Community interest that such regulations should not be set aside without proper guarantees. The national court must, where it is minded to give interim relief, give the relevant Community institution an opportunity to express its views. The national court must consider in this respect whether the Community act will be deprived of all effectiveness if not immediately implemented, and when making this calculus should factor in the cumulative effect if other national courts were also to adopt interim measures. If the grant of interim relief poses a financial risk for the Community then the national court must require adequate financial guarantees or other security.

The national court should also, when assessing whether to grant interim relief, respect what the Community courts have decided on the relevant issue. The national court must respect any relevant ruling on interim relief given by the Community courts. It must also do so where the validity of the regulation has already been considered by the Community courts. Where this was so the national court cannot order interim measures, and must revoke any already granted, unless the grounds of illegality alleged differ from those that have already been ruled on. It was especially important that national courts respect a decision of the Community courts concerning an assessment of the Community interest and the balance between that interest and the relevant economic sector.

C. Assessment

The central elements of the test for interim relief in direct and indirect actions, the need to show a *prima facie* case and serious and irreparable damage, are common in many legal systems. Much turns on how rigorously they are applied. It is clear from the jurisprudence on direct actions that the Community courts will not lightly accede to pleas for suspension of a Community norm or for interim measures. It should, however, be recognized that applicants for this kind of relief will also face significant burdens of proof in national legal systems. The common feature is that courts generally set the hurdles relatively high precisely because the applicant in such cases is seeking to suspend the operation of what is *prima facie* a valid law. It should nonetheless be acknowledged that the Community courts' view that financial loss will only very exceptionally qualify as irreparable, and then only when the applicant can show that it is likely to go out of business or suffer some very marked fall in its market value, is limiting of claims in this area and unduly so.

The nature of the test as applied in direct and indirect actions is generally the same. The factors added to the case law concerning interim relief and indirect actions are mainly directed towards ensuring that the national court takes proper account of the Community interest and relevant Community case law when making its decision. The obligation cast on national courts to take account of the effect on the Community norm if other national courts also award interim measures is, however, impractical to say the very least. The national court will generally be in no position to assess whether similar claims for interim relief are made in other national legal systems, or what the cumulative effect of such claims might be on the efficacy of the Community measure.

While the test applied in direct and indirect actions is generally the same it should nonetheless be recognized that there are bound to be some differences in its practical application. This is principally because where suspension or interim relief are sought before the Court of First Instance (CFI) or ECJ the judge deciding the application has in-depth knowledge of Community law and is therefore better placed to decide whether there is a *prima facie* case than the national judge in an indirect action.

3. ANNULMENT

It is important, in any system of administrative law, to be aware of the consequences of a finding that a contested decision is illegal or invalid. This is equally so in relation to EU administrative law. It is necessary in this respect to distinguish between direct and indirect actions involving challenge to Community action.

A. Direct Actions: Articles 231 and 233 EC

Where a Community measure has been challenged successfully,[22] there are two principal Treaty provisions that determine the consequences of illegality. Article 231 EC provides that if the action under Article 230 EC is well founded, the ECJ shall declare the act void. This is then modified by the second paragraph of Article 231 which provides that, in the case of a regulation, the ECJ shall, if it considers it necessary, state which of the effects of the regulation declared void shall be considered as definitive. Article 233 EC complements this by stating that the institution whose act has been declared void, or whose failure to act has been declared contrary to the Treaty, shall be required to take the necessary measures to comply with the ECJ's judgment.

[22] The Commission cannot avoid a challenge by withdrawing the contested measure when it is challenged before the ECJ, while seeking to preserve the effects it has produced, Case C-89/96, *Portuguese Republic v Commission* [1999] ECR I-8377.

B. Direct Actions: Article 231 EC

Article 231 provides that where a measure has been found to be illegal under Article 230 it is void.[23] The Community courts have no power to substitute their own reasoning for that of the author of the contested measure.[24]

It is, however, clear that it is the Community courts that will decide whether an error is of a kind to warrant annulment of the contested measure. The *Hercules* case is a fitting example.[25] The ECJ ruled that access to the file in competition cases should be regarded as part of the rights of the defence. Infringement of the right of access could therefore constitute a ground for annulment if it led to breach of the rights of defence. It could not be remedied merely by the fact that access to the file was made possible at a later stage of the proceedings, such as when annulment of the original decision was sought in an annulment action. However infringement of the right of access would only lead to annulment if the applicant could show that it could have used the documents to which it was denied access as part of its defence. The same principle is apparent in *Limburgse Vinyl*,[26] where the CFI ruled that infringement of the general principle of European Community (EC) law that decisions following administrative proceedings relating to competition policy must be adopted within a reasonable time would lead to annulment only if it contravened the undertakings' rights of defence, such as where it was established that the undue delay affected the ability of the undertakings to defend themselves.

It is equally clear that the Community courts will determine the effects of an error on the overall validity of the measure being challenged. Thus in *Limburgse Vinyl* the CFI held that where a Commission decision in breach of the competition rules was annulled because of a procedural defect that occurred at the final stage of adoption of the decision and which affected only the manner in which it was adopted, for example lack of authentication, the annulment did not affect the validity of the measures taken preparatory to the decision before the defect was found.[27]

The general principle is that nullity is retroactive: once the act is annulled

[23] Normally an act will have to be challenged for its illegality to be established. There are, however, certain limited instances in which the act will be treated as absolutely void or non-existent, where the act may be treated as if it were never adopted. In general, however, proceedings will be required to establish the illegality of the act.

[24] Case C-164/98 P, *DIR International Film Srl and others v Commission* [2000] ECR I-447, at paras. 48–49.

[25] Case C-51/92 P, *Hercules Chemicals NV v Commission* [1999] ECR I-4235.

[26] Cases T-305–7, 313–6, 318, 325, 328–9, and 335/94, *Limburgse Vinyl Maatschappij NV and others v Commission* [1999] ECR II-931.

[27] Ibid. See also, Case C-415/96, *Spain v Commission* [1998] ECR I-6993.

under Article 230 it is void *ab initio*.[28] This principle can, however, cause hardship, particularly in those instances where the measure is a regulation, which has been relied on by many, and which may be the basis of other measures adopted later.

This is the rationale for the second paragraph of Article 231, which allows the Court to qualify the extent of the nullity. It provides that in the case of a regulation the ECJ shall, if it considers this necessary, state which of the effects of the regulation it has declared void shall be considered as definitive. This has been used to limit the temporal effect of the Court's ruling when it annuls a regulation.[29] Although the second paragraph of Article 231 is framed in terms of regulations, the ECJ has extended it to directives[30] and decisions.[31] Considerations of legal certainty will often be paramount in this respect. The ECJ will be inclined to apply the second paragraph of Article 231 in order to retain in force the contested measure until a new measure can be adopted in order to avoid the drastic consequences that can be attendant on retroactive nullity.[32]

Thus in *Commission v Council*[33] the Court annulled part of a regulation concerning staff salaries. However, if the regulation had been annulled retroactively then the staff would not have been entitled to any salary increases until a new regulation had been adopted. The Court therefore ruled that the regulation should continue to have effect until a new regulation, in accord with the Court's judgment, had been promulgated. The consequences of retroactive nullity would have been far-reaching in *European Parliament v Council*.[34] The ECJ found illegalities in relation to the budget for a particular financial year, but this decision was made when most of the period had elapsed. The need to ensure continuity in the public service of the EU, combined with legal certainty, led the ECJ to exercise the power under the

[28] Case C-228/92, *Roquette Frères SA v Hauptzollamt Geldern* [1994] ECR I-1445, at para. 17; Cases T-481 and 484/93, *Vereniging van Exporteurs in Levende Varkens v Commission* [1995] ECR II-2941, at para. 46; Case T-171/99, *Corus UK Ltd v Commission* [2001] ECR II-2967, at para. 50.

[29] In addition to the power to limit the temporal effect of its rulings, the Court may also find that the illegality affects only part of the measure in question.

[30] Case C-295/90, *European Parliament v Council* [1992] ECR I-4193; Case C-21/94, *European Parliament v Council (Road Taxes)* [1995] ECR I-1827.

[31] Case C-360/93, *European Parliament v Council (Government Procurement)* [1996] ECR I-1195, at paras. 32–36; Case C-22/96, *European Parliament v Council (Telematic Networks)* [1998] ECR I-3231.

[32] Case 51/87, *Commission v Council (Generalized Tariff Preferences)* [1988] ECR 5459, at paras. 21–22; Case C-392/95, *European Parliament v Council* [1997] ECR I-3213, at paras. 25–27; Case C-1159/96, *Portugal v Commission* [1998] ECR I-7379, at paras. 52–53; Case C-445/00, *Austria v Council* [2003] ECR I-8549, at paras. 103–106; Case C-93/00, *European Parliament v Council* [2001] ECR I-10119, at paras. 47–48.

[33] Case 81/72, [1973] ECR 575.

[34] Case C-41/95, *European Parliament v Council* [1995] ECR I-4411, at paras. 43–45.

second paragraph of Article 231 and declare those parts of the budget that should nonetheless be regarded as definitive. The need to limit the effects of nullity was equally apparent in *Commission v European Parliament and Council*.[35] The ECJ annulled the application of the regulatory committee procedure to an environmental regulation on the ground that it should *prima facie* have been the management committee procedure and the Council had not given adequate reasons for use of the former. The Commission, which had sought the annulment, argued, however, that the effects of the regulation should, for reasons of legal certainty, be maintained in force until its amendment. This was in order to protect measures passed pursuant to the regulatory committee procedure prior to this action. The ECJ accepted the imperative of legal certainty in the instant case. The Community courts will also be minded to limit the impact of nullity where this would defeat the very purpose of the courts' finding. Thus in *Timex* an anti-dumping duty was annulled because it was too low. The impact of this judgment would clearly not have been enhanced by a finding of retroactive voidness and therefore the ECJ held that the existing measure should retain its validity until a new, higher duty was imposed.[36] The ECJ will, by way of contrast, be less inclined to limit the temporal effect of its rulings where retroactive annulment does not deleteriously affect the rights of traders.[37]

C. Direct Actions: Article 233 EC

We have seen that Article 233 EC provides that the institution whose act has been declared void, or whose failure to act has been declared contrary to the Treaty, shall be required to take the necessary measures to comply with the ECJ's judgment.[38]

It is important to understand that Article 233 does not create an autonomous remedy. Thus to take *Gondrand Frères*[39] as a recent example the CFI ruled that it was not for the Community courts to issue directions to the

[35] Case C-378/00, *Commission v European Parliament and Council* [2003] ECR I-937, at paras. 73–77.

[36] Case 264/82, *Timex Corporation v Council and Commission* [1985] ECR 849, at para. 32.

[37] Case C-239/01, *Germany v Commission* [2003] ECR I-10333, at para. 78.

[38] Toth, 'The Authority of Judgments of the European Court of Justice: Binding Force and Legal Effects' (1984) 4 *YBEL* 1, at 49.

[39] Case T-104/02, *Société Français de Transports Gondrand Frères v Commission*, judgment of 21 September 2004, not yet published, at para. 20. See also, Case T-114/92, *Bureau Européen des Medias de l'Industrie Musicale v Commission* [1995] ECR II-147, at para. 33; Case T-67/94, *Ladbroke Racing Ltd v Commission* [1998] ECR II-1, at para. 200; Case T-127/98, *UPS Europe SA v Commission* [1999] ECR II-2633, at para. 50; Case T-126/99, *Graphischer Maschinenbau GmbH v Commission* [2002] ECR II-2427, at para. 17; Case T-125/01, *Jose Marti Peix, SA v Commission* [2003] ECR II-865, at para. 42.

Community institutions or assume the role assigned to them when a measure was annulled under Article 230. It was for the relevant Community institution to take pursuant to Article 233 the measures to give effect to the Court's judgment. It was not therefore open to the CFI to grant remission of an anti-dumping duty. Similarly in *Holcim*[40] the applicant sought to recover the cost of bank charges incurred to guarantee the payment of a fine imposed by the Commission under Article 81 EC, after the imposition of the fine was annulled. The CFI held that this claim could not be based on Article 233, since it did not constitute an autonomous remedy. The appropriate method of ensuring compliance with the obligation in Article 233 was by way of a further action under Article 230 or 232 depending on the circumstances of the case. It was not for the Community court to substitute its view for that of the Commission and decide the measures that the latter should have taken under Article 233, although it was open to the ECJ and CFI to review such measures or the lack of them under Articles 230 or 232. There may therefore be a further action under Article 230 or 232 where the applicant is dissatisfied with the measures taken pursuant to an act found to be void.[41] An action based on Article 232 will be appropriate where the applicant claims that the Community institution has failed, pursuant to Article 233, to take action in relation to other measures that were not challenged in the initial annulment action.[42] The decision in *CT Control* is a corollary of these principles: in a direct action against a Community institution the ECJ will not rule on the obligations of national authorities that have implemented a Community act that has been annulled.[43]

While Article 233 does not establish an autonomous remedy it has nonetheless been interpreted broadly. There is a duty to put an end to the infringement within a reasonable period of time.[44] Article 233 may involve eradication of the effects of the measure found to be void,[45] and the taking of adequate steps to restore the applicant to its original position prior to the

[40] Case T-28/03, *Holcim (Deutschland) AG v Commission*, judgment of 21 April 2005, not yet published, at paras. 32–37. See also, Cases 191, 212–214/98, *Atlantic Container Lines AB v Commission* [2003] ECR II-3275, at para. 1643; Case T-224/00, *Archer Daniels Midland Company and Archer Daniels Midlands Ingredients Ltd v Commission* [2003] ECR II-2597, at para. 356.

[41] Case T-387/94, *Asia Motor France SA v Commission* [1996] ECR II-961.

[42] Cases T-297–298/01, *SIC-Sociedade Independente de Communicacao, SA v Commission* [2004] ECR II-743, at para. 32.

[43] Cases C-121–122/91, *CT Control (Rotterdam) BV and JCT Benelux BV v Commission* [1993] ECR I-3873, at paras. 55–57.

[44] Case C-21/94, *European Parliament v Council (Road Taxes), supra* n. 30, at para. 33.

[45] Cases T-480 and 483/93, *Antillean Rice Mills NV v Commission* [1995] ECR II-2305; Case T-196/01, *Thessalonikis v Commission* [2003] ECR II-3987, at para. 226; Case T-307/01, *Jean-Paul François v Commission* [2004] ECR II-1669, at para. 109.

illegality.[46] It may also require the Commission to refrain from adopting an identical measure. This was so in *Asteris*[47] where the ECJ held that when a measure had been annulled compliance with the judgment required the Community institution to have regard not only to the operative part of the judgment, but also to the grounds on which it was based, in order to identify the precise provision held to be illegal and the reasons underlying this finding. The primary obligation in such cases was for the Community institution to remedy the illegality through adoption of a measure replacing that which had been annulled. There could however, said the ECJ, be other obligations flowing from annulment. Thus the new measure should contain no provisions having the same effect as that held to be illegal.[48] Moreover, because annulment was retroactive to the date when the annulled measure was enacted, it was incumbent on the Community institution to ensure that no other measure enacted after that date, but prior to the annulment, was tainted by the same defect as that held to be illegal.

In *Asteris* the measure annulled was a regulation. The precise implications of annulment may however differ where the measure annulled is a decision and this has consequential implications for the nature of the duty on the Community institutions under Article 233. This is apparent from *Kraft Products.*[49] The applicants had been fined by the Commission for taking part in the wood pulp cartel. They did not challenge this Commission decision, which was, however, contested by other members of the cartel. The ECJ annulled the Commission's cartel decision in certain important respects and the Commission pursuant to Article 233 repaid most of the fines imposed on those who had taken part in this legal challenge in accord with the ECJ's judgment. The applicants in *Kraft Products* argued that the Commission should also, pursuant to Article 233, repay fines imposed on them even though they had not taken part in the challenge to the cartel decision. The Commission refused, and the applicants sought the annulment of this decision. The ECJ found for the Commission. The original Commission decision concerning the cartel was treated as a bundle of individual decisions addressed to each member of the cartel, with a fine being calculated for each such

[46] Case T-211/02, *Tideland Signal Ltd v Commission* [2002] ECR II-3781, at para. 44.

[47] Cases 97, 99, 193 and 215/86, *Asteris AE and Hellenic Republic v Commission* [1988] ECR 2181. See also, Case C-458/98 P, *Industrie des Poudres Sphèriques v Council and Commission* [2000] ECR I-8147, at para. 81; Case T-206/99, *Métropole Télévision SA v Commission* [2001] ECR II-1057, at para. 35; Case T-89/00, *Europe Chemi-Con (Deutschland) GmbH v Council* [2002] ECR II-3651, at para. 32; Case C-41/00 P, *Interporc Im- und Export GmbH v Commission* [2003] ECR I-2125, at paras. 29–30.

[48] See also, Cases C-199–200/01 P, *IPK-München GmbH v Commission* [2004] ECR I-4627, at para. 83.

[49] Case C-310/97 P, *Commission v AssiDomän Kraft Products AB* [1999] ECR I-5363, at para. 56.

member.[50] The ECJ held that while the *erga omnes* authority of its earlier annulment ruling attached to both the operative part and the *ratio decidendi* of its judgment,[51] it did not, however, entail annulment of an act not challenged before the ECJ, even where it was alleged to be vitiated by the same illegality. The authority of an earlier annulment could not, therefore, apply to persons that were not parties to those proceedings 'and with regard to whom the judgment cannot therefore have decided anything whatever'.[52] It followed said the ECJ that while Article 233 required the Community institution to ensure that any act designed to replace the annulled act was not vitiated by the same irregularities as those identified in the judgment annulling the original act, it did not require the Commission at the request of interested parties to re-examine identical or similar decisions allegedly affected by the same irregularity, addressed to persons other than the applicants.[53]

Although Article 233 does not create an autonomous remedy or allow the Community courts to issue directions to the Community institutions, the judgments may nonetheless provide specific guidance as to what the institutions should do to comply with the court's decision.[54] Thus in *Hirsch* the CFI ruled, in line with established orthodoxy, that it could not order the European Central Bank (ECB) to pay tuition fees or declare an entitlement for an educational allowance for the sons of an applicant. This would be to encroach on the prerogatives of the defendant institution, which was required under Article 233 to take the necessary steps to comply with the CFI's judgment.[55] The CFI upheld the applicants' claim and stated that it was for the ECB to give effect to the judgment under Article 233 by modifying the scheme of education allowances in the light of the judgment so that they were in accord with the principle of equal treatment, and by reviewing under this modified scheme the applicants' request for an education allowance for their children.[56] The CFI thereby gave fairly specific indications as to what was required of the ECB.

D. Indirect Actions: The Analogous Application of Articles 231 and 233

A finding of invalidity pursuant to Article 234 EC is, in theory, different from a decision made pursuant to Article 230 EC. The former is addressed

[50] Ibid. at para. 49. [51] Ibid. at para. 54. [52] Ibid. at para. 55.

[53] Ibid. at para. 56. See also, Cases T-305–7, 313–6, 318, 325, 328–9, and 335/94, *Limburgse Vinyl, supra* n. 26, at para. 100; Case T-211/02, *Tideland, supra* n. 46, at para. 44; Case C-239/99, *Nachi Europe GmbH v Hauptzollamt Krefeld* [2001] ECR I-1197, at paras. 25–26.

[54] Case T-310/01, *Schneider Electric SA v Commission* [2002] ECR II-4071, at para. 465.

[55] Cases T-94, 152, and 286/01, *Hirsch, Nicastro and Priesemann v ECB* [2003] ECR IA-1, at para. 15.

[56] Ibid. at para. 73.

only to the national court which requested the ruling. However the Court held in the *ICC* case[57] that its rulings on Article 234 references concerning validity of Community acts have an *erga omnes* effect. These rulings provide a sufficient reason for any other national court to treat that act as void, although the national court may make a reference on the same point if it is unclear about the scope, grounds, or consequences of the original ruling. Moreover, the ECJ has applied the principles of Articles 231 and 233, which technically only operate in the context of Articles 230 and 232, by analogy to cases arising under Article 234. This has further eroded any distinction between the effects of a judgment given under Articles 230 and 234.

The rationale for the application of Article 231 in the context of preliminary rulings was provided in *Société de Produits de Maïs*.[58] The ECJ held that its power to impose temporal limits on the effects of a declaration that a Community act was invalid in the context of a preliminary ruling was justified by the need to ensure consistency of treatment between Article 230 and Article 234, which were the two methods for reviewing the legality of Community acts. It must therefore be possible to impose temporal limits on the effects of the invalidity of a Community regulation, irrespective of whether the action was brought under Article 230 or 234. The judicial discretion to decide pursuant to the second paragraph of Article 231, which specific effects declared void should nonetheless be considered as definitive, applied therefore in relation to preliminary rulings. It was for the Court, where it made use of this possibility under Article 234, to decide whether an exception to that temporal limitation of the effect of its judgment could be made in favour of the party that brought the action before the national court or of any other trader that took similar steps before the declaration of invalidity or whether, conversely, a declaration of invalidity applicable only to the future constituted an adequate remedy even for traders who took action at the appropriate time with a view to protecting their rights. Considerations of legal certainty will be of decisive importance here, just as they are in direct actions. Such considerations involving all interests, public as well as private, with a stake in the case may well preclude calling into question the charging or payment of money made on the basis of the measure found invalid in respect of the period prior to the date of the judgment.[59]

[57] Case 66/80, *International Chemical Corporation v Amministrazione delle Finanze dello Stato* [1981] ECR 1191.

[58] Case 112/83, *Société de Produits de Maïs v Administration des Douanes* [1985] ECR 719. See also, Case 145/79, *SA Roquette Frères v France* [1980] ECR 2917; Case 4/79, *Société Coopérative 'Providence Agricole de la Champagne' v ONIC* [1980] ECR 2823; Case 41/84, *Pinna v Caisse d'allocations familiales de Savoie* [1986] ECR 1; Cases C-38, 151/90, *R v Lomas* [1992] ECR I-178; Case C-228/92, *Roquette Frères, supra* n. 28.

[59] Case 41/84, *Pinna, supra* n. 58, at para. 28; Case C-228/99, *Silos e Mangimi Martini SpA v Ministero delle Finanze* [2001] ECR I-8401, at para. 35.

The ECJ used similar reasoning in *ONIC*[60] to justify the application of the principle underlying Article 233 in the context of Article 234. The obligation on the Community institutions to take the measures necessary to comply with the Court's judgment applies therefore where the finding of invalidity is made pursuant to Article 234 just as much as when it is made under Article 230.[61] The jurisprudence considered above on the application of Article 233 in the context of direct actions would by parity of reasoning also be applicable in the context of indirect actions.

E. Assessment

It is axiomatic that the interrelationship between courts and administration runs throughout administrative law. The precise nature of that interrelationship differs depending on the particular topic that is in issue. It is clear nonetheless that the consequence of illegality/invalidity raises such issues that are of importance both practically and theoretically. This is readily apparent from the preceding discussion.

It is equally apparent that legal systems differ in their approach to the problems considered above. Thus, to take an example, the UK courts have generated much complex and confusing case law when dealing with the temporal effect of invalidity, but have shown no compunction in principle about issuing orders or directions to the administration resulting from a finding of invalidity.[62]

This stands in contrast to the position in EU law. The second paragraph of Article 231 has surely helped the Community courts to deal with the problems of retroactive nullity, since it embodies an explicit discretionary power to determine that certain effects of a void measure shall be definitive. The Community courts have on the whole made good and sensible use of this provision. They have taken proper account of the imperative of legal certainty in deciding whether to qualify the retroactive consequences of annulment.

The EU approach embodied in Article 233 and the interpretation given to that Article by the Community courts reflects general civilian assumptions about remedies. Courts declare acts to be void and it is then for the relevant Community institution to take the measures necessary to comply with the court's judgment. It is not for the court to issue specific instructions in this regard. If the successful claimant is dissatisfied with the action taken or not taken then recourse should be had to Articles 230 and 232 respectively. It is,

60 Case 4/79, *ONIC, supra* n. 58, at para. 44.
61 Ibid.
62 P.P. Craig, *Administrative Law* (Sweet & Maxwell, 5th ed., 2003), Chaps. 20, 22.

however, as we have seen, open to the Community courts, if they choose to do so, to give fairly specific guidance as to what should be done by the Community institutions pursuant to a finding of illegality/invalidity. The judicial reluctance to exercise more formal powers in this respect may well be influenced not only by civilian assumptions concerning the roles of court and administration consequent on a finding of illegality, but also by factors that are especially pertinent in the Community context. Thus where a regulation is annulled the 'necessary measures' to comply with the court's judgment may not be immediately self-evident. There may be various ways in which the problem identified could be met, and these decisions are therefore best left to the Community administration, subject to the possibility of further recourse to the Community courts should the person affected be dissatisfied with the outcome.

4. DAMAGES LIABILITY: SCOPE

The discussion thus far has been concerned with the setting aside of Community action that is invalid or illegal. The applicant may, however, have suffered loss and seek redress. Legal systems will commonly make provision for recovery of losses caused by governmental action, although the criteria for liability may vary significantly in different countries. Article 288(2) EC lays down the test for actions against the Community.

In the case of non-contractual liability, the Community shall, in accordance with the general principles common to the laws of the Member States, make good any damage caused by its institutions or by its servants in the performance of their duties.

The basic limitation period for such actions is five years.[63] The Community courts have made it clear that the term institutions will be interpreted broadly, to cover not only the institutions listed in Article 7 EC, but also other Community bodies established by the Treaty that are intended to contribute to attainment of Community objectives.[64] They have properly held that it would be contrary to principle if the Community when it acts through a body established pursuant to the Treaty could escape the consequences of Article 288(2). This coheres with earlier authority holding the Community liable for acts performed by bodies to which the Communities have delegated governmental functions.[65] It should also be noted that

[63] Art. 46 of the Statute of the Court of Justice. For discussion as to when the period begins, see, Case T-201/94, *Kusterman v Council and Commission* [2002] ECR II-415; Case T-261/94, *Schulte v Council and Commission* [2002] ECR II-441.

[64] Case C-370/89, *SGEEM and Etroy v EIB* [1992] ECR I-6211; Case T-209/00, *Lamberts v Commission* [2002] ECR II-2203.

[65] Case 18/60, *Worms v High Authority* [1962] ECR 195.

Community legislation will often make specific provision for damages liability for agencies and the like.[66] Thus the enabling regulations for agencies contain provisions identical to Article 288(2).[67]

5. DAMAGES AND ANNULMENT

It is clear that Article 288(2) leaves the ECJ considerable room for interpretation. It initially held in *Plaumann*[68] that annulment of the relevant norm was a necessary condition precedent to using Article 288(2) EC. If this requirement had been retained then Article 288(2) would have been of little use, given the difficulty that non-privileged applicants face in proving *locus standi* for annulment.[69] This condition has, however, generally been discarded, and the action for damages is regarded as independent and autonomous. The fact that the contested provision has not been annulled will not therefore normally bar a damages action.[70]

This general rule is, however, subject to exceptions. Thus a damages action will be held inadmissible if it is aimed at securing withdrawal of a measure that has become definitive where the damages action would in effect nullify the legal effects of that measure. This would be the case where the applicant sought payment in a damages action of an amount precisely equal to a duty paid by it pursuant to a measure that had become definitive.[71]

Subject to this caveat, a damages action can be pursued even if the relevant

[66] See, e.g., Council Regulation (EC) 58/2003 of 19 December 2002, Laying Down the Statute for Executive Agencies to be Entrusted with Certain Tasks in the Management of Community Programmes, OJ 2003 L11/1, Art. 21(1); Council Regulation 1210/90/EEC of 7 May 1990, On the Establishment of the European Environment Agency, OJ 1990 L120/1, Art. 18.

[67] See above, Chap. 5.

[68] Case 25/62, *Plaumann v Commission* [1963] ECR 95.

[69] See above, Chap. 10.

[70] Case 5/71, *Aktien-Zuckerfabrik Schöppenstedt v Council* [1971] ECR 975; Cases 9 and 11/71, *Compagnie d'Approvisionnement de Transport et de Crédit SA et Grands Moulins de Paris SA v Commission* [1972] ECR 391; Case T-178/98, *Fresh Marine Company SA v Commission* [2000] ECR II-3331, at paras. 45–49; Case T-99/98, *Hameico Stuttgart GmbH v Council and Commission* [2003] ECR II-2195, at paras. 37–38.

[71] Case 543/79, *Birke v Commission* [1981] ECR 2669, at para. 28; Cases C-199 and 200/94, *Pesqueria Vasco-Montanesa SA (Pevasa) and Compania Internacional de Pesca y Derivados SA (Inpesca) v Commission* [1995] ECR I-3709, at paras. 27–28; Case T-93/95, *Laga v Commission* [1998] ECR II-195; Case C-310/97 P, *Commission v AssiDomän Kraft Products AB* [1999] ECR I-5363, at para. 59; Case T-178/98, *Fresh Marine, supra* n. 70, at para. 50; Cases T-44, 119, 126/01, *Eduardo Vieira SA, Vieira Argentina SA and Pescanova SA v Commission* [2003] ECR II-1209, at paras. 214–216; Mead, 'The Relationship between an Action for Damages and an Action for Annulment: The Return of *Plaumann*', in T. Heukels and A. McDonnell (eds), *The Action for Damages in Community Law* (Kluwer Law International, 1997), Chap. 13.

measure has not been annulled. This leads directly to the test for liability, a matter on which Article 288(2) provides scant guidance. The Community courts have developed different tests for liability depending upon whether the decision-maker has discretion or not. We will begin by considering the jurisprudence on damages liability for discretionary acts.

6. DAMAGES LIABILITY: DISCRETIONARY ACTS

A. The *Schöppenstedt* Test

The *Schöppenstedt* case[72] established the general test for recovery in those cases where the decision-maker has some meaningful discretion.

In the present case the non-contractual liability of the Community presupposes at the very least the unlawful nature of the act alleged to be the cause of the damage. Where legislative action involving measures of economic policy is concerned, the Community does not incur non-contractual liability for damage suffered by individuals as a consequence of that action, by virtue of the provisions contained in Article 215, second paragraph, of the Treaty, unless a sufficiently flagrant violation of a superior rule of law for the protection of the individual has occurred. For that reason the Court, in the present case, must first consider whether such a violation has occurred.

The *Schöppenstedt* test will most commonly apply where Community legislation is enacted in circumstances where there is some significant discretion, as exemplified by regulations and directives made in relation to the Common Agricultural Policy (CAP). It is, however, clear that the test will also be applicable where the contested provision is not legislative in form, but where the primary decision-maker nonetheless possessed some real discretion.

This is apparent from *Bergaderm*.[73] The applicant sought damages for losses suffered by the passage of a Directive, which prohibited the use of certain substances in cosmetics. It claimed, *inter alia*, that the Directive should be regarded as an administrative act, since it only concerned the applicant and therefore it should suffice for damages to show illegality *per se*, rather than having to prove a sufficiently serious breach. The ECJ rejected the argument, stating that 'the general or individual nature of a measure taken by an institution is not a decisive criterion for identifying the limits of the discretion enjoyed by the institution in question'.[74] The same point

[72] Case 5/71, *Aktien-Zuckerfabrik Schöppenstedt*, *supra* n. 70, at para. 11.

[73] Case C-352/98 P, *Laboratoires Pharmaceutiques Bergaderm SA and Goupil v Commission* [2000] ECR I-5291.

[74] Ibid. at para. 46. See also, Case C-472/00 P, *Commission v Fresh Marine A/S* [2003] ECR I-7541, at para. 27; Case C-312/00 P, *Commission v Camar Srl and Tico Srl* [2002] ECR I-11355, at para. 55.

emerges from *Antillean Rice.*[75] The applicants challenged, *inter alia*, aspects of the basic Council Decision which governed the relationship between the overseas countries and territories (OCTs) and the EC. They also challenged a Commission Decision, which introduced safeguard measures for rice originating in the Dutch Antilles, for breach of the Council Decision. The applicants argued before the ECJ that the CFI was wrong to have required proof of a sufficiently serious breach, since the contested measures were decisions. The ECJ rejected the claim. It held that the Commission enjoyed a wide discretion in the field of economic policy, which meant that liability was dependent on showing a sufficiently serious breach of a superior rule of law for the protection of the individual. The fact that the contested measure took the form of a Decision was not decisive, since the test for damages liability depended on the nature of the measure in question and not its form.

It follows that whether an act is subject to the *Schöppenstedt* test will be dependent upon the substance of the measure, and not the legal form in which it is expressed.[76] This means that it is always open to an applicant in an Article 288(2) action to claim that the measure, although called a regulation, was in reality an administrative decision.[77] The converse is also true: it is possible for a measure to be a decision for some purposes, but to be a legislative act for the purposes of Article 288(2).[78] Moreover, the mere fact that an applicant has a sufficient interest for a challenge under Article 230 EC will not necessarily mean that the measure is not legislative for the purposes of the Article 288(2) action.[79]

B. Superior Rule of Law

It is clear from the *Schöppenstedt* case[80] that the applicant must show that the damage resulted from breach of a superior rule of law for the protection of the individual. Superior sometimes seems to be equated with 'important', and sometimes with a more formalistic conception of one rule being hierarchically superior to another, as in the case of the regulation being in breach

[75] Case C-390/95 P, *Antillean Rice Mills NV v Commission* [1999] ECR I-769, at paras. 56–62. See also, Case C-312/00 P, *Camar*, *supra* n. 74, at paras. 55–56.

[76] Case C-390/95 P, *Antillean Rice*, *supra* n. 75, at para. 60; Arnull, 'Liability for Legislative Acts under Article 215(2) EC', in Heukels and McDonnell, *supra* n. 71, at 131–136.

[77] Case C-119/88, *Aerpo and Others v Commission* [1990] ECR I-2189; Case T-472/93, *Campo Ebro and Others v Commission* [1995] ECR II-421.

[78] Cases T-481/93 and 484/93, *Vereniging van Exporteurs in Levende Varkens v Commission (Live Pigs)* [1995] ECR II-2941; Case C-390/95 P, *Antillean Rice*, *supra* n. 75, at para. 62.

[79] Cases T-480 and 483/93, *Antillean Rice Mills v Commission* [1995] ECR II-2305; Case C-390/95 P, *Antillean Rice*, *supra* n. 75, at para. 62.

[80] Case 5/71, *Aktien-Zuckerfabrik Schöppenstedt*, *supra* n. 70, at para. 11.

of a parent regulation. It is apparent from the case law that three differing types of norm can, in principle, qualify in this respect.[81]

First, it is clear that many Treaty provisions fall within this category. One of the most commonly cited grounds in cases under Article 288(2) is the ban on discrimination contained in Article 34(3) EC, in the context of the CAP. This is not surprising, given that many of the damages actions are brought pursuant to regulations made under the CAP.[82]

A second ground of claim is that a regulation is in breach of a hierarchically superior regulation.[83] The regulations which are made pursuant to, for example, the CAP, may be 'one-off' provisions, but they may also relate to a prior network of regulations on the same topic. There may therefore be regulations which are made pursuant to more general regulations on the same topic.

A third ground which has been held capable of sustaining the claim in damages is where the Community legislation is held to infringe certain general principles of law such as proportionality, legal certainty, or legitimate expectations.[84]

It is of course perfectly possible to rely on more than one ground in order to convince the court that there has been a breach of a superior rule of law, as exemplified by the *CNTA* case.[85] The applicant claimed that it had suffered loss because a Regulation had withdrawn certain monetary compensatory amounts (MCAs). The system of MCAs was designed to compensate traders for fluctuations in exchange rates. The Regulation abolished the MCAs for colza and rape seeds because the Commission decided that the market situation had altered, thereby rendering them unnecessary. The applicant had, however, entered into contracts before the Regulation was passed, even though these contracts were to be performed after the ending of the scheme. It argued that it had made the contracts on the assumption that the MCAs would still be payable, and that it had set the price on that hypothesis. The sudden termination of the system in this area, without warning, was said by

[81] Rules of the World Trade Organization (WTO) cannot generally be relied on in this context, Case C-149/96, *Portugal v Council* [1999] ECR I-8395; Case T-18/99, *Cordis Obst und Gemüse Grosshandel GmbH v Commission* [2001] ECR II-913; Case T-3/99, *Banatrading GmbH v Council* [2001] ECR II-2123; Case C-377/02, *Léon Van Parys NV v BIRB* [2005] ECR I-1465.

[82] See e.g. Case 43/72, *Merkur-Aussenhandels-GmbH v Commission* [1973] ECR 1055; Case 153/73, *Holtz und Willemsen GmbH v Commission* [1974] ECR 675.

[83] Case 74/74, *Comptoir National Technique Agricole (CNTA) SA v Commission* [1975] ECR 533.

[84] The duty to give reasons does not appear to qualify as a superior rule of law for these purposes: Case 106/81, *Julius Kind KG v EEC* [1982] ECR 2885; Case C-119/88, *Aerpo, supra* n. 77, at para. 19; Cases T-466, 469, 473, 474, 477/93, *O'Dwyer v Council* [1996] ECR II-207, at para. 72.

[85] Case 74/74, *CNTA, supra* n. 83.

the applicant to have caused it loss. The applicant argued that the Regulation withdrawing the MCAs infringed the more basic Regulation governing this area. The ECJ rejected this argument on the facts. It held, however, that the withdrawal with immediate effect and without warning had infringed the principle of legitimate expectations, which was a superior rule of law.[86]

C. Flagrant Violation/Serious Breach: The Early Case Law

It is clear from *Schöppenstedt* that the individual must prove not only that there has been breach of a superior rule of law for the protection of the individual, but also that the breach was flagrant. This has been the most important control device used by the courts. Its meaning has altered over time and it is necessary to consider some of the earlier case law in order to appreciate the shift in the more recent jurisprudence. Analysis of the older case law reveals two senses of the term flagrant violation/serious breach.

In some cases this condition was used to deny recovery where *the loss was not deemed to be sufficiently serious.* This is exemplified by *Bayerische.*[87] There was a milk surplus in the EC, which took the form of large stocks of skimmed-milk powder. In order to reduce these stocks Council Regulation 563/76 was passed, which imposed an obligation to purchase skimmed-milk powder for use in certain feeding-stuffs. The applicant claimed that this rendered the costs of feeding its animals more expensive. In earlier cases the ECJ held that the Regulation was void, because the obligation to purchase at a disproportionate price was equivalent to a discriminatory distribution of the burden of the costs between the various agricultural sectors.[88] In *Bayersiche* the applicants' claimed damages. The ECJ reiterated the *Schöppenstedt* principle, emphasizing the rationale that the legislative authority could not be hindered in making its decisions by the prospect of damages claims whenever it had to adopt legislative measures in the public interest that might adversely affect the interests of individuals.[89] It followed, said the ECJ, that individuals might be required to accept 'within reasonable limits certain harmful effects on their economic interests as a result of a legislative measure without being able to obtain compensation from public funds'.[90] The ECJ held that there was no flagrant violation primarily because the effects of the Regulation on the price of feedingstuffs was small, causing only a price increase of 2 per cent. This increase was small, moreover, in

[86] See above, at 639.
[87] Cases 83, 94/76, 4, 15, 40/77, *Bayerische HNL Vermehrungsbetriebe GmbH & Co KG v Council and Commission* [1978] ECR 1209.
[88] See e.g. Case 116/76, *Granaria BV v Hoofdproduktschap voor Akkerbouwprodukten* [1977] ECR 1247.
[89] Cases 83, 94/76, 4, 15, 40/77, *Bayerische, supra* n. 87, at para. 4.
[90] Ibid. at para. 5.

comparison with price increases resulting from other factors during the relevant period. The ECJ therefore concluded that 'the effects of the Regulation on the profit-earning capacity of the undertakings did not ultimately exceed the bounds of economic risks inherent in the activities of the agricultural sectors concerned'.[91]

In other cases, however, the ECJ interpreted the requirement of flagrant violation to refer *to the seriousness of the breach*. *Amylum* provides a good example.[92] The applicants produced isoglucose, a sweetener made from starch, which competed with sugar. There was a sugar surplus, and it was subject to production constraints. The producers of isoglucose were therefore perceived as having an economic advantage, and it was decided that they too should be subject to a production levy. The system for levies was introduced by Council Regulation 1111/77 and Commission Regulation 1468/77. In an earlier case the ECJ held that Regulation 1111/77 was invalid because the particular production levy was in breach of Article 34 EC, although the Court added that the Council could nonetheless devise appropriate measures to ensure that the market in sweeteners functioned properly.[93] The applicants in *Amylum* sought compensation for the reduction in profits due to the fact that the companies replaced sales of isoglucose with less profitable sales of starch, and because of lost production in their factories. The ECJ denied the claim. It pointed out that in the earlier decision about nullity the Court had not declared invalid any isoglucose production levy, but only the method of calculation adopted and the fact that the levy applied to the whole of the isoglucose production. Given that an appropriate levy on isoglucose was justified, the errors in the calculation of the levy 'were not of such gravity that it may be said that the conduct of the institutions in this respect was verging on the arbitrary and was thus of such a kind as to involve the Community in non-contractual liability',[94] more especially so since the levy was adopted to deal with an emergency situation.

It seems that the conditions in *Bayerische* and *Amylum* were cumulative, given that the losses in the latter case were undeniably serious. Thus an applicant would have to show both that the *effects* of the breach were serious, in terms of the quantum of loss suffered, and also that the *manner* of the breach was arbitrary. These hurdles were not easy to surmount, particularly the second. It will be rare for the Community to promulgate a regulation that is wholly unrelated to the general ends they are entitled to advance in, for

[91] Ibid. at para. 6.

[92] Cases 116 and 124/77, *Amylum NV and Tunnel Refineries Ltd v Council and Commission* [1979] ECR 3497.

[93] Cases 103 and 145/77, *Royal Scholten-Honig (Holdings) Ltd v Intervention Board for Agricultural Produce; Tunnel Refineries Ltd v Intervention Board for Agricultural Produce* [1978] ECR 2037.

[94] Ibid. at para. 19.

example, the agricultural sphere. The mistakes are likely to be the carrying out of general, legitimate policies in an erroneous manner. Claimants did, however, occasionally win.[95]

D. Flagrant Violation/Serious Breach: The Current Test

There have, however, been significant shifts in the ECJ's more recent jurisprudence. Thus it is now clear that the possibility of a large number of applicants claiming damages as a result of the same illegality will not, in itself, rule out an Article 288(2) action.[96]

It is equally apparent that the ECJ has modified its stance as to the meaning of flagrant violation/serious breach. It made it clear in *Stahlwerke*[97] that fault in the nature of arbitrariness was not required for liability.[98] The major shift in direction came however with *Bergaderm*.[99] When considering state liability in damages the ECJ, in *Brasserie du Pêcheur/Factortame*,[100] held that the test should not be different from that used to determine the EC's liability under Article 288(2). This cross-fertilization between the test for the Community's damages liability and that of the Member States was carried further in *Bergaderm*, where the ECJ completed the circle by explicitly drawing on the factors mentioned in *Brasserie du Pêcheur/Factortame* to determine the meaning of flagrant violation for the purposes of liability under Article 288(2).

Thus in *Bergaderm* the ECJ held that the rules for liability under Article 288(2) take account, as do those in relation to state liability in damages, of 'the complexity of situations to be regulated, difficulties in the application or interpretation of the texts and, more particularly, the margin of discretion available to the author of the act in question'.[101] It affirmed that the test for damages liability was in general the same irrespective of whether the Community or the Member State inflicted the loss: the rule of law infringed must be intended to confer rights on individuals; there must be a sufficiently serious breach; and there had to be a direct causal link between the breach

[95] Cases 64, 113/76, 167, 239/78, 27, 28, 45/79 *Dumortier Frères SA v Council* [1979] ECR 3091.

[96] Cases C-104/89 and 37/90, *Mulder v Council and Commission* [1992] ECR I-3061.

[97] Case C-220/91 P, *Stahlwerke Peine-Salzgitter AG v Commission* [1993] ECR I-2393. See also Case T-120/89, *Stahlwerke Peine-Salzgitter v Commission* [1991] ECR II-279. However, compare Cases T-481 and 484/93, *Live Pigs*, *supra* n. 78 above, at para. 128, where the CFI used the language of arbitrariness in deciding upon the liability of the Commission.

[98] See also, Case C-282/90, *Industrie-en Handelsonderneming Vreugdenhil BV v Commission* [1992] ECR I-1937, at paras. 17–19.

[99] Case C-352/98 P, *Laboratoires Pharmaceutiques Bergaderm*, *supra* n. 73.

[100] Cases C-46 and 48/93, *Brasserie du Pêcheur SA v Germany*; *R v Secretary of State for Transport, ex p Factortame Ltd* [1996] ECR I-1029.

[101] Case C-352/98 P, *Laboratoires Pharmaceutiques Bergaderm*, *supra* n. 73, at para. 40.

and the damage.[102] This means that under Article 288(2) the seriousness of the breach will be dependent upon factors articulated in the case law on state liability such as the relative clarity of the rule which has been breached; the measure of discretion left to the relevant authorities; whether the error of law was excusable or not; and whether the breach was intentional or voluntary. Where the Member State or the Community institution in question has only considerably reduced, or even no discretion, the mere infringement of Community law may be sufficient to establish the existence of a sufficiently serious breach. The decisive issue for the purposes of damages liability is not the individual or general nature of the act adopted, but the discretion available to the institution when it was adopted. This approach has been followed in later cases.[103]

Commentators might well have differing views concerning the current test. My own view is that there are valid reasons for the test adopted by the ECJ. Many of the major cases arise out of the CAP, under which the Community institutions have to make difficult discretionary choices. This will often entail a complex process designed to balance the conflicting variables identified in Article 33 EC. A test for liability based on illegality *per se* would render the decision-makers susceptible to a potentially wide liability, and would run the risk that the Court might 'second-guess' the decisions made by the Council and Commission as to how the variables within Article 33 should be balanced in any particular instance. Such a strict test for damages liability might also deter the courts from finding illegality.

If this is accepted the crucial issue is how the phrase 'flagrant violation' or 'serious breach' should be interpreted. The interpretation in the early case law required something akin to arbitrary action and this was too restrictive. The approach in *Brasserie du Pêcheur/Factortame*, which was adopted in *Bergaderm*, is therefore to be welcomed. The existence of a serious breach requires attention to the factors which the ECJ identified in those cases. Where loss has been caused by sufficiently serious illegal action the applicant should not, however, have to prove that the loss was particularly serious. The applicant should have to show that the illegality caused the loss, but there should be no requirement over and above this. The ordinary 'economics of litigation' should ensure that claims are, in general, only pursued when it is economically worthwhile to do so. There are, however, instances where liability continues to be denied, in part at least, because the loss did not exceed the economic risk inherent in the activity undertaken by the applicant.[104]

[102] Ibid. at para. 41–42.

[103] Case C-472/00 P, *Fresh Marine A/S, supra* n. 74; Case C-312/00 P, *Camar, supra* n. 74.

[104] Case T-57/00, *Banan-Kompaniet AB and Skandinaviska Bananimporten AB v Council and Commission* [2003] ECR II-607, at para. 70.

7. DAMAGES LIABILITY: NON-DISCRETIONARY ACTS

A. The Test

The nature of the test that applies to liability for non-discretionary acts has been subtly altered in the recent jurisprudence. The traditional approach, prior to *Bergaderm*, was that where the contested measure did not entail any meaningful discretionary choice then it would normally suffice to show illegality, causation, and damage.[105] Discretionary measures, by way of contrast, would be subject to the further requirement of showing a sufficiently serious breach.

The more recent jurisprudence continues to distinguish between discretionary and non-discretionary acts, but does so within the unitary framework of the sufficiently serious breach test. The modern formulation, set out in *Bergaderm* and applied in subsequent cases by the ECJ, is as follows. It is necessary for the applicant to prove that the rule of law infringed was intended to confer rights on individuals, there must be a sufficiently serious breach, and a causal link between the breach and the resultant harm. Where, however, the Community institution has considerably reduced or no discretion, the mere infringement of Community law may be sufficient to establish the existence of the sufficiently serious breach.[106]

The ECJ therefore continues to distinguish between the test for liability for discretionary and non-discretionary acts, but within the framework of the sufficiently serious breach test. Where there is no or considerably reduced discretion, the mere breach of Community law *may* suffice to establish the existence of the sufficiently serious breach.

[105] Cases 44–51/77, *Union Malt v Commission* [1978] ECR 57; Cases T-481 and 484/93, *Live Pigs, supra* n. 78 above; Case 26/81, *Oleifici Mediterranei v EEC* [1982] ECR 3057, at para. 16; Case C-146/91, *KYDEP v Council and Commission* [1994] ECR I-4199; Cases C-258 and 259/90, *Pesquerias de Bermeo SA and Naviera Laida SA v Commission* [1992] ECR I-2901; Case T-175/94, *International Procurement Services v Commission* [1996] ECR II-729, at para. 44; Case T-336/94, *Efisol v Commission* [1996] ECR II-1343, at para. 30; Case T-178/98, *Fresh Marine, supra* n. 70, at para. 54; Cases T-79/96, 260/97, 117/98, *Camar Srl and Tico Srl v Commission* [2000] ECR II-2193, at paras. 204–205; van der Woude, 'Liability for Administrative Acts under Article 215(2)', in Heukels and McDonnell, *supra* n. 71, at Chap. 6.

[106] Case C-352/98 P, *Laboratoires Pharmaceutiques Bergaderm, supra* n. 73, at paras. 42–44; Case C-472/00 P, *Fresh Marine A/S, supra* n. 74, at paras. 26–27; Case C-312/00 P, *Camar, supra* n. 74, at paras. 54–55; Cases T-198/95, 171/96, 230/97, 174/98, and 225/98, *Comafrica SpA and Dole Fresh Fruit Europa Ltd & Co v Commission* [2001] ECR II-1975, at paras. 134–136; Case T-283/02, *EnBW Kernkraft GmbH v Commission*, judgment of 16 March 2005, not yet published, at para. 87; Case T-139/01, *Comafrica SpA and Dole Fresh Fruit Europe & Co Ltd v Commission* [2005] ECR II-409, at para. 142.

B. Discretionary and Non-Discretionary Acts

It follows, as we have seen, from *Bergaderm*[107] and *Antillean Rice*[108] that the general or individual nature of the measure is not a decisive criterion when identifying the limits of discretion possessed by an institution. This is correct in terms of principle. Many administrative measures involve discretionary choices that are just as difficult as those made in the context of legislative action.[109] The very line between the two may be difficult to draw in particular cases.

This is exemplified by *Schröder*.[110] The CFI held that in relation to administrative action any infringement of law constitutes illegality giving rise to damages liability. The CFI was, however, willing to consider whether the challenged norms, which were Commission *decisions*, really were administrative or legislative. The Commission Decisions were made pursuant to a Directive dealing with veterinary checks applicable to live trade in animals. These Decisions imposed a ban on the export of pigs from Germany because of swine fever. The CFI decided that they were legislative because of their generalized application, their discretionary nature, and the need to balance the free movement of animals with the protection of health. Liability could therefore only be incurred if there was a manifest and serious breach of a superior rule of law. The same approach is evident, as we have seen, in *Antillean Rice*:[111] the sufficiently serious breach test should be applied, even though the subject matter of the damages action was a Commission Decision, since this Decision was made in the area of economic policy where the Commission had broad discretion. It was the nature of the measure, and not its legal form, that was determinative of the test to be applied in a damages action.

C. The Meaning of Illegality

It should also be recognized that even where the Community courts decide that there is no meaningful discretion, and therefore that on the modern approach the mere infringement of Community law may suffice to establish a sufficiently serious breach, issues may still arise concerning the meaning of

[107] Case C-352/98 P, *supra* n. 73, at para. 46; Case T-178/98, *Fresh Marine, supra* n. 70, at para. 57.

[108] Case C-390/95 P, *Antillean Rice, supra* n. 75, at paras. 56–62.

[109] See e.g. in the context of the UK, *X (Minors) v Bedfordshire CC* [1995] 2 AC 633.

[110] Case T-390/94, *Aloys Schröder v Commission* [1997] ECR II-501. See also, Cases T-458 and 523/93, *ENU v Commission* [1995] ECR II-2459; Case T-178/98, *Fresh Marine, supra* n. 70, at para. 57; Case T-79/96, *Camar Srl, supra* n. 105, at para. 206; Case C-64/98, *Petrides Co. Inc. v Commission* [1999] ECR I-5187, at paras. 26–28.

[111] Case C-390/95 P, *Antillean Rice, supra* n. 75.

illegality. There are certainly judicial statements that in the field of administrative action any infringement of Community law constitutes illegality for these purposes.[112] It is moreover possible to list a variety of errors which *might* lead to liability. These will include: failure to gather the facts before reaching a decision, taking a decision based on irrelevant factors, failure to accord appropriate procedural rights to certain individuals before making a decision, and inadequate supervision of bodies to whom power has been delegated. The mere proof of such an error will not, however, always ensure success in a damages action. It is always open to a court to construe illegality narrowly, or to define it so as to preclude liability unless there has been some culpable error, or something equivalent thereto.

This is exemplified by *Richez-Parise*.[113] The applicants were Community officials who had been given incorrect information concerning their pensions. The information given was based on an interpretation of the relevant regulation, which was believed to be correct at that time. The department which gave the information later had reason to believe that its interpretation of the regulation was incorrect, but no immediate steps were taken to inform the applicants of this. This was done only at a later stage, by which time the applicants had already committed themselves as to the way in which they would take their pension entitlements. The ECJ held that the adoption of the incorrect interpretation did not constitute in itself a wrongful act for the purposes of damages liability, but that the department's delay in rectifying their interpretation was such as to render the Community liable.

We see the same general point in *Fresh Marine*.[114] The applicant sought damages because the Commission had erroneously decided that the company was in breach of an undertaking it had given in relation to the dumping of salmon. The CFI held that a mere infringement of Community law would suffice for liability, because the alleged error did not involve complex discretionary choices by the Commission. However it then defined the relevant error leading to illegality to be lack of ordinary care and diligence by the Commission, and took account of the applicant's contributory negligence.[115]

8. DAMAGES LIABILITY: CAUSATION AND DAMAGE

An applicant must show causation and damage in any action, irrespective of whether the contested measure is discretionary or non-discretionary in nature.

[112] Case T-79/96, *Camar Srl, supra* n. 105, at para. 205.
[113] Cases 19, 20, 25, 30/69, *Denise Richez-Parise v Commission* [1970] ECR 325.
[114] Case T-178/98, *supra* n. 70, at para. 61.
[115] Ibid. at paras. 57–61, 82. See also, Cases T-198/95, 171/96, 230/97, 174/98, and 225/98, *Comafrica, supra* n. 106, at paras. 144, 149.

A. Causation

Causation can give rise to difficult problems in any legal system where recovery is sought for monetary loss. The EU is no exception in this respect. Claims for damages have often fallen at this hurdle. Toth provides a succinct explanation of the difficulties facing applicants in this respect.[116]

> T]he establishment of the necessary causality may give rise to difficult problems in practice. This is particularly so in the field of economic and commercial relations where the cause of an event can usually be traced back to a number of factors, objective as well as subjective, operating simultaneously or successively and producing direct as well as indirect effects. Broadly speaking, it may be said that there is no causality involving liability where the same result would have occurred in the same way even in the absence of the wrongful Community act or omission in question. The converse proposition, i.e., that the requisite causality exists whenever it can be shown that the damage would not have occurred without the Community action, is, however not always correct. Although in theory it is true that any circumstance, near or remote, without which an injury would not have been produced may be considered to be its cause, the fact that a Community act or omission is one only of several such circumstances may not in itself be sufficient to establish a causal connection entailing non-contractual liability. For that purpose, the causality must be 'direct, immediate and exclusive' which it can be only if the damage arises directly from the conduct of the institutions and does not depend on the intervention of other causes, whether positive or negative.

The difficulties of proving that it was the Community's action which caused the loss can be exemplified by *Dumortier*.[117] The case concerned losses suffered as a result of the discriminatory abolition of certain production refunds. Some applicants claimed that they should be compensated because they were forced to close their factories. The ECJ rejected the claim, stating that 'even if it were assumed that the abolition of the refunds exacerbated the difficulties encountered by those applicants, those difficulties would not be a sufficiently direct consequence of the unlawful conduct of the Council to render the Community liable to make good the damage'.[118] Similarly in *Scan Office Design* the applicant failed in its damages claim, because although it had established some serious faults by the Commission in procurement procedure, it could not show that it should have been awarded the contract.[119]

[116] Toth, 'The Concepts of Damage and Causality as Elements of Non-Contractual Liability', in Heukels and McDonnell, *supra* n. 71, at 192.

[117] Cases 64, 113/76, 167, 239/78, 27, 28, 45/79, *Dumortier Frères SA v Council* [1979] ECR 3091.

[118] Ibid. at para. 21.

[119] Case T-40/01, *Scan Office Design SA v Commission* [2002] ECR II-5043.

The applicant must show not only that the Community action caused the loss,[120] but also that the chain of causation has not been broken by either the Member State or the applicant. The ECJ has held that where the loss arises from an independent or autonomous act by the Member State, the Community is no longer liable.[121] If, however, this conduct has been made possible by an illegal failure of the Commission to exercise its supervisory powers, then it will be this failure that will be considered to be the cause of the damage.[122] The EU will also bear the liability where Member State action was premised on the need to comply with EU rules and it is the Commission's inaction that has caused the loss.[123] Similarly, the EU will be liable where it committed the wrong, and hence any damage caused by implementation of the invalid Community act by national authorities that had no discretion will be attributable to the Community.[124] There may be instances where both the Community and the Member State are responsible. This complex issue will be considered below.

It is not entirely clear what type of conduct by the applicant will break the chain of causation. Negligence, or contributory negligence, will suffice either to defeat the claim or to reduce the damages.[125] If the individual ought to have foreseen the possibility of certain events which might cause loss, then the possibility of claiming damages will be diminished or lost.[126] The ECJ has also encouraged individuals who believe that a wrongful act of the Community has caused loss to challenge the measure via Article 234.[127]

B. Damage

The general objective when awarding compensation for loss in the context of non-contractual liability is to provide restitution for the victim, in the sense of placing the victim in the situation that would have pertained if the

[120] Cases C-363–4/88, *Finsider v Commission* [1992] ECR I-359, at para. 25; Case T-57/00, *Banan-Kompaniet, supra* n. 104, at para. 40; Case T-333/01, *Karl Meyer v Commission* [2003] ECR II-117, at para. 32.

[121] Case 132/77, *Société pour l'Exportation des Sucres SA v Commission* [1978] ECR 1061, 1072–3; Case T-261/94, *Schultze v Commission* [2002] ECR II-441, at para. 57.

[122] Cases 9 and 12/60, *Vloeberghs v High Authority* [1961] ECR 197, 240; Case 4/69, *Alfons Lütticke GmbH v Commission* [1971] ECR 325, at 336–338.

[123] Cases T-344–345/00, *CEVA Santé Animale SA and Pharmacia Enterprises SA v Commission* [2003] ECR II-229, at paras. 107–108.

[124] Case T-210/00, *Etablissments Biret et Cie SA v Council* [2002] ECR II-47, at paras. 36–37.

[125] Case 145/83, *Adams v Commission* [1985] ECR 3539, 3592; Case T-178/98, *Fresh Marine, supra* n. 70.

[126] Case 59/83, *SA Biovilac NV v EEC* [1984] ECR 4057; Case T-514/93, *Cobrecaf v Commission* [1995] ECR II-621, at 643; Case T-572/93, *Odigitria v Council and Commission* [1995] ECR II-2025, at 2051–2052; Case T-184/95, *Dorsch Consult* [1998] ECR II-667.

[127] Cases 116, 124/77, *Amylum, supra* n. 92.

wrong had not been committed.[128] It is nonetheless clear that while Article 288(2) speaks of the duty of the Community to make good 'any damage', losses will only be recoverable if they are certain and specific, proven and quantifiable.[129]

While the damage claimed must in general be *certain*, the Court held in *Kampffmeyer* that it is possible to maintain an action 'for imminent damage foreseeable with sufficient certainty even if the damage cannot yet be precisely assessed'.[130] The rationale was that it might be necessary to pursue an action immediately in order to prevent even greater damage.

The idea that the damage suffered must be *specific*, in the sense that it affects the applicant's interests in a special and individual way, is found in various guises in ECJ decisions. Thus, in the *Bayerische* case the Court emphasized that the effects of the regulation did not exceed the bounds of economic risk inherent in the activity in question.[131] Similar themes concerning the special nature of the burden imposed on a particular trader, or group of traders, can be found in the case law concerning the possible recovery for lawful governmental action.[132] The question whether an applicant should have to prove abnormal or special damage in a case concerning unlawful Community action has already been discussed.

The applicant will have the onus of *proving* that the damage occurred. In general the individual will have to show that the injury was actually sustained.[133] This may not be easy, and it is not uncommon for cases to fail for this reason.[134] Subject to this caveat, losses will take account of the effluxion of time between the event causing the damage and the date of payment, and hence the fall in the value of money through inflation will be factored into the award,[135] and so too will default interest from the date of the judgment establishing the duty to make good the damage.[136]

[128] Case C-308/87, *Grifoni v EAEC* [1994] ECR I-341, at para. 40; Cases C-104/89 and 37/90, *Mulder and others v Council and Commission* [2000] ECR I-203, at paras. 51, 63; Case T-260/97, *Camar Srl v Council*, judgment of 13 July 2005, not yet published, at para. 97.

[129] Toth, *supra* n. 116, at 180–191; Case T-139/01, *Comafrica*, *supra* n. 106, at paras. 163–168; Case T-99/98, *Hameico Stuttgart*, *supra* n. 70, at para. 67.

[130] Cases 56–60/74, *Kampffmeyer v Commission and Council* [1976] ECR 711, 741; Case T-79/96, *Camar Srl*, *supra* n. 105, at para. 207; Case T-260/97, *Camar Srl*, *supra* n. 128, not yet published, at para. 91.

[131] Cases 83, 94/76, 4, 15, 40/77, *Bayerische*, *supra* n. 87.

[132] See below, at 781–782.

[133] Case 26/74, *Roquette Frères v Commission* [1976] ECR 677, at 694, Trabucchi AG.

[134] See, e.g., Case 26/68, *Fux v Commission* [1969] ECR 145, at 156; Case T-1/99, *T. Port GmbH & Co. KG v Commission* [2001] ECR II-465.

[135] Cases C-104/89 and 37/90, *Mulder*, *supra* n. 128, at paras. 51–52; Case T-260/97, *Camar Srl*, *supra* n. 128, at para. 138.

[136] Cases C-104/89 and 37/90, *Mulder*, *supra* n. 96, at para. 35; Case T-260/97, *Camar Srl*, *supra* n. 128, at paras. 143–144;

The damage must also be *quantifiable*. In order to decide whether the loss is indeed quantifiable, one needs to know what *types* of damage are recoverable. Advocate General Capotorti put the matter in the following way:[137]

It is well known that the legal concept of 'damage' covers both a material loss *stricto sensu*, that is to say, a reduction in a person's assets, and also the loss of an increase in those assets which would have occurred if the harmful act had not taken place (these two alternatives are known respectively as *damnum emergens* and *lucrum cessans*) . . . The object of compensation is to restore the assets of the victim to the condition in which they would have been apart from the unlawful act, or at least to the condition closest to that which would have been produced if the unlawful nature of the act had not taken place: the hypothetical nature of that restoration often entails a certain degree of approximation . . . These general remarks are not limited to the field of private law, but apply also to the liability of public authorities, and more especially to the non-contractual liability of the Community.

The ECJ will grant damages for losses actually sustained and will exceptionally award for non-material damage.[138] It is willing in principle also to give damages for lost profits, but is reluctant to do so. Thus, in the *Kampffmeyer* case, while the Court admitted that lost profit was recoverable, it did not grant such damages to traders who had abandoned their intended transactions because of the unlawful act of the Community, even though these transactions would have produced profits.[139] In the *CNTA* case it was held that lost profits were not recoverable where the claim was based on the concept of legitimate expectations, the argument being that that concept only served to ensure that losses were not suffered owing to an unexpected change in the legal position; it did not serve to ensure that profits would be made.[140] However, in *Mulder*[141] the ECJ was prepared to compensate for lost profit, although it held that any such sum must take into account the income which could have been earned from alternative activities, applying the principle that there is a duty to mitigate loss.

In quantifying the loss suffered by the applicant the Community institutions have argued that damages should not be recoverable if the loss has been passed on to the consumers. This was accepted in principle by the ECJ in the *Quellmehl and Gritz* litigation.[142] Toth has justly criticized this reasoning. He

[137] Case 238/78, *Ireks-Arkady v Council and Commission* [1979] ECR 2955, at 2998–2999.

[138] Case T-84/98, *C v Council* [2000] ECR IA–113, at paras. 98–103; Case T-307/01, *Jean-Paul François v Commission* [2004] ECR II-1669, at paras. 107–111; Case T-48/01, *François Vainker and Brenda Vainker v European Parliament*, judgment of 3 March 2004, not yet published, at para. 180.

[139] Cases 5, 7, 13–24/66, *Kampffmeyer v Commission* [1967] ECR 245, 266–267. See also, Case T-160/03, *AFCon Management Consultants v Commission*, judgment of 17 March 2005, not yet published, at paras. 112–114.

[140] Case 74/74, *supra* n. 83, at 550.

[141] Cases C-104/89 and 37/90, *Mulder*, *supra* n. 96.

[142] Case 238/78, *supra* n. 137, at 2974.

pointed out that whether a firm could pass on a cost increase to consumers would depend upon many variables, which might operate differently for different firms, and which would be difficult to assess. He argued, moreover, that such an idea was wrong in principle, since it would mean that losses would be borne by consumers, rather than by the institutions which had committed the wrongful act.[143]

9. DAMAGES LIABILITY: COMMUNITY SERVANTS

Article 288(2) specifically allows for loss to be claimed where it has been caused either by the Community institutions or by the acts of its servants 'in the performance of their duties'. It is clear that not every act performed by a servant will be deemed to be an act in the performance of his or her duties. It is equally clear that the ECJ has construed this provision narrowly.

Thus in *Sayag*[144] an engineer employed by Euratom was instructed to take Leduc, a representative of a private firm, on a visit to certain installations. He drove him there in his own car, having obtained a travel order enabling him to claim expenses for the trip from the Community. An accident occurred and Leduc claimed damages in the Belgian courts against Sayag. It was argued that Sayag was driving the car in the performance of his duties, and that therefore the action should have been brought against the Community. The ECJ held that the Community was only liable for those acts of its servants which, by virtue of an internal and direct relationship, were the necessary extension of the tasks entrusted to the institutions. A servant's use of his private car for transport during the course of his duties could only satisfy this condition in exceptional circumstances, notwithstanding the fact Sayag had obtained a travel order for the journey. The range of acts done by its servants for which the Community will accept responsibility is therefore more limited than in most Member States. No justification for the limited nature of this liability is provided by the ECJ.

If the Community is not liable then an action can in principle be brought against the servant in his or her personal capacity in a national court and governed by national law. However, Article 291 EC provides that the Communities shall enjoy in the Member States such privileges and immunities as are necessary for the performance of its tasks, under the conditions laid down by the 1965 Protocol on the Privileges and Immunities of the European Communities as amended.[145] Article 12(a) of the Protocol provides that servants have immunity from suit in national courts in relation to 'acts

[143] Toth, *supra* n. 116, at 189–190. For consideration of the analogous situation in relation to unlawful charges levied by Member States, see below at 810–811.

[144] Case 9/69, *Sayag v Leduc* [1969] ECR 329.

[145] [1967] OJ L152/13.

performed in their official capacity'. One would expect that where the Community is liable under Article 288(2), because the servant is acting in the performance of her duties, then it would follow that the servant would not be personally liable, since he or she would be deemed to be acting in an official capacity. The interrelationship between these two provisions may, nonetheless, be more problematic, and the ECJ has held that the servant's personal immunity and the scope of the Community's liability for the acts of the servant are separate issues.[146] There is nonetheless much to be said for the view proffered by Schermers and Swaak[147] that acts 'in the performance of their duties', which lead to EC liability, include but are not limited to acts 'performed by them in their official capacity', which lead to the servants' immunity.

10. DAMAGES LIABILITY: LAWFUL ACTS

The discussion thus far has been concerned with liability in damages for unlawful acts. Individuals may, however, suffer loss flowing from lawful Community acts, more especially because of complex regulatory structures such as the CAP.[148] The problem of loss being caused by lawful governmental action is not peculiar to the Community. Thus, French law recognizes a principle of *égalité devant les charges publiques*, and German law the concept of *Sonderöpfer*, allowing loss caused by lawful governmental action to be recovered, albeit in limited circumstances.[149]

The difficulties of deciding when to grant such compensation should not be underestimated.[150] Legislation will often explicitly or implicitly aim to benefit one section of the population at the expense of another. This may be in the form of tax changes or in a decision to grant selective assistance to one industry rather than another. Any recognition of liability for losses flowing from lawful legislation requires, therefore, the drawing of a difficult line between cases where the deleterious effect on a firm was the aim of the legislation or a necessary effect thereof, and where legislation was passed that incidentally affects a particular firm in a serious manner, but where there is no legislative objection to compensating the firm for the loss suffered. The drawing of such a line in the context of, for example, the CAP may be especially difficult, given that there will often be 'winners and losers' as the

[146] Case 5/68, *Sayag v Leduc* [1968] ECR 395, 402.

[147] Schermers and Swaak, 'Official Acts of Community Servants and Article 215(4)', in Heukels and McDonnell, *supra* n. 71, at 177.

[148] Bronkhorst, 'The Valid Legislative Act as a Cause of Liability of the Communities', in Heukels and McDonnell, *supra* n. 71, Chap. 8.

[149] Ibid. at 155–159.

[150] Craig, 'Compensation in Public Law' (1980) 96 *LQR* 413, at 450.

result of the institutions' attempts to give effect to the often conflicting imperatives which lie at the heart of that policy.[151] At the very least, it serves to explain why the Community is reluctant to admit such claims.

Claims to recover for lawfully caused loss have been advanced on a number of occasions, and have been rejected.[152] The leading case is now *Dorsch Consult.*[153] The case arose out of the Gulf war. The EC, acting pursuant to a UN Security Council resolution, passed a regulation banning trade with Iraq. The Iraqi government retaliated with a law that froze all assets of companies doing business in Iraq, where those companies were based in countries that imposed the embargo. The applicant was such a company. It argued, *inter alia*, that it should be compensated by the EC for the loss it had incurred, even if the EC had acted lawfully. The CFI emphasized that if liability for lawful acts were recognized by EC law, it was necessary for the applicant to prove damage and causation. Such liability could only be incurred if the damage affected a particular circle of economic operators in a disproportionate manner in comparison with others (unusual damage) and exceeded the economic risks inherent in operating in the sector concerned (special damage), where the legislative measure that gave rise to the alleged damage was not justified by a general economic interest. The CFI concluded that the applicant had not met these criteria.

11. RESTITUTION

Most legal systems recognize liability in restitution, in addition to that based on contract or tort. The precise nature of this liability continues to divide academics, but the better view is that it is distinct from both contract and tort. The essence of the argument is that restitution is not based upon a promise, but rather on unjust enrichment by the defendant; hence its difference from contractual liability. Restitution does not normally require the

[151] See above, Chap. 3.

[152] Cases 9 and 11/71, *Compagnie d'Approvisionnement de Transport et de Crédit SA and Grands Moulins de Paris SA v Commission* [1972] ECR 391, at para. 45; Cases 54–60/76, *Compagnie Industrielle et Agricole du Comté de Loheac v Council and Commission* [1977] ECR 645, at para. 19; Case 59/83, *SA Biovilac NV v EEC* [1984] ECR 4057, at 4080–4081; Case 265/85, *Van den Bergh & Jurgens BV and Van Dijk Food Products (Lopik) BV v EEC* [1987] ECR 1155; Case 81/86, *De Boer Buizen v Council and Commission* [1987] ECR 3677.

[153] Case T-184/95, *Dorsch Consult Ingenieurgesellschaft mbH v Council* [1998] ECR II-667, upheld on appeal, Case C-237/98 P, *Dorsch Consult Ingenieurgesellschaft mbH v Council* [2000] ECR I-4549. See also, Case T-99/98, *Hameico Stuttgart, supra* n. 70, at para. 60; Case T-170/00, *Förde-Reederie GmbH v Council and Commission* [2002] ECR II-515, at para. 56; Cases T-64–65/01, *Afrikanische Frucht-Compagnie GmbH and Internationale Fructhimport Gesellschaft Weichert & Co v Council and Commission* [2004] ECR II-521, at paras. 150–156.

proof of a wrongful act by the defendant, in the sense of fault or a breach of a duty of care, and the measure of recovery is normally determined by the extent of the defendant's unjust enrichment rather than the extent of the plaintiff's loss, hence its difference from most forms of tort liability.

Article 288(2) is framed in terms of 'non-contractual liability', which can clearly cover restitution, notwithstanding the fact that the requirement to 'make good any damage caused' by its institutions, does not fit perfectly with the idea of a restitutionary action. Moreover, if the ECJ were to find that it had no jurisdiction over such actions, then Article 240 EC would mean that relief could be sought in an action against the Community in national courts. It is doubtful whether the ECJ would wish to be in a position where it had 'no control' over the development of appropriate restitutionary principles involving Community liability.

The ECJ has applied restitutionary principles where there has been unjust enrichment by an individual against the Community, as exemplified by staff cases.[154]

A common restitutionary claim by an individual arises where payments are made to public bodies that have no right to the money.[155] It can arise in two types of situation. There can be cases where a Member State has, for example, imposed a levy which is illegal under EC law. In such cases, the matter will be remitted to the national court, once the ECJ has found that the levy was in breach of Community law. It will be for the national court to devise a remedy that gives effect to the Community right, and this will often be return of the sum paid to the national authority.[156]

There can also be cases where an illegal charge has been levied by the Community. The Community courts have held that unjust enrichment is a general principle of Community law.[157] Thus where a fine imposed for breach of the competition rules is annulled there is an obligation to return the money plus interest.[158] This is in accord with principle. A remedy should be available in favour of an individual, where the Community has been unjustly enriched at the individual's expense, as where the EC has imposed an unlawful charge. Given that a levy imposed by a Member State is

[154] See e.g. Case 18/63, *Wollast v EEC* [1964] ECR 85, at 98; Case 110/63, *Willame v Commission* [1965] ECR 649, at 666; Case 36/72, *Meganck v Commission* [1973] ECR 527; Case 71/72, *Kuhl v Council* [1973] ECR 705.

[155] A. Jones, *Restitution and European Community Law* (Mansfield Press, 2000); R. Williams, *Unjust Enrichment and Public Law, A Comparative Study of England, France and the EU* (Hart, forthcoming 2007), Chaps. 6–7.

[156] See below, at Chap. 21.

[157] Case C-259/87, *Greece v Commission* [1990] ECR I-2845, at para. 26; Case T-171/99, *Corus, supra* n. 28, at para. 55; Case T-7/99, *Medici Grimm KG v Council* [2000] ECR II-2671, at para. 89; Case T-28/03, *Holcim, supra* n. 40, at paras. 127–130.

[158] Case T-171/99, *Corus, supra* n. 28, at paras. 53–55.

recoverable where it is unlawful under EC law, so too should an illegal charge levied by the Community.

The matter is, however, complicated. There is, as will be seen below, ECJ case law stipulating that, in many such instances, the action should be commenced in the national court against the national collecting agency, even where the funds are treated as Community funds.

12. JOINT LIABILITY OF THE COMMUNITY AND THE MEMBER STATES

The preceding analysis has assumed that the Community committed the unlawful act. There can, however, be cases where the Community and the Member States share liability.[159] The traditional starting point of the Community courts has been that where a charge levied by a national intervention agency may not be due because the regulation on which the charge was imposed is illegal the initial recourse for recovery of the charge must be against the national agency.[160]

A. Procedural Issues

In procedural terms Article 235 EC confers jurisdiction in relation to Article 288(2) on the ECJ and, while it does not state that this jurisdiction is exclusive, this is implied by Article 240 EC.[161] Conversely, it is not possible for an individual to bring an action for damages against a Member State directly before the ECJ, since there is no provision for this in the Treaty.

When an action is brought before the ECJ under Article 288(2) Community law is applied. An action brought against a Member State in the national court will be governed by national law. This will, however, include Community law. The national courts are under an obligation to provide an effective remedy for the enforcement of directly effective Community provisions; and the rights against the state in such suits must be no less favourable than those which exist in domestic matters.[162]

[159] Durand, 'Restitution or Damages: National Court or European Court?' (1975–6) 1 *ELRev* 431; Hartley, 'Concurrent Liability in EEC Law: A Critical Review of the Cases' (1977) 2 *ELRev* 249; Wils, 'Concurrent Liability of the Community and a Member State' (1992) 17 *ELRev* 191; Oliver, 'Joint Liability of the Community and the Member States', in Heukels and McDonnell, *supra* n. 71, at Chap. 16.

[160] Case 26/74, *Roquette Frères*, *supra* n. 133, at para. 11 and Trabucchi AG at 690–691.

[161] Cases 106–120/87, *Asteris v Greece and EEC* [1988] ECR 5515; Case T-18/99, *Cordis*, *supra* n. 81, at para. 27.

[162] See below, Chap. 21.

B. Substantive Issues: Wrongful Authorization of National Action

Issues of joint liability can arise where the Community wrongfully authorizes national action that is in breach of Community law, such as in *Kampffmeyer*.[163] The facts were complex, but in essence the Commission wrongfully confirmed a decision taken by the German government that suspended zero-rated import licences for maize, in circumstances where firms had acted in reliance on the zero-rating and had concluded contracts to buy maize on that assumption. The decision was annulled[164] and the applicants sought compensation from the Commission under what is now Article 288.

The ECJ held that the Commission acted unlawfully so as to give rise to damages liability. It decided, however, that the extent of the Community's liability should be determined after the conclusion of actions in the German courts brought by certain of the firms affected. This aspect of the case has been criticized on the ground that there was no reason to require the applicants to proceed initially in the German courts, and that the ECJ's rationale was based implicitly on the assumption that the German authorities were primarily liable, with the Community bearing only a residual liability.[165]

We should, however, distinguish the claim for the return of the levies paid from the more general tort action. Primary liability for the former should rest with Germany, given that it imposed the levy and received the funds. There is, however, no reason in relation to the latter why the liability of the Community should be seen as secondary to that of the Member State.

C. Substantive Issues: Application of Unlawful Legislation by a Member State

Issues concerning joint liability can also arise where the Member State applies unlawful Community legislation. This can occur, for example, in the context of the CAP, where Community regulations will often be applied by national intervention boards. The general rule is that it is the national intervention boards, and not the Commission, which are responsible for the application of the CAP, and that an action must normally be commenced in the national courts.

This is exemplified by *Haegeman*.[166] The applicant was a Belgian company that imported wine from Greece, which was at the time outside the EC. It claimed the loss flowing from a countervailing charge imposed on the import of wine from Greece to Belgium. This charge was imposed by a Council

[163] Cases 5, 7, 13–24/66, *Kampffmeyer v Commission* [1967] ECR 245.
[164] Cases 106 and 107/63, *Toepfer v Commission* [1965] ECR 405.
[165] See Oliver, *supra* n. 159.
[166] Case 96/71, *R. and V. Haegeman Sprl v Commission* [1972] ECR 1005.

regulation and levied by the Belgian authorities. The ECJ held that the dispute should be resolved initially by the national courts, which could have recourse to Article 234 where the validity of a Community regulation was in issue. The decision can be criticized since the money levied went into the Community's funds. The mere fact that the sums were collected by national authorities should make no difference, given that these sums were imposed by the Community and were collected on behalf of the Community by the Member State.[167]

The ECJ has also held that an action must be commenced in the national courts where a trader is seeking payment of a sum to which he believes himself to be entitled under Community law, although this decision was heavily influenced by the wording of the relevant Community regulations.[168] This principle applies even where the Commission has sent telexes to the national board setting out its interpretation of the relevant regulations.[169] The Member State may, however, be able to recover from Community funds where they have paid for losses which are the EC's responsibility.[170]

There are, however, a number of situations in which it is possible to proceed against the Community directly.

First, if the Commission sends a telex which is interpreted, in the context of the relevant legislation, as an instruction to the national agency to act in a particular manner, then an action may be brought against the Commission for damages.[171]

Secondly, an applicant can proceed against the Community where there would be no remedy available in the national courts. Thus, in *Unifrex*, an applicant sought damages before the ECJ because of the Commission's failure to pass a regulation that would have granted the applicant a subsidy for exports to Italy when the Italian lira was devalued. It was held that the action could proceed before the ECJ, since the national court could not have helped the applicant: even if the relevant Community rules had been declared illegal pursuant to Article 234, 'that annulment could not have required the

[167] See T. C. Hartley, *The Foundations of European Community Law* (Oxford University Press, 4th ed., 1998), at 479.

[168] Case 99/74, *Société des Grands Moulins des Antilles v Commission* [1975] ECR 1531.

[169] Case 133/79, *Sucrimex SA and Westzucker GmbH v Commission* [1980] ECR 1299; Case 217/81, *Compagnie Interagra SA v Commission* [1982] ECR 2233; Case T-160/98, *Firma Léon Van Parys NV and Pacific Fruit Company NV v Commission* [2002] ECR II-233.

[170] This may be possible in the context of the CAP. The basis for shifting the loss to the Community was bound up with the operation of the EAGGF (the European Agricultural Guarantee and Guidance Fund). For discussion of this issue, see Oliver, *supra* n. 159, at 306–308; J. A. Usher, *Legal Aspects of Agriculture in the European Community* (Oxford University Press, 1988), at 104–106, 150–152.

[171] Case 175/84, *Krohn & Co. Import-Export GmbH & Co. KG v Commission* [1986] ECR 753.

national authorities to pay higher monetary compensatory amounts to the applicant, without the prior intervention of the Community legislature'.[172]

Thirdly, it is possible to bring a claim in the ECJ where the Community has committed a tortious wrong to the applicant. This is exemplified by the *Dietz* case[173] in which the essence of the claim was that the Community authorities had introduced a levy without transitional provisions and had thereby caused loss in breach of the applicant's legitimate expectations. This claim could be pursued in the ECJ since the wrong alleged was entirely directed towards the Community's behaviour, and not that of the Member State.

13. DAMAGES LIABILITY: ASSESSMENT

It was the ECJ that took the bare wording of Article 288(2) and fashioned a test for Community liability that it has refined and altered over the ensuing years, and the CFI now plays an increasingly important role in the interpretation and application of this Article.

The jurisprudence displays a chequered history. The *Schöppenstedt* test was applied in the early years in such a way that rendered it extremely difficult for any applicant to succeed. The combination of the need to prove serious loss and a breach that verged on the arbitrary meant that the Community coffers rarely had to pay out where losses were caused by legislative measures entailing the balancing of economic variables. Applicants were more successful where there was no discretion. The courts upheld such claims where the applicant could show illegality, causation, and resulting damage, but even here many claims failed because the applicant could not prove the requisite causation or proof of the loss.

The jurisprudence has, however, become more liberal and clearer since *Bergaderm*. It is no longer necessary to prove that the Community action verged on the arbitrary in order to satisfy the serious breach test. The ECJ emphasized the parity between the tests for Community and state liability and applied the test for serious breach in *Brasserie du Pêcheur/Factortame* to Community liability. The ECJ in *Bergaderm* also made it clear that the decisive criterion for the application of this test was whether the institution exercised discretionary power, and not the form through which this was expressed. These are positive developments.

[172] Case 281/82, *Unifrex v Commission and Council* [1984] ECR 1969; Case 20/88, *Roquette Frères v Commission* [1989] ECR 1553; Case T-167/94, *Nölle v Council and Commission* [1995] ECR II-2589; Case T-18/99, *Cordis, supra* n. 81, at para. 28.

[173] Case 126/76, *Dietz v Commission* [1977] ECR 2431; Case T-18/99, *Cordis, supra* n. 81, at para. 26. The principle in *Dietz* may not apply if the national authorities were partially to blame for the loss caused to the applicant as in Cases 5, 7, 13–24/66, *Kampffmeyer, supra* n. 163.

It remains to be seen whether the Community courts intend to modify their approach in relation to non-discretionary acts. The test for liability hitherto was illegality, causation, and damage. The formulation in *Bergaderm* and subsequent cases is subtly different. The ECJ continues to distinguish between the test for liability for discretionary and non-discretionary acts, but within the framework of the sufficiently serious breach test. Where there is no or considerably reduced discretion, the mere breach of Community law *may* suffice to establish the existence of the sufficiently serious breach. It would certainly be regrettable if this new formulation were to render it more difficult than hitherto to recover for loss where there is illegality and no discretion.

21

Remedies II: Member States

1. INTRODUCTION

The previous chapter considered remedies against the Community. The discussion now turns to the availability of relief against the Member States, this being in certain respects a more complex topic.

This is because relief against Member States that violate Community law will normally be sought in national courts. The action will *prima facie* have to conform to national procedural and remedial rules concerning matters such as time limits, quantum of recovery, and the like. This raises the issue of the extent to which Community law imposes constraints on such national rules. A complex jurisprudence has built up around this topic and it will be analysed in the first half of the chapter.

The Community courts have, however, also developed a Community cause of action for damages that is applicable against all Member States. This will be examined in the second half of the chapter, with consideration being given to the conceptual foundations of the cause of action, its subsequent modification, and the relationship between the Community courts and the national courts in the application of the criteria for recovery.

2. NATIONAL REMEDIAL AUTONOMY: THE INITIAL LIMITS

The previous chapter analysed actions brought against the Community, whether directly under Article 230 EC, or indirectly under Article 234 EC, and the consequences of finding that the contested measure is illegal.

It may, however, be Member State action that is challenged as being in breach of Community law. Such actions will normally begin and end in the national courts, with recourse to the European Court of Justice (ECJ) via Article 234 EC where the national court feels that this is necessary in order to determine whether the state action was in breach of Community law. Such actions have raised difficult issues concerning the extent to which Community law should impose constraints on the remedies available within the national courts and how far national remedial autonomy should be limited.

The ECJ's initial approach was cautious and imposed limited constraints on national procedural autonomy.[1] This is exemplified by the early decision in *Rewe-Zentralfinanz*.[2] The applicants sought a refund, including interest, of charges they had paid in Germany for import inspection costs, these charges having been found to be in breach of Community law. The national time limit for challenging the validity of national administrative measures had passed, and the applicants argued that Community law nonetheless required that they should be given the remedy sought. The ECJ held that in the absence of Community rules on the issue, it was for the Member State to determine the procedural conditions governing actions intended to ensure the protection of directly effective Community rights. In the absence of harmonization these rights should therefore be exercised before the national courts in accordance with the conditions set out in the national rules.

This was subject to two caveats. The national procedural conditions could not be less favourable than those relating to similar actions of a domestic nature. Those conditions and time limits must not make it impossible in practice to exercise the rights which the national courts were obliged to protect, and the ECJ held that this condition was not violated where the limitation period was reasonable. These twin caveats therefore embodied some minimum constraint on national remedial autonomy, cast in terms of equivalence and practical impossibility.

The corollary of this early approach was that Community law did not, in the absence of harmonization, require the creation of new national remedies. Thus in *Rewe-Handelsgesellschaft Nord*[3] the applicants contested the legality of 'butter-buying cruises' for the purchase of tax-free butter that were allowed under German law. They argued that the cruises were contrary to Community tax and customs law, and that their economic interests were adversely affected by the Member State's failure to apply Community rules to third party competitors. The ECJ held that the Treaty was not intended to create new remedies in the national courts to ensure the observance of Community law other than those already laid down by national law. It was therefore open to Member States to apply their own procedural rules and conditions without being required to create new national remedies, although these rules remained subject to the twin principles of equivalence and practical possibility.

[1] Case 6/60, *Humblet v Belgium* [1960] ECR 559; Case 13/68, *Salgoil v Italian Ministry for Foreign Trade* [1973] ECR 453.

[2] Case 33/76, *Rewe-Zentralfinanz eG and Rewe-Zentral AG v Landwirtschaftskammer für das Saarland* [1976] ECR 1989. See also, Case 45/76, *Comet BV v Produktschap voor Siergewassen* [1976] ECR 2043; Case 179/84, *Bozetti v Invernizzi* [1985] ECR 2301.

[3] Case 158/80, *Rewe-Handelsgesellschaft Nord mbH v Hauptzollamt Kiel* [1981] ECR 1805.

3. NATIONAL REMEDIAL AUTONOMY AND EFFECTIVENESS OF COMMUNITY LAW

The ECJ's early approach was modified in later case law. The driving force behind this modification was the effectiveness of Community law, which led to greater limitations being imposed on national remedial autonomy. One manifestation of this was the way in which concern for the effectiveness of Community law could require Member States to expand the scope of existing remedies.

A. Effectiveness and 'New' Remedies

The scope of the principle that Community law would not demand the creation of new national remedies was thrown into question even in the relatively early case law. Thus in cases concerned with the repayment of charges levied in breach of European Community (EC) law, the ECJ appeared to hold that a right to repayment should be available under national law. In *San Giorgio* the ECJ reasoned that 'entitlement to the repayment of charges levied by a member state contrary to the rules of Community law is a consequence of, and an adjunct to, the rights conferred on individuals by the Community provisions prohibiting charges having an effect equivalent to customs duties or, as the case may be, the discriminatory application of internal taxes'.[4] The ECJ went on to state that repayment must be sought within the framework laid down by national law, subject to the conditions of equivalence and the need to ensure that the national rules did not render virtually impossible the exercise of rights conferred by Community law. This case law concerning unlawfully levied charges nonetheless appeared to involve either the ECJ imposing a particular remedy,[5] or alternatively requiring, as a matter of EC law, that such a specific remedy be available in principle in national legal systems.

The extent to which the Community courts were willing to demand the provision of new remedies in national law was thrown into sharp relief by *Factortame*.[6] Factortame and other companies, most of the directors and shareholders of which were Spanish nationals, were incorporated under UK law and owned or operated fishing vessels registered as British vessels under

[4] Case 199/82, *Amministrazione delle Finanze dello Stato v San Giorgio* [1983] ECR 3595, at para. 12; Case C-192/95, *Comateb v Directeur Général des Douanes et Droits Indirects* [1997] ECR I-165.

[5] Dougan 'Cutting your Losses in the Enforcement Deficit: A Community Right to the Recovery of Unlawfully Levied Charges?' (1998) 1 *CYELS* 233.

[6] Case C-213/89, *R v Secretary of State for Transport, ex p Factortame Ltd* [1990] ECR I-2433.

the Merchant Shipping Act 1894. The 1988 Merchant Shipping Act was adopted to require all fishing vessels to register anew, and the applicants did not satisfy the new registration conditions. They argued that these conditions, including requirements as to nationality and residence, were in breach of Community law. They claimed interim relief until final judgment was given because of the harm that they would suffer from not being able to fish while the litigation was pending. The House of Lords held that interim relief was not available against the Crown, but referred the case to the ECJ, which held that the absence of such relief was not compatible with EC law.

The cornerstone of the ECJ's reasoning was *Simmenthal*.[7] Any provision of a national legal system and any legislative, administrative, or judicial practice, which might impair the effectiveness of Community law by withholding from the national court having jurisdiction to apply such law the power to do everything necessary at the moment of its application to set aside national legislative provisions which might prevent, even temporarily, Community rules from having full force and effect, was itself incompatible with Community law.[8] This principle was then applied to the facts of the instant case. The ECJ concluded that the full effectiveness of Community law would be just as much impaired if a rule of national law could prevent a court seized of a dispute governed by Community law from granting interim relief in order to ensure the full effectiveness of the judgment to be given on the existence of the rights claimed under Community law. It followed that a court which in those circumstances would grant interim relief, if it were not for a rule of national law, was obliged to set aside that rule.[9]

The pre-existing orthodoxy that EC law did not require the creation of new remedies was modified, to say the very least, by *Factortame*. When the case went from the House of Lords to the ECJ the position under UK law was that there was an injunctive remedy, there could be an interim as well as a final injunction, but there could be no interim injunction against the Crown. The ECJ decided in *Factortame* that such relief should nonetheless be available as a matter of principle, and that its absence was itself a breach of Community law. The effect of this ruling at a minimum was that, provided the type of relief sought by the applicant was recognized by national law, in this instance the injunction, the fact that it was not previously available against the Crown would be regarded as an example of ineffective protection of Community rights, with the consequence that the national law must be changed, if possible by the courts in the case at hand. The driving force behind the ECJ's reasoning in *Factortame* might well have been the effectiveness of Community law, based on *Simmenthal*, but the effect of that reasoning was to

[7] Case 106/77, *Amministrazione delle Finanze dello Stato v Simmenthal SpA* [1978] ECR 629.
[8] Case C-213/89, *Factortame*, *supra* n. 6, at para. 20.
[9] Ibid. at para. 21.

require a national legal system to change its rules about the availability of a particular remedy.

B. Effectiveness of Community Law: Proportionality and Adequacy of National Remedies

The emphasis placed on the effectiveness of Community law in *Factortame* and its impact on national remedial autonomy was echoed and reflected in other cases. Its impact differed depending on the nature of the case.

In some cases the ECJ held that the duty of cooperation under Article 10 EC meant that where Community legislation did not provide a remedy for infringement of its provisions it was for national law to take all necessary measures to ensure the effectiveness of Community law. For that purpose, while the choice of remedy remained within the discretion of the Member State, it had to ensure not only that the remedy was similar to that applicable for infringements of a similar nature under national law, but also that the penalty was effective, proportionate, and dissuasive.[10] The same principle applies where the Community legislation lays down particular penalties, but does not exhaustively prescribe the penalties that a Member State can impose.[11]

The effectiveness of Community law could in other instances limit the type of penalty that a Member State could impose. This is exemplified by *Sagulo*,[12] where the applicants were French and Italian nationals resident in Germany who had failed to comply with the administrative formalities to obtain resident permits to which they were entitled under EC law and were penalized under German law. The ECJ held that although Member States were entitled to impose reasonable penalties for infringement of the obligation to obtain a valid identity card or passport, such penalties should not be so severe as to cause an obstacle to the freedom of entry and residence provided for in the Treaty. The penalties imposed could not be disproportionate to the nature of the offence committed.

The importance attached to the effectiveness of Community law could in yet other cases lead the ECJ to assess the adequacy of the remedy chosen by a national legal system in order to ensure that it was effective to achieve the objective required by Community law. *Von Colson* provides a fitting example.[13]

[10] Case 68/88, *Commission v Greece* [1989] ECR 2965; Case C-383/92, *Commission v UK* [1994] ECR I-2479; Case C-354/99, *Commission v Ireland* [2001] ECR I-7657, at para. 46; Cases 387, 391, and 403/02, *Criminal Proceedings against Silvio Berlusconi and others* [2005] ECR I-3565, at para. 53.

[11] Case C-186/98, *Criminal Proceedings against Nunes and de Matos* [1999] ECR I-4883.

[12] Case 8/77, *Sagulo, Brenca, and Bakhouche* [1977] ECR 1495. See also, Case C-186/98, *Nunes and de Matos*, *supra* n. 11.

[13] Case 14/83, *Von Colson and Kamann v Land Nordrhein-Westfalen* [1984] ECR 1891.

The plaintiffs were women who had applied for posts as social workers at a German prison. They were unsuccessful and two men were appointed. The plaintiffs were successful in their action for sex discrimination and sought as a remedy to be appointed to a post in the prison, or to be awarded six months salary. The Arbeitsgericht considered that under German law it could allow only the claim for 'reliance loss', this being only repayment of travelling expenses of one of the plaintiffs, who argued that this limited remedy was not sufficient to fulfil the state's obligations under the Equal Treatment Directive 76/207. The ECJ held that although full implementation of the Directive did not require any specific form of sanction for unlawful discrimination, it did require that the sanction guaranteed real and effective judicial protection. It followed that while the Directive left the choice of sanction to the Member State, if it chose to penalize breach of the Directive by the award of compensation, then in order to ensure that it was effective and had a deterrent effect, the compensation had to be adequate in relation to the damage sustained and more than purely nominal compensation of the kind offered by the German authorities in this case. The same concern for the adequacy of the national remedy in order to ensure that it properly effectuated the Community right is evident in other cases,[14] with the ECJ emphasizing the importance of a judicial remedy in order to secure effective protection for the Community right.[15]

C. Effectiveness of Community Law: The Temporal Effect of Preliminary Rulings

The ECJ also kept firm control over the temporal effect of preliminary rulings concerning the compatibility of national law with EC law. It made clear that the general principle was that the ruling defined the legal position as it must have been understood from the time when the relevant EC norm came into force.[16] The Community norm must, therefore, be applied by national courts to situations that occurred before the ECJ's ruling was given, provided that the conditions enabling an action relating to that rule to be brought before the courts having jurisdiction are satisfied. This proposition would only be qualified in exceptional circumstances, for example, where there was a risk of serious economic repercussions owing to the large number

[14] Case 222/84, *Johnston v Chief Constable of the RUC* [1986] ECR 1651; Cases C-87–89/90, *Verholen v Sociale Verzekeringsbank Amsterdam* [1991] ECR I-3757.

[15] Case 222/86, *UNECTEF v Heylens* [1987] ECR 4097; Case C-185/97, *Coote v Granada Hospitality Ltd* [1998] ECR I-5199; Case C-120/97, *Upjohn v The Licensing Authority established by the Medicines Act 1968* [1999] ECR I-223; Case C-228/98, *Dounias v Ypourgio Oikonomikon* [2000] ECR I-577.

[16] Cases 66, 127 and 128/79, *Salumi v Amministrazione delle Finanze* [1980] ECR 1237, at paras. 9–10; Case C-50/96, *Deutsche Telekom AG v Schröder* [2000] ECR I-743, at para. 43.

of legal relationships entered into in good faith on the basis of the rules considered to be validly in force, and where the individuals and national authorities had adopted practices which did not comply with EC law because of uncertainty about what EC law required, to which the conduct of the Commission might have contributed.[17]

4. NATIONAL REMEDIAL AUTONOMY AND EFFECTIVENESS OF COMMUNITY LAW: JUDICIAL EXPANSION

The 1990s saw the ECJ build on the foundations that it had created. The focus fell ever more sharply on the adequacy and effectiveness of the national remedies and the extent to which they properly protected the relevant Community right and thereby ensured the effectiveness of Community law.

A. The Adequacy of the National Monetary Remedy

In some cases the issue was the adequacy of the monetary remedy provided under national law. The ECJ was willing to override national limits even though they did not render exercise of the right practically impossible. This is exemplified by *Marshall*.[18] The case was concerned with assessment of compensation for gender discrimination in breach of Directive 76/207.[19] The UK Industrial Tribunal assessed compensation at £18,405 including £7,710 as interest. UK legislation, however, set £6,250 as the maximum that could be awarded and it was uncertain whether the Industrial Tribunal could award interest in this case. The ECJ considered whether these limits were compatible with the Member State's obligations under the Directive.

It affirmed that Article 6 of the Directive obliged Member States to take the necessary measures to enable those who considered themselves wronged by discrimination to pursue their claims by judicial process. This obligation implied that the measures should be sufficiently effective to achieve the objective of the Directive. The Member State was free to choose between different solutions suitable for achieving the objective of the Directive. The objective was, however, to achieve real equality of opportunity, and this

[17] Cases C-197 and 252/94, *Société Bautiaa v Directeur des Services Fiscaux des Landes* [1996] ECR I-505; Case 61/79, *Denkavit Italiana* [1980] ECR 1205; Case C-137/94, *R v Secretary of State for Health, ex p Richardson* [1995] ECR I-3407; Case C-359/67, *Commission v UK* [2000] ECR I-6355.

[18] Case C-271/91, *Marshall v Southampton and South-West Hampshire Area Health Authority II* [1993] ECR I-4367.

[19] Council Directive 76/207/EEC of 9 February 1976, On the Implementation of the Principle of Equal Treatment for Men and Women as Regards Access to Employment, Vocational Training and Promotion, and Working Conditions, OJ 1976 L39/40.

could not be attained in the absence of measures appropriate to restore such equality when it had not been observed. Where there was a discriminatory dismissal contrary to Article 5(1) of the Directive, equality could not be restored without either reinstating the victim of discrimination or, in the alternative, granting financial compensation for the loss and damage sustained. When financial compensation was the measure adopted to achieve real equality of opportunity, it had to be adequate in the sense that it had to enable the loss and damage actually sustained as a result of the discriminatory dismissal to be made good in full in accordance with the applicable national rules.

It followed, said the ECJ, that 'the fixing of an upper limit of the kind at issue in the main proceedings cannot, by definition, constitute proper implementation of Article 6 of the directive, since it limits the amount of compensation *a priori* to a level which is not necessarily consistent with the requirement of ensuring real equality of opportunity through adequate reparation for the loss and damage sustained as a result of discriminatory dismissal'[20]. It followed also in relation to award of interest that full compensation for discriminatory dismissal could not leave out of account factors such as the effluxion of time, which might reduce its value and 'the award of interest, in accordance with the applicable national rules, must therefore be regarded as an essential component of compensation for the purposes of restoring real equality of treatment'.[21]

The ECJ was therefore willing to find that national remedial rules imposing limits on the amount of compensation were not adequate to protect the Community right contained in the Directive, and its ruling contrasts with earlier case law in which decisions as to whether to award interest on the reimbursement of sums wrongly levied under Community law were left to national law.[22] The ruling in *Marshall II* led to revision of the Equal Treatment Directive,[23] but the more general principles from that case have, as will be seen, nonetheless been narrowed by later case law.

B. Substantive Conditions Attached to the National Remedy

In other cases the effectiveness of Community law impacted on the adequacy of the national remedy by placing limits on the conditions attached to that remedy. This was in effect the situation in *Dekker*.[24] The applicant sought

[20] Case C-271/91, *Marshall*, *supra* n. 18, at para. 30. [21] Ibid. at para. 31.

[22] Case 6/60, *Humblet*, *supra* n. 1; Case 26/74, *Société Roquette Frères v Commission* [1976] ECR 677.

[23] Directive 2002/73 of the European Parliament and of the Council of 23 September 2002, Amending Council Directive 76/207/EEC, OJ 2002 L269/15, Art. 5, amending Art. 6 of Dir. 76/207.

[24] Case C-177/88, *Dekker v Stichting Vormingscentrum voor Jong Volwassenen (VJV-Centrum) Plus* [1990] I-ECR 3941.

damages before the Dutch courts for the defendant's refusal to employ her on grounds of her pregnancy. The ECJ held that this constituted unlawful sex discrimination and then turned its attention to the remedy. It reiterated the principle from *Von Colson* that although full implementation of the Equal Treatment Directive did not require any specific form of sanction for unlawful discrimination, it did entail that the sanction chosen must guarantee real and effective judicial protection and have a real deterrent effect on the employer.

It followed, said the ECJ, that if the employer's liability for infringement of the principle of equal treatment were subject to proof of a fault attributable to him and also to there being no ground of exemption recognized by the applicable national law, the practical effect of those principles would be weakened considerably. Thus where a Member State opted for a sanction forming part of the rules on civil liability, any infringement of the prohibition of discrimination should suffice to make the defendant fully liable, and regard should not be had to grounds of exemption provided for by national law.[25]

The principle of the effectiveness of Community law therefore placed limits on the conditions that could be attached to the national remedy in order for that remedy to be regarded as adequate. Conditions in national rules on civil liability pertaining to fault could not be applied in the instant case. This was so even though the national rule did not violate the equivalence test; there was no discrimination between situations involving Community law and domestic law. The fault requirement would moreover probably not have rendered exercise of the Community right impossible, though it would have made it more difficult.

C. Sustainability of National Time Limits

There were yet other cases in which the effectiveness of Community law was held to have an impact on the national time limits within which an action could be brought. *Emmott* is the best known example of this.[26] The applicant had been discriminated against on the grounds of sex. She sought payment retrospectively for a disability benefit for the period during which Council Directive 79/7[27] had not been implemented in Ireland. She was informed by the relevant government department that no decision could be made in her case until the ECJ had ruled on another case pending before it. However,

[25] Ibid. at para. 26.

[26] Case C-208/90, *Emmott v Minister for Social Welfare and Attorney General* [1991] ECR I-4269.

[27] Council Directive 79/7/EEC of 19 December 1978, On the Progressive Implementation of the Principle of Equal Treatment for Men and Women in Matters of Social Security, OJ 1979 L6/24.

when she did seek judicial review of the decisions concerning her social security benefit the department argued that her delay in beginning proceedings was a bar to the action.

The ECJ reiterated the principle of national procedural autonomy, as qualified by the conditions of equivalence and practical possibility, and stated that reasonable national time limits for the bringing of actions would generally satisfy these conditions. The situation was, however, different in relation to directives. Where a directive had not been properly transposed into national law, individuals could not ascertain the full extent of their rights. That uncertainty subsisted even after the ECJ delivered a judgment finding that the Member State had not fulfilled its obligations under the directive, and this was so even if the ECJ held that a particular provision of the directive was sufficiently precise and unconditional to be relied upon before a national court. It followed that until the directive had been properly transposed a defaulting Member State could not rely on an individual's delay in initiating proceedings against it in order to protect rights conferred by the provisions of the directive. The national time limits for bringing an action could not begin to run before then.

Emmott did not force the Member State to change its rules on time limits. The ECJ did, however, stipulate the point from which time could begin to run and the principal rationale for this was so as to ensure the effectiveness of the rights contained in the directive. There is little doubt that the ECJ was influenced in reaching its conclusion by the fact that the state was seeking to rely on its own default, its failure to implement the directive coupled with the misleading advice, to defeat the applicant's claim. Similar considerations have influenced the ECJ in other cases.[28] The *Emmott* ruling has, however, been interpreted narrowly, and particular emphasis has been laid on the misleading conduct of the national authorities, as we shall from the cases discussed below.

It is nonetheless interesting to reflect on the rationale for the ECJ's more strident jurisprudence during this period. Dougan proffers a number of suggestions.[29]

> First it was clear that the Court was wrong to have so much faith in the adequacy of national rules; in fact, as the dispute in *Factortame* demonstrated, they often offered less than adequate levels of protection. Secondly, more and more Community claims were coming before the domestic courts, making the problem more visible. Thirdly, the character of such claims was changing significantly. As well as the economic interests of big business, the Court was being confronted with ordinary citizens

[28] Case C-377/89, *Cotter and McDermott v Minister for Social Welfare and Attorney General* [1991] ECR I-1155.

[29] M. Dougan, *National Remedies before the Court of Justice, Issues of Harmonisation and Differentiation* (Hart, 2004), at 230.

asserting their right to the social benefits of Community membership. Bearing in mind the drive for 'Europe with a human face', coupled with the natural tendency of a system of decentralised enforcement to emphasise the role of the individual, this change may well have increased the Court's inclination to increase the levels of protection guaranteed by Community law. Finally, the Court's repeated requests for legislative intervention to address the 'problem' of national remedies had gone largely unheeded. So, if any thing was to be done to help the increasing number of citizens invoking the Community's aid, the initiative lay with the judiciary.

5. NATIONAL REMEDIAL AUTONOMY AND EFFECTIVENESS OF COMMUNITY LAW: JUDICIAL RETREAT

The case law discussed in the previous section signalled willingness on the part of the ECJ to scrutinize closely the national remedial provisions and intervene if they did not provide adequate and effective protection for the relevant Community right.[30] There was little by way of deference to national remedial rules. Subsequent case law has, however, indicated a measure of retreat in this regard.[31]

A. The Limiting of *Marshall II*

The approach in *Marshall II* to the adequacy of national monetary remedies was distinguished and limited by the ruling in *Sutton*.[32] The applicant successfully challenged the refusal by the Member State to grant her an invalid care allowance, on the ground that this was in breach of Directive 79/7 on equal treatment in social security. She was awarded arrears of benefit, but not the payment of interest, because national law did not provide for the payment of interest on social security benefits. The applicant argued that the wording of Article 6 of Directive 79/7 was very close to that of Article 6 of

[30] See also, Cases C-312/93, *Peterbroeck, Van Campenhout & Cie v Belgian State* [1995] ECR I-4599, at para. 12; Cases C-430–431/93, *Van Schijndel & Van Veen v Stichting Pensioenfonds voor Fysiotherapeuten* [1995] ECR I-4705, at para. 17.

[31] Ward, 'Effective Sanctions in EC Law: A Moving Boundary in the Division of Competence' (1995) 1 *ELJ* 205; Chiti, 'Towards a Unified Judicial Protection in Europe(?)' (1997) 9 *ERPL* 553; Himsworth, 'Things Fall Apart: The Harmonisation of Community Judicial Protection Revisited' (1997) 22 *ELRev* 291; Craufurd Smith, 'Remedies for Breaches of EU Law in National Courts: Legal Variation and Selection', in P. Craig and G. de Burca (eds), *The Evolution of EU Law* (Oxford University Press, 1999), Chap. 8; A. Ward, *Judicial Review and the Rights of Private Parties in EC Law* (Oxford University Press, 2000), Chaps. 2–4; P. Craig and G. de Burca, *EU Law, Text, Cases and Materials* (Oxford University Press, 3rd ed., 2002), Chap. 6; Dougan, *supra* n. 29, at Chap. 5.

[32] Case C-66/95, *R v Secretary of State for Social Security, ex p Eunice Sutton* [1997] ECR I-2163.

Directive 76/207 which was in issue in *Marshall II*, and that since both provisions were concerned with equal treatment payment of interest should therefore be awarded here as it had been in *Marshall II*.

The ECJ disagreed. *Marshall II* concerned the award of interest on amounts payable by way of reparation for loss and damage sustained as a result of discriminatory dismissal. The present action concerned the right to receive interest on amounts payable by way of social security benefits, and since these payments did not constitute reparation for loss or damage sustained the reasoning in *Marshall II* was not applicable. Since social security benefits were not compensatory in nature, payment of interest could not be required on the basis either of Article 6 of Directive 76/207 or of Article 6 of Directive 79/7.

The reasoning in *Sutton* appeared to confine *Marshall II* to cases of discriminatory dismissal under Directive 76/207, or at the very least it suggested that the extent to which the ECJ would intrude on national remedies would depend on the nature of the Community right that had been infringed. Social security benefits are certainly factually different from money received by way of compensation for loss or damage. It is, however, more questionable whether this difference should have led to the consequences in *Sutton*, where the ECJ gave much less regard to the idea of an adequate remedy under national law as compared to its reasoning in *Marshall II*.

B. The Limiting of *Emmott*

The ECJ also retracted from the broader implications of *Emmott* in the *Steenhorst-Neerings case*.[33] The applicant brought an action for retrospective payment of disability benefits, because the EC Social Security Directive had not been properly implemented in to Dutch law. The national law stated, however, that such benefits should not be payable retroactively for more than one year.

The ECJ held that the right to claim incapacity benefits for work under the same conditions as men, conferred on married women by the direct effect of Article 4(1) of Directive 79/7, must be exercised under conditions determined by national law, provided that they were no less favourable than those relating to similar domestic actions, and that they were not framed so as to render virtually impossible the exercise of rights conferred by Community law. It held that the national rule restricting the retroactive effect of a claim for benefits for incapacity for work satisfied these conditions.

[33] Case C-338/91, *Steenhorst-Neerings v Bestuur van de Bedrijfsvereniging voor Detailhandel, Ambachten en Huisvrouwen* [1993] ECR I-5475. See however Case C-246/96, *Magorrian and Cunningham v Eastern Health and Social Services Board* [1997] ECR I-7153 and Case C-78/98, *Preston v Wolverhampton Healthcare NHS Trust* [2000] ECR I-3201.

The Commission argued by way of analogy from *Emmott* that time limits for actions brought by individuals who sought to avail themselves of their rights were applicable only when a Member State had properly transposed the Directive, and contended that the same principle should govern this case.

The ECJ rejected the analogy. It reasoned that the national rule in this case was concerned not with the time limits for bringing an action, but merely limited the retroactive effect of claims made for the purpose of obtaining the relevant benefits. The ECJ accepted that *Emmott* established that the policy behind time limits could not prevail over the need to protect the rights conferred on individuals by the direct effect of provisions in a directive so long as the defaulting Member State responsible for those decisions has not properly transposed the provisions into national law. The ECJ held, however, that the policy behind the rule restricting the retroactive effect of claims was designed to ensure sound administration, in the sense of enabling the administration to ascertain whether the claimant satisfied the conditions for eligibility, so that the degree of incapacity, which might vary over time, could be fixed. It also preserved financial balance, in the sense that the scheme was predicated on the assumption that claims submitted by those insured in the course of a year should in principle be covered by contributions collected during that same year.

The judgment in *Steenhorst-Neerings* clearly limited the force of the reasoning in *Emmott*.[34] It is true that there is a factual difference between a mandatory time bar and a rule that limits the retroactive period for which a benefit can be claimed. It is equally clear that the ECJ in *Steenhorst-Neerings* was willing to allow this difference to mask or trump the deeper point of congruence between that case and *Emmott*. The applicant in *Steenhorst-Neerings* was unlawfully prevented from claiming benefits to which she was entitled under a Directive that had not been improperly implemented at that time by the Member State, and the national rule now limited the extent to which she could claim that benefit retroactively. This rule weakened the effectiveness of the Directive and significantly reduced the adequacy and effectiveness of the available remedy by restricting her remedy to one year's benefit only. There were to be sure policy reasons behind the state's rule. However whereas in *Emmott* the ECJ acknowledged the policy reasons behind the time bar rule, but was willing to override them in circumstances where the Directive had not been implemented, in *Steenhorst-Neerings* the ECJ was unwilling to take the same step, notwithstanding the fact that the contested state rule limited the benefits that she would have obtained if the Directive had been properly implemented at the right time. The broader principle articulated in *Emmott*

[34] Flynn, 'Whatever Happened to *Emmott*? The Perfecting of Community Rules on National Time Limits', in C. Kilpatrick, T. Novitz, and P. Skidmore (eds), *The Future of Remedies in Europe* (Hart, 2000), Chap. 2.

that a Member State could not rely on domestic procedural restrictions to inhibit an applicant's claim to rights under a directive until that directive had been properly implemented was abandoned.

Emmott was further limited in subsequent cases. The ECJ reinforced its ruling in *Steenhorst-Neerings* in *Johnson II*, holding that even where a Member State's concerns relating to administrative convenience and financial balance were not in issue, a provision restricting the retroactive effect of a claim for a non-contributory incapacity benefit to one year was compatible with Community law.[35] It stressed that the solution in *Emmott* was justified by its particular circumstances, where a time bar deprived an applicant of any opportunity whatever to rely on her right to equal treatment under the Directive.[36] This was also the reading of *Emmott* in *Fantask A/S*.[37] The applicant sought to recover charges levied by Denmark in breach of a Community Directive, but fell outside the five-year limitation period. The ECJ rejected the applicant's argument that the start of the time limit should by parity of reasoning with *Emmott* be postponed until Denmark had correctly implemented the Directive. The ECJ emphasized once again the specific circumstances of *Emmott* and was unwilling to apply it to the case at hand.

Emmott now seems limited to instances where there has been some misrepresentation or misleading advice by the person seeking to rely on the time limit. Advocate General Jacobs[38] suggested that the fact that the Member State itself was at fault in *Emmott* and misled the applicant was especially pertinent. This factor has been emphasized in later cases. Thus in *Levez*[39] the ECJ held that Community law precluded the application of a national rule that limited an employee's entitlement to arrears of remuneration or damages for breach of the principle of equal pay to a period of two years prior to the date on which the proceedings were instituted, with no possibility of extending the period, where the delay in bringing the claim was attributable to the fact that the employer deliberately misrepresented to the employee the level

[35] Case C-410/92, *Johnson v Chief Adjudication Officer* [1994] ECR I-5483. See also, Case C-394/93, *Alonso-Pérez v Bundesanstalt für Arbeit* [1995] ECR I-4101; Case C-231/96, *Edis v Ministero delle Finanze* [1998] ECR I-4951.

[36] Case C-410/92, *Johnson, supra* n. 35, at para. 26; Cases C-114–115/95, *Texaco A/S v Havn* [1997] ECR I-4263, at para. 48; Case C-90/94, *Haahr Petroleum v Havn* [1997] ECR I-4085, at paras. 51–52; Case C-229/96, *Aprile v Amminstrazione delle Finanze dello Stato* [1998] ECR I-7141, at paras. 35–41.

[37] Case C-188/95, *Fantask A/S v Industriministeriet* [1997] ECR I-6783; Case C-88/99, *Roquette Frères SA v Direction des Services Fiscaux du Pas-de-Calais* [2000] ECR I-10465.

[38] Case C-62/93, *BP Supergas v Greece* [1995] ECR I-1883, at paras. 55–59; Case C-2/94, *Denkavit International BV v Kamer van Koophandel en Fabrieken voor Midden-Gelderland* [1996] ECR I-2827, at para. 74; Jacobs, 'Enforcing Community Rights and Obligations in National Courts: Striking the Balance', in J. Lonbay and A. Biondi (eds), *Remedies for Breach of EC Law* (Wiley, 1997), at 25, 29.

[39] Case C-326/96, *Levez v Jennings (Harlow Pools) Ltd* [1998] ECR I-7835, at para. 34.

of remuneration received by persons of the opposite sex performing like work. To allow this to occur would, said the ECJ, be manifestly incompatible with the principle of effectiveness.[40] Similar considerations were at play in *Santex*,[41] although the behaviour of the defendant was not as egregious as in the previous case. The applicant objected to a condition contained in an invitation to tender on the ground that it was inconsistent with the Directive on public procurement.[42] The defendant public authority told tenderers that it would not be treated as an absolute condition for eligibility, but then changed its position and excluded all those that did not conform to the terms of the original notice. The applicant could not seek judicial review since it was outside the 60-day limitation period that ran from the date of the original notice. The ECJ held that while the 60-day limitation period would generally be regarded as ensuring the effective protection of the relevant Community right, this case was different because it was the conduct of the public authority that rendered it practically impossible for the applicant to bring its claim within the limitation period.

C. The Implications for *Marshall II*

Steenhorst-Neerings not only limited *Emmott*, but also had negative implications for the principle of adequacy of compensation established in *Marshall II*. It was not clear why the reasoning in *Marshall II* that the limits on the quantum of compensation and the lack of power to award interest fell below the required standards of adequacy and effectiveness of national remedies, should not also have been applicable in *Steenhorst-Neerings*, given that the restriction of the retroactive effect of the claim for benefits could, in relative terms, have an equally significant impact on the quantum of money received by the applicant.[43]

6. NATIONAL REMEDIAL AUTONOMY AND EFFECTIVENESS OF COMMUNITY LAW: A NUANCED APPROACH

Community law often ebbs and flows, with periods of activism followed by restraint or retreat, to be followed yet again by the development of a middle

[40] Ibid. at para. 32.

[41] Case C-327/00, *Santex SpA v Unita Socio Sanitaria Locale n.42 di Pavia, Sca Molnlycke SpA, Artsana SpA and Fater SpA* [2003] ECR I-1877.

[42] Council Directive 93/36/EEC of 14 June 1993, Coordinating Procedures for the Award of Public Supply Contracts, OJ 1993 L199/1.

[43] Dougan, *supra* n. 29, at 270–271; Fitzpatrick and Szyszczak, 'Remedies and Effective Judicial Protection in Community Law' (1994) 57 *MLR* 434; Coppel, 'Time up for *Emmott*?' (1996) 25 *ILJ* 153; Prechal, 'EC Requirements for an Effective Remedy', in Lonbay and Biondi, *supra* n. 38, Chap. 1.

way. There are indications of this in the present context. The ECJ continues to apply the principles of equivalence and effectiveness, but it does so in a nuanced manner. The approach was initially identified by de Búrca when discussing whether national courts could be compelled to consider Community law points of their own motion.[44] The essence of the method is that the ECJ will look closely at the national remedial provision pertaining to the enforcement of the Community right, and will examine whether the provision viewed against the specific circumstances of the case and the nature of the Community right renders the exercise of that right excessively difficult. The purpose of the national rule will therefore be examined and weighed against the degree to which it restricts enforcement of the Community right. This entails, as de Búrca notes, a kind of proportionality test for weighing the impact of a national rule on a particular Community right against the legitimate aim served by that rule, and Dougan also perceives analogies between this method and the objective justification model developed in the context of free movement and equal treatment.[45] The approach outlined above accurately captures Community judicial doctrine and can be seen at work in a number of areas.

A. National Courts and Consideration of Community Law at their own Motion

The way in which national procedural rules might impact on the exercise of the Community right was central in the case law concerning the capacity of national courts to consider points of Community law of their own motion. The issue arose in *Van Schijndel*[46] and in *Peterbroeck*.[47]

In *Van Schijndel* the applicants argued that the national appeal court ought to have considered, if necessary of its own motion, the compatibility of a compulsory pension fund provision with EC competition law, even though they had not previously raised any point of EC law. Under Dutch law, this plea involving a new argument could only be made where no factual examination was required, and the court could not raise such points of law of its own motion.

The ECJ began by setting out the basic notion of national procedural autonomy, qualified by the principles of equivalence and practical effectiveness. It then stated that 'each case which raises the question whether a national procedural provision renders application of Community law impossible or

[44] De Búrca, 'National Procedural Rules and Remedies: The Changing Approach of the Court of Justice', in Lonbay and Biondi, *supra* n. 38, at Chap. 4.

[45] Dougan, *supra* n. 29, at 30.

[46] Cases C-430–431/93, *Van Schijndel & Van Veen v Stichting Pensioenfonds voor Fysiotherapeuten* [1995] ECR I-4705.

[47] Case C-312/93, *Peterbroeck, Van Campenhout & Cie v Belgian State* [1995] ECR I-4599.

excessively difficult must be analysed by reference to the role of that provision in the procedure, its progress and its special features, viewed as a whole'.[48] This was so for basic principles of the domestic judicial system, such as the protection of the rights of the defence, the principle of legal certainty, and the proper conduct of procedure.

The ECJ acknowledged that national limits concerning the extent to which a court could raise points of its own motion were premised on certain precepts, these being that a court should keep to the subject matter of the dispute; that it should base its decision on the facts before it; and that in a civil suit it was for the parties to take the initiative, the court being able to act of its own motion only in exceptional cases where the public interest requires its intervention. This thereby safeguarded the rights of the defence and ensured proper conduct of proceedings.[49] Community law did not therefore require national courts to raise a matter of Community law of their own motion where that would:

> oblige them to abandon the passive role assigned to them by going beyond the ambit of the dispute defined by the parties themselves and relying on facts and circumstances other than those on which the party with an interest in application of those provisions bases his claim.[50]

While the ECJ therefore upheld the national rule in the instant case, it is the approach that is of interest here. The objective of the national rule preventing courts from raising matters of their own motion was examined and the purposes thus identified were then factored into the decision as to whether that rule rendered the exercise of the Community right excessively difficult.

The ECJ reached the opposite conclusion on the facts in *Peterbroeck*.[51] The case concerned a procedural provision of the Belgian Tax Code that prevented the parties and the court from raising a point of EC law after 60 days. The rationale for the provision was to ensure legal certainty and the proper conduct of the proceedings. The ECJ concluded that while the 60-day period was reasonable, the application of the rule in the particular circumstances of the case rendered the exercise of the Community right excessively difficult, because no court in the proceedings had had the opportunity to raise the point of EC law and refer it to the ECJ.[52]

[48] Cases C-430–431/93, *Van Schijndel*, *supra* n. 46, at para. 19. See also, Case C-327/00, *Santex*, *supra* n. 41, at para. 56; Case C-63/01, *Evans v Secretary of State for the Environment, Transport and the Regions and the Motor Insurers' Bureau* [2003] ECR I-14447, at para. 46.

[49] Ibid. at paras. 20–21.

[50] Ibid. at para. 22.

[51] Case C-312/93, *Peterbroeck*, *supra* n. 47

[52] For detailed analysis of these cases, see, de Búrca, *supra* n. 44.

The ECJ has considered the same issue on other occasions.[53] The nature of the Community right at stake, and the extent to which the national procedural rule limits the effectiveness of that right, is central to the ECJ's reasoning. The *Océano* case is especially interesting in this respect. The ECJ held that the aims of the Unfair Contract Terms Directive would not be ensured if the consumer were obliged to raise the unfair nature of such terms. The national court must therefore acknowledge that it had 'power to evaluate terms of this kind of its own motion'.[54] The need to ensure the effectiveness of the Community right, the protection of consumers, meant that the national court must at least have the power to raise points of its own motion. This reasoning was extended in *Cofidis*[55] where the ECJ held that a national rule that prohibited a national court, on expiry of a limitation period, from finding on its own motion or following a plea raised by the consumer that a contract term sought to be enforced by the seller was unfair, would render application of the protections in the Unfair Contract Terms Directive excessively difficult.[56]

B. Limitation Periods

The approach identified by de Búrca is also evident in relation to judicial treatment of limitation periods. The general principle is that national limitation rules will be accepted provided that they are not less favourable than those governing similar domestic actions, the principle of equivalence, and do not render exercise of the Community right excessively difficult or impossible, the principle of effectiveness. Reasonable limitation periods will therefore be compatible with Community law.[57] It is moreover clear that the principle of equivalence does not oblige a Member State to extend its most favourable rules governing recovery under national law to all actions for

[53] Case C-72/95, *Aannemersbedrijf P. K. Kraaijeveld BV v Gedeputeerde Staten van Zuid-Holland* [1996] ECR I-5403; Case C-446/98, *Fazenda Pública v Camara Municipal do Porto* [2000] ECR I-11435, at para. 48.

[54] Cases C-240–244/98, *Océano Grupo Editorial v Rocio Murciano Quintero* [2000] ECR I-4491, at para. 26.

[55] Case C-473/00, *Cofidis SA v Fredout* [2002] ECR I-10875, at paras. 35–38.

[56] See also, Case C-126/97, *Eco Swiss China Time Ltd v Benetton International NV* [1999] ECR I-3055, at paras. 36–37. In the Commission Notice on Co-operation between the Commission and Courts of EU Member States in the Application of Articles 81 and 82 EC, OJ 2004 C101/54, at para. 3, the Commission accepts the judicial passivity principle from *Van Schijndel*, but also states that where a national court has discretion to raise a point of its own motion this must be exercised to raise a point of EC Competition law.

[57] See, e.g., Case C-231/96, *Edis v Ministero delle Finanze* [1998] ECR I-4951, at paras. 34–35; Case C-126/97, *Eco Swiss China Time Ltd v Benetton International NV* [1999] ECR I-3055; Case C-30/02, *Recheio-Cash and Carry SA v Fazenda Pública/Registo Nacional de Pessoas Colectivas and Ministerio Público* [2004] ECR I-6051, at paras. 17–18.

repayment of charges or dues levied in breach of Community law. It is open to a Member State, for example, to lay down, alongside the limitation period applicable under ordinary law to actions between private individuals for the recovery of sums paid but not due, special rules, which are less favourable, governing claims and legal proceedings to challenge the imposition of charges and other levies. The principle of equivalence would be violated only if the rules imposing less favourable time limits applied solely to actions based on Community law for the repayment of such charges or levies.[58]

The ECJ will therefore normally accept the national limitation period. It will not, however, do so if it feels that it violates the principle of equivalence, or if it is of the opinion that it renders the exercise of the Community right excessively difficult.

In *Levez* the pertinent issue was the equivalence of the national remedy.[59] It will be remembered that the case concerned an employee who sought damages for arrears in payment denied to her in breach of the equal pay provision of the Treaty, and that the ECJ held that the two-year limit on arrears of damages could not be applied because the employer's deception caused the delay. The UK argued that the time limit should nonetheless apply, because there was an alternative remedy before the County court in an action for deceit against her employer and an action based on the Equal Pay Act. The ECJ accepted that the alternative remedies meant that exercise of her right was not rendered ineffective,[60] and then considered the issue of equivalence. It was for the national court to determine compliance with the principle of equivalence in the light of the purpose and essential characteristics of allegedly similar domestic actions. When deciding whether a national procedural rule was less favourable than the rules governing similar domestic actions, the national court should take into account the role played by that provision in the procedure as a whole, as well as the operation and any special features of that procedure before the different national courts.[61] It was therefore necessary to identify actions that could be regarded as similar under national law and decide whether the applicable procedural rules were less favourable. It was appropriate to consider whether, for example, the applicant, if asserting her Community rights before the County court, would incur additional costs and delay by comparison with a claimant who, because she was relying on a similar right under domestic law, could proceed before the Industrial Tribunal.[62]

[58] Case C-231/96, *Edis, supra* n. 57, at paras. 36–37; Case C-260/96, *Ministero delle Finanze v Spac* [1998] ECR I-4997, at paras. 20–21; Case C-229/96, *Aprile, supra* n. 36, at paras. 20–21; Case C-343/96, *Dilexport v Amministrazione delle Finanze dello Stato* [1999] ECR I-579; Case C-88/99, *Roquette Frères SA v Direction des Services Fiscaux du Pas-de-Calais* [2000] ECR I-10465, at paras. 29–30.

[59] Case C-326/96, *Levez, supra* n. 39. See also, Case C-78/98, *Preston v Wolverhampton Healthcare NHS Trust* [2000] ECR I-3201, at paras. 62–63.

[60] Ibid. at para. 38.

[61] Ibid. at paras. 43–44.

[62] Ibid. at para. 51.

In *Pflücke* the pertinent issue was effectiveness rather than equivalence.[63] The ECJ considered whether it was permissible for Germany to impose a two-month time limit for payments by the national guarantee institution set up to administer a Directive designed to protect workers in the event of insolvency.[64] The Directive was silent as to time limits, but the ECJ concluded that it was permissible for states to impose such limits, provided that they complied with the principles of equivalence and effectiveness. Reasonable time limits were compatible with Community law. It should nonetheless be recognized, said the ECJ, that salary claims were very significant for an individual and therefore the shortness of the time limit should not have the practical result that the individual would not be able to comply and therefore fail to obtain the benefits of the Directive. The ECJ noted that the time limits in other Member States were significantly longer. It was left to the national court to decide whether the German rule was really justified by overriding considerations of legal certainty, but the ECJ made it clear that it disagreed with a number of the justificatory arguments for the rule put forward by the German government, and the expectation was that the ECJ's reasoning in this respect would be taken into account by the national court. In *Preston* the ECJ went further, holding that the principle of effectiveness precluded a national procedural rule requiring a claim for membership of an occupational pension scheme to be brought within six months of the end of each contract of employment to which the claim related, where there had been a stable employment relationship resulting from a succession of short-term contracts in respect of the same employment to which the pension scheme applied.[65]

Levez, *Pflücke*, and *Preston* provide good examples of the approach adumbrated above. While the ECJ will generally accept national limitation periods, it is also willing to look more closely at such provisions for compliance with equivalence and effectiveness. When it does so it will examine the purpose of the national rule and this will be weighed against the degree to which it restricts enforcement of the Community right.

C. Recovery of Interest

The same approach is apparent in other areas, such as recovery of interest. This has, as we have seen, occupied the ECJ on more than one occasion. It was presented with the issue once again in *Metallgesellschaft & Hoechst*.[66] The

[63] Case 125/01, *Pflücke v Bundesanstalt für Arbeit* [2003] ECR I-9375.

[64] Council Directive 80/987/EEC of 20 October 1980, On the Approximation of the Laws of the Member States Relating to Protection of Employees in the Event of the Insolvency of their Employer, OJ 1980 L283/23.

[65] Case C-78/98, *supra* n. 33, at paras. 64–72.

[66] Cases C-397 and 410/98, *Metallgesellschaft & Hoechst v Inland Revenue and Attorney General* [2001] ECR I-1727.

plaintiffs challenged the discriminatory imposition of advance corporation tax (ACT) on subsidiaries whose parent companies were not resident within the Member State. The essence of their claim was the interest they would have accrued if they had not been subject to discriminatory advance taxation.

The ECJ accepted that it was for the national court to classify the nature of the action, either as restitution or compensation for damage. It was also for national law to settle ancillary questions such as the rate of interest and the date from which it should be calculated. It held, however, that payment of interest covering the cost of loss of the use of the sums paid by way of ACT was not ancillary, but was the plaintiffs' very objective. In such circumstances, 'where the breach of Community law arises, not from the payment of the tax itself but from its being levied prematurely, the award of interest represents the "reimbursement" of that which was improperly paid and would appear to be essential in restoring the equal treatment guaranteed by Article 52 of the Treaty'.[67]

It brushed aside the national court's concern as to whether English law provided for restitution for damage arising from loss of the use of money where no principal sum was due, with the terse response that in such a restitution action the principal sum due was the interest that would have been generated by the sum, the use of which was lost as a result of the premature levy of the tax.

The ECJ acknowledged that it had not always held recovery of interest to be an essential component of the relevant right, *Sutton* being the obvious example.[68] However, the ECJ regarded the case as akin to *Marshall II*,[69] where the award of interest was held to be an essential component of the compensation Community law required to be paid for discriminatory dismissal. So too here, the award of interest was essential to remedy the damage caused by breach of the Treaty, and hence was the essential component of the Treaty right conferred on them.[70]

The reasoning in this case is instructive. The ECJ began with the nature of the substantive Community right and reasoned from that to the adequacy of the national remedy. It was this as opposed to national procedural autonomy that provided the focus of the Court's judgment. To put the same point the other way round, the national rule was weighed against the degree to which it restricted enforcement of the Community right, and given that the essence of the Community right in the instant case was payment of interest then a national rule that precluded this could not stand.

The *Evans* case is equally instructive.[71] The applicant argued that

[67] Ibid. at para. 87.

[68] Ibid. at para. 93; Case C-66/95, *Sutton*, *supra* n. 32.

[69] Case C-271/91, *Marshall*, *supra* n. 18.

[70] Cases C-397 and 410/98, *Metallgesellschaft*, *supra* n. 66, at paras. 93–94.

[71] Case C-63/01, *Evans*, *supra* n. 48, at paras. 65–71.

Community Directives on the provision of compensation for those injured by an unidentified vehicle required the payment of interest, even though the relevant Directive contained no express provision for payment of interest. The ECJ nonetheless held that compensation for loss was intended to provide restitution for the accident victim and that in accord with *Marshall II* such compensation could not leave out of account factors such as effluxion of time, which might reduce its value. It was for the Member State to decide how to take account of this factor. It might do so by payment of interest or payment of an aggregate sum that took the passage of time into account.

D. Recovery of Sums Unduly Levied

We have already seen that the ECJ was especially concerned about the recovery of charges and taxes levied in breach of Community law.[72] The general principle is that such charges should be repaid. This is subject to the qualification that the Member State might decline to reimburse where this would amount to unjust enrichment to the trader because he had passed on the charges to third parties, although even in such instances it is open to the trader to argue that he has suffered loss because the demand for his products and hence his profits have fallen as a result of the charge being passed on to consumers.[73] Many of the cases have been concerned with provisions of national law dealing with this issue, and it is unsurprising that the Community courts have looked at them closely in order to determine whether they render exercise of the Community right excessively difficult.[74]

Thus in *Dilexport*[75] the ECJ considered a provision of Italian law concerning the recovery of charges levied by the state in breach of Community law, which stipulated that such charges could be recovered unless they had been passed on to others. The ECJ held that if there was a presumption that such duties or charges had been passed on to third parties and could not therefore be recovered unless the person who had paid the charge rebutted that presumption, this would be contrary to Community law, since it would make recovery excessively difficult. If, by way of contrast, it was for the administration to show by any form of evidence generally accepted under national law that the charge had been passed on to third parties then this would not be contrary to Community law.

[72] Case 199/82, *San Giorgio, supra* n. 4; Case C-192/95, *Comateb, supra* n. 4.

[73] Case C-192/95, *Comateb, supra* n. 4.

[74] R. Williams, *Unjust Enrichment and Public Law, A Comparative Study of England, France and the EU* (Hart, forthcoming 2007), Chap. 7; A Jones, *Restitution and European Community Law* (Mansfield Press, 2000).

[75] Case C-343/96, *Dilexport, supra* n. 58, at paras. 52–55; Cases C-441–442/98, *Kapniki Michailidis AE v Idryma Koinonikon Asfaliseon (IKA)* [2000] ECR I-7145, at paras. 27–42.

The same provision of Italian law came before the Community courts once again in *Commission v Italy*,[76] on this occasion in the context of an action under Article 226 EC and hence it was for the ECJ to decide whether the practice of the Italian courts led to a presumption that such charges had been passed on or otherwise rendered recovery excessively difficult. The ECJ held that where such national legislation had been interpreted differently by national courts, some of the interpretations being consonant with Community law, others not so, then at the very least this meant that the national legislation was not sufficiently clear to ensure its application in conformity with EC law.[77] It found moreover that the Corte Suprema di Cassazione did in effect apply a presumption that charges levied in breach of Community law would be passed on and the ECJ held that this was contrary to Community law.[78] The ECJ then considered various other conditions for repayment applied by the Italian courts, such as the production of accounting documents, and considered whether such conditions rendered exercise of the Community right excessively difficult.[79]

E. Recovery of Sums Unduly Paid

The ECJ's willingness to accept national remedial provisions that impact on the recovery of sums paid to individuals under Community law which they should not have received has also been influenced by the nature of the Community right in issue.[80]

The ECJ has made it clear that the obligation to recover sums that should not have been paid, although this might be stipulated by a particular agricultural regulation, flowed more fundamentally from the duty of cooperation in Article 10 EC.[81] The ECJ has, however, been willing to accept national remedial provisions in relation to the recovery of agricultural subsidies that should not have been paid. Thus in *Steff-Houlberg*[82] it held that Community law did not preclude a national rule that prevented recovery of Community

[76] Case C-129/00, *Commission v Italy* [2003] ECR I-14637.

[77] Ibid. at para. 33. [78] Ibid. at para. 35.

[79] See also, Case C-147/01, *Weber's Wine World Handels-GmbH v Abgabenberufungskommission Wien* [2003] ECR I-11365.

[80] Williams, *Unjust Enrichment and Public Law*, *supra* n. 74, at Chap. 7.

[81] Case C 54/81, *Firma Wilhelm Fromme v Bundesanstalt für Landwirtschaftliche Marktordnung* [1982] ECR 1449.

[82] Case C-366/95, *Landbrugsministeriet – EF-Direktoratet v Steff-Houlberg Export* [1998] ECR I-2661. See also, Cases 205–215/82, *Deutsche Milch-Kontor GmbH v Germany* [1983] ECR 2633, at para. 33; Case C-298/96, *Oelmühle Hamburg v Bundesanstalt für Landwirtschaft und Ernährung* [1998] ECR I-4767.

export refunds paid under the Common Agricultural Policy (CAP), where regard was had to criteria such as the negligence of the national authorities and the elapse of time since payment of the aid. This was subject to the provisos that the recipient of the funds acted in good faith, that the same conditions applied to recovery of Community funds as to national funds, and that the interest of the Community was fully taken into account.

The ECJ has, by way of contrast, been far more reluctant to accept limits on recovery that might be imposed by national law in the context of state aids. The Community imperative to prohibit illegal state aid is especially strong, with the corollary that illegal aid should be recovered. In *Bug-Alutechnik*[83] it held that recipients of state aid could not have a legitimate expectation that the aid was lawful unless it had been granted in accordance with the procedure in Article 88 EC. National concepts such as legitimate expectations could not be relied upon if the effect was to make it impossible to recover the aid, such as where national doctrine set time limits for the revocation of administrative acts. The circumstances in which recovery of illegal aid should not be ordered were very exceptional.[84]

F. Cause of Action

The linkage between the substantive Community right and the remedy at national level is apparent again in the ECJ's willingness to stipulate that a particular Community right requires a cause of action in damages.

Thus in *Crehan*[85] the ECJ held that the full effectiveness of Article 81 EC would be put at risk if it were not open to any individual, even a party to the agreement, to claim damages for loss caused by a contract, or by conduct liable to distort competition. There should not therefore be any absolute bar in national law to such actions, even by parties to the agreement. It was, however, open to national law to prevent a party from being unjustly enriched, or profit from his unlawful conduct. The national court should take into account, *inter alia*, the respective bargaining strength of the contracting parties, and the extent to which a contracting party had responsibility for the breach of Article 81.

[83] Case C-5/89, *Re State Aid to Bug-Alutechnik GmbH: Commission v Germany* [1990] ECR I-3437; Case C-24/95, *Land Rheinland-Pfalz v Alcan Deutschland GmbH* [1997] ECR I-1591.

[84] Case C-354/90, *Fédération Nationale du Commerce Exterieur des Produits Alimentaires v France* [1991] ECR I-5505; Cases T-116 and 118/01, *P & O European Ferries (Vizcaya), SA and Diputación Foral de Vizcaya v Commission* [2003] ECR II-2957, at paras. 201–213.

[85] Case C-453/99, *Courage Ltd v Crehan* [2001] ECR I-6297, at paras. 26–36.

7. NATIONAL REMEDIAL AUTONOMY AND EFFECTIVENESS OF COMMUNITY LAW: AN ASSESSMENT

The case law considered in the preceding pages is complex. It is therefore all the more important to stand back and consider the extent to which Community law ought to intrude on national remedies. There are not surprisingly differing views on this.

Some have argued that the uniformity of Community law requires close control over national procedures and remedies. Procedures vary from state to state and so do the broader remedial provisions of national law. To allow any significant measure of remedial autonomy would therefore lead to inequality and unfairness in the protections provided by Community law and jeopardize its uniform application.[86] The solution proffered varies. It is generally recognized that the creation of a single European judicial system that would obviate these problems is not feasible, politically or legally. A more realistic option would be to press for greater harmonization of procedural and remedial provisions to be administered by the existing national legal systems. The most plausible way forward in this respect would be for Community legislation that applies within different sectoral areas to specify the procedures and remedies that should be provided with greater exactitude than hitherto. The Community legislature has, however, not generally done this[87] and as we have seen from the previous analysis the Community judiciary have not generally sought to fill this legislative gap.

Others have questioned the need for or desirability of increased Community intervention over procedures. There has been concern that excessive reliance on the principle of effectiveness of Community law could undermine values embodied in national procedures, whether these are legal certainty, judicial passivity, or the quantum of damages that should be properly recoverable for a certain violation.[88] There is the related but distinct argument that the imposition of Community principles for the grant of remedies could interfere with the cultural plurality of the legal systems that make up the Community.[89] A more far-reaching challenge to the need for greater Community intervention in relation to remedies has been put by Dougan,

[86] Bridge, 'Procedural Aspects of the Enforcement of European Community Law through the Legal Systems of Member States' (1984) 9 *ELRev* 28; Chiti, *supra* n. 31.

[87] Dougan, *supra* n. 29, at 101–104.

[88] Hoskins, 'Tilting the Balance: Remedies and National Procedural Rules' (1996) 21 *ELRev* 365; Dougan, *supra* n. 29, at 105–110.

[89] Harlow, 'A Common European Law of Remedies?', in Kilpatrick, Novitz, and Skidmore, *supra* n. 34, Chap. 3; Harlow, 'Voices of Difference in a Pluralist Community', in P. Beaumont, C. Lyons, and N. Walker (eds), *Convergence and Divergence in European Public Law* (Hart, 2002), Chap. 11.

who questions the very imperative of uniformity and argues that differentiation in a whole range of areas is now accepted as part of the Community legal and political order and that it is desirable that this should be so.[90] Dougan acknowledges that the imperative of uniformity is still important in certain areas. He suggests therefore that uniformity should be interpreted at a sectoral level, 'selectively matching the required level of remedial and procedural harmonization to the actual degree of substantive approximation achieved within any given policy area, and therefore to the variegated nature of the Community's current programmes for supranational integration'.[91]

The literature on this topic is rich and diverse,[92] and there is much to be said for the differing points of view. My own view is as follows. It is axiomatic that rights demand effective remedies. There are two dimensions to this in the EU.

There is the extent to which the procedures, whatsoever they might be, operate uniformly across the Member States. There can be difficulties in framing Community legislation designed to enhance uniformity in a particular area. In the absence of such legislation it is problematic for this to be done by courts in any systematic manner. They would have to decide on the nature of the uniform procedural requirements that should be imposed, define the areas to which they would apply, and achieve this in a way that was acceptable to national legal orders. Adjudication is inherently ill-suited to this task, more especially because particular national procedures will normally be part of a broader framework of civil procedure in which the particular rules interact.

There is a related but separate issue of the nature of the procedure provided for in any one Member State, and the extent to which it impacts on the effectiveness of the relevant Community right. This has been the ECJ's principal focus throughout. The ebbs and flows in the jurisprudence relate to the extent to which the ECJ has been willing to limit national remedial autonomy in order to ensure the effectiveness of the Community right. It is of course true that a by-product of this case law might be a degree of uniformity across the Member States. Thus, other things being equal, the more vigorously the Court scrutinizes national procedural rules to determine whether they unduly limit the Community right, the more likely it is to be that the resulting principle will be capable of application in other Member States. Thus *Emmott*, before being curtailed, stood for the principle that national procedural rules limiting actions could not preclude an action before a directive had been implemented.

While the ECJ's case law can therefore have an indirect harmonizing impact, the thrust of this jurisprudence has been to ensure that the procedure

[90] Dougan, *supra* n. 29, at 111–2, Chaps. 3–4. [91] Ibid. at 202.

[92] See, e.g., in addition to the literature cited above, Weatherill, 'Addressing Problems of Imbalanced Implementation in EC Law: Remedies in an Institutional Perspective', in Kilpatrick, Novitz, and Skidmore, *supra* n. 34, Chap. 4; Arnull, 'Rights and Remedies: Restraint or Activism', in Lonbay and Biondi, *supra* n. 38, Chap. 2.

applied in the particular Member State does not impact unduly on the effectiveness of the Community right. The key issue then becomes how vigorously the ECJ should scrutinize the national rules to determine the answer to this inquiry, an issue on which views will not unnaturally differ. My own view is that the ECJ's case law even in its most activist period as represented by *Emmott/Marshall II/Dekker* was legitimate. The reasoning in these cases was forceful, but the result did not entail untoward incursion into national remedial autonomy. To be sure these judicial decisions meant that national procedural values had to be modified to some degree, but membership of a Community naturally entails modification of substantive values and there is no reason why procedural values should be immune in this regard. In any event, I am also content with the nuanced approach found in recent case law. An approach that considers the purpose of the national procedural rule and considers whether this should be upheld in the light of its impact on the Community right is well-suited to balance the contending interests in these cases, even if the nature of the test means that there will inevitably be a degree of uncertainty as to its application.[93]

8. STATE LIABILITY: THE *FRANCOVICH* FOUNDATIONS

The discussion thus far has been concerned with the extent to which Community law impinges on national remedial autonomy. Member State liability is, however, also dependent upon the extent to which Community law fashions its own causes of action that must be applied in all states. The best known example of this is the principle of state liability in damages.

The seminal decision was of course *Francovich*.[94] The applicants sued the Italian state because of the government's failure to implement Directive 80/987 on the protection of employees in the event of their employer's insolvency.

[93] EC law should not however demand better enforcement of Community law by national courts than that provided at European level. This was recognized in Case C-120/97, *Upjohn Ltd v The Licensing Authority Established by the Medicines Act 1968* [1999] ECR I-223, at para. 35, and by Case C-352/98 P, *Laboratoires Pharmaceutiques Bergaderm SA and Goupil v Commission* [2000] ECR I-5291, at para. 41.

[94] Cases C-6/90 and C-9/90, *Francovich and Bonifaci v Italy* [1991] ECR I-5357; Curtin, 'State Liability under Private Law: A New Remedy for Private Parties' [1992] *ILJ* 74; Lewis and Moore, 'Duties, Directives and Damages in European Community Law' [1993] *PL* 151; Ross, 'Beyond *Francovich*' (1993) 56 *MLR* 55; Craig, '*Francovich*, Remedies and the Scope of Damages Liability' (1993) 109 *LQR* 595; Steiner, 'From Direct Effects to *Francovich*: Shifting Means of Enforcement of Community Law' (1993) 18 *ELRev* 3; Dougan, 'The *Francovich* Right to Reparation: Reshaping the Contours of Community Remedial Competence' (2000) 6 *EPL* 103.

Their employer had become insolvent, but they were unable to recover their wages because Italy had not implemented the Directive. They argued that the state was liable to pay them the sums owed. The ECJ held that although the Directive lacked sufficient precision to be directly effective, it was nevertheless intended to confer rights on these individuals. The ECJ continued by stating that 'the full effectiveness of Community rules would be impaired and the protection of the rights which they grant would be weakened if individuals were unable to obtain compensation when their rights are infringed by a breach of Community law for which a Member State can be held responsible'.[95] It followed that 'the principle of State liability for harm caused to individuals by breaches of Community law for which the State can be held responsible is inherent in the system of the Treaty'.[96] Further foundation for this obligation was located in Article 10 EC, requiring Member States to take all appropriate measures to ensure fulfilment of their Community obligations. This included 'the obligation to nullify the unlawful consequences of a breach of Community law'.[97]

The ECJ in *Francovich*, however, gave little guidance as to the specific conditions for liability. It held that these conditions could vary depending on the nature of the breach of Community law. In relation to non-implementation of a directive, the result prescribed by the directive should entail the grant of rights to individuals; it should be possible to identify the content of those rights from the directive; and there should be a causal link between the breach of the State's obligation and the harm suffered by the injured parties. It was then for national law to determine the detailed procedural rules for such legal proceedings, subject to the caveat that such rules should not be less favourable than those relating to similar internal claims and should not be so framed as to make it virtually impossible or excessively difficult to obtain compensation.

It is common to talk of *Francovich* and later case law as instantiating state liability in damages. A monetary remedy is indeed the most common form of relief sought. We should nonetheless pause and take account of Dougan's argument that *Francovich* might not always demand a financial remedy, but might in certain circumstances be satisfied by relief that is non-stipendiary in character.[98] There is force in this observation. It should, however, be noted that in most instances financial relief of some kind will be a central facet of the claim.

[95] Cases C-6/90 and C-9/90, *Francovich*, *supra* n. 94. at para. 33.

[96] Ibid. at para. 35.

[97] Ibid. at para. 36.

[98] Dougan, *supra* n. 29, at 256–258.

9. STATE LIABILITY: THE *BRASSERIE DU PÊCHEUR/FACTORTAME* CRITERIA

A. The Three Part Test

It was the ECJ's judgment in *Brasserie du Pêcheur/Factortame*[99] that developed the criteria for state liability. In *Brasserie du Pêcheur* a French company sued the German government for losses resulting from not being able to sell beer into Germany, this prohibition being contrary to EC law on free movement of goods. In *Factortame* the applicants sued the UK for losses suffered by being unable to fish in certain areas because of the Merchant Shipping Act 1988, which was held to be contrary to EC law on freedom of establishment.

The ECJ clarified the nature and extent of state liability.[100] It made it clear that the action could apply even where the provision of Community law that was broken had direct effect. Direct effect was seen as a minimum form of protection and the right to reparation was held to be a corollary of direct effect.[101] The ECJ held, moreover, that liability could be imposed irrespective of which organ of the state was responsible for the breach, the legislature, the executive, or the judiciary.[102]

The ECJ then provided guidance as to the conditions under which the state could incur liability. It followed Advocate General Tesauro who argued that the test for state and Community liability should be linked. The ECJ held that the conditions for state liability should cohere with the Article 288(2) EC case law,[103] since the protection individuals derived from Community law could not, in the absence of some particular justification, vary depending upon whether a national authority or a Community institution was responsible for the breach.[104] The liability rules under Article 288(2)

[99] Cases C-46 and 48/93, *Brasserie du Pêcheur SA v Germany, R v Secretary of State for Transport, ex p Factortame Ltd* [1996] ECR I-1029.

[100] Van Gerven, 'Bridging the Unbridgeable: Community and National Tort Laws after *Francovich* and *Brasserie*' (1996) 45 *ICLQ* 507; Harlow, 'The Problem of the Disobedient State' (1996) 2 *ELJ* 199; Emiliou, 'State Liability under Community Law: Shedding More Light on the *Francovich* Principle' (1996) 21 *ELRev* 399; Convery, 'State Liability in the UK after *Brasserie du Pêcheur*' (1997) 34 *CMLRev* 603; Craig, 'Once More unto the Breach: The Community, the State and Damages Liability' (1997) 113 *LQR* 67; Deards, 'Curiouser and Curiouser? The Development of Member State Liability in the Court of Justice' (1997) 3 *EPL* 117; Steiner, 'The Limits of State Liability for Breach of European Community Law' (1998) 4 *EPL* 69; Tridimas, 'Liability for Breach of Community Law: Growing Up and Mellowing Down?' (2001) 38 *CMLRev* 301; Dougan, 'What is the Point of *Francovich*?', in T. Tridimas and P. Nebbia (eds), *European Union Law for the Twenty-First Century: Rethinking the New Legal Order* (2004), Chap. 14.

[101] Cases C-46 and 48/93, *Brasserie du Pêcheur, supra* n. 99, at para. 22.

[102] Ibid. at para. 32. [103] Ibid. at para. 42. [104] Ibid. at para. 42.

took account, said the Court, of the wide discretion possessed by the Community institutions in implementing Community policies. Member States did not always possess such discretion when acting under EC law, but when they did the conditions for damages liability must be the same as those applying to the Community itself.[105] In the present cases the national legislatures had, said the ECJ, a wide discretion in the relevant areas and were faced with choices comparable to those made by the Community institutions when the latter adopted legislative measures pursuant to a Community policy.[106] Given that this was so, the right to damages was dependent upon three conditions.[107]

First, the rule of law infringed must have been intended to confer rights on individuals. This was held to be satisfied in the instant cases since Articles 28 and 43 EC were intended to confer rights on individuals.[108] In more general terms, whether the Treaty article, regulation, directive, or decision was intended to confer rights will be determined, *inter alia*, by construction of the relevant provision and claims may fall at this hurdle.[109]

Secondly, the breach of this rule of law must have been sufficiently serious. As regards both Community liability under Article 288(2) and state liability in damages, the decisive test for deciding whether the breach was sufficiently serious was whether the Community or the Member State had manifestly and gravely disregarded the limits of its discretion.[110] The following factors should be taken into account:[111] the clarity and precision of the rule breached; the measure of discretion left by the rule to the national or Community authorities; whether the breach and consequential damage were intentional or voluntary; whether any error of law was excusable or inexcusable; whether the position adopted by a Community institution contributed to the act or omission causing loss committed by the national authorities; and whether on the facts the national measures had been adopted or retained contrary to Community law. A breach of EC law would be sufficiently serious if the state persisted in its behaviour notwithstanding an ECJ judgment finding the infringement to have been established. It would be equally so where there was settled case law of the Court making it clear that the Member State action was in breach of Community law.[112] There was moreover no requirement to prove fault over and beyond the finding of a serious breach.[113]

Thirdly, there must be a direct causal link between the breach of the obligation imposed on the state and the damage sustained by the injured

[105] Ibid. at para. 47. [106] Ibid. at paras. 48–50. [107] Ibid. at paras. 51.
[108] Ibid. at para. 54.
[109] Case C-222/02, *Peter Paul, Sonnen-Lütte and Christel Mörkens v Bundesrepublik Deutschland* [2004] ECR I-9425.
[110] Cases C-46 and 48/93, *Brasserie du Pêcheur, supra* n. 99, at para. 55.
[111] Ibid. at para. 56. [112] Ibid. at para. 57. [113] Ibid. at paras. 78–79.

parties.[114] It was for national courts to determine whether the requisite causal link had been established.[115] The damages should in general be commensurate with the loss or damage suffered.[116] In the absence of Community rules, it was for the Member States to establish the criteria for determining the extent of the reparation, subject to the criteria of equivalence and effectiveness.[117] The ECJ nonetheless gave legal guidance on specific issues concerning damages, such as mitigation;[118] the type of recoverable loss;[119] the availability of exemplary damages;[120] and the date from which the obligation to make reparation began to run.[121]

B. The Relevance of Discretion

It is clear from *Brasserie du Pêcheur/Factortame* and subsequent cases that the application of the sufficiently serious breach test will depend on the degree of discretion that exists in relation to the power exercised in the instant case. Where there is meaningful discretion the existence of a serious breach will be determined by the factors set out in *Brasserie du Pêcheur/Factortame.* Where there is no meaningful discretion an infringement of EC law may suffice to establish the existence of a serious breach for the purposes of damages liability.[122]

It is, however, the nature of the discretion that is relevant, rather than the body that exercises it. In that sense whether the contested measure is, in formal terms, legislative, executive, administrative, or judicial is not determinative. This is consistent with *Bergaderm*,[123] where, as we saw in the previous chapter, the ECJ stressed the interconnection between Community and state liability in damages and made it clear that the crucial issue was the measure of discretion, not the general or individual nature of the provision in which it was embodied. This is surely right in principle. The very classification of legislative, administrative, or executive action is beset with difficulty. It can be entirely fortuitous whether a state operates through one medium or another. It should, moreover, be recognized that exercise of executive or administrative discretionary power can be just as complex as a discretionary choice made by the legislature.

[114] Smith and Woods, 'Causation in *Francovich*: The Neglected Problem' (1997) 46 *ICLQ* 925.

[115] Cases C-46 and 48/93, *Brasserie du Pêcheur, supra* n. 99, at para. 65.

[116] Ibid. at para. 82. [117] Ibid. at para. 83. [118] Ibid. at para. 85.

[119] Ibid. at paras. 86–87. [120] Ibid. at para. 89. [121] Ibid. at para. 94.

[122] Case C-5/94, *R v Ministry of Agriculture, Fisheries and Food, ex p Hedley Lomas (Ireland) Ltd* [1996] ECR I-2553, at para. 28; Case C-127/95, *Norbrook Laboratories Ltd v Ministry of Agriculture Fisheries and Food* [1998] ECR I-1531, at para. 109; Case C-424/97, *Haim v Kassenzahnärztliche Vereinigung Nordrhein* [2000] ECR I-5123, at para. 38.

[123] Case C-352/98 P, *Bergaderm, supra* n. 93, at paras. 40–46.

It should also be recognized that the type of discretion can vary depending on the provision of EU law that is in issue. This is apparent from the factors listed by the ECJ in *Brasserie du Pêcheur/Factortame* to determine whether there was a serious breach. The 'measure of discretion left by the rule to the national authorities' is an acknowledgement that there can be national legislative or executive discretion in relation to the application of EU law, such as when a state implements a directive and exercises choice as to the manner through which the objectives should be attained. Reference to the 'clarity and precision of the rule breached' and whether the 'error of law was excusable or inexcusable' also reflect what may be termed interpretative judgment. Community norms may be cast in general terms and it may therefore be debatable whether they apply to a particular situation. Real interpretative difficulties may also arise when the contested norm is more detailed. The meaning of particular provisions of a regulation or a directive may be unclear, and open to a spectrum of reasonable interpretations. These interpretative difficulties can beset the Community authorities, as recognized in *Bergaderm* where the ECJ spoke of the Article 288 test reflecting, *inter alia*, 'difficulties in the application or interpretation of the texts'.[124] They can also beset the Member States, as exemplified by *British Telecom* and *Brinkmann*.[125] The results of the interpretative choice thus made may be expressed in national legislation, but need not be. The choice may be equally expressed through an administrative or executive act, which may itself be relatively formal or informal. It is fitting that cases involving such interpretative judgment should be subject to the serious breach test. It is often assumed that such cases are less problematic than those involving legislative or executive discretionary power. This is mistaken. The difficulties entailed can be equally great. Interpretative judgment may involve the weighing of complex variables in order to decide which interpretation best effectuates the aims of the relevant provision; the exercise of legislative or executive discretionary power will often be affected, explicitly or implicitly, by interpretative judgments which are made as to the meaning of the variables that have to be balanced.

C. Interpretation and Application: The ECJ's 'Guidance'

The traditional division of function between the ECJ and national courts is that the former interprets Community law, and the latter then applies that interpretation to the facts of the case. The malleability of the divide between interpretation and application was nonetheless apparent when the ECJ stated

[124] Ibid. at para. 40.

[125] Case C-392/93, *R v HM Treasury, ex p British Telecommunications plc* [1996] ECR I-1631; Case C-319/96, *Brinkmann Tabakfabriken GmbH v Skatteministeriet* [1998] ECR I-5255.

in *Brasserie du Pêcheur/Factortame* that it would be helpful for the national courts if it, the ECJ, indicated a number of circumstances which the national courts should take into account.[126] This 'guidance' effectively resolved certain crucial issues in the two cases. Thus in *Brasserie du Pêcheur* the ECJ held that the breach of Community law could not be excusable, since prior case law made it clear that the German laws on beer purity would be incompatible with Article 28 EC. In *Factortame* the ECJ stated that the nationality condition under the Merchant Shipping Act 1988 was directly discriminatory and manifestly contrary to EC law, and that the conditions concerning residence and domicile for vessel owners were also *prima facie* contrary to Article 43 EC.[127]

10. STATE LIABILITY POST *BRASSERIE DU PÊCHEUR/FACTORTAME*: JUDICIAL ACTS

The ECJ in *Brasserie du Pêcheur/Factortame* made it clear that state liability could attach irrespective of the organ of the state that committed the breach, whether this was the legislature, executive, or the courts. This caused a significant 'stir' at the time, even insofar as it entailed the imposition of liability for legislative acts, given that this was not possible in many Member States. The idea that state liability could attach to judicial acts was viewed with a mixture of caution and scepticism. There was the lingering feeling that when the ECJ was really faced with the issue it would pull back from this particular brink, re-evaluate its prior case law, and find some justification for excluding judicial action from the remit of state liability. The issue finally arose for real in *Köbler*[128] and the ECJ, sitting as a full Court, did not pull back from the brink, notwithstanding interventions from national governments warning of the dire consequences of such liability.

The ECJ affirmed that state liability could apply irrespective of the entity that caused the breach. The state was viewed as a single entity for the purposes of liability in international law, and this was equally true in relation to the EC, given that all state authorities were bound to comply with EC law. The full effectiveness of individual rights would therefore be called in question if it were not possible to obtain reparation where the breach of EC law

126 Cases C-46 and 48/93, *Brasserie du Pêcheur, supra* n. 99, at para. 58.

127 The UK had sought to justify the conditions in the light of the Community fisheries policy, but this was rejected in Case C-221/89, *R v Secretary of State for Transport, ex p Factortame Ltd* [1991] ECR I-3905. The UK's argument was nonetheless relatively strong, Noirfalisse, 'The Community System of Fisheries Management and the *Factortame* case' (1992) 12 *YBEL* 325.

128 Case C-224/01, *Köbler v Austria* [2003] ECR I-10239.

was committed by a national court of last instance.[129] It was for the national legal systems to designate the courts that were competent to hear such actions, and to decide on the applicable procedural rules, subject to the principles of effectiveness and equivalence.[130] The three conditions for state liability were held to be equally applicable in this context, although the ECJ stressed that liability would attach only in the exceptional case where the national court had manifestly infringed EC law.[131]

The ECJ acknowledged the importance of the principle of *res judicata*, but held that this did not preclude the imposition of state liability in relation to final courts. Proceedings for state liability did not necessarily involve the same parties as the initial decision, nor did such liability necessarily require or entail the revision of the judicial decision responsible for the damage, but merely the provision of reparation.[132] The ECJ was unconvinced by the argument that state liability would compromise the independence of the judiciary, since liability would fall on the state, not the judge or court that gave the decision.[133] It was equally unconvinced that such liability would diminish the authority of national courts, stating by way of reply that the provision of reparation could enhance the quality of the national legal system and the authority of the judiciary.[134]

11. STATE LIABILITY POST *BRASSERIE DU PÊCHEUR/ FACTORTAME*: SERIOUS BREACH

A. The Serious Breach Test: The ECJ Resolves the Issue

The ECJ continues to acknowledge that application of the *Brasserie du Pêcheur/Factortame* criteria is for the national court. The reality is, however, that in the majority of later cases the ECJ has effectively resolved the issue of liability by deciding whether there has been a serious breach. It has also on occasion decided issues of causation rather than leaving them to national courts.[135] The ECJ has thereby retained maximum control over the development of the cause of action, stating that it will determine the seriousness of the breach for itself where it has all the necessary information on which to do so.

British Telecom[136] concerned the incorrect transposition of Directive 90/351 on procurement procedures in the utilities sector, flowing from a mistaken

[129] Ibid. at paras. 32–36.
[130] Ibid. at paras. 46–47, 58.
[131] Ibid. at paras. 52–55.
[132] Ibid. at paras. 38–40.
[133] Ibid. at paras. 41–42.
[134] Ibid. at para. 43.
[135] Case C-319/96, *Brinkmann*, *supra* n. 125; Case C-140/97, *Rechberger v Austria* [1999] ECR I-3499.
[136] Case C-392/93, *British Telecommunications plc*, *supra* n. 125.

interpretation as to the meaning of an Article therein. The ECJ, having found that the UK had misconstrued the Article, then proceeded to deny the damages claim. There had been no serious breach of EC law, given that the Article of the Directive was imprecisely worded and was reasonably capable of bearing the meaning given to it by the UK and other governments, and there was no guidance from past rulings of the Court or the Commission.[137] In *Denkavit*[138] an incorrect transposition by Germany of Directive 90/435 on the taxation of parent companies and subsidiaries in different states, was held by the ECJ not to amount to a sufficiently serious breach, since almost all other Member States had adopted the same interpretation of the Directive as Germany and there was no existing case law on the provision in question.[139] Similarly in *Brinkmann*[140] the ECJ held that an interpretation of Directive 79/32 by the national authorities that had erroneously classified a certain product as a cigarette for taxation purposes did not amount to a sufficiently serious breach because the relevant provisions of the Directive were open to a 'number of perfectly tenable interpretations'[141] and the interpretation actually given was not manifestly contrary to the wording of the Directive or its aims. The ECJ also retained control over the cause of action in *Köbler*, stating once again that while the application of the *Brasserie du Pêcheur* criteria was in principle for the national court, the ECJ nonetheless had all the materials to enable it to decide whether there had been a serious breach.[142] This was unsurprising given the nature and sensitivity of the case. The ECJ found that there had been no serious breach, which was almost certainly a generous conclusion on the facts.

The retention of the power to decide whether there has been a serious breach has also led the ECJ to conclude that such a breach existed on the facts of the instant case. Thus in *Dillenkofer*[143] Germany had failed to implement Directive 90/314 on package holidays. The ECJ ruled that *Francovich* established that non-transposition of a directive within the required time constituted *per se* a sufficiently serious breach.[144] The ECJ reached the same result in *Rechberger*,[145] even though in this instance the case turned on incorrect transposition of Directive 90/314. It ruled that there was no discretion in relation to Article 7 of the Directive and hence that the limitation of the

137 Ibid. at paras. 43–45.

138 Cases C-283, 291, and 292/94, *Denkavit International v Bundesamt für Finanzen* [1996] ECR I-5063.

139 Ibid. at paras. 51–52.

140 Case C-319/96, *Brinkmann*, *supra* n. 125, at paras. 30–32.

141 Ibid. at para. 32.

142 Case C-224/01, *Köbler*, *supra* n. 128, at paras. 101–102.

143 Cases C-178–179/94, 188–190/94, *Dillenkofer and others v Federal Republic of Germany* [1996] ECR I-4845.

144 Ibid. 21–27.

145 Case C-140/97, *Rechberger*, *supra* n. 135, at paras. 51–53.

protection provided by this Article to holidays with a departure date of 1 May 1995 or later constituted a sufficiently serious breach of Community law. The same reasoning was apparent in *Hedley Lomas*,[146] where the UK had refused to grant licences for the export of live sheep to Spain, on the ground that Spanish slaughterhouses were not complying with the terms of an EC Directive. The UK government acknowledged that it was in breach of Article 29 EC on export restrictions, but argued justification under Article 30 EC for the protection of animal welfare. The ECJ held that the lack of discretion left to Member States following the Directive, the clarity of the Treaty provision breached, and the absence of a properly verified ground of justification pointed to the existence of a sufficiently serious breach.[147] The ECJ has also been ready to find that there was no meaningful discretion and hence that there had been a sufficiently serious breach of Community law where, as in *Larsy*,[148] there had been a prior ECJ ruling on the issue.

B. The Serious Breach Test: The ECJ Leaves the Issue to the National Court

There are, however, also cases where the ECJ chooses to leave resolution of the serious breach test to the national courts. It will tend to do so where there is no obvious answer as to whether there has been such a breach in the light of the factors laid down in *Brasserie du Pêcheur/Factortame*. Thus in *Evans*[149] the applicant argued that the UK had defectively implemented Directive 84/5 concerning compulsory civil liability in respect of motor vehicles and more specifically the provisions concerning damage caused by unidentified vehicles. The ECJ held that it was for the national court to determine in the light of the *Brasserie du Pêcheur* criteria whether there had been defective implementation and if so whether this was sufficiently serious for the purposes of damages liability.

12. STATE LIABILITY POST *BRASSERIE DU PÊCHEUR/FACTORTAME*: THE RELATIONSHIP WITH NATIONAL REMEDIAL REGIMES

The *Francovich* principle, as elaborated by *Brasserie du Pêcheur/Factortame*, established a Community principle of state liability, which was to be given

[146] Case C-5/94, *Hedley Lomas*, *supra* n. 122.

[147] Ibid. at paras. 28–29. See also, Case C-150/99, *Stockholm Lindöpark Aktiebolag v Sweden* [2001] ECR I-493, at paras. 39–42.

[148] Case C-118/00, *Larsy v INASTI* [2001] ECR I-5063, at para. 44.

[149] Case C-63/01, *Evans*, *supra* n. 48, at paras. 84–88. See also, Case C-127/95, *Norbrook*, *supra* n. 122, at paras. 105–112.

effect within the national legal systems. This has generated a number of issues concerning the relationship between the Community principle and the national remedial regimes.

A. Who Pays

One such issue concerns the body liable to make the reparation. The ECJ made it clear in *Brasserie du Pêcheur/Factortame* that the state could be liable irrespective of whether the breach was caused by the legislature, the executive, the administration, or the judiciary. In that sense it adopted a unitary conception of the state. The rationale for this approach was not hard to divine. The objective was to provide a damages remedy for individuals against the state. The ECJ clearly did not wish to get into complex arguments as to which organ of the state was actually responsible for the breach of Community law, with all the attendant problems that this could involve. The Member State itself would therefore be liable and it would be for the state to make consequential apportionment of loss to particular organs if it wished to do so. This approach has been maintained, but the ECJ has also been willing to make certain qualifications.[150]

In *Konle*[151] the ECJ reiterated the principle that it was for the Member State to ensure that individuals could obtain compensation for breach of EC law irrespective of the public authority that was responsible for the breach and irrespective of the public authority that was liable to make reparation under national law. The Member State could not, therefore, plead the national distribution of powers and responsibilities in order to free itself from liability. Subject to that reservation, EC law did not, however, require Member States to change the distribution of responsibilities between public bodies in their territory, provided that Community legal rights were effectively protected and received equivalent protection to rights derived from domestic law. It followed that in a Member State with a federal structure it was not necessary that reparation be provided by the federal authorities.

This reasoning was developed further in *Haim*.[152] The ECJ followed *Konle* and held that the reasoning therein could also be applied to Member States without a federal structure, where certain legislative or administrative tasks were devolved to territorial bodies with a certain degree of autonomy or to any other public law body legally distinct from the state. In such states reparation for the breach of Community law could be made by such bodies.[153]

[150] Anagnostaras, 'The Allocation of Responsibility in State Liability Actions for Breach of Community Law: A Modern Gordian Knot?' (2001) 26 *ELRev* 139.

[151] Case C-302/97, *Konle v Austria* [1999] ECR I-3099, at paras. 62–64.

[152] Case C-424/97, *Haim, supra* n. 122, at para. 38.

[153] Ibid. at para. 31.

Nor did EC law preclude a public law body in addition to the state itself from being liable to make reparation for losses caused by measures taken in breach of Community law.[154]

B. Equivalence and Effectiveness

It is important to recognize the duality inherent in the cause of action for state liability. The right to reparation is, on the one hand, founded directly on Community law. The ECJ will therefore establish the conditions for liability, as exemplified by the three criteria laid down in *Brasserie du Pêcheur/ Factortame*. It is also open to the ECJ, as we have seen, to retain control over the cause of action by deciding for itself whether there has been a serious breach. The ECJ has, moreover, ruled definitively on certain aspects of the loss that can be recovered, the impact of mitigation, exemplary damages, and the like. It is in this sense open to the ECJ to define with more or less exactitude aspects of the cause of action.[155]

The application of this cause of action is, on the other hand, a matter for national courts, which may have different rules on matters such as time limits, causation, mitigation of loss, and assessment of damages. The issues not addressed by the ECJ are governed by national law, subject to the principles of equivalence and effectiveness.[156] This necessarily means that the ECJ may be asked whether particular national rules are compatible with these conditions.

This can be exemplified by the Italian cases that arose in the aftermath of *Francovich*. The Italian government passed legislation to implement Directive 80/987 on the protection of employees in the event of their employer's insolvency, and established a compensation scheme for those who had suffered loss as a result of the earlier failure to implement. The ECJ considered a number of cases where the litigants argued that the implementing legislation breached the principles of effectiveness and equivalence.

Palmisani provides a fitting example.[157] The applicant was refused compensation under the Italian scheme, because she had not brought her compensation claim within the one-year time limit set by the national legislation.

[154] Ibid. at para. 32.

[155] See, e.g., Cases C-397 and 410/98, *Metallgesellschaft Ltd and Hoechst AG and Hoechst (UK) Ltd v Commissioners of Inland Revenue and HM Attorney General* [2001] ECR I-1727, at paras. 102, 107.

[156] Cases C-6/90 and C-9/90, *Francovich, supra* n. 94. at paras. 41–43; Cases C-46 and 48/93, *Brasserie du Pêcheur, supra* n. 99, at paras. 67, 70, 71, 73, 83, 87, 90, 99; Case C-127/95, *Norbrook Laboratories, supra* n. 122, at para. 111; Case C-424/97, *Haim, supra* n. 122, at para. 33.

[157] Case C-261/95, *Palmisani v INPS* [1997] ECR I-4025. See also, Cases C-94–95/95, *Bonifaci and Berto v Istituto Nazionale della Previdenza Sociale (INPS)* [1997] ECR I-3969; Case C-373/95, *Maso and Gazzetta v INPS* [1997] ECR I-4051.

The general time limit for cases of non-contractual liability brought under the Italian Civil Code was five years. The ECJ held that reasonable time limits were consistent with legal certainty. In this case the one-year time limit did not breach the principle of effectiveness, since it did not make it excessively difficult for an applicant to obtain reparation, more especially because the beneficiaries of the scheme knew the full extent of their rights and the conditions under which loss flowing from belated transposition would be made good.[158]

The ECJ then considered whether the Italian scheme complied with the principle of equivalence. It distinguished between claims for wages under the national measure implementing the Directive, and claims for damages for loss caused by the late implementation of the Directive. The former were akin to a social security benefit where the appropriate comparator might be national pension rules. The latter were designed to compensate for late implementation of the Directive, and hence the appropriate comparator was the ordinary system of non-contractual liability, which was intended to guarantee reparation of the loss or damage sustained as a result of the conduct of the perpetrator. The ECJ, however, felt that it did not have sufficient information to decide on the comparability of the two systems and therefore left the matter for the Italian courts to decide.[159] It nonetheless signalled that it could well be contrary to the principle of equivalence for there to be a five-year time limit for domestic actions for non-contractual liability and a one-year limit for actions for compensation due to the State's non-implementation of a directive.[160]

13. STATE LIABILITY: AN ASSESSMENT

The ECJ has been at its most creative in this area, reasoning in a teleological manner when it created the principle in *Francovich* and when it defined it further in *Brasserie du Pêcheur/Factortame*. There are unsurprisingly differences of view as to the cogency of the reasoning in *Francovich* and the desirability of the result. The reasoning in *Francovich* was teleological and it was based on broad principles, but this is commonly so for case law that breaks new ground. The principles that informed the judgment were foundational. The need for effective remedies to safeguard Community rights is reflective of the principle *ubi ius, ibi remedium* that is found and applied in many national legal systems. The duty incumbent on Member States to take all appropriate measures to ensure fulfilment of their Community obligations is especially salient in a polity such as the EU, but resonates with analogous obligations that exist in federal or confederal systems.

[158] Case C-261/95, *Palmisani*, *supra* n. 157, at paras. 28–29.
[159] Ibid. at para. 38. [160] Ibid. at para. 39.

The test for liability, distinguishing as it does between discretionary and non-discretionary acts, is soundly based for the reasons given in the previous chapter when discussing the Community's liability.[161] The ECJ has refined and developed this test in subsequent case law on state liability. It has, moreover, proved adept at retaining resolution of the core components of the case in its own hands when it wished to do so, in order that it could make the all-important judgment as to whether there had been a serious breach on the facts of the case. There will be instances where commentators disagree with the way in which the test was applied in a particular case. That is inevitable.

Any assessment of *Francovich* and its progeny should also take account of the insistence on parity between Member State and Community liability. The ECJ properly resisted the calls of some at the time when *Brasserie du Pêcheur/Factortame* was being litigated that Member State liability should be more extensive than that of the Community. These calls were unwarranted in normative terms and unwise in terms of practical politics. The reality has been that the cause of action for state liability has developed in a symbiotic manner with that for Community liability considered in the previous chapter. In *Brasserie du Pêcheur* the ECJ made the important policy choice that the conditions for Community and state liability should be parallel, and therefore drew on the jurisprudence on Community liability when devising the criteria for state liability. In *Bergaderm* the influence ran in the opposite direction, with the ECJ importing the more sophisticated test for serious breach developed in the context of state liability and applying it to the Community's liability under Article 288(2).

There are nonetheless differences between the two causes of action, which stem primarily from the fact that Community liability will be resolved by the Community courts. The application of the principles of state liability will, by way of contrast, be left to national courts. It is true as we have seen that key issues can be retained by the ECJ, which can also shape the cause of action by rulings on matters such as mitigation, recoverable loss, and the like. It is nonetheless the case that matters such as time limits and procedural rules will be determined by the national court, subject to the principles of effectiveness and equivalence. There may therefore be divergence in the conditions for recovery in different national legal systems. This raises the tension between uniformity and diversity that we discussed earlier in this chapter. It should, however, be recognized that there will inevitably be a degree of diversity, precisely because the ECJ has made it clear that the test for state liability is a minimum, and does not prevent a Member State from imposing on its state authorities more far-reaching rules of liability if it chooses to do so.[162]

[161] See above, 771–772.

[162] Cases C-46 and 48/93, *Brasserie du Pêcheur, supra* n. 99, at para. 66; Case C-224/01, *Köbler, supra* n. 128, at para. 57.

22

The Ombudsman*

The Treaty of Maastricht introduced the European Ombudsman into the institutional landscape of the Union. The emergence of an extra-judicial mechanism geared towards overseeing the administrative behaviour of the Community bureaucracy served a two-fold objective. In legal terms, it sought to enhance the protection of citizens' rights and interests in the Union space by establishing an alternative route to administrative litigation. In political terms, it was employed as a tool to put a beneficient face to a largely distant and impersonal Community structure, soothe the growing uneasiness of the Union citizenry, and sugar the pill of further European integration.

The analysis will proceed in the following manner. There will be a brief discussion of the historical emergence of the Ombudsman. The focus will then shift to the powers of the European Ombudsman and the restraints placed thereupon. This will be followed by analysis of the way in which the Ombudsman has defined and applied the concept of maladministration. Specific aspects of the institutional relationship between the Ombudsman and the Community judiciary will then be addressed. The chapter will conclude with some general remarks pertaining to the institutional evolution of the Ombudsman in the Union's political and legal order.

1. THE INSTITUTIONAL HISTORY OF THE OMBUDSMAN

The Ombudsman concept entered the realm of Community politics in September 1974, when it was briefly discussed in a policy document of the European Conservative Group.[1] A series of written questions were subsequently addressed by MEPs to the Commission and the Council exploring

* This chapter was written by Dr. Alexandros Tsadiras.

[1] On the genesis of the European Ombudsman see Moreiro Gonzalez, 'El defensor del pueblo en el tratado de la Union europea' [1992] *Gaceta juridica de la CEE* 167; Hummer 'Opinion on the Position and Duties of the Ombudsman of the European Parliament' EOI; Magliveras, 'Best intentions but empty words: the European Ombudsman' (1995) 20 *ELRev* 401, P. Magnette, *La citoyenneté européenne : droits, politiques, institutions* (l'Université de Bruxelles, 1999).

the possibility of setting up a European Ombudsman office.[2] The European Parliament's (EP) sympathy for the creation of a European Ombudsman culminated in the adoption of the Resolution of 1979.[3] Drawing extensively on the report that its Legal Affairs Committee had recently delivered (known as the Walker-Smith report),[4] the EP underlined the desirability of introducing a Community Ombudsman scheme and instructed its Committee on the Rules of Procedure and Petitions to report on the procedure to be followed. The rationale for the adoption of a European Ombudsman was rooted in the shortcomings of the Community judicial system and the Ombudsman's effectiveness as an extra-judicial mechanism for control over the executive.

The first euro elections by direct and universal suffrage, which took place only days after the Resolution of 1979 had been passed, signalled the beginning of a political process that would eventually lead to the metamorphosis of the EP from an enthusiastic proponent to an opponent of the Ombudsman concept. The elected MEPs of the 1980s, self-confident in their enhanced numbers and augmented powers, felt that the EP was now fully fledged to do the job for which their weaker predecessors of the 1970s were willing to introduce a distinct institutional scheme. They were influenced in this respect by the fear that the Ombudsman would rob the Petitions Committee of part of its institutional power and gave relatively little attention to his utility in improving the protection of citizens' rights and interests. Trapped within this reasoning, the EP kept on weighing and evaluating the Ombudsman project in terms of its costs and benefits to the petition option, the latter having been raised to the level of an undisputed yardstick against which the desirability of the Ombudsman's existence would be tested. Viewed from this angle, the institutional interrelationship between the Petitions Committee and the European Ombudsman was perceived as a zero-sum game, whereby each player's loss was the other player's gain.

It was fortunate that during the 1980s the EP lost the monopoly over discussions concerning the creation of a European Ombudsman. It is worth recalling that in the preceding decade the Parliament was basically the unique institutional actor proactively pursuing the Ombudsman cause rather than reactively dealing with it. This picture changed in June 1985 when the European Council in Milan not only approved the much celebrated Commission's White Paper on the completion of the internal market by 1992,[5] but also adopted the second and final report by the Committee on a People's

[2] Written Questions No. 663/74, OJ 1975 C86/85; No. 562/74, OJ 1975 C55/13; No. 751/76, OJ 1977 C70/14.

[3] Resolution on the appointment of a Community Ombudsman by the European Parliament, OJ 1979 C140/153.

[4] Document 29/79, PE 57.508/def.

[5] Completing the Internal Market, COM(85) 310

Europe (known as the Adonnino Committee), which listed the European Ombudsman scheme amongst the means to counterbalance the citizens' isolation from Brussels-based decision-making and foster their participation in the European enterprise.[6] This broadening of interest in the Ombudsman concept was of paramount importance, since it meant that the fate of the Ombudsman project no longer lay exclusively with the EP, or more precisely its Committee on the Rules of Procedure and Petitions.

The political discourse in the opening years of the 1990s displayed a renewed interest in the incorporation of an Ombudsman scheme into the Union structure. On 24 September 1990 the Spanish delegation to the Intergovernmental Conference on Political Union issued a memorandum entitled 'The Road to European Union', suggesting that the introduction of Union citizenship ought to go hand-in-hand with the creation of a special body whose objective would be to safeguard the rights attached to citizenship.[7] In response to the Spanish initiative, the Danish government tabled a less ambitious proposal on 4 October 1990 calling for the adoption of an Ombudsman scheme oriented towards overseeing the administrative behaviour of Community authorities. Endorsing in principal the idea of a European Ombudsman, the European Council in Rome (14–15 December 1990) stated in the conclusions of its meeting that 'consideration should be given to the possible institution of a mechanism for the defence of citizen's rights as regards Community matters ("ombudsman")'.[8] On 21 February 1991, and within the context of the political dialogue on the rights linked to Union citizenship, the Spanish government presented a new and elaborated proposal suggesting the appointment of a mediator in each Member State who would be entrusted with the task of aiding European citizens to assert their rights against the bureaucracy of both the Union and its Member States. A month later, the Danish delegation repeated its submission of 4 October 1990, and, drawing extensively on the Danish experience, produced draft Treaty provisions on a European Ombudsman whose mission would be restricted to overseeing the delivery of administrative services by Community authorities.

The EP, supported by ombudsmen and petition committees operating at national and sub-national level, vehemently opposed these initiatives. The MEPs of the early 1990s had apparently been affected by the same fear of institutional disempowerment that possessed their predecessors in the 1980s and fiercely fought to safeguard their status. Their resistance reached its peak on 14 June 1991, when the EP, amidst talks favouring varying European

[6] Report submitted to the Milan European Council (Milan, 28–29 June 1985), Bulletin of the European Communities, March 1985, No 3, at 18–30.

[7] See Agence Europe No. 5337, 27 September 1990, at 3. A few months before, on 4 May 1990, the Spanish Prime Minister had already addressed a letter to the other European Council members suggesting the idea of a Union citizenship.

[8] Point I(7) of the conclusions, Bull. 12–1990, at 10.

Ombudsman schemes, adopted a Resolution calling for their rejection, and advocated instead the promotion of the Petitions Committee solution.[9] Notwithstanding the EP's stance, the plans for the creation of a European Ombudsman went ahead. On 18 June 1991 the Luxembourg's Presidency put forward a draft Treaty text establishing a European Ombudsman, who would be functionally independent from, but institutionally affiliated with the EP, and whose jurisdictional ambit would be confined to the horizontal dimension of the Community legal order, without power over the domestic administrative structures of the Member States. This model, which represented for some a solution midway between the Spanish and Danish proposals,[10] while for others it resonated with the Danish view,[11] was eventually incorporated in the Treaty on European Union signed on 7 February 1992 in Maastricht.[12] The conclusion of a tripartite political agreement amongst the EP, the Council, and the Commission in October 1993 paved the way for the adoption of the Ombudsman's Statute in March 1994.[13] Following three consecutive proposals for amendment of the appointing procedure and a series of three voting rounds in the Plenary of the EP, the first European Ombudsman was finally elected on 12 July 1995 and took office on 27 September 1995.

2. THE POWERS OF THE EUROPEAN OMBUDSMAN

The discussion in this section will focus on the powers of the Ombudsman. The term 'power' will be used in three ways. Firstly, it refers to the authority of the European Ombudsman to initiate inquiries either in response to complaints he has received or on his own volition. Secondly, it pertains to the investigative tools he can make use of to determine the factual basis of the cases he examines. Thirdly, it is concerned with the means of remedial action he has at his disposal in order to address instances of Community maladministration. Each of these components will be examined in turn.

[9] Resolution on the deliberations of the Committee on Petitions during the parliamentary year 1990–1991, OJ 1991 C183/448

[10] Marias 'The European Ombudsman: Competences and Relations with the Other Community Institutions and Bodies', in E. Marias (ed), *The European Ombudsman* (EIPA Maastricht, 1994), at 75.

[11] K. Heede, *European Ombudsman: Redress and Control at Union Level* (Kluwer Law International, 2000), at 13.

[12] OJ 1993 L293/61.

[13] Resolution 94/262/ECSC,EC,Euratom of the European Parliament of 9 March 1994, OJ 1994 C113/15 (hereafter 'the Statute').

A. The Initiation of Inquiries

A cursory examination of the relevant Community legal framework reveals that there are two methods for setting the Ombudsman's mechanism in motion. The European Ombudsman is authorized to conduct inquiries either reactively on the basis of complaints launched with him or proactively on his own initiative.

(1) The Reactive Role: Responding to Complaints

Article 195 EC empowers the European Ombudsman to investigate complaints filed by any citizen of the Union or any natural or legal person residing or having its registered office in a Member State. Citizenship and, alternatively, residence (or registered office for legal persons) constitute the decisive factors in determining the standing of complainants. If the natural person holds the citizenship of any of the Member States, he or she can file a complaint irrespective of the place of residence. If the natural person is not an EU national, that person cannot access the Ombudsman, unless residence is taken up in the EU. The same restriction applies to legal persons, whose registered office has to be established in a Member State. Complaints launched by natural persons who are neither EU nationals nor EU residents, or by legal persons with a registered office outside the Union territory are rejected as inadmissible,[14] and can only be considered if they raise issues important enough to justify the commencement of an own initiative inquiry by the Ombudsman.[15]

The notion of 'residence' has been liberally interpreted. It does not imply the existence of permanent or usual habitation. It can be the place where a natural person lives sporadically without having the intention to make it the centre of his social relations or professional activities. Nor is it necessary that the residence be established in a legal manner. Once the complainant is physically present within the Union territory, the question of whether his entry and stay is legal or not becomes irrelevant.[16] It follows that illegal immigrants have access to the European Ombudsman. The term 'legal person' has also received an expansive reading. It does not presuppose the endowment of the person with legal personality and it has been employed as a residual notion embracing the complainants that cannot be classified as

[14] Complaint 978/97/XD [1997] EOAR 18; Complaint 398/98/HL [1998] EOAR 16.

[15] Complaint 1150/97/OI/JMA [1998] EOAR 268, OI/4/99/OV [2001] EOAR 18, OI/2/2003/GG available at <http://www.euro-ombudsman.eu.int/decision/en/03oi2.htm>, OI/4/2003/ADB [2003] EOAR 33, 205, OI/2/2004/GG available at <http://www.euro-ombudsman.eu.int/decision/en/04oi2.htm>.

[16] Complaint 972/24.10.96/FMO/DE/DT [1996] EOAR 15.

'natural persons'. The European Ombudsman has thus far agreed to take up complaints filed by companies,[17] associations,[18] federations,[19] foundations,[20] unions,[21] funds,[22] charities,[23] non-governmental organizations,[24] interest and initiative groups,[25] city councils,[26] municipalities,[27] regional ombudsmen,[28] and national courts[29]. Against this background, it is a defensible thesis to argue that national governments and state authorities, e.g. police and tax offices, or even Community institutions and bodies are entitled to launch a complaint with the European Ombudsman.

The author and the object of the complaint must be identified.[30] A complaint can be launched either by one person (individual complaint) or by two or more (joint or collective complaint).[31] An initially individual complaint can turn into a joint complaint, if a person wishes to associate himself with an already filed complaint while the inquiries are still under way.[32] Complainants can access the Ombudsman either directly or indirectly through a MEP. The submission of a complaint indirectly does not set aside the requirement for EU citizenship or residence. *Actio popularis* complaints are admissible.[33] Contrary to the position with respect to petitions to the EP,[34] the admissibility of complaints to the European Ombudsman is not dependent upon the complainant proving personal interest in the subject matter of the case that is filed. The complainant needs neither to have been affected by the alleged instance of maladministration, nor to derive any benefit from the

[17] Complaint 821/2000/GG [2001] AR 152.

[18] Complaint 1101/16.12.96/CFUI/IT/JMA [1998] AR 88; Complaint 1554/99/ME [2001] AR 47.

[19] Complaint 1042/25.10.96/SKTOL/FIN/BB [1997] AR 40; Complaint 133/97/VK [1998] AR 93.

[20] Complaint 601/99/IJH [2000] AR 113; Complaint 511/99/GG [2001] AR 120.

[21] Complaint 659/24.6.96/AEKA/FIN/IJH [1997] AR 232.

[22] Complaint 384/97/JMA [1998] AR 143.

[23] Complaint 245/98/OV [1999] AR 116.

[24] Complaint 669/98/JMA [1999] AR 118.

[25] Complaint 943/14.10.96/Open Line/GR/BB/OV [1998] AR 74; Complaint 506/97/JMA [1999] AR 158; Complaint 1043/99/(IJH)/MM [2000] AR 116; Complaint 1194/2000/JMA [2001] AR 161.

[26] Complaint 555/17.4.96/ALDM/ES/PD [1997] AR 218; Complaint 533/98/OV [2000] AR 34.

[27] Complaint 457/2001/OV [2001] AR 85.

[28] Complaint 478/97/JMA [1998] AR 274.

[29] Complaint 615/98/BB [1998] AR 29.

[30] Art. 2.3 of the Statute.

[31] E.g. Complaint 132/21.9.95/AH/EN [1996] AR 67; Complaint 37/97/JMA [1997] AR 176.

[32] Complaint 74/97/PD [1998] AR 36.

[33] The term '*actio popularis*' is used for the first time in [1997] EOAR 40.

[34] Arts. 21(1) and 194 EC.

outcome of the inquiry.[35] The disengagement of the admissibility question from the existence of personal interest of the complainant gives rise to cases where the inquiries of the Ombudsman are undertaken without, or even contrary to the consent of the person who is directly and personally affected by the alleged instance of maladministration.[36]

The European Ombudsman has jurisdiction to oversee the administrative behaviour of Community institutions and bodies when performing tasks falling within the first and third pillar of the Union structure.[37] Three consequences follow from this. Firstly, the second pillar falls outside the Ombudsman's reach.[38] Secondly, entities set up by international law are excluded from the Ombudsman's mandate.[39] Thirdly, authorities established by national law escape the Ombudsman's remit, even when they implement Community policies.[40]

It is worth noting that according to the statistical data provided in the Annual Reports from 1995 until 2003 inclusive, on average 71.25 per cent of the complaints launched every year with the European Ombudsman are outside his mandate and 92 per cent thereof do not concern a Community

[35] Complaint 142/97/PD [1997] EOAR 262. See however Complaint 1323/2002/IJH [2001] EOAR 21.

[36] See, e.g., Complaint 794/5.8.1996/EAW/SW/VK [1997] AR 129; Complaint 1219/99/ME [2000] AR 90 and the speech by the Ombudsman 'The role of the European Ombudsman', Jerusalem, 9–11 September 1997, point 1, available at <http://www.euro-ombudsman.eu.int/speeches/pdf/en/jerus_en.pdf>.

[37] See however Complaint 1795/2002/IJH against the European Convention available at <http://www.euro-ombudsman.eu.int/decision/en/021795convention.htm> which appears to defy this rule.

[38] Pursuant to Art. 41 TEU, as amended by the Treaty of Amsterdam, Art. 195 EC applies to third pillar issues. On the contrary, Art. 28 TEU does not provide for Art. 195 EC to apply to the provisions relating to the areas falling within the second pillar.

[39] See [1995] EOAR 18. Examples include the European Schools (Complaint 199/23.10.95/EP/B/KT [1996] EOAR 36); the Technical Centre for Agricultural and Rural Co-operation (Complaint 218/98/OV [1998] EOAR 17); the Centre for the Development of Industry (Complaint 41/97/OV [1999] EOAR 41); the European Molecular Biology Laboratory (Complaint 374/15.01.96/MV/UK/PD [1997] EOAR 19); the European Commission of Human Rights ([1995] EOAR 19); and the European University Institute in Florence (Complaint 2225/2003/(ADB)PB available at <http://www.euro-ombudsman.eu.int/decision/en/032225.htm> overturning a previous decision on Complaint 659/2000/GG [2000] EOAR 99).

[40] [1995] EOAR 18. See e.g. Complaint 187/17.10.95/FS/B/IJH [1997] EOAR 53 and Complaint 943/14.10.96/Open Line/GR/BB/OV [1998] EOAR 74. It is telling that in cases where the subject matter of challenge is the administrative behaviour of the European Commission towards citizen complainants in the enforcement proceedings against Members States allegedly in breach of EC law (hereafter 'Art. 226 complaints'), the European Ombudsman repeatedly stresses that his inquiries are exclusively directed at the Commission's performance of its assigned duties and not the activity of national authorities, see Complaint 298/97/PD [1999] EOAR 47 and Complaint 396/99/IP [2000] EOAR 66.

institution or body. It follows that 65.5 per cent of the incoming complaints are directed against authorities over which the Ombudsman has no competence. It is difficult to determine the precise number of cases that concern national authorities performing Community tasks, however a rough estimate on the basis of the transfers of complaints to the competent institution and the advice given to complainants suggests that at least one in every six complaints filed with the Ombudsman raises questions of indirect Community administration. This figure underlines the importance of the established liaison network linking the European Ombudsman with his national peers, which has enabled the reciprocal transfer of complaints,[41] facilitated the dealing with of queries,[42] and could in future lead to the launching of common investigations or even the presentation of joint reports.[43]

The European Ombudsman is not authorized to investigate complaints relating to the judicial role of the European Court of Justice (ECJ) and the Court of First Instance (CFI).[44] The precise scope of the term 'judicial role' is not clear and the Ombudsman appears to have endorsed an unjustifiably expansive definition thereof.[45] The Ombudsman is barred from investigating facts that are or have been the subject of legal proceedings[46] and he may not intervene in cases before courts or question the soundness of a court's ruling.[47]

The complaint must be made within two years of the date when the facts on which it is based came to the attention of the complainant and must have been preceded by appropriate administrative approaches to the institution or body concerned.[48] In the case of complaints concerning work relationships between the institutions and bodies and their officials and servants, the possibilities for submission of internal administrative requests and complaints must have been exhausted before the case is brought before the

[41] See e.g. [1997] EOAR 282.

[42] See e.g. Q1/1999/PD [1999] EOAR 243.

[43] Statement by the European Ombudsman, following his re-election, Strasbourg, 11 January 2005, available at <http://www.euro-ombudsman.eu.int/speeches/en/2005–01–11.htm>.

[44] Art. 195(1) EC.

[45] Complaint 126/97/VK [1998] EOAR 17.

[46] Art. 195(1) EC, indent 2, Arts. 1.3 and 2(7) of the Statute. See [1995] EOAR 19, where reference is made to Complaints 105 and 110, Complaint 216/8.11.95/MH/A [1996] EOAR 16; Complaint 458/27.2.96/HS/B/KT [1997] EOAR 170; Complaint 463/28.2.96/RK/CH/PD [1997] EOAR 170; Complaint 739/98/ADB [1999] EOAR 20, 115; Complaint 867/99/GG [1999] EOAR 21, 116; Complaint 1055/99/VK [2000] EOAR 20; Complaint 224/99/IP [2000] EOAR 20.

[47] Art. 1(3) of the Statute. See Complaint 223/98/IJH [1998] EOAR 24.

[48] Art. 2(4) of the Statute. On the two year time limit see: Complaint 937/97/OV [1997] EOAR 27; Complaint 525/25.3.96/HDC/FR/PD/IJH/XD [1997] EOAR 174; Complaint 1275/99/(OV-MM-JSA)IJH [2001] EOAR 34. On the prior administrative approaches see: Complaint 1136/97/IJH [1997] EOAR 28; Complaint 1316/2000/GG [2000] EOAR 19; Complaint 557/2001/IJH [2001] EOAR 20.

Ombudsman.[49] Even when declared admissible, complaints will not be investigated, unless they provide grounds for inquiries.[50] Such grounds are, for example, wanting when the complaint raises issues that can be more effectively addressed by another, more specialized oversight body than the Ombudsman himself,[51] or where it has already been dealt with as a petition by the Committee on Petitions of the European Parliament and no new evidence is presented.[52]

From 1995 until 2003 inclusive, 13,523 complaints have been launched with the European Ombudsman. On average, only 13 per cent of these satisfy the admissibility criteria, successfully pass the 'grounds for inquiry' test, and eventually lead to a reasoned decision. 90 per cent of the complaints have been filed by individual citizens and 8 per cent by legal persons. The European Ombudsman's Annual Reports do not provide information as to which Community institutions and bodies are targeted by the incoming complaints, however such data are available for those of the complaints that finally led to a reasoned decision. As intuitively expected, it is the Commission that easily tops the list of the Ombudsman's 'clientele' with 76 per cent. Next comes the EP with 10 per cent and the Council with 4 per cent.

With respect to the types of maladministration complained of, there appears to be a high concentration focused on questions of openness, transparency, and public accessibility to the EU institutions.[53] An overall decline is also registered in the number of 'Article 226 complaints', a fact that could be interpreted as a telltale sign of the improvement of the Commission's record of compliance with the principles of good administration in the specific field of infringement procedures.[54]

As to geographical origins of the complaints, the placing of the Member States on the ranking scale largely reflects their demographic gravity, except for two countries which are 'overrepresented' in the Ombudsman's docket,

[49] Art. 2.8 of the Statute. See Complaint 483/4.3.96/DG/L/KT [1997] EOAR 35; Complaint 754/23.7.96/LS/IT/DT [1997] EOAR 127; Complaint 1056/2000/JMA [2001] EOAR 187.

[50] Art. 195(1) EC, Art. 3(1) of the Statute.

[51] See 4th Report of the House of Lords Select Committee on the European Communities, (HL 18; 1997–1998) and Complaint 630/6.6.96/CJ/UK/IJH [1997] EOAR 226; Complaint 971/24.10.96/UK/PD [1998] EOAR 129; Complaint 620/98/IJH [1999] EOAR 189; Complaint 734/99/(VK)/IJH [2000] EOAR 76.

[52] Complaint 851/3.9.96/ALC/ES/VK [1997] EOAR 45; Complaint 1152/97/OV [1999] EOAR 89.

[53] Harden, 'The European Ombudsman's Efforts to Increase Openness in the Union', in V. Deckmyn (ed), *Increasing Transparency in the EU?* (EIPA, 2002).

[54] See speech by the European Ombudsman 'The European Ombudsman: The Guardian of Good Administration', Athens, 8 October 2004, available at <http://www.euro-ombudsman.eu.int/speeches/en/2004–10–08.htm>.

namely Belgium, the 'Mecca' of EU administrative bureaucracy, and Finland, the home country of the first incumbent of the Ombudsman Office.

(2) The Proactive Role: Own Initiative Inquiries

Article 195 EC, in conjunction with Article 3(1) of the Ombudsman Statute and Article 9 of the Implementing Provisions,[55] entrusts the European Ombudsman with the power to activate his oversight apparatus on his own volition. Just over six months into his tenure, the Ombudsman made an important policy statement spelling out the normative foundations of his proactive philosophy. After stressing that the two-year time bar applies to complaints launched with him, but not to his own initiative investigations,[56] he stated that:[57]

> The Ombudsman's primary duty . . . is to deal with the complaints that are addressed to him. The right to conduct own initiative inquiries, though important, should not be used too frequently. It might be used, for example, where a series of complaints had focused attention on a specific body or a particular type of administrative activity, providing grounds to think that a more general inquiry should be conducted.

This compass setting has remained unaltered since 1996 and has been subsequently reiterated on several occasions.[58] It is readily apparent that there are two main attributes to the Ombudsman's proactive strategy.

The first feature pertains to the number of own initiative investigations and introduces a quantitative factor with obvious qualitative implications: the proactive mechanism is to be used infrequently, on the ground that excessive use could diminish its value and practical utility. The second feature concerns the origins of the own initiative inquiries. It appears that the Ombudsman's proactive function is constructed in a predominately complaint-based manner. Own initiative investigations are mainly conceived as

[55] Decision of the European Ombudsman adopting implementing provisions adopted on 8 July 2002 and amended by decision of the Ombudsman of 5 April 2004, available at <http://www.euro-ombudsman.eu.int/lbasis/en/provis.htm>.

[56] [1995] EOAR 20. [57] [1995] EOAR 21.

[58] [1996] EOAR 66; [1997] EOAR 15; [1998] EOAR 10; [1999] EOAR 15; [2000] EOAR 17; [2001] EOAR 17; [2002] EOAR 17; [2003] EOAR 20, 25, 33. See also Söderman, 'A Thousand and One Complaints: The European Ombudsman en Route' (1997) 3 *EPL* 351, at 354; Söderman, 'The Role of the European Ombudsman', speech at the 6th Meeting of European National Ombudsmen, Jerusalem, 9–11 September 1997, at 7, <http://www.euro-ombudsman.eu.int/speeches/pdf/en/jerus_en.pdf>; Söderman, 'The Effectiveness of the Ombudsman in the Oversight of the Administrative Conduct of Government', speech at the 7th International Ombudsman Institute Conference, Durban, 30 October–3 November 2000, under the heading 'Own-initiative inquiries', <http://www.euro-ombudsman.eu.int/speeches/en/durban1.htm>.

tools to circumvent technical aspects of the reactive method of engaging the Ombudsman. This entails examination of complaints whose authors' identities ought to be protected, or where the admissibility requirements are not satisfied, because the complainant, for example, is not a person entitled to contact the Ombudsman or the complaint is time-barred. In addition, the proactive option can be used to tackle significant instances of structural administrative malfunctioning revealed through distinct reactive investigations.

Empirical evidence supports this view. A careful analysis of the Ombudsman's record reveals that he has made measured use of his proactive machinery. From 1995 until 2003 inclusive, he initiated only 25 investigations on his own volition, which, if compared to the 1,700 reactive inquiries launched within the same time period, accounted for a bit less than 1.5 per cent of his overall investigative activity. On average, one own initiative inquiry commences every four months and, in principle, not more than five such inquiries are open at any given moment. Most importantly, the overwhelming majority of the own initiative inquiries appear to originate directly from a reactive background: nine investigations were initiated following waves of complaints pinpointing high risk areas of institutionalized administrative malfunction;[59] five investigations sought to enable the examination of otherwise inadmissible complaints;[60] one investigation was launched in order to protect the anonymity of the complainant;[61] another investigation was used as a means of bringing remedial pressure on the recalcitrant institution to honour the commitments it had agreed to undertake in a previous complaint-triggered decision;[62] another inquiry began following the transmission to the Ombudsman of the file on a petition which the Petitions Committee had examined;[63] finally one investigation was initiated after a national ombudsman disagreed with the reply that a Community institution had given to his query.[64]

[59] 616/PUBAC/F/IJH [1996] EOAR 81; 303/97/PD [1997] EOAR 270; 626/97/BB [1998] EOAR 259; 1004/97/(PD)/GG [2000] EOAR 206; OI/1/98/OV [2000] EOAR 207; OI/1/99/IJH [1999] EOAR 245; OI/5/99/(IJH)/GG [2001] EOAR 215; OI/3/2001/SM [2001] EOAR 221; OI/5/2003 <http://www.euro-ombudsman.eu.int/decision/en/03oi5.htm>.

[60] 132/21.9.95/AH/EN [1996] EOAR 69; 1150/97/OI/JMA [1998] EOAR 268; OI/4/99/OV [2001] EOAR 18; OI/2/2003 <http://www.euro-ombudsman.eu.int/recommen/en/oi030002.htm>, OI/4/2003/ADB 2003 [EOAR] 33, 205. See also 'Note' to Case 398/98/HL [1998] EOAR 16.

[61] 674/COMLA/F/PD [1997] EOAR 269.

[62] OI/1/2000/OV [2000] EOAR 204.

[63] OI/1/99/IJH/COM <http://www.euro-ombudsman.eu.int/decision/en/99oi1ec.htm>.

[64] OI/3/99/(IJH)/PB [2000] EOAR 197. See also [1999] EOAR 17.

B. Investigative Powers

In the course of the discussions on the European Ombudsman's Statute the precise nature and scope of his investigative powers emerged as a central matter of contention between the EP on one side and the Commission and the Council on the other, with the former favouring and the latter opposing the strengthening of the Ombudsman's investigative capacity. The resulting scheme is characterized by two key features.

The first is the fundamental, albeit not absolute, principle that the Ombudsman can employ any investigative tool he considers suitable for the examination of any particular case.[65] This is complemented by Article 5(5) of the Implementing Provisions, which stipulates that the Ombudsman may commission any studies or expert reports he finds necessary to the success of an inquiry.

The second feature is that the Ombudsman has two types of investigative powers, which are horizontal and vertical in nature. On the horizontal plane, the Ombudsman is entitled to contact Community institutions and bodies and ask for information or files that originate from them. The default position in these cases is that the Community institution or body contacted is bound to comply with the Ombudsman's request.[66] This is reinforced by the Implementing Provisions, which oblige the Community bureaucracy to supply, within a reasonable time, information or documents for the purposes of an inquiry, make arrangements for on-the-spot investigations, and allow the taking of photocopies in the course of file inspections.[67] By way of exception, 'duly substantiated grounds of secrecy' can be resorted to with a view to legitimately evading the fulfilment of these obligations.[68] Along the same lines, 'officials and other servants of Community institutions and bodies must testify at the request of the Ombudsman; they shall speak on behalf of and in accordance with instructions from their administrations and shall continue to be bound by their duty of professional secrecy'.[69]

Moving on to the vertical dimension, the Ombudsman's powers are of two kinds. There are what may be termed direct investigative powers that pertain to the relations between the Ombudsman and the national authorities. The latter are 'obliged to provide [the former], whenever he may so request, via the Permanent Representations of the Member States to the European Communities, with any information that may help to clarify instances of maladministration by Community institutions or bodies unless such information is covered by laws or regulations on secrecy or by provisions preventing

[65] Art. 3(1) of the Statute. [66] Art. 3(2) subpara. 1 of the Statute
[67] Art. 5(1), 5(4) and 5(2) of the Implementing Provisions respectively.
[68] Art. 3(2) subpara. 1 of the Statute.
[69] Art. 3(2) subpara. 5 of the Statute. See also Art. 5(3) of the Implementing Provisions.

its being communicated'.[70] There are also what may be termed indirect investigative powers, which are concerned with the question of access to documents that originate in a Member State, but are in the possession of a Community institution or body.[71] These documents are accessible to the Ombudsman only after the Member State concerned has been informed, unless they are classified as secret by law or regulation, in which case the Member State has to give its prior agreement.[72]

This horizontal and vertical classification is important since certain consequences follow in relation to the breadth and degree of the investigative powers. First, the Statute does not appear to allow for the taking of testimony from officials of national authorities, a tool that is expressly provided for investigations undertaken at the horizontal level. In the unlikely event that such an issue arises, e.g. in the context of an 'Article 226 complaint', it is questionable whether any relevant obligation on the part of the Member State could directly be deduced from Article 10 EC. Second, the horizontal and the indirectly vertical investigative powers share the same degree of intrusiveness, given that both can be limited only if grounds of secrecy are properly advanced and substantiated. It follows that confidentiality considerations cannot limit the investigative authority of the Ombudsman when he utilizes the foregoing types of powers. The directly vertical investigative powers are by way of contrast the most constrained, since they are subject to limitations that are not only based on secrecy sensitivities, but extend also to 'information . . . covered . . . by provisions preventing its being communicated', wording that can be understood to permit invocation of confidentiality arguments.

It is also important to examine empirically the way in which the investigative powers are used. It should be noted at the outset that it is the horizontal investigative powers which have been most commonly employed and the use of these powers has raised practical questions in a variety of cases, whereas the indirectly vertical powers have been mainly related to 'Article 226 complaints' and their application has not been problematic.[73] No directly vertical powers have been used to date.

It is further worthy of note that the Ombudsman's investigative practice consists chiefly in gathering and assessing factual data and written observations submitted by the complainant and the targeted institution. In only a few instances, and mostly in the course of own initiative inquiries, did the

[70] Art. 3(3) of the Statute.

[71] It has been suggested that this type of power was the most hotly debated issue in the discussions of the Ombudsman's Statute in the Luxembourg Interinstitutional Conference, Corbert, 'Governance and Institutional Developments' (1994) 23 *JCMS* 27, at 33.

[72] Art. 3(2) indents 3 and 4 of the Statute.

[73] 1045/21.11.96/BH/IRL/JMA [1998] EOAR 154; 1338/98/ME [2001] EOAR 65; 995/98/OV [2001] EOAR 116. See also the Ombudsman's Note prepared for Mrs A. Garrett concerning the possible revision of Art. 3 (2) of the Statute of the Ombudsman, Brussels, 24 May 2000, <http://www.euro-ombudsman.eu.int/speeches/en/cac240500.htm>.

Ombudsman resort to other investigative tactics, like an on-the-spot visit in response to an invitation from the targeted institution,[74] public appeals for submission of observations in relation to ongoing inquiries,[75] and commission of a research study for the purposes of an investigation under way.[76]

Another striking finding is that in the overwhelming majority of cases the Ombudsman appears to consider the information and explanations provided by the targeted institution sufficiently accurate and complete. As a consequence, file inspections and witness hearings, the two most highly controversial and hotly debated of the Ombudsman's investigative powers, have proven in quantitative terms to play a relatively small role in the Ombudsman's investigations: from 1995 until 2003 inclusive, files have been inspected in less than 40 cases and oral evidence has been taken in only five.[77] Those are figures which, if compared to the 1,725 inquiries carried out either proactively or reactively within the foregoing period, account for less than 3 per cent of the total investigative activity.

In qualitative terms file inspections have demonstrated their utility in three main types of case, namely access to documents,[78] Article 226 EC enforcement proceedings,[79] and recruitment competitions.[80] As to the taking of

[74] OI/3/2001/SM [2001] EOAR 222.

[75] See OI/5/99/(IJH)/GG [2001] EOAR 215, where an invitation was addressed to the public for comments on problems arising from late payment by the Commission (Press Release No. 15/99 <http://www.euro-ombudsman.eu.int/release/en/late1.htm>), and OI/3/2003, where a similar invitation was made in the context of an investigation into the measures implemented by the Commission to ensure that persons with disabilities are not discriminated against in their relations with the institution (Press Release No. 15/2004 <http://www.euro-ombudsman.eu.int/release/en/2004–04–29.htm> and <http://www.euro-ombudsman.eu.int/disabilities/en/default.htm>).

[76] See OI inquiry 626/97/BB [1998] EOAR 260, where the Ombudsman contacted the ECJ with a view to asking its Research and Documentation Division to prepare a research note on the application of age limits in the Member States.

[77] In some cases both inspection of documents and hearing of witnesses were necessitated, see 1140/97/IJH [1999] EOAR 83; 995/98/OV [2001] EOAR 116; 1230/2000/GG [2002] EOAR 79. The first inspection of documents was carried out on 5 November 1996 (132/95/AH [1996] EOAR 70, 91), whereas the first hearing of a witness took place three years later, on 24 June 1999 (1140/97 [1999] EOAR 83). Both inquiries were directed against the Commission and concerned the way it had exercised its role as guardian of the Treaty under Art. 226 EC.

[78] 1087/10.12.96/STATEWATCH/UK/IJH [1998] EOAR 41; 1045/21.11.96/BH/IRL/JMA [1998] EOAR 154; 620/97/PD and 306/98/PD [1999] EOAR 64; 648/2002/IHJ [2003] EOAR 134. See also 754/23.7.96/LS/IT/DT [1997] EOAR 128 and 172/2003/IP [2003] EOAR 70, where the inspection of confidential documents by the Ombudsman was essential in clarifying the issues raised.

[79] 132/21.9.95/AH/EN [1996] 70, 91; 1140/97/IJH [1999] EOAR 83; 995/98/OV [2001] EOAR 116.

[80] 365/97/JMA [1999] EOAR 53; 466/97/PD [1999] EOAR 135; 647/2002/OV [2003] EOAR 47.

testimony, it has not only failed most of the times to produce a marked impact on the deliberative process owing to the draconian restrictions imposed on those testifying, but has also given rise to a protracted, wearisome, and fruitless dispute over whether Commissioners are and, if not, should be obliged to be heard as witnesses at the Ombudsman's request.[81]

Community institutions and bodies that have been confronted with the Ombudsman's investigative machinery have for the most part cooperated reasonably well and have either actively supported[82] the investigation or passively tolerated it.[83] The notable exception has been, unsurprisingly, the Commission, which on some occasions delayed considerably the investigative process by refusing to allow the Ombudsman to inspect crucial documents on the basis of a perversely expansive reading of the secrecy clause.[84] The Ombudsman's efforts to have this clause removed have not been successful thus far.[85]

C. Remedial Powers

It is necessary to have a clear understanding of the structure of the Ombudsman's remedial regime. This can be outlined as follows.

Once the investigation has produced conclusive evidence that an instance of maladministration has indeed occurred, the Ombudsman must seek to reach a friendly solution with the targeted institution or body in order to rectify the administrative irregularity at issue and satisfy the complainant.[86] If

[81] 995/98/OV [2001] EOAR 116, Ombudsman's remarks to the Committee on Constitutional Affairs on the modification of Art. 3 of the Ombudsman's Statute, Brussels, 5 March 2001, <http://www.euro-ombudsman.eu.int/speeches/en/2001–03–05.htm> and Harden, 'When Europeans Complain: The Work of the European Ombudsman' (2000) 3 *CYELS* 199, at 217.

[82] 1087/10.12.96/STATEWATCH/UK/IJH [1998] EOAR 41.

[83] 844/8.8.96/HL/FIN/IJH/BB <http://www.euro-ombudsman.eu.int/decision/en/960844.htm>.

[84] See 132/21.9.95/AH/EN [1996] EOAR 70, 91, 531/97/PD and 535/97/PD [1999] EOAR 58, especially 365/97/JMA [1999] EOAR 53 and 1140/97/IJH [1999] EOAR 83 as well as the Ombudsman's introductory remarks to the Committee on Petitions concerning his first mandate, Brussels, 28 September 1999, available at <http://www.euro-ombudsman.eu.int/speeches/en/cop280999.htm>, the Ombudsman's Note prepared for Mrs A. Garrett concerning the possible revision of Art. 3 (2) of the Statute of the Ombudsman, Brussels, 24 May 2000 <http://www.euro-ombudsman.eu.int/speeches/en/cac240500.htm>, and the Ombudsman's remarks to the Committee on Constitutional Affairs on the modification of Art. 3 of the Ombudsman's Statute, Brussels, 5 March 2001, <http://www.euro-ombudsman.eu.int/speeches/en/2001–03–05.htm>. By way of contrast see 754/23.7.96/LS/IT/DT [1997] EOAR 128, where the Commission contributed very positively to the investigative effort.

[85] Council Note 14782/02 OMBUDS 29 of 26 November 2002, [2002] EOAR 25.

[86] Art. 3(5) of the Ombudsman's Statute, Art. 6 of the Implementing Provisions.

a friendly settlement cannot be achieved, either because it is considered to be inappropriate in the specific case,[87] or because the targeted institution or body rejects it, the Ombudsman will have to choose between closing the matter with a critical remark and keeping the case open by issuing a draft recommendation.[88]

The former will be chosen when it is no longer possible for the institution or body concerned to eliminate the instance of maladministration and where the maladministration has no general implications.[89] If either of these conditions is not satisfied, the Ombudsman will make a draft recommendation to which the institution or body at issue shall respond within three months by sending a detailed opinion that might signify acceptance of the Ombudsman's recommendations, together with a description of the measures taken to implement them.[90] If the Ombudsman finds the opinion satisfactory, he will close the matter. In the event, however, that the Community bureaucracy refuses to comply with the recommendations addressed to it, the Ombudsman will either confine himself to making a critical remark, if he thinks fit to terminate the case with no further action, or draw up a special report to the EP repeating the recommendations he has already put forward.[91] The Committee on Petitions is responsible for dealing with the Ombudsman's special reports and drafting its own reports thereon that could at a later stage be endorsed by the Plenary in the form of a Resolution.[92]

The Ombudsman is also obliged to submit to the EP an annual report on his activities as a whole which includes the outcome of his inquiries and may contain specific recommendations aiming at improving the functioning of the Community administrative apparatus.[93] Recent years have witnessed a sustained and concerted effort on the part of the Ombudsman to enhance his remedial competence by suggesting that he be vested with the authority to

[87] The grounds on which the Ombudsman has until now based his decision to refrain from pursuing a friendly solution vary and include the following: the complainant expressly excludes any such possibility (Complaint 1319/2003/ADB, available at <http://www.euro-ombudsman.eu.int/decision/en/031319.htm>); the complaint is related to past events that cannot be undone (Complaint 1571/2003/OV, available at <http://www.euro-ombudsman.eu.int/decision/en/031571.htm>, Complaint 1367/2003/OV, available at <http://www.euro-ombudsman.eu.int/decision/en/031367.htm>); the complaint is '*actio popularis*' (Complaint 2216/2003/(BB)MHZ, available at <http://www.euro-ombudsman.eu.int/decision/en/032216.htm>).

[88] Art. 6(3) of the Implementing Provisions.

[89] Art. 7 of the Implementing Provisions.

[90] Art. 3(6) of the Ombudsman's Statute, Art. 8 of the Implementing Provisions.

[91] Art. 3(7) of the Ombudsman's Statute, Art. 8(4) of the Implementing Provisions.

[92] Art. 195 EC and Annex VI, XX of the Rules of Procedure of the European Parliament. See also [1997] EOAR 13 and 16, [1999] EOAR 16.

[93] Art. 3(8) of the Ombudsman's Statute, Arts. 11 and 16 of the Implementing Provisions.

refer to the Court of Justice cases concerning violations of fundamental rights that could not be solved through a normal ombudsman investigation.[94]

In normative terms, it is readily apparent that the Ombudsman's remedial powers are premised on a conciliatory ethos. Thus the Ombudsman's primary task, once an instance of maladministration is established, is to seek a friendly solution between the Community administration and the aggrieved complainant. Moreover the Ombudsman's decisions are not legally binding and do not create enforceable rights for the complainant. It is left to the targeted Community institution or body to take the measures necessary to rectify the administrative error and prevent its recurrence in future. If the Community institution or body concerned refuses to enter a friendly settlement and rejects the critical remarks or draft recommendation addressed to it, the Ombudsman can do nothing formally beyond submitting a special report to the Parliament and criticizing the relevant authorities in his annual report. This lack of formal legal authority on the part of the European Ombudsman to award a remedy should not lead to the supposition that his investigative efforts are futile. The truth is that the Ombudsman's decisions are in principle accepted by the targeted institution or body.[95] These decisions have resulted in varying forms of remedial redress at both the micro level of specific complaints seeking the correction of an individual error,[96] and the macro level of wide-ranging investigations aimed at altering established departmental practices and procedures.[97]

In practical terms, a close look at the application of the Ombudsman's remedial scheme yields a number of interesting findings. From 1995 until 2004 inclusive, an amicable solution was reached in approximately 25 cases, which accounts for less than 1.5 per cent of the total number of inquiries closed with a reasoned opinion. The prime cause for such a low figure is the fact that a large number of cases are settled by the Community institution or body itself before any amicable solution is proposed by the Ombudsman. To this it should be added that in many instances the nature of the action under investigation is related to a completed set of past events that cannot be altered

[94] See the speeches the European Ombudsman addressed to the European Convention in Brussels: 24 April 2003, available at <http://www.euro-ombudsman.eu.int/speeches/en/2003–04–24.htm> and on 24 June 2003, available at <http://www.euro-ombudsman.eu.int/speeches/en/2002–06–24.htm>. See also the European Ombudsman's proposals for Treaty changes, Article D(2), available at <http://www.euro-ombudsman.eu.int/letters/en/20020712–1.htm> and the Ombudsman's Statement following his re-election, Strasbourg, 11 January 2005, available at <http://www.euro-ombudsman.eu.int/speeches/en/2005–01–11.htm>.

[95] [2002] EOAR 12.

[96] E.g. Complaint 2111/2002/(BB)MF available at <http://www.euro-ombudsman.eu.int/decision/en/022111.htm>.

[97] OI/2/2002/IJH [2003] EOAR 201.

and thus any corrective attempt is not possible. Friendly settlements have been achieved with the European Commission,[98] the European Parliament,[99] as well as the European Personnel Selection Office (EPSO).[100] The overwhelming majority of these settlements are concerned with money claims[101] and there is a secondary line of cases relating to disputes over access to documents.[102] Critical remarks have been made in 235 cases, which amounts to 15 per cent of the total number of inquiries closed with a reasoned opinion. As intuitively expected, the European Commission has been the target of most of the Ombudsman's criticism, followed by the EP and the Council. The subject matter of the decisions varies and a considerable range of Community administrative activity seems to have been covered. Draft recommendations have been issued in 70 cases, representing less than 4.5 per cent of the number of investigations closed with a reasoned opinion. Critical remarks following draft recommendations turned down by the Community administration have been made on a handful of occasions.[103] Nine investigations, four of which were commenced on the Ombudsman's own volition, have been concluded with submission of a special report to the EP:[104] six related to transparency questions,[105] whereas the other three were focused on

[98] See e.g. Complaint 1320/2003/(ADB)ELB, available at <http://www.euro-ombudsman.eu.int/decision/en/031320.htm>, Complaint 1552/2002/OV, available at <http://www.euro-ombudsman.eu.int/decision/en/021552.htm>, as well as [1997] EOAR 32.

[99] Complaint 760/24.7.96/JC/UK/IJH [1998] EOAR 150; Complaint 375/2001/IJH, available at <http://www.euro-ombudsman.eu.int/decision/en/010375.htm>.

[100] Complaint 1917/2003/(BB)MHZ, available at <http://www.euro-ombudsman.eu.int/decision/en/031917.htm>; Complaint 1423/2003/(BB)MHZ, available at <http://www.euro-ombudsman.eu.int/decision/en/031423.htm.>

[101] See e.g. Complaint 1317/2001/PB, available at <http://www.euro-ombudsman.eu.int/decision/en/011317.htm> and Complaint 860/99/(IJH)MM, available at <http://www.euro-ombudsman.eu.int/decision/en/990860.htm>.

[102] See e.g. Complaint 1045/21.11.96/BH/IRL/JMA [1998] EOAR 154; Complaint 415/2003/(IJH)TN available at <http://www.euro-ombudsman.eu.int/decision/en/030415.htm>.

[103] See e.g. Complaint 511/99/GG, available at <http://www.euro-ombudsman.eu.int/recommen/en/990511.htm>; Complaint 1689/2000/GG, available at <http://www.euro-ombudsman.eu.int/recommen/en/001689.htm>; Complaint 232/2001/GG, available at <http://www.euro-ombudsman.eu.int/recommen/en/010232.htm>; Complaint 1435/2002/GG, available at <http://www.euro-ombudsman.eu.int/recommen/en/021435.htm>; Complaint 1889/2002/GG, available at <http://www.euro-ombudsman.eu.int/recommen/en/021889.htm>.

[104] On the principle that Special Reports be infrequently used see [1997] EOAR 32.

[105] Cases 616/PUBAC/F/IJH, available at <http://www.euro-ombudsman.eu.int/special/pdf/en/970616.pdf>; 1004/97/PD, available at <http://www.euro-ombudsman.eu.int/special/pdf/en/971004.pdf>; 713/98/IJH, available at <http://www.euro-ombudsman.eu.int/special/pdf/en/980713.pdf>; 917/2000/GG, available at <http://www.euro-ombudsman.eu.int/special/pdf/en/000917.pdf>; 341/2001/(BB)IJH, available at <http://www.euro-ombudsman.eu.int/special/pdf/en/010341.pdf>; 1542/2000/(PB)SM available at <http://www.euro-ombudsman.eu.int/special/pdf/en/001542.pdf>.

the Code of Good Administrative Behaviour,[106] sex discrimination,[107] and staff issues[108] respectively.

3. THE NOTION OF MALADMINISTRATION

The concept of maladministration performs a dual function within the Ombudsman system. It delineates the outer boundaries of the Ombudsman's jurisdiction and is therefore employed as a criterion for determining the admissibility of complaints that are filed. It also constitutes the yardstick against which the administrative behaviour of the Community bureaucracy is assessed and hence serves as the basis on which the merits of each case are considered. Neither the drafters of the EC Treaty nor the framers of the Ombudsman's Statute made any effort to define maladministration, thus leaving this task to the European Ombudsman subject to the superior interpretative authority of the ECJ. In his Annual Report for 1995 the Ombudsman produced a non-exhaustive list of conduct that would amount to maladministration and included therein administrative irregularities and omissions, abuse of power, negligence, unlawful procedures, unfairness, malfunction or incompetence, discrimination, avoidable delay, and lack or refusal of information.[109] Following an invitation by the European Parliament to develop a precise and clear definition of maladministration,[110] the Ombudsman proclaimed in his Annual Report for 1997 that: 'maladministration occurs when a public body fails to act in accordance with a rule or principle which is binding upon it'.[111] This definition was complemented by a statement that 'when the Ombudsman investigates whether a Community institution or body has acted in accordance with the rules and principles which are binding upon it, his first and most essential task must be to establish whether it has acted lawfully'.[112]

A close look at the Ombudsman's statements and investigative record reveals that his perception of maladministration is governed by a dual logic. There is the concept of legality, which emerges as the chief definitional

[106] Case OI/1/98/OV, available at <http://www.euro-ombudsman.eu.int/special/pdf/en/oi980001.pdf>.

[107] Case 242/2000/GG, available at <http://www.euro-ombudsman.eu.int/special/pdf/en/000242.pdf>.

[108] Case OI/2/2003/GG, available at <http://www.euro-ombudsman.eu.int/special/pdf/en/oi030002.pdf>.

[109] [1995] EOAR 17.

[110] Resolution of the European Parliament on the Annual Report on the Activities of the European Ombudsman in 1996, C4–0293/97- A4–0211/1997, at point 4.

[111] [1997] EOAR 23.

[112] [1997] EOAR 24.

component of maladministration.[113] Contrary to the objections that have been sporadically raised by the Commission,[114] the Ombudsman has consistently held that the wrongful interpretation or application of Community norms constitutes an instance of maladministration.[115] The Community norms whose infringement will lead to a finding of maladministration consist of the Treaties, legally binding provisions of Community legislation, and the whole corpus of the judgments of the ECJ and the CFI.[116] Particularly important for the Ombudsman's work are the general administrative law principles, both procedural and substantive, that have been established and elaborated by the Community judiciary.[117] These include: provision of accurate information;[118] diligent and impartial examination of grievances;[119] respect of the right to be heard;[120] duty to give adequate and coherent reasons for decisions;[121] protection of legitimate expectations;[122] equality of treatment;[123] and transparency.[124]

[113] This approach has not gone uncontested, see speech by the European Ombudsman at the Ceremony for the award of the Alexis de Tocqueville Prize 2001 available at <http://www.euro-ombudsman.eu.int/speeches/en/2001–11–21.htm> and Complaint 916/2000/GG [2001] EOAR 193, where the Council maintained that the review of the legality of administrative decisions falls outside the remit of the Ombudsman's competence.

[114] See [1999] EOAR 12, 17, OI/3/99/(IJH)PB [2000] EOAR 197 and Complaint 449/96/20.2.96/HKC/PD [1998] EOAR 46, where the Commission sought to challenge the Ombudsman's competence by arguing respectively that the interpretation of a Regulation and the application of competition rules are not matters falling under the rubric of maladministration.

[115] See e.g. Complaint 996/5.11.96/JC/IRL/BB [1997] EOAR 138 (interpretation and application of a Directive); Complaints 256/23.11.95/EA/B-FR *et al.* [1996] EOAR 51, 132/21.9.1995/AH/EN [1996] EOAR 67, 531/97/PD *et al.* [1999] EOAR 58 (interpretation of Directives); Complaints 308/96/PD [1997] EOAR 72, 1060/28.11.96/BK/DK/PD [1997] EOAR 143, 26/97/VK [1998] EOAR 90, 298/99/(IJH)BB [2001] EOAR 39 (interpretation of Regulations); and Complaint 1053/25.11.96/STATEWATCH/UK/IJH [1998] EOAR 167 (interpretation of a Decision).

[116] [1995] EOAR 23.

[117] On these principles see Usher, 'The "Good Administration" of Community Law' [1985] *CLP* 278; L. Reif, *The Ombudsman, Good Governance and the International Human Rights System* (Martinus Nijhoff, 2004), at 379 and the bibliographical references in n. 83, as well as L. Senden *Soft Law in European Community Law* (Hart, 2004).

[118] Complaint 1051/25.11.96/AF/B/VK [1998] EOAR 164; Complaint 16/97/JMA [1998] EOAR 182; Complaint 1011/99/BB [2000] EOAR 137.

[119] Complaint 852/3.9.96/SJB/UK/IJH [1998] EOAR 137.

[120] Complaint 475/7.3.96/SH/ROM/KT [1997] EOAR 84; Complaint 1250/2000/(JSA)IJH [2001] EOAR 101.

[121] Complaint 23/97/KH [1998] EOAR 230; Complaint 1250/2000/(JSA)IJH [2001] EOAR 101.

[122] Complaint 288/99/ME [2000] EOAR 132; Complaint 548/2002/GG [2003] EOAR 115.

[123] Complaint 109/98/ME [2000] EOAR 185; Complaint 1365/2002/OV [2003] EOAR 57; Complaint 1536/2002/OV [2003] EOAR 67.

[124] OI/1/99/IJH [1999] EOAR 245.

The concept of maladministration is not, however, exhausted by the concept of legality. It also includes rules and principles that for the purposes of the Ombudsman's investigations are considered to restrain the Community administrative behaviour even though they lack any legally binding force. This is, for example, the case when the European Ombudsman employs his previous decisions,[125] the Code of Good Administrative Behaviour[126] and the Charter of Fundamental Rights,[127] as yardsticks against which the

[125] See speech by the European Ombudsman to the Committee on Petitions concerning the presentation to the European Parliament of his Annual Report for 2002, Brussels 24 March 2003, available at <http://www.euro-ombudsman.eu.int/speeches/en/2003–03–24.htm> and OI/1/2000/OV [2000] EOAR 204.

[126] On the efforts of the Ombudsman to promote the Code see OI/1/98/OV [1999] EOAR 213; [2000] EOAR 207; [2002] EOAR 194. On 6 September 2001 the European Parliament invited the Ombudsman to apply the code in examining whether maladministration occurred, [2001] EOAR 11 and 19, European Parliament resolution on the annual report for 2000 on the activities of the European Ombudsman, C5–0302/2001–A5–0280/2001, at point 7. On the application of specific provisions of the Code in concrete cases see: Complaint 1840/2002/GG [2003] EOAR 173 (Art. 6); Complaint 39/2002/OV [2002] EOAR 164 (Art. 9); Complaint 754/2003/GG [2003] EOAR 159 (Art. 10(1)); Complaint 1237/2002/(PB)OV [2003] EOAR 151 (Art. 10(2)); OI/1/2002/OV [2002] EOAR 204 (Art. 12); Complaint 1565/2002/GG [2003] EOAR 129 (Art. 12(1)); Complaint 852/2003/OV [2003] EOAR 169 (Arts. 12(1) and 12(3)); Complaint 1200/2003/OV [2003] EOAR 141 (Art. 13); Complaint 1751/2001/GG [2002] EOAR 170 (Arts. 14 and 17); OI/1/99/IJH [1999] EOAR 245 (Art. 18); Complaint 1346/98/OV [2000] EOAR 150 (Art. 18); Complaint 1117/2003/GG [2003] EOAR 81 (Arts. 19 and 23); Complaint 1015/2002/(PB)IJH [2003] EOAR 195 (Art. 22).

[127] [2003] EOAR 27. Cases where provisions of the Charter have been relied upon include Complaint 1128/2001/IJH [2002] EOAR 189 (Art. 11); OI/1/2001/GG [2002] EOAR 196 (Art. 11); Complaint 1402/2002/GG [2003] EOAR 123 (Arts. 11 and 42); OI/2/2001/(BB)OV [2002] EOAR 207 (Arts. 15(1) and 21(1)); Complaint 845/2002/IJH [2003] EOAR 181 (Arts. 24(2) and 41); OI/3/2003/JMA available at <http://www.euro-ombudsman.eu.int/letters/en/20031119–1.htm> (Art. 26); OI/4/2001/ME [2002] EOAR 201 (Art. 33(2)); Complaint 1250/2000/(JSA)IJH [2001] EOAR 101 (Arts. 39 and 41); Complaint 1100/2001/GG [2002] EOAR 147 (Art. 41(1)); Complaint 1272/2001/SM [2002] EOAR 156 (Art. 41); Complaint 406/2003/(PB)IJH [2003] EOAR 37 (Art. 41); Complaint 1200/2003/OV [2003] EOAR 141 (Art. 41); OI/1/2002/OV [2002] EOAR 204 (Art. 43); Complaint 1351/2001/(ME)(MF)BB [2003] EOAR 144 (Art. 43). See also the following speeches by the Ombudsman: 'El Defensor del Pueblo Europeo y la Defensa de los Derechos Humanos', Madrid, 8 October 2001, available at <http://www.euro-ombudsman.eu.int/speeches/es/2001–10–08.htm>; 'La Charte des Droits Fondamentaux de l'Union européenne', Andorre, 14–18 October 2001, available at <http://www.euro-ombudsman.eu.int/speeches/fr/2001–10–17.htm>; 'The Convention and the Charter of Fundamental Rights', Brussels, 25 February 2003, available at <http://www.euro-ombudsman.eu.int/speeches/en/2003–02–25.htm>; 'Le Médiateur européen, les droits fondamentaux et la future Constitution pour l'Europe', Tunisia, 14–17 October 2003, available at <http://www.euro-ombudsman.eu.int/speeches/fr/2003–10–14.htm>; 'The European Ombudsman: the guardian of good administration', Athens, 8 October 2004, available at <http://www.euro-ombudsman.eu.int/speeches/en/2004–10–08.htm>; 'The European Ombudsman and the European Constitution', The Hague, 15 October 2004, available at <http://www.euro-ombudsman.eu.int/speeches/en/2004–10–15.htm>.

bureaucratic activity of Community institutions and bodies is assessed. It is worth noting that human rights are protected under the rubric of maladministration[128] and the cases that have arisen to date relate to freedom of expression,[129] age limits,[130] parental leave,[131] and discrimination on the basis of gender,[132] race,[133] and physical disability.[134]

The European Ombudsman has construed maladministration such that it limits his mandate in three distinct ways. Firstly, in cases pertaining to contractual relationships regulated by national law, the Ombudsman will not seek to determine whether there has been a breach of contract by any of the parties, but rather confines himself to assessing whether the targeted Community institution or body provided a coherent account of the legal basis for its actions and explained the reasons why it believed that its view of the contractual position was justified.[135] Secondly, when in carrying out its administrative tasks Community bureaucracy is vested with discretionary powers, the Ombudsman will only examine whether the institution or body concerned has acted within the limits of its legal authority without questioning the merits of the discretionary administrative decision made.[136] Thirdly, decisions of a political rather than administrative nature fall beyond the Ombudsman's jurisdictional reach.[137] As a result, the Ombudsman has declined to investigate complaints relating to the political work of the EP[138]

[128] [1995] EOAR 17, speech by the Ombudsman, 'El Defensor del Pueblo Europeo y la Defensa de los Derechos Humanos,' Madrid, 8 October 2001, available at <http://www.euro-ombudsman.eu.int/speeches/es/2001–10–08.htm>, Gregory and Giddings, 'Citizenship, Rights and the EU Ombudsman', in R. Bellamy and A. Warleigh (eds), *Citizenship and Governance in the European Union* (2001).

[129] Complaint 794/5.8.1996/EAW/SW/VK [1997] EOAR 129; Complaint 219/99/ME [2000] EOAR 90; OI/1/2001/GG [2002] EOAR 196.

[130] Case 626/97/BB [1998] EOAR 259; OI/2/2001/(BB)OV [2002] EOAR 207.

[131] OI/4/2001/ME [2002] EOAR 201.

[132] Special Report in Complaint 242/2000/GG [2001] EOAR 224.

[133] 777/2001/IJH, available at <http://www.euro-ombudsman.eu.int/decision/en/010777.htm>.

[134] OI/3/2003/JMA, available at <http://www.euro-ombudsman.eu.int/letters/en/20031119–1.htm>.

[135] [1997] EOAR 24. See e.g. Complaint 768/26.7.96/CP/UK/IJH [1998] EOAR 199; Complaint 568/98/PD [1999] EOAR 98; Complaint 506/99/GG [2000] EOAR 70; Complaint 821/2000/GG [2001] EOAR 152; Complaint 1689/2000/GG [2002] EOAR 106; Complaint 1141/2002/GG [2003] EOAR 93. See also Complaint 993/2002/GG [2002] EOAR 44, where similar reasoning was applied in a case concerning an alleged abuse of monopolistic position.

[136] [1997] EOAR 26; Complaint 754/23.7.96/LS/IT/DT [1997] EOAR 127; Complaint 568/98/PD [1999] EOAR 98; Complaint 1338/98/ME [2001] EOAR 61; Complaint 506/99/GG [2002] EOAR 70; Complaint 905/99/GG [2002] EOAR 85; Complaint 500/2001/IJH [2003] EOAR 29.

[137] [1995] EOAR 17 and Söderman 'A Thousand and One Complaints', *supra* n. 58, at 353.

[138] [1997] EOAR 26; Complaint 760/24.7.96/JC/UK/IJH [1998] EOAR 150, 153.

and, more specifically, to the formal positions it adopts as an institution,[139] the decisions of its Committees,[140] the allocation of powers amongst its services,[141] and its internal organization.[142] Complaints against the merits of Community legislative acts such as regulations and directives have suffered the same fate.[143]

4. THE EUROPEAN OMBUDSMAN AND THE COMMUNITY COURTS

International experience shows that the institution of Ombudsman has been successfully employed as a vehicle for providing a speedy, free of charge, and informal alternative to administrative litigation. This holds also true of the European Ombudsman. Article 195 EC styles him as extra-judicial machinery through which grievances concerning poorly performed Community administrative services can be inexpensively voiced and processed. No-cost accessibility, procedural flexibility, and deliberative promptness figure amongst the most obvious attractions of the Ombudsman scheme. Unlike the European Ombudsman, Community courts lack any proactive

[139] [1995] EOAR 20, where reference is made to Complaint 281, which was declared inadmissible, because it concerned the position taken by the EP in respect of the French nuclear tests in the Pacific.

[140] [1995] EOAR 18: '[F]or example, Complaints against the political work of the European Parliament or its organs, such as decisions of the Committee on petitions, [are regarded as inadmissible]'. See also [1995] EOAR 20 and 29, [1997] EOAR 26, as well as Complaint 1152/97/OV et al. [1999] EOAR 89, 93. Complaint 332/2001/AT (not reported) was declared inadmissible given that it concerned a decision of the Committee on Civil Liberties, Justice and Home Affairs of the European Parliament.

[141] Complaint 1243/2000/PB [2000] EOAR 18.

[142] Complaint 420/9.2.96/PLMP/B [1996] EOAR 15, where the administrative handling of petitions by the Petitions Committee was considered to be a matter falling within the EP's responsibility to organize its own services and as such was deemed to raise issues of a political nature rather than questions of maladministration. See, however, Complaint 569/97/IJH [1997] EOAR 177 in conjunction with Complaint 287/99/ADB [2000] EOAR 96, at 98 and Complaint 1250/2000/(JSA)IJH [2001] EOAR 101, at 104, where matters of internal organization were fully investigated. The running of competitions for the selection of temporary agents by the Parliament's political groups constitutes an administrative activity falling within the Ombudsman's ambit, Complaint 1163/97/JMA [1999] EOAR 27.

[143] [1995] EOAR 18. See also, Complaint 262/27.11.95/APF/PO/EF-po [1997] EOAR 206, at 208; Complaint 829/22.8.96/FDR/D/PD [1998] EOAR 62, at 67; Complaint 1048/21.11.96/FPR/ES/JMA [1998] EOAR 80, at 82; Complaint 579/99/JMA [2001] EOAR 29, at 30. Complaint 1375/2001/AT (not reported) was declared inadmissible for it concerned the merits of the Community provisions regulating the administrative treatment of EU nationals residing in a Member State other than that of their origin. On the question of determining whether the measure under investigation is legislative or administrative see Complaint 1487/99/IJH [2000] EOAR 126, at 128.

capacity and their adjudicative role is therefore confined within the limits of the issues raised by litigation. Contrary to what is the case with courts, the Ombudsman's investigative authority is limited by secrecy-related considerations and his coercive remedial competence is non-existent.

One of the key issues pertaining to the institutional relationship between the European Ombudsman and the Community judiciary is the dovetailing of their respective jurisdictional areas. The concept of maladministration results in a jurisdictional divide based on the geometric logic of concentric circles. The inner ring relates to matters falling under the rubric of legality and it is shared by the Ombudsman and the Community courts. The concern here is the duplication of investigations and the dangers attendant upon such a practice, including the formulation of differing sets of values to assess the same factual circumstances and the dissimilar application of a single set of values. Both the EC Treaty and the Statute address the problem of jurisdictional conflict by according the judicial interpretation precedence over that of the Ombudsman. It has already been stressed that the Ombudsman is authorized neither to inquire into the judicial activities of the Community courts nor to investigate facts that are or have been the subject of legal proceedings. If such proceedings are in progress or have been concluded, the Ombudsman has to declare the complaint inadmissible or terminate its consideration, and file definitively the outcome of any enquiries he has carried out up to that point. It should also be recalled that the Ombudsman may not intervene in cases before courts or question the soundness of a court's ruling. The combined effect of the foregoing institutional restraints is that once a case is brought before the ECJ or the CFI, the latter assert jurisdictional superiority over the Ombudsman who is barred from challenging the judicial wisdom.

The outer ring of the concentric circle pertains to issues regulated by the non-legally binding rules and principles that for the purposes of the Ombudsman's inquiries ought to be respected by the Community administrative machinery. The Ombudsman enjoys full monopoly over this jurisdictional area and has consistently sought to stretch its boundaries outwards through the introduction of an expanding array of soft law obligations on Community bureaucracy.[144] This is exemplified by a line of cases pertaining to the role of individual parties in the infringement proceedings under Article 226 EC. Notwithstanding the acknowledged importance of the individual complainant for the infringement procedure,[145] the Commission has consist-

[144] Bonnor, 'The European Ombudsman: A Novel Source of Soft Law in the European Union' (2000) 25 *ELRev* 39.

[145] 20th Annual Report on Monitoring the Application of Community law for 2002, COM(2003) 669, available at <http://europa.eu.int/comm/secretariat_general/sgb/droit_com/pdf/rapport_annuel/20_rapport_annuel_en.htm>.

ently viewed the law enforcement mechanism of Article 226 as a bilateral bargaining game between itself and the defaulting Member State, rather than a triangular construct whereby private parties are treated as equal and respectable institutional interlocutors.[146] Similarly, the Community judiciary refused to recognize procedural rights to individuals as they were not formally seen as parties to the infringement procedure and left the Commission with a wide margin of discretion as to its final decision.[147] The Ombudsman, unlike Community courts, did not confine himself to addressing the issue of what was legally demanded of the Commission, the inner jurisdictional circle, but extended his investigation to the question of what was ethically expected of it, the outer jurisdictional circle. Through the initiation of an inquiry of his own volition[148] and through his reactive dealing with complaints, the Ombudsman managed to reshape the Commission's perception of the role that individual parties play in the enforcement procedure and established a series of commitments that the Commission ought to fulfil in the everyday handling of citizens' complaints concerning the compliance of Member States with EU norms.[149] Thus far the Commission has committed itself to registering the complaints and informing their authors accordingly,[150] obtaining replies from the Member States,[151] concluding the investigation of complaints within one year except in special cases,[152] keeping the complainants informed of the action taken in response to their complaints,[153]

[146] Rawlings, 'Engaged Elites Citizen Action and Institutional Attitudes in Commission Enforcement' (2000) 6 *ELJ* 4.

[147] Case T-191/99, *Petrie v Commission* [2001] ECR II-3677.

[148] OI 303/97/PD [1997] EOAR 270.

[149] Commission Communication to the European Parliament and the European Ombudsman, On Relations with the Complainant in Respect of Infringements of Community Law, COM(2002) 141 final, OJ 2002 C 244/5; Harden, 'What Future for the Centralized Enforcement of Community law?' [2002] *CLP* 496; Munoz, 'La participation du plaignant a la procédure en infraction au droit communautaire diligentée par la Commission' (2003) 472 *Revue du Marché Commun et de L'Union Européenne* 610.

[150] Complaint 1267/99/ME [2001] EOAR 132; Complaint 1194/2000/JMA [2001] EOAR 161; Complaint 1767/2001/GG [2002] EOAR 161.

[151] Complaint 259/27.11.95/PL/UK/PD [1997] EOAR 59; Complaint 583/3.5.96/MFCL/IT/KT [1997] EOAR 105.

[152] Complaint 190/97/DT [1997] EOAR 151; Complaint 1060/97/OV [1999] EOAR 75; Complaint 1075/97/IJH [1999] EOAR 118; Complaint 783/1.8.96/LBR/ES/KH(JMA) [1999] EOAR 212; Complaint 715/98/IJH [2000] EOAR 39; Complaint 1237/2002/(PB)OV [2003] EOAR 151.

[153] Complaints 206/27.10.95/HS/UK et al [1996] EOAR 59; Complaint 132/21.9.95/AH/EN [1996] EOAR 67; Complaint 259/27.11.95/PL/UK/PD [1997] EOAR 59; Complaint 956/18.10.96/RM/B/PD [1997] EOAR 245; Complaint 651/97/IJH [1999] EOAR 111; Complaint 472/6.3.96/XP/ES/PD [1999] EOAR 191; Complaint 250/97/OV [1999] EOAR 236; Complaint 715/98/IJH [2000] EOAR 39; Complaint 396/99/IP [2000] EOAR 66; Complaint 879/99/IP [2000] EOAR 114; Complaint 1288/99/OV [2002] EOAR 98.

stating adequate, clear, and sufficient reasons for its decisions,[154] and providing the complainants with sufficient information and time to prepare and submit observations before the closure of their cases.[155] The Ombudsman also considers that it is not only the procedural treatment of the complainant, but also the substantive assessment of the complaint that falls within his oversight purview.[156]

A further central aspect of the institutional relationship between the European Ombudsman and the Community judiciary is the susceptibility of the Ombudsman's decisions to judicial review. A possible way to challenge the Ombudsman's findings directly is the action for annulment in Article 230 EC. However the Ombudsman does not figure in the list of institutions that can be defendants in a legality challenge. Even if this hurdle could be overcome through an expansive reading of Article 230(1),[157] the question that would arise would be whether the Ombudsman's decisions fall within the range of acts that are reviewable. The *ACSV* case provides us with some helpful guidance in this respect.[158] The case was concerned with a failure to act under Article 232 EC. The CFI concluded that the European Ombudsman did not qualify as a Community institution for the purposes of Article 232(3) and that his reports following investigations were not amenable to annulment proceedings and, by extension, to actions for failure to act by reason of the fact that they did not produce any legal effects vis-à-vis the complainant or third parties.[159] It is worthy of note that this concerns the reports that the Ombudsman drafts after he has concluded his investigations and established an instance of maladministration. It does not seem to extend to decisions declaring, for example, a complaint to be inadmissible. In such cases it could be argued that the decisions of the Ombudsman do produce legal effects and should therefore be considered reviewable given that they prevent the complainant from asserting his right to have his grievances examined pursuant to Article 195 EC.

The legality of the Ombudsman's decisions can also be indirectly examined through an action for damages under Article 288(2) EC, provided that the applicant can show that the conditions for liability are fulfilled. Thus the applicant will need to prove a sufficiently serious breach of a rule of law intended to confer rights on individuals, damage, and a causal link between

[154] Complaint 323/97/PD [1999] EOAR 145; Complaint 396/99/IP [2000] EOAR 66; Complaint 995/98/OV [2001] EOAR 116; Complaint 493/2000/ME [2001] EOAR 144.

[155] Complaint 396/99/IP [2000] EOAR 66; Complaint 995/98/OV [2001] EOAR 116.

[156] Complaint 764/9.7.96/TH/DK/PD [1998] EOAR 51; Complaint 831/98/(PD)GG [2000] EOAR 49; Complaint 879/99/IP [2000] EOAR 114; Complaint 1288/99/OV [2002] EOAR 98; Complaint 39/2002/OV [2002] EOAR 164.

[157] Case 294/83, *Parti Ecologiste 'Les Verts' v European Parliament* [1986] ECR 1339.

[158] Case T-103/99, *Associazione delle Cantine Sociali Venete v European Ombudsman and Parliament* [2000] ECR II-4165

[159] Ibid. at paras. 47–51.

the two previous elements.[160] The CFI and ECJ left little doubt that actions seeking to establish extra-contractual liability for decisions of the Ombudsman were admissible in principle.[161] However the wide discretion the Ombudsman enjoys when dealing with complaints and assessing their merits renders it difficult to prove a sufficiently serious breach, thereby reducing the chances of a successful action. Notwithstanding this, it is, as the CFI and ECJ held, possible that in very exceptional circumstances the Ombudsman might commit a flagrant and manifest error in the performance of his duties that could causally result in damage to an individual.[162] Such cases might more readily arise when the cause of the alleged damage is not the Ombudsman's substantive findings, but his procedural conduct, for example, conclusion of inquiries with unreasonable delay[163] and disclosure of confidential information relating to his investigations.[164]

5. CONCLUSION

There will be no attempt to summarize the analysis presented above. It is, however, important to reflect on the evolution of the Ombudsman within the Union institutional system. Within less than a decade the European Ombudsman has succeeded in accumulating an increasing degree of political acceptance and institutional respect, which has allowed the office of Ombudsman to change over time. The office has evolved from being contested within the Union constitutional framework in the middle 1990s, to a position in the first half of the 2000s in which the Ombudsman is the largely uncontested protagonist in the field of extra-judicial protection against Community maladministration. It is undoubtedly true that the impact of the Ombudsman's investigations on the administrative functioning of the Union is hard to quantify, and the question of whether his record to date falls short of the results hoped for still remains a question open to debate. It is, however, difficult to deny that the European Ombudsman has contributed towards improving the protection of citizen's rights and interests in the Union, and has fostered the fashioning of a healthier administrative ethos for Community governance, considerable achievements the importance of which should not be underestimated.

160 See, e.g., Case C-472/00 P, *Commission v Fresh Marine* [2003] ECR I-7541.

161 Case T-209/00, *Frank Lamberts v European Ombudsman* [2002] ECR II-2203, at paras. 45–60; Case C-234/02 P, *European Ombudsman v Frank Lamberts* [2004] ECR I-2803, at paras. 31–71. See also, E. Combreros Mendazona, 'Responsabilidad Patrimonial del Defensor del Pueblo Europeo?' (2002) 159 *Revista de Administracion Publica* 209.

162 Case T-209/00, *Lamberts, supra* n. 161, at para. 57 and Case C-234/02 P, *Lamberts, supra* n. 161, at para. 52.

163 Case T-209/00, *supra* n. 161, at paras. 73–77.

164 Case C-234/02 P, *supra* n. 161, at para. 35.

CONCLUSION

Index

AAR 24
ABM Steering Group 25
abuse of administrative power
see also **judicial review**
control by courts 30
access 313–47
see also **process**
consultation 316–18
agencies 327–28
Community legislation according 322–24
soft law 324–27
generally 313–14
initial determination
consultation 316–18
generally 314
individual decisions 314–16
legislative norms 316–18
participation 316–18, 322–24
political process 322–31
principle and policy 318–22
right to be heard 314–16, 322
soft law 324–27
meaning 313
participation 316–18, 322–24
agencies 327–28
Community legislation according 322–24
political process 328–30
soft law 324–27
standing *see* standing
acte clair
preliminary reference procedure 303
activity-based management
ABM Steering Group 25
Commission 22, 25
meaning 25
politically meaningful activities 25
priority setting 25
White Paper on the Reform of the Commission 22
Adonnino Committee 831
affirmative action
sex discrimination 595–98
age discrimination 603
agencies
accountability
Agency Regulation 164–65
Commission, agencies created by 164–65
composition 170–73
Constitutional Treaty 165–67
contractual liability 164
Council, agencies created by 165
criteria, specification of 169–70
financial accountability 180–82
internal appeals 164
judicial review 167–68
legal 164–68
networks 176–79
non-contractual liability 164
participation of agencies 179–80
political 168–80
references to Commission 165
reporting 169–70
tasks, specification of 169–70
transparency 175–76
work programme, agency 173–75
administrative board 170–71
appointments 172, 187
basis of creation 150
classification 152–60
alternative view 154–60
Commission view 153–54
decision-making agencies 155
executive agencies 153
information and coordination agencies 156–60
quasi-regulatory agencies 155–56

agencies (*cont.*):
classification (*cont.*):
reasons for classification 152
regulatory agencies 153–55
Commission Communication 146, 162
Community Fisheries Control Agency (CFCA) 150
Community Plant Variety Office (CPVO) 149, 153
composition 170–73
administrative board 170–71
appointments 172
Community agencies 171–72
Council agencies 172–73
director 172
future regime 187–88
general structure 170
governing board 170–71
management board 170–71
Constitutional Treaty 163, 165–67
consultation 327–28
Council origins of 151
decision-making agencies 155
director 172
Draft Interinstitutional Agreement 162, 171–72
Eurojust 151, 158, 172
European Agency for Safety and Health at Work (EU-OSHA) 149, 157, 165, 171–72
European Agency for the Management of Operational Cooperation at the External Borders (FRONTEX) 152
European Agency for Reconstruction (EAR) 149
European Aviation Safety Agency (EASA) 153, 155, 164, 169–70, 172, 174, 177, 179, 180, 327–28
European Centre for the Development of Vocational Training (Cedefop) 148–49
European Centre for Disease Prevention and Control (ECDC) 150, 165, 177
European Chemicals Agency (ECA) 150
European Defence Agency (EDA) 151, 152, 172
European Environment Agency (EEA) 149, 157
European Food Safety Authority (EFSA) 149–50, 153, 175, 176, 177, 179
European Foundation for the Improvement of Living and Working Conditions (EUROFOUND) 149
European Maritime Safety Agency (EMSA) 150, 157, 173, 174, 178
European Medicines Agency (EMEA) 149, 153
European Monitoring Centre for Drugs and Drug Addiction (EMCDDA) 149
European Monitoring Centre on Racism and Xenophobia (EUMC) 149, 150, 164, 177, 541
European Network and Information Security Agency (ENISA) 150, 158, 179
European Parliament and 150–51
European Police College (Cepol) 151, 152
European Railway Agency (ERA) 150
European Training Foundation (ETF) 149
European Union Agency for Fundamental Rights 150
European Union Institute for Security Studies (EUISS) 151, 152, 172
European Union Satellite Centre (EUSC) 151, 152, 172
Europol 151, 152, 158, 173
evolution 148–52
executive *see* **executive agencies**
existing regime 182–83
financial accountability 180–82

Financial Regulation, new 180–82
first wave 148–49, 150
food safety 149, 150
future regime
generally 183
legal constraints 185–86
political constraints 186–90
rationale for EU agencies 183–85
governing board 170–71
increased use 143
information and coordination agencies 156–60
judicial review 167–68
legal limits 160–62
legal personality 164
legislative veto 189–90
limits
Constitutional Treaty 163
delegation, unlawful 160–62
generally 160
legal 160–62
Meroni principle 160–62, 164
political 162–64
management board 170–71
Meroni principle 160–62, 164, 183–85, 186, 190
nation states, rationale in 143–45
networks 176–79
Office for Harmonization in the Internal Market (OHIM) 149, 153, 155, 164
participation 179–80, 327–28
political limits 162–64
quasi-regulatory agencies 155–56
rationale
EU agencies 145–48
nation state, in 143–45
regulatory 153–155
regulatory impact assessment 188–89
reporting 169–70, 187
second wave 149, 150
tasks, specification of 169–70, 186
third wave 149–50
Translation Centre for Bodies of the European Union (CdT) 149
transparency 175–76
work programme 173–75
Agency for Trans-Mediterranean Networks (ARTM) 7–8
Agenda 2000
Common Agricultural Policy 59, 60
agriculture
Common Agricultural Policy *see* **Common Agricultural Policy**
European Agricultural Fund for Rural Development (EAFRD) 68
European Agricultural Guidance and Guarantee Fund (EAGGF) 19, 60–61, 64, 70
single farm payment 60
air safety
European Aviation Safety Agency (EASA) 153, 155, 164, 169–70, 172, 174, 177, 179, 180, 327–28
AMPs 24
Annual Activity Report (AAR) 24, 29
Annual Management Plans (AMPs) 24
Annual Policy Strategy Decision (APS) 24
annulment
see also **remedies**
Art 231 EC 755, 756–58, 761–63
Art 233 EC 755, 758–63
assessment 763–64
damages 765–766
direct actions
Art 231 755, 756–58
Art 233 EC 755, 758–61
indirect actions 761–63
meaning 749
anti-dumping
proportionality 665–66
APS 24
ARTM 7
audit
Audit Progress Committee 23, 28
Internal Audit Service *see* **Internal Audit Service**

audit (*cont.*):
White Paper on the Reform of the Commission 22, 23

Barrosso Commission 24
Belle Group 66
blasphemy 489
broadcasting
rights 489
Budget Commissioner 27

***Calpak* test** 332–33
CAP *see* **Common Agricultural Policy**
causation
damages 775–77
CdT 149
Cedefop 148–49
CEEP 236
Central Financial Service 27
centralized management *see* **direct/centralized management**
Cepol 151, 152
certainty, legal *see* **legal certainty**
CF 70, 74
CFCA 150
CFI *see* **Court of First Instance (CFI)**
CFS 73–74, 76, 77, 79, 83
Charter of Fundamental Rights 487
abuse of rights 496
application, scope of 504–505
Articles 495–97
background 492–94
Citizens' Rights 496
competence and power of EU, effect on 506–08
Constitutional Treaty 497
consultation on 494
content 494–97
Dignity 495
direct and vertical effect distinguished 498–501, 505
draft 493
ECHR, relationship with 523–32
absence of accession 525–31
accession 531–32
corresponding rights 523–24
modification of ECHR rights 524
same meaning and scope given to Charter rights 524–25
effect 498–501
Equality 495, 498
Freedoms 495
General Provisions 496
genesis 492–94
horizontal effect 505
implementation 502–503
institutional structure 493
institutions and bodies of the Union 498–99
international law, relationship with 535–37
interpretation
Community legislation and 518–20
consistent interpretation 517–23
courts' jurisprudence 520–22
ECHR, relationship with 523–32
existing EU law 517–23
international law, relationship with 535–37
limitation clause 496, 512–17
national constitutions, relationship with 532–35
replication in Charter 522–23
rights and principles 508–12
Treaty rights and 518
Justice 496
legal status 538–39
level of protection 496, 533–35
limitation clause 496, 512–17
national constitutions, relationship with 532–35
generally 532
interpretative obligation 533
substantive obligation 533–35
normative argument 499–501
outline 494–97
position prior to 488–92
process 385–87
remedies 537–38
replication in 522–23

rights and principles 508–12
scope of guaranteed rights 496
sex discrimination 587
Solidarity 495–96
standing 346–47
status 538–39
subsidiarity 498
vertical impact 498–01, 505

Charter of the Internal Audit Service 37

chemicals
European Chemicals Agency (ECA) 150

citizenship 565–76

co-decision procedure
creation 108
Treaty on European Union (TEU) 108

Code of Conduct for Commissioners 17

Code of Good Administrative Behaviour 280–81
introduction of 23

Cohesion Fund (CF)
Structural Funds 70, 74–75, 77

comitology
advisory committee procedure 114
approaches 113
basic committee procedures 107–108
birth of 104–105
Common Agricultural Policy 104
consensual deliberation 116–17
constitutional hierarchy of norms 124–26
Constitutional Treaty 112–13, 124–26
content of secondary rules 100–101
delegated regulations 126–28
controls over 128–31
ex ante control 128–29
ex post control 129–31
deliberative supranationalism
consensual deliberation 116–17
European Parliament 117–19
participatory rights 119–21
thesis 114–15
democracy 131–40
paradigm 99–100
European Parliament view 108–109, 117–19
First Comitology Decision 106–108
generally 99
hierarchy of norms 124–26
implementing Acts 127–28
legislative mandate 131–34
legitimation
bottom, from 134–40
top, from 131–34
Luxembourg Crisis 104
management committee procedure 104–105
legitimacy 105–106
methodology 105
methods of making secondary norms 100
nature of problem 99–102
'original intent' 102–104
participation rights 119–21, 134–40
political choice 101
primary legislation, subject matter of 100
regulations 126–27
Second Comitology Decision 110–11
Single European Act (SEA) 106–108
technocracy 121–24
Treaty of Amsterdam 110
Treaty on European Union (TEU) 108
Treaty of Nice 111–12

Comitology Committee
creation 74
executive agencies 38

Commission
ABM Steering Group 25
activity-based management 22, 25
Annual Activity Report (AAR) 24, 29
annual planning cycle 24
Annual Policy Strategy Decision (APS) 24
Audit Progress Committee 28

Commission (*cont.*):
Budget Commissioner 27
Central Financial Service 27
Code of Good Administrative Behaviour 23, 280–81
comitology *see* **comitology**
Committee of Independent Experts *see* **Committee of Independent Experts**
culture based on service and ethical standards 23–24
DECODE exercise 21
direct management *see* **direct/centralized management**
Directorate-General
Annual Activity Report (AAR) 24
Annual Management Plans (AMPs) 24
efficient use of resources 21–22, 24–25
enforcement actions *see* **enforcement actions**
ethical and professional standards 23–24
externalization policy 22
financial management and control 22–23, 25–28
Audit Progress Committee 28
Budget Commissioner 27
Central Financial Service 27
centralized management *see* **direct/centralized management**
constitutionalization 26
decentralized management 27–28
direct management 26
Financial Regulation, new *see* **Financial Regulation, new**
Internal Audit Service 23, 28
shared management 26, 27
see also **shared management**
Financial Regulation, new *see* **Financial Regulation, new**
Group of Resource Directors 25
Internal Audit Service 23, 28
internal coordination 17
Interservice Coordination Group 25
Legislative and Work Programme 24
policy coordination 25
priority setting 17, 24–25
Prodi Commission *see* **Prodi Commission**
public access to documents 23–24
reform 23–28
responsibilities 17
Rules of Procedure, revision under Prodi Commission of 17
Santer Commission, fall of 3–12
see also **Committee of Independent Experts**
service delivery
contracting out 15–16
staff shortages 12, 13–15
staff
appraisal 25
discipline 24, 25
early retirement 25
mobility 25
pay 25
pensions 25
policy 25
promotion 25
Regulations 25
serious wrongdoing 24
shortages 12, 13–15
under-performance 24
Synthesis Report 24
Task Force for Administrative Reform (TFRA) 17
White Paper on the Reform of the Commission *see* **White Paper on the Reform of the Commission**
working groups 17
Commissioners
code of conduct 17
Committee of Independent Experts 28
background 3–4
Common Agricultural Policy 65
contracting out 15–16, 18, 32, 53
service delivery, as 15–16

convening 3–4
core of minimum standards 4
detailed critique 6–11
direct management 18
direct/centralized management 18–19, 35
European Community Humanitarian Office (ECHO) 8–9, 12
executive agencies 37
First Report
conclusions 11–12
effect 4
function 5
importance 12
media reaction 4–5
production of 4
reflections on 12–16
fraud 4, 6, 20
Leonardo da Vinci programme 9–10, 12
mandate 4
MED programmes 7–8, 12
mismanagement 4
nepotism 4
nuclear safety 10–11
origin 3–4
reaction of Commission 53
Santer Commission, fall of 3–12
Second Report 5, 17, 18–20
contracting out 18
control environment 20
direct management 18–19
European Agricultural Guidance and Guarantee Fund (EAGGF) 19
fraud 20
implementing agencies 19
importance 18
internal audit systems 20
publication 18
recommendations 18–20
shared management 19–20
Structural Funds 19–20
technical assistance offices 18
shared management 19–20, 57
staff shortages 12, 13–15
Structural Funds 78, 79
technical assistance offices 18
terms of reference 4
tourism 6–7
White Paper on the Reform of the Commission 21
committees
comitology *see* **comitology**
Common Agricultural Policy (CAP)
accreditation of paying agencies 61–62, 63, 65, 68–69
administrative reforms 68
Agenda 2000 59, 60
certified accounts 62, 63
collective interest and individual Member States' interests, tensions between 62
comitology 104
Committee of Independent Experts 65
conciliation procedure 65–66
discretion in operation 658–64
discrimination 58
ECJ, contribution of 66–68
equality 579–80
European Agricultural Fund for Rural Development (EAFRD) 68
European Agricultural Guidance and Guarantee Fund (EAGGF) 60–61, 64, 68
export refunds 63
foundations 579
fraud 3
future of 68–69
General Agreement on Tariffs and Trade (GATT) and 59
income support 58–60
irregularities, discovery and recovery of 63–64
law and 62–69
conciliation procedure 65–66
design, legislative 63–64
ECJ, contribution of 66–68
formal legal change, effectiveness of 64–65
incentives for compliance 63–64

Common Agricultural Policy (CAP) (*cont.*):
law and (*cont.*):
objectives, legislative 62
pressure from Member States 64
tensions 62
undermining 64
new regime 60
non-discrimination 579–80
objectives 58, 659
powers of Commission 69
price support 58, 59
production and marketing aids 58
proportionality 658–64
quotas 59
reform 60
regulations governing 29–30
shared management 57, 58–69
accreditation of paying agencies 61–62
certified accounts 62
clearance of accounts 61
ECJ, contribution of 66–68
enabling provision 61
European Agricultural Guidance and Guarantee Fund (EAGGF) 60–61
framework 60–62
future of CAP 68–69
income support 59–60
law and 62–69
objectives of CAP 58
price support 58–60
timetables for accounting compliance 62
Treaty foundations 58
single farm payment 60
storage arrangements 58
timetables for accounting compliance 62
Treaty foundations 58
World Trade Organization (WTO) negotiations 60

Common Foreign and Security Policy (CFSP)
European Union Satellite Centre (EUSC) 151, 152, 172
Community Fisheries Control Agency (CFCA) 150
Community Plant Variety Office (CPVO) 149, 153
Community Support Framework (CFS) 73–74, 76, 77, 79, 83
compensation *see* **damages**
competence
attributed power 401
Constitutional Treaty
external competence 416–18
internal competence 403–404
Convention on the Future of Europe 402, 403
division of 401–404
external
Constitutional Treaty 416–18
cooperation 415–16
early case law 410–12
ERTA ruling 413–15
exclusive, whether 412–15, 416–18
express competence 411
generally 410
implied competence 411–12
legal basis of adoption of international agreement 411
legal personality of EC 410
legal personality of EU 410
limits 412–13
mixed agreements 416
negotiation of international agreements 411
Open Skies case 413–15
shared competence 415–16
WTO case 412–13
generally 401
grant 402–403
implied power 406–407
internal
divisions between 401–404
generally 401

implied power 406–407
meaning 401–404
shared competence 401–404
Treaty articles 404–406
mixed agreements 416
necessity 407–10
power
Community objectives 407–410
implied 406–407
necessity 407–410
shared
external competence 415–16
internal competence 401–404
competition
manifest error 473, 478
process 375–76, 388–91
conciliation procedure
Common Agricultural Policy 65–66
conflict of interest
contracting out 53
Constitutional Treaty
agencies 163, 165–67
Charter of Fundamental Rights 497
comitology 112–13, 124–26
competence
external competence 416–18
internal competence 403–404
ratification 165
rights 543
standing 344–46
subsidiarity 424–25
White Paper on European Governance 112–13
constitutionalization
financial management and control 26
meaning 26
consultation
access 316–18
agencies 327–28
contracting out
authorizing officer 53
award of contracts 53
bodies to whom tasks can be assigned 52
Commission, by 15–16
Committee of Independent Experts 15–16, 18, 32, 53
conflict of interest 53
direct/centralized management 32–33, 34–35, 52–53
European Community Humanitarian Office (ECHO) 15
excluded tasks 52
executive agencies 52
Financial Regulation, new 52–53
fraud 53
implementing tasks 52
Leonardo da Vinci programme 15
MED programmes 15, 32
nuclear safety 32
private sector bodies 52
problems 15–16, 32, 52
reasons 32
reforms 52
service delivery via 15–16
specification of terms of contract 53
supervision 15
tender 53
terms of contract 53
types of activities 52
White Paper on the Reform of the Commission 16, 33
Convention on the Future of Europe
see also **Constitutional Treaty**
competence 402, 403
cooperation, principle of
judicial review 277–78
Council
public access to documents 23–24
role 29
Structural Funds, control over 70
Court of Auditors
audit recommendations, implementation of 23
generally 283–84
standing 331–32
Court of First Instance (CFI)
see also **courts**
caseload 286–90
competence 285–86

Court of First Instance (CFI) (*cont.*):
creation 284
direct actions 293–96
ECJ, relationship with 292–99
expertise 284
future of 292
jurisdictional responsibility 284–85, 291–99
precautionary principle 718
preliminary rulings 296–99
state aids 294

courts
see also **access; Court of Auditors; Court of First Instance (CFI); European Court of Justice (ECJ); national courts; process; standing**
caseload 286–90
delays 287
direct actions 288
enforcement actions 288
intensity of judicial oversight, limiting 290
judicial mechanism for limiting 288–90
preliminary references 288–89
rationale for problem 287–88
reform of judicial system 286
standing 28
techniques for reducing 289–90
Constitutional Treaty 310–12
distribution of jurisdictional competences 284–85, 291–92
reform objectives 291–92
structural features 284–85

CPVO 149, 153

damages
see also **remedies**
annulment 765–66
assessment of provisions 787–88
causation 775–77
Community servants 780–81
criteria for liability 764
damage 777–80
discretionary acts
current test 771–72
early case law 769–72
flagrant violation 769–72
general principles of law, infringement of 768
general test for recovery 766–67
hierarchically superior regulation, breach of 768
Schöppenstedt case 766–67, 769
superior rule of law 767–69
lawful acts 781–82
limitation period 764
non-contractual liability 764
non-discretionary acts
discretionary test and 773, 774
illegality, meaning of 774–75
test 773
traditional approach 773
Schöppenstedt case 766–67, 769
scope 764–65
servants, Community 780–81
significance as remedy 749
specific provision for 765
superior rule of law 767–69
test for actions against Community 764

decentralized management
financial management and control 27–28

Declaration of Fundamental Rights and Freedoms 487

DECODE exercise 21

defence
European Defence Agency (EDA) 151, 152, 172

democracy
social partners
associative democracy 252–53
Community democratic model 249–51
directly-deliberative polyarchy 253–54
functional democracy 254–55

neo-corporatism 254–55
participatory democracy 251–52

direct actions
annulment
Art 231 EC 755, 756–58
Art 233 EC 755, 758–61
caseload 288
European Court of Justice (ECJ) 293–96
interim measures 750–52
standing 288
Treaty provision 264

direct effect
Treaties 498

direct/centralized management 31–55
authorization of expenditure 35–36
collection of revenue 35
Commission, management by 34–37
Committee of Independent Experts 18–19, 35
contracting out 32–33, 34–35, 52–53
delivery 32–33
emergency aid 32
executive agencies, management by 37–50
see also **executive agencies**
financial management and control 26–27
Financial Regulation, new 26–27, 31, 33–34
authorization of expenditure 35–36
collection of revenue 35
conditions of delegation 33
contracting out 52–53
executive agencies, management by 37–50
see also **executive agencies**
framework 34
general principles 33–34
implementing tasks, clear delegation of 33
internal auditor 36–37
national public bodies 50–51
private sector bodies 34
proper control and accounting procedures 33–34
transparency 33
five choices of 34
framework 34
general principles 33–34
increase 32
initiatives, Commission 32
internal auditor 36–37
management tasks 34
meaning 32
MED programmes 32
modes 34
Commission, management by 34–37
contracting out 52–53
executive agencies, management by 37–50
see also **executive agencies**
five 34
national public bodies 50–51
network management 50–51
national public bodies 50–51
network management 50–51
nuclear safety 32
PHARE programme 32
private sector bodies 34
rationale 31–32
TACIS programme 32
tourism 32
traditional Community administration 31–32
transparency 33
vocational training 32
White Paper on the Reform of the Commission 35, 50

discrimination
age 603
citizenship 565–76
Common Agricultural Policy 58
equality
citizenship 565–76
economic rationale 559–60
four freedoms 547–49
Gravier case 565–67

discrimination (*cont.*):
equality (*cont.*):
implementation of Community legislation 564–65
interpretative device, Art 12 EC as 560–62
protector of objectives underlying four freedoms, Art 12 EC as 562–64
social rationale 559–60
Framework Directive 603
nationality *see* **nationality discrimination**
racial 602–603
religious 603
sex *see* **sex discrimination**
sexual orientation 599–602, 603
disease prevention and control
European Centre for Disease Prevention and Control (ECDC) 150, 165, 177
documents
public access 23–24
drugs
European Monitoring Centre for Drugs and Drug Addiction (EMCDDA) 149
Due report 293, 294, 296, 300, 302, 304, 306, 307, 308

EAFRD 68
EAGGF *see* **European Agricultural Guidance and Guarantee Fund (EAGGF)**
EAR 149
EASA 153, 155, 164, 169–70, 172, 174, 177, 179, 180, 327–28
ECA 150
ECDC 150, 165, 177
ECHO 8–9
ECJ *see* **European Court of Justice (ECJ)**
Economic and Monetary Union (EMU)
Open Method of Coordination 191
EDA 151, 152, 172
Educational, Audiovisual and Culture Executive Agency 47–49
EEA 149, 157
effectiveness, principle of
judicial review 277–78
EFSA 149–50, 153, 175, 176, 177, 179
EMCDDA 149
EMEA 149, 153, 174
emergency aid
direct/centralized management 32
employment
Open Method of Coordination 201–205
placement services 586
sex discrimination *see* **sex discrimination**
EMSA 150, 157, 173, 174, 178
enforcement actions
caseload 288
discretion of Commission 288
ENISA 150, 158, 179
enlargement of EU
Structural Funds 75
environment
precautionary principle and compliance of Member States with directives on 731–33
EP *see* **European Parliament**
equal pay 588–93
proportionality 698–701
equal treatment
equality 547–49
four freedoms 547–59
limits 595–600
proportionality 695–98
regulatory role 578–80
Common Agricultural Policy (CAP) 579–80
ECSC 579
sex discrimination 593–600
affirmative action 595–98
Directive 594–95
exceptions 594
gender reassignment 599–600

indirect discrimination 595
introduction of provisions 594
limits 595–600
sexual orientation 599–600

equality
age 603
arbitrariness 582–84
Art 12 EC
assessment of 576–78
Bidar case 573–75
citizenship 567–76
Collins case 575–76
economic rationale 559–60
Gravier case 565–67
Grzelczyk case 572–75
implementation of Community legislation 564–65
interpretative device 560–62
Martinez Sala case 569–72
scope of application of Treaty 565–76
social rationale 559–60
Trojani case 571–72
Art 13 EC 600–602
Art 141 EC *see* **sex discrimination**
Collins case 575–76
Common Agricultural Policy (CAP) 579–80
comparability and objective justification
arbitrariness 582–84
Royal Scholten-Honig 581–82
Ruckdeschel 581–82
conceptions 545
consistency, as 545
disability 603
discrimination
CAP 579–80
citizenship 565–76
economic rationale 559–60
four freedoms 547–49
Gravier case 565–67
implementation of Community legislation 564–65
interpretative device, Art 12 EC as 560–62
protector of objectives underlying four freedoms, Art 12 EC as 562–64
social rationale 559–60
express provision for 545
formal 545
four freedoms
benefits given to workers 551–555
discrimination 547–49
economic rationale 546–47
equal treatment 547–59
Gravier case 565–67
nationality discrimination 547–49
protector of objectives underlying, Art 12 EC as 562–64
public service exception 555–59
social rationale 546–47
worker, definition of 549–51
Framework Directive 603
generally 545–46
Gravier case 565–67
Grzelczyk case 572–75
Martinez Sala case 569–72
meaning 545
nationality discrimination 547–49
opportunity 545–46
Race Directive 602–603
regulatory role of equal treatment 578–80
Common Agricultural Policy (CAP) 579–80
ECSC 579
religion 603
results, of 545
Royal Scholten-Honig 581–82
Ruckdeschel 581–82
sex discrimination *see* **sex discrimination**
sexual orientation
economic rationale of Art 13 EC 600–602
social rationale of Art 13 EC 600–602
Trojani case 571–72

equality (*cont.*):
workers
benefits 551–55
definition 549–51
public service exception 555–59
ERA 150
ERDF 70
ESF 70
establishment, freedom of 692–94
ETF 149
ethical and professional standards
Code of Conduct 24
Commission 23–24
ETUC **236**
EU Network of Independent Experts on Fundamental Rights 540–41
EU-OSHA 149, 157, 165, 171–72, 177
EUISS 151, 152, 172
EUMC 149, 150, 164, 177
EUROFOUND 149
Eurojust
competence 159–60
establishment 151, 158
management board 173
purpose 159
European Agency for Safety and Health at Work (EU-OSHA) 149, 157, 165, 171–72, 177
European Agency for the Management of Operational Cooperation at the External Borders (FRONTEX) 152
European Agency for Reconstruction (EAR) 149
European Agricultural Fund for Rural Development (EAFRD)
Common Agricultural Policy 68
European Agricultural Guidance and Guarantee Fund (EAGGF)
Common Agricultural Policy 60–61, 64, 68
Guarantee section 19
Structural Funds 70
European Anti Fraud Office (OLAF) 182
European Aviation Safety Agency (EASA) 153, 155, 164, 169–70, 172, 174, 177, 179, 180, 327–28
European Central Bank
standing 332
European Centre for the Development of Vocational Training (Cedefop) 148–49
European Centre for Disease Prevention and Control (ECDC) 150, 165, 177
European Centre of Enterprises with Public Participation and of Enterprises of General Economic Interest (CEEP) 236
European Chemicals Agency (ECA) 150
European Community Humanitarian Office (ECHO)
Committee of Independent Experts 8–9, 12
contracting out 15
European Convention on Human Rights (ECHR)
see also **rights**
accession of Community to 486, 491
Charter of Fundamental Rights, relationship with 523–32
absence of accession 525–31
accession 531–32
corresponding rights 523–24
modification of ECHR rights 524
same meaning and scope given to Charter rights 524–25
EC, relationship with 490–91
European Court of Justice (ECJ)
see also **courts**
CFI, relationship with 292–99
Common Agricultural Policy, decisions on 66–68
competence 285–86

decentralized judicial bodies, proposal for creation of 307–10
direct actions 293–96
failure to act 294
jurisdictional responsibility 284–85, 291–92
precautionary principle 718–19
preliminary reference procedure 285–86, 288–90, 296–99
Structural Funds, case law on 91–93
workload 284, 286–90
European Defence Agency (EDA) 151, 152, 172
European Employment Strategy 191, 201–205
European Environment Agency (EEA) 40, 149, 157
European Food Safety Authority (EFSA) 149–50, 153, 175, 176, 177, 179
European Foundation for the Improvement of Living and Working Conditions (EUROFOUND) 149
European Union Institute for Security Studies (EUISS) 151, 152, 172
European Maritime Safety Agency (EMSA) 150, 157, 173, 174, 178
European Medicines Agency (EMEA) 149, 153, 174
European Monitoring Centre for Drugs and Drug Addiction (EMCDDA) 149
European Monitoring Centre on Racism and Xenophobia (EUMC) 149, 150, 164, 177, 541
European Network and Information Security Agency (ENISA) 150, 158, 179
European Ombudsman *see* **Ombudsman**
European Parliament
agencies and 150–51
comitology, view on 108–109, 117–19
Declaration of Fundamental Rights and Freedoms 487
Open Method of Coordination and 218–21
public access to documents 23–24
role 29
European Police College (Cepol) 151
European Political Community (EPC) 484
European Racism and Xenophobia Information Network (Raxen) 177
European Railway Agency (ERA) 150
European Regional Development Fund (ERDF) 70
see also **Structural Funds**
European Security and Defence Policy
European Defence Agency (EDA) 151, 172
European Social Fund (ESF) 70
see also **Structural Funds**
European Strategy for Employment
Structural Funds 77
European Training Foundation (ETF) 149
European Union Agency for Fundamental Rights 150, 541–43
European Union Satellite Centre (EUSC) 151, 152, 172
Europol 151, 152, 158
Convention 159
management board 173
objectives 159
EUSC 151, 152, 172
excessive deficit procedure 197–201
executive agencies 153
see also **agencies**
approval 38
authorizing officer 40
capacity, legal 38
Comitology Committee 38
Committee of Independent Experts 37

executive agencies (*cont.*):
conjunction of power and responsibility 42
contracting out 52
contractual liability 40
cost-benefit analysis 38
creation 37
damages liability 40–41
delegation 39
direct/centralized management 37–50
director 38
Educational, Audiovisual and Culture Executive Agency 47–49
establishment 37–38
European Environment Agency 40
Executive Agency for the Public Health Programme 49–50
financial arrangements 39–40
Financial Regulation, new 37
first agencies 43–50
grounds for review 41–42
head of 38
Intelligent Energy Executive Agency 43–47
internal review of decisions 41–42
legal design issues 42–43
legal status 38
lifetime 38
location 38
meaning 37
meetings 38
Meroni principle 42
non-contractual liability 40
origins 37
regulation on 37
review of legality 40–43
staff 38
Steering Committee 38
tasks 38–39
temporary 38
winding-up 38

Executive Agency for the Public Health Programme 49–50

failure to act
European Court of Justice (ECJ) 294
Treaty provision 263

financial management and control
see also **audit**
Budget Commissioner 27
Central Financial Service 27
centralized management 26–27
Commission 22–23, 25–28
Audit Progress Committee 28
Budget Commissioner 27
Central Financial Service 27
centralized management *see* **direct/centralized management**
constitutionalization 26
decentralized management 27–28
direct management *see* **direct/centralized management**
Financial Regulation, new *see* **Financial Regulation, new**
Internal Audit Service 23, 28
shared management 26, 27
constitutionalization 26
decentralized management 27–28
Financial Regulation, new 25, 26, 28, 29
Internal Audit Service 23
shared management 26, 27
see also **shared management**
White Paper on the Reform of the Commission 22, 25

Financial Regulation, new
agencies 180–82
authorization of expenditure 35–36
collection of revenue 35
contracting out 52–53
direct/centralized management 26–27, 31, 33–34
authorization of expenditure 35–36
collection of revenue 35
conditions of delegation 33
contracting out 52–53
executive agencies, management by 37–50
see also **executive agencies**

framework 34
general principles 33–34
implementing tasks, clear delegation of 33
internal auditor 36–37
national public bodies 50–51
network management 50–51
private sector bodies 34
proper control and accounting procedures 33–34
transparency 33
executive agencies, management by 37–50
see also **executive agencies**
financial management and control 25, 26, 28, 29
general principles 33–34
internal auditor 36–37
proper control and accounting procedures 33–34
shared management
generally 57
food safety
agencies 149, 150
European Food Safety Authority (EFSA) 149–50, 153, 175, 176, 177, 179
precautionary principle 743–46
four freedoms
discrimination 547–49
equality
benefits given to workers 551–55
discrimination 547–49
economic rationale 546–47
equal treatment 547–59
Gravier case 565–67
nationality discrimination 547–49
protector of objectives underlying, Art 12 EC as 562–64
public service exception 555–59
worker, definition of 549–51
establishment 692–94
goods
precautionary principle 719
proportionality 689–92
nationality discrimination 560–62
persons 692
precautionary principle 733–35
proportionality
establishment 692–94
generally 687–89
goods 689–92
persons 692
services, provision of 692–94
workers 692
protector of objectives underlying four freedoms, Art 12 EC as 562–64
services, provision of 692–94
fraud
Committee of Independent Experts 4, 6, 20
Common Agricultural Policy 3
contracting out 53
legal certainty 617
meaning 4
Member States' responsibility to counter 20
misappropriation of funds 4
free movement *see* **four freedoms**
FRONTEX 152
fundamental rights
see also **Charter of Fundamental Rights; European Convention on Human Rights (ECHR); rights**
European Union Agency for Fundamental Rights 150, 541–43
proportionality 674–78

GATT *see* **General Agreement on Tariffs and Trade (GATT)**
gender reassignment
sex discrimination 599–600
General Agreement on Tariffs and Trade (GATT)
Common Agricultural Policy and 59
***Gravier* case** 565–67
Group of Resource Directors 25

hard look doctrine 475–77
health and safety
European Agency for Safety and Health at Work (EU-OSHA) 149, 157, 165, 171–72, 177
heard, right to be 314–16, 322, 349
see also **access; process**
access to the file 365–69
causation 372–73
content 361–63
cross-examination 369–70
respond, right to 363–65
separation of functions 370–72
human resources
see also **staff**
appraisal 25
career structure 22
Commission 21, 22, 25
promotion 25
White Paper on the Reform of the Commission 21, 22, 25
human rights *see* **Charter of Fundamental Rights; European Convention on Human Rights (ECHR); rights**

Independent Audit Service 20
Intelligent Energy Executive Agency 43–47
Interactive Policy Making (IPM) 215
interim measures
application 751–52
assessment 754–55
burden of proof 751
direct actions 750–52
indirect actions 752–54
serious and irreparable damage 751
suspension of operation, application for 751
Internal Audit Service 23, 27–28
Charter 37
establishment 23, 28, 36–37
Financial Regulation, new 37
role 36
White Paper on the Reform of the Commission 23

IPM 215

judicial review
access *see* **access; standing**
access to information 264
acts producing legal effects 267–69
administrative efficacy 278–79
agencies 167–68
background principles 270–79
administrative efficacy 278–79
cooperation, principle of 277–78
effectiveness, principle of 277–78
institutional balance 273–77
rule of law 270–73
case law 266
Code of Good Administrative Behaviour 280–81
comptence *see* **competence**
cooperation, principle of 277–78
courts *see* **Court of First Instance (CFI); courts; European Court of Justice (ECJ)**
damages liability 278
discretion 266
see also law, fact and discretion *below*
classic 439–40, 442–44
contrast and similarity 444
jurisdictional 440–44
jurisdictional discretion plus classic discretion 442–44
manifest error 477–81
meaning 433–34
normative reflections on 445–46
positive reflections 445
secondary 440
substantive review 474–75
substitution of judgment 440
effectiveness, principle of 277–78
equality *see* **equality**
foundations 263–81
grounds 265–66
infringement of EC Treaty 265
infringement of essential procedural requirement 265

lack of competence 265
sources 265–266
infringement of EC Treaty 265
infringement of essential procedural requirement 265, 266
institutional balance 273–77
institutional capacity 473–74
justification 263–64
law, fact and discretion
constancy 446–64
discretion 433–34
fact 431–32, 464–74
see also standard of review *below*
generally 429–30
law 431
legal issues, review of 435–39
qualifications 438–39
substitution of judgment 435–38, 440
legal certainty *see* **legal certainty**
legal issues, review of 435–39
legitimate expectations *see* **legitimate expectations**
manifest error 266
Airtours case 452–53
common policies 458–60, 472
competition 473, 478
discretion 477–81
future of test 471
legitimacy 481
meaning 467–70
modern application 478–80
Pfizer case 447–52
risk regulation 473, 478
State aids 460–62
structural funds 462
Tetra Laval 453–57
misuse of power 462–64
non-discrimination 264–65
process *see* **process**
reasons, duty to give 264
remedies *see* **remedies**
reviewable acts 266–70
rights *see* **rights**
role 30
rule of law 270–73
sources of law 264–65
standard of review
applied by court 466–67
clarity, need for 471
differential test 471–73
future prospects 470–74
manifest error *see* **manifest error**
primary decision-maker, required of 465–66
proof, standard of 470–71
standing *see* **standing**
State aids 460–62
structural funds 462
subsidiarity *see* **subsidiarity**
substitution of judgment 435–38, 440, 478
use 30

Kok Task Force 193

law
limits 30
role of 29–30
legal certainty
see also **legitimate expectations**
actual retroactivity 607–10
arguments against allowing 607–608
basic principle 608
Community objective, pressing 609–10
construction, principle of 608–609
meaning 607
national rules implementing Community law 610
necessary 608
Racke case 608
rule of construction 608–609
rule of law 607–608
substantive constraints 609
apparent retroactivity 610–14
cases involving 611
fairness in public administration argument 612
fostering good administration 613

legal certainty (*cont.*):
apparent retroactivity (*cont.*):
impact 611
meaning 610–11
rationale for legal protection 611–12
reliance argument 612–13
rule of law 613
trust in government 613
change of policy 619–21
conditional decisions 618–19
fraud 617
misrepresentation 617
prospective revocation 626–27
revocation of lawful decisions
conditional decisions 618–19
consent to revocation 617
fraud 617
general principle 614–17
misrepresentation 617
revocation of unlawful decisions
balancing test 623–26
confidence in legality of measure 624–25
development of case law 623
extent of reliance before revocation 624
factors affecting 623–24
false or misleading information 624
illegality and legality, divide between 622
legality v justice 621–22
nature of problem 621–22
obvious illegality 625–26
public interest 621
reasonable time, within 624
SNUPAT case 623–24
rule of law 607–08, 613
use of concept 607
Legislative and Work Programme, Commission 24
legitimate expectations
see also **legal certainty**
alteration of policy 613–14
apparent retroactivity 610–14
cases involving 611
fairness in public administration argument 612
fostering good administration 613–14
impact 610
meaning 610–11
rationale for legal protection 611–12
reliance argument 612–13
rule of law 613
trust in government 613
balancing exercise
application of test 651–52
generally 649
nature of legal test 649–51
overriding public interest, whether 649–51
proportionality 651
reasoning of court 650–51
significant imbalance 650–51
standard of review 649
changes in policy
assurances 637–39
balancing exercise 639–41
bargain between individual and authorities 637–39
general principle 635–37
mutability 635–37
overriding public interest 639–41
public interest 639–41
departure from existing policy/guidelines
discretion inherent in or left by guidelines 648–49
fines 643–44, 648–49
general principle of binding guidelines 641–44
importance of guidelines/notices 642
judicial construction of guidelines 644–47
open textured guidelines 648
practice, policy established through 643–44

qualification to the general principle 647–48
scope of guidelines 647–48
state aids 642–43, 644–48
individual/specific representations made, departure from
conduct of representee 631–35
expectation not legitimate 634–35
form of representation 628
general framework of Community law, assessment within 633–34
irreversible investments made 630
legitimacy of the claim 633–35
nature of problem 628–31
precise and specific assurance 628–31
provisional statements 629
prudent trader 631–33
representee, conduct of 631–35
state aids 631
wrongdoing of applicant 634
policy changes
assurances 637–39
balancing exercise 639–41
bargain between individual and authorities 637–39
general principle 635–37
mutability 635–37
overriding public interest 639–41
public interest 639–41
proportionality 651
prospective revocation 626–27
proving existence of expectation 614
revocation of lawful decisions
conditional decisions 618–19
consent to revocation 617
fraud 617
general principle 614–17
misrepresentation 617
revocation of unlawful decisions
balancing test 623–24
confidence in legality of measure 624–25
development of case law 623
extent of reliance before revocation 624
factors affecting 623–24
false or misleading information 624
no reliance proven 626
obvious illegality 625–26
reasonable time, within 624
SNUPAT case 623–24
unproven expectation 625
rule of law 613
state aids 642–43, 644–48
substantive 612
unlawful representations
normative considerations 653–54
positive law 652–53
use of concept 607
Leonardo da Vinci programme 32
Committee of Independent Experts 9–10, 12
contracting out 15
Luxembourg Crisis 104

manifest error
Airtours case 452–53
common policies 458–60, 472
competition 473, 478
discretion 477–81
future of test 471
legitimacy 481
meaning 467–70
modern application 478–80
Pfizer case 447–52
risk regulation 473, 478
State aids 460–62
structural funds 462
Tetra Laval 453–57
margin of appreciation
rights 489
maritime safety
European Maritime Safety Agency (EMSA) 150, 157, 173, 174, 178
MED programmes
Agency for Trans-Mediterranean Networks (ARTM) 7–8
Committee of Independent Experts 7–8, 12

MED programmes (*cont.*):
conflicts of interest 8
contracting out 15, 32
criticism 7
direct/centralized management 32
purpose 7
technical assistance offices (TAOs) 7
***Meroni* principle**
agencies 160–62, 164, 183–85, 186, 190
executive agencies 42
mismanagement
Committee of Independent Experts 4
meaning 4
misrepresentation
legal certainty 617
misuse of power
judicial review 462–64

national courts
see also **courts**
Community courts, relationship with
decentralized judicial bodies, proposal for creation of 307–10
filtering mechanism for preliminary rulings 301–304
generally 299–300
judgment, giving 305–307
preliminary reference procedure 300–304
proposed reply to preliminary reference 304–305
enforcers of Community law 284
features 284
jurisdictional responsibility 285
preliminary reference procedure 300–301
proportionality, role in inquiry into 711–15
National Strategic Reference Framework (NSRF) 77, 78
nationality discrimination 547–49
Art 12 EC
economic rationale 559–60
interpretative device for four freedoms 560–62
social rationale 559–60
free movement 486–87, 547–49
protector of objectives underlying, Art 12 EC as 562–64
rights 486–87
network management
direct/centralized management 50–51
White Paper on the Reform of the Commission 50
non-discrimination
judicial review 264–65
NSRF 77, 78
nuclear safety
Committee of Independent Experts 10–11
contracting out 32
direct/centralized management 32

Office for Harmonization in the Internal Market (OHIM) 149, 153, 155
legality review 164
review of decisions 40
OHIM *see* **Office for Harmonization in the Internal Market (OHIM)**
OLAF 182
Ombudsman
Community courts 851–55
history 829–32
initiation of inquiries 833–39
introduction 829
investigative powers 840–43
maladministration
examples 847–48
legality, concept of 849–51
meaning 847
origins of concept 829–30
own initiative inquiries 838–39
powers 832–47
initiation of inquiries 833–39
investigative 840–43
own initiative inquiries 838–39
remedial 843–47

responding to complaints 833–38
remedial powers 843–47
responding to complaints 833–38
OMC *see* **Open Method of Coordination**
Open Method of Coordination
broad economic policy guidelines (BEPGs) 194, 195
Brussels European Council 193–94
Charter of Rights, relationship with 233
deliberation and learning 224–26
Economic and Monetary Union (EMU) 191
economic policy 195–201
excessive deficit procedure 197–201
harder version of coordination 197–98
importance of coordination 195–96
multilateral surveillance procedure 196–97, 200
sound money, sound finance paradigm 196
Stability and Growth Pact 196, 197, 200, 201
employment policy 201–205
European Employment Strategy 201–205
rationale for EU involvement 201–203
European Employment Strategy 191, 201–205
European Parliament and 218–21
evaluation 215–28
features 192
future of 229–33
generally 191
impact 228
integrated guidelines 194
Kok Task Force 193
launch and relaunch of 191–95
Lisbon Summit 191–92, 193, 194
national reform programmes 194
Nice European Council 192–93
origins 191–95
Parliamentary involvement 218–21
participation 221–24
peer pressure 227–28
procedural impact 228
public debate 218
reform of process 231–33
revised strategy 194
rights 542
social exclusion 205–208
social partners 241
soft law v hard law 209–13
streamlining procedures 208–209
substantive impact 228
traditional Community method contrasted 213–15
transparency 217–18

pay
equal 588–93, 698–701
PHARE programme 10, 32
***Plaumann* test** 332
police
European Police College (Cepol) 151, 152
Europol 148, 151, 152
policy coordination
Commission 25
Interservice Coordination Group 25
precautionary principle
academic discourse 738–41
application 724–27, 728–30
Artegodan 727–30
best available technology 740
Commission Communication 735–38
controversy over 717
Court of First Instance (CFI) 718
criticism 739–40
development 719–21
environmental directives 731–33
European Court of Justice (ECJ) 718–19
food safety 743–46
foundations 718–19

precautionary principle (*cont.*):
four freedoms 733–35
free movement of goods 719
generally 717
interpretation of Community legislation 735
interpretation of principle 722–24, 727–28
legal decision-making in EU 746–48
margin of safety 740
Member State action, review of 731–35
environmental directives 731–33
four freedoms 733–35
interpretation of Community legislation 735
Monsanto 730–31
non-preclusion 740
Pfizer 722–27
political decision-making in EU
evaluative strategy 741–42
food safety 743–46
prohibitory 740
review of Community action 723
application of principle 724–27, 728–30
apportionment of burden of proof 724
Artegodan 727–30
consultation, importance of 728–29
factual errors on contested legislation 724–26
interpretation of the precautionary principle 722–24, 727–28
manifest error of assessment 726
Monsanto 730–31
Pfizer 722–27
proportionality 727
risk assessed, identification of 723
success of challenge 724
versions of 740
preliminary reference procedure
acte clair 303
caseload 288–89
Court of First Instance (CFI) 296–99
decentralized judicial bodies, proposal for creation of 307–10
Due Report 296
European Court of Justice (ECJ) 285–86, 288–90, 296–99
filtering mechanism 301–304
judgment given by national court, proposal for 305–307
length of time taken to complete 300
limiting, method for 300–301
national courts 300–304
proportionality 711
proposed reply to reference 304–305
statement of reasons 289
temporal effect of preliminary rulings 794–95
private sector bodies
contracting out 52
direct/centralized management 34
process
see also **access**
Charter of Fundamental Rights 385–87
competition 375–76, 388–91
diligent and impartial examination 349
competition 375–76
development of principle 378–81
limitation of principle 378–81
recognition of principle 373–75
State aids 376–78
due care *see* diligent and impartial examination *above*
generally 349–50
hearing
access to the file 365–69
applicability 349, 360–61
causation 372–73
content of right to be heard 361–73
cross-examination 369–70
generally 360
notice 363–65

respond, right to 363–65
separation of functions 370–72
interrelationship between rights 349, 393–96
reasons, duty to give 349, 381–85
relationship between rights 349, 393–96
sector-specific legislation 350, 387–96
competition 388–91
generally 387–88
State aids 392–93
separate consideration of rights 393–94
source of rights 349
State aids 392–93
substantive review 396–98
transparency 349
And see **transparency**
Community courts 353–59
EU Treaty 351–53
values served by 350–51

Prodi Commission 16–23
Formation of the New Commission 17
implementation of reforms 23–28
initial reforms 16–17
Operation of the Commission 17
Task Force for Administrative Reform (TFRA) 17
White Paper on the Reform of the Commission 21

proportionality
anti-dumping 665–66
application of Community legislation 701–703
Art 10 EC 703
Common Agricultural Policy (CAP) 658–64
common policies
Common Agricultural Policy (CAP) 658–64
transport 664–65
cooperation, duty of 703
development of concept 655–58
discretionary policy choices 658–72
anti-dumping 665–66
Common Agricultural Policy (CAP) 658–64
common arguments made 658
guiding principle 658
inter-institutional controls 666–68
manifest disproportionality 668–70
necessity 668–70
rights 674–78
stricto sensu proportionality 670–72
substitution of judgment 658
suitability 668–70
transport 664–65
ECSC case law 656
equal pay 698–701
equal treatment 695–98
four freedoms
establishment 692–94
generally 687–89
goods 689–92
persons 692
services, provision of 692–94
workers 692
fundamental rights 674–78
German law 656
identification of interests 656
importance of principle 655
intensity of application of concept 657
intensity of review 704–10
inter-institutional controls 666–68
justification for strict scrutiny 704–706
legitimate expectations 651
manifest disproportionality 668–70
meaning 655–58
national courts, role of 711–15
national values, sensitivity to 706–708
differences in national values 708–10
necessary measure 656
necessity 668–70

proportionality (*cont.*):
penalties/financial burden 681–85
evaluation of courts' jurisprudence 684–85
general approach 681–82
legislative objectives 682–84
unlimited jurisdiction 684
preliminary reference procedure 711
rights 672–81
Community legislation, rights enshrined in 672–73
discretionary policies 674–78
evaluation of Courts' jurisprudence 678–81
fundamental rights 674–78
Treaty rights 672–73
routes of cases involving 711
stricto sensu 657, 670–72
Structural Funds 77
suitability 668–70
transport 664–65
types of cases involving 657–58
use of principle 655

quotas
Common Agricultural Policy 59

racism
discrimination 602–603
European Monitoring Centre on Racism and Xenophobia (EUMC) 149, 150, 164, 177, 541
railways
European Railway Agency (ERA) 150
Raxen 177
reasons, duty to give 349, 381–85
regulatory impact assessment
agencies 188–89
religious discrimination 603
remedies
annulment *see* **annulment**
compensation *see* **damages**
damages *see* **damages**
effectiveness of Community law 791–95
adequacy of national remedies 793–94
assessment 813–15
cause of action 812
limitation periods 806–808
new remedies 791–93
own motion, consideration of Community law 804–806
proportionality 793–94
recovery of interest 808–10
temporal effect of preliminary rulings 794–95
unduly levied, recovery of 810–11
unduly paid, recovery of sums 811–12
generally 749
interim measures
application 751–52
assessment 754–755
balancing interests 751
burden of proof 751
criteria for award 750–51
direct actions 750–52
indirect action 752–54
serious and irreparable damage 751
suspension of operation, application for 751
joint liability of Community and Member States
application of unlawful legislation by Member State 785–87
generally 784
procedural issues 784
wrongful authorization of national action 785
Member States', against 789–28
adequacy of national monetary remedy 795–96
adequacy of national remedies 793–94
approach 803–12
assessment 813–15

cause of action 812
effectiveness of Community law 791–15
Emmott, limiting 800–803
limitation periods 806–808
Marshall II, limiting 799–800
national remedial autonomy 789–15
'new' remedies 791–93
own motion, consideration of Community law 804–806
proportionality 793–94
recovery of interest 808–10
State liability 815–28
substantive conditions attached to the national remedy 796–97
temporal effect of preliminary rulings 794–95
time limits, sustainability of national 797–99
unduly levied, recovery of 810–11
unduly paid, recovery of sums 811–12
restitution 782–84
State liability 815–28
assessment 827–28
Brasserie du Pêcheur 817–21
discretion, relevance of 819–20
Factortame 817–21
Francovich 815–17
interpretation and application, ECJ guidance on 820–21
judicial acts 821–22
national remedial regimes, relationship with 824–27
post-*Brasserie du Pêcheur*/*Factortame* 821–22
serious breach test 822–24
three part test 817–19
resources
Commission 21–22, 24–25
efficient use by Commission of 21–22, 24–25
Group of Resource Directors 25
White Paper on the Reform of the Commission 21–22
restitution 782–84
rights
abortion 489
blasphemy 489
broadcasting 489
Charter of Fundamental Rights *see* **Charter of Fundamental Rights**
coherent policy, need for 491–92
Constitutional Treaty 543
Declaration of Fundamental Rights and Freedoms 487
differing views of Member States on 488
EU Network of Independent Experts on Fundamental Rights 540–41
European Convention on Human Rights *see* **European Convention on Human Rights (ECHR)**
European Monitoring Centre on Racism and Xenophobia (EUMC) 149, 150, 164, 177, 541
European Political Community (EPC) 484
evolution of fundamental rights
Amsterdam Treaty 487–88
charters 487
declarations 487
early case law 484–86
ECJ approach 484–86
hard law approach 487
judicial contribution to 484–86
legislative contribution 486–88
original Treaties 484
political contribution 486–88
position prior to Charter of Fundamental Rights 488–92
soft law approach 487
Treaty on European Union 487–88

rights (*cont.*):
Fundamental Rights Agency (FRA) 150, 541–43
general principles, rights as 490
generally 483–84
Human Rights Agency 541
margin of appreciation 489
market rights, bias towards 489
national differences and 488–89
nationality, non-discrimination on grounds of 486–87
Open Method of Coordination 542
policy for human rights in EU 539–43
position prior to Charter of Fundamental Rights 488–92
relationship between EC and ECHR 490–91
Single European Act 487
Social Charter 487
soft law approach 487
specific requirements approach 490
surrogacy 489
taking rights seriously 489
rule of law
judicial review 270–73
legal certainty 607–608, 613
legitimate expectations 613

Santer Commission
see also **Committee of Independent Experts**
fall of 3–12, 28, 31, 53, 153
resignation 3–12, 28
sex discrimination
affirmative action 595–98
Charter of Fundamental Rights 587
complexity of issues 585
comptence of EC over 585
development 587
economic rationale of provisions 585–87
equal pay 588–93
equal treatment 593–600
affirmative action 595–98
Directive 594–95
exceptions 594
gender reassignment 599–600
indirect discrimination 595
introduction of provisions 594
limits 595–600
sexual orientation 599–600
gender reassignment 599–600
indirect discrimination 595
limits of equal treatment 595–600
market-integration model 585, 586
original rationale for Art 141 586
sexual orientation 599–602
social citizenship model 587
social policy models 585–86
social rationale of provisions 585–87
sexual orientation
Art 13 EC 600–602
discrimination 599–602, 603
sex discrimination 599–602
shared management
Committee of Independent Experts 19–20, 57
Common Agricultural Policy 57, 58–69
and see **Common Agricultural Policy**
accreditation of paying agencies 61–62
certified accounts 62
clearance of accounts 61
ECJ, contribution of 66–68
enabling provision 61
European Agricultural Guidance and Guarantee Fund (EAGGF) 60–61
framework 60–62
future of CAP 68–69
income support 59–60
law and 62–69
objectives of CAP 58
price support 58–60
timetables for accounting compliance 62
Treaty foundations 58
definition 57

financial management and control 26, 27
Financial Regulation, new
generally 57
importance 57
Structural Funds 57, 69–96
and see **Structural Funds**
framework 78
law and 78–96
policy 70–72
Treaty foundations 69–70
Single European Act (SEA)
comitology 106–08
single farm payment 60
social dialogue
see also **social partners**
emergence 235–36
importance 236
origins 235–36
social agenda, goal of attaining 236
Val Duchesse process 236
social exclusion
Open Method of Coordination 205–08
social partners
see also **social dialogue**
agreements brokered by
better governance 248–55
democracy 248–55
representation 243–47
subisidiarity 247–48
agreements and law 238–40
autonomous agreements 257–58
consultation 238
democracy
associative democracy 252–53
Community democratic model 249–51
directly-deliberative polyarchy 253–54
functional democracy 254–55
generally 248–49
neo-corporatism 254–55
participatory democracy 251–52
directives, implementation of 238
European Centre of Enterprises with Public Participation and of Enterprises of General Economic Interest (CEEP) 236
European Council 242–43
European Trade Union Confederation (ETUC) 236
joint opinions 258–59
OMC, role in 235
Open Method of Coordination 241
process-orientated texts 240–41, 258–59
Protocol on Social Policy 236
role 237
sectoral social dialogue 258–59
social dialogue, emergence of 235–36
social policy, furtherance of 237
subisidiarity 247–48
Treaty framework 237–43
Tripartite Social Summit for Growth and Employment 241–42
Union of Industrial and Employers' Confederations of Europe (UNICE) 236
Val Duchesse process 236
Stability and Growth Pact 196, 197, 200, 201
staff
Commission
appraisal 25
discipline 24, 25
early retirement 25
mobility 25
pay 25
pensions 25
policy 25
professional incompetence 24
promotion 25
Regulations 25
serious wrongdoing 24
shortages 12, 13–15
under-performance 24
whistle-blowing 24
executive agencies 38

staff (*cont.*):
under-performance
Commission 24
whistle-blowing 24
standing
background 331–35
Calpak test 332–33
Charter of Fundamental Rights 346–47
Codorniu case 333
complexity of law 331
Constitutional Treaty 344–46
Court of Auditors 331–32
direct challenge 342–44
European Central Bank 332
generally 331
indirect challenge 340–42
Jego-Quere 339–40
non-privileged applicants
Calpak test 332–33
Codorniu case 333
difficulty of direct challenge 332–33
intervention rights 334–35
Plaumann test 332
Plaumann test 332
Treaty provision 331–32
UPA case
Advocate General's Opinion 335–37
ECJ decision 337–39
state aids
Court of First Instance (CFI) 294
diligent and impartial examination principle 376–78
judicial review 460–62
legitimate expectations 642–43, 644–48
manifest error 460–62
process 392–93
Structural Funds
1988 reforms 72–74
1993 reforms 74–75
1999 reforms 75–76
2007 reforms 76–78
additionality 73, 74, 75, 76, 79, 82–83
administration 19–20
certification of payments 86
Cohesion Fund (CF) 70, 74–75, 77
Committee of Independent Experts 78, 79
Community Support Framework (CSF) 73–74, 76, 77, 79, 83
compliance incentives 83–84
concentration 73, 74, 76, 77
Council and 70
documentation 77
ECJ case law 91–93
Economic Policy Guidelines 77
economic strategy 77
enlargement of EU 75
European Agricultural Guidance and Guarantee Fund (EAGGF) 70
European Regional Development Fund (ERDF) 70
European Social Fund (ESF) 70
European Strategy for Employment 77
irregularities, correction of 88–91
judicial review 462
law and 78–96
certification of payments 86
checking 87
collective interest and individual interests of Member States, tension between 78–80
compliance incentives 83–84
control systems 84–88
design, legislative 80–91
ECJ case law 91–93
formal law 93–94
irregularities, correction of 88–91
legislative objectives 78–80
liability for sums unduly paid 88–89
payment 83–84
prevention of irregularities 89–91
project selection 80–83
recovery of amounts lost 88
reporting 86–87

soft law 94–96
manifest error 462
National Strategic Reference Framework (NSRF) 77, 78
objectives 72–73, 74, 75–76, 77
partnership 73, 74, 75, 76, 80–82
payments 83–84
policy 70–72, 78
programming 73, 74, 76
project selection 80–83
proportionality 77
regulations governing 30
reporting 86–87
reports 70
shared management 57, 69–96
ECJ case law 91–93
framework 78
law and 78–96
policy 70–72
Treaty foundations 69–70
soft law 94–96
strategic guidelines 77
subsidiarity 77
TEU reforms 74
Treaty foundations 69–70
subsidiarity
Charter of Fundamental Rights 498
Constitutional Treaty 424–25
court's role 425–27
exclusive competence, meaning of 420–22
impact 423–24
importance of concept 419
Inter-institutional Agreement 422
meaning 419, 422–25
Protocol on Application of Principles 422–23
rationale 419
social partners 247–48
state rights 402
Structural Funds 77
Treaty provision 419
Synthesis Report 24

TACIS programme 10, 32
Task Force for Administrative Reform (TFRA) 17
technical assistance offices
Committee of Independent Experts 18
use 18–19
tender
contracting out 53
TFRA 17
consultation document (2000) 21
Thomson Report 71
tourism
Committee of Independent Experts 6–7
direct/centralized management 32
training
European Training Foundation (ETF) 149
Translation Centre for Bodies of the European Union (CdT) 149
transparency 349
agencies 175–76
assessment of provisions 359–60
Community courts 353–59
direct/centralized management 33
EU Treaty 351–53
exceptions in Regulation 1049/2001 356–59
features 351
importance 350, 351
Open Method of Coordination 217–18
protection of reality of access 355
purpose 350–51
Regulation 1049/2001 and 354–59
values served by 350–51
transport policies
proportionality 664–65

UNICE 236
Union of Industrial and Employers' Confederations of Europe (UNICE) 236

United States
discretion, substantive review of 475–76
'hard look' 475–77, 479–80

Val Duchesse process 236
vocational training
direct/centralized management 32

whistle-blowing
staff 24
White Paper on European Governance
Community method 113
Constitutional Treaty 112–13
White Paper on the Reform of the Commission 5, 28
Action Plan 21
activity-based management 22
audit 22, 23
Committee of Independent Experts 21
contracting out 16, 33
direct/centralized management 35, 50
externalization policy of Commission 22
financial management and control 22, 25
human resources 21, 22, 25
implementation of reforms 23–28
Internal Audit Service 23
network management 50
Part I 21
Part II 21
priority setting 21
Prodi Commission 21
publication 21
resources, efficient use of 21–22
theme of 21
winding-up
executive agencies 38
World Trade Organisation (WTO)
accession of EC to 491
Common Agricultural Policy, negotiations and 60
WTO *see* **World Trade Organisation (WTO)**